Lecture Notes in Computer Science 4096

Commenced Publication in 1973
Founding and Former Series Editors:
Gerhard Goos, Juris Hartmanis, and Jan van Leeuwen

Edwin Sha   Sung-Kook Han
Cheng-Zhong Xu   Moon Hae Kim
Laurence T. Yang   Bin Xiao (Eds.)

Embedded and Ubiquitous Computing

International Conference, EUC 2006
Seoul, Korea, August 1-4, 2006
Proceedings

Springer

Volume Editors

Edwin Sha
University of Texas at Dallas, USA, e-mail: edsha@utdallas.edu

Sung-Kook Han
Won Kwang University, Korea, e-mail: skhan@wku.ac.kr

Cheng-Zhong Xu
Wayne State University, Detroit, USA, e-mail: czxu@wayne.edu

Moon Hae Kim
Konkuk University, Seoul, Korea, e-mail: mhkim@konkuk.ac.kr

Laurence T. Yang
St. Francis Xavier University, Antigonish, Canada, e-mail: lyang@stfx.ca

Bin Xiao
Hong Kong Polytechnic University, Hong Kong, e-mail: csbxiao@comp.polyu.edu.hk

Library of Congress Control Number: 2006929849

CR Subject Classification (1998): C.2, C.3, D.4, D.2, H.4, H.3, H.5, K.4

LNCS Sublibrary: SL 3 – Information Systems and Application, incl. Internet/Web and HCI

ISSN 0302-9743
ISBN-10 3-540-36679-2 Springer Berlin Heidelberg New York
ISBN-13 978-3-540-36679-9 Springer Berlin Heidelberg New York

Springer is a part of Springer Science+Business Media

springer.com

Printed in Germany

Typesetting: Camera-ready by author, data conversion by Scientific Publishing Services, Chennai, India
Printed on acid-free paper SPIN: 11802167 06/3142 5 4 3 2 1 0

Preface

Embedded and ubiquitous computing is an exciting new paradigm that provides computing and communication services all the time, everywhere. Now we can attach computing and communication devices to human bodies to monitor our health, embed computing chips into brains to cure memory losses, or make smart fabrics so they can change colors or generate heat. All these new devices are created to the benefits or convenience of human lives. We need creativity as well as the advance of technology. This emergence is an outcome of research and technological advances in embedded software, embedded hardware, pervasive computing and communications, wireless networks, mobile computing, distributed computing and agent technologies, etc.

The EUC 2006 conference provided a forum for engineers and scientists in academia, industry, and government to address challenges and to present and discuss their ideas, results, work in progress, and experience. The Technical Program Committee of EUC 2006 was led by the TPC Chair, Edwin Shan, and 13 TPC Vice Chairs. A strong international Technical Program Committee was then formed to review, evaluate the submissions, and select the papers to be presented.

EUC 2006 had a very large number of submissions, more than 500 submissions from all over the world. After the TPC Chair asked authors to consider resubmitting their papers to EUC workshops, 50 submissions were withdrawn and resubmitted to EUC workshops. Finally, 467 submissions entered the EUC conference review process. Each paper was reviewed by at least three TPC members or external reviewers. It was extremely difficult to select papers to be accepted for presentations because there were so many excellent and interesting submissions. We finally accepted 117 papers in which 113 papers are published in these proceedings. We believe that all of these accepted papers are of very high quality and can also stimulate future research innovations in the area of embedded and ubiquitous computing.

We wish to thank the Program Committee members for the time and thought that they gave to create a first-class program, especially considering that they worked under a very tight schedule with a surprisingly huge number of submissions. To all the authors who submitted the papers and made this conference a success, we thank you.

We are also grateful to the Organizing Committee for organizing the conference, and to the keynote speakers who agreed to give exciting speeches.

April 2006

Edwin H.-M. Sha, Sung-Kook Han, Cheng-Zhong Xu
Moon-Hae Kim, Laurence T. Yang and Bin Xiao
EUC 2006 Program and Organization Chairs

Preface

Organization

EUC 2006 was organized and supported by the International Federation for Information Processing (IFIP). It was held in cooperation with the IEEE Computer Society, Korea Information Science Society and *Lecture Notes in Computer Science* (LNCS) of Springer.

Executive Committee

General Chairs:	Sung-Kook Han, Wonkwang University, Korea
	Cheng-Zhong Xu, Wayne State University, USA
	Moon-Hae Kim, Konkuk University, Korea
Program Chair:	Edwin Sha, University of Texas at Dallas, USA
Program Vice Chairs:	Tei-Wei Kuo, National Taiwan University, Taiwan
	Jihong Kim, Seoul National University, Korea
	Jenq-Kuen Lee, National Tsing-Hua University, Taiwan
	Jun Yang, University of California at Riverside, USA
	Morris Chang, Iowa State University, USA
	Ting-Chi Wang, National Tsing-Hua University, Taiwan
	Jiannong Cao, Hong Kong Polytechnic University, Hong Kong
	Franco Zambonelli, University of Modena and Reggio Emilia, Italy
	Cho-Li Wang, The University of Hong Kong, Hong Kong
	Chu-Sing Yang, National Sun Yat-Sen University, Taiwan
	Jie Li, University of Tsukuba, Japan
	Li Jianzhong, Harbin Institute of Technology, China
	Yoohwan Kim, University of Nevada, Las Vegas, USA
Steering Chairs:	Minyi Guo, University of Aizu, Japan
	Laurence T. Yang, St. Francis Xavier University, Canada
Local Organizing Chairs:	Young-Sik Jeong, Wonkwang University, Korea
	Jeong-Bae Lee, Sunmoon University, Korea
Workshop Chairs:	Xiaobo Zhou, University of Colorado at Colorado Springs, USA
	Oleg Sokolsky, University of Pennsylvania, USA

Publication Chair:	Bin Xiao, Hong Kong Polytechnic University, Hong Kong
	Xiaobo Zhou, University of Colorado at Colorado Springs, USA
Publicity Chairs:	Makoto Takizawa, Tokyo Denki University, Japan
	Kyung Dong Ryu, Arizona State University, USA
Panel Chairs:	Su-Chong Joo, Wonkwang University, Korea
	Seongsoo Hong, Seoul National University, Korea

Program Committee

Sanjoy Baruah	University of North Carolina, USA
Pete Beckman	Argonne National Lab., USA
Claudio E. Casetti	Politecnico di Torino, Italy
Chaitali Chakrabarti	Arizona State University, USA
Naehyuck Chang	Seoul National University, Korea
Rong-Guey Chang	National Chung-Cheng University, Taiwan
Chantana Chantrapornchai	Silpakorn University, Thailand
Pascal Chatonnay	Université de Franche-Comte, France
Sao-Jie Chen	National Taiwan University, Taiwan
Yih-Farn Chen	AT&T Research Labs, USA
Ray-Guang Cheng	National Taiwan University of Science and Technology, Taiwan
Sang Young Cho	Hankuk University of Foreign Studies, Korea
Lynn Choi	Korea University, Korea
Slo-Li Chu	Chung-Yuan Christian University, Taiwan
Hao-Hua Chu	National Taiwan University, Taiwan
Sung Woo Chung	University of Virginia, USA
Yeh-Ching Chung	National Tsing-Hua University, Taiwan
Siobh. Clarke	Trinity College Dublin, Ireland
Gerard Damm	Alcatel USA, USA
Mark d'Inverno	University of Westminster, UK
Lan-Rong Dung	National Chiao Tung University, Taiwan
Stephen A. Edwards	Columbia University, USA
Javier Garcia-Villalba	University of Madrid, Spain
Dan Feng	Huazhong University of Science and Technology, China
Xiang Feng	Microsoft Corporation, USA
Hong Gao	Harbin Institute of Technology, China
Marie-Pierre Gleizes	IRIT-Université Paul Sebatier Toulouse, France
Hani A K Hagras	University of Essex, UK
David Hales	Università di Bologna, Italy
Dong-Won Han	ETRI, Korea
Taisook Han	KAIST, Korea

Program Committee (continued)

Youn-Hee Han	Korea University of Technology and Education
Salima Hassas	Université de Lyon, France
Bo Hong	Drexel University, USA
Jiman Hong	Kwangwoon University, Korea
Pao-Ann Hsiung	Chung Cheng University, Taiwan
Ching-Hsien Hsu	Chung Hua University, Taiwan
Feng-Hsiung Hsu	Microsoft Research Asia, China
Hui-Huang Hsu	Tamkang University, Taiwan
Fei Hu	Rochester Institute of Technology, USA
Weichih Hu	Chung-Yuan Christian University, Taiwan
Michael C. Huang	University of Rochester, USA
Shih-Hsu Huang	Chung-Yuan Christian University, Taiwan
Wei Huang	Iowa State University, USA
Yo-Ping Huang	Tatung University, Taiwan
Ren-Hung Hwang	National Chung Cheng University, Taiwan
Wen-Jyi Hwang	National Taiwan Normal University, Taiwan
Yin-Tsung Hwang	National Chung Hsing University, Taiwan
Tohru Ishihara	Kyushu University, Japan
Rong-Hong Jan	National Chiao Tung University, Taiwan
Ravindra Jejurikar	Sun Microsystems, USA
Dongwon Jeong	Kunsan National University, Korea
Zhiping Jia	Shandong University, China
Ju-Yeon Jo	California State University, Sacramento, USA
David B. Johnson	Rice University, USA
Roy Ju	Google Inc., USA
Shiguang Ju	Jiangsu University, China
Mahmut Kandemir	Pennsylvania State University, USA
Soon Ju Kang	Kyungpook National University, Korea
Doohyun Kim	Kokkuk University, Korea
Jae-Hyun Kim	Ajou University, Korea
Jung Guk Kim	Hankuk University of Foreign Studies, Korea
Sun-Ja Kim	ETRI, Korea
Hsien-Hsin (Sean) Lee	Georgia Institute of Technology, USA
Dong Chun Lee	Howon University, Korea
Jaejin Lee	Seoul National University, Korea
Wonjun Lee	Korea University, Korea
Woo Hyong Lee	Samsung Co., Korea
Minglu Li	Shanghai Jiantong University, China
Qing Li	City University of Hong Kong, Hong Kong
Xiang-Yang Li	IIT, USA
Xiaoming Li	Peking University, China
Xuandong Li	Nanjing University, China
Yingshu Li	Georgia State University, USA

Program Committee (continued)

Wanjiun Liao	National Taiwan University, Taiwan
Vincenzo Liberatore	Case Western Reserve University, USA
Yao-Nan Lien	National Chengchi University, Taiwan
Chae-Deok Lim	ETRI, Korea
Ee-Peng Lim	Nanyang Technological University, Singapore
Sung-Soo Lim	Kookmin University, Korea
Frank Yeong-Sung Lin	National Taiwan University, Taiwan
Phone Lin	National Taiwan University, Taiwan
Xuemin Lin	University of New South Wales, Australia
Tok Wang Ling	National University of Singapore, Singapore
Chia-Tien Dan Lo	University of Texas at San Antonio, USA
Shi-Wu Lo	National Chung Cheng University, Taiwan
Yung-Hsiang Lu	Purdue University, USA
Mon-Yen Luo	Cheng Shiu University, Taiwan
Pyung-Soo Ma	ETRI, Korea
Rabi N. Mahapatra	Texas A&M University, USA
Marco Mamei	Università di Modena e Reggio Emilia, Italy
Gokhan Memik	Northwestern University, USA
Byoung-Joon Min	Incheon University, Korea
Sang Lyul Min	Seoul National University, Korea
Pablo Noriega	IIIA-CSIC, Spain
Andrea Omicini	Universitá di Bologna, Italy
Timothy O'Neil	University of Akron, USA
Chan Yeol Park	KISTI, Korea
Doo-Soon Park	Soonchunhyang University, Korea
Jung-Ho Park	Sunmoon University, Korea
Neungsoo Park	Konkuk University, Korea
Seung-Min Park	ETRI, Korea
Nelson Passos	Midwestern State University, USA
Massimo Poncino	Politecnico di Torino, Italy
Yi Qian	University of Puerto Rico at Mayagez, USA
Vijay Raghunathan	NEC Labs America, USA
Michael Rovatsos	University of Edinburgh, UK
Pedro M. Ruiz	University of Murcia and ICSI Berkeley, Spain
Zili Shao	The Hong Kong Polytechnic University, Hong Kong
Onn Shehory	IBM Haifa Research Labs, Israel
Shashi Shekhar	University of Minnesota, USA
Timothy Sherwood	University of California, Santa Barbara, USA
Yuanchun Shi	Tsinghua University, China

Program Committee (continued)

Ce-Kuen Shieh	National Cheng Kung University, Taiwan
Wei-Kuan Shih	National Tsing-Hua University, Taiwan
Dongkun Shin	Samsung Electronics, Korea
Yan Solihin	North Carolina State University, USA
Bala Srinivasan	University of Melbourne, Australia
Witawas Srisa-an	University of Nebraska-Lincoln, USA
Jaideep Srivastava	University of Minnesota, USA
Ching-Lung Su	National Yunlin University of Science and Technology, Taiwan
Hyo-Joong Suh	The Catholic University of Korea, Korea
Min-Te Sun	Auburn University, USA
Yuqing Sun	Shandong University, China
Rajshekhar Sunderraman	Georgia State University, USA
David Surma	Indiana University at South Bend, USA
Robert Tolksdorf	Free University of Berlin, Germany
Hiroyuki Tomiyama	Nagoya University, Japan
Sissades Tongsima	NSTDA, Thailand
Chien-Chao Tseng	National Chiao-Tung University, Taiwan
Putchong Uthayopas	Kasetsart University, Thailand
Ramakrishna Vishnuvajjala	Lucent Technologies, USA
Chun-Yao Wang	National Tsing Hua University, Taiwan
Guojung Wang	Central South University, China
Jinling Wang	NEC Lab, China
Li-C. Wang	University of California, Santa Barbara, USA
Li-Chun Wang	National Chiao Tung University, Taiwan
Ling Wang	Harbin Institute of Technology, China
Yan Wang	Macquarie University, Australia
Zhijun Wang	Hong Kong Polytechnic University, Hong Kong
Hongxing Wei	BeiHang University, China
Gang Wu	Shanghai Jiaotong University, China
Jun Wu	China University of Technology, Taiwan
Kui Wu	University of Victoria, Canada
Zhaohui Wu	Zhejiang University, China
Bin Xiao	Hong Kong Polytechnic University, Hong Kong
Yuan Xie	Pennsylvania State University, USA
Jianliang Xu	Hong Kong Baptist University, Hong Kong
Ming Xu	National University of Defense and Technology, China
Jason Xue	University of Texas at Dallas, USA
Dong Xuan	Ohio State University, USA
Haijin Yan	Motorola, USA
Mei Yang	University of Nevada, Las Vegas, USA
Yang Yang	University of College London, UK

Program Committee (continued)

Xu Jeffrey Yu	Chinese University of Hong Kong, Hong Kong
Qin-an Zeng	University of Cincinnati, USA
Youtao Zhang	University of Texas at Dallas, USA
Zhao Zhang	Iowa State University, USA
Huiyang Zhou	University of Central Florida, USA
Da Yong Zhou	University of Oklahoma, USA
Xiaofang Zhou	University of Queensland, Australia
Xingshe Zhou	Northwestern Polytechnical University, China
Zhichun Zhu	University of Illinois at Chicago, USA

Additional Reviewers

Juan A. Botia
Ben-Jye Chang
Lu-Tsung Chang
Yu-How Chang
Yuan-Hao Chang
Hong-Yueh Chen
Jian-Jia Chen
Min-Xiou Chen
Wei Chen
Ya-Shu Chen
Youdong Chen
Shin-Ming Cheng
Chun-Mok Chung
Cormac Driver
Abdulazis Eker
Yunsi Fei
Rung-Hung Gau
Fei Guo
Rui Gao
Yuanchen He
Jen-Wei Hsieh
Pi-Cheng Hsiu
Yuan-Ying Hsu
Yu Hua
Di-Wei Huang
J. H. Huang
Kuei-Li Huang
Wen-Shyang Hwang
Xiaowei Jiang
Cheol Hong Kim
Seongbeom Kim
Young-Jin Kim
Yen-Cheng Lai
Chih-Hung Lee
Seong-Won Lee
Yu-Cheng Lin
Eamonn Linehan
Kathy Liszka
De-Kai Liu
Qing Liu
Tsung-Hsien Liu
C. H. Lu
Yung-Feng Lu
Yi Luo
Praveen Madiraju
Arindam Mallik
Andronikos Nedos
Yow-Tyng Nieh
Serkan Ozdemir
Nei-Chiung Perng
Karthik Raghavan
Navin Rongratana
Juan A. Sanchez
Kristal Sauer
Kulpreet Singh
Kuen-Yuan Shieh
Yung-Chien Shih
Sung Hoon Shim
Pei-lun Suei
Chiung-Ying Wang
Haibin Wang
Jui-Tang Wang
Miaomiao Wang
Shupeng Wang
Kuo-Wei Wen
J. Y. Wu
Minji Wu
Carmen M. Yago
Chuan-Yue Yang
Lei Yang
Yi-Ping You
Bo Yu
Yidong Yuan
Nai-Xin Zhang
Qing Zhang
Ying Zhang

Table of Contents

Keynote

On Securing Networked Real-Time Embedded Systems
Kang G. Shin 1

Towards Self-coordinating Ubiquitous Computing Environments
Franz J. Rammig 2

Frontier of Digital Technology and Future Strategy
Hyun Jin Ko 14

Power Aware Computing

SAQA: Spatial and Attribute Based Query Aggregation in Wireless Sensor Networks
Yang Jie, Yan Bo, Sungyoung Lee, Jinsung Cho 15

Efficent Algorithm of Energy Minimization for Heterogeneous Wireless Sensor Network
Meikang Qiu, Chun Xue, Zili Shao, Qingfeng Zhuge, Meilin Liu, Edwin H.-M. Sha 25

Power-Aware Instruction Scheduling
Tzong-Yen Lin, Rong-Guey Chang 35

Minimising the Energy Consumption of Real-Time Tasks with Precedence Constraints on a Single Processor
Hui Wu, Sridevan Parameswaran 45

Power Aware H.264/AVC Video Player on PAC Dual-Core SoC Platform
Jia-Ming Chen, Chih-Hao Chang, Shau-Yin Tseng, Jenq-Kuen Lee, Wei-Kuan Shih 57

Dynamic Repartitioning of Real-Time Schedule on a Multicore Processor for Energy Efficiency
Euiseong Seo, Yongbon Koo, Joonwon Lee 69

Security and Fault Tolerance 1

A Secure Key Agreement Scheme in Low-Energy Wireless Sensor Networks
Taeyeon Kim, Gicheol Wang, Gihwan Cho 79

Person-Wise Privacy Level Access Control for Personal Information Directory Services
Hyung-Jin Mun, Keon Myung Lee, Sang-Ho Lee 89

An Efficient Computing-Checkpoint Based Coordinated Checkpoint Algorithm
Chaoguang Men, Dongsheng Wang, Yunlong Zhao 99

A Parallel GNFS Algorithm Based on a Reliable Look-Ahead Block Lanczos Method for Integer Factorization
Laurence T. Yang, Li Xu, Man Lin, John Quinn 110

SPDA: A Security Protocol for Data Aggregation in Large-Scale Wireless Sensor Networks
Jin Wook Lee, Yann-Hang Lee, Hasan Cam 121

Efficient and User Friendly Inter-domain Device Authentication/Access Control for Home Networks
Jin-Bum Hwang, Hyung-Kyu Lee, Jong-Wook Han 131

Agent and Distributed Computing 1

A Programming Model for the Automatic Construction of USN Applications Based on Nano-Qplus
Kwangyong Lee, Woojin Lee, Juil Kim, Kiwon Chong 141

Hierarchical and Dynamic Information Management Framework on Grid Computing
Eun-Ha Song, Yang-Seung Jeon, Sung-Kook Han, Young-Sik Jeong 151

Kalman Filter Based Dead Reckoning Algorithm for Minimizing Network Traffic Between Mobile Nodes in Wireless GRID
Seong-Whan Kim, Ki-Hong Ko 162

A Conceptual Framework for Agent-Based Information Resource Management
Charles C. Willow 171

Advanced Stochastic Host State Modeling to Reliable Computation in Global Computing Environment
EunJoung Byun, HongSoo Kim, SungJin Choi, MaengSoon Baik, SooJin Goo, Joon-Min Gil, HarkSoo Park, Chong-Sun Hwang 183

Dynamic Buffer Allocation for Conserving Disk Energy in Clustered Video Servers Which Use Replication
Minseok Song 193

Wireless Communications 1

LBN: Load-Balancing Network for Data Gathering Wireless Sensor Networks
Wenlu Yang, Chongqing Zhang, Minglu Li 204

Multi-user Diversity for IEEE 802.11 Infrastructure Wireless LAN
Sung Won Kim 214

Performance Analysis of DS-BPAM UWB System over Fading Channels–Uncoded and Coded Schemes
Zhiquan Bai, Shaoyi Xu, Weihua Zhang, Kyungsup Kwak 224

Protocol Design for Adaptive Video Transmission over MANET
Jeeyoung Seo, Eunhee Cho, Sang-Jo Yoo 234

mSCTP-DAC: Dynamic Address Configuration for mSCTP Handover
Dong Phil Kim, Seok Joo Koh, Sang Wook Kim 244

TCP-New Veno: The Energy Efficient Congestion Control in Mobile Ad-Hoc Networks
Namho Cho, Kwangsue Chung 254

Real-Time Systems

A Real-Time Message Scheduling Scheme Based on Optimal Earliest Deadline First Policy for Dual Channel Wireless Networks
Junghoon Lee, Mikyung Kang, Gyung-Leen Park, Ikchan Kim, Cheolmin Kim, Jong-Hyun Park, Jiman Hong 264

On Multiprocessor Utility Accrual Real-Time Scheduling with Statistical Timing Assurances
Hyeonjoong Cho, Haisang Wu, Binoy Ravindran, E. Douglas Jensen 274

Linux/RTOS Hybrid Operating Environment on Gandalf Virtual Machine Monitor
Shuichi Oikawa, Megumi Ito, Tatsuo Nakajima 287

Optimizing Code Size for Embedded Real-Time Applications
Shao-Yang Wang, Chih-Yuan Chen, Rong-Guey Chang 297

Dual-Mode r-Reliable Task Model for Flexible Scheduling in Reliable Real-Time Systems
Kyong Hoon Kim, Jong Kim, Sung Je Hong 308

Security and Fault Tolerance 2

Securing Internet Gateway Discovery Protocol in Ubiquitous Wireless Internet Access Networks
Bok-Nyong Park, Wonjun Lee, Christian Shin 318

Data Integrity Related Markup Language and HTTP Protocol Support for Web Intermediaries
Chi-Hung Chi, Lin Liu, Xiaoyin Yu 328

Efficient Batch Verification for RSA-Type Digital Signatures in a Ubiquitous Environment
Seungwon Lee, Yookun Cho 336

Secure User Authentication Mechanism in Digital Home Network Environments
Jongpil Jeong, Min Young Chung, Hyunseung Choo 345

Agent and Distributed Computing 2

Scalable Message Routing for Mobile Software Assistants
Paweł T. Wojciechowski 355

Grid Resource Management Based on Functional Dependency
Doan Thanh Tran, Eunmi Choi 365

Distributed Proximity-Aware Peer Clustering in BitTorrent-Like Peer-to-Peer Networks
Bin Xiao, Jiadi Yu, Zili Shao, Minglu Li 375

Distributed Invocation of Composite Web Services
Chang-Sup Park, Soyeon Park 385

Embedded Software Optimization

System Software for Flash Memory: A Survey
Tae-Sun Chung, Dong-Joo Park, Sangwon Park, Dong-Ho Lee, Sang-Won Lee, Ha-Joo Song 394

Loop Striping: Maximize Parallelism for Nested Loops
Chun Xue, Zili Shao, Meilin Liu, Meikang Qiu, Edwin H.-M. Sha 405

Efficient Error Control for Scalable Media Transmission over 3G Broadcast Networks
Kyungtae Kang, Joonho Lee, Yongwoo Cho, Heonshik Shin 415

Implementation Synthesis of Embedded Software Under Operating Systems Supporting the Hybrid Scheduling Model
Zhigang Gao, Zhaohui Wu, Hong Li 426

Designing Dynamic Software Architecture for Home Service Robot Software
Dongsun Kim, Sooyong Park 437

Embedded Systems

A Processor Extension for Cycle-Accurate Real-Time Software
Nicholas Jun Hao Ip, Stephen A. Edwards 449

Next Generation Embedded Processor Architecture for Personal Information Devices
In-Pyo Hong, Yong-Joo Lee, Yong-Surk Lee 459

A Secret Image Sharing Scheme Based on Vector Quantization Mechanism
Chin-Chen Chang, Chi-Shiang Chan, Yi-Hsuan Fan 469

A Framework for Managing the Solution Life Cycle of Event-Driven Pervasive Applications
Johnathan M. Reason, Han Chen, ChangWoo Jung, SunWoo Lee, Danny Wong, Andrew Kim, SooYeon Kim, JiHye Rhim, Paul B. Chou, KangYoon Lee 479

A Fast Instruction Set Evaluation Method for ASIP Designs
Angela Yun Zhu, Xi Li, Laurence T. Yang, Jun Yang 489

An ARM-Based Embedded System Design for Speech-to-Speech Translation
Shun-Chieh Lin, Jhing-Fa Wang, Jia-Ching Wang, Hsueh-Wei Yang 499

Multimedia and Data Management 1

Human Computer Interaction for the Accelerometer-Based Mobile Game
Jonghun Baek, Ik-Jin Jang, KeeHyun Park, Hyun-Soo Kang, Byoung-Ju Yun 509

Using Automatic Facial Expression Classification for Contents Indexing Based on the Emotional Component
Uwe Kowalik, Terumasa Aoki, Hiroshi Yasuda 519

A Framework for Data Management and Transfer in Grid Environments
Haojie Zhou, Xingwu Liu, Liqiang Cao, Li Zha 529

MMSDS: Ubiquitous Computing and WWW-Based Multi-modal Sentential Dialog System
Jung-Hyun Kim, Kwang-Seok Hong 539

A Speech and Character Combined Recognition Engine for Mobile Devices
Min-Joung Kim, Soo-Young Suk, Ho-Youl Jung, Hyun-Yeol Chung ... 549

Scalable Fingerprinting Scheme Using Statistically Secure Anti-collusion Code for Large Scale Contents Distribution
Jae-Min Seol, Seong-Whan Kim 560

Mobile Computing 1

Broadcasting Group Information to Ensure Consistency and Correctness in Mobile Computing Environments
Daein Kim, Buhyun Hwang 570

A Fuzzy-Based Service Adaptation Middleware for Context-Aware Computing
Ronnie Cheung, Jiannong Cao, Gang Yao, Alvin Chan 580

Next Generation Mobile Service Environment and Evolution of Context Aware Services
JungSook Bae, Jae Yong Lee, Byung Chul Kim, Seungwan Ryu 591

Efficient Routing Protocol Using Virtual Connection and Load Balancing for Network Mobility
SungHo Kim, Sunshin An 601

Network Mobility in MIPv6 Considering Arrival Time
Sun Ok Yang, SungSuk Kim 610

Service-Oriented Device Anycasting Using Quality First Search in Wireless Personal Area Network
Chien-Chung Su, Kuo-Shiang Lu, Mong-Fong Horng, Chao-Lieh Chen, Yau-Hwang Kuo, Jang-Pong Hsu, Wen-Hsin Cheng ... 620

Wireless Communications 2

BaseStation Assisted TCP: A Simple Way to Improve Wireless TCP
Shaoen Wu, Saâd Biaz, Yiming Ji, Bing Qi ... 630

Modeling Asymmetric Slot Allocation for Mobile Multimedia Services in Microcell TDD Employing FDD Uplink as Macrocell
Dong-Hoi Kim ... 642

Dynamic Clustering for Coverage-Time Maximization in Two-Tiered Hierarchical Sensor Network Architectures
Joongheon Kim, Wonjun Lee, Dongshin Kim, Eunkyo Kim, Hyeokman Kim, Sanghyun Ahn ... 652

An Enhanced Hybrid Rerouting Scheme for Handoff in Wireless ATM Networks
Bih-Hwang Lee, Su-Shun Huang, Hsin-Pei Chen ... 662

Bridging Nodes Density: A Connection Stability Heuristic for Dynamic Ad-Hoc Networks
Stefan Penz, Martin Wenig ... 672

A Base Station Centralized Simple Clustering Protocol for Sensor Networks
Giljae Lee, Minsun Lee, Woojin Seok, Junguk Kong, Okhwan Byeon ... 682

Embedded System Design Automation

Simulation Cost Reduction Strategies for Behavioral Model Verification in Bayesian Based Stopping Rule
Kang Chul Kim, Chang-Gyoon Lim, Jae Hung Yoo, Seok Bung Han ... 692

Low Power Hardware-Software Partitioning Algorithm for Heterogeneous Distributed Embedded Systems
Tianyi Ma, Jun Yang, Xinglan Wang ... 702

Refactoring-Based Stepwise Refinement in Abstract System-Level Design
Ryosuke Yamasaki, Kazutaka Kobayashi, Nurul Azma Zakaria, Shuji Narazaki, Norihiko Yoshida 712

Custom Instruction Generation Using Temporal Partitioning Techniques for a Reconfigurable Functional Unit
Farhad Mehdipour, Hamid Noori, Morteza Saheb Zamani, Kazuaki Murakami, Koji Inoue, Mehdi Sedighi 722

Scheduling of Transactions Based on Extended Scheduling Timed Petri Nets for SoC System-Level Test-Case Generation
JinShan Yu, Tun Li, Yang Guo, QingPing Tan 732

Automatic Generation of Hardware/Software Interface with Product-Specific Debugging Tools
Jeong-Han Yun, Gunwoo Kim, Choonho Son, Taisook Han 742

Embedded Architectures

Fault-Tolerant VLIW Processor Design and Error Coverage Analysis
Yung-Yuan Chen, Kuen-Long Leu, Chao-Sung Yeh 754

Interconnect Estimation for Mesh-Based Reconfigurable Computing
Haibin Shen, Rongquan You, Yier Jin, Aiming Ji 766

Efficient Logic Circuit for Network Intrusion Detection
Huang-Chun Roan, Chien-Min Ou, Wen-Jyi Hwang, Chia-Tien Dan Lo 776

A Multi-protocol Baseband Modem Processor for a Mobile RFID Reader
Seok Joong Hwang, Joon Goo Lee, Seon Wook Kim, Sunshin Ahn, Si-Gyung Koo, Jihun Koo, Kyung Ho Park, Woo Shik Kang 785

Write Back Routine for JFFS2 Efficient I/O
Seung-Ho Lim, Sung-Hoon Baek, Joo-Young Hwang, Kyu-Ho Park . . . 795

Register Array Structure for Effective Edge Filtering Operation of Deblocking Filter
Jongwoo Bae, Neungsoo Park, Seong-Won Lee 805

Network Protocols 1

Quantitative Service Differentiation: A Square-Root Proportional Model
Xiaobo Zhou, Cheng-Zhong Xu 814

Power-Efficient Route Discovery (PERDP) for ODMA Systems
Ray-Guang Cheng, Jia-Yang Hung, Yao-Yuan Liu ... 824

Energy Efficient Routing for Wireless Sensor Networks with Grid Topology
Hock Guan Goh, Moh Lim Sim, Hong Tat Ewe ... 834

Performance Evaluation of Mobile IP Agents' Auto-reconfiguration Mechanisms in MANET
Cláudia J. Barenco Abbas, Georges Amvame-Nze, L. Javier García Villalba ... 844

Formulas and Protocols for Broadcasting in Mobile Ad Hoc Networks
Chang Wu Yu, Cheng Yao Tseng ... 854

Traffic Adaptive IEEE 802.15.4 MAC for Wireless Sensor Networks
Younggoo Kwon, Yohan Chae ... 864

Wireless Communications 3

An Efficient Relay Sensors Placing Algorithm for Connectivity in Wireless Sensor Networks
Jyh-Huei Chang, Rong-Hong Jan ... 874

Performance Analysis of IEEE 802.15.4 with Non-beacon-enabled CSMA/CA in Non-saturated Condition
Tae Ok Kim, Hongjoong Kim, Junsoo Lee, Jin Soo Park, Bong Dae Choi ... 884

Cross-Layer Duty Cycle Scheduling with Data Aggregation Routing in Wireless Sensor Networks
Yean-Fu Wen, Frank Yeong-Sung Lin ... 894

A Link Stability Model and Stable Routing for Mobile Ad-Hoc Networks
Min-Gu Lee, Sunggu Lee ... 904

Energy-Aware Routing with Limited Route Length for Multimedia Applications
Cheolgi Kim, Kisoo Chang, Joongsoo Ma ... 914

Iterative Decoding-Based Phase Estimation for OFDM Systems at Low Operating SNR
A. Sh. Fayziyev, Kwonhue Choi 924

Middleware and P2P

Semi-lock: An Efficient Cheat-Proof Synchronization Mechanism for Peer-to-Peer Game Systems
Huaping Shen, Sajal K. Das, Mohan Kumar, Zhijun Wang 935

A Case Study on Message-Oriented Middleware for Heterogeneous Sensor Networks
Sangim Ahn, Kiwon Chong 945

A Proxy-Enabled Service Discovery Architecture to Find Proximity-Based Services in 6LoWPAN
Shafique Ahmad Chaudhry, Won Do Jung, Chaudhary Sajjad Hussain, Ali Hammad Akbar, Ki-Hyung Kim 956

PosCFS: An Advanced File Management Technique for the Wearable Computing Environment
Woojoong Lee, Shine Kim, Jonghwa Shin, Chanik Park 966

Control of Information Appliances Using Instant Messaging
Seong Joon Lee, Kwang Seon Ahn 976

Hybrid Dissemination Based Scalable and Adaptive Context Delivery for Ubiquitous Computing
Lenin Mehedy, Md. Kamrul Hasan, Young Koo Lee, Sungyoung Lee, Sang Man Han 987

Multimedia and Data Management 2

A Neuroscientific Approach to Emotion System for Intelligent Agents
Gunn-Yong Park, Seung-Ik Lee, Joong-Bae Kim 997

Automatic Decision Method of Effective Transform Coefficients for Face Recognition
Jean Choi, Yun-Su Chung, Ki-Hyun Kim, Jang-Hee Yoo 1007

Finding the Perfect Projection System – Human Perception of Projection Quality Depending on Distance and Projection Angle
Jochen Ehnes, Michitaka Hirose 1017

Context Reasoning Technologies in Ubiquitous Computing Environment
Sun Jie, Wu ZhaoHui 1027

X-Tree Diff+: Efficient Change Detection Algorithm in XML Documents
Suk Kyoon Lee, Dong Ah Kim 1037

wear-UCAM: A Toolkit for Mobile User Interactions in Smart Environments
Dongpyo Hong, Youngjung Suh, Ahyoung Choi, Umar Rashid, Woontack Woo 1047

Network Protocols 2

A Sensing Resolution-Based Energy Efficient Communication Protocol for Wireless Sensor Networks
Poyuan Li, Soon-Gyu Jeong, Sang-Jo Yoo 1058

Impact of Node Cheating on Gossip-Based Protocol
Nan Zhang, Yuanchun Shi, Bin Chang 1068

Energy-Efficient Clustering Algorithm in Wireless Sensor Networks
DaeHwan Kim, SangHak Lee, We Duke Cho 1078

Enhanced Multipath Routing Protocol Using Congestion Metric in Wireless Ad Hoc Networks
Chunsoo Ahn, Jitae Shin, Eui-Nam Huh 1089

Virtual Hierarchical Architecture Integrating Mobile IPv6 and MANETs for Internet Connectivity
Hyemee Park, Tae-Jin Lee, Hyunseung Choo 1098

Mobile Computing 2

A Comprehensive Study on Handover Performance of Hierarchical Mobile IPv6
Youn-Hee Han, Dongwon Jeong 1108

Adaptive Error Recovery in cdma2000 1xEV-DO Mobile Broadcast Networks
Kyungtae Kang, Yongwoo Cho, Hosang Park, Heonshik Shin 1119

A Novel Approach for Sharing White Board Between PC and PDAs with Multi-users
Xin Xiao, Yuanchun Shi, Weisheng He 1129

Semi-soft FMIPv6 for 802.11 Network
Hyon-Young Choi, Sung-Gi Min, Youn-Hee Han, Hee-Jin Jang 1139

An Optimized Scheme for Mobile IPv6 Handover Between Domains Based on AAA
Seonggeun Ryu, Youngsong Mun 1148

Interoperation of Home and Mobile Network Devices Employing a Jini-Agent System
Sang Tae Kim, Hyun Deok Kim 1158

Author Index 1167

On Securing Networked Real-Time Embedded Systems

Kang G. Shin

Department of Electrical Engineering and Computer Science
The University of Michigan
Ann Arbor, MI 48109-2121, U.S.A.
kgshin@umich.edu

Abstract. There has been an exponential growth of applications that rely on diverse types of embedded real-time end systems and devices, such as smart phones, play stations, home appliances, consumer and industrial electronics, smart sensors and actuators. These applications require diverse types of Quality-of-Service (QoS) including timeliness, dependability, security and privacy, from the end systems/devices which are usually networked together via heterogeneous networking technologies and procotols.

We now know how to guarantee timeliness and, to a lesser extent, how to provide fault-tolerance, on both end systems and their interconnection networks. However, how to secure them is far less known, despite the growing importance of protecting information stored in the end systems/devices and exchanged over their interconnection networks. Morever, timeliness, fault-tolerance, security and privacy—which I will call simply QoS—must be supported simultaneously, often with a tight resource budget such as memory, computation and communication bandwidth, and battery power. Also, different applications require different combinations of QoS components, and hence, one-fits-all solutions are not acceptable.

This talk will start with generic aspects of QoS and then detail how to secure a sensor network for surveillance applications. Sensor networks, usually built with a large number of small, low-cost sensor devices, are characterized by their large-scale and unattended deployment that invites many critical attacks, thereby necessitating high-level security support for their intended applications and services. However, making sensor networks secure is challenging due mainly to the fact that sensors are battery-powered and it is often very difficult to change or recharge their batteries. To meet this challenge, we have been developing Lightweight Security Protocols (LiSP) that cooperatively build a unified, energy-efficient security framework for sensor networks.

E. Sha et al. (Eds.): EUC 2006, LNCS 4096, p. 1, 2006.

Towards Self-coordinating Ubiquitous Computing Environments

Franz J. Rammig

Heinz Nixdorf Institute
University of Paderborn
Paderborn, Germany
franz@upb.de

Abstract. We are surrounded by an enormous amount of microprocessors. Their quantity outnumbers the human population by a factor of more than three. These microprocessors enable most technological artifacts to become intelligent *"things that think"* and a majority of these intelligent objects will be linked together to an *"Internet of things"*. This omnipresent virtual *"organism"* will provide ubiquitous computing to an amount which goes far beyond all presently existing systems. To master this emerging virtual organism, completely new paradigms of operation have to evolve. In this paper we present our vision of establishing self-coordination as the dominant paradigm of operation of future ubiquitous computing environments. This vision is looked at from four different points of view. First of all techniques to model self-coordinating distributed systems in an adequate manner is discussed. Then the principle of self-coordination is applied to individual intelligent objects. In a next step such objects have to be arranged in a networked manner. Again the potential of self-coordination, now applied to communication infrastructures is studied. Finally self-coordination is applied to next generation interfaces between human beings an artificial ones. In this paper we do not attempt to provide a complete discourse of the area. Instead of this we try to illustrate the four aspects mentioned above by proper examples.

Keywords: Self-coordination, Organic Computing, ant-colony algorithms.

1 Introduction

In the world of information technology it is no longer the computer in the classical sense where the majority of IT applications are executed; computing is everywhere. More than 20 billion processors have already been fabricated and the majority of them can be assumed to still be operational. These microprocessors enable most technological artifacts to become intelligent *"things that think"*. At the same time virtually every PC worldwide is connected via the Internet. This combination of traditional and embedded computing creates an artifact of a complexity, heterogeneity which is rarely manageable by classical means. Metaphorically speaking, the emerging ubiquitous computing environment may be treated as an organism made up of computers, networks, system software, applications, and, most importantly, human beings.

E. Sha et al. (Eds.): EUC 2006, LNCS 4096, pp. 2 – 13, 2006.

This virtual organism as it exists today is still in a state of adolescence. Each of our technical artifacts with a built-in processor can be seen as a "*Thing that Thinks*", a term introduced by MIT's Thinglab. It can be expected that in the near future these billions of *Things that Think* will become an "*Internet of Things*", a term originating from ETH Zurich. This means that (using the above metaphor) we will be constantly surrounded by a virtual *"organism"* of *Things that Think.*

In order to deal with such kinds of ubiquitous computing environments, novel principles, methods, and tools to design such a virtual organism and its constituents are needed. A very promising solution may be seen in handing over a large amount of design activities to the system itself. This means that a large portion of decisions which traditionally take place in the design phase, now are handed over to the operational phase. Even more important, these decisions no are made by the system itself, based on information about its environment and its own nature. To a certain degree, the objects and the resulting virtual organism develop themselves. The bare size of the virtual organism to be handled makes any attempt of a centralized solution senseless. Instead of this, self-coordinating principles have to be established on the majority of the individual objects constituting the entire system, and even more important on the interconnection structure. In the sequel various aspects of introducing self-coordination as the basic paradigm of future ubiquitous computing environments are discussed.

In any scientific discipline it is hardly possible to deal with objects which can not be modeled. Therefore a well adapted modeling paradigm for self-coordinating, highly distributed systems is a major step towards establishing the paradigm of self-coordination. This aspect will be discussed in section "Modeling". Some main principles are explained before the basic ideas are illustrated by an example.

If the concept of self-coordination is to be applied to the entire field of ubiquitous computing environments, both the individual constituents and the network made out of theses objects should follow this paradigm. In section "Self-Coordinating Objects" basic principles are discussed, how future intelligent object can be empowered to act in a self-coordinating manner. Again an example of some already completed work is used to illustrate this principle.

An even higher potential of self-coordination arises if the global interaction of such objects is envisioned. By analyzing solutions found in biological systems, especially in ant colonies, approaches can be looked for, how such communication structures and problem solving strategies can be handled by means of self-coordination. This topic is covered by section "Self-Coordinating Networked Objects". Here again, results from previous work is used as example to illustrate the basic approach.

Finally, these intelligent objects that form a virtual organism are, in and of themselves, of no value. They need to be able to serve human needs. In the end, artificial assistants offering intelligent services have to come into existence. To achieve this level of service provisioning, a discipline that may be characterized as *Anthropomatics* (a term originating from the Univ. of Karlsruhe and used by the German Organic Computing initiative) has to evolve. Communication of human beings is not restricted to a bare intellectual level. In addition, emotions play an important role. If intelligent artifacts shall be accepted by humans as adequate communication partners and friendly servants, this aspect of emotions has to be considered as well. I.e. an intelligent artifact or some virtual "organism" must be able to express emotions (without having ones, of course) and to recognize emotions of human communication partners. In section "Self-Coordinated Anthropomatics" this aspect is exemplified using some previous work.

2 State of the Art

Modeling of Self-coordinating Distributed Systems
Some theoretical work has been published characterizing the emergence of global behavior patterns based on local rules. A prominent, currently extensively studied area is given by game-theoretical approaches initiated by Koutsoupias and Papadimitriou [12]. However, it is still unclear how local rules can be designed for a given target behavior, what their possibilities/restrictions in comparison to global rules are, and how to deal with real-time limitations.

Concerning description techniques, methods, and tools needed for the practical construction of such systems, software engineering has developed model-based development and formal analysis techniques for analysis and transformation of requirements and system design down to executable code. However, they are more or less only applicable before the system is deployed – in no way do they address the inherent dynamics in problem-solving and reconfiguration of structures and algorithms or scalability properties needed here. The necessity to model systems where the constituents act strictly individually and only based on local information (i.e. in absence of any kind of global control), is reflected by the basic principle of Petri nets and derivatives.

The initiatives Autonomic Computing [11], Organic Computing [20], and parts of the European Complex Systems Initiative [5, 7] are interesting attempts to attack the mentioned challenges. These initiatives use inspirations from biological systems, transferring such principles into the engineering domain. However, both initiatives rarely deal with the coordination paradigm and systems of highly dynamic structure are investigated only marginally.

Self-coordinating Objects
Self-coordinating objects can be found in user-oriented IT-systems, IT-based games [KRP04], logistics, robotics, just to mention some examples. In the IT-area first systems following the self-x paradigms of Autonomic Computing have been reported in the area of servers and information systems.

The various *Robocup* contests may serve as interesting experimental environments where self-coordinating "intelligent" agents have to be developed [17]. These agents have to act autonomously and in a team-oriented manner together with their team mates. Methods from various research traditions like artificial intelligence, cognition, smart sensors, mechatronics, ad-hoc networks, etc. have to be combined to obtain good results.

Various results concerning evolutionary virtual creatures have been published, e.g. [19, 13, 14]. Systems are reported that allow the creation and the evolution of virtual creatures that adapt to varying environments or that compete for rare resources. Even physical the realization of such creatures has been reported [14].

Self-coordinating Networked Objects

Networking became an important area of systems-oriented research (e.g., self-organization as typically found in MANETs [15]). New systems concepts such as cooperative networking or in-network processing have appeared, mostly in sensor networks (e.g., distributed source/network coding). Although algorithm theory has resulted in excellent solutions in the area of routing (e.g. [16]), self-coordinating techniques are applied as well. Based on Marco Dorigo's pioneering work [6] various attempts have been made. In [9], e.g., the authors directly apply this technique to a reactive, hop-by-hop routing protocol. Approaches to build overlay networks with the aid of ant colony algorithms have been reported as well, e.g. [8]. Following this paradigm, highly adaptive and emergent network construction and optimization techniques can be established.

Self-coordinating Anthropomatics

In an aging population the development of interactive artificial assistants is of great relevance. In this field, one can observe the convergence of different research topics (e.g. machine learning, statistics, reasoning, neuroscience, computer science, and engineering) into a new field called *Anthropomatics*. Artificial assistants interact constantly with their human users; therefore they will be cognitive systems that can reason and learn from their experience. As they are aware of their own capabilities and reflect on their own behavior they can be seen as instances of Organic Computing. To make the interaction with humans more natural, these artificial assistants should be able to express emotions and to recognize emotions of their communication partners. This aspect has been identified long ago [2]. More recent publications address this aspect from various points of view [1, 3].

3 Aspects of Self-coordinating Ubiquitous Computing

3.1 Modeling of Self-coordinating Distributed Systems

The volatility of the upcoming new pervasive and ubiquitous systems, the lack of global control, their emergent behavior, and their stringent requirements on dependability and security require a kind of new *"System Theory for Self-coordinating Systems"* and, in particular, an improved understanding of coordination paradigms.

Most of today's methods are limited to essentially static cases where the behavior of the composed system can be predicted beforehand. In the future, however, we can instead endow generic components with more or less strict rules on how to behave, how to interact with other components, and even how to change these rules if necessary. These components need to act in a self-coordinated way to reach application goals in a volatile environment.

Numerous completely new research questions arise to address these issues. As the entire research, basic and applied one, depends on adequate modeling techniques, in this paper only the modeling aspect is addressed.

Models and Modeling Techniques

Model-based design and development is widely accepted as the most promising way to master complexity in today's system design. Certainly it will remain indispensable for the new types of systems. Unlike for traditional static systems, modeling realistic behavior of these systems is challenging. Most of the established techniques relay on the existence of global states. In highly distributed systems and especially in such ones that are based on local decisions without global control, global states do not exist at all or at least of no importance at all. Therefore modeling techniques are needed that are communication centric, that are not dependent on global states and that are based on local transitions. At the same time a profound mathematical foundation is required.

Modeling techniques are necessary for expressing models and their dynamics at different abstraction levels based on sound semantic foundation and mathematical elegance. This technique needs a "calculus" to enable model manipulation, e.g., refinement between abstraction levels or verification. Multi-dimensional modeling in an integrated manner, including non-functional and mobility aspects is an important part of such techniques. This requires languages operating on meta-level, integrating models written in different languages. A new dimension in the definition of language semantics is a consequence of this approach, i.e. the semantics of the meta-model depend on the semantics of the underlying models. Using such modeling techniques, realistic models have to be constructed for the dynamic volatile behavior of specific classes of systems. They must support application-oriented system as well as design and analysis of algorithms. They should provide new ways to understand and abstract from properties of such systems, such as profiling methods that become the basis for generating formal models suitable for solid experimental and theoretical analysis, e.g., models for user movement that are not only amenable to simulation but also to mathematical analysis. The most demanding property, however, of such a modeling technique is the ability to describe self-modification in an elegant and easy to understand way.

Example: Self Modifying Extended Predicate/Transition Nets

The main properties requested for modeling self-coordinating ubiquitous computing environments can be summarized as:

- Communication centric,
- Local control,
- Absence of global state,
- Asynchronous,
- Modeling support for complex systems,
- Heterogeneity,
- Support of self-modification.

It can be observed that the first 4 properties are already present in case of Petri nets. Higher order Petri nets like Predicate/Transition nets even support the description of complex and heterogeneous systems, at least when hierarchy is added, as done by work at our group. Therefore it seems to be a good advice to follow the path of higher order Petri nets as the basis for the needed modeling technique. The main open gap is self-modification. As it will be shown, even this gap can be closed in an elegant manner.

Petri nets are bipartite directed graphs $PN = (P, T, f, g)$ augmented by a marking M and firing rules. The Petri net graph consists of a finite set of places P, a finite set of transitions T, directed edges $f \subseteq P \times T$ from places to transitions and $g \subseteq T \times P$ from transitions to places. Places model conditions. For this purpose they may be marked by tokens. Driven by specific firing rules a transition can fire based on the local marking of those places it is directly connected with. By firing, the marking of these places is modified.

In the case of High-Level nets the tokens are typed individuals. The other net components are annotated accordingly: places with data types, edges with variable expressions and transitions with a guard and a set of variable assignments. Now a transition can fire only if the formal edge expressions can be unified with actually available tokens and this unification passes the guard expression of the transition. By firing, the input tokens are consumed and calculations associated with the transition are executed. By this new tokens are produced that are routed to output places according to variable expressions annotating the output edges of the transition.

Pr/T–Nets are very powerful, offering the modeling power of Turing machines. To support easy modeling of highly complex systems in our research group we additionally added a hierarchy concept that combines hierarchy over places (following Harel's hierarchy concepts for *StateCharts* [10]) and over transitions (in accordance with the concepts of *Structured Nets* by Cherkasova/Kotov [4]).

Finally we added description means for timing to Pr/T–Nets. By this we obtained an elegant, adequate and powerful modeling means that serves as foundation of our entire work on design systems for distributed embedded systems. However up to now this modeling technique is adequate only for structurally static systems. Structurally dynamic systems demand for some further extensions that are to be described in the sequel.

In the case of static systems the resulting system can be modeled in advance. In the case of a dynamically reconfigurable one, only the generating system of a set of potentially resulting systems can be provided. Obviously this is an even more demanding task. Resulting systems are modeled by extended Pr/T–Nets in our case. By reasons of intended elegance and in order to achieve a self-contained concept we decided to use an extension of these modeling means to describe the generation process as well [18].

For realizing dynamic reconfiguration, we propose to apply the mechanism of net refinement – usually only used during the specification of a system – at run-time. Technically, changes to the refinement of components are associated to the firing of certain transitions. For this purpose, we allow to annotate transitions with a rule for the refinement of other nodes in the surrounding Petri net specification.

Usually it is not reasonable to specify rules applicable to arbitrary transitions. Therefore, restrictions on the application of a rule can be specified. On the one hand, a scope may be specified, that is a subnet in which the transformation may take place. On the other hand, attributes of the component, whose refinement is changed, can be specified in the guard of a transition. That way it is possible for instance, to specify precisely to which transition the transformation should be applied by specifying its fully qualified path name.

Using refinements for net modifications combines two advantages. On the one hand, Petri net refinements are a thoroughly elaborated concept for developing a specification in a well-structured way. They allow for defining transformations that preserve certain relevant properties of the specification. On the other hand they are powerful enough for describing a variety of dynamic modifications. However, in some cases it is necessary to extend the limited set of refinement operations. We therefore offer a generic approach in addition to the one described above. We allow annotating transitions with rules as they are used in High-Level replacement systems. Annotating an arbitrary transition *TMod* of a Petri net *N* with this rule specifies that, after firing of *TMod*, a subnet *Left* of *N* is replaced by the net *Right*. As for the transitions annotated with refinement rules, also for transitions with replacement rules the firing rule is extended. In addition to the standard checking for fireability of transitions it is checked whether the left hand side of the rule is part of the current Petri net. During transition firing, the rule is executed in addition to the standard firing actions.

3.2 Self-coordinating Objects

Numerous IT-based objects are enhanced by built-in intelligence. This means that a sense-decide-act loop is included in such systems. By exploring the environment using smart sensor functionalities decisions can be made how to behave in the current situation. These decisions depend not only on actual environmental information but also on a certain history of both, input from the environment and internal state. The latter means that the system has to have certain reflective capabilities. Based on this reflective knowledge, information from the environment including previous environmental reaction on activities of the system, and some global knowledge the system is able to learn and by this self-optimize its behavior. Systems of this kind are emerging in the areas of smart user interfaces, in gaming, and in the field of mechatronics.

Possible applications are robotics, driver assistant systems, advanced vehicle dynamics control, traffic systems with coordinated vehicle control, energy management, and route planning. Cognitive actuators with integrated smart sensors and inherent intelligence will take over major parts of the sense-decide-act loop. An intelligent actuator will be able to supervise itself and to take care of its health. All these constituents of embedded software have to be seen as a whole. Today's reconfigurable hardware and the upcoming developments in this field allow making late decisions whether control algorithms have to be implemented in HW or SW. This distribution even may change at runtime, dependent on the actual value of various resources.

Example: Self-emerging Virtual Creatures

Imagine a virtual creature that can adapt itself to become able to match a certain objective. There is some research into this direction, e.g. as reported in [3, 13, 14]. In the latter case (the Golem project) even physical realizations of such virtual creatures are looked at. In a thesis at our lab, Tim Schmidt concentrated on an automated design procedure for such creatures. The basic principle can be characterized by an evolutionary algorithm where all constituents of such a virtual creature (morphology, dynamics, sensing, and control) are object to this evolutionary process. Even more than other work, Tim Schmidt provides a powerful simulation environment that allows observing and evaluating the evolutionary process easily during the design process.

The virtual creatures considered are formed by a tree structure of cubic solids connected by joints. Number, shape, and dimensioning of the solids are object to evolution. The joints may allow any degree of movement in all three axles. Joints may be located at any location on the surface of the solids. The only actuators are motors inside the joints. They may provide movements at any speed into any direction within an assignable limit. Sensors, too, may be located at any location on the surface of solids. They just sense contacts between solids and other solids or between solids and the environment.

The control system of these creatures is a distributed one. It consists of a set of Limited Recurrent Neural Networks. There is a local controller per joint. It controls the rotation of the two connected solids relatively to each other. The controllers observe the values gathered by the relevant sensors. In addition the various controllers communicate in order to provide their control services. So a completely self-coordinating system is obtained.

Construction of the virtual creatures takes place using a genetic algorithm. The morphology of creatures is coded using *Binary String Covering*. The leaf nodes of a creature (all creatures are tree-structured) are coded by constants while the inner node coding is calculated by application of appropriate functions. Based on such a gene coding, the usual genetic operations like mutation and crossover are applied. The resulting creatures are evaluated concerning the respective objective. Promising creatures form the next generation of the population.

3.3 Self-coordinating Networked Objects

The most dramatic change in systems' nature comes up if services are provided by **networks** in the most general sense. In history any kind of traffic (i.e. networking) was one of the most important driving factors in enhancing culture and technology. Therefore it can be expected that omnipresent and seamless networking of technical artifacts will have a comparable impact on modern technology. The service-providing entities are usually considered as autonomous and cooperating towards a common goal, but competition and selfishness of various kinds is also present. There is a wide range of "helper" disciplines engaged to improve such services; for example, optimization theory has found its application in virtually every kind of network. In most cases, a central resource planning is usually not feasible, nor is a static planning – perturbations in network structure and requests have to be accounted for and corrected.

Services and networks need to be composed. Networks usually do not exist in isolation; rather, they come in contact with each other. A team of soccer playing robots [17] may serve as an example. The natural computing architecture of future ubiquitous computing systems is that of a distributed, concurrent, and communicating set of processing nodes (sensors, actuators, controller units). To meet the demands of high reliability and hard real-time processing of such complex heterogeneous networks, integrated software/hardware architectures have to be explored together with optimally matching operating system services. Self-coordination is mandatory for resource-efficient design and management of such distributed controller architectures. Operating systems themselves will become network-based. I.e. the whole set of offered services will no longer be provided by each single instance of the OS by a cluster of instances as a whole. The same techniques to migrate application software from one computing node to another can also be applied to the OS. This turns such a network-based OS into a volatile, self coordinating artifact.

Example: Self-coordinating Operating Systems / Communication Structures
Ordinary operating systems (OS) are forced to provide all services that might be asked for by any application as the set of possible application over the OS's lifetime is not predictable. In embedded systems, usually exactly these services are provided that are really needed by the set of (a priori known) applications. This saves a lot of resources, especially concerning memory. In the case of self-coordinating systems, however, the set of possible applications is no longer fixed and cannot be predicted off-line. In order to avoid the overhead of general purpose operating systems, techniques of self-adaptation, now applied to the OS are used. An extreme approach into this direction is Paderborn University's NanoOS. This OS is especially tailored towards swarms of tiny nodes, e.g. sensor networks. The basic idea of NanoOS is to use an entire swarm of instances running on top of a swarm of nodes as the service provider. This means that a broad band of services is available, however not necessarily entirely on a specific node. Rarely requested services may be distributed sparsely over the network. When such a service is requested and it is not available at the location of request it may be activated remotely on another node of the respective cluster. A cluster in this context is defined as the set of OS instances that provides the entire set of services.

Of course the distribution of services over the network is crucial. In the case of NanoOS ant colony algorithms are applied to approach an optimal distribution of services. Whenever a service is requested remotely all nodes on the path from the requesting node to the providing one is marked by *"pheromone"*. Services now have a tendency to move into the direction of the highest "pheromone" concentration.

Similar techniques are used to provide a self-coordinating communication structure in between the nodes of such a swarm. Ant colony algorithms are used to construct a less dense (and therefore less power consuming) backbone net. Again special ant colony algorithms are used to adapt the network dynamically to any kind of distortion. Shortest paths can be found using Dorigo's "classical" algorithm simulating the nest – food source behavior of ants.

3.4 Self-coordinating Anthropomatics

The term *anthropomatics* describes a scientific field that uses methods of computer, electrical, and mechanical engineering to develop models of interaction of humans with artificial agents, artifacts, servants, or assistants. Future technical systems will learn about the user and the environment without the user's explicit input to the machine. Recognition of the intention of the user by analyzing prior actions and his/her emotions together with the generation of intuitive feedback will constitute more enjoyable man-machine interaction. Methods for natural communication, emphasizing higher-level cognitive functions have to be applied. The coordinated combination of these techniques will allow humans to communicate in a situation-specific and context-sensitive manner with artificial assistants that are endued with cognitive capabilities.

The recognition of speech can be enhanced by the extensive use of vision to analyze gestures and postures of the user. To enhance haptic communication with cognitive systems, advanced sensors will have to be designed. A flexible electronic skin, e.g., could give robots an almost-human sense of touch. The processing of the input of olfactory sensors will allow a further step into total immersion technologies. The resulting vicarious interactive participation in activities and the carrying out of physical work will bring benefits to a wide range of users. Examples include emergency and security services, entertainment and education industries, and those of restricted mobility such as the disabled or elderly.

Example: Expression and Recognition of Emotions
Human beings communicate not only based on pure facts but also express and recognize emotions. This additional communication "channel" seems to be extremely efficient. Therefore any communication which does not include this aspect is experienced as un-natural by humans. A human-centric man – machine communication therefore should include the aspect of emotions. The problem, however is, that obviously a machine has no emotions at all. But this does not mean that a machine cannot express emotions. What is needed is an internal model of emotions and how they can be stimulated.

C-LAB, the cooperation between Paderborn University and SIEMENS, has developed MEXI. This is an artificial head that is able to express emotions like joy, demand for contacting humans, desire to play, anger. Of course MEXI does not have such emotions. But is carries an internal model of them and is able to express the respective modeled emotional state by properly moving mouth, eyes, ears, or the entire head. The internal model includes rules, how basic emotions are triggered by specific stimuli from the outside and on the other hand how they fade away by a decay process. Elementary emotions then are overlaid to result in complex ones.

Human emotions are not only triggered by external stimuli but also by cyclic moods or drives. In MEXI, this cyclic behavior is modeled as well. The resulting values provide an additional overlay level. By this an even more realistic expression of emotions is obtained.

If we have a model of emotions and if we know how they are expressed by facial patterns, this can also be used to recognize emotions of humans. From psychology the basics are known. Relatively few patterns are sufficient to conclude rather precisely which emotional state a person is in. In the case of C-LAB's research, a combination of facial patterns and speech is used for analysis.

4 Summary

Self-coordination will play a dominant role in future IT systems which will consist of billions of interconnected things that think. Completely new approaches are needed to design and operate such intelligent IT environments. Substantial theoretical research is necessary to develop a "System Theory of Self-coordinating Systems". On the other hand real systems of this kind have to be developed, built, and investigated. Both, self-coordinating objects and networks made out of them have to be studied. Finally the human being has to remain the central point of consideration. Preliminary results are already available. Some examples of such already existing approaches have been shown in the paper.

Acknowledgments. This paper summarizes from the authors' view point the results of intensive discussions with his co-workers and students. Especially the examples used originate from joint work with these persons. The author would like to thank especially Carsten Rust for his work on self-modification of enhanced Predicate/Transition nets, Christian Geiger and Tim Schmidt for their work on evolutionary virtual creatures, Tales Heimfarth and Peter Janacik for their results on self-coordinating operating systems and communication structures. Finally we would like to thank Bernd Kleinjohann and Natascha Esau for their pioneering work on emotion modeling and emotion recognition.

We also would like to thank our colleagues Wilhelm Dangelmaier, Friedhelm Meyer auf der Heide, Odej Kao, Holger Karl, Bärbel Mertsching, and Ansgar Trächtler for fruitful discussions about the presented research area.

References

1. R.C. Arkin, M. Fujita, T. Takagi, and R. Hasegawa: An ethological and emotional basis for human-robot interaction. In: Robotics and Autonomous Systems, vol. 42, no. 3, pp. 191-201, Elevier, 2003
2. J. Bates: The role of emotion in believable agents. CACM, 37(7), pp 122-125, 1992
3. C. Breazeal: Affective interaction between humans and robots. In: Proc of ECAL01, pp. 582-591, Prague, 2001
4. L. A. Cherkasova and V. E. Kotov: Structured Nets. In J. Gruska and M. Chytil, editors, LNCS 118, Springer Verlag, 1981.
5. The European Complex Systems Initiative, http://www.cordis.lu/ist/fet/co.htm , 2003
6. M. Dorigo and G. DiCaro: The Ant Colony Optimization Meta-Heuristic. New Ideas in Optimization, McGraw Hill, pp.11-32, 1999
7. The DELIS project, http://delis.upb.de/ , 2004
8. S. Goss, S. Aron, J.-L. DeNeubourg, and J. M. Pasteels: Self-organized Short-cuts in the Argentine Ant. Naturwissenschaften, 76, pp. 579-581, 1989
9. M. Günes, U. Sporges, and I. Buazizi: ARA – The Ant-Colony Based Routing Algorithm for MANETs. In: Proc. IWAHN'02, pp. 79-85, 2002
10. D. Harel. Statecharts: A visual formalism for complex systems. In: Science of Computer Programming, 8(3), pp. 231–274,June 1978.
11. The Vision of Autonomic Computing, http://www.research.ibm.com/autonomic/manifesto/, 2003
12. E. Koutsoupias and C. H. Papadimitriou: Worst-case Equilibria. Symposium on Theoretical Aspects of Computer Science STACS 1999, Springer, 1999
13. M. Komusinski, Sz. Ulatowski: Framesticks: towards a simulation of a nuture-like world, creatures and evolution. In: Proc. Of the 5th European Conference on Artificial Life (ECAL99), Springer Verlag, pp. 261-265, 1999

14. Hod Lipson, Jordan B. Pollack: Automatic Design and Manifacture of Robotic Lifeforms, Nature 406, pp. 974-978, 2000
15. M. Mauve, J. Widmer, and H. Hartenstein: A Survey on Position-based Routing for Mobile Wireless Ad-Hoc Networks. IEEE Network 15(6), 2001
16. P. Papadimitratos, Z.J. Haas, and E.G. Sirer: Path Set Selection in Mobile Ad Hoc Networks. Proc. Of ACM Mobihoc'02, 2002
17. RoboCup Official Site. http://www.robocup.org/
18. C. Rust and F. Rammig: A Petri Net Based Approach for the Design of Dynamically Modifiable Embedded Systems. In Proc. IFIP DIPES2004, Kluwer, 2004
19. Karl Sims: Evolving 3D Morphology and Behaviour by Competition. Artificial Life, pp. 353-372, MIT Press, 1994
20. DFG SPP 1183 Organic Computing: http://www.organic-computing.de/spp , 2004

Frontier of Digital Technology and Future Strategy

Hyun Jin Ko

Korea IT Industry Promotion Agency
President and CEO
hjko@software.or.kr

Abstract. Digitalization has become the unavoidable trend all around the world. The digital future holds infinite possibilities. The obvious questions are who will win and who can survive in this fast-changing world, not only in devices but also in services and contents.

Digital technology is the key locomotive that promotes the development of digital device, services and contents. The power of digital technology is getting stronger everyday in this digital era. For example, digital devices and services have merely been capable of responding to demanded requests. But now we are entering an era where the digital technology is capable of actively getting into our life, getting things done smoothly and silently. New forms of human-computer interface, such as wearable computers that are communicating with innumerable sensors deployed almost everywhere, will be common in the very near future. As ubiquitous computing evolves into an essential component of our daily lives, we need to address a variety of issues regarding social infrastructure, legal and political problems, etc. as well as technological capability.

The world has witnessed Korea turning what sounded like science fiction into everyday life. Korea is the world leader in applying new digital technologies and creating added value from them. To seize this unique opportunity for Korea, technological and social consensus among government, industry, academia, and other social bodies are needed. What are our technological strategies in developing new value-creating opportunities? What should be the role of the government in responding to the emerging digital trends? I hope that EUC will provides new insights into these challenging questions.

E. Sha et al. (Eds.): EUC 2006, LNCS 4096, p. 14, 2006.

SAQA: Spatial and Attribute Based Query Aggregation in Wireless Sensor Networks

Yang Jie[1], Yan Bo[2], Sungyoung Lee[1,*], and Jinsung Cho[1]

[1] Department of Computer Engineering
Kyung Hee University, Korea
{yangjie, sylee}@oslab.khu.ac.kr, chojs@khu.ac.kr
[2] Intelligent Engineering Lab
Institute of Software, Chinese Academy of Sciences, China
yan_bo04@mails.gucas.ac.cn

Abstract. In most wireless sensor networks, applications submit their requests as queries and wireless sensor network transmits the requested data to the applications. However, most existing work in this area focuses on data aggregation, not much attention has been paid to query aggregation. For many applications, especially ones with high query rates, query aggregation is very important. In this paper, we design an effective query aggregation algorithm SAQA to reduce the number of duplicate/overlapping queries and save overall energy consumption in the wireless sensor networks. This new aggregation algorithm focuses on the duplicate/overlapping spatial and attribute information in the original queries submitted by the applications. Our performance evaluations show that by applying our query aggregation algorithm, the overall energy consumption can be significantly reduced and the sensor network lifetime can be prolonged correspondingly.

1 Introduction

Wireless sensor networks consist of large numbers of devices, each capable of some limited computation, communication and sensing, operating in an unattended mode. One unifying view is to treat them as distributed databases. The applications and these distributed databases will communicate through a set of queries, which is quite similar to the concept of SQL queries in the traditional database context.

Traditionally, applications forward queries to the base station which processes the queries one by one and sends queries to proper regions of the sensor network using the underlying routing infrastructure. However, query rate can be high due to a large number of applications sending queries. These applications heavily rely on the query search so that the energy consumption spent on sending and routing queries may far exceed that due to sending the response data. In these cases, optimizing query dissemination is critical to improve the overall performance of the sensor networks.

AODV [3] (used in Cougar [9]) is a reactive routing protocol for ad-hoc mobile networks. It builds a route between two nodes only on the demand of the source node.

* Corresponding author.

E. Sha et al. (Eds.): EUC 2006, LNCS 4096, pp. 15 – 24, 2006.

Directed Diffusion [4] is a data-centric communication paradigm that integrates application-specific semantics into the routing layer. Data is named as attribute-value pairs and is disseminated from source nodes to the node of a query along multiple paths for reliability. In comparison, AQUIRE [7] uses random walks which adopt a look-ahead mechanism in each step to answer one-shot, non-aggregate, complex, replicate data queries.

In TAG [8] in TinyDB approach, an aggregate is computed bottom-up in the routing tree and many optimization techniques are used to improve the performance, e.g., snooping over the shared radio channel to reduce message load and improve accuracy of aggregates, hypothesis testing and adaptive network topology maintenance. Jonathan Beaver, et al. TiNA [1] provides further optimizations over TAG. It exploits temporal coherency tolerances. The approach is to send the data only when there is a significant change in the data value. A data value can be ignored if the variation from the previous value is within the range specified by the *tct* condition.

In [2], our work has some similarities to techniques proposed. The authors proposed a multi-layered overlay-based framework consisting of a query manager and access points (nodes), where the former provides the query aggregation plan and the latter executes the plan. The main goal is to minimize the number of queries sent out, to dispatch the aggregated queries to proper regions and to prevent data transmission in the same region happening multiple times. To achieve this goal, they present an effective query aggregation algorithm, which is mainly based on reducing the duplicate/overlapping spatial information of the original queries sent by the applications.

However, there is still some redundancy in the aggregated queries. We can easily find that not only the spatial information can be duplicated/overlapped, but also the attribute information. Thus, we propose our query aggregation algorithm SAQA based on the spatial and attribute information to help consolidate the queries and reduce the overall energy consumption for query dissemination and data transmission.

The remainder of this paper is organized as follows. Section 2 introduces the query model we use in our aggregation mechanism. In Section 3, we formalize the query aggregation problem and propose our algorithm SAQA for query aggregation. In Section 4, performance evaluation and analysis results are given. Finally we conclude our study with scope for future work in Section 5.

2 Query Model

In this section, we give the query models used to conduct query aggregation.

First we make the following assumptions about the network: 1) a location-based routing scheme is supported by the sensor network; 2) we assume that there is a centralized base station that connects to applications; 4) we assume that that multiple applications can simultaneously send a number of queries to the sensor network.

Applications request information from a sensor network through queries. Depending on the nature of the application, many types of queries can be delivered on the sensor network. In general, these queries can be summarized by the following tuple [2]:

$Q = < S, V, T, F, D >$, where

S = Spatial information, indicating the geographical locations that the application is interested in.

V = Attribute information, indicating the list of attributes which the application is interested in.

T = Temporal information, indicating the duration of the query.

F = Frequency information, indicating the frequency at which the data should be reported.

D = Deadline restriction information, indicating the urgency at which the data should be reported.

In the example: *"Report regularly temperature level and wind speed from region S_1, S_2 and S_3 from time T_1 to T_2 every second"*, where $S = \{ S_1, S_2 \}$, $V = \{$ temperature level, wind speed $\}$, $T = \{T_1$ to $T_2\}$, $F = 1$ second, and $D = \{$not urgent$\}$.

In order to conduct query aggregation, we make the following assumptions about the query model: *1) Query content*: each query can ask for one or several spatial information (S) and attributes (V). The list of attributes and geographical locations will be referred to as $\{V_1, V_2 \dots V_n\}$ and $\{S_1, S_2 \dots S_n\}$ respectively in this paper. We assume that most of the queries have spatial information. A query without spatial information can be processed through the traditional query processing techniques such as flooding or direct diffusion [4], etc. *2) Query arrival rate*: we assume that queries are coming at a relatively high rate, or in other words, the deadline restriction level (D) of queries is not high so that we can temporarily buffer queries for aggregation. *3) Query temporal information*: we assume that the majority of queries are snap-shot queries, i.e. queries that ask for current value of the sensors as opposed to continuous queries, which asks for sensor values during a period of time.

3 Query Aggregation Design

A. Problem Definition

We first identify problems with the current query dissemination schemes.

Generally, when receives queries from applications, the base station directly forward them to the sensor network. The transmission of these queries may naively be flooding or follow some logic that the intermediate sensor nodes apply [4] [5]. When the queries are routed to proper sensors, the sensors start sending data back to the base station, which will deliver data to the applications accordingly. When there are multiple queries from applications, this process repeats until all the queries have been satisfied. At base station or some intermediate nodes, some caching algorithms may be performed to avoid redundant query forwarding.

Fig. 1 shows some of the problems of the above scheme, where queries can be location specific and contain multiple attributes. When two queries Q_1 *and* Q_2 come simultaneously and the queried information is not available in the base station local database, both queries will be transmitted to the network. In this case, the base station just needs to send Q_1. The information of Q_2 can be inferred from Q_1. For Q_1 and Q_3, they ask for partially different attributes in overlapped query areas, recombining into three simple queries as $< (S_2, S_3)\ (V_1, V_2, V_3) >$, $< (S_1)\ (V_1, V_2) >$ and $< (S_4,)\ (V_2, V_3) >$ will be beneficial. It reduces the energy overhead of sending separate duplicate query messages to the same region and more importantly avoids much disturbing other intermediate nodes (and node in overlapped region) in the location-based routing process. When sending the queries to their corresponding regions, the combined query will be routed to a proper node (such as the cluster head) in one of these regions only once. After that, this node will separate the combined query. From here, the query part corresponding to the other region will be routed to its destination and different attributes can be collected at the same time in the same region to satisfy the original queries. Compared to the original case, the number of intermediate nodes (and nodes in the overlapping region) involved in the routing process will therefore be reduced. As the last example, when Q_1 and Q_4 ask for different attributes on the same region. Instead of sending two different queries, we can combine them into two queries as < (S_1, S_2) (V_1, V_2, V_3) > and < (S_3) (V_1, V_2) >.

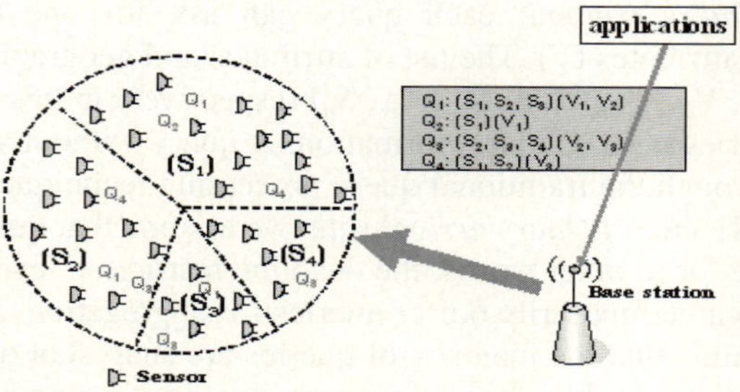

Fig. 1. Query example

As illustrated by this example, our motivation in this paper is to 1) perform the query aggregation efficiently and dispatch the aggregated queries to proper regions so that the routing process will disturb a minimal number of intermediate nodes, and 2) prevent data transmission of sensor nodes in the same region from happening multiple times, 3) collect information for different attributes at the same time to satisfy different queries when they are querying the same area. By achieving these objectives, we can reduce the overall energy overhead for both query transmission and data delivery. Thus, the lifetime of the sensor network can be prolonged.

There are N queries: $Q_1 \ldots Q_N$ denoted by set Q. For the query aggregation operation, we mainly use two important concepts, union and intersection, in set theory. In the next section, we study the algorithms in detail.

B. SAQA

The following examples show us how our algorithm works.

Suppose we have one query Q = < (S_1, S_2, S_3), (V_1, V_2) >. According to the set theory, there are only three relationships between two sets: Disjoint, Intersectant and Inclusive.

We will give the following four queries as examples to do the aggregation, which uses the above set operations.

$$Q_1 = < (S_1, S_2), (V_1, V_2, V_3) >;$$
$$Q_2 = < (S_4, S_5), (V_1, V_2) >;$$
$$Q_3 = < (S_2, S_3, S_5), (V_2, V_3) >;$$
$$Q_4 = < (S_2, S_3), (V_2) >.$$

For Q_1, the aggregated query consists of two sub queries:

$$< (S_1, S_2), (V_1, V_2, V_3) \ldots >; < (S_3), (V_1, V_2) \ldots >$$

Since (S_1, S_2) is included in (S_1, S_2, S_3), we can separate the area to two parts, one is the intersection part, the other is the set of elements outside the intersected area. Also, (V_1, V_2) is included in (V_1, V_2, V_3), we integrate them to only one set. After aggregation, two queries will be sent to two areas in wireless sensor network. One are is (S_1, S_2), and the other one is S_3. Nodes in these two areas will be disturbed only once, but still gather the necessary information.

For Q_2, no aggregation is needed in that the spatial information in Q and Q_2 is disjoint information.

For Q_3, the aggregated query consists of three sub queries:

$$< (S_2, S_3), (V_1, V_2, V_3) \ldots >; < (S_1), (V_1, V_2) \ldots >; < (S_5), (V_2, V_3) \ldots >$$

As for the spatial information, Q and Q_3 have one intersection (S_2, S_3). That's why we aggregate the two queries into three parts, one is the intersection, and the other two are the rest part of Q and Q_3. Then for the attribute information, in the case of (S_2, S_3), we unify the two parts from Q and Q_3 to get one set (V_1, V_2, V_3). That is, what we have introduced, the union operation. And for the rest two areas S_1 and S_5, the attribute in the new aggregated queries will be the same as in the original queries.

For Q_4, the aggregated query consists of two sub queries:

$$< (S_1, S_2, S_3), (V_1, V_2) \ldots >$$

(S_2, S_3) is included in (S_1, S_2, S_3) and also (V_2) is included in (V_1, V_2), Q_4 can be fully aggregated into Q. So there is only one query after aggregation.

The above examples list all the possibilities of query aggregating operations. The key issue here is to efficiently find the good query merge order. In fact, as the base station has the information of all query information, it can globally calculate all overlapping regions in the whole query space and find the zones with the heaviest overlapping (calculated by as weight). Based on the overlapping weight, the queries located near to the heaviest overlapping zone will be merged together with higher priority. Thus, efficient query merge order can be easily achieved with reasonable performance.

The detail of SAQA is given in figure 2 which also shows the flowchart of SAQA:

Parameters:

Q: set of input queries with cardinality $|Q|$, each query $Q_i \in Q$ is denoted by $<S_i, V_i>$, where S_i represents the query region and Vi represents the query attributes

Y: set of output aggregated queries by SAQA algorithm

4 Performance Evaluation

In this section, we use simulation to evaluate the performance of the system that uses our algorithm. We will first describe the experimental model and then report performance results.

Spatial and Attribute based Query Aggregation algorithm (SAQA)

```
Begin:
    //Process the input queries in set Q by filtering queries with full cover property
    For queries Q_i, Q_j ∈ Q, where i ≠ j,
        If queries are overlapping, i.e., S_i ∩ S_j ≠ Ø
        //Calculate the overlapping zone and assign the weight for each zone
        //Sort the weights and assign the query merge order
Do aggregation:
    For queries Q_a, Q_b ∈ Q, where a ≠ b, //Q_a and Q_b have the largest weight of overlapping zone
        If    S_a ⊂ S_b, the same with S_b ⊂ S_a
              S_ab = S_a ∩ S_b
              V_ab = V_a ∪ V_b
              S_rb = S_b - S_ab   //S_rb is the rest part of Q_b after aggregation
              V_rb = V_b
              Y = Q_ab + Q_rb
        Else
              if     S_a = S_b
                     S_ab = S_a
                     V_ab = Va ∪ V_b
                     Y = Q_ab
              Else
                     S_ab = S_a ∩ S_b
                     V_ab = V_a ∪ V_b
                     S_rb = S_b - S_ab   //S_rb is the rest part of Q_b after aggregation
                     V_rb = V_b
                     S_ra = S_a - S_ab   //S_ra is the rest part of Q_a after aggregation
                     V_rb = V_a
                     Y = Q_ab + Q_rb + Q_ra
```

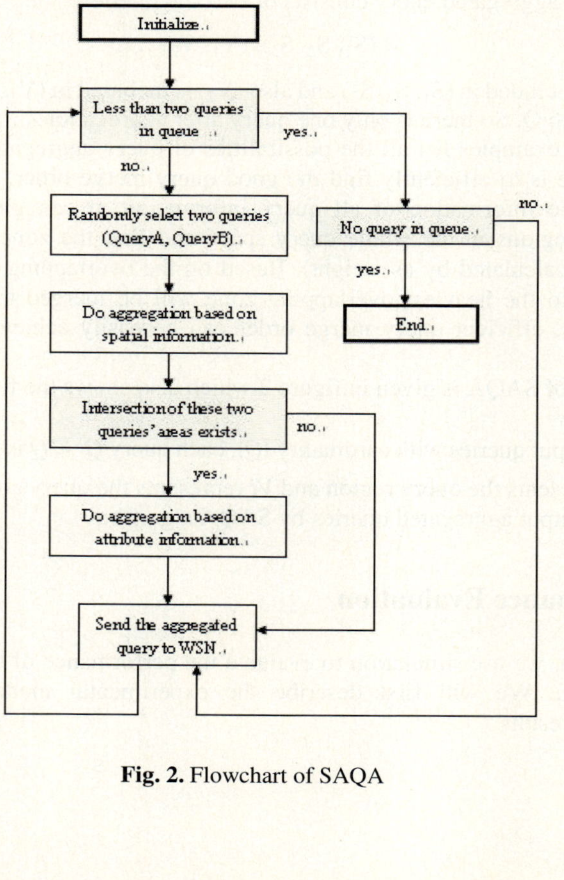

Fig. 2. Flowchart of SAQA

A. Experimental Model

1) Network and Energy Model

We assume that there are *N* queries, each of which is *m*-bit long. The queries uniformly request data from the whole network. We assume that each sensor works in free space mode with some experimental data introduced in [6]: the energy consumption of sending message is calculated by $E_{tx}(a, b) = E * a + E * a * b^2$ and the energy consumption of receiving a message is calculated by $E_{rx}(a, b) = E_{elet} * a$, where *a* is the message size and *b* is the message transmission distance between the sender and receiver, *E*= 50 *nJ*/bit, and *E* = 100PJ/bit*m^2 (1 *nJ* = 1000 *pJ* and 1 *MnJ* = 1000 *nJ*). Since the energy consumed for processing queries and sensing data consists of only a very small portion of the overall energy consumption (node that energy consumed to process 100 million instructions almost equals that to transfer 10 bits of data), we do not take it into account in our calculation.

2) Evaluation System

We define the *Query region overlapping degree R* as the ratio of overlapping region size and the original query region size. For example, two queries Q_1 (query region size S_1) and Q_2 (query region size S_2) have the overlapping region with size S_{12}. In this case, $R = S_{12} / (S_1 + S_2)$. The range of *R* is [0, 0.5], where 0 represents the case where the query regions do not overlap and 0.5 represents the case where the query regions are exactly the same. We also define the *Query attribute overlapping degree T* as the ratio of overlapping attribute number and the original query attribute number. The range of *T* is also [0, 0.5], where 0 represents the case where the query attribute do not overlap and 0.5 represents the case where the query attributes are exactly the same.

We compare the following query processing approaches with our SAQA:

1) Pure query processing (PQP): In this approach, the base station just simply forwards queries to the sensor network without any aggregation. Obviously, this approach is not optimal because intermediate sensor nodes do not have a global view of the whole network. Sensor nodes in an overlapping region may have to send the same data multiple times to reply for different queries asking for attribute in the same region.

2) Spatial based query aggregation (SQA): In this approach, the base station acts as a manager in a normal centralized system, it makes the query aggregation decision based on the spatial information of all the input queries. As a result, a number of queries which are not sharing any common regions are generated. The queries are sent to corresponding regions and executed locally. Data from sensors will be sent back to the base station by each region. No query or data forwarding between regions is implemented. The main advantage of this scheme is its simplicity and ease in implementation. However, it can generate a larger number of new queries and disturb more sensor nodes in both query dissemination and data transmission process. Besides, the queries can be aggregated more based on the attribute information in the original queries, so that the number and size of the aggregated queries can be reduced.

B. Performance Results

We report the performance results comparing the following metrics. The conclusions we draw generally hold for many other cases which we have evaluated.

1) The Sensitivity of Query Number

Fig. 3 shows the data on the sensitivity of energy performance for different input query numbers. In this Figure, *X* axis represents the total number of input queries and Y axis represents the total energy consumption. From this figure, we have the following observations: i) overall, our SAQA outperforms both PQP and SQA algorithms. For example, with a large number of queries, i.e., from 100 to 200, the SAQA can achieve around 80%-350% performance improvement over the PQP and SQA. The result matches our expectation because as SAQA adequately consolidates the queries. The energy cost for both query transmission and data delivery has been significantly reduced. ii) SQA performs better than PQP. The reason is because SQA conducts the query aggregation at the centralized base station. It can reduce the energy consumption by removing the redundant queries for the overlapping regions. iii) The overall energy consumption is sensitive to the number of queries. A larger N generally implies more queries, and therefore, more energy consumption. However, in SAQA, this problem is alleviated because, when the number of queries increases, there will be more chances of overlaps between query regions, which can be effectively reduced by our query aggregation approach.

2) The Sensitivity of Query Region Size

Fig. 4 shows the data on the sensitivity of energy performance for different query region sizes. In this figure, the X axis represents the different query region sizes and Y axis represents the total energy consumption. As the query size is enlarged, the overall energy consumption also increases. This is because a larger region size means that more sensor nodes are involved, or more query/data transmissions are performed. Regardless of the query size, our SAQA performs better than the other 2 schemes with the same reasons given above.

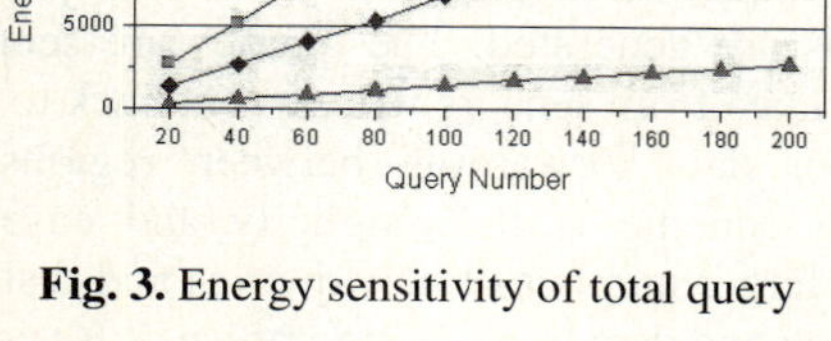

Fig. 3. Energy sensitivity of total query

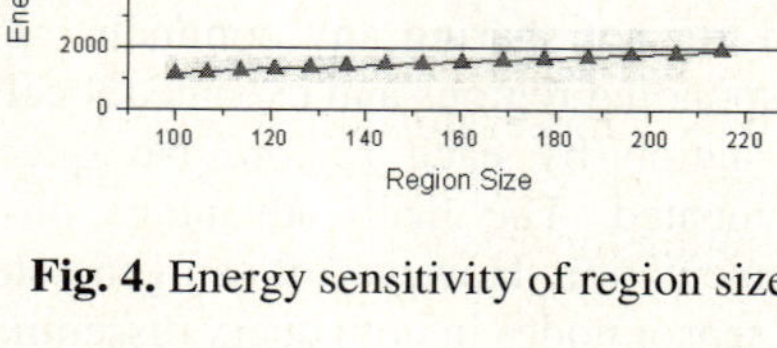

Fig. 4. Energy sensitivity of region size

3) The Sensitivity of Query Region Overlapping Degree

Fig. 5 shows the data on the sensitivity of energy performance for different query region overlapping degrees. In this figure, the X axis represents the different query region overlapping degrees and Y axis represents the total energy consumption. When the query regions are not overlapping, SAQA can not take advantage of query aggregation. Therefore, performance of SAQA is almost the same as other algorithms.

However, as query regions become highly overlapped, SAQA shows significant improvement. As shown in this figure, when the overlapping degree becomes 0.1, overall energy consumption of SAQA reduced dramatically. The behavior of SQA is explainable because, although SQA can prevent the duplicate queries for overlapping regions, duplicated attribute information not compressed require extra energy cost for the query/data transmission.

4) The Sensitivity of Query Attribute Overlapping Degree
Fig. 6 shows the data on the sensitivity of energy performance for different query attribute overlapping degrees. In this figure, the X axis represents the different query attribute overlapping degrees and Y axis represents the total energy consumption. We can easily find that besides the spatial information, the attribute information can also be aggregated to reduce both the number and size of queries, which will consequently reduce the energy consumption of query/data transmission.

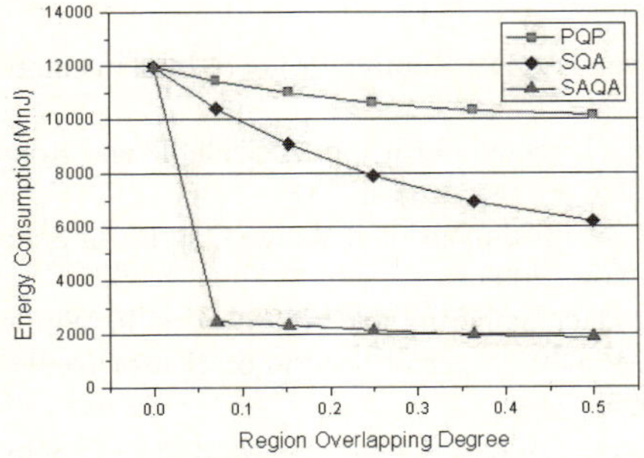

Fig. 5. Energy sensitivity of region overlapping degree

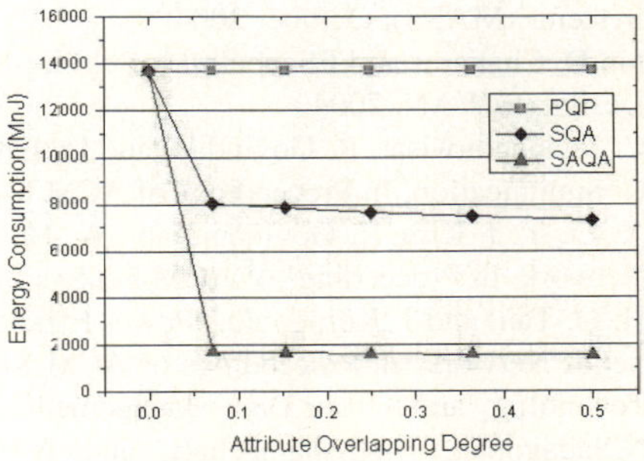

Fig. 6. Energy sensitivity of attribute overlapping degree

5 Conclusion and Future Work

In this paper, we propose an effective query aggregation algorithm SAQA to reduce overall energy overhead for the data services in the sensor network. To the best of our knowledge, this is the first study that leverages existing research work and address the issues in this aspect. We conduct extensive performance evaluations on different algorithms. Our evaluation results show that by applying our query aggregation algorithm, we can significantly reduce the amount of query traffic and energy consumption for data services.

There are several directions to extend our study. First, in the original model, we implicitly assume that the underlying architecture supports location-based routing. Extending our algorithm so that it can support other routing protocols would be one direction. Second, in the query aggregation algorithm, we construct our zones based on the input query zones and do not consider the existing topology and distribution of sensors in the network. Such as, adjacent spatial information can be combined together in that they may share part of the route for query dissemination. Combining both dimensions (input query zones and network topology) in our algorithm will certainly produce better results. Finally, find an efficient way to decide the query merge order is also an important issue we should consider about.

Acknowledgement

This work was supported by IITA Professorship for Visiting Faculty Positions in Korea from Ministry of Information and Communications.

References

1. Jonathan Beaver, Mohamed A. Sharaf, Alexandros Labrinidis, Panos K. Chrysanthis.: Power-Aware In-Network Query Processing for Sensor Data, MobiCom 2003
2. W. Yu, T. Le, Dong Xuan and W. Zhao.: Query Aggregation for Providing Efficient Data Services in Sensor Networks, in Proc. of IEEE Mobile Sensor and Ad-hoc and Sensor Systems (MASS), October 2004
3. Ian D. Chakeres and Elizabeth M. Belding-Royer.: AODV Routing Protocol Implementation Design. WWAN, 2004
4. C. Intanagonwisat, R. Govindan, and D. Estrin.: Directed Diffusion: A Scalable and Robust Communication, In Proceedings of ACM MobileCom'00, August 2000
5. X. Li, Y. J. Kim, R. Govindan, and W. Hong.: Multi-dimensional Range Queries in Sensor Network, In Proceedings of ACM SenSys'03, Nov., 2003
6. H. O. Tan, and I. Korpeoglu.: Power Efficient Data Gathering and Aggregation in Wireless Senor Network, In Proceedings of ACM SIGMOD'03, Special Section on Sensor Network Technology and Sensor Data Management, 2003
7. N.Sadagopan, B.Krishamachari, and A.Helmy.: Active Query Forwarding in Sensor Networks, Accepted to Journal of Ad-hoc Networks, ELSEVIER, August, 2003
8. Samuel Madden, Michael J. Franklin, Joseph M.Hellerstein, and Wei Hong.: TAG: a Tiny Aggregation Service for Ad-Hoc Sensor Networks. OSDI, 2002
9. Yong Yao and Johannes Gehrke.: Query Processing for Sensor Networks. CIDR, 2003

Efficent Algorithm of Energy Minimization for Heterogeneous Wireless Sensor Network*

Meikang Qiu[1], Chun Xue[1], Zili Shao[2], Qingfeng Zhuge[1], Meilin Liu[1], and Edwin H.-M. Sha[1]

[1] Univ. of Texas at Dallas,
Richardson, Texas 75083, USA
{mxq012100, cxx016000, qfzhuge, mxl024100, edsha}@utdallas.edu
[2] Hong Kong Polytechnic Univ.,
Hung Hom, Kowloon, Hongkong
cszshao@comp.polyu.edu.hk

Abstract. Energy and delay are critical issues for wireless sensor networks since most sensors are equipped with non-rechargeable batteries that have limited lifetime. Due to the uncertainties in execution time of some tasks, this paper models each varied execution time as a probabilistic random variable and incorporating applications' performance requirements to solve the MAP (Mode Assignment with Probability) problem. Using probabilistic design, we propose an optimal algorithm to minimize the total energy consumption while satisfying the timing constraint with a guaranteed confidence probability. The experimental results show that our approach achieves significant energy saving than previous work. For example, our algorithm achieves an average improvement of 32.6% on total energy consumption.

1 Introduction

Recent advances in heterogeneous wireless communications and electronics have enabled the development of low cost, low power, multifunctional sensor nodes that are small in size and communicate in short distances. These tiny sensor nodes have capability to sense, process data, and communicate. Typically they are densely deployed in large numbers, prone to failures, and their topology changes frequently. They have limited power, computational capacity, bandwidth and memory. As a result of its properties traditional protocols cannot be applied in this domain. Sensor networks have wide applications in areas such as health care, military, collecting information in disaster prone areas and surveillance applications [1, 2, 3, 4].

Lifetime of distributed micro sensor nodes is a very important issue in the design of sensor networks. The wireless sensor node, being a microelectronic device, can only be equipped with a limited power source ($\leq$ 0.5 Ah, 1.2 V).

* This work is partially supported by TI University Program, NSF EIA-0103709, Texas ARP 009741-0028-2001, NSF CCR-0309461, NSF IIS-0513669, and Microsoft, USA.

E. Sha et al. (Eds.): EUC 2006, LNCS 4096, pp. 25–34, 2006.

In some application scenarios, replenishment of power resources might be impossible. Hence, power conservation and power management take on additional importance [5]. Optimal energy consumption, i.e., minimizing energy consumed by sensing and communication to extend the network lifetime, is an important design objective. In the data transmisson, real-time is a critical requirement for many application for wireless sensor network. There are three modes (active, vulnerable, and sleep) for a sensor network. We call it as *Mode Assignment with Probability* (MAP) problem. For example, in a Bio-sensor, we sample the temperature every minutes. The data collected will go through a fixed topology to the destination. Assume we need the data transmisson within 20 seconds. Given this requirement, we need to minimize the total energy consumed in each transmisson. Due to the transmisson line situation and other overheads, the execution time of each transmision is not a fix number. It may tranmit a data in 1 seconds with 0.8 probability and in 3 seconds with 0.2 probability. The mode of a sensor node will affect both the energy and delay of the node.

This paper presents assignment and optimization algorithms which operate in probabilistic environments to solve the MAP problem. In the MAP problem, we model the execution time of a task as a random variable [6]. For heterogeneous systems, each node has different energy consumption rate, which related to area, size, reliability, etc. [7]. Faster one has higher energy consumption while slower one has lower consumption. This paper shows how to assign a proper mode to each node of a *Probability Data Flow Graph* (PDFG) such that the total energy consumption is minimized while the timing constraint is satisfied with a guaranteed confidence probability. With confidence probability P, we can guarantee that the total execution time of the DFG is less than or equal to the timing constraint with a probability that is greater than or equal to P.

Our contributions are listed as the following: 1) our algorithm *MAP_Opt* gives the optimal solution and achieves significant energy saving than *MAP_CP* algorithm. 2) Our algorithm not only is optimal, but also provides more choices of smaller total energy consumption with guaranteed confidence probabilities satisfying timing constraints. In many situations, algorithm *MAP_CP* cannot find a solution, while ours can find satisfied results. 3) Our algorithm is practical and quick.

The rest of the paper is organized as following: The models and basic concepts are introduced in Section 2. In Section 3, we give a motivational example. In Section 4, we propose our algorithms. The experimental results are shown in Section 5, and the conclusion is shown in Section 6.

2 System Model

System Model: *Probabilistic Data-Flow Graph* (PDFG) is used to model a DSP application. A ***PDFG G*** $= \langle V, E, T, R\rangle$ is a *directed acyclic graph* (DAG), where $\mathbf{V} = \langle v_1, \cdots, v_i, \cdots, v_N\rangle$ is the set of nodes; $\mathbf{M} = \langle M_1, \cdots, M_j, \cdots, M_R\rangle$ is a mode set; the execution time $\mathbf{T_{R_j}(v)}$ is a random variable; $\mathbf{E} \subseteq V \times V$ is the edge set that defines the precedence relations among nodes in V. There is a timing constraint L and it must be satisfied for executing the whole PDFG.

In sensor netowrk, we know that there are three kinds of mode, ie. active, vulnerable, and sleep modes. We assume under same mode, the energy consumption is same, while the execution time can be a random variable. Also, we assume that from source to destionation there is a fixed steps to go through before a node stop working. The Data Flow Graph is assumed to be a DAG (Directed Acyclic Graph), that is, there is no cycle in it.

Definitions: We define the ***MAP (Mode Assignment with Probability)*** problem as follows: Given R different voltage levels: M_1,M_2,$\cdots$,M_R, a PDFG $G = \langle V, E \rangle$ with $T_{M_j}(v)$, $P_{M_j}(v)$, and $C_{M_j}(v)$ for each node $v \in V$ executed on each mode M_j, a timing constraint L and a confidence probability P, find the mode for each node in assignment A that gives the *minimum total energy consumption C with confidence probability P under timing constraint L.*

3 Motivational Example

In our model, under the same mode (M), the execution time (T) of a task is a random variable, which is usually due to condition instructions or operations that could have different execution times for different inputs. The energy consumption (C) depends on the mode M. Under different modes, a task has different energy consumptions. The execution time of a node in active mode is less than that of it in vulnerable mode, and they both are less than the execution time of it in sleep mode; The relations of energy consumption are just the reverse. This paper shows how to assign a proper mode to each node of a *Probabilistic Data-Flow Graph* (PDFG) such that the total energy consumption is minimized while satisfying the timing constraint with a guaranteed confidence probability.

An exemplary PDFG is shown in Figure 1(a). Each node can select one of the three different modes: M_1 (active), M_2 (vulnerable) , and M_3 (sleep). The execution times (T), corresponding probabilities (P), and energy consumption (C) of each node under different modes are shown in Figure 1(b). The input DAG (*Directed Acyclic Graph*) has five nodes. Node 1 is a multi-child node, which has three children: 2, 3, and 5. Node 5 is a multi-parent node, and has three parents: 1, 3, and 4. The execution time T of each node is modeled as a random variable. For example, When choosing M_1, node 1 will be finished in 1 time unit with probability 0.8 and will be finished in 2 time units with probability 0.2. Node 1 is the source and node 5 is the destination or the drain.

In sensor network application, a real-time system does not always has hard deadline time. The execution time can be smaller than the hard deadline time with certain probabilities. So the hard deadline time is the worst-case of the varied smaller time cases. If we consider these time variations, we can achieve a better minimum energy consumption with satisfying confidence probabilities under timing constraints.

For Figure 1, the minimum total energy consumptions with computed confidence probabilities under the timing constraint are shown in Table 1. The results are generated by our algorithm, *MAP_Opt*. The entries with probability that is equal to 1 (see the entries in boldface) actually give the results to the hard

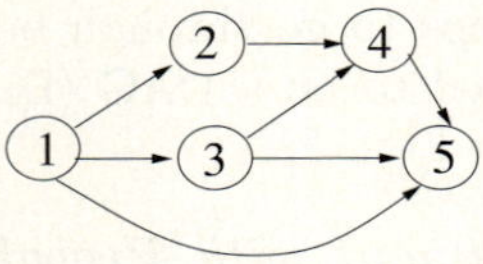

(a)

Nodes	M1 T	M1 P	M1 C	M2 T	M2 P	M2 C	M3 T	M3 P	M3 C
1	1	0.8	9	3	0.9	3	5	0.7	1
	2	0.2		4	0.1		6	0.3	
2	1	1.0	8	2	1.0	6	3	1.0	2
3	1	1.0	8	2	1.0	6	3	1.0	2
4	1	0.7	8	2	0.9	4	5	0.9	2
	3	0.3		4	0.1		6	0.1	
5	1	0.9	10	3	0.8	3	5	0.8	1
	2	0.1		4	0.2		6	0.2	

(b)

Fig. 1. (a) A sensor network topology. (b) The times, probabilities, and energy consumptions of its nodes in different modes.

Table 1. Minimum total energy consumptions with computed confidence probabilities under various timing constraints

T	(P , C)	(P , C)	(P , C)	(P , C)	(P , C)
4	0.50, 43				
5	0.65, 39				
6	0.65, 35	0.81, 39			
7	0.65, 27	0.73, 33	0.81, 35	0.90, 39	
8	0.81, 27	0.90, 35	**1.00, 43**		
9	0.58, 20	0.73, 21	0.81, 27	0.90, 32	**1.00, 39**
10	0.72, 20	0.81, 21	0.90, 28	**1.00, 36**	
11	0.65, 14	0.90, 20	**1.00, 32**		
12	0.81, 14	0.90, 20	**1.00, 28**		
13	0.65, 12	0.90, 14	**1.00, 20**		
14	0.81, 12	0.90, 14	**1.00, 20**		
15	0.50, 10	0.90, 12	**1.00, 14**		
16	0.72, 10	0.90, 12	**1.00, 14**		
17	0.90, 10	**1.00, 12**			
18	0.50, 8	0.90, 10	**1.00, 12**		
19	0.72, 8	**1.00, 10**			
20	0.90, 8	**1.00, 10**			
21	**1.00, 8**				

real-time problem which shows the worst-case scenario of the MAP problem. For each row of the table, the C in each (P, C) pair gives the minimum total energy consumption with confidence probability P under timing constraint j. For example, using our algorithm, at timing constraint 12, we can get (0.81, 14) pair. The assignments are shown in Table 2. We change the mode of nodes 2 and 3 to be M_2. Hence, we find the way to achieve minimum total energy consumption 14 with probability 0.81 satisfying timing constraint 12. While using the heuristic algorithm *MAP_CP* [8], the total energy consumption obtained is 28. Assignment $A(v)$ represents the voltage selection of each node v. We will prove that the results obtained by algorithm *MAP_Opt* are always optimal.

Table 2. The assignments of algorithms *MAP_Opt* and *MAP_CP* with timing constraint 12

		Node id	T	M	Prob.	Consum.
Ours	$A(v)$	1	3	M_2	0.90	3
		2	3	M_3	1.00	2
		3	3	M_3	1.00	2
		4	2	M_2	0.90	4
		5	4	M_2	1.00	3
	Total		12		0.81	14
MAP_CP	$A(v)$	1	2	M_1	1.00	9
		2	2	M_2	1.00	6
		3	2	M_2	1.00	6
		4	4	M_2	1.00	4
		5	4	M_2	1.00	3
	Total		12		1.00	28

4 The Algorithms for MAP Problem

4.1 Definitions and Lemma

To solve the MAP problem, we use dynamic programming method traveling the graph in a bottom up fashion. For the easiness of explanation, we will index the nodes based on bottom up sequence. For example, Figure 2 (a) shows nodes indexed in a bottom up sequence After topological sorting the Figure 1 (a), that is, $v_1 \rightarrow v_2 \rightarrow v_3 \rightarrow v_4 \rightarrow v_5$.

Given the timing constraint L, a PDFG G, and an assignment A, we first give several definitions as follows: 1) $\mathbf{G^i}$: The sub-graph rooted at node v_i, containing all the nodes reached by node v_i. In our algorithm, each step will add one node which becomes the root of its sub-graph. For example, G^3 is the graph containing nodes 1, 2, and 3 in Figure 2 (a). 2) In our algorithm, table $\mathbf{D_{i,j}}$ will be built. Each entry of table $D_{i,j}$ will store a link list of (Probability, Consumption) pairs

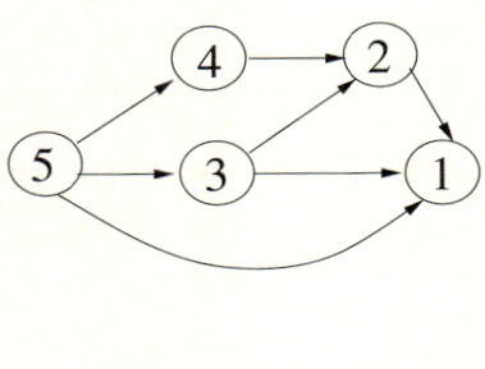

(a)

Nodes	M1 T	M1 P	M1 C	M2 T	M2 P	M2 C	M3 T	M3 P	M3 C
5	1	0.8	9	3	0.9	3	5	0.7	1
	2	0.2		4	0.1		6	0.3	
4	1	1.0	8	2	1.0	6	3	1.0	2
3	1	1.0	8	2	1.0	6	3	1.0	2
2	1	0.7	8	2	0.9	4	5	0.9	2
	3	0.3		4	0.1		6	0.1	
1	1	0.9	10	3	0.8	3	5	0.8	1
	2	0.1		4	0.2		6	0.2	

(b)

Fig. 2. (a) The resulted DAG after topological sorting of Figure 1 (a). (b) The times, probabilities, and energy consumptions of its nodes in different modes.

sorted by probability in an ascending order. Here we define the **(Probability, Consumption) pair ($\mathbf{P_{i,j}}$, $\mathbf{C_{i,j}}$)** as follows: $C_{i,j}$ is the minimum energy consumption of $C_A(G^i)$ computed by all assignments A satisfying $T_A(G^i) \leq j$ with probability $\geq P_{i,j}$.

We introduce the ***operator* "$\oplus$"** in this paper. For two (Probability, Consumption) pairs H_1 and H_2, if H_1 is ($P^1_{i,j}$, $C^1_{i,j}$), and H_2 is ($P^2_{i,j}$, $C^2_{i,j}$), then after applying the $\oplus$ operation between H_1 and H_2, we get pair ($P^{'}$, $C^{'}$), where $P^{'}$ = $P^1_{i,j}$ * $P^2_{i,j}$ and $C^{'}$ = $C^1_{i,j}$ + $C^2_{i,j}$. We denote this operation as "$\mathbf{H_1 \oplus H_2}$".

$D_{i,j}$ is the table in which each entry has a link list that stores pair ($P_{i,j}$, $C_{i,j}$) sorted by $P_{i,j}$ in an ascending order. Here, i represents a node number, and j represents time. For example, a link list can be (0.1, 2)→(0.3, 3)→(0.8, 6)→(1.0, 12). Usually, there are redundant pairs in a link list. We use Lemma 1 to cancel redundant pairs.

Lemma 1. *Given ($P^1_{i,j}$, $C^1_{i,j}$) and ($P^2_{i,j}$, $C^2_{i,j}$) in the same list:*

1. *If $P^1_{i,j} = P^2_{i,j}$, then the pair with minimum $C_{i,j}$ is selected to be kept.*
2. *If $P^1_{i,j} < P^2_{i,j}$ and $C^1_{i,j} \geq C^2_{i,j}$, then $C^2_{i,j}$ is selected to be kept.*

For example, if we have a list with pairs (0.1, 2) → (0.3, 3) → (0.5, 3) → (0.3, 4), we do the redundant-pair removal as following: First, sort the list according $P_{i,j}$ in an ascending order. This list becomes to (0.1, 2) → (0.3, 3) → (0.3, 4) → (0.5, 3). Second, cancel redundant pairs. Comparing (0.1, 2) and (0.3, 3), we keep both. For the two pairs (0.3, 3) and (0.3, 4), we cancel pair (0.3, 4) since the cost 4 is bigger than 3 in pair (0.3, 3). Comparing (0,3, 3) and (0.5, 3), we cancel (0.3, 3) since 0.3 < 0.5 while 3 ≥ 3. There is no information lost in redundant-pair removal. Using Lemma 1, we can cancel many redundant-pair ($P_{i,j}$, $C_{i,j}$) whenever we find conflicting pairs in a list during a computation.

In every step of our algorithm, one more node will be included for consideration. The information of this node is stored in local table $\mathbf{E_{i,j}}$, which is similar to table $D_{i,j}$, but with accumulative probabilities only on node v_i. A local table only store information, such as probabilities and consumptions, of a node itself. Table $E_{i,j}$ is the local table only storing the information of node v_i. In more detail, $E_{i,j}$ is a local table of link lists that store pair ($p_{i,j}$, $c_{i,j}$) sorted by $p_{i,j}$ in an ascending order; $c_{i,j}$ is the energy consumption only for node v_i with timing constraint j, and $p_{i,j}$ is CDF (cumulative distributive function) F(j).

4.2 The MAP_CP Algorithm

In this subsection, we first design an heuristic algorithm for sensor network according to the *DFG_Assign_CP* algorithm in [8], we call this algorithm as *MAP_CP*.

The MAP_CP Algorithm

A critical path (CP) of a DAG is a path from source to its destionation. To be a leagl assignment for a DFG (*Data Flow Graph*), the execution time for any critical path should be less than or equal to the given timing constraint.

Algorithm 4.1. Heuristic algorithm for the MAP problem when the PDFG is DAG (*MAP_CP*)

Require: R different mode types, a DAG, and the timing constraint L.
Ensure: a mode assignment to minimize energy while satisfying L.

```
Assign the best energy type to each node and mark the type as assigned.
Find a CP that has the maximum execution time among all possible paths based
  on the current assigned types for the DAG.
For every node v_i in CP,
    for every unmarked type p,
        change its type to p,
        calculate r = cost_increase/time_reduce
        select the minimum r.
        if (T > L)
            contiune
        else
            exit      /* This is the best assignment */
```

In algorithm *MAP_CP*, we only consider the hard execution time of each node, that is, the case when the probability of the random variable T equals 1. This is a heuristic solution for hard real-time systems. We find the CP with minimized energy consumption first, then adjust the energy of the nodes in CP until the total execution time is $\leq L$.

4.3 The MAP_Opt Algorithm

We propose our algorithm, *MAP_Opt*, for sensor network, which shown as follows.
The MAP_Opt Algorithm
Require: R different modes, a DAG, and the timing constraint L.
Ensure: An optimal mode assignment

1. Topological sort all the nodes, and get a sequence A.
2. Count the number of multi-parent nodes t_{mp} and the number of multi-child nodes t_{mc}. If $t_{mp} < t_{mc}$, use bottom up approach; Otherwise, use top down approach.
3. For bottom up approach, use the following algorithm. For top down approach, just reverse the sequence.
4. If the total number of nodes with multi-parent is t, and there are maximum K variations for the execution times of all nodes, then we will give each of these t nodes a fixed assignment.
5. For each of the K^t possible fixed assignments, assume the sequence after topological sorting is $v_1 \rightarrow v_2 \rightarrow \cdots \rightarrow v_N$, in bottom up fashion. Let $D_{1,j} = E_{1,j}$. Assume $D'_{i,j}$ is the table that stored minimum total energy consumption with computed confidence probabilities under the timing constraint j for the sub-graph rooted on v_i except v_i. Nodes $v_{i_1}, v_{i_2}, \cdots, v_{i_R}$ are all child nodes of node v_i and R is the number of child nodes of node v_i, then

$$D'_{i,j} = \begin{cases} (0,0) & \text{if } R = 0 \\ D_{i_1,j} & \text{if } R = 1 \\ D_{i_1,j} \oplus \cdots \oplus D_{i_R,j} & \text{if } R \geq 1 \end{cases} \quad (1)$$

6. Then, for each k in $E_{i,k}$.

$$D_{i,j} = D'_{i,j-k} \oplus E_{i,k} \quad (2)$$

7. For each possible fixed assignment, we get a $D_{N,j}$. Merge the (Probability, Consumption) pairs in all the possible $D_{N,j}$ together, and sort them in ascending sequence according probability.
8. Then use the Lemma 1 to remove redundant pairs. Finally get $D_{N,j}$.

In algorithm *MAP_Opt*, we exhaust all the possible assignments of multi-parent or multi-child nodes. Without loss of generality, assume we using bottom up approach. If the total number of nodes with multi-parent is t, and there are maximum K variations for the execution times of all nodes, then we will give each of these t nodes a fixed assignment. We will exhausted all of the K^t possible fixed assignments. Algorithm *MAP_Opt* gives the optimal solution when the given PDFG is a DAG. In equation (1), $D_{i_1,j} \oplus D_{i_2,j}$ is computed as follows. let G' be the union of all nodes in the graphs rooted at nodes v_{i_1} and v_{i_2}. Travel all the graphs rooted at nodes v_{i_1} and v_{i_2}. For each node a in G', we add the energy consumption of a and multiply the probability of a to $D'_{i,j}$ for only once, because each node can only have one assignment and there is no assignment conflict. The final $D_{N,j}$ we get is the table in which each entry has the minimum energy consumption with a guaranteed confidence probability under the timing constraint j.

In algorithm *MAP_Opt*, there are K^t loops and each loop needs $O(|V|^2 * L * R * K)$ running time. The complexity of *Algorithm MAP_Opt* is $O(K^{t+1} * |V|^2 * L * R)$. Since t_{mp} is the number of nodes with multi-parent, and t_{mc} is the number of nodes with multi-child, then $t = min(t_{mp}, t_{mc})$. $|V|$ is the number of nodes, L is the given timing constraint, R is the maximum number of modes for each node, and K is the maximum number of execution time variation for each node. The experiments show that algorithm *MAP_Opt* runs efficiently.

5 Experiments

This section presents the experimental results of our algorithms. We conduct experiments on a set of DAGs. Three different modes, M_1, M_2, and M_3, are used in the system, in which a node with mode M_1 (active) is the quickest with the highest energy consumption and a node with type M_3 (sleep) is the slowest with the lowest energy consumption. The execution times, probabilities, and energy consumptions for each node are randomly assigned. The experiments are performed on a Dell PC with a P4 2.1 G processor and 512 MB memory running Red Hat Linux 9.

Figure 3 shows a DAG with 21 nodes. We assume this is the topology of a sensor network. S is the source and D is the destination. Each node has three

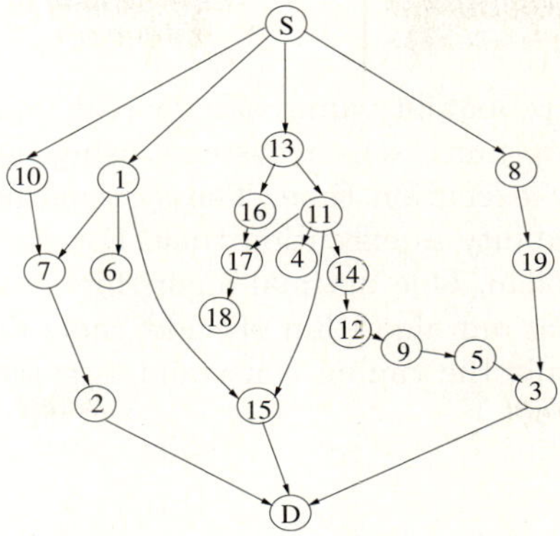

Fig. 3. The Data Flow Graph of exp1

Table 3. Experimental results of algorithms *MAP_CP* and *MAP_Opt* for exp1

TC	*MAP_CP*	*MAP_Opt*					
		0.7		0.8		0.9	
	Energy	Energy	Saving	Energy	Saving	Energy	Saving
30	×	5202		×		×	
40	×	5190		5191		5192	
50	×	4721		4725		5188	
60	**5186**	3602	30.5%	3994	23.0%	3995	23.0%
70	**5180**	2646	48.9%	3112	39.9%	3586	30.8%
80	**2395**	1042	59.8%	1512	58.0%	2072	13.6%
100	**3111**	1042	66.4%	1509	49.3%	1509	38.6%
120	**3109**	1042	66.5%	1042	66.5%	1509	51.5%
136	**1509**	1042	30.9%	1042	30.9%	1042	30.9%
137	**1042**	1042		1042		1042	
Average Saving			51.5%		43.8 %		32.6 %

modes with different execution times and energy consumptions. The collected data need to go through the topology to the destination within a timing constaint. Exclude the source and destination node, this DAG has 3 multi-child nodes and 4 multi-parent nodes. Using top-down approach, we implemented all $3^3 = 27$ possibilities. The experimental results for exp1 is shown in Table 3. Column "TC" stands for the timing constraint of the DAG. Column "Saving" shows the percentage of reduction on system energy consumptions, compared the results for soft real-time with those for hard real-time. The average percentage reduction is shown in the last row "Average Saving" of the table. The entry with "×" means no solution available. Under timing constraint 30 in Table 3, there is no solution for hard real-time using MAP_CP algorithm. However, we can find solution 5202 with probability 0.9 that guarantees the total execution time of the DFG is less than or equal to the timing constraint 30.

6 Conclusion

This paper proposed a probability approach for real-time sensor network applications to assign and optimize sensor systems using heterogeneous functional units with probabilistic execution time. The systems become very complicate when considering probability in execution time. For the *Mode assignment with probability* (MAP) problem, One optimal algorithms was proposed to solve it. Experiments showed that our algorithm provides more design choices to achieve minimum total cost while the timing constraint is satisfied with a guaranteed confidence probability.

References

1. Akyildiz I.F., Su W., Sankarasubramaniam Y., Cayirci E.: A Survey on Sensor Networks. IEEE Communications Magazine, Vol. 40, No. 8, (Aug. 2002) 102–116
2. Tan H., Lu I.: Power efficient data gathering and aggregation in wireless sensor networks. ACM SIGMOD Record, SPECIAL ISSUE: Special section on sensor network technology and sensor data management, Vol. 4, No. 3, (2003) 66–71
3. Law Y. W., Hoesel L. , Doumen J. , Havinga P.: Sensor networks: Energy-efficient link-layer jamming attacks against wireless sensor network MAC protocols. Proceedings of the 3rd ACM workshop on Security of ad hoc and sensor networks SASN '05, Alexandria, VA, USA (Nov. 2005) 76–88
4. Chatzigiannakis I., Kinalis A., Nikoletseas S.: Power Conservation Schemes for Energy Efficient Data Propagation in Heterogeneous Wireless Sensor Networks. Proceedings of the 38th annual Symposium on Simulation, (Apr. 2005) 60–71
5. Kumar S., Lai T. H., Balogh J.: On k-coverage in a mostly sleeping sensor network. Proceedings of the 10th Annual International Conference on Mobile Computing and Networking (Mobicom '04) (2004) 144–158
6. Tongsima S., Sha Edwin H.-M., Chantrapornchai C., Surma D., Passose N.: Probabilistic Loop Scheduling for Applications with Uncertain Execution Time. IEEE Trans. on Computers, Vol. 49, (Jan. 2000) 65-80
7. Li W. N., Lim A., Agarwal P., Sahni S.: On the Circuit Implementation Problem. IEEE Trans. on Computer-Aided Design of Integrated Circuits and Systems, Vol. 12, (Aug. 1993) 1147–1156
8. Shao Z., Zhuge Q. , Xue C., Sha Edwin H.-M.: Efficient Assignment and Scheduling for Heterogeneous DSP Systems. IEEE Trans. on Parallel and Distributed Systems, Vol. 16, (Jun. 2005) 516–525

Power-Aware Instruction Scheduling

Tzong-Yen Lin and Rong-Guey Chang*

Department of Computer Science
National Chung Cheng University
Chia-Yi, Taiwan
lty93@cs.ccu.edu.tw, rgchang@cs.ccu.edu.tw

Abstract. This paper presents an innovative DVS technique to reduce the energy dissipation. Our objective is to minimize the transitions between power modes by maximizing the idle periods of functional units with instruction scheduling. Our work first analyzes the control flow graph of the application, which contains many regions. Second, we collect the power information and build its power model for each region. Then two regions with the same functional units will be merged if no dependencies exist between them. The process is repeated until no further mergings can be performed. Next, the idle functional units will be turned off and each region will be assigned a power mode based on the power model. Finally, the application is rescheduled to merge the regions to reduce the transitions between power modes. The experimental results show that our work can save the energy by 26%.

1 Introduction

As most embedded systems are portable, how to reduce the energy dissipation when running applications to extend the lifetimes of batteries has become a crucial issue. The energy dissipation is closely related to voltage and clock frequency [11]. The architectures of modern processors provide several power modes to reduce energy dissipation by adjusting the voltage and the clock frequency at run time.

Previous work showed the switching overheads of power modes make a significant impact on energy dissipation [1,14]. In this paper, we reduce the energy dissipation with instruction scheduling to minimize the transitions between power modes by maximizing the idle periods of functional units. To exploit the maximum potential for instruction scheduling, for an application, we first use the SUIF compiler infrastructure to build its control flow graph (CFG) and data flow graph (DFG) [9,14]. Then these graphs are divided into many basic blocks. Each basic block is composed of several regions, each of which will contain at least one functional unit. The power model of the application is also built in this step by profiling the CFG. Second, to minimize the transitions between power modes, two regions that contain the same functional units will be merged if no dependencies exist between them by referring to DFG. Then for each region, the idle functional units in it will be turned off and it is

* This work was supported in part by National Science Council, Taiwan, under Grant NSC 94-2220-E-194-011-

E. Sha et al. (Eds.): EUC 2006, LNCS 4096, pp. 35 – 44, 2006.

assigned one power mode by referring to the power model. Afterward, instruction scheduling is applied again so that the regions with the same power modes will be merged if no dependencies exist in them. Finally, we assign the power modes to basic blocks to further optimize energy and performance. The experiments will show how much this potential can be exploited for our benchmarks.

The remainder of this paper is organized as follows. Section 2 presents our main idea with a motivating example. Section 3 describes our compilation flow, system architecture, and the algorithm in detail. The experimental results are shown in Section 4. Section 5 is the related work. Finally, section 6 concludes our work briefly.

2 Motivating Example

Figure 1 shows a motivating example to explain the basic idea of our work. Figure 1b is the optimized code segment for Figure 1a. In Figure 1a, There are four regions: two loops and two multiplication expressions. We assume that the adder is turned on, the multiplier is turned off, the default power mode is the normal mode, and two loops are assigned power down mode. To reduce energy dissipation, the functional units will be turned off. In Figure 1a, the adder will be turned on and the multiplier will be turned off in two loops, and the adder will be turned off and the multiplier will be turned on when doing multiplications. In Figure 1b, two loops and two expressions can be merged into two regions respectively since they contain the same functional unit and no dependences exist in them. Then the multiplier is turned off in the newly loop then the adder is turned off in the expressions. Finally, we assign the loop region power down mode and the expression region normal mode. In contrast with Figure 1a, Figure 1b can reduce more power consumption since it maximize the idle periods of functional units and save two transitions of power modes.

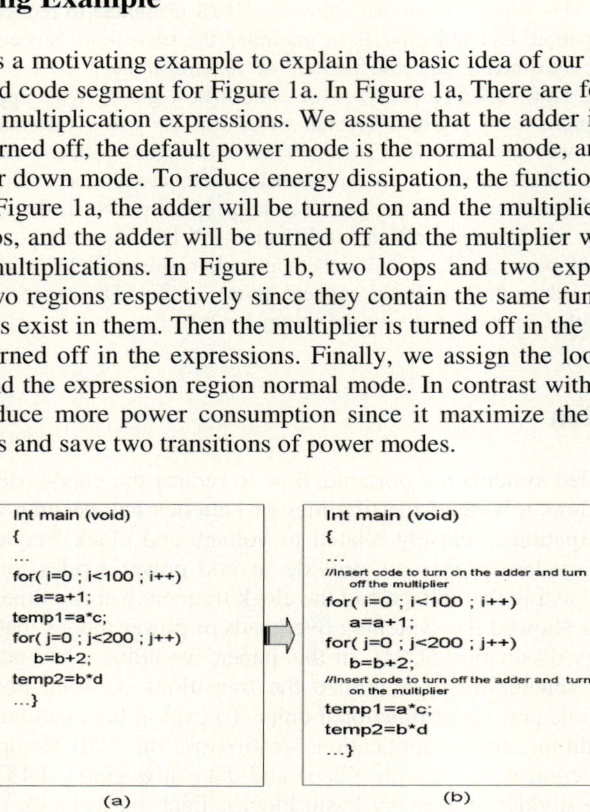

Fig. 1. Motivating example

3 Power-Aware Compilation

In this section, we first describe compilation flow and system architecture of our work and then present our algorithm.

3.1 Compilation Flow and System Architecture

Figure 2 shows our compilation flow and system architecture. Our approach is implemented on the basis of the SUIF2 compiler infrastructure and the Wattch simulator. SUIF2 helps us to build the control flow graph (CFG) and the data flow graph (DFG) and then we perform our low-power optimizations. First, we build the power model by profiling the graphs of the application. Meanwhile, the control flow graph will be divided into many regions according to the usage of functional units. Then each region will be assigned a power mode by referring to its power model. Next, the idle functional units in a region will be turned off. Then two regions will be merged to reduce the transitions of power modes with instruction scheduling, if the functional units in them have the same statuses, they have the same power modes, and no dependencies exist in them. The process will repeat until no further mergings can be performed. Finally, the resulted DVS'ed program is compiled and linked with runtime library to produce an executable code running on the Wattch simulator [3].

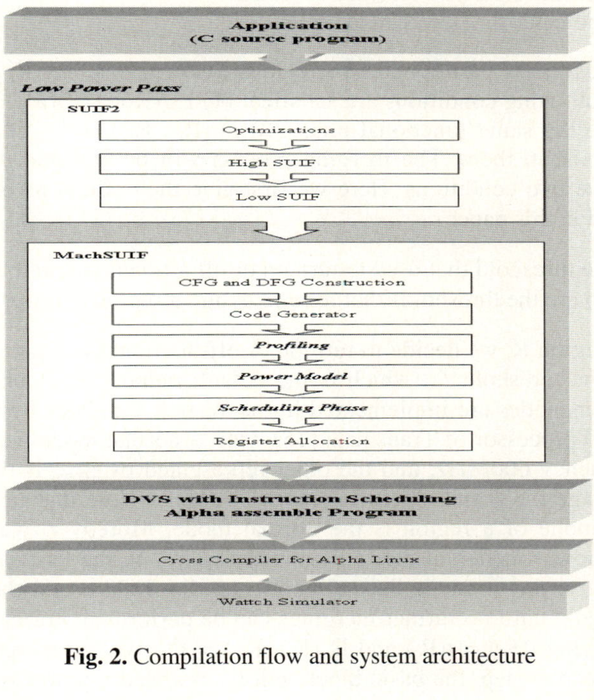

Fig. 2. Compilation flow and system architecture

3.2 Architectural Support

To turn on and off the functional units, we add new instructions into the Alpha instruction set in the Wattch simulator, which is listed below. In this paper, we only consider the adders and the multipliers for integer and floating point.

alu.on	switch ON one integer ALU functional unit
alu.off	switch OFF one integer ALU functional unit

mdu.on	switch ON one integer multiplier/divide functional unit
mdu.off	switch ON off integer multiplier/divide functional unit
alu.s.on	switch ON one float ALU functional unit
alu.s.off	switch OFF one float ALU functional unit
mdu.s.on	switch ON one float multiplier/divide functional unit
mdu.s.off	switch OFF one float multiplier/divide functional unit

In our algorithm, to perform the optimizations on an application, we define the following symbols that are used in this paper. For a basic block B and a region R in the basic block B,

N(B) is the number of times when B is executed,
FU(B) is the set of functional unit used in B,
FU(R) is the set of functional unit used in R,
f_{mem} is the ratio of memory accesses to total instructions in B,
Tper(R) is the ratio of the execution time to that of B,
f (B) indicates the power mode of B, and
f (R) indicates the power mode of R.

After the program is partitioned into regions, two regions, say R_i and R_j, will be merged if the following conditions are satisfied. (1) FU(R_i) = FU(R_j). It implies these two regions use the same functional units. (2) D (R_i , R_j) = ∅ . It means that no dependencies exist in them. The merging process will be repeated until no regions satisfy the above two conditions. Here we first give the definitions of the following parameters used in this paper.

γ is the threshold that used to turn on or off a functional unit and
α and β are the thresholds that used to assign a region a power mode.

Next, for a region R, we decide to turn on or off the functional units in it if $T_{per}(R)$ is larger than the threshold γ , which is the default number of clock cycles. In our work, two power modes are implemented in the Wattch simulator by referring to the Crusoe TM5800 processor of Transmeta [15]. One is normal mode with voltage 1.5V and clock frequency 600MHz, and the other represented by f_{down} is the power down mode with voltage 0.3V and clock frequency 300MHz. Note that in this paper, the default power mode of a region is the normal mode. Moreover, we determine the assignment of power modes in the following two steps. In the first step, we first assign each region a power mode depending on the threshold α and then perform the merging repeatedly until no further mergings can be performed. Formally, the regions R_i and R_j satisfying f(R_i) = f(R_j) and D (R_i , R_j) = ∅ will be merged across basic blocks. In the second step, the basic block will be assigned a power mode depending on the threshold β.

Now we use a code segment selected from 8x8 IDCT, which is used frequently in digital signal processing, as an example to demonstrate our idea. Figure 3 shows its control flow graph and power model. For simplicity, we use another code segment selected from 8x8 IDCT shown in Figure 4 to explain our algorithm. The original code segment shown in Figure 4a consists of five regions. Notice that regions R_1, R_3 and R_5 use adder only, and regions R_2 and R_4 use both adder and multiplier. Initially,

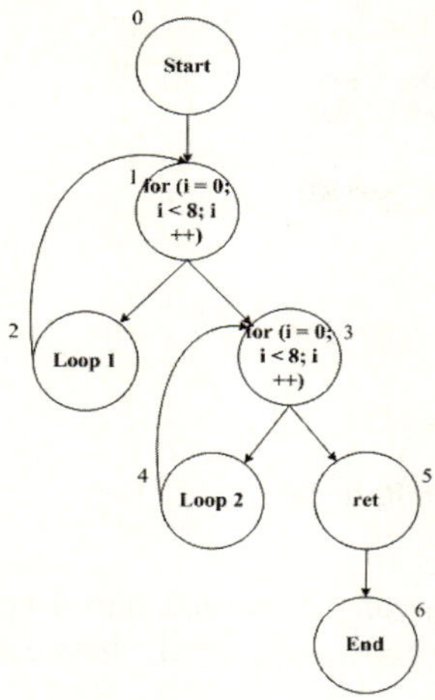

B_i	R_{ij}	N(B_i)	$T_{per}(R_{ij})$
B_0	N/A	1	N/A
B_1	R_0: Integer ALU	8	R_0 : 0.02
B_2	R_1: Integer ALU R_2: Integer ALU Integer multiplier/divide R_3: Adder R_4: Integer ALU Integer multiplier/divide R_5: Adder	8	R_1: 0.07 R_2: 0.07 R_3: 0.04 R_4: 0.18 R_5: 0.05
B_3	R_6: Integer ALU	8	R_6 :0.01
B_4	...	8	...
B_5	...	1	...
B_6	N/A	1	N/A

Fig. 3. Control flow graph and power model for a code segment selected from 8x8 IDCT

```
//R1
x8 = x7 + x1;
x1 -= x7;
x7 = x0 + x4;
x0 -= x4;
x4 = x1 + x5;
x1 -= x5;
x5 = x3 + x8;
x8 -= x3;
//R2
x3 = ir2c6 * (x2 + x6);
x6 = x3 + (- ir2c6 - ir2s6) * x6;
x2 = x3 + (- ir2c6 + ir2s6) * x2;
//R3
x3 = x7 + x2;
x7 -= x2;
x2 = x0 + x6;
x0 -= x6;
//R4
x6 = ic3 * (x4 + x5);
x5 = (x6 + (- ic3 - is3) * x5) >> 6;
x4 = (x6 + (- ic3 + is3) * x4) >> 6;
x6 = ic1 * (x1 + x8);
x1 = (x6 + (- ic1 - is1) * x1) >> 6;
x8 = (x6 + (- ic1 + is1) * x8) >> 6;
//R5
x7 += 512;
x2 += 512;
x0 += 512;
x3 += 512;
```

(a)

```
//R1
// turn off multiplier
x8 = x7 + x1;
x1 -= x7;
x7 = x0 + x4;
x0 -= x4;
x4 = x1 + x5;
x1 -= x5;
x5 = x3 + x8;
x8 -= x3;
//turn on multiplier
//R2
x3 = ir2c6 * (x2 + x6);
x6 = x3 + (- ir2c6 - ir2s6) * x6;
x2 = x3 + (- ir2c6 + ir2s6) * x2;
//R3-5
// turn off multiplier
x3 = x7 + x2;
x7 -= x2;
x2 = x0 + x6;
x0 -= x6;
x7 += 512;
x2 += 512;
x0 += 512;
x3 += 512;
//turn on multiplier
//R4
x6 = ic3 * (x4 + x5);
x5 = (x6 + (- ic3 - is3) * x5) >> 6;
x4 = (x6 + (- ic3 + is3) * x4) >> 6;
x6 = ic1 * (x1 + x8);
x1 = (x6 + (- ic1 - is1) * x1) >> 6;
x8 = (x6 + (- ic1 + is1) * x8) >> 6;
```

(b)

Fig. 4. The sample and optimized code segment selected from 8x8 IDCT

we assume that the adder is turned on since some instructions such as load and store will use it to calculate the target address and the multiplier is turned off.

According to the DFG of Figure 4a, we can merge R_3 and R_5 into a new region $R_{3\text{-}5}$ shown in Figure 4b after applying our approach to it. R1 cannot be merged with R_3 and R_5 due to the dependences, although they use the same functional unit. In addition, region R_2 and $R_{3\text{-}5}$ cannot be merged further into a region. Figure 5 shows the dependence graph between R_2 and $R_{3\text{-}5}$ and it explains why they cannot be merged. Thus, we can apply our algorithm to reschedule the code so that the regions with the

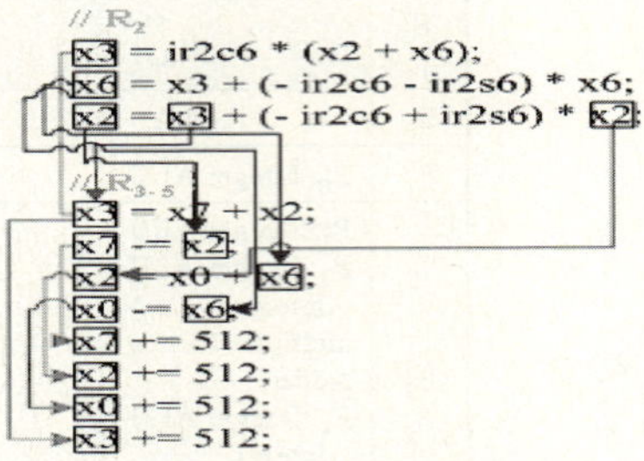

Fig. 5. Dependence graph between R_2 and $R_{3\text{-}5}$

same statuses can be merged. However, R_3 and R_5 can be merged into a new one, because multiplier can be shut down in them and no dependences exist between them. Figure 4b shows the optimized code segment.

4 Experimental Results

In this section, we present the experimental results of our work. Our work is implemented on the basis of the SUIF2 compiler infrastructure and the Wattch simulator. The applications are complied into the Alpha 21264 instructions by a cross compiler. The Alpha 21264 is one of the most advanced processors. It has four ALUs, aggressive branch predictor, two-level cache, TLB (translation look-aside buffer), and other modern designs [2]. The experiments are measured using SPEC2000, DSPstone, and Mediabench as benchmarks by setting three thresholds α = 0.3, β = 10, and γ = 3. With our experiences, these settings are better choices after applying our work to the above benchmarks. The impact of the settings on our work will be discussed further in the near future. In this section, we use "with scheduling" to represent all optimizations of our work and "without scheduling" to represent the optimizations without applying instruction scheduling.

4.1 Energy Evaluation

To demonstrate the effect of our work, we first show the power reductions after applying our approach to Dspstone, SPEC 2000, and Mediabench benchmarks, which are plotted with columns on the left axis of Figure 6 to Figure 8.

In Figure 6, our work can achieve an average energy reduction of 24% with scheduling and an average energy reduction of 19% without scheduling. For DSPstone, the effect of scheduling is small since the code sizes of applications in it are smaller. Basically, for a benchmark, our method will save more energy if its complexity is higher or its length is longer. For the matrix, the energy reduction caused by using scheduling can achieve up to 23% since it has a higher instruction level parallelism. It contains a 10 x 10 x 10 nested loop that calculates the multiplication of matrices. In this loop, several multiplications are calculated in different places. Our algorithm can work very well for "matrix" by grouping these multiplications together to maximize the idle period of the multiplier. So we can reduce the energy dissipation of a

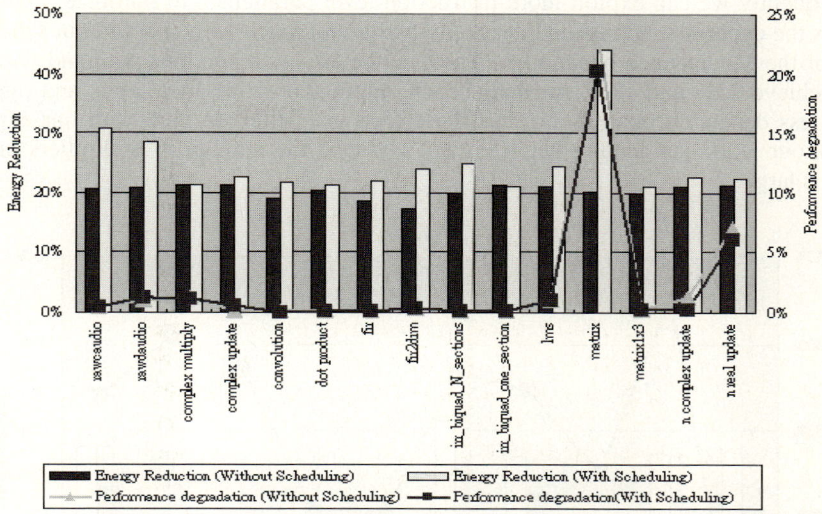

Fig. 6. Energy reduction and performance evaluation for DSPstone

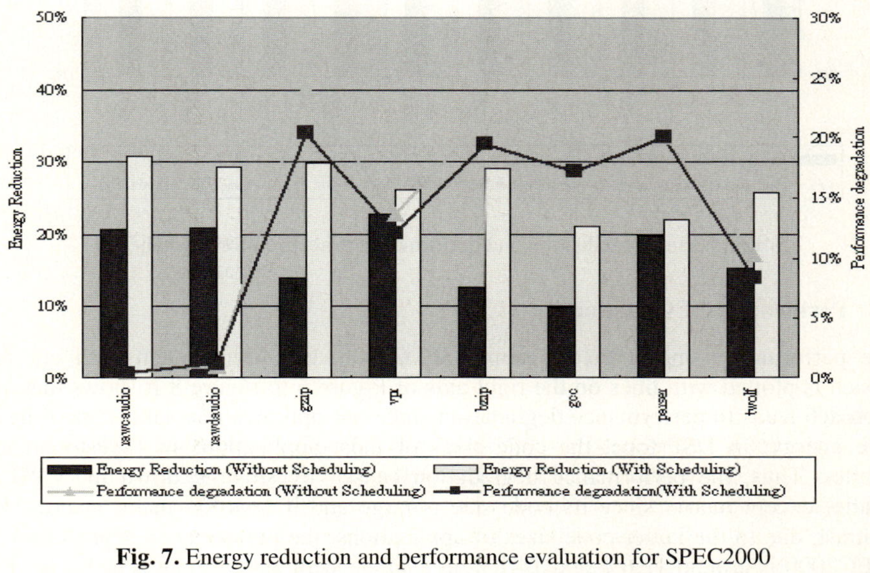

Fig. 7. Energy reduction and performance evaluation for SPEC2000

program. Figure 7 shows the experimental results after applying our approach with and without scheduling for the SPEC2000 benchmark. On average, the energy reduction can achieve up to 27%. The average energy reduction caused by the scheduling is around 11% that is larger than that of DSPstone. The reason is that the code sizes of applications in SPEC2000 are larger in comparison with those of DSPstone and consequently we can exploit more instruction level parallelism to optimize. Figure 8 shows the experimental results after applying our approach with and without scheduling for the Mediabench benchmark. The average energy reductions with and without can achieve 25% and 18%. In Mediabench, applications like Jpeg, epic, and pgpwit have less dependences in them, thus the effects are better. In fact, with our experiences, our work can acquire better energy saving if the number of multipliers in the CPU is large.

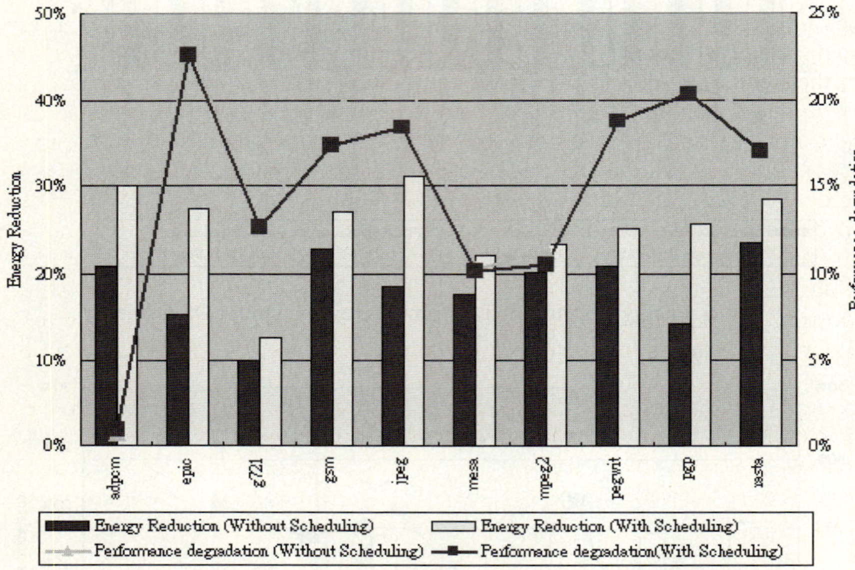

Fig. 8. Energy reduction and performance evaluation for Mediabench

4.2 Performance Evaluation

The performance impact on Dspstone, SPEC2000, and Mediabench with our approach is plotted with lines on the right axis of Figure 6 to Figure 8 It shows that our approach leads to performance degradation since our optimizations take some time to save energy. In DSPstone, the code sizes of most applications in DSPstoneit are smaller. Thus, the performance degradation caused by slowing down the CPU is smaller except matrix since its code size is large and it uses too many macros. By contrast, due to the larger code sizes of applications, the performance degradation of SPEC2000 is around 12.6% and 14.1% on average with and without scheduling. For Mediabench, the code sizes of most applications in it are larger, which results in worse performance. On average, the performance degradations are 14.9% and 16.4% with and without scheduling, respectively. The performance degradation of adpcm is better since its size is very small. In our experiments, no performance degradations of benchmarks will exceed 20% if "with scheduling" is applied. For the remaining cases, the performance degradations are under 10% except 'gzip'. In addition, with our knowledge, no previous DVS algorithms that use compilation techniques have shown the impact on the performance.

5 Related Work

Previous work reduced the energy dissipation by proposing various DVS techniques [1,4,6,7,8,10,12,13,14]. Some work [8,10] focused on scheduling the tasks using DVS to meet the real-time constraint to lower energy consumption. Shin et al. also aimed at the intra-task scheduling under the real-time constraint based on the power information generated by compiler [12]. Previous work addressed the DVS issue by slowing down the frequency with a low voltage in the regions containing many memory accesses [6,7]. In their work, the issue was modeled as the minimization problem with the performance and the transition constraints. Although they took the transition overheads into account, they did not reschedule the program to exploit the potential of reducing the transitions between power modes. Rele et al. devised a region-based approach to reduce the energy dissipation by turn off the idle functional units for superscalar processors [11]. Their work only showed the impacts on the utilization of functional units and performance after applying their work to programs, but it did not demonstrate the experimental results about power dissipation. By contrast, on the one hand our work extends the period of idle functional units and on the other hand we performs instruction scheduling on the programs to reduce the number of transitions between power modes. In comparison with previous work [5,6], they also divided an application into regions and adjust voltages and frequencies of power modes, but their approaches did not consider turning off the idle functional units and the transitions between power modes to save energy. You et al. presented three low-power optimizations with respect to a basic block [16]. One is to turn off the idle functional units in a basic block and the other two are to adjust the voltage of an execution path according to their two different power constraints. Their approach is partially similar to ours. But ours differs with theirs in the following two ways. (1) Our work targets at Alaph 21264 with four ALUs, while theirs was performed on a virtual architecture proposed by themselves. (2) Our work can maximize the idle periods of functional units with instruction scheduling and minimize the transitions between power modes, while theirs just turned off the idle functional unit without doing further optimizations.

6 Conclusions and Future Work

This paper presents an effective DVS approach at compiler time to reduce energy dissipation by attempting to minimize the transitions between power modes by maximizing the idle periods of functional units with instruction scheduling. To reduce energy dissipation when executing an application, we first implement new instructions to turn off the idle functional units and two power modes to adjust voltage and clock frequency of CPU. Then we apply instruction scheduling to maximize the idle periods of functional units and minimize transitions between power modes .Our work is performed with DSPstone, SPEC2000, and Mediabench benchmarks on the basis of the SUIF2 compiler infrastructure and the Wattch simulator. On average, the experimental results show that our work can save the energy by around 26% and lead to the performance degradation less than 18% for most benchmarks. Our future research will focus on the settings of three thresholds to see how they influence the optimizations of our work.

References

1. N. AbouGhazaleh, D. Moss'e, B. Childers, and R. Melhem. Toward the placement of power management points in real time applications. In Proceedings of the Workshop on Compilers and Operating Systems for Low Power, September 2001
2. 2. Alpha , Alpha 21264 Processor Technical Reference Manual, http://www.alpha.com.
3. D. Brooks , V. Tiwari , and M. Martonosi. Wattch: A Framework for Architectural Level Power Analysis and Optimizations. In International Symposium on Computer Architecture (ISCA) , Vanconver , British Columbia , 2000
4. T. Burd and R. Brodersen. Design issues for dynamic voltage scaling. In Proceedings of 2000 International Symposium on Low Power Electronics and Design, July 2000
5. C.H. Hsu and U. Kremer. Compiler-directed dynamic voltage scaling based on program regions. Technical Report DCS-TR-461, Department of Computer Science,Rutgers University, November 2001
6. C.H. Hsu and U. Kremer. Single region vs. multiple regions: A comparison of different compiler-directed dynamic voltage scheduling approaches. In Workshop on Power-Aware Computer Systems, 2002
7. C.H. Hsu and U. Kremer. The Design, Implementation, and Evaluation of a Compiler Algorithm for CPU Energy Reduction. In Proceedings of the ACM SIGPLAN Conference on Programming Languages Design and Implementation, June 2003
8. C.M. Krishna and Y.-H. Lee. Voltage-clock-scaling adaptive scheduling techniques for low power in hard real-time systems. In Proceedings of the 6th Real Time Technology and Applications Symposium (RTAS'00), May 2000
9. MachSuif: A Framework built on top of SUIF for building back-ends http://www.eecs.harvard.edu/~hube
10. A. Manzak and C. Chakrabarti. Variable voltage task scheduling for minimizing energy or minimizing power. In Proceeding of the International Conference on Acoustics, Speech and Signal Processing, June 2000
11. K. Roy. Leakage Power Reduction in Low-Voltage CMOS Design. In IEEE International Conference on Circuits and Systems , Pages 167-173, 1998
12. Sannella, M. J. Constraint Satisfaction and Debugging for Interactive User Interfaces. Ph.D. Thesis, University of Washington, Seattle, WA, 1994
13. D. Shin, J. Kim, and S. Lee. Intra-task voltage scheduling for low-energy hard real-time applications. IEEE Design and Test of Computers, 18(2), March/April 2001
14. SUIF. Stanford University Intermediate Format. http://suif.stanford.edu
15. Transmeta, Crusoe TM5800 Processor Technical Reference Manual http://transmeta.com/
16. Yi-Ping You, Chingren Lee, and Jenq Kuen Lee, Compilers for Leakage Power Reduction," accepted, ACM Transactions on Design Automation of Electronic Systems.

Minimising the Energy Consumption of Real-Time Tasks with Precedence Constraints on a Single Processor

Hui Wu and Sridevan Parameswaran

School of Computer Science and Engineering
The University of New South Wales
{huiw, sridevan}@cse.unsw.edu.au

Abstract. Energy-aware task scheduling is critical for real-time embedded systems. Although dynamic power has traditionally been a primary source of processor power consumption, leakage power is becoming increasingly important. In this paper, we present two optimal energy-aware polynomial-time algorithms for scheduling a set of tasks with release times, deadlines and precedence constraints on a single processor with continuous voltages. Our algorithms are guaranteed to minimise the total energy consumption of all tasks while minimising their maximum lateness under two power models: the dynamic power model where the dynamic power dominates the processor power consumption and the dynamic and leakage power model where both dynamic power and leakage power are significant sources of the processor power consumption. The time complexities of both algorithms are $O(n^3)$, where n is the number of tasks.

1 Introduction

In mobile real-time embedded systems, energy is a precious resource. Minimising the energy consumption while satisfying the performance constraints is a key issue in the design of such systems. Energy reduction is also important in other real-time embedded systems. A real-time system with less energy consumption generates less heat and therefore has a longer lifetime.

Traditionally, dynamic power is the main source of processor power consumption. There are two techniques, namely DVS (Dynamic Voltage Scaling) and DPM (Dynamic Power Management) that can be used to reduce the dynamic power consumption of processors. In DVS, different tasks are run at different voltages and clock frequencies to fill up the idle periods in the schedule, while still satisfying the performance constraints. DPM aims to shut down system components not currently in use. DVS is more efficient than DPM in reducing the energy consumption of processors. DPM is used only if DVS is not applicable.

A lot of work has been done in DVS for real-time embedded systems. In the case of a single processor, many algorithms and heuristics have been proposed. Yao et al [1] studied the problem of scheduling a set of independent tasks with

E. Sha et al. (Eds.): EUC 2006, LNCS 4096, pp. 45–56, 2006.

individual release times and deadlines on a single processor with continuous voltage such that the energy consumption of the processor is minimised. They proposed an optimal EDF-based (Earliest Deadline First) algorithm for static scheduling and suboptimal algorithms for online scheduling. Kwon and Kim [16] proposed a static scheduling algorithm for the same problem with discrete voltages. Li and Yao [2] proposed a faster algorithm for the same problem solved by Kwon and Kim.

Ishihara and Yasuura [3] proposed a model of dynamically variable voltage processor and a static voltage scheduling algorithm formulated as an integer linear programming problem. In addition to task execution times and deadlines, their algorithm also requires the average switched capacitance for each task. However, their algorithm does not consider precedence constraints and release times.

Hong et al [4] proposed an energy-aware on-line algorithm for scheduling both periodic tasks and sporadic tasks. Their algorithm guarantees the deadlines of all periodic tasks and tries to maximise the number of aperiodic tasks that can be finished by their deadlines.

Quan et al [6] studied the problem of minimising the total energy consumption of a set of tasks with individual release time and deadline on a single processor using fixed priority scheduling. They proposed a heuristic for this problem. Yun and Kim [15] also studied the same problem. They proved the NP-hardness of the problem and proposed an approximation algorithm.

Sinha and Chandrakasan [5] proposed an energy-aware SEDF (Slack Earliest Deadline First) algorithm for scheduling a set of independent tasks with release times and deadlines on a single processor. Their algorithm is stochastically optimal in minimising processor energy consumption and maximum lateness.

Shin et al [9] proposed an intra-task scheduling approach that can further reduce energy consumption of tasks by partitioning a task into several segments, each assigned with a separate a voltage.

As technology feature size continues to scale, leakage power is increasing and will limit power savings obtained by DVS alone. Therefore, the optimisation objective of task scheduling is to minimise the sum of dynamic energy and leakage energy. Recently, a number of researchers studied the problem of combining DVS and adaptive body biasing (ABB) to simultaneously optimise both dynamic energy consumption and leakage energy consumption.

Quan et al [8] proposed a scheduling technique that can effectively reduce the overall energy consumption for hard real-time systems scheduled according to a fixed priority scheme. Experimental results show that a processor using their strategy consumes as less as 15 percent of the idle energy of a processor employing the conventional strategy.

Andrei et al [12] investigated the problem of overhead-aware voltage selection for dynamic and leakage energy reduction of time-constrained systems where tasks are subject to deadline and precedence constraints. They optimally solved the continuous voltage selection problem by using non-linear programming and proved NP-hardness in the discrete case.

Jejurikar et al [13] proposed a leakage-aware algorithm for scheduling periodic tasks on a single processor. Their algorithm uses EDF scheduling strategy. Unlike our algorithms, their algorithm does not consider critical task sets. Instead, it computes the execution speed of each task individually. Jejurikar and Gupta [14] proposed leakage-aware algorithms for fixed-priority systems. Both algorithms are not guaranteed to minimise the total energy consumption of all tasks.

In this paper, we propose polynomial-time task scheduling algorithms for minimising the total energy consumption of a set of real-time tasks with individual release times, deadlines and precedence constraints on a single processor with continuous voltages. Assuming that the voltage transition overheads are negligible, our algorithms are guaranteed to minimise the total energy consumption of all tasks under two power models: the dynamic power model where the dynamic power dominates the processor power consumption and the dynamic power and leakage power model where both dynamic power and leakage power are significant sources of the processor power consumption. In addition, our algorithms are guaranteed to minimise the maximum lateness of all tasks.

We make the following significant contributions.

1. Under the dynamic power and leakage power model our algorithm is the first algorithm for minimising the total energy consumption of a set of tasks with release times, deadlines and precedence constraints on a single processor. The previous algorithm proposed by Jejurikar et al [13] is not guaranteed to minimise the total energy consumption of all tasks and does not consider the precedence constraints. [1]
2. Under the dynamic power model our algorithm generalises Yao's algorithm [1] by considering additional precedence constraints.

2 Power Models and Definitions

2.1 Dynamic Power Model

Under the dynamic power model, the processor power is dominated by the dynamic power [17] which is given by:

$$P_{dynamic} = C_{eff} V_{dd}^2 f \tag{1}$$

where C_{eff} is the effective switching capacitance, V_{dd} is the supply voltage and f is processor clock frequency.

Processor clock frequency f, is almost linearly related to the supply voltage:

$$f = \frac{(V_{dd} - V_{th})^{\alpha}}{kV_{dd}} \tag{2}$$

[1] The algorithm proposed by Jejurikar et al considers periodic tasks without any precedence constraint and uses EDF scheduling strategy. Since a periodic task can be represented by a set of non-periodic tasks with individual release times and deadlines, the problem they studied is a special case of our problem where no precedence constraint exists.

where k is a constant, V_{th} is the threshold voltage and $1 < \alpha \leq 2$. Based on the SPICE simulation of the Berkley predictive models for a $0.07\mu m$ process [18], the threshold voltage [10] is given by the following equation:

$$V_{th} = V_{th1} - k_1 V_{dd} - k_2 V_{bs} \tag{3}$$

where V_{th1}, k_1 and k_2 are constants and V_{bs} is body bias voltage.

Substitute (3) into (2) gives the expression of f in terms of V_{dd} and V_{bs}.

$$f = \frac{((1+k_1)V_{dd} + k_2 V_{bs} - V_{th1})^{\alpha}}{kV_{dd}} \tag{4}$$

Substituting (4) into (1), we have the dynamic power function $P(V_{dd})$ where the dynamic voltage V_{dd} is the only variable:

$$P(V_{dd}) = \frac{C_{eff}}{k} V_{dd}((1+k_1)V_{dd} + k_2 V_{bs} - V_{th1})^{\alpha} \tag{5}$$

Note that $P(V_{dd})$ is a convex function.

2.2 Dynamic and Leakage Power Model

Under dynamic power model, the processor power dissipation is dominated by both dynamic power and leakage power [17], where the leakage power [11] can represented as:

$$P_{leakage} = I_s(\frac{W}{L})V_{dd}e^{\frac{-V_{th}}{nV_T}} + |V_{bs}|(I_j + I_b) \tag{6}$$

where I_s and n are technology parameters, W and L are device geometries, I_j is drain-body junction leakage current, I_b is source-body junction leakage current, and V_T is the thermal voltage.

Substituting (3) into (6), we have:

$$P_{leakage} = k_3 V_{dd} e^{k_4 V_{dd} + k_5 V_{bs}} + |V_{bs}|(I_j + I_b) \tag{7}$$

where k_3, k_4 and k_5 are new constants. Therefore, the total power consumption can be represented by:

$$\begin{aligned} P &= P_{dynamic} + P_{leakage} \\ &= C_{eff}V_{dd}^2 f + k_3 V_{dd} e^{k_4 V_{dd} + k_5 V_{bs}} + |V_{bs}|(I_j + I_b) \end{aligned} \tag{8}$$

From Equation (4), we have

$$V_{bs} = k_6 V_{dd} + k_7 (fV_{dd})^{\frac{1}{\alpha}} + k_8 \tag{9}$$

where k_6, k_7 and k_8 are new constants.

Substituting (9) into (8), we have the dynamic and leakage power function $P(V_{dd}, f)$ where V_{dd} and f are the only two variables:

$$\begin{aligned} P(V_{dd}, f) = &C_{eff}V_{dd}^2 f + k_9 V_{dd} e^{k_{10} V_{dd} + k_{11}(fV_{dd})^{\frac{1}{\alpha}}} \\ &+ k_{12} V_{dd} + k_{13}(fV_{dd})^{\frac{1}{\alpha}} + k_{14} \end{aligned} \tag{10}$$

where $k_9 - k_{14}$ are new constants. Note that $P(V_{dd}, f)$ is a convex function.

2.3 Problem and Definitions

In this section, we propose two optimal algorithms for energy-aware real-time task scheduling on a single processor. We assume two power models: the dynamic power model and the dynamic and leakage power model. Under the dynamic power model, the dynamic power is the main source of the processor power consumption and the leakage power is negligible. Under the dynamic and leakage power model, both dynamic power and leakage power are significant sources of the processor power consumption.

A problem instance P consists of a set $V = \{T_1, T_2, \cdots, T_n\}$ of n tasks with the following constraints:

1. Worst case execution times. The worst case execution time of task T_i, denoted by c_i, is the longest execution time of T_i when the processor runs at the maximum frequency.
2. Release times. Each task T_i has a pre-assigned release time r_i.
3. Deadlines. Each task T_i has a pre-assigned deadline d_i.
4. Precedence constraints represented by a DAG (Directed Acyclic Graph) $G = (V, E)$, where $E = \{(T_i, T_j) : T_i \text{ precedes } T_j\}$.
5. A single processor with continuous voltages.

The energy-aware single processor scheduling problem is described as follows. Given a problem instance P, find a valid schedule with minimum lateness for all the tasks such that the total energy consumption of all tasks is minimised. A schedule is called a valid schedule if it satisfies all release times and precedence constraints.

Definition 1. *Given a schedule σ for a problem instance P and a task T_i, the lateness of T_i is $f_i - d_i$, where f_i is the completion time of T_i in σ.*

Definition 2. *Given a problem instance P and a task T_i, the edge-consistent release time of T_i, denoted by r'_i, is recursively defined as follows: $r'_i = max\{r_i, max$ $\{ r'_j + c_j$: T_j is an immediate predecessor of $T_i\}\}$*

Definition 3. *Given a problem instance P and a task T_i, the edge-consistent deadline of T_i, denoted by d'_i, is recursively defined as follows: $d'_i = min\{d_i, min$ $\{ d'_j - c_j$: T_j is an immediate successor of $T_i\}\}$*

Definition 4. *Given a set S of tasks with individual release times and deadlines and a partial schedule for S on a single processor, a time interval $[a, b]$ is a forbidden interval if it is fully occupied by one or more tasks in the partial schedule. A time interval $[a, b]$ is a maximum forbidden interval if it is a forbidden interval and there exists d such that neither $[a-d, a]$ nor $[b, b+d]$ is a forbidden interval.*

Since all forbidden time intervals are occupied by the tasks already scheduled, they cannot be used by other tasks.

Definition 5. *Given a set S' of independent tasks with individual release times and deadlines, a partial schedule σ for S' and a set S of unscheduled tasks, the processor utilisation of S is defined to be:*

$$U(S) = \frac{\sum_{T_j \in S} c_j}{d_{max} - r_{min} - l(S)}$$

where r_{min} is the minimum release time of all tasks in S, d_{max} is the maximum deadline of all tasks in S, and $l(S)$ is the total length of all maximum forbidden intervals within $[r_{min}, d_{max}]$.

Definition 6. *Given a set S' of independent tasks with individual release times and deadlines, a partial schedule σ for S', a subset S of unscheduled tasks is a critical subset if S has the greatest processor utilisation among all subsets of unscheduled tasks.*

Definition 7. *Given a set S of tasks with individual release times and deadlines, the interval of S is $[r_{min}, d_{max}]$, where r_{min} and d_{max} are the minimum release time and the maximum deadline of all tasks, respectively.*

3 Optimal Scheduling Algorithm

3.1 Optimal Task Execution Speed

Our scheduling algorithms are underpinned by critical task subsets. If dynamic voltage and body bias voltage take continuous values, we can show that in an optimal schedule all the tasks in a critical task subset must have the same speed. We call this speed optimal speed. The optimal speed is dependent on the power model. Next we show how to compute the optimal speed $f_{opt}(S')$ for all tasks in a critical task subset $S' = \{T_{i_1}, T_{i_2}, \cdots, T_{i_k}\}$.

Under the power model where the dynamic power is the main source of processor power consumption, $f_{opt}(S')$ is the slowest speed at which the interval of S' is fully occupied by all tasks in S'. Specifically, $f_{opt}(S')$ is equal to $U(S')f_{max}$, where f_{max} is the maximum frequency of the processor. After assigning the optimal speed to all tasks in the critical task set, the interval of S' becomes a forbidden interval.

Under the power model where both dynamic power and leakage power are the significant sources of the processor power consumption, the optimal speed may not be the slowest speed due to the leakage power. Let F_{opt} be the optimal processor frequency which minimises the total power $P(V_{dd}, f)$ of the processor. F_{opt} can be computed by using gradient search [20]. Given a processor, F_{opt} is a constant. When computing the optimal speed $f_{opt}(S')$ for all tasks in S', we need to consider the following two cases:

1. $U(S')f_{max} < F_{opt}$. Since the power function $P(V_{dd}, f)$ is a convex function and F_{opt} is the speed which minimises $P(V_{dd}, f)$, $f_{opt}(S')$ is equal to F_{opt}.
2. $U(S')f_{max} \geq F_{opt}$. In this case, by the convexity of the power function $P(V_{dd}, f)$, $P(V_{dd}, f)$ decreases as f increases within $[f_{min}, F_{opt}]$, where f_{min} is the minimum processor frequency. As a result, $f_{opt}(S')$ is equal to $U(S')f_{max}$.

In the case where $U(S')f_{max} < F_{opt}$ holds, the interval of S' will contain non-forbidden intervals after all tasks in S' are scheduled. This is because the interval of S' cannot be fully used by all tasks in S'. In the case where $U(S')f_{max} \geq F_{opt}$ holds, since all tasks in S' will fully use the interval, the interval of S' will become a forbidden interval after all tasks in S' are scheduled.

3.2 Minimum Energy Scheduling Algorithms

Our scheduling algorithms consist of the following two main steps.

1. Transform the original problem instance P into a precedence-free scheduling problem instance P' as follows.
   (a) Compute the edge-consistent release time for each task and set its release time to its edge-consistent release time.
   (b) Compute the edge-consistent deadline for each task and set its deadline to its edge-consistent deadline.
   (c) Compute a schedule σ for the original problem instance P on the single processor running at the maximum frequency by using EDF strategy.
   (d) Create a precedence-free problem instance P' as follows:
      – For each task T_i, set its release time to its start time in σ and its deadline to $\max\{d_i, e_i\}$, where e_i is the finish time of T_i in σ.
2. Find a minimum energy schedule for the precedence-free problem instance P' as follows. Let V be a set of all tasks in P. Repeat the following steps until V is empty.
   (a) Find a critical task subset S' of V.
   (b) Compute the optimal speed for all tasks in S' as described in the previous subsection.
   (c) Compute a partial schedule for S' using EDF strategy and the optimal speed.
   (d) $V = V - S'$.

The minimum energy schedule for P' is a union of partial schedules for all critical task subsets. As we will prove in the next section, it is also a minimum energy and minimum lateness schedule for the original problem instance P.

Under the dynamic power model, we can use Yao's algorithm [1] to compute all critical task subsets. Under the dynamic and leakage power model, the interval of a critical task subset may not be fully used. Therefore, the whole interval cannot be removed. As a result, Yao's algorithm is not applicable to the dynamic and leakage power model.

Next, we describe an efficient implementation of our algorithm for computing critical task sets under the dynamic and leakage power model. Given a problem instance P which consists of a set of independent tasks with individual release times and deadlines and a single processor, the critical task subsets are computed as follows:

1. Find a critical task subset S for P as in [1].
2. Compute the optimal speed for S.

3. Compute a partial schedule σ for S using EDF strategy.
4. Find all maximum forbidden intervals in $[r_{min}, d_{max}]$, where r_{min} and d_{max} are the minimum release time and the maximum deadline, respectively, of all tasks in S. Let $[a_1, b_1]$, $[a_2, b_2]$, $\cdots$, $[a_k, b_k]$ be the k maximum forbidden intervals in $[r_{min}, d_{max}]$ with $a_i < b_i$ $(i = 1, 2, \cdots, k)$ and $b_i < a_{i+1}$ $(i = 1, 2, \cdots, k-1)$.
5. Remove all tasks in S from P.
6. Modify the release time of each task T_i in P as follows:
   (a) If $r_i \geq d_{max}$, set the new release time of T_i to $r_i - \sum_{j=1}^{k}(b_j - a_j)$.
   (b) If $r_i \geq r_{min}$ and $r_i < d_{max}$, there are two cases.
      i. Case 1: r_i is within a maximum forbidden interval $[a_s,\ b_s]$. Set the new release time of T_i to $r_i - \sum_{j=1}^{s}(b_j - a_j)$.
      ii. Case 2: r_i is not within any maximum forbidden interval in $[r_{min}, d_{max}]$. Let $[a_t, b_t]$ be the maximum forbidden interval such that t is the largest integer satisfying $b_t < r_i$. Set the release time of T_i to $r_i - \sum_{j=1}^{t}(b_j - a_j)$.
7. Modify the deadline of each task T_i in P as follows:
   (a) If $d_i \geq d_{max}$, set the new deadline of T_i to $d_i - \sum_{j=1}^{k}(b_j - a_j)$.
   (b) If $d_i \geq r_{min}$ and $d_i < d_{max}$, there are two cases.
      i. Case 1: d_i is within a maximum forbidden interval $[a_s, b_s]$. Set the new deadline of T_i to $a_s - \sum_{j=1}^{s-1}(b_j - a_j)$.
      ii. Case 2: r_i is not within any maximum forbidden interval in $[r_{min}, d_{max}]$. Let $[a_t, b_t]$ be the maximum forbidden interval such that t is the largest integer satisfying $b_t < d_i$ and set the new deadline of T_i to $d_i - \sum_{j=1}^{t}(b_j - a_j)$.
8. Repeat the above steps until there is no task in P.

4 Optimality Proof and Time Complexity Analysis

We will use the following property of convex functions in our optimality proof.

Lemma 1. *Given a convex function f(X) in the n−dimensional space, the following inequality holds:*

$$\sum_{i=1}^{m} \lambda_i f(X_i) \geq f(\sum_{i=1}^{m} \lambda_i X_i)$$

where $X_1, X_2, \cdots, X_m$ are m points in the n-dimensional space and $\sum_{i=1}^{m} \lambda_i = 1$ and $\lambda_i \geq 0 (i = 1, 2, \cdots, m)$

Theorem 1. *Given a set of tasks with individual release times, deadlines and precedence constraints, our scheduling algorithm is guaranteed to find a schedule with minimum lateness on a single processor with continuous voltages.*

Proof. It is known that earliest edge-consistent deadline first strategy is guaranteed to find a schedule with minimum lateness [19]. We just need to prove that in a schedule σ for P' computed by our algorithm, no task will miss its new deadline P'. Suppose that a task T_i misses its new deadline in σ. T_i must be in a critical task subset S' and S' must have at least two tasks, including T_i. Otherwise, T_i cannot miss its new deadline in σ. Since T_i misses its new deadline, its processor utilisation must be greater than that of S'. By the definition of a critical task subset, T_i cannot be included in S', which leads to a contradiction.

Theorem 2. *Given a set of tasks with individual release times, deadlines and precedence constraints, our scheduling algorithm is guaranteed to find a schedule with minimum energy consumption on a single processor with continuous voltages.*

Proof. Let S' be a critical task subset computed by our algorithm, T_1, T_2, $\cdots$, T_m be all tasks in S' and σ be an optimal schedule for S'. We distinguish two power models.

1. Under the power model where the dynamic power is the dominant source of the processor power consumption, there is no idle time within the interval of S' in σ. The total energy consumption W of all tasks in σ is $\sum_{i=1}^{m} \frac{P(v_i)c_i f_{max}}{f_i}$, where v_i and f_i are the dynamic voltage and the clock frequency, respectively, of the processor when task T_i is running. Let $c = \sum_{i=1}^{m} \frac{c_i f_{max}}{f_i}$ and $\eta_i = \frac{c_i f_{max}}{f_i c}$. Note that $\sum_{i=1}^{m} \eta_i = 1$ and $c = d_{max} - r_{min} - l(S')$, where d_{max} and r_{min} are the maximum deadline and minimum release time, respectively, of all tasks in S' and $l(S')$ is the total length of all forbidden intervals in $[r_{min}, d_{max}]$. By the property of convex functions, we have
$$W = \sum_{i=1}^{m} \frac{P(v_i)c_i f_{max}}{f_i} = c\sum_{i=1}^{m} \eta_i P(v_i)$$
$$\geq cP(\sum_{i=1}^{m} \eta_i v_i) \geq cP(v_{opt})$$
Where v_{opt} is the dynamic voltage which corresponds to the slowest processor frequency for S' i.e. $\frac{\sum_{i=1}^{m} c_i}{c} f_{max}$.
Note that $cP(v_{opt})$ is the total energy consumption of all tasks in our schedule for S'. Therefore our schedule for S' is a minimum energy schedule.
2. Under the power model where both the dynamic power and leakage power are the dominant sources of the processor power consumption, idle time may exist within the interval of S' in σ. The total energy consumption W of all tasks in σ is $\sum_{i=1}^{m} \frac{P(v_i, f_i)c_i f_{max}}{f_i}$, where v_i and f_i are the dynamic voltage and the clock frequency, respectively, of the processor when task T_i is running. Let $c = \sum_{i=1}^{m} \frac{c_i f_{max}}{f_i}$ and $\eta_i = \frac{c_i f_{max}}{f_i c}$. Note that $\sum_{i=1}^{m} \eta_i = 1$. By the property of convex functions, we have

$$W = \sum_{i=1}^{m} \frac{P(v_i, f_i) c_i f_{max}}{f_i} = c \sum_{i=1}^{m} \eta_i P(v_i, f_i)$$
$$\geq cP(\sum_{i=1}^{m} \eta_i v_i, \sum_{i=1}^{m} \eta_i f_i)$$

which implies that a single processor frequency for all tasks in a critical task set is the necessary condition for minimising the total energy consumption of all tasks in a critical task set. Since our algorithm computes an optimal processor clock frequency for all tasks in S' which minimises the power function, our schedule for S' is a minimum energy schedule.

Next we analyse the time complexities of our algorithms. First, we analyse the time complexity of transforming the original problem instance P to the precedence-free problem instance P' as follows.

1. The edge-consistent release times and deadline of all tasks can be computed by using breadth-first search, which takes $O(e)$ time, where e is the number edges in the precedence graph.
2. The EDF schedule for P can be computed using a priority queue, which takes $O(n \log n)$, where n is the number of tasks.
3. It takes $O(n)$ time to set the release times and deadlines for all tasks in P'.

Therefore, it takes $O(e + n \log n)$ time to construct the precedence-free problem instance P'.

Under the dynamic power model, we can use Yao's algorithm to compute the critical task sets. The time complexity of Yao's algorithm is $O(n^3)$. [2] Therefore, the time complexity of our algorithm for the dynamic power model is $O(n^3)$.

To facilitate the analysis of the time complexity of our algorithm for the dynamic and leakage power model, we assume that there are m critical task subsets for a problem instance P. Let S_1, S_2, $\cdots$, S_m be the m critical task subsets, k_i the number of remaining tasks in P and p_i the number of forbidden intervals when S_i is computed. We analyse the time complexity of our algorithm for computing the optimal speed for all tasks in each critical task subset $S_i (i = 1, 2, \cdots, m)$ as follows.

1. The time complexity for finding a critical task subset is $O(n^2)$ [1].
2. When modifying the release time and the deadline for each remaining task in P, we can sort all maximum forbidden intervals and use binary search to determine which case is applicable. Therefore, it takes $O(p_i \log p_i + k_i \log p_i)$ to modify the release times and deadlines for all tasks in S_i.

Therefore, the time complexity for computing all critical intervals is $O(mn^2) + O(\sum_{i=1}^{m} (p_i \log p_i + k_i \log p_i)) = O(n^3)$.

[2] The time complexity of Yao's algorithm was said to be reducible to $O(n \log^2 n)$, but the claim was withdrawn in [2].

5 Conclusion

We proposed two polynomial-time algorithms for finding a minimum energy schedule for a set of tasks with individual release times, deadlines and precedence constraints on a single processor with continuous voltages. Our algorithms are guaranteed to find a schedule with both minimum lateness and minimum energy consumption under two power models. Under the first power model, the dynamic power is the dominant source of the processor power consumption and the leakage power is negligible. Under the dynamic and leakage power model, both the dynamic power and the leakage power are significant sources of the processor power consumption. Under the dynamic power model, the time complexities of both algorithms are $O(n^3)$, where n is the number of tasks.

In this paper, voltage transition overheads are ignored. It is not known if the problem can also be optimally solved in polynomial-time if voltage transition overheads are included. Another interesting problem is how to generalise our algorithms to multiple processor scheduling. In the existing work on leakage-aware DVS scheduling for multiple processor real-time systems, the execution speed of each task is computed individually. By the property of convex functions, more energy would be saved if all tasks in a critical subset are executed at the same speed.

References

1. Frances Yao, Alan Demers and Scott Schenker. A Scheduling Model for Reduced CPU Energy. The proceedings of Annual Symposium on Foundation of Computer Science,1995, Pages 374-382.
2. Minming Li and Frances Yao. An Efficient Algorithm for Computing Optimal Discrete Voltage Schedules. Siam Journal on Computing, 35(3), 2005, Pages 658-671.
3. Tohru Ishihara and Hiroto Yasuura. Voltage Scheduling Problem for Dynamically Variable Voltage Processors. Proceedings of International Symposium on Low Power Electronics and Design, 1998, Pages 197-202.
4. Inki Hong, Miodrag Potkonjak, Mani B. Srivastava. On-line Scheduling of Hard Real-Time Tasks on Variable Voltage Processor. Proceedings of International Conference on Computer-Aided Design, November 1998, Pages 458-470.
5. Amit Sinha and Anantha P. Chandrakasan. Energy Efficient Real-Time Scheduling. Proceedings of International Conference on Computer-Aided Design, 2001, Pages 458-470.
6. Gang Quan and Xiaobo Hu. Energy Efficient Fixed-Priority Scheduling for Real-Time Systems on Variable Voltage Processors. Proceedings of Design Automation Conference, 2001, Pages 828-833.
7. Yumin Zhang, Xiaobo Sharon Hu, and Danny Chen. Task Scheduling and Voltage Selection for Energy Minimisation. Proceedings of Design Automation Conference, June 2002.
8. Gang Quan, Linwei Niu, Xiaobo Sharon H and Mochocki, B. Fixed Priority Scheduling for Reducing Overall Energy on Variable Voltage Processors. Proceedings of Real-Time Systems Symposium, 2004.

9. D. Shin, J. Kim and S. Lee. Low-Energy Intra-Task Voltage Scheduling Using Static Timing Analysis. Proceedings of Design Automation Conference, June, 2001, Pages 438-443.
10. S. M. Martin, K. Flautner, T. Mudge and D. Blauuw. Combined Dynamic Voltage Scaling and Adaptive Body Biasing for Low Power Microprocessors under Dynamic Workloads. Proceedings of International Conference on Computer-Aided Design, Nov. 2002, Pages 721-725.
11. Le Yan, Jiong Luo and Niraj K. Jha. Combined Dynamic Voltage Scaling and Adaptive Body Biasing for Heterogeneous Distributed Real-Time Embedded Systems. Proceedings of 2003 International Conference on Computer-Aided Design, Nov. 2003, Pages 30-38.
12. Alexandru Andrei, Marcus Schmitz, Petru Eles, Zebo Peng, Bashir M. Al-Hashimi: Overhead-Conscious Voltage Selection for Dynamic and Leakage Energy Reduction of Time-Constrained Systems. Proceedings of 2004 Design, Automation and Test in Europe Conference and Exposition (DATE 2004), Pages 518-525.
13. Ravindra Jejurikar, Cristiano Pereira, Rajesh K. Gupta: Leakage aware dynamic voltage scaling for real-time embedded systems. Proceedings of Design Automation Conference, June, 2004, Pages 275-280.
14. Ravindra Jejurikar, Rajesh K. Gupta: Procrastination scheduling in fixed priority real-time systems. Proceedings of ACM SIGPLAN/SIGBED Conference on Languages, Compilers, and Tools for Embedded Systems, June, 2004, Pages 57-66.
15. Han-Saem Yun and Jihong Kim. On Energy-Optimal Voltage Scheduling for Fixed Priority Hard Real-Time Systems. ACM Transactions on Embedded Computing Systems, Vol. 2, No. 3, August 2003, Pages 393-430.
16. Woo-Cheol Kwon and Taewhan Kim. Optimal Voltage Allocation Techniques for Dynamically Variable Voltage Processors. ACM Transactions on Embedded Computing Systems, Vol. 4, No. 1, February 2005, Pages 211-230.
17. N. H. E Weste and K. Eshraghian. Principle of CMOS VLSI Design. Addison Wesley, 1993.
18. http://www-device.eecs.berkley.edu/ ptm/introduction.html
19. Peter Brucker. Scheduling Algorithms. Springer, 2004.
20. Stephen Boyd and Lieven Vandenberghe. Convex Optimisation. Cambridge University Press, 2001.

Power Aware H.264/AVC Video Player on PAC Dual-Core SoC Platform

Jia-Ming Chen[1], Chih-Hao Chang[2], Shau-Yin Tseng[2], Jenq-Kuen Lee[1], and Wei-Kuan Shih[1]

[1] Department of Computer Science, National Tsing Hua University, Hsinchu, Taiwan
jonathan@rtlab.cs.nthu.edu.tw, {jklee, wshih}@cs.nthu.edu.tw
[2] SoC Integration Division of STC, ITRI, Hsinchu, Taiwan
{chchang, tseng}@itri.org.tw

Abstract. This paper proposes a novel power-aware scheme of H.264/AVC video player for the PAC SoC platform based on its modern dual-core architecture with DVFS capability. Energy/power is saved by the global view of power state transitions on the dual-core subsystem according to a user's behaviors of playing a video. When the user stays in continuous video decoding, a fine-grain power-aware scheme is devised to save the energy/power in advance. Especially the fine-grain model is suitable for any standard coded H.264/AVC video without extra modifications. We also discuss a workable reduction technique when imprecise video decoding time is permitted under soft real-time constraint. For a similar SoC platform with the dual-core architecture and DVFS capability, the idea presented here is, to the best of our knowledge, the first power-aware design of H.264/AVC video player.

Keywords: Power-aware, Dual-Core SoC, DVFS, H.264/AVC.

1 Introduction

Multimedia applications on mobile/portable devices, such as PDAs, smart phones, and Portable Media Players (PMPs) become more and more popular nowadays. Due to these portable devices are battery-operated, one imperative objective is conserving energy consumption to lengthen the battery service time. Especially within these multimedia applications, video services play an important role such as video conferences, video phones, digital TV broadcasting, and DVD players. However, processing video data requires a huge amount of computation and energy. Based on the state-of-the-art video coding standard, H.264/AVC [1, 2], many researches [3, 4, 5] revealed that there is a great variances in computational complexity between sub-procedures during video decoding, which is mainly induced by different frame types and variation of moving objects among scenes. This characteristic makes further investigation of reducing energy consumption during video decoding possible.

E. Sha et al. (Eds.): EUC 2006, LNCS 4096, pp. 57 – 68, 2006.

Traditional low power techniques, such as clock gating, power gating and dynamic voltage and frequency scaling (DVFS) have been commonly used in modern hardware and software designs, and have been proved to be a powerful and practical solution on power/energy reductions. The main idea of these techniques is to provide just enough computation power without degrade the system performance while seeking possible for minimizing power/energy dissipation. Thus, many researchers have applied DVFS technique to reduce power for video decoding. Based on prediction models for the decoding time of oncoming frames, the processor can be set to the proper voltage and frequency to minimize the power consumption without violating the quality of video streaming. These studies have been compared and summarized in [6]. Similarly, [7] has further investigated the prediction through decomposition of video workloads together with a methodology, called "inter-frame compensation" to reduce the predication errors. In addition, since prediction methods essentially evoke errors, and are harmful to video decoding with hard real-time constraints, [8] proposed a power-aware video decoding scheme according to information of non-zero coded macroblocks, where these information need to be recoded in video streams.

In general, most researches of power-aware video decoding by DVFS techniques only concentrated on a single processor. However, in recent trends of hardware design for portable devices, system designers [9, 10, 11] often integrate a RISC processor with a coprocessor (DSP or ASIC) into one SoC chip by taking advantages of modern VLSI design processes in order to achieve higher cost-effective hardware solutions. The primary reason for this design is that customers require more complex functionalities on smaller portable devices. At the same time, while concerning saving more energy/power, built-in a DVFS technology into a dual-core SoC platform is a promising solution. For example, Texas Instrument Inc. will provide the SmartReflex™ technology on their next generation OMAP™ 2 architecture [12]. Likewise, the PAC (Parallel Architecture Core) SoC platform, which is developing in an on-going project held by STC/ITRI organization at Taiwan [13], provides another comparable solution.

Unfortunately, in regard to these modern SoC platforms with dual-core architecture, previous researches cannot simply be adopted to efficiently solve the power-saving problems for video decoding. Therefore, in this paper, we first propose a valuable power-aware scheme of H.264/AVC video player, and demonstrate how to apply this technology onto the PAC SoC platform. In fact, the principle of the proposed methodology can be also applied to similar platforms (e.g., a dual-core platform with DVFS capability) without or with minor modifications.

The remainder of this paper is organized as follows: The architecture of PAC dual-core SoC platform with DVFS capability is introduced in Section 2. Then based on this platform, a coarse-grain power-aware scheme for H.264/AVC video player is presented in Section 3 and a fine-grain power-aware scheme for continuous video decoding process is devised in Section 4. After that, in Section 5, we proposed a workable reduction techniques based on the devised scheme in Section 4 when imprecise decoding time are admitted under soft real-time constraint and some experiments are given. Finally, conclusions are made in Section 6.

2 The PAC SoC Platform

Before proposing the power-aware scheme of H.264/AVC video player, we briefly introduce the DVFS capability of the PAC SoC platform in this section. Detail information can be found in [13]. The core of PAC SoC platform is divided into eight power domains: MPU, DSP-Logic, DSP-Memory, on-chip memory, AHB modules, APB modules, analog modules (e.g., PLLs), and others (with fixed voltage), where DSP, MPU, and AHB modules have DVFS capabilities, which can be triggered by the DVFS controller. According to the DVFS capabilities of MPU and DSP, their operation modes can be further classified into *active*, *inactive*, *pending* and *sleep* as shown in Table 1.

Thus from the viewpoint of the dual-core subsystem, the interactions of global power states between MPU and DSP can be illustrated in Fig. 1(a). For example, when some functions are implemented on DSP and is activated right away, the power state may be transited from Active state 3 (i.e., MPU is in active and DSP is in sleep) to Active state 1 (i.e., both MPU and DSP are in active). Furthermore, in the Active state 1, MPU and DSP have different voltage and frequency settings (as shown in Table 1) for their power-saving purposes. Along with taking advantage of this feature, we can devise our power-aware scheme for H.264/AVC video player, explained in the next section.

Table 1. Power and action states of MPU and DSP

Power mode	Operation condition		Power consumption(II)	Computation power(I)	Transition latency(us)
	Freq.(MHz)	Voltage(V)			
MPU_active-1	228	1.2	100%	1	1
MPU_active-2	152	1.2	76%	2	1
MPU_active-3	114	1.2	65%	3	1
MPU_inactive	0	1.2	<30%	None	1
MPU_sleep	0	0	<1%	None	120
DSP_active-1	228	1.2	100%	1	120
DSP_active-2	152	1.0	60%	2	120
DSP_active-3	114	0.8	50%	3	120
DSP_inactive	0	1.2	<30%	None	1
DSP_pending	0	0.8	<30%	None	120
DSP_sleep	0	0	<1%	None	120

(I): 1>2>3; (II): theoretical value

3 Power-Aware H.264/AVC Video Player

Fig. 1(b) displays the behaviors mapping onto Fig. 1(a) when a typical H.264/AVC video player is running on the PAC SoC platform. Once the video player changes its behavior, the dual-core subsystem may switch its power states. For example, while the video player changes its behavior from "Play" to "Pause within 15 min", the dual-core subsystem switches its power state from "Active state 1" to "Active sate 2", in which

MPU keeps in active mode, but DSP switches from active mode into inactive mode. At this moment, the frequency of DSP is turned off by the DVFS controller to save the dynamic power dissipation. As a result, through this mapping policy H.264/AVC video player can indicate the DVFS controller to dynamically adjust the supply voltage/frequency of dual-core subsystem in order to conserve the energy of the whole system.

In experience, as soon as H.264/AVC video player enters "Play" behavior, it would keep quite a long time staying in that behavior due to users' habits. Many researches [14, 15] have been presented to convince that power consumption is reduced by about 30%~40% during continuously video decoding in a single processor. Likewise, when dual-core subsystem stays in "Active state 1" to proceed H.264/AVC video decoding, fine-grain frame-based voltage/frequency adjustment for DSP can further save energy consumption (i.e., switching between 3 active modes, 228MHz, 152MHz and 114MHz for DSP depending on the required computation power). Therefore, in the following sections, we explain how to achieve this purpose to complete our power-aware scheme for H.264/AVC video player on PAC SoC platform.

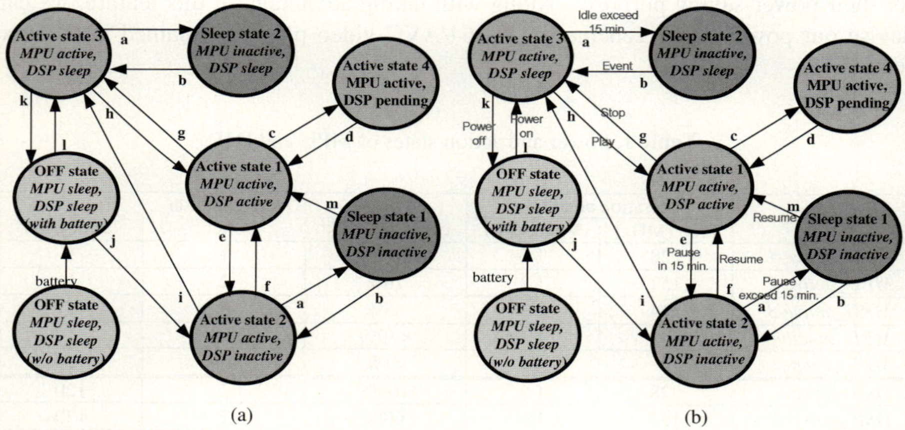

Fig. 1. (a) States of power transition for dual-core subsystem; (b) Mapping a typical video player into states of power transition for dual-core subsystem

4 Power-Aware H.264/AVC Video Decoding

First, we describe how to achieve the fine-grain power-aware H.264/AVC decoding by introducing a partition scheme of H.264/AVC decoding algorithm based on the dual-core architecture. Then, we inlay the power-aware video decoding technique into the system via DVFS capability.

4.1 Partitioning and Mapping Scheme

As shown in Fig. 2(a), the decoding flow of H.264/AVC is classified into four main procedures: Entropy Decoding (ED), Inverse Quantization/Inverse Transformation (IQ/IT), Predictive Pixel Compensation (PPC), and Deblocking Filter (DF). First, the ED procedure decodes and reorders the compressed bitstream from the NAL to produce a set of quantized DCT coefficients X. Second, the IQ/IT procedure scales and inverse transforms X to D'_n (residual data). Third, the PPC procedure creates a prediction block PRED via Motion Compensation (MC) using reference data F'_{n-1} or Intra prediction where the decision is made by the header information decoded from the bitstream. Finally, PRED is added to D'_n to produce uF'_n which is filtered to produce decoded block F'_n by the DF procedure.

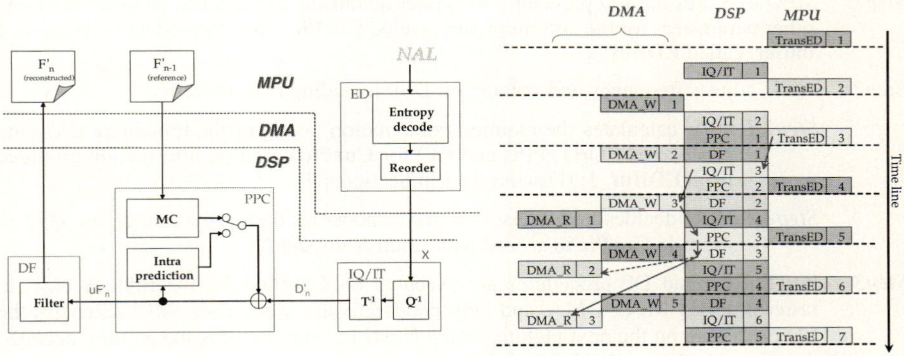

(a) (b)

Fig. 2. (a) H.264 decoding algorithm and partitioning; (b) Parallel execution of decoding a picture via MB-by-MB basis

To map the decoding procedure onto PAC SoC platform, we partitioned the decoding procedures into two parts: the **MPU_Part** and the **DSP_Part**. The **MPU_Part** includes the ED and Reference Picture Management (RPM) procedures while the **DSP_Part** includes the IQ/IT, PPC, and DF procedures. There are two primary reasons for MPU to execute the ED and RPM procedures instead of DSP. First, on the one hand the innate behavior of the ED procedure performs back and forth between bit extraction and table-look-up operations, and on the other, the RPM procedure is I/O-intensive as compared with the IQ/IT, PPC, and DF procedures. Both procedures are superior to executing on MPU (large memory) rather than on DSP (less memory). Second, the information gathered during executing the ED procedure on a picture benefits the calculations of computation power for DSP so that it is better to keep the ED and RPM procedures executed on MPU and the other procedures on DSP.

4.2 Execution Flow of Decoding Process with Power-Aware Technique

Based on the partition scheme described in Section 4.1, we propose the decoding flow of H.264/AVC with power-aware technique as explained in Fig. 3. Note that in ***Step3***, the data transfer between MPU and DSP are parallel executed in pipeline concept using the TransED, DMA_Ref, and DMA_Out procedures as described in Table 2. Fig. 2(b) displays the executing flow, where every MB is processed in TransED, IQ/IT, DMA_Ref, PPC, DF, and DMA_Out order (as depicted in Fig. 2(b) by arrow solid lines). Consecutive MBs are also pipelining executed. For instance, when executing the TransED on MB 4, the DF on MB 1, the PPC and DMA_Ref on MB 2, and the IQ/IT on MB 3 are executed in parallel. At this moment, MPU only executes the TransED so that it can utilize the leisure time to execute the ED procedure on the next picture.

Step1 MPU executes the ED procedure to extract quantized coefficients, MVs of MBs and other parameters for the current picture, called **CurPic**. Then those data is stored on a buffer, called **EDBuf_1**.

Step2 MPU adjusts frequency and voltage for DSP including two substeps:

- ***Step2.1*** MPU calculates the required computation power of the remaining decoding procedures (IQ/IT, PPC and DF) for **CurPic** based on information provided from **EDBuf_1**; (Discuss later in Section 4.3);
- ***Step2.2*** MPU decides and adjusts the most moderate frequency/voltage for DSP to decode **CurPic** in accord with result from ***Step2.1***;

Step3 IQ/IT, PPC and DF procedures are executed on **CurPic** with macroblock basis in raster order by MPU, DMA, and DSP cooperatively. Meanwhile, MPU executes the ED procedure on the next picture, called **NextPic,** and produces the entropy decoded data into a buffer, called **EDBuf_2**.

Step4 After DSP has completely decoded **CurPic** and MPU has already prepared **EDBuf_2** for **NextPic**, Step2~3 are applied to **EDBuf_2** repeated, and the entropy decoded data of **NextPic** is restored in the **EDBuf_1.**

Fig. 3. Decoding flow of H.264/AVC with power-aware technique on PAC SoC platform

Table 2. Procedures of data transfer between DSP and MPU

Procedure	Description
TransED	MPU transfers quantized coefficients data of one MB from entropy decoded buffer (**EDBuf_1**) to DSP memory.
DMA_Ref	DMA transfers required reference data (gathered from reconstructed inter or intra pictures) and its related parameters (e.g., luma CBP, MB type information, MVs…) when DSP executes PPC and DF procedures for one MB.
DMA_Out	DMA transfers reconstructed MB (finished by DSP) to MPU memory.

Next, we explain how to calculate the required computation power for ***Step2.1*** and derive the equation in order to apply DVFS technique to DSP.

4.3 Determination of Clock Frequency and Supply Voltage for DSP

Generally, in the proposed scheme as stated in Section 4.2, the calculation of the proper supply frequency f_{dsp} (in MHz) for DSP in ***Step2*** can be formulated as Eq. (1), where $T_{IQ/IT}$, T_{PPC}, and T_{DF} are decoding time (in clock cycles per picture) spent by IQ/IT, PPC, and DF procedures respectively. Besides, since DSP and MPU cooperate to decode the picture in parallel fashion and MBs of a picture must follow the execution order as described in ***Step3*** of Section 4.2, we introduce a control flow procedure in DSP to handle this matter, which spends T_{Ctrl} time (in clock cycles per picture). Furthermore, the parameter $\mathbf{FrameRate_{video}}$ (in fps) is the frame rate provided by the video stream (for example, 30fps in real-time). It is a conservative estimation because the ED procedure for decoding a picture is slack-stealing and is executed by MPU instead of by DSP (as described in ***Step3*** of Section 4.2). Particularly note that during decoding a picture, the overhead of transferred procedures (i.e., DMA_Out, DMA_Ref, and TransED) are not counted here since they are hidden from overlapped parallel fashion as depicted in Fig. 2(b). In Eq. (1), we omit the overhead of executing the TransED procedure on the first MB because it can be compensated by the conservative estimation of aforementioned overlapping executing procedure between MPU and DSP.

$$f_{dsp} = (T_{IQ/IT} + T_{PPC} + T_{DF} + T_{Ctrl}) \times \mathbf{FrameRate}_{\mathbf{video}} \times 10^{-6} \tag{1}$$

Previous research [16] proved that apparently different computation power is required when decoding distinct type of pictures (e.g., I/B/P/SI/SP-types). It implies that IQ/IT, PPC, and DF procedures for decoding each picture may consume different power. Here, in order to simplify but not limited to our work, we merely focus on the baseline profile of H.264/AVC decoding, which only contains I-type and P-type pictures. Thus, we can further distinguish Eq. (1) into two cases as follows:

Case1. Decoding an I-type picture

According to H.264/AVC standard, an I-type picture only contains intra-coded MBs such that only three modes, intra 4x4 mode (i.e., a luma MB with 4x4 intra prediction), intra 16x16 mode (i.e., a luma MB with 16x16 intra prediction) and intra 8x8 mode (i.e., a chroma MB with 8x8 intra prediction), are supported. Based on the values of coded block pattern (CBP) for each MB which is known during executing the ED procedure, we can further decompose Eq. (1) into Eq. (2).

$$f_{dsp} = (T^{I}_{IQ/IT} + T^{I}_{intra} + T^{I}_{DF} + T_{Ctrl}) \times \mathbf{FrameRate}_{\mathbf{video}} \times 10^{-6}, \tag{2}$$

where

$$\begin{aligned} T^{I}_{IQ/IT} = {} & N^{I}_{4x4CBP} \times T_{4x4IQ/IT} + N^{I}_{16x16CBP} \times (17 \times T_{4x4IQ/IT}) \\ & + N^{I}_{ChrCBP} \times (8 \times T_{4x4IQ/IT} + 2 \times T_{2x2IQ/IT}) \end{aligned} \tag{2.1}$$

$$T^{I}_{intra} = N^{I}_{intra4} \times (16 \times T_{4x4PRED}) + N^{I}_{intra16} \times (16 \times T_{4x4PRED}) + N^{I}_{intraChr} \times (4 \times T_{4x4PRED}) \quad (2.2)$$

$$T^{I}_{DF} = N_{bS3} \times T_{bS3} + N_{bS4} \times T_{bS4} \quad (2.3)$$

Eq. (2.1) represents the IQ/IT procedure applying on a picture containing intra 4x4 mode, intra 16x16 mode and intra 8x8 mode MBs (including chroma blue and chroma red). We implement a subroutine of IQ/IT operation on a 4x4 block since IQ/IT operations on 4x4 AC or 4x4 DC blocks (no matter luma or chroma MBs) have the same cycle counts. The cycle counts spent in intra 16x16 mode which contain 16 4x4 AC blocks and 1 4x4 DC block can be summarized to 17 times of $T_{4x4IQ/IT}$. Similarly, cycle counts spent in intra 8x8 mode can be summarized to 8 times of $T_{4x4IQ/IT}$ plus 2 times of $T_{2x2IQ/IT}$ for 8 4x4 AC blocks and 2 2x2 DC blocks respectively. Especially note that N^{I}_{4x4CBP}, $N^{I}_{16x16CBP}$, and N^{I}_{ChrCBP} parameters for each prediction mode only count the frequencies for nonzero coefficient blocks which are known from corresponding CBP values (i.e., CBP=1 if a block contains nonzero coefficients) during executing ED procedure.

In the same way, we consider the cycle counts spent in intra prediction mode for the PPC procedure which is conducted by Eq. (2.2). Parameters N^{I}_{intra4}, $N^{I}_{intra16}$, and $N^{I}_{intraChr}$ stand for the occurrences of three distinct modes in an I-type picture respectively. Moreover, we implement each subroutine for various prediction types (e.g., *DC*, *vertical*, *horizontal*, *planar* and etc.) on a 4x4 block basis. In the H.264/AVC standard, there are 9 types in intra 4x4 mode, 4 types in intra 16x16 mode for luma, and 4 types in intra 8x8 modes for chroma. In order to meet the precisely timing requirement for video decoding, we choose the maximum one as the parameter $T_{4x4PRED}$ (i.e., the *planar* type in our implementation). The values 16, 16, and 4 represent the frequencies of calling subroutines for intra 4x4, intra 16x16 and intra 8x8 modes respectively.

Finally, within an I-type picture, only bS (boundary strength) value equals 3 or 4 occurs in the DF procedure. Therefore, two subroutines (for bS=3, and bS=4) are applied and N_{bS3} and N_{bS4} stand for their occurrence respectively.

Case2. Decoding a P-type picture

Relatively, with the information of CBPs, MB types, and MVs extracted from the ED procedure, Eq. (1) can be decomposed into Eq. (3).

$$f_{dsp} = (T^{P}_{IQ/IT} + T^{P}_{intra} + T^{P}_{inter} + T^{P}_{DF} + T_{Ctrl}) \times \mathbf{FrameRate_{Video}} \times 10^{-6}, \quad (3)$$

where

$$\begin{aligned} T^{P}_{IQ/IT} = {} & N^{P}_{4x4CBP} \times T_{4x4IQ/IT} + N^{P}_{16x16CBP} \times (17 \times T_{4x4IQ/IT}) \\ & + N^{P}_{ChrCBP} \times (8 \times T_{4x4IQ/IT} + 2 \times T_{2x2IQ/IT}) \end{aligned} \quad (3.1)$$

$$T^{P}_{intra} = N^{P}_{intra4} \times (16 \times T_{4x4PRED}) + N^{P}_{intra16} \times (16 \times T_{4x4PRED}) + N^{P}_{intraChr} \times (4 \times T_{4x4PRED}) \quad (3.2)$$

$$T^{P}_{inter} = \sum_{i=0}^{8} \sum_{j=0}^{7} N_{inter(i,j)} \times T_{inter(i,j)} + \sum_{i=0}^{8} \sum_{j=0}^{7} N_{interChr(i,j)} \times T_{interChr(i,j)} \quad (3.3)$$

$$T^{P}_{DF} = N_{bS1} \times T_{bS1} + ... + N_{bS4} \times T_{bS4} \tag{3.4}$$

Eq. (3.1) and Eq. (3.2) have the similar meanings as Eq. (2.1) and Eq. (2.2) in **Case1** except for the various execution frequencies of each subroutine. Moreover, the PPC procedure of **Case2** introduces additional motion compensated (MC) inter prediction mode as formulated in Eq. (3.3). It can be divided into 72 subroutines by applying 9 variances of interpolation operations (according to distinct MVs) to 8 distinct MB partitions (including the skip mode) by our implementation in DSP codes. Finally, during the DF procedure, we need to take bS = 1, 2, 3, and 4 into consideration due to the coexistences of inter and intra-coded MBs in a P-type picture. The definitions of symbols in each equation are summarized in Table 3.

Table 3. Definition of subroutines and cycle counts used in Eq. (2) and Eq. (3)

Symbol	Meaning
$T^{I}_{IQ/IT}$,$T^{P}_{IQ/IT}$	Total cycle counts spent in IQ/IT procedures for I-type and P-type picture respectively
$T_{4x4IQ/IT}$	Cycle counts spent in IQ/IT operation for a 4x4 block
$T_{2x2IQ/IT}$	Cycle counts spent in IQ/IT operation for a 2x2 block
T^{I}_{Intra} , T^{P}_{Intra}	Total cycle counts spent in intra-coded MBs (including luma and chroma) for I-type and P-type pictures respectively
$T_{4x4PRED}$	Cycle counts spent in the maximum prediction type operation for a 4x4 block (i.e., the planar type)
T^{P}_{inter}	Total cycle counts spent in inter-coded MBs for P-type pictures
$T_{inter(I,j)}$	Cycle counts spent in interpolation on each inter-coded luma MB or subMB, there are totally 72 cases (9x8) where i=0,..,8 indicates 9 variances of interpolation based on MVs (*) j=0,..,7 indicates 16x16,16x8,8x16,8x8,8x4,4x8,4x4 MB partitions and skipped mode
$T_{interChr(i,j)}$	Similar to above $T_{inter(i,j)}$, but proceed on chroma MB or sub-MB
T^{I}_{DF} , T^{P}_{DF}	Total cycle counts spent in DF procedures for I-type and P-type pictures respectively
T_{bS1}, .., T_{bS4}	Cycle counts spent per 4x4 block for bS=1, 2, 3, 4 respectively within DF procedure (luma and chroma MBs are considered together)

(*) {(0,0)}, {(1/2,0)}, {(1/4,0), (3/4,0)}, {(0,1/2)}, {(0,1/4),(0,3/4)}, {(1/4,1/4),(3/4,3/4),(3/4,4/1),(1/4,3/4)}, {(1/4,1/2),(3/4,1/2)}, {(1/2,1/4),(1/2,3/4)}, {(1/2,1/2)} totally 9 variances for i=0,..,8; We can group several MVs together since their cycles are the same in our implementation on DSP.

Consequently, during executing the ED procedure on a picture, MPU can calculate the computation power required by DSP through Eq. (2) and Eq. (3). As a result, the proper supply voltage/frequency for DSP to execute the remainder decoding procedures is determined and triggered via DVFS controller according to the action states of DSP as listed in Table 1.

5 Saving Energy for MPU Under Soft Real-Time Constraint

The methodology proposed in Section 4.3 exactly seeks for saving energy by estimating the required frequency of DSP under the hard real-time constraint that the frame rate indicated by the parameter **FrameRate$_{video}$** cannot miss. However, by taking a closer look at Eq. (2) and Eq. (3), $T^{I}_{IQ/IT}$, $T^{P}_{IQ/IT}$, and T^{P}_{inter} consider the calculations of all different cases of prediction modes and macroblock types such that they bring MPU significant computation power. It indicates that MPU may stay in the highest frequency (e.g., *MPU_active-1* in Table 1) and consume large power. On the contrary, if the video decoding only requires satisfying soft real-time constraint and the imprecise estimation are allowed, we can simplify several subroutines in Eq. (1) and Eq. (2) to let MPU stay in lower frequency to save its power dissipation. We summarized the techniques in the following paragraphs.

First, the IQ/IT procedure is simplified by estimating $N^{I}_{16x16CBP}$, N^{I}_{ChrCBP}, $N^{P}_{16x16CBP}$, and N^{P}_{ChrCBP} in Eq. (2.1) and (3.1) based on the profiling results as shown in Table 4(a). Eq. (2.1) is reduced to Eq. (2.1.1), where N^{I}_{16x16}, N^{I}_{8x8} are the total amount of MBs in intra 16x16 mode and intra 8x8 mode for luma and chroma, and P_{16x16}, P_{Cb}, P_{Cr} are extracted from Table 4(a), which individually indicate the probabilities of N^{I}_{16x16} and N^{I}_{8x8} with nonzero coded blocks. Eq. (3.1) is similarly reduced to Eq. (3.1.1). Second, the PPC procedure is simplified in two cases: (i) average value is used for $T_{4x4PRED}$ in Eq. (2.2) and Eq. (3.2), instead of using the maximum one, for the purpose of saving more power of DSP, and (ii) the calculations of MVs for various MB partitions in Eq. (3.3) is simplified by replicating the MVs of subMBs to other subMBs through the policies as shown in Fig. 4. For instance, a MB partition with 16 4x4 luma subsamples is treated as having 4 MVs instead of 16 MVs. Finally, the DF procedure is simplified by unifying the T_{bS1}, T_{bS2}, T_{bS3}, and T_{bS4} in Eq. (2.3) and (3.4) into average value such that we only execute the DF procedure on each MB depending on the bS value (i.e., skip the calculation when bS=0).

We have evaluated the aforementioned mechanisms by investigating the imprecise estimation of DSP. In the experiment, all test sequences are baseline profile in *IPPPPIPP...* frame sequences and ±16 search range including 6 video sequences: (i) container – QCIF, 100 frames, (ii) silent – QCIF, 100 frames, (iii) foreman – QCIF, 100 frames, (iv) news – QCIF, 100 frames, (v) mobile – CIF, 100 frames, and (vi) football – CIF, 90 frames. The result revealed that MPU has chance to switch its frequency into lower level but incurred estimation errors of DSP as listed in Table 4(b). Take the peek error in 246 cycles/MB (i.e., the football in Table 4(b)) as the worse case with D1 (totally 1350 MBs) resolution encoded in real-time (30 fps), the total estimation error is within $246 \times 1350 \times 30 = 9.96$ MHz/sec, which is quite acceptable comparing to the topmost frequency of DSP (228 MHz).

$$T^{I}_{IQ/IT} = \left[N^{I}_{4x4CBP} + N^{I}_{16x16} \times (16 \times P_{16x16} + 1) + N^{I}_{8x8} \times 8 \times (\frac{P_{Cb} + P_{Cr}}{2}) \right] \times T_{4x4IQ/IT} + N^{I}_{8x8} \times 2 \times T_{2x2IQ/IT} \quad (2.1.1)$$

$$T^{P}_{IQ/IT} = \left[N^{P}_{4x4CBP} + N^{P}_{16x16} \times (16 \times P_{16x16} + 1) + N^{P}_{8x8} \times 8 \times (\frac{P_{Cb} + P_{Cr}}{2}) \right] \times T_{4x4IQ/IT} + N^{P}_{8x8} \times 2 \times T_{2x2IQ/IT} \quad (3.1.1)$$

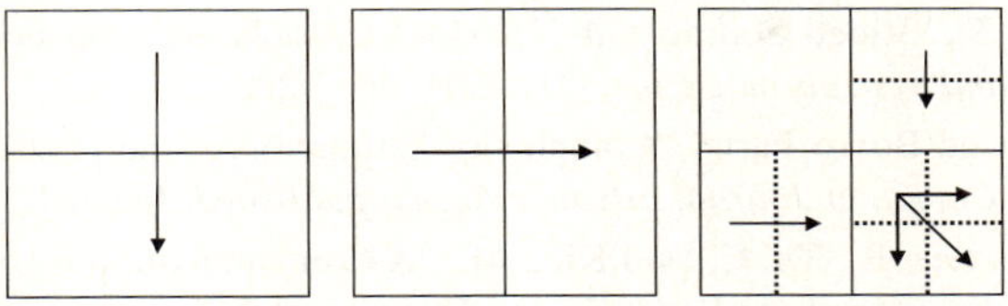

Fig. 4. Policy for reducing MV calculations according to distinct MB partitions

Table 4. (a) Probabilities for nonzero 4x4 blocks of a luma MB in intra 16x16 mode, and nonzero 4x4 blocks of a chroma MB in intra 8x8 mode; (b) Estimation errors of each test sequence for DSP

(a)

Test sequence	Probabilities (%)		
	luma	chroma	
		Cb	Cr
Container	84.5	47.6	42.4
Silent	87.5	43.5	43.8
News	67.2	41.3	37.9
Foreman	66.4	43	40
Mobile	61.6	38.5	39.7
Football	84.1	43.8	44.2

(b)

Test sequence	Max. Error (cycle/MB)	Avg. Error (cycle/MB)
Container	62	13
Silent	85	33
Foreman	105	41
News	89	27
Mobile	138	86
Football	246	55

6 Conclusion

In this paper, we proposed a novel power-aware scheme of H.264/AVC video player for PAC SoC platform based on its dual-core architecture and DVFS capability. The power-aware scheme is derived from a coarse-grain model according to a user's behaviors on playing a video and a fine-grain model along with continuous video decoding. A workable reduction scheme is also proposed to seek for further energy-saving under soft real-time constraint. Our work provides a valuable solution for designing a state-of-the-art H.264/AVC video player on similar platforms, such as PAC SoC platform, which is a promising hardware solution in modern VLSI design process.

References

[1] Wiegand, T., Sullivan, G.J., Bjntegaard, G., and Luthra, A, "Overview of the H.264/AVC video coding standard," *IEEE Transactions on Circuits and Systems for Video Technology*, vol. 12, issue 7, July 2003, pp. 560-576.

[2] G. J. Sullivan, P. Topiwala, and A. Luthra, "The H.264/AVC Advanced Video Coding Standard: Overview and Introduction to the Fidelity Range Extensions," *SPIE Conference on Applications of Digital Image Processing*, vol. 5558, part 1, Aug. 2004, pp. 454-474.

[3] Horowitz, M., Joch, A., Kossentini, F., and Hallapuro, A., "H.264/AVC baseline profile decoder complexity analysis," *IEEE Transactions on Circuits and Systems for Video Technology*, vol. 13, issue 7, July 2003, pp. 704-716.

[4] Ostermann, J., Bormans, J., List, P., Marpe, D., Narroschke, M., Pereira, F., Stockhammer, T., and Wedi, T., "Video Coding with H.264/AVC: tools, performance, and complexity," *IEEE Circuit and Systems magazine*, Q1, 2004, pp. 7-28.

[5] Hari Kalva 1 and Borko Furht, "Complexity Estimation of the H.264 Coded Video Bitstreams," *The Computer Journal Advance Access published*, June 24, 2005.

[6] Nurvitadhi, E., Lee, B., Yu, C., and Kim, M., "A Comparative Study of Dynamic Voltage Scaling Techniques for Low-Power Video Decoding," *International Conference on Embedded Systems and Applications*, June 2003, pp. 23-26.

[7] Kihwan Choi, Ramakrishna Soma, and Massoud Pedram, "Off-chip latency-driven dynamic voltage and frequency scaling for an MPEG decoding," *Proceedings of the 41st annual conference on Design automation*, June 2004, pp. 07-11.

[8] Seongsoo Lee, "Low-Power Video Decoding on Variable Voltage Processor for Mobile Multimedia Applications," *ETRI Journal*, vol.27, no.5, Oct. 2005, pp.504-510.

[9] Song, J.; Shepherd, T.; Minh Chau; Huq, A.; Syed, L.; Roy, S.; Thippana, A.; Shi, K.; Ko, U., "A Low Power Open Multimedia Application Platform for 3G Wireless," *Proceedings of IEEE International SoC Conference*, 17-20 Sept. 2003, pp. 377-380.

[10] Knight, W., "Two heads are better than one [dual-core processors]," *IEE Review*, vol.51, no.9, Sept. 2005, pp. 32- 35.

[11] Zhaowei Teng; Peng Liu; Liya Lai, "Physical design of dual-core system-on-chip," *Proceedings of IEEE International Workshop on VLSI Design and Video Technology*, May 2005, pp. 36- 39.

[12] Texas Instruments Inc., white paper of SmartReflex™ Technologies, "SmartReflex™ power and performance management technologies — reduced power consumption, optimized performance", Sept. 2005. *http://focus.ti.com/pdfs/wtbu/smartreflex_whitepaper.pdf*

[13] Juin-Ming Lu et al., "DVFS SoC Architecture and Implementation," *SoC Technology Journal, Taiwan*, vol. 3, Nov. 2005, pp. 84-91.

[14] J. Pouwelse, K. Langendoen, R. Lagendijk, and H. Sips, "Power Aware Video Decoding," *Proc. Picture Coding Symposium*, 2001, pp. 303-306.

[15] K. Choi, K. Dantu, W. Cheng, and M. Pedram, "Frame-Based Dynamic Voltage and Frequency Scaling for a MPEG Decoder," *Proc. Int'l Conf. Computer-Aided Design*, 2002, pp. 732-737.

[16] A.C. Bavier, A.B.Montz, and L.L.Peterson, "Predicting MPEG execution times," in *Proceedings of ACM SIGMETRICS'98*, 1998, pp. 131-140. 97.

Dynamic Repartitioning of Real-Time Schedule on a Multicore Processor for Energy Efficiency*

Euiseong Seo[1], Yongbon Koo[2], and Joonwon Lee[1]

[1] Dept. of CS, Korea Advanced Institute of Science and Technology
[2] Electronics and Telecommunications Research Institute
ses@calab.kaist.ac.kr, ybkoo@etri.re.kr, joon@kaist.ac.kr

Abstract. Multicore processors promise higher throughput at lower power consumption than single core processors. Thus in the near future they will be widely used in hard real-time systems as the performance requirements are increasing. Though DVS may reduce power consumption for hard real time applications on single core processors, it introduces a new implication for multicore systems since all the cores in a chip should run at the same performance. Blind adoption of existing DVS algorithms may result in waste of energy since a core which requires low performance should run at the same high frequency with other cores. Based on the existing partitioning algorithms for the multiprocessor hard real-time scheduling, this article presents dynamic task repartitioning algorithm that balances task loads among cores to avoid the phenomena dynamically during execution. Simulation results show that in general cases our scheme makes additional energy saving more than 10% than that without our scheme even when the schedules are generated by WFD partitioning algorithm which is known as the best energy efficient partitioning algorithm.

1 Introduction

The use of real-time systems are getting wider and the target applications are getting more complex. Thus more powerful processors are demanded for real-time systems. To improve processor performance the processor vendors have competed to raise the operating frequencies of their processors. However the power consumption of a processor is increased proportionally to the cubic of its operating frequency f. Hence the power consumption of processors have been increased dramatically. However The concern for energy efficiency has been increased as the use of mobile equipments grows.

Multicore architecture[1] which integrates a few processor cores in a single chip draws attention because it provides more throughput without increasing f.

* This research was supported by the MIC(Ministry of Information and Communication), Korea, under the ITRC(Inofrmation Technology Research Center) support program supervised by the IITA(Institute of Information Technology Assessment) (IITA-2005-C1090-0502-0031).

E. Sha et al. (Eds.): EUC 2006, LNCS 4096, pp. 69–78, 2006.

Similar to symmetric multiprocessors, multicore systems achieve linear speed-up because each core has independent processing element and cache. Thus the throughput increase of a multicore processor is expected to be linear with respect to the increase of power consumption.

DVS(dynamic voltage scaling) is an another feature that changes V_{dd} and f of a processor during its operation. Many of multicore processors are to be expected to employ DVS. Current multicore technology offers a DVS feature that allows only the same frequency for all cores because individual voltage regulator for each core costs too much in both design and production. This limitation is expected to remain for foreseeable future[2].

Then the energy efficient scheduling of real-time tasks in this environment emerges. This problem is similar to that of the energy efficient real-time scheduling on multiprocessors of having DVS function. It is known as a NP-hard problem that scheduling hard real-time tasks for multiprocessors[3]. Thus many heuristic algorithms are introduced to solve this. Among many heuristics, partitioning scheduling [4,5,6] is one of the representative schemes which statically distributes tasks onto each processor. By partitioning scheduling the problem is transformed into single processor real-time scheduling problems which can be solved by using existing real-time schedulers like EDF(earliest deadline first)[5] or RM(rate-monotonic)[6].

Adding energy efficiency to the real time task schedule for a multiprocessor system has been a challenging problem. Most approaches depend on the idea[4,7] of using existing single processor DVS algorithms[8,9,10] in each processor that has its own task set which is given by a certain partitioning algorithm. Applying those approaches to a multicore processor underperforms due to the aforementioned limitation of using DVS in multicore processor. Hence this paper suggests a dynamic repartitioning algorithm to reduce the difference of demanded performance among cores.

The rest of this paper is organized as follows. Section 2 reviews existing related work especially on the DVS algorithm for the real-time schedule on a processor. Section 3 describes the dynamic repartitioning problem and a heuristic algorithm for it. Section 4 presents the simulation results of the suggested algorithm. And section 5 summarizes our conclusions.

2 Related Work

EDF is an optimal algorithm in scheduling periodic real-time tasks on a processor. The utilization of a task is defined as its WCET(worst case execution time) divided by its period and the utilization of a task set is the sum of the utilizations of tasks in it. By using EDF it is guaranteed that the task set which have the processor utilization under 1.0 is always feasible to schedule. The decrease of the processor performance will increase WCET of each task. Thus lowering processor performance will increase the utilization of the task set too. Due to the property of EDF we can lower processor performance till the utilization of the task set becomes 1 while the dead-lines are still kept. Based on this concept Pillai et.

Table 1. Example task set

Task	Period	WCET	Load	1st Exec. Time	2nd Exec. TIme
τ_1	8 ms	3 ms	0.375	2 ms	1 ms
τ_2	10 ms	3 ms	0.300	1 ms	1 ms
τ_3	14 ms	1 ms	0.071	1 ms	1 ms

al.[10] suggested three heuristics, *static, cycle-conserving* and *look-ahead,* which adjust processor performance for the real-time schedules that were generated by EDF or RM algorithms.

static adjust performance to make the utilization of the task set to 1 and stay in the decided performance level all the time. For example the utilization of the task set described in Table 1 is 0.746 and let the maximum frequency of the processor is 1.0. The lowered frequency of 0.746 make the utilization of the task set 1.

In general the actual execution time of a task shows much difference from the WCET of the task. The early completion of a task makes room for more energy saving. For example let there be a task set described in Table 1, there occur considerable amount of idle time with *static* algorithm. To exploit these idle periods from the early completions of the tasks, when a task is completed *Cycle-conserving* algorithm updates the utilization of the task as the actual execution time divided by its period. Thus after the updates the performance will be lowered according to the updated utilization and the updated value will be used till the next release of that task. After the next release of the task, the utilization of the task should be restored to its initial value to keep the dead-line. This algorithm improves energy efficiency much in case that the actual execution times tend to be much different from the WCETs. Figure 1 shows using *cycle-conserving* algorithm for the example task set in 1.

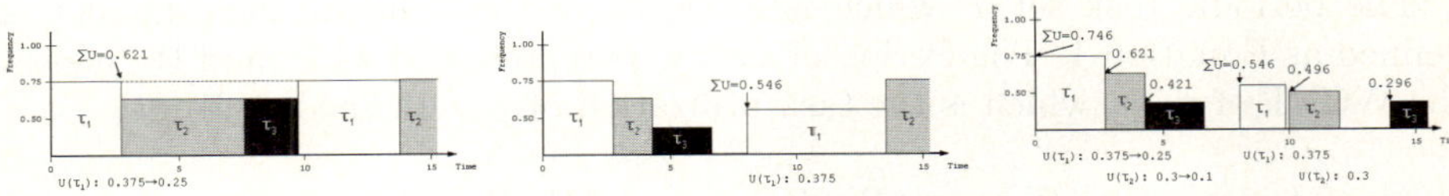

(a) After end of τ_1 (b) After end of τ_2 and τ_3 (c) Actual execution flow

Fig. 1. Cycle-conserving scheduling of example task set[10]

Because *cycle-conserving* algorithm dynamically utilizes the idle period from the early completion of the tasks, it saves more energy than *static* algorithm. However as depicted in Figure 1 (c) the tasks are executed at high performance at the starting and the performance had decreased as time flowed and this made idle time again. If most of the tasks are finished in much less than WCET, it is more effective to execute a task with lowered performance at the starting time and to execute the task with raised performance after certain threshold to keep the dead-line. *Look-ahead* algorithm is based on this idea.

In addition to this research, many DVS algorithms on periodic hard real-time systems are suggested. Aydin et. al.[8] suggested GDRA(generic dynamic reclaiming algorithm) and AGR(aggressive speed adjustment) algorithms to exploit the situation that the actual execution times are less than WCETs. The basic concept of GDRA is similar to *cycle-conserving* and AGR tries performance adjusting based on the execution history of tasks. The algorithm suggested by Gruian[9] starts to execute a task at low performance and based on the probability distribution of the execution time, it gradually raises the performance as the execution of the task goes on.

For the DVS scheduling on multiprocessor environment the basic approach is that adopting the existing single processor DVS algorithms onto the results from the partitioning algorithms. Aydin et. al.[4] also evaluated several partitioning heuristics for the energy efficiency and the result showed that Worst-Fit-Decreasing is the best energy efficient partitioning algorithm.

Yang et. al.[2] suggested an energy efficient static scheduling algorithm of hard real-time tasks on the multicore processors including DVS which is the same assumption in this paper. However it is based on the assumption that all the tasks have same periods and the execution time will be always same.

3 DVS Scheduling on a Multicore Processor

3.1 Dynamic Repartitioning Problem

The aim of this work is devising an algorithm that reduces the waste of energy due to the difference of performance demand among cores for executing periodic real-time tasks on a multicore processor in which cores have same V_{dd}. The real-time scheduling is assumed to be done by the partitioning approach. And our algorithm will work on the resulting schedule dynamically during the execution.

The periodic task set $\mathcal{T}$ which is executed in the assumed environment is defined as Equation 1. The Period of task τ_i is represented as P_i and W_i means the WCET of τ_i. u_i which is the task utilization of τ_i is defined as W_i/P_i.

$$\mathcal{T} = \{\tau_1(P_1, W_1), \ \ldots, \ \tau_n(P_n, W_n)\} \tag{1}$$

The dead-lines of each task are assumed to be same as their periods. Tasks have no dependency among them. The preemption and the migration of the tasks among cores are possible. The cost for the preemption and migration is assumed to be free because it can be considered in the actual implementation stage.

A multicore processor is defined as Equation 2. Processor S have m cores C in it.

$$\mathcal{S} = \{C_1, \ldots, C_m\} \tag{2}$$

Each core has a dedicated partitioned task set $\mathcal{T}_m$. The utilization sum U_m of $\mathcal{T}_m$ belonged to a certain core m does not exceed 1.0. To be simple if cores are operated at a relative performance p and the power consumption in a core is $g(p)$, at a certain point the power consumption in the processor is $mg(max(U_1, ..., U_m))$. In real the cores in the idle period from unexpected early completion consume only leakage power at the corresponding V_{dd}.

Performance of all cores are assumed to be decided by *cycle-conserving* algorithm. Among the performance demand of *cycle-conserving* algorithm for each core, the maximum is chosen for the performance of the whole cores. The additional power consumption compared to the multiprocessor systems occurs when the performance demands of cores are different from those of each other. And by using *cycle-conserving* the difference is dynamically changing according to the actual execution time of the tasks. Thus we define dynamic utilization L_n of core n as Equation 3. cc_i means the last execution time of τ_i at that time. Thus the power consumption of a certain point is $mg(max(L_1, ..., L_m))$. Energy consumption is the product of time and power. As a result our aim can be defined as maintaining L of all cores to have similar value all the time by dynamically migrating tasks between cores because the execution times of each tasks are meaningless as far as the dead-lines are kept.

$$L_n = \sum_{\forall completed\ \tau_i} \frac{cc_i}{P_i} + \sum_{\forall incompleted\ \tau_i} \frac{W_i}{P_i} \tag{3}$$

3.2 A Heuristic Approach

In this section we suggest dynamic repartitioning heuristic algorithm as a solution to the problem in section 3.1. Algorithm 1 is the pseudo code of dynamic repartitioning algorithm. Basic idea of the suggested algorithm is migrating tasks from the cores which have high L to the cores having low L until all the cores have similar L. This repartitioning occurs at the completion and the release of the tasks.

Cores can be categorized into donator or grantee group. The two groups are exclusive. In other words if a core is in donator group then it can not be in grantee group. A core in donator group have tasks which is initially partitioned to that core but migrated to some cores in grantee group. A core in grantee group have tasks to run at that time which is not initially partitioned to that core. By separating these two groups, the situations that a core give its task to others and get tasks from others can be easily prevented. This makes the algorithm work more effectively and in understandable manner.

As shown in line 28 and 35, L of a core is updated when tasks are completed and released. If a task is released, algorithm checks that updated L is not over 1.0. When L is over 1.0 there should be migrated tasks from other cores in the core. Thus all the migrated tasks are returned to their original cores. After this procedure repartitioning function will be called. Repartitioning function which is described from line 12 to line 26 is actually doing migration job. It decides the source core as the core with the highest L. If the source core in grantee group then the source core should return the task with minimum utilization in the source core to the initially partitioned core of the task. If the source core is not grantee group then the source core will migrate the task which have the lowest utilization in the source core to the destination core which is the minimum utilization core among the cores not in the donator group. This procedure will be repeated until L of the destination exceeds L of the source. When it happens it can be thought that all cores have less differences of L than the lowest task utilization in the core which has the minimum utilization at that time.

Whenever a migration occur or a task is released the algorithm checks that L of the core with the incident does not exceed 1.0. If L of a certain core becomes to exceed 1 then the migrated tasks in it will be restored to the cores in which the tasks were scheduled initially. Thus suggested algorithm never breaks the dead-lines by the property of EDF algorithm.

4 Evaluation

The suggested algorithm is evaluated by simulations. Our simulator uses several partitioning algorithms like NFD(Next-Fit-Decreasing), FFD(First-Fit-Decreasing), BFD(Best-Fit-Decreasing) and WFD. For comparison all the simulations were done both with and without dynamic repartitioning algorithm.

There are many factors which affect the energy consumption. Based on the related researches[10,7,4,8,9] we extracted major factors described in Table 2 which were changed to simulate the different situations. α means the upper limit of the utilization which a task can get. The utilizations of tasks are randomly generated and they follow the uniform distribution.

Table 2. Parameters used in the evaluations

Parameters	Values
α	0.1, 0.3, 0.5
Number of Cores (m)	2, 4, 8, 16
Task Load ($\sum_{i=1}^{m} \frac{U_i}{m}$)	0.1, 0.5, 0.9
Execution time (cc)	Normal distribution with μ: {20, 50, 80}% of WCET and σ: 1/6

Figure 2 shows the difference of energy consumption according to the partitioning heuristics and the combination of each heuristic and the suggested algorithm. The results are normalized to that of WFD without dynamic repartitioning. With the result we found that WFD performs better than the other heuristics in multicore systems too. However with dynamic repartitioning the energy consumption of all heuristics become similar. By using dynamic repartitioning algorithm combined with NFD which shows the worst energy efficiency 42% of energy was saved.

As shown in Figure 2 in the low load the dynamic repartitioning did not produce good results. Under low load all cores had low performance demands. Thus there were little differences among the performance demands of the cores. Due to that the benefits from dynamic repartitioning were little there.

Algorithm 1. Dynamic task repartitioning algorithm

```
C_max and C_min each returns the core with the highest and the lowest L
Γ(C) returns a task τ_r such that:
      ∀i where Π(τ_i) = Φ(τ_i) = C, (u_i <= u_r) ∧ (r ∈ i) ∧ (τ_r is ready to run)
Π(τ) means the core where τ is partitioned initially
Φ(τ) means the core where τ is currently located
D is the set of C such that:
      ∃τ where Φ(τ) = C, Π(τ) ≠ C                               /* Donator */
G is the set of C such that:
      ∃τ where Π(τ) = C, Φ(τ) ≠ C                               /* Grantee */

migrate(τ, C):
      Φ(τ) ⟵ C;

repartitioning():
      do
            C_src ⟵ C_max;
            if C_src ∈ G
                  τ_l ⟵ Γ(C_src);
                  C_dst ⟵ Π(τ);
                  migrate(τ_l, C_dst);
            else
                  τ_l ⟵ Γ(C_src);
                  C_dst ⟵ C_min where C_min ∉ D;
                  if (L_dst + u_l) > 1
                        migrate(τ, C_dst);
                  else
                        break;
      while (L_{C_src} > L_{C_dst});

upon task_release(τ_i):
      L_i ⟵ W_i/P_i;
      if (L_{Φ(τ_i)} > 1)
            for each task τ' in Φ(τ_i)
                  if Π(τ') ≠ Φ(τ_i)
                        migrate(τ', Π(τ'));
      repartitioning();

upon task_completion(τ_i):
      L_i ⟵ cc_i/P_i;                          /* cc_i := actual used cycles */
      repartitioning();
```

In case that the task loads were over 0.5, as shown in Figure 3 (a),(b),(c) and (d) the dynamic repartitioning worked better as the difference between cc and $WCET$ grew. This is because that more differences causes more changes of L and thus the load balance among cores were more spoiled. We also found that bigger α made dynamic repartitioning more effective. Small α means that the length of WCET is relatively short compared to the period. Thus there is relatively low margin of cc variance. Moreover the number of tasks increased when the α decreased because the task load was fixed. The actual execution time of a task is randomly decided at every rounds. If the number of task grows, in macro view there is less change of L because more samples produce more stable average value and L is an aggregation value of the random values.

The differences of demanding performance among cores tend to be greater when the number of cores grows because many cores mean many different demanding performances at a certain time. Figure 4 shows the tendency. With

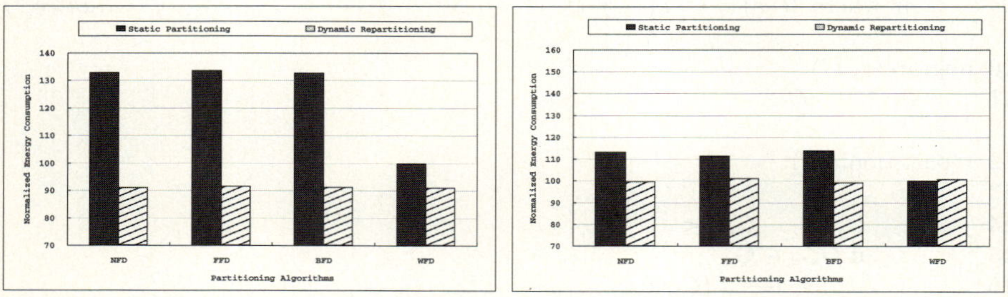

(a) Task load = 0.5 (medium load)   (b) Task load = 0.1 (low load)

Fig. 2. Normalized energy consumption according to the partitioning algorithms (m = 4, α = 0.1, μ of cc = 20% of WCET)

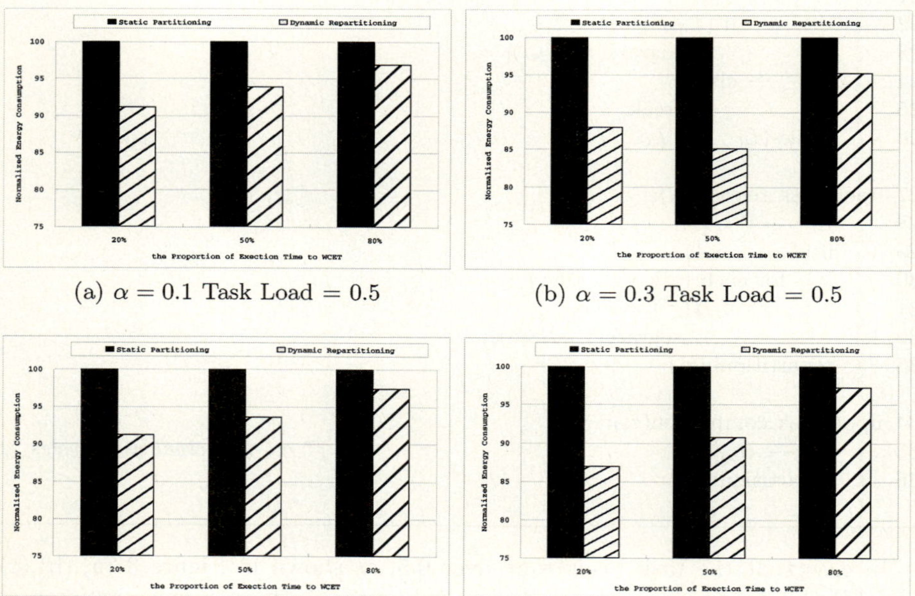

(a) $\alpha = 0.1$ Task Load = 0.5   (b) $\alpha = 0.3$ Task Load = 0.5

(c) $\alpha = 0.1$ Task Load = 0.9   (d) $\alpha = 0.3$ Task Load = 0.9

Fig. 3. Normalized energy consumption (m = 4, WFD partitioned)

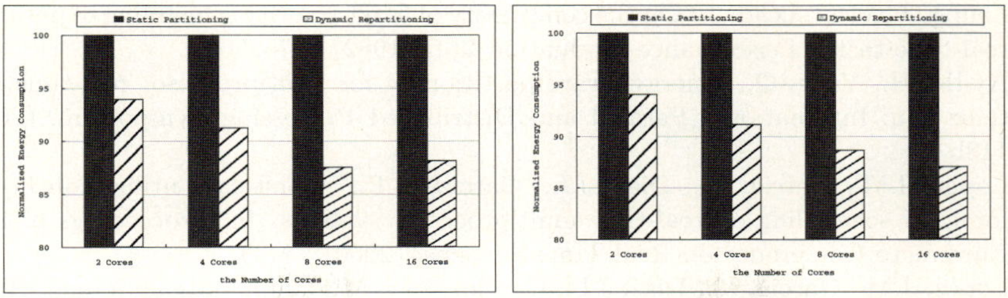

(a) Task load = 0.9 (b) Task load = 0.5

Fig. 4. Normalized energy consumption corresponding to the number of cores ($\alpha = 0.1$, WFD partitioned, μ of cc = 20% of WCET)

this result we can tell that while the number of cores grows, the benefit from dynamic repartitioning also grows.

5 Conclusion

This paper introduces the problem of using DVS on a multicore processor which has the limitation that all cores should run at the same performance level. As far as we know this problem is introduced in this paper for the first time. And as a solution to that problem we suggest dynamic repartitioning algorithm based on the partitioned schedule which have been used on the multiprocessor systems. To reduce the energy consumption from unbalanced load of the cores the suggested algorithm migrates tasks from high load cores to low load cores based on the dynamically updated load when a task is released and completed.

The simulation results show that in general cases more than 10% of additional energy is saved even with WFD partitioning, the best energy efficient partitioning algorithm. Moreover with other partitioning algorithm, up to 42% of additional energy saving was achieved. No matter which partitioning method is employed at the beginning, our scheme results in the same level of energy consumption which is always more efficient than the best energy efficient partitioning.

However the algorithm presented in this paper is blind to the purpose of a system. Considering the fact that most mobile embedded system is targeted for a specific purpose, each system is expected to have a specific set of tasks to run. In the further work, we will develop more intelligent algorithms which are tailored for the purpose of the target system.

References

1. Inc., A.M.D.: Multi-core processors - the next evolution in computing. White paper, Advanced Micro Devices, Inc. (2005)
2. Yang, C., Chen, J., Luo, T.: An approximation algorithm for energy-efficient scheduling on a chip multiprocessor. In: Proceedings of the Design, Automation and Test in Europe Conference and Exhibition. (2005) 468–473

3. Leung, J., Whitehead, J.: On the complexity of fixed-priority scheduling of periodic, real-time tasks. Performance Evaluation **2**(4) (1982) 237–250
4. Aydin, H., Yang, Q.: Energy-aware partitioning for multiprocessor real-time systems. In: International Parallel and Distributed Processing Symposium. (2003) 113b
5. Lopez, J.M., Garcia, M., Diaz, J.L., Garcia, D.F.: Worst-case utilization bound for EDF scheduling on real-time multiprocessor systems. In: Proceedings of 12th Euromicro Conference on Real-Time Systems. (2000) 25–33
6. Lopez, J.M., Garcia, M., Diaz, J.L., Garcia, D.F.: Minimum and maximum utilization bounds for multiprocessor RM scheduling. In: Proceedings of 13th Euromicro Conference on Real-Time Systems. (2001) 67–75
7. Anderson, J.H., Baruah, S.K.: Energy-aware implementation of hard-real-time systems upon multiprocessor platforms. In: Proceedings of the 16th International Conference on Parallel and Distributed Computing Systems. (2003) 430–435
8. Aydin, H., Melhem, R., Mosse, D., Mejia-Avarez, P.: Power-aware scheduling for periodic real-time tasks. IEEE Transactions on Computers **53**(5) (2004) 584–600
9. Gruian, F.: Hard real-time scheduling for low-energy using stochastic data and DVS processors. In: Proceedings of the 2001 international symposium on Low power electronics and design. (2001) 46–51
10. Pillai, P., Shin, K.G.: Real-time dynamic voltage scaling for low-power embedded operating systems. In: Proceedings of the 18th ACM Symposium on Operating Systems. (2001) 89–102

A Secure Key Agreement Scheme in Low-Energy Wireless Sensor Networks

Taeyeon Kim[1], Gicheol Wang[2], and Gihwan Cho[3]

[1] Dept. of Computer Science and Information Communications,
Seonam University, Namwon, Jeonbuk, 590-711, Republic of Korea
kcopper7@hanmail.net
[2] CAIIT, Chonbuk National University, Jeonju,
Jeonbuk, 561-756, Republic of Korea
gcwang@dcs.chonbuk.ac.kr
[3] CAIIT, Division of EIE, Chonbuk National University,
Jeonju, Jeonbuk, 561-756, Republic of Korea
ghcho@dcs.chonbuk.ac.kr

Abstract. Ubiquitous computing environment provides users with information access anytime and anywhere. In particular, sensor networks must be broadly deployed in real world and utilized to ensure the safety of the human life. In cryptography aspect, key agreement protocol is very important element to exchange messages safely between sensor nodes. This concern originates from the fact that sensor nodes are highly vulnerable to faults, energy depletions, and security attacks. The open problems are how to verify the identity of communicating nodes, how to set up a session key between communicating nodes, and how to minimize any information about the keys disclosed to the other side of key agreement. To solve above problems, we propose a secure key agreement scheme for low-energy sensor networks. Our scheme is based on the MRS scheme and enhances the security by hiding unshared keys and the number of shared keys. Besides, it resolves the weak points in encryption mechanism of MRS by employing multiple random numbers. Performance and security analyses have proven that our scheme is suitable for sensor networks in terms of availability and security aspects.

1 Introduction

Wireless Sensor Network (WSN) is known as a new communication infrastructure for the future computing era. Usually it requires no centralized center or fixed network infrastructure, and can be deployed quickly and inexpensively as needed. The sensor nodes collaborate to collect, process, analysis, and disseminate the sensed data in hostile environments, eventually in order to provide users information access anytime and anywhere. However, the individual sensor node suffers from limited resources, battery, memory, processor, network bandwidth, and so on.

Many studies focus on the routing, fault recovery, energy-efficient communication, and security issues for WSN [1]. Due to the resource scarcity, these concerns are originated from the fact that nodes are highly vulnerable to faults of sensor nodes,

E. Sha et al. (Eds.): EUC 2006, LNCS 4096, pp. 79 – 88, 2006.

energy depletions, and security attacks. Therefore, it is important to invent a communication protocol which satisfies the security requirements as well as the energy saving of nodes. For example, malicious nodes can easily listen to the traffic, impersonate one of the nodes, or provide misleading information to other nodes intentionally. Therefore, the communication between nodes in hostile environments should be authenticated and encrypted.

It is natural that common key management techniques using asymmetric cryptographic algorithms are not appropriate for WSN due to limited resources; it is natural to use symmetric cryptographic algorithms in WSNs because they are relatively fast and induce low cost for cryptographic processes.

Almost all of key pre-distribution schemes [2-6] assumed that a random graph $G(n, P)$ is a graph of n nodes for which the probability that a link exists between two nodes is P. And each one fully trusts the other side during the key pre-distribution. Without a doubt, nodes disclose their key information to neighboring nodes which held a random subset of keys of the key pool. At any rate, the existing protocols, which are based on random key pre-distribution, can not perfectly satisfy requirement of the key management due to some drawbacks. The open problems are how to authenticate the key information of communicating nodes, how to securely set up a session key between communicating nodes, and how to minimize the amount of disclosed information about the keys to the other side.

To solve the first problem, almost all the schemes so far rely on three phases as followings: key pre-distribution, shared-key discovery and path-key establishment. But the second and the third problems are big challenges that are not yet solved.

In the existing schemes, if two nodes share at least one key, they consider each other to be worthy of confidence and generate a session key for further communication between them. But if an adversary accidentally generates the same key(s) that any key(s) in the key pool to impersonate one of legitimate nodes, he can get a session key after completing shared-key discovery phase.

Recently, Chan [7] proposed a key agreement scheme where each node can find keys shared with a communicating node without revealing the unshared keys. However, in this scheme, some security problems are discovered. For example, before completing shared-key discovery phase, a malicious node can know how many keys in the key chain held by itself are shared with the other side without receiving the other side's response. Also, it can guess some of the keys held by the other side due to the weakness of encrypted values received from the other side.

In security aspect, disclosure of a secret key itself causes a lot of threats to legitimate nodes. This paper proposes a novel key agreement scheme which resolves the second and third problem caused during the key discovery phase in WSNs. It includes some methods by which each node authenticates the secret keys received from the other side, prevents the disclosure of unshared keys as well as the exposure of number of shared keys, and strengthens a cryptographic algorithm.

The rest of the paper is organized as follows. In section 2 and 3, we present the modified Rivest's scheme and the secure key agreement scheme for WSNs. In section 4, the performance results and security analyses are described. Finally, section 5 concludes this paper.

2 Modified Rivest's Scheme (MRS)

In the rest of this paper, we use the following notation.

- n : size of network
- z, s, m : size of the key space, the key pool and the key chain respectively
- SK : session key generated between authorized nodes
- KA, KB : secret key of node A and B
- $E^K(M)$, $D^K(M)$: message M encrypted and decrypted with key K
- $h()$: one-way hash function
- p, q : prime numbers
- r (or r_i), s (or s_i) : random numbers, $0 \le i < m$.

Before we describe our scheme, we review the modified Rivest's scheme which is based on a scheme in [8]. A detailed scheme is described in [7]. The key pre-distribution phase ensures that each node is assigned a random subset of keys, *m*, from a key pool before deployment. And in shared-key discovery phase, each node finds the keys shared with the other side node. It does not disclose any information about the keys that the other side does not have. The algorithm for the encryption and decryption of a message and the shared-key discovery phase are performed as follows.

[Encryption] To encrypt a message $M \in Z_n$, the following steps are performed:

- Break down M into a number of arbitrary pieces - $(a_1, a_2, ..., a_k)$ in such a way that $M = \sum_{i=1}^{k} a_i \bmod (p \times q)$.
- Randomly choose $r_i < p$ and $s_i < q$, $\forall_i \in [1, k]$ (which are kept secret).
- Apply the encryption function like the following.

$$E_{p,q,r_i,s_i}(M) = ((a_1 r_1 \bmod p, a_1 s_1 \bmod q), ..., (a_k r_k \bmod p, a_k s_k \bmod q))$$
$$= ((x_1, y_1), (x_2, y_2), ..., (x_k, y_k))$$

[Decryption] Given $X = ((x_1, y_1), (x_2, y_2), ..., (x_k, y_k))$, the decryption steps are as follows:

- $E_{p,q,r_i,s_i}(M) = ((x_1 r_1^{-1} \bmod p,\ y_1 s_1^{-1} \bmod q), ..., (x_k r_k^{-1} \bmod p,\ y_k s_k^{-1} \bmod q))$
- Use Chinese Remainder Theorem to find $(a_1, a_2, ..., a_k \pmod{(p \times q)})$.
- Sum up a_i's to recover M. In such a way that $M = \sum_{i=1}^{k} a_i \bmod (p \times q)$

MRS ensures which the componentwise addition and multiplication (mod (p×q)) of the ciphertexts are the same as the encrypted values of the addition and multiplication of the corresponding plaintexts, and a value should have a number of different possible representations in the ciphertext domain.

When MRS scheme is used in the shared-key discovery phase, each node makes use of a polynomial expression. For example, suppose that Alice wants to find out the common keys with Bob, and Alice has the key set $A = \{a_1, a_2, ..., a_m\}$ and Bob has the key set $B = \{b_1, b_2, ..., b_m\}$. Alice forms a polynomial expression:

$$f_A(x) = (x - a_1)(x - a_2)...(x - a_m) = x^m + A_{m-1}x^{m-1} + ... + A_1x + A_0$$

and sends the encrypted coefficients of $f_A(x)$ to Bob.

Alice $\rightarrow$ Bob : $E^K(A_0), E^K(A_1), ..., E^K(A_{m-1})$, where K is a secret key which she has only.
Bob forms the following polynomial expression using the received message:

$$f_A^{'}(x) = x^m + E^K(A_{m-1})x^{m-1} + ... + E^K(A_1)x + E^K(A_0)$$

To generate a list of encrypted values (i.e., $rE^K(B_0), rE^K(B_1), ..., rE^K(B_{m-1})$), he applies his keys to the expression (2). Here, $E^K(B_i)$ is $f_A^{'}(B_i)$ and r is a random number.

$$\text{Bob} \rightarrow \text{Alice} : rE^K(B_0), rE^K(B_1), ..., rE^K(B_{m-1})$$

She applies $D^K(rE^K(B_{i-1}))$ and can get $rf_A(b_i))$ for $1 \le i \le m$. Since she has no knowledge about r, she does not know what b_i is. But, if anything in $rf_A(b_i))$ is zero, she knows that two nodes share at least one key. Otherwise, she knows that they share no keys with each other. Also, for $rf_A(b_i)) \ne 0$, since there are $u+1$ unknowns in non-linear equations(for some $u \le m$), it would not be possible for Alice to find b_i in the information theoretic sense. When the protocol is still in process, since Bob does not know two large primes p and q, and random number r_i and s_i, he also cannot know which one in a list of encrypted values is an encrypted zero. Consequently, after the shared-key discovery, each node can find shared keys only without revealing unshared keys.

3 Secure Key Agreement Scheme

The proposed scheme leverages Eschenauer and Gligor's scheme [2] and Modified Rivest's Scheme [7]. Sensor networks consist of base stations and sensor nodes. The base station is assumed to be computationally robust and installed in a fixed and secure location. In the remainder of this paper, we make use of their algorithm as the underlying scheme. The path-key establishment phase will not be described since it is assumed that our scheme employs the same protocol as the scheme [2] proposed.

3.1 Key Pre-distribution Phase

In the initialization phase, the base station picks a random key pool out of the total possible key space. Also, a key information in the key pool is combined a secret key (K_i) in the key space with a one-way hash function (h_i), (K_i, h_i), $0 \le i \le z-1$. Each node randomly picks a key chain (i.e., $(K_i, h_i), i = 1, ..., m$) from the key pool before deployment. The key chain is utilized to generate a session key between two nodes during the key discovery phase. And the hash function is utilized to authenticate the secret keys (K_i). It is for the sake of decreasing the possibility that malicious nodes intentionally generate a random key chain.

3.2 Key Agreement Phase

3.2.1 Negotiatory Keys (NKs)

After deployment, each node needs to find whether it shares any key with its neighbors. To do this, each node generally generates m non-linear equations with the secret keys it carries as expression (1) and broadcasts the message containing the encrypted coefficients of $f_A(x)$.

But in this paper, we make use of negotiatory keys so as to enhance security. The generation of negotiatory keys is as follows. For example, let Alice has the key set $A = \{a_1(= a_{11} \parallel a_{12}), a_2(= a_{21} \parallel a_{22}), ..., a_m(= a_{m1} \parallel a_{m2})\}$, Bob has the key set $B = \{b_1(= b_{11} \parallel b_{12}), b_2(= b_{21} \parallel b_{22}), ..., b_m(= b_{m1} \mid b_{m2})\}$, and $h()$ generates the value of limited length. Also, r_i and $r_i^{'}$ are random numbers where $r_{i-1} \neq r_i$ and $r_{i-1}^{'} \neq r_i^{'}$ for $1 \leq i \leq m$. We yield a negotiatory key by concatenating the first half of the key and a hash function's value, and in reverse. That is, the half of Alice's negotiatory keys consists of $\{s_{11}(= a_{11} \parallel h(a_{11})), s_{21}(= a_{21} \parallel h(a_{21})), ..., s_{m1}(= a_{m1} \parallel h(a_{m1}))\}$. The other half consists of $\{s_{12}(h(a_{12}) \parallel a_{12}), s_{22}(h(a_{22}) \parallel a_{22}), ..., s_{m1}(h(a_{m2}) \parallel a_{m2})\}$. Similarly, the first half of Bob's negotiatory keys consists of the following. $\{t_{11}(= b_{11} \parallel h(b_{11})), t_{21}(= b_{21} \parallel h(b_{21})), ..., t_{m1}(= b_{m1} \parallel h(b_{m1}))\}$. Also, the second half consists of $\{t_{12}(= h(b_{12}) \parallel b_{12}), t_{22}(= h(b_{22}) \parallel b_{22}), ..., t_{m2}(= h(b_{m2}) \parallel b_{m2})\}$.

3.2.2 Shared-Key Discovery

In this section, we describe the way how two nodes calculate their session key. Alice who wants to establish a session key generates negotiatory keys and adapts them to expression (3). Then she encrypts coefficients of $f_A(x)$ with her secret key (*KA*) (i.e. $E^{KA}(A_0), E^{KA}(A_1), ..., E^{KA}(A_{m-1})$) and broadcasts them to neighboring nodes. In reverse, when she receives a requesting message from the other side (i.e. Bob), she applies her negotiatory keys to expression (6) in order to generate a list of encrypted values (i.e. $r_0 f_B^{'}(s_{12}), r_1 f_B^{'}(s_{22}), ..., r_{l-1} f_B^{'}(s_{m2})$) and sends them to Bob. Bob also generates negotiatory keys and adapts them to expression (5). Then he encrypts coefficients of $f_B(x)$ with his secret key (*KB*) (i.e. $E^{KB}(B_0), E^{KB}(B_1), ..., E^{KB}(B_{m-1})$) and broadcast them to neighboring nodes. In reverse, when he receives a requesting message from other side (i.e. Alice), he applies his keys to expression (4) in order to generate a list of encrypted values (i.e. $r_0^{'} f_A^{'}(t_{12}), r_1^{'} f_A^{'}(t_{22}), ..., r_{m-1}^{'} f_A^{'}(t_{m2})$) and sends them to Alice.

However, two nodes decrypt $r_i^{'} f_A^{'}(t_{i1})$ and $r_i f_B^{'}(s_{i2})$ with their secret key respectively. And Alice sends an *m*-bit bitmap with 1 at bits where $D^{KA}(r_i^{'} f_A^{'}(t_{i1})) = 0$ to Bob, and Bob sends an *m'*-bit bitmap with 1 at bits where $D^{KB}(r_i f_B^{'}(s_{i2})) = 0$ to Alice. To strengthen security, each node reduces the number of bits with 1 in its bit bitmap by one-half. The detailed description is as follows.

$$f_A(x) = (x - s_{11})(x - s_{21})...(x - s_{m1}) = x^m + A_{m-1}x^{m-1} + ... + A_1 x + A_0 \tag{1}$$

$$f_A^{'}(x) = x^m + E^{KA}(A_{m-1})x^{m-1} + ... + E^{KA}(A_1)x + E^{KA}(A_0) \tag{2}$$

$$f_B(x) = (x - t_{12})(x - t_{22})...(x - t_{m2}) = x^m + B_{m-1}x^{m-1} + ... + B_1 x + B_0 \tag{3}$$

$$f_B^{'}(x) = x^m + E^{KB}(B_{m-1})x^{m-1} + ... + E^{KB}(B_1)x + E^{KB}(B_0) \tag{4}$$

1) Alice calculates encrypted coefficients of $f_A(x)$ in expression (3), $E^{KA}(A_0), E^{KA}(A_1), ..., E^{KA}(A_{m-1})$ and sends them to Bob.

2) ⓐ Bob, on receiving the encrypted coefficients, applies them to expression (4) and gets $f_A^{'}(t_{i1})$, for $1 \le i \le m$. To strengthen security, Bob chooses random numbers $r_i^{'}$ and calculates $M^{'} = r_1^{'} f_A^{'}(t_{11}), r_2^{'} f_A^{'}(t_{21}), ..., r_m^{'} f_A^{'}(t_{m1})$. Where $r_i^{'}$ are different values and nonzero.
ⓑ As the above, he calculates encrypted coefficients of $f_B(x)$ in expression (5), $E^{KB}(B_0), E^{KB}(B_1), ..., E^{KB}(B_{m-1})$.
ⓒ He sends $M^{'}$ and the encrypted coefficients to Alice.

3) ⓐ Alice decrypts $M^{'}$, $D^{KA}(r_i^{'} f_A^{'}(t_{i1}))$, and calculates an *m*-bit bitmap with 1 at bits where $D^{KA}(r_i^{'} f_A^{'}(t_{i1}))$ is 0 and 0 elsewhere. A 1 at the *i*-th bit indicates to Bob that she also has t_{i1}. To enhance security, if the number of bits with 1 in *m*-bit bitmap (i.e. *W*) is more than 1, she randomly adjusts it to w $(= \left\lceil \frac{W}{2} \right\rceil < m)$.
ⓑ She applies the other side's encrypted coefficients to expression (6) and gets $f_B^{'}(s_{i2})$, for $1 \le i \le m$. Alice chooses random numbers r_i and calculates $M = \{r_1 f_B^{'}(s_{12}), r_2 f_B^{'}(s_{22}), ..., r_m f_B^{'}(s_{m2})$, where r_i s are different values and nonzero.
ⓒ She sends M and an *m*-bit bitmap to Bob.

4) ⓐ Bob decrypts M, $D^{KB}(r_i f_B^{'}(s_{i2}))$ and calculates an *m'*-bit bitmap with 1 at bits where $D^{KB}(r_i f_B^{'}(s_{i2}))$ is 0 and 0 elsewhere. To enhance security, if the number

of bits with 1 in m'-bit bitmap (i.e. W') is more than 1, he randomly adjusts it to $w' (= \left\lceil \frac{W'}{2} \right\rceil < m)$.

ⓑ He sends the m'-bit bitmap to Alice.

5) Each node generates a session key using both m-bit and m'-bit bitmap. That is, a new session key SK is generated as the hashed value of the concatenation of shared keys (i.e. $SK = h(K_1 \| K_2 \| ... \| K_{w'})$).

4 Performance and Security Analysis

4.1 Probability of Sharing at Least One Key

An event-driven simulator has been developed to evaluate availability and security of proposed scheme. Our approach is compared with MRS proposed by Chan [7]. In our simulations, we induced two metrics to evaluate the availability and the security of the proposed scheme. One metric is the actual probability that any two neighboring nodes share at least one key during a key agreement phase. The other metric is the rate that all session keys are exposed to an attacker under the existence of one compromised node. For the sake of presentation, our scheme is hereafter referred to as SKS (Secure Key agreement Scheme).

The network model for our simulation assumed as follows; (a) 200 nodes were randomly placed in a 100m × 100m area. (b) the length (r) of the key chain varied in 2, 6, and 10. (c) number of cases that, in key pool, the first half of key is same to others is varied in 0% and 30%.

As shown Fig. 1, as the size of key pool increases, the probability that any two neighboring nodes share at least one key also decreases. In both schemes, if the first half of the keys are not the same to others', the key sharing probability is identical (see Fig. 1(a)). However, as the cases that the first half of keys are same to others increased to 30% (See Fig. 1(b)), the key sharing probability makes a little difference between two schemes, although very little.

Next, to evaluate the security of the proposed scheme, we estimated the exposure rate of session keys during a key agreement under the existence of one compromised node by an attacker. In our simulations, the compromised nodes were randomly selected. Fig. 2 shows the session key exposure rate when a node is compromised by an attacker. As shown in Fig. 2, even though a node is compromised by an attacker, the proposed scheme is much less affected than the MRS. This is because the proposed scheme hides the keys unshared with other nodes. Therefore, the proposed scheme is robust against the compromise of nodes.

4.2 Key Authentication

Upon and after network initialization, in order to increase the communication and computation overhead of networks, a malicious node can broadcast a random key chain falsified by itself to neighboring nodes. If any keys in the falsified key chain are in common with the other side, the attacker can establish a secure link with the

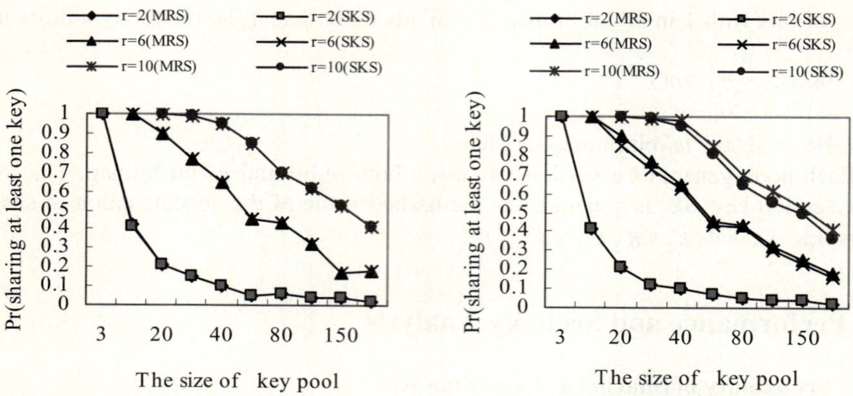

(a) Number of cases = 0% (b) Number of cases = 30%

Fig. 1. Key sharing probability vs. key pool size (zero and 30% match case)

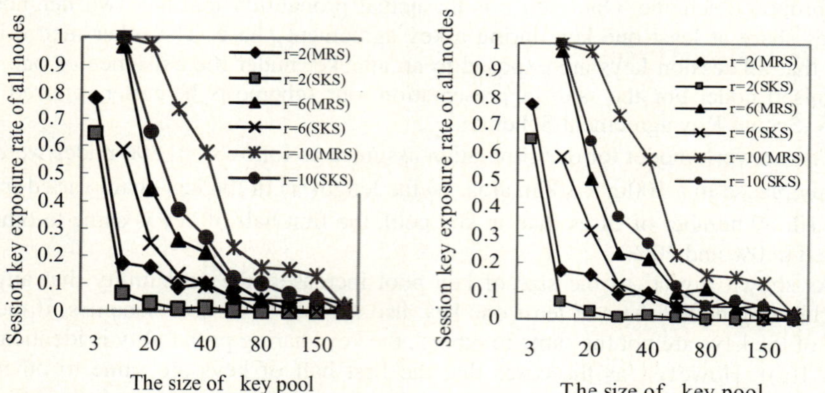

(a) Number of cases = 0% (b) Number of cases = 30%

Fig. 2. Session key exposure rate vs. key pool size (zero and 30% math case)

legitimate node. However, since our scheme makes use of negotiatory key to provide the authentication of key information, it guarantees the key authentication. Even if an attacker luckily generates a key shared with a legitimate node, it can not generate a session key for further communication between two nodes. This is because it has no corresponding one-way hash function.

4.3 Reducing the Number of Disclosing Shared Keys

Before completing the MRS protocol, malicious node can know how many keys of the key chain are in common with the other side without the other side's response. In the worst case, it is not difficult to guess any shared keys while the ratio of the shared keys to unshared keys is by far higher than the reverse of it. Eventually, other side may suffer from potential attacks even if the shared-key discovery is completed before finishing an attack.

Also, after finishing the shared-key discovery phase in MRS, each pair of nodes can know all the shared keys but they can not know unshared keys. However, if one node of them is compromised by adversaries later, the other side also is easy to suffer from attacks by malicious nodes. And one of the two nodes can use random messages in order to search any keys among the other side's keys. That is, to mount an exhaustive discovery for keys held by his neighboring nodes by intentionally, the node may encrypt coefficients using random secret keys and broadcast them. After a completion of key discovery process, it would be possible to know any secret keys held by his neighboring nodes.

To surmount these problems, we made use of negotiatory keys instead the secret keys that is generally used by the existing schemes and mechanism which restricts the number of disclosed shared keys. Consequently, if some nodes are captured, the probability that a session key between any two nodes is affected by malicious nodes is decreased considerably.

4.4 Preventing Attack of Ciphertexts

Simple encryption of a message does not absolutely assure that the message will not be revealed during or after key discovery. That is, if MRS scheme is used in the shared-key discovery phase, nodes face to another threat caused by guessing secret keys and striking weak points of encryption. After an adversary receives all the messages from anyone in the network, the node can guess any secret keys held by the other side due to a weakness of encrypted values, which received from the other side. Let's suppose that an adversary received a list of encrypted values (i.e. $rE^K(D_0), rE^K(D_1), ..., rE^K(D_{m-1})$) from any legitimate node. If two parties have any common key (i.e., c_i) in their key chains, the encrypted value(s) which corresponds to it are decrypted to zero. Otherwise all encrypted values are decrypted to nonzero. However, even if node A has no knowledge about r, he can obtain factorization expressions as follows:

$$D^K(rE^K(D_i)) = r \times (Y_i)^m, i = 0...m-1 \tag{5}$$

It is not easy to guess two numbers (r and Y_i) from m different values as the expression (7). On the other hand, it is not difficult to guess them. That is, the node can generate any keys, Y_i, that held by the other side using his secret key K, two large prime numbers p and q, and a random number r. If the number of $D^K(rE^K(D_i)) \neq 0$ is more than 3, it becomes easier.

Therefore, the number r needs to be managed deliberately. To do this, we made use of different random numbers instead of a random number. As a result, it is not easy for a malicious node to find a value c_i or any secret key held by other side because it is very difficult to guess the relationship between different random numbers and Y_i.

5 Conclusions

In this paper, we proposed a secure key agreement scheme for low-energy wireless sensor networks. We made use of negotiatory keys instead of the secret keys that used in almost all the schemes developed so far, and different random numbers instead of a random number. The negotiatory keys prevent the entities of key agreement from revealing unshared secret keys and the number of shared keys. Also, the proposed scheme resolves the weakness of the cryptographic algorithm by exploiting multiple random numbers during a key agreement phase. Consequently, the proposed scheme guarantees that two nodes agree a session key in a secure method and provides the robustness against the compromise of nodes. Simulation results have proven that it does not reduce the key sharing probability between any two nodes providing the high robustness against a node compromise. Also, security analyses indicate that it is more secure than the simple MRS scheme. That is, judging from the security and availability of the proposed scheme, our protocol is extremely suitable for WSNs. In our future work, we will study the communication and computational overhead caused by the proposed scheme and devise an improved scheme for reducing the overheads. Also, the implementation of these techniques on real sensor platforms will be another future research item.

References

1. Cam, H., Ozdemir, S., Muthuavinashiappan, D., Nair, P.: Energy-Efficient Security Protocol for Wireless Sensor Networks. Proc. of IEEE VTC Fall 2003Conference, Oct. 4-9, Orlando, (2003) 2981-2984
2. Eschenauer, L., Gligor, V.D.: A Key-management Scheme for DistributedSensor Networks. Proc. of the 9th ACM Conference on Computer and Communications Security, (2002) 41-47
3. Du, W., Deng, J., Han, Y.S., Varshney, P.K.: A Pairwise Key Pre-distribution Scheme for Wireless Sensor Networks. Proc. of ACM Conference on Computer and Communications Security (CCS'03) (2003) 42-51
4. Chan, H., Perrig, A., Song, D.: Random Key Predistribution Schemes for Sensor Networks. IEEE Symposium on Research in Security and Privacy, May 11-14 (2003) 197-213
5. Du, W., Deng, J., Han, Y.S., Varshney, P.K.: A Key Management Scheme for Wireless Sensor Networks Using Deployment Knowledge. IEEE INFOCOM (2004) 586-597
6. Liu, D., Ning, P., Du, W.: Group-Based Key Pre-distribution in Wireless Sensor Networks. Proc. of 10th ACM Conference on Computer and Communications Security (CCS'03), (2003) 11-20
7. Chan, A.C-F.: Distributed Symmetric Key Management for Mobile Ad hoc Networks. IEEE INFOCOM (2004) 2414-2424
8. Rivest, R.L., Adleman, L., Dertouzos, M.L.: On Data Banks and Privacy. In Foundations of Secure Computation, eds. R. A. DeMillo et al., Academic Press, (1978) 169-179.

Person-Wise Privacy Level Access Control for Personal Information Directory Services*

Hyung-Jin Mun, Keon Myung Lee, and Sang-Ho Lee

School of Electrical and Computer Engineering,
Chungbuk National University, Korea
hjmun@cbnu.ac.kr

Abstract. This paper proposes a policy-based access control mechanism for the personal information directory service systems which prevents the information users from illegally accessing the personal information and enables the information subjects to control access to their own information. In the proposed mechanism, the individuals' personal information which is encrypted with different keys is stored into the directory repository. In order to control access to her own personal information, information subject sets up the access control policy for it and the access control is practiced out by providing encryption keys to the legal users according to the subject's policy.

1 Introduction

With the advance of the information technology and the diversity of society, lots of personal information has been collected and distributed. To provide the quality services for the individuals, the organizations and the companies try to use the information of the customers, the employees, the partners, and so on. The collected personal information could be used without the permission of the information subjects. The unprotected personal information could infringe on personal rights and sometimes could financially damage the information subjects. Therefore, there have been increasing concerns to the individuals about their personal information. Now the personal information protection becomes one of important issues in the various computing and communication environments. [2-11].

In order to protect personal information, some organizations and companies employ the access control techniques. Sometimes the information subjects might want to control access to their personal information even though it is provided through the directory services. The traditional access control skills have difficulty in providing fine-grained person-wise access control to the personal information. This paper is concerned with the person-wise access control mechanism in which information subjects could determine who can access which personal information in what context.

In the proposed person-wise access control mechanism, the underlying idea is for each individual to use different encryption keys for each attribute of her/his

* This work was supported by the Regional Research Centers Program of the Ministry of Education & Human Resources Development in Korea.

E. Sha et al. (Eds.): EUC 2006, LNCS 4096, pp. 89–98, 2006.

own record. They write their own access policies and register them into the directory service system. The directory service system hands the encryption keys to the information users when they are allowed to access the designated personal information according to the information subjects' policy.

2 Related Works

Encryption techniques have been employed to protect the e-mail messages, stored files, on-line communication, and so on.[1-5] Once encryption is done, only the legal actors have the keys for the encrypted data and thus can access it.

The mandatory access control(MAC) is a technique that controls the users' access according to the rules enforced by the restricted number of security managers in the military or highly restricted environments. The discretionary access control(DAC) is a technique to enables the information owners to delegate or revoke the access rights to other users at their disposal. Therefore it is more flexible than MAC and can perform the distributed access control. However, both MAC and DAC is inappropriate to manage the various strategies of the organizations or the companies. Therefore, as an alternative, the role-based access control(RBAC) is proposed by R. Sandhu, et al.[6] RBAC takes into account the complicated structure of the organizations and could satisfy the different security and policy requirements. RBAC grants the access rights according to the users' role and restricts the access to the data which do not fit with the role of the users. The activity-based access control(ABAC) is an access control technique for the cooperative working environments such as workflows.[7] The task role-based access control(TRBAC) is an access control technique which combines both RBAC and TRBAC.[8,9,10] TRBAC fits with the organizations or the companies that have the complicated organizational structures, various kinds of users and information.

HP research center proposed a technique that protects a large volume of the personal information systematically stored in a database of the organizations or companies[11]. In the model, a specific piece of personal information is encrypted and stored into the database, and the Privacy Management Service module maintains the keys. The Privacy Management Service module provides the decryption keys to the users when they are allowed to access the requested data according to the enforced policy. In the model, an attribute shares the same encryption key across all records and thus it is impossible to control the access rights to the record attributes in a person-wise way. In addition, the allowed policy rules can hardly express contextual condition such as *John's current location information is available to his boss only on-duty.*

3 The Proposed Person-Wise Access Control Model

The proposed person-wise access control model, named P^2MS(Person-wise Policy-based access Management System), allows the information subjects to control access to their own information according to their policy. The model takes the strategy to encrypt each attribute for each individual with different keys and to endow the decryption keys for the allowed attributes to the information users according to the information subjects' policy.

3.1 The Application Environment

Individuals, i.e., information subjects(IS), is supposed to give their personal information to the companies or organizations. The personal information is managed by the database management system and published through the directory service system. Information users(IU) try to access the stored personal information(PI) on their own demand. The individuals write their own policy about who can access which pieces of their information in what context. The directory service system maintains the information subjects' policy and enforces them when an IU asks some pieces of PI. It is supposed that only allowed IU can access the allowed pieces of PI. Figure 1 shows the situations in which IUs access PI according to the endowed access rights by the information subjects' policy.

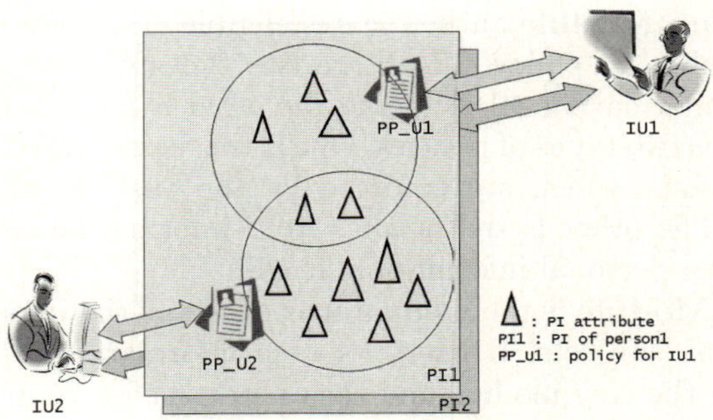

Fig. 1. Access Control of Information User for Personal Information

3.2 The Person-Wise Privacy Level Access Control Model

The proposed model consists of the PI access client(PIA), the P^2MS, and the Data Repositories as shown in the Figure 2.

The PI Access Client. An information subject provides her own information through PI access client and makes their policy to prevent illegal access of the information users. Through PI access client, IU accesses the information by receiving the authentication and requesting it. PI access client consists of Access Module, Decryption Module.

Access Module. The module accesses P^2MS, requests the information list, and then gets the encryption keys. It also plays the role of getting the encrypted information from the Data Repositories.

Decryption Module. The module is to decrypt the encrypted personal information with the received keys from P^2MS.

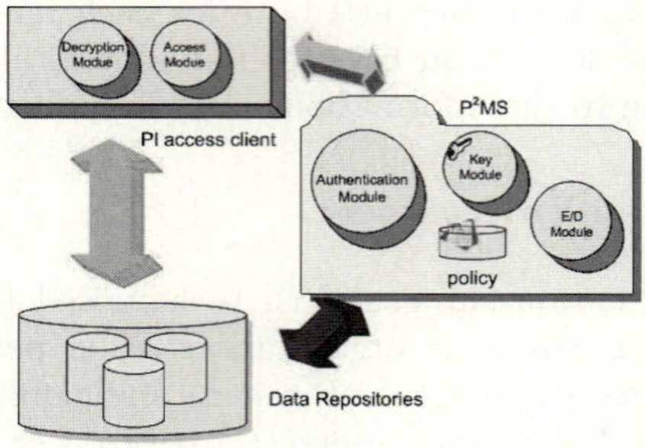

Fig. 2. The Proposed Person-wise Privacy Level Access Control Model

The P^2MS. P^2MS plays the role of protecting the personal information according to personal policies written by the information subjects through PI access client. IUs and ISs can access P^2MS only through PIA. P^2MS consists of the Authentication Module, the Policy database, the Encryption/Decryption modules, and the Key module.

Authentication Module authenticates eligible information users according to information subjects' policy. There are two types of authentications one of which is for the information subjects and the other is for the information users.

Policy contains two types of policies. One is the access control policies written by the organizations, which are enforced by the customs and regulations to protect privacy. The other is the policies from information subjects to control access to their own personal information at will.

Encryption Module is the module that encrypts the information provided by the information subjects. It encrypts each information attribute using the keys generated in the Key module and then sends the encrypted information to Data Repositories.

Decryption Module is the module that decrypts the retrieved encrypted PI. When some person's policy or the organization's policy has been changed, the corresponding PI should re-encrypted with different keys. At that situation, P^2MS retrieves the encrypted PI to be re-encrypted from DR, and recovers and encrypts it with new keys, and then stores it to DR.

Key Module comprises Key generation module and Key DB. In the proposed model, each field of a record is encrypted by different keys. Therefore, it is crucial to effectively maintain keys. *Key generation module* generates a master key for each person and generates attribute keys from the master key. *Key DB* is the storage that securely stores generated master keys.

Data Repositories. The Data Repositories(DR) is in charge of storing the personal information. In the DR, each record of a person consists of the hashed value of her ID and the encrypted sentences for her PI. The attributes are encrypted with different keys which are maintained by P^2MS. When PI access client requests some personal information, DR sends the encrypted personal information for which decryption keys could be provided from P^2MS.

3.3 Data Format in Data Repositories

The personal information is stored into DR in an encrypted format. Each individual has a record to store her PI as shown in Figure 3(a). P^2MS encodes such records into encrypted records as shown in Figure 3(b), and then stores them into DR.

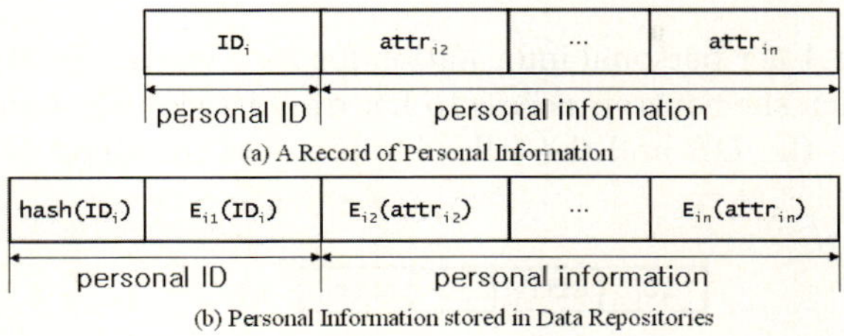

Fig. 3. Structure of Personal Information stored in the DB

Instead of IS's ID, ID_i, the pair of its hashed value $(hash(ID_i))$ and its encrypted data $(E_{i1}(ID_i))$ is stored. The hashed value plays the role of an index for the encrypted database, with which record retrieval is enabled. All the other personal information such as phone number, address and so on are encrypted using different key, respectively. IU can search the records with the hashed values of IS's ID of interest. Due to inherent properties of hashed functions, it is nearly impossible for the DB administrator to recover the real IDs from the encrypted records, and thus the information subject's privacy can be successfully protected.

4 The Protocols Employed in the Proposed Model

This section presents how the proposed method generates keys and maintains them, how information subjects register their personal information, how information users retrieve others' personal information, how information subjects modify their personal information stored in DR, the situations in which personal information should be re-encrypted, and what the policy looks like.

4.1 Key Management

To protect PI safely, the proposed model allows each attribute of PI to be encrypted with different keys. In the model, the key generation module generates a master key(K_{ID_i}) for each IS i, which is later used to build attribute keys for encrypting the attributes of IS i's PI. In the attribute key generation, both the PI's ID and random number R_j are used as follows: $key_{ij} = E_{K_{ID_i}}(ID_i|R_j)$. The generated attribute keys are symmetric cipher keys, which are advantageous in encryption time and key size, and only the master keys but attribute keys are stored in the Key DB. When an IU requests the keys for the allowed attributes, P^2MS provides the keys which are generated at the moment from the stored master key. The number of keys stored in Key DB is equal to that of subjects. The master keys are secure because they are used only in the attribute key generation. P^2MS provides the permitted IU with a ticket which contains the information about which attributes are allowed to retrieve and their valid access time period. The tickets are signed with the P^2MS's private key for their verification.

4.2 Personal Information Registration

An IS sends PIA her personal information for its registration. An IS writes her policy with which she controls access to her own PI. Figure 4 shows how an IS stores her PI in the DR and the following presents the steps:

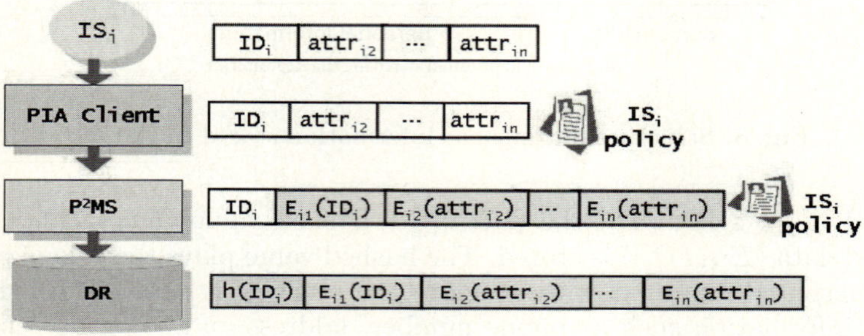

Fig. 4. Personal Information Registration

1. An IS i provides her information $DataSet_i$ for PIA.
   $ISi \rightarrow PIA : [DataSet_i]$ where $DataSet_i = (ID_i | \bigcup_{j=2}^{n} attr_{ij})$
2. IS i writes her access policy POL_i with help of PIA.
3. PIA sends both $DataSet_i$ and POL_i to P^2MS.
   $PIA \rightarrow P^2MS : [DataSet_i | POL_i]$
4. P^2MS encrypts each attribute value $attr_{ij}$ of $DataSet_i$ with a different key key_{ij} generated from the master key K_{ID_i} for IS i, computes the hashed value $h(ID_i)$ for ID_i, and in addition stores POL_i into the policy DB.
5. P^2MS stores the encrypted information into the DR.
   $P^2MS \rightarrow DR : [h(ID_i) | E_{K_{i1}}(ID_i) | \bigcup_{j=2}^{n} E_{K_{ij}}(attr_j)]$

4.3 Information Retrieval

When an IU intends to get the PI for a person ISs, the steps take place:
1. An IU u sends P^2MS the ID ID_s of the IS s and the attribute list AL_u of interest for IS s, and the access intent AI_u about how to use it, along with the her certificate $Cert_{ID_u}$ on her ID.
   $IU \rightarrow P^2MS : [Cert_{ID_u} | ID_s | AL_u | AI_u]$
2. P^2MS authenticates the ID of the IU.
3. P^2MS looks up the policies of the organization and that of ISs, and then decides which attributes fr_{AL} to be allowed to be accessible with reference to AL_u and AI_u at the moment, and the valid access time period TP_{su}. Then

it encrypts fr_{AL}, TP_{su} with the P^2MS's private key KP_{P^2MS}, and issues a ticket $T = E_{KP_{P^2MS}}(fr_{AL}|TP_{us})$. Then, it encrypts the ticket T and the key list $KL_{fr_{AL}}$ for fr_{AL} with IU_u's key KS_{ID_u} which is shared with the PIA of IUu.

$P^2MS : E_{KS_{ID_u}}(T|KL_{fr_{AL}})$

4. P^2MS sends the message $E_{KS_{ID_u}}(T|KL_{fr_{AL}})$ to PIA.

$P^2MS \rightarrow PIA : [E_{KS_{ID_u}}(T|KL_{fr_{AL}})]$

5. PIA decrypts the received message with KS_{ID_u} and sends both IS's ID ID_s and ticket T to DR.

$PIA \rightarrow DR : [ID_s|T]$

6. DR verifies the ticket's validity, and checks the requested attribute list AL_u and the ticket's valid period TP_{su}. And then it generates the hashed values $h(ID_s)$ of ID_s and searches the DB for the records with $h(ID_s)$.
7. DR sends PIA the retrieved records with $h(ID_s), E_{K_{s1}}(ID_s), E_{K_{sj}}(attr_j)$ for $attr_j \in fr_{AL}$ as far as the ticket T is valid.

$DR \rightarrow PIA : [h(ID_s), E_{K_{s1}}(ID_s), E_{K_{sj}}(attr_j)$ for $attr_j \in fr_{AL}]$

8. PIA decrypts the received records using the keys KL_{AL} and recovers the corresponding IS's PI.
9. PIA sends the recovered PI to the IU.

4.4 Personal Information Modification

When an information subject tries to modify her information, the following steps take place.

1. An IS s sends P^2MS her ID ID_s, her certificate $Cert_{ID_s}$ and the attribute list MR_{AL} to be modified.

$IS \rightarrow P^2MS : [Cert_{ID_s}|ID_s|MR_{AL}]$

2. P^2MS authenticates ID_s.
3. P^2MS sends PIA a ticket $T = E_{KP_{P^2MS}}(MR_{AL}|TP_{sp})$ and the keys $K_{MR_{AL}}$ for attributes in MR_{AL} which are encrypted with the ID_s's key KS_{ID_s} which is shared with P^2MS.

$P^2MS \rightarrow PIA : [E_{KS_{ID_s}}(K_{MR_{AL}}|T)]$

4. PIA sends ID_s, T, and MR_{AL} to DR.

$PIA \rightarrow DR : [ID_s|T|MR_{AL}]$

5. DR checks the validity of the ticket T. If so, retrieve the record(s) corresponding to the hashed value $h(ID_s)$.
6. DR sends PIA the retrieved record(s) corresponding to MR_{AL}.
7. PIA identifies the ID_s's record by decrypting the encrypted ID field with the key received from P^2MS.
8. PIA sends $ISID_s$ the ID_s's information record to modify.
9. IS ID_s modifies its information in the record and sends it to PIA.
10. ID_s sends P^2MS the modified record $newVMR_{AL}$ encrypted by the shared key KS_{sp}.

$IS \rightarrow P^2MS : [E_{KS_{sp}}(newVMR_{AL})]$

11. P^2MS generates a new key and encrypts the modified information from ID_S.
12. P^2MS sends the encrypted information to DR.

$P^2MS \rightarrow DR : [h(ID_s)|E_{K_{s1}}(ID_s)|\bigcup_{j=2}^{n} E_{K_{sj}}(attr_j)]$ where $attr_j$ indicates the updated one, if updated.
13. DR updates ID_s's information with the received one.

4.5 Re-encryption of Personal Information

When an IU requests some pieces of information for an individual, P^2MS provides the decryption keys for the allowed pieces. Once an IU has the keys, IU could retrieve the individual's corresponding data from DR at any time. Therefore, P^2MS takes charge of re-encrypting the PI at each expiration of issued tickets, to keep safe the PI.

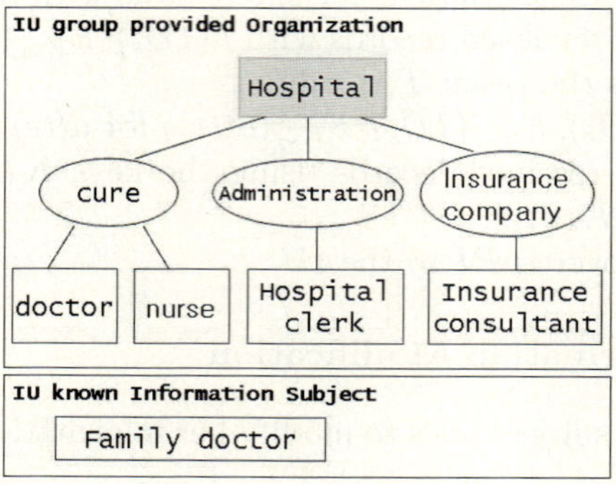

Fig. 5. IU group category

```
- <xsd:schema xmlns:xsd="http://www.w3.org/2001/XMLSchema">
  - <xsd:element name="Hong's Policy">
    - <xsd:complexType>
      - <xsd:sequence>
          <xsd:element name="Info_user" type="xsd:string" />
          <xsd:element name="ID" type="xsd:string" />
          <xsd:element name="name" type="xsd:string" />
          <xsd:element name="tel" type="xsd:string" />
          <xsd:element name="health_checkup" type="xsd:string" />
          <xsd:element name="job" type="xsd:string" />
          <xsd:element name="sex" type="xsd:string" />
          <xsd:element name="medical_fee" type="xsd:string" />
          <xsd:element name="prescription" type="xsd:string" />
          <xsd:element name="disease_name" type="xsd:string" />
          <xsd:element name="disease_history" type="xsd:string" />
        </xsd:sequence>
      </xsd:complexType>
    </xsd:element>
  - <xsd:Policy Info_user="doctor">
    - <xsd:AttributeInformation>
        <xsd:Attribute ID="read" />
        <xsd:Attribute tel="read" />
        <xsd:Attribute disease_name="modify" />
        <xsd:Attribute job="read" />
        <xsd:Attribute health_checkup="read" />
      </xsd:AttributeInformation>
    - <xsd:Constraint>
        <xsd:Time>AM 9:00~PM 6:00</xsd:Time>
      </xsd:Constraint>
    </xsd:Policy>
  - <xsd:Policy Info_user="nurse">
    - <xsd:AttributeInformation>
        <xsd:Attribute ID="read" />
        <xsd:Attribute prescription="read" />
      </xsd:AttributeInformation>
    - <xsd:Constraint>
        <xsd:timeDuration>under medical treatment</xsd:timeDuration>
      </xsd:Constraint>
    </xsd:Policy>
  - <xsd:Policy Info_user="hospital clerk">
    - <xsd:AttributeInformation>
        <xsd:Attribute prescription="read" />
        <xsd:Attribute tel="read" />
        <xsd:Attribute medical_fee="write" />
      </xsd:AttributeInformation>
    </xsd:Policy>
  - <xsd:Policy Info_user="Insurance consultant">
    - <xsd:AttributeInformation>
        <xsd:Attribute name="read" />
        <xsd:Attribute tel="read" />
        <xsd:Attribute address="read" />
        <xsd:Attribute job="read" />
        <xsd:Attribute medical_fee="read" />
      </xsd:AttributeInformation>
    - <xsd:Constraint>
        <xsd:Time>AM 9:00~PM 6:00</xsd:Time>
      </xsd:Constraint>
    </xsd:Policy>
  - <xsd:Policy Info_user="family doctor">
    - <xsd:AttributeInformation>
        <xsd:Attribute ID="read" />
        <xsd:Attribute tel="read" />
        <xsd:Attribute health_checkup="modify" />
        <xsd:Attribute disease_history="modify" />
        <xsd:Attribute disease_name="write" />
      </xsd:AttributeInformation>
    - <xsd:Constraint>
        <xsd:IPaddress>192.168.0.100</xsd:IPaddress>
        <xsd:Time>AM 9:00~PM 5:00</xsd:Time>
        <xsd:timeDuration>2006.6.31</xsd:timeDuration>
      </xsd:Constraint>
    </xsd:Policy>
</xsd:schema>
```

Fig. 6. Person-wise policy

4.6 Policy Registration

Each IS is supposed to write the access control policy about her own information. To write a policy effectively, the organizations or companies could provide subject with IS's group categories like Figure 5. An IS writes the group-wise access authorization policies as well as policies for some known users. When some policy for an individual user contradicts with that for a user group, the policy of individual users has a higher priority to group-wise policies.

Figure 6 shows an example of person-wise policy using the group categories in a medical application. The policy tells that a family doctor can access such sensitive information as disease history, and so on.

5 Privacy Preservation Strength of the Model

In order to analyze the privacy preservation strength of the proposed model, we compare the proposed model with the HP model in the following four aspects:

First, the proposed model can fully respect the information subjects' intention in the access control of their personal information, whereas the HP model protects the personal information only according to the organization policy and thus it is very difficult to finely control the access to the personal information according to the information subjects' intention.

Second, the proposed model allows the elaborate access control to the personal information with the consideration of contextual information such as time, location, relationship, and so on. The HP model does the access control by the role and the duty, whereas the proposed model does the access control with the information subjects' policy as well as the organization policy.

Third, the proposed model can protect the personal information even from the database administrator since the key management part is separated from the database and the personal identity information is encrypted in the database. In the HP model, the identity information is recorded in a plain text in order to allow the search service.

Fourth, in the proposed model, each attribute of a record comes to have a different key even though all attribute encryption keys are generated from the master key of an individual. Therefore, even a key is exposed in public by accident or by incident, the damage incurred is so small. However, the HP model each attribute shares a key across the records of a table. Compared to the proposed model, the risk incurred by the loss of a key is severe.

6 Conclusion

The organizations and companies employ the encryption techniques and access control techniques to protect personal information maintained by themselves, yet the personal information subjects do not feel comfortable in that their information is stored somewhere. The privacy protection guidelines and regulation ask the information management authorities to get the permission from the information subjects, and to give the information subjects the access control rights to their own information.

In this paper we proposed an access control model in which the information subjects write the access control policy for their personal information and the policies are enforced in a secure way. In the model, each attribute of an information subject is encrypted with different encryption keys, respectively. The allowed information users can acquire the decryption keys for the allowed attributes according the information subject's policy. In order to improve the privacy preservation level, the key management part is separated from the database which stores the encrypted personal information. The personal identify information is also not exposed to the unintended information users, even to the database administrator. The proposed model has to maintain as many keys as the number of attributes times that of records. In order to resolve this problem, the model takes the approach to assign a single master key to each record and to generate attribute encryption keys from the master key. This strategy avoids the potential key management problem. The proposed model is expected to be used in the personal information directory service systems such as e-government systems in which personal information need to be provided to authorized parties with the permission of the information subjects.

References

1. Stallings, W.: Cryptography and Network Security. 3rd edn. Prentice-Hall, New Jersey (2003)
2. Fischer-Hubner, S.: IT-Security and Privacy : Design and Use of Privacy Enhancing Security Mechanism. Lecture Notes in Computer Science, LNCS 1958 (May 2001)
3. Chaum, D.L.: The Dining Cryptographers Problem: Unconditional Sender and Recipient Untraceability. Journal of Cryptology. 1(1). (1988) 65-75
4. Rither, M.K., Rubin, A.D.: Crowds : Anonymity for Web Transactions. ACM Transactions on Informatino and System Security. 1(1). (1998) 66-92
5. Chaum, D.L.: Untraceble Electronic Mail Return Address, and Digital Pseudonyms. Communications of the ACM. 24(2) (1981) 84-88
6. Sandhu, R.S., Coyne, E.J., Feinstein, H.L., Youman, C.E.: Role-Based Access Control Models. IEEE Computer. 29(2) (1996) 38-47
7. Huang, W.K., Atluri, V.: SecureFlow: A secure Web-enabled Workflow Management System. Proc. Of 4th ACM Workshop on Role-based Access Control (1999)
8. Thomas, P.K., Sandhu, R.S. : Task-based Authorization Control(TBAC): A Family of Models for Active and Enterprise-oriented Authorization Management. Proc. of the IFIP WG11.3 Workshop on Database Security (1997)
9. Oh, S., Park, S.: An Integration Model of Role-based Access Control and Activity-based Access Control Using Task. Proc. of 14th Annual IFIP WG11.3 Working Conference on Database Security (Aug. 2000)
10. Oh, S., Park, S.: A Process of Abstracting T-RBAC Aspects from Enterprise Environment. Proc. DASFAA'01 (Apr. 2001)
11. Mont, M.C., Pearson, S., Bramhall. P.: An Adaptive Privacy Management System for Data Repositories. http://www.hpl.hp.com/techreports/2004/HPL-2004-211.html (2004)

An Efficient Computing-Checkpoint Based Coordinated Checkpoint Algorithm

Men Chaoguang[1,2], Wang Dongsheng[1,2], and Zhao Yunlong[2]

[1] Department of Computer Science and Technology, Tsinghua University, Beijing 100084, P.R. China
{mencg, wds}@tsinghua.edu.cn
[2] Research Center of High Dependability Computing Technology, Harbin Engineering University, Harbin, Heilongjiang, 150001, P.R. China

Abstract. In this paper, the concept of "computing checkpoint" is introduced, and then an efficient coordinated checkpoint algorithm is proposed. The algorithm combines the two approaches of reducing the overhead associated with coordinated checkpointing, which one is to minimize the processes which take checkpoints and the other is to make the checkpointing process non-blocking. Through piggybacking the information including which processes have taken new checkpoint in the broadcast committing message, the checkpoint sequence number of every process can be kept consistent in all processes, so that the unnecessary checkpoints and orphan messages can be avoided in the future running. Evaluation result shows that the number of redundant computing checkpoints is less than 1/10 of the number of tentative checkpoints. Analyses and experiments show that the overhead of our algorithm is lower than that of other coordinated checkpoint algorithms.

1 Introduction

Checkpointing and rollback-recovery has been an attractive technique for providing fault-tolerance in distributed computing system. When a fault occurs, the processes can reload the checkpoints state to recover the system [1-2]. Due to its simple, domino-free, and the minimal requirement for storage, coordinated checkpointing is efficient. Two approaches are used to reduce the overhead of coordinated checkpoint algorithm: one is to minimize the number of checkpoints [3-6]; the other is to make the checkpointing process non-blocking [7-8]. To reduce the overhead of coordinated checkpoint algorithm, the concept of computing checkpoint is introduced. And, an efficient coordinated checkpoint algorithm based on computing checkpoint is proposed.

The paper is organized as follows: Section 2 introduces the system model and definitions. Section 3 presents an efficient low-cost non-blocking coordinated checkpoint algorithm (*LNCC*). Section 4 gives its correctness proofs. Section 5 evaluates the number of redundant computing checkpoints. Section 6 shows the experiment results. Section 7 compares *LNCC* with some earlier relative coordinated checkpoint schemes. Section 8 draws a conclusion.

E. Sha et al. (Eds.): EUC 2006, LNCS 4096, pp. 99 – 109, 2006.

2 Preliminaries

The distributed computation consists of N sequential processes denoted by P_1 ,P_2,... , P_N running concurrently on fail-stop. Processes do not share a common memory or a common clock. Message passing is the only way for the processes to communicate with each other. The computation is asynchronous, i.e., each process progresses at its own speed and messages are exchanged through reliable communication channels, whose transmission delays are finite but arbitrary. The messages generated by the underlying distributed application will be referred to as computation messages. The messages generated by the processes to advance checkpoints will be referred to as system messages. A process can execute internal, send and delivery statements. Each process P_i produces a sequence of events $e_{i,1}$, ..., $e_{i,s}$, ..., which can be finite or infinite. Every process P_i has an initial local state denoted $\sigma_{i,0}$. The sequence of events $e_{i,1}$, ..., $e_{i,s}$ applied to the initial state $\sigma_{i,0}$ result the state $\sigma_{i,s}$. Every process saves its local state on stable memory to produce its local checkpoint and each checkpoint taken by a process is assigned a unique checkpoint sequence number (*CSN*). The checkpoint taken by the initiator or a process on which the initiator depends is called basic checkpoint. The ith ($i \geq 0$) checkpoint of process P_k is assigned a sequence number i and is denoted by $C_{k,i}$. Any event $e_{k,x}$ exist between $C_{k,i-1}$ and $C_{k,i}$ is said "$e_{k,x}$ belongs to $C_{k,i}$". The ith checkpoint interval of process P_p denotes all the computation performed between its ith and $(i+1)^{th}$ checkpoint, including the ith checkpoint but not the $(i+1)^{th}$ checkpoint, denoted as $I(p,i)$. In distributed systems, orphan messages and in-transit messages may result in the inconsistency.

Orphan messages: A message M sent by process P_i to process P_j is called an orphan message with respect to the ordered pair of local checkpoints ($C_{i,x}$,$C_{j,y}$), if the delivery of M belongs to $C_{j,y}$ while its sending event does not belong to $C_{i,x}$.

In-transit messages: A message M sent by process P_i to process P_j is called an in-transit message with respect to the ordered pair of local checkpoints ($C_{i,x}$,$C_{j,y}$), if the sending of M belongs to $C_{i,x}$ while its delivery does not belong to $C_{j,y}$.

If a fault occurs, in-transit messages will be lost. By logging and replaying them out when process recovering, the in-transit messages lost can be avoided. An orphan message will result in the system becoming inconsistent when rollback recovery.

Definition 1, dependency relation: A process P_i sends a message to process P_j with respect to the ordered pair of local checkpoints ($C_{i,x}$,$C_{j,y}$), we say that P_j at its yth checkpoint interval depends on P_i at its xth checkpoint. Simply we say P_j depends on P_i, denoted as $R_j(i)$=1. If P_j depends on P_k, and P_k depends on P_i, we say P_j transitively depends on P_i. We simply call the two cases P_j depends on P_i.

Definition 2, computing checkpoint: Assume that P_i has taken its $(x+1)^{th}$ tentative checkpoint and sends a computation message M to P_j. Before receiving M, P_j knows P_i in its xth checkpoint. Hence P_j must take forced checkpoint before delivering M. The checkpoint taken by P_j is called a computing checkpoint.

Definition 3, global consistent checkpoint: A global checkpoint is a set of local checkpoints, one from each process. A global checkpoint is consistent if no message is orphan with respect to any pair of its local checkpoints [9-10].

3 The Low-Cost Non-blocking Coordinated Checkpointing (*LNCC*)

Two-phase scheme and computing checkpoint are used to improve the efficiency of algorithm. When a process takes a computing checkpoint, it does not request these processes on which it depends to take checkpoints. A computing checkpoint should be transformed to a tentative checkpoint or be discarded according to the process receiving request or not. In the second phase, the initiator broadcasts committing message to all processes in the system, piggybacking the information including which processes have taken checkpoints. According to the information, each process can ensure the *CSNs* of all processes are consistent so that orphan message and unnecessary checkpoint can be avoided. When the checkpoints are taken, the dependent relations of the processes will be updated to avoid taking unnecessary checkpoints [11].

3.1 The Data Structure of *LNCC*

R_i: a Boolean array. $R_i(j)$=1 means P_i depends on P_j. R_i is initialized to 0, but $R_i(i)$=1.
Tem_R_i: a Boolean array. It is used to save temporary dependent relation when taking tentative checkpoint. It is initialized to 0, but $Tem\_R_i(i)$=1 in every P_i.
Rep_R_i: a Boolean array. It is used to save which process has taken a new checkpoint.
$CSN_i[j]$: an integer array. $CSN_i[j]=X$ means process P_j takes *Xth* checkpoint that P_i expects. *CSN* is initialized to 0 in every process.
Cp_state: a Boolean variable. Cp_state_i=1 marks a process in its checkpointing.
Com_state: a Boolean variable, marking a process takes a computing checkpoint.
Weight: a non-negative variable of type real with maximum value of 1. It is used to detect the termination of the checkpointing.
Trigger: a tuple (*pid,inum*). *pid* indicates the checkpoint initiator that triggered this node to take its latest basic checkpoint. *inum* indicates the *CSN* at node *pid* when it takes its local basic checkpoint on initiating consistent checkpointing.

3.2 The *LNCC* Algorithm Description

A formal description of the two-phase checkpoint algorithm is given in Fig.1.

3.3 An Example of *LNCC* Algorithm

Fig.2 is an example of *LNCC* executing. Solid line means transmitting computing message and dashed line means request message. P_4, as the initiator, takes checkpoint $C_{4,1}$ and sends request to the processes on which it depends. After taking checkpoint $C_{3,1}$, P_3 sends *M4* to P_2 with $CSN_3(3)$=1. Due to $CSN_2(3)$=0 and $CSN_2(3)<CSN_3(3)$, P_2 takes computing checkpoint $C_{2,1}$ before delivering *M4*. Due to $CSN_1(2)$=0 and $CSN_2(2)$=1, P_1 takes computing checkpoint $C_{1,1}$ before delivering *M5*. After receiving request, P_1 makes computing checkpoint $C_{1,1}$ tentative and sends request to P_2. P_2 makes computing checkpoint $C_{2,1}$ tentative. The system is consistent. When receiving committing message, P_6 cancels the dependent relation of P_6 depending P_5. P_6 increases $CSN_6(5)$, $CSN_6(4)$, $CSN_6(3)$, $CSN_6(2)$, $CSN_6(1)$.

Actions taken when P_i sends a computation message to P_j :

If P_i is in its checkpointing, P_i sends message with its *CSN* and *Trigger*.

Actions for the initiator P_j :

The initiator P_j increases its $CSN_j[j]$, sets *weight*:=1, *trigger*:=(P_j, $CSN_j[j]$), marks that it is in its checkpointing and takes local checkpoint. The initiator sends request message with a half of its residuary *weight* to the processes on which the initiator depends to request them take checkpoints too.

Actions at process P_i , on receiving a checkpoint request from P_j :

If P_i has taken a computing checkpoint, it makes computing checkpoint basic tentative, propagates the checkpoint request to these processes with a half of its residuary *weight* on which it depends but P_j does not depend. P_i replies message with residuary *weight* to the initiator. If P_i doesn't take computing checkpoint and $CSN_j[j]>CSN_i[j]$, P_i increases $CSN_i[i]$, takes tentative checkpoint, propagates the checkpointing requiring with a half of its residuary *weight* to the processes on which it depends but P_j does not depend. P_i replies message with residuary *weight* to the initiator.

Actions at process P_i, on receiving a computation message from P_j :

P_i receives a computation message from P_j with $CSN_j[j]$ and *trigger*. If $CSN_j[j]>CSN_i[j]$ then P_i takes a computing checkpoint, increases $CSN_i[i]$, then delivers the message.

Actions in the second phase for the initiator P_i:

If the sum of *weight* which piggyback in every reply messages is equal to one, it means all processes on which initiator depends have taken checkpoints, the initiator broadcasts committing message with the information including which processes have taken checkpoint; otherwise initiator broadcast negative message. The initiator updates the dependent relations.

Actions at other process P_j on receiving a broadcast message from P_i:

If a process receives a committing message, the receiver makes tentative permanent or discards computing checkpoint. The receiver updates the dependent relations and the *CSN*s of each process according to the information that which processes have taken checkpoints. If a process receives a negative message, the receiver discards tentative checkpoint or computing checkpoint, and updates the dependent relations and *CSN*s of each process.

Fig. 1. The *LNCC* algorithm description

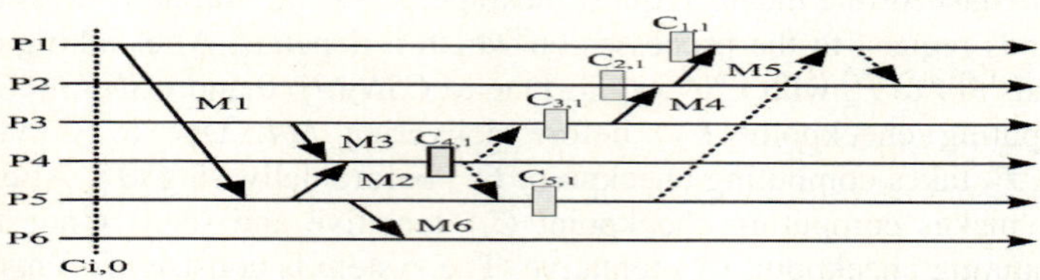

Fig. 2. An example of a distributed system with *LNCC* algorithm

4 Correctness of the Algorithm

Theorem 1. Computing checkpoint is necessary.

Proof: Assume that P_j sends M piggybacking $CSN_j[j]$ to P_i. If $CSN_j[j]>CSN_i[j]$, it means P_j has taken a checkpoint before sending M. Assume that P_i doesn't take computing checkpoint before delivering M. Since the future running situations of processes are unforeseen, later, P_i may receive a request from another process P_k. P_i will take checkpoint, M becomes an orphan. If P_i takes computing checkpoint before delivering M, when receiving a checkpoint request, P_i will transform the computing checkpoint to basic tentative checkpoint, so M is avoided to become an orphan. After making computing checkpoint tentative, P_i propagates request of taking checkpoint to the processes on which it depends but P_k does not depend. If P_i doesn't receive any request message, the computing checkpoint will be discarded, and the system still is consistent. □

Theorem 2. An initiator P_i takes checkpointing, all the processes on which P_i depends should take relative checkpoints too.

Proof. If initiator P_i directly depends on a process P_j, there is $R_i(j)$=1. P_j will receive a request from P_i. So P_j will take tentative checkpoint caused by P_i. If the initiator P_i transitively depends on P_j, there must be processes P_1, P_2, …, P_n, having P_i directly depends on P_1, P_1 directly depends on P_2, …, P_n directly depends on P_j. P_j will receive the request and take tentative checkpoint. □

Theorem 3. *LNCC* is a consistent checkpoint algorithm.

Proof. Assume that there is an inconsistent after the *LNCC*. There is a message M sent from P_i to P_j such that P_j saves the event of delivering M and P_i doesn't save the event of sending M. P_j is an initiator or a process on which initiator depends because of its taking a checkpoint. M is sent from P_i to P_j, so there is $R_j(i)$=1. If P_j takes checkpoint, P_i must take checkpoint too. Contradiction. □

5 Evaluating the Redundant Computing Checkpoints

A computing checkpoint that isn't transformed into a tentative is a redundant checkpoint. If there is not any redundant computing checkpoint, the checkpoint algorithm is a minimum algorithm. We analyze the proportion of redundant computing checkpoint among all checkpoints.

5.1 The Model and Assumption

A checkpoint interval can be denoted by two parts: the period of not taking checkpointing (denoted as T_{NC}) and the period of taking checkpointing (denoted as T_C) as shown in Fig.3.

Obviously there is T_{NC}>>T_C. P_{sc} initiates checkpointing and the processes on which P_{sc} depends take checkpoint too. The set N_D includes the processes on that P_{sc} depends and the set $\overline{N_D}$ includes the processes on that P_{sc} does not depend. Computing checkpoints are produced in period of T_C only. The computing checkpoints that are produced in N_D will be transformed into tentative and the computing checkpoints that are produced in $\overline{N_D}$ are redundant computing checkpoints. In order to compute the redundant checkpoint, denoted as N_{comp}, assume that the message sending and receiving rate are the same, denoted as λ_M, and receiver receives message in no delay.

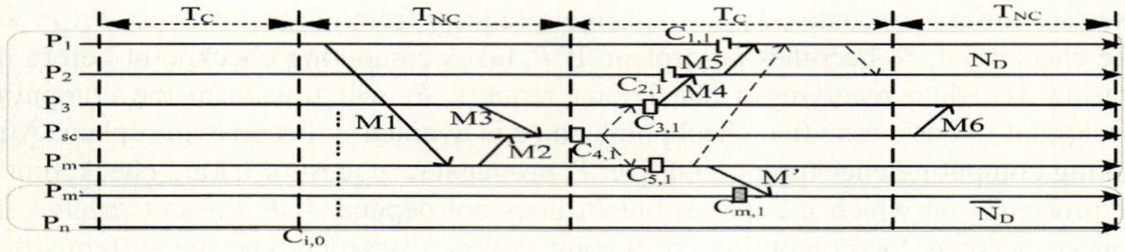

Fig. 3. The example of redundant computing checkpoints

5.2 The Number of Processes on That Initiator Does Not Depend

In the last T_{NC} period, the number of messages received by P_{sc}, $N_{SC}(T_{NC})$, is:

$$P\{N_{SC}(T_{NC})=m\}=\frac{(\lambda_M T_{NC})^m}{m!}e^{\lambda_M T_{NC}} \quad (1)$$

The expectation number, N_{SC}, is:

$$\begin{aligned} N_{SC} &= E(N_{SC}(T_{NC}))=\sum_{m=0}^{\infty} m\frac{(\lambda_M T_{NC})^m}{m!}e^{\lambda_M T_{NC}} \\ &= \lambda_M T_{NC} e^{-\lambda_M T_{NC}} \times e^{\lambda_M T_{NC}} = \lambda_M T_{NC} \end{aligned} \quad (2)$$

The probability that P_{sc} receives a message from P_i is $\rho = 1/(N-1)$. The probability that P_{sc} does not receive a message from P_i is:

$$\rho(0)=(1-\rho)^{N_{sc}}=(1-1/(N-1))^{\lambda_M T_{NC}} \quad (3)$$

The probability that K out of $(N-1)$ processes does not send messages to P_{sc} is:

$$P(x=K)=\binom{N-1}{K}\rho(0)^K(1-\rho(0))^{N-1-K} \quad (4)$$

Its expectation number is:

$$\begin{aligned} N_{ND} = E(K) &= \sum_{K=0}^{K=N-1} KP(K)=\sum K\binom{N-1}{K}\rho(0)^k(1-\rho(0))^{N-1-K} \\ &= (N-1)\rho(0)=(N-1)(1-1/(N-1))^{\lambda_M T_{NC}} \end{aligned} \quad (5)$$

That is, in the last T_{NC} period, the expectation number of processes that have not sent any message to P_{sc} equals to N_{ND}. Assume that there are two sets, S_{S1}={P_i|P_i has sent a message to P_{sc} in the last T_{NC} period} and S_{NS1}={P_i|P_i has not sent any message to P_{sc} in the last T_{NC} period}. Assume that $P_i \in S_{NS1}$ in the last T_{NC} period, the probability that the message sent by P_i has not sent to S_{S1} is:

$$\rho_{ND} = N_{ND} / N \quad . \tag{6}$$

In the last T_{NC} period, the expectation number of processes that belong to set S_{NS1} and have not sent any message to set S_{S1} is N_{ND1}.

$$\begin{aligned} N_{ND1} &= N_{ND}\rho = N_{ND}(\rho_{ND})^{\lambda_M T_{NC}} \\ &= (N-1)(1-1/(N-1))^{\lambda_M T_{NC}}((N-1)(1-1/(N-1))/N)^{\lambda_M T_{NC}} \quad . \end{aligned} \tag{7}$$

In turn, the processes which belong to S_{NS1} can be parted into two sets, S_{S2}={P_i|P_i has sent a message to S_{S1} in the last T_{NC} period} and S_{NS2}={P_i|P_i has not sent any message to S_{S1} in the last T_{NC} period}. $|S_{NS2}|= N_{ND1}$ .The number of processes which belong to S_{NS2} and not send message to S_{S1} is N_{ND2}.

$$N_{ND2} = N_{ND1}\rho_2 \quad . \tag{8}$$

Thereinto,

$$\rho_2 = (\rho_{ND2})^{\lambda_M T_{NC}} \quad . \tag{9}$$

$$\rho_{ND2} = N_{ND1} / N \quad . \tag{10}$$

In turn, the processes which belong to $S_{NS(i-1)}$ can be parted into two set, S_{Si}={P_i|P_i has sent a message to $S_{S(i-1)}$ in the last T_{NC} period} and S_{NSi}={P_i|P_i has not sent any message to $S_{S(i-1)}$ in the last T_{NC} period}. The probability of a process P_i which belongs to S_{NSi} and does not send message to $S_{S(i-1)}$ is:

$$\rho_{NDi} = N_{ND(i-1)} / N \quad . \tag{11}$$

The probability of the processes which belong to S_{NSi} and don't send message to $S_{S(i-1)}$ is:

$$\rho_i = (\rho_{NDi})^{\lambda_M T_{NC}} \quad . \tag{12}$$

The expectation number of processes which belong to S_{NSi} and don't send message to $S_{S(i-1)}$ is:

$$N_{ND(i+1)} = N_{NDi}\rho_i \quad . \tag{13}$$

If $(N_{NDi}-N_{ND(i+1)}) \leq 1$, the number of processes on which P_{SC} does not depends is $N_{ND(i+1)}$. Set $N_{ID}= N_{ND(i+1)}$, N_{ID} is the number of processes on which P_{SC} does not depend.

5.3 The Number of Redundant Computing Checkpoints

Assume that there are two sets, S_{ID}={P_i|P_{SC} does not depend on P_i directly or indirectly} and S_D={P_i|P_{SC} depends on P_i directly or indirectly}.

In the T_C period, P_i that belongs to S_{ID} receives a message sent by a process P_j that belongs to S_D. If the *CSN* which is appended by P_j is larger than the *CSN* which P_i expects P_j has, P_i must take computing checkpoint. This computing checkpoint is redundant computing checkpoint that should be discarded in the future. If the *CSN* which is appended by P_j isn't larger than the *CSN* which P_i expects P_j has, P_i does not take computing checkpoint. For simplifying analysis, we consider the worst situation that P_i takes computing checkpoint when it receiving a message sent from P_j, regardless its *CSN* and the appended *CSN*.

The ratio that the processes belonged to S_{ID} receive the messages sent from the processes belonged to S_D is λ_D.

$$\lambda_D = ((N - N_{ID}) / N)\lambda_M \quad . \tag{14}$$

In the T_C period, the probability of taking computing checkpoint is:

$$\rho_C = 1 - e^{-\lambda_D T_C} \quad . \tag{15}$$

The expectation number of redundant computing checkpoints is:

$$\begin{aligned} N_{comp} &= E(K_C) = \sum_{K=0}^{N_{ID}} K \binom{N_{ID}}{K} \rho_C{}^K (1-\rho_C)^{N_{ID}-K} \\ &= N_{ID}\rho_C = N_{ID}(1 - e^{-((N-N_{ID})/N)\lambda_M T_C}) \quad . \end{aligned} \tag{16}$$

Table 1 shows the redundant computing checkpoints ratio（*E%*） to tentative checkpoints under *N*=20.

Table 1. The efficiency of *LNCC* algorithm under parameters

T_{NC}	300	300	600	600	300	300	600	600
T_C	10	10	10	10	20	20	20	20
λ_M	0.01	0.001	0.01	0.001	0.01	0.001	0.01	0.001
N_{ID}	11.97	18.12	7.29	17.27	11.97	18.12	7.29	17.27
ρ_C	0.04	0.00046	0.061	0.0014	0.07	0.0019	0.12	0.0027
N_{comp}	0.48	0.08	0.45	0.23	0.84	0.034	0.86	0.047
E (%)	5.6	4	3.4	7.8	9.5	1.8	6.3	1.7

Table 1 shows that the number of redundant computing checkpoints depends on the values of T_{NC}, T_C and λ_M, but it is always less than 10% of the total tentative checkpoints. The computing checkpoints ratio is in the worst situation. In fact the real ratio is less than the ratio listed in table 1, because the action of taking computing checkpoint relies on the *CSNs* of processes too.

6 Experiment

A system with 16 nodes is simulated, the nodes are connected through a LAN which has 100Mbps bandwidth and each node has one process running on it. The length of each computation message is 1KB, and the length of each system message is 50Bytes. The computer's CPU is PⅣ2.4GHz, memory is 512MB. The rate of memory bus with 64bit width is 100MHz. The length of checkpoint is 1MB. Fig.4 shows the number of

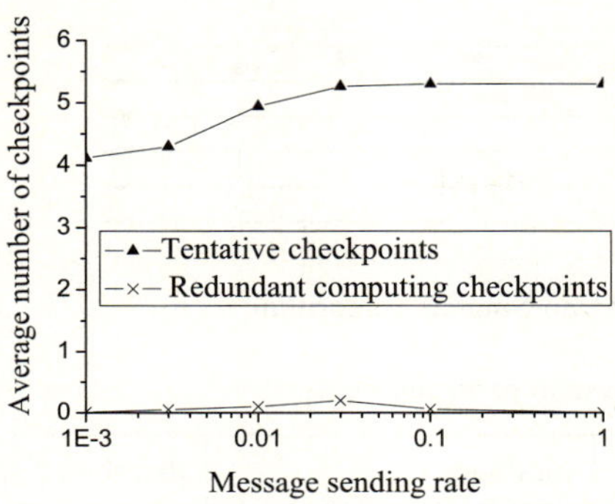

Fig. 4. The comparison of redundant computing checkpoints and tentative checkpoints

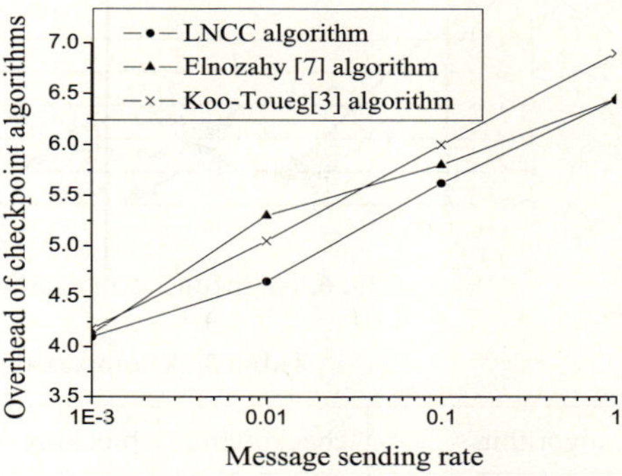

Fig. 5. The comparison of the overhead of checkpoint algorithms

redundant computing checkpoints and tentative checkpoints change with the change of message sending rate.

As shown in Fig.4, when the massage sending rate increasing, the number of redundant computing checkpoints increases at first, then gets its maximum, and then decreases. This can be explained as follows: a process takes a computing checkpoint only when it receives a computation message from a process that has taken a tentative checkpoint. If the message sending rate is low, processes have low probability of sending messages and they have low probability of receiving messages during the T_C time. Thus, processes have low probability of taking computing checkpoints. So, the number of redundant computing checkpoints is less too. If the message sending rate enhancing, it is more likely for a process to receive a message and take a computing checkpoint during the T_C time. If the message sending rate enhancing further, the initiator is more likely to depend on other processes. The computing checkpoints are also more likely to be turned into tentative checkpoint. The number of redundant computing checkpoint decreases. If the message sending rate is large enough, the number of redundant computing checkpoint will be zero. Simulations show that the number of redundant computing checkpoints always less than 5 percent of the tentative checkpoints, less than the number computed in table 1. Because we assume that a process always takes a computing checkpoint when the process receives a computation message from another process that has taken tentative checkpoint in table 1, in despite of the *CSN* of them. Fig.5 shows the comparison result of the algorithms' overhead. As shown in Fig.5, *LNCC* has the low overhead than other algorithms.

7 Comparisons with Existing Work

Many coordinated checkpointing schemes have been proposed for the distributed computing. In ref.[3], a min-process coordinated checkpointing scheme has been proposed, in which only minimal processes need to take new consistent globe checkpoint while others needn't change their old checkpoints. But it must block processes when taking checkpointing. Blocking algorithms may dramatically degrade system performance [7]. To address this issue, non-blocking algorithms are proposed [7-8].

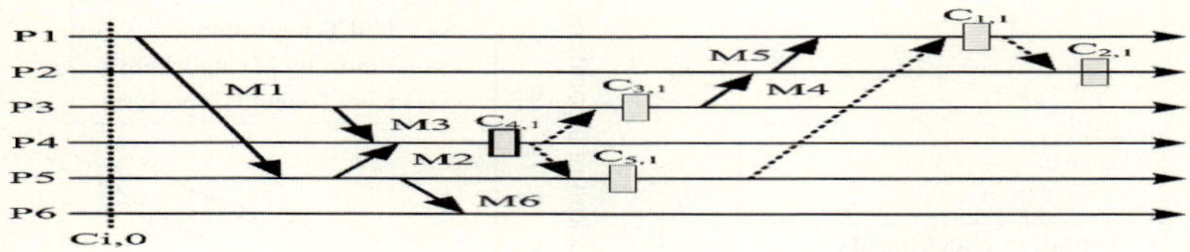

Fig. 6. An inconsistent example of Cao-Singhal's algorithm

Table 2. A comparison of system performance

algorithm	checkpoints	blocking time	messages	distributed
Koo–Toueg[3]	N_{min}	$N_{min}*T_{ch}$	$3*N_{min}*N_{dep}*C_{uni}$	yes
Cao-Singhal [6]	N_{min}	$2*T_{msg}$	$C_{broad}+2*C_{uni}*(N+N_{min})$	yes
Elnozahy [7]	N	0	$2*C_{broad}+N*C_{uni}$	no
LNCC	$N_{min}+N_{comp}$	0	$\approx 2*C_{uni}*N_{min}+C_{broad}$	yes

In the algorithms, processes use a checkpoint sequence number to identify orphan messages. However, these algorithms require all processes to take checkpoints during checkpointing, even though many of them may not be necessary.

Prakash–Singhal's algorithm was the first algorithm to attempt to combine these two approaches [12]. It only forces minimum number of processes to take checkpoints and does not block the underlying computation during the checkpointing. However, this algorithm may result in an inconsistency [6,11]. Cao-Singhal improves Prakash–Singhal's algorithm by using mutable checkpoint [11]. According to Cao-Singhal's algorithm, when P_i receives a computation message M from P_j, P_i should take a mutable checkpoint if following three conditions have been satisfied: (1) P_j is in checkpointing process before sending M; (2) P_i has sent a message since last checkpoint; (3) P_i has not taken a checkpoint associated with the initiator [11]. But there is still an inconsistency in some situations.

Fig.6 illustrates the inconsistency of Cao-Singhal's algorithm. P_4 (as an initiator) takes checkpoint and asks P_3 and P_5 to take checkpoints (dashed represents request messages). After taking a checkpoint, P_3 sends M_4 to P_2, and P_2 sends M_5 to P_1. Condition 2 isn't satisfied, so P_2 needn't take mutable checkpoint. Due to transmission delays, later, P_1 may receive a checkpoint request after receives M_5. Then P_1 takes a checkpoint and requires P_2 to take checkpoint. Then M_4 becomes an orphan.

In table 2, we use four parameters to compare *LNCC* with other algorithms: the number of tentative checkpoints required during a checkpointing process, the blocking time (in the worst case), the system message overhead, whether the algorithm is distributed or not.

C_{uni}: cost of sending a message from one process to another process; C_{broad}: cost of broadcasting a message to all processes; T_{disk}: delay incurred in saving a checkpoint on the stable storage; T_{data}: delay incurred in transferring a checkpoint to the stable storage; T_{msg}: delay incurred by transferring system messages during a checkpointing process; T_{ch}: the checkpointing time, $T_{ch}=T_{msg}+T_{data}+T_{disk}$; T_{comp}: delay incurred in saving a computing checkpoint; N_{min} is the number of processes that need to take checkpoints using the Koo–Toueg algorithm [3], N is the total number of processes in the system, N_{comp} is the number of redundant computing checkpoints during a checkpointing, N_{dep} is the average number of processes on which a process depends.

Since a computing checkpoint can be saved on the main memory, the delay of saving computing checkpoint can be ignored comparing with the delay of saving tentative checkpoint. The overhead of *LNCC* is $N_{min}*T_{disk}+N_{comp}*T_{comp}+2*C_{uni}*N_{min}+C_{broad}$, which is less than the overhead of other algorithms.

8 Conclusion

In this paper, a low-cost non-blocking coordinated checkpoint algorithm is presented. Through using computing checkpoint and piggybacking the information including which processes have taken checkpoint in the broadcast committing message, the unnecessary checkpoints and orphan messages can be avoided in the future running. The algorithm is consistent coordinated checkpoint algorithm which combines the two approaches of reducing the overhead associated with coordinated checkpointing. Analyses and simulations show that our algorithm is better than other coordinated checkpoint algorithms.

References

1. E.N.Elnozahy, L.Alvisi, Y.M.Wang and D.B.Johnson: A Survey of Rollback-Recovery Protocols in Message-Passing Systems. ACM Computing Surveys. 2002, 34(3):375-408.
2. S.Kalaiselvi, V.Rajaramana: A Survey of Checkpointing Algorithms for Parallel and Distributed Computers. Sadhana Academy Proceedings in Engineering Sciences. 2000, 25(5):489-510.
3. R.Koo, S.Toueg: Checkpointing and Rollback-Recovery for Distributed Systems. IEEE Transactions on Software Engineering. 1987:13:23–31.
4. J.L.Kim, T.Park. An Efficient Protocol for Checkpointing Recovery in Distributed Systems. IEEE Transactions on Parallel and Distributed Systems. 1993, 5(8):955–960.
5. Y.Deng, E.K.Park: Checkpointing and Rollback-Recovery Algorithms in Distributed Systems. Journal of Systems Software. 1994, 4:59–71.
6. Cao Guohong, M.Singhal: On the Impossibility of Min-Process Non-Blocking Checkpointing and an Efficient Checkpointing Algorithm for Mobile Computing Systems. Proceedings of the 27th int'l International Conference on Parallel Processing, Minneapolis, USA. 1998:37-44.
7. E.N.Elnozahy, D.B.Johnson, W.Zwaenepoel: The Performance of Consistent Checkpointing. Proceedings of the 11th Symposium on Reliable Distributed Systems, Houston. 1992:39-47.
8. L.M.Silva, J.G.Silva: Global Checkpointing for Distributed Programs. Proceedings of the 11th Symposium on Reliable Distributed Systems, Houston. 1992:155–162.
9. J.M.Helery, A.Mostefaoui, M.Raynal: Communication-Induced Determination of Consistent Snapshots. IEEE Transactions on Parallel and Distributed Systems. 1999, 10(9):865-877.
10. J.M.Helary, A.Mostefaoui, R.H.B.Netzer and M.Raynal: Preventing Useless Checkpoints in Distributed Computations. Proceedings of the 16th Symposium on Reliable Distributed Systems. 1997:183-190.
11. Cao Guohong, M.Singhal: Checkpointing with Mutable Checkpoints. Theoretical Computer Science. 2003,290:1127–1148.
12. R.Prakash, M.Singhal: Low-Cost Checkpointing and Failure Recovery in Mobile Computing Systems. IEEE Transactions on Parallel Distributed System. 1996, 7(10):1035–1048.

A Parallel GNFS Algorithm Based on a Reliable Look-Ahead Block Lanczos Method for Integer Factorization

Laurence T. Yang[1,2], Li Xu[2], Man Lin[2], and John Quinn[2]

[1] Department of Computer Science and Engineering
Jiangsu Polytechnic University
Changzhou, Jiangsu Province, 213164, P.R. China
[2] Department of Computer Science
St. Francis Xavier University
Antigonish, Nova Scotia, B2G 2W5, Canada
{lyang, x2002uwf, mlin, jquinn}@stfx.ca

Abstract. The Rivest-Shamir-Adleman (RSA) algorithm is a very popular and secure public key cryptosystem, but its security relies on the difficulty of factoring large integers. The General Number Field Sieve (GNFS) algorithm is currently the best known method for factoring large integers over 110 digits. Our previous work on the parallel GNFS algorithm, which integrated the Montgomery's block Lanczos method to solve large and sparse linear systems over GF(2), is less reliable. In this paper, we have successfully implemented and integrated the parallel General Number Field Sieve (GNFS) algorithm with the new look-ahead block Lanczos method for solving large and sparse linear systems generated by the GNFS algorithm. This new look-ahead block Lanczos method is based on the look-ahead technique, which is more reliable, avoiding the break-down of the algorithm due to the domain of GF(2). The algorithm can find more dependencies than Montgomery's block Lanczos method with less iterations. The detailed experimental results on a SUN cluster will be presented in this paper as well.

1 Introduction

Today, the Rivest-Shamir-Adleman (RSA) algorithm [21] is the most popular algorithm in public-key cryptosystem and it also has been widely used in real-world applications such as: internet explorer, email systems, online banking, cell phones etc. The security of this algorithm mainly relies on the difficulty of factoring large integers. Many integer factorization algorithms have been developed. Examples are: Trial division [22], Pollard's p-1 algorithm [19], Lenstra Elliptic Curve Factorization (ECM) [13], Quadratic Sieve (QS) [20] and General Number Field Sieve (GNFS) [1,2,3,15] algorithm. GNFS is the best known method for factoring large composite numbers over 110 digits so far.

Although the GNFS algorithm is the fastest algorithm so far, it still takes a long time to factor large integers. In order to reduce the execution time, one natural solution is to use parallel computers. The GNFS algorithm contains several

E. Sha et al. (Eds.): EUC 2006, LNCS 4096, pp. 110–120, 2006.

steps. The most time consuming step is sieving which is used to generate enough relations. This step is very suitable for parallelization because the relation generations are independent. Another step that could benefit from parallel processing is the Montgomery's block Lanczos method [16]. It is used to solve large and sparse linear systems over GF(2) generated by the GNFS algorithm. The disadvantage of this block Lanczos method is its unreliability. The look-ahead block Lanczos method proposed in [8] has overcome this disadvantage and improved the overall reliability of block Lanczos algorithm. There are numerous references available on the look-ahead block Lanczos method [6,7,9,18], but none of those methods can be applied to GF(2) field directly. The algorithm we are developing and implementing is very suitable for solving the generated large and sparse linear systems over small finite fields such as GF(2). In this paper we have successfully developed and implemented the look-ahead block Lanczos method, and integrated together with the GNFS algorithm for integer factorization.

The rest of the paper is organized as follows: we first briefly describe the original GNFS algorithm in section 2. Then we present two block Lanczos methods, namely Montgomery's block Lanczos method [16] and look-ahead block Lanczos method [8] in section 3 and 4 respectively. Section 5 shows the detailed implementation and corresponding parallel performance results.

2 The GNFS Algorithm

The General Number Field Sieve (GNFS) algorithm [2,3,15] is derived from the number fields sieve (NFS) algorithm, developed by Lenstra et al. [14]. It is the fastest known algorithm for integer factorization. The idea of GNFS is from the congruence of squares algorithm [12].

Suppose we want to factor an integer n where n has two prime factors p and q. Let's assume we have two integers s and r, such that s^2 and r^2 are perfect squares and satisfy the constraint $s^2 \equiv r^2 (mod\ n)$. Since $n = pq$, the following conditions must hold [2]:

$$\begin{aligned} pq|(s^2\text{-}r^2) \ &\Rightarrow pq|(s\text{-}r)(s+r) \\ &\Rightarrow p|(s\text{-}r)(s+r) \ and \ q|(s\text{-}r)(s+r). \end{aligned}$$

We know that, if $c|ab$ and $gcd(b,c) = 1$, then $c|a$. So p, q, r *and* s must satisfy $p|(s\text{-}r)$ or $p|(s+r)$ and $q|(s\text{-}r)$ or $q|(s+r)$. Based on this, it can be proved that we can find factors of n by computing the greatest common divisor $gcd(n,(s+r))$ and $gcd(n,(s\text{-}r))$ with the possibility of $2/3$ (see [2]).

Therefore, the essence of GNFS algorithm is based on the idea of factoring n by computing the $gcd(n,\ s+r)$ and $gcd(n,\ s\text{-}r)$. There are six major steps [15]:

1. Selecting parameters: choose an integer $m \in Z$ and a polynomial f which satisfies $f(m) \equiv 0\ (mod\ n)$.
2. Defining three factor bases: rational factor base R, algebraic factor base A and quadratic character base Q.

Table 1. The composite number n and the results after integer factorization

name	number
$tst100_{30}$	727563736353655223147641208603 = 743774339337499•978204944528897
$F7_{39}$	680564733841876926926749214863536422914 = 5704689200685129054721•59649589127497217
$tst150_{45}$	799356282580692644127991443712991753990450969 = 32823111293257851893153•24353458617583497303673
$Briggs_{51}$	556158012756522140970101270050308458769458529626977 = 1236405128000120870775846228354119184397•449818591141
$tst200_{61}$	1241445153765162090376032461564730757085137334450817128010073 = 1127192007137697372923951166979•1101360855918052649813406915187
$tst250_{76}$	3675041894739039405533259197211548846143110109152323761665377505538520830273 = 69119855780815625390997974542224894323•53169119831396634916152282437374262651

3. Sieving: generate enough pairs *(a,b)* (relations) to build a linear dependence.
4. Processing relations: filter out useful pairs *(a,b)* found from sieving.
5. Building up and solve a large and sparse linear system over GF(2).
6. Squaring root: use the results from the previous step to generate two perfect squares, then factor n.

Based on the previous studies, the most time consuming step is step 3, sieving. In our previous work [23,24], we have successfully implemented the sieving in parallel with very scalable performance. In this paper, we are focusing on another time consuming part, namely solving the large and sparse linear systems over GF(2) in parallel.

3 Montgomery's Block Lanczos Method

Montgomery's block Lanczos method was proposed by Montgomery in 1995 [16]. This block Lanczos method is a variant of the standard Lanczozs method [10,11]. Both Lanczos methods are used to solve large and sparse linear systems. In the standard Lanczos method, suppose we have a symmetric matrix $A \in R^{n\times n}$. Based on the notations used in [16], the method can be described as follows:

$$\begin{aligned} w_0 &= b, \\ w_i &= Aw_{i-1} - \sum_{j=0}^{i-1} \frac{w_j^T A^2 w_{i-1}}{w_j^T A w_j}. \end{aligned} \tag{1}$$

The iteration will stop when w_i*=0*. $\{w_0,\ w_1,\ \ldots\ w_{i-1}\}$ are a basis of *span*$\{b,$ $Ab,\ A^2b,\ \ldots\}$ with the properties:

$$\forall 0 \le i < m, \quad w_i^T A w_i \neq 0, \tag{2}$$

$$\forall 0 \le i < j < m, \quad w_i^T A w_j = w_j^T A w_i = 0. \tag{3}$$

The solution x can be computed as follows:

$$x = \sum_{j=0}^{m-1} \frac{w_j^T b}{w_j^T A w_j} w_j. \tag{4}$$

Furthermore the iteration of w_i can be simplified as follows:

$$w_i = Aw_{i-1} - \frac{(Aw_{i-1})^T(Aw_{i-1})}{w_{i-1}^T(Aw_{i-1})} w_{i-1} - \frac{(Aw_{i-2})^T(Aw_{i-1})}{w_{i-2}^T(Aw_{i-2})} w_{i-2}.$$

The total time for the standard Lanczos method iss $O(dn^2)+O(n^2)$, d is the average number of nonzero entries per column.

The Montgomery's block Lanczos method is an extension of the standard Lanczos method applied over field GF(2). The major problem for working on GF(2) is that inner products are very likely to become zero because of the binary entries, then the algorithm breaks down accordingly, can not proceed easily. The Montgomery's block Lanczos method is the first attempt to avoid such break down by using N vectors at a time (N is the length of the computer word). Instead of using vectors for iteration which easily leads to inner products to zero, we are using the subspace instead. First we generate the subspace:

$$\begin{aligned} \mathcal{W}_i \qquad & is A - invertible, \\ \mathcal{W}_j^T A \mathcal{W}_i = \{0\}&, \{i \neq j\}, \\ A\mathcal{W} \subseteq \mathcal{W}, \quad & \mathcal{W} = \mathcal{W}_0 + \mathcal{W}_1 + \ldots + \mathcal{W}_{m-1}. \end{aligned} \tag{5}$$

Then we define x to be:

$$x = \sum_{j=0}^{m-1} W_j (W_j^T A W_j)^{-1} W_j^T b, \tag{6}$$

where W is a basis of $\mathcal{W}$. The iteration in the standard Lanczos method will be changed to:

$$\begin{aligned} W_i &= V_i S_i, \\ V_{i+1} &= AW_i S_i^T + V_i - \sum_{j=0}^{i} W_j C_{i+1,j} \quad (i \geq 0), \\ \mathcal{W}_i &= \langle W_i \rangle, \end{aligned} \tag{7}$$

in which

$$C_{i+1,j} = (W_j^T A W_j)^{-1} W_j^T A (AW_i S_i^T + V_i). \tag{8}$$

This iteration will stop when $V_i^T AV_i$=0 where $i = m$. The iteration can also be further simplified as follows:

$$V_{i+1} = AV_i S_i S_i^T + V_i D_{i+1} + V_{i-1} E_{i+1} + V_{i-2} F_{i+1}.$$

where $D_{i+1}, E_{i+1}, F_{i+1}$ are:

$$D_{i+1} = I_N - W_i^{inv}(V_i^T A^2 V_i S_i S_i^T + V_i^T A V_i),$$
$$E_{i+1} = -W_{i-1}^{inv} V_i^T A V_i S_i S_i^T,$$
$$F_{i+1} = -W_{i-2}^{inv}(I_N - V_{i-1}^T A V_{i-1} W_{i-1}^{inv})(V_{i-1}^T A^2 V_{i-1} S_{i-1} S_{i-1}^T + V_{i-1}^T A V_{i-1}) S_i S_i^T.$$

$\mathbf{S}_i$ is an $N \times N_i$ projection matrix (N is the length of computer word and $N_i < N$). The cost of the Montgomery's block Lanczos method will be reduced to $O(n^2)+O(dn^2/N)$.

4 Look-Ahead Block Lanczos Method

In this paper, the look-ahead block Lanczos method over small finite fields such as GF(2) we are developing is mainly based on the method proposed in [8]. There are some advantages of such look-ahead block Lanczos method compared with Montgomery's block Lanczos method: first of all, this method is bi-orthogonalizing, so the input matrix generated from GNFS does not need to be symmetric. In order to apply Montgomery's block Lanczos method, we need to multiply the coefficient matrix A with A^T. However over GF(2), the rank of the product $A^T A$ is, in general, much less than that of A. Thus, when applied to find elements of the nullspace of A, the Montgomery's block Lanczos method may find many spurious vectors. Secondly, also more importantly, it solves the problem of break down we mentioned before, namely ($\mathcal{W}_i{}^T A \mathcal{W}_i = \{0\}$).

Due to the limited space, we only outline the algorithm in the paper. First we choose v_0 and u_0 from $\mathbb{K}^{n \times N}$. Then we will compute $v_1, v_2, \cdots, v_{m-1}$ and $u_1, u_2, \cdots, u_{m-1}$. We try to achieve the following conditions:

- $K(A^T, u_0) = \bigoplus_{i=0}^{m-1} \langle u_i \rangle$ and $K(A, v_0) = \bigoplus_{i=0}^{m-1} \langle v_i \rangle$.
- Each subspace $\langle u_i \rangle$ and $\langle v_i \rangle$ is of dimension at most N.
- For all $0 \le i < m$, $u_i^T A v_i$ is invertible.
- For all $0 \le i, j \le m$ with $i \ne j$, $u_i^T A v_j = 0$ and $u_j^T A v_i = 0$.

Then we can decompose the vector spaces $\langle u_i \rangle$ and $\langle v_i \rangle$. Define variables $\bar{v}_i$, $\bar{u}_i$, $\hat{v}_i$, $\hat{u}_i$, $\check{v}_i^i$, $\check{u}_i^i$, σ_i^v and σ_i^u have the properties:

- $\hat{v}_i^T A v_i = 0$.
- $u_i^T A \hat{v}_i = 0$.
- $\bar{u}_i^T A \bar{v}_i$ is invertible.

and

$$\check{u}_i^i := \{\bar{u}_i^i | \hat{u}_i^i\} = u_i \sigma_i^u, \quad (9)$$

$$\check{v}_i^i := \{\bar{v}_i^i | \hat{v}_i^i\} = v_i \sigma_i^v, \quad (10)$$

σ_i^v and σ_i^u are two invertible matrices in $\mathbb{K}^{N \times N}$. This may be computed by performing a Gauess-Jordan decomposition of the matrix $u_i^T A v_i$ and using the output to select the independent row and column vectors, which then correspond to the columns of $\bar{v}_i$ and $\bar{u}_i$, respectively. The matrices σ_i^u and σ_i^v permute these columns to the front and apply row and column dependencies, respectively, to give $\hat{u}_i$ and $\hat{v}_i$. We define $\check{u}_i$ and $\check{v}_i$ to be the matrices representing this decomposition: $\check{v}_i = v_i\sigma_i^v$, $\check{u}_i = u_i\sigma_i^u$. Through this, then v_{i+1} and u_{i+1} can be computed by:

$$v_{i+1} = Av_i - \sum_{k=0}^{i} \bar{v}_k (\bar{u}_k^T A \bar{v}_k)^{-1} \bar{u}_k^T A^2 v_i, \tag{11}$$

$$u_{i+1} = A^T u_i - \sum_{k=0}^{i} \bar{u}_k (\bar{v}_k^T A^T \bar{u}_k)^{-1} \bar{v}_k^T (A^T)^2 u_i. \tag{12}$$

In computing u_{i+2} and v_{i+2} in next iteration, we have the following situations:

$$(\check{u}_{i-1}|\check{u}_{i-1})^T A(\check{v}_{i-1}|\check{v}_i|v_{i+1}|Av_{i+1}) = \left(\begin{array}{c|c|c|c} r_{i-1,i-1} & & & u_{i-1}^T A^2 v_{i+1} \\ \hline & r_{ii} & & s_{i+1,i+2} \\ & 0 & r_{i,i+1} & r_{i+1,i+2} \end{array}\right) \tag{13}$$

Since $r_{i-1,i-1}$ and $r_{i,i}$ are assumed invertible (modifying to operate in the case where it is not invertible is straightforward), elimination steps to zero $u_{i-1}^T A^2 v_{i+1}$ and $s_{i+1,i+2}$ are performed. For the cases of $r_{i,i+1}$ has full rank or not, we cope differently. We continue the same manner until all rows corresponding to u_i have an associated invertible minor. The iterative formula has been simplified as follows:

$$u_{i+1} = A^T u_i - \sum_{k=0}^{i} \dot{u}_k^i ((\bar{v}_k^i)^T A^T \dot{u}_k^i)^{-1} (\bar{v}_k^i)^T (A^T)^2 u_i, \tag{14}$$

$$v_{i+1} = Av_i - \sum_{k=0}^{i} \dot{v}_k^i ((\bar{u}_k^i)^T A \dot{v}_k^i)^{-1} (\bar{u}_k^i)^T A^2 v_i. \tag{15}$$

The elimination and decomposition steps presented above do not yield sufficient orthogonality conditions to allow computation of a candidate system solution easily. We would continue the elimination and decomposition until it has a permuted block diagonal structure, in which the non-zero parts are as closely clustered around the diagonal as possible. Please refer to [8] for details. Eventually, the solution x can be calculated by:

$$x = \sum_{i=0}^{m-1} \dot{v}_i^m ((\bar{u}_i^m)^T A \dot{v}_i^m)^{-1} (\bar{u}_i^m)^T b. \tag{16}$$

5 Parallel Implementation Details

As we mentioned before, the most time consuming part in GNFS is sieving. This part has already been parallelized in our previous work [23,24]. This paper is build on top of the our previous parallel implementation. Our overall parallel code is built on the sequential source GNFS code from Monico [15].

5.1 Hardware and Programming Environment

The whole implementation is built on two software packages, the sequential GNFS code from Monico [15] (Written in ANSI C) and the sequential Look-ahead block Lanczos code from Hovinen [8] (Written in C++). For parallel implementation, MPICH1 (Message Passing Interface) [5] library is used, version 1.2.5.2. The GMP 4.x is also used [4] for precision arithmetic calculations. We use GUN compiler to compile whole program and MPICH1 [17] for our MPI library. The cluster we use is a Sun cluster from University of New Brunswick Canada whose system configurations is:

- Model: Sun Microsystems V60.
- Architecture: x86 cluster.
- Processor count: 164.
- Master processor: 3 GB registered DDR-266 ECC SDRAM.
- Slave processor: 2 to 3 GB registered DDR-266 ECC SDRAM.

In the program, each slave processor only communicates with the master processor. Figure 1 shows the flow chart of our parallel program.

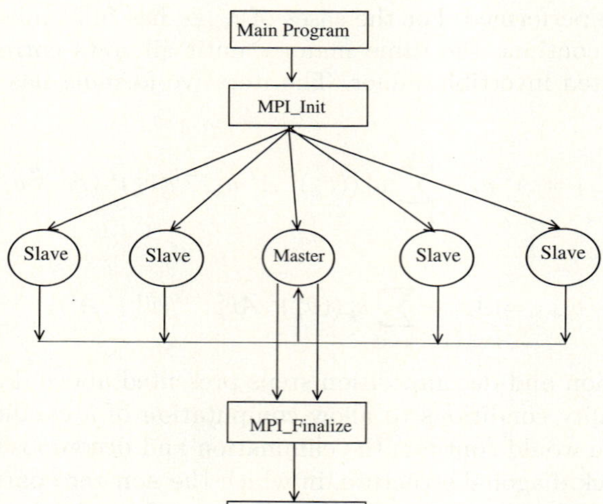

Fig. 1. Each processors do the sieving at the same time, and all the slave nodes send the result back to master node

6 Performance Evaluation

We have six test cases, each test case have a different size of n, all are listed in Table 1.

The sieving time increases when the size of n increases. Table 2 shows the average sieving time for each n with one processor. Table 3 shows the number

Table 2. Average sieving time for each n

name	number of sieve	average sieve time(s)
$tst100_{30}$	1	35.6
$F7_{39}$	1	28.8
$tst150_{45}$	5	50.6
$Briggs_{51}$	3	85.67
$tst200_{61}$	7	560.6
$tst250_{76}$	7	4757.91

Table 3. Number of processors for each test case

name	number of slave processors
$tst100_{30}$	1,2,4,8,16
$F7_{39}$	1,2,4,8,16
$tst150_{45}$	1,2,4,8,16
$Briggs_{51}$	1,2,4,8,16
$tst200_{61}$	1,2,4,8,16
$tst250_{76}$	1,2,4,8,16

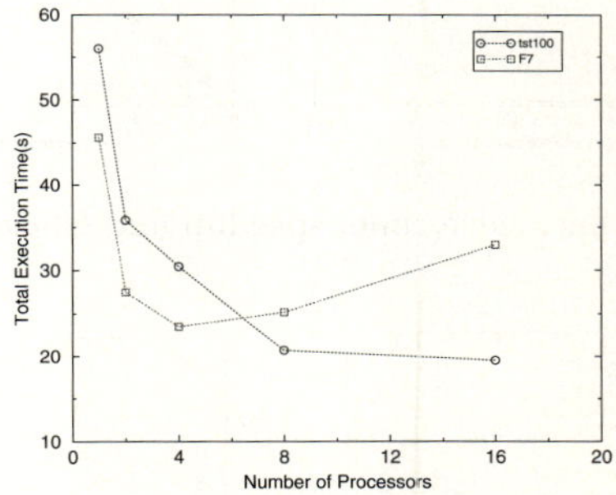

Fig. 2. Execution time for tst100 and F7

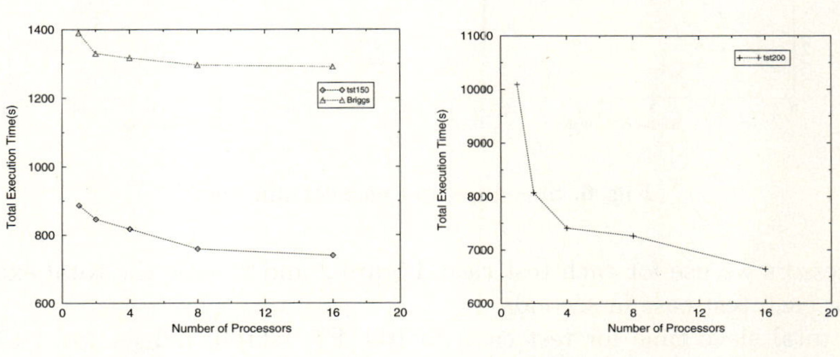

Fig. 3. Execution time for tst150, Briggs and tst200

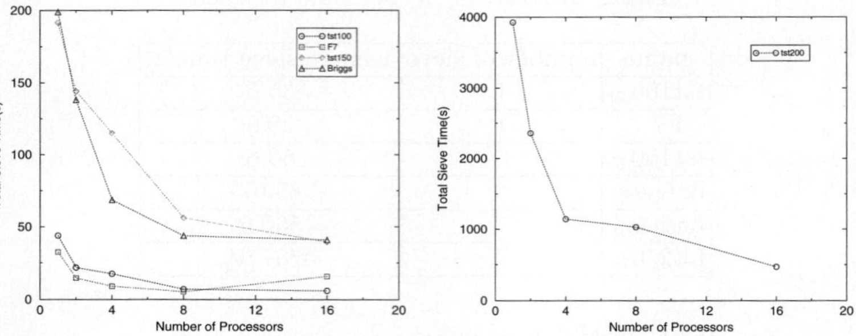

Fig. 4. Sieve time for tst100, F7, tst150, Briggs and tst200

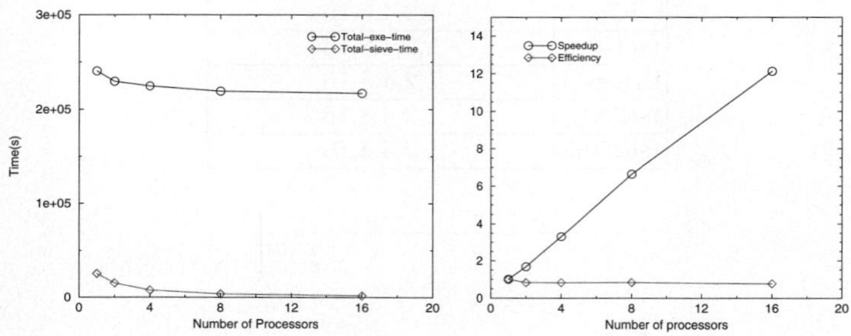

Fig. 5. Total execution time, sieve time, speedup and efficiency for test case tst250

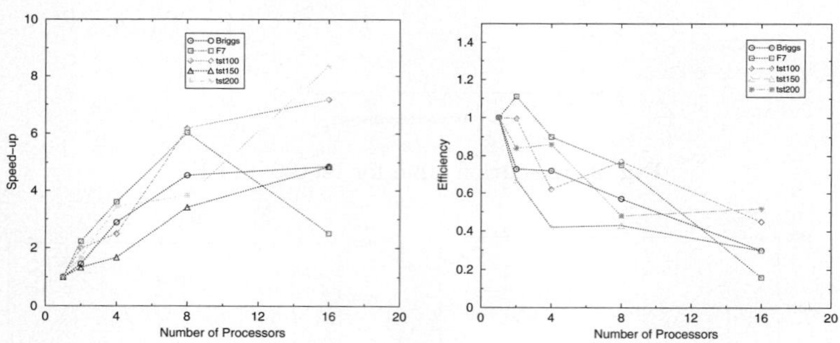

Fig. 6. Speedups and parallel efficiency

of processors we use for each test case. Figure 2 and 3 show the total execution time for each test case in seconds.

The total sieve time for test case: tst100, F7, tst150, Briggs and tst200 are presented in Figure 4. Figure 5 gives the total execution time, sieve time, speed-ups and parallel efficiency with different processor numbers. Figure 6 gives the speed-ups and parallel efficiency for each test case with different processor numbers.

Additionally, based on our comparisons on a few limited test cases, the method can find more dependencies than Montgomery's block Lanczos method with less iterations. We will report the details in future publications.

Acknowledgements

We would like to thank C. Monico of Texas Tech University and B. Hovinen of University of Waterloo. Our work is based on their sequential source codes. They also helped us with some technical problems through emails. Dr. Silva from IBM advised us many good ideas for our parallel program.

References

1. M. E. Briggs. An introduction to the general number field sieve. Master's thesis, Virginia Polytechnic Institute and State University, 1998.
2. M. Case. A beginner's guide to the general number field sieve. Oregon State University, ECE575 Data Security and Cryptography Project, 2003.
3. J. Dreibellbis. Implementing the general number field sieve. pages 5–14, June 2003.
4. T. Granlund. *The GNU Multiple Precision Arithmetic Library.* TMG Datakonsult, Boston, MA, USA, 2.0.2 edition, June 1996.
5. W. Gropp, E. Lusk, and A. Skjellum. *Using MPI: Portable Parallel Programming with the Message-Passing Interface.* MIT Press, 1994.
6. M. H. Gutknecht. Block krylov space methods for linear systems with multiple right-hand sides. In *The Joint Workshop on Computational Chemistry and Numerical Analysis (CCNA2005)*, Tokyo, Dec 2005.
7. M. H. Gutknecht and T. Schmelzer. A QR-decomposition of block tridiagonal matrices generated by the block lanczos process. In *Proceedings IMACS World Congress*, Paris, July 2005.
8. B. Hovinen. Blocked lanczos-style algorithms over small finite fields. Master Thesis of Mathematics, University of Waterloo, Canada, 2004.
9. R. Lambert. *Computational Aspects of Discrete Logarithms.* PhD thesis, University of Waterloo, 1996.
10. C. Lanczos. An iteration method for the solution of the eigenvalue problem of linear differential and integral operators. In *Journal of Research of the National Bureau of Standards*, volume 45, pages 255–282, 1950.
11. C. Lanczos. Solutions of linread equations by minimized iterations. In *Journal of Research of the National Bureau of Standards*, volume 49, pages 33–53, 1952.
12. A. K. Lenstra. Integer factoring. *Designs, Codes and Cryptography*, 19(2-3):101–128, 2000.
13. H. W. Lenstra. Factoring integers with elliptic curves. *Annals of Mathematics(2)*, 126:649–673, 1987.
14. H. W. Lenstra, C. Pomerance, and J. P. Buhler. Factoring integers with the number field sieve. In *The Development of the Number Field Sieve*, volume 1554, pages 50–94, New York, 1993. Lecture Notes in Mathematics, Springer-Verlag.
15. C. Monico. General number field sieve documentation. GGNFS Documentation, Nov 2004.
16. P. L. Montgomery. A block lanczos algorithm for finding dependencies over gf(2). In *Proceeding of the EUROCRYPT '95*, volume 921 of *LNCS*, pages 106–120. Springer, 1995.

17. MPICH. http://www-unix.mcs.anl.gov/mpi/mpich/.
18. B. N. Parlett, D. R. Taylor, and Z. A. Liu. A look-ahead lanczos algorithm for unsymetric matrics. *Mathematics of Computation*, 44:105–124, 1985.
19. J. M. Pollard. Theorems on factorization and primality testing. In *Proceedings of the Cambridge Philosophical Society*, pages 521–528, 1974.
20. C. Pomerance. The quadratic sieve factoring algorithm. In *Proceeding of the EUROCRYPT 84 Workshop on Advances in Cryptology: Theory and Applications of Cryptographic Techniques*, pages 169–182. Springer-Verlag, 1985.
21. R. L. Rivest, A. Shamir, and L. M. Adelman. A method for obtaining digital signatures and public-key cryptosystems. Technical Report MIT/LCS/TM-82, 1977.
22. M. C. Wunderlich and J. L. Selfridge. A design for a number theory package with an optimized trial division routine. *Communications of ACM*, 17(5):272–276, 1974.
23. L. Xu, L. T. Yang, and M. Lin. Parallel general number field sieve method for integer factorization. In *Proceedings of the 2005 International Conference on Parallel and Distributed Processing Techniques and Applications (PDPTA-05)*, pages 1017–1023, Las Vegas, USA, June 2005.
24. L. T. Yang, L. Xu, and M. Lin. Integer factorization by a parallel gnfs algorithm for public key cryptosystem. In *Proceddings of the 2005 International Conference on Embedded Software and Systems (ICESS-05)*, pages 683–695, Xian, China, December 2005.

SPDA: A Security Protocol for Data Aggregation in Large-Scale Wireless Sensor Networks

Jin Wook Lee[1], Yann-Hang Lee[2], and Hasan Cam[2]

[1] Networking Lab.,
Samsung Advanced Institute of Technology, P.O. 111, Suwon, Korea 440-600
[2] Department of Computer Science and Engineering,
Arizona State University, Tempe, AZ 85287-8809, USA

Abstract. In this paper we propose a new key establishment protocol enabling any data aggregation protocol to be operated securely. This is accomplished by a bidirectional key distribution scheme based on *Forward Key Setup* and *Backward Key Setup* developed by using synchronized broadcast and multi-level key concept. Our protocol, called SPDA(Security Protocol for Data Aggregation) is well suited for any data aggregation algorithms and applications. Our analysis results prove SPDA's efficiency meaning that its communication cost is manageable.

1 Introduction

The issue of security in sensor networks has been addressed at various levels. In order to prevent unauthorized entities from intercepting, decrypting, or hijacking data communications, data should be encrypted with either symmetric or asymmetric keys. The keys must be protected and managed appropriately between the base station and all sensor nodes and must satisfy several security and functional requirements. To support secured data aggregation in sensor networks, there must be a key management scheme between each sensor node and its correspondent data aggregation node. Thus, the collected data are encrypted at each sensor node and then decrypted at the data aggregation node for aggregation processing. This paper focuses on a simple key establishment for data aggregation in sensor networks. The objective is to construct an efficient key management for data aggregation mechanism that can give confidentiality and integrity against malicious intruders. To eliminate the security loophole open to malicious intruders, we present a mechanism to set up pair-wise symmetric keys for data aggregation operations. The core of a Security Protocol for Data Aggregation (SPDA) mechanism is the ***bidirectional key setup scheme*** that stochastically makes a unique symmetric key between a sensor node and a correspondent aggregation node in the sensor network.

2 Related Works

So far the issue of security in sensor networks has been addressed at various levels. Secure data aggregation schemes have been introduced in recent literatures [1] [2] [3] [4] [5]. In the papers [3] [4], the authors attempted to make data aggregation secure by designing alternate data aggregation schemes such as pattern-based data aggregation and reference-based data aggregation. They employed a kind of group key management

E. Sha et al. (Eds.): EUC 2006, LNCS 4096, pp. 121–130, 2006.

scheme, so a group header becomes an aggregator to perform the aggregation algorithm. However, such schemes also have their limitations in performing specific data aggregation algorithms and specific applications. In another work [2], Przydatek et al. recently proposed secure information aggregation. Their scheme is also dedicated to specific applications. Lee et al. [1] proposed a key management for data aggregation and pointed out that the disadvantage of their scheme was that more data needed to be passed through the key setup message and stored at each node. Worse yet, compromising a node allows an adversary to understand all data communications originating from the node's neighboring nodes. A similar paper to ours is proposed by Hu et al. [5], but they don't discuss key management issues in detail. Unlike other works, we provide a security platform that conforms to any data aggregation scheme and any application scenarios.

3 SPDA Protocol

Our aim is to construct a key establishment mechanism which enable a node to have a unique symmetric key agreed with the correspondent aggregator. Our idea is to allow each node to compute a key with seeds originating from both the Forward Key and Backward Key sent by aggregators. Our design goal is to devise a simple key establishment scheme well suited to any data aggregation algorithm by using pre-defined aggregators. Only aggregators have a data aggregation algorithm to perform and have more security information for key generation. Throughout the paper, we use several terms to describe the protocol as defined in Table 1.

Table 1. Glossary

Glossary	*Description*
FKeySetup	A protocol packet. Only the base station can generate the initial FKeySetup packet. All the nodes start the operation by receiving a FKeySetup packet firstly.
BKeySetup	A protocol packet. Only the aggregators can generate their own BKeySetup packets. All the sensor nodes create their own BKeySetup packet to send data messages to aggregators.
FLK	Forward Level Key. A key hint of the base station.
BLK	Backward Level Key. A key hint of the aggregator.
PubK	Public key of the base station. This public key is shared by all nodes.
SPK	Secret key, partially selected bits of PubK.
PrvK	Private key that the base station and aggregators share.
CK	Combination key. This key is generated by forward and backward key setups and is used by aggregators and sensor nodes.
hc	Hop Count. Logical hop count from the base station
bhc	Backward Hop Count. Logical hop count from an aggregator

3.1 Definition of Keys and Functions

Our approach to key generating functions is motivated by the need to establish a symmetric key of each node as efficient in communication cost as possible. Our idea of key generation introduces symmetry of key with two asymmetric keys. Combining two different keys produces a high probability of having a virtually unique key in the network if each of the two different keys is not carelessly generated. One key is propagated from the base station to sensor nodes. The other key is propagated from aggregators to the base station. The keys are propagated by the relaying procedure of each node. The relayed keys should not be easily guessed, so we suggest the use of a one-way hash function as a key relaying function. Each sensor node receives two different keys from two different neighboring nodes by relaying keys in opposite directions.

We define and use three types of crypto keys and two types of seed keys as below:

- Crypto key
  - Public Key (PubK)
  - Private Key (PrvK) of the base station and aggregator
  - Sub-Public Key (SPK)
  - Combination Key (CK)
- Seed key
  - Forward Level Key (FLK)
  - Backward Level Key (BLK)

All nodes maintain the public key (PubK) of the base station. This public key offers data confidentiality of a broadcast message during announcement at the base station. SPK is partially selected bits of PubK (i.e. most significant 64 bits of PubK) and is used as a secret key among all nodes. The public key processing is costly; sensor node's public key processing is performed only during key establishment. Once a sensor node finishes the key establishment, PubK and SPK are no longer used for data confidentiality so this public key mechanism does not significantly affect the network performance. We choose 64 bits for a symmetric key and 512 bits for a public key, so the size of all symmetric keys in this work is 64 bits. Combination Key (CK) is a core cryptographic key in this protocol; it is computed in each node to use for sensed data message confidentiality. Each CK for each sensor node has a high probability of being unique in a network. Additionally, aggregators have the private key (PrvK) of the base station that is pre-installed, so aggregators are said to have the same security power as the base station and can also use this to establish secure channels to other aggregators. During the key establishment, performing Forward and Backward Key Setup enables each sensor node to compute its CK by itself and to use it for data encryption afterwards. Forward Level Key (FLK) and Backward Level Key (BLK) are combined to generate the CK. The first FLK is created only by the base station, whereas the generating BLK is started by all aggregators. We are going to explain how to generate and propagate FLK and BLK in the next subsection.

We suggest applying two one-way hash functions and a combining function to perform the protocol. All nodes have two key-generating functions and one key-combining function as below:

- One-way function
  - Forward Key Generating Function (FFunc)
  - Backward Key Generating Function (BFunc)
- Combining function
  - Combination Function (CFunc)

3.2 Key Establishment

Our key establishment is done in two stages, *Forward Key Setup and Backward Key Setup*. The base station starts a key establishment phase by broadcasting a message enclosing *The Seed of Forward Level Key*(FLK^l), where l is the level of the base station. We now address the two key setup stages in greater detail, using Figure 1 to help explain the Forward and Backward Key Setup protocol.

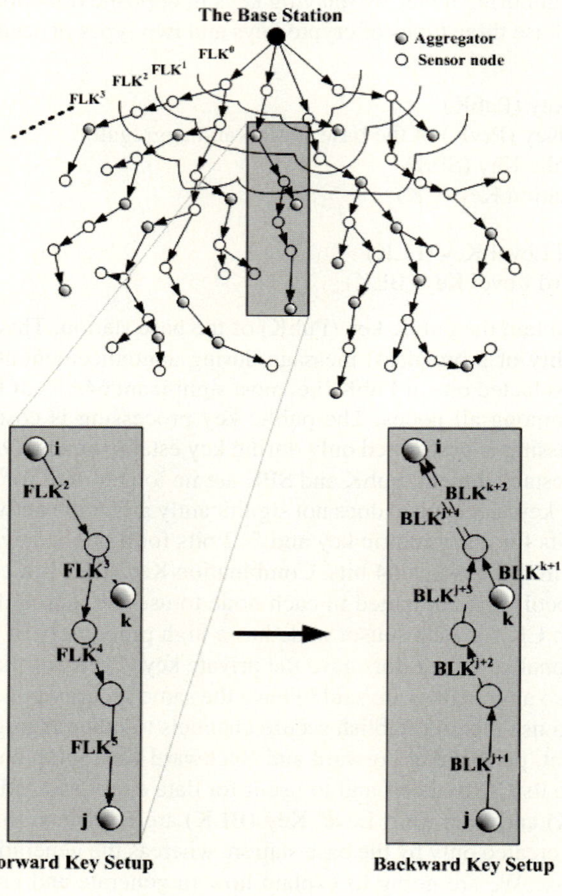

Fig. 1. Network Illustration of Forward and Backward Key Setup

Forward Key Setup. Key distribution for wireless sensor networks should not ignore scalability. In order to achieve scalability, a flooding-based broadcast is commonly used for distributing keys. The base station starts the Forward Key Setup stage by sending a $FKeySetup$ packet containing the commitment code of the *Forward Level Key* (FLK^n, where n is a big enough number and the last element of the key chain. For notation, we use superscript for hop count or level) to all adjacent nodes, which prevents an adversary from compromising the base station. In the Forwarding Key Setup stage, the concept of '$level$' is important, meaning that those who have the same hop count from the base station locate in the same level and have the same FLK. The format of the first FKeySetup packet is shown below:

Base Station $\xrightarrow{broadcast}$ ***Neighbors*** : $FKeySetup^0$

$$E_{PrvK}\{\ FLK^n \mid n \mid G\ \}$$
$$\mid E_{SPK}\{\ FLK^0 \mid hc^0\ \}$$
$$\mid MAC_{SPK}(\ FLK^n \mid n \mid G\ ),$$

where G is a gap value of hop-count assigned by the base station.

On receiving the FKeySetup packet, a node starts performing the protocol. The node naively decrypts the packet with PubK and computes the MAC of the decrypted content with SPK. The node then verifies the packet with two procedures, MAC comparison and Commitment key validation. Firstly, the integrity and authenticity of the packet could be validated by comparison of the computed MAC with the received MAC; however, MAC comparison, with the syntax verification method is not enough, since a malicious node that steals SPK is able to forge the whole packet by changing random bits of the content and computing corresponding MAC with SPK. In such a case, MAC comparison could not detect this abnormality. Commitment key validation solves the problem. Provided that *hc* starts with 0 and $increases\ by\ one$, the node applies FFunc with FLK, '$n - G \cdot hc$' times to verify FLK^n. Applying a gap value, G, between two consecutive *hc* prevents an attacker having no G from generating the next FLK properly.

If the verification fails, the node stops the protocol; otherwise, the node becomes a level-1 node and prepares its own FKeySetup packet based on application of FFunc for the next Forward Level Key ($FLK^1 = FFunc^G(FLK^0)$, meaning G times FFunc application). After an appropriate time, all level-1 nodes transmit their FKeySetup packet as below. Nodes that receive these kinds of packets for the first time become a part of the network as level-2 nodes.

Level-1 nodes $\xrightarrow{broadcast}$ ***Neighbors*** : $FKeySetup^1$

$$\text{RELAY}[E_{PrvK}\{\ FLK^n \mid n \mid G\ \}]$$
$$\mid E_{SPK}\{\ FLK^1 \mid hc^1\ \}$$
$$\mid \text{RELAY}[MAC_{SPK}(\ FLK^n \mid n \mid G\ )],$$

where hc^1 is $hc^0 + 1$.

As a result of completion of the Forward Key Setup stage, all nodes including aggregators have FLK^l, where l is a relative hop distance from the base station.

Backward Key Setup. Aggregators may start the Backward Key Setup stage right after they receive a FKeySetup while sensor nodes wait to receive a Backward Key Setup packet to start the Backward Key Setup stage. Backward Key Setup is performed with unicast communication started by aggregators. Once each aggregator receives a FKeySetup packet, it is ready to start the Backward Key Setup stage by generating the BKeySetup packet as follows (For notation, we use subscript for node ID):

$$\textbf{\textit{Aggregator i}} \xrightarrow{unicast} \textbf{\textit{Its parent node j}} : BKeySetup_i$$
$$E_{PubK}\{\ Seed_i \mid bhc_i^0 \mid i \mid hc_i\ \}$$
$$\mid E_{SPK}\{\ BLK_i^0 \mid bhc_i^0\ \}$$
$$\mid MAC_{SPK}(\ Seed_i \mid bhc_i^0 \mid i \mid hc_i\ )$$

An aggregator, i, chooses a random number as the Seed of the Backward Key, then applies a one-way function once to make its BLK_i^0. We suggest choosing an arbitrary number for bhc instead of zero. This technique prevents an adversary who compromises SPK from knowing the relative location of an aggregator by calculating bhc. The $Seed$ and bhc are encrypted with PubK and reported to an upper-level aggregator which will use them to compute proper CKs of intermediate sensor nodes in the routing path between two aggregators. Assume that each node chooses one of its neighboring nodes as the next hop node to reach the base station. An aggregator unicasts its BKeySetup to its next hop node (say, node j).

On receiving this BKeySetup packet, sensor node j decrypts $E_{SPK}\{BLK_i^0 \mid bhc_i^0\}$ with SPK and makes its own $BKeySetup_j$, which contains updated $bhc_j^1 (= bhc_i^0 + 1)$ and BLK_j^1 (the output of $BFunc(BLK_i^0)$) as below:

$$\textbf{\textit{Sensor Node j}} \xrightarrow{unicast} \textbf{\textit{Its parent node k}} : BKeySetup_j$$
$$\text{RELAY}[E_{PubK}\{\ Seed_i \mid bhc_i^0 \mid i \mid hc_i\ \}]$$
$$\mid E_{SPK}\ \{\ BLK_j^1 \mid bhc_j^1\ \}$$
$$\mid \text{RELAY}[MAC_{SPK}(\ Seed_i \mid bhc_i^0 \mid i \mid hc_i\ )]$$

Only aggregators having PrvK are capable of understanding all the contents of the BKeySetup. Whenever an aggregator receives a BKeySetup packet, it decrypts the whole packet with PrvK and then keeps the source ID, bhc_i^0, and $Seed_i$ of the source aggregator in the aggregator list.

3.3 Combination Key Generating

The main purpose of Forward and Backward Key Setup is to allow a node to be able to have a secret key agreed with an aggregator for data message confidentiality, which is *Combination Key (CK)*. Once a node generates CK, it could encode a data message to give to an aggregator lightly and securely. Now we explain how each kind of node computes its own CK. There are two sorts of nodes in the protocol, such as aggregator and sensor nodes. Each kind of node does apply differently CK generation functions. A sensor node which receives FLK and BLK uses them as inputs of CFunc as $CK_j = CFunc(FLK_j, BLK_j)$. This key combination is quite unique in the network and also can be computed with seeds of each key. All aggregators share PrvK and are able to compute other aggregator's CK generated with PrvK and their ID as below for aggregator i: $CK_i = CFunc(PrvK, i)$. The reason that an aggregator incorporates its ID into CK is to differentiate CK of other aggregators. Having ID of other aggregators grants an aggregator the CK generation of others.

3.4 Key Usage

Two different kinds of nodes build the first data message with three different message fields usage, as below:

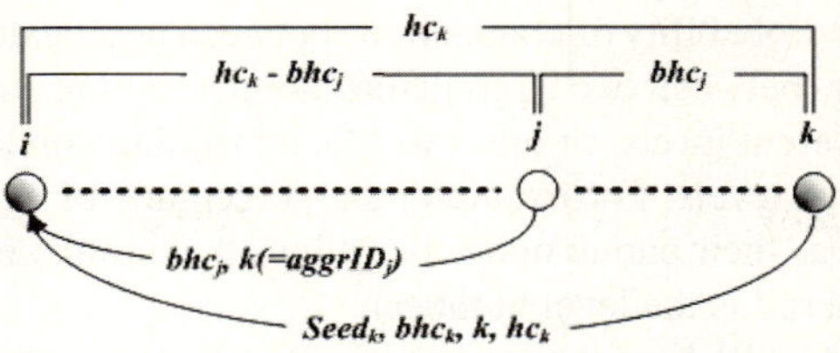

Fig. 2. Finding relative distance of a source node

Node k $\xrightarrow{unicast}$ ***Aggregator i*** :

$$E_{CK_k}\{Message\} \mid E_{SPK}\ \{k|0|k\} \mid MAC_{CK_k}(Message) \text{ for aggregators}$$
$$\text{or } E_{CK_k}\{Message\} \mid E_{SPK}\ \{k|bhc_k|aggrID_k\ \} \mid$$
$$MAC_{CK_k}(Message|bhc_k|aggrID_k\ ) \text{ for sensor nodes,}$$

where $aggrID_k$ is the source aggregator ID of bhc that node k receives.

When an aggregator receives the first data message from a node, it searches the source ID, say k, in the aggregator list. If k is found in the aggregator list, the ID is used to compute CK_k. The aggregator figures out the generation of proper CK for sensor nodes.

With aggrID, an aggregator can calculate the length of the path between two aggregators and also locate the message source node with *bhc*. Therefore, the aggregator is able to find the relative distance of the message source node from aggregators and calculate its FLK and BLK, as illustrated in Figure 2.

As mentioned above, CK calculation is done only once. After that, all nodes send smaller sized messages as below:

Node k $\xrightarrow{unicast}$ ***Aggregator*** :

$$E_{CK_k}\ \{\ Message\ \} \mid k \mid MAC_{CK_k}(Message).$$

4 Analysis

In this section, we show the performance of SPDA through approximate numerical analysis and provide simulation results to validate our numerical analysis. We choose communication cost as the performance metric because the number of communications is critical in wireless sensor network. Communication cost is defined as the additional number of communications per non-aggregator for Backward key setup. We first derive the basic calculation of the number of nodes. During the Forward key setup, the tree-structured network is formed level by level. The percentage of aggregators (denoted by α) on each level is expected to be the same under uniform distribution. Let $N(l)$ denote the number of nodes on level l. Thus, the number of aggregators, $N_{agg}(l)$, is $\alpha \cdot N(l)$. With a maximum level number of a network, h, the total number of nodes in a whole network, T_N, and the total number of aggregators, T_{agg}, can be calculated respectively as:

$$T_N = \sum_{i=1}^{h} N(i), T_{agg} = \alpha \cdot \sum_{i=1}^{h} N(i).$$

Now we calculate the probability of connections between aggregators. To find the number of non-aggregators between two aggregators along a routing path, we note that they are all located on different levels. In other words, all routing connections between two nodes are between two levels. For example, the percentage of aggregators on a level that have aggregators as their parent nodes is α times the number of aggregators on the level ($\alpha \cdot N_{agg}(l)$ where l is the level number).

Not all nodes receive a BLK necessary to generate CK. In the tree-structured network we target, some nodes are not destined to receive BLK because they are not located in the routing path of any aggregators. We define a *tail node* as a node that has no chance of receiving any BLK from any aggregators and does not contribute the network security. The number of tail nodes contributes directly to the protocol performance as a whole so the number of tail nodes should be found. The number of tail nodes can be derived like this. Intuitively, all non-aggregators on the maximum level l are tail nodes because there is no possibility of getting them to receive a Backward key. In the same way, some non-aggregators on level $l-1$ are going to be tail nodes since they are not selected as parents by aggregators on level l. In the same way, the number of tail nodes on a level with h, maximum level number, can be derived as:

$$N_{tail}(l) = (1-\alpha)^{h-l}(1-\alpha)N(l).$$

The total number of tail nodes in network is

$$T_{tail} = \sum_{i=1}^{h} N_{tail}(i) = \sum_{i=1}^{h}(1-\alpha)^{h-i}(1-\alpha)N(i).$$

We suggest three scenarios for aggregator's BLK forwarding to reduce the number of tail nodes in a network. We categorize three different scenarios for the behavior of an aggregator: (1) An aggregator unicasts a BLK to only its parent node(Say, Scenario I). (2) An aggregator unicasts a BLK to all its parent level nodes, not to just the parent node(Scenario II). (3) An aggregator unicasts a BLK to all its neighbor nodes except its child level nodes(Scenario III).

In an ideal case, just one Backward key is sufficient for the computation of a non-aggregator's CK. However, a node may be expected to relaying several Backward keys to the upper level in SPDA. Note that Backward key setup communication commences from an aggregator and ends at another aggregator. In order to count the number of additional communications for Backward key distribution, we first find the sum of all intermediate non-aggregators that relay the Backward key for aggregators. t_n represents the number of aggregators in the network that travel through n, the number of non-aggregators, to reach another aggregator. t_n can be derived with α and N_{agg} as below.

$$t_0 = \sum_{l=2}^{h} \alpha N_{agg}(l) + N_{agg}(1)$$

$$t_1 = \sum_{l=3}^{h}(1-\alpha)\alpha N_{agg}(l) + (1-\alpha)N_{agg}(2)$$

$$\ldots = \ldots$$

$$t_i = \sum_{l=i+2}^{h} (1-\alpha)^i \alpha N_{agg}(l) + (1-\alpha)^i N_{agg}(i+1)$$

$(1-\alpha)^2\alpha N_{agg}(4)$, for instance, represents the case when that many aggregators on level 4 send a Backward key; there are 2 non-aggregators relaying the key until the key reaches an aggregator. Therefore, the total number of additional communications necessary for Backward key setup of all non-aggregators is calculated thus:

$$T_{forward} = p \cdot \sum_{i=0}^{h-1} (i \cdot t_i) = p \cdot \sum_{i=0}^{h} (i \cdot (\sum_{l=i+2}^{h-1} ((1-\alpha)^i \alpha^2 N(l)) + \alpha(1-\alpha)^i N(i+1)).,$$

where p is the scenario factor. For scenario I, p is 1. p is going to be $0.3N$ and $0.7N$ for scenario II and scenario III, respectively. N is the average number of neighbors. $0.3N$ is the approximate average number of parent level nodes per an aggregator and $0.7N$ is the approximate average number of parent and sibling level nodes per an aggregator.

In conclusion, the average number of forwarding communication per each non-aggregator, $A_{forward}$, is

$$A_{forward} = \frac{T_{forward}}{T_{non}}.$$

where T_{non} is $T_N - T_{agg} - T_{tail}$.

Now we can calculate the communication cost if we know the network parameters, such as the average number of neighbor nodes(N), the average number of sensor nodes in a level($N(l)$), the number of aggregators(α), and the maximum number of levels(h). The results of numerical analysis and simulation are shown in Figure 3(a) and 3(b). We set the average number of neighbors, N with 10 and maximum number of level in a network, h with 14 for numerical analysis. We see the numerical results is similar to the simulation results.

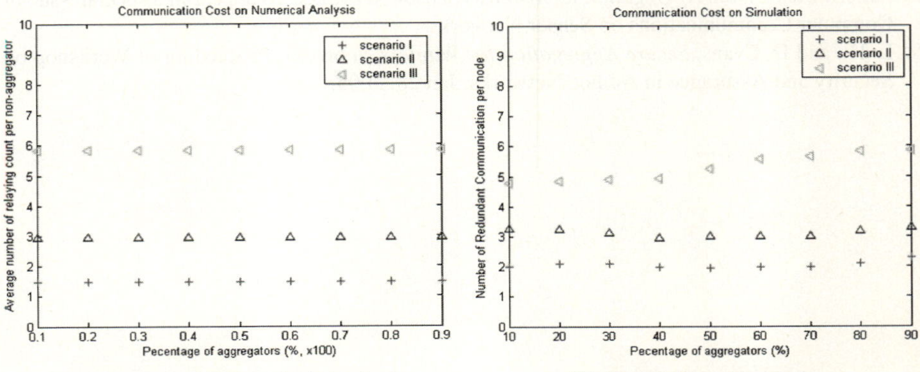

(a) Result from Numerical Analysis (b) Result from Simulation

Fig. 3. Communication Cost

5 Conclusion

In this paper we proposed SPDA, a security protocol for data aggregation, to offer a lightweight key establishment and adaptability of any aggregation algorithms for large-scale tree-structured sensor networks. The protocol provides data integrity and confidentiality by applying a secret key mechanism established with a key generation and distribution scheme. The concept of Forward and Backward Key establishment that plays a key role is presented. By using the protocol, a network administrator is able to build secure networks for data aggregation. In SPDA, a sensor node generates its own crypto-key, CK, realizing its uniqueness in a network with a high probability.

There are two main points concerning the proposed protocol. First, SPDA is totally 'distributed'; i.e. there is no central manager for the protocol, such as a cluster-head or group-head. Hence, it is advantageous for scalability and also adding or deleting a sensor node is easy. Second, SPDA is independent of a data aggregation algorithm. Any data aggregation algorithm could be used together with this protocol. Aggregators should be pre-defined before deployment, at the expense of aggregation efficiency., however.

References

1. Y. H. Lee, A. Deshmukh, V. Phadke and J. W. Lee, *Key Management in Wireless Sensor Networks*, Proceedings of the first European Workshop, ESAS 2004.
2. B. Przydatek, D. Song and A. Perrig, *SIA: Secure Inforamtion Aggregation in Sensor Networks*, Proceedings of the 1st ACM International Conference on Embedded Networked Sensor Systems (SenSys 2003), 2003.
3. H. O. Sanli, S. Ozdemir and H. Cam, *SRDA: Secure Reference-Based Data Aggregation Protocol for Wireless Sensor Networks*, Proceedings of IEEE VTC Fall 2004 Conference, Sept. 26-29, 2004.
4. H. Cam, S. Ozdemir, P. Nair, D. Muthuavinashiappan and H. O. Sanli, *Energy-Efficient Secure Pattern Based Data Aggregation for Wireless Sensor Networks*, To appear in a special issue of Computer Communications on Sensor Networks.
5. L. Hu and D. Evans, *Secure Aggregation for Wireless Networks*, Proceeding of Workshop on Security and Assurance in Ad hoc Networks, Jan 28, 2003.

Efficient and User Friendly Inter-domain Device Authentication/Access Control for Home Networks

Jin-Bum Hwang, Hyung-Kyu Lee, and Jong-Wook Han

University of Science & Technology, Korea
Electronics and Telecommunications Research Institute, Korea
161 Gajeong-dong, Yuseong-gu, 305-350, Korea
{hjb64253, leehk, hanjw}@etri.re.kr

Abstract. Device authentication can reinforce the security of the home network services by ensuring that only specific authorized devices by specific authorized users can access the services. And it is also a mandatory technology for context-aware services in which users do not participate in the service flow. In this paper, we propose a device authentication and access control scheme based on two-layered PKI approach for efficient communication and user convenience. The two layers of our model are Global PKI layer and Localized PKI layer. Global PKI layer uses conventional PKI model. There is only one global root CA, and certificate verification is performed by validating the certificate-chain linked to the root CA. Otherwise, in Localized PKI layer, each home gateway takes a role of root CA which is responsible for issuing device certificates to the devices belong to its domain. We use Global PKI layer for device registration and authentication of inter-home-network, but use Localized PKI layer to authenticate each end-device. Based on this separating, our model provides secure, efficient and user friendly multi-domain device authentication protocols. We also provide a convenient access control scheme using Attribute Mapping Certificate.

1 Introduction

The home network is an emerging technology which provides residents more comfortable and convenient living environment. Home networks consist of many networked devices and the devices provide users variable services such as home automation, data sharing, and context-aware service. Security in home networks is a more important problem than in traditional network environment, because the services provided in home networks is very closely related with the resident's privacy and safety (e.g. door lock/unlock, gas valve control, and remote healthcare) and compromising of the services can result in vast damages to the residents' property and body directly. Therefore, the security in home networks needs to be considered more carefully.

Authentication is a fundamental security mechanism that verifies principal's claimed identity. Generally, user authentication process verifies a user identity through variable means such as password, identity certificate, smart cards, or biometrics. However, these user authentication mechanisms are prone to be easily compromised due to

E. Sha et al. (Eds.): EUC 2006, LNCS 4096, pp. 131 – 140, 2006.

their intrinsic vulnerabilities or the users' inattention. Device authentication is one way that can complement these weaknesses. Device authentication ensures that only specific authorized devices by specific authorized users can access the services. This means that even if password or other user credential is compromised, the security between two parties is still protected as long as the authorized device is not used. Besides this, the device authentication is a mandatory technology that enables emerging context-aware services providing service automatically through device cooperation without user intervention, and DRM systems also need the device authentication [1,2].

So far, several mechanisms have been proposed for this purpose. Some industries suggest hardware fingerprint based approach [3,4] that extracts the secret information from the unique hardware fingerprint and trusts the device by verifying the secret. Bluetooth [5] and Zigbee [6] provide device authentication mechanism based on shared symmetric key, and CableLab [7] also provides PKI based one. Personal CA [8] and UPnP [9,10] provides localized PKI model. However, to the best of our knowledge none of them are applicable for multi-domain environment; they are not scaleable and not user friendly in multi-domain environment for several reasons [11].

In our previous work [11], we proposed a two-layered PKI model for device authentication in multi-domain home networks to solve existing problems, but it lacks relating the authentication scheme to an access control scheme. In this paper, we suggest a device authentication and access control mechanism based on the two-layered PKI model.

The rest of this paper is organized as follows. In Section 2 we explain the architecture of the two-layered PKI model for device authentication in multi-domain home networks. Next in Section 3, we describe our design of multi-domain device authentication model, and we show our device access control model in Section 4. Then we conclude and discuss our future work In Section 5.

2 Architecture of Two Layered PKI Model

We present two layered PKI model, which consist of Global PKI layer and Localized PKI layer, for device authentication applicable to multi-domain home network environment. Fig 1 shows the architecture of our model.

The main principal of our architecture and protocol design is minimizing the end-device's operations, user intervention, and communication time delay in overall device authentication procedure for user friendly, efficient, and scalable device authentication. Generally, home gateways have uniform and more powerful computational capabilities than generic home devices, and they are always on, connected to Internet, and deployed only one at a home domain. These characteristics of the home gateway make it feasible to use the conventional PKI model in authentication process between them. In proposed model, Global root CA issues X.509 certificates to home gateways and manufacturer server, and conventional PKI management protocols are work among them. We named this conventional PKI layer as "Global PKI layer" against "Localized PKI Layer." Global PKI layer is responsible for authentication between manufacturer server and a home gateway during device registration process and authentication among home gateways during domain association process which will be described later.

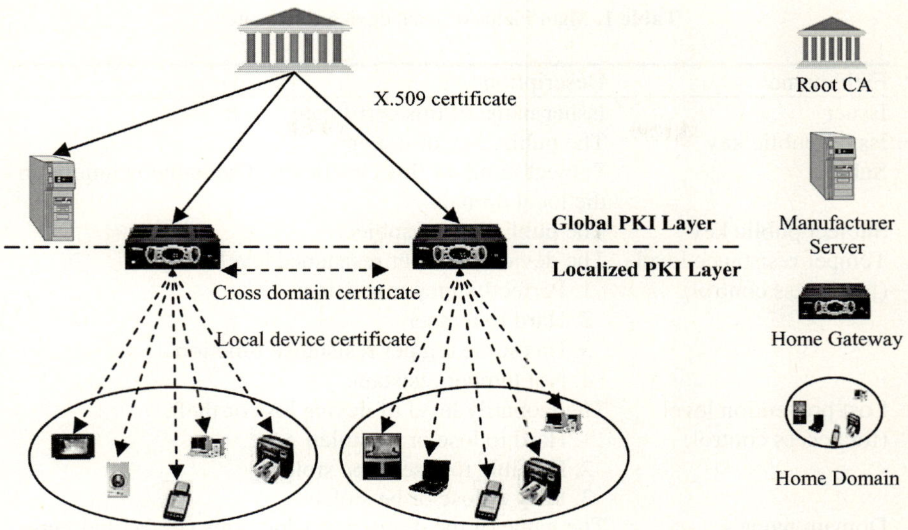

Fig. 1. Proposed device authentication model is consists of Global and Localized PKI Layer. The root CA issues X.509 certificate to Home gateway and Manufacturer Server (Subordinated CAs are omitted to simplify the figure.) Home gateway or Manufacture Server uses this certificate to authenticate each other in proposed protocols. The Home gateway has a role of CA in home domain and it issues a newly defined local device certificate to each home device.

Contrary to the home gateway, end-devices have variable characteristics according to their functions, and many of them have limited capabilities in computational power and memory, although some devices, such as PC and media servers, have powerful computational power and large memory. In addition to this, the large number of deployed end-devices is a big obstacle to use the conventional PKI model in authentication of the devices due to the several reasons [11]. Therefore, we suggest localized PKI model for end-devices and provide safe, efficient and user friendly inter-domain authentication protocols. This is a Localized PKI layer. Two characteristics, always on and connected to Internet, enable the home gateway to have a role of root CA in this layer. The home gateway is responsible for issuing and managing local device certificates for end-devices and cross-domain certificate for other home gateways in Localized PKI layer. The cross-domain certificate makes the communication time delay optimized by eliminating the need of inter-domain communications. Table 1 shows the main fields of local device certificates.

Finally, the manufacturer server is responsible for storing and providing device related information to the home gateway one of whose domain resident purchase the device. The information includes device security level and device public key information. The manufacturer server also acts as a trusted third party between the device and the home gateway during device registration process.

The details of the protocols will be described in next section.

Table 1. Main Fields of local device certificate

Field name	Description
Issuer	Issuer name of this certificate
Issuer public key	The public key of issuer
Subject	Subject name of this certificate. The name is unique in the local domain.
Subject public key	The public key of subject
Temper resistance level (for access control)	The device's temper resistance level. 1. Perfectly temper resistant 2. Hard to temper 3. Has some temper resistance function 4. Not temper resistant
Lost prevention level (for access control)	The jeopardy level of device loss or theft. 1. Hard to lose or be stolen 2. Possible to lose or be stolen 3. Easy to lose or be stolen
Domain name	The name of the domain to which this subject belongs
Domain URL	The URL of the Domain
Validate	The expiration date of this certificate

3 Device Authentication

In this section, we illustrate proposed device authentication based on our two layered PKI architecture. Table 2 shows the notations we will use.

3.1 Device Registration

Device registration is a mutual authentication process between a device and a home gateway for imprinting device and issuing local device certificate to the device. The device sets the home gateway's public key as the root public key after authenticates it, and the home gateway issues a local device certificate to the device also after authenticates its identity.

We use the manufacturer as a trusted third party in this process. The manufacturer has two well fitted features for this role. First, it can easily embed a secret shared between a device and itself to the device at manufacturing time, and also easily contact a user through out of band or authenticated channel to inform a *SecretID* of the device when the user purchases the device. This characteristic makes the device registration more simple and user friendly. Through the manufacturer server, the user is only responsible for entering *SecretID* received from the manufacturer in overall device registration process. Second, the manufacturer has qualification to certify the device's security characteristics. For example, it knows the device's temper resistance level and jeopardy level of lost or theft because it produces the device. This information can be used for device access control which will be described later.

Table 2. Notations for proposed protocols

Symbol	Denotation
$Gcert_X$	A X.509 certificate that the global CA issues to X.
$Ccert_{XY}$	A cross domain certificate that domain X issues to domain Y
$Lcert_{XY}$	A local device certificate that a home gateway X issues to Y
N_X	A nonce that X creates to prevent a replay attack.
K_{XY}	A symmetric key shared between X and Y
K_X	A public key of X
$(\ )K_{XY}$	An encryption using symmetric key K_{XY}
$(\ )K_X$	An encryption using X's public key
$(\ )K_{X^{-1}}$	A signature using X's private key
M	Manufacturer Server
D	A device
H	A home gateway
C	A client device
S	A service device
H_X	A home gateway to which X belongs

Table 3. Device registration protocol

From → To	Message
1: $D \rightarrow H$	*Registration request*
2: $H \rightarrow D$	N_H
3: $D \rightarrow H$	$(D_{ID}, N_D, N_H)K_{MD}$
4: $H \rightarrow M$	$(D_{ID}, N_D, N_H)K_{MD}, (N_H, N_D, SecretID)K_{H^{-1}}, Gcert_H$
5: $M \rightarrow H$	$(K_H, N_D)K_{MD}, DevInfo, (N_H, DevInfo)K_{M^{-1}}, Gcert_M$
6: $H \rightarrow D$	$(K_H, N_D)K_{MD}, Lcert_{HD}$

Now, we describe the device registration protocol. The purposes of this protocol are securely transferring the root public key to a device and issuing local device certificate of Localized PKI layer to the appropriate device. For these purposes, the manufacturer server mediates the device and the home gateway to authenticate each other. Table 3 shows the device registration protocol and the detailed description can be found in [11].

3.2 Device Authentication

In the case of authentication between the devices that belong to different domains, there are two states according to the relation between the two domains each device belongs to; "*Association Unestablished*" and "*Association Established.*" *Association Unestablished* state is the one that the two domains have no security related information about each other. In this state, a device can't authenticate other domain's device. On the other hand, *Association Established* state is the one in which the two domains have a security association, and one domain's device can authenticate another domain's device based on this association. Two domains in *Association Unestablished* state can move to *Association established* state by issuing cross certificates each other and storing the domain name and public key. When a device requests a service to other device which belongs to different domain and the two domains are in *Association Unestablished*, the protocol, which establishes security association between two domains, is executed. We called this protocol "Inter-domain association protocol." Table 4 shows the messages exchanged in this protocol.

At first, the client requests authentication to the service domain home gateway with Nonce N_C and its local certificate. Then, the home gateway confirms whether it and the client domain home gateway are in *Association Established* state or not. If they are not, the service domain home gateway sends its global certificate to the client domain home gateway. Then, the client domain home gateway verifies the certificate, and if it is valid, issues cross domain certificate to the service domain home gateway and sends its global certificate together. Upon the receiving the certificate, the service domain home gateway verifies the certificate and stores the client domain home gateway's domain name and public key.

Table 4. Inter-domain association protocol

From → To	Message
1: $C \rightarrow H_S$	$N_C, Lcert_{H_C C}$
2: $H_S \rightarrow H_C$	$Gcert_{H_S}$
3: $H_C \rightarrow H_S$	$Gcert_{H_C}, Ccert_{H_C H_S}$

Once the two domains enters into *Relation established* state, two devices belongs to each domain can authenticate each other without Global PKI layer until the cross domain certificates are revoked. This is "Inter-domain device authentication protocol" and table 5 shows the flow of this protocol.

At first, the client requests authentication to the service domain home gateway with Nonce N_C and its local certificate. Then, the home gateway confirms whether it and the client domain home gateway are in *Association Established* state or not. If they are, the service domain home gateway verifies the client's local certificate using the client domain home gateway's public key stored during the Inter-domain association protocol, and sends the cross domain certificate, signed message with its private key, and Attribute Mapping Certificate ($AttMappingCert$). Attributed Mapping Certificate will be described in next section. Then, the client device verifies the cross domain certificate and the signature of messages.

Table 5. Inter-domain device authentication protocol

From → To	Message
1: $C \rightarrow H_S$	$N_C, Lcert_{H_C C}$
2: $H_S \rightarrow C$	$Ccert_{H_C H_S}, (N_C)K_{H_S^{-1}}, AttMappingCert$

4 Device Access Control

4.1 Access Control Metrics

Access control is a process that decides whether grant or deny a request to access a specific service. After authenticating the client device, service domain's home gateway can know about the following client's information.

- *Device name*
- *Device's domain name*
- *Temper resistance level*
- *Lost prevention level*

The service device administrator can decide whether permit or deny the access to the device's service based on the confidence of the client device's domain. For example, if the domain is same with the one the service device belongs to, the client device can be granted access to most of the services. On the other hands, if the domain is a neighbor, the client device can access to limited services but it can access more services than unknown domain's device. The device name makes the decision more specific. The administrator can add or remove access authorities of the device according to the device's name. Although two devices are from same domain, one device can use more services than those permitted to the domain, but another can use fewer services than those according to the specific policies for the devices.

Device's temper resistance level and lost prevention level provide information how credible the device is. The secret such as private key can be easily compromised by physical attack if temper resistance technologies are not provided. The temper resistance level means that how well the device can resist against the physical attack to compromise the device's secret. Although the device's domain and the device itself are confident, the low temper resistant level device must not totally be trusted because it may be an adversary who already compromised the device's secret and impersonate the device. The lost prevention level is also important because the user of the device may be an adversary who stole the device from the owner. The low lost prevention level means that the device is likely to be stolen easily. So, the administrator should forbid the access to the critical services from low lost prevention level devices.

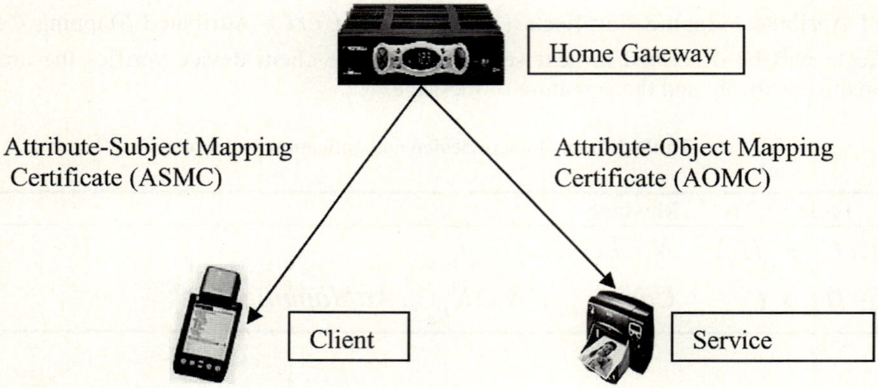

Fig. 2. The domain's Home gateway issues Attribute-Object Mapping to its domain's service devices and issues Attribute-Subject Mapping Certificate to a client

ObjectID	
Attribute1	Permissions
:	:
AttributeN	Permissions
Validity	
Signature	

a) Attribute-Object Mapping Certificate (AOMC)

SubjectPublicKey
Attribute1
:
AttributeN
Validity
Signature

b) Attribute-Subject Mapping Certificate (ASMC)

Fig. 3. ObjectID in AOMC is the service device identifier who is issued this certificate. AOMC can include several attributes and permissions allowed to the attribute. Validity is the expiration date of this certificate. SubjectPublicKey in ASMC is the client's public key. ASMC can have several attributes.

For this access control, we use two kinds of Attribute Mapping Certificates. Figure 2 shows the certificate issuing from a home gateway to end-devices.

At the first, the service domain's home gateway issues the AOMC to its domain's service devices. And upon receiving the request, the home gateway issues an ASMC to the client after authentication according to its access control policy for the client. The elements of these two certificates are shown in the figure 3.

The role of these certificates is that enforce the service devices to provide its service to the client who have the attributed described in the certificate. For example, a client who has an ASMC in which gold and silver attributes are described, it can use the services provided by the service devices who have the AOMC in which gold or silver attributes is described.
The access control protocol is as follows;

1. Client requests a service to a service device.
2. Service sends a nonce to the client and request to present its certificates.
3. Client signs the request message using it private key and send this message with its ASMC.
4. Service device verify the signature of the ASMC using its domain home gateway's public key. Then, if the certificate is valid and it includes a required attribute, the service device provides requested service to the client.

With the Attribute-Mapping Certificate the client can use all of the domain's service authorized to it without the authentication on the domain's home gateway. And the service can authorize the client without the detail information about client and the home gateways help. This can simplify the management of the access control policy.

5 Conclusions

We have suggested a device authentication and access control model for multi-domain home network environments. The main goals of our architecture and protocol design are minimizing the end-device's operations, user interventions, and communication time delay in over all device authentication and access control process. For these purposes, our model uses two layered PKI approach for scalable, efficient, and user friendly device registration and authentication. Global PKI layer participate on the device registration protocol and inter-domain association protocol, and Localized PKI layer is in charge of the authentication between end-devices. The X.509 certificate, which Global PKI layer uses, enables user friendly device registration and inter-domain authentication, and the Local device certificate and the Cross domain certificate makes the end-device authentication efficient and scalable in multi-domain environment. And the attribute mapping certificates makes the access control policy management of service devices simple and convenient. In our model, the device registered to one domain can be authenticated and authorized in other domains without other registration process, and the authentication and access control protocol between two end-devices executed only in local domain without inter-domain communications.

References

1. Yeonjeong Jeong, Kisong Yoon, and Jaesheol Ryou, A Trusted Key Management Scheme for Digital Rights Management, ETRI Journal, vol.27, no.1, Feb. 2005, pp.114-117.
2. Junseok Lee, et al., A DRM Framework for Distributing Digital Contents through the Internet, ETRI Journal, vol.25, no.6, Dec. 2003, pp.423-436.
3. Device Authentication. http://www.safenet-inc.com
4. TrustConnector 2. http://www.phoenix.com
5. Bluetooth Core Specification v2.0. http://www.bluetooth.org/spec/, 2004
6. ZigBee Specification v1.0, December 2004, http://www.zigbee.org/en/spec_download/
7. OpenCable Security Specification. http://www.opencable.com/specifications/, 2004
8. Gehrmann, C., Nyberg, K., and Mitchell, C.J.: The personal CA - PKI for a personal area network. [Conference Paper] IST Mobile and Wireless Telecommunications Summit 2002, pp.31-5, 2002.
9. Universal Plug and Play Forum, http://www.upnp.org/
10. Ellison, C.: UPnP Security Ceremonies Version 1.0. UPnP Forum, 2003.
11. Jin-Bum Hwang, Do-Woo Kim, Yun-Kyung Lee and Jong-Wook Han, Two Layered PKI Model for Device Authentication in Multi-Domain Home Networks, Proc. of 10th International Symposium on Consumer Electronics (ICSE), June 2006

A Programming Model for the Automatic Construction of USN Applications Based on Nano-Qplus*

Kwangyong Lee[1], Woojin Lee[2], Juil Kim[2], and Kiwon Chong[2]

[1] Ubiquitous Computing Middleware Team, ETRI, Daejeon, Korea
kylee@etri.re.kr

[2] Department of Computing, Soongsil University, Seoul, Korea
{bluewj, sespop}@empal.com, chong@ssu.ac.kr

Abstract. A programming model for the automatic construction of USN applications based on Nano-Qplus is proposed in this paper. Nano-Qplus is a sensor network platform developed by ETRI. Programs of nodes such as sensors, routers, sinks and actuators in a sensor network are automatically generated through the technique of this paper. Developers can implement USN applications from models of sensor networks. The configuration information of each node is automatically generated from a model. Then, the execution code is automatically generated using the configuration information. Through the technique of this paper, developers can easily implement USN applications even if they do not know the details of low-level information. The development effort of USN applications also will be decreased because execution codes are automatically generated. Furthermore, developers can consistently construct USN applications from USN models using the proposed tool.

1 Introduction

Recent advances in wireless communications and electronics have enabled the development of lowcost, low-power, multifunctional sensor nodes. These sensor nodes, which consist of sensing, data processing, and communicating components, leverage the idea of sensor networks [1]. Ubiquitous sensor network (USN) is a wireless network which consists of a lot of lightweight, low-powered sensors. A lot of sensors which are connected to a network sense geographical and environmental changes of the field. Through USN, things can recognize other things and sense environmental changes, so users can get the information from the things and use the information anytime, anywhere. The sensor networks can be used for various application areas such as military, home, health, and robot.

However, it is difficult to construct USN applications. Resources of nodes in a sensor network are limited and wireless communication between nodes is unreliable. Nodes should also perform low-power operations. Developers should consider these facts, so it is very difficult to construct USN applications. Therefore, it is need to

* This work was supported by the Soongsil University Research Fund.

E. Sha et al. (Eds.): EUC 2006, LNCS 4096, pp. 141 – 150, 2006.

make developers can simply design USN applications by abstracting the details of low-level communication, data sharing, and collective operations.

Accordingly, a programming model for automatic construction from a model of USN application is proposed in this paper. Programs of nodes such as sensors, routers, sinks and actuators in a sensor network are automatically generated from an USN model. Therefore, developers can easily develop USN applications even if they do not know the details of low-level communication, data sharing, and collective operations. The technique of this paper brings focus to USN application on a sensor network platform known as Nano-Qplus [2, 3]. Nano-Qplus is a sensor network platform developed by ETRI. It is a scalable and reconfigurable Nano-OS. It supports a variety of scheduling methods and various energy-efficient power management schemes in order to meet application specific goals.

2 Related Works

In this section, existing works for generation of USN applications are described. The difference between existing works and the technique of this paper is also described.

Cheong et al. [4] have proposed TinyGALS which is a globally asynchronous and locally synchronous model for programming event-driven embedded systems. This programming model is structured such that all asynchronous message passing code and module triggering mechanisms can be automatically generated from a high-level specification. They have implemented the programming model and code generation facilities on a wireless sensor network platform known as the Berkeley motes. Welsh et al. [5] have simplified application design by providing a set of programming primitives for sensor networks that abstract the details of low-level communication, data sharing, and collective operations. Newton et al. [6] have proposed a functional macroprogramming language for sensor networks, called Regiment. The goal of Regiment is to write complex sensor network applications with just a few lines of code.

Boulis et al. [7] have proposed a framework to define and support lightweight and mobile control scripts that allow the computation, communication, and sensing resources at the sensor nodes to be efficiently harnessed in an application-specific fashion. Their framework, SensorWare, defines, creates, dynamically deploys, and supports such scripts. The SensorWare architecture is based on a scriptable lightweight run-time environment, optimized for sensor nodes that have limited energy and memory.

Greenstein et al. [8] have proposes a new configuration language, component and service library, and compiler that make it easier to develop efficient sensor network applications. Their goal is the construction of smart application service libraries: high-level libraries that implement concepts like routing trees and periodic sensing, and that combine automatically into efficient programs. Their language, library, and compiler are collectively called SNACK (Sensor Network Application Construction Kit). Ramakrishna Gummadi et al. [9] have proposed Kairos. Kairos is a natural next step in sensor network programming in that it allows the programmer to express, in a centralized fashion, the desired global behavior of a distributed computation on the entire sensor network. Kairos' compile-time and runtime subsystems expose a small set of programming primitives, while hiding from the programmer the details of distributed-code generation and instantiation, remote data access and management, and inter-node program flow coordination. Kairos is a simple set of extensions to a programming language that allows programmers to express the global behavior of a distributed computation. Kairos extends the programming language by providing three simple abstractions.

Developers who use the technique of Cheong et al. [4] should write high-level specifications in order to generate sensor network applications. Developers who use the technique of Welsh et al. [5] should develop sensor network applications using the given APIs. Developers who use the techniques of Newton et al. [6], Greenstein et al. [8] and Greenstein Ramakrishna Gummadi et al. [9] should develop sensor network applications using the given languages. Developers who use the technique of Boulis et al. [7] should write script codes in order to generate sensor network applications. On the other hand, developers who use the technique of this paper can automatically generate sensor network applications from models of the applications. They only write USN models using a tool. Therefore, they can easily develop sensor network applications. But, the technique of this paper supports only sensor network applications based on Nano-Qplus platform.

3 A Programming Model for the Automatic Construction of USN Applications

A programming model to construct USN applications based on Nano-Qplus is presented in this section. It is compared to the existing programming models for USN applications. Moreover, the modeling & design of an application using a tool is presented. The algorithm for automatic construction of the application is also presented.

3.1 Concepts of the USN Programming

Figure 1 presents the concept of USN programming described in existing works [4, 5, 6, 7, 8, 9].

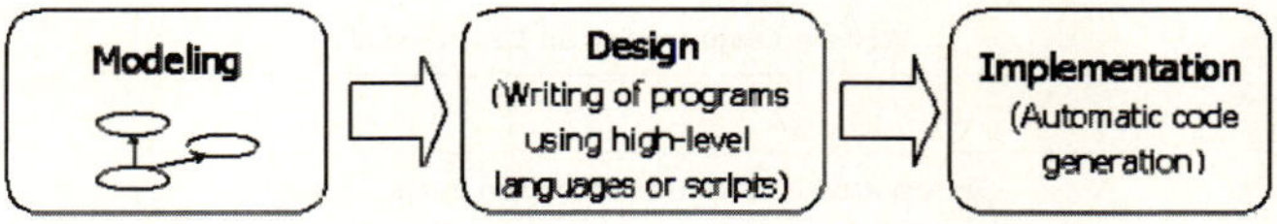

Fig. 1. The concept of USN programming in the existing works

A modeling is done and a simple program based on the model is written using the high level language or the simple script. Then the code is automatically generated according to the program. It is important that the program is written using the high level language or the script. The high level language or the script helps users to construct applications, even though they do not know the details of low-level information of USN. A specification-level language, a script language, or APIs were proposed in order to abstract the low-level information in the related works. However, users should learn the proposed language, the script language or APIs in order to develop USN applications using these techniques.

A technique to complement the existing techniques for the construction of USN applications is proposed in this paper.

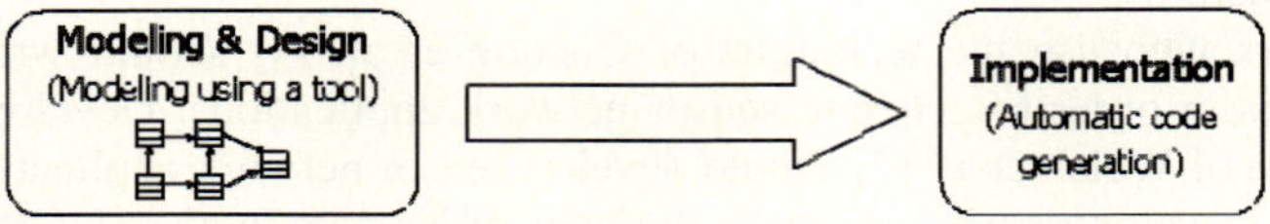

Fig. 2. The concept of USN programming in this paper

Figure 2 presents the concept of USN programming proposed in this paper. Developers can implement USN applications by automatically generating execution code of each node in the sensor networks after they do modeling and design the sensor networks using a tool. The execution code is automatically generated from the model. Therefore, users can construct USN applications without learning a language or APIs.

3.2 The Modeling and Design of USN Applications

The following is the process for the modelling & design of USN applications.

Step 1 – Write an USN model for an USN application using a tool.
Step 2 – Set up attribute values of nodes in the model using a tool.
Step 3 – Generate the model information using XML in order to automatically generate the configuration information of nodes.
Step 4 – Generate configuration information of nodes from the XML in order to automatically generate execution codes of nodes.

Figure 3 presents the process for the modelling & design of USN applications.

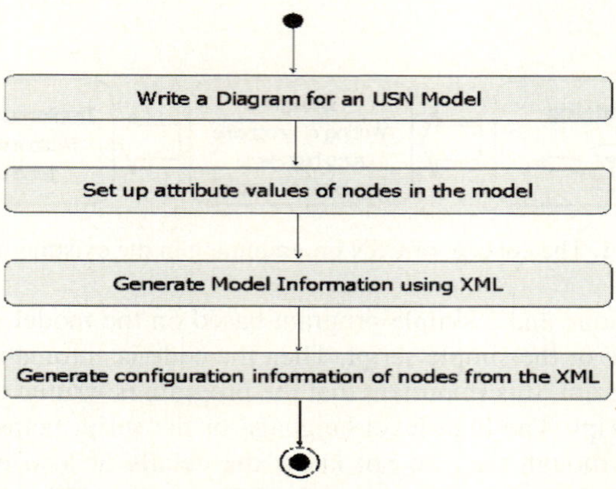

Fig. 3. The process for the modelling & design of USN applications

The tool presented in figure 4 is proposed in this paper in order to model and design of USN applications. The user can write a diagram for an USN model and set attribute values of each node in the model using the tool. The tool generates a XML file which stores the model information. Figure 5 shows the XML file generated by the tool.

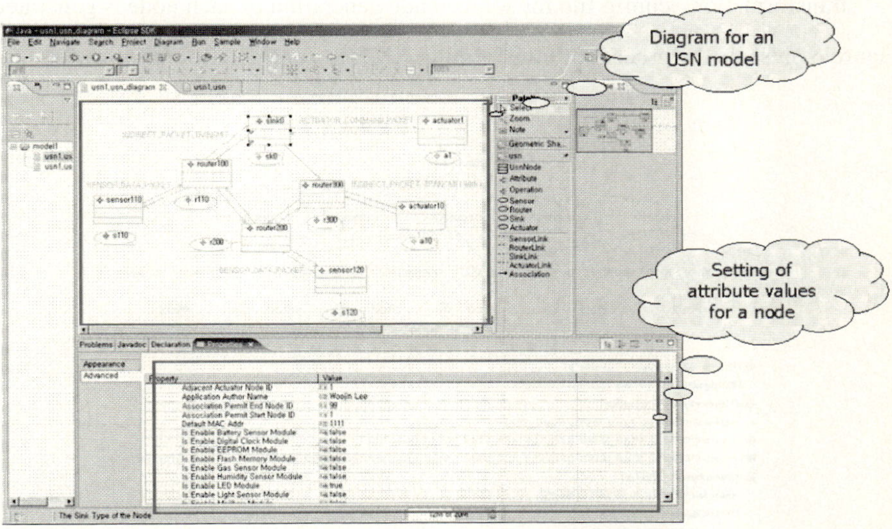

Fig. 4. The modeling & design using a tool

```xml
<?xml version="1.0" encoding="UTF-8"?>
<usn:Usn xmlns:usn="http://www.example.eclipse.org/Usn">
  <nodes>
    <name>sensor110</name>
    <sensorType>#//@sensors.0</sensorType>
    <target>#//@nodes.1</target>
  </nodes>
  <nodes>
    <name>router100</name>
    <routerType>#//@routers.1</routerType>
    <target>#//@nodes.2</target>
    <target>#//@nodes.4</target>
  </nodes>
  <nodes>
    <name>sink0</name>
    <sinkType>#//@sinks.0</sinkType>
    <target>#//@nodes.7</target>
    <target>#//@nodes.3</target>
  </nodes>
  <nodes>
    <name>actuator1</name>
    <actuatorType>#//@actuators.1</actuatorType>
  </nodes>
  <sensors>
    <name>s110</name>
    <applicationAuthorName>Woojin Lee</applicationAuthorName>
    <nodeID>110</nodeID>
    <isEnableNON_BEACON>true</isEnableNON_BEACON>
    <defaultMACAddr>1111</defaultMACAddr>
    <scheduler>Preemption-RR</scheduler>
    <zigbeeRFModule>Star-MeshRoute</zigbeeRFModule>
    <isEnableLightSensorModule>true</isEnableLightSensorModule>
    <isEnableGasSensorModule>true</isEnableGasSensorModule>
  </sensors>
  <routers>
    <name>r100</name>
    <applicationAuthorName>Woojin Lee</applicationAuthorName>
    <nodeID>100</nodeID>
    <isEnableNON_BEACON>true</isEnableNON_BEACON>
```

Fig. 5. An example of a XML file generated by the tool

The tool generates .config files from the XML file. The .config files store the configuration information of nodes, and the files are used to automatically generate an USN application. The following is the process for transformation XML to configuration information.

Step 1 – Parse the XML file. Parser generates the parsing tree based on the XML file.
Step 2 – Get the information of each node from the parsing tree.
Step 3 – Generate the configuration information of each node. The information of the parsing tree is transformed to the configuration information. As a result of transformation, .config file for source code generation of each node is generated.

Figure 6 presents the process of transforming XML to configuration information.

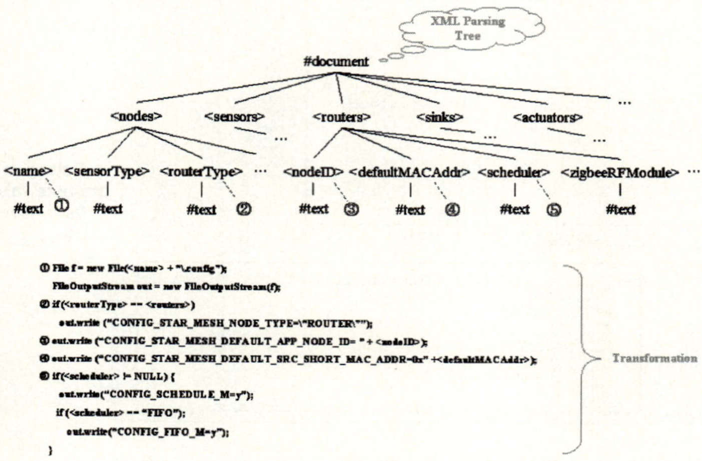

Fig. 6. The process of transforming XML to configuration information

The configuration information showed in figure 7 has been automatically generated by the tool in order to generate the source code of a node.

```
#
# ETRI-SSN(or MINI) Menu
#
# CONFIG_EEPROM_M is not set
# CONFIG_FLASHMEM_M is not set
CONFIG_TIMER_M=y
# CONFIG_DIGITAL_CLOCK_M is not set
CONFIG_UART_M=y
CONFIG_PRINTF_M=y
# CONFIG_SCANF_M is not set
CONFIG_ACTUATOR_M=y
CONFIG_LED_M=y
# CONFIG_ADC_M is not set
CONFIG_SCHEDULE_M=y
# CONFIG_FIFO_M is not set
CONFIG_PREEMPTION_RR_M=y
# CONFIG_PWM_M is not set
CONFIG_ZIGBEE_RF_M=y
CONFIG_ZIGBEE_M=y
CONFIG_IEEE_802_15_4_MAC_M=y
CONFIG_STAR_MESH_ROUTE_M=y
CONFIG_STAR_MESH_NODE_TYPE="SINK"
CONFIG_STAR_MESH_DEFAULT_RF_CHANNEL="25"
CONFIG_STAR_MESH_DEFAULT_APP_NODE_ID="0"
CONFIG_STAR_MESH_ADJACENT_ACTUATOR_NODE_ID="1"
CONFIG_STAR_MESH_THIS_NODE_PAN_COORDINATION_ENABLE="TRUE"
CONFIG_STAR_MESH_COORDINATOR_TYPE="NON_BEACON_ENABLE"
CONFIG_STAR_MESH_DEFAULT_SRC_SHORT_MAC_ADDR="0x1111"
# CONFIG_STAR_MESH_USE_DEFAULT_EXTENDED_MAC_ADDR is not set
CONFIG_START_MESH_ASSOCIATION_PERMIT_NODEID_START="1"
CONFIG_START_MESH_ASSOCIATION_PERMIT_NODEID_END="99"
# CONFIG_RSSI_M is not set
# CONFIG_ITC_M is not set
# CONFIG_UTILITY_M is not set
CONFIG_LOG_M=y
```

Fig. 7. An example of automatically generated configuration information of a node

3.3 The Automatic Construction of USN Applications

The following is the process for generating source code to control each node.

Step 1 – Read Config_Info(.config) file in order to get the attribute values of a node.
Step 2 – Parse Config_info(.config) file and find out selected modules. Then read headers, data and function codes from the DynamicTemplate class according to the selected modules and save them to the template.
Step 3 – Read main code from the HashTable_Main class based on selected modules and save it to the template.

```
Templet Transformation(Config_Info config_info) {
    templet = getTemplet(config_Info.NODETYPE);
    templet.setAttribute(config_info.Attribute);

    DynamicTemplate dynamicTemplate = new DynamicTemplate();
    HashTable_Main hashTable_Main = new HashTable_Main();

//  Set the NODETYPE of HashTable_Module
    dynamicTemplate.setType(config_info.NODETYPE);

// Construct code according to the config_info of each node
    Iterator iterator = Parser.getIterator(conifg_info);
    while( iterator.hasNext() ) {
            // Set the name of selected module
            dynamicTemplate.setModuleName(iterator.ModuleName);

            templet.addHeader(dynamicTemplate.getHeader() );
            templet.addData(dynamicTemplate.getData() );
            templet.addFunction(dynamicTemplate.getFunction() ) ;
            templet.addMain( hashTable_Main.getMain() );
            iterator.next();
    }
}
```

Fig. 8. An algorithm for generating USN application

```
public class DynamicTemplate {
        //&1 == node type, &2 == module name, &3 == header, data, or function name
        private String moduleTemplate = "&1_&2_&3";
        private String moduleFileName = "";

        private final String HEADER = "H";
        private final String DATA = "D";
        private final String FUNCTION = "F";

        public void setType(String nodeType) {
                moduleTemplate = moduleTemplate.replaceFirst ("&1", nodeType);
        }
        public void setModuleName(String moduleName) {
                moduleFileName = moduleTemplate.replaceFirst("&2", moduleName);
        }
        public String getHeader(String moduleName) {
                return moduleFileName.replaceFirst("&3", HEADER.);
        }
        public String getData(String moduleName) {
                return moduleFileName.replaceFirst("&3", DATA);
        }
        public String getFunction(String moduleName) {
                return moduleFileName.replaceFirst("&3", FUNCTION);
        }
};
```

Fig. 9. DynamicTemplate class

Figure 8 presents the algorithm for generating source code of each node. Headers, data and function codes are generated by calling the functions of the DynamicTemplate class according to the type of the target node.

The DynamicTemplate class used in the algorithm is presented in figure 9. The class includes setType(), setModuleName(), getHeader(), getData() and getFunction()

to generate the program for each node. These functions use the *moduleTemplate* field in order to get source codes. The DynamicTemplate class generates the proper source code using the *moduleTemplate* field dynamically because the codes of headers, data and functions are dependent upon the type of node and module.

The type of the *moduleTemplate* field is "String", and the initial value is "&1_&2_&3". Strings such as "&1", "&2" and "&3" are dynamically replaced according to the type of module and node. When the type of each node is determined, the string "&1" is replaced with the type through the setType() method. The string "&2" is replaced with the name of a module provided by Nano-Oplus through the setModuleName() method. The string "&3" is replaced with "H" (means Header), "D" (means Data) or "F" (means Function) based on the type of required module. For example, the value of the *moduleTemplate* field is replaced as follows by calling functions of the DynamicTemplate class if the type of a node is SINK and Zigbee_Simple module for radio frequency communication of the node is selected.

setType("SINK"); → "SINK_&2_&3"
setModuleName("Zigbee_Simple"); → "SINK_Zigbee_Simple_&3"
getHeader("Zig_Simple") → "SINK_Zigbee_Simple_H"
getFunction("Zig_Simple") → "SINK_Zigbee_Simple_F"

"SINK_Zigbee_Simple_H" is the name of a file which contains header codes of the Zigbee_Simple module for a sink node, and "SINK_Zigbee_Simple_F" is the name of a file which contains function codes of the Zigbee_Simple module for a sink node.

The main function code of each node is generated by the HashTable_Main class. The HashTable_Main class generates the main function code using the hash table presented in table 1. The key of the hash table is the name of a module provided by Nano-Qplus. The main function code is generated according to the type of selected module using the key value of the hash table.

Table 1. Structure of hash table for the main function code

Key	Value
Zigbee_Simple	"mlme_start_request(MY_MAC_ADDRESS, rf_recv_data)"
Zigbee_MAC	"mlme_ll_link_start(NULL, rf_recv_data)"
Zigbee_MAC_StarMesh	"mlme_ll_link_start(NULL, rf_recv_data)"
Scheduler_FIFO	"(*start)((void *)0);"

Scheduler_PreemptionRR	"uint8_t int_handle;
	int_handle = thread_disable_int();
	thread_enable_ints(int_handle);
	pthread_create(NULL, rf_recv_data);
	start_threads();"

4 Case Study with Light Sensing System

An USN application for Light Sensing System such as figure 10 has been developed using the proposed technique in this paper. The Light Sensing System is composed of sensor nodes which sense light data, router nodes which transmit the received data to other nodes, a sink node which is connected to the monitoring system and determines the action command, and a light bulb which contains an actuator to turn the light bulb on.

A USN model was designed for the Light Sensing System. In the model, sensor nodes sense light data and transmit the data to router nodes. The router nodes receive the data and transmit it to the sink node. The sink node receives the data, computes it and transmits it to the actuator node. The actuator node performs an action according to the threshold value.

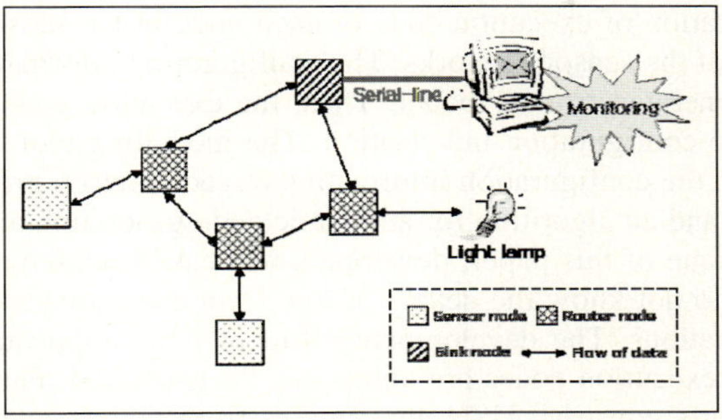

Fig. 10. Block diagram of Light Sensing System

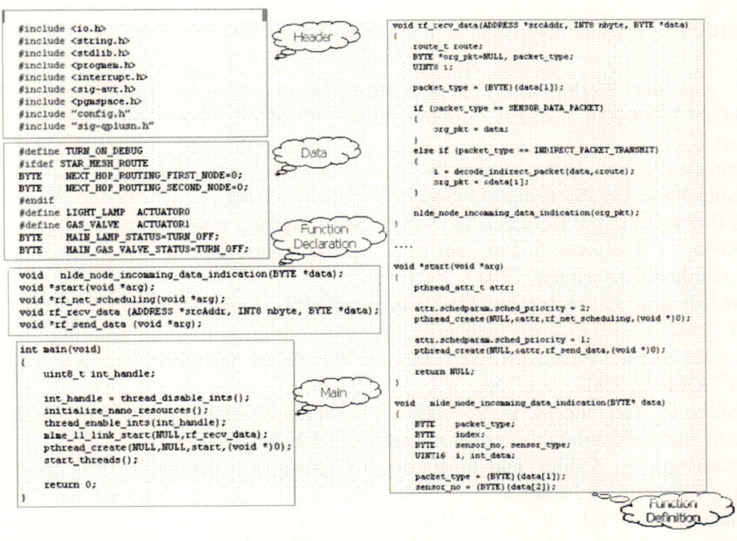

Fig. 11. An example of automatically generated code

The system of figure 10 was developed after the application was automatically generated from the designed model. Result that applies, sensing light data was forwarded from sensor node to router node and router node sent forwarded data to sink node. An action command according to the light value was forwarded from sink node to router node and router node sent forwarded the action command to actuator. Actuator turned the light bulb on or off according to the action command.

Figure 11 is the source code of sink node automatically generated based on the configuration information presented in figure 7.

5 Conclusion

A programming model for the automatic construction of USN applications based on Nano-Qplus is proposed in this paper. Developers can implement USN applications by automatic generation of execution code of each node in the sensor networks after they make models of the sensor networks. The configuration information of each node is automatically generated from a model. Then, the execution code is automatically generated using the configuration information. The modelling tool to make an USN model and generate the configuration information of each node is proposed in this paper. The templates and an algorithm for automatic code generation are also presented. Through the technique of this paper, developers will easily implement USN applications even if they do not know the details of low-level communication, data sharing, and collective operations. The development effort of USN applications also will be decreased because execution codes are automatically generated. Furthermore, developers can consistently construct USN applications from USN models using the proposed tool.

References

[1] Ian F. Akyildiz, Weilian Su, Yogesh Sankarasubramaniam, and Erdal Cayirci, "A Survey on Sensor Networks," IEEE Communications Magazine, Volume 40 Issue 8, pp.102-114, August 2002.

[2] Kwangyong Lee et al., "A Design of Sensor Network System based on Scalable & Reconfigurable Nano-OS Platform," IT-SoC2004, October 2004.

[3] ETRI Embedded S/W Research Division, "Nano-Qplus," http://qplus.or.kr/

[4] E. Cheong, J. Liebman, J. Liu, and F. Zhao, "Tinygals: a programming model for event-driven embedded systems," SAC, 2003.

[5] M. Welsh and G. Mainland, "Programming sensor networks using abstract regions," NSDI, 2004.

[6] R. Newton and M. Welsh, "Region streams: Functional macroprogramming for sensor networks," DMSN, 2004.

[7] A. Boulis, C. Han, and M. B. Srivastava, "Design and implementation of a framework for efficient and programmable sensor networks," MobiSys, 2003.

[8] B. Greenstein, E. Kohler, and D. Estrin, "A sensor network application construction kit (SNACK)," SenSys, 2004.

[9] Ramakrishna Gummadi, Omprakash Gnawali, and Ramesh Govindan, "Macro-programming Wireless Sensor Networks Using Kairos," LNCS 3560, pp. 126–140, 2005.

Hierarchical and Dynamic Information Management Framework on Grid Computing*

Eun-Ha Song, Yang-Seung Jeon, Sung-Kook Han, and Young-Sik Jeong**

Dept. of Computer Eng., Wonkwang Univ., 344-2 Shinyoung-Dong,
Iksan, 570-749, Korea
{ehsong, globaljeon, skhan, ysjeong}@wku.ac.kr

Abstract. This paper presents a GridIMF framework that provides support for adaptive grid services in response to the change of resource supplies and demands in a dynamic computing environment. The framework features a 3-tier hierarchical resource management structure. At the top is a global information manager that serves as a service broker between resource requesters and providers. Resource providers form virtual organizations, each of which is controlled by a local resource manager. The resource managers schedule the execution of tasks adaptively for efficiency and fault tolerance according to the dynamic resource availability information. The framework provides a common API through an application proxy. The proxy decouples grid applications from the implementation details of the framework.

1 Introduction

Grid is in the center of Virtual Organizations and the member of Virtual Organizations is an environment using not only a computing but also distributed computation or information resource as a virtual computer. In order to solve a grand challenge problem inside this paradigm, it is required to decide a policy or mechanism which can make the approach of grid[1][2]. Grid computing environment should take the feature that has unlimited number of resources, is spread into the area and organization and is heterogeneous system and the state of resources is variable. Grid User needs to the efficient grid resource management by integrating such resources in order to use them consistently[3][4][5]. The construction of framework which can support the upper level of requirement and include the facility to control grid work and information representation of grid resource is also needed in the grid computing environment.

Grid information includes metadata composing grid resource, grid resources and virtual organization which forms group of grid resources[6]. This paper adapts to variableness of grid information and establishes GridIMF(Grid Information Management Framework) which supports the requirement of user. GridIMF designs 3-tier hierarchical information management model classifying role and management policy of grid information functionally and logically. This provides scalability of grid

* This paper was supported by Wonkwang University in 2004.

** Corresponding author.

E. Sha et al. (Eds.): EUC 2006, LNCS 4096, pp. 151 – 161, 2006.

information. GridIMF offers effective grid information management by designing the remote object reference for directly delivering an information saving model pursuant to the definition of an entry structure as well as computation results according to communication model pursuant to the definition of a connection object and a protocol object. GridIMF supports solubility of service with optimum selection of virtual organization and auto-recovery strategy in the virtual organization. It also improves the performance with adaptive performance-based task allocation method which supports load balancing and fault tolerance inside virtual organization. Grid users have different workload, requirement and job specification. This paper provides GridIMF and application proxy which divides the structure having minimum relation between them. Finally, it analyzes adaptability and executability of grid by applying grid application in GridIMF[7][8][9].

2 Related Works

The current study related to grid is actively on the progress in research institutions over the world and Globus Toolkit is the most representing model[10]. Globus Toolkit connects and manages diversified heterogeneous resources of the lower layer in order to use them in the grid job and provides necessary service required in upper layer. Globus Toolkit is not a single system which cannot be separated but suggests the necessary service in grid as an independent element. It is very similar to GridIMF which was established in this paper from the point of view of reducing degradation between different systems and providing the integration function. But it is inefficient in the matter of management for metadata as it has the uniformed change and delivery cycle which ignore the characteristic of data. Thus, this Globus Toolkit can cause the degradation of grid performance.

Table 1. Globus vs. GridIMF

System / Activity Functions	Globus	GridIMF	Remark
Scalability of grid	●	●	3-tier hierarchical resource management model
Dynamic VO configuration	▲	●	
Availability for service	●	●	Optimum virtual organizations choosing method and Auto-recovery method
Deletion of replication operation at fault	×	●	
Resource state monitoring	●	●	PDH Library, Virtual Observer
Load balancing strategy	▲	●	Performance-based Task Allocation Method
Fault tolerance strategy	▲	●	
Independency among application	●	●	Application Proxy
User access interface	●	▲	Java Applet

(●: support, ▲: a partial support, ×: nonsupport)

GridIMF modeled in this paper accepts the information service of Globus Toolkit and service function of resource management as much as possible. GridIMF provides the Globus toolkit's MDS and GRAM supporting function with GVMS(Grid Virtual Management System) and GRMS(Grid Resource Management System). Service of GVMS considers scalability of grid by hierarchical node structure. User minimizes the load with optimum selection of virtual organization for the use of grid resource. Virtual organization suggests virtual organization auto-recovery strategy technology for server fault. GRMS service periodically receives the state of metadata included in local resource through Virtual Observer and accepts the load balancing and fault with adaptive performance-based task allocation method which operates scheduler in the virtual organization. Especially, GridIMF has the additional monitoring technology to understand the state of grid information in real-time and share and utilize them efficiently. Table 1 shows the comparison of Globus toolkit and supportive system which was presented in this system.

3 Grid Information Management Framework

3.1 Function Model of the GridIMF Components

GridIMF divides the components of grid into RR(Resource Requester), RP(Resource Provider), LRM(Local Resource Manager) and GIM(Global Information Manager) depending on the intention and purpose of participation. Fig. 1 shows the structure of architecture layer and control stream of suggested GridIMF components.

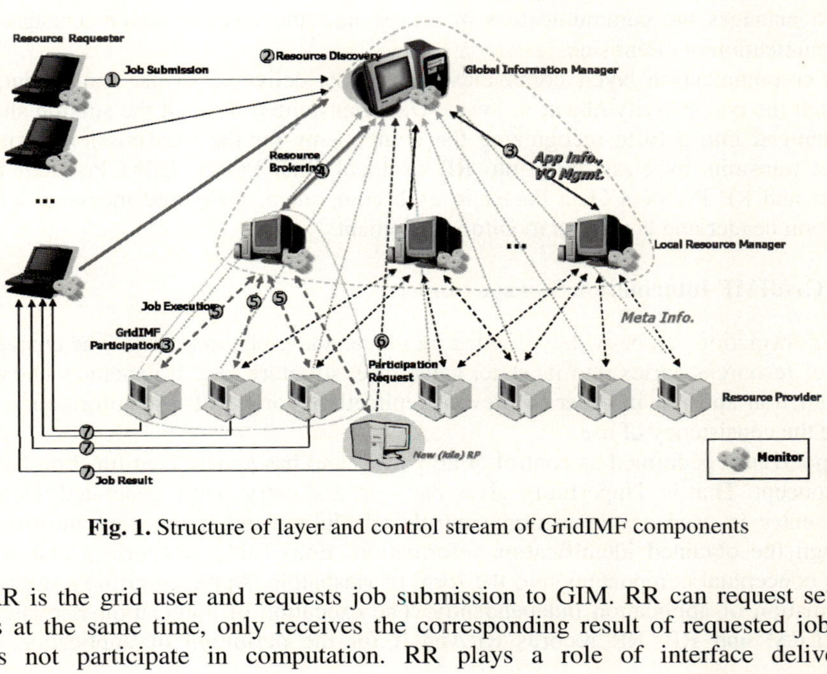

Fig. 1. Structure of layer and control stream of GridIMF components

RR is the grid user and requests job submission to GIM. RR can request several jobs at the same time, only receives the corresponding result of requested job and does not participate in computation. RR plays a role of interface delivering information of independent application. GIM is the top level manager and is a kind of resource brokering proxy connecting between resource and user who wants to use grid in remote. GIM manages the connection by providing common interface of components and executes job submission and control management as proxy. GIM is a super scheduler which brings the list of LRM satisfying based on job specification of specific application and permits the connection. LRM gets the delegation collecting resource and allocating task for requested job. LRM selects RP through resource discovery, intermediate the connection between RP and RR and makes core scheduling between remote resources. RP is a group which permits the execution for a part of task instead of huge scale of job and collects the information of metadata. RP delivers the executable resource, performs the operation and transmits the result.

3.2 GridIMF Communication Model

The components of GridIMF require to consistent in receiving data, command or query. For this, communication model is defined to provide activation of data exchange between information and active association of grid information. GridIMF communication model can be classified into Connectivity Object for connection between recourses and Protocol Object for generating and translating requirements such as command or query.

Depending on the hierarchical information management, LRM is a client for the position of GIM and performs two roles as a server for the position of RP. In order to prevent replication, GridIMF defines these connections as session with the complexity of lower communication. A session is classified into SessionProvider which processes the initial connection of components and has the server socket, ManagerSession which manages the communication of server side and Session which manages the communication of client side.

In communication layer, commands or requests delivered to the components go through the connectivity object in lower. Data transmitted through the session should be changed into a form recognizing the components for the transmission. Protocol object transmits by classifying into RR Protocol Data Parser, LRM Protocol Data Parser and RP Protocol Data Parser in each component. Delivered message defines common header and is used as monitoring element.

3.3 GridIMF Information Storage Model

Grid information can be widely divided into local and global resource. The characteristic of resources varies into its state, value, use, structure, etc. It generates entry for the function and use in order to prevent replication storage of grid information and make the consistency of use.

UpperEntry is defined as control of all entries and has generalized function having the concept. That is, UpperEntry gives entry_id and entry_name generated. Concertized entry is used as connection control, scheduling and monitoring information through the obtained identification information. EntryTable categorizes and stores same conceptual components into the form of Hashtable. ApplicationEntry stores the information of application independently. The execution of application is related to RR, LRM and RP. RR records RRAppUI for the definition of application user interface as RP records for ProProxyInterfaceName processing common application proxy and LRM records for SchedulerName taking the reference data and make the scheduling. RREntry records ActiveApplication which is the name of application that currently corresponding RP executes and TaskResult which is the name of class for receiving the result of operation by remote object reference. LRMEntry records TotCpuSpeed, TotCpuNum, NumOfRP, etc. which are the benchmarking information of RPs. RPEntry is used as monitoring element and records ResourceFactor which is the element of metadata of RP, StateOfRP which is the state information and SizeOfTask which is the workload.

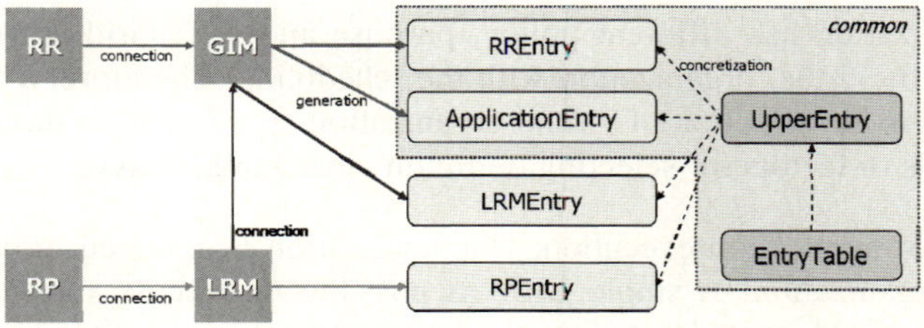

Fig. 2. Structure of GridIMF Entry

3.4 GridIMF Remote Object Reference

Remote object reference is the mechanism reducing the load of LRM by transmitting the result of RP to RR directly. LRM generates RefBinder which is the list of RREntry and then binds the remote interface by exchanging it into RRRefBroker. The result of binding looks up RR and RP related to LRM. RR transmits remote object reference

```
public interface GridIMF_RRRefBroker extends Remote{          // the LRM side Interface
  public void GridIMF_SetRRRemoteReference(int iRRID, GridIMF_RemoteTaskResult
                                    nRRReceiverRef)  throws RemoteException;
  public void GridIMF_SetRRRemoteReference(GridIMF_RemoteTaskResult
                                    nRRReceiverRef)  throws RemoteException;
  public GridIMF_RemoteTaskResult GridIMF_GetRRRemoteReference(int iRRID)
                                    throws RemoteException;
  public GridIMF_RemoteTaskResult GridIMF_GetRRRemoteReference()
                                    throws RemoteException;
}
public interface GridIMF_RemoteTaskResult extends Remote {      // the RR side Interface
  public void SetProcessJobResult(
        int nRPID,         // RP ID
        int iTaskID,       // Task ID
        String sResult,    // Job Result
        int nStreamSize,   // Stream Data Size
        byte btStream[]    // Stream Data
    ) throws RemoteException;
}
```

Fig. 3. Interface of LRM and RR side for remote object reference value to LRM through the interface of RemoteTaskResult with the class of TaskReceiver which is the class receiving the result. RR registers remote result processing class from RefBinder class generated by LRM and RR receives the class from RRReferBroker and sends the task result to RR. Fig. 3 is the interface of LRM and RR side defined for remote object reference.

4 GridIMF Dynamic Information Management

4.1 Task Brokering Rule

Virtual organization has different policy, purpose and size. Grid application is finished its task by virtual organization with the scheduling. Therefore, the performance of application is the selection of virtual organization appropriate to the task. GridIMF defines 4 kinds of factors for selecting optimum virtual organization:

▸ Possibility of application execution: One application is assumed to be executed by one virtual organization. A single LRM is possible to execute various applications independently. GIM provides a list of application which is already executed and should be executed. LRM selects application which can be executed. The first stage selection depends on LRM which knows the capability and size of its virtual organization.

▸ Idle State: GIM senses the wait state by LRM virtual observer that is going to execute the requested task and then decides the possibility of execution.

▸ Application Power: The operation result of grid application is recorded as log file. The attribute of log file is the application name, execution time, LRM information, number of LRM and RP, total amount of static CPU speed, etc.

▸ LRM Performance Index: This performance index can be obtained by the analysis of application log file. Performance index selects a value close to the expected value in proportion to the average speed of CPU and number of nodes for executing requested application.

4.2 LRM State Control and Auto-recovery Strategy

GIM is the manager of dynamic LRM so that transmission of control message is frequent related to LRM. GridIMF makes LRM virtual observer that gathers information of LRM and plays communication broker, and separates operation and control. LRM virtual observer is the monitor which makes scheduling the task and manages RPs inside virtual organization.

LRM auto-recovery method senses the LRM fault and secures the availability of service by obtaining the corresponding resource from another LRM. RR can be possible to use the grid information and to change the specification of executing application until the connection of GridIMF is disconnected. The fault information of LRM is accomplished by LRM virtual observer. When LRM fault is found, it looks for a new LRM in idle state. RR sends address, remote object reference and task table for the reference and operation is automatically executed by a new LRM. When the search for LRM is failed, RR is in wait state and added into the waiting list. The management of RR task table and remote object reference do not have replicated operation of LRM which generated fault.

4.3 Task Allocation Algorithm

GridIMF makes the counter measure and suggests DPTA(Dynamic Performance-based Task Allocation) and APTA(Adaptive Performance-based Task Allocation) for minimizing the cost of resource. Table 2 is the suggested task allocation method.

Table 2. Task Allocation Method of GridIMF

Task Allocation Method	Performance Evaluation & Reallocation Factor	Remark
Dynamic Performance-based Task Allocation	▪ CPU Speed ▪ Job History	▪ Fault Detection ▪ Append Processor ▪ State Monitoring
Adaptive Performance-based Task Allocation	▪ CPU Speed ▪ CPU Usage ▪ Proportional Factor	▪ Fault Detection ▪ Append Processor ▪ Realtime State Monitoring

DPTA is a method allocating and reallocating task according to the ratio of performance by considering RP performance. Performance index use CPU speed which are the static resource factor of RP and job history. Assuming total job amount for the application is $TotJobSize$ and CPU speed value of RPs is $\{sRP_0, sRP_2, \Lambda, sRP_{NumRP-1}\}$, the job size of random RP_i is allocated as follows.

$$JobRP_i = \frac{sRP_i}{\sum_{k=0}^{NumRP-1} sRP_k} \times TotJobSize, \qquad i = 0 \sim NumRP - 1$$

The factor of job history is the factor measuring expectation of each RP performance and dynamically expects the job size per performance. The size of reallocated job for RP is as follows.

$$\mathrm{Re}AllocJobRP_i = pRateIncomRP_i \times (JobIncomRP_j - ComJobIncomRP_j)$$

$$pRateIncomRP_i = \frac{sComRP_i}{sComRP_i + sIncomRP_j \times \dfrac{ComJobIncomRP_j}{JobIncomRP_j}}$$

where, $sComRP_i$: Finished RP performance for the allocated job

$sIncomRP_j$: Unfinished RP performance for the allocated job

$JobsIncomRP_j$: Unfinished size of initially allocated RP job for allocated job

$ComJobsIncomRP_j$: Size of job performed by RP which did not finish the allocated job

$pRateIncomRP_j$: RP performance index occurring performance change

Table 3. Proportional Factor in different section

Section	User CPU Usage	PF(Proportional Factor)
A	0~10%	2.10
B	10~20%	1.91
C	20~30%	1.67
D	30~40%	1.40
E	40~60%	1.09
F	60% over	1.00

APTA is a method which monitors the static and dynamic performance of RP and allocates the job adaptively. This establishes a standard based on the performance executing real allocated task not a physical performance for the RP performance. RP performance value applies proportional factor and CPU speed. Proportional Factor(PF) is a standard value as CPU usage rate used by RP user or internal system differs in the degree of total execution time depending on the range. Table 3 is the proportional factor in different section.

Assuming CPU speed value of RPs is $\{sRP_0, sRP_2, \Lambda, sRP_{NumRP-1}\}$, the expectation of total CPU usage is $CPUUsageAvg$ at the time of reallocation and expectation of job processor usage rate is $JobUsageAvg$, the performance value of random RP_i is as follows.

$$RP_i Performance = (100 - (CPUUsageAvg - JobUsageAvg)) \times PF \times sRP_i \times 0.01$$

APTA uses RPPerformance value not the job history information and its reallocation is similar to DPTA. Reallocated job size of RP is as follows.

$$\mathrm{Re}\,AllocJobRP_i = pRateIncomRP_i \times (JobIncomRP_j - ComJobIncomRP_j)$$

$$pRateIncomRP_i = \frac{pComRP_i}{pComRP_i + pIncomRP_j \times \dfrac{ComJobIncomRP_j}{JobIncomRP_j}}$$

where, $pComRP_i$: value of RP which finished the allocated job

$pIncomRP_j$: value of RP which did not finish the allocated job

Fig. 4 is the comparison of task allocation method that user gives random CPU usage rate to 4 RPs with different specification. For the case if user CPU usage rate is below 10%, there is no difference in task allocation methods. This implies that performance changes almost did not in RPs and it did not influence on the task performance rate. On the contrary, the case of user CPU usage rate increasing to 20~30% and 30~40%, the total job performance time of APTA considering total CUP usage rate is low. That is, user CPU usage rate of RP influenced on job performance rate of total CPU usage rate.

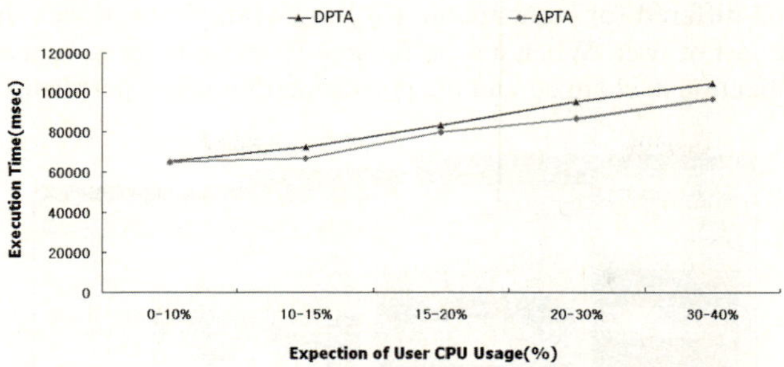

Fig. 4. Comparison of task allocation method according to the change of user CPU usage rate

5 GridIMF Implementation and Performance Result

5.1 Application Architecture

Application is implemented with the verification of strategy suggested in GridIMF. Grid user has different request depending on application so that the application architecture is structurally divided only with minimum correlation.

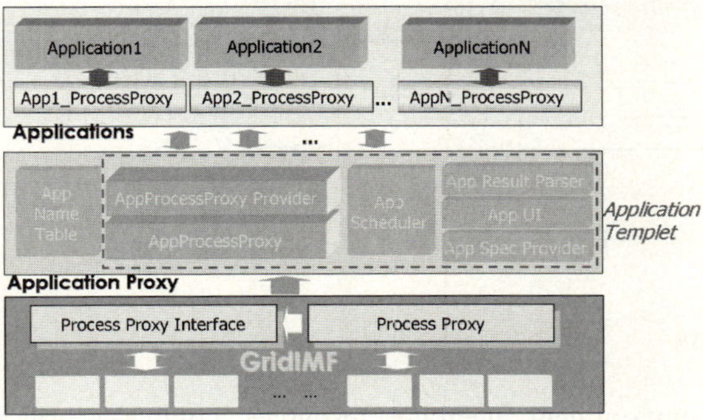

Fig. 5. Application Architecture of GridIMF

For the mechanism minimizing interdependence between different application and GridIMF, Application Proxy is designed as shown in Fig. 5. Application Proxy is a standardized common API and includes core function for interacting between application and GridIMF. Application proxy is an Application Name of plug-in for accessing specific application and the object is generated dynamically by Application Templet.

5.2 Implementation of Application and Result of Performance

Implemented application is Mandelbrot's Fractal Image Processing depending on LSM coloring method as shown in Fig. 6. Task allocation algorithm is APTA and new two RPs participate in operation one after the other while the job is performed by initial two RPs. (c) shows the occurrence of reallocation by additional RP and the coloring method differed for comparison. (d) is an example of processing reoperation changed by request of user. When a specific area is set up by drag function, the specification of application is changed and the corresponding job is performed again.

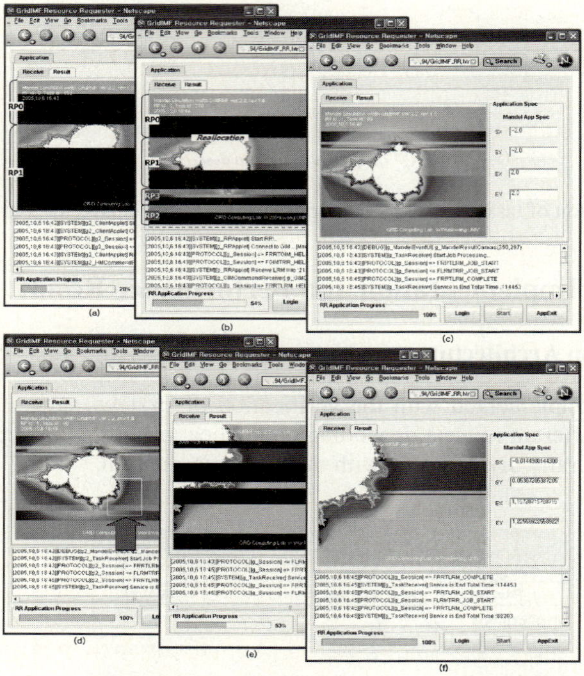

Fig. 6. Process of fractal image generation

6 Conclusions

Grid computing environment integrates resources, composes grid information and becomes a single huge system by forming one virtual organization for the purpose and characteristic. This paper established GridIMF in order to use the grid information consistent used by user and implemented a real grid application.

GridIMF designed 3-tier hierarchical information management mode dividing into GIM, LRM, RP and RR depending on the characteristic of grid information. For the efficient operation of components, management domain was classified into GVMS and GRMS. GVMS suggested optimum virtual organization selection method for job brokering of application and virtual organization. Also, it suggested LRM auto-recovery strategy considering request change of user and replication of operation even though fault of virtual organization occurred. GRMS suggested APTA task allocation method for the change, participation and fault of grid information state, and evaluated its performance. Also application proxy was designed for satisfying the characteristic of grid application and supporting minimum code modification as standardized API. Then, Fractal image generation was applied for analyzing performance of GridIMF and grid application. The main contributions of this paper are as followed; scalability(3-tier hierarchical resource management structure), adaptive(dynamic virtual organization, task allocation), availability of service, deletion of replication operation and independent of applications.

With the further study, interdependent application between detailed jobs or other specific application can be implemented by adding the user access interface function which can process detailed job procedure for user in the point of GridIMF access suggested in this paper.

References

1. I. Foster, C. Kesselman, "The Grid: Blueprint for a New Computing Infrastructure", Morgan Kaufmannn, 1999.
2. I. Foster, C. Kesselman, S. Tueche, "The Anatomy of the Grid: Enabling Scalable Virtual Organizations", International Journal Supercomputer Applications, Vol. 15, No. 3, 2001.
3. I. Foster, "The Grid: A New Infrastructure for 21st Century Science," Physics Today.org, 2002.
4. Dr. Bernhard R. Katzy, "Design and Implementation of Virtual Organizations," University St. Gallen and Erasmus University Rotterdam
5. Rashmi Bajaj and Dharma P. Agrawal, Fellow, "Improving Scheduling of Tasks in a Heterogeneous Environment," IEEE Trans. Parallel and Distributed Systems, Vol. 15, No. 2, pp. 107-118, 2004.
6. A. Takefusa, H. Casanova, and S. Matsuoka, F. Berman, "A Study of Deadline Scheduling for Client-Server Systems on the Computational Grid," High Performance Distributed Computing, 2001. Proceedings 10th IEEE International Symposium, Aug. 2001
7. Rajkumar Buyya, Steve Chapin, and David DiNucci, "Architectural Models for Resource Management in the Grid," Grid Computing GIRD 2000. First IEEE/ACM International Workshop Bangalore, India, pp. 20-33, 2000.
8. Haban, D. Shin, K. G, "Application of RealTime Monitoring to Scheduling Tasks with Random Execution Times," IEEE Transactions on Software Engineering, Vol. 16, pp. 1374-1389, Dec. 1990
9. D. Angulo, I. Foster, C. Liu, and L. Yang., "Design and Evaluation of a Resource Selection Framework for Grid Applications," Proceedings of IEEE International Symposium on High Performance Distributed Computing (HPDC-11), Edinburgh, Scotland, July 2002.
10. I. Foster, C. Kesselman, "Globus: A Metacomputing Infrastructure Toolkit, " International Journal supercomputer Applications, Vol. 11, No. 2, pp. 115-128, 1997

Kalman Filter Based Dead Reckoning Algorithm for Minimizing Network Traffic Between Mobile Nodes in Wireless GRID

Seong-Whan Kim and Ki-Hong Ko

Department of Computer Science, Univ. of Seoul, Jeon-Nong-Dong, Seoul, Korea
Tel.: +82-2-2210-5316; fax: +82-2-2210-5275
swkim7@uos.ac.kr, jedigo@venus.uos.ac.kr

Abstract. Conventional GRID service is static (no mobility), and it has many drawbacks such as continuous connection, waste of bandwidth, and service overloading. Wireless GRID supports mobility, however it should consider geographic position to support efficient resource sharing and routing. When the devices in the GRID are highly mobile, there will be much traffic to exchange the geographic position information of each mobile node, and this makes adverse effect on efficient battery usage. To minimize the network traffic between mobile users, we use dead reckoning algorithm for each mobile nodes, where each node uses the algorithm to estimates its own movement (also other node's movement), and when the estimation error is over threshold, the node sends the UPDATE (including position, velocity, etc) packet to other devices. As the estimation accuracy is increased, each node can minimize the number of UPDATE packet transmission. To improve the prediction accuracy of dead reckoning algorithm, we propose Kalman filter based dead reckoning approach. To experiment our scheme, we implement a popular network game (BZFlag) with our scheme added on each mobile node, and the results show that we can achieve better prediction accuracy and reduction of network traffic by 12 percents.

Keywords: Dead reckoning, Kalman filter, Wireless GRID.

1 Introduction

Conventional GRID service supports no mobility, and results in many drawbacks such as continuous connection, waste of bandwidth, and service overloading. Wireless GRID supports mobility and it should consider geographic position to support efficient resource sharing and routing [1]. However, if the device in the GRID is highly mobile, there will be much traffic to manage the geographic position of each mobile node, and this make adverse effect on efficient battery usage. To minimize the network traffic between networking mobile devices, dead reckoning technique is used [2]. Each mobile device uses the algorithm to estimates its movement and other devices' movement, thereby, each device can minimize the transmission of its information (position, velocity, etc) to other entities. R. Gossweiler and R. J. Laferriere introduced the dead reckoning algorithm for the multi-user game [2], and S. Aggarwal and

E. Sha et al. (Eds.): EUC 2006, LNCS 4096, pp. 162 – 170, 2006.

H. Banavar proposed the use of globally synchronized clocks among the participating players and a time-stamp augmented dead reckoning vector that enables the receiver to render the entity accurately [3]. In addition, W. Cai and F. B.S. Lee proposed a multi-level threshold scheme that adaptively adjusted, based on the relative distance between entities to reduce the rate of transmitting UPDATE packets [4].

To improve the prediction accuracy of dead reckoning algorithm, we propose the Kalman filter based dead reckoning approach. To simulate the mobility of mobile device scenarios in wireless GRID, we use a simple analogy, network game (BZFlag). In section 2, we review the dead reckoning and Kalman filter. In Section 3, we propose a Kalman filter based dead reckoning algorithm. In Section 4, we apply our Kalman approach on BZFLAG game; show the experimental results with minimized UPDATE packets between game players. We conclude in section 5.

2 Related Works

The networking server technique can be implemented using three methods: (1) peer to peer, (2) client server architecture, and (3) distributed server architecture. In peer to peer, each entity transmits the occurred information to each other. It is suitable for the small-scale network. In client server (CS) architecture, the server collects all of the data from the clients, stores the changes in some data, and then sends the results to each participating client. For large-scale networks, we need distributed server architecture. To distribute server, we can use load distribution method or map server method. Networking techniques should minimize (1) network bandwidth and (2) network delay.

2.1 Location Awareness in Wireless Mobile Networks

In the wireless mobile GRID, the GRID protocol's core concept partitions the geographic area into several squares in GRIDs. Each GRID is elected the GRID's leader (so called gateway), and GRID leaders perform routing GRID by GRID. This protocol is location awared because it exploits location information in routing. Geographic location awareness can be GeoCast, GeoTora, and GeoGrid methods [10].

- GeoCast: GeoCast sends a message to all mobile devices within a designated geographic area (so called a geo-cast region). This protocol differs from traditional multicast, because the it uses two zones: forwarding zone and multicast region. In the forwarding zone, the data packet is sent by unicast to each other's device, and in the multicast region, the data packet is sent by multicast to each other's device.
- GeoTora: GeoTora derives from TORA (temporally ordered routing algorithm). TORA maintains a DAG (directed acyclic graph) with the destination device as sink; the data packet is forwarded by the DAG's direction to sink. GeoTora divides into TORA (DAG region) and GeoCast region. In GeoCast regions, mobile devices perform the flooding, and in the DAG region, mobile devices perform an anycast from the source to any host.
- GeoGrid: GeoGrid is derived by the GRID protocol that have the GRID leader. GeoGrid uses two methods such as the flooding-based geo-casting and ticket-based geo-casting. The flooding-based geo-casting allows any grid leader in the forwarding zone to rebroadcast the messages, and the ticket-based geo-casting allows only ticket-holding grid leaders to rebroadcast.

2.2 Reviews on Dead Reckoning Algorithms

Since each mobile device is physically distributed, updating states (e.g. each mobile device's position, etc) of the mobile devices may generate a large amount of communication and thus saturate network bandwidth. To reduce the number of state UPDATE packets, the DR technique is used [4]. In addition to the high fidelity model that maintains the accurate position about its entities, each mobile device also has a dead reckoning model that estimates the position of all entities (both local and remote). Therefore, instead of transmitting state UPDATE packets, the estimated position of a remote mobile device can be readily available through a simple and localized computation [4]. The mobile device compares real position with DR position. If the difference between real position and DR position is greater than a threshold, the mobile device informs others remote entities to update their ghost object position [2]. We can describe the simple dead reckoning algorithm as follows.

```
Algorithm : Dead Reckoning

for every received packet of remote entity do
  switch received packet type {
    case UPDATE
      fix ghost position of remote entity
      break;
    case PLAYER_QUITING
      remove remote entity
      break;
  }

[Extrapolation] Extrapolate all ghost position based
on the past state information;

if (local entity's true position - local entity's
extrapolated position) > Threshold {
  Broadcast an UPDATE packet to the group
}
Draw all ghost
```

3 Kalman Filter Based Dead Reckoning Algorithm

In wireless GRID environment, each mobile device is geographically distributed. A technique referred to as dead reckoning (DR) is commonly used to exchange information about movement among the mobile devices [6, 7, 8]. Each mobile device sends information about its movement as well as the movement of the entities it controls to the other mobile devices using a dead reckoning vector (DRV). A DRV typically contains information about the current position of the entity in terms of x, y and z coordinates (at the time the DRV sent) as well as the trajectory of the entity in terms of the velocity component in each of the dimensions [3].

In this paper, we use the mobility of network game users to simulate the real geographically distributed mobile device environments. For the network game, we present a Kalman filter based dead reckoning to optimize the network traffic. A Kalman filter is a recursive procedure to estimate the states s_k of a discrete-time controlled process governed by the linear stochastic difference equation, from a set of measured observations t_k. The mathematical model is shown in in Equation (1) and Equation (2).

$$\boldsymbol{s}_k = \boldsymbol{A}\boldsymbol{s}_{k-1} + \boldsymbol{w}_{k-1} \tag{1}$$

$$\boldsymbol{t}_k = \boldsymbol{H}\boldsymbol{s}_k + \boldsymbol{r}_k \tag{2}$$

The NxN matrix A represents an state transition matrix, w_k is an Nx1 process noise vector with N(0, σ_w^2), t_k is Mx1 measurement vector, H is MxM measurement matrix, and r_k is Mx1 measurement noise vector with N(0, σ_r^2). To estimate the process, Kalman filter uses a form of feedback control as shown in Figure 1 [5]. We define $\hat{s}_k^-$, $\hat{s}_k$, p_k^- and p_k as the priori state estimate, posteriori state estimate, priori estimate error covariance, and posteriori estimate error covariance, respectively. K is the Kalman gain.

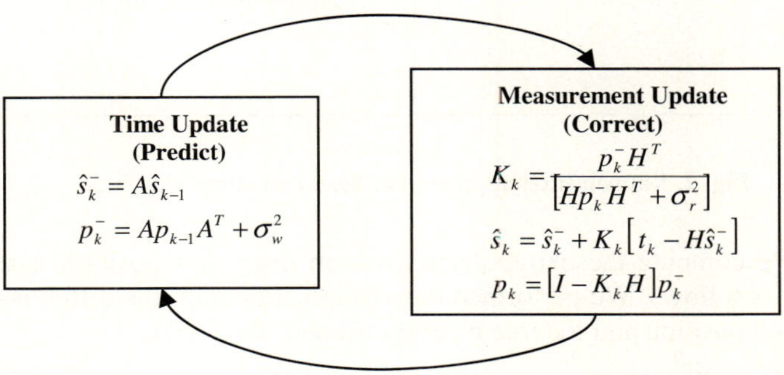

Fig. 1. Kalman filter cycle [5].

To evaluate our scheme, we used simple dead reckoning scenarios (scheme 1) and optimized dead reckoning algorithm for game logic (scheme 3) for comparison. For scheme 1 and scheme 3, we use Kalman filter approach (scheme 2 and scheme 4) to improve the prediction performance of scheme 1 and scheme 3 as shown in Figure 2.

Scheme 1 and scheme 2 use DRV, which includes only position and velocity information of each mobile device. In scheme 3 and scheme 4, we added the angle which is a direction of mobile device for prediction improvements, and the DRV is (x, y, z, vx, vy, vz, angle, t). Scheme 3 is real dead reckoning algorithm, which is optimized for BZFlag game logic. The details of each schemes are as follows.

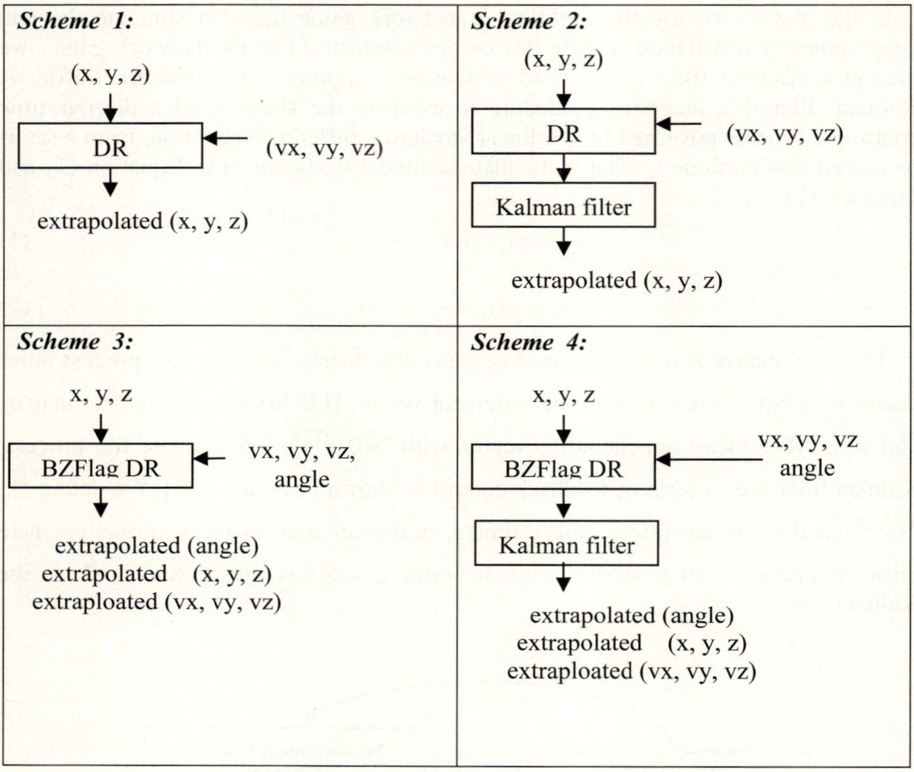

Fig. 2. Kalman filter approach for dead reckoning algorithm

Scheme 1: We compute the extrapolated position using last position, last velocity, and time step as follows. We performed the extrapolation until the difference between the extrapolated position and the true position is under threshold.

```
Extrapolated position = last position + last velocity *
time step;
```

Scheme 2: Scheme 2 uses Kalman filter after computing the extrapolated position as scheme 1. We performed the extrapolation until the difference between the extrapolated position and the true position is under threshold.

```
Extrapolated position = Kalman Filter (last position +
last velocity * time step);
```

Scheme 3: To get a new extrapolated position, the scheme uses two equations depending on the game entity's motion type as follows. We performed the extrapolation until the difference between the extrapolated position and the true position is under threshold.

```
if (linear motion) {
  extrapolated position = last position + last velocity
* time step;
} else {
  extrapolated position = BZFlag function(angle);
}
```

Scheme 4: Scheme 4 adds Kalman filter after computing the extrapolated (position, velocity, and angle) as scheme 3. Our dead reckoning algorithm (scheme 4) is described as follows.

```
float speed = (vx * cosf(angle)) + (vy * sin(angle));
// speed relative to the tank's direction
radius = (speed / angular_velocity);

float inputTurnCenter[2]; // tank turn center
float inputTurnVector[2]; // tank turn vector
inputTurnVector[0] = +sin(last_angle) * radius;
inputTurnVector[1] = -cos(last_angle) * radius;
inputTurnCenter[0] = last_position-inputTurnVector[0];
inputTurnCenter[1] = last_position-inputTurnVector[1];

// compute new extrapolated angle using Kalman filter
float angle = Kalman (time step * angular_velocity);
float cos_val = cosf(angle);
float sin_val = sinf(angle);

// compute new extrapolated position
const float* tc = inputTurnCenter;
const float* tv = inputTurnVector;
new_x = tc[0]+((tv[0] * cos_val) - (tv[1] * sin_val));
new_y = tc[1]+((tv[1] * cos_val) + (tv[0] * sin_val));
new_z = last_position + (vz * time step);

// compute new extrapolated velocity
float vx = Kalman ((vx * cos_val) - (vy * sin_val));
float vy = Kalman ((vy * cos_val) + (vx * sin_val));
float vz = Kalman (vz);
```

4 Experimental Results

In this paper, we use a simple analogy: a popular on-line game BZFlag to simulate geographically distributed mobile devices. BZFlag (Battle Zone Flag) is a first-person shooter game where the players in teams drive tanks and move within a battlefield. The aim of the players is to navigate and capture flags belonging to the other team and bring them back to their own area. The players shoot each other's tanks using "shooting bullets" The movements of the tanks (players) as well as that of the shots (entities) exchanged among the players using DR vectors [3, 9].

The experimental data are the position value and the velocity value gotten in BZFlag game. We used the experimental data of 8301 numbers, and the threshold to 0.09. We compared the number of DRV packet transmission and the average prediction error E as shown in (3). (x, y, z) represent the true position, (newx, newy, newz) represent the extrapolated position, and (n) represent the number of data.

$$E = \frac{\sum_{i=1}^{n=8301} \sqrt{(x_i - newx_i)^2 + (y_i - newy_i)^2 + (z_i - newz_i)^2}}{n} \tag{3}$$

Table 1 shows the experimental result. Table 1 shows that the number of DRV transmission of scheme 2 and scheme 4 is smaller than that of scheme 1 and scheme 3, respectively.

Table 1. Font sizes of headings. Table captions should always be positioned *above* the tables.

	Scheme 1	Scheme 2	Scheme 3	Scheme 4
# of DRV transmission	4657	3965	703	611
E	4.511	2.563	0.4745	0.4048

In BZFlag game, it uses the game optimized dead reckoning algorithm, which means that it considers the two more vectors (orientation and angle) to predict the position more accurately. Scheme 3 improves the simple dead reckoning approaches: scheme 1 and scheme 2. In scheme 4, we used Kalman filter prediction on velocity and angle, and Figure 3 compares the scheme 3 and scheme 4 over 8000 time steps.

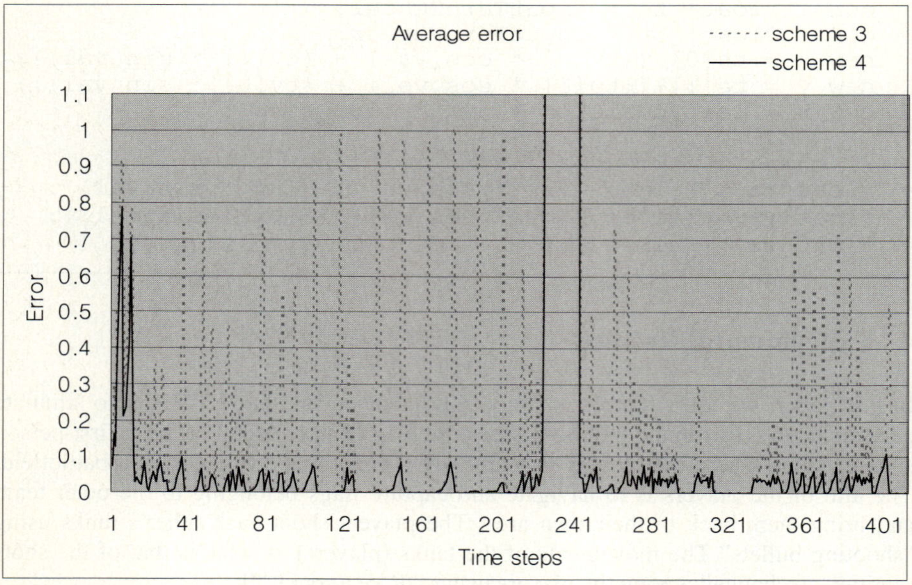

Fig. 3. Comparison of prediction accuracy for 8301 time step duration

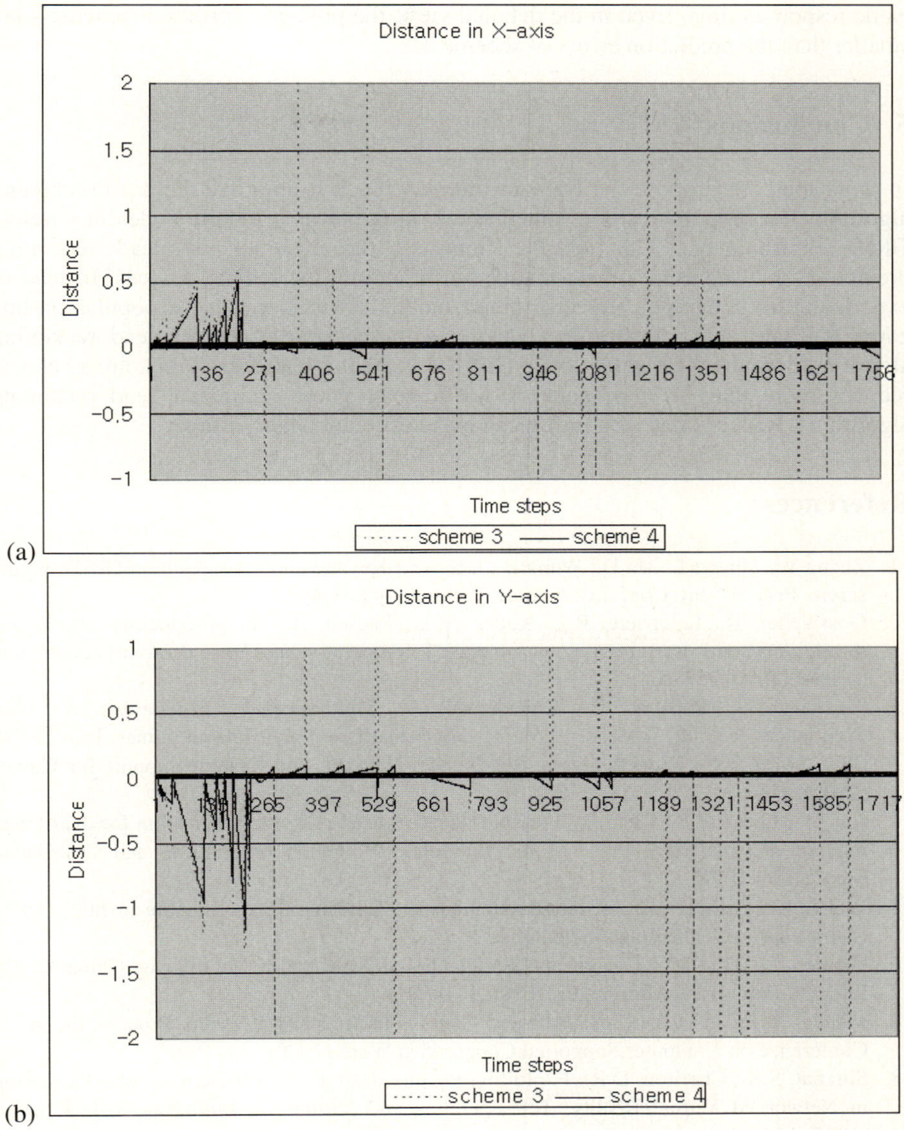

Fig. 4. Error in X and Y prediction: (a) errors in X direction, (b) errors in Y direction

For better comparison, we computed moving average for each 20 samples. *The dotted line* and *the solid line* show the result of scheme 3 and scheme 4, respectively.

Figure 4 shows the prediction errors in X and Y direction, respectively. Scheme 3, which uses BZFlag game optimized logic, shows fluctuations, and when the prediction error is over than 0.9, the BZFlag clients should send dead reckoning packets. Minimizing dead reckoning packets also minimized network latency and the game responses time. Even in the detailed view, the prediction errors of scheme 4 are smaller than the prediction errors of scheme 3.

5 Conclusions

In this paper, we propose the Kalman filter approach to improve the dead reckoning algorithm for geographically oriented networking between mobile nodes in wireless GRID environments. Our scheme improves the accuracy of dead reckoning prediction, and minimizes the network traffic among the mobile devices. Instead of experimenting geographically distributed mobile devices, we use a popular on-line game BZFlag, and compare our scheme with the state-of-the-art dead reckoning algorithm optimized for game logic. Our Kalman filter based dead reckoning scheme reduces more than 10% of network traffic over game optimized dead reckoning algorithms. Reduced network traffic can make efficient battery usage.

References

1. Zhang W., Zhang J., Ma D., Wang B., Chen Y.: Key technique research on GRID mobile servie. Proc. 2nd Int. Conf. Information Technology (2004)
2. Gossweiler, R., Laferriere, R.J., Keller, M.L., Pausch, R.: An introductory tutorial for developing multi-user virtual environments. Tele-operators and Virtual Environments, vol. 3. no. 4 (1994) 255-264
3. Aggarwal, S., Banavar, H., Khandelwal, A., Mukherjee, S., Rangarajan, S.: User experience: accuracy in dead-reckoning based distributed multi-player games. Proc. ACM SIGCOMM 2004 Workshops on Net-Games. Network and System Support for Games (2004)
4. Cai, W., Lee, F.B.S., Chen, L.: An auto-adaptive dead reckoning algorithm for distributed interactive simulation. Proc. of the thirteenth Workshop on Parallel and Distributed Simulation (1999)
5. Welch, G., Bishop, G.: An introduction to the Kalman filters. available in http://www.cs.unc.edu/~welch/Kalman/index.html
6. Gautier, L., Diot, C.: Design and Evaluation of MiMaze, a Multiplayer Game on the Internet. Proc. IEEE Multimedia. ICMCS (1998)
7. Mauve, M.: Consistency in Replicated Continuous Interactive Media. Proc. of the ACM Conference on Computer Supported Cooperative Work (2000) 181–190
8. Singhal, S.K., Cheriton, D.R.: Exploiting Position History for Efficient Remote Rendering in Networked Virtual Reality. Tele-operators and Virtual Environments. vol. 4. no. 2 (1995) 169-193
9. Schoeneman, C., Riker, T.: BZFlag (Battle Zone capture Flag), available in http://www.bzflag.org
10. Tseng, Y.-C., Wu, S.-L., Liao, W.-H., Chao, C.-M.: Location awareness in ad hoc wireless mobile networks. IEEE Computer. vol. 34, no. 6, (2001) 46-52

A Conceptual Framework for Agent-Based Information Resource Management

Charles C. Willow

Management Information Systems, Monmouth University, West Long Branch, NJ 07764-1898, U.S.A.
cwillow@monmouth.edu
www.monmouth.edu/~cwillow

Abstract. The information systems manager is often constrained by maintaining a certain threshold amount of memory for an organization. However, this requires more than technical and managerial resolutions, encompassing knowledge management for the group, eliciting tacit knowledge from the end users, and pattern and time series analyses of utilization for various applications.

This paper proposes a framework for building an automated intelligent agent for memory management under the client-server architecture. The emphasis is on collecting the needs of the organization and acquiring the application usage patterns for each client involved in real time. Due to dynamic nature of the tasks, incorporation of a neural network architecture with tacit knowledge base is suggested.

Keywords: Information resource management, automatic intelligent agent, automata, knowledge management, neural networks.

1 Introduction

This paper discusses problems associated with Information Resource Management (IRM), and suggests a development framework for reconfiguring the server as well as clients for moderately large-scale information systems.

Among others, one of the difficulties concerning IRM from the standpoint of the administrator is the correct forecast of overall memory needs for the organization. In particular, the manager is often confronted with maintaining a certain threshold amount of memory for a prolonged period of time. One may argue that the cost of memory is declining rapidly, and its management may not be a factor effecting IRM. Contrary to this common misbelief, however, a number of authors suggest there be a certain threshold for memory management [2, 7, 8, 9, 15, 18, 19] within a prescribed time window, analogous to budgetary considerations. In essence, memory management affects overall performance for both *client-server* and *peer-to-peer* architectures of the information system.

Major contribution of this paper lies in the development of framework for building multiple agents for the mail server, with emphasis on memory management. By far, agent-based autonomous systems (*i.e.* automata) have been adopted as one of the

E. Sha et al. (Eds.): EUC 2006, LNCS 4096, pp. 171 – 182, 2006.

better methods for managing virtual organizations in various applications [7, 15, 16, 22]. They range from e-commerce such as on-line travel arrangements to system diagnostics including on-line data quality audits and remote trouble-shooting.

Organization of this paper follows. In section 2, knowledge management for eliciting, building, and managing end-user preference and email usage patterns is discussed. Section 3 follows to illustrate the core system, 'multiple agents'. Suggestions for construction of the proposed framework are made in section 4, subsequently followed by conclusions in section 5.

2 Knowledge Management

The key to maintaining accuracy of the proposed multi-agent system lies in managing highly subjective knowledge for sharing and customizing/personalizing end-user memory usage patterns across the organization. Information Technology (IT) may support Knowledge Management (KM) in two classes: codification and personalization [8]. In essence, the codification approach manages structured knowledge, whereas personalization manages unstructured, tacit knowledge. Because email usage patterns for end-users may entail both types of knowledge, separate knowledge base or repository is suggested for the framework of this research. That is, there may be common patterns of email management among end users such as removing messages which are more than 36 months old or organizing their mail folders in every 30 days, and so forth on the one hand. On the other hand, each user may have highly subjective patterns which may not be consistent with those *codified* knowledge. Lansdale [9] emphasized the need for Cognitive Interface Tools (CITs) to collect, organize, build, and share both types of knowledge for the office system in his early research. However, not many literatures have been dedicated to solving this problem to date.

2.1 Knowledge Management Attributes

As noted in Lansdale [9], the process of information retrieval in the human mind is fundamentally different from filing or library system, in which items are accessed by location rather than their meaning. The first notion is that people recall chronological information about information: what else was happening at roughly the same time. Consequently, 'time stamp' of emails may be a good source of structured information or knowledge.

Association is another means by which humans retrieve information. Each email message is associated with four pieces of tacit information: recipient or sender, event or subject, attachment(s), and significance of the message. Table 1 summarizes the attributes for KM concerning email usage.

A set of six generic attributes associated with emails, as described in Table 1, is to be employed in the suggested framework of this paper. Notice that the first two attributes, time stamp and size, are structured information, which may be available for both the server and clients. By contrast, each client may manage her/his email messages based on one or more of the four tacit attributes: recipient/sender, event/subject, attachment(s), and significance. Given a certain restriction of memory size, say 100MB per email account holder, one client may choose to either remove or archive (on local memory store) emails based on recipient/sender, event/subject, attached file(s), significance, or any combination of the four, so far as tacit knowledge management is concerned. Alternatively, s/he may simply choose to archive or remove emails with regard to structured information such as time stamp and/or size. It is precisely this knowledge associated with each email client, which is expected to be elicited by the automated multiple agents proposed in this paper, preferably in real time.

Table 1. Attributes of Knowledge Management for Email Usage

Attributes	Type of Knowledge
Time Stamp	Structured
Size (KB)	Structured
Recipient / Sender	Tacit / Unstructured
Event / Subject	Tacit / Unstructured
Attachment	Tacit / Unstructured
Significance	Tacit / Unstructured

3 Intelligent Automated Agents

Under a certain memory constraint for each email client, the administrator of the information system (*i.e.* mail server) may choose to adopt a 'brute-force' approach, based on structured information such as time stamp or size of the message. As a consequence, clients – without their consent – may often realize their emails unavailable at times, once they have reached the memory quota set by the system. However, this aggressive method is not effective, due to its user-service if not legal implications. Thus, an automated system which may *advise* the clients in real time about their email usage patterns is considered as an attractive alternative for information resource management. Once the client is logged onto the system, the automatic intelligent agent generates a list of email messages which are to be removed, as well as those which are highly likely to be candidates for local archives. In addition, another agent system is suggested for the server to advise the administrator(s) of potential preventative measures. In essence, a conceptual framework for a multi-agent system is proposed in this paper. Similar ideas are being incorporated into the web and applications servers in Willow [25, 26] at present.

Neural networks (NN) are employed as the inference engine for the proposed multi-agent system. A Neural Network typically processes large-scale problems in terms of dimensionality, amount of data handled, and the volume of simulation or neural hardware processing [24]. It emerged as an area of Artificial Intelligence (AI) to mimic the human neurons in both perception and learning. It is interesting to note, however, that a conceivably disparate area within information science classified as 'knowledge representation' had brought the attention of researchers to pursue classes of 'computing and processing', such as neural networks. Object-oriented paradigm emerged as one of the better models for knowledge representation. In fact, the motivation for NN research was to seek an improved methodology in *machine learning*, and more specifically, in the area of *planning* algorithm, thereby augmenting the techniques available at the time. However, as the research progressed, more obstacles in emulating the human neurons were realized. To this end, the jargon NN at present, is more appropriate if it were to be replaced with *parallel, distributed simulation*. An excellent taxonomic view of NN models is provided by Willow [24].

3.1 Adaptive Resonance Theory

Adaptive Resonance Theory (ART), as illustrated in Zurada [28], is a unique *unsupervised* class of neural network algorithm. It has the novel property of controlled discovery of clusters. Further, the ART network may accommodate new clusters without affecting the storage or recall capabilities for clusters which were already learned, fit for the scope of the problem of this paper.

Nomenclature of the model follows:

Subscripts and Superscripts

i Subscript for input variable, x; $i = 1, \ldots, n$.

j Subscript for output clusters, $j = 1, \ldots, M$.

m Subscript for output neuron, y or neuron of hidden layer; $m = 1, \ldots j, \ldots, M$.

k Superscript for neuron y at layer k; $k \geq 0$.

Parameters

M Total number of clusters set by the decision maker.

n Total number of variables for input vector/tuple, $\mathbf{x} = [x_1, \ldots, x_n] = < x_1, \ldots, x_n>$.

Variables

$\mathbf{x}$ Input vector; $\mathbf{x} = [x_1, \ldots, x_n]$.

$\mathbf{w}$ Weight of the input vector; $\mathbf{w} = [w_1, \ldots, w_n]$.

$\mathbf{y}$ Output vector; $\mathbf{y}^k = [y_1, \ldots, y_M]$.

ρ Controlled vigilance factor indicating closeness of input to a stored cluster prototype to provide a desirable match ; $0 < \rho < 1$. The ART net will seek a perfect match for $\rho=1$ and loosely coupled matches for lower values of ρ.

$\mathbf{v}$ Weight vector for verifying cluster exemplar proximity; $\mathbf{v} = [v_1, \ldots, v_n]$.

t Update index for weights, $\mathbf{w}$ and $\mathbf{v}$.

Algorithm for ART is referenced to Zurada [28], and is summarized as follows:

Step 1: Initialization

The vigilance threshold, ρ, is set.

Weights are initialized for n-tuple input vectors and M top-layer neurons. $(M \times n)$ matrices $\mathbf{W}$ and $\mathbf{V}$ each are initialized with identical

$$\mathbf{W} = \left[\frac{1}{1+n}\right] \tag{1}$$

$$\mathbf{V} = [1] \tag{2}$$

$$0 < \rho < 1 \tag{3}$$

Step 2: Input Neuron Processing

Binary unipolar input vector **x** is presented at input nodes, $x_i = 0, 1$ for $i = 1, 2, \ldots, n$.

Step 3: Matching Score Computation

All matching scores are computed as follows:

$$y_m^o = \sum_{i=1}^{n} w_{im} x_i \,, \quad \text{for } m = 1, \ldots, M. \tag{4}$$

In this step, selection of the best matching existing cluster, *j*, is performed according to the maximum criterion, as follows:

$$y_j^o = \max_{j=1,\ldots,M} (y_m^o) \tag{5}$$

Step 4: Resonance

The similarity test for the winning neuron *j* is performed as follows:

$$\frac{1}{\|x\|} \sum_{i=1}^{n} v_{ij} x_i > \rho \tag{6}$$

where, the norm is defined as

$$\|x\| \equiv \sum_{i=1}^{n} |x_i| \tag{7}$$

If the test as illustrated in equation (6) is passed, the control is passed on to Step 5. Upon failing the test, Step 6 is followed only if the top layer has more than a single active node left. Otherwise, Step 5 is followed.

Step 5: Vigilance Test

Entries of the weight matrices are updated for index *j* passing the test of Step 4. The updates are only for entries (*i*, *j*), where $i = 1, 2, \ldots, M$, and are computed as follows:

$$w_{ij}(t+1) = \frac{v_{ij}(t) x_i}{0.5 + \sum_{i=1}^{n} v_{ij}(t) x_i} \tag{8}$$

$$v_{ij}(t+1) = x_i v_{ij}(t) \tag{9}$$

This updates the weights of the *j*-th cluster, newly generated or existing. The algorithm returns to Step 2.

Step 6: Cluster Generation

The node j is deactivated by setting y_j to 0. Thus this mode does not participate in the current cluster search. The algorithm goes back to Step 3, and will attempt to establish a new cluster different from j for the pattern under test.

Clusters are generated by the network itself if such clusters are identified in input data, and store the clustering information about patterns or features in the absence of *a priori* information about the possible number and type of clusters. In essence, ART computes the input-pattern-to-cluster matching score (y), which represents the degree of similarity of the present input to the previously encoded clusters. The vigilance threshold, ρ, where $0 < \rho < 1$, determines the degree of required similarity, or 'match', between a cluster or pattern already stored in the ART network and the current input in order for this new pattern to *resonate* with the encoded one. If no match is found, then a new class or cluster is created.

Applications of ART to the proposed multi-agent system follow in sections 3.2 and 3.3.

3.2 Client Agent Architecture with ART

The ART architecture for the suggested client agent follows. The major purpose of the client agent is to provide real-time knowledge regarding email management for each client end-user. Fig. 1 follows to illustrate.

For each email message, an input vector comprised of the following 7-tuple attribute is produced; $\mathbf{x} = <x_1, \ldots, x_7>$:

x_1 Age of the message. It is automatically computed as system-generated time (TNOW) – (Time_Stamp).

x_2 Size of the email, generally measured in kilobytes (KB).

x_3 Recipient information in smtp address format (To: johndoe@xyz.com).

x_4 Sender information in smtp address format (From: janedoe@xyz.com). Note that x_3 and x_4 are mutually exclusive, and may have *null* values associated. That is, each message is either received from or strictly sent to an smtp address.

x_5 Subject of the message (character strings).

x_6 Attachment to the message. A unique four-digit code encompassing the number of attachments between 0 and 99 (first two digits) and their file types is assigned for x_6. To simplify the data structure, file types are restricted to three most common on the Internet; ASCII .txt (1), Microsoft .doc (2), and Adobe .pdf (3). Examples of x_6 values are:

0000 No attachments.
0103 One attachment in .pdf format.
9923 Ninety-nine attachments in mixtures of .doc and .pdf files.

x_7 Significance of the email message, set by the end user. It ranges from 1 to 5, 5 being the most significant, and 1 being the least. Note that this value is applicable exclusively for the *body* of the email. For instance, a message with $x_7 = 1$ does not warrant automatic removal from the mailbox. Instead, the user may choose to archive it due to the importance of its attachment(s), x_6, for example.

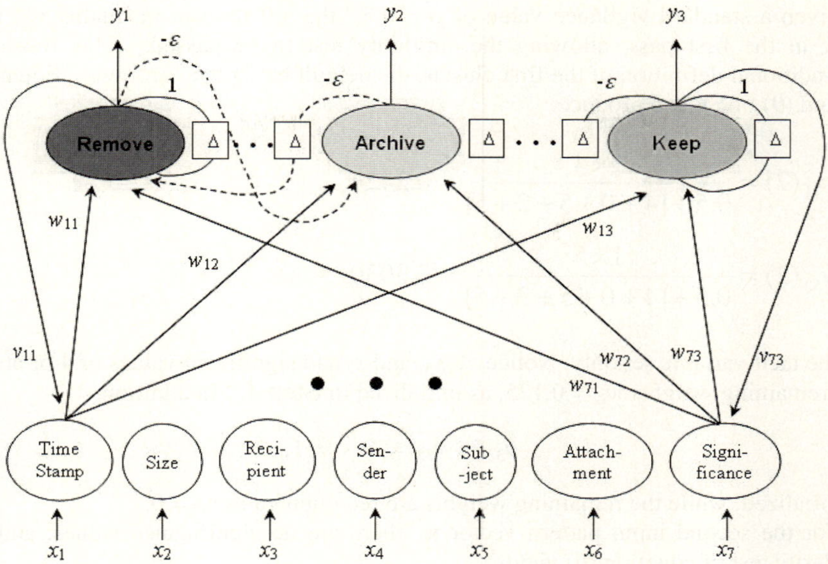

Fig. 1. ART for the Client Agent

A simplified numerical example follows to illustrate. Consider the following three messages for a client:

Message #1 $= \langle x_1, \ldots, x_7 \rangle$
= <60, 2000, *jmis@xyz.edu*, null, "publication consideration", 0203, 5>
Message #2
= <02, 20, null, *jdoe@usa.com*, "Greetings", 0000, 1>
Message #3
= <14, 250, *family@home.org*, null, "get together", 0000, 5>

Thus, each message forms an input pattern vector, **x**. Tacit input values are converted into a utility scale of 1 to 5 for neural processing, based on interactions with the knowledge base. This pertains to the attributes, x_3, x_4, and x_5. As a consequence, the input vectors are:

$$\mathbf{x_1} = \langle 60,\ 2000,\ 4,\ \text{null},\ 5,\ 02,\ 5\rangle$$
$$\mathbf{x_2} = \langle 02,\ 20,\ \text{null},\ 5,\ 1,\ 00,\ 1\rangle$$
$$\mathbf{x_3} = \langle 14,\ 250,\ 5,\ \text{null},\ 1,\ 00,\ 5\rangle$$

When $\mathbf{x_1}$ is presented, the steps of the ART algorithm are:

$$M = 3; \quad n = 7; \quad w_{ij} = \frac{1}{n+1} = 1/8 = 0.125;$$

$v_{ij} = 1, \quad i = 1, \ldots, 7, \quad j = 1, 2, 3$ for Remove, Archive, Keep.

Given a standard vigilance value of $\rho = 0.5$, the left term in inequality (6) is of unity in the first pass, allowing the similarity test to be passed. This results in unconditional definition of the first cluster, the default being the 'Archive'. Equations (8) and (9) of Step 5 produce:

$$w_{32}(2) = \frac{1 \times 4}{0.5 + [4 + 0 + 5 + 2 + 5]} = 0.2424$$

$$w_{52}(2) = \frac{1 \times 5}{0.5 + [4 + 0 + 5 + 2 + 5]} = 0.3030 = w_{72}$$

for the tacit variable set only. Notice x_3, x_5, and x_7 had significant values of 4 or above. The remaining weights $w_{i2} = 0.125$, as initialized in Step 1. In addition,

$$v_{32} = v_{52} = v_{72} = 1,$$

as initialized, while the remaining weights are recomputed as $v_{i2} = 0$.

For the second input pattern vector $\mathbf{x}_2$, there are no significance values, and the similarity test of equation (6) yields

$$\frac{1}{\|x\|}\sum_{i=1}^{7} v_{ij} x_i > \rho = 0 < 0.5$$

Due to the failure of the vigilance test and the absence of other nodes for further evaluation and for potential disabling, pattern $\mathbf{x}_2$ is treated as another new cluster. Further, a null value for the left-hand side of (6) is classified as the 'Remove' cluster.

In essence, the ART-based neural network processing is expected to advise the email clients of possible action(s) for each (email) message, while self-organizing the (neural) network dynamically.

3.3 Server Agent Architecture with ART

The Adaptive Resonance Theory (ART) model may also be employed for another set of agent system dedicated to assisting the email server administrator(s). The two systems of agents, targeting individual clients as well as administrators, may then communicate in real time by accessing the integrated knowledge base. However, the server agent architecture is relatively more complicated due to differences in network protocols. Two major methods employed are: **I**nternet **M**essage **A**ccess **P**rotocol (IMAP) and **P**ost **O**ffice **P**rotocol (POP). IMAP integrates messages on the shared mail server, and permits client email programs to access remote message stores as if they were local. Thus, the memory burden on the server is far greater for IMAP than for POP. However, complete monitoring of client emails is possible under the IMAP scheme. That is, a single server-side agent system may suffice for the IMAP, whereas a single client-agent may fit systems with POP being implemented. Table 2 follows to illustrate.

Table 2. Classes of Information Availability based on Email Application Protocols

Email Protocols / Information Process	IMAP *(central)*	POP *(distributed)*
Server-based	Server only	**Mixed*
User-based	**Mixed*	Client only

4 Implementation

A *generalized* Multi-Agent System (MAS) architecture entitled RETSINA has been presented by Sycara et al. [21], in which three classes of agents are proposed: *interface*, *task*, and *information* agents.

The architecture of the proposed MAS for mail server management is built similar to the RETSINA architecture. Fig. 2 shows the proposed architecture, and its components are briefly described below.

In the application domain of mail server memory management, it is interesting to note that the users or clients themselves act as information source. That is, the input pattern vector **x**, to be incorporated into the Adaptive Resonance Theory (ART) algorithm used by the four task agents, represented by shaded hexagons, is collected by each corresponding interface agent for a user. In essence, the interface agents function as both interacting and information agents. There may be as many as m number of interface agents for the n number of clients, where $n \geq m$, since some users may choose to decline the automated service that tracks and manages their email messages. Instead, they will be liable for managing their memory quota manually. Dashed arrows indicate access to the knowledge repository, in which patterns of email usage for each client are retained in the form of rules.

Three task agents, 'Input Weight Vector', 'Output Weight Vector', and 'Vigilance Factor' dynamically interact with knowledge bases to adjust themselves asynchronously in real time. In effect, the neural network based on ART learns without supervision, and a unique cluster is generated for each email message. Possible clusters were illustrated in Fig. 1.

Implementation of the proposed architecture has been initiated with Dell PowerEdge™ 1850 server with Intel Xeon processor at clock speed up to 3.0GHz and 1.0GB RAM. At present, a closed proprietary network with two clients is being tested for building the prototype multi-agent system. Network Operating System (NOS) of choice is Linux, with Visual C++ as the major development platform.

In building a technical infrastructure, the following obstacles are expected, among others:

- Difficulty of data mining: Execution of a *spyware* is inevitable on the client machine, which may develop legal implications. At present, cookies are being considered as the quick implementation vehicle.
- Network Utilization: Running a multi-agent system in real time may decrease the network performance in terms of bandwidth utilization and reliability to a critical level.

- Portability/Scalability: There is a constant portability problem of this proposed agent system with respect to operating system and/or hardware platform. Platforms running operating systems other than Linux have to be simulated and tested for, once this prototype completes its pilot run.

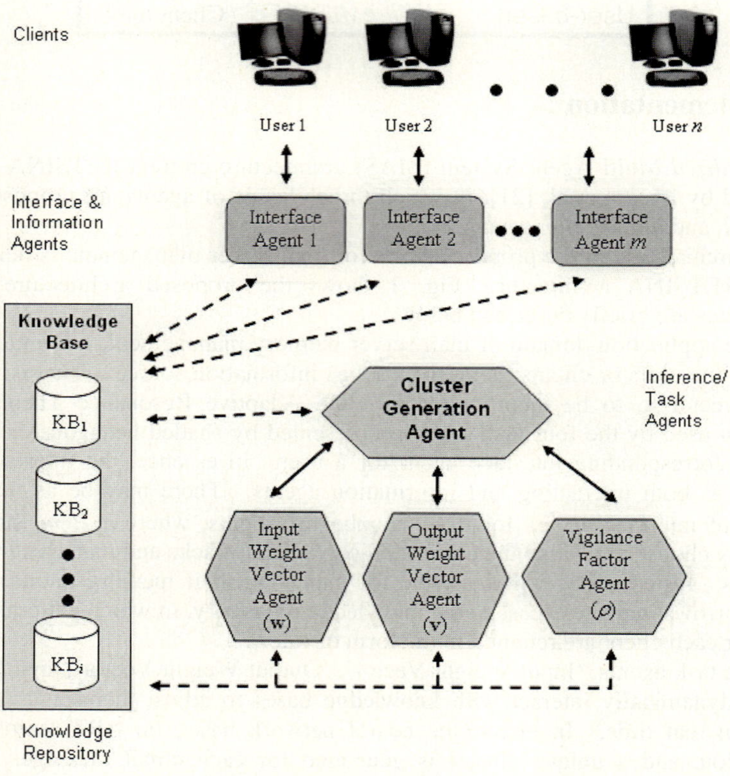

Fig. 2. Multi-Agent System Architecture for Mail Server Management

5 Conclusions

A conceptual framework for real-time multi-agent system built with neural network and knowledge base has been presented in this paper, with emphasis on Information Resource Management (IRM). Managing client as well as server knowledge concerning emails was selected as the scope of this research due to its significance as a major communication vehicle in the *e*-economy.

Adaptive Resonance Theory (ART) was the primary algorithm of choice for the neural-network engine due to its capability to achieve *unsupervised* learning. A simplified numerical example was provided to illustrate the effectiveness of ART applied to the problem domain.

Marked differences are discovered for the two major email protocols for the server: IMAP and POP. The suggested multi-agents are expected to be most effective for managing client knowledge under the IMAP and for managing server knowledge under the POP structure.

Challenges of implementing the proposed framework include but not restricted to data mining, network utilization, portability, and security.

Acknowledgments. This paper was in part supported by the 2005-2006 Research Grant from the Business Council and in most part by the 2005-2006 Faculty Grants-in-Aid for Creativity funds of the Monmouth University, West Long Branch, New Jersey, U.S.A.

References

1. Ahuja, M. K.: Network Structure in Virtual Organizations. Journal of Computer-Mediated Communication. 3 (1998) [online journal]
2. Applen, J. D.: Technical Communication, knowledge management, and XML. Technical Communication. 49 (2002) 301-313
3. Davenport, T. H., Prusak, L.: Working Knowledge: How organizations manage what they know. Harvard Business School Press, Boston (1998)
4. Dutta, S.: Strategies for implementing knowledge-based systems. IEEE Transactions on Engineering Management. 22 (1997) 79-90
5. Gold, A. H., Malhotra, A., Segars, A. H.: Knowledge management: an organizational capabilities perspective. Journal of Management Information Systems. 18 (2001) 185-214
6. Grudin, J.: Why CSCW applications fail: problems in the design and evaluation of organizational interfaces. Proceedings of the 1988 ACM Conference on Computer Supported Cooperative Work. New York (1988) 85-93
7. Kanawati, R., Malek, M.: A Multi-agent system for collaborative bookmarking. Proceedings of the First ACM International Joint Conference on Autonomous Agents and Multi-agent Systems: Part 3. Bologna, Italy (2002) 1137-1138
8. Kankanhalli, A., Tanudidjaja, F., Sutanto, J., Tan, C. Y.: The role of IT in successful knowledge management initiatives. Communications of the ACM. 46 (2003) 69-73
9. Lansdale, M.: The psychology of personal information management. Applied Ergonomics. 19 (1988) 55-66
10. Laurillau, Y., Nigay, L.: Clover Architecture for Groupware. Proceedings of the 2002 ACM Conference on Computer Supported Cooperative Work. (2002) 236-245
11. Majchrzak, A., Rice, R. E., Malhotra, A., King, N.: Technology adaptation – the case of a computer-supported inter-organizational virtual team. MIS Quarterly. 24 (2000) 569-600
12. Malek, M.: Hybrid approaches integrating neural networks and case based reasoning – from loosely coupled to tightly coupled models. In: Sankar, K. P., Tharam, S. D., Daniel, S. Y. (eds): Soft Computing in Case-based Reasoning. Springer, New York (2000) 73-94
13. Markus, M. L., and Connolly, T.: Why Computer Supported Collaborative Work applications fail – problems in the adoption of interdependent work tools. Proceedings of the International Conference on Computer Supported Collaborative Work (CSCW '90). Association for Computing Machinery, New York (1990) 371-380

14. Markus, M. L.: Toward a theory of knowledge reuse: types of knowledge reuse situations and factors in reuse success. Journal of Management Information Systems. 18 (2001) 57-93
15. Mathe, N., Chen, J. R.: Organizing and sharing information on the World-Wide Web using a multi-agent systems. Proceedings of ED-MEDIA '98 Conference on Educational Multimedia and Hypermedia. Freiburg, Germany (1998)
16. Murch, R.: Autonomic Computing. Prentice-Hall, New York (2004)
17. Nonaka, I., Takeuchi, H.: The Knowledge-creating company – How Japanese companies create Dynamics of Innovation. Oxford University Press, New York (1995)
18. Pinelle, D., Gutwin, C., Greenberg, S.: Task analysis for groupware usability evaluation – modeling shared-workspace tasks with the mechanics of collaboration. ACM Transactions on Computer-Human Interaction. 10 (2003) 281-311
19. Roos, L. L., Soodeen, R-A., Bond, R., Burchill, C.: Working more productively – tools for administrative Data. Health Services Research. 38 (2003) 1339-1357
20. Roseman, M., Greenberg, S.: Building real-time groupware with GroupKit, a groupware toolkit. ACM Transactions on Computer-Human Interaction. 3 (2001) 66-106
21. Sycara, K., Pannu, A., Williamson, M., Zeng, D., Decker, K.: Distributed Intelligent Agents. IEEE Intelligent Systems. 11 (1996) 36-46
22. Taylor, W. A.: Computer-mediated knowledge sharing and individual user differences – an exploratory study. European Journal of Information Systems. 13 (2004) 52-64
23. Wiesenfeld, B. M., Raghuram, S., Garud, R.: Communication Patterns as Determinants of Organizational Identification in a Virtual Organization. Journal of Computer-Mediated Communication. 3 (1998) [online journal]
24. Willow, C. C.: A Feedforward Multi-layer Neural Network for Machine Cell Formation in Computer Integrated Manufacturing. Journal of Intelligent Manufacturing. 13 (2002) 75-87
25. Willow, C. C.: Neural Network-based Multiple Agent System for Web Server Management. MU WP No. W05-02, Management Information Systems, School of Business Administration, Monmouth University, NJ (2005a)
26. Willow, C. C.: Neural Network-based Multiple Agent System for Application Server Management. MU WP No. W05-03, Management Information Systems, School of Business Administration, Monmouth University, NJ (2005b)
27. Ye, Y., Fischer, G., Reeves, B.: Integrating Active Information Delivery and Reuse Repository Systems. Proceedings of the Eighth ACM SIGSOFT International Symposium on Foundations of Software Engineering – 21 Century Applications. San Diego (2000) 60-68
28. Zurada, J. M.: Introduction to Artificial Neural Systems. West Press, St. Paul (1992)

Advanced Stochastic Host State Modeling to Reliable Computation in Global Computing Environment*

EunJoung Byun[1], HongSoo Kim[1], SungJin Choi[1], MaengSoon Baik[2], SooJin Goo[1], Joon-Min Gil[3], HarkSoo Park[4], and Chong-Sun Hwang[1]

[1] Dept. of Computer Science & Engineering, Korea University
{vision, hera, lotieye, softsj, hwang}@disys.korea.ac.kr
[2] IT Research & Development Center
SAMSUNG SDS
maengsoon.baik@samsung.com
[3] Dept. of Computer Science Education, Catholic University of Daegu
330 Geumnak, Hayang-eup, Gyeongsan-si, Gyeongbuk 712-702, Korea
jmgil@cu.ac.kr
[4] Supercomputing Center, KISTI, Korea
hspark@kisti.re.kr

Abstract. To design a stable global computing environment supporting reliable job execution and covering unanticipated state changes of hosts, the dynamic characteristics (i.e. volatilities) of hosts should be considered. Since a host is not dedicated to the system, voluntary hosts are free to leave and join autonomously in the middle of execution. As current systems do not relate volatility to a scheduling procedure, global computing systems suffer from performance degradation, reliability loss, job interruption, and execution time delays. For dependable computation, we propose Advanced Stochastic Host State Modeling (ASHSM), which is based on Markov model relating to execution availability quantifying duration and regularity of execution patterns of each host. Through the model, the system predicts desktop activities and allocates jobs according to the host features. Furthermore ASHSM alleviates unreliability due to unstable resource provision and job suspension during execution.

1 Introduction

Global computing[9], [2] is a computing paradigm harnessing idle cycles through the Internet. It processes massive computational application through the participation of idle computing resources on the edge of the Internet. The main goals of the global computing systems are achieving high throughput and high performance, and providing huge computational resources by harvested cycles. Most of the global computing systems up to now are based on a cycle stealing scheme

* This work was supported by the Korea Institute of Science and Technology Information.

E. Sha et al. (Eds.): EUC 2006, LNCS 4096, pp. 183–192, 2006.

that uses these available cycles. Such systems are also known as peer-to-peer Grid, desktop Grid[8], meta computing[3], or volunteer computing [1]. Global computing constitutes large-scale computing power based on a proliferation of personal computers and the rapid growth of the Internet. SETI@home[4] is a well-known example for achieving tremendous computing power harnessed from the Internet.

The individual computing resources, however, are not devoted to global computing systems and, therefore, the systems experience blocked job execution and delayed execution time. Previous attempts cannot solve problems such as delayed total execution time, unpredictable execution patterns of the host, and system instability and unreliability because existing global computing systems do not consider the volatile aspects of volunteer hosts. System performance and reliability is reduced as a result of these autonomous and dynamic host properties (i.e. volatilities).

Volatility means the state in which a resource is unavailable for use. Volatility is created by individual physical machine crashes, software failures, user intermittence, and temporal disconnection of the physical communication link. This volatility is the main cause of degradation in terms of reliability and makespan increase. As a result of volatility, systems cannot guarantee that participants will finish jobs in the requested time period or that the workloads will be executed in a stable manner.

Availability indicates how well hosts act and how frequently nodes perish. It helps to identify the volatile features of volunteer hosts. Therefore, availability can be used to measure the dynamic characteristics of volunteer nodes. In this paper, appropriate availability, described in our previous work[13] on measuring the dynamic properties of hosts, is used. Since hosts are extremely dynamic in global computing environments, systems must be adaptive to dynamic changes. To develop a reliable global computing system, ASHSM is proposed to solve these problems originating from volatility by considering past experience of host execution in host selection. The ASHSM enables the system to improve performance and reliability by using a Markov model based on availability that takes into account the volatile aspects of each host.

2 Related Work

While several existing research studies focus on the CPU clock, memory capacity, and network bandwidth to select a resource, we concentrate on patterns of execution such as availability rather than the physical capacity to overcome the highly dynamic and uncertain activities of a host that usually causes task failure, performance deterioration, and system instability. Generally, availability is defined as the property that a system is ready to be used immediately. It may be represented by the probability that the system will operate correctly at any given time. Availability has recently become an important issue in global computing systems and peer-to-peer networks, which consist of personal computers as a main resource.

The concept of availability is introduced in global computing systems to cope with volatile hosts. In [12], the scheduling scheme mainly concerns the capability of the volunteer host to select eligible workers for job executions. As shown in [16], the algorithms allocating available capacity required long periods when owners do not use their stations. The workstations were available for more than 75% of the time observed, according to analyzed usage patterns. The distribution of availability in global computing environments is described in [6] where experimental measurements and mathematical distributions are compared. However, they do not take into account intermittent job execution caused by users.

[11] and [10] use a simple metric, the percentage of available CPU cycles of host machines. These studies, however, suffer from job suspension during execution because they do not consider user intermittence such as keyboard or mouse activities. [8] not only has insight into the detailed temporal structure of CPU availability of global computing system resources, but also offers extensive measurements of an enterprise's global computing with a real platform. The researchers divide availability into host availability and CPU availability to separate the practical execution state from the turning-on state. However, they cannot solve the aforementioned problems caused by volatilities by using simple statistical measurement. In Peer-to-Peer systems, [5],[6], and [7] separate resources by whether they are usable at the time or not. The existing systems neither consider availability nor utilize appropriate availability reflecting host execution manner because they use simple statistical availability. The simple concepts of availability are inadequate to both represent the dynamic features of volunteers and guarantee execution stability and completeness. The activities of hosts connected by the Internet are difficult to predict based on simple statistical values. To understand the dynamic properties of hosts, we propose a more precise stochastic model to represent host execution patterns.

3 System Model

3.1 System Environment

In global computing, the systems are largely composed of clients, central server, and voluntary hosts. Large-scale jobs can be coordinated with the distributed individual nodes using efficient scheduling and management. The job consists of data and operation codes. The clients entrusts large-scale jobs to the central server. The server independently divides the job into sub-jobs, so-called workload or task. Each workload is distributed to and executed by a host. The server performs allocation, including the reallocation process. In practice, the clients are modules to find large-scale computational power and commit a job to the central server. The central server is a module that manages individual hosts, jobs, and job scheduling. The hosts are personal computers or workstations that compute the jobs. They execute allocated workloads and return the result upon workload completion. Finally, the central sever integrates the workload results from each volunteer and returns the final result.

3.2 Desktop Availability

There is a need for measuring the host execution characteristics for global computing systems. The existing measurements of availability are not only inadequate but also unsuitable as they lack proprietary availability to explain the dynamic properties. In this paper, we use a novel definition according to our previous work[13] of availability to draw execution patterns. The study involves a newly defined proprietary availability of volunteer hosts as a quantity of state that can accept requests for use. The study roughly divided volunteer availability into spatial availability and temporal availability. Spatial availability represents physical capacity, including CPU capacity, memory capacity, and network bandwidth, while temporal availability is related to the time of availability of the host. As shown in **Figure 1**, temporal availability, based on statistical time series analysis, is categorized into Host Availability (HA) and Execution Availability (EA). Each HA is composed of EA and Execution Unavailability (EU). HA measures how much the host participates in execution with regularity and EA measures how much the volunteer executes a job with predictability. Host Unavailability (HU) means an inactive period of participation in the system and EU means an unavailable period for execution. Each volunteer's HA and EA is measured by an amount of time as sum of the differences between start time and end time that represents the pair of t_s^i and t_e^i such as $O^n = [t_s^i, t_e^i]$. t_s^i means n*th* availability of start time while t_e^i means n*th* availability of end time. Each HA, HU, EA, and EU are recorded in the profile on the host.

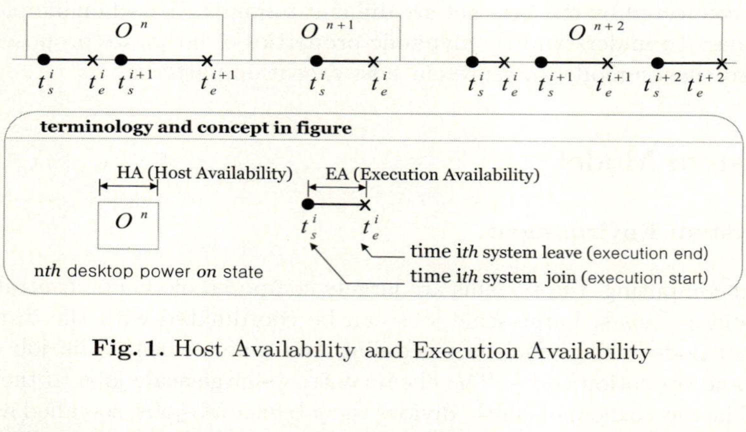

Fig. 1. Host Availability and Execution Availability

4 Advanced Stochastic Scheduling Scheme Using Markov Chain Based on Availability

4.1 Markov Modeling

Even if various statistical scheduling algorithms to predict availability of host are used, these studies cannot represent execution patterns of volunteers accurately. We model temporal availability of nodes with a stochastic approach to measure dynamic aspects of the volunteer based on analysis of time variations. The proposed scheduling scheme supports a more reliable execution environment because the stochastic model is used to provide information on volunteer characteristics and reflect the characteristics in the scheduling scheme. The proposed availability model is developed to assess the impact of time-based and predictive scheduling schemes on volunteer availability. In this paper, the scheduler uses the stochastic process modeled with the Markov chain to solve problems caused by the volatility of each host. The scheduler selects a suitable volunteer for the workload relying on a stochastic process, which measures node availability. In global computing systems, one of the major concerns is reliability. A more accurate basis for decision-making is a stochastic model representing a change of host execution state instead of a simple statistical model. The proposed scheduling scheme is an appropriate solution to system reliability problems faced by host volatility through the modeling of temporal analysis of each host. The systems become exceedingly complex to manage when most participating hosts dynamically fluctuate in the course of execution. Therefore, host behavior is uncertain in the presence of host departures and job obstructions, particularly in highly dynamic environments or during serious disasters. Some studies, however, have been used to provide a limited degree of reliability and stability, by associating availability with a simple statistical value [14]. To address the issues of dynamism and uncertainty, we use a heuristic approach that provides a reliable means to control volatility. The existing availability has a stationary probability for the state of the host that suggests whether it can be accessed or not. In addition, availability is difficult to predict because the dynamism of participant activity comes from the autonomy of each node. Also, using simple availability is often inaccurate or insufficient as characteristics vary over time. The characteristics of availability associated with participation could be roughly categorized by statistical values. Instead of using availability directly, we modeled availability using a Markov chain to measure patterns of participation and execution more accurately. The Markov Chain measures how much a given volunteer is dedicated to the global computing system. Also, the Markov chain suggests properties of hosts such as suspension rate, regularity, pattern deviation, and so on. Using the distribution of availability of volunteers where volunteers are unstable, the Markov model helps to predict the duration of host execution, considering change of availability, and selects the appropriate volunteer based on past host activity. The Markov scheduler can accurately capture the intent of all state changes made by the node user by using time-travel-like activities of host execution[15]. The Markov chain is built anew for each time unit. The proposed Markov model suggests a simple way to process the multiple sequences that would be very difficult to manipulate otherwise. In the model, the state of each host was checked and updated every thirty minutes with three different states: Idle (I), Use (U), and Stop (S). I state indicates a state enabling job execution without user intervention. The reason why we use units of thirty minutes is based on [6] that most subtask units require from twenty to thirty minutes. U state indicates a state unable to work because of user occupancy or intervention even when the machine is active. S state denotes a disabled state caused by machine crash, system termination, network disconnection, and so on. The EA is related to I state and EU considers S state and U state. The Markov Chain is updated every day, repeating the process where each volunteer host is modeled with the states being checked every thirty minutes. Then the volunteer calculates the probability of each state transition.

In addition, the Markov model provides a simple way to process the multiple sequences that would be very difficult to manipulate otherwise. **Figure 2** shows a Markov chain modeled with 48 time units sequenced in twenty-four hours representing each 30-minute time period. As represented in **Figure 2**, I_i means I state in i*th* time unit while $P_{I_i I_j}$ indicates transition probability from I state in i*th* time unit to I state in j*th* time unit. Each transition in the state diagram of the Markov chain has a transition probability associated with it. The matrix of transition probability is shown in **Equation 1**. The sum of each column is one.

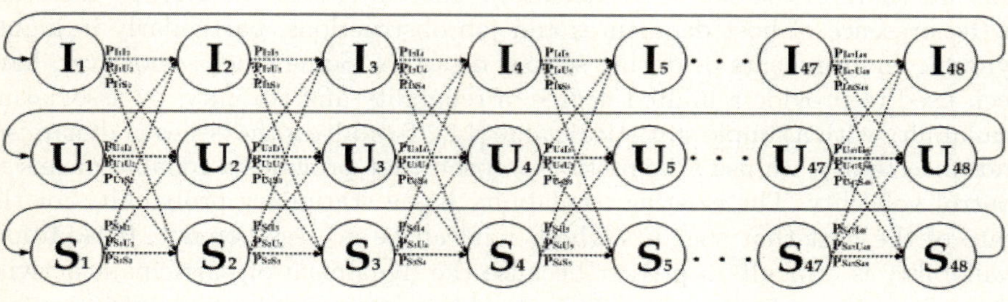

Fig. 2. Markov Chain

The state transition probability, $P_{State_j State_k}$, is given

$$P_{State_j State_k} = \begin{pmatrix} P_{I_j I_k} & P_{I_j U_k} & P_{I_j S_k} \\ P_{U_j I_k} & P_{U_j U_k} & P_{U_j S_k} \\ P_{S_j I_k} & P_{S_j U_k} & P_{S_j S_k} \end{pmatrix} \tag{1}$$

Viterbi algorithm[17] is used to draw an accumulated likelihood score in a given observation sequence. The Markov models apply Viterbi to find the most likely state sequence and the likelihood score of this sequence. The credit suggests most-likely probability which indicates a reliable value for the state. The probability of all paths going through I state are computed by multiplying the Forward Credit (FC) by the Backward Credit (BC). Finally the FC by the BC creates the credit of i*th* stage. The FC is the calculated sum of the multiplied credit of the previous stage by the sum of the transition probability from the previous i-1*th* time unit to the current i*th*time unit. In contrast, the BC is time reverse version of FC. The state of the host calculated probability of the state in each time unit helps to estimate and predict the next state of the host.

Forward credit of I_i:

$$FC\_I_i = C\_I_{i-1} * P_{I_{i-1} I_i} + C\_U_{i-1} * P_{U_{i-1} I_i} + C\_S_{i-1} * P_{S_2 I_3} \tag{2}$$

Backward credit of I_i:

$$BC\_I_i = C\_I_{i+1} * P_{I_i I_{i+1}} + C\_U_{i+1} * P_{U_i I_{i+1}} + C\_S_{i+1} * P_{S_i I_{i+1}} \quad (3)$$

The Credit of I_i:

$$C\_I_i = FC\_I_i \times BC\_I_i. \quad (4)$$

Finally C_I_i is a representative credit that probability value of all paths going through I_i is calculated using the follow equation.

In the initial generation of the Markov chain, the FC at the first stage without forward transition probabilities in the windows is given by rate of frequency. The BC at the last stage without backward transition probabilities is given by same manner.

We measure this durable and predictable credit factor by using HA and EA based on heuristics through profiling. Each of the host records and preserves the state in the profile every thirty minutes and then sends the current state to the central server. The central server updates the Markov Chain for the credit values based on availability upon receiving the information about the state of the node. ASHSM helps to solve unstable resource provision and frequent job resubmission by presenting the probability that a computing unit is executed at any given point in time.

4.2 Scheduling Algorithm

The scheduling scheme is most formidable in global computing systems since performance is highly dependent on the scheme. There is a need for a scheduling scheme to cover the volatile aspects of volunteers, where each volunteer is a computing resource with fluctuating participation and execution with time variations. Especially, stability and reliability are more required for timely completion of mission-critical applications. We demonstrate ASHSM, which helps to achieve predictable and reliable execution performance. This paper considers the scheduling problem of allocating a specific workload to a host with different participation and execution patterns. The existing schemes, for example, simple scheduling scheme or eager scheduling scheme are inadequate to handle the problems previously mentioned owing to volatility. We overcome these limitations by applying the Markov model to scheduling. The scheduling algorithm follows four fundamental steps that we refer as the "Four E's Rule": Estimation, Eligibility, Execution, and Evaluation. In the each step, Markov Job Scheduler makes a decision concerning selection based on the Markov Chain. In the Estimation step, the Markov scheduler estimates each credit value of the host state as described in the previous section. Next, the scheduler selects an appropriate volunteer according to the given job and allocates the job to a node in the Eligibility step. Then, in the Execution step, the host executes the allocated job where not only the execution state but also the results of success and failure are recorded and reported. Finally, the scheduler evaluates the volunteer based on the record of execution behavior and updates the Markov Chain in the Evaluation step.

5 Performance Evaluation

In this section, we provide a mathematical analysis of the extent of ASHSM leverage on system performance. We choose two metrics, probability of execution success and average throughput.

5.1 Success Probability of Execution

[6] indicates that the hyperexponential or Weibull distribution model effectively represents host availability in enterprise and Internet computing environments. We assume that the availability of each volunteer fits a hyperexponential distribution. We compare the proposed Markov model-based scheduling scheme with FCFS, eager scheduling, and a previously proposed scheme in terms of success probability. Success probability of execution is shown in **Equation 5** through **Equation 8**.

$$P\{S_{EXE}^{FCFS}\} = \sum_{i=1}^{n} p_i \lambda_i e^{-\lambda_i(\Delta+(1-(\alpha+\beta))\Delta)} \tag{5}$$

$$P\{S_{EXE}^{Eager}\} = \sum_{i=1}^{n} p_i \lambda_i e^{-\lambda_i(\Delta+(1-\alpha)\Delta)} \tag{6}$$

$$P\{S_{EXE}^{SSDR}\} = \sum_{i=1}^{n} p_i \lambda_i e^{-\lambda_i \Delta} \tag{7}$$

$$P\{S_{EXE}^{ASHSM}\} = \sum_{i=1}^{n} p_i \lambda_i e^{-\lambda_i \Delta}, \lambda_i = min\{\lambda_1, \lambda_2, ...\} \tag{8}$$

λ means execution stop rate and Δ means an indeed time to execute a workload. The FCFS scheme requires reallocation time and delay time; α and β, respectively in **Equation 5**. **Equation 6** shows that eager scheduling exceeds execution time because it makes Δ increase by requiring additional reallocation time, denoted as α. In these schemes, the execution time slows as the workload is reallocated repeatedly. This results in consecutively low execution success probability. In **Equation 7**, as SSDR maintains initial execution time, it may promise a high execution success probability since SSDR considers the quality of execution, (i.e. duration of availability) in advance. ASHSM gets a good success probability by reaching $min\{\lambda_1, \lambda_2, ...\}$ as shown in **Equation 8**.

As shown in **Figure 3**, the curve of proposed ASHSM is remarkably high in a success probability more than the curve of other schemes. Especially, ASHSM performs highly during low stop rate. In addition, Success probability of execution decreases moderately, goes on increasing in stop rate of execution. These results present that ASHSM helps reliable and stable execution even each host is volatile unpredictable.

5.2 Average Throughput

Consider the host with n identical independent EA where the length of successive node EAs follows an exponential distribution with mean $1/\mu$ and that successive EUs are also independent exponentially distributed variables with mean $1/\lambda$. At

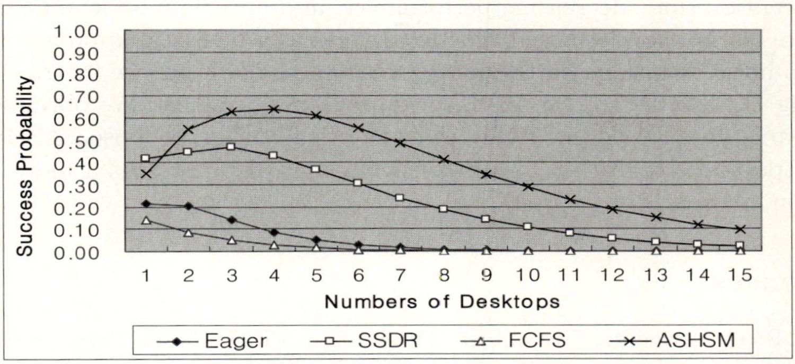

Fig. 3. Comparisons of Total Execution Time

the end of EA follows EU with probability $q_1(q_0+q_1=1)$ where $q_0$is the success probability and q_1 is the failure probability. Waiting is performed with rate λ and Execution is served with rate λ, μ: $EU = 1/\mu$, $EA = 1/\lambda$. It is similar to the M/M/1 queueing model. At the end of workload completion, another workload is executed. Given the number of workloads in EA, i, where $0 \le i \le n$ and denoting $\frac{\lambda}{\mu q_1}$ by ρ, we see that the steady-state probabilities are given by

$$\pi_i = (\frac{\lambda}{\mu q_1})^i \pi_0 = \rho^i \pi_0, and \pi_0 = \frac{1}{\sum_{i=0}^{n} \rho_i} \tag{9}$$

so that

$$\pi_0 = \begin{cases} \frac{1-\rho}{1-\rho^{n+1}}, & \rho \neq 1 \\ \frac{1}{n+1}, & \rho = 1 \end{cases} \tag{10}$$

The utilization of EA is given by

$$U_{EA} = 1 - \pi_0 \begin{cases} \frac{\rho-\rho^{n+1}}{1-\rho^{n+1}}, & \rho \neq 1 \\ \frac{n}{n+1}, & \rho = 1 \end{cases} \tag{11}$$

The average host throughput, T_{D_i} in the steady-state is given by

$$T_{D_i} = \mu q_0 U_{EA} \tag{12}$$

Job execution is completed with μ, and a q_0 contributing to the throughput. For fixed values of μ and q_0, T_{D_i} is proportional to the utilization of EA, U_{EA}. ASHSM achieves high throughput by increasing ρ since ρ indicates the relative measure of the EA versus EU of a host because we have plotted U_{EA} as a function of the balance factor ρ and the number of EAs (i.e. most probable I state). If $\rho < 1$, then the host is in EU and otherwise if $\rho > 1$, then the host is in EA.

6 Conclusions

In this paper, we proposed ASHSM to guarantee reliable and persistent execution. ASHSM helps to alleviate problems in existing systems such as increasing total execution time, decreasing performance, and uncertain job completion. We specify a Markov model based scheduling taking a heuristic approach to solve unstable host execution. Furthermore, we suggest more precise metrics, credits including FC and BC of the host, to improve performance. We obtained good performance both experimentally and analytically. The proposed ASHSM not only outperforms the other existing schemes but also provides a more reliable execution environment.

References

1. Luis F. G. Sarmenta, "Volunteer Computing", Ph.D. thesis. Dept. of Electrical Engineering and Computer Science, MIT, Mar, 2001.
2. G. Fedak, C. Germain, V. Neri and F. Cappello. "XtremWeb : A Generic Global Computing System", Workshop on Global Computing on Personal Devices, CCGRID2001, May 2001.
3. A. Baratloo, M. Karaul, Z. Kedem, and P. Wyckoff. "Charlotte: Metacomputing on the web", In proceedings of 9th Conference on Parallel and Distributed Computing System, 1996.
4. D. P. Anderson, J. Cobb, E. Korpela, M. Lebofsky, D. Werthimer, "SETI@home: an experiment in5 public-resource computing", Communications of the ACM, Vol.45, No. 11, Nov. 2002.
5. Bhagwan, Savage, and Voelker, "Understanding availability", IPTPS 2003
6. John Brevik, Daniel Nurmi, Rich Wolski, "Modeling machine availability in enterprise and wide-area distributed computing environment", Technical Report CS2003-28, Oct. 2003.
7. Jacky Chu, Kevin Labonte, and Brian Neil Levine, "Availability and Popularity Measurements of Peer-to-Peer File systems", Technical report 04-36, Jun. 2004.
8. Derrick Kondo, Michela Taufer, John Karanicolas, Charles L. Brooks, Henri Casanova and Andrew Chien, "Characterizing and Evaluating desktop Grids - An Empirical Study", in Proceedings of IPDPS 04, Apr. 2004.
9. D. Kondo, H. Casanova, F. Berman, "Models and Scheduling Mechanism in Global Computing Applications", in Proceedings of IPDPS 02, Apr. 2002.
10. H. Casanova, A. Legrand, D. Zagorodnov, and F. Berman. Heuristics for Scheduling Prameter Sweep Applications in Grid Environments. In Proceedings of the 9th Hrogeneous Computing Workshop, May 2000.
11. R. Wolski, N. Spring, and J. Hayes. "The Network Weather Service: A Distributed Resource Performance Forecasting Service for Metacomputing." Journal of Future Generation Computing Systems, 1999.
12. L. F. Lau, A.L. Ananda, G. Tan, W. F. Wong, "Gucha : Internet-based parallel computing using Java", ICA3PP, Dec. 2000.
13. EunJoung Byun, S. J. Choi, M. S. Baik, C. Y. Park, S. Y. Jung, and C. S. Hwang, "Scheduling Scheme based on Dedication Rate", ISPDC, 2005.
14. J. Schopt and F. Berman, "Stochastic Scheduling", Proceedings of SC99, Nov., 1999.
15. L. R. Rainer, "A Tutorial on Hidden Markov Models and Selected Application", IEEE AS3P Magagine, Jan. 1986.
16. M. W. Mutka, M. Livny, *The Available Capacity of a Privately Owned Workstation Environmont*, Performance Evaluation, vol.12, no.4, pp. 269-284, 1991.
17. G. D. Forney Jr., "The Viterbi Algorithm", IEEE Proceedings of TT, Mar. 1973.

Dynamic Buffer Allocation for Conserving Disk Energy in Clustered Video Servers Which Use Replication

Minseok Song

School of Computer Science and Engineering,
Inha University, Korea
mssong@inha.ac.kr

Abstract. Reducing energy consumption is a key concern in video data centers, in which disk arrays consume a significant portion of the total energy. Disks typically support multiple power modes including a low-power mode in which they use considerably less energy than in any other mode. Therefore, extending the length of time that disks stay in low-power mode is important for energy conservation. We propose a new energy-aware buffer allocation scheme for clustered video servers which use replication. We first present a data retrieval scheme which adaptively retrieves data from the primary and backup copies so as to allow disks to go into low-power mode. We then analyze the relationship between the retrieval period and the buffer size assigned to a cluster, and examine how buffer allocation influences total energy consumption. Based on this, we propose a new buffer partitioning scheme in which the retrieval period for each cluster can be dynamically changed to adjust disk utilization, with the aim of increasing the number of disks that enter low-power mode. Simulations demonstrate that our scheme saves between 22% to 43% of the energy required for conventional video server operation.

1 Introduction

Recent advances in multimedia and network technologies make it feasible to provide multimedia-on-demand (MOD) services for application areas such as digital libraries, education-on-demand, distance learning and movie-on-demand. In a MOD system, video data is housed in a storage server and delivered to clients where requested. Due to the high bandwidth and large storage requirements of video data, video servers are built on disk arrays which may consist of hundreds of disks.

The increasing demands for multimedia data makes the energy consumption of servers a significant problem. *Energy User News* [6] recently suggests that the power requirements of typical service providers are now 150-200 W/ft^2 and will be 200-300 W/ft^2 in the near future. These growing power demands are a serious economic problem for service providers. For instance, a medium-sized 30,000 ft^2 data center requires 15 MW, which currently costs $13 million per year [10,11]. Another problem with such high power consumption is *heat* [4,7]. It has been

E. Sha et al. (Eds.): EUC 2006, LNCS 4096, pp. 193–203, 2006.

shown that running at 15 °C above ambient can double the failure rate of a disk drive [4]. But cooling systems for high heat densities are prohibitively expensive and the cooling system itself adds significantly to the power cost of a data center.

Among the components of a server, storage is one of the biggest energy consumers. A recent report [7] indicates that storage devices consume 27% of the total power. It has also been shown [7] that the energy consumed by a disk array can easily surpass that of the rest of the system, depending on the array size. This problem is exacerbated by the availability of faster disks which need more power. To reduce power consumption, modern disks have multiple power modes [4,10,11]: in *active mode* the platters are spinning and the head is reading or writing data; in *seek mode* the head is seeking; in *idle* mode the disk spins at full speed but there is no disk request; and in *low-power* or *standby* mode the disks stops spinning completely and consumes much less energy than in any other mode. A commonly used method of energy reduction is to transition a disk into low-power mode after the disk has been idle for a while. If a request arrives while a disk in low-power mode, then it immediately transitions to active mode to service the request. But this method of power saving is not readily applicable to video servers because the length of a video usually exceeds 1 hour and the server rarely goes to low-power mode.

We propose a new energy-aware buffer allocation (EBA) scheme for clustered video servers which use replication. We will first present a data retrieval scheme which adaptively retrieves data from the primary and backup copies so as to allow disks to go to low-power mode. We will then analyze the relationship between the retrieval period and the buffer size allocated to each cluster, and examine how buffer allocation affects energy consumption. Finally, we go on to propose a dynamic buffer partitioning algorithm in which the buffer size for each cluster is dynamically changed with the aim of minimizing the total energy consumption.

The rest of this paper is organized as follows. We explain the background to our work in Section 2. We propose a energy-aware buffer allocation scheme in Section 3. We validate the proposed scheme through simulations in Section 4 and conclude the paper in Section 5.

2 Background

2.1 Multimedia-on-Demand Servers

We use round-based scheduling for video data retrieval: time is divided into equal-sized periods, called rounds, and each client is served once in each round. We partition a video object into blocks and distribute them over multiple disks. We will refer to this scheme as *striping*, and a segment denotes the maximum amount of contiguous data that is stored on a single disk. To reduce seek overhead, data retrieved during a round are grouped into a segment, and each segment is stored in a round-robin fashion across the disks [9]. In addition, for scalability, the disk array is generally partitioned into several clusters, each of which independently forms a striping group, and each video is then striped within a cluster [3].

For fault-tolerance, we use a replication technique where the original data is duplicated on separate disks. We refer to the original data as the primary copy and call the duplicated data the backup copy. The server retrieves data from the primary copy when all disks are operational; but in degraded mode when a disk fails, it reads the backup copy. Among various replication schemes, chained declustering (CD) shows the best performance [9]. Suppose that each cluster consists of Q homogeneous disks and that the number of clusters is C. In the CD scheme, a primary copy on D_k^i, the ith disk of cluster k will have a backup copy on $D_k^{(i+1) \bmod Q}$. We place the backup copy on one disk as in the CD scheme. Let us assume that a video V_i is divided into finite numbers of sequential segments ($S_{i,1}$, $S_{i,2}$, ...). We can now see, in Fig. 1, how data placement works using the CD scheme, with videos, V_i stored in cluster 1 and V_j, in cluster 2.

	cluster 1				cluster 2			
	D_1^1	D_1^2	D_1^3	D_1^4	D_2^1	D_2^2	D_2^3	D_2^4
primary copy	$S_{i,1}$ $S_{i,5}$ ...	$S_{i,2}$ $S_{i,6}$ ...	$S_{i,3}$ $S_{i,7}$ ...	$S_{i,4}$ $S_{i,8}$ ...	$S_{j,1}$ $S_{j,5}$ ...	$S_{j,2}$ $S_{j,6}$ ...	$S_{j,3}$ $S_{j,7}$ ...	$S_{j,4}$ $S_{j,8}$ ...
backup copy	$S_{i,4}$ $S_{i,8}$ ...	$S_{i,1}$ $S_{i,5}$ ...	$S_{i,2}$ $S_{i,6}$ ...	$S_{i,3}$ $S_{i,7}$ ...	$S_{j,4}$ $S_{j,8}$ ...	$S_{j,1}$ $S_{j,5}$ ...	$S_{j,2}$ $S_{j,6}$ ...	$S_{j,3}$ $S_{j,7}$ ...

Fig. 1. An example of data placement using the CD scheme in a clustered video server with $Q = 4$ and $C = 2$

2.2 Conventional Power Management in Servers

Even though disk power management in mobile devices has been studied extensively, relatively few attempts have been made to reduce the energy consumption of storage servers. Most existing schemes involve switching disks to low-power mode whenever that is possible without affecting performance. These schemes primarily aim to extend the period during which a disk is in low-power mode [4,7,10,11]. However, because returning from low-power to active mode involves spinning up the disk, the energy saved by putting the disk into low-power mode needs to be greater than the energy needed to spin it up again; we call the shortest idle period which justifies the energy cost of spinning up again the *break-even time*.

As we have already described, saving power by going to low-power mode is hardly relevant to current video servers, due to the long duration of video streams. To emphasize this, let us consider a video that lasts for an hour and playing on a server configuration like that shown in Fig. 1, with a round length of 2 seconds and disks which have a break-even time of 16 seconds. Even if there is only one request for the video, no disk can go to low-power mode because the server needs to access each disk once every 8 seconds.

3 Energy-Aware Buffer Allocation

3.1 Adaptive Data Retrieval

We now present an adaptive data retrieval scheme that permits to video server disks to enter low-power mode by supporting dynamic data retrieval from either the primary copy or the backup copy depending on the disk loads. Let CDU_k^i be the disk bandwidth utilization of D_k^i, the ith disk of cluster k, in the situation that all data is being retrieved from the primary copy ($k = 1, ..., C$ and $i = 1, ..., Q$). We define two states: if $\forall i$, $CDU_k^i \leq 0.5$, then cluster k is in *energy reduction (ER)* state; otherwise, cluster k is in *normal* state. In the normal state, data is retrieved from the primary copy on every disk in the cluster; while in the ER state, data is retrieved only from odd-numbered disks. Since the data on disk D_k^i is replicated as a backup copy on $D_k^{(i+1) \bmod Q}$, the disk loads incurred in reading the primary copies on D_k^{2i} are shifted to the backup copies on disks $D_k^{(2i+1) \bmod Q}$, $(i = 1, ..., \lfloor \frac{1}{2}Q \rfloor)$. D_k^{2i} is able to go into low-power mode because it is not being accessed. Even though $D_k^{(2i+1) \bmod Q}$ now carries the load from D_k^{2i}, its utilization does not exceed 1 because $\forall i$ $CDU_k^i \leq 0.5$. Fig. 2 illustrates how disk loads are shifted at the moment when the server changes from normal to ER states, and we see that D_k^2, D_k^4 and D_k^6 can all go to low-power mode because they are not being accessed.

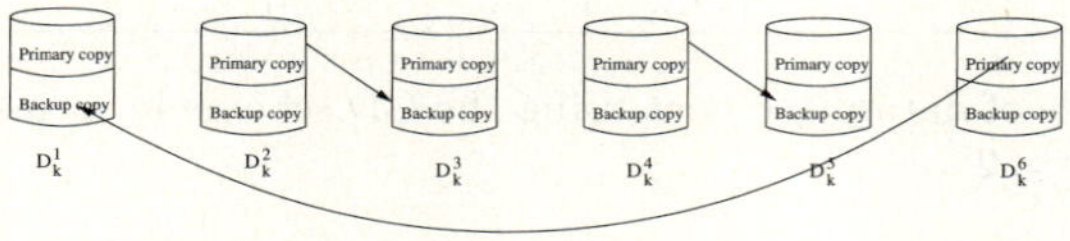

Fig. 2. Example movement of disk loads when changing from normal to ER state

3.2 The Variation of Energy Consumption with the Round Length

The round length plays an important role in determining the requirements for server resources (i.e. disk bandwidth and buffer) [5,9]. Increasing the round length decreases disk bandwidth utilization because retrieving a large amount of data during a single round reduces the impact of disk latency; but this increases buffer requirements because a lot of buffer space is needed to store the data retrieved during a round. Reducing disk bandwidth utilization below 0.5 allows a transition to the ER state, so it is clear that a long round is advantageous in terms of energy conservation.

The main idea of our scheme is to divide the entire buffer space into C partitions, one for each cluster, and to allocate buffer space dynamically with the aim of minimizing the total energy consumption. This approach is motivated by the observation that extending the round length is profitable in terms of energy reduction but increases the buffer overhead. This means that assigning more buffer space to a cluster may allow it to go to the ER state. But this requires judicious buffer partitioning methods, because buffer space is limited and is shared by clusters.

Changing the round length may also incur an additional seek overhead because the data retrieved during a round may not be stored contiguously. To remedy this, we split a data segment $S_{i,m}$ into NS sub-segments $ss^n_{i,m}$ ($n = 1, ..., NS$), where the size of each sub-segment corresponds to the data retrieved during a basic round of length BR. The NS sub-segments are stored contiguously to constitute a segment, and each segment is placed in round-robin fashion, as depicted in Fig. 1. Fig. 3 illustrates the sub-segments that makes up a segment $S_{i,m}$ when $NS = 8$.

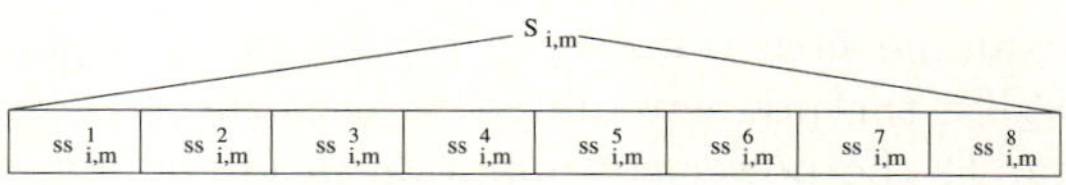

Fig. 3. A segment and its associated sub-segments

We will use dv_j to the jth divisor of NS ($j = 1, ..., ND$), where ND is the number of divisors for NS, and the set of feasible round lengths $FS = \{fr_j | fr_j = BR \times dv_j\}$. We will assume that the elements of FS are sorted in ascending order. For example, if $NS = 6$, then $FS = \{fr_1 = BR, fr_2 = 2BR, fr_3 = 3BR, fr_4 = 6BR\}$. The selection of round lengths other than fr_j is not allowed because this may lead to the occurrence of two seeks for one read.

Let us see how the buffer and disk bandwidth requirements for a video V_i with data rate dr_i (bits/sec) depends on the round length. To ensure the continuous playback of all streams, the total time spent retrieving the streams must not exceed the round duration. The bandwidth utilization for a disk is usually defined as the ratio of the total service time to the round length [1]. We use a typical seek time model in which a constant seek time of T_s and a rotational delay of T_d are required for one read of contiguous data [1]. Retrieving a video stream V_i incurs an overhead of $T_s + T_d$ and a reading time of $fr_j \times \frac{dr_i}{tr}$, where tr is the data transfer rate of the disk. For ease of exposition, we are assuming that disk loads are evenly distributed across disks in the same cluster. If the round length is fr_j, and there are Q disks in a cluster, then servicing a video stream V_i increases the bandwidth utilization for a cluster by $DU_i(j)$, where

$$DU_i(j) = \frac{T_s + T_d + fr_j \times \frac{dr_i}{tr}}{fr_j \times Q}. \tag{1}$$

Let B be the total buffer size. We assume that SCAN scheduling is used to reduce the seek overhead. Since double buffering is used for SCAN scheduling [1], servicing a video stream V_i increases the buffer utilization by $BU_i(j)$, where

$$BU_i(j) = \frac{fr_j \times dr_i}{B}. \tag{2}$$

We now suppose that a client CL^m_i requests a video stream V_i. We partition the clients into C client groups (say CG_1,...,CG_C) where the clients in group

CG_k receive streams from cluster k. We can now determine the disk bandwidth utilization $DS_k(j)$ for cluster k, as follows:

$$DS_k(j) = \sum_{CL_i^m \in CG_k} DU_i(j). \tag{3}$$

We also obtain the buffer utilization $BS_k(j)$ for cluster k as follows:

$$BS_k(j) = \sum_{CL_i^m \in CG_k} BU_i(j). \tag{4}$$

We will now examine how the energy consumption depends on the round length, fr_j. Let P_s be the power required to perform a seek, P_a the power to read or write data, P_i the power consumption in idle mode, and P_l the power consumption in low-power mode. We now formulate the following energy properties for a cluster k:

1. The total seek time during fr_j is $\sum_{CL_i^m \in CG_k} T_s$. Thus, the energy required to perform seeks during fr_j denoted by $E_k^s(j)$, is $\sum_{CL_i^m \in CG_k} T_s \times P_s$.
2. The energy required for reading or writing during fr_j, denoted by $E_k^a(j)$, is $\sum_{CL_i^m \in CG_k}(fr_j \times \frac{dr_i}{tr}) \times P_a$.
3. If no disk activity is taking place or a disk is waiting for a sector to arrive underneath a head, it is considered to be passive, and its energy consumption must be calculated in different ways depending on whether the server is in the normal or the ER state.
   – In the normal state, no disk goes to low-power mode so the energy consumed by passive disks during fr_j, denoted by $E_k^n(j)$, may be expressed as:

$$E_k^n(j) = P_i \times (\underbrace{Q \times fr_j}_{\text{total round length for Q disks}} - \underbrace{\sum_{CL_i^m \in CG_k} (T_s + fr_j \times \frac{dr_i}{tr})}_{\text{read or seek time}}).$$

   – In the ER state, $\lfloor \frac{1}{2}Q \rfloor$ disks go to low-power mode, and the energy consumed by passive disks during fr_j, denoted by $E_k^e(j)$, may be expressed as:

$$E_k^e(j) = \underbrace{P_i \times (\lceil \frac{1}{2}Q \rceil \times fr_j - \sum_{CL_i^m \in CG_k} (T_s + fr_j \times \frac{dr_i}{tr}))}_{\text{energy for disks in idle mode}} + \underbrace{P_l \times \lfloor \frac{1}{2}Q \rfloor}_{\text{energy for disks in low-power mode}}.$$

If $DS_k(j) > 0.5$, cluster k is in the normal state; otherwise, it is in the ER state. Based on the expressions above, we can now how the total energy consumption during BR, denoted by $E_k(j)$, depends on the round length fr_j:

$$E_k(j) = \begin{cases} (E_k^s(j) + E_k^a(j) + E_k^n(j)) \times \frac{BR}{fr_j} & \text{if } DS_k(j) > 0.5, \\ (E_k^s(j) + E_k^a(j) + E_k^e(j)) \times \frac{BR}{fr_j} & \text{if } DS_k(j) \le 0.5. \end{cases}$$

3.3 A Dynamic Buffer Partitioning Algorithm

Let SL_k be a selection parameter indicating that the $SL_k{}^{\text{th}}$element of FS, fr_{SL_k}, is selected as the round length for cluster k. For example, if $FS = \{BR, 2BR, 3BR, 6BR\}$ and $SL_k = 2$, then $2BR$ is selected as the round length. From Equations (1), (2), (3) and (4), we can easily see that higher values of fr_j decrease $DS_k(j)$ but increase $BS_k(j)$. Since decreasing the value of $DS_k(j)$ below 0.5 leads to the cluster entering the ER state, higher values of SL_k may produce the ER state in circumstances under which lower values of SL_k would result in the normal state. Since higher values of SL_k also increases the buffer requirements, SL_k should be selected carefully.

Our goal is to minimize the total energy consumption during a round BR while satisfying the disk bandwidth constraint $\forall\ k$, $DS_k(SL_k) \leq 1$, $(k = 1, ..., C)$ without exceeding the buffer limits $\sum_{k=1}^{C} BS_k(SL_k) \leq 1$. We now define this more formally as the buffer allocation problem.

Definition 1. The Buffer Allocation Problem ($\mathcal{BAP}$)
The $\mathcal{BAP}$ is to find SL_k $(SL_k = 1, ..., ND)$ for every cluster k $(k = 1, ..., C)$, which minimizes $\sum_{k=1}^{C} E_k(SL_k)$ while satisfying $\sum_{k=1}^{C} BS_k(SL_k) \leq 1$ and $\forall\ k$, $DS_k(SL_k) \leq 1$, $(k = 1, ..., C)$.

Note that $\mathcal{BAP}$ is a variant of the multiple-choice knapsack problem, in which each object has a finite set of items, and exactly one item from each object must be selected so as to maximize the total profit. Since the multiple-choice knapsack problem is NP-hard [8], $\mathcal{BAP}$ is also NP-hard, which implies that a heuristic approach will be necessary, especially as the values of SL_k must be determined quickly, so that the admission of new clients in not noticeably delayed. We will now outline our solution.

The server first checks whether changing the round length to fr_j would violate the disk bandwidth constraint, $DS_k(j) \leq 1$. Let SV_k be the smallest value of j that satisfies $DS_k(j) \leq 1$. We start by defining a set of parameters, $DF_k(m)$, $(m = SV_k, ..., ND - 1)$ for cluster k, as follows:

$$DF_k(m) = \frac{E_k(m) - E_k(ND)}{BS_k(ND) - BS_k(m)}.$$

In this formulation the denominator represents the decrease in buffer requirements, while the numerator represents the increase in energy consumption for cluster k when selection parameter SL_k is decreased from ND to m. Based on this, we propose Algorithm 1, which we call a dynamic buffer partitioning algorithm (DBPA).

The array SD is a set of $DF_k(m)$ parameters and initially contains those of every video (line 1). DBPA initializes the value of SL_k to ND (line 4). Next, it chooses the lowest value of $DF_k(l)$ in SD and removes it from SD. If $l < SL_k$ (line 6), the value of SL_k is reduced to l. These steps are then repeated while $IS > B$ and $SD \neq \phi$ (lines 5-12).

Algorithm 1. DBPA (Dynamic Buffer Partitioning Algorithm)

Set of values of $DF_k(m)$: SD;
Temporary variable: IS;
$IS \leftarrow \sum_{i=1}^{NC} BS_k(ND)$;
$SL_k \leftarrow ND$;
while $IS > B$ and $SD \neq \phi$ **do**
  Find the lowest value, $DF_k(l) \in SD$;
  $SD \leftarrow SD - \{DF_k(l)\}$;
  if $l < SL_k$ **then**
    $IS \leftarrow IS - BS_k(SL_k) + BS_k(l)$;
    $SL_k \leftarrow l$;
  end if
end while

4 Experimental Results

To evaluate the effectiveness of our scheme, we performed several simulations. Our server has 160 disks, each of which employs an IBM Ultrastar36Z15 disk [10], with the parameters shown in Table 1. The server is divided into 40 clusters, each of which composed of 4 disks. The arrival of client requests is assumed to follow a Poisson distribution. We also assume that all videos are 90 minutes long, and have the same bit-rate of 4.5MB/sec. The access probability follows a Zipf distribution with $\alpha = 0.271$ [2]. We calculated the round length that achieves a balanced use of disk bandwidth and buffer, as described in [9]; the resulting value of BR, is 0.85 seconds. The cluster location of each movie is chosen randomly. NS is assumed to be 8. To evaluate the efficacy of the EBA scheme, we will compare it with four other methods:

1. PRS: operates like a conventional video server, in that it does not allow data retrieval from the backup copy. The round length used for PRS is BR.
2. ORS: permits data retrieval from the backup copy depending on the disk utilization, but does not allow adaptive round adjustment. The round length used for ORS is BR.
3. RAN: allows adaptive round adjustment, but randomly assigns SL_k to each cluster subject to buffer constraints.
4. UNI: allows adaptive round adjustment but, unlike DBPA, initially assigns SL_k to SV_k. Then it uniformly increases the value of SL_k subject to buffer constraints.

Note that the number of admitted clients is lower for PRS and ORS than for the UNI, RAN and EBA schemes. This is because PRS and ORS do not permit adaptive round adjustment so server resources may not be fully utilized. To reflect this, we assess the total energy consumption per client admitted. Fig. 4 shows how the energy consumption of the four schemes depends on the inter-arrival time of requests, compared to PRS. The EBA scheme exhibits the best performance under all workloads with an energy saving of between 22%

Table 1. Parameter values for our video server

Transfer rate (tr)	55 MB/s
Typical disk seek time (T_s)	7 ms
Typical disk rotation time (T_r)	4 ms
Storage space for each disk	18 GB
Idle power	10.2 W
Standby power (low-power mode)	2.5 W
Active power	13.5 W
Total buffer size (B)	8 GB

to 43% compared to the conventional PRS scheme. This is because the EBA scheme allows up to half of the disks to go to low-power mode when the level of utilization permits. As the inter-arrival time increases, the performance gap increases because EBA gives the disks more opportunities to go to ER state when it is lightly loaded. EBA uses between 19% and 36% less energy than ORS. This is because EBA adjusts the round length, which results in more time in low-power mode. EBA also saves between 4.6% to 18% more energy than RAN, and 1.4% to 17% more than UNI, which implies that buffer allocation has a significant impact on energy consumption.

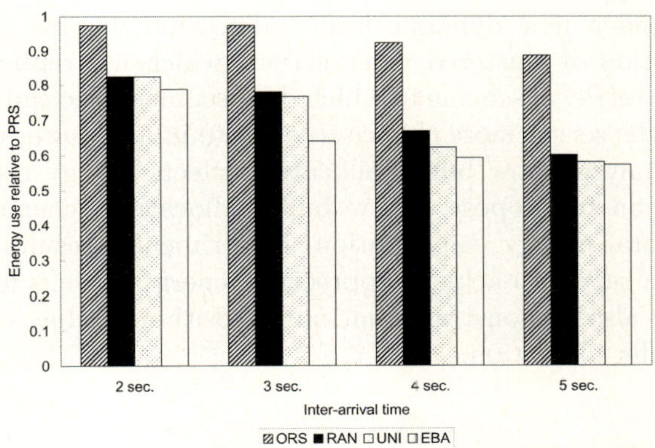

Fig. 4. Energy consumption per client relative to PRS for various inter-arrival times

To evaluate the effectiveness of our heuristic algorithm, let us consider another partitioning algorithm called LB: this method relaxes the integrality constraints on variables (here, SL_k) and then calculates the energy consumption. Its performance corresponds to a lower bound on $\mathcal{BAP}$ [8][1]. Whenever a client requests or closes a video stream, we calculate the lower bound on $\mathcal{BAP}$ using the LB method, and then find the average value of that bound over 24 hours. We also examine the average energy consumption of DBPA, UNI and RAD over 24 hours.

[1] A relaxed version of $\mathcal{BAP}$ can be reduced to a linear multiple-choice knapsack problem for which the optimal solution can be obtained in polynomial time [8].

Table 2 shows the energy consumption relative to the LB method for DBPA, UNI and RAD as a function of inter-arrival time. From the table, we observe that the energy consumption of DBPA is very close to the lower bound. We also see that, compared with the lower bound, RAD consumes between 4.7% to 16.9% more energy, UNI uses between 2.5% to 14.7% more. Note that no algorithm can produce a better result than the lower bound obtained by the LB method, which implies that DBPA is a near-optimal solution to $\mathcal{BAP}$.

Table 2. Energy consumption relative to the LB method

inter-arrival time	DBPA	UNI	RAD
1 second	1.007	1.065	1.065
2 seconds	1.007	1.070	1.077
3 seconds	1.007	1.147	1.169
4 seconds	1.001	1.086	1.113
5 seconds	1.0002	1.025	1.047

5 Conclusions

We have proposed a new dynamic buffer allocation scheme for reducing the energy consumption of clustered video servers which use replication. We have presented a data retrieval scheme in which data segment size can be dynamically selected to give the server more chance to operate in low-power mode. Based on this, we have analyzed how buffer allocation affects energy consumption. We have then gone on to propose a new buffer allocation scheme with the aim of minimizing total energy consumption. Experimental results show that our scheme enables a server to achieve appreciable energy savings under a range of workloads. They also demonstrate that our algorithm produces a practical and near-optimal buffer allocation.

Acknowledgements

This work was supported by INHA UNIVERSITY Research Grant. (INHA-33917).

References

1. E. Chang. *Storage and Retrieval of Compressed Video.* PhD thesis, University of California at Berkeley, 1996.
2. A. Dan, D. Sitaram, and P. Shahabuddin. Dynamic batching policies for an on-demand video server. *ACM/Springer Multimedia Systems Journal*, 4(3):112–121, 1996.

3. L. Golubchik, J. Lui, and M. Papadopouli. A survey of approaches to fault tolerant vod storage servers: Techniques, analysis, and comparison. *Parallel Computing*, 24(1):123–155, January 1998.
4. S. Gurumurthi. *Power Management of Enterprise Storage Systems.* PhD thesis, Pennsylvania State University, 2005.
5. K. Lee and H. Yeom. A dynamic scheduling algorithm for large scale multimedia server. *Information Processing Letters*, 68(5):235–240, March 1998.
6. B. Moore. Taking the data center power and cooling challenge. *Energy User News*, 27, August 2002.
7. E. Pinheiro and R. Bianchini. Energy conservation techniques for disk-array-based servers. In *Proceedings of the ACM/IEEE Conference on Supercomputing*, pages 88–95, June 2004.
8. D. Pisinger. *Algorithms for Knapsack Problems.* PhD thesis, University of Copenhagen, 1995.
9. M. Song and H. Shin. Replication and retrieval strategies for resource-effective admission control in multi-resolution video servers. *Multimedia Tools and Applications Journal*, 28(3):89–114, March 2006.
10. Q. Zhu, Z. Chen, L. Tan, Y. Zhou, K. Keeton, and J. Wilkes. Hibernator: helping disk arrays sleep through the winter. *ACM Operating Systems Review*, 39(5):177–190, 2005.
11. Q. Zhu and Y. Zhou. Power aware storage cache management. *IEEE Transactions on Computers*, 54(5):587–602, 2005.

LBN: Load-Balancing Network for Data Gathering Wireless Sensor Networks

Wenlu Yang[1,2], Chongqing Zhang[2], and Minglu Li[2]

[1] Department of Electronic Engineering,
Shanghai Maritime University, Shanghai, China
[2] Department of Computer Science and Engineering,
Shanghai Jiaotong University, Shanghai, China
wenluyang@online.sh.cn, zhangchongqing@sjtu.edu.cn

Abstract. Hotspots of energy consumption and network congestions can be caused by load imbalance among sensor nodes in wireless sensor networks. This may lead to loss of data packets and premature death of sensor nodes which may cause the premature death of entire network. Load-balancing techniques can prolong the lifetime of sensor networks and avoid the occurrence of packet congestions. This paper proposes an approach that using load-balancing network to balancing the load in a static data gathering wireless sensor network. Experiments show the effectiveness of our approach.

1 Introduction

Many wireless sensor networks are deployed for monitoring applications. Examples of such kind of applications include monitoring the temperature of a vineyard, monitoring the pH value of a farmland's soil [1], etc. In such applications, sensor nodes are required to sense the monitored objects periodically and send the sensed data to the base station. The base station serves as the data aggregation point or the data sink of the WSN. Such wireless sensor networks are characterized by many-to-one traffic patterns [2] and called data gathering wireless sensor networks [8].

A Typical WSN may consist of a large number of sensor nodes. As the size of a WSN scales up, load unevenness may happen. Load unevenness may cause network congestion and even loss of data packet. What is more, some nodes with heavy load burden may run out of their energy rapidly and make the network become disconnected. By averaging the energy consumption of sensor nodes, load balancing can prolong the expected lifetime of the WSN. In addition, load balancing is also useful for avoiding congestion in network, thereby reducing wireless collisions [3].

Previous work has researched load balancing issue in WSNs. For example, R. C. Shah et al in [3] proposed an energy-aware routing multiple paths routing mechanism to balancing the load of sensor nodes. However, the WSN model they used is not many-to-one model. In [4], M. Perillo et al tried to solve unbalanced load distribution by transmission range optimization technique. Yet in their WSN model all sensor nodes can communication with the base station directly.

E. Sha et al. (Eds.): EUC 2006, LNCS 4096, pp. 204 – 213, 2006.

Constructing a WSN into a load-balancing tree is a way to solve load unevenness problem in WSNs for monitoring applications. P. H. Hsiao et al in [5] designed a load-balancing routing algorithm which achieves the balancing goal by constructing top balancing trees for wireless access networks. Because the flow in a WSN is totally different from the flow in a wireless access network, their work cannot be applied to wireless sensor networks. And their algorithm is designed for networks with mesh topology which is not common in most applications. In [6], H. Dai et al designed a node-centric algorithm that constructs a load-balancing tree fro WSNs. However, their algorithm is a centralized algorithm and is only applied to WSNs with grid topology.

Load-balance cannot be achieved by constructing only one static load-balancing tree in many cases. The can be illustrated by a simple example presented in Fig. 1. As for such a WSN, two load-balancing trees, as shown by Fig. 1 (a) and Fig. 1 (b) respectively, can be constructed. Yet none of them is a load-balancing tree. To solve such a problem, in Refs [7], H. Yang et al propose DQEB (Dynamic Query-tree Energy Balancing) protocol to dynamically adjust the tree structure to balance energy consumption for cluster-based WSNs. By their approach, a WSN will change its tree structure when working. As a result, their approach is energy-consumed because of the readjustment of the tree structure.

In this paper, we try to solve the load-balancing problem by constructing a load-balancing supply and demand network for a WSN. The routing structure that our algorithm builds is not a tree, but a network. The idea of our approach comes from the supply and demand network of commodity. In our approach a WSN is regarded as a market composed of a buyer and many producers and conveyancers. The base station which acts as the data collector is the only buyer and nodes are data producers and conveyancers. The buyer buys data from all the data producers. We propose a distributed algorithm to organize these buyer and conveyancers into a load-balanced network.

The remainder of this paper is organized as follows. In Section 2, WSN model and an overview of the approach are presented. In Section 3, we present the algorithm. In Section 4, the approach is evaluated and compared with several other load-balancing approaches. Finally, we conclude and give directions for future work in Section 5.

2 Network Model and Overview of LBN

2.1 Wireless Sensor Network Model

The WSN model used in this paper is based on following assumptions:

1) A WSN is composed of a base station and a large number of sensor nodes that are uniformly scattered on a plane. Each node is assigned a unique ID.

2) Sensor nodes are energy-constrained; while the base station is not energy-constrained.

3) The communication range of sensor nodes is fixed. After being deployed, all the base station and sensor nodes remain stationary. The nodes may organize into a flat WSN or a hierarchical WSN, for example, a cluster-based WSN.

4) A sensor node sense the monitored objects periodically every a fixed interval, and this is called a round. In each round a data packet is generated by a node and sent to the base station [8].

2.2 Overview of LBN

The main idea of LBN comes from the market mechanism, that is, the supply and demand network of commodity. A WSN can be regarded as a market composed of a buyer and many producers and conveyancers. In our approach, the measurement data is commodity. The base station which acts as the data collector is the only buyer and the nodes are data producers and conveyancers. The buyer buys data from all the data producers. All nodes are classified into different levels according to the least hop count that a node takes to send the data generated by this node to the base station.

The base station can only communicate directly with its direct neighbors. In this paper, the nodes that can communicate with the base station are called critical nodes. Correspondingly, the nodes that cannot communicate with the base station are called non-critical nodes. In a WSN, the critical nodes are most heavily burdened because these nodes need to relay data packets generated by other nodes to the base station. The base station can only make deals with the critical node and it pays same amount of money to the critical nodes. After that, the neighbors of the base station use the money it receives from the base station to buy data from their sons. Using proper strategy, we can ensure that the sons are assigned nearly same amount of money. In succession, a node uses the money it receives from its topper layer nodes to buy data from its lower layer nodes. In such a way, all nodes at the same level cost nearly identical amount of money. And as a result, the loads of the nodes at the same level are nearly identical. By making deals, the energy cost of the nodes can be balanced.

Although using deals to balance energy consumption as discussed above is applicable, exchanging deals information costs energy. To save energy, it is appropriate for the nodes to form fixed bargaining relations. We use a balanced bargaining network to meet this end. A bargaining tree constructed by our approach has following features:

1. The loads of nodes at the same level are nearly identical.
2. Loads of critical nodes are biggest, which means that the nodes that can communicate with the base station directly have the heaviest load and will deplete their energy earlier than other nodes.

A load-balancing network is constructed from the base station of a WSN. As described by Fig. 1 (a), each node is assigned one product and the base station is assigned the money that amounts to the number of the nodes firstly. To do this, the base station needs to know the number of the sensor nodes in the WSN. Then as Fig. 1 (b) describes, the base station sends every critical node a money message containing a number equal to $\lfloor (n / c_n) \rfloor$ or $\lceil (n / c_n) \rceil$, where n is the number of sensor nodes in the WSN and c_n is the number of neighbors of the base station. $\lfloor x \rfloor$ stands for the biggest integer of the integers that are smaller than or equal to the real number x, and $\lceil x \rceil$ stands for the smallest integer of the integers that are bigger than or equal to x. The number contained in the message represents the money that the base station used to buy data from it children. After a neighbor of the base station receives the message, if its product number is 1, then it deletes 1 from the number and resends the money to its children using certain strategy. In the end, all the nodes are organized into a load-balancing network which is depicted by Fig. 1 (c).

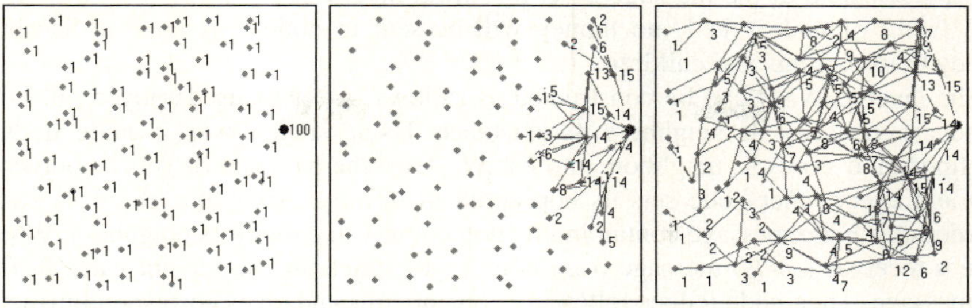

(a) (b) (c)

Fig. 1. Constructing Load-balancing Network from the Base station

3 Algorithm

Two steps are involved in constructing a flat WSN into a load-balancing network. The first step is initializing the WSN so as to organize the nodes into a layered network. Based on the layered network constructed in the first step, the second step uses a distributed algorithm to organize the nodes into a load-balancing network. Then the nodes begin to work and send the data packets to the base station using the load-balancing network constructed by the algorithm.

3.1 Initialization

A WSN can be viewed as a graph $G = (V, E, g)$ in which each member of set $V \setminus \{g\}$ stands for a sensor node, an edge (u, v) is included in E if sensor nodes u and v can communicate with each other directly, and node $g \in V$ represents the base station. First, we need to organize the WSN into a layered WSN according to the least hop counts of sensor nodes to the base station. Each node maintains several lists: the list of its parent nodes *PL*, the list of its children nodes *CL*, the list of its sibling nodes *SL*, and the list of its neighbor nodes *NL*.

For a node u, its four lists can be defined as:
$v \in PL$, if $v \in V$ and $(u, v) \in E$ and $h_u = h_v + 1$;
$v \in CL$, if $v \in V$ and $(u, v) \in E$ and $h_u = h_v - 1$;
$v \in SL$, if $v \in V$ and $(u, v) \in E$ and $h_u = h_v$;
$v \in NL$, if $v \in V$ and $(u, v) \in E$;

where v is a neighbor node of node u; h_u and h_v are the hop count of node u and v respectively. A member of these lists is a structure defined as: *<nodeID*, *moneyTo*, *moneyFrom*, *productTo*, *productFrom*, *isFull>*, where *nodeID* is the ID of the member node in the list; *moneyTo* denotes the amount of money that node u sends to node v; *moneyFrom* denotes the amount of money that node u receives from node v; *productTo* denotes the amount of product that node u sends to node v; *productFrom* denotes the amount of product that node u receives from node v; *isFull* denotes if the money of node v exceeds the upper bound. If node u receives a money message that the *isReturn* field of the message is set to 1 from node *v*, then *isFull* is set to 1. If the field *isFull* of node *v* is 1, no money will be sent to node *v* as node u distributes money to its siblings and children.

The layered WSN can be constructed as follows. After being deployed, all nodes broadcast to notify its neighbors its existence. Using such a way, a node finds its neighbors and stores its neighbors into list *NL*. Then the base station sets its hop count to 0 and every other node sets its hop count to infinity. After that, the base station broadcasts a *hello* message containing its hop count value to all its neighbors. When a node *u* receives a *hello* message from node *v*, it extracts the hop count value h_v from the message. Then node *u* does following comparisons and takes corresponding action based on the comparison results:

1. If $h_v = h_u$, node *u* adds *v* into *SL*.
2. If $h_v = h_u + 1$, node *u* adds *v* into *CL*.
3. If $h_v > h_u - 1$, node *u* does nothing.
4. If $h_v = h_u - 1$, node *u* adds node *v* into *PL*.
5. If $h_v < h_u - 1$, node *u* deletes all the nodes from *PL* and adds node *v* into *PL*. Then, node *u* sets $h_u = h_v + 1$, and re-broadcasts the hello message with hop count value h_u to its neighbors.

By broadcasting *hello* messages and comparing h with hu step by step, the layered network can be constructed. An example of such a layered network is shown in Fig. 2. Parent-children relations are displayed in Fig. 2 (a); Sibling relations are exhibited by Fig. 2 (a); and Fig. 2 (c) is the combination of Fig. 2 (a) and Fig. 2 (b). It can easily be seen that *PL* list of the base station is empty. There is only one member, the base station, in the *PL* list of a critical node. And the *CL* list of a leaf node is empty.

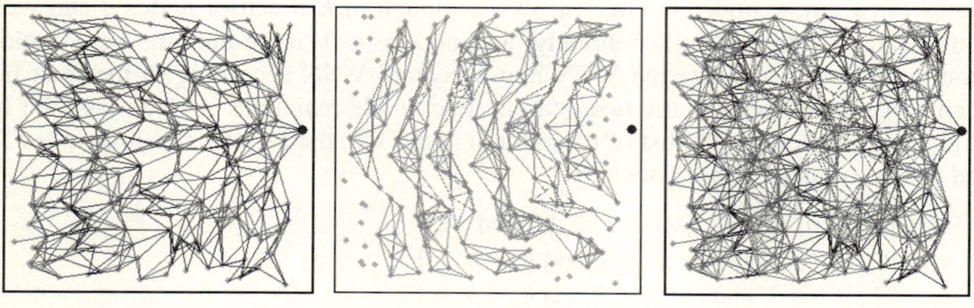

(a) (b) (c)

Fig. 2. The Use of Siblings

3.2 Constructing an LBN

Five types of message, *hello*, *count*, *register*, *money* and *deal*, are used to build a load-balancing network. A message is defined as: <msgType, senderID, value, upperBound, isReturn>, where msgType can be *mtHello*, *mtCount*, *mtRegister*, *mtMoney*, or *mtDeal*; *senderID* is the source node of the message; *value* refers to the hop count if *msgType* is *mtHello*, the mount of money if *msgType* is *mtMoney* and the amount of product if *msgType* is *mtDeal*; *upperBound* is used to avoid the load of a non-critical node exceeding the load of any critical nodes. *isReturn* indicates whether or not a money message is returned back.

After the construction of the layered WSN, then the base station sends a *money* message containing the amount of money to each of the critical nodes. Before doing this, the base station needs to know how many nodes are there in the WSN. To do this, the base station floods a *count* message to all the nodes. A node sets one variable *product* to 1 and two variable *moneyAccept* and *moneyTotal* to be 0, and then it replies with a *register* message to the base station to report its existence. After counting the number of the *register* it receives, the base station can know the total number of sensor nodes in the WSN.

After the base station gets the number of nodes in the WSN, it sends a message containing the amount of money to each of its children. The amount is calculated as follows: let n be the number of nodes in the WSN; let c_n be the number of critical nodes. If n can be divided by c_n exactly, then $m_n = n / c_n$; otherwise the base station send some nodes with $m_n = \lfloor (n / c_n) \rfloor$, and other nodes with $\lceil (n / c_n) \rceil$ randomly. $\lfloor x \rfloor$ stands for the biggest integer that is smaller than x, and $\lceil x \rceil$ stands for the smallest integer that is bigger than x.

A node u has two list, *moneyList* and *dealList*. List *moneyList* is used to manage the money node u receives. List *dealList* is used manage the deals node u makes or the deal message it receives. Members of these two lists have same structure as: <*value*, *nodeID*>, where *value* refers to the amount of *money* or *product*; nodeID refers to the node that node u receives money from or sends deals to.

```
if (v in PL) or ((v in SL) and (msg->isReturn != 1) {
    if msg->upperBound <= moneyTotal
       return the money back to v;
    if (msg->upperBound - moneyTotal - msg->value)<0 {
            return partial money back to v;
            add a money record into money list;
    }
else
            add a money record into money list;
    if product = 1 {
            make a deal and send deal message to v;
            add a money record into deal list;
    }
}
if (v in CL) or ((v in SL) and (msg->isReturn == 1)
    mark the link as full;
if (moneyAccept >0) and (ifFull field of some child or sibling = 0) then {
    Select a node whose isFull is 0 randomly and send pmsg to it;
}
else { // return money back to v
    return money to v;
    delete corresponding record from money list;
}
```

Fig. 3. Processing Algorithm for a Money Message

After a node *u* receives a money message from node *v*, node *u* does following actions as shown in Fig. 3. Compared to the handling of a *money* message, the handling of a *deal* message is very easy. The processing algorithm for a *deal* message is shown in Fig. 4.

```
if (node u is not the base station) {
niv->productFrom = niv->productFrom + 1;
Find the oldest money record;
nix->productTo = nix->productTo + 1;
}
else
niv->productFrom = niv->productFrom + 1;
```

Fig. 4. Processing Algorithm for a Deal Message

After the completion of the algorithm, each node has a deal list. The node collates the deal list and produces a list in which each member is a probability associated with a parent. When a node receives a data packet as it is working, it use this probability list to judge to which parent it should send the data packet.

4 Experimental Results

In this section we will show through simulations that LBN can prolong the lifetime of a WSN and avoid traffic congestion in the WSN. Our simulations do not consider the MAC or physical layer. The sensors are randomly deployed on regions with different size and shape. For each instance of deployment, we calculate the lifetime for the static network. The result is averaged over 50 instances for each set of network size and density. All simulations are implemented using a standalone VC++ program.

4.1 WSN Model

As Fig. 5 (a), one of the simulation scenes, shows, a WSN used in the experiments consists of 200 sensor nodes scattered on a 300m×300m square area. All nodes have same transmission ranges of 50 meters. The initial energy of a sensor node is 50 joules, and the energy of the base station is infinite. The WSN is deployed to monitor the environment in the sensing field. The sensor nodes are required to send their sensing data to the base station every 20 seconds. The size of a data packet is 10 bytes. In our simulations, the energy needed for a sensor node to sense, receive and transmit a packet is 2×10-5 joule, 2×10-5 joule and 1×10-4 joule respectively. These values of power consumption are calculated based on information presented in [12]. As Fig. 5 (b) and (c) show, the base station is located at the border of the simulation area or in the middle of the monitoring field. These two figures give two load-balancing networks constructed by LBN. In the experiments, we use these two kinds of WSNs that have different base station positions to compare the performances of different load-balancing approaches.

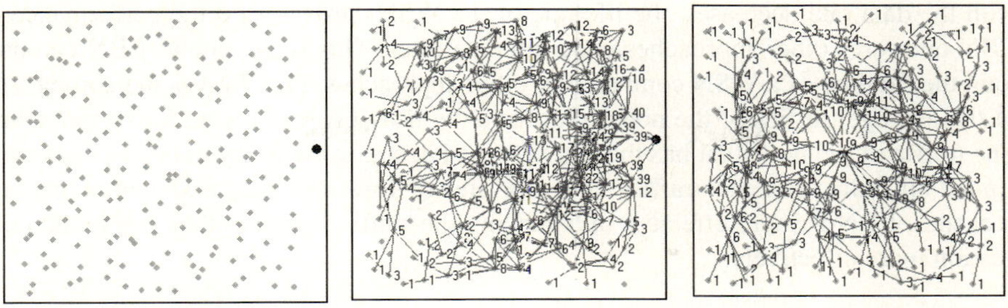

(a) (b) (c)

Fig. 5. Load-balancing Network for Hierarchichal WSNs

4.2 Approaches Compared and Performance Metrics

Four approaches are compared in the experiment: 1) the most energy saving approach which is denoted as MESA (stands for most energy saving approach). In MESA every node sends it data packets to the base station using a most energy saving route; 2) the approach using static load-balancing trees, and this approach is denoted as SLBT (stands for static load-balancing tree); 3) the approach using dynamic load-balancing tree to balance loads, and this approach is denoted as DLBT (stands for dynamic load-balancing tree); 4) the forth approach is our approach which is denoted as LBN.

Two metrics, the lifetime of WSNs and the average traffic of the node that has the heaviest load, are used to evaluate the performances of different approaches. The lifetime of a WSN is defined as the time span from the moment the WSN begins to work to the moment that the first sensor node runs out of its energy. The average traffic of the node that has the maximum load is used to reflect the congestion degree of the traffic flows in the network. The higher the value is, the severer is the congestion degree.

4.3 Performance Results

In this section, the comparison results of the performances of different approaches are presented. Two kinds of WSNs, WSNs that the base stations locate at the border of the monitoring area and WSNs that the base stations locate at the center of the monitoring area, are used in the experiments. 20 WSNs are used for each kind of WSNs. Four data sensing rates, 10 seconds, 20 seconds, 30 seconds and 40 seconds are used, that is to say, a node may generate and send a data packet to the base station every 10, 20, 30 or 40 seconds. For each data rata, the network lifetime and the average traffic of the node that has the maximum load is figured out. For the WSNs under same data rate, we average the network lifetimes and average traffics of the node that has the maximum load, compare these averages and present comparison results in the following figures.

Based on the WSNs that the base station locates at the border of the monitoring area, Fig. 6 compares the network lifetime of the four approaches. From the figure, with the data rate decreases, the lifetime of the WSNs grows. And the performance of LBN outscores other approaches under all data rates. This figure shows LBN can prolong the lifetime of a WSN compared to other approaches. Fig. 7 gives the comparison of the average traffics of the nodes that have the heaviest load of the four approaches. The traffic of the node that has the heaviest load decreases with the data rate decreases. Under all data rates the traffics of LBN are all lowest. Compared with other approaches, LBN is more effective in balancing the traffic load and thus can avoid congestion more effectively.

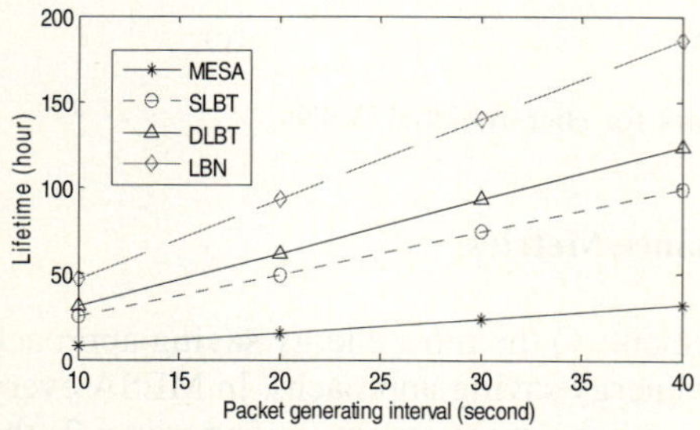

Fig. 6. Lifetime Comparison of All Approaches

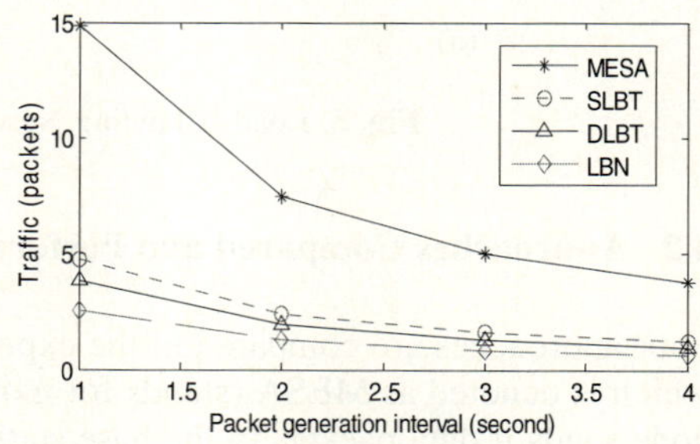

Fig. 7. Traffic Comparison of All Approaches

Base on the WSNs that the base station lies at the center of the monitoring area, Fig. 8 compares the network lifetime of the four approaches. From the figure, with the data rate decreases, the lifetime of the WSNs grows. And the performance of LBN outscores other approaches under all data rates. This figure shows LBN can prolong the lifetime of a WSN compared to other approaches. Fig. 9 gives the comparison of the average traffics of the nodes that have the heaviest load of the four approaches. The traffic of the node that has the heaviest load decreases with the data rate decreases. Under all data rates the traffics of LBN are all lowest. Compared with other approaches, LBN is more effective in balancing the traffic load and thus can avoid congestion more effectively.

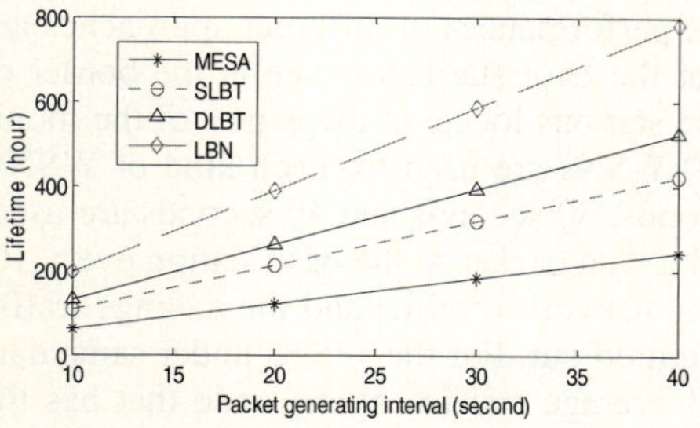

Fig. 8. Lifetime Comparison of All Approaches

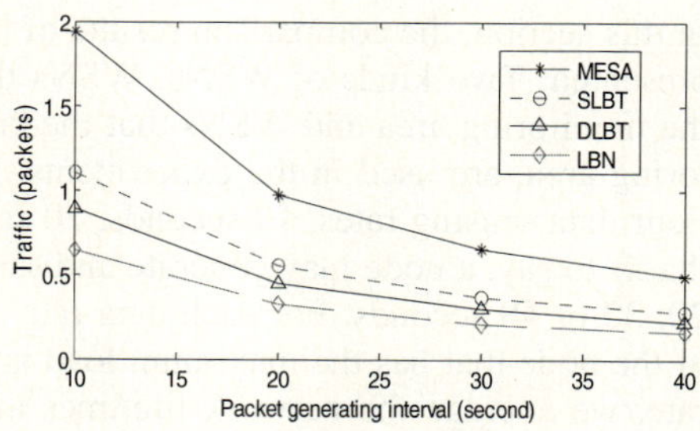

Fig. 9. Traffic Comparison of All Approaches

5 Conclusion and Future Work

Hotspots of energy consumption and network congestions can be caused by load imbalance among sensor nodes in wireless sensor networks. This will lead to loss of data packets and premature death of sensor nodes which may cause the premature death of entire network. Load-balancing techniques can prolong the lifetime of sensor networks and avoid the occurrence of packet congestions. This paper proposes an approach that using load-balancing network to balancing the load in a static data gathering wireless sensor network. Experiments show the effectiveness of our approach. The approach can be adjusted to meet the need of WSNs in which the transmission range of nodes is adjustable.

References

[1] F. Akyildiz, W. Su, Y. Sankarasubramaniam, E. Cayirci. “A survey on sensor networks. Computer Networks”, Computer Networks, 38(4): 393-422, March 2002.

[2] S. Tilak, N. B. Abu-Ghazaleh, and W. Heinzelman. “A taxonomy of sensor network communication models”. Mobile Computing and Communication Review, 6:28--36, 2002.

[3] R. C. Shah, J. M. Rabaey. “Energy Aware Routing for Low Energy Ad Hoc Sensor Networks”. IEEE WCNC 2002.

[4] M. Perillo, Zhao Cheng, and W. Heinzelman. “On the Problem of Unbalanced Load Distribution in Wireless Sensor Networks”. Globecom 2004.

[5] P. H. Hsiao, A. Hwang, H. T. Kung, and D. Vlah. “Load-Balancing Routing for Wireless Access Networks”. IEEE Infocom 2001.

[6] H. Dai and R. Han. “A Node-Centric Load Balancing Algorithm for Wireless Sensor Networks”, IEEE GlobeCom 2003.

[7] H. Yang, F. Ye and B. Sikdar. “References A Dynamic Query-tree Energy Balancing Protocol for Sensor Networks”, IEEE WCNC 2004.

[8] S. Lindsey, C. Raghavendra, and K. Sivalingam, “Data Gathering in Sensor Networks using the Energy*Delay Metric”. IEEE Transactions on Parallel and Distributive Systems, special issue on Mobile Computing, pp. 924-935, April 2002.

[9] F. Zhao, L. Guibas. “Wireless Sensor Networks : An Information Processing Approach”. Boston: Elsevier-Morgan Kaufmann; 2004.

[10] O. Younis and S. Fahmy, "HEED: A Hybrid, Energy-Efficient, Distributed Clustering Approach for Ad-hoc Sensor Networks". IEEE Transactions on Mobile Computing, volume 3, issue 4, pp. 366-379, Oct-Dec 2004.

[11] W.R. Heinzelman, A. Chandrakasan, H. Balakrishnan. “Energy-efficient communication protocol for wireless microsensor networks”. IEEE HICSS. Jan, 2000.

[12] J. Hill, R. Szewczyk, A. Woo, S. Hollar, D. Culler, K. Pister. “System architecture directions for networked sensors”. ACM ASPLOS-IX 2000.

Multi-user Diversity for IEEE 802.11 Infrastructure Wireless LAN

Sung Won Kim

School of Electrical Engineering and Computer Science, Yeungnam University, Gyeongsangbuk-do, 712-749, Korea
ksw@ieee.org

Abstract. To realize high data rate wireless communication systems, much attention is being payed to multi-user diversity due to large bandwidth availability. Multi-user diversity based opportunistic scheduling is a modern view communication over fading wireless channels, whereby, unlike rate adaptation based schemes, channel variations are exploited rather than mitigated. This paper proposes a multi-user diversity scheme for IEEE 802.11 infrastructure wireless LAN to enhance the throughput. Numerical investigations show the throughput superiority of the scheme over IEEE 802.11 standard and other method.

1 Introduction

The transmission medium used by wireless data networks is inherently time-varying due to e.g. multipath propagation, user mobility, and non-stationary clutter. Also, the wireless resource is scarce and expensive, requiring optimized usage to maximize the throughput (spectral efficiency). Achieving overall throughput maximization requires scheduler to momentarily postpone scheduling packets to a node with poor link quality until its link hits near its peak. Opportunistic scheduling, used to extract multi-user diversity gain, was first proposed in [1] and then extended to many wireless communication systems [2][3]. An opportunistic scheduling algorithm that exploits the inherent multi-user diversity has been implemented as the standard algorithm in the third-generation cellular system IS-856 [4] (also known as high data rate, HDR). To enable the opportunistic multi-user communications, timely channel information of each link is required for an effective scheduling. Feedback of predicted link quality of each active node that is required in opportunistic scheduling is usually integrated into wireless systems. Usually, each receiver measures the received signal-to-noise ratio (SNR) on the channel and then feeds it back to the transmitter.

When it comes down to wireless local area networks (WLANs), it is difficult to utilize the multi-user diversity. The access point (AP) cannot track the channel fluctuations of each link because of the single shared medium and the distributed Carrier Sense Multiple Access with Collision Avoidance (CSMA/CA) Medium Access Control (MAC) protocol. Wang et al. [5] presented the opportunistic packet scheduling method for WLANs. The key mechanism of the method is

E. Sha et al. (Eds.): EUC 2006, LNCS 4096, pp. 214–223, 2006.

the use of multicast RTS (Request-To-Send) and priority-based CTS (Clear-To-Send) to probe the channel status information. Since their method requires the modification of RTS and CTS in the standard, the scheme cannot be directly applied into widely deployed IEEE 802.11 typed WLANs.

On the other hand, this form of the multi-user wireless system produces asymmetric traffic loads where most of the traffic loads converge into APs. For example, Internet access or mobile computing uses transmission control protocol (TCP) or user datagram protocol (UDP) in which the offered traffic load is strongly biased toward the downlink (from AP to nodes) against the uplink (from nodes to AP) or the direct link (from nodes to nodes). Thus, these traffic flows for the downlink are completely blocked due to the CSMA/CA MAC protocol in distributed environments.

To alleviate this downlink bottleneck problem, some resource allocation algorithms between the uplink and the downlink are proposed in [6]–[8]. In [6], the authors observe a significant unfairness between the uplink and the downlink flows when DCF is employed in a WLAN. The reason is that in a WLAN with N nodes there are N uplink CSMA/CA instances contending with only one downlink CSMA/CA instance. Thus, when the downlink has much more offered traffic load than that of the uplink, the downlink becomes bottleneck of the system capacity and much more APs should be deployed to accommodate such nodes. The TCP fairness issue between the uplink and the downlink in WLANs has been studied in [7]. The authors are interested in a solution that results in uplink and downlink TCP flows having an equal share of the wireless bandwidth. Because this solution operates on the TCP layer, it is not effective when there exist traffic flows other than TCP. In [8][9], we proposed FAIR that is a dynamic resource allocation method between the uplink and the downlink. FAIR estimates the utilization ratio between the uplink and the downlink to determine the AP access method. FAIR does not consider the throughput improvement by using the multi-user diversity. Moreover, the parameter estimation method proposed in FAIR is not stable.

To mitigate the bottleneck problem in the downlink and to increase the throughput in WLANs, we propose a MAC protocol that exploits the multi-user diversity. The remainder of this paper is organized as follows. The next section presents system model. Section 3 describes the proposed method. In Section 4, we investigate the enhancement of the proposed method with some numerical results. Finally, the paper is concluded in Section 5.

2 System Model

2.1 Infrastructure WLAN

MAC protocol in the IEEE 802.11 standard [10] consists of two coordination functions: mandatory Distributed Coordination Function (DCF) and optional Point Coordination Function (PCF). In DCF, a set of wireless nodes communicates with each other using a contention-based channel access method, CSMA/CA. CSMA/CA is known for its inherent fairness between nodes and robustness. It is quite effective in supporting symmetric traffic loads in ad hoc networks where the traffic loads between nodes are similar.

DCF achieves automatic medium sharing between compatible nodes through the use of CSMA/CA. Before initiating a transmission, a node senses the channel to determine whether or not another node is transmitting. If the medium is sensed idle for a specified time interval, called the distributed interframe space (DIFS), the node is allowed to transmit. If the medium is sensed busy, the transmission is deferred until the ongoing transmission terminates.

If two or more nodes find that the channel is idle at the same time, a collision occurs. In order to reduce the probability of such collisions, a node has to perform a backoff procedure before starting a transmission. The duration of this backoff is determined by the Contention Window (CW) size which is initially set to CW_{min}. The CW value is used to randomly choose the number of slot times in the range of $[0, CW - 1]$, which is used for backoff duration. In case of an unsuccessful transmission, the CW value is updated to $CW \times 2$ while it does not exceed CW_{max}. This will guarantee that in case of a collision, the probability of another collision at the time of next transmission attempt is further decreased.

A transmitter and receiver pair exchanges short RTS and CTS control packets prior to the actual data transmission to avoid the collision of data packets. An acknowledgement (ACK) packet will be sent by the receiver upon successful reception of a data packet. It is only after receiving an ACK packet correctly that the transmitter assumes successful delivery of the corresponding data packet. Short InterFrame Space (SIFS), which is smaller than DIFS, is a time interval between RTS, CTS, data packet, and ACK. Using this small gap between transmissions within the packet exchange sequence prevents other nodes from attempting to use the medium. As a consequence, it gives priority to completion of the ongoing packet exchange sequence.

Fig. 1 illustrates the system model of an infrastructure WLAN. The AP plays the important role for relaying the traffic between the mobile nodes (wireless

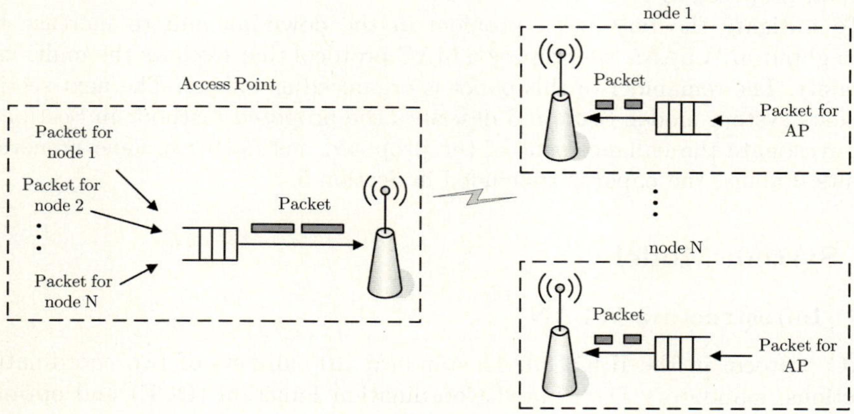

Fig. 1. System model for an infrastructure WLAN

stations) and the wired network which results in asymmetric traffic load between the AP and single mobile node in the infrastructure WLANs. Although PCF is designed for infrastructure networks, the problem is that currently most of the WLAN cards do not support the PCF mode. With DCF mode, the CSMA/CA mechanism makes the AP and mobile nodes have the same priority to access the medium. This leads to the significant unfair WLAN bandwidth distribution between uplink and downlink flows.

2.2 Rate Adaptation

The auto-rate fallback (ARF) protocol for IEEE 802.11 has been presented in [11]. Specifically, if the ACKs for two consecutive data packets are not received by the sender, the sender reduces the transmission rate to the next lower data rate and starts a timer. When the timer expires or ten consecutive ACKs are received, the transmission rate is raised to the next higher data rate and the timer is canceled. However, if an ACK is not received for the immediately next data packet, the rate is lowered again and the timer is restarted. The ARF protocol is simple and easy to incorporate into the IEEE 802.11. However, as pointed out in [12], it is purely heuristic and cannot react quickly when the wireless channel conditions fluctuate.

In the above algorithm, the rate adaptation is performed at the sender. However, it is the receiver that can perceive the channel quality, and thus determine the transmission rate more precisely. Observing this, the authors in [13] have presented a receiver-based auto-rate (RBAR) protocol assuming that the RTS/CTS mechanism is there. The basic idea of RBAR is as follows. First, the receiver estimates the wireless channel quality using a sample of the SNR of the received RTS, then selects an appropriate transmission rate for the data packet, and piggybacks the chosen rate in the responding CTS packet. Then, the sender transmits the data packet at the rate advertised by the CTS. The simulation results in [13] show that the RBAR protocol can adapt to the channel conditions more quickly and in a more precise manner than does the ARF protocol, and thus it improves the performance greatly.

3 Proposed MAC Protocol

3.1 Downlink Channel Access

Each node can directly communicate only with the AP (uplink or downlink), since we focus on AP-coordinated infrastructure WLANs. The AP manages the downlink packet queues for each node as shown in Fig. 1. We propose that the AP determines the downlink channel access method according to the operation mode, that is *normal mode* and *opportunistic mode*. In normal mode, nodes and AP use the DCF mechanism with RTS/CTS handshaking, where each node should wait for DIFS and backoff window time after previous ACK packet.

Let N be the number of active nodes except AP. Then the probability that the successful packet transmission is performed by node n is given as

$$P_n = \frac{1}{N+1}, \quad \text{for } n = 1, 2, ..N. \tag{1}$$

The same probability applies to the AP. Let Γ be the maximum available system throughput. Then, the system throughput allocated to the downlink, Γ_d, and the uplink, Γ_u, are given as

$$\Gamma_d = \Gamma \times P_n = \Gamma \frac{1}{N+1}, \tag{2}$$

$$\Gamma_u = \Gamma \times \sum_{n=1}^{N} P_n = \Gamma \frac{N}{N+1}, \tag{3}$$

where the packet size is assumed to be the same. The ratio between the uplink throughput and the downlink throughput is given as

$$\frac{\Gamma_d}{\Gamma_u} = \left(\frac{\Gamma}{N+1}\right) / \left(\frac{\Gamma N}{N+1}\right) = \frac{1}{N}. \tag{4}$$

Thus, in DCF, the allocated downlink throughput decreases as the number of nodes increases because the system throughput is shared equally between nodes. This method is not efficient when the traffic load is asymmetric between the uplink and the downlink such as TCP and UDP. Even in the case of symmetric traffic load, the downlink traffic in DCF gets less throughput than that of the uplink and this causes the increased delay of the downlink traffic. To solve this problem, the opportunistic mode is used in the AP.

In the opportunistic mode, the AP waits only for SIFS interval instead of DIFS and backoff interval. By shorting the interval period, the AP can access the channel without collision because all other nodes should wait at least DIFS period which is longer than SIFS period. By using the opportunistic mode, more throughput can be allocated to the downlink.

For the change of the operation mode, the AP has counters for the uplink and the downlink, denoted by ST_u and ST_d, respectively. The counter values increase by one whenever there is a successful packet transmission in the uplink and the downlink, respectively. When $ST_d \geq ST_u$, which means the accumulated number of the successful downlink packet transmission is equal to or larger than that of the uplink, the operation mode of the AP is set to the normal mode. On the contrary, when $ST_d < ST_u$, the operation mode of the AP is changed to the opportunistic mode to allocate more throughput to the downlink. The two counters, ST_u and ST_d, also run in the opportunistic mode and the operation mode will be changed to the normal mode as soon as it becomes $ST_d \geq ST_u$. The mode change algorithm is illustrated in Fig. 2.

3.2 Packet Scheduling Algorithm

In the normal mode, the packet scheduling algorithm adopts the first-in first-out (FIFO) algorithm. In the opportunistic mode, the AP schedules the packet based on the channel quality. The link with better channel quality is given higher

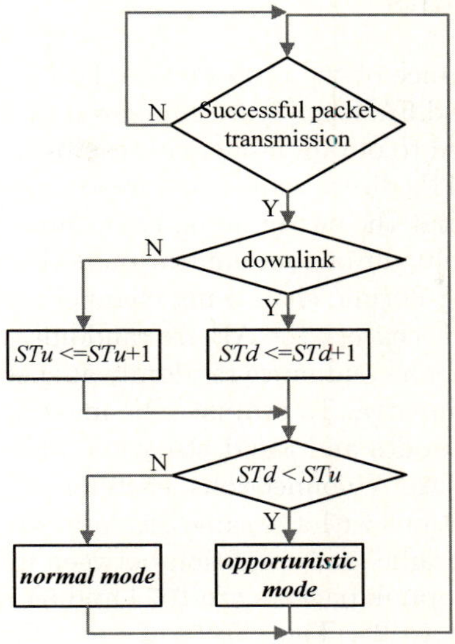

Fig. 2. Mode change algorithm

priority in packet scheduling. In order to track the latest channel quality, it is necessary to send the control packet to the node. However, this method will increase the overhead and need the modification of the IEEE 802.11 standard. Our design goal is that the scheduling method can be implemented without the modification of the nodes already deployed in the system. Thus, we propose that the AP updates the channel quality of each link after every successful packet transmissions. The channel quality is reported from the physical layer of AP by measuring the SNR of the received packets, e.g. CTS and ACK packets for the downlink traffic. This estimation of the channel quality may not be the timely information. However, the estimation error is in the acceptable range as will be shown in the next section. Moreover, the proposed method can be implemented without the modification of the deployed nodes.

The AP lists all the communication links according to the estimated channel quality. When the AP is in the opportunistic mode, the link that recorded the best channel quality in the previous successful packet transmission is given the first chance to transmit the packet in the queue. When there is no packet in the queue for that link, the next communication link in the list is given the second chance to transmit the packet.

One of the problems in the previous opportunistic scheduling method is the unfairness between the nodes [5]. The node that has the better channel quality gets more throughput and this may lead to the starvation problems for other nodes. However, in our method, opportunistic scheduling is compromised with FIFO scheduling and this alleviates the unfairness problem.

4 Numerical Results

We evaluate the performance of the proposed method by computer simulations. The IEEE 802.11 DCF and FAIR in [8] are compared with the proposed method. The parameter values used to obtain numerical results of the simulation runs are based on the IEEE 802.11b direct sequence spread spectrum (DSSS) standard [10]. To reflect the fact that the surrounding environmental clutter may be significantly different for each pair of communication nodes with the same distance separation, we use the log-normal shadowing channel model [14].

We assume that all nodes except the AP are randomly distributed in the circle area with diameter 150 meters and move randomly at speed 0.1 m/sec. The AP is located at the center of the area. To evaluate the maximum performance, traffic load is saturated in each nodes and the destination addresses of the packets are the AP. In the AP, there are N connections, each for one node, and packets are generated for each connections with the same distrubution as those in each nodes. To make an asymmetric traffic load condition between uplink and downlink, the size of the downlink and uplink packets are 1024 and 64 bytes, respectively. The number of node N is set to 25. The effects of the uplink packet size and the number of nodes on the performance are also evaluated by the simulation.

In FAIR, the system resource is allocates based on the dynamic estimation of the number of nodes and FIFO scheduling algorithm is used. Simulation results of the dynamic update method of the number of downlink and uplink nodes in FAIR are shown in Fig. 3. The ideal value for the downlink and uplink ratio is one because the number of downlink flows and that of uplink flows are the same in the simulation. However, the estimated values are different for three simulation runs, R_1, R_2, and R_3. Thus, the throughput allocation ratio between uplink and downlink may be far from the ideal value in some cases.

The time wasted by the packet collision of the proposed method is compared with those of DCF and FAIR in Fig. 4. The proposed method is denoted by MUD

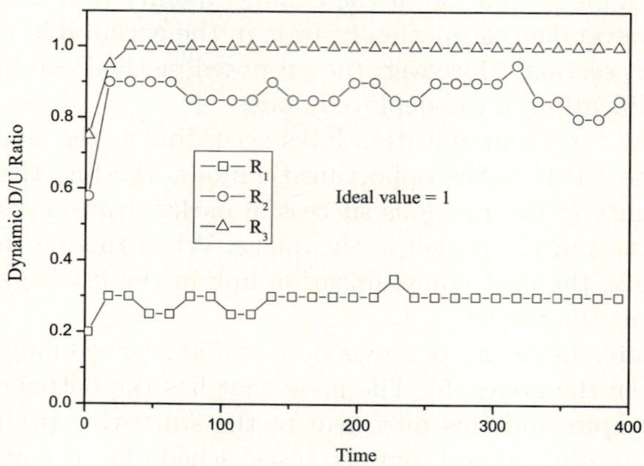

Fig. 3. Dynamic parameter estimation of Down/Up ratio in FAIR

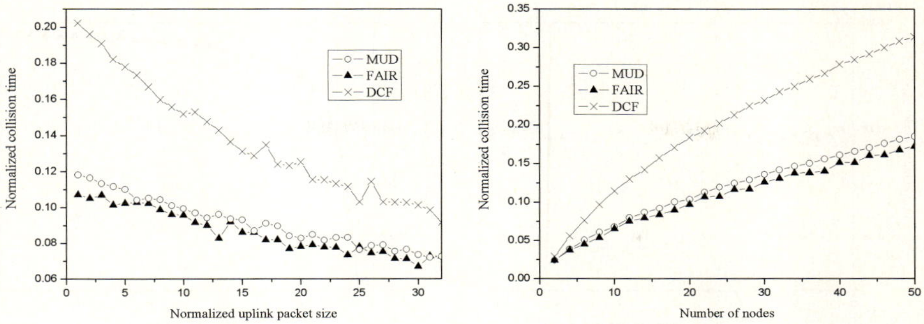

Fig. 4. Normalized collision time as a function of normalized uplink packet size and number of nodes

in the figure. The collision time is normalized to the total simulation time and the uplink packet size is normalized to 64 bytes. The collision time decreases as the uplink packet size increases because the data packet length per a transmission increases. The probability of the packet collision increases as the number of nodes increases. FAIR and MUD show less collision time than DCF because they provide the access method without the collision. FAIR shows less collision time than MUD. It is because MUD utilizes the multi-user diversity during the opportunistic mode which increases the throughput of the opportunistic mode. Thus, more time for the channel access can be allocated to the normal mode in MUD. This will be shown again in the next figure.

The channel access number of the opportunistic mode divided by total channel access number in the proposed method is compared with FAIR in Fig. 5. There is not the opportunistic mode in FAIR and the similar concept, called downlink compensation access, is compared in the figure. The opportunistic mode ratio does not change by the uplink packet size because the access method is changed by the number of channel access. As the number of nodes increases, uplink flows can easily get more throughput as explained in (4). Thus, more opportunistic mode is required to compensate the unfairness. Note that the opportunistic mode ratio is not 0.5 because the AP transmits packets both in normal mode and opportunistic mode. The opportunistic mode ratio of MUD is less than that of FAIR because of the same reason in Fig. 4.

The system throughput of the proposed method is compared with those of DCF and FAIR in Fig. 6. The system throughput increases as the uplink packet size increases because of the reduced overhead per a transmission. The system throughput of DCF decreases as the number of nodes increases because of the increased collisions. However, the system throughput of FAIR and MUD are not changed by the number of nodes because the opportunistic mode ratio is controlled by the number of nodes as shown in Fig. 5. The system throughput of MUD is larger than that of FAIR because of the multi-user diversity gain during the opportunistic mode.

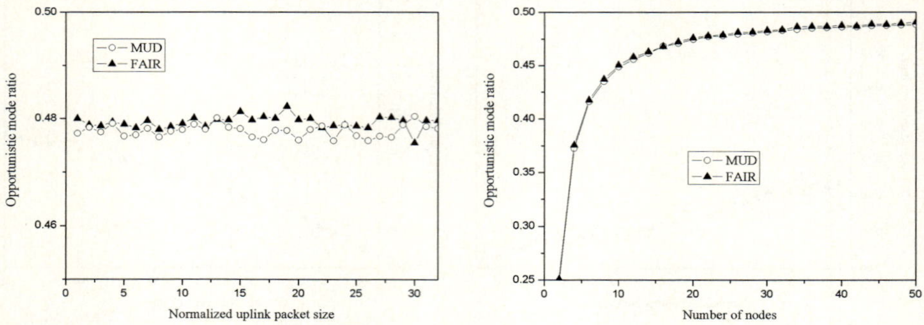

Fig. 5. Opportunistic mode ratio as a function of normalized uplink packet size and number of nodes

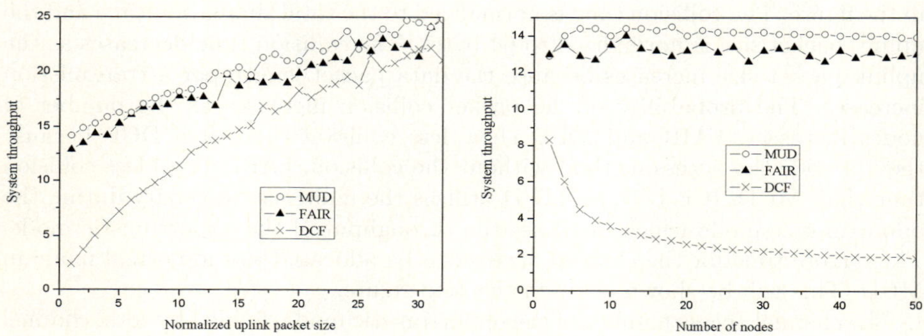

Fig. 6. System throughput as a function of normalized uplink packet size and number of nodes

5 Conclusion

We have proposed a multi-user diversity method to enhance the system throughput of the IEEE 802.11 DCF. Moreover, the proposed method alleviates the throughput unbalance between uplink and downlink. The proposed method can be implemented without the modification of the IEEE 802.11 standard for nodes that are widely deployed.

The efficiency of the proposed system has been demonstrated by computer simulation. The results show that the proposed method enhances the system throughput for asymmetric traffic load. This, in turn, reduces the blocking probability of multimedia data packets in the proposed systems compared with that in the IEEE 802.11 DCF where most of bandwidth is occupied by the uplink.

References

1. Knopp, R., Humblet, P.A.: Information capacity and power control in single cell multiuser communications. In: Proc. IEEE ICC 1995. (1995) 331–335
2. Ajib, W., Haccoun, D.: An overview of scheduling algoriths in MIMO-based fourth-generation wireless systems. IEEE Network **19** (2005) 43–48
3. Gyasi-Agyei, A.: Multiuser diversity based opportunistic scheduling for wireless data networks. IEEE Commun. Lett. **9** (2005) 670–672
4. IS-856: CDMA 2000 standard: High rate packet data air interface specification. (2000)
5. Wang, J., Zhai, H., Fang, Y.: Opportunistic packet scheduling and media access control for wireless LANs and multi-hop ad hoc networks. In: Proc. IEEE WCNC'04, Atlanta, Georgia (2004) 1234–1239
6. Grilo, A., Nunes, M.: Performance evaluation of IEEE 802.11e. In: Proc. IEEE PIMRC'02, Lisboa, Portugal (2002)
7. Pilosof, S., Ramjee, R., Raz, D., Shavitt, Y., Sinha, P.: Understanding TCP fairness over wireless LAN. In: Proc. IEEE Infocom'03, San Francisco, CA, USA (2003)
8. Kim, S.W., Kim, B., Fang, Y.: Downlink and uplink resource allocation in IEEE 802.11 wireless LANs. IEEE Trans. Veh. Technol. **54** (2005) 320–327
9. Kim, S.W., Kim, B.: Reource allocation based on traffic load over relayed wireless access networks. In: Proc. ICESS'05, Xian, China (2005) 441–451
10. IEEE Std 802.11b-1999: Wireless LAN Medium Access Control (MAC) and Physical Layer (PHY) Specifications: Higher-Speed Physical Layer Extension in the 2.4 GHz Band. (1999)
11. Kamerman, A., Monteban, L.: WaveLAN-II: A high-performance wireless LAN for the unlicensed band. Bell Labs Tech. J. **2** (1997) 118–133
12. Qiao, D., Choi, S., Shin, K.G.: Goodput analysis and link adaptation for IEEE 802.11a wireless LANs. IEEE Trans. Mob. Comput. **1** (2002) 278–292
13. Holland, G., Vaidya, N., Bahl, P.: A rate-adaptive MAC protocol for multi-hop wireless networks. In: Proc. IEEE/ACM MOBICOM'01, Boston, MA, USA (2001) 236–251
14. T. S. Rappaport: Wireless communications: principles and practices, 2nd Ed. Prentice Hall (2002)

Performance Analysis of DS-BPAM UWB System over Fading Channels— Uncoded and Coded Schemes

Zhiquan Bai, Shaoyi Xu, Weihua Zhang, and Kyungsup Kwak

UWB Wireless Communications Research Center (INHA UWB-ITRC),
Graduate School of Information Technology and Telecommunications,
Inha University, 402-751, Incheon, Korea
{sdzqbai, shaoyixu, zhweihua}@hotmail.com
kskwak@inha.ac.kr

Abstract. This paper investigates the performance of two direct sequence ultra wideband (DS-UWB) communication systems over multipath fading channels. The first system is the classic DS-UWB system and the second is obtained by adding a forward error control code (FEC), convolutional code. For the two systems, bipolar pulse amplitude modulation (BPAM) is applied. In the receiver end, the selective diversity combining receiver-SRake receiver is used as a feasible receiver. In the proposed coded scheme, we use soft output Viterbi algorithm (SOVA). The analysis shows that the coded DS-UWB system outperforms the conventional DS-UWB system significantly with the increase of the SRake fingers. The effective order of processing gains achieved by the coded scheme is the product of the number of SRake branches and the free distance of the code applied.

Keywords: Direct sequence (DS), Ultra wideband (UWB), Convolutional codes, Soft Output Viterbi algorithm (SOVA), Multipath fading channel, SRake receiver.

1 Introduction

Ultra Wideband radio presented in [1]-[2] is already used in military applications. Now it has attracted much interest for indoor high rate communications for its significant characteristics. In UWB system, data is transmitted directly using sub-nanosecond baseband pulses and the occupied frequency band is about several gigahertzes. Because of the large bandwidth, UWB technology can achieve high throughput and has the ability of robustness to co-channel interference and narrowband interference, and greater spectrum sharing. The characteristics of low cost and low power usage make it promising for mobile applications. UWB system can provide the fading robustness; wideband nature of the signal reduces time varying amplitude fluctuations (fading). Two popularly considered multiple access techniques for an impulse radio system are time hopping (TH), where users are distinguished by their pulse arrival time sequence, and direct sequence (DS) where users are distinguished by their pulse polarity sequence.

In [3]-[4], the coded and uncoded schemes of TH Pulse Position Modulation (TH-PPM) UWB communication systems were proposed over AWGN channel. The

E. Sha et al. (Eds.): EUC 2006, LNCS 4096, pp. 224 – 233, 2006.

performance of the coded TH-PPM UWB system over multipath fading channels was presented in [5]. It is shown the coded scheme can achieve better performance. In our knowledge, there are no much literatures about the analysis of coded and uncoded scheme of DS-BPAM UWB system. In this paper, the bit error rate (BER) of the two systems is analyzed in detail over UWB multipath fading channels. For the coded system, we use convolutional encoder and the soft output Viterbi algorithm (SOVA) is considered here. The computer simulations show that the coded DS-BPAM UWB system can get better performance with the acceptable complexity compared with the uncoded scheme.

The organization of this paper is as follows. In Section II, an overview of the DS-BPAM UWB system model is provided and the performance analysis is given in detail over multipath fading channels and SRake receiver. Section III presents the proposed coded DS-UWB system and also gives the upper bound and lower bound of the coded scheme. Section IV describes the simulation results obtained and interpretations. Finally, conclusions are presented in Section V.

2 DS UWB System Description

The performance analysis of the direct sequence spread spectrum UWB system over multipath fading channels is presented in this section. The transmitter of DS-BPAM UWB system is shown in Fig.1. This DS-BPAM UWB system is similar with [6]. We assume that desired user has a unique pseudo-noise (PN) sequence with N_c chips per message symbol period T_f such that $T_f = N_c T_c$, where N_c is the spread spectrum processing gain. A typical transmitted signal can be expressed as

$$s_{tr}(t) = \sum_{j=-\infty}^{\infty} \sum_{n=0}^{N_c-1} d_j c_n w_{tr}\left(t - jT_f - nT_c\right), \quad (1)$$

where $w_{tr}(t)$ is the transmitted monocycle waveform, seen in [1], $\{D_j\}$ is the binary information bit and $\{d_j\}$ is the modulated data symbols with $d_j = 2D_{\lfloor j/N_s \rfloor} - 1$, N_s is the pulse repetition time, $\{c_n\}$ is the spread chips with duration T_c . We show the modulated waveforms of the DS-BPAM UWB modulation waveforms in Fig.2, where the DS sequence is $\{+1,-1,-1,+1\}$ with $N_c = 4$ and $N_s = 1$.

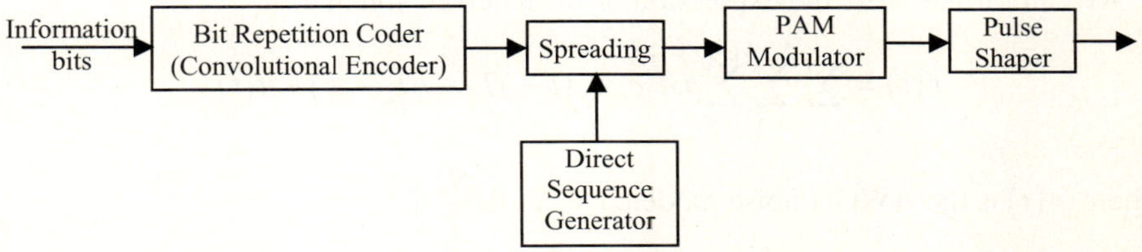

Fig. 1. Transmitter diagram of DS-BPAM-UWB (Uncoded/Coded) System

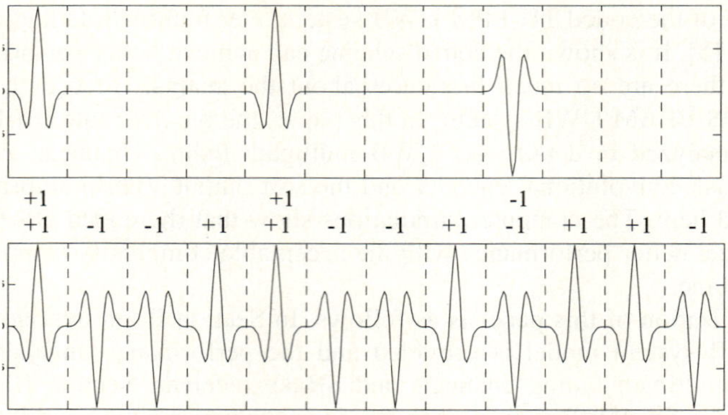

Fig. 2. DS-BPAM UWB modulation waveform (N_c=4, N_s=1)

In this paper, we consider a simple L-tap multipath channel model instead of the clustered multipath channels in order to simplify the analysis and high light the benefit of SRake receiver [7]. The channel mpulse response can be expressed by

$$h(t)=\sum_{l=0}^{L-1} a_l \delta(t-\tau_l), \tag{2}$$

where a_l and τ_l are the amplitude attenuation and time delay of the lth path, respectively, and L is the number of the corresponding branches in the SRake receiver.

An ideal channel and antenna system is known to modify the shape of the transmitted monocycle $w_{tr}(t)$ to $w_{rec}(t)$ at the output of the receiver antenna. For the purpose of analysis, we have assumed that the true transformed pulse shape $w_{rec}(t)$ is known at the receiver.

Through the UWB multipath fading channels, the received signal $r(t)$ can be expressed as [8]

$$r(t)=s_{rec}(t)*h(t)+n(t), \tag{3}$$

where $s_{rec}(t)=\sum_{j=-\infty}^{\infty}\sum_{n=0}^{N_c-1} d_j c_n w_{rec}\left(t-jT_f-nT_c\right)$.

We can further write the expression of the received signal as

$$r(t)=\sum_{j=-\infty}^{\infty}\sum_{n=0}^{N_c-1}\sum_{l=0}^{L-1} a_l d_j c_n w_{tr}\left(t-jT_f-nT_c-\tau_l\right)+n(t), \tag{4}$$

where $n(t)$ is the AWGN noise modeled as $N\left(0,\frac{N_0}{2}\right)$.

SRake receiver with MRC (maximum ratio combination) is employed in the receiver. The diagram of SRake receiver is shown in Fig.3. We can make the decision

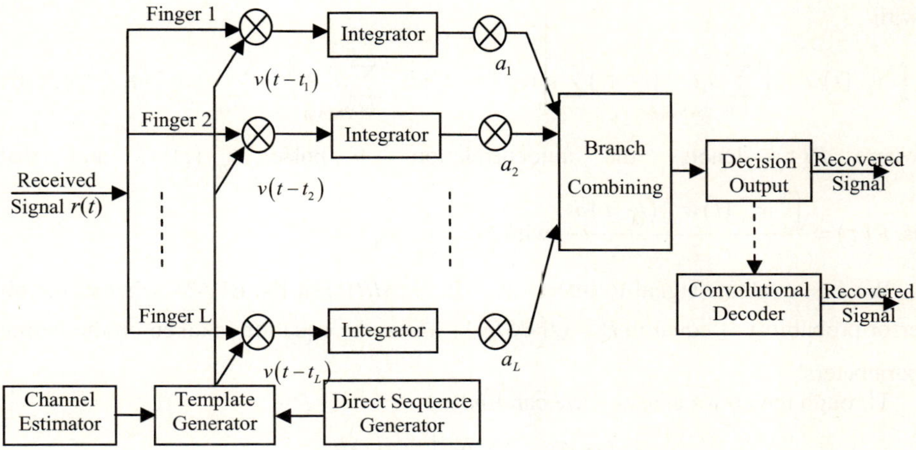

Fig. 3. Rake receiver diagram of DS-BPAM UWB (Uncoded and Coded) System

of the received information bit according to the output of branch combining. Since we assume that the receiver has achieved perfect synchronization for the signal transmitted by the transmitter. According to the estimated channel impulse response, the template can be set as

$$v_{bit}(t)=\sum_{n=0}^{N_c-1}c_n w_{rec}\left(t-jT_f-nT_c\right)*h(t)=\sum_{l=0}^{L-1}\sum_{n=0}^{N_c-1}a_l c_n w_{rec}\left(t-jT_f-nT_c-\tau_l\right). \tag{5}$$

The SRake correlation output can be expressed as

$$\alpha=\sum_{j=0}^{N_s-1}\int_0^T r(t)v_{bit}(t)dt=\sum_{j=0}^{N_s-1}\int_0^T r(t)\sum_{l=0}^{L-1}a_l\sum_{n=0}^{N_c-1}c_n w_{rec}\left(t-jT_f-nT_c-\tau_l\right)dt. \tag{6}$$

For the quantity a_l, we assume the order $a_1>a_2>...>a_L$. $[0,T]$ is the time interval includes the selected L paths.

The decision consists of

$$if\ \ \alpha>0, D_j=1;\ if\ \ \alpha<0, D_j=0. \tag{7}$$

In the following, we assume that the received waveform satisfies the relation $\int_{-\infty}^{+\infty}w_{rec}(t)dt=0$.

Let $\alpha_{\pm1}$ and $\sigma_{\pm1}^2$ be the mean and variance of the correlation output conditioned on $D_j=1$ and $D_j=0$, respectively. We calculate these two values as follows:

$$\alpha_1=-\alpha_{-1}=N_sN_c\int_0^T v_{bit}^2(t)dt, \tag{8}$$

$$\sigma_1^2=\sigma_{-1}^2=\frac{N_sN_cN_0}{2}\int_0^T v_{bit}^2(t)dt, \tag{9}$$

with

$$\int_{T_1}^{T_2} v_{bit}^2(t)dt = \int_0^T \sum_{l=0}^{L-1} a_l w_{rec}(t-\tau_l) \sum_{k=0}^{L-1} a_l w_{rec}(t-\tau_k)dt = \sum_{l=0}^{L-1} a_l^2 + \sum_{l=0}^{L-1} \sum_{k=0, l\neq k}^{L-1} a_l a_k R(\tau_l - \tau_k), \quad (10)$$

where $R(\tau)$ denotes the autocorrelation of pulse $w_{rec}(t)$, and that is, $R(\tau) = \dfrac{\int_{-\infty}^{\infty} w_{rec}(t) w_{rec}(t-\tau)dt}{E_w}$ with $E_w = \int_{-\infty}^{\infty} w_{rec}^2(t)dt$.

We first evaluate signal to interference ratio (*SIR*). For the BPAM scheme, the bit error probability is equal to $P_b = Q\left(\sqrt{SIR}\right)$, where the equation is taken on the fading parameters.

Through the above analysis, we can find

$$SIR = \frac{(\alpha_{\pm 1})^2}{\sigma_{\pm 1}^2} = \frac{2N_s N_c \int_0^T v_{bit}^2(t)dt}{N_0}. \quad (11)$$

The bit error probability of the system is given by

$$P_b = Q\left(\sqrt{SIR}\right) = Q\left(\sqrt{\frac{2N_s N_c}{N_0} \int_0^T v_{bit}^2(t)dt}\right)$$
$$= Q\left(\sqrt{\frac{2N_s N_c E_w}{N_0}\left[\sum_{l=0}^{L-1} a_l^2 + \sum_{l=0}^{L-1} \sum_{k=0, l\neq k}^{L-1} a_l a_k R(\tau_l - \tau_k)\right]}\right), \quad (12)$$

where $Q(\;)$ is the Gaussian probability integral.

When the channel attenuation is assumed to be normalized to one, $\sum_{l=0}^{L-1} a_l^2 = 1$ with $\sum_{l=0}^{L-1} \sum_{k=0, l\neq k}^{L-1} a_l a_k R(\tau_l - \tau_k) = 0$, then the BER reduces to be

$$P_b = Q\left(\sqrt{\frac{2N_s N_c E_w}{N_0}}\right). \quad (13)$$

3 Coded DS-UWB System Model

In this section, we consider the proposed coded DS-BPAM UWB system. We show the proposed receiver diagram of the convolutional coded system in Fig.3. In order to give the comparison of these two systems, in the DS-UWB system, we will assume that each data bit is transmitted by N_s repetition pulses. We consider it as a simple repetition block code with rate $1/N_s$. In the coded DS-UWB system, we will use an orthogonal convolutional code with constraint length K. For each input bit, we can get 2^{k-2} coded bits, here we set $N_s = 2^{k-2}$ in order to compare with the uncoded system. In the receiver end, we will apply soft output viterbi decoding algorithm.

For each encoded bit, the correlator output can be written as:

$$\alpha_j = \int_0^T r(t)\sum_{l=0}^{L-1} a_l \sum_{n=0}^{N_c-1} c_n w_{rec}\left(t - jT_f - nT_c - \tau_l\right)dt . \tag{14}$$

In the proposed SOVA scheme, we will normalize the correlator output α_j to the input of the decoder. The metric of SOVA is generated according to the correlator output α_j. According to the characteristics of the correlator output, the SOVA is the optimal decoding algorithm for this system. The decoding complexity grows linearly with *K*. Since in the practical system, the value of *K* is relatively low, the coded system is completely practical. In this paper, we use a simple convolutional encoder with code rate being 1/2.

According to the generating function of this kind of convolutional encoder given in [4], [9]

$$T_{SO}(\gamma,\beta) = \frac{\beta W^{K+2}(1-W)}{1-W\left[1+\beta\left(1+W^{K-3}-2W^{K-2}\right)\right]}, \tag{15}$$

where γ and β in each term of the polynomial indicate the number of paths and output-input path weights, respectively. We set $W=\gamma^{2^{K-3}}=Z^{2^{K-3}}$ and $Z=\int_{-\infty}^{+\infty}\sqrt{p_0(y)p_1(y)}dy$, where $p_0(y)$ and $p_1(y)$ are the probability density functions of pulse correlator output. The free distance of this code can be expressed as $d_f = 2^{K-3}(K+2) = N_s(\log_2 N_s + 4)/2$. The bit error probability can be obtained as [9],

$$P_b = Q\left(\sqrt{2\frac{E_s}{I_0}d_f}\right)\sum_{k=d_f}^{\infty} b_k e^{-k\left(\frac{E_s}{I_0}\right)} e^{d_f\left(\frac{E_s}{I_0}\right)}, \tag{16}$$

where $\frac{E_s}{I_0} = \frac{N_c E_w}{N_0}\left[\sum_{l=0}^{L-1} a_l^2 + \sum_{l=0}^{L-1}\sum_{k=0,l\neq k}^{L-1} a_l a_k R(\tau_l - \tau_k)\right]$.

For a uniform power delay profile (PDP), we obtain the following upper bound P_e on P_b according to (16), it can be expressed as below [4], [9]:

$$\begin{aligned} P_e &\le e^{d_f\left(\frac{E_s}{I_0}\right)} Q\left(\sqrt{2\left(\frac{E_s}{I_0}\right)d_f}\right)\frac{dT(Z,\beta)}{d\beta}\Bigg|_{\beta=1,Z=e^{-\left(\frac{E_s}{I_0}\right)},Z=\gamma} \\ &= \gamma^{-d_f} Q\left(\sqrt{2\left(\frac{E_s}{I_0}\right)d_f}\right) W^{K+2}\left(\frac{1-W}{(1-2W)\left(1-W^{K-2}\right)}\right)^2 \\ &= Q\left(\sqrt{2\left(\frac{E_s}{I_0}\right)d_f}\right)\left(\frac{1-W}{(1-2W)\left(1-W^{K-2}\right)}\right)^2, \end{aligned} \tag{17}$$

$$P_e \le Q\left(\sqrt{\frac{2d_f N_c E_w}{N_0}\left[\sum_{l=0}^{L-1} a_l^2 + \sum_{l=0}^{L-1}\sum_{k=0,l\neq k}^{L-1} a_l a_k R(\tau_l - \tau_k)\right]}\right)\left(\frac{1-W}{(1-2W)(1-W^{K-2})}\right)^2 . \quad (18)$$

The lower bound in this case can be obtained as

$$P_e > Q\left(\sqrt{\frac{2d_f N_c E_w}{N_0}\left[\sum_{l=0}^{L-1} a_l^2 + \sum_{l=0}^{L-1}\sum_{k=0,l\neq k}^{L-1} a_l a_k R(\tau_l - \tau_k)\right]}\right). \quad (19)$$

From the above equation, it can be realized that in the coded scheme, the effective order of the processing gains is the product of L (the number of branches in SRake receiver) and the free distance of the code. This product plays an important role in deciding the bit error performance and it makes the different performance of the coded and uncoded system. In order to get better BER performance, we can increase the SRake branches to gather more multipath components, but the system complexity will be increased correspondingly.

4 Simulations Results

In this section, we present some computer simulation results about these two systems. Like the same example in [1], the received pulse is modeled as $w_{rec}(t) = \left[1 - 4\pi\left(\frac{t}{\tau_m}\right)^2\right]\exp\left[-2\pi\left(\frac{t}{\tau_m}\right)^2\right]$, shown in Fig.4, where $\tau_m = 0.2$ ns, $T_w = 0.5$ ns. The gold code sequence used here has the characteristics with length $N_c = 7$ and chip duration $T_c = 20$ ns. For each information bit, we repeat it twice for the comparison of the two systems. The information bit rate is $R_b = 1/T_f = 1/(N_s N_c T_c)$ *bps*.

The channel impulse response of the IEEE model [10] can be expressed as follows:

$$h(t) = X\sum_{n=1}^{N}\sum_{k=1}^{K(n)} \alpha_{nk}\delta(t - T_n - \tau_{nk}), \quad (20)$$

Table 1. Parameters for IEEE UEB channel scenarios

Channel Model (CM1~4)	Λ	λ	Γ	γ	σ_ξ	σ_ζ	σ_g
Case 1 LOS (0-4m)	0.0233	2.5	7.1	4.3	3.3941	3.3941	3
Case 2 NLOS (0-4m)	0.4	0.5	5.5	6.7	3.3941	3.3941	3
Case 3 NLOS (4-10m)	0.0667	2.1	14	7.9	3.3941	3.3941	3
Case 4 NLOS Multipath Channel	0.0667	2.1	24	12	3.3941	3.3941	3

where X is a log-normal random variable representing the amplitude gain of the channel, N is the number of observed clusters, K(n) is the number of multipath contributions received within the n-th cluster, α_{nk} is the coefficient of the k-th multipath contribution of the n-th cluster, T_n is the time arrival of the n-th cluster, and τ_{nk} is the delay of the k-th multipath contribution within the n-th cluster. The IEEE suggested an initial set of values for the parameters of UWB channel. The list of parameters for different environment scenarios is provided in Table 1.

We have the parameters defined as:

- The cluster average arrival rate Λ,
- The pulse average arrival rate λ,
- The power decay factor Γ for clusters,
- The power decay factor γ for pulses within a cluster,
- The standard deviation σ_ξ of the fluctuations of the channel coefficients for clusters,
- The standard deviation σ_ζ of the fluctuations of the channel coefficients for pulses within each cluster,
- The standard deviation σ_g of the channel amplitude gain.

In the simulation, we consider the channel model is CM3 and CM4 suggested by IEEE and the number of SRake branches is 3 and 5. The BER performance of the coded and uncoded DS-UWB systems with different SRake branches (SRake=3 and 5) is shown in Fig.5 and Fig.6, respectively. When SRake=3 and BER is around 10^{-4}, the coded scheme can get about 1dB gains compared with the uncoded scheme under CM3 and CM4. When SRake=5, the coded scheme can get about 1dB or 3dB gains around the BER being 10^{-4} with CM=3 and CM=4, respectively. From these two figures, the performance of the coded DS-BPAM UWB scheme is better than the uncoded one with the increase of SRake branches.

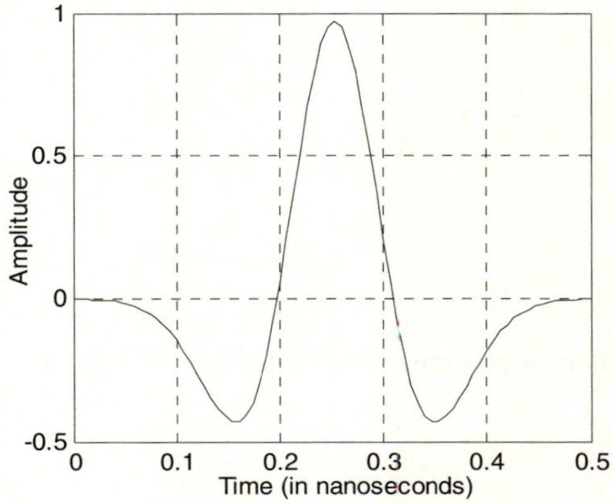

Fig. 4. Transmit Gaussian Waveform

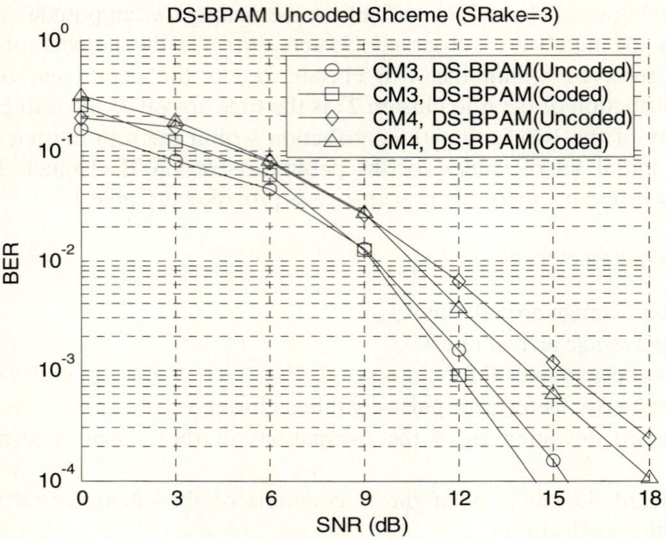

Fig. 5. BER performance of DS-UWB (SRake=3)

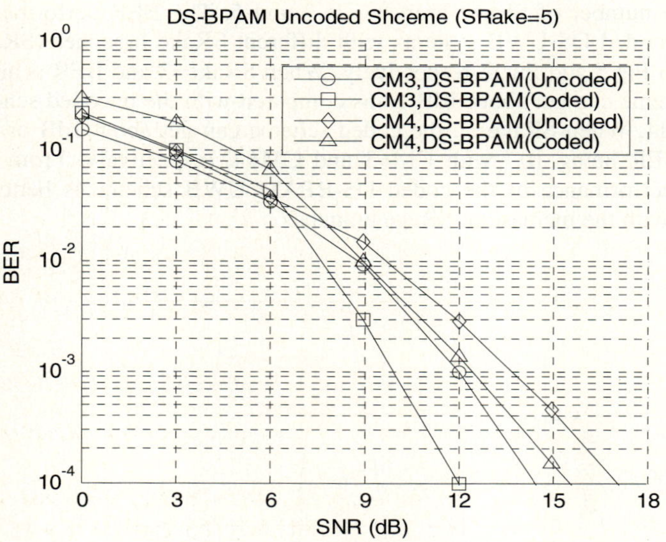

Fig. 6. BER performance of Coded DS-UWB (SRake=5)

5 Conclusions

In this paper, the performance of coded and uncoded DS-UWB system is analyzed over UWB multipath fading channel. In order to minimize the power consumption and get better performance, bipolar modulation is used here. A useful BER expression is deduced for uncoded DS-UWB scheme; for coded DS-UWB scheme, an upper bound and lower bound of BER are achieved. The analysis and simulation results show that the coded scheme is outperform the uncoded system significantly with acceptable complexity improvement. From the bit error probability expression of the coded scheme, we can see that the free distance d_f and the number of SRake fingers play an important role in deciding the system performance.

References

1. R. A. Scholtz: Multiple access with time-hopping impulse modulation. IEEE Military Communications Conf. (1993) 11–14.
2. M. Z. Win and R. A. Scholtz: Impulse radio: How it works. IEEE Commun. Lett., Vol. 2 (1998) 36–38.
3. A. R. Forouzan, M. Nasiri-Kenari and J. A. Salehi: Performance analysis of time-hopping spread-spectrum multiple-access systems: uncoded and coded schemes. IEEE Transactions on Wireless Communications, Vol. 1, Issue 4. (2002) 671–681.
4. A. R. Forouzan, M. Nasiri-Kenari and J. A. Salehi: Low-rate convolutionally encoded time-hopping spread spectrum multiple access systems. IEEE PIMRC 2000, Vol. 2 (2000) 1555–1558.
5. H. R. Ahmadi and M. Nasiri-Kenari: Performance analysis of time-hopping ultra-wideband systems in multipath fading channels (uncoded and coded schemes). The 13th IEEE PIMRC, Vol. 4 (2002) 1694–1698.
6. N. Boubaker and K. B. Letaief: Ultra wideband DSSS for multiple access communications using antipodal signaling. IEEE ICC 2003, Vol. 3 (2003) 2197–2201.
7. R. D. Wilson and R.A. Scholtz: Comparison of CDMA and modulation schemes for UWB radio in a multipath environment. IEEE GLOBECOM 2003, Vol. 2 (2003) 754–758.
8. F. Ramirez-Mireles: On the performance of ultra-wideband signals in Gaussian noise and dense multipath. IEEE Trans. Veh. Technol., Vol. 50 (2001) 244–249
9. A. J. Viterbi: CDMA: Principles of Spread Spectrum Communications. Addison-Wesley (1995).
10. Maria-Gabriella Di Benedetto and Guerino Giancola: Understanding Ultra Wide Band Radio Fundamentals, Prentice Hall PTR (2004).

Protocol Design for Adaptive Video Transmission over MANET*

Jeeyoung Seo, Eunhee Cho, and Sang-Jo Yoo

Graduate School of Information Technology & Telecommunications Inha University, 253 YongHyun-dong, Nam-ku, Incheon 402-751, Korea
eseseo@naver.com, euny1002@hotmail.com, sjyoo@inha.ac.kr
http://multinet.inha.ac.kr

Abstract. In this paper, we propose an efficient video data transmission protocol using the cross-layer approach in ad hoc networks. Due to node movement, the MANET is frequently changing path and each path has different transmission rate so that it shows low performance when transmitters select a constant transmission late at the encoding time regardless path condition. So, we need an effective video transmission method that considers physical layer channel statistics, node's energy status, and network topology changes at the same time unlike the OSI layered protocol in that each layer is independent and hard to control adaptively video transmission according to the network conditions. In the proposed CVTP protocol, a source node selects an optimal path using multilayer information such as node's residual energy, channel condition and hop counts to increase path life time and throughput. And a video source can determine an adequate video coding rate to achieve high PSNR and loss packet loss ratio.

1 Introduction

Conventional wireless networks require as prerequisites some form of fixed network infrastructure and centralized administration for their operation. In contrast, the so-called MANET (Mobile Ad hoc Network), consisting of a collection of wireless nodes, all of which may be mobile, dynamically creates a wireless network among them without using any such infrastructure or administrative support. MANET is affected by wireless transmission channel conditions like that interference and fading, so it is necessary to effectively utilize in limited wireless resources. Also MANET is generally running by limited energy, an efficient energy management is required to increase network life time and network throughput.

Because existing MANET uses layered protocol such as OSI (Open Systems Interconnection) reference model, each layer has independent and detached characteristics. It is difficult to adaptively control different layers at the same time and integrated manner so that the existing layered approach shows low performance especially in ad hoc environments in which network conditions and topologies frequently changes. Cross-layer design architecture [1][2] is attractive in ad-hoc networks, because layer information can be easily exchanged and each layer can accommodate other layer's

* This work was supported by Korea Research Foundation Grant (KRF-2005-202-D00321).

E. Sha et al. (Eds.): EUC 2006, LNCS 4096, pp. 234 – 243, 2006.

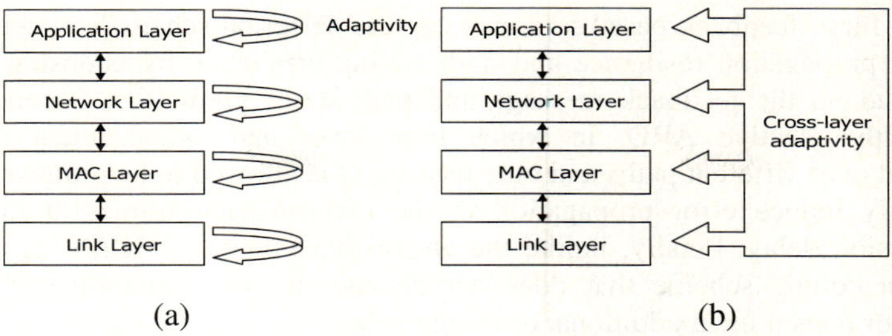

Fig. 1. OSI layered and adaptive cross-layer structures

conditions for performance increase in terms of network life time, node's residual energy, data rate, network throughput. A Difference between OSI and cross layer design structure is shown in Figure1.

This paper proposes optimum routing path selection and video transmission rate decision methods in MANET environment using the cross-layer design architecture. In the proposed method, we use multilayer information such as node's residual energy, wireless channel condition and hop count. And video source selects a path to the destination based on possible channel speed and its energy stability. In accordance with dynamic path change and node or network status varying, video encoder computes the maximum coding rate and changes quantization parameter (QP) value.

The remainder of the paper is organized as follows. Section 2 explains existing video transmission methods in MANET and cross-layer design architecture. In Section 3 we propose a new cross-layer video transmission protocol (CVTP) for effective video transmission in MANET. Section 4 shows our experimental results and in Section 5 we conclude this paper.

2 Cross Layer Design Approach

In ad-hoc network, there are frequent topology changes due to the node movements and energy shortages. Therefore, packet loss and overdue delivery plentifully occur in such network environments. These characteristics make receivers difficult to correctly decode received video data or continuously display real-time video with high quality. To overcome this difficulty, several cross layer methods which jointly consider various layers including video coding, error control, transport mechanisms, and routing were suggested.

Among various approaches, multipath transport mechanism is a popular field of research. It uses multiple paths from a video source to a destination to transmit a video program. Because multipath transport has advantages such as load balancing, fault-tolerance, and higher aggregate bandwidth, it can be suitable for transmission of real-time video that is burst and delay sensitive. If this mechanism is combined other mechanisms such as video coding or error control, its performance can be improved. For example, in [3][4], multipath transport mechanism is combined with some schemes, which are feedback based reference picture selection, layered coding with selective automatic repeat request (ARQ) and multiple description motion compensation coding

(MDMC). First, feedback based reference picture selection scheme can achieve both high error propagation resilience and high coding efficiency by choosing reference frame based on the feedback message and path status prediction. Second, layered coding with selective ARQ, in which base layer and enhancement layers are transmitted over different paths and only base layer is allowed to be retransmitted, can significantly reduce error propagation in the reconstructed frames at the cost of retransmission delay. Finally, unlike the above two schemes, MDMC is a multiple description coding scheme that does not depend on the availability of feedback channel, nor does it incur additional decoding delay.

However, these advantages of multipath transmission mechanism come at the cost of higher coding redundancy, higher computation complexity, and higher control traffic overhead in network. It is because more streams may increase the video bit rate for the same video quality, and delay during traffic partitioning and re-sequencing, and maintaining multiple paths in the dynamic ad hoc network environment involves higher control traffic overhead and more complex routing algorithm.

And some feedback-based mechanism with single path were proposed [5][6]. They control the source bit rate in accordance with hop count information. A crucial factor affecting ad-hoc channel performance is the deterioration of the network throughput as the number of transmission hops increases. As soon as a new route is established, the application layer upon receiving the hop-counts information from a routing layer would be able to adjust QP parameter for effective transmission. This mechanism allows an application layer to adapt itself to changes in a network layer condition. However, this method only considers hop count to adjust video coding rate. In fact, there are several network characteristics that impact on video quality and desirable behaviors such as node's residual energy, path's expected life time, channel speed, hop count, and so on.

3 Proposed Effective Cross-Layer Video Transmission Protocol

In wireless ad-hoc video application, providing good video quality without service breaks or termination for a given video service time is very important. In this paper, we define T_v as the desirable video service time by users and during this time video should be transmitted incessantly. In ad-hoc network, the actual video transmission time through a selected routing path is limited by residual energy level of participating nodes, video transmission rate, channel speeds of all links of the path, and hop count. When a video is transmitted with a constant quality through the selected path by a conventional ad-hoc routing protocol, since some wireless links on the path may not support the source transmission rate, there will be lots of packet retransmissions (or packet losses) and large delay. And even worse some nodes can consume all their energies before the desirable video service time T_v so that the service can be disrupted and the source node needs to find whether there is a new path to the destination or not.

Therefore, in this paper we propose an effective cross-layer design architecture and protocol that can select an optimal path and adaptively determine the adequate video coding rate by means of multilayer information such as node's residual energy, channel condition and hop counts. In the proposed cross-layer video transmission protocol (CVTP), multilayer information between network and physical layers are collected through routing message exchanges and used for selection of optimal and reliable transmission path in routing layer. Also this information is utilized for calculation of adaptive and optimum transmission rate in application layer by means of video encoder that adaptively changes QP value. CVTP consists of three phases: optimum path selection, effective video coding rate decision, and adaptive coding rate adjustment.

a) Optimum Path Selection

In Figure 2, an example ad-hoc network structure is shown. Source *S* want to communicate with destination *D*, and three candidate paths are currently found via a routing protocol. $Path_i$ means *i*'th path among the all paths from source to destination. In ad-hoc network, each node's residual energy level impacts on the network or path life time. In CVTP, routing messages carry each node's residual energy on a path. A $minREnergy_i$ (minimal residual energy of path *i*) is defined as (1).

$$minREnergy_i = \min\{REneregy_j, \forall j \in \mathbf{V}_{path_i}\} \quad (1)$$

where, $REnergy_j$ is the residual energy of node *j*; $\mathbf{V}_{path_i}$ is the set of nodes of path *i*.

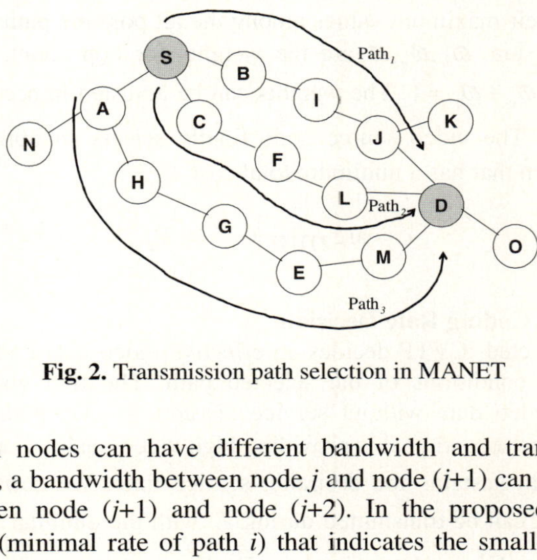

Fig. 2. Transmission path selection in MANET

Links between nodes can have different bandwidth and transmission rates in MANET. Namely, a bandwidth between node *j* and node (*j*+1) can be different from a bandwidth between node (*j*+1) and node (*j*+2). In the proposed CVTP, we have defined $minRate_i$ (minimal rate of path *i*) that indicates the smallest link bandwidth from the all links of path *i*.

$$minRate_i = \min\{Rate_l, \forall l \in \mathbf{E}_{path_i}\} \quad (2)$$

where $Rate_l$ is the bandwidth of link *l*; $\mathbf{E}_{path_i}$ is the set of links of path *i*.

To select an optimal path that can provide long path life time and high path bandwidth, we define a total cost function C_i for each routing path *i* as (3). In ad-hoc network, the larger hop count from source to destination, we have the higher probabilities of link or node failure and path partitioning due to node movements. Therefore, as in (3) the path total cost includes hop count, minimal residual energy, and minimal rate of the path.

$$C_i = \omega_h \cdot HOP_i^N + \omega_e \cdot \frac{1}{minREnergy_i^N} + \omega_r \cdot \frac{1}{minRate_i^N} \quad (3)$$

where

$$HOP_i^N = \frac{HOP_i}{\max\left[HOP_p, {}^{\forall} p \in \mathbf{P}_{s-d}\right]}, \; HOP_i = \text{hop count of path } i$$

$$minREnergy_i^N = \frac{minREnergy_i}{\max\left[minREnergy_p, {}^{\forall} p \in \mathbf{P}_{s-d}\right]}$$

$$minRate_i^N = \frac{minRaate_i}{\max\left[minRate_p, {}^{\forall} p \in \mathbf{P}_{s-d}\right]}$$

$\mathbf{P}_{s-d}$ = set of paths from the source s to the destination d

ϖ = weight

In (3), each path's hop count, minimal residual energy, and minimal rate are normalized with their maximum values among the all possible paths to make them be in an equal dimension. $\varpi_h, \varpi_e, \varpi_r$ are the weights for hop count, energy, and rate, respectively; $\varpi_h + \varpi_e + \varpi_r = 1$. The weights can be adjusted in accordance with each item's importance. The video source node finally selects an optimal path i^* from source to destination that has a minimum total cost C_i.

$$i^* = \arg\min_i \left\{C_i, {}^{\forall} i \in \mathbf{P}_{s-d}\right\} \quad (4)$$

b) Effective Video Coding Rate Decision

Once a path is selected, CVTP decides an effective video data coding rate based on channel and node conditions of the selected path. The first goal of this step is transmitting the video data without service disruptions during the desirable video service time T_v. The second goal is providing high video quality (i.e., high bit rate) as possible as the path sustains the desirable service time. We define the number of packets (N_{Pkt}^E) that can be transmitted during T_v with the minimal residual energy of the selected path i^*. N_{Pkt}^E is determined as (5). E_{Pkt} is a sum of the required energies for receiving, processing, and transmitting a packet as (6). Because a source can know the average video packet size $(AvgSize_{Pkt})$, we assume that a source node can calculate the required energy to relay a packet in advance. Therefore N_{Pkt}^E is the maximum packet numbers that can be transmitted through the selected path without any node's energy exhaustion.

$$N_{Pkt}^{E} = \frac{minREnergy_{i^*}}{E_{Pkt} \times T_v} \quad (5)$$

$$E_{Pkt} = E_{Pkt}^{R} + E_{Pkt}^{P} + E_{Pkt}^{T} \quad (6)$$

Also, we define the number of packets $\left(N_{Pkt}^{R}\right)$ that can be transmitted at the minimum rate of the selected path during the service time T_v. Consideration of the minimum link speed of the path is important to the real-time applications. If the source node transmits its video data at higher rate than the minimum rate of the path, then many packets can be delayed and lost at the bottleneck nodes.

$$N_{Pkt}^{R} = \frac{minRate_{i^*} \times T_v}{AvgSize_{Pkt}} \quad (7)$$

In the proposed CVTP, video application layer computes the maximum number of packets to be transmitted during the service time in terms of energy and link bandwidth as (8).

$$N_{Pkt}^{*} = \min\left\{N_{Pkt}^{E}, N_{Pkt}^{R}\right\} \quad (8)$$

Finally, the application layer decides the maximum video coding rate at the encoder with (9). OH_{Pkt} is an amount of a packet overhead in network, data link, and physical layers.

$$maxCRate_{i^*} = \frac{N_{Pkt}^{*} \times \left(AvgSize_{Pkt} - OH_{Pkt}\right)}{T_v} < minRate_{i^*} \quad (9)$$

Coding rate of a sender is controlled by changing QP value and the coding rate is always less than the minimum rate of the selected path.

c) Adaptive Coding Rate Adjustment

In ad-hoc network, because nodes can move and be used as relay nodes for other data flows, the selected path can be partitioned and node failure can be happened due to the energy exhaustion. In the proposed CVTP, source periodically sends a route discovery packet and performs the procedure of (a). Therefore, when the current path is not available any more, a new optimal path can be selected again using Equation (4). If a new path is selected at time t after its service starting time, the source node should readjust its maximum coding rate $maxCRate_{i^*}(t)$ based on the new selected path's energy and link rate conditions as (10).

$$maxCRate_{i^*}(t) = \frac{N_{Pkt}^{*} \times \left(AvgSize_{Pkt} - OH_{Pkt}\right)}{T_v - t} \quad (10)$$

In conclusion, CVTP decides an optimum path by means of physical and network layer information that were acquired at routing time and adaptively calculates application layer video coding rate. Therefore, it has advantages that a connection can be continuously and stably maintained during the desirable service time and quality of received video is improved because of little packet losses and delay. The proposed path selection and coding rate decision can decrease frequent path re-establishments due to energy exhaustion of nodes before the expected service time so that routing overhead also can be reduced. Figure 3 shows the functional and procedural structure of the proposed CVPT at the video source node.

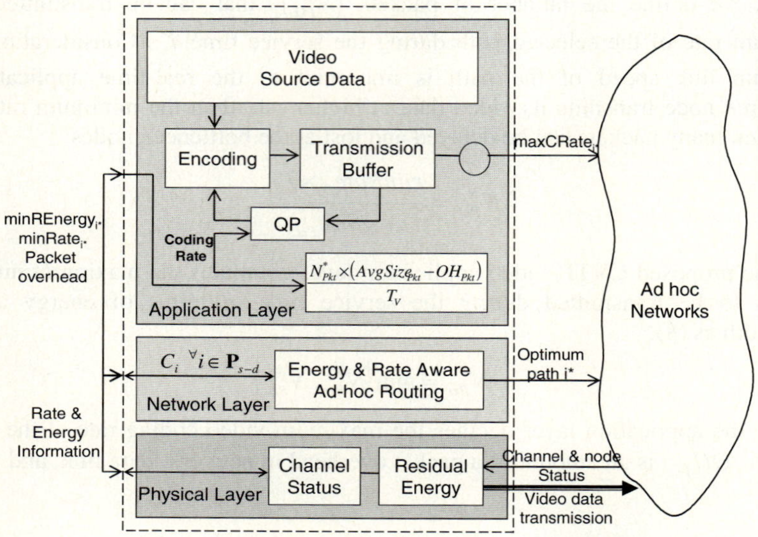

Fig. 3. Functional and procedural structure of CVPT

4 Experimental Results

In this section, we demonstrate performance of proposed CVPT. NS2 (Network Simulator 2) is used to make a simulation environment as Table1. In this experiment sources and destinations are randomly selected and the packet overhead (OH_{Pkt}) is ignored. For CVPT all weights are the same $(\varpi_h = \varpi_e = \varpi_r = 1/3)$.

Table 1. Simulation Environment

Simulation area	600 m× 600 m
Number of nodes	10~35
Buffer size at each node	50 packets
Node velocity	0~30 m/s (0~108 km/h)
Average packet size	512 bytes
Energy of nodes	15~25 kJ (random)
Link bandwidth	50 ~ 80 kbps (random)
Simulation time	300 sec

H.263 codec that it can adaptively change QP value is used for video data compression. The codec is implemented by UBC and the version is TMN5. This codec has simple function of error concealment. For comparison, we implemented two methods that are different from the proposed method on the decision of video coding rate and optimal path selection. For the video coding rate, one method (NgbMin) uses the minimum link bandwidth among the links between a source and its all one hop neighbors. Another method (NgbAvg) uses the average bandwidth between a source and all its one hop neighbors. For the two compared methods, video transmitting paths were determined using the conventional AODV [7] protocol. The source and destination nodes are randomly selected.

Figure 4 shows the video data transmitting rate (i.e., coding rate) changes according to the number of nodes. As increasing number of nodes, the minimum path's link bandwidth and minimum path's residual energy will generally decrease. This means that the required hop count from the source to the destination is increasing and network condition is getting worse by increasing the number of nodes. As we can see, the proposed CVTP adaptively control its coding rate in accordance with channel condition. The video transmitting rate is similar NgbMin and lower than NgbAvg. The large node count, CVTP decreases its rate to reduce possible packet losses on the path.

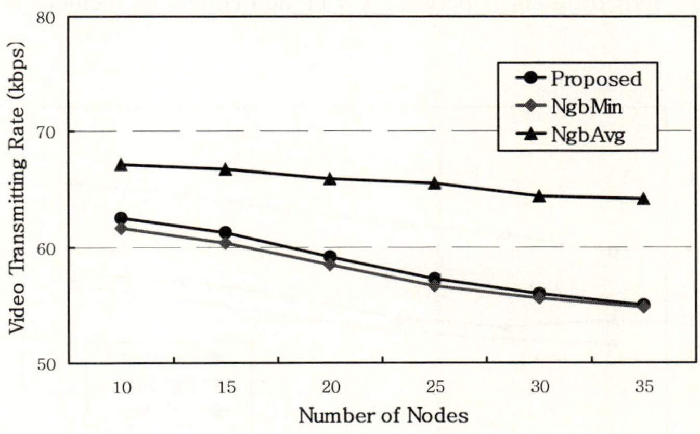

Fig. 4. Video data transmitting rates by increasing nodes

Figure 5 shows the packet loss rate by increasing node numbers. For the small number of node case, there was longer path break time than that of the large number of node case. When the number of nodes is small, if one of the nodes one the path moves out, there is a path break and it takes a long time to recover the path with a new node appearance that interconnects the broken paths. However for the case of the large number of nodes, when a path is broken, because there are many candidate nodes to interconnect the broken paths, shorter path recovery time is required. All packets during the path break time are lost. And as shown in Figure 5 the packet loss ratio of CVTP is also maintained lower level than those of compared methods.

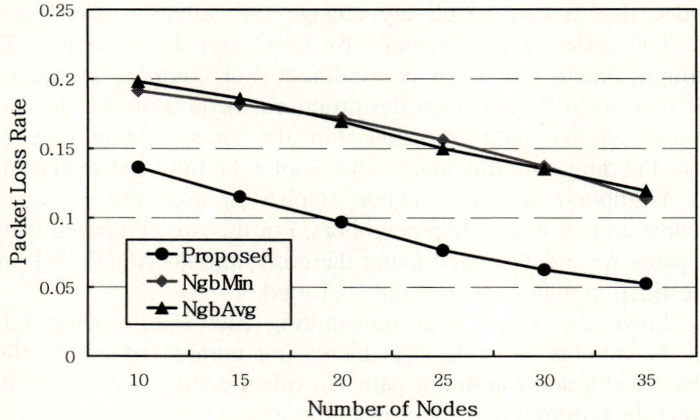

Fig. 5. Packet loss ratio by increasing nodes

Figure 6 shows the average PSNR changes at a decoder according to the number of nodes. The proposed CVTP shows higher average PSNR for all node number conditions than those of the compared two methods. For the larger node number condition, the PSNR differences between CVTP and compared methods are also the larger.

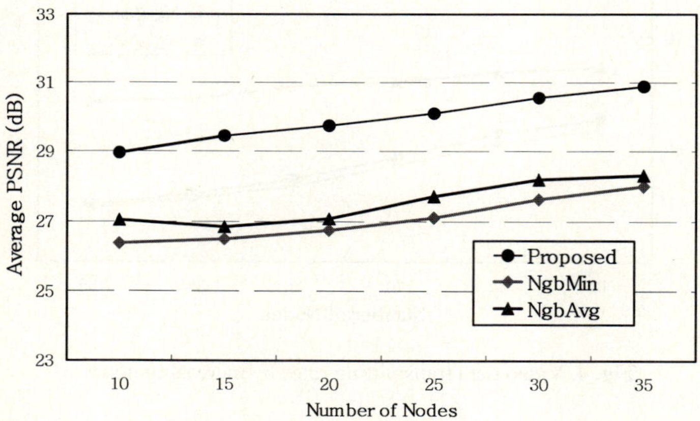

Fig. 6. Observed PSNR by increasing nodes

Figure 7 shows transmitting rate changes of the proposed protocol for one example experiment (20 nodes) during the simulation time. The transmitting rate of CVTP is recomputed whenever path reconstruction is required. As we can see, the CVTP can control transmission rate adaptively based on the new path's channel and energy status.

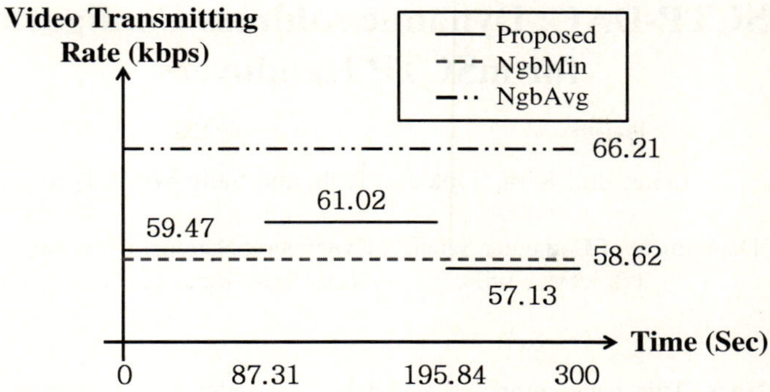

Fig. 7. During simulation time, observed video transmitting rate

5 Conclusion

Video transmission application in ad-hoc network is restrained by node's mobility, frequently topology changes, various node's energy capacity, and transmission path conditions compared with video transmission in general wired or wireless networks. So, in this paper, we propose a new cross-layer protocol for effective video transmission in wireless ad-hoc network. The proposed CVTP decides an optimum path by means of information in terms of minimal residual energy, link bandwidth, and hop count of a path that are collected at routing time. This optimal path selection method can increase path life time and transmission speed. With help of physical and network layer in CVTP a video source adaptively decides its video coding rate for reducing packet losses and at the same time achieving maximum video quality.

References

[1] Conti M., Maselli G., Giovanni, Turi, Silvia, Giordano, "Cross-layering in mobile ad hoc network design", IEEE Computer, Vol. 37, No. 2, pp. 48-51, February 2004.

[2] Goldsmith A.J., Wicker S.B., "Design challenges for energy-constrained ad hoc wireless networks", IEEE Wireless Communications, Vol. 9, No 4, pp. 8-27, August 2002.

[3] Shunan Lin, Yao Wang, Shiwen Mao, Shivendra Panwar, "Video transport over ad-hoc networks using multiple paths", IEEE ISCAS 2002, vol. 1,pp. 57-60,May 2002.

[4] Shiwen Mao, Shivendar S. Panwar, Emere Celebi, "Video transport over ad hoc networks : multistream coding with mul-tipath transport", IEEE Journal on Selected Areas in Communications, Vol. 21, No. 10, pp.1721-1735, December 2003.

[5] Gharavi, H., Ban, K. "Dynamic packet control for video communications over ad-hoc networks" IEEE Int. Conf. on Communications (ICC 2004), pp.3086-3090, June 2004.

[6] Gharavi H., Ban K., "Rate adaptive video transmission over ad hoc networks", IEE Electronics Letters, vol. 40, No 19, pp. 1177-1178, September 2004.

[7] Chales E. Perkins, Elizabeth M. Royer, "Ad-hoc on-demand distance vector routing", Proceedings of the 2nd IEEE Workshop on Mobile Computing Systems and Applications, pp.90-100, February 1999.

mSCTP-DAC: Dynamic Address Configuration for mSCTP Handover*

Dong Phil Kim, Seok Joo Koh, and Sang Wook Kim

Department of Computer Science, Kyungpook National University, Korea
{dpkim, sjkoh, swkim}@cs.knu.ac.kr

Abstract. This paper proposes a dynamic IP address configuration (DAC) scheme for mSCTP handover, which exploits the information from the link layer to support SCTP handover between heterogeneous access networks. The proposed DAC scheme enables a mobile terminal to automatically add a new IP address in the newly visited region, change the primary path, and delete the old IP address so as to support the mSCTP handover. For experimental analysis of mSCTP handover, we consider the handover scenarios for 3G-BWA and 3G-WLAN over Linux platforms. From experimental results, it is shown that the throughput and handover latency of the mSCTP handover would be affected by the timing of primary-change and the overlapping period.

Keywords: mSCTP, Link Layer, Handover, Mobility, Latency.

1 Introduction

Stream Control Transmission Protocol (SCTP), as defined in the IETF RFC 2960 [1], is an end-to-end, connection-oriented transport layer protocol, next to TCP and UDP. In particular, the SCTP multi-homing feature enables SCTP endpoints to support multiple IP addresses in an association. Each SCTP endpoint can send and receive messages from any of the several IP addresses. One of the several IP addresses is designed as the primary address during the SCTP initiation.

On the other hand, IP handover has been one of the challenging issues to support mobility between heterogeneous networks such as 3G-BWA (Broadband Wireless Access; IEEE 802.16(e)) and 3G-WLAN(Wireless LAN; IEEE 802.11) [2]. The mobile Stream Control Transmission Protocol (mSCTP) [3] can be used to support the soft handover for mobile terminals with the help of the SCTP multi-homing feature and ADDIP extension [4].

This paper describes a scheme of Dynamic IP Address Configuration using the link layer information for mSCTP handover (mSCTP-DAC). We especially propose the mSCTP-DAC scheme that can be used to dynamically and automatically configure the relevant IP addresses for the on-going SCTP session by using the status

* This research was supported by the MIC(Ministry of Information and Communication), Korea, under the ITRC (Information Technology Research Center) support program supervised by the IITA(Institute of Information Technology Assessment).

E. Sha et al. (Eds.): EUC 2006, LNCS 4096, pp. 244 – 253, 2006.

information of network interface, whenever a mobile terminal moves into a new region.

The recent works on SCTP include the capability of dynamic IP address reconfiguration during an association in the SCTP protocol level, which is called ADDIP extension [4]. While an SCTP association goes on, the ADDIP extension enables the SCTP to add a new IP address (ADD-IP), to delete an unnecessary IP address (DEL-IP) and to change the primary IP address (P-C) for the association. In this paper, we define mSCTP as SCTP with the ADDIP extension.

Figure 1 sketches the mSCTP handover for a Mobile Terminal (MT) between two different IP networks, where the MT is moving from Base Station (BS) A to B [3].

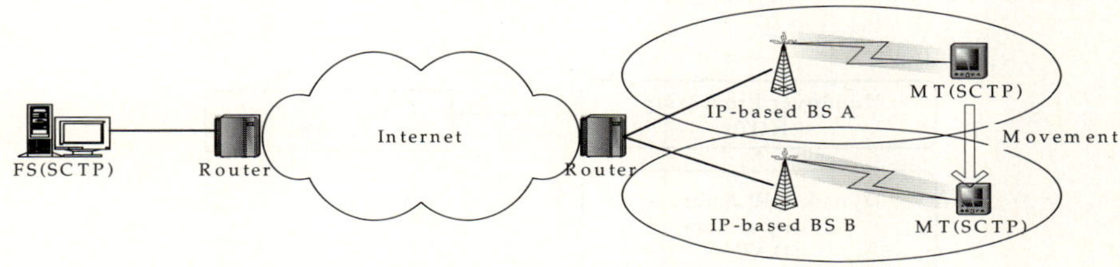

Fig. 1. mSCTP handover

In the figure, it is assumed that an MT initiates an SCTP session with a Fixed Server (FS). After initiation of an SCTP association, the MT moves from BS A to BS B, as shown in the figure. Refer to [4] for details of mSCTP handover procedures.

Some works [5-8] have been made on mSCTP handvoer. Those works in [5, 6, 7] have experimented the mSCTP handover by using manual (static) IP configuration. More especially, the works in [8] performed the experimental analysis by using the NS-2 simulator about when to add a new IP address and when to delete the existing IP address.

In this paper, we describe a 'dynamic (automaic)' IP address configuration scheme, rather than a 'manual (static)' scheme, for mSCTP handover. For experimental analysis, we use the NISTNET [9] network emulator to perform the mSCTP handover across heterogeneous networks such as 3G-BWA and 3G-WLAN. We consider the handover latency and throughput as the performance metrics.

This paper is organized as follows. In Section 2, we present the proposed dynamic IP address configuration scheme for mSCTP handover. Section 3 describes the mSCTP handover based on the proposed mSCTP-DAC scheme. Section 4 describes the experimental analysis of mSCTP handover over Linux platforms. Finally, Section 5 concludes this paper.

2 Dynamic IP Address Configuration Scheme for mSCTP Handover

To support the mSCTP handover for an MT, we need to detect movement of an MT and to determine when to perform the handover. This section describes the dynamic IP address configuration scheme for mSCTP handover (mSCTP-DAC). mSCTP-DAC interacts with the data link, IP and transport (SCTP) layer. More especially, mSCTP-DAC monitors status information on the attached link, determines when to trigger the handover, and then enables mSCTP to dynamically configure the IP addresses required for handover.

Figure 2 shows an overview of mSCTP-DAC operations. In the figure, mSCTP-DAC consists of three modules: Link Layer Information Monitoring (LLM), Dynamic IP Address Configuration (DAC), and Handover Processing (HOP). The LLM module collects state information at the link layer and IP layer, and sends it to the DAC module. DAC determines when to trigger HOP to perform mSCTP handover. HOP performs mSCTP handover at the transport layer with the SCTP protocol stack. The specific description for each module is given in the succeeding sections.

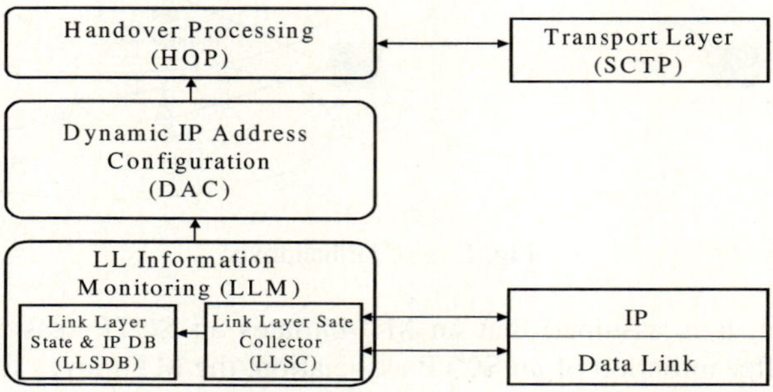

Fig. 2. Overview of mSCTP-DAC operations

2.1 Link Layer Information Monitoring (LLM)

The Link Layer information Monitoring (LLM) consists of the following two sub-modules: Link Layer State Collector (LLSC) and Link Layer State DB (LLSDB).

LLSC gathers state information of network links, and LLSDB contains the gathered information, and then transmits the state information, including IP addresses, to the DAC. In LLSC, it is assumed that MT has two different NIC (Network Interface Cards). LLSC first probes all the network interfaces attached to MT. It then monitors the status of link-up/down of the detected network interfaces. For example, if 'link-up' of 1st network interface is detected by LLSC, the corresponding link information and IP address will be recorded into LLSDB. In addition, the same procedures are applied to the link-down of network interfaces.

On the other hand, LLSDB transmits the information into the DAC module. It may include the following four fields: Interface ID, IP address, Signal Strength, and Link State. Interface ID indicates the interface name of the network link. IP address and Signal Strength field indicate the IP address and signal strength of link-up interface. In addition, Link State indicates whether the network interface is up or down. This information will be used to determine when to perform mSCTP handover by MT.

2.2 Dynamic IP Address Configuration (DAC)

The Dynamic IP Address Configuration (DAC) module can be used to determine when to perform mSCTP handover by analyzing state transition of link status, and requests the HOP module to trigger mSCTP handover. In order to determine when to perform mSCTP handover, the DAC module refers to link states of network interface.

The description of the associated states and events is given in Table 1.

Table 1. States and events used to trigger handover

STATE	DESCRIPTION	EVENT	DESCRIPTION
CLOSED	No link is up.	IF1_UP	LLM detects link-up of IF1
		IF2_UP	LLM detects link-up of IF2
IF1_SH	IF1 link is only link-up.	IF1_DOWN	LLM detects link-down of IF1
		IF2_DOWN	LLM detects link-down of IF2
IF2_SH	IF2 link is only up.	IF1_INIT_REQ	DAC request initiation of IF1 to HOP
		IF2_INIT_REQ	DAC request initiation of IF2 to HOP
		IF1_ADD_REQ	DAC request ADD-IP of IF1 to HOP
		IF2_ADD_REQ	DAC request ADD-IP of IF2 to HOP
IF_DH	Both IF1 and IF2 links are up.	IF1_DEL_REQ	DAC request DEL-IP of IF1 to HOP
		IF2_DEL_REQ	DAC request ADD-IP of IF1 to HOP
		IF1_P-C_REQ	DAC request P-C to HOP
		IF2_P-C_REQ	DAC request P-C to HOP

In Table 1, DAC defines four states and nine events used for handover. In the table, 'state' indicates the current link state of network interface, and 'event' indicates link state information of the corresponding interface, or message generated while the state is transited. In the table, CLOSED state means that there is no link-up of network interface. IF1_SH and IF2_SH mean that either 1st network or 2nd network interface is link-up. In addition, IF_DH means that both two network interfaces are link-up at the same time. For example, IF1_UP or IF1_DOWN event makes the 1st network interface link-up or link-down.

Based on these states and events, Figure 3 shows the state transition diagram used for mSCTP handover. As seen in Figure 3, the state transition diagram starts at the CLOSE state. CLOSE state means that the communication between MT and FS has not been initiated yet. DAC receives the link state event from LLSDB, and then makes state transmit from CLOSED into IF1_SH or IF2_SH state, if LLM detects a new link-up. When the state moves from CLOSED into IF1_SH or IF2_SH, either IF1_INIT_REQ or IF2_INIT_REQ event is generated and sent to the HOP module for initializing an SCTP session with the corresponding IP address. After that, if the DAC detects IF1_UP or IF2_UP event from the IF1_SH or IF2_SH state, the state moves into IF_DH. At this point, IF1_ADD_REQ or IF2_ADD_REQ event will be generated and sent to the HOP module for requesting addition of a newly assigned IP address to the SCTP session.

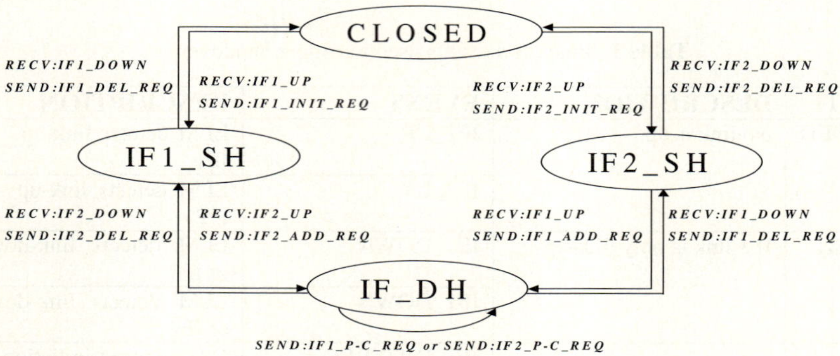

Fig. 3. State Transition Diagram of mSCTP-DAC

In the IF_DH state, the MT is in the overlapping area between the existing region and the new region. Moreover, when the signal strength of the new link-up interface is stronger than the threshold configured by system administrator, the IF1_P-C_REQ or IF2_P-C_REQ event may be generated and sent to the HOP module for requesting change of primary path, which will occur when the MT continuously moves toward the new region. From these events, MT uses the new IP address as the primary path.

After then, if the IF1_DOWN or IF2_DOWN event is sent from LLSDB, the state of DAC transits from IF_DH into IF1_SH or IF2_SH. In this case, the IF1_DEL_REQ or IF2_DEL_REQ is generated and sent to the HOP module for requesting deletion of the old IP address. At this state, it is considered that MT just left the existing region and is in the new region.

2.3 Handover Processing (HOP)

Handover Processing (HOP) is used to handle the SCTP ASCONF/ASCONF-ACK chunks required for mSCTP handover, with the help of the SCTP APIs. Initially, HOP initiates an SCTP association. If IF1_ADD or IF2_ADD, and IF1_DEL_REQ or IF2_DEL_REQ event are delivered from DAC, the HOP then sends the ASCONF (Address Configuration) chunk by calling sctp_bindx(). It then processes the corresponding ASCONF-ACK, and will call the sctp_recvmsg(). Moreover, when IF1_P-C_REQ or IF2_P-C_REQ events are received, the HOP module sends an ASCONF chunk for changing the primary path by calling setsockopt().

3 mSCTP Handover with mSCTP-DAC

To describe the operations of the mSCTP handover with mSCTP-DAC, we assume that an MT with the two different network interfaces tries to move across between heterogeneous networks.

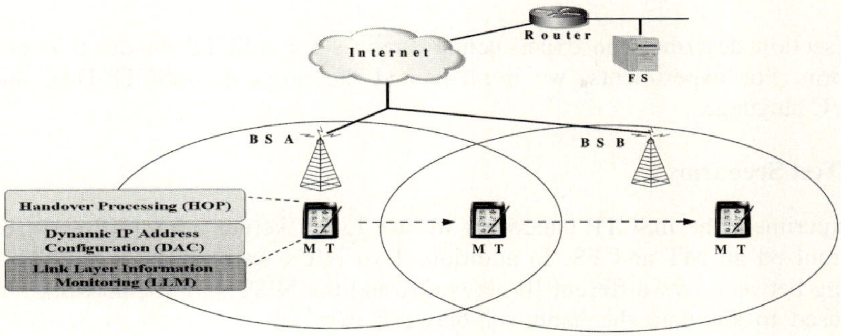

Fig. 4. The mSCTP handover with mSCTP-DAC module

In Figure 4, there are two heterogeneous networks, and an MT communicates with FS through Internet. Both MT and FS have the SCTP stack, and the MT additionally has the mSCTP-DAC module proposed in this paper. The mSCTP handover is performed as follows:

① When an MT enables the mSCTP-DAC mdule, an mSCTP session is initiated by MT. LLM Firstly collects the link-up of 1st network interface and records the information into DB. The state of mSCTP-DAC is transited from CLOSED to IF1_SH, and sends then the IF1_INIT_REQ event to the HOP module for adding the correspondent IP address. HOP then tries to initiate an SCTP association with the FS.

② When the MT moves toward a new region and then detects the new signal from the BS B, the 2nd network interface is link-up. The correspondent link state information is recorded into DB, and the state is transited from IF1_SH into IF_DH. At this time, DAC sends IF2_ADD_REQ event to HOP for adding the correspondent IP address to the SCTP session. The HOP generates an ASCONF chunk and sends it to the FS for ADD-IP, and receives the ASCONF-ACK chunk from the FS.

③ When the MT continuously moves toward the new region, and then the signal strength gets stronger than the pre-configured threshold, DAC sends IF2_P-C_REQ event to HOP module for requesting Primary-Change. HOP then sends ASCONF to FS for Primary-Change, and receives the ASCONF-ACK. If once the primary address is changed, the FS will send the outgoing data over the new primary IP address.

④ When LLM detects the link-down of 1st network interface as the MT progresses to move toward the new region, DAC transits the state from

IF_DH to IF2_SH, and then sends IF1_DEL_REQ to HOP for DEL-IP. The HOP module sends ASCONF to FS, and receives ASCONF-ACK.

⑤ The procedural steps for seamless handover described above will be repeated, whenever the MT moves to a new region.

4 Experimental Analysis of mSCTP-DAC

This section describes the experimental analysis for mSCTP handover over Linux platform. For experiments, we implemented the proposed mSCTP-DAC modules using C language.

4.1 Test Scenarios

To experiment the mSCTP handover, we use Linux kernel 2.6.8 [10] and LKSCTP [11] tool on an MT and FS. In addition, Two NICs were used for the MT that is moving between two different IP networks, and the NISTNET [9] network emulator was used to simulate the handover between two networks such as 3G-BWA and 3G-WLAN.

We have experimented the following two test scenarios, as shown in Figure 5.

A. Scenario A: mSCTP handover between 3G and BWA (see Fig. 5(a))
For the 3G-BWA scenario, an MT has two NICs and goes from 3G to BWA networks. When MT moves from 3G to BWA network, it tries to add the new IP address assigned from BWA, and delete the existing IP address assigned from 3G networks. In this case, the primary-change is performed in the overlapping region.

B. Scenario B: mSCTP handover between 3G and WLAN (see Fig. 5(b))
For the 3G-WLAN scenario, an MT has two NICs and goes from 3G to WLAN networks, and then it also goes from WLAN to 3G. It is noted that the primary-change for 3G-WLAN is performed twice in the experiments.

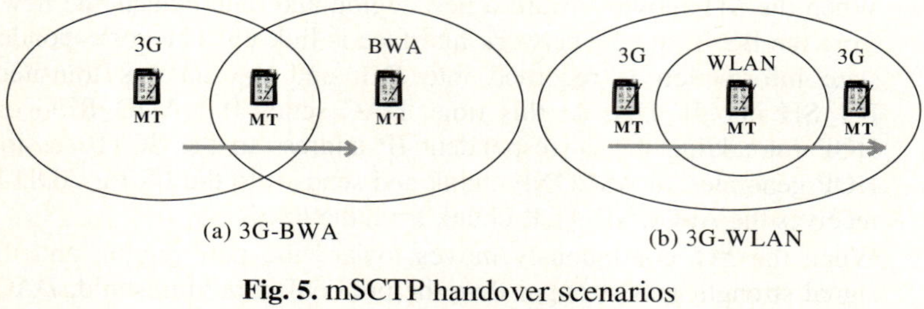

Fig. 5. mSCTP handover scenarios

On the other hand, the testbed environment consists of two hosts, one router for DHCP server, and a PC router for NISTNET. PC router has two NICs, which have an IP address "192.168.62.1" for 192.168.62.0 network and an IP address "192.168.1.1" for 192.168.1.0 network. An FS has an IP address "192.168.1.2". IP addresses of the MT are assigned from the DHCP server connected to the PC router. In the testbed network, the MT is initially connected to the 3G networks with the link bandwidth of 1.2 Mbps. After handover, the MT has the bandwidth of 5.4 Mbps to BWA or 8 Mbps to WLAN.

4.2 Experimental Results

We consider the throughput and handover latency as the performance metrics. We will analyze how the primary-change timing and the overlapping period can affect the mSCTP throughput and handover latency, respectively.

A. Throughput of mSCTP-DAC by Primary-Change

Figure 6 shows the experimental results of mSCTP-DAC handover in terms of the throughput for the two test scenarios: 3G-BWA and 3G-WLAN. In the figure, the number of transmitted packets exchanged between MT and FS are plotted, as the elapsed time goes on. For each experiment, we performed the primary-change (P-C) operations at three different time 5.5, 7.5, and 9.5 second. It is noted that the ADD-IP is performed at the time of 4.5 second for all the experiments.

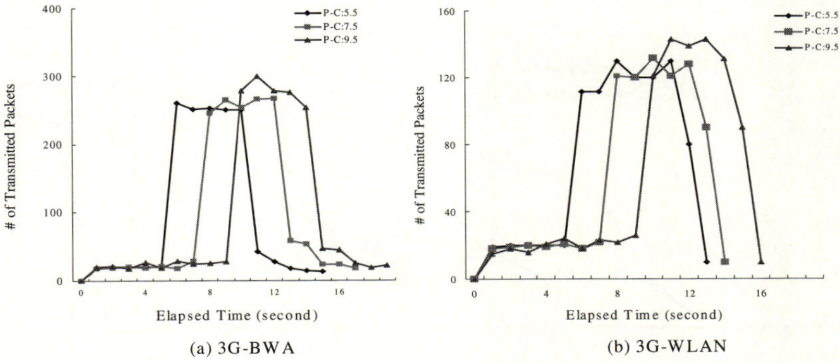

Fig. 6. Results on Throughput by mSCTP-DAC

Figure 6(a) depicts the results of throughput by mSCTP-DAC for three different Primary-Change scenarios. In the figure, we note that the # of transmitted packets rapidly increases after the primary-change operation (i.e., the transmitted packet count gets much larger after the P-C operation). This is because the MT moves from the old link of 3G with bandwidth of 1.2 Mbps to the new link of BWA with bandwidth of 5.4Mbps. We also note that the case with an earlier P-C operation has completed the data transmission faster.

On the other hand, Figure 6(b) shows the results on throughput by mSCTP-DAC for handover from 3G to WLAN, and again to 3G, for three different P-C scenarios. It is shown in the figure that the # of transmitted packets gets larger just after the primary-change operation (when the MT is in the WLAN network), and then falls back to the normal throughput of 3G Network.

In summary, we can see from Figure 6 that the mSCTP throughput is affected by the time when the primary-change operation is performed. It is better to perform the primary-change operation quickly when the MT goes into the network with a higher bandwidth.

B. Handover Latency of mSCTP-DAC by Overlapping Period

Figure 7 compares the handover latency of the mSCTP-DAC handover for the different times of the primary-change operation, given that the MT is staying in the overlapping region at the fixed period of 4.5 or 2.5 second. Figure 7(a) and 7(b) show the handover latency of the mSCTP handover between 3G and BWA, and between 3G and WLAN, respectively. As shown in the figure, the handover latency of mSCTP gets larger, as the time for the primary-change operation is delayed (after the ADD-IP operation). This implies that it is better for the MT to perform the primary-change operatin as soon as possible, in order to reduce the handover latency.

On the other hand, we can also see in the figure that the handover latency can be reduced for the larger overlapping period. In particular, when the MT is staying in the overlapping region enough to complete the primary-change operation (or when the MT is moving with a slower speed), the handover latency becomes nearly 'zero' if the primary-change operation is completed within the overlapping period, as shown at the P-C time of 1-3 second in Figure 7(a) and 7(b).

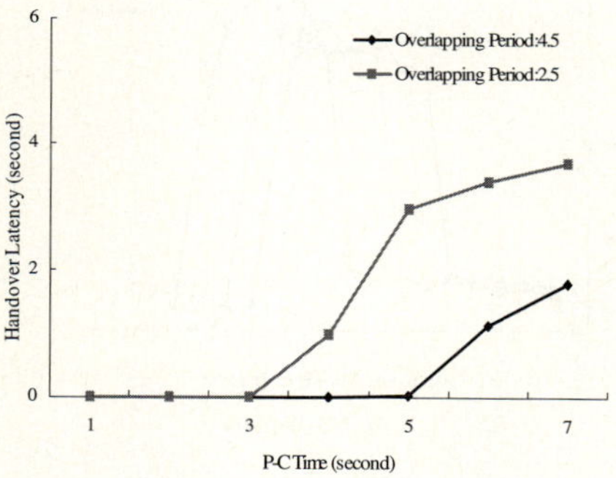

(a) 3G-BWA

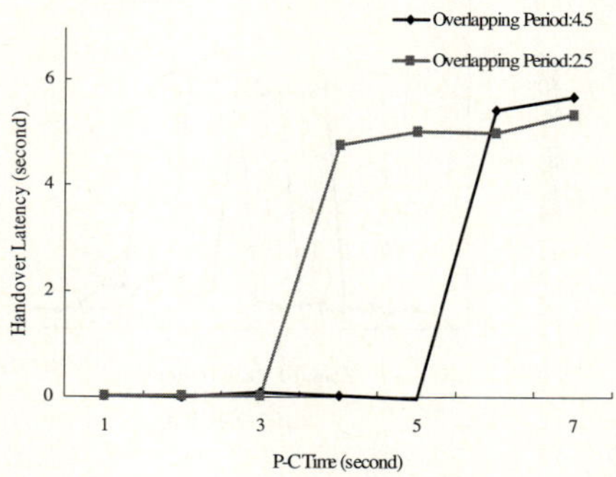

(b) 3G-WLAN

Fig. 7. Handover Latency by Primary-Change

As shown in the figure, the handover latency of mSCTP gets larger, as the time for the primary-change operation is delayed (after the ADD-IP operation). This implies that it is better for the MT to perform the primary-change operatin as soon as possible, in order to reduce the handover latency.

On the other hand, we can also see in the figure that the handover latency can be reduced for the larger overlapping period. In particular, when the MT is staying in the overlapping region enough to complete the primary-change operation (or when the MT is moving with a slower speed), the handover latency becomes nearly 'zero' if the primary-change operation is completed within the overlapping period, as shown at the P-C time of 1-3 second in Figure 7(a) and 7(b).

5 Conclusions

In this paper, we proposed a dynamic IP address configuration scheme using link-layer information for mSCTP handover (mSCTP-DAC), and performed the experimental analysis of mSCTP handover. The proposed dynamic IP address configuration scheme can be used to configure dynamically and automatically the relevant IP addresses for the on-going SCTP session by using the status information of network interface during the movement of an MT. For these experiments, we implemented mSCTP-DAC under Linux platform, and made some scenarios to show performance of mSCTP handover. Moreover, we used NISTNET network emulator to simulate the handover for 3G-BWA and 3G-WLAN environments.

From the experiments, it is shown that the throughput of the mSCTP handover becomes degraded, as the primary-change is delayed. We can also see that the handover latency of mSCTP becomes nearly zero if the primary-change operation can be completed within the overlapping period. Accordingly, we note that it is better to perform the primary-change operation as quickly as possible, when the MT goes into the network with a higher bandwidth.

References

1. Stewart R., et al., Stream Control Transmission Protocol, IETF RFC 2960, October 2000.
2. ITU-T Supplement to Recommendations Q.sup52, Technical Report on Mobility Management Requirement for Systems Beyond IMT-2000, 2005.
3. Koh, S., et al., "mSCTP for Soft Handover in Transport Layer," IEEE Communications Letters, Vol. 8, No.3, pp.189-191, March 2004.
4. Stewart R., et al., Stream Control Transmission Protocol (SCTP) Dynamic Address Reconfiguration, IETF Internet Draft, draft-ietf-tsvwg-addip-sctp-13.txt, November 2005.
5. Koh, S., et al., "mSCTP for Vertical Handover Between Heterogeneous Networks," LNCS 3597, pp. 28 – 36, July 2005.
6. Ma, L., *et al.*, "A New Method to Support UMTS/WLAN Vertical Handover Using SCTP," IEEE Wireless Comm., pp. 44-51, August 2004.
7. Jinyang S., *et al.*, "Experimental Performance Studies of SCTP in Wireless Access Networks," Proceedings of IEEE International Conference on Communication Technology (ICCT'03), vol.1, pp.392-395, April 2003.
8. Chang M., *et al.*, "Transport Layer Mobility Support Utilizing Link Signal Strength Information," IEICE Transactions on Communications, Vol. E87-B, No. 9, pp. 2548-2556, September 2004.
9. NISTNET network emulation package, Available from http://snad.ncsl.nist.gov/itg/nistnet
10. Linux Kernel Archives, Available from http://www.kernel.org/
11. Linux Kernel SCTP Project, Available from http://lksctp.sourceforge.net/

TCP-New Veno: The Energy Efficient Congestion Control in Mobile Ad-Hoc Networks

Namho Cho and Kwangsue Chung

School of Electronics Engineering, Kwangwoon University, Korea
nhcho@adams.kw.ac.kr, kchung@daisy.kw.ac.kr

Abstract. In recent years, there have been many researches about Mobile Ad-hoc Networks (MANETs) which is available to communicate freely between mobile devices by using multi-hop without any support of relay base or access point. TCP that used the most widely transport protocol in the Internet repeats packet loss and retransmission because it increases congestion window size by using reactive congestion control until packet loss occurs. As a result of this, the energy of mobile device is wasted unnecessarily.

In this paper, we propose TCP-New Veno in order to improve the energy efficiency of mobile device. According to the network state, the scheme adjusts appropriate size of congestion window. Therefore, the energy efficiency of mobile device and utilization of bandwidth are improved by the scheme. From the simulation by using ns-2, we could see more improved energy efficiency with TCP-New Veno than those with TCP in MANETs.

Keywords: Mobile Ad-hoc Networks (MANETs), TCP, Energy efficiency, Congestion control, Packet loss.

1 Introduction

In recent years, there have been many researches about Mobile Ad-hoc Networks (MANETs) which is available to communicate freely between mobile devices by using multi-hop without any support of relay base or access point. Unlike wired networks, there are some unique characteristics of MANETs. These characteristics include the lossy wireless channels due to noise, fading and interference, and the frequent route breakages and changes due to node mobility. Moreover, mobile nodes in MANETs can be an important part of MANETs because they can function as not only end-host but also intermediate node. Therefore, the lifetime of mobile nodes is closely related to the lifetime of MANETs [1,2].

TCP employs reactive congestion control. This congestion control repeats packet losses and retransmissions for recovery of the lost packet. Repeated retransmissions are not the problem in wired networks, but lead to waste the limited battery power of mobile nodes in MANETs. As a result, networks could be collapsed because the lifetime of mobile nodes is closely related to the lifetime of MANETs. Moreover, TCP can not distinguish between congestion loss and

E. Sha et al. (Eds.): EUC 2006, LNCS 4096, pp. 254–263, 2006.

link error loss. TCP unnecessarily invokes congestion control when a packet is lost due to link error. Since TCP wastes the limited bandwidth of MANETs, its performance is worse in MANETs.

In this paper, we propose TCP-New Veno in order to improve the performance of TCP in MANETs. According to the network state, the scheme adjusts appropriate size of congestion window. Moreover, when packet loss has occurred, the scheme invokes appropriate congestion control according to a cause of packet loss. Therefore, the energy efficiency of mobile device and utilization of bandwidth are improved by our proposed scheme.

The rest of this paper is organized as follows. Section 2 describes the problem with TCP in MANETs and the proposed work. The following section outlines the principles of our TCP-New Veno. The subsequent section presents the simulation results, and lastly we conclude the work.

2 Related Work

If TCP is used without modification in MANETs, the performance of TCP is seriously dropped. In this section, we describe the problem with TCP in MANETs and the related works.

2.1 The Problem with TCP in MANETs

TCP employs reactive congestion control. The congestion window is adjusted on the basis of the collective feedback of ACKs and DUPACKs generated at the receiver. TCP probes for the available bandwidth by continuously increasing the congestion window size gradually until the network reaches the congestion state. When packet loss has occurred, TCP will then fall back to a much slower transmission rate for reducing the congestion. TCP increases the congestion window size without taking the network capacity into consideration. In this sense, congestion and packet loss is inevitable. Therefore, the congestion control of TCP repeats packet losses and retransmissions for recovery of the lost packet. As a result, repeated retransmission is not the problem in wired networks, but leads to waste the limited battery power of mobile device in MANETs.

In MANETs, packet losses is usually caused by high bit error rate. However, TCP can not distinguish between congestion loss and link error loss. Whenever a packet is lost, TCP assumes that network congestion has happened since it is designed for wired networks originally. It then invokes the congestion control such as reducing congestion window. When packet loss has occurred due to link error, TCP interprets the packet loss as congestion. In this case, TCP unnecessarily invokes congestion control. As a result, its performance suffers from the unnecessary congestion control, causing reduction in throughput and link utilization [3,4].

2.2 TCP-Veno

The algorithm of TCP-Veno is mostly based on the algorithm of TCP-Vegas. In TCP-Vegas, the sender measures the *Expect Throughput* and *Actual*

Throughput as described in Figure. 1, where *cwnd* is the current congestion window size, *BaseRTT* is the minimum of measured round-trip times, *RTT* is the smoothed round-trip time measured, and N is the backlog at the bottleneck queue. TCP-Vegas attempts to keep N to small range by adjusting the congestion window size. If N exceeds $\beta(=3)$, TCP-Vegas assumes that the network is congested [5].

$$Expect\ Throughput = cwnd\ /\ BaseRTT$$
$$Actual\ Throughput = cwnd\ /\ RTT$$
$$N = (Expect\ Throughput - Actual\ Throughput) \times BaseRTT$$

Fig. 1. TCP-Vegas Algorithm

TCP-Veno modifies the AIMD(Additive Increase Multiplicative Decrease) of TCP-Reno based on the algorithm of TCP-Vegas. When *cwnd* exceeds *ssthresh* (slow-start threshold), TCP-Veno reduces the increase rate of *cwnd* to avoid congestion as defined in Figure 2. If N is below β, TCP-Veno assumes that the available bandwidth is not fully utilized. Therefore, TCP-Veno increases the *cwnd* by one after each round-trip time. If N exceeds β, TCP-Veno assumes that the available bandwidth is fully utilized. Therefore, TCP-Veno increases the *cwnd* by one after two round-trip times [6].

```
if(cwnd ≥ ssthresh)
    if(N < β)
        cwnd = cwnd + 1
    else
        cwnd = cwnd + 1/2
```

Fig. 2. TCP-Veno Additive Increase Algorithm

Moreover, TCP-Veno can distinguish between the congestion loss and the link error loss. When the sender receives the 3 duplicative ACKs in AI(Additive Increase) phase, TCP-Veno adjusts *ssthresh* as designed in Figure 3. If N exceeds β, TCP-Veno assumes that the packet loss has occurred due to congestion. Therefore, TCP-Veno adjusts the *ssthresh* and *cwnd* to a half of *cwnd* for alleviating the congestion. If N is below β, TCP-Veno assumes that the packet loss has occurred due to link error. In this case, TCP-Veno reduces the *ssthresh* and *cwnd* by a smaller amount.

In this manner, TCP-Veno effectively avoids repeated packet losses, retransmissions, and the unnecessary congestion control by using the dynamic adjustment of congestion window. However, like TCP-Vegas, TCP-Veno can also save the problem of incorrect *BaseRTT*. The *BaseRTT* is the smallest *RTT* without competitive flow in the network. Therefore, it is hard that the *BaseRTT* is correctly estimated. Because of this problem, TCP-Veno can not monitor the

```
if(N > β)
    cwnd = cwnd / 2          //Congestion Loss
else
    cwnd = cwnd / 0.8        //Link Error Loss
```

Fig. 3. TCP-Veno Multiplicative Decrease Algorithm

network state. In addition, the low utilization of bandwidth and the inaccuracy of discrimination loss type are caused by the inaccurate *BaseRTT* [7,8].

3 TCP-New Veno

In this section, we propose TCP-New Veno for improving the performance of TCP-Veno and describe the monitoring algorithm and the congestion control of TCP-New Veno.

3.1 The Monitoring Algorithm of the Network State

TCP-New Veno adds the monitoring algorithm of the network state for solving the problem of *BaseRTT*. Our TCP-New Veno classifies the network state into three states, that is, stable, congestion increase, and congestion decrease.

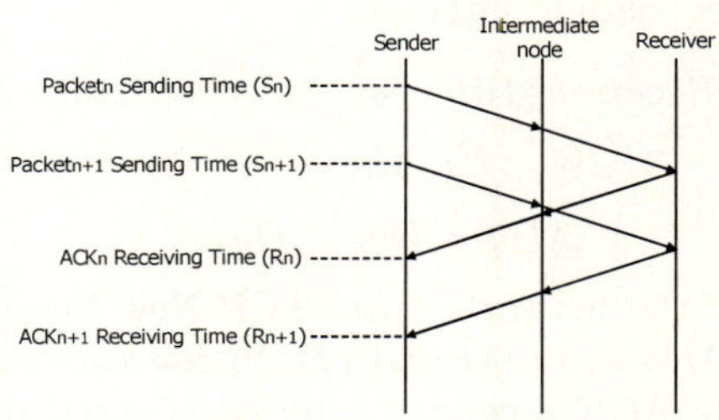

Fig. 4. Stable State of Network

Figure 4 shows the stable state of network. In this state, the sender sends $packet_n$ and $packet_{n+1}$ to receiver without queuing delay at S_n and S_{n+1} respectively. Then, the sender receives the ACKs for $packet_n$ and $packet_{n+1}$ at R_n and R_{n+1} respectively. Because of no queuing delay, the ACK receiving interval $R_{n+1} - R_n$ is equal to the packet sending interval $S_{n+1} - S_n$.

Figure 5 shows the congestion increase state of network. In this state, the packet is queued due to the congestion increase in the queue of immediate node. Since the packet queuing delay is increased, the ACK receiving interval is increased. Therefore, the ACK receiving interval exceeds the packet sending interval.

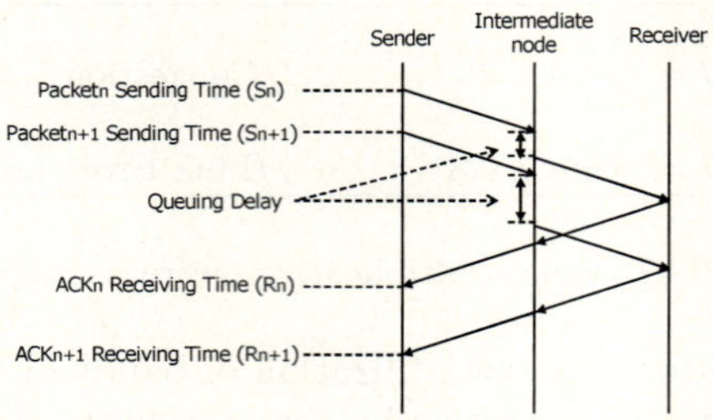

Fig. 5. Congestion Increase State of Network

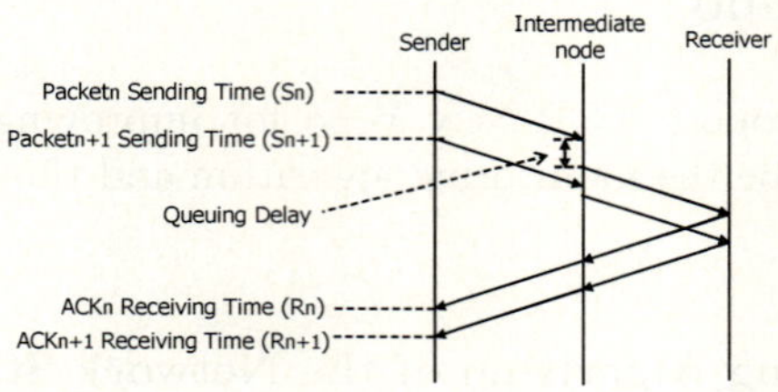

Fig. 6. Congestion Decrease State of Network

Figure 6 shows the congestion decrease state of network. Since the congestion decrease, the packet queuing delay is decreased. The ACK receiving interval is shorter than the packet sending interval.

$$\begin{aligned} Dq &= ACKReceivingInterval - PacketSendingInterval \\ &= (R_n - R_{n-1}) - (S_n - S_{n-1}) \end{aligned} \tag{1}$$

$$\Delta Dq = Dq_n - Dq_{n-1} \tag{2}$$

In order to monitor the network state, TCP-New Veno defines Dq(Relative Queuing Delay) and ΔDq as in (1) and (2). In the stable state of network, Dq is the zero because the ACK receiving interval is equal to the packet sending interval. In the congestion increase state of network, Dq has a positive value because the ACK receiving interval exceeds the packet sending interval. In the congestion decrease state of network, Dq has a negative value because the ACK receiving interval is below the packet sending interval. ΔDq, the difference of Dq, means the degree of the congestion increase rate. Figure 7 and Figure 8 show the summary of these concepts.

$Dq < 0$	//Congestion Decrease State
$Dq = 0$	//Stable State
$Dq > 0$	//Congestion Increase State

Fig. 7. Network State Classification Based on Dq

$\Delta Dq < 0$	//Congestion Degree Decrease State
$\Delta Dq = 0$	//Stable State
$\Delta Dq > 0$	//Congestion Degree Increase State

Fig. 8. Network State Classification Based on ΔDq

3.2 The Congestion Control

TCP-Veno estimates the network state by using N and β. TCP-Veno still inherits the *BaseRTT* problem from TCP-Vegas. Thus, TCP-Veno can't accurately estimate the network state. To solve the problem, TCP-New Veno introduces the concept of Dq and ΔDq. By using these parameters, TCP-New Veno modifies the AIMD defined in TCP-Veno.

```
if (N < β)
    set cwnd = cwnd + 1
if (N ≥ β)
    if (Dq < 0)            // Highly Aggressive Phase
        set cwnd = cwnd + 1
    if (Dq = 0)            // Aggressive Phase
        if (ΔDq ≤ 0)
            set cwnd = cwnd + 1
        if (ΔDq > 0)
            set cwnd = cwnd + 1/2
    if (Dq > 0)            // Conservative Phase
        if (ΔDq ≤ 0)
            set cwnd = cwnd + 1/4
        if (ΔDq > 0)
            set cwnd = cwnd
```

Fig. 9. Additive Increase Algorithm in TCP-New Veno

Figure 9 shows the additive increase algorithm of TCP-New Veno. If N is below β, TCP-New Veno increases the *cwnd* by one after each round-trip time because the available bandwidth is not full. If N exceeds β, TCP-New Veno classifies the *cwnd* adjustment in three phases, that is, highly aggressive, aggressive, and conservative, based on the value of Dq. First, in the highly aggressive phase, network congestion is getting better. In this phase, TCP-New Veno increases the *cwnd* by one after each round-trip time. Second, the network state is stable in aggressive phase. Since TCP-Reno increases aggressively the *cwnd* in the stable state of network, TCP-New Veno also increases aggressively the *cwnd*, based on ΔDq, to compete with TCP-Reno. Third, the conservative phase means that the available bandwidth is nearly full. Therefore, if ΔDq is the negative, TCP-New Veno increases conservatively the *cwnd*. If ΔDq is the positive, TCP-New Veno keeps the current *cwnd*.

Figure 10 shows the multiplicative decrease algorithm of TCP-New Veno. In TCP-Veno, when the sender receives three duplicative ACKs, it tries to find

```
if (N ≥ β)
    if (Dq > 0)          // Congestion Loss
        set ssthreshold = cwnd / 2
        set cwnd = ssthreshold
else
    Keep all parameters
```

Fig. 10. Multiplicative Decrease Algorithm in TCP-New Veno

the cause of the packet loss by using N and β. However, due to the problem of inaccurate $BaseRTT$, TCP-Veno can't accurately find the came out. To solve the problem in TCP-Veno, TCP-New Veno introduces the concept of Dq. If N exceeds β and Dq is the positive, TCP-New Veno assumes that the network is congested. Therefore, when packet loss is detected in this state, TCP-New Veno invokes the congestion control, like TCP-Reno.

TCP-New Veno modifies the AIMD employed in TCP-Veno by introducing new parameters, Dq and ΔDq. According to Dq and ΔDq, TCP-New Veno adjusts dynamically the *cwnd*. It can also discriminate the cause of packet loss. Therefore, TCP-New Veno can avoid repeating the packet loss and retransmission, and invoking the unnecessary congestion control. As the results, TCP-New Veno improves significantly the energy efficiency of mobile device and the bandwidth utilization.

4 Performance Evaluation of TCP-New Veno

In this section we evaluate the TCP-New Veno based on the ns-2 simulator [9]. This evaluation has been carried out to show some improvements on the throughput and the energy efficiency of TCP-New Veno in experimental networks. The performance of TCP-New Veno is compared with the performance of TCP-Reno and TCP-Veno.

4.1 Simulated Environment

The network configuration for the simulation is shown in Figure 11. The simulation is based on mobile nodes according to IEEE 802.11 with 2Mbps and a nominal transmission radius of 250m on the link layer [10]. We used the Ad-hoc On-demand Distance Vector(AODV) routing protocol [11]. Since we focus on performance in presence of link errors, the mobility of mobile node is excluded in this simulation. To generate the link errors, the intermediate node(S1) drops compulsively the packets as the packet loss rate. The ranges of packet loss rate is 0∼10 % . The source node(S0) sends continuously packet to the destination node(S2). The initial energy of the mobile nodes set to 100J(Joule). All nodes consume the 0.6W(Watt) for transmitting a packet and 0.3W for receiving a packet.

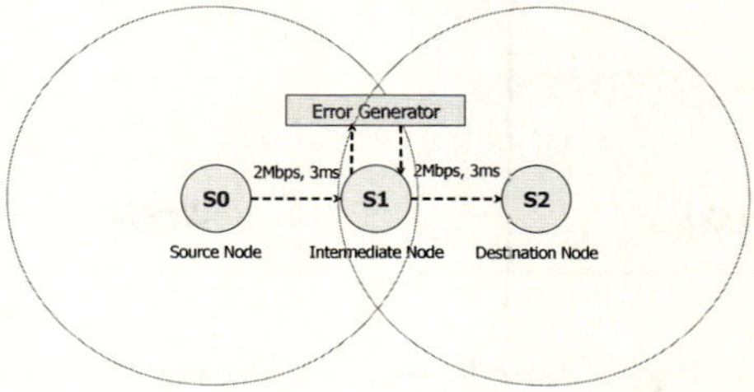

Fig. 11. Network Configuration for Simulations

4.2 Simulation Results

When packet losses have occurred due to the link error, Figure 12 shows the throughput of TCP-Reno, TCP-Veno and TCP-New Veno according to packet loss rate each. For 2% packet loss rate, Figure 12 (a) shows that TCP-New Veno performs better than TCP-Reno and nearly same as TCP-Veno. However, in Figure 12 (b) for 5% packet loss rate, TCP-New Veno performs much better than TCP-Reno and TCP-Veno. In Figure 12 (c) at 0~10% packet loss rate, the performance of TCP-New Veno is better than TCP-Reno and TCP-Veno since TCP-New Veno can discriminate accurately the cause of packet loss and avoid effectively the unnecessary congestion control. As the packet loss rate increases higher than 5% the performance of TCP-New Veno is decreased as TCP-Reno and TCP-Veno. It is because that timeout is invoked due to the ACK loss.

$$\text{Energy Efficiency}(\eta) = \frac{Throughput}{Consumed\ Energy}(Kb/sJ) \tag{3}$$

We also investigated the energy efficiency of each protocol in a lossy link situation. The energy efficiency of TCP-Reno, TCP-Veno and TCP-New Veno are shown in Figure 13. To evaluate the energy efficiency, we use the (3). It means the amount of bit that sender can send by a Joule. During the whole simulation time, 150sec, TCP-New Veno accomplishes better energy efficiency than TCP-Reno and TCP-Veno. The improvement is approximately about 20% $\sim$ 90% . At 5% packet loss rate, the throughput of TCP-Reno, TCP-Veno and TCP-New Veno are each of about 0.5Mbps, 1.3Mbps and 1.6Mbps. And the consumed energy of them is each of about 41J, 44J and 43J. Here, TCP-Reno has the low energy efficiency as the low throughput and high consumed energy. It means that TCP-Reno retransmits the large amount of packets. The consumed energy of TCP-New Veno is similar to TCP-Veno but the throughput of TCP-New Veno is higher than TCP-Veno. Therefore, TCP-New Veno has the better energy efficiency than TCP-Veno. This result shows that TCP-New Veno can avoid effectively the repeated retransmissions since it adjusts accordingly the *cwnd* by Dq and ΔDq.

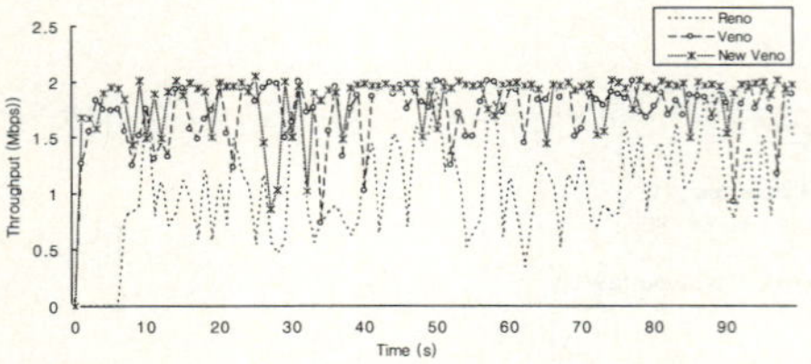

(a) Throughput at 2 % Packet Loss Rate

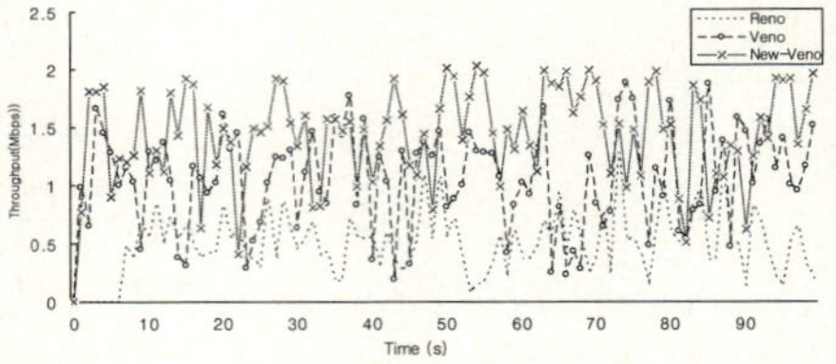

(b) Throughput at 5 % Packet Loss Rate

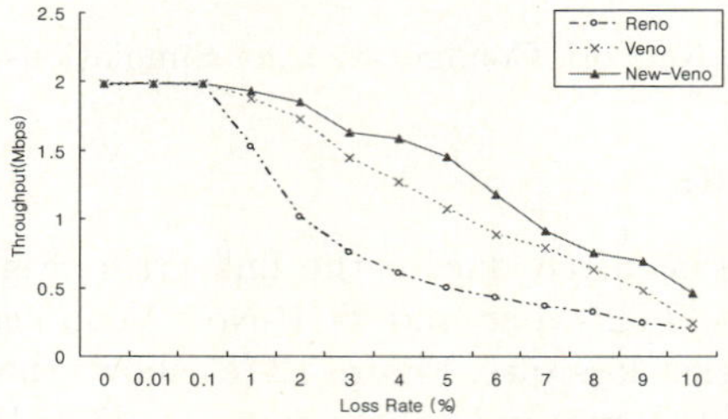

(c) Average Throughput vs Packet Loss Rate

Fig. 12. Throughput vs Packet Loss Rate

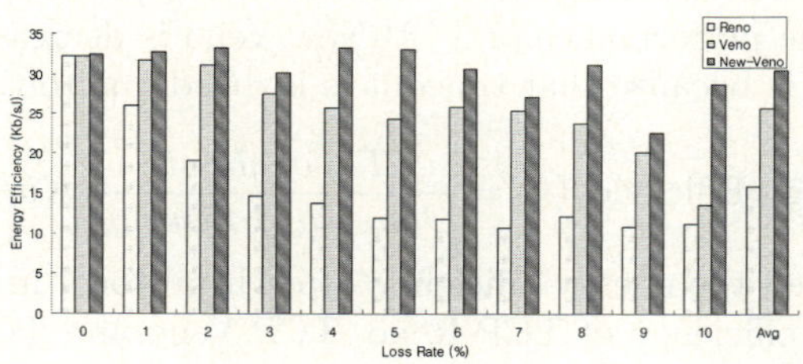

Fig. 13. Energy Efficiency VS Packet Loss Rate

5 Conclusion and Future Work

The performance of TCP degrades in MANETs since it can not distinguish between causes of packet losses. TCP does not also consider the energy of mobile node. In this paper, we propose the new transport protocol, called TCP-New Veno, to solve the problems of TCP in MANETs. The performance enhancement and and the energy efficiency in TCP-New Veno are obtained by avoiding the repeated retransmissions, by distinguishing between causes of packet loss, and by adjusting the *cwnd* to the current network state. The simulation results prove that TCP-New Veno has a better performance than TCP-Reno and TCP-Veno in MANETs.

In the future, we will focus our attention on the extension of TCP-New Veno such as mobility support and route change.

Acknowledgement

This research is supported by the MIC(Ministry of Information and Communication), Korea, under the ITRC(Information Technology Research Center) support program supervised by the IITA(Institute of Information Technology Assessment). This research also has been conducted by Korea Science and Engineering Foundation under contract number R01-2005-0000-10934-0.

References

1. The Internet Engineering Task Force: Mobile Ad-hoc Networks Discussion Archive-Data. http://www1.ietf.org/mail-archive/working-groups/manet/current/maillist.html
2. H. Balakrishnan, V. N. Padmanabhan, S. Seshan, and R. H. Katz: A Comparison of Mechanisms of Improving TCP Performance over Wireless Links. ACM Transactions On Networking. (1997)
3. H. Singh, S. Saena, and S. Singh: Energy Consumption of TCP in Ad Hoc Networks. Wireless Networks. (2004)
4. G. Holland and N. Vaidya: Analysis of TCP Performance over Mobile Ad Hoc Networks. ACM MOBICOM'99. (1999)
5. L. Brakmo and L. Peterson: TCP Vegas: End-to-end Congestion Avoidance on a Global Internet. IEEE Journal on Selected Areas in Communications. (1995)
6. C. P. Fu and S. C. Liew: TCP Veno: TCP Enhancement for Transmission over Wireless Access Networks. IEEE Journal of Selected Areas in Communications. (2003)
7. T. Henderson and E. Sahouria: On Improving the Fairness of TCP Congestion Avoidance. IEEE GLOBECOM'99. (1999)
8. W.Feng and S. Vanichpun: Enabling Compatibility Between TCP Reno and TCP Vegas. The Symposium on Applications and the Internet'2003. (2003)
9. UCB LBNL VINT: Network Simulator(ns-2). http://www.isi.edu/nanam/ns/
10. C. E. Perkins and E. M. Royer: Ad-hoc On-Demand Distance Vector Routing. IEEE Workshop on Mobile Computing Systems and Applications. (1999)
11. M. Gast: 802.11 Wireless Networks: The Definitive Guide. O'REILLY (2002)

A Real-Time Message Scheduling Scheme Based on Optimal Earliest Deadline First Policy for Dual Channel Wireless Networks*

Junghoon Lee[1], Mikyung Kang[1], Gyung-Leen Park[1], Ikchan Kim[1], Cheolmin Kim[2], Jong-Hyun Park[3], and Jiman Hong[4,**]

[1] Dept. of Computer Science and Statistics, Cheju National University
[2] Dept. of Computer Education, Cheju National University
[3] Telematics Research Group, Telematics and USN Laboratory, ETRI
[4] School of Computer Science and Engineering, Kwangwoon University
690-756, Jeju Do, Republic of Korea
{jhlee, mkkang, glpark, ickim, cmkim}@cheju.ac.kr, jhp@etri.re.kr, gman@daisy.kw.ac.kr

Abstract. This paper addresses the problem of scheduling time sensitive messages on dual channel wireless sensor networks. Besides the bandwidth expansion, partitioning evenly the transmission time makes it possible to inherit the optimality of EDF scheduling scheme on the dual channels based on fixed-size time slots synchronized across the two channels. Slot rearrangement also maximizes the number of switchable pairs, so the allocation can be switched dynamically between the channels according to the current channel status, enhancing the reliability of timely message delivery. Simulation results show that the rearrangement scheme can generate 70 % of switchable pairs even when the utilization reaches the saturation point, improving the ratio of successful transmission by up to 18 % when the packet error rate exceeds 0.4, compared with global EDF or NCASP.

1 Introduction

Wireless media such as WLAN (Wireless Local Area Network) have become increasingly important in today's computer and communications industry [1]. In addition to traditional data services, WLAN is creating new opportunities for the deployment of advanced multimedia services such as broadband VoD (Video on Demand). Meanwhile, one of the promising application areas of wireless technology is the wireless sensor network, where the periodically sampled data are delivered to the appropriate station within a reasonable deadline to produce meaningful data [2]. The message of sampled data has a real-time constraint that it should be transmitted within a bounded delay as long as the channel stays in good state. Otherwise, the data are considered to be lost, and

* This research was supported by the MIC, Korea, under the ITRC support program supervised by the IITA (IITA-2005-C1090-0502-0009).

** Corresponding author.

E. Sha et al. (Eds.): EUC 2006, LNCS 4096, pp. 264–273, 2006.

the loss of a real-time message may jeopardize the correctness of execution result or system itself. Accordingly, a real-time message stream strongly demands the guarantee from the underlying network that its time constraints are always met in advance of the system operation or connection setup.

However, the guarantee scheme is not sufficient to satisfy such time constraints as the wireless network is subject to unpredictable location-dependent and bursty errors, which make a real-time traffic application fail to send or receive some of its real-time packets [3]. In the mean time, the wireless network has an advantage that it can be easily duplicated, or a cell is able to operate dual channels, as a cell can have up to 3 channels according to the IEEE 802.11 standard. In this system, each sensor station may be equipped with a transmitter and a receiver that can tune to either channel, giving the flexibility to transmit and receive on both channels. After all, the dual channel system enables various ways to improve the reliability of the message delivery.

The dual network architecture is analogous to the dual processor system in that both network and processor can be considered as an active resource. However, real-time scheduling for dual or multiple resource system is known to be an NP-hard problem [4], while the uniprocessor system has an optimal scheduling solutions such as RM (Rate Monotonic) for static scheduling as well as EDF (Earliest Deadline First) for dynamic scheduling. Applying RM or EDF method to multiple resource system is not optimal in scheduling preemptable jobs due to its work conserving nature [5]. Existing multichannel scheduling schemes such as MULTI-FIT cannot be applied directly to the real-time communication, as they didn't directly take into account the timeliness requirement [4].

In wireless sensor network, each message usually has no data dependency, so the optimality of EDF scheme can be sustained also for the dual networks by evenly partitioning each stream rather than grouping streams into two sets. Moreover, the dual channels can efficiently cope with network errors without violating the time constraints of messages, if the transmission order is rearranged lest the same stream should be scheduled on the concurrent time slots of two channels. Then, the allocation can be switched dynamically between the channels according to the current channel status. With these assertions, we are to propose and analyze the performance of a bandwidth allocation scheme for real-time sensor messages on the dual channel wireless networks, aiming at keeping the optimality of EDF scheduling scheme as well as maximizing the capability of coping with wireless channel errors. In this paper, the infrastructure mode IEEE 802.11 WLAN is assumed to be the target communication architecture [6].

The rest of this paper is organized as follows: Section 2 will introduce backgrounds and related works on real-time message scheduling for multiple networks, and then Section 3 explains the scope of this paper and basic assumptions on network, message, and error models. Section 4 will describe the proposed scheduling scheme in detail along with a relevant example. After exhibiting the performance measurement result in Section 5, Section 6 concludes this paper and briefly describes future works.

2 Background and Related Works

The IEEE 802.11 was developed as a MAC (Medium Access Control) standard for WLAN, and the standard consists of both an essential DCF (Distributed Coordination Function) and an optional PCF (Point Coordination Function) [6]. The DCF exploits collision-based CSMA/CA (Carrier Sense Multiple Access with Collision Avoidance) protocol for non-real-time messages, aiming at enhancing not only their average delivery time but also overall network throughput. However, packet collisions, intrinsic to CSMA and its variants, make it impossible for a node to predictably access the network. In the other hand, PCF mode makes one AP (Access Point) take the initiative of the traffic flow from all stations onto the network medium. The AP polls all stations to determine which station has the right to transmit during a given time slice, and it can prioritize traffic from specific stations, as well as guarantee the bounded latency for data transmission. In addition, the available wireless spectrum is divided into several channels. The IEEE 802.11b standard specifies 11 channels operating in the 2.4 GHz band with 80 MHz of reusable spectrum. Even though the number of simultaneous channels in a cell is limited to 3 due to the channel overlap problem, it is possible to create multiple channels from the wireless spectrum in a cell.

As the most prominent dynamic priority scheduling mechanism for the uniresource real-time system, EDF algorithm assigns priorities to individual jobs in the tasks according to their absolute deadlines. M. Caccamo et al. have proposed a MAC that supports deterministic real-time scheduling via the implementation of TDMA (Time Division Multiple Access) to apply the EDF scheme to the WLAN [7]. Referred as *implicit contention*, their scheme makes every station concurrently run the common real-time scheduling algorithm to determine which message can access the medium. Each message implicitly contends for the medium through the scheduling algorithm, for example, with priorities, rather than explicitly on the physical medium, thus it can save power and time.

Traditionally, there have been two approaches for scheduling periodic tasks in dual or multiprocessors, namely, *partitioning* and *global scheduling* [4]. The partitioning scheme assigns each stream to a single network, on which messages are scheduled independently. The main advantage of partitioning approaches is that they reduce a multiprocessor scheduling problem to a set of uniprocessor ones. However, finding an optimal assignment to networks is a bin-packing problem, which is NP-hard in the strong sense. For another example, Lee et al. have proposed a bandwidth allocation scheme for real-time traffic on dual channel WLANs, which decides the polling vector based on the weighted round robin policy for CFP (Contention Free Period) [8]. Though their scheme can efficiently overcome the deferred beacon problem that significantly deteriorates the schedulability of WLAN for real-time messages, it did not consider how to cope with the channel error at all.

In global scheduling, all eligible tasks are stored in a single priority-ordered queue while the global scheduler selects the highest priority task for execution from this queue. For example, CASP (Contiguous Algorithm for Single Priority) maintains an allocation vector V, where V_i represents the partial sum of slots currently allocated to channel i [9]. For a given request, the scheduling algorithm allocates the request contiguously on the channel which has the least partial sum of allocation. In contrast, NCASP (Non-continuous Algorithm for Single Priority) defines an overflow amount Φ, and if an assignment makes V_i exceed Φ, it is split and then the overflown part is assigned to another resource. However, how to decide Φ brings another complex case-sensitive problem.

3 Basic Assumptions

3.1 Network and Error Models

To begin with, each cell is assumed to consist of an AP and multiple (mobile) SSs (sensor stations) as shown in Fig. 1. Each member of a cell has interfaces to two respective channels, and transmits or receives data on two channels in parallel. AP may be linked to a wired backbone or other wireless channel. In a cell, every station shares medium on the common frequency band and accesses according to the predefined MAC protocol. Whether each flow is ether an uplink (SS to AP) or downlink (AP to SS), AP coordinates the overall network operations. This paper exploits the contention-free polling-based access policy as in most of previous works [3,4,10], for the real-time guarantee cannot be provided without developing a deterministic access schedule, as well as the contention resolution via packet collisions consumes the precious communication energy. Moreover, the mobility of sensor station can be reinforced by an appropriate hand-off mechanism [11].

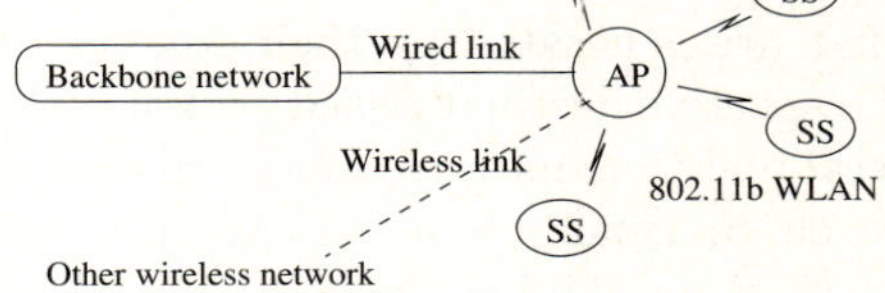

Fig. 1. Network model

Each station is associated with a channel link which has either of two states, namely, *error state* and *error-free state* at any time instant. A channel link is defined between each mobile and the AP, and it can be modeled as a Gilbert channel [12]. We can denote the transition probability from state *good* to state *bad* by p and the probability from state *bad* to state *good* by q, as shown in Fig. 2. The pair of p and q representing a range of channel link conditions, has been obtained by using the trace-based channel link estimation. The average error probability and the average length of a burst of errors are derived as $\frac{p}{p+q}$ and $\frac{1}{q}$, respectively. A packet is received correctly if the channel link remains in state *good* for the whole duration of packet transmission. Otherwise, it is received in error. Channel links between the AP and respective stations are independent

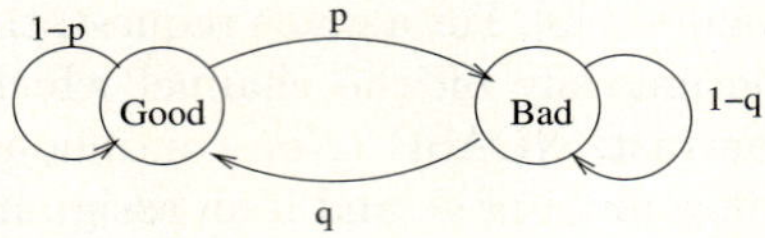

Fig. 2. Error model

of one another in their error characteristics. Correspondingly, while error-free transmission may be possible between a given host and the AP, transmission between another host and the AP may be corrupted by errors.

3.2 Message Model

A station, currently inactive, can be activated by an upper layer query command that wants to monitor or process the data flow from the sensor station [13]. The query may also specify sampling period as well as precision level of needed data to determine the message length. In case of a change in the active flow set, the network schedule should be regenerated [5]. The destination of a message can be either within a cell or outside a cell, and the outbound messages are first sent to the AP and then forwarded to the remote destination, while internal messages are also relayed by the AP. Hence, AP also acts as another source of message stream and is treated as such with an exception that it is just virtually polled. In addition, WLAN mandates the ACK from the receiver for every unicast transmission, but it consumes not a little network time and is meaningless, as the retransmission is only possible upon the polling from AP, not a sender station. Accordingly, even for the point-to-point streaming, multicast mode transmitting is assumed to deactivate the mandatory ACK.

The traffic of sensory data is typically *isochronous* (or synchronous), consisting of message streams that are generated by their sources on a continuing basis and delivered to their respective destinations also on a continuing basis [5]. This paper follows the general real-time message model which has n streams, namely, S_1, S_2, ..., S_n, and each S_i generates a message not more than C_i at each beginning of its period P_i, while the first message of each stream arrives at time 0. Each packet must be delivered to its destination within D_i time unit from its generation or arrival at the source, otherwise, the packet is considered to be lost. D_i usually coincides with P_i to ensure that the transmission completes before the generation of the next message. However, sometimes, D_i is larger than P_i, and in this case, more errors can be recovered within message deadline. Finally, each stream belongs to a specific station, so if a slot is assigned to a stream, it means that AP should poll that station at the slot time.

4 Dual Channel Operation

4.1 Bandwidth Management

The network time is divided into a series of fixed-size slots, and each of them is exclusively assigned to a real-time station, completely removing a contention procedure such as CSMA/CA, for the sake of both real-time guarantee and power saving, as mentioned earlier. The slot length, say L, is as large as the basic unit of wireless data transmission and every traffic is also segmented to fit the slot size. On WLAN, such network access can be implemented by making AP poll each station according to the predefined schedule during the CFP, while each station transmits for as long as L. To describe the goal of slot assignment, let $< f_i^1, f_i^2 >$ be the i-th slots of channel 1 and channel 2. If f_i^1 and f_i^2 are allocated to different streams, say A and B, respectively, switching their transmission channels does not violate their time constraints. We define a *switchable pair* if f_i^1 and f_i^2 are allocated to different streams, or any one of f_i^1 and f_i^2 is left unassigned. The purpose of bandwidth allocation, or slot assignment is to maximize the number of switchable pairs, as it can overcome channel errors as already explained in Section 1.

For AP to decide the polling order for a stream set, each stream S_i submits tuple of (P_i, C_i) information to AP. For simplicity, we assume that every P_i as well as C_i is an integer multiple of L. The bandwidth allocation consists of 3 steps, namely, stream partition, EDF based reservation, and slot rearrangement. At Step 1, to inherit the optimality of EDF in a single resource system, the allocation scheme first partitions the given stream set into two identical sets so that each of them has the same period but the transmission time of every stream is reduced by half. Namely,

$$\Theta : \{(P_i, C_i)\} \rightarrow \Theta_1 : \{(P_i, \tfrac{C_i}{2})\}, \Theta_2 : \{(P_i, \tfrac{C_i}{2})\}$$

Then, the schedulability of message streams is tested by the following sufficient condition [5]:

$$\textstyle\sum_{i=1}^{n} \frac{C_i}{P_i} + \Delta \leq 1.0,$$

which assumes that there are n streams and that all the messages are sorted by increasing relative deadlines, while Δ denotes the overhead term originated from the network management such as polling/probing overhead, beacon packet broadcast, interframe space, and so on. As Δ is fixed for a stream set, we can calculate per-slot overhead, and merge it into C_i. Hence, Δ can be assumed to be 0, enabling us to concentrate on the problem of slot allocation.

Next at Step 2, the transmission is reserved for a fixed number of time slots by a station. The AP should create a polling table for the entire polling sequence. For S_i, every message arrival is estimated at 0, P_i, $2P_i$, and so on, while each invocation needs $\lceil \frac{C_i}{L} \rceil$ slots. Based on these estimations, the scheduling is virtually performed at each slot boundary to build a polling order table. The scheduler selects the message whose deadline is closest and allocates the next slot to it. If no slot request is pending at a slot boundary, the scheduler leaves the slot unassigned. The schedule for Θ_1 and Θ_2 is determined by EDF policy, both schedules being identical. The table-driven reservation scheme seems to demand a lot of memory space to store the polling order information. However, since the invocation behavior for a set of periodic tasks repeats itself once every T time units, where T, called the *planning cycle* of the task set, is the least common multiple of the periods of all periodic tasks, we only need to consider all the task invocation in a planning cycle.

Finally in Step 3, the allocation in Θ_2 is rearranged to maximize the number of switchable pairs. When the allocation scheme generates the schedule of Θ_2, it also creates the list of range to which an allocation can be migrated. The earliest time of movement, E_t, is the arrival time of message associated with slot t, while the amount of backward movement is marked as its laxity, L_t. The E_t and L_t of unassigned slot are set to 0 and T, respectively, as it can be relocated anywhere within the planning cycle. From the last slot, f_t^1 and f_t^2 are investigated whether they are equal, namely, they are allocated to the same station. If so, the rearrangement procedure attempts to change f_t^2 as follows:

```
for slot i from E_t to t
  if (f_i^2 == f_t^2) continue; // same station
  if (L_i < t) continue; // cannot be deferred
  else exchange f_i^2 and f_t^2 and break;
```

[Example] The example stream set consists of 3 streams, A(6,2), B(3,2), and C(4,4). Their utilization is 2.0, the length of planning cycle being 12. At Step 1, the given stream set is partitioned into Θ_1 : {(6,1), (3,1), (4,2)} and Θ_2 : {(6,1), (3,1), (4,2)}. Then EDF generates same network schedules for two networks as shown in Fig. 3(a). The figure also shows that the earliest relocatable slot and slack time by which the allocation can be deferred. The rearrangement procedure begins from slot 11 backward to slot 0. As shown in Fig. 3(a), f_{11}^1 and f_{11}^2 are both C, so it is desirable to relocate C in f_{11}^2. Among slots from 8 (decided by E_{11}) to 11, as f_8^2 is A and $L_8 + 8 \geq t$, f_8^2 and f_{11}^2 are exchanged, making $< f_{11}^1, f_{11}^2 >$ a switchable pair. This procedure will be repeated up to slot 0 and Fig. 3(b) shows the final allocation. In this example, every slot pair turned into the switchable one.

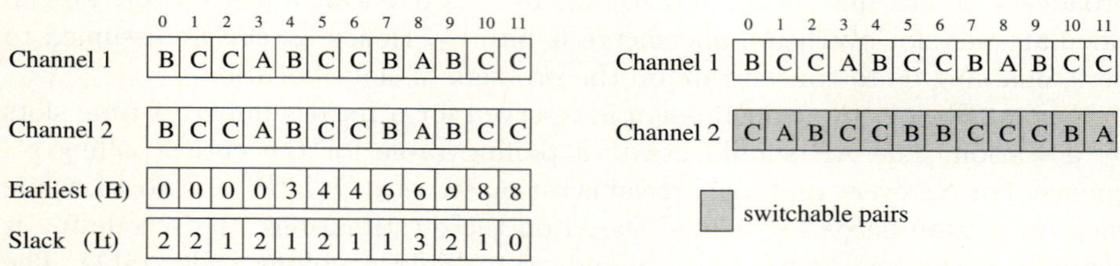

(a) Step 1 : partition (b) Step 2 : rearrangement

Fig. 3. Example of scheduling procedure

4.2 Runtime Scheduling

Before polling a station, the AP transmits a probing control packet to the scheduled station, which then returns the control packet to the AP [10]. If the AP does not receive the probing control packet correctly from the station, the channel is estimated to be bad. Even though the probing indicates the channel is good, the ensuing transmission can fail if a state transits to the bad state during the transmission. Let's assume that AP is to start slot i which is originally allocated to A on channel 1 as well as B on channel 2, namely, $< A, B >$. AP first probes the channel condition from itself to A and B on all two channels. Thus each slot should inevitably contain two probing latencies. Table 1 shows the probing result and corresponding actions. As shown in row 1, AP can reach A on channel 1 and also B on channel 2, AP polls each station as scheduled. In row 2, all connections from AP are good except the one to B through channel 2. If we switch $< A, B >$ to $< B, A >$, both streams can successfully send their messages. Otherwise, only A can send on channel 1, so in this case, we can save one transmission loss. Row 8 describes the situation that AP can reversely reach A only on channel 2 while B on channel 1. By switching polls between the two channels, AP can save the 2 transmissions that might fail on ordinary schedule.

Table 1. Channel status and transmission

No.	Ch1–A	Ch2–B	Ch1–B	Ch2–A	Ch1	Ch2	save
1	Good	Good	X	X	A	B	0
2	Good	Bad	Good	Good	B	A	1
3	Good	Bad	Good	Bad	A	–	0
4	Good	Bad	Bad	X	A	–	0
5	Bad	Good	Good	Good	B	A	1
6	Bad	Good	Good	Bad	–	B	0
7	Bad	Good	Bad	X	–	B	0
8	Bad	Bad	Good	Good	B	A	2
9	Bad	Bad	Good	Bad	B	–	1
10	Bad	Bad	Bad	Good	–	A	1
11	Bad	Bad	Bad	Bad	–	–	0

X : don't care

5 Performance Evaluation

This section measures the performance of the proposed scheme in terms of switchable pairs and corresponding success ratio according to the packet error rate via simulation using ns-2 event scheduler [14]. For the first experiment, we fixed the length of planning cycle to 24 as well as the number of streams to 3, and generated every possible stream sets whose utilization ranges from 0.2 to 2.0, aiming at measuring how many the rearrangement scheme can generate switchable pairs. Fig. 4 plots the measurement result sorted by the utilization of stream sets. Even when the utilization is 2.0, 17 out of 24 slots are rearranged to switchable pairs on average. As the utilization gets lower, the number of switchable pairs increases, since the number of unassigned slots also grows. Global EDF generates the switchable pair only by unassigned slots, so the number of switchable pairs proportionally decreases as the utilization increases. The gap between the two schemes becomes large on the higher utilization.

Fig. 5 shows the success ratio according to the packet error rate along with utilization to demonstrate the effect of slot rearrangement. The success ratio means the ratio of timely delivered real-time packets to all generated packets. The packet error rate is the function of packet length and bit error rate, and it ranges from 0.0 to 0.4, considering the error-prone wireless channel characteristics. This experiment compared the success ratio of the proposed scheme with those of global EDF and NCASP. The value of Φ is ideally chosen to 12. As shown in Fig. 5, first of all, when the packet error rate is 0.0, every transmission succeeds both in our scheme and in global EDF regardless of utilization. However, NCASP misses some deadlines because it cannot optimally schedule the real-time packets when utilization exceeds 1.3. The proposed scheme outperforms the global EDF by around 18 % at maximum due to the difference in the number of switchable pairs when the packet error rate is over 0.4. The performance gap gets larger according to the increase of packet error rate. On lower utilization, NCASP shows almost same performance as the proposed scheme since it assigns a series of slots to stream, maximizing the number of switchable pairs. However, the limitation of real-time scheduling capability causes performance degradation on high utilization.

Actually, we have also measured the effect of deadline length to the success ratio. However, even in the case the deadline is longer than the period, the rearrangement within a planning cycle did not result in a significant performance improvement. The rearrangement across the planning cylce will bring another difficult problem.

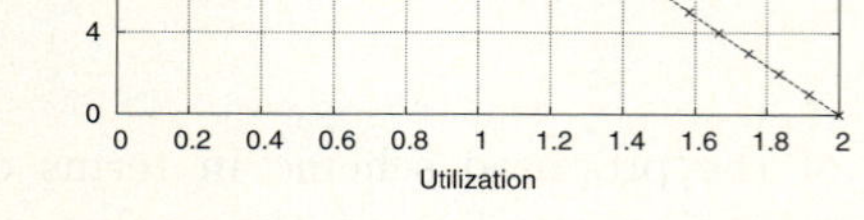

Fig. 4. Number of switchable slots

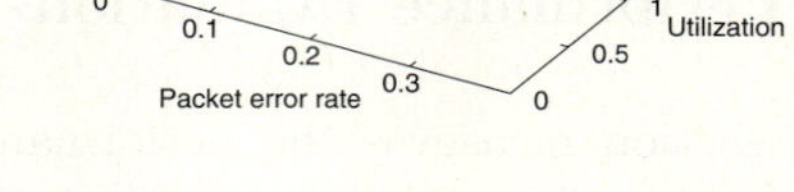

Fig. 5. Success ratio

6 Conclusion

This paper has proposed and analyzed the performance of real-time message scheduling scheme for dual channel wireless sensor networks. The proposed scheme solves NP-hard complexity of multiple resource scheduling by evenly partitioning the stream set into two identical sets to apply EDF policy that is optimal under uniprocessor environment for dynamic preemptive real-time scheduling. In addition, slot rearrangement maximizes the number of switchable pairs, so the AP can dynamically select the error-free channel for two streams. Simulation results show that the proposed scheme can generate 70 % of switchable pairs even when the utilization reaches the saturation point, improving the ratio of timely delivery by up to 18 % when the packet error rate exceeds 0.4.

As a future work, we will extend the allocation scheme to combine the error control functions such as the retransmission of damaged packets as well as reclaim the unused slot to reassign to other reachable stations. For example, the polling table in Table 1 has some entries marked as '-', which means AP cannot poll A or B. In this case, it seems better to poll another station, and the way to select this station is to be investigated.

References

1. Rangnekar, A., Wang, C., Sivalingam, K., Li, B.: Multiple access protocols and scheduling algorithms of multiple channel wireless networks. Handbook of Algorithms for Mobile and Wireless Networking and Computing (2004)
2. Li, H., Shenoy, P., Ramamritham, K.: Scheduling communication in real-time sensor applications. Proc.10th IEEE Real-time Embedded Technology and Applications Symposium (2004) 2065–2080
3. Adamou, M., Khanna, S., Lee, I., Shin, I., Zhou, S.: Fair real-time traffic scheduling over a wireless LAN. Proc. IEEE Real-Time Systems Symposium (2001) 279–288
4. Carpenter, J., Funk, S., Holman, P., Srinivasan, A., Anderson, J., Baruah, S.: A categorization of real-time multiprocessor scheduling problems and algorithms. Handbook of Scheduling: Algorithms, Models, and Performance Analysis. Chapman Hall/CRC Press (2003)
5. Liu J.: Real-Time Systems. Prentice Hall (2000)
6. IEEE 802.11-1999: Part 11-Wireless LAN Medium Access Control (MAC) and Physical Layer (PHY) Specifications (1999)
7. Caccamo, M., Zhang, L., Sha, L., Buttazzo, G.: An implicit prioritized access protocol for wireless sensor networks. Proc. IEEE Real-Time Systems Symposium (2002)
8. Lee, J., Kang, M., Park, G.: Design of a hard real-time guarantee scheme for dual ad hoc mode IEEE 802.11 WLANs. Lecture Notes in Computer Science, Vol. 3738. Springer-Verlag, Berlin Heidelberg New York (2005) 141–152
9. Damodaran, S., Sivalingam, K.: Scheduling algorithms for multiple channel wireless local area networks. Computer Communications (2002)
10. Choi, S., Shin, K.: A unified wireless LAN architecture for real-time and non-real-time communication services. IEEE/ACM Trans. on Networking **8** (2000) 44–59
11. Kang, M., Lee, J., Hong, J., Kim, J.: Design of a fast handoff scheme for real-time media application on the IEEE 802.11 wireless LAN, accepted to at LNCS: International Conference on Computational Science (2006)
12. Shah, S., Chen, K., Nahrstedt, K.: Dynamic bandwidth management for single-hop ad hoc wireless networks. ACM/Kluwer Mobile Networks and Applications (MONET) Journal **10** (2005) 199-217
13. Madden, S., Franklin, M., Hellerstein, J., Hong, W.: The design of an acquisitional query processor for sensor networks. ACM SINGMOD (2003)
14. Fall, K., Varadhan, K.: Ns notes and documentation. Technical Report. VINT project. UC-Berkeley and LBNL (1997)

On Multiprocessor Utility Accrual Real-Time Scheduling with Statistical Timing Assurances

Hyeonjoong Cho[1], Haisang Wu[2], Binoy Ravindran[1], and E. Douglas Jensen[3]

[1] ECE Dept., Virginia Tech, Blacksburg, VA 24061, USA
{hjcho, binoy}@vt.edu
[2] Juniper Networks, Inc., Sunnyvale, CA 94089, USA
hswu@ieee.org
[3] The MITRE Corporation, Bedford, MA 01730, USA
jensen@mitre.org

Abstract. We present the first Utility Accrual (or UA) real-time scheduling algorithm for multiprocessors, called gMUA. The algorithm considers an application model where real-time activities are subject to time/utility function time constraints, variable execution time demands, and resource overloads where the total activity utilization demand exceeds the total capacity of all processors. We establish several properties of gMUA including optimal total utility (for a special case), conditions under which individual activity utility lower bounds are satisfied, a lower bound on system-wide total accrued utility, and bounded sensitivity for assurances to variations in execution time demand estimates. Our simulation experiments confirm our analysis and illustrate the algorithm's effectiveness.

1 Introduction

Multiprocessor architectures (e.g., Symmetric Multi-Processors or SMPs, Single Chip Heterogeneous Multiprocessors or SCHMs) are becoming more attractive for embedded systems primarily because major processor manufacturers (Intel, AMD) are making them decreasingly expensive. This makes such architectures very desirable for embedded system applications with high computational workloads, where additional, cost-effective processing capacity is often needed. But this exposes the critical need for multiprocessor real-time scheduling, which has recently received significant attention.

Pfair algorithms [3] have been shown to achieve a schedulable utilization bound (below which all tasks meet their deadlines) that equals the number of processors. Due to their higher overhead, algorithms other than Pfair (e.g., global EDF) have also been studied. With M processors, EDF's utilization bound is shown to be $M - (M-1)\,u_{max}$, where u_{max} is the maximum individual task utilization. This work was later extended for the case of deadlines less than or equal to periods in [2]. In [4], it is shown that the utilization bound in [2] does not dominate the bound in [10], and vice versa.

Timeliness objectives other than the hard real-time objective have also received attention. For example, tardiness bounds are established for a suboptimal Pfair algorithm in [14], an EDF-based partitioning scheme and scheduling algorithm in [1], and global EDF in [8].

E. Sha et al. (Eds.): EUC 2006, LNCS 4096, pp. 274–286, 2006.

1.1 Contributions

In this paper, we consider embedded real-time systems that operate in environments with dynamically uncertain properties. These uncertainties include transient and sustained resource overloads due to context-dependent activity execution times and arbitrary activity arrival patterns. Nevertheless, such systems' desire the strongest possible assurances on activity timeliness behavior. Another important distinguishing feature of these systems is their relatively long execution time magnitudes—e.g., in the order of milliseconds to minutes. Some example systems that motivate our work include [7, 6].

When overloads occur, meeting deadlines of all activities is impossible as the demand exceeds the supply. The urgency of an activity is typically orthogonal to the relative importance of the activity—-e.g., the most urgent activity can be the least important, and vice versa; the most urgent can be the most important, and vice versa. Hence when overloads occur, completing the most important activities irrespective of their urgency is often desirable. Thus, a clear distinction has to be made between urgency and importance. During under-loads, such a distinction need not be made, because deadline-based scheduling algorithms such as EDF are optimal (on one processor).

Deadlines by themselves cannot express both urgency and importance. Thus, we consider the time/utility function (TUF) model that express the utility of completing an activity as a function of its completion time [12]. We specify deadline as a binary-valued, downward "step" shaped TUF; Figure 1(a) shows examples. Note that a TUF decouples importance and urgency—i.e., urgency is measured as a deadline on the X-axis, and importance is denoted by utility on the Y-axis.

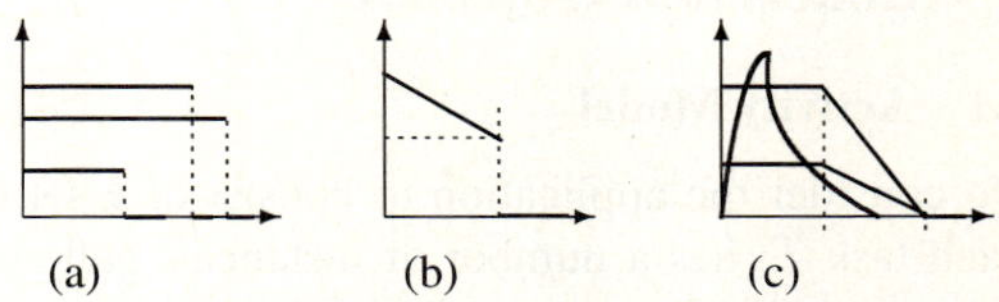

Fig. 1. Example TUFs: (a) Step TUFs; (b) AWACS TUF [6]; and (c) Air defense TUFs [13]

Many real-time systems also have activities that are subject to *non-deadline* time constraints, such as those where the utility attained for activity completion *varies* (e.g., decreases, increases) with completion time. Figures 1(a)-1(c) show example TUFs from two real applications. When time constraints are specified using TUFs, the scheduling criteria is based on accrued utility, such as maximizing sum of the activities' attained utilities. We call such criteria, *utility accrual* (or UA) criteria, and scheduling algorithms that optimize them, as UA scheduling algorithms.

We consider the problem of global UA scheduling on an SMP system with M number of identical processors. We consider global scheduling (as opposed to partitioned scheduling) because of its improved schedulability and flexibility [11]. Further, in many embedded architectures (e.g., those with no cache), its migration overhead has a lower impact on performance [4]. Moreover, applications of interest to us [7, 6] are often subject to resource overloads, during when the total application utilization demand exceed the total processing capacity of all processors. When that happens, we hypothesize that global scheduling can yield greater scheduling flexibility, resulting in greater accrued activity utility, than partitioned scheduling.

We consider repeatedly occurring application activities that are subject to TUF time constraints, variable execution times, and overloads. To account for uncertainties in activity execution behaviors, we consider a stochastic model, where activity execution demand is stochastically expressed. Activities repeatedly arrive with a known minimum inter-arrival time. For such a model, our objective is to provide statistical assurances on activity timeliness behavior.

This problem has not been previously studied. We present a polynomial-time, heuristic algorithm called the *global Multiprocessor Utility Accrual scheduling algorithm* (or gMUA). We show that gMUA achieves optimal total utility (for a special case), probabilistically satisfies individual activity utility lower bounds, and lower bounds the system-wide total accrued utility. Thus, the paper's contribution is the gMUA algorithm. We are not aware of any past efforts that solve the problem solved by gMUA.

The rest of the paper is organized as follows: Section 2 describes our models and scheduling objective. In Section 3, we discuss the rationale behind gMUA and present the algorithm. We describe the algorithm's properties in Section 4 and report our simulation studies in Section 5. The paper concludes in Section 6.

2 Models and Objective

2.1 Activity Model

We consider the application to consist of a set of tasks, denoted **T**=$\{T_1, T_2, ..., T_n\}$. Each task T_i has a number of instances, called jobs, and these jobs may be released either periodically or sporadically with a known minimal inter-arrival time. The jth job of task T_i is denoted as $J_{i,j}$. The period or minimal inter-arrival time of a task T_i is denoted as P_i. All tasks are assumed to be independent. The basic scheduling entity that we consider is the job abstraction. Thus, we use J to denote a job without being task specific, as seen by the scheduler at any scheduling event.

A job's time constraint is specified using a TUF. Jobs of the same task have the same TUF. A task T_i's TUF is denoted by $U_i()$; thus job $J_{i,j}$'s completion at time t will yield an utility $U_i(t)$. We focus on *non-increasing* unimodal TUFs, as they encompass majority of the time constraints in our motivating applications.

Each TUF U_i of $J_{i,j}$ has an initial time $I_{i,j}$ and a termination time $X_{i,j}$, which are the earliest and the latest times for which the TUF is defined, respectively. We assume that $I_{i,j}$ is the arrival time of job $J_{i,j}$, and $X_{i,j} - I_{i,j}$ is the period or minimal inter-arrival time P_i of the task T_i. If $J_{i,j}$'s $X_{i,j}$ is reached and execution of the corresponding job has not been completed, an exception is raised, and the job is aborted.

2.2 Job Execution Time Demands

We estimate the statistical properties of job execution time demand, instead of the worst-case, because our motivating applications exhibit a large variation in their *actual* workload. Thus, the statistical estimation of the demand is much more stable and hence more predictable than the actual workload.

Let Y_i be the random variable of a task T_i's execution time demand. Estimating the execution time demand distribution of the task involves two steps: (1) profiling its execution time usage, and (2) deriving the probability distribution of that usage. A number of measurement-based, off-line and online profiling mechanisms exist (e.g., [16]). We assume that the mean and variance of Y_i are finite and determined through either online or off-line profiling. We denote the *expected* execution time demand of a task T_i as $E(Y_i)$, and the variance on the demand as $Var(Y_i)$.

2.3 Statistical Timeliness Requirement

We consider a task-level statistical timeliness requirement: Each task must accrue some percentage of its maximum possible utility with a certain probability. For a task T_i, this requirement is specified as $\{\nu_i, \rho_i\}$, which implies that T_i must accrue at least ν_i percentage of its maximum possible utility with the probability ρ_i. This is also the requirement of each job of T_i. Thus, for example, if $\{\nu_i, \rho_i\} = \{0.7, 0.93\}$, then T_i must accrue at least 70% of its maximum possible utility with a probability no less than 93%. For step TUFs, ν can only take the value 0 or 1.

This statistical timeliness requirement on the utility of a task implies a corresponding requirement on the range of task sojourn times. Since we focus on non-increasing unimodal TUFs, upper-bounding task sojourn times will lower-bound task utilities.

2.4 Scheduling Objective

We consider a two-fold scheduling criterion: (1) assure that each task T_i accrues the specified percentage ν_i of its maximum possible utility with at least the specified probability ρ_i; and (2) maximize the system-level total attained utility. We also desire to obtain a lower bound on the system-level total attained utility. Also, when it is not possible to satisfy ρ_i for each task (e.g., due to overloads), our objective is to maximize the system-level total utility.

This problem is $\mathcal{NP}$-hard because it subsumes the $\mathcal{NP}$-hard problem of scheduling dependent tasks with step TUFs on one processor [5].

3 The gMUA Algorithm

3.1 Bounding Accrued Utility

Let $s_{i,j}$ be the sojourn time of the jth job of task T_i, where the sojourn time is defined as the period from the job's release to its completion. Now, task T_i's statistical timeliness requirement can be represented as $Pr(U_i(s_{i,j}) \geq \nu_i \times U_i^{max}) \geq \rho_i$. Since TUFs are assumed to be non-increasing, it is sufficient to have $Pr(s_{i,j} \leq D_i) \geq \rho_i$, where D_i is the upper bound on the sojourn time of task T_i. We call D_i "critical time" hereafter, and it is calculated as $D_i = U_i^{-1}(\nu_i \times U_i^{max})$, where $U_i^{-1}(x)$ denotes the inverse function of TUF $U_i()$. Thus, T_i is (probabilistically) assured to accrue at least the utility percentage $\nu_i = U_i(D_i)/U_i^{max}$, with the probability ρ_i.

Note that the period or minimum inter-arrival time P_i and the critical time D_i of the task T_i have the following relationships: (1) $P_i = D_i$ for a binary-valued, downward step TUF; and (2) $P_i \geq D_i$, for other non-increasing TUFs.

3.2 Bounding Utility Accrual Probability

Since task execution time demands are stochastically specified, we need to determine the actual execution time that must be allocated to each task, such that the desired utility accrual probability ρ_i is satisfied. Further, this execution time allocation must account for the uncertainty in the execution time demand specification (i.e., the variance factor).

Given the mean and the variance of a task T_i's execution time demand Y_i, by a one-tailed version of the Chebyshev's inequality, when $y \geq E(Y_i)$, we have:

$$Pr[Y_i < y] \geq \frac{(y - E(Y_i))^2}{Var(Y_i) + (y - E(Y_i))^2} \quad (1)$$

From a probabilistic point of view, Equation 1 is the direct result of the cumulative distribution function of task T_i's execution time demands—i.e., $F_i(y) = Pr[Y_i \leq y]$. Recall that each job of task T_i must accrue ν_i percentage of its maximum utility with a probability ρ_i. To satisfy this requirement, we let $\rho_i' = \frac{(C_i - E(Y_i))^2}{Var(Y_i)+(C_i-E(Y_i))^2} \geq \rho_i$ and obtain the minimum required execution time $C_i = E(Y_i) + \sqrt{\frac{\rho_i' \times Var(Y_i)}{1-\rho_i'}}$.

Thus, gMUA allocates C_i execution time units to each job $J_{i,j}$, so that the probability that $J_{i,j}$ requires no more than the allocated C_i time units is at least ρ_i—i.e., $Pr[Y_i < C_i] \geq \rho_i' \geq \rho_i$. We set $\rho_i' = (\max\{\rho_i\})^{\frac{1}{n}}$, $\forall i$ to satisfy requirements. Supposing that each task is allocated C_i time within its P_i, the actual demand of each task often vary. Some jobs of the task may complete its execution before using up its allocated time and the others may not. gMUA probabilistically schedules the jobs of a task T_i to provide assurance ρ_i' ($\geq \rho_i$) as long as they satisfy a certain schedulability test.

3.3 Algorithm Description

gMUA's scheduling events include job arrival and job completion. To describe gMUA, we define the following variables and auxiliary functions:

- ζ_r: current job set in the system including running jobs and unscheduled jobs.
- σ_{tmp}, σ_a: a temporary schedule; σ_m: schedule for processor m, where $m \leq M$.
- $J_k.C(t)$: J_k's remaining allocated execution time.
- `offlineComputing()` is computed at time $t = 0$ once. For a task T_i, it computes C_i as $C_i = E(Y_i) + \sqrt{\frac{\rho_i \times Var(Y_i)}{1-\rho_i}}$.
- `UpdateRAET(`ζ_r`)` updates the remaining allocated execution time of all jobs in the set ζ_r.
- `feasible(`σ`)` returns a boolean value denoting schedule σ's feasibility; `feasible(`J_k`)` denotes job J_k's feasibility. For σ (or J_k) to be feasible, the predicted completion time of each job in σ (or J_k), must not exceed its critical time.
- `sortByECF(`σ`)` sorts jobs of σ in the order of earliest critical time first.
- `findProcessor()` returns the ID of the processor on which the currently assigned tasks have the shortest sum of allocated execution times.
- `append(`J_k`,`σ`)` appends job J_k at rear of schedule σ.
- `remove(`J_k`,`σ`)` removes job J_k from schedule σ.

- `removeLeastPUDJob(σ)` removes job with the least *potential utility density* (or PUD) from schedule σ. PUD is the ratio of the expected job utility (obtained when job is immediately executed to completion) to the remaining job allocated execution time, i.e., PUD of a job J_k is $\frac{U_k(t+J_k.C(t))}{J_k.C(t)}$. Thus, PUD measures the job's "return on investment." Function returns the removed job.
- `headOf(σ_m)` returns the set of jobs that are at the head of schedule σ_m, $1 \leq m \leq M$.

Algorithm 1. gMUA

1 **Input** : T=$\{T_1,...,T_n\}$, ζ_r=$\{J_1,...,J_N\}$, M:# of processors
2 **Output**: array of dispatched jobs to processor p, Job_p
3 **Data**: $\{\sigma_1, ..., \sigma_M\}$, σ_{tmp}, σ_a
4 `offlineComputing`(**T**);
5 Initialization: $\{\sigma_1, ..., \sigma_M\} = \{0, ..., 0\}$;
6 `UpdateRAET`(ζ_r);
7 **for** $\forall J_k \in \zeta_r$ **do**
8     $J_k.PUD = \frac{U_k(t+J_k.C(t))}{J_k.C(t)}$;
9 σ_{tmp} = `sortByECF`(ζ_r);
10 **for** $\forall J_k \in \sigma_{tmp}$ *from head to tail* **do**
11   **if** $J_k.PUD > 0$ **then**
12   m = `findProcessor`();
13   `append`(J_k, σ_m);
14 **for** $m = 1$ ***to*** M **do**
15     $\sigma_a = null$;
16   **while** *`!feasible(`* σ_m*`)` and `!IsEmpty(`* σ_m *`)`* **do**
17   t = `removeleastPUD`(σ_m);
18   `append`(t, σ_a);
19   `sortByECF`(σ_a);
20   σ_m += σ_a;
21 $\{Job_1, ..., Job_M\}$ = `headOf`($\{\sigma_1, ..., \sigma_M\}$);
22 **return** $\{Job_1, ..., Job_M\}$;

A description of gMUA at a high level of abstraction is shown in Algorithm 1. The procedure `offlineComputing()` is included in line 4, although it is executed only once at $t = 0$. When gMUA is invoked, it updates the remaining allocated execution time of each job, which is decreasing for running jobs and a constant for unscheduled jobs. The job PUDs are then computed.

The jobs are then sorted in the order of earliest critical time first (or ECF), in line 9. In each step of the for loop from line 10 to line 13, the job with the earliest critical time is selected to be assigned to a processor. The processor that yields the shortest sum of allocated execution times of all jobs in its local schedule is selected for assignment (procedure `findProcessor()`). The rationale for this choice is that the shortest summed execution time processor results in the nearest scheduling event for completing a job after assigning each job. Then, the job J_k with the earliest critical time is inserted into the local schedule σ_m of the selected processor m.

In the for-loop from line 14 to line 20, gMUA attempts to make each local schedule feasible by removing the lowest PUD job. In line 16, if σ_m is not feasible, then gMUA removes the job with the least PUD from σ_m until σ_m becomes feasible. All removed jobs are temporarily stored in a schedule σ_a and then appended to each σ_m in ECF order. Note that simply aborting the removed jobs may result in decreased accrued utility. This is because, the algorithm may decide to remove a job which is estimated to have a longer allocated execution time than its actual one, even though it may be able to accrue utility. For this case, gMUA gives the job another chance to be scheduled instead of aborting it, which eventually makes the algorithm more robust. Finally, each job at the head of $\sigma_m, 1 \leq m \leq M$ is selected for execution on the respective processor.

4 Algorithm Properties

4.1 Timeliness Assurances

We establish gMUA's timeliness assurances under the conditions of (1) independent tasks that arrive periodically, and (2) task utilization demand satisfies any of the schedulable utilization bounds for global EDF (GFB, BAK, BCL) in [4].

Theorem 1. *Suppose that only step shaped TUFs are allowed under conditions (1) and (2). Then, a schedule produced by global EDF is also produced by gMUA, yielding equal total utilities. This is a critical time-ordered schedule.*

Proof. We prove this by examining Algorithm 1. In line 9, the queue σ_{tmp} is sorted in a non-decreasing critical time order. In line 12, the function `findProcessor()` returns the index of the processor on which the summed execution time of assigned tasks is the shortest among all processors. Assume that there are n tasks in the current ready queue. We consider two cases: (1) $n \leq M$ and (2) $n > M$. When $n \leq M$, the result is trivial — gMUA's schedule of tasks on each processor is identical to that produced by EDF (every processor has a single task or none assigned). When $n > M$, task T_i $(M < i \leq n)$ will be assigned to the processor whose tasks have the shortest summed execution time. This implies that this processor will have the earliest completion for all assigned tasks up to T_{i-1}, so that the event that will assign T_i will occur by this completion. Note that tasks in σ_{tmp} are selected to be assigned to processors according to ECF. This is precisely the global EDF schedule, since gMUA's critical times correspond to EDF's deadlines. Under conditions (1) and (2), EDF meets all deadlines. Thus, each processor always has a feasible schedule, and the if-block from line 16 to line 18 will never be executed. Thus, gMUA produces the same schedule as global EDF.

Some important corollaries about gMUA's timeliness behavior can be deduced from EDF's behavior under conditions (1) and (2).

Corollary 2. *Under conditions (1) and (2), gMUA always completes the allocated execution time of all tasks before their critical times.*

Theorem 3. *Under conditions (1) and (2), gMUA meets the statistical timeliness requirement $\{\nu_i, \rho_i\}$ for each task T_i.*

Proof. From Corollary 2, all allocated execution times of tasks can be completed before their critical times. Further, based on the results of Equation 1, among the actual processor time of task T_i's jobs, at least ρ_i of them have lesser actual execution time than the allocated execution time. Thus, gMUA can satisfy at least ρ_i critical times—i.e., the algorithm accrues ν_i utility with a probability of at least ρ_i.

Theorem 4. *Under conditions (1) and (2), if a task T_i's TUF has the highest height U_i^{max}, then the system-level utility ratio, defined as the utility accrued by gMUA with respect to the system's maximum possible utility, is at least* $\frac{\rho_1\nu_1 U_1^{max}/P_1+\ldots+\rho_n\nu_n U_n^{max}/P_n}{U_1^{max}/P_1+\ldots+U_n^{max}/P_n}$.

Proof. We denote the number of jobs released by task T_i as m_i. Each m_i is computed as $\frac{\Delta t}{P_i}$, where Δt is a time interval. Task T_i can accrue at least ν_i percentage of its maximum possible utility with the probability ρ_i. Thus, the ratio of the system-level accrued utility to the system's maximum possible utility is $\frac{\rho_1\nu_1 U_1^{max} m_1+\ldots+\rho_n\nu_n U_n^{max} m_n}{U_1^{max} m_1+\ldots+U_n^{max} m_n}$. Thus, the formula comes to $\frac{\rho_1\nu_1 U_1^{max}/P_1+\ldots+\rho_n\nu_n U_n^{max}/P_n}{U_1^{max}/P_1+\ldots+U_n^{max}/P_n}$.

4.2 Dhall Effect

The *Dhall effect* [9] shows that there exists a task set that requires nearly 1 total utilization demand, but cannot be scheduled to meet all deadlines under global EDF and RM even with infinite number of processors. Prior research has revealed that this is caused by the poor performance of global EDF and RM when the task set contains both high utilization tasks and low utilization tasks together. This phenomena, in general, can also affect UA scheduling algorithms' performance, and counter such algorithms' ability to maximize the total attained utility. We discuss this with an example inspired from [15]. We consider the case when the execution time demands of all tasks are constant with no variance, and gMUAi estimates them accurately.

Example A. Consider $M+1$ periodic tasks that are scheduled on M processors under global EDF. Let task τ_i, where $1 \le i \le M$, have $P_i = D_i = 1, C_i = 2\epsilon$, and task τ_{M+1} have $P_{M+1} = D_{M+1} = 1+\epsilon, C_{M+1} = 1$. We assume that each task τ_i has a step shaped TUF with height h_i and task τ_{M+1} has a step shaped TUF with height H_{M+1}. When all tasks arrive at the same time, tasks τ_i will execute immediately and complete their execution 2ϵ time units later. Task τ_{M+1} then executes from time 2ϵ to time $1+2\epsilon$. Since task τ_{M+1}'s critical time — we assume here it is the same as its period — is $1+\epsilon$, it begins to miss its critical time. When $M \to \infty$, $\epsilon \to 0$, $h_i \to 0$ and $H_{M+1} \to \infty$, we have a task set, whose total utilization demand is near 1 and the maximum possible total attained utility is infinite, but that finally accrues zero total utility even with infinite number of processors. We call this phenomena as the *UA Dhall effect*. Conclusively, one of the reasons why global EDF is inappropriate as a UA scheduler is that it is prone to suffer this effect. However, gMUA overcomes this phenomena.

Example B. Consider the same scenario as in Example A, but now, let the task set be scheduled by gMUA. In Algorithm 1, gMUA first tries to schedule tasks like global EDF, but it will fail to do so as we saw in Example A. When gMUA finds that τ_{M+1} will miss its critical time on processor m (where $1 \le m \le M$), the algorithm will select a task with lower PUD on processor m for removal. On processor m, there should be two tasks, τ_m and τ_{M+1}. τ_m is one of τ_i where $1 \leq i \leq M$. When $h_i \to 0$ and $H_{M+1} \to \infty$, τ_m's PUD is almost zero and that of task τ_{M+1} is infinite. Therefore, gMUA removes τ_m and eventually accrues infinite utility as expected.

Under the case when *Dhall effect* occurs, we can establish *UA Dhall effect* by assigning extremely high utility to the task that will be removed by global EDF. In this sense, *UA Dhall effect* is a special case of the *Dhall effect*. It also implies that the scheduling algorithm suffering from *Dhall effect* will likely suffer from *UA Dhall effect*, when it schedules the tasks that are subject to TUF time constraints.

The fact that gMUA is more robust against *UA Dhall effect* than global EDF can be observed in our simulation experiments (see Section 5).

4.3 Sensitivity of Assurances

gMUA is designed under the assumption that task expected execution time demands and the variances on the demands — i.e., the algorithm inputs $E(Y_i)$ and $Var(Y_i)$ – are correct. However, it is possible that these inputs may have been miscalculated (e.g., due to errors in application profiling) or that the input values may change over time (e.g., due to changes in application's execution context). To understand gMUA's behavior when this happens, we assume that the expected execution time demands, $E(Y_i)$'s, and their variances, $Var(Y_i)$'s, are erroneous, and develop the sufficient condition under which the algorithm is still able to meet $\{\nu_i, \rho_i\}$ for all tasks T_i.

Theorem 5. *Let gMUA satisfies $\{\nu_i, \rho_i\}, \forall i$, under correct $E(Y_i)$'s and their correct $Var(Y_i)$'s. When incorrect expected values, $E'(Y_i)$'s, and variances, $Var'(Y_i)$'s, are given as inputs, gMUA satisfies $\{\nu_i, \rho_i\}, \forall i$, if $E'(Y_i) + (C_i - E(Y_i))\sqrt{\frac{Var'(Y_i)}{Var(Y_i)}} \geq C_i, \forall i$, and the task execution time allocations, computed using $E'(Y_i)$'s and $Var'(Y_i)$, satisfy any of the schedulable utilization bounds for global EDF.*

Proof. We assume that if gMUA has correct $E(Y_i)$'s and $Var(Y_i)$'s as inputs, then it satisfies $\{\nu_i, \rho_i\}, \forall i$. This implies that the C_i's determined by Equation 1 are feasibly scheduled by gMUA satisfying all task critical times:

$$\rho_i = \frac{(C_i - E(Y_i))^2}{Var(Y_i) + (C_i - E(Y_i))^2}. \tag{2}$$

However, gMUA has incorrect inputs, $E'(Y_i)$'s and $Var'(Y_i)$, and based on those, it determines C_i's by Equation 1 to obtain the probability $\rho_i, \forall i$:

$$\rho_i = \frac{(C_i' - E'(Y_i))^2}{Var'(Y_i) + (C_i' - E'(Y_i))^2}. \tag{3}$$

Unfortunately, C_i' that is calculated from the erroneous $E'(Y_i)$ and $Var'(Y_i)$ leads gMUA to another probability ρ_i' by Equation 1. Thus, although we expect assurance with the probability ρ_i, we can only obtain assurance with the probability ρ_i' because of the error. ρ' is given by:

$$\rho_i' = \frac{(C_i' - E(Y_i))^2}{Var(Y_i) + (C_i' - E(Y_i))^2}. \tag{4}$$

Note that we also assume that tasks with C_i' satisfy the global EDF's utilization bound; otherwise gMUA cannot provide the assurances. To satisfy $\{\nu_i, \rho_i\}, \forall i$, the actual probability ρ_i' must be greater than the desired probability ρ_i. Since $\rho_i' \geq \rho_i$,

$$\frac{(C_i' - E(Y_i))^2}{Var(Y_i) + (C_i' - E(Y_i))^2} \geq \frac{(C_i - E(Y_i))^2}{Var(Y_i) + (C_i - E(Y_i))^2}.$$

Hence, $C' \geq C_i$. From Equations 2 and 3,

$$C_i' = E'(Y_i) + (C_i - E(Y_i))\sqrt{\frac{Var'(Y_i)}{Var(Y_I)}} \geq C_i. \tag{5}$$

5 Experimental Evaluation

Performance with Constant Demand. We consider an SMP machine with 4 processors. A task T_i's period $P_i(= X_i)$ and its expected execution time $E(Y_i)$ are randomly generated in the range [1,30] and [1, $\alpha \cdot P_i$], respectively, where α is defined as $max\{\frac{C_i}{P_i}|i = 1, ..., n\}$ and $Var(Y_i)$ are zero. According to [10], EDF's utilization bound depends on α and the number of processors, which means that irrespective of the number of processors, there exists task sets with total utilization demand (UD) close to 1.0, which cannot be feasibly scheduled under EDF. Generally, the performance of global schemes tends to decrease when α increases.

We consider two TUF shape patterns: (1) all tasks have step shaped TUFs, and (2) a heterogeneous TUF class, including step, linearly decreasing and parabolic shapes. Each TUF's height is randomly generated in the range [1,100].

The number of tasks are determined depending on the given UD and the α value. We vary the UD from 3 to 6.5, including the case where it exceeds the number of processors. We set α to 0.4, 0.7, and 1. For each experiment, more than 1000,000 jobs are released. To see the generic performance of gMUA, we assume $\{\nu_i, \rho_i\} = \{0, 1\}$.

Figure 2 shows the AUR and CMR of gMUA and EDF, respectively, under increasing UD (from 3.0 to 6.5) and for the three α values. AUR (accrued utility ratio) is the ratio of total accrued utility to the total maximum utility, and CMR (critical time meet ratio)

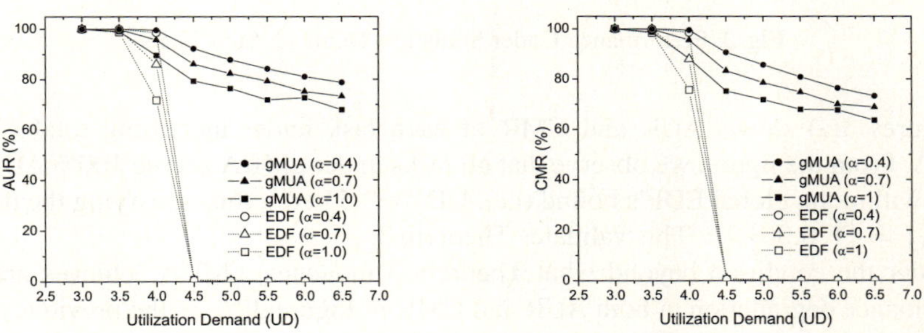

(a) AUR (b) CMR

Fig. 2. Performance Under Constant Demand, Step TUFs

is the ratio of the number of jobs meeting their critical times to the total number of job releases. For a task with a step TUF, its AUR and CMR are identical. But the system-level AUR and CMR can be different due to the mix of different utility of tasks.

When all tasks have step TUFs and the total UD satisfies the global EDF's utilization bound, gMUA performs exactly the same to EDF. This validates Theorem 1. EDF's performance drops sharply after $UD = 4.0$ (for step TUFs), which corresponds to the number of processors in our experiments. This is due to EDF's domino effect that occurs when UD exceeds the number of processors. On the other hand, gMUA's performance gracefully degrades as UD increases and exceeds 4.0, since it selects as many feasible, higher PUD tasks as possible.

Observe that EDF begins to miss deadlines much earlier than when $UD = 4.0$, as indicated in [4]. Even when $UD < 4.0$, gMUA outperforms EDF in both AUR and CMR. This is because, gMUA is likely to find a feasible or at least better schedule even when EDF cannot find a feasible one, as discussed in Section 4.2.

We also observe that α affects EDF's and gMUA's AUR and CMR. Despite this, gMUA outperforms EDF for the same α and UD for the reason that we describe above.

We observed similar and consistent trends for tasks with heterogeneous TUFs; these are omitted here for brevity.

Performance with Statistical Demand. We now evaluate gMUA's statistical timeliness assurances. For each task T_i's demand Y_i, we generate normally distributed execution time demands. Task execution times are changed along with the total UD. We consider both step and heterogeneous TUF shapes as before.

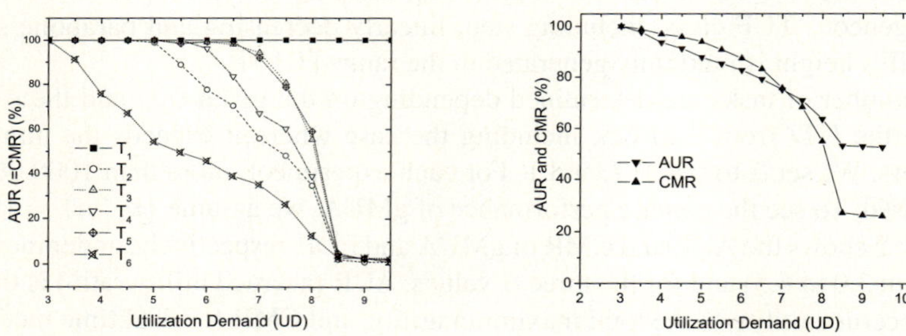

(a) Task-level (b) System-level

Fig. 3. Performance Under Statistical Demand, Step TUFs

Figures 3(a) shows AUR and CMR of each task under increasing total UD of gMUA. From the figure, we observe that all tasks under gMUA accrue 100% AUR and CMR within the global EDF's bound (i.e., UD$<\approx$2.5 here), thus satisfying the desired $\{\nu_i, \rho_i\} = \{1, 0.96\}, \forall i$. This validates Theorem 3.

Under the condition beyond what Theorem 3 indicates, gMUA achieves graceful performance degradation in both AUR and CMR in Figure 3(b), as the previous experiment. In Figure 3(a), gMUA achieves 100% AUR and CMR for T_1 over all range of UD. This is because, T_1 has a step TUF with higher height. Thus, gMUA favors T_1 over others to obtain more utility when it cannot satisfy the critical time of all tasks.

According to Theorem 4, the system-level AUR must be at least 96%. (For each task $T_i, \nu_i = 1$, because all TUFs are step shaped.) We observe that AUR and CMR of gMUA under the condition of Theorem 4 are above 99.0%. This validates Theorem 4.

A similar trend was observed for heterogeneous TUFs.

6 Conclusions and Future Work

We present a global UA scheduling algorithm for SMPs, called gMUA. The algorithm considers tasks that are subject to TUF time constraints, variable execution time demands, and resource overloads. We establish that gMUA achieves optimal total utility (for a special case), probabilistically satisfies task utility lower bounds, and lower bounds system-wide total accrued utility. We also show that gMUA's utility lower bound satisfactions have bounded sensitivity to variations in execution time demand estimates, and that the algorithm is robust against a variant of the Dhall effect. Our simulation experiments validate our analysis and confirm the algorithm's effectiveness.

Examples directions for further research include relaxing the sporadic task arrival model to allow a stronger adversary (e.g., the unimodal arbitrary arrival model) and allowing greater task utilizations for satisfying utility lower bounds.

References

1. J. Anderson, V. Bud, and U. C. Devi. An edf-based scheduling algorithm for multiprocessor soft real-time systems. In *IEEE ECRTS*, pages 199–208, July 2005.
2. T. P. Baker. Multiprocessor edf and deadline monotonic schedulability analysis. In *IEEE RTSS*, pages 120–129, Dec. 2003.
3. S. Baruah, N. Cohen, C. G. Plaxton, and D. Varvel. Proportionate progress: A notion of fairness in resource allocation. In *Algorithmica*, volume 15, page 600, 1996.
4. M. Bertogna, M. Cirinei, and G. Lipari. Improved schedulability analysis of edf on multiprocessor platforms. In *IEEE ECRTS*, pages 209– 218, 2005.
5. R. K. Clark. *Scheduling Dependent Real-Time Activities*. PhD thesis, Carnegie Mellon University, 1990.
6. R. K. Clark, E. D. Jensen, et al. An adaptive, distributed airborne tracking system. In *IEEE WPDRTS*, April 1999.
7. R. K. Clark, E. D. Jensen, and N. F. Rouquette. Software organization to facilitate dynamic processor scheduling. In *IEEE WPDRTS*, April 2004.
8. U. C. Devi and J. Anderson. Tardiness bounds for global edf scheduling on a multiprocessor. In *IEEE RTSS*, 2005.
9. S. K. Dhall and C. L. Liu. On a real-time scheduling problem. *Operations Research*, 26(1):127140, 1978.
10. J. Goossens, S. Funk, and S. Baruah. Priority-driven scheduling of periodic tasks systems on multiprocessors. *Real-Time Systems*, 25(2-3):187–205, 2003.
11. P. Holman and J. H. Anderson. Adapting pfair scheduilng for symmetric multiprocessors. In *Journal of Embedded Computing*, to appear.
12. E. D. Jensen, C. D. Locke, and H. Tokuda. A time-driven scheduling model for real-time systems. In *IEEE RTSS*, pages 112–122, December 1985.
13. D. P. Maynard et al. An example real-time command, control, and battle management application for alpha. Technical report, CMU CS Dept., Dec. 1988. Archons Project TR 88121.

14. A. Srinivasan and J. Anderson. Efficient scheduling of soft real-time applications on multiprocessors. In *IEEE ECRTS*, pages 51–59, July 2003.
15. O. U. P. Zapata and P. M. Alvarez. Edf and rm multiprocessor scheduling algorithms: Survey and performance evaluation. `http://delta.cs.cinvestav.mx/~pmejia/multitechreport.pdf`. Last accessed October 2005.
16. X. Zhang, Z. Wang, et al. System support for automated profiling and optimization. In *ACM SOSP*, pages 15–26, October 1997.

Linux/RTOS Hybrid Operating Environment on Gandalf Virtual Machine Monitor

Shuichi Oikawa[1], Megumi Ito[1], and Tatsuo Nakajima[2]

[1] Department of Computer Science, University of Tsukuba
1-1-1 Tennodai, Tsukuba, Ibaraki 305-8573, Japan
[2] Department of Computer Science, Waseda University
3-4-1 #61-505, Okubo, Shinjuku, Tokyo 169-8555, Japan

Abstract. This paper presents our Linux/RTOS hybrid operating environment constructed upon Gandalf VMM. Gandalf can host multiple RTOSes along with Linux, and RTOSes and Linux execute within their own isolated protection domains; thus, they can be spatially and temporally protected from each other. We design Gandalf from scratch as a simple and efficient VMM in order to minimize overheads incurred by virtualization. The simplicity and efficiency are achieved by the hybrid of para- and nearly full-virtualization approaches. The implementation of the presented hybrid operating environment is on the PC/AT compatible platform with the Intel IA-32 processor with μITRON as an RTOS. From the measurement results, we make clear that the benefits of using a VMM to construct a hybrid environment exceed shortcomings by showing the impact on performance is limited.

1 Introduction

The current embedded systems, especially consumer electronics products, contain a number of complicated requirements for their operating environments that are difficult to satisfy them together at once by a single operating system (OS). Consumer electronics products need to be easy-to-use to appeal not only to enthusiastic users but to a wide range of ordinary people; thus, they are nowadays equipped with many applications along with fancy GUI. On the other hand, they have essential functionality that must work reliably in a timely manner. Those functionality requires real-time processing, and their requirements for real-time processing tend to be difficult to be satisfied by an OS that can provide fully featured GUI.

In order cope with such conflicting requirements imposed by complex embedded systems, the hybrids of a general purpose OS and a real-time operating system (RTOS) have been developed. While a general purpose OS is good at the provision of GUI with its rich set of middleware support, an RTOS covers real-time processing. Those hybrids have a general purpose OS kernel and an RTOS's application tasks share the same most privileged level of a processor without protection. This hybrid model may work well if a system is designed from scratch having applications properly classified into real-time and non real-time tasks. In reality, however, the existing software resources inherited from the past products need to be reused; thus, undesired programs are also brought into the most privileged level to run on an RTOS, and can become sources of problems because of lack of protection.

E. Sha et al. (Eds.): EUC 2006, LNCS 4096, pp. 287–296, 2006.

This paper presents our hybrid operating environment constructed upon Gandalf virtual machine monitor (VMM). As an RTOS and a general purpose OS hosted on Gandalf, we use μITRON [14] and Linux, respectively. The implementation of this hybrid operating environment is on the PC/AT compatible platform with the Intel IA-32 processor. We designed Gandalf from scratch as a simple and efficient VMM in order to minimize overheads incurred by virtualization. Unlike the existing approach described above, only Gandalf executes at the most privileged level, and has them execute within their own isolated protection domain; thus, hosted OSes can be spatially and temporally protected from each other and from a general purpose OS. Additionally, Gandalf can host multiple RTOSes along with a general purpose OS. We chose μITRON and Linux because of their popularity. Since in Japan μITRON is the RTOS that has been the most widely used in a variety of products, industries have a huge amount of the existing software resources. Linux's popularity is recently increasing for larger embedded systems.

The features of this system are summarized as follows:

- The provision of spatially and temporally protection is enabled by constructing a hybrid of an RTOS and a general purpose OS on a VMM.
- The hybrid of para- and full-virtualization approaches is implemented in Gandalf VMM in order to balance implementation cost and runtime cost.
- We introduce nearly full-virtualization, by which we allow a few straightforward modifications to bring up Linux on Gandalf. Nearly full-virtualization enables the significant reduction of both implementation and runtime costs.

1.1 Background and Related Work

Making hybrids of an RTOS and a general purpose OS is not a new idea. As a practical approach to deal with complex systems, several of them have been developed, and some are widely used. [3] introduced the executive that support the co-residence of an RTOS and a general purpose OS. RTLinux [1] and RTAI [8], which are poplar among Linux users, have Linux kernel execute on a RTOS kernel. There are some commercial products, such as Accel-Linux and Linux on NORTi, that enable μITRON to run aside of Linux kernel.

All of them take the same approach, which is that an RTOS, RTOS's application tasks, and a general purpose OS kernel share the same most privileged level; thus, there is no protection among them. Such lack of protection may not be a problem if a system is designed from scratch having applications properly classified into real-time and non real-time tasks. After proper classification, there should be only a small number of RTOS's application tasks that specifically require real-time execution. It is, however, problematic if the existing applications on an RTOS are simply reused by taking advantage of the hybrid of an RTOS and a general purpose OS. In such a system, there tend to be a lager number of RTOS's application tasks. Their misbehavior is directly connected to system malfunction or a crash. A general purpose OS kernel also can be a source of problems because of its execution at the most privileged level. A general purpose OS kernel for the hybrid with an RTOS is usually modified not to touch hardware's interrupt controlling functions, so that interrupts are not disabled for a indeterministically long time. Since a general purpose OS kernel is still allowed to disable interrupts by controlling hardware, there are chances to introduce kernel modules that are not properly modified for the hybrid; thus, they cause temporal malfunction.

Our approach is that Gandalf VMM hosts RTOSes and a general purpose OS. This approach enables the provision of spatial and temporal protection. Spatial protection is implemented by having OSes run within their own protection domains. Since there is no means provided to corrupt or steal the programs or data of the other OSes, OSes' misbehavior does not affect the execution of the other OSes. Temporal protection is realized by limiting hardware access by OSes. The OSes hosted on Gandalf execute at a less privileged level, at which only limited hardware access is allowed; thus, the hosted OSes cannot directly disable interrupts at hardware's interrupt controller. Therefore, temporal malfunction incurred by disabling interrupts can be avoided.

The development of VMMs has a long history beginning with IBM CP/67 [10] followed by IBM VM/370 [5] and its alikes for mainframe computers. Since a few years ago VMMs revived to be a hot research and development topic because of VMMs' capability to accommodate multiple operating systems in a single machine. Researchers and developers consider VMMs to deal with increasing reliability and security. In order to achieve better performance on commodity platforms, which cannot be virtualized efficiently, para-virtualization was introduced [15]. With para-virtualization, VMM developers define easily and efficiently virtualizable hardware as interface with a VMM. Para-virtualization can be used for only I/O devices [13] or platforms [2]. In contrast to para-virtualization, which defines virtual non-existing hardware, the approach first taken by mainframe VMMs is called full-virtualization, which defines the same interface as the existing real hardware.

Gandalf VMM takes the hybrid of para- and full-virtualization approaches. Gandalf exports a virtual processor interface for RTOSes while it enables a general purpose OS to run on it with limited modifications. Such a hybrid approach can balance implementation cost and runtime cost.

1.2 Paper Organization

The rest of this paper is organized as follows. The next section describes the overall architecture of our hybrid operating environment constructed upon Gandalf VMM. Section 3 describes the presented system's design and implementation in more detail. Section 4 describes the current status of the implementation and shows the preliminary evaluation results. Finally, Section 5 summarizes the paper.

2 Overall Architecture

This section describes the overall architecture of our Linux/RTOS hybrid operating environment constructed upon Gandalf VMM.

Figure 1 depicts that Gandalf implements protection domains in order to isolate the execution environments of μITRON RTOS and Linux. Realizing protection domains is hardware dependent. Since this hybrid operating environment is implemented on the Intel IA-32 processor, segments associated with protection levels can provide protection domains. Gandalf, RTOSes, and Linux execute within their own segments. The segments of RTOSes and Linux do not overwrap; thus, their memory access is contained

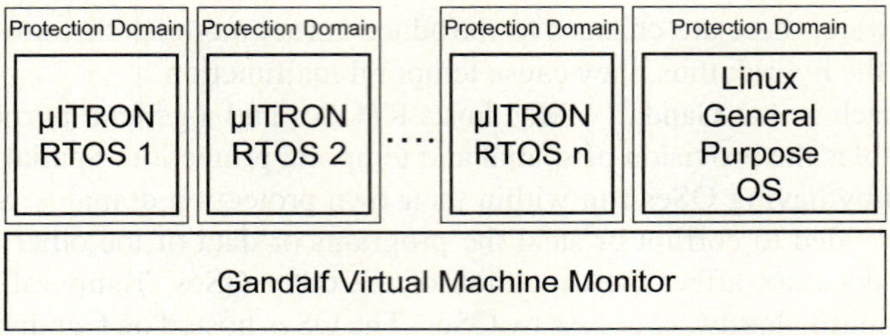

Fig. 1. Overall Architecture of Linux/RTOS Hybrid Operating Environment on Gandalf

within their segments. Gandalf executes at the most privileged level while RTOSes and Linux executes at the less privileged level; thus, only limited hardware access by RTOSes and Linux is allowed. Physical memory is statically partitioned at a time of configuration, and the fixed amounts of memory are allocated for Gandalf, RTOSes, and Linux at a boot time.

Gandalf VMM takes the hybrid of para- and full-virtualization approaches. We choose para-virtualization for RTOSes and full-virtualization for a general purpose OS in order to balance implementation cost and runtime cost. A general purpose OS is huge and very complicated software. It tends to be actively updated in order to incorporate new features and to fix their bugs. Applying para-virtualization to such an OS significantly increases implementation cost. It is also hard to maintain the source code modified for para-virtualization since it needs to keep up with rapid updates. On the other hand, the implementation of RTOSes is considerably simpler than a general purpose OS, and it tends to be stable for a long time because keeping reliability is more important than adding new features; thus, once their source code base is modified for para-virtualization, the amount of its maintenance work is limited. Therefore, its implementation cost is negligible. In fact, runtime cost is more important for RTOSes. In order to have unmodified OSes execute at a less privileged level, full-virtualization emulates a subset of hardware. Such emulation costs at runtime. Para-virtualization can decrease the overheads of emulation; thus, using para-virtualization is desired for RTOSes in terms of both implementation and runtime costs.

3 Detailed Design and Implementation

This section describes the detailed design and implementation of our hybrid operating environment implemented on the PC/AT compatible platform with the Intel IA-32 processor.

3.1 Address Map, Segments, and Protection

As described in the previous section, physical memory is statically partitioned at a time of configuration, and the fixed amounts of memory are allocated for Gandalf VMM, μITRON instances, and Linux at a boot time. In a physical address map, Linux takes the first part of physical memory, then μITRON instances comes next, and Gandalf

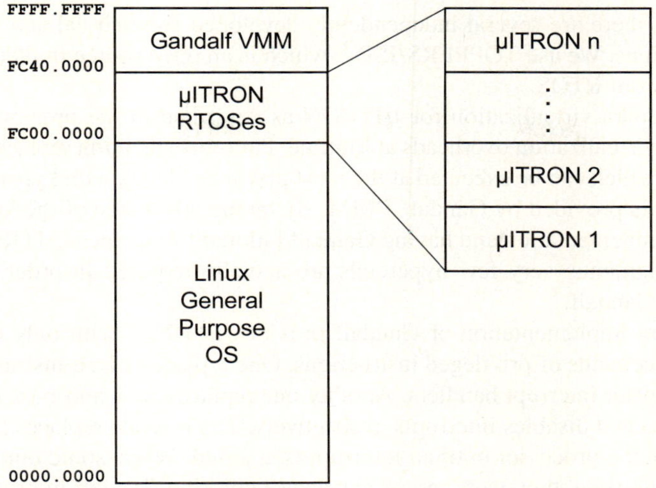

Fig. 2. Virtual Address Map

takes the last part. There can be multiple μITRON instances hosted on Gandalf. They, however, do not share physical memory.

The layout of Linux, μITRON instances, and Gandalf in physical memory is reflected in virtual memory but at different addresses. At this moment, virtual memory is also statically partitioned at a time of compilation. The partitioning can be easily changed by parameters. Figure 2 depicts their current layout in virtual memory. Linux uses the first part from virtual address `0x0` to `0xfbff.ffff`.[1] μITRON instances are located from `0xfc00.0000` to `0xfc3f.ffff`. Gandalf uses the top part from `0xfc40.0000` until the end of virtual address `0xffff.ffff`. Limiting a virtual address range available for Linux requires a simple modification to Linux's source code.

Protection domains of OSes and Gandalf are realized by segments of the Intel IA-32 processor. Each segment has its base address and size, and memory access is allowed only within the current segment. Gandalf allocates two segments, one for program code and another for data, to each of OSes and Gandalf. Only Gandalf has control of segments. Gandalf's segments cover the whole virtual memory from `0x0` to `0xffff.ffff`; thus, it can access any part of virtual memory. Linux's segments start at `0x0` and end at `0xfbff.ffff`. The segments of the first μITRON instance start at `0xfc00.0000`, and the last ones end at `0xfc3f.ffff`. Since the segments of RTOSes and Linux do not overwrap, hosted OSes are spatially protected from each other by segments.

3.2 μITRON RTOS

μITRON is actually a specification of a simple embedded RTOS that provides real-time tasks, synchronization and communication mechanisms, system services, and device

[1] A 32-bit address is denoted with a pair of 16-bit numbers connected with a period for better readability.

drivers; thus, there are several independently developed commercial and open source implementations. We use TOPPERS/JSP [2], which is an open source implementation of μITRON, for our RTOS.

We chose para-virtualization for μITRON as described in the previous section in favor of less virtualization overheads at runtime. Para-virtualization replaces privileged instructions, which can be executed at the most privileged level, with hypercalls, which are systemcalls provided by Gandalf VMM. By taking advantage of the knowledge of μITRON's implementation and having Gandalf tailored to execute a μITRON instance in specific segments, very few hypercalls are actually required in order to bring up μITRON on Gandalf.

The current implementation of Gandalf provides μITRON with only three hypercalls as replacements of privileged instructions. One replaces `lidt` instruction, which is used to register interrupt handlers. Another one replaces `sti` and `cli` instructions, which enables and disables interrupts, respectively. The last one replaces `hlt` instruction, which halt a processor until an interrupt is asserted. While some other privileged instructions are used, they were removed because tailoring Gandalf to provide an execution environment expected by μITRON makes them no longer needed.

3.3 Linux General Purpose OS

We use Linux as a general purpose OS. We chose full-virtualization to support Linux since Linux kernel is huge and complicated software and is actively updated to incorporate new features and to fix their bugs. Truly full-virtualization, however, costs quite expensive to implement a VMM and to execute an unmodified OS on it. It requires a fully virtualizable processor [11], or it is made possible only in return for the overheads of virtualizing all computing resources. For example, an OS kernel is designed to utilize the whole virtual address space made available by a processor. If a processor is not fully virtualizable as most of the current processors, there is no room in the same virtual address space left for locating a VMM in a way that the it is protected from its guest OS kernel and user processes.

In this case, a VMM requires another virtual address space, and heavy context switching between a OS kernel and a VMM happens at every time the VMM's intervention is needed. Such intervention includes the emulation of privileged instructions, handling interrupts and exceptions, and so on. There are many other virtualization overheads caused by full-virtualization. Achieving practical performance that matches commercial VMMs, such as VMware [13] and Microsoft VirtualPC, requires many techniques including on-the-fly binary translation [12]; thus, the provision of truly full-virtualization is considered to be cumbersome.

We therefore decided to allow a few straightforward modifications to bring up Linux on Gandalf. We call this approach *nearly* full-virtualization. Allowing a few modifications enables the significant reduction of both implementation and runtime costs. For example, by reducing the virtual address range used by Linux, we can create room for μITRON and Gandalf in the same virtual address space. It removes the necessity to switch virtual address spaces at each time when Gandalf is invoked. Such reduction

[2] http://www.toppers.jp/

of the virtual address range can be done only by modifying a single line in a Linux source code file. Thirteen lines in seven files are currently modified to achieve nearly full-virtualization of Linux on Gandalf.

3.4 Gandalf Virtual Machine Monitor

Gandalf is a virtual machine monitor designed and built from scratch. Our design principle of Gandalf is simplicity. In order to follow this principle, Gandalf takes the hybrid of para- and full-virtualization approaches, but full-virtualization is approximated as nearly full-virtualization. While the hybrid of two virtualization approaches may seem to add complexity, it actually simplifies the implementation since the distinction of callee OSes is made at the entry point to Gandalf and there is no need to differentiate them at each operation. Applying nearly full-virtualization to bring up Linux on Gandalf also makes Gandalf significantly simpler than real full-virtualization as described previously.

Gandalf is responsible for the provision of the execution environments of μITRON RTOS and Linux. For that purpose, Gandalf provides three functionalities, 1) a boot loader for Linux and μITRON, 2) the emulation of privileged instructions for Linux, and 3) the hypercalls for μITRON. First, Gandalf works as a boot loader for Linux and μITRON. We use GRUB as an actual boot loader, which loads Gandalf, Linux, and μITRON into memory, and transfers the execution to Gandalf. GRUB passes to Gandalf the information about the memory locations of Gandalf itself, Linux, and μITRON. By using the passed information, Gandalf performs the initialization to set up the physical and virtual memory maps as described in Section 3.1. Gandalf first boots up μITRON and then Linux.

Gandalf emulates privileged instructions executed by Linux. Since Linux kernel executes at a less privileged level, its issuing a privileged instruction causes an exception. The type of such an exception is a general protection fault in case of the Intel IA-32 processor. Gandalf registers an exception handler for a general protection fault, so that Gandalf handles it when it occurs. Gandalf's exception handler for a general protection fault examines the instruction at the address where an exception occurred. If the instruction is a privileged instruction, Gandalf emulates it accordingly.

μITRON uses the hypercalls instead of privileged instructions. Gandalf implements only three hypercalls as replacements of privileged instructions, such as `lidt`, `sti/cli`, and `hlt`, as described in Section 3.2.

4 Current Status and Evaluation Results

We have implemented Gandalf and constructed the our Linux/RTOS hybrid operating environment upon it. The rest of this section shows the preliminary evaluation results obtained from the current implementation. All measurements reported below were performed on the Dell Precision 470 Workstation with Intel Xeon 2.8GHz CPU.[3] Hyper-threading was turned off. Please note that since there is no benchmark program that is

[3] Linux reports this CPU as 2794.774 MHz. We use this number to convert cycle counts obtained from `rdtsc` instruction to micro seconds for accuracy.

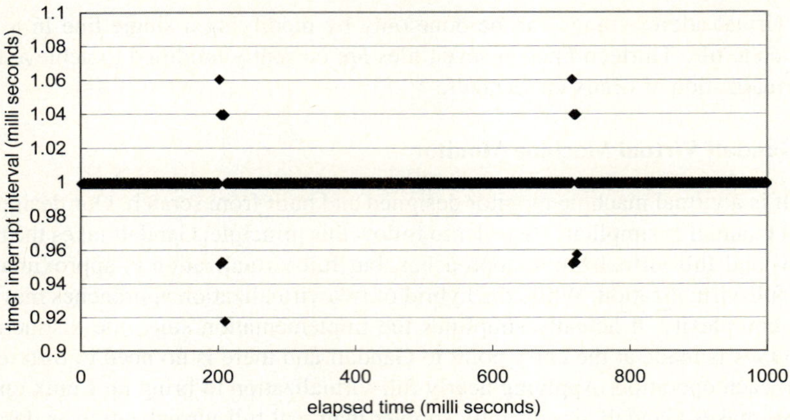

Fig. 3. Timer Interrupt Intervals in μITRON

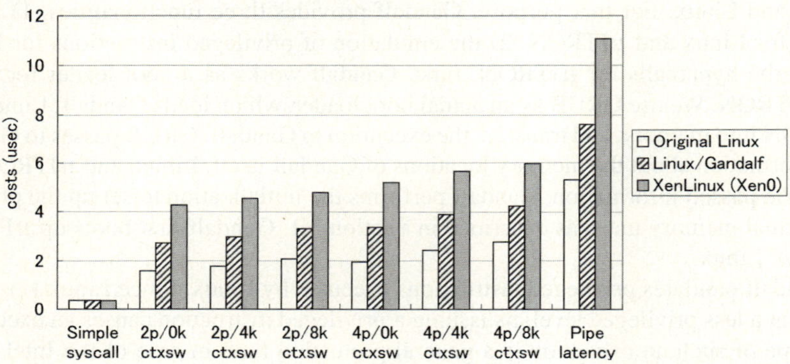

Fig. 4. Linux Performance Comparison (1)

appropriate for the evaluations of a hybrid environment, we are currently developing evaluation programs for this purpose.

First, we measured the switching cost between μITRON and Linux. It was measured by using a pair of `hlt` instruction in Linux and its replacement hypercall in μITRON. Gandalf was instrumented to switch to the other OS when they were executed. We used cycle counts obtained from `rdtsc` instruction for this measurement. The average cost to switch from μITRON to Linux and then back to μITRON, which means that two OS switchings are involved, is 1.02 μ seconds after repeating 10,000 times.

Second, we measured the timer interrupt intervals in μITRON. We used cycle counts obtained from `rdtsc` instruction for this measurement, too. Figure 3 shows the measurement result.

The measured timer interrupt intervals are mostly the same at 1 millisecond as the timer device was configured to periodically raise an interrupt every 1 millisecond. There are, however, some spikes around 200 and 700 milliseconds in elapsed time. We need more investigations to be performed in order to find out a cause of these spikes.

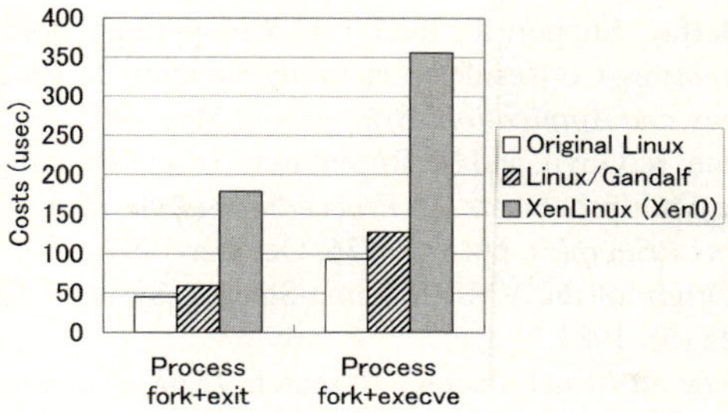

Fig. 5. Linux Performance Comparison (2)

Finally, in order to evaluate our nearly full-virtualization approach used for Linux, we ran several programs included in lmbench benchmark suite [9]. Figure 4 and 5 show the results of lmbench programs. We ran the same programs on the original Linux (without virtualization) and XenLinux (Dom0) for comparison of performance.

The measurement results show that nearly full-virtualization approach reduces the runtime costs significantly as Linux on Gandalf outperforms XenLinux in all cases. The costs of process fork and exec are close to the original non-virtualized Linux and significantly better than XenLinux.

5 Summary

We presented our Linux/RTOS hybrid operating environment constructed upon Gandalf VMM. we use μITRON as an RTOS. Since RTOSes and Linux execute within their own isolated protection domains, they can be spatially and temporally protected from each other. We designed Gandalf from scratch as a simple and efficient VMM in order to minimize overheads incurred by virtualization. The simplicity and efficiency were achieved by the hybrid of para- and nearly full-virtualization approaches. The presented hybrid operating environment was implemented on the PC/AT compatible platform with the Intel IA-32 processor.

From the measurement results described in the previous section, we showed that the impact on performance by using a VMM to construct a hybrid environment is limited. The benefits to use a VMM, by which spatial and temporal protection can be provided, exceed the limited performance loss. Therefore, our Linux/RTOS hybrid operating environment on Gandalf, which is constructed upon the hybrid of para- and nearly full-virtualization approaches, is considered to be very practical and useful.

References

1. M. Barabanov and V. Yodaiken. Real-Time Linux. *Linux Journal*, March 1996.
2. P. Barham, B. Dragovic, K. Fraser, S. Hand, T. Harris, A. Ho, R. Neugebauer, I. Pratt, and A. Warfield. Xen and the Art of Virtualization. In *Proceedings of the 19th ACM Symposium on Operating System Principles*, pp. 164–177, October 2003.

3. G. Bollella and K. Jeffay. Support for Real-Time Computing within General Purpose Operating Systems - Supporting Co-Resident Operating Systems. In *Proceedings of the 1st IEEE Real-Time Technology and Applications Symposium*, May 1995.
4. E. Bugnion, S. Devine, K. Govil, and M. Rosenblum. Disco: Running Commodity Operating Systems on Scalable Multiprocessors. In *Proceedings of the 16th ACM SIGOPS Symposium on Operating Systems Principles*, pp. 143–156, October 1997.
5. R. J. Creasy. The Origin of the VM/370 Time-Sharing System. *IBM Journal of Research and Development*, 25 (5), 1981.
6. R. P. Goldberg. Survey of Virtual Machine Research. *IEEE Computer*, pp. 34–45, June 1974.
7. Intel Corporation. IA-32 Intel Architecture Software Developer's Manual.
8. P. Mantegazza, E. Bianchi, L. Dozio, and S. Papacharalambous. RTAI: Real Time Application Interface. *Linux Journal*, April 2000.
9. L. McVoy and C. Staelin. lmbench: Portable Tools for Performance Analysis. In *Proceedings of the USENIX Annual Technical Conference*, pp. 279–294, January 1996.
10. R. Meyer and L. Seawright. A Virtual Machine Time Sharing System. *IBM Systems Journal*, 9 (3), pp. 199–218, 1970.
11. G. Popek and R. Goldberg. Formal Requirements for Virtualizable 3rd Generation Architectures. *Communications of the A.C.M.*, 17(7):412–421, 1974.
12. M. Rosenblum and T. Garfinkel. Virtual Machine Monitors: Current Technology and Future Trends. *IEEE Computer*, pp. 39–47, May 2005.
13. J. Sugerman, G. Venkitachalam, and B. H. Lim. Virtualizing I/O Devices on VMware Workstation's Hosted Virtual Machine Monitor. In *Proceedings of 2001 USENIX Annual Technical Conference*, 2001.
14. H. Takada ed. μITRON4.0 Specification. TRON Association, 1999. (In Japanese)
15. A. Whitaker, M. Shaw, and S. D. Gribble. Scale and Performance in the Denali Isolation Kernel. In *Proceedings of the 5th Symposium on Operating Systems Design and Implementation*, pp. 195–210, December 2002.

Optimizing Code Size for Embedded Real-Time Applications

Shao-Yang Wang, Chih-Yuan Chen, and Rong-Guey Chang*

Department of Computer Science National Chung Cheng University
Chia-Yi, Taiwan
{wsya92, chancy, rgchang}@cs.ccu.edu.tw

Abstract. This paper presents an efficient technique for code compression. In our work, a sequence of instructions that occurs repeatedly in an application will be compressed to reduce its code size. During compression, each instruction is first divided into the operation part and the register part, and then only the operation part is compressed. For reducing the run-time overhead, we propose an instruction prefetching mechanism to speed the decompression. Moreover, we devise some optimization techniques to improve the code size reduction and the performance, and show their impacts. The experimental results show that our work can achieve a code size reduction of 33% on average and a low overhead in the process of decompression at run time for these benchmarks.

1 Introduction

Many memories have been incorporated into embedded systems to execute application programs. In some embedded systems, the application programs are expected to completely fit in the memory of the chip. In other embedded systems such as portable devices, the code sizes of application programs must be as small as possible to reduce the cost and decrease the weight. However, the memory required by an application program is determined by the size of its data and instructions. Therefore, how to compress the code size of an application program to shrink the amount of memory required has become a crucial issue in embedded systems.

In this paper, we address the code compression of an application program by compressing its repeated instruction sequences. Here, repeated instruction sequences represent the instruction sequences that occur more than once in an application. In our method, each instruction of an application is divided into the operation part and the register part. Then the operation part is profiled and compressed by reducing the number of its repeated sequences. This process will be applied to the newly operation part recursively until no further compressions can be performed. Note in above process the register part is not compressed. The compression information of operation part and register part is put into the instruction table and the register bank respectively. The information about how to access the items in the instruction table and the register bank

* This work was supported in part by National Science Council, Taiwan, under Grant NSC 94-2220-E-194-005-.

E. Sha et al. (Eds.): EUC 2006, LNCS 4096, pp. 297 – 307, 2006.

is systematically stored in the index table. During execution, the compressed program is decompressed instruction by instruction through accessing these tables. Previous work [8,10] showed that there is a tradeoff between the compression ratio and the performance. Thus, we propose an instruction prefetching mechanism to speed decompression and some optimization techniques to remedy this issue. Our work is performed on the basis of the ARM instructions and the experimental results show that our method is quite effective in achieving a high code size reduction and a low overhead in decompression.

The remainder of this paper is organized as follows. Section 2 describes the related work. We first introduce the compression approach in Section 3 and then present the details of our decompression approach in Section 4. Section 5 shows our experimental results without optimization. In Section 6, we propose our optimization techniques and show their impacts. Finally, we conclude this paper briefly.

2 Related Work

Some researchers addressed this issue by using specific architectural support. ARM Thumb [1,2] provides a compressed 16-bit instruction set to reduce the code size, each of which can be translated to its corresponding 32-bit instruction with a hardware decompressor during execution. In addition, MIPS compresses the code in a similar way by also providing a shorter instruction set called MIPS16 [11]. IBM CodePack uses Huffman encoding [7] for their code compression, partitioning the code word into two parts and applying Huffman encoding to these two parts separately [9]. The code size reductions of these approaches range from 30% to 40%.

Other researchers addressed this issue in terms of software. Evans and Fraser devised an approach for compressing a stack-machine bytecode and achieved a code size reduction of up to 29% [6]. Debray and Evans addressed this issue by proposing a profile-guided code compression on the basis of the 80-20 rule [4]. Bell et al. solved this problem by using a dictionary table, assigning each of the frequently occurring instructions to an index in the dictionary table [3]. Other works provided code compression by improving the dictionary method [12,13]. Ernst et al. applied a hybrid technique to address this issue, presenting two code compressors to handle transmission and memory bottlenecks independently [5]. Keith et al. compressed the code with compilation techniques, but the code size reduction was only 5% on average [10].

3 Compression Approach

In this section we first present the basic idea with an example and we then describe our prefetching mechanism.

For ARM instructions, the register fields of bit 16 to bit 19, bit 12 to bit 15, and bit 0 to bit 3 are used to indicate the register part; the remaining bits are the operation part. In our work, only the operation part is compressed and for simplicity, we use assembly codes to represent binary codes as examples. Our compression concept is shown in Figure 1. In Figure 1b, we first find that the instruction sequence in Figure 1a, two consecutive add instructions, is the one that occurs most frequently, so these two add instructions are compressed as "add, add". The process is repeated to check whether other instruction sequences can be compressed. The sequence, the rsb followed by "add, add", is compressed as the "rsb, add, add" instruction again and the final result is shown in Figure 1c. In contrast with Figure 1a, the length of the code shown in Figure 1c is shorter. The whole process can be represented as the binary tree illustrated in Figure 1d.

The compressed code is stored in three parts: instruction table, register bank, and index table, as shown Figure 2.

In compression, each opcode in the operation part is represented as an index number and these opcodes and indices are put into the instruction table and the index table. The instruction table contains two parts, as shown in Figure 3. They can be distinguished

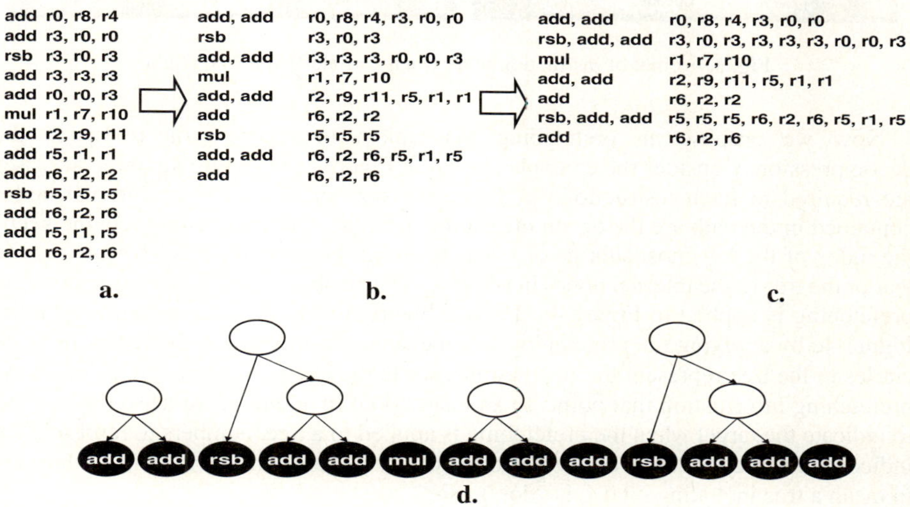

Fig. 1. Motivating example

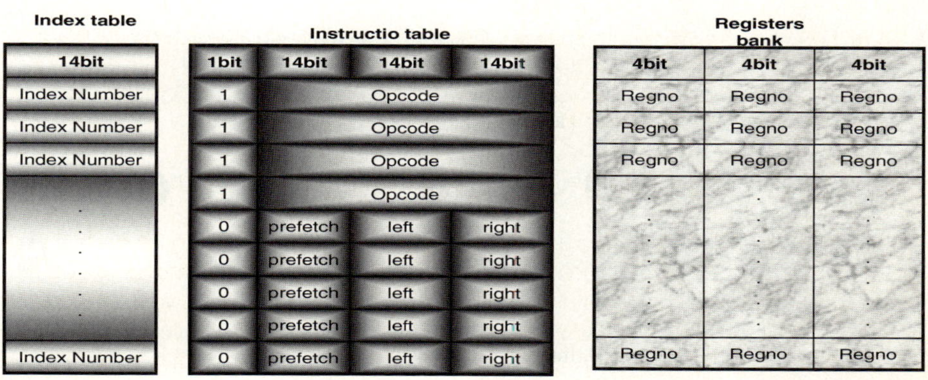

Fig. 2. Compression architecture

from the T bit. The left part contains the opcodes of the instructions used in a program and the right part represents the combination information of the compressed instructions. The sources of compressed instructions may come from the opcodes of the left part, other compressed instructions, or a mixture of both. The Left and Right fields of the case T = 0 represent the sources in the normal case, and the prefetch field is used to optimize the decompression performance. The register operands are stored in the register bank. The entries of the index table point to the addresses of the opcode sources in the instruction table and the addresses of the register operands in the register bank. In decompression, we access the entries in the index table in order to fetch the opcodes and the registers. Thus we can compress a code and then easily decompress it instruction by instruction at run time.

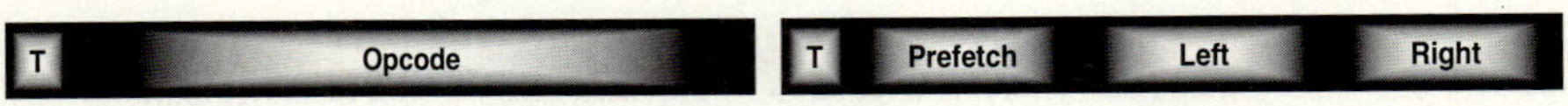

Fig. 3. Format of instruction table when T=1 (left) and T=0 (right)

Now we propose an prefetching mechanism in compression to speed the decompression. Consider the example shown in Figure 4. In Figure 4a, three accesses are required to fetch instruction "a" from the root. In this case, the internal nodes contained in the path are the decompression overheads. Our prefetching scheme keeps the index of the left-most subtree or a leaf (that will be executed first) by moving the leaf or the tree to the internal nodes in advance. Figure 4b is the tree after the instruction prefetching is applied to Figure 4a. In fact, Figure 4b can be further optimized to be Figure 4c by applying the prefetching scheme again. In this paper, the letters in black circles in the tree represent the instructions, while the letters in white circles mean the prefetching information that points to an instruction. In addition, we use a dashed line to indicate the target when the prefetching is applied to a tree, numbers to represent the indices in instruction table, dot nodes to indicate a tree is "don't care", and slash nodes to mean a tree including NULL is "don't care".

Consider the example shown in Figure 5. The operation part and the register part are first put in the instruction table and the register bank. Next the repeated instruction

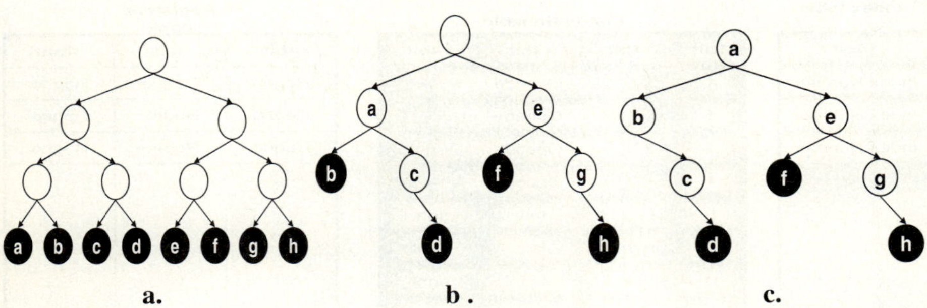

Fig. 4. Instruction prefetching scheme

sequence "MOVI, SUB" has been compressed with index 6, and T bit is set to false. The T bit of index 1 is set true, and prefetch = 1, left = NULL, right = 4. The combination (1+4) is inserted into entry 6 in the instruction table. These steps will be applied repeatedly and 1+4, 1+5, 7+7, 6+8, 6+6, 1+2 is inserted sequentially. In prefetching, four cases must be handled to optimize the compression. First, the left subtree is a leaf, thus it will be prefetched. Second, the left is NULL and the right is a leaf, then the prefetching information is stored in the root. If the right is an internal node, the prefetching information must be kept for further executions. Third, the prefetch is a leaf, the prefetching information is not kept and the prefetch points to a tree. Finally, the prefetch is the same as the prefetch of left subtree since the information kept in prefetch is a left-most tree. In our approach, if a node and its prefetch are not leaves, then it is called a *Redundant Node*, abbreviated R-node. In this case, we are not able to acquire any leaf information during decompression.

Index	Opcode	comment
1	000100000000	MOVI
2	001001100011	STW
3	000000000000	MOV
4	000100010010	SUB
5	000100100010	ADD
6	1+4	MOVI+SUB
7	1+5	MOVI+ADD
8	7+7	(MOVI+ADD)*2
9	6+8	OVI+SUB)+(MOVI+ADD)*
10	1+2	MOVI+STW
11	6+6	(MOVI+SUB)*2

a.

```
movi    r0, #32768
movi    sp, #4096
stw     r0, [sp, #52]
mov     r6, r0
movi    r1, #0
stw     r1, [sp, #48]
movi    r11, #0
movi    r3, #3072
sub     r3, r3, #231
movi    r4, #2048
add     r4, r4, #360
movi    r5, #1024
add     r5, r23, #84
movi    r6, #2048
add     r6, r6, #228
movi    r7, #3584
sub     r7, r7, #178
movi    r8, #4096
sub     r8, r8, #79
movi    r9, #1024
sub     r9, r9, #225
movi    r2, #1536
add     r2, r28, #32
movi    r10, #3584
add     r10, r10, #200
```

b.

Fig. 5. Example for ARM instructions

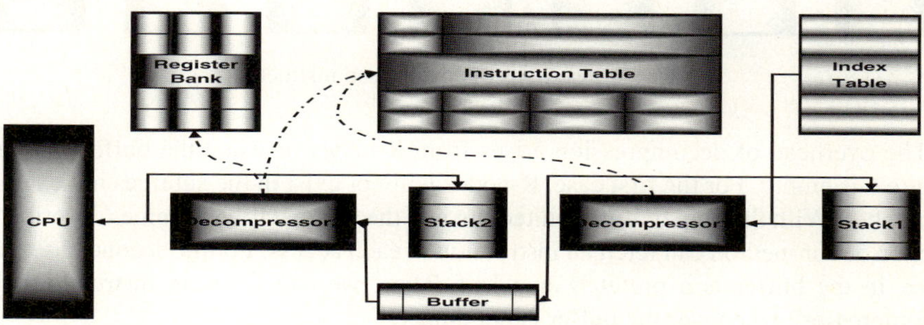

Fig. 6. Architecture of the Decompression System

4 Decompression Approach

In decompression, the prefetching is performed only in the root and the right subtree. We use the two decompressors synchronously shown in Figure 6 to reduce the decompression overhead. One decompresses the indices from the instruction table into buffer and the other decompresses the data from buffer into the CPU. Figure 7 shows an example of our decompression scheme. For decompressor 1, the index 9 is first acquired from the index table and its root is set to true. As the T bit of the index 9 is false, index 8 is pushed into the stack and the root of its right side is set to true. Then the index 4, to the left of index 9, is pushed into the stack and its root is set to false. Next, the prefetch of index 9, index 1, is put in the buffer and the root is set to true since the root of index 9 is true. Then the stack is not empty and the process will return to the beginning of this step and acquire an index from the stack. Now we acquire the index 4 and its T bit is true, thus it is put in the buffer and the root is set to true. The above steps will be repeated and the content of buffer will be (1,4,1,5,1,5). Now we use the above buffer to explain the action of decompressor 2. First, we acquire the item index = 1 from the buffer. Second, we can access the registers based on the program counter and combine them together into one item because the T bit of index = 1 is true. Then the new item is delivered to the CPU and the process is rpeated because the stack is still empty. These steps will be performed recursively and the instructions (movi, sub, movi, add, movi, add) will be delivered to the CPU in order.

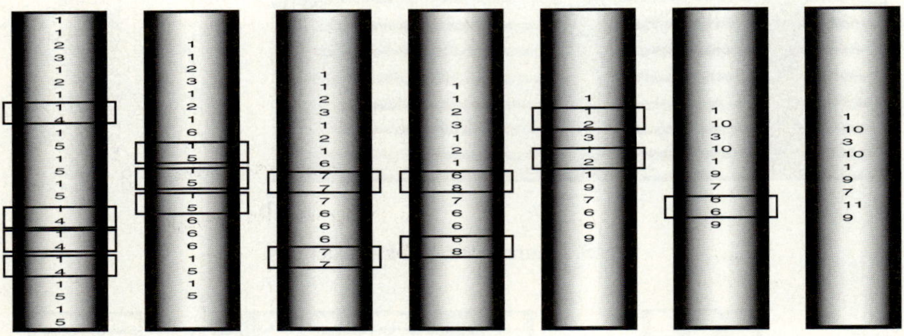

Fig. 7. Insertions of compressed instructions

The overhead of decompression arises from R-nodes or when the buffer shown in Figure 6 is empty. For the first case, R-nodes will not exist in the subtrees indicated by prefetches. With the help of this architecture and the optimization schemes described in Section 5, our method can fetch an instruction in each access. For the second case, each index in the buffer is a prefetch or a leaf. Thus, we can fetch an instruction from decompressor2 whenever the buffer is not empty.

5 Experimental Result

The experiments are performed on the ARM simulator running the RedHat9.0 operating system and compiled with a GNU compiler with default settings. The testing sets consist of SPEC2000, MediaBench, DSPstone benchmarks.

5.1 Compression Ratio Evaluation

The bars in Figure 8 show the compression ratio of four benchmarks calculated by the following equation.

$$\left(\frac{(compressed\_instruction \cdot compressed\_width) + (instruction\_counts \cdot 12) + instruction\_table\_size}{instruction\_counts \cdot 32}\right)$$

The compression ratio ranges between 54% and 81%. With our experiences, the width is limited to 14 bits. In addition, the instruction savings of applications in SPEC2000 and MediaBench are around 30% and 36%, respectively. However, in DSPstone, the instruction saving is low because its applications are quite small. For MPEG4, the instruction saving is between 28% and 68%. In particular, the "bitstream" has the best result because there are many macros used in it. Consider ghostscript in MediaBench as an example, which is the largest program in all benchmarks. It has 304124 instructions and its compressed code only contains 5415 opcodes. Therefore, the width and the length of the index table are 13 bits and 189545, the width and the length of the instruction table are 40 bits and 8192, and the width and the length of the register bank are 12 bits and 304124. The compression ratio is $(13 \times 189545 + 40 \times 8192 + 12 \times 304124) / 32 \times 304124 = 0.66$.

5.2 Performance Evaluation

The experiments are performed in the ARM simulator running on RedHat9.0 to count the cycles needed to decompress the compressed codes. In the experiments, the sizes of buffer and the two stacks are limited to 16 slots. The curves in Figure 14 show the performance degradations. The ratio of performance degradation is calculated from the number of cycles during decompression to those executed in the normal cases. The range of the performance loss is below 25%. For DSPstone, the average performance levels are worse because the average heights of the compression trees in it are higher than those of other benchmarks. The average performance in Xvid is better except the bitstream. Its performance is bad because it use many macros, which increases the height of the tree.

6 Optimizations

In this section, we propose some optimizations to enhance our method in compression ratio and performance. They are described in the following and the results are shown in Figure 9 and Figure 10.

6.1 Performance Enhancement

There are some optimizations performed on the instruction table to improve the performance without increasing the size. First, in the first part of the instruction table (T = 1), the opcode is shorter than the length of entries. For a large application, it is very possible to utilize the remaining space of entries to occupy another opcode. In this way, a single leaf can contain two opcodes and we can fetch two instructions each time to

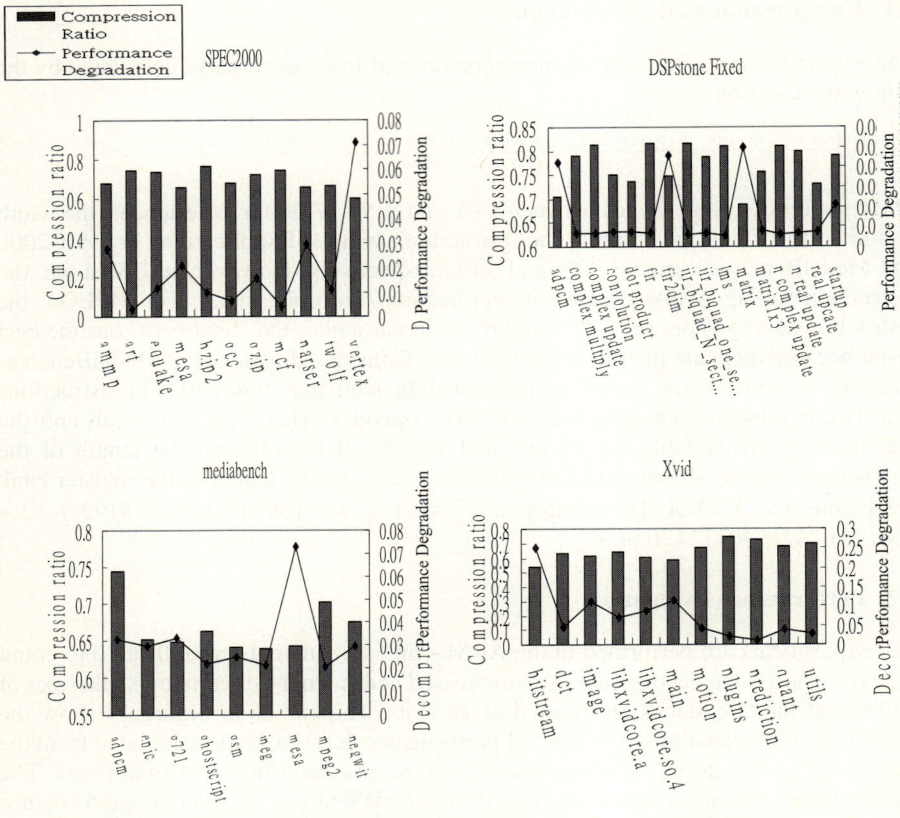

Fig. 8. Results of compression ratio and performance degradation

improve the performance. Second, if the width of the left field and the prefetch field is longer than that of opcode, the left must be NULL, and the prefetch must be a leaf, we can put the opcode of prefetch in the left field and the prefetch field. We can use one bit to specify that the content is an index or an opcode. Therefore, the performance will be improved. The result is shown in Figure 9 with the line 'Opcode in prefetch and left'. Moreover, the case in Figure 10b can be further optimized to be that in Figure 10c. Its performance can be improved by applying the above techniques to it. We can ensure that the prefetch will point to a leaf or a tree. In this case, as the left of a tree is NULL, the decompressor2 can deliver more than one instruction each fetch. The defect of this way might cause the increase of R-nodes and degrade the performance loss. The curve 'Optimization on instruction table' in Figure 9 shows the performance after all methods described in this section are applied.

If the width of the prefetch in the instruction table can be extended to contain an opcode, then the performance will be almost the same as that of the original program. This is because it is unnecessary to look up the prefetches. In addition, we still need one bit to specify that the content of the prefetch is an opcode or an index, but it will

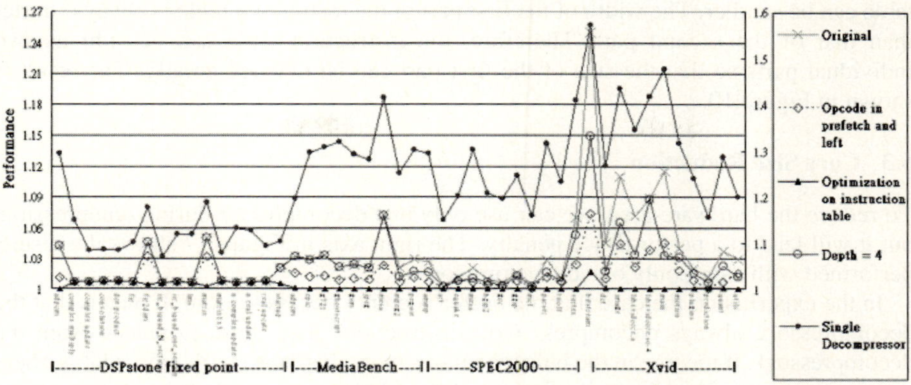

Fig. 9. Performance with optimizations

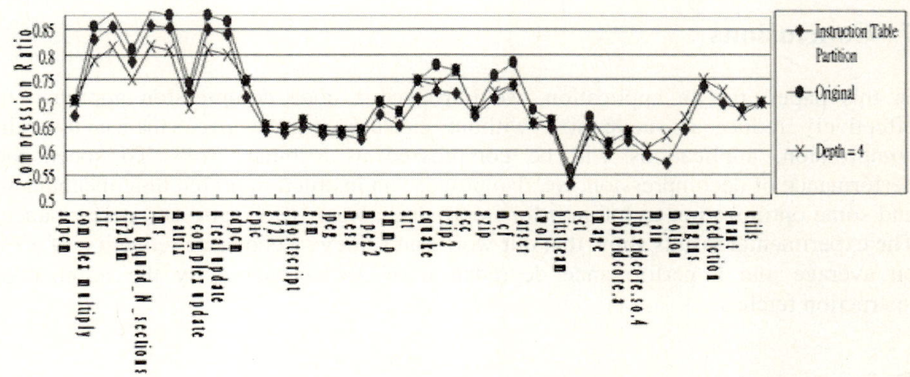

Fig. 10. Compression ratio with optimizations

increase the size of instruction table. For example, in the case of application 'mesa' in the MediaBench, the size of the instruction table will be increased from 40KB to 47KB.

In the experiment, we found that the number of R-nodes has a close relationship with the depth of a tree. Therefore, in the process of compressing an instruction sequence, we can check first if the depth of the new tree is higher to stop the merging. In this way, we can improve the performance by reducing the R-nodes. We limit the depth of the tree to 4 and show the performance result in Figure 9 and the compression result in Figure 10 with the line 'Depth = 4'.

6.2 Compression Optimization

In our work, we use T-bit in the instruction table to tell whether the entry is an opcode or not. Indeed, we can use one register or one counter to specify that entries belong to which part instead of using the T-bit for each entry. Thus, the size of the instruction table can be smaller. The width of the first part of the instruction table is always shorter than that of the second part. Therefore, the instruction table can be split as two individual parts so that the size of the first part can be reduced greatly. The result is shown in Figure 10.

6.3 Core Size Reduction

To reduce the hardware area, we can use only one decompressor during compression, but it will lead to a performance penalty. The right axis in Figure 17 shows the results performed with using only one decompressor.

In the experiment, the case that the buffer is empty occurs seldom. It means that the decompressor2 always decompress more instructions than those produced from the decompressor1. If the tree in the buffer contains more than one instruction, that is, there are not too many R-nodes in it, the size of the buffer can be reduced to optimize the memory required. The experimental results show that the performances are the same no matter the size of the buffer is 4, 8 or 16. Thus, the buffer may be not very large.

7 Conclusions

In this paper, for an application, we introduce a code compression approach to effectively reduce its code size without causing a great performance loss. In compression, applications will be compressed as a binary tree. To speed the performance of decompression, we also propose an instruction prefetching mechanism and some optimization techniques for improving compression ratio and performance. The experimental results show that our work can achieve a code size reduction of 33% on average and a performance degradation of 3% measured by the number of instruction fetches.

References

1. ARM. ARM7TDMI (Rev4) Technical Reference Manual. Advanced RISC Machines Ltd., (15 May 2003).
2. ARM. An Introduction to Thumb. Advanced RISC Machines Ltd., (March 1995).
3. T. Bell, J. Cleary, and I. Witten. Text Compression. Prentice Hall, (1990).
4. Saumya Debray, and William Evans: Profile-Guided Code Compression, Proceedings of the 2002 ACM SIGPLAN Conference on Programming Language Design and Implementation (PLDI).
5. Jens Ernst, William Evans, Christopher W. Fraser, Steven Luco, and Todd A. Proebsting: Code Compression, Proceedings of the 1997 ACM SIGPLAN Conference on Programming Language Design and Implementation (PLDI).
6. William S. Evans and Christopher W. Fraser: Bytecode Compression via Profiled Grammar Rewriting, Proceedings of the 2001 International Conference on Programming Language Design and Implementation (PLDI).
7. R.M. Fano: Transmission of Information. Cambridge, MA: MIT Press 1961.C.
8. W. Fraser, T. A. Proebsting: Custom Instruction Sets for Code Compression. Unpublished. Available at http://www.cs. arizona.edu/people/todd/papers/pldi2.ps, Oct. 1995.

9. IBM. CodePack PowerPC Code Compression Utility User's Manually Version 3.0. 1998.
10. Keith, D. Cooper and Nathaniel McIntosh. Enhanced Code Compression for Embedded RISC Processors. Proceedings of the 1999 International Conference on Programming Language Design and Implementation (PLDI).
11. K. Kissell. MIPS16: High-Density MIPS for the Embedded Market. Silicon Graphics MIPS Group, (1997).
12. C. Lefurgy, P. Bird, I.-C. Chen, and T. Mudge: Improving Code Density Using Compression Techniques. Proceedings of the 30th Annual International Symposium on Microarchitecture, (December 1997).
13. S. Liao, S. Devadas, and K. Keutzer: Code Density Optimization for Embedded DSP Processors Using Data Compression Techniques. Proceeding of the 15th Conference on Advanced Research in VLSI.(March 1995).

Dual-Mode r-Reliable Task Model for Flexible Scheduling in Reliable Real-Time Systems

Kyong Hoon Kim, Jong Kim, and Sung Je Hong

Department of Computer Science and Engineering
Pohang University of Science and Technology (POSTECH)
Pohang, Korea
{jysh, jkim, sjhong}@postech.ac.kr

Abstract. Recent research in real-time systems has much focused on new task models for flexible scheduling and fault-tolerant real-time systems. In this paper, we propose a novel task model for the purpose of flexible scheduling in reliable real-time systems. In the proposed dual-mode r-reliable task model, a task periodically releases fast mode jobs or reliable mode jobs with the constraint that reliable mode jobs must be executed at least once for any r consecutive periods to guarantee the reliability of task. We also propose scheduling algorithms and compare performance through simulation results.

1 Introduction

Real-time systems are the systems in which the completion time of task affects systems as well as the correct result of task. Traditional real-time systems are classified into hard and soft real-time systems. In hard real-time systems, missing task deadlines is fatal for the task. By contrast, in soft real-time systems, a few missed deadlines do not cause serious problems, but the task has some diminished value for the failure of deadlines. Recent research in real-time systems, however, has focused on new task models for the purpose of the flexibility of task scheduling or the reliability of systems.

For more flexible scheduling, (m, k)-*firm* task model [1], s-*skippable* task model [2], and window-constrained task model [3] were proposed. Bernat et al. [4] generalized those task models and introduced *weakly hard* real-time systems. Weakly hard real-time systems are hard but permit occasional misses of task deadlines, so that tasks have their own bounded numbers to tolerate missed deadlines during any consecutive window of time. Moreover, Mok and Chen [5] proposed the *multiframe* task model, which allows the execution time of a task to vary from one instance to another with a known pattern. Another flexible task models are Imprecise Computation (IC) [6,7] and Increased-Reward-with-Increased-Service (IRIS) [8]. A task in IC model consists of a mandatory part and an optional part. In IRIS model, each task receives a reward that depends on the amount of service received prior to deadline.

In addition to flexible scheduling, much research on fault-tolerant real-time systems has been conducted. In critical real-time systems, tasks must meet their

E. Sha et al. (Eds.): EUC 2006, LNCS 4096, pp. 308–317, 2006.

deadlines in spite of some failures. Fault-tolerant real-time scheduling algorithms have been proposed with both *forward recovery* and *backward recovery* schemes. For forward recovery in fault-tolerant real-time systems, the scheduling algorithms in [9,10,11] considered task replications and Ghosh et al. [12] analyzed the Rate Monotonic scheduling with task duplications. Punnekkat et al. [13] analyzed checkpointing for backward recovery of fault-tolerant real-time systems.

There have been recent works related on flexible and reliable real-time control systems. The Simplex architecture [14,15] is a flexible and reliable software architecture that uses analytically redundant controllers. In the Simplex architecture, a device is controlled by two different versions of programs, a high-assurance controller and a high-performance controller. The high-assurance controller provides high reliability with low performance. The high-performance controller, however, shows good performance but low reliability. Chandra et al. [16] presented a method that finds the optimal frequencies for systems using analytically redundant controllers on the assumption that the failure rates are known.

In this paper, we introduce a new task model in which a task must execute at least one reliable job during the bounded window of time. A task periodically releases jobs which may be in *fast* mode or *reliable* mode. The fast mode job is the normal execution process to accomplish the goal of task, while the reliable mode job adds more dependable process for the reliability of task. In wireless real-time communication, for instance, reliable job data may be sent with a large amount of redundant bits to tolerate packet loss, while fast mode job data are sent with few redundant bits. Besides two different job modes, we specify the minimum number of reliable mode jobs to be executed. A task with the bound of r must execute at least one reliable job for any r consecutive jobs, which will be defined by *r-reliable constraint*. Thus, the proposed task model is named the *dual-mode r-reliable* task model. The applications of the proposed task model include reliable real-time communication, fault-tolerant real-time scheduling, and QoS or multimedia related applications. This paper will also suggest several priority-driven scheduling algorithms for the proposed task model.

The remainder of this paper is organized as follows. In Section 2, we specify the new task model and discuss the scheduling problem. The scheduling algorithms for the proposed task model are described in Section 3 and simulation results of those algorithms are given in Section 4. Finally, this paper is concluded with Section 5.

2 Dual-Mode r-Reliable Real-Time Systems

The dual-mode r-reliable real-time system is a real-time system which consists of the dual-mode r-reliable tasks. This section defines dual-mode r-reliable task model and the scheduling problem to solve.

2.1 Dual-Mode r-Reliable Task Model

A dual-mode r-reliable real-time task can be explained by three terminologies: *real-time, dual-mode*, and *r-reliable*. Since we assume a task is periodic, a

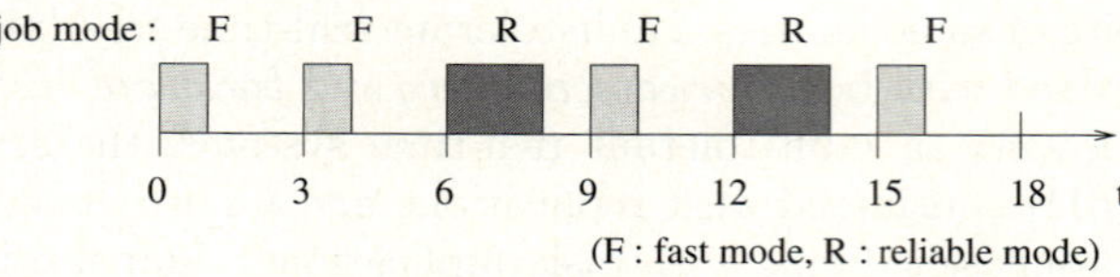

Fig. 1. Example of a dual-mode r-reliable task $\tau(2, 1, 3, 3)$

real-time task means that the task periodically creates jobs which must be finished before the next job releases. *Dual-mode* means that the computation mode of each job is either in *fast* mode or *reliable* mode. Lastly, *r-reliable* notifies the constraint that at least one job of every r consecutive jobs of the task is in reliable mode. Thus, a dual-mode r-reliable real-time task τ is defined by four parameters (c^R, c^F, p, r).

- c^R : the execution time of reliable mode job
- c^F : the execution time of fast mode job
- p : the period of jobs released
- r : r-reliable constraint

A task τ releases a job every p time units. Each job of the task can be executed as soon as it is released and its relative deadline is p. As stated above, a job is either in fast mode or reliable mode. According to the computation mode, the required execution time of the job is c^F or c^R in each. In general, the reliable mode job requires more processing time so that we assume the execution time of the reliable mode job is larger than that of the fast mode job ($c^R > c^F$). The parameter r indicates how often the reliable mode job should be executed for the reliability of the task. Thus, we represent the reliability of a task with this *r-reliable constraint.*

For example, the task $\tau(2, 1, 3, 3)$ can be scheduled as shown in Figure 1. The task creates a job every 3 time units, and the job is either in fast mode or reliable mode. While the fast mode job is executed for one time unit, the reliable mode job is executed for two time units. Since at least one reliable job is executed during every three consecutive periods, the schedule in Figure 1 meets the 3-reliable constraint.

The reliable mode job of a task can be modeled in two different manners. The first is an additional computation which is independent of the fast mode job and requires ($c^R - c^F$) computation times. The second approach of the reliable mode job is to execute more reliable process different from the fast mode job. One such example is the MPEG decoding process, in which I-frame in MPEG decoding differs from P-frame decoding and takes more time. Reliable real-time communications using FEC (Forward Error Correct) schemes are also an example. A low rate-coded massage with less redundant information corresponds to the fast mode job, while a high rate-coded message with more redundant information corresponds to the reliable mode job. In this paper, we assume the latter case so that the computation process of the reliable mode job is different from that of the fast mode job.

The main applications of dual-mode r-reliable task model are reliable real-time communication, fault-tolerant real-time scheduling, and QoS or multimedia related applications. In reliable real-time communication, it is necessary to send data with more redundant bits to tolerate packet loss but we cannot send such data every time for the lack of network bandwidth. These data can be represented with a reliable mode job in the proposed task model and its minimum distance corresponds to the r-reliable constraint. We may apply the model to fault-tolerant real-time scheduling using backward error recovery scheme with checkpointing. That is, a normal job added with checkpointing process is modeled as a reliable mode job and the checkpointing period indicates the r-reliable constraint. Moreover, many real-time applications related on QoS or multimedia can use the r parameter in such a manner that tasks with higher qualities are assigned with lower r's. For example, the standard H.261 and H.263 ITU video codecs have two different frame types, Intraframe (I-frame) and Interframe (P-frame). Data size of P-frame is smaller than that of I-frame since it is based on the previous frame (I-frame or P-frame). Thus, both H.261 and H.263 bitstreams are modeled with dual-mode r-reliable tasks and the minimum interval between I-frames corresponds to th r-reliable constraint.

The proposed dual-mode r-reliable task can be modeled with previous task models [17,5,1]. A dual-mode r-reliable task can be modeled as the task with the worst-case execution time c^R in the L&L task model [17], or the multiframe task with one reliable job and $(r-1)$ consecutive fast mode jobs in the multiframe task model [5]. However, these are so pessimistic that their schedulabilities are low. The $(m,\ k)$-firm task model [1] can also be used for modeling a dual-mode r-reliable task by decomposing the task into $(1,\ 1)$-firm task with execution time c^F and $(1,\ r)$-firm task with execution time $(c^R - c^F)$. It is only suitable for the case that the reliable mode job is an additional process independent of the fast mode job. However, as we assume the reliable mode job is different process from the fast mode job, the $(m,\ k)$-firm task model does not exactly model the proposed task.

2.2 Scheduling Problem

Before turning to the scheduling problem, we address the feasibility. A schedule of a given dual-mode r-reliable task set is *feasible* if the schedule makes all jobs meet their deadlines and each task meet its r-reliable constraint. Also, a dual-mode r-reliable task set T is said to be *feasible* if and only if there exists a scheduling algorithm to generate a feasible schedule of the task set.

Quan and Hu [18] proved that the scheduling problem of the (m,k)-firm task model is NP-hard. In the assumption that all the computation times of fast mode jobs are zero, the scheduling problem of dual-mode r-reliable tasks is equal to that of corresponding $(1,r)$-firm tasks. Thus, the scheduling problem of the dual-mode r-reliable task model is NP-hard in the weak sense.

The *minimum effective utilization* of a dual-mode r-reliable task $\tau(c^R, c^F, p, r)$ is defined by $\frac{c^F}{p} + \frac{c^R - c^F}{p \times r}$. The minimum effective utilization of the task τ is the minimum fraction of time that the task τ keeps a processor busy, since τ requires

c^F time units every p periods and at least $(c^R - c^F)$ times are allocated to τ's reliable jobs for $p \times r$ time units. The minimum effective utilization $U^e(T)$ of a dual-mode r-reliable task set T is the summation of minimum effective utilization of the individual tasks within it.

Lemma 1. *Given a dual-mode r-reliable task set* $T = \{\tau_i = (c_i^R, c_i^F, p_i, r_i) | 1 \leq i \leq n\}$, *if* $U^e(T)$ *is larger than 1, then* T *is not feasible.*

Proof. Even if we fully utilize the processor to execute the task set, the utilization is 1. Since $U^e(T) > 1$, a task exists which cannot be scheduled. Thus, the task set T is not feasible. □

The task set satisfying the condition in Lemma 1 cannot be scheduled by any algorithm due to its over-utilization. By contrast, if the utilization of a task set is small enough to schedule every job as a reliable mode job, the task set is always schedulable. The following lemma tells the condition to guarantee that every task in the task set is schedulable.

Lemma 2. *Given a dual-mode r-reliable task set* $T = \{\tau_i = (c_i^R, c_i^F, p_i, r_i) | 1 \leq i \leq n\}$, T *is feasible if* T *satisfies* $\sum_{\tau_i \in T} \frac{c_i^R}{p_i} \leq 1$.

Proof. Consider the EDF algorithm and assume all tasks always release their jobs in the reliable mode. Since the EDF is optimal, all reliable mode jobs of tasks are schedulable if $\sum_{i=1}^{n} \frac{c_i^R}{p_i} \leq 1$. Furthermore, all jobs meet their r-reliable constraints. Thus, T is feasible. □

By Lemmas 1 and 2, scheduling algorithms in the next section concentrate on scheduling the task set T such that $U^e(T) \leq 1$ and $\sum_{\tau_i \in T}(c_i^R/p_i) > 1$.

3 Scheduling Algorithms

In this section, we propose one fixed priority-based algorithm and three dynamic priority-based algorithms for dual-mode r-reliable real-time systems. The fixed priority-based algorithm described in Section 3.1 is based on the RM, and dynamic priority-based algorithms in Section 3.2 are based on the EDF.

3.1 Fixed Priority-Based Algorithm

DR-RM (Dual-mode r-Reliable Rate Monotonic) assigns priorities to tasks according to the Rate Monotonic policy [17]: the shorter period, the higher priority. In DR-RM, the reliable mode job pattern of the task with r-reliable constraint is determined in such a manner that every r-th job is in reliable mode. For instance, the job mode pattern of a 4-reliable task is FFFRFFFR$\cdots$ (F : fast mode, R : reliable mode).

As we fix the reliable mode job pattern of a task, a dual-mode r-reliable task $\tau(c^R, c^F, p, r)$ is modeled as the multiframe [5] task with period p and r execution time list which consists of $(r-1)$ c^F's and one c^R. The *critical instance test* for testing the schedulability of multiframe tasks [5] is applicable to test the schedulability of dual-mode r-reliable tasks. Therefore, Theorem 1 follows.

Theorem 1. *Suppose that a dual-mode r-reliable task set* $T = \{\tau_i(c_i^R, c_i^F, p_i, r_i) | 1 \leq i \leq n\}$ *is given and tasks are sorted such that* $p_1 \leq p_2 \leq \ldots \leq p_n$. *Let us define the worst-case execution time* $W_i(t)$ *as follows:*

$$W_i(t) = c_i^R + \sum_{j=1}^{i-1} \left(\left\lceil \frac{t}{p_j} \right\rceil \cdot c_j^F + \left\lceil \frac{t}{p_j \times r_j} \right\rceil \cdot (c_j^R - c_j^F) \right)$$

If, for all $1 \leq i \leq n$, *some* $t \leq p_i$ *exists such that* $W_i(t) \leq t$, *then all the tasks in the task set* T *are schedulable by the DR-RM and their r-reliable constraints are met.*

Proof. Let us define $R_j(t)$ be $\left\lceil \frac{t}{p_j} \right\rceil \cdot c_j^F + \left\lceil \frac{t}{p_j \times r_j} \right\rceil \cdot (c_j^R - c_j^F)$ so that $W_i(t)$ is the sum of c_i^R and $\sum_{j=1}^{i-1} R_j(t)$. Consider the reliable mode job of task τ_i. The critical instance of task τ_i is when all reliable mode jobs of higher-priority tasks than τ_i are released at the same time. Then, $R_j(t)$ is the computation times of task τ_j until t because task τ_j requires c_j^F times for every p_j times and additional $c_j^R - c_j^F$ times for every $p_j \times r_j$ times. Thus, $W_i(t)$ becomes the sum of the computation times of the reliable mode job of task τ_i and the computation times of all jobs with higher-priority than τ_i at time t.

Therefore, if $t < p_i$ exists such that $W_i(t) \leq t$, then the reliable mode job of τ_i will meet its deadline. Since the reliable mode job of task τ_i meets its deadline, fast mode jobs also meet their deadlines. Moreover, DR-RM generates every r_i-th job with a reliable mode job so that the r_i-reliable constraint is met. Hence, task τ_i is schedulable and the theorem follows since i can be any number. □

3.2 Dynamic Priority-Based Algorithms

Dynamic priority-based algorithms do not fix priorities of tasks so that the scheduler always executes the highest-priority job among available jobs. In this paper, we select the EDF policy for assigning the priorities of jobs. Thus, the earlier the deadline of the job, the higher the priority. Figure 2 shows the scheduling algorithm based on the dynamic priority scheme.

In Figure 2, the algorithm **Queue-Schedule** executes the job with the earliest absolute deadline in the *wait_queue* and the algorithm **Job-Release** releases every job among given tasks. At the time of releasing a job, the job mode is determined by the function *Determine_Mode*. In this paper, three different algorithms are used to determine job mode patterns. The following subsections describe those algorithms.

(1) FIX Algorithm

The FIX algorithm determines the job mode patterns in the same manner as that of DR-RM. That is, every r-th job is in reliable mode and others are in fast mode.

```
Algorithm Scheduling_Dual-mode_r-reliable
/* - t : current time
   - wait_queue : the queue of current available jobs
*/
Concurrently execute Queue-Schedule and Job-Release.

Queue-Schedule
Execute the job which has the earliest absolute deadline in wait_queue.

Job-Release
for each task τi do
   if t mod pi == 0 then
      mode = Determine_Mode (τi)
      if mode == RELIABLE then
         Create a reliable mode job of τi and insert it in wait_queue.
      else /* FAST mode */
         Create a fast mode job of τi and insert it in wait_queue.
      endif
   endif
endfor
```

Fig. 2. Dynamic priority-based algorithm

(2) DBP Algorithm

We modify the DBP (Distance-Based Priority) assignment scheme [1] to generate computation modes of tasks. Each task maintains $state_i$ which indicates the state of task τ_i in the state transition diagram of the DBP assignment [1]. The state transition diagram of a dual-mode r-reliable task is shown in Figure 3. At every state, when the task releases the reliable mode job, its state becomes $r-1$. When the r-reliable task of state j ($j > 0$) releases the fast mode job, its state becomes $j-1$. If the task of state 0 releases the fast mode job, its state remains at state 0, and at that time the task cannot meet the r-reliable constraint.

The DBP job mode determining algorithm assigns the task τ_i of the lowest $state_i$ to be in reliable mode. To prevent tasks from missing the r-reliable constraint, the task in state 0 always releases the reliable mode job.

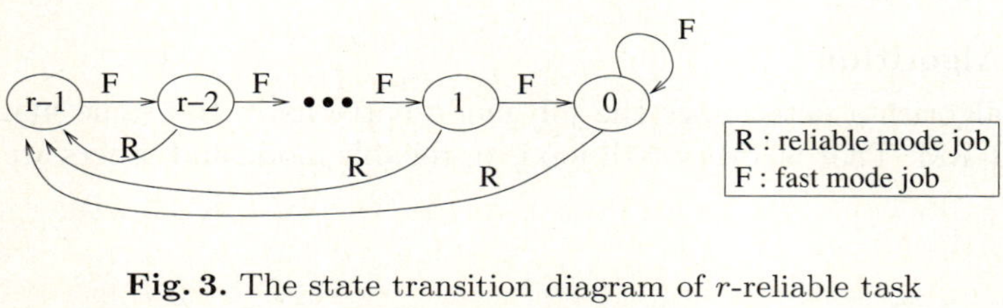

Fig. 3. The state transition diagram of r-reliable task

(3) SS Algorithm

The SS (Slack Stealing) algorithm for determining the job mode is based on generic slack stealing techniques for scheduling aperiodic and sporadic jobs. This paper references the work of Chetto and Chetto [19].

For a given dual-mode r-reliable task set T, we define e_i and Δ_i. e_i is the distinct i-th arrival time of jobs in system and Δ_i is the length of idle time between e_{i-1} and e_i under the EDF schedule of tasks in T assuming that all jobs are in fast mode. Chetto and Chetto [19] derive the equation for calculating Δ_i without scheduling the EDF until time e_i. Since we schedule all jobs of tasks with fast modes, the length of the idle time between e_{i-1} and e_i is given by the following equation.

$$\Delta_i = \max\{0,\ e_i - \sum_{j=1}^{n} \lceil \frac{e_i}{p_j} \rceil c_j^F - \sum_{k=1}^{i-1} \Delta_k\}, \qquad i = 1, 2, \ldots$$

The SS algorithm manages $dist\_reliable_i$ to indicate the distance to a reliable mode job. When $dis\_reliable_i$ is non-zero, the task τ_i creates a fast mode job and $dis\_reliable_i$ decreases by one. When $dis\_reliable_i$ is zero, the task τ_i releases a reliable mode job and then decides the next $dist\_reliable_i$. The brief algorithm to determine the next $dist\_reliable_i$ is finding the last-fit period in which enough idle times for the reliable mode job exists among the next r_i periods. If the summation of Δ_i's during each period is larger than or equal to $c_i^R - c_i^F$, then we can schedule the reliable mode job at that period.

4 Simulation Results

In this section, we present simulation results to compare the proposed algorithms in dual-mode r-reliable real-time systems. The simulation in this section is performed as follows: we randomly generate 500 feasible task sets for each minimum effective utilization bound. Each task set consists of at least five tasks. To generate a feasible task set, we start the empty task set and add a randomly generated task to the task set one by one. The randomly generated task is examined to test for schedulability, including tasks in the task set so that only the task to succeed in the schedulability test is added to the task set. We perform the schedulability test for the task by scheduling it with tasks in the task set until the least common multiple of $r_i \times p_i$'s of all tasks.

In the experiment of Figure 4, the period p_i of each task is given in the range from 4 to 25 and the reliable constraint r_i is in the range from 2 to 10. For the computation time, we randomly select c_i^R between 3 and p_i and then randomly generate c_i^F in the range from 2 to $c_i^R - 1$. The characteristics of feasible task sets in the experiment is shown in Table 1. Since dynamic priority-based algorithms proposed in the previous section are all based on the EDF policy, they are named FIX-EDF, DBP-EDF, and SS-EDF according to the job mode pattern algorithm.

Figure 4 shows the success ratio of scheduling dual-mode r-reliable task sets in percentile. The success ratios of dynamic priority-based algorithms are higher

Table 1. Characteristics of feasible task sets

Effective Util.	$0.4 \sim 0.5$	$0.5 \sim 0.6$	$0.6 \sim 0.7$	$0.7 \sim 0.8$	$0.8 \sim 0.9$
# of tasks / set	5.0	5.0	5.0	5.0	5.0
average c^R	4.5	4.8	5.1	5.0	4.7
average c^F	2.1	2.3	2.5	2.7	2.7
average p	21.2	20.1	19.4	18.5	17.6
average r	6.8	6.6	6.3	6.2	6.0

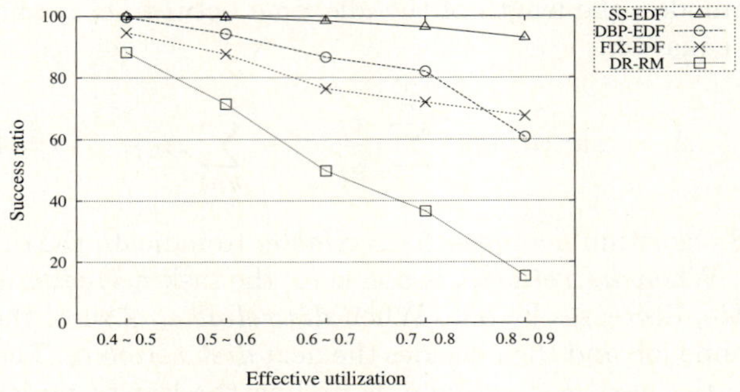

Fig. 4. The success ratios of algorithms

than that of fixed priority-based algorithm DR-RM. SS-EDF shows the highest success ratio among dynamic priority-based algorithms.

5 Conclusions

In this paper, we proposed a dual-mode r-reliable real-time task model, which is a novel task model for flexible scheduling in reliable real-time systems. A dual-mode r-reliable task has two different mode jobs and its reliable mode job must be executed at least once for any r consecutive periods. The task model can be applied to many recent real-time applications, including reliable real-time communication, fault-tolerant real-time systems, and QoS related applications. We also suggested priority-driven scheduling algorithms for the proposed task model and compared performance throughout simulation results.

Acknowledgement

This research was supported by the MIC (Ministry of Information and Communication), Korea, under the ITRC (Information Technology Research Center) support program supervised by the IITA (Institute of Information Technology Assessment) (IITA-2005-C1090-0501-0018).

References

1. Hamdaoui, M., Ramanathan, P.: A dynamic priority assignment technique for streams with (m,k)-firm deadlines. IEEE Transactions on Computers **44(12)** (1995) 1443–1451
2. Koren, G., Shasha, D.: Skip-Over: algorithms and complexity for overloaded systems that allow skips. Proceedings of Real-Time Systems Symposium (1995) 110–117
3. West, R., Poellabauer, C.: Analysis of a window-constrained scheduler for real-time and best-effort packet streams. Proceedings of Real-Time Systems Symposium (2000) 239–248
4. Bernat, G., Burns, A., Llamosi, A.: Weakly hard real-time systems. IEEE Transactions on Computers **50(4)** (2001) 308–321
5. Mok, A.K., Chen, D.: A multiframe model for real-time tasks. IEEE Transactions on Software Engineering **23(10)** (1997) 635–645
6. Lin, K.-J., Natarajan, S., Liu, J. W.-S.: Imprecise results: utilizing partial computations in real-time systems. Proceedings of Real-Time Systems Symposium (1987) 210–217
7. Liu, J. W.-S., Lin, K.-J., Shih, W.-K., Yu, A. C.-S., Chung, C., Yao, J., Zhao, W.: Algorithms for scheduling imprecise computations. IEEE Computers **24(5)** (1991) 58–68
8. Dey, J. K., Kurose, J., Towsley, D.: On-line scheduling policies for a class of IRIS (Increasing Reward with Increasing Service) real-time tasks. IEEE Transactions on Computers **45(7)** (1996) 802–813
9. Liestman, A. L., Campbell, R. H.: A fault-tolerant scheduling problem. IEEE Transactions on Software Engineering **12(11)** (1986) 1089–1095
10. Krishna, C., Shin, K.G.: On scheduling tasks with a quick recovery from failure. IEEE Transactions on Computers **35(5)** (1986) 448–455
11. Han, C.-C., Shin, K.G., Wu, J.: A fault-tolerant scheduling algorithm for real-time periodic tasks with possible software faults IEEE Transactions on Computers **52(3)** (2003) 362–372
12. Ghosh, S., Melhem, R., Mossé, D., Sarma, J. S.: Fault-tolerant rate-monotonic scheduling. Journal of Real-Time Systems **15(2)** (1998) 149–181
13. Punnekkat, S., Burns, A., Davis, R.: Analysis of checkpointing for real-time systems. Journal of Real-Time Systems **20(1)** (2001) 83–102
14. Seto, D., Krogh, B., Sha, L., Chutinan, A.: Dynamic control systems upgrade using Simplex architecture. IEEE Control Systems (1998) 72–80
15. Sha, L.: Dependable system upgrade. Proceedings of Real-Time Systems Symposium (1998) 440–448
16. Chandra, R., Liu, X., Sha, L.: On the scheduling of flexible and reliable real-time control systems. Journal of Real-Time Systems **24(2)** (2003) 153–169
17. Liu, C.L., Layland, J.W.: Scheduling algorithms for multi-programming in a hard real-time environment. Journal of ACM **20** (1973) 46–61
18. Quan, G., Hu, X.: Enhanced fixed-priority scheduling with (m,k)-firm guarantee. Proceedings of Real-Time Systems Symposium (2000) 79–88
19. Chetto, H., Chetto, M.: Some results of the earliest deadline scheduling algorithm. IEEE Transactions on Software Engineering **15(10)** (1989) 1261–1269

Securing Internet Gateway Discovery Protocol in Ubiquitous Wireless Internet Access Networks*

Bok-Nyong Park[1], Wonjun Lee[1,**], and Christian Shin[2]

[1] Dept. of Computer Science and Engineering,
Korea University, Seoul, Republic of Korea
wlee@korea.ac.kr
[2] Department of Computer Science
State University of New York at Geneseo, USA

Abstract. Ubiquitous wireless Internet access networks (UWIANs) integrate mobile ad hoc networks into the Internet to achieve ubiquitous Internet connectivity. The Internet connectivity is provided by Internet gateways in the UWIANs. Most of the Internet connectivity research has not considered a malicious environment. However, UWIANs will not be able to succeed without an effective security solution due to wireless links and energy constraints. Thus, security is a critical factor to the success of ubiquitous Internet connectivity. In this paper, we propose a secure Internet gateway discovery protocol in order to provide the secure Internet connectivity. A registration mechanism is also proposed to secure a foreign network and an ad hoc mobile node when it connects within the network. The efficiency of the protocol is shown via simulation.

1 Introduction

As various wireless/mobile networks evolve into the next generation, we need a new network technology that provides better services. In order to realize the next generation network, we introduce a ubiquitous wireless Internet access network (UWIAN) that is a mobile ad hoc network (MANET) integrated with the Internet. Ubiquitous wireless Internet access networks consist of Internet gateways (IGs) and ad hoc mobile nodes (AMNs) interconnected by multihop path. These characteristics can provide flexibility and scalability. In the area of integration with Internet and MANET, IGs may be deployed in order to provide the Internet connectivity. An Internet gateway acting as a bridge between a wired network and a MANET can provide ubiquitous Internet connectivity for AMNs. Thus, the Internet gateway discovery is an important research issue in the UWIAN.

Most of the research so far has focused on efficiency with security being given a lower priority [5]. Existing schemes are carried out in a trusted environment in which all nodes are honest. Without adequate security, however, unauthorized

* This work was supported by grant No. R01-2005-000-10267-0 from the Korea Science and Engineering Foundation in the Ministry of Science and Technology.

** Corresponding author.

E. Sha et al. (Eds.): EUC 2006, LNCS 4096, pp. 318–327, 2006.

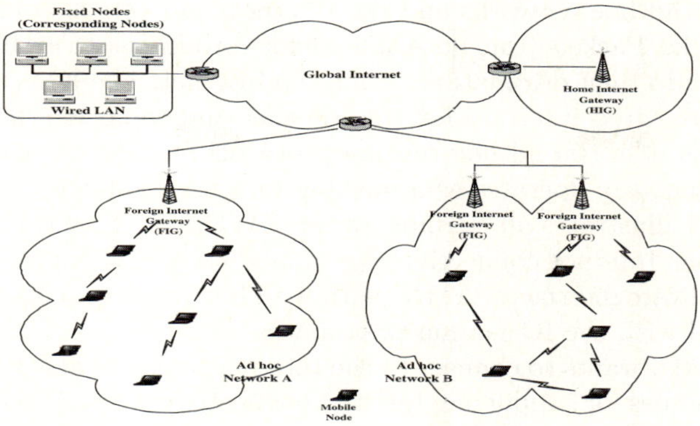

Fig. 1. System Architecture for ubiquitous wireless Internet access networks

access and usage may violate the Internet connectivity. The nature of broadcasts in wireless networks potentially results in more security exposures. The physical medium of communication is inherently insecure. In general, attacks on the Internet connectivity are caused by malicious nodes that modify, drop or generate messages related to mobile IP such as advertisement, registration request or reply that disrupt the ubiquitous Internet connectivity. Hence, security mechanisms for the secure Internet connectivity are needed. In order to support the secure Internet connectivity, we propose a secure Internet gateway discovery (SDP) protocol for ubiquitous wireless Internet access networks. In the secure IG discovery process, an AMN first registers its public/private key pair to a home Internet gateway, and then the AMN finds paths to an IG in a foreign domain. After the AMN finds an optimal path to the IG, it registers to the foreign IG. The Internet gateways serve as a distributed trust entity. The secure IG discovery protocol uses the modified ISMANET protocol [2] that utilizes identity-based signcryption with a paring over an elliptic curve [8].

The rest of this paper is organized as follows. Section 2 provides an overview of the ubiquitous wireless Internet access networks. Section 3 proposes a secure Internet gateway discovery protocol. In Sections 4 we present our performance evaluation and our analysis of the efficiency and safety of the proposed protocol, respectively. Finally, we draw out our conclusions in Section 5.

2 Ubiquitous Wireless Internet Access Networks

Mobile ad hoc networks (MANETs) allow users to establish low-cost, limited coverage networks for the purpose of sharing data among devices. They can be used to extend the coverage of WLANs or cellular networks. An Internet gateway (IG) in ubiquitous wireless Internet access networks (UWIANs) provides Internet connectivity for ad hoc mobile nodes (AMNs), and enables ubiquitous Internet services. AMNs are typically connected to the Internet via IGs. The IG is part of both ad hoc networks and the Internet, and acts as a bridge between the two networks. Packets from an AMN are forwarded first to an IG that further transmits them to their destination within the Internet. The IG is equipped with both interfaces: wired interface for the Internet and radio interface for ad hoc networks. Thus, IGs run ad hoc routing protocols in order to act as an AMN, and it simultaneously operates as a member of a fixed subnet connected to the Internet. Fig. 1 illustrates an example of the UWIAN architecture. The IG provides ubiquitous Internet connectivity to mobile users without having to rewire or change hardware interfaces. AMNs within ad hoc networks communicate with each other and with the IG via multihop paths.

When an AMN wants to connect to the Internet, it can connect to an Internet gateway. Key issues for supporting Internet connectivity include the IG discovery and selection. A number of research have proposed IG discovery mechanisms based on proactive, reactive, and hybrid approaches [7,10,11,12]. In the proactive approach, IGs broadcast periodic advertise messages during a time interval that are flooded through the whole. Thus, the proactive scheme costs more overhead, but it allows good connectivity with low delay because it instantly knows better paths to IGs. On the contrary, the reactive approach incurs fewer overhead than the proactive approach because AMNs request IG information by sending out request messages only when necessary. However, whenever there is a need for sending a packet, AMNs must find IGs if the IGs are not already known. This IG discovery process may cause considerable delay. As a result, it causes longer delay and lower ratio of packet delivery. The hybrid approach combines the proactive and reactive approaches, reaping the best of both schemes: good connectivity and low delay. After discovering multiple relay routes, AMNs select the best IG to communicate with Internet hosts outside the ad hoc networks. An AMN needs to consider several metrics when selecting an optimal IG that maximizes the network performance among the available IGs.

3 Secure Ubiquitous Internet Connectivity

In this section, we propose a secure Internet gateway discovery protocol (SDP) for ubiquitous wireless Internet access networks, and discuss authentication method for secure registration.

3.1 Basic Operations

Ubiquitous wireless Internet access networks (UWIANs) consist of ad hoc mobile nodes (AMNs) and Internet gateways (IGs). Each AMN shares a security association (SA) with an IG within its own home network. For example, An AMN always shares a trust relationship with its home Internet gateway (HIG) even when it moves to a foreign domain. We assume that authorization information is always handled by a foreign IG (FIG) in the visited network. Most likely, the authorization information is obtained originally from an HIG in AMN's home networks. The secure IG discovery process for the UWIAN includes three phases:

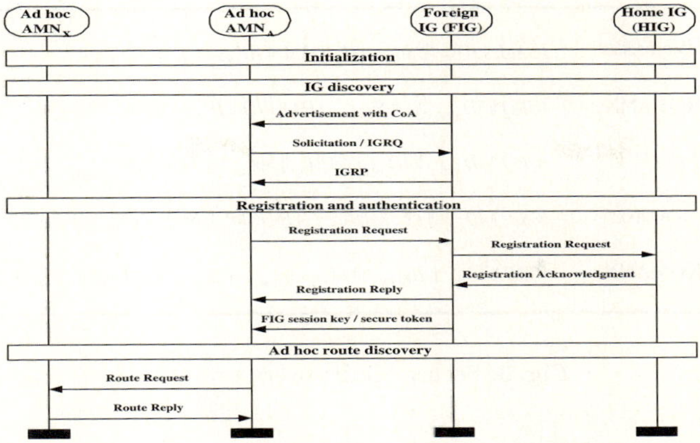

Fig. 2. Sequence diagram for the secure ubiquitous Internet connectivity

Table 1. Notations used for the Proposed Protocol

Symbol	Definition	Symbol	Definition
ID_X	Identification of node X	$H(m)$	One-way hash function
SK^*	System master key	SK_X, PK_X	Private key and public key of X
t	Secure token	K	Shared secret key
$\hat{e}(P,Q)$	Bilinear map based on the Weil	P, P_{pub}	Generator, Master secret key $\cdot$ P

i) the initialization phase, ii) secure discovery phase, and iii) registration with FIG phase. Before an AMN gains its successful mobile IP registration and a secret key from a FIG, it cannot participate in ad hoc routing protocol. After the AMN registers with the FIG successfully, the FIG issues a secret key to the AMN. Meanwhile the FIG is responsible for verifying AMNs' information at the request of an AMN. Each AMN shares a system master key with its HIG and a secret key with its FIG for the calculation and validation of a secure token which uses Message Authentication Code (MAC). Table 1 lists the notations used for the development of the proposed protocol. The sequence diagram in Fig. 2 illustrates the basic process of the secure connectivity in the UWIAN. In the following sections, each step is discussed in detail.

3.2 Initialization

Initialization phase is the operation that an AMN must complete before it can connect to the network. Initialization through HIG registration takes place between an AMN and its home Internet gateway. After the HIG registration process, each AMN and its HIG share a security association to create a secure token for the IG discovery and registration. The secure token is computed as follows:

$$t = (H(ID_{AMN} \parallel SK^*))$$

1.	FIG -> broadcast:	$IGAM \parallel ID_{FIG} \parallel Sig_{FIG}\{H(IGAM \parallel ID_{FIG} \parallel t_{FIG})\}$
2.	AMNs -> AMNx:	$IGRQ \parallel ID_{AMN_S} \parallel t \parallel Sig_{AMN_S}\{H(IGRQ \parallel ID_{AMN_S} \parallel t)\}$
3.	AMNs -> FIG:	$IGRQ \parallel ID_{AMN_S} \parallel ID_{AMN_X} \parallel t \parallel t_X \parallel Sig_{AMN_S}\{H(IGRQ \parallel ID_{AMN_S} \parallel t)\}$
4.	FIG -> AMNx:	$IGRP \parallel ID_{FIG} \parallel t \parallel t_{FIG} \parallel Sig_{FIG}\{H(IGRP \parallel ID_{FIG} \parallel t \parallel t_{FIG})\}$
5.	AMNx -> AMNs:	$IGRP \parallel ID_{FIG} \parallel ID_{AMN_X} \parallel t \parallel t_{FIG} \parallel t_{AMN_X} \parallel Sig_{FIG}\{H(IGRP \parallel ID_{FIG} \parallel t \parallel t_{FIG})\}$

Fig. 3. Secure IG discovery protocol

HIGs act as an authentication server for AMNs by sharing security association between the HIG and AMN or FIG. Key establishment among participations uses the ECDH key exchange. The ECDH [8] key exchange allows two entities to exchange keys on an unsecured communication path.

3.3 Secure Internet Gateway Discovery

Before the FIG discovery, an AMN establishes public-private keys with a HIG (PK_{AMN}, SK_{AMN}). The AMN starts route discovery to a FIG. In the secure discovery protocol, we follow the ISMANET protocol [2] which uses identity-based signcryption to discover IG, and all intermediate nodes must be registered. Fig. 3 shows the process of the secure IG discovery.

IGs periodically announce their presence in an ad hoc network by broadcasting Internet Gateway Advertisement Messages (IGAMs) containing their state information and authentication information at every periodic interval:

$$< IGAM \parallel ID_{FIG} \parallel Sig_{FIG}\{H(IGAM \parallel ID_{FIG} \parallel t_{FIG})\} >$$

where t_{FIG} is $H(ID_{FIG} \parallel SK^*)$ which FIG's secure token, and IGAM is including FIG's address, sequence number, CoA, etc. To prevent flooding the network, these advertisements are limited within n-hop neighborhood using a time-to-live (TTL) field. This range determines the FIG's discovery scope, called a proactive area. In [3], we proposed a load-adaptive Internet gateway discovery (LAID) scheme which dynamically adjusts the range of proactive IG advertisements. The proposed discovery protocol is based on the LAID. AMN_S within the proactive area of x hops receive the periodic IGAM messages from IGs. If they are out of range, the AMN_S broadcast Internet Gateway Request messages (IGRQ). The AMN_S chooses a random number r, and computes $k = \hat{e}(P, P_{pub})^r$ for the message's origin. The AMN_S sends IGRQ, a secure token, and created values, all of which are signed. The signature Sig is defined as follows: Sig=$Signcrypt$(*security parameters, private key, message*). Notice that signing does not involve any pairing calculations and thus it can be done very quickly even on low-end processors.

When an intermediate node AMN_X receives the IGRQ, the AMN_X first verifies the signature of source node, and then the node computes $k' = \hat{e}(P, SK_{AMN_S})\cdot$

$\hat{e}(P_{pub}, PK_{AMN_S})^r$ for the message's origin and checks $t = H(ID_{AMN_S} \parallel SK^*)$ for the validity of sender node. The verification of signature is defined as follows: *valid=Unsigncrypt(Sig, public key, security parameters, message)*. *Valid* is a binary value that is set to 0 if the signature is invalid and to 1 if the signature is valid. If the confirmation is successful, the AMN_S and the AMN_X will trust each other and this process completes successfully. After authentication, the intermediate node computes t_{AMN_X} using the same method above with its ID_{AMN_X} and the system master key. Finally, the node broadcasts the message to the next nodes. When the FIG receives the message, it verifies the signature and computes t and t_{AMN_X}. If the authentication is successful, the FIG is ready to reply a message. Otherwise, packet is dropped. Then, AMN_X inside the proactive area of a FIG responds with Internet Gateway Response messages (IGRP) to the soliciting AMN or relays the IGRQ to IGs. Upon receipt of IGRQ messages, IGs send an IGRP message which contains the IGs' prefix and other authentication information back to the soliciting AMN. The computation method of the authentication information in the discovery reply follows the similar say in IGRQ. When the AMN_S receives the IGRP packet with a message for authentication, it verifies authentication information returned by the FIG as well as the FIG's signature. If the verification of the digital signature and the secure token is successful, the secure route to FIG can be established over the channel. An AMN collects all IGAM messages sent from the available IGs in the foreign network. From these IGAM messages, the AMN can obtain information for each FIG (e.g. the hop count, network load, and security association). Using the IG information, the AMN makes an available FIG list and registers to an FIG with optimal metric. The secure token is introduced for a preliminary check in order to start the registration request without having to wait for re-authentication and re-authorization results from the HIG.

3.4 Secure Registration

When an AMN sends a registration request to a new FIG in a foreign network, it includes the system master key in the secure token so that the FIG can check this master key distributed from the HIG through the secure token. This operation begins with AMN broadcasting the registration request. The FIG checks the security information of the AMN and decides whether to forward the signaling message. If this simple check is passed, the FIG regards the AMN as a registered and credible node and starts its registration process. Before an AMN gains its successful registration from a FIG, it cannot participate in ad hoc routing protocol. Upon successfully registration, the AMN will obtain the FIG information such as ID_{FIG}, shared secrets, etc. from the FIG, and set the FIG to be its default IG.

3.5 Secure Ad Hoc Route Discovery

On receiving an ad hoc route discovery message from a neighbor, an AMN checks the neighbor's ID. Then the AMN computes the secure token by using the extracted ID and the system master key to verify neighbor nodes. After the verification is successful, the AMN checks the signature of the route message by using the neighbor's public key. If the signature is matched, it shows that the neighbor is a certified node. Otherwise the neighbor with its ID is invalid, and the received packet must be discarded during the processing of ad hoc route discovery. The secure ad hoc route discovery is based on the ISMANET [2].

4 Performance Evaluation

The goal of the simulation is to evaluate the effects of integration of the secure discovery protocol into load-aware IG discovery (LAID) scheme [3]. In this section, we show the simulation results of the secure discovery protocol.

4.1 Simulation Setup

We used the ns-2 simulator [9] for our evaluation. The LAID protocol [3] is used as a benchmark to study the performance evaluation of the proposed secure discovery protocol. The radio model uses characteristics similar to a commercial radio interface, Lucent's WaveLAN [4]. WaveLAN is a shared-media radio with a nominal bit-rate of 2Mb/sec and a nominal radio range of 250 meters. The number of source-destination pairs and packet sending rate varies for modeling different network loads. As a mobility model, we used the random waypoint model in rectangular field with 700m×700m where a node starts its journey from a random location to a random destination with a randomly chosen speed. Each node moves at a speed is 10 m/s. Seven different pause times were used: 0, 10, 50, 100, 200, 400, and 800 seconds. Constant Bit Rate (CBR) traffic sources are used with different packet generation rates. The data packet size is 512 bytes. The set of experiments uses differing numbers of sources with a moderate packet rate and varying pause times. For the 50 node experiments, we used 5 and 20 traffic sources and a packet rate of 4 packets/s. We simulated some simple scenarios by varying pause times in order to see the throughput in 900 second simulation time. We varied the pause time where high pause time means low mobility and small pause time means high mobility. The IG is placed in the middle of the grid [i.e., coordinate (350, 350)] for the simulation scenarios. To manage AMNs' mobility between ad hoc networks, AMNs as well as IGs run MIP [6], where MIP FA and HA are hosted in the IG.

4.2 Simulation Results

To compare IG discovery approaches, a set of simulations has been performed in terms of three metrics: packet delivery ratio, end-to-end delay, and normalized routing overhead. Various mobility and offered load scenarios have been simulated to understand their effects. We conducted the simulations to compare the existing Internet gateway discovery protocols without any security method to the proposed secure IG discovery protocol (SDP). Figs 4, 5, and 6 show the

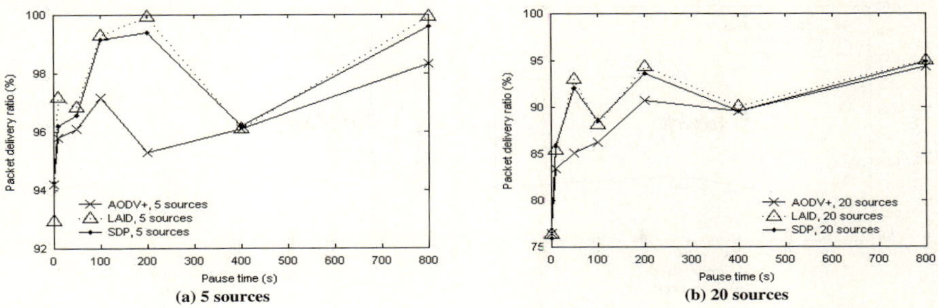

Fig. 4. Packet delivery ratio (%) for the 50-node model with various numbers of sources

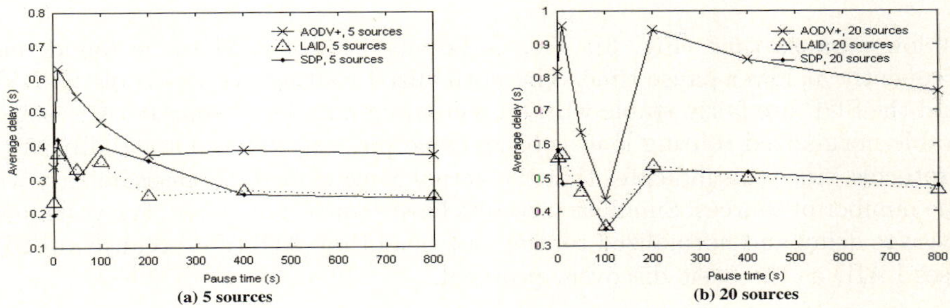

Fig. 5. Average data packet delays for the 50-node model with various numbers of sources

simulation results for the hybrid Internet gateway discovery (AODV+) [1], load-aware Internet gateway discovery (LAID), and the proposed secure IG discovery protocol (SDP). The goal of our study is to illustrate that our scheme works effectively in addressing many security issues with routing protocols without causing any substantial degradation in the network performance.

In Fig. 4, the results show that our SDP protocol works well because the effect of throughput of the network is small around 2-10%. The packet delivery ratios for LAID and SDP are very similar with 5 and 20 sources. However, if other realistic scenarios, such as disaster scenarios, battlefield scenario, or very high-speed scenarios, use our scheme, the effect of network throughput may be reduced even more. Fig. 5 shows the effect of different mobility on the average end-to-end delay. The average data packet delays are fairly low both with authentication (SDP) and without authentication (LAID) extension. SDP and LAID have similar delays with 5 and 20 sources. There is a small increase with 5 sources (Fig. 5(a)) due to the exchange of packets during the authentication phase of security process. In Fig. 6, the normalized overhead of the SDP is significantly larger than that of the LAID. The number of routing packets increases when our scheme is incorporated. The increase in routing load is higher

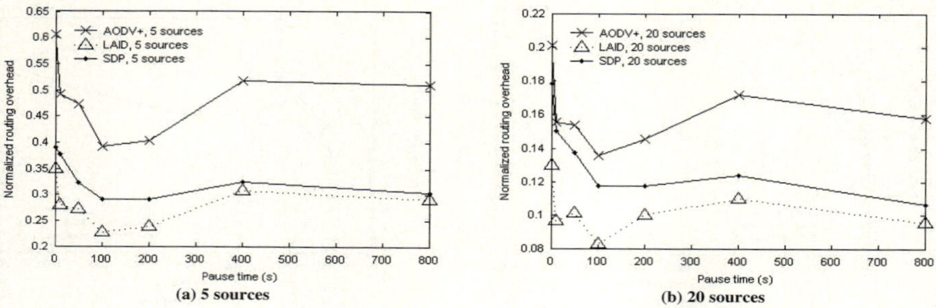

Fig. 6. Normalized routing overheads for the 50-node model with various numbers of sources

at lower pause time (Fig. 6). This is because routes need to be found more frequently at lower pause time. The normalized routing overheads of the LAID and the SDP are fairly stable with an increasing number of sources. A relatively stable normalized routing load is a desirable property for the scalability of the protocols, since this indicates that the actual routing load increases linearly with the number of sources. Simulation results have shown that the SDP gives a lower average delay and normalized routing overhead than AODV+ because our SDP uses LAID as the basic discovery protocol.

4.3 Safety Analysis

Security includes the protection of the information and the resources from both inside and outside of a network. The FIG discovery process establishes a secure path between a FIG and an AMN by using authenticated nodes. It avoids those unregistered malicious nodes that mislead route or drop registration-related messages with the intention of hindering the AMN registration. The proposed discovery protocol can authenticate all nodes of routes with a secure token t. The t is computed by the system master key. Each node can verify the ID and the secure token of each node so that malicious nodes cannot hide their identity. In addition, the malicious nodes cannot fabricate the messages since they don't know the secret key of the message signed by the source. As a result, the proposed protocol is safe from fabrication attacks. Similarly, it can provide robust protection from modification. When they modify the IGAM, IGRQ, or IGRP packets, they cannot generate the correct hash value since they do not know the security parameters. By sharing a secret key between an AMN and a FIG in order to calculate a secure token, registration messages are protected from modification. Because of a shared secret key a malicious node could not register successfully with a FIG even if it can masquerade itself with a bogus CoA.

5 Conclusions

In the ubiquitous wireless Internet access network (UWIAN), security is a primary research challenge. In the UWIAN system, AMNs can access the Internet via IGs which serve distributed entities. In this paper we have proposed a secure IG discovery protocol as well as authentication method for registration in order to protect the Internet connectivity. The protocol have been developed to authenticate an ad hoc mobile node and to distribute the shared secret key. In order to secure both the foreign IG and the AMN, they mutually authenticate each other with the help of the home IG. The secure discovery protocol avoids unregistered malicious nodes and provide the secure Internet connectivity.

References

1. AODV+: "The Network Simulator: Contributed Code". *http://www.isi.edu/nsnam/ns/ ns-contributed.html.*
2. B. Park and W. Lee, "ISMANET: A Secure Routing Protocol using Identity-based Signcryption Scheme for Mobile Ad-hoc Networks," IEICE Transaction on Communications, Vol. E88-B, No. 6, June 2005.
3. B. Park, W. Lee, C. Lee, J. Hong, and J. Kim, "LAID: Load-Adaptive Internet Gateway Discovery for Ubiquitous Wireless Internet Access Networks," Proceedings of the International Conference on Information Networking (ICOIN) 2006. January 2006.
4. B. Tuch, "Development of WaveLAN, and ISM Band Wirelees LAN," AT&T Tech. H. Vol. 82, no. 4, pp. 27-33, July/Aug 1993.
5. B. Xie and A. Kumar, "A Framework for Integrated Internet and Ad hoc Network Security," Proceedings of International Symposium on Computer Communication, pp. 318-324, Egypt, June 2004.
6. C. E. Perkins, "IP Mobility Support," RFC 3311 in IETF, August 2002.
7. E. M. Belding-Royer, Y. Sun, and C. E. Perkins, "Global Connectivity for IPv4 Mobile Ad-hoc Network," IETF Internet-Draft, draft-royer-manet-globlav4-00.txt, November 2001.
8. J. Lopez and R. Dahab, "Performance of Elliptic Curve Cryptosystems," Technical Report IC-00-08, 2000.
9. K. Fall and K. Varadhan, Eds., "ns Notes and Documentation," 2003; available from *http://www.isi.edu/nanam/ns/*.
10. P. Ratanchandani and R. Kravets, "A hybrid approach to Internet connectivity for mobile ad hoc networks," Proceedings of IEEE Wireless Communications and Networking Conference (WCNC) 2003, March 2003.
11. R. Wakikawa, J. T. Maline, C. E. Perkins, A. Nilsson, and A. H. Tuominen, "Global Connectivity for IPv6 Mobile Ad-hoc Networks," IETF Internet-Draft, draft-wakikawa-manet-gflobalv6-03.txt, October 2003.
12. U. Jonsson, F. Alriksson, T. Larsson, P. Johnasson, and G. Q. Maguire, "MIP-MANET: Mobile IP for Mobile Ad-hoc Network," Proceedings of the First Annual Workshop on Mobile Ad Hoc Networking & Computing (MobiHoc), Auguest 2000.

Data Integrity Related Markup Language and HTTP Protocol Support for Web Intermediaries*

Chi-Hung Chi[1], Lin Liu[1], and Xiaoyin Yu[2]

[1] School of Software, Tsinghua University, Beijing, China 100084
[2] School of Computing, National University of Singapore, Singapore
chichihung@mail.tsinghua.edu.cn

Abstract. In this paper, we propose the markup language framework and its associated HTTP protocol extension to support data integrity for active web intermediaries. There are three aspects that our language framework would like to focus on. Firstly, the content server can specify its intended authorization and task to multiple web intermediary proxies in its content objects easily. Secondly, a web intermediary performing value-added services through content adaptation needs to leave its modification footprints for possible verification by client. Thirdly, a client is facilitated to verify the received message with the server's authorizations and intermediaries' footprints without affecting his perceived web latency. We demonstrate the feasibility and practicability of this language framework through its actual implementation.

1 Introduction

Recently, one key direction to provide better web quality services in heterogeneous pervasive web environment is the real-time adaptive content delivery. Basically, the research of focus is to investigate technologies and practical systems to provide more efficient and effective value-added services through real-time content adaptation in the network. Examples of these services include: image transcoding, media conversion (e.g. image to text), language translation, encoding format (e.g. lossless data compression), and local advertisement uploading.

The prosperity of the research on real-time content transformation by active web intermediaries draws great attention to the problem of data integrity. Since the same set of technologies supports the modification of a message on its way from a server to a client, independent of the authorization of the web intermediaries by the content server, how can the client trust the receiving message and how can the server ensure that what the client receives is what it intends to respond? In this paper, we would like to address this data integrity problem through the support of markup language and HTTP protocol extension. With the complete definition of our data integrity language framework and its associated HTTP extension, we demonstrate the accuracy, feasibility and practicability of our approach through its actual implementation.

---

* This research is supported by the funding 2004CB719400 of China.

E. Sha et al. (Eds.): EUC 2006, LNCS 4096, pp. 328 – 335, 2006.

2 Related Work

There have been proposed solutions for data integrity but their context is quite different from the new active web intermediary environment here. In HTTP/1.1, integrity protection [7] is a way for a client and a server to verify not only each other's identity but also the authenticity of the data they send. Secure Sockets Layer [7] does a good job for the integrity of the transferred data since it ensures the security of the data through encryption. However, these methods do not meet the need of active web intermediary services because they do not support legal content modification in the data transmission process, even by the authorized intermediaries.

Recently, there are new proposals being put forward in the area of content delivery and real-time content adaptation on the web. To meet the need of data integrity for delta-encoding [4], [4] defines a new HTTP header "Delta-MD5" to carry the digest value of the reassembling HTTP response from several individual messages. However, this solution is proposed only for delta-encoding exclusively and is not suitable for active web intermediaries. VPCN [1] is another proposal to solve the integrity problem brought by OPES. It makes use of the concept similar to Virtual Private Networks (VPN) to ensure the integrity of the transport of content among network nodes. It also supports transformation on content provided that the nodes are inside the virtual private content network. Its main problems are the potential high overhead and the restriction of performing value-added web services by a small predefined subset of proxy gateways only. Other proposals [6] draft the requirements of data integrity solution in the active web intermediary environment. [2] proposes a XML-based service model to define the data integrity solution formally. However, these works are at their preliminary stages; they are just drafts or proposals without actual implementation to demonstrate the system feasibility and performance.

3 Language Support in Data Integrity Framework

In this section, we will first give the basic format/structure of the language for our data integrity framework, followed by the detailed description of how a content server can use it to express its intention to web intermediaries for content modification.

3.1 Overview

Our data integrity framework follows naturally the HTTP response message model to transfer data-integrity messages. Under this framework, a data-integrity message contains an entity body so that a server can declare its authorization on a message, active web intermediaries can modify the message and clients can verify it. However, it should also be backward compatible such that a normal HTTP proxy can process the non-integrity part of the response without error.

```
HTTP Status_Line
General \ Response \ Entity Headers
CRLF
(Manifest)+
(Part Headers
  Part Body)+
(Notification)*
```

Fig. 1. Message Format where "+" denotes one or more occurrences and "*" denotes zero or more occurrences

The format for the data-integrity message in our framework is shown in Figure 1. Their details are as follows:

- *Status Line*
  The status line in a data-integrity message is defined in the same way as that in a normal HTTP response message. The semantics of the status codes also follows those in HTTP/1.1 for status communication.
- *Headers*
  Generally speaking, the message headers are consistent with those defined in HTTP/1.1 [3]. However, some headers might lose their original meanings due to the change of the operating environment from object homogeneity to heterogeneity. As will be seen later in this section, we will analyze all the HTTP headers and propose the concept of "Part Headers" in Section 3.4 in our data-integrity language. Furthermore, we also need "DIAction", an extended HTTP response header field to indicate the intent of a data-integrity message.
- *Message Body*
  The entity body consists of one or more "manifests", one or more "parts", and zero or more "notifications". They are the important components of our language.

  Manifest: A server should provide a manifest to specify its intentions for authorizing intermediary proxies to perform value-added services on the message (See Section 3.2). A manifest might also be provided by an intermediary proxy who is authorized by the server for further task delegation.

  Part: A part is the basic unit of data content for manipulation by an intermediary. The party who provides a manifest should divide the object (or fragment of an object) into parts, each of which can be manipulated and validated separately from the rest. An intermediary proxy should modify content in the range of an authorized part, and a client might verify a message in the unit of a part. A part consists of part headers and a part body. (See Section 3.3)

  Notification: A notification is the footprint about the content modification of a part that an authorized proxy performs. Details about this concept will be discussed in Section 4.2).

  Note that the entity body of a message body might be encoded via the method specified in the "Transfer-Encoding" header field (See [3] for details).

Next, we will discuss how a server makes use of Manifest, Part and Headers to express its authorizations.

3.2 Manifest

Both a server and delegated proxies can provide manifests. The elements and the functionalities of proxies' manifests are almost the as server's one. We will cover proxies' manifests in Section 4.2 and server's manifest in this section. A manifest has two important functionalities. One is for a server to specify its authorizations. The other is to prevent its intentions from being tampered.

3.2.1 Authorization Information

We have mentioned that a server should partition its object into parts and use the part as the authorization unit. So we use a pair of tags < PartInfo > and < / PartInfo > to mark up authorizations on a part. The server should identify which part it intends to authorize via the element "PartID" and specify its authorizations on this part. Since the server may authorize others to do a variety of services on the part, each authorization on this part is confined via a pair of tags < Permission > and < /Permission >.

Table 1. Action, Interpretation and Roles n.a.: not applicable; c.o.: content owner; p.: presenter; a.o.: authorization owner

Action	Interpretation	Possible Roles
None	No authorization is permitted on the part	n.a.
Replace	Replace content of the part with new content	c.o.
Delete	Cut off all the content of the part	c.o.
Transform	Give a new representation of the content of the part	p.
Delegate	Do actions or authorize others to do actions	c.o., p., a.o.

In an authorization, i.e., between < Permission > and < /Permission >, three aspects of information should be given: (i) What action(s) can be done? (ii) Who should do the action(s)? (iii) With what restriction(s) the action(s) should be done?

- Action
  This element gives an authorized service. By now, our language supports four types of feasible services. The keywords "Replace", "Delete", "Transform" and "Delegate" stand for these services respectively. A keyword is also needed for the server to express a part not in demands of any services. These keywords and their corresponding meanings are listed in Table 1. If a new type of service is available, the language can be extended to support it easily.
- Editor
  The element provides an authorized proxy. Here, we propose to use the URL host name of an intermediary proxy to identify it.
- Restricts
  All the constraints should be declared here to confine the authorization. Usually, the constraints are related to the content's properties. For example, the server can limit the type, format, language or length of a new content provided by proxies. But for "Delegate" action, its meaning is much more than this. The constraints

should give answers to at least these three questions. Can a delegated proxy `A` authorize a proxy `B` to do services? Can the proxy `A` (without delegation from the server) authorize the proxy `B` to do a certain service? If the answer is "yes" to the first two questions, can the proxy `B` further authorize others to do its authorized services? The answers of these questions are given by the sub-elements of the "`Restricts`" element, "`Editor`", "`Action`", and "`Depth`". (See more in Section 4.2). Note that although "`Action`" and "`Editor`" elements can have only one value, it is possible for an authorization to contain multiple of these elements. In this case, all the specified editors will do the specified actions on a part with the same restrictions.

Two elements, "`PartDigestValue`" in a part information and "`Roles`" in an permission, have not been introduced yet. The first element is one of the protection measures against malicious intermediaries. The element "`Roles`" depicts what roles an editor might play on the data integrity framework due to their services permitted on a data integrity message. Note that for every role or service that a data-integrity intermediary does, there will be a corresponding responsibility in the data integrity framework. For example, an intermediary proxy uploading local information to a part needs to be responsible for its freshness and data validation.

Now, let us analyze what might be changed by each of the support services and conclude their possible roles in the data integrity framework below. We also list the possible roles of an action in Column 3 of Table 1.

- *Content*
  From the interpretations of "`Replace`" and "`Delete`", they modify the original content of a part. If a delegated proxy does "`Replace`" or "`Delete`" action by itself, "`Delegate`" action will also change the content of the authorized part. In these cases, an authorized proxy will play the role of `Content Owner`.
- *Representation*
  "`Transform`" action might only change the representation of an authorized part but not its content. Also, "`Delegate`" action will bring a new representation to a delegated part if a delegated proxy itself transforms the content of the part through "`Transform`" action. In these cases, an authorized proxy will play the role of `Presenter`.
- *Authorization*
  Only "`Delegate`" action might change authorizations on a part. A delegated proxy becomes an `Authorization Owner` if it authorizes others to do some services on its delegated part.

3.3 Part

A server uses < `Part` > and < `/Part` > tags to mark up a part of an object, which is defined as the basic entity for ownership and content manipulation. To decompose an object into parts, while a server might have its own rules, there are three general guidelines that we would like to suggest.

The first guideline is that each part should be independent of the other in the object. If dependency occurs between two parts, errors might occur. For example, a server asks proxies A and B to do language translation on the content of two parts a and b respectively. If there is content dependency between the two parts a and b, errors or at least inaccuracy translation might occur because separate translation might cause some of the original meanings to be lost.

The second guideline is related to the malicious proxy attack. It is advisable for a server to mark up *all* the parts of an object in lest the unmarked parts might be attacked. In this way, the integrity of the whole object can be ensured.

Lastly, the properties (or attributes) of a part need to be specified carefully. For example, the content of the object in a part is also the content of the part. < Content > and < /Content > tags are used to mark it up and "PartID" element is used to identify a part. Furthermore, it is necessary to give out properties of a part via "Headers" element.

3.4 Message and Part Headers

Under the current HTTP definition, headers are used to describe the attributes of an object. It is defined by the tag < Headers > and < /Headers >. One basic assumption behind is that the same attribute value can be applied to every single byte of the object. However, with the introduction of content heterogeneity by active web intermediaries, this assumption might not be valid to some of the headers' values. A given attribute (reflected in the header) might have different values to different parts in the same object. In this section, we would like to introduce the concept of "homogeneous" message headers and "heterogeneous" part headers for an object and define the relationship between them.

A *message header* is a HTTP header which describes a property (or attribute) of a whole web object and its value will not be affected by any intermediary's value-added services to individual parts of the object. That is, the attribute can be applied to *all* parts of an object. On the other hand, a *part header* is a HTTP header which describes a property (or attribute) of a part, defined by the tag pair < Part > and < /Part > in a web object. These headers are specified in the header line, starting with <Headers? tag and ending with <\Headers> tag. With decomposition of the object into parts for web intermediaries to work on, the attribute of interest might have different values for different parts.

On top of the current HTTP headers, there are four new headers that we introduce for a part. They are: "Content-Owner", "Presenter", "Authorization-Owner", and "URL". The first three headers record which intermediary does the services on the part and describes its role/responsibility. A data-integrity intermediary should also specify its host name in these headers if it plays the corresponding roles. The "URL" header is used to locate the part. These four headers will be very useful when a part is cached and it needs to be validated for reuse.

There is one intrinsic relationship between these two types of headers. Whenever an attribute of a part is described by both the message header and the part header at the same time, the latter one will override the former one. That is, the message header will lose its effect in this situation. This property is to give flexibility in the actual implementation of the system architecture and the application deployment. Note that headers specified in one part do not affect the properties of the other sibling parts.

4 Footprints of Intermediary Proxies

One important requirement of a good data-integrity framework is for the intermediary proxies to leave footprints (or what they have done) in the message that passes through them. In the language support, the footprint will be mapped into information in three locations: part headers, notification, and possible manifests.

4.1 Data-Integrity Intermediary's Manifest

A data-integrity intermediary's manifest is an important component in our language definition for data integrity framework. Its delegated proxy's manifest plays the same role as a server's manifest. It provides authorizations to the subsequent intermediary proxies clearly and accurately. Thus it is made up of both authorization information and protection measures. Despite the similarities, however, there are two basic differences between the server's (parent's) manifest and delegated proxy's (child's) manifest.

- *Authorization Information*
  The basic units for authorization in the two manifests are different. While a delegated proxy's manifest works on one part of an object, a server's manifest works on the whole object. Thus, what the "`MessageURL`" element refers to is the URL of the authorized part, but not the object. On the other hand, although the tags " `<PartInfo>`" and "`</PartInfo>`" in the proxy's manifest mark up only some sub-part of the authorized part, the basic components of the authorization information inside is still the same. The only extra information required is the "`PartID`" element, which describes the relationship between the parent and the child manifests. A sub-part is given an ID with a suffix "`.x`", where the ID stands for the parent manifest's ID and the suffix "`.x`" indicates which sub-part in this parent manifest is being described. In the case where the proxy does not partition its authorized part, the part ID will have a "`.0`" suffix.
- *Protection Measures*
  Compared to the protection measures in a server's manifest, one new key element introduced the delegated proxy's manifest is the "`ParentManifestDigest-Value`", which specifies who authorizes the proxy to give such a manifest. On the other hand, the element "PartDigestValue" for each sub-part might be omitted. Since the proxy's manifest is generated on-on-the-fly and should be streamed from the proxy just like the server's manifest, we propose to put off the calculation of the digest value of each sub-part to the notification by the intermediary proxy. The proxy should provide both a manifest and a notification if the digest value of a sub-part is specified. However, the proxy need not give a notification if it just delegates the authorized part identified by the suffix "`.0`".

Note that despite the differences, information extracted from a delegated proxy's manifest is the same as, if not more than, as a server's manifest.

4.2 Notification

Notification is another key footprint element of the intermediary proxies that the data-integrity framework introduces. There are at least four considerations to construct such notification. Firstly, with the element "`ManifestDigestValue`", the client can find out which manifest authorizes an intermediary proxy to do the action. Secondly, the elements "`Editor`", "`Action`" and "`PartID`" can be used to ensure the consistency of the manifest: Who does what action on which part. Thirdly, to assure that the part received by the client is exactly what the proxy should put in the message, the proxy fills in the "`PartDigiestValues`" with the digest value of the part. Finally, in order to prove that the notification is really from the proxy, the proxy should sign the notification just as the server signs its manifest.

Besides the components introduced above, a notification might also include "`InputDigestValue`" and "`PartDigestValues`" elements. To assure that the authorized part received by the proxy that does the "`Transform`" action is not tempered by malicious intermediaries, the proxy should put the digest value of the part before transformation into the "`InputDigestValue`" element. The element "`PartDigestValues`" is for the intermediary proxy that does the "`Delegate`" action to record each sub-part's digest value.

5 Conclusions

In this paper, we proposed a data integrity framework with the following functionalities that a server can specify its authorizations, active web intermediaries can provide services in accordance with the server's intentions, and more importantly, a client is facilitated to verify the received message with the server's authorizations and intermediaries' traces. Our main contributions are to define a data integrity framework, its associated language specification and its associated system model to solve the data integrity problem in active, content transformation network. We also built a prototype of our data integrity model to show the practicability of our proposal.

References

1. A. Barbir, N. Mistry, R. Penno, and D. Kaplan, "A framework for OPES end to end data integrity: Virtual private content networks (VPCN)," Nov 2001. http://standards. nortelnetworks. com/ opes/non-wg-doc/draft-barbir-opes-vpcn-00.txt
2. C.-H. Chi, and Y. Wu, "An XML-based data integrity service model for web intermediaries," *Proc. International Workshop on Web Content Caching and Distribution*, August 2002.
3. R. Fielding, J. Gettys, J. Mogul, H. Frystyk, L.Masinter, P. Leach, and T. Berners-Lee, "Hypertext Transfer Protocol – HTTP/1.1," 1999. [Online]. Available: http://www.ietf.org/ rfc/rfc2616.txt
4. J. C. Mogul, F. Douglis, A. Feldmann, and B. Krishnamurthy, "Potential benefits of delta encoding and data compression for HTTP," in *Proc. SIGCOMM*, 1997, pp. 181–194.
5. J. C. Mogul, F. Douglis, A. Feldmann, and B. Krishnamurthy, "Potential benefits of delta encoding and data compression for HTTP (corrected version)," Dec 1997. http://citeseer. nj. nec.com/ mogul97potential.html
6. H. K. Orman, "Data integrity for mildly active content," Aug 14 2001.http://standards. nortelnetworks.com/opes/non-wg-doc/opes-data-integrityPaper.pdf
7. S. Thomas, *HTTP Essentials*. Wiley, John and Sons, 2001.

Efficient Batch Verification for RSA-Type Digital Signatures in a Ubiquitous Environment

Seungwon Lee and Yookun Cho

School of Computer Science and Engineering, Seoul National University
Seoul, 151-742, Korea

Abstract. The paper addresses batch verification to reduce large computational cost when many digital signatures are verified together, and then presents bad signature identification in the batch verification of signatures too when there is one bad signature in the batch. Our method, *EBV* (Exponent Based Verifier), can verify a batch of signatures and identify a bad signature using one modular exponentiation and $2n + 3\sqrt{n}/2$ modular multiplications where n is the number of signatures in the batch instances. Simulation results also show the proposed method reduces considerably the number of modular multiplications compared with the existing methods.

1 Introduction

Ubiquitous computing environments generally consist of mobile, small, embedded, and portable devices, which have limited computational resources. There are many security issues in the ubiquitous environments, including confidentiality, authentication, integrity, authorization, and non-repudiation. On the environments, efficient utilization of the computational resources is much more important than the normal environment and a proper security strategy has to be devised and implemented depending on the type of data and the cost of possible loss, modification, and stolen data.

As the secure transactions such as m-commerce and e-government are commonly used in ubiquitous computing environments, the electronic payment systems require a powerful security mechanism for creating and verifying lots of digital signatures with a low cost. Therefore, it is very important to develop an efficient verification method for digital signatures in batches.

Recently, much work has been conducted to verify multiple signatures in batches [1,2,3,4,5]. Batch verification is an attractive approach for efficient signature validation to improve the system performance by reducing number of modular exponentiation operations in signature verification. However, batch verification brings about another issue of identifying bad signatures when there are invalid signatures. It is possible to verify each signature individually for identifying bad signatures, which is rather inefficient. Better approach would be batch identification. One of existing batch identification methods, divide-and-conquer verifier, takes a contaminated batch and splits it repeatedly until all

E. Sha et al. (Eds.): EUC 2006, LNCS 4096, pp. 336–344, 2006.

bad signatures are identified [6]. Another method, Hamming Code verifier, creates subsets according to a parity check matrix based Hamming Codes. And it applies generic test to each subset and calculates the position of a bad signature.

In this paper, we investigate a method, *EBV* (Exponent Based Verifier), which verifies efficiently digital signatures in batch for secure transactions in ubiquitous computing like m-commerce. The proposed method can also identify quickly the bad signature when there is one bad signature in the batch. Our method first assigns a unique exponent to each signature according to its position in the batch and computes an equation. By looking at the resulting value, we can tell whether there exist one or more bad signatures. If there exists only one bad signature, we can find out its location. In most cases, since it is known that there is at most one invalid signature in a batch[6], our work is a help to construct secure transactions. Simulation results show our method reduces the number of modular multiplication operations significantly compared with conventional methods.

The rest of the paper is organized as follows. Section 2 gives an introduction on the prior methods to identify bad signatures in batches. In Section 3, we propose a new method for identifying a bad signature efficiently. Section 4 compares our method with the previous method in the number of the number of modular multiplications. The paper concludes in section 5.

2 Related Work

Digital signatures can be classified as either DSA-type signatures or RSA-type signatures [6]. In this paper, we mainly focus on RSA-type signatures. In a RSA-type signature scheme with a message m and its signature s, the following equation must hold.

$$m \equiv s^e \bmod N \tag{1}$$

In the equation, e is a relative prime to $(p-1) \times (q-1)$ and N is $p \times q$ where p and q are large prime numbers. A batch instance $x = ((m_1, s_1), (m_2, s_2), \cdots ,(m_n, s_n))$ with n signatures can be verified by checking if it satisfies the following equation [4,6].

$$\prod_{i=1}^{n} m_i \equiv \left(\prod_{i=1}^{n} s_i\right)^e \bmod N \tag{2}$$

In the equation, m_i is a message and s_i is m_i's signature. When all of the signatures $s_1, s_2, \cdots, s_n$ in x are valid, Eq. (2) is satisfied. Unfortunately, there is a possibility that Eq. (2) can be satisfied even if there are two or more bad signatures in the same batch instance x [3].

To decrease this possibility, Bellare et al. presented batch verification tests [3]. These batch verification tests, denominated as *GT* (Generic Test) in previous study [6], make use of a probabilistic algorithm and is defined as follows:

GIVEN : $((m_1, s_1), (m_2, s_2), \cdots, (m_n, s_n))$ and a security parameter l.

Random Subset (RS) Test : Repeat the following atomic test, independently l times, and returns "true" if all sub-tests return "true":

i) For each $i = 1, \ldots, n$ pick $b_i \in \{0, 1\}$ at random
ii) Let $S = \{i : b_i = 1\}$
iii) Compute $m = \prod_{i \in S} m_i$ and $s = \prod_{i \in S} s_i$
iv) If $m \equiv s^e \bmod N$ then return "true", else return "false".

Small Exponents (SE) Test :

i) Pick $h_1, \ldots, h_n \in \{0, 1\}^l$ at random
ii) Compute $m = \prod_{i=1}^{n} {m_i}^{h_i}$ and $s = \prod_{i=1}^{n} {s_i}^{h_i}$
iii) If $m \equiv s^e \bmod N$ then return "true", else return "false".

Fig. 1. Batch verification tests for RSA

Definition 1 (GT). *Given a batch instance $x = ((m_1, s_1), \cdots, (m_n, s_n))$ and security parameter l. The GT takes x and*

i) returns "true" whenever all signatures are valid. The test never makes mistakes for this case.
ii) returns "false" whenever there is at least one bad signature. In this case the test makes mistakes with probability 2^{-l}.

To implement GT, the random subset test and the small exponents test were proposed in the previous study [7]. The two batch verification tests are described in Figure 1.

When the test fails, (i.e. $GT(x, n)$ = "false"), the verifier is faced with the problem of identifying bad signatures. Identification of bad signatures can be performed by so called divide-and-conquer verifier (DCV_α), which is defined as follows:

Definition 2 (DCV_α). *Given a batch instance $x = ((m_1, s_1), \cdots, (m_n, s_n))$.*

i) If n=1, then run $GT(x, 1)$. If $GT(x, 1)$ is "true", return "true" and exit. Otherwise return x as the bad signature.
ii) If $n \neq 1$, then run $GT(x, n)$. If $GT(x, n)$ is "true", return "true" and exit. Otherwise go to the step 3.
iii) Divide instance x into α batch instances$(x_1, x_2, \cdots, x_\alpha)$ containing $\frac{n}{\alpha}$ signatures each. Apply DCV_α to each α sub instances, i.e. $DCV_\alpha(x_1, \frac{n}{\alpha})$, $\cdots$, DCV_α $(x_\alpha, \frac{n}{\alpha})$.

Another method, Hamming verifier, divides a batch instance into sub instances based on Hamming Code for identifying a single bad signature [6]. Hamming Code is described with a block length n and r parity check equations where $n = 2^r - 1$. It allows a quick identification of the error position as the error *syndrome* is the binary index of the position in which the error occurs [8]. Hamming Code verifier(HCV) is defined as follows:

Definition 3 (*HCV*). *Given a batch instance $x = ((m_1, s_1)\ , \cdots\ ,(m_n, s_n))$ of length $n = 2^r - 1$ for some positive r and a parity check matrix H which contains r rows and n columns. HCV tries to*

i) Apply GT on the input instance. If $GT(x, n)$ = "true", exit. Otherwise, go to the next step.
ii) Create r sub instances. i.e.

$$x_i = \{(m_j, s_j)|h_{i,j} = 1\}$$

for $i = 1, \cdots, r$ where x_i is a sub instance composed from elements of x chosen whenever $h_{i,j}$ is equal to 1(elements of x for which $h_{i,j} = 0$ are ignored).
iii) Run $GT(x_i, 2^{r-1}) = \sigma_i$ for $i = 1, \cdots, r$ where $\sigma_i = 0$ if the test returns "true" or $\sigma_i = 1$ if it returns "false". The syndrome$(\sigma_1, \cdots, \sigma_r)$[8] identifies the position of the bad signature.
iv) Apply GT on the input instance without the bad signature. If the batch instance is accepted, return the index of the bad signature. Otherwise, return "false" and exit.

HCV needs the smaller number of *GT* than DCV_α needs that of *GT* when there is one bad signature in a batch instance.

3 Proposed Method

We present a method, denominated as *EBV* (Exponent Based Verifier), that identifies a bad signature for the case when there exists one bad signature in a batch instance. *EBV* returns "true" when all signatures are valid. *EBV* returns an integer as the index of a bad signature when only a bad signature exists in a batch instance and it returns "false" when two or more bad signatures exist. *EBV* is defined as follows:

Definition 4 (*EBV*). *Given a batch instance $x = ((m_1, s_1)\ , \cdots\ ,(m_n, s_n))$ of length n. EBV tries to*

i) Apply GT on the input batch instance and store the intermediate values of $\prod_{i=1}^{n} m_i$ and $\prod_{i=1}^{n} s_i$.
ii) If $GT(x, n)$ = "true", return "true" and exit.Otherwise, go to the next step.
iii) Compute $\prod_{i=1}^{n} {m_i}^i$ by multiplication of all intermediate values of $\prod_{i=1}^{n} m_i$ like as $m_n \times m_n m_{n-1} \times \cdots \times m_n m_{n-1} \cdots m_2 m_1$ and $\prod_{i=1}^{n} {s_i}^i$ by multiplication of all intermediate values of $\prod_{i=1}^{n} s_i$ like as $s_n \times s_n s_{n-1} \times \cdots \times s_n s_{n-1} \cdots s_2 s_1$.
iv) Compute $(\prod_{i=1}^{n} {s_i}^i)^e$.
v) Find a integer k which satisfied the following equation where $1 \le k \le n$.

$$\left(\frac{(\prod_{i=1}^{n} s_i)^e}{\prod_{i=1}^{n} m_i}\right)^k \equiv \frac{(\prod_{i=1}^{n} {s_i}^i)^e}{\prod_{i=1}^{n} {m_i}^i} \bmod N \qquad (3)$$

If the integer k exist, go to the next step. Otherwise, return "false" and exit.

vi) Apply GT on the input instance without the k-th signature. If the batch instance is accepted, return k as the index of the bad signature. Otherwise, return "false" and exit.

The main parts of *EBV* are step *iv*) and *v*), that is Eq. (3). We will elaborate what Eq. (3) implies in Theorem 1.

Theorem 1. *Given a batch instance of length n which has one bad signature. If an integer k $(1 \le k \le n)$ satisfies Eq. (3), then (m_k, s_k) is the bad signature in the batch instance.*

Proof. Assuming that the j-th signature s_j is invalid in a batch instance x. Since all signatures except (m_j, s_j) satisfies Eq. (1), we can reduce the fractions $(\frac{(\prod_{i=1}^n s_i)^e}{\prod_{i=1}^n m_i}$ and $\frac{(\prod_{i=1}^n {s_i}^i)^e}{\prod_{i=1}^n {m_i}^i}$) to their lowest terms as follows:

$$\frac{(\prod_{i=1}^n s_i)^e}{\prod_{i=1}^n m_i} \equiv \frac{(s_1)^e}{m_1} \cdots \frac{(s_j)^e}{m_j} \cdots \frac{(s_n)^e}{m_n} \equiv \frac{(s_j)^e}{m_j} \bmod N$$

$$\frac{(\prod_{i=1}^n {s_i}^i)^e}{\prod_{i=1}^n {m_i}^i} \equiv \frac{(s_1)^e}{m_1} \cdots \frac{(s_j)^{je}}{{m_j}^j} \cdots \frac{(s_n)^{ne}}{(m_n)^n} \equiv \frac{(s_j)^{je}}{(m_j)^j} \bmod N.$$

By substituting $\frac{{s_j}^e}{m_j}$ and $\frac{({s_j}^e)^j}{(m_j)^j}$ for $\frac{(\prod_{i=1}^n s_i)^e}{\prod_{i=1}^n m_i}$ and $\frac{(\prod_{i=1}^n {s_i}^i)^e}{\prod_{i=1}^n {m_i}^i}$ in Eq. (3) respectively, we can derive the equation $\left(\frac{{s_j}^e}{m_j}\right)^k \equiv \frac{({s_j}^e)^j}{(m_j)^j}$. This implies that k is equal to j, which is the index of the bad signature. □

In step *iii*), we can get $\prod_{i=1}^n {m_i}^i$ and $\prod_{i=1}^n {s_i}^i$ in the middle steps of n modular multiplications. Specifically, while computing $\prod_{i=1}^n m_i$ and $\prod_{i=1}^n s_i$ in step *i*),we can obtain the intermediate values such as $m_n, m_n m_{n-1}, \cdots, m_n\, m_{n-1} \cdots m_2 m_1$ and $s_n, s_n s_{n-1}, \cdots, s_n s_{n-1} \cdots s_2 s_1$. Then by multiplying all the intermediate values of $\prod_{i=1}^n m_i$ like as $m_n \times m_n m_{n-1} \times \cdots \times m_n m_{n-1} \cdots m_2 m_1$ and multiplying all the intermediate values of $\prod_{i=1}^n s_i$ like as $s_n \times s_n s_{n-1} \times \cdots \times s_n s_{n-1} \cdots s_2 s_1$, we can obtain $\prod_{i=1}^n {m_i}^i$ and $\prod_{i=1}^n {s_i}^i$.

Let g denote $\frac{(\prod_{i=1}^n s_i)^e}{\prod_{i=1}^n m_i}$ and h denote $\frac{(\prod_{i=1}^n {s_i}^i)^e}{\prod_{i=1}^n {m_i}^i}$. Then Eq. (3) can be abbreviated as $g^k \equiv h \bmod N$. This problem is a kind of the *discrete logarithm problem* (*DLP*) [9,10]. It is generally known that there is no polynomial time algorithm to solve the *DLP*. However, the proposed *EBV* is in a restricted domain of *DLP*, that is, k lies in the certain interval of integer, say $[1,n]$. Some efficient algorithms have been proposed for this case. To solve *EBV* efficiently, we employ Shanks' baby-step giant-step algorithm [11]. Figure 2 shows Shanks' baby-step giant-step algorithm. It can compute k in at most $2\sqrt{n}$ modular multiplications ($3\sqrt{n}/2$ on the average case) [10]. As a result, *EBV* requires one modular exponentiation and $2n + 3\sqrt{n}/2$ modular multiplications.

4 Performance Analysis

To compare the performance of our method (*EBV*) and the previous methods (DCV_α and *HCV*), we first analyze the number of *GT* invoked during batch

INPUT : $\frac{(\prod_{i=1}^{n} s_i)^e}{\prod_{i=1}^{n} m_i}, \frac{(\prod_{i=1}^{n} {s_i}^i)^e}{\prod_{i=1}^{n} {m_i}^i}, n$
OUTPUT : k

```
x1 ← (∏_{i=1}^n s_i)^e / ∏_{i=1}^n m_i , y1 ← (∏_{i=1}^n s_i^i)^e / ∏_{i=1}^n m_i^i , β ← ⌈√n⌉
for j ← 1, 2, ···, β do
  for i ← 1, 2, ···, β do
    if y_j ≡ x_i then
      return k ← (j − 1) × β + i
    else
      if j ≡ 1 then
        x_{i+1} ← x_i × x_1
      end if
    end if
  end for
  y_{j+1} ← y_j / x_β
  i ← 1
end for
return k ← 0
```

Fig. 2. Shanks' baby-step giant-step algorithm

verification for the each methods. Next, we estimate the performance of each method when there is one bad signature. The basic metric of the performance is the number of modular multiplications required at each method.

Table 1. The Computational cost of *EBV*, *HCV* and DCV_α according to the invoked number of *GT*

	Computational Cost
EBV	$2CostGT_l(n)$
HCV	$2CostGT_l(n) + \log_2 n \times CostGT_l(\frac{n}{2})$
DCV_α	$CostGT_l(n) + 2\sum_{i=1}^{\log_\alpha n} CostGT_l(\frac{n}{\alpha^i})$

If there is one bad signature in a batch instance of size n, *EBV* calls *GT* only twice to identify it, while DCV_α calls *GT* $2log_\alpha n + 1$ times and *HCV* calls *GT* $\log_2 n + 2$ times [6]. The cost of *GT* depends on the length of a given batch instance and a security parameter. So, we present the computational cost of *EBV*,DCV_α and *HCV* in terms of the computational cost of *GT*. Let $CostGT_l(n)$ denote the computational cost of *GT* when the length of a given batch instance is n and security parameter is l. Table 1 shows the comparison of computational cost.

Next, we convert the computational cost of *GT* into the number of modular multiplications under two different assumptions. In first assumption, the random subset test [7] is used as *GT*. *GT* requires l modular exponentiations and $2 \times l \times (c-1)$ modular multiplications where l is a security parameter and c is the

Table 2. The number of modular operations to perform EBV, HCV and DCV_2 where the random subset test is used as GT

	Computational Cost	
	modular exponentiation	**modular multiplication**
EBV	$2l + \mathbf{1}$	$2ln + \mathbf{2n} + \mathbf{3\sqrt{n}/2}$
HCV	$l \log_2 n + 2l$	$l/2 \times n \log_2 n + 2ln$
DCV_2	$2l \log_2 n + l$	$3ln - 2l$

order of S in Figure 1. c is $n/2$ in average case where n is the size of a batch instance. In the second assumption, the small exponents test [7] is used as GT. We can compute $m = \prod_{i \in S} {m_i}^{h_i}$ and $s = \prod_{i \in S} {s_i}^{h_i}$ with $l + nl/2$ modular multiplication respectively in Figure 1. So, the computational cost of GT is one modular exponentiation and $2l + nl$ modular multiplications when the small exponents test is used as GT. Note that l is commonly set to 60 [12,7].

Table 3. The number of modular operations to perform EBV, HCV and DCV_2 where the small exponent test is used as GT

	Computational Cost	
	modular exponentiation	**modular multiplication**
EBV	$2 + \mathbf{1}$	$4l + 2ln + \mathbf{2n} + \mathbf{3\sqrt{n}/2}$
HCV	$\log_2 n + 2$	$4l + 2ln + l \log_2 n(2 + n/2)$
DCV_2	$2 \log_2 n + 1$	$3ln + 4l \log_2 n$

Table 2 and Table 3 show the number of modular operations to perform EBV, HCV, and DCV_2. Table 2 shows the number of modular operations when the random subset test is used as GT and Table 3 shows the number of modular operations when the small exponents test is used as GT. We assign 2 to α in DCV_α(2 is optimal value when there is one bad signature in a batch instance [6]). The bold characters in Table 2 and Table 3 represent the additional modular operations of EBV.

To represent the computational cost of a modular exponentiation as the number of modular multiplications, we suppose that a modular exponentiation is implemented as the sliding-window algorithm [13]. One modular exponentiation in RSA can be computed by 17 modular multiplications where key length is 1024 bits and public key value is 65537 [14,15].

Figure 3 and Figure 4 show the comparison of average computational cost for performing EBV, HCV, and DCV_2. The figures show that EBV outperforms conventional methods where the random subset test or the small exponents test is used as GT. In Figure 3, we can observe that, when n is 1024, EBV reduces the number of modular multiplications by 38.2% and 71.3% compared with DCV_2 and HCV respectively. Also, we can observe from Figure 4 that, when n is 1024, EBV reduces the number of modular multiplications by 33.0% and 71.0% compared with DCV_2 and HCV respectively.

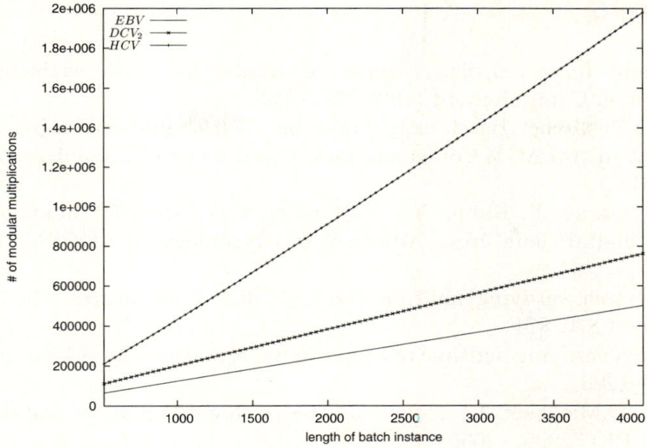

Fig. 3. The average number of modular multiplications of EBV,HCV and DCV_2 where the random subset test is used as GT

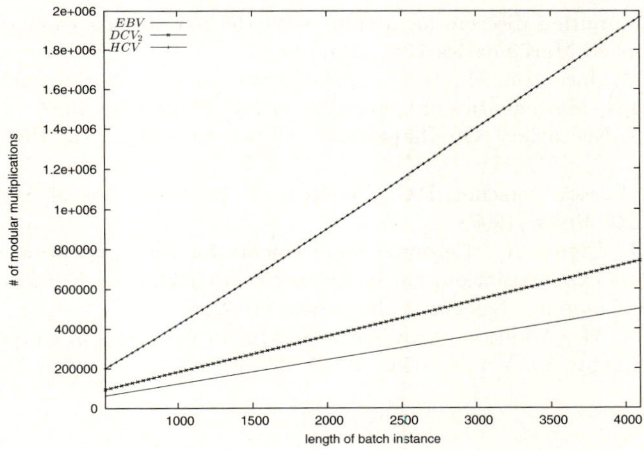

Fig. 4. The average number of modular multiplications of EBV,HCV and DCV_2 where the small exponent test is used as GT

5 Conclusion

In this paper, we have proposed a new batch identification method called EBV. When there is one bad signature in a batch, EBV finds out it by invoking GT twice. Moreover, figures show that EBV is more efficient than DCV_α and HCV when the random subset test or the small exponents test is used as a GT.

References

1. S.Yen, C.Laih: Improved digital signature suitable for batch certification. IEEE Transactions on Computers **44** (1995) 957–959
2. D.Marihi, D.Naccache: Batch exponentiation - a fast dlp-based signature generation strategy. In: 3rd ACM Conference on Computer and Communications Security. (1996) 58–61
3. Bellare, M., Garay, J., Rabin, T.: Fast batch verification for modular exponentiation and digital signatures. Advances in Cryptology-EUROCRYPT'98 (1998) 236–250
4. Harn, L.: Batch verifying multiple dsa-type digital signatures. In: Electronics Letters. (1998) 870–871
5. L.Harn: Batch verifying multiple rsa-type digital signatures. In: Electronics Letters. (1998) 1219–1220
6. J.Pastuszak, D.Michalek, J.Pieprzyk, J.Seberry: Identification of bad signatures in batches. In: PKC'2000. (2000)
7. Bellare, M., Garay, J.A., Rabin, T.: Batch verification with applications to cryptography and checking. Lecture Notes in Computer Science **1380** (1998)
8. Berlekamp, E.: Algebraic Coding Theory. McGraw-Hill (1968)
9. Schneier, B.: Applied Cryptography: Protocols, Algorithms, and Source Code in C. Wiley (1996)
10. E.Teske: Computing discrete logarithms with the parallelized kangaroo method. Discrete Applied Mathematics **130** (2003) 61–82
11. Buchmann, J., Jacobson, M., Teske, E.: On some computational problems in finite abelian groups. Mathematics of Computation **66** (1997) 1663–1687
12. J-S.Coron, D.Naccache: On the security of rsa screening. In: PKC99. (1999) 197–203
13. Menezes, A.J., van Oorschot, P.C., Vanstone, S.A.: Handbook of Applied Cryptography. CRC Press (1997)
14. Sauerbrey, J., Dietel, A.: Resource requirements for the application of addition chains modulo exponentiation. In: In Advances in Cryptology-Eurocrypt'92, Lecture Notesin Computer Science. Volume 658. (1992)
15. J.Bos, Coster, M.: Addition chain heuristics. In: In Advances in Cryptology Proceedings of Crypto 89. Volume 658. (1989) 400–407

Secure User Authentication Mechanism in Digital Home Network Environments*

Jongpil Jeong, Min Young Chung, and Hyunseung Choo**

Intelligent HCI Convergence Research Center
Sungkyunkwan University
440-746, Suwon, Korea
Tel.: +82-31-290-7145
{jpjeong, mychung, choo}@ece.skku.ac.kr

Abstract. The home network is a new IT technology environment for making an offer of convenient, safe, pleasant, and blessed lives to people, making it possible to be provided with various home network services by constructing home network infrastructure regardless of devices, time, and places. This can be done by connecting home devices based on wire and wireless communication networks, such as mobile communication, Internet, and sensor network. However, there are many risks involved, for example user privacy violations and service interference. Therefore, security service is required to block these risk elements, and user authentication is an essential component for secure home network service. It enables non-authorized persons not to use home network. In this paper, an authentication protocol for secure communications is proposed for secure home network environments. The proposed authentication protocol is designed to accept existing home networks based on public key infrastructure (PKI) and Authentication, Authorization, and Accounting (AAA), which both use Kerberos.

1 Introduction

Not that the home network is entirely new network system, but that existing network system is applied to home. That is, the home network is that various home appliances communicate with each other and the home members use outdoor network services supplied by internet service providers at indoor. The home network supplies to us convenient and secure life. For example, turn off our home's gas valve, turn on/off the light, and control the temperature of boiler or air conditioner by remote control at indoor or outdoor. And we can use internet banking services through TV stations, use T-commerce, and use remote medical treatment. These infrastructure building is the purpose of the home network. For

* This research was supported by the Ministry of Information and Communication (MIC), Korea, under the Information Technology Research Center (ITRC) support program supervised by the Institute of Information Technology Assessment (IITA), IITA-2005-(C1090-0501-0019).

** Corresponding author.

E. Sha et al. (Eds.): EUC 2006, LNCS 4096, pp. 345–354, 2006.

security and privacy protection of the home network users, the home network security is necessary.

As various mobile sensing technologies, remote control and ubiquitous infrastructure are developing and expectations on quality of life are increasing, a lot of researches and developments on home network technologies and services are actively on going. There are several wired-based network technologies for networking between devices in the home, such as HomePNA technology, constructing a high-speed in-home network using the existing telephone line, power-line communication (PLC) technology and networking technology with peripheral devices such as Universal Serial Bus (USB), Ethernet technology which is in use widely in local area networks, and IEEE 1394 technology to transfer multimedia data of Audio/Video digital devices, due to high-speed serial transmission. There are also several wireless network technologies such as Wireless LAN technology, Wireless PAN technology (e.g. Bluetooth), Zigbee, and ultra wideband (UWB) [1]. In addition, integrated home gateway technology exists [2][3], in order to accept heterogeneous networks. Security technologies are the first consideration for making the home network phenomenon possible. For example, a home network user's privacy can be violated if an attacker forcibly enters the home network and inspects the inside of a home with a web-camera. In addition, if attackers can control information appliances, these attackers may execute actions resulting in a loss to home users, possibly blocking home network services. There are many risk elements for different attack types, due to network extension.

For home network environments, information security technology is gathering strength as a critical issue. Security issues from information security requirements are very important, for example, mutual authentication between devices, user authentication services and access control services. In the case of wireless communication, wireless security aspects are extremely important because radio waves are continuously open.

The rest part of the paper is organized as follows. In Section 2, related works is presented. The definition of home network security requirements is presented in Section 3. In Section 4, an authentication protocol suitable for home network environments is proposed. Finally, this paper is concluded, and future directions are noted in Section 5.

2 Related Works

In home networks, several networking technologies exist, such as wired/wireless network technology, access network technology for communication between information appliances in home, and gateway technology for integration between outside networks and home networks. Network configuration equipments such as in-home information appliances, electronic appliances, home automation appliances, home gateway devices, and PDA/ Smart Phone/ Notebook/ PC are used for accessing the home network from outside.

Fig. 1 presents an example of the home network architecture, consisting of various technologies and equipments. Integrated Authentication Server (IAS)

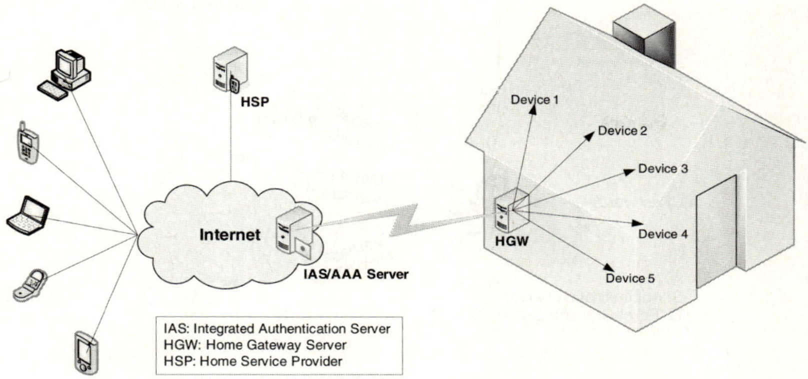

Fig. 1. Home Network architecture

has interfaces for several devices, making it possible to use the Internet, control networking technologies, and manage the home gateway. In addition, it not only performs transmission of home network service software to the home gateway, but also performs authentication, granting the privilege, accounting for home network users, and forwarding accounting information to Home Service Provider (HSP) [4]. Home Gateway (HGW) requires an open architecture platform to communicate with heterogeneous networks. This platform should be independent of hardware and software vendors. In addition, address transition, protocol transition, and seamless data transition, for supporting interconnection and compatibility with heterogeneous networks should be guaranteed. This platform should connect with existing entire networks, and accept new networks in the future.

Open Service Gateway Initiative (OSGi) [3][7][8], one of the home gateway standardization organizations, distributes the OSGi Service Platform and maintains a framework standard for home network services, indicating the direction of several methods such as ID/PW, PKI, and Token card, for security related user authentication.

If node A desires secure communications with node B, node A receives the session key and the ticket that can only be decrypted by correspondent node B from Trusted Third Parties (TTP). Node A transmits its ticket and session key to node B. Thus, secure communication between nodes A and B is made after that the session key received by node B. There are two representative protocols for reusing tickets within the ticket's valid time; the Neuman-Stubblebine authentication protocol [5] and the Kerberos authentication protocol [6] developed by MIT. [5] takes advantage of its ability to prevent replay attacks, within a ticket's valid time, by not requiring synchronization of the time stamp with each party. Fig. 2 shows the operation flow of Kerberos authentication protocol. [6] consists of Authentication Server (AS) and Ticket Granting Server (TG). If node A user desires communication with the Service Server securely, node A receives a service issue ticket from TG after user authentication from authentication server. Node A achieves service

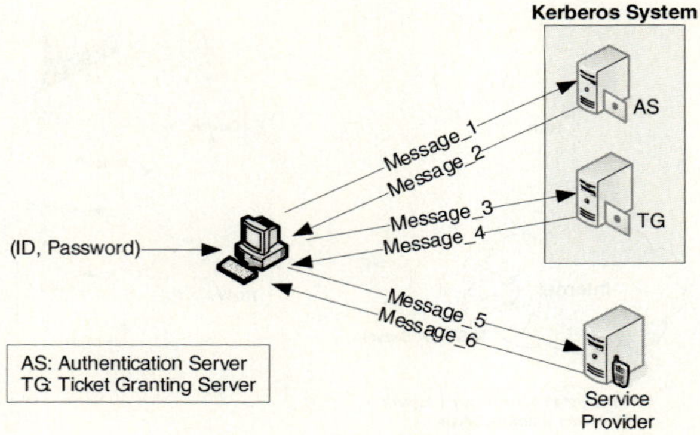

Fig. 2. Kerberos authentication protocol

privileges from the Service Server using this ticket. Node A keeps the privileges for the service, without communicating with the Kerberos system within the ticket's valid time. The Kerberos authentication mechanism is based on distributed environments receiving the server's service over the network, eliminating the user's inconvenience of repeatedly entering the password, in addition to providing authentication for clients and performing mutual authentication for the authentication server and ticket granting server.

3 Home Network Security Requirements

In home networks, the security requirements can be varied as the corresponding home network configuration. If the network is connected with a PC using a cable modem, users can execute their network security services. However, the home network consists of heterogeneous networks that connect to the Internet, therefore situations at outside home are considered for secure communication.

3.1 Entity Authentication

In home networks, entity authentication is classified into two types, user authentication for verifying right users and device authentication for verifying information appliances consisting of home networks in inter-device communication. Fig. 3 presents the authentication architecture for users to access information appliances in the home through a home gateway. It is necessary for users to be authenticated a minimum of 3 times to access information appliances between User-IAS, User-HGW, and HGW-Information appliances. Mutual authentication is conducted to prevent impersonation attack from malicious users.

It is required to apply the concept of single sign on (SSO) for providing user's convenience. In other words, when a user logs on to a home gateway as a legitimate user, any additional operation should not be required to access additional resources in the home network [8].

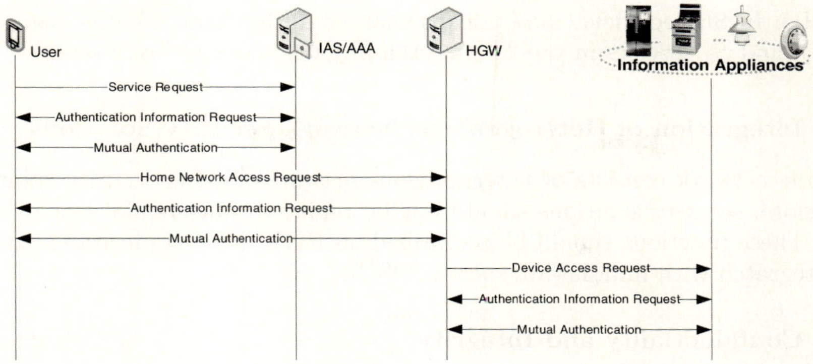

Fig. 3. Home Network authentication architecture

3.2 Privilege Delegation

Home network users should grant specific privileges to programs. Therefore, programs should have access to the resources authenticated by users. In addition, a master user who has home network service privileges, should be granted all services accessed to users. The privilege granting function is performed by the privilege granting service command to HGW after master user access to HGW. For these methods, there are functional limitations for each entity.

If the authentication process is completed with legitimate keys, information appliances should be required to know what an authenticated entity could achieve. For this method, access control list (ACL) is considered. This is to provide limited services, after finding a user ID in the ACL and checking a user's capabilities. It is stored in HGW, and can be updated by HGW with the master user privilege granting command. Table 1 represents the ACL specification. Functional limitation method is having lists of applicable functions explicitly, making it possible to list one function or group of functions.

Table 2 presents ACL specification to limit functions. This demonstrates the functions that can be performed with a specified ID. After service users authenticated by the home gateway, and they can take suitable service privileges for

Table 1. ACL specification

Subject	Identifier of entities able to be accessed
Authentication	Indicator to decide what functions to perform
Validity	Indication of entity validation, such as a timestamp

Table 2. Functional limitation

Subject	*none*	B_2	B_3	B_4
Authentication	S_1, S_2, S_3	S_1, S_4, S_5	S_1, ... , S_n	S_1, S_5, S_6
Validity	T_1	T_2	T_3	T_4

each ID. In Subject field, *none* means that an authenticated entity can access S_1, S_2, and S_3 services in the T_1 timestamp, for home gateway access.

3.3 Integration of Heterogeneous Network Security Solutions

A home network consists of heterogeneous networks having security solutions. Therefore, security solutions should not be replaced, but should provide mapping. These functions should be performed on HGW-*built* applications and can be integrated with middleware such as OSGi.

3.4 Confidentiality and Integrity

It is necessary to provide confidentiality and integrity services for secure data communication control of each system. For these services, it is required to share the secure private key between information appliances, service users and authentication server, authentication server and home gateway, and users and home gateway. The secure key is shared between information appliances in the home network. It is simply verified by using the message authentication code (MAC) validation function for providing integrity services for data. Also, it can be used to authenticate information appliances in the home network.

4 Security in Home Network Environments

4.1 Authentication Mechanism Between HGW and IAS

HGW downloads the home network service modules from IAS and installs them, during the boot-strapping process that initializes the home gateway. At this time, HGW requires a secure mechanism for downloading home network services from IAS, in order to prevent illegal falsification from service software errors and attacks during the mutual authentication or the sharing of the secure key. This secure mechanism can be implemented through the public key infrastructure (PKI) [9] or symmetric key algorithm. In general, PKI algorithm is superior to symmetric key in managing and distributing keys. However, this PKI algorithm require the complicated operation for data encryption/decryption and the additional certificate verification. Thus, PKI algorithm cause a longer delay than symmetric key algorithms.

4.2 User Authentication Protocol

Service subscribers require mutual authentication between IAS and HGW, in order to access home network services. In addition, they must be able to operate service access control when privilege services are granted. Users, authenticated through SSO, can access other home services without additional authentication procedures. Fig. 4 illustrates the user authentication mechanism.

In this section, it is assumed that IAS is located on the outside of the home network environment, manages the home gateway, and performs AAA functions.

Table 3. Notation

Notation	Meaning
R_1	Number calculated by IAS using U_{ID} and Password
R_2	Random Number generated by IAS
$E_{P-IAS}(-)$	Encryption using IAS's public key
S_{key}	Shared Session Key between Client and HGW
U_{ID}	User's Identifier
IAS_{ID}	IAS's Identifier
$E_{IAS-HGW}(-)$	Encryption using Symmetric key between IAS and HGW
$E_K(-)$	Encryption using K
T	Timestamp to decide Session key's validation

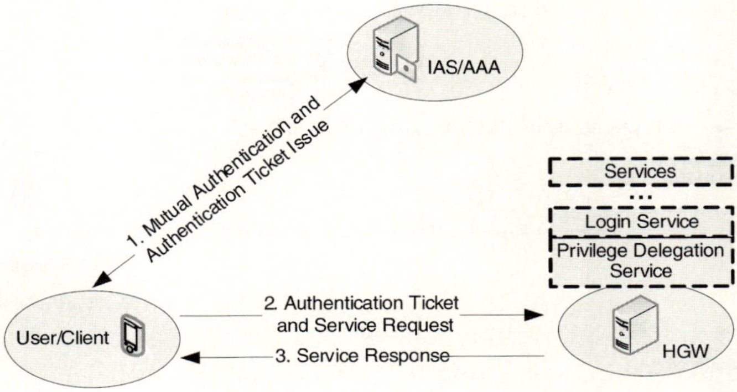

Fig. 4. User authentication mechanism

Another assumption is that clients have already taken and validated the IAS certificate. A suitable user authentication protocol is proposed for home network environments, focusing on authentication for users receiving the home service and controlling the service privilege.

The proposed authentication scenario is described in Fig. 5, the protocol is outlined in each step as follows.

1. Client transmits U_{ID} and $Password$ to IAS/AAA. Here, $Password$ is encrypted using IAS's public key. IAS verifies U_{ID} and $Password$ after decrypting the message using IAS's private key, and then authenticates client. Also, R_1 calculated as $h(U_{ID}, Password)$.
2. IAS delivers the authentication ticket $E_{IAS-HGW}(U_{ID}, IAS_{ID}, R_1, R_2, T)$ and the encrypted message by R_1. In case of having the right IAS's private key, R_1 could be decrypted by IAS and S_{key} also could be calculated by IAS, thus client implicitly authenticates IAS. In other words, client decrypt the encrypted message $E_{R_1}(IAS_{ID}, U_{ID}, R_2, h(S_{key}, U_{ID}), T)$ from IAS using R_1, and obtain R_2 and U_{ID}. After calculating of S_{key}, client verify the value of $h(S_{key}, U_{ID})$ and then validate U_{ID} and S_{key}.

Fig. 6 demonstrates that IAS indicates the authentication to access point (AP) in wireless network, after transmission of key material to AP and AP handshakes with client, keys for encryption/decryption are established on the MAC layer [10],[16].

3. Client transmits the authentication ticket $E_{IAS-HGW}(U_{ID}, IAS_{ID}, R_1, R_2, T)$, U_{ID} and *Services* encrypted using S_{key} to HGW. HGW compares U_{ID} of authentication ticket and U_{ID} of $E_{S_{key}}(U_{ID}, Services)$ and then implicitly authenticates client.

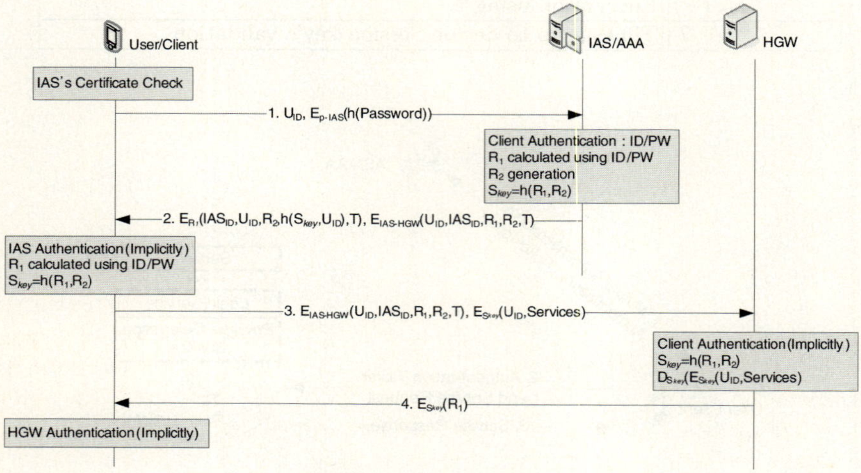

Fig. 5. Proposed authentication protocol

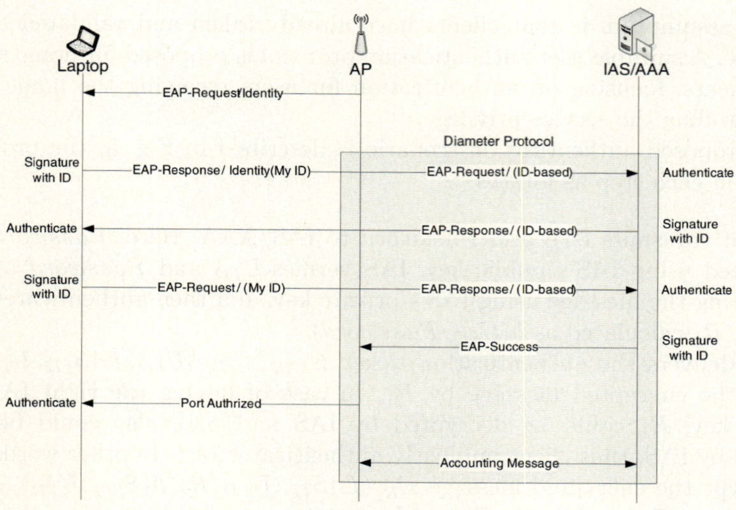

Fig. 6. Wireless LAN access authentication

4. HGW transmits R_1 encrypted using S_{key} to the client, and then authenticates HGW implicitly.

4.3 Security Analysis

The proposed protocol is designed under the assumption that public key or symmetric key infrastructure is used according to HGW's storage and computation capabilities, the symmetric key is shared between IAS and HGW. In addition, it is assumed that IAS exists outside the home network, it manages the home gateway, authenticates users, grants privileges, and controls accounting as the home gateway operator. Another assumption is that service users trust IAS. Actually, the OSGi operator exists in OSGi framework, it is outside the home network as the home gateway manager for managing the home gateway and authenticating users.

HGW knows that the authentication server is legitimate using the PKI-*based* public key algorithm or symmetric algorithm as a mechanism to authenticate IAS in the home network. In addition, the user authentication mechanism is based on U_{ID} and *Password*, and can transmit *Password* securely, using a public key algorithm with the certificate received from the authentication server (IAS). In addition, it encrypts the challenge with the *Password* transmitted from senders, and prevents the replay attack from attackers. Authentication between HGW and users employ the authentication ticket granted from the authentication server, and users can request and receive services with a valid authentication ticket after single authentication, there is no requirement to login each time when requesting services. Authentication ticket's validation can verify with its time-stamp, satisfied with authentication requirements as mentioned earlier. In addition, as U_{ID} is checked in authentication ticket after login, it can control whether having service privileges. ACL is stored as table format for U_{ID} privileges list in HGW's policy file, the purpose is to supply suitable services in response to user identification information.

5 Conclusion

Home network is defined as environments where users can receive home network services for anytime and anywhere access through any device, connected with a wired/wireless network to home information appliances including the PC. In this environment, there is many security threats that violate users privacy and interfere with home services. In addition, the home network consists of several networks with each network being inter-connected, so network security for each network is required. This means that there are a number of security threats to other networks when a security threat occurs in any network. Also, users in home network are needed security mechanism, for receiving home services from attackers and sharing information between home information appliances.

In this paper, the security requirements in home network environments are defined, and a user authentication mechanism between a home gateway and user is proposed, an authentication mechanism between home gateway and home gateway operator (IAS) can perform AAA functions. Authentication technologies in the wireless network are investigated and are acceptable in home network environments. In this paper, integration of home network environments and authentication servers in wireless networks are discussed, regarding methods of authenticating wireless networks effectively.

There is still progress in the standardization of home network architecture, which is required to be researched in the future. In addition, research regarding the integration of authentication servers for 3G-WLAN and authentication servers in home networks needs to be conducted.

References

1. K. Choi *et al.*, "Trends of Home Networking Standardization in Korea," KETI Journal, 2003.
2. Y. Park *et al.*, "Home Station Architecture based on Digital Convergence toward U-Home age," ETRI Journal, 2003.
3. "OSGi Service Platform, Release 4 Specification," http://www.osgi.org, October 2005.
4. S. Lim *et al.*, "Home Network Protocol Architecture for Ubiquitous Communication," Journal of KIPS, vol.10, 2003.
5. B. Clifford Neuman, Stuart G. Stubblebie, "A Note on the Use of Timestamps as Nonces Operating Systems Review," 1993.
6. B. Clifford Neuman, Theodore Is'o, "Kerberos: An Authentication Service for computer Network." IEEE, Computer Magazine, September 1994.
7. OSGi, "RFC 18 - Security Architecture. Specification," Draft, 2001.
8. K. Jeon *et al.*, "User Authentication Mechanism in OSGi Service Framework Enviroments," Journal of KISS, vol.9, 2003.
9. CCITT Recommendation X.509. The Directory Authentication Framework, CCITT, December 1998.
10. IEEE P802.11i/D9.0 "Medium Access Control(MAC) Security", 2004.
11. J. Gu *et al.*, "Security Clustering: A Network-wide Secure Computing Mechanism in Pervasive Computing," Networking 2004, pp.1326-1331, May 2004.
12. H. Jo, H. Youn, "A Secure User Authentication Protocol Based on One-Time-Password for Home Network," ICCSA 2005, vol.3480, p.519, May 2005.
13. MIT Media Lab: Things That Think Consortium, http://ttt.media.mit.edu
14. Microsoft Research: Easy Living, http://research.microsoft.com/easyliving
15. Y. Chen, L. Yeh, "An Efficient Authentication and Access Control Scheme Using Smart Cards," Parallel and Distributed Systems, 2005. Proceedings. 11th International Conference (ICPADS'05), vol.2(20-22) , p.78-82, July 2005.
16. B. Aboba *et al.*, "Extensible Authentication Protocol (EAP)," RFC 3748, June 2004.

Scalable Message Routing for Mobile Software Assistants

Paweł T. Wojciechowski

Poznań University of Technology
60-965 Poznań, Poland
ptw@cs.put.poznan.pl

Abstract. In this paper we define an algorithm for location-independent communication of mobile software Personal Assistants (PAs). The algorithm extends the Query Server with Caching algorithm that we proposed earlier, with support of message routing in the wide-area networks. Our algorithm is suitable for two kinds of PAs collaboration: (1) within a local group of mobile individuals, who can communicate frequently using different computers connected to a local-area network (possibly via a wireless medium), and (2) some individuals may also communicate via the global network and move to other groups.

Keywords: Mobile agents, distributed computing, protocols, middleware, P2P.

1 Introduction

The ongoing growth of wide-area networks has brought up considerable interest in *mobile agents* [1,2,3,4]; mobile agents are units of executing code that can migrate between machines and perform tasks locally. It has been widely argued [4,3,5] that mobile computation provides a useful enabling technology for wide-area applications, such as web services, scientific computation, and collaborative work.

To ease application writing one would like to be able to use high-level *location independent* communication facilities, allowing the parts of an application to interact without explicitly tracking each other's movements. To provide these above standard network technologies (which directly support only location-dependent communication) requires some distributed infrastructure. Sewell, Wojciechowski, and Pierce [6] argued that the choice or design of an infrastructure must be somewhat application-specific – any given *infrastructure algorithm* will only have satisfactory performance for some range of migration and communication behaviour; the algorithms must be matched to the expected properties of applications and the communication network.

In [7], we described the *Personal Assistant (PA)* – an application that uses mobile agents to support collaborative work of mobile individuals. The PA application uses the *Query Server with Caching (QSC)* infrastructure algorithm for

E. Sha et al. (Eds.): EUC 2006, LNCS 4096, pp. 355–364, 2006.

location-independent communication. We have prototyped our application using *Nomadic Pict* [6,7] – a statically-typed, distributed programming language, which is based on the π-calculus [8] extended with distribution and agent mobility. The QSC algorithm however does not scale to wide-area networks, nor to many groups of PA agents, which would be required in the full-scale, practical implementation of the PA application.

In this paper, we therefore extend the QSC algorithm to support wide-area collaboration. We have done so with the following model of collaboration in mind: (1) mobile individuals within a local working group can communicate frequently using different computers connected to a local-area network (possibly via a wireless medium), and (2) some individuals may also communicate via the global network and move to other groups. This model of collaboration covers many real-world scenarios, e.g. think of people working closely on the same project or task within a local (indoor or outdoor) area, who may occasionally contact a distant expert or manager, or migrate to other working group.

We propose a *Federated Query Server with Caching (FQSC)* algorithm that fits well into the above model of collaboration. The algorithm uses a federation of servers. Each federated server is responsible for managing communication within a local group of PAs, and maintaining a dynamic forwarding pointers chain used for communication between groups. The FQSC algorithm behaves as well as the optimal-within-LAN QSC algorithm proposed in [7]. However, it avoids a single point of failure. Furthermore, cache information and compaction techniques are used so that also the communication between LANs requires only one network message in the common case.

Our paper is aimed at developers of mobile agent applications, and researchers interested in distributed (or peer-to-peer) algorithms. The algorithm has been specified formally as an executable encoding in Nomadic Pict; due to lack of space, we omitted this description in the paper but we made it available in the technical report [9]. The formal specification is concise but gives enough details to be directly translated by application programmers using their language of choice.

The paper is organized as follows. Section 2 presents the PA application. Section 3 describes the FQSC algorithm in several steps, beginning with two simple, centralized algorithms. Then we present our distributed algorithm. Section 4 proposes several extensions. Section 5 discusses related work, and Section 6 concludes.

2 The Personal Assistant Application

We consider the support of collaborations within (say) a large computer science department, spread over several buildings. Most individuals will be involved in a few collaborations, each of 2–10 people. Individuals move frequently between offices, labs and public spaces; impromptu working meetings may develop anywhere. Individuals would therefore like to be able to *summon* their working state (which may be complex, consisting of editors, file browsers, tests-in-progress etc.)

to any machine. These summonings should preserve any communications that they are engaged in, for example audio/video links with other members of the project. To achieve this, the user's working state can be encapsulated in a mobile agent, an electronic *personal assistant (PA)*, that can migrate on demand.

We also consider the support of remote collaborations. Individuals can either visit other institutions and summon their personal assistants there, or the PAs can be temporarily *delegated* to other groups. For example, a personal assistant agent encapsulating a buggy program (which may include source files, makefiles, and test data) can be delegated to language experts, who can analyse the program while interacting remotely with the program developer who launched the PA agent, then modify code, check the modified code using the original test data, and finally send the PA (with corrected program) back to the developer.

A usable infrastructure for location-independent communication of PA agents can only be designed in the context of detailed assumptions, both about the system properties and about the expected behaviour of the PA agents. We assume that the application is running over a collection of large LANs, which are connected to a wide-area network, or intranet. In each LAN reliable messaging can be provided by lower-level protocols and all machines are at roughly the same communication cost distance from each other. Machines are also basically reliable, although from time to time it is necessary to reboot or turn off.

We suppose that the number of PA agents is of the same order as the number of people in the labs. Each PA will migrate infrequently, with minutes or hours between migrations. The path of migrations is unpredictable – it may range over the whole LAN, some PAs may occasionally migrate between LANs. The migrations of different PAs are essentially uncorrelated in time. It is common for people to work for extended periods at machines out of their offices. PAs communicate between each other frequently, with significant bandwidth – e.g. audio/video messages or streams, and other data (that must be delivered reliably).

3 Design of Appropriate Infrastructure

We develop our infrastructure in several steps, beginning with two simple, centralized algorithms. Then we present our distributed algorithm.

3.1 Central Server and Query Server with Caching

The *Central Server* algorithm has a single server that records the current site of every agent. Agents synchronize with the server before and after migrations. The location-independent, application messages are sent via the server. The central server is however a bottleneck for all inter-PA communication. Furthermore, all application messages must make two hops (and these messages make up the main source of network load).

Adapting the Central Server so as to reduce the number of application-message hops required, we have the *Query Server with Caching* algorithm, described in [7]. As before, it has a server Q that records the current site of every

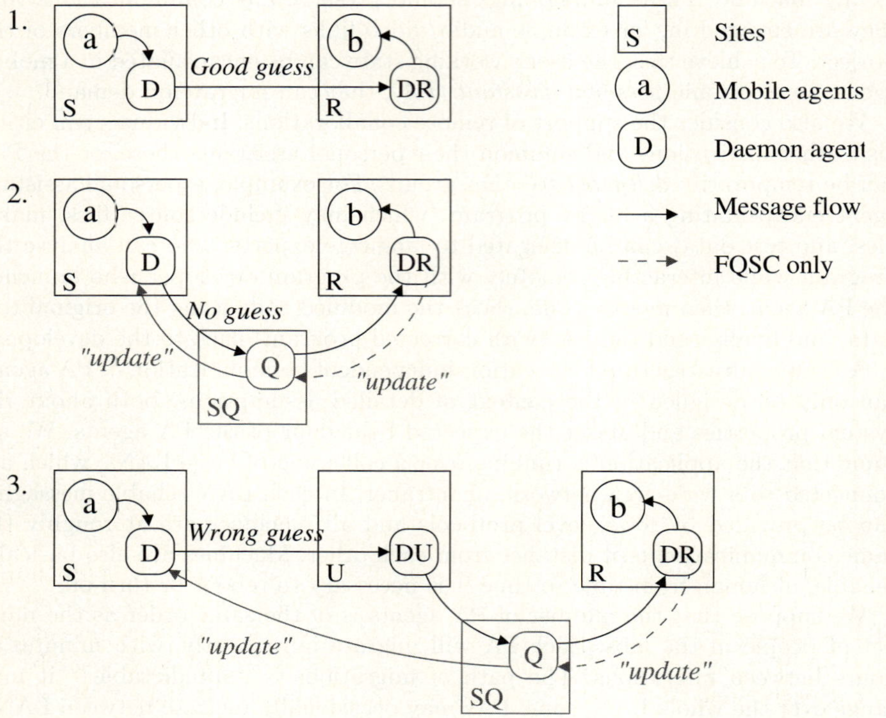

Fig. 1. The QSC and FQSC algorithms: the delivery of a message from agent a to b

agent, and agents synchronize with it on migrations. In addition, each site has a daemon that maintains a cache of location data.

Consider the delivery of an application message from agent a to agent b. The message (see Fig. 1-1) is first sent to a daemon D on the current site S, which then forwards the message to the daemon DR on the target site R, which delivers the message to b. When a daemon D does not know the agent b (see Fig. 1-2), or when a daemon DU receives a mis-delivered message, for an agent b that has left its site U (see Fig. 1-3), the message is forwarded to server Q. The server both forwards the message on to the agent's current site R and sends a cache-update message to the originating daemon. In the common case application messages will here take only one hop (the "good guess" case in Fig. 1-1).

3.2 Federated Query Server with Caching

The QSC algorithm however does not scale to a large number of PAs and a global network. Consider PA migration to a remote working group. The obvious defect in this case is the need to send control messages between the daemon and the server over the Internet, even if migrations and communications of the PA would be local within a LAN of the new group. Furthermore, the QSC

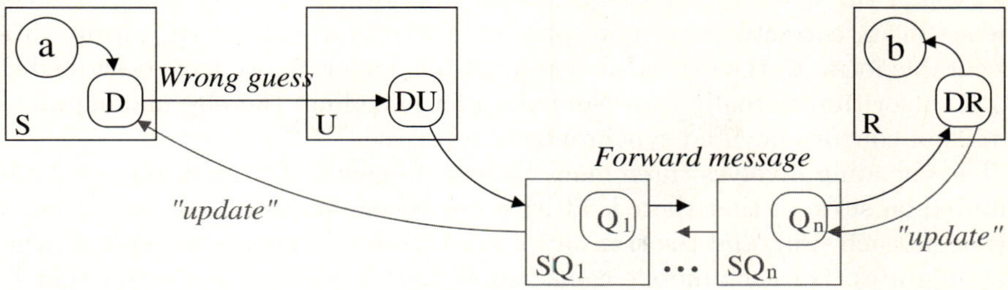

Fig. 2. The FQSC algorithm: the delivery of a message in the "wrong-guess" scenario

algorithm has single point of failure. To overcome these drawbacks, we may have many servers, each one dealing with agents of a single user or collaborative group. Mobile computation introduces however an interesting problem: how to synchronize migrations and communications on these servers, so that the number of messages between servers and daemons is optimized ?

In this paper, we therefore propose the *Federated Query Server with Caching (FQSC)* algorithm, which removes the bottleneck. It employs a collection of query servers Q_1, ..., Q_n for the specific migration and communication pattern of PA agents. Each server maintains locations of agents that are present in a local domain, where a *domain* can range from a single computer to a LAN.

For each agent there is at least one server, which records the current site of the agent; a *local server* in agent's current domain is an example of such a server. Agents synchronize with the local server before and after migrations. When an agent migrates away to a new domain, it must register at the query server in this new domain, which now becomes the agent's new local server.

As before, each site has a daemon that maintains a cache of location data. Application messages are sent via the daemons, much like in the QSC algorithm (see Fig. 1, 1-3). When a message cannot be delivered using cache information, the message is forwarded by query servers, using forwarding pointer chains that are collapsed when possible upon receipt of an "update" message (see Fig. 2). By compaction of the pointer chains, in the common case application messages are delivered in only one hop, as in the case of QSC.

If a server has no pointer for the destination agent b, then it will forward the message to b's home server, which has the pointer. An agent's *home server* is the query server on which the agent was originally registered upon its creation. The address of this server is recorded as part of the agent's high-level ID.

This may seem well-suited to the PA application, but the textual description omits many critical points – it does not unambiguously identify a single algorithm. For example, it is difficult to explain in prose the following details:

- How are the migrations and communications synchronized (if at all) ?
- What data about agents are actually locked and for how long ?
- How to collapse the pointer chain on servers without loosing messages ?

To explain the details of the FQSC algorithm and to develop reasonable confidence in its correctness, a more precise description is required, ideally in an executable form. In the extended version of this paper [9], we have described the FQSC algorithm formally as a Nomadic Pict encoding, thereby making all the details of concurrency and synchronization precise.

The encoding involves three main classes of agents: the query servers `Q` (distributed on sites, so that there is at least one server in each LAN), the daemons `D` (one on each site), and the translations of high-level application agents (which may migrate). For each mobile agent name there is at least one server that has the site and daemon where the agent *is* currently located; servers store these data in a map `m`. Each daemon maintains its own map `m` from agent names to the site and daemon where they *guess* the agent is located. This is updated only when a message delivery fails. The encoding of each high-level agent records its current site and daemon, and the name and site of the local server. This is kept accurate when agents are created or migrate.

The messages sent between agents fall into three groups, implementing the location-independent messages, the high-level agent creation, and agent migration. Below we describe the first group of messages in more details.

Message delivery. To send a location-independent message the translation of a high-level agent simply asks the local daemon to send it. Consider an output of a message in agent `a` on site `S` to agent `b`, where the local daemon is `D`. The message will be reliably delivered to agent `b`, irrespective of the current site of `b` and of any migrations. Suppose `b` is on site `R`, where the daemon is `DR`. There are three cases to describe. Either `D` has the correct site/daemon of `b` cached, or `D` has no cache data for `b`, or it has incorrect cache data.

In the first case (see Figure 1-1) `D` sends a message to `DR` which delivers the message to `b` atomically. For the PA application this should be the common case, including the cross-domain communication; it requires only one network message.

In the cache-miss case (see Figure 1-2) daemon `D` sends a message to the local query server `Q`, which forwards the message to a daemon `DR` at site `R`, which then delivers successfully and sends an `update` message back to `D` via `Q` (both `D` and `Q` update their cache). The query server's lock is kept until the message is delivered, thus preventing `b` from migrating until then. Two other variants are possible. If the forwarding pointer for the agent `b` is not found, `Q` forwards the message to `b`'s home server (the server's name/site are encoded as part of the name `b`). Similarly, if `b` has moved between domains and there has been no communication to `b` since then (and so no cache updates), `Q` will contain a pointer to the query server in the domain visited by `b`. In this case, the `message` message is forwarded between query servers until it eventually reaches `DR` (see Figure 2). The forwarding pointer chain is collapsed by sending the `update` messages which update caches with `b`'s current location.

Finally, the incorrect-cache-hit case (see Figure 1-3). Suppose `D` has a mistaken pointer to `DU` at `U`. It will send a message to `DU` which will be unable to deliver the message. DU will then send the message to the query server, much as before (except that the cache update message still goes to D, not to DU).

4 Further Extensions

The FQSC algorithm avoids sending too many cache updates over the Internet. As long as agent migrations are local, a cache-update message to other query servers is sent only in the case of incorrect-cache-hits from these servers. Consequently, the cost of forwarding a message to agents in other domains is paid only for the first message. Then, the forwarding pointer chain is collapsed and any subsequent messages (from the same location) are sent directly.

The above design choice reflects the expected behaviour of the PA agents: communications are more frequent than migrations, and the inter-domain migrations, which correspond to delegation or a physical movement of individuals, are less frequent than migrations within a local domain. If PA behaviour would be different, it may be worth to collapse the forwarding pointer chains more often. For example, upon each cross-domain migration, the cache of *several* daemons and servers could be updated, not just those last visited.

One can also analyse the application further. In fact, migrations of the PA agents may usually be within a small group of machines, e.g. those of a project group. More sophisticated infrastructures might use some heuristics to take advantage of this. For a critical application a quantitative analysis may be required. An exhaustive discussion is beyond the scope of this paper.

This paper does not explicitly address questions of security, fault-tolerance, or administrative domains. These should be addressed in the full-size implementation of the PA infrastructure. In order to tolerate machine crashes, the (logical) query servers can be replicated on several machines (e.g. using the *group communication* middleware [10]).

5 Related Work

Many authors present strategies for *locating* mobile objects and devices (see, e.g., surveys [11,12]). Similar to locating objects are mechanisms for resource discovery, e.g. Dimakopoulos and Pitoura [13] describe cached-based distributed flooding approaches to locate a peer that provides a particular resource, with cache updates propagated either upon resource lookup or change.

Our work builds on the above, but is focused on the location-independent *message delivery*, which provides stronger properties than a pair of unsynchronized agent lookup and message sending actions. For instance, the FQSC algorithm guarantees that messages are not lost irrespective of agent migrations, and the upper bound on the number of hops required to deliver a message in case of local (within domain) migrations is known.

A number of agent systems provide a form of location independence; we briefly review some of them below. Comparisons are difficult, in part because of the lack of clear levels of abstraction and descriptions of algorithms – without these, it is hard to understand the performance and robustness properties of the infrastructures. Some mobile agent infrastructure algorithms are for locating agents only, which – as we explained above – provides weaker guarantees.

For instance, Mobile Objects and Agents (MOA) [14] supports four schemes for locating agents; these are used as required to deliver location-independent messages. Stream communication between agents is also described, with communicating channel managers informing each other on migration.

The MASIF proposal [15] also involves four locating schemes, but appears to build communication facilities on top. This excludes a number of reasonable infrastructures; it contrasts with our approach here, in which location-independent message delivery is taken as primary (some infrastructures do not support a location service).

The infrastructure work of Aridor and Oshima [16] provides three main forms of message delivery: location-independent using either forwarding pointers or location servers, and location dependent (they also provide other mechanisms for *locating* an agent).

Roth and Peters [17] propose a scalable global service for locating mobile agents, with encryption and decryption capabilities to prevent security attacks through agent impersonating.

The Join Language [18] provides location-independent messages using a built-in infrastructure, based on forwarding pointer chains that are collapsed when possible.

The Mobile Object Workbench [19] provides location independent interaction, using a hierarchical directory service for locating clusters of objects that have moved. There is a single infrastructure, although it is stated that the architecture is flexible enough to allow others.

Moreau [20] describes formally an algorithm for routing messages to migrating agents, which is based on distributed location directory service, with forwarding pointer chains that are collapsed when possible. In [21], he describes the directory extended with pointer redundancy to tolerate node crashes; the algorithm has been verified using the proof assistant Coq.

Our model assumes direct message routing, while other approaches are also possible, e.g. Murphy and Picco [22] present a distributed-snapshot-based algorithm. It attempts to deliver a message to every agent in the system using broadcast, and only the agents whose IDs match the message target actually accept the message. Cao *et al.* [23,24] propose to separate agents and movable *mailboxes*, i.e. receivers of location-independent messages, with push and pull techniques that can be used by agents to obtain messages from their mailbox. They also discuss schemes to make the communication tolerant to mailbox crashes [23], and path compression for better performance [24].

The use of home servers in our FQSC algorithm resembles the *Internet Mobile Host Protocol (IMHP)* proposed by Perkins *et al.* [25] for transparent routing of IP packets to mobile hosts. By enabling sites to also cache bindings for mobile hosts (or mobile agents in FQSC) both protocols provide mechanisms for better routing which bypasses the default reliance on routes through the home server, and so they eliminate the likelihood that the home server would be a bottleneck. However, cache updates are performed differently, with FQSC optimizing the specific migration and communication pattern of PA agents. The FQSC protocol normally delivers messages to mobile agents in one-hop, while IMHP must route messages to mobile hosts via *care-of address* (which corresponds to the current local server of the target mobile agent in FQSC).

6 Conclusion

In this paper we have proposed a distributed algorithm for scalable location-independent message delivery to mobile agents, that is suitable for the Personal Assistants application. The algorithm reflects the expected behaviour of the Personal Assistant agents: communications are more frequent than migrations, and the inter-domain migrations, which correspond to delegation or a physical movement of individuals, are less frequent than migrations within a local domain.

Acknowledgments. We would like to thank Peter Sewell and Asis Unyapoth for many useful discussions. This work was supported in part by the State Committee for Scientific Research (KBN), Poland, under KBN grant 3 T11C 073 28.

References

1. D. Chess, C. Harrison, and A. Kershenbaum. Mobile agents: Are they a good idea? In *Mobile Object Systems – Towards the Programmable Internet*, LNCS 1222, pages 25–48. Springer, 1997.
2. Dejan Milojičić, Frederick Douglis, and Richard Wheeler, editors. *Mobility: Processes, Computers, and Agents.* Addison-Wesley, 1999.
3. David Kotz, Robert Gray, and Daniela Rus. Future directions for mobile agent research. *IEEE Distributed Systems Online*, 3(8), August 2002.
4. Luca Cardelli. Abstractions for mobile computation. In *Secure Internet Programming: Security Issues for Mobile and Distributed Objects*, LNCS 1603, pages 51–94. Springer, 1999.
5. Anand Tripathi, Tanvir Ahmed, and Neeran M. Karnik. Experiences and future challenges in mobile agent programming. *Microprocessors and Microsystems*, 25(2):121–129, April 2001.
6. Peter Sewell, Paweł T. Wojciechowski, and Benjamin C. Pierce. Location-independent communication for mobile agents: A two-level architecture. In *Internet Programming Languages*, LNCS 1686, pages 1–31. Springer, 1999.
7. Paweł T. Wojciechowski and Peter Sewell. Nomadic Pict: Language and infrastructure design for mobile agents. *IEEE Concurrency*, 8(2):42–52, April-June 2000.
8. R. Milner, J. Parrow, and D. Walker. A calculus of mobile processes, Parts I and II. *Information and Computation*, 100(1):1–77, 1992.
9. Paweł T. Wojciechowski. Scalable message routing for mobile software assistants. Technical Report RA-2006, Institute of Computing Science, Poznań University of Technology, May 2006. Available electronically at `http://www.cs.put.poznan.pl/pawelw`.

10. Sergio Mena, André Schiper, and Paweł T. Wojciechowski. A step towards a new generation of group communication systems. In *Proc. Middleware '03*, LNCS 2672, June 2003.
11. Vincent Wong and Victor Leung. Location management for next generation personal communication networks. *IEEE Network*, 14(5):8–14, Sept./Oct. 2000.
12. Evaggelia Pitoura and George Samaras. Locating objects in mobile computing. *IEEE Transactions on Knowledge and Data Engineering*, 13(4):571 – 592, July/August 2001.
13. Vassilios V. Dimakopoulos and Evaggelia Pitoura. A peer-to-peer approach to resource discovery in multi-agent systems. In *Proc. CIA '03: the 7th Workshop on Cooperative Information Agents*, LNCS 2782, August 2003.
14. Dejan S. Milojičić, William LaForge, and Deepika Chauhan. Mobile Objects and Agents (MOA). In *Proc. COOTS '98: the 4th USENIX Conference on Object-Oriented Technologies and Systems*, April 1998.
15. D. Milojicic, M. Breugst, I. Busse, J. Campbell, S. Covaci, B. Friedman, K. Kosaka, D. Lange, K. Ono, M. Oshima, C. Tham, S. Virdhagriswaran, and J. White. MASIF: The OMG Mobile Agent System Interoperability Facility. In *Proc. 2nd Int. Workshop on Mobile Agents*, LNCS 1477, September 1998.
16. Yariv Aridor and Mitsuru Oshima. Infrastructure for mobile agents: Requirements and design. In *Proc. 2nd Int. Workshop on Mobile Agents*, LNCS 1477, September 1998.
17. Volker Roth and Jan Peters. A scalable and secure global tracking service for mobile agents. In *Proc. of the 5th Int. Workshop on Mobile Agents*, LNCS 2240, pages 169–181, December 2001.
18. Cédric Fournet, Georges Gonthier, Jean-Jacques Lévy, Luc Maranget, and Didier Rémy. A calculus of mobile agents. In *Proc. CONCUR '96: the 7th Int. Conference on Concurrency Theory*, LNCS 1119, August 1996.
19. Michael Bursell, Richard Hayton, Douglas Donaldson, and Andrew Herbert. A Mobile Object Workbench. In *Proc. the 2nd Int. Workshop on Mobile Agents*, LNCS 1477, September 1998.
20. Luc Moreau. Distributed directory service and message router for mobile agents. *Science of Computer Programming*, 39(2–3):249–272, 2001.
21. Luc Moreau. A fault-tolerant directory service for mobile agents based on forwarding pointers. In *Proc. SAC '02: the 17th Symp. on Applied Computing: Track on Agents, Interactions, Mobility and Systems*, March 2002.
22. Amy L. Murphy and Gian Pietro Picco. Reliable communication for highly mobile agents. In *Proc. ASA/MA '99: 1st Int. Symposium on Agent Systems and Applications / 3rd Int. Symposium on Mobile Agents*, October 1999.
23. Jiannong Cao, Liang Zhang, Jin Yang, and Sajal K. Das. A reliable mobile agent communication protocol. In *Proc. ICDCS '04: the 24th Int. Conference on Distributed Computing Systems*, March 2004.
24. Jiannong Cao, Liang Zhang, Xinyu Feng, and Sajal K. Das. Path compression in forwarding-based reliable mobile agent communications. In *Proc. ICPP '03: the 32nd Int. Conference on Parallel Processing*, October 2003.
25. Charles Perkins, Andrew Myles, and David B. Johnson. IMHP: a mobile host protocol for the Internet. *Computer Networks and ISDN Systems*, 27(3):479–491, December 1994.

Grid Resource Management Based on Functional Dependency*

Doan Thanh Tran and Eunmi Choi**

School of Business IT, Kookmin University
Jeongneung-dong, Seongbuk-gu, Seoul, 136-702, Korea
td_thanh@yahoo.com, emchoi@kookmin.ac.kr

Abstract. In this paper, we propose a resource management system in Grid computing in order to specify system Quality of Service (QoS) requirements for dynamic and complex emerging applications. Our approach is based on the *functional dependency* among application components to specify the probability of system QoS requirements for the emerging application. Experimental results show that our application scheduling based on *functional dependencies* can achieve scheduling and managing emerging applications to satisfy a client's quality of service in Grid computing. The results also show significant improvement of performance comparing to cluster distribution and random distribution scheduling approaches.

1 Introduction

Large-scale grids are complex systems composed of thousands of components from disjoined domains. Planning the capacity to guarantee quality of service (QoS) in such environments is a challenge because global service-level agreements (SLAs) depend on local SLAs. Thus, resource management is the major concern in Grid. The resource management system (RMS) is central to the operation of a Grid. Resources are the entities such as processors and storage that are managed by the RMS. The set of services provided by a RMS varies depending on the intended purpose of the Grid. The resource management system should predict the impact of applications' requests on the overall resource pool and quality of service guarantees.

Condor [1] is the typical one, not using the prediction method but using the policy rules for matching between requestors and providers. In the prediction and heuristic approach, PBS (Portable Batch System) [2] and LSF (Load Sharing Facility) [3] are two typical schedulers and both are supports batch jobs scheduling. Batch rescheduling allows potentially more effective utilization of the Grid resources since more requests can be considered at one time.

This paper proposes a resource management system with the online application modeling approach for Grid Resource Management. The application components are modeled with resource requirement and functional dependency. The resource

* This work was supported by the Korea Science and Engineering Foundation (KOSEF) under Grant No. R04-2003-000-10213-0. This work was also supported by the Brain Korea 21 project in 2006.

** Corresponding author.

E. Sha et al. (Eds.): EUC 2006, LNCS 4096, pp. 365 – 374, 2006.

requirement considers CPU utilization, network load, and storage allocation. The functional dependency is applied to composite web services. The approach to extract dependency structures among application service in this paper is pragmatic and based on a static dependency analysis that yields information on entities within a system. The analysis shows that dependency information is stored in built-in repository of all standard operating systems. Based on the application model, we propose a complete architecture for application service management. This architecture supports resource management and scheduling for composite web services or emerging complex applications, which include many functional dependency components. Through this system, we can achieve scheduling and managing applications to optimize resource utilization while satisfying client's quality of service in Grid computing.

The rest of the paper is organized as follows. We first show the shortcoming of current approaches in Grid Resource Management and propose a new method of application modeling based on functional dependencies in Section 2. In Section 3, we describe the architecture for application service management and scheduling based on the functional dependencies. Finally, we present experimental results of our scheduling approach in Section 4, and conclude this paper in Section 5.

2 Application Modeling Based on Functional Dependency

Normally, resource management applied in Grid computing is used for single application. Compared to the old method of resource management is not applicable in complicated applications, our approach focuses on solving the resource management for dynamic and complex emerging applications.

In this approach, as well as the resource requirements of application components, we consider the online characterization of dependencies. Applying these two requirements to individual application, we create an Online Model Instance for each of application components and, based on this, we estimate the system QoS requirements.

The application model for application services includes: *R,* which is the set of System QoS requirement per application service, and *D,* which is Functional dependency structure among application services. We have the application model with the two vectors be presented as the following expression: $QoSModel = F(D, R)$.

For *R* vector, we use Resource Specification Language provided in Globus Toolkits 4.0 [5] as the standard structure to describe the Grid resources and job requests. For *D* vector, we adopt the functional dependency of application services that presented in [4]. In [4], the authors consider the fact that majority of application services run on UNIX and Windows NT based systems and it is worth of analyzing the degree to which information regarding application services is already contained in the operating system. The system administrators successfully deploy application services without having to access to detailed and application-specific management instrumentation because they have this information. We called this information the application service dependencies.

3 The Architecture for Application Service Management

Our objective is to create an automated solution of resource management for resource utilization increased while guaranteeing service level agreement to end users. In this section, we describe the architecture for application service management, the execution flow, and the details of admission control and resource assignment.

The architecture for application service management is shown in Figure 1. As a result of the static analysis during application installation and provisioning, each application service offering has associated with a list of resources that provide the basis of that service. This data is kept in dependency repository and maintained by the application dependency analysis process discussed in previous section and depicted in upper part of Figure 1.

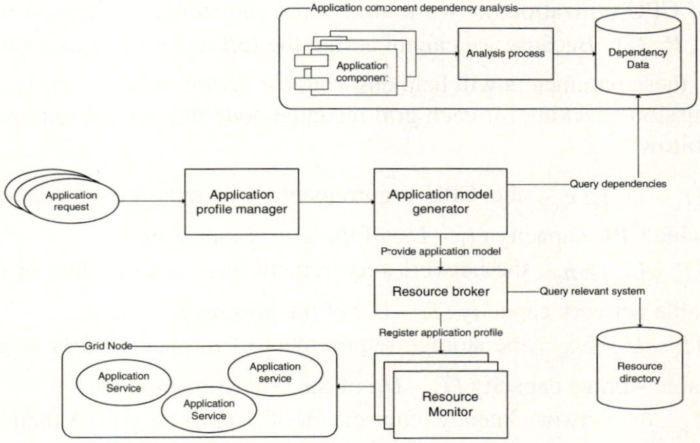

Fig. 1. The Architecture for Application Service Management

In the architecture, we have four major components:

- *Application profile manager* is in charge of choosing application requests from end users and submitting it to *Application model generator*.
- *Application model generator* receives application profile from *Application profile manager* and query dependency structure from *Dependency repository* to generate the application model $F(D,R)$. Then it submits the application model to *Resource broker*.
- *Resource broker* receives an application model from *Application model generator*, extracts separate application service component a_i from *R,* and finds suitable grid nodes to process it from *Resource directory.* After choosing best-fit grid node for the application service component, *Resource broker* registers it to *Resource monitor* of that grid node. The application service components are consequently processed by *Resource broker* depending on the dependency structure *D*.
- *Resource monitor* is in charge of executing an application service components registered by *Resource broker* and retrieving resource utilization information to update to *Resource directory*.

3.1 Admission Control

The *Resource broker* performs the admission control for each application service component a_i with resource requirement $\{c, n, s, l_n, l_s\}_{a_i} \in R$ in the request where c is CPU utilization requirement, n is network utilization requirement, s is storage utilization requirement, l_n is network access latency, and l_s is storage access latency.

Supposed that at each grid resource node we have T_c, U_c, T_n, U_n, T_s, U_s which are the total capacity (T) and the utilized capacity (U) of CPU, network bandwidth, and storage. P_C, P_N, P_S are the weight parameters to reserve the resources for unexpected workload of CPU utilization, network utilization, and storage utilization respectively. $0 \le P_C, P_N, P_S \le 1$. Because we cannot assign the full resource capacity for a well-fit job request, these parameters will help ensuring the system work properly.

The admission checking for each grid resource node that has all required resources will be as follow:

- $P_c \times (T_c - U_c) \ge c_{a_i}$, the CPU requirement of a_i must be less or equal to the available CPU capacity $(T_c - U_c)$ of the grid resource node.
- $P_n \times (T_n - U_n) \ge n_{a_i}$, the network requirement of a_i must be less or equal to the available network capacity $(T_n - U_n)$ of the grid resource node.
- $P_s \times (T_s - U_s) \ge s_{a_i}$, the storage requirement of a_i must be less or equal to the available storage capacity $(T_s - U_s)$ of the grid resource node.
- $l_n \le l_{na_i}$, the network latency requirement of a_i must be greater than the network latency of the grid resource node.
- $l_s \le l_{sa_i}$, the storage latency requirement of a_i must be greater than the storage latency of the grid resource node.

3.2 Resource Assignment

Resource assignment is optimized for minimizing wait-time and maximizing utilization of servers. Considering utilization of a server, we need to measure the utilization of CPU, network capacity, and storage capacity. The differences of priority of these resources depend on the application services, the environment, and the policy of the system. Therefore, we try to give a general metric to consider all the resources' utilization as follow

- Fitting metric for each grid node that passes admission checking

Supposed that at each grid resource node we have T_c, U_c, T_n, U_n, T_s, U_s, which are the total capacity and the utilized capacity of CPU, network bandwidth, and storage. The terms c_a, n_a, s_a are the CPU, network, and storage requirement of application a. We have the available capacities of this node: T_c-U_c, T_n-U_n, T_s-U_s. Therefore the utilization rates of CPU, network, and storage of application a on the remaining capacities are $\frac{c_a}{T_c - U_c}, \frac{n_a}{T_n - U_n}$, and $\frac{s_a}{T_s - U_s}$ where $\frac{c_a}{T_c - U_c}, \frac{n_a}{T_n - U_n}, \frac{s_a}{T_s - U_s} \le 1$. The simple metric is the sum of these utilization rates. However, in many real cases, the priorities of requirements are various. Depending on these priorities, we can set the weights for each utilization rate. For that reason, we choose the fitting metric for an application *a* as follow:

$$M_{fit} = Wc_f \times \frac{c_a}{T_c - U_c} + Wn_f \times \frac{n_a}{T_n - U_n} + Ws_f \times \frac{s_a}{T_s - U_s} \leq 1$$

where $Wc_f + Wn_f + Ws_f \leq 1$, and Wc_f, Wn_f, and Ws_f are weight of CPU, network, and storage. These weights are chosen to optimize wait-time and utilization of servers. Depending on different type of grid resources and application request, we can choose the suitable weights. For example, for the computational grid, the CPU optimization is the most significant. Therefore, we can set the value of Wc_f high for this type of Grid. For the grid requires heavy network communication, we can set the Wn_f high.

- Best fit criterion: Supposed that we have *n* nodes to pass the admission check, the chosen Grid resource node is the node that satisfy the following expression:

$$M_{fit} = \max_{i=1}^{n} M_{fit_i}$$

The idea of this metric is a simple greedy algorithm. The key point is that with weights of requirements, we can optimize the utilization of the system by choosing suitable weights depending on the system and the application types.

4 Experiment Results and Evaluation

In this section, we evaluate the performance of our application allocation approach against cluster allocation approach and random allocation approach. The GridSim simulator [5] is used in our study. For evaluating the system, we consider three criteria: the system throughput, the Grid node utilization, and the job's waiting time.

Table 1. The QoS Model of the Standard Application Requests

Request Type	CPU Utilization	Network bandwidth	Storage	Duration in wall clock time
Heavy composite web service request	15% Guarantee on a 3Ghz machine	15Mbps	15MB	6 hours
Light composite web service request	10% Guarantee on a 3Ghz machine	10Mbps	10MB	1 hour
Heavy batch job request	Minimum threshold of 35% on a 3Ghz machine	0Mbps	300MB	4 hours
Light batch job request	Minimum threshold of 5% on a 3Ghz machine	0Mbps	100MB	3 hours

The major application requests we used in the simulation are composite web service requests. In some test cases, we choose mixed workload of batch and composite web services in accordance with realistic workload cases. We consider two scenarios in the realistic workload cases: day time experiment and night time experiment.

During day time, the workload of a batch job request is light. Only small number of jobs is submitted. The workload of a composite web service request is heavy during day time, so a large number of composite web services are submitted. The arrival rate of these requests has Poisson distribution. During night time, the workload of a batch job request is heavy. They are submitted in large number. In contrast, the workload of a composite web service request is light. There are very few requests submitted.

For the composite web service request, we assume that the relations are hand-drafted and auto-provided to the *Application model generator*. We have two types of Composite Web service request structures for two different light and heavy composite web service requests. Table 1 shows the QoS model for the standard application requests in experiment. For the diversity of our request, we apply normal distribution with the random variation of 0-20% of the standard requirements.

All simulation scenarios run in the system which composes 100 Grid resource nodes. Each node has the resource capabilities as follows: Intel Pentium 4 (D850EMVR, 3.06GHz, Hyperthreading Technology Enabled), Operating system Windows 2003 Sever, SPEC/MIPS rating: 1099, Network share: 100Mbps, Storage share: 700MB, Resource manager type: Time-shared. To ensure that the system runs properly, we set the limitation of utilization of each type of resources at 90% of the resource capability. The 10% resource capability is reserved for overhead.

4.1 Composite Web Service Request Simulation

In this type of experiment, we generate only composite web service requests. We compare the request processing with and without using functional dependency. The purpose of this experiment is to compare the performance of our approach of compartmentalizing the composite web service request into a set of sub application services with the performance of cluster allocation and random allocation approaches.

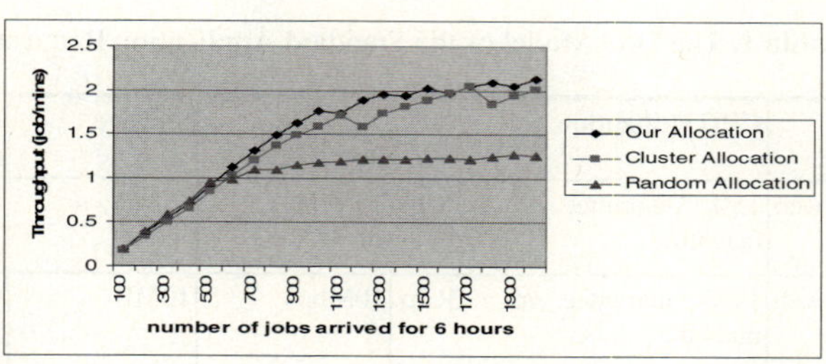

Fig. 2. Throughput Results of Our Allocation, Cluster Allocation, and Random Allocation

The input data is heavy request type only and the requirements vary using normal distribution with the variation of 0-20% of those of the standard request described in Table 1. The depth of dependency request is two or three. The requests are sent for six

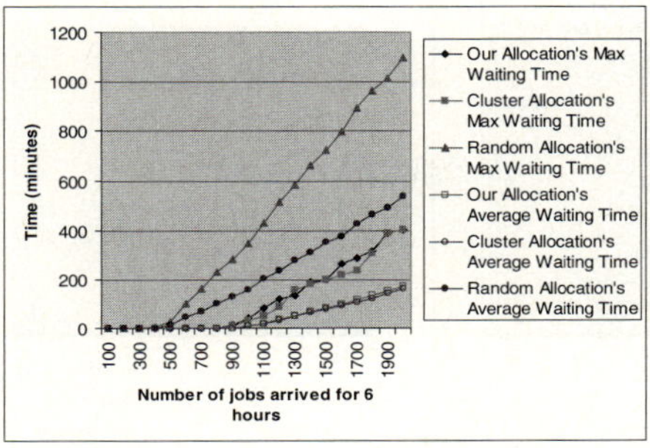

Fig. 3. Waiting Time Results of Our Allocation, Cluster Allocation, and Random Allocation

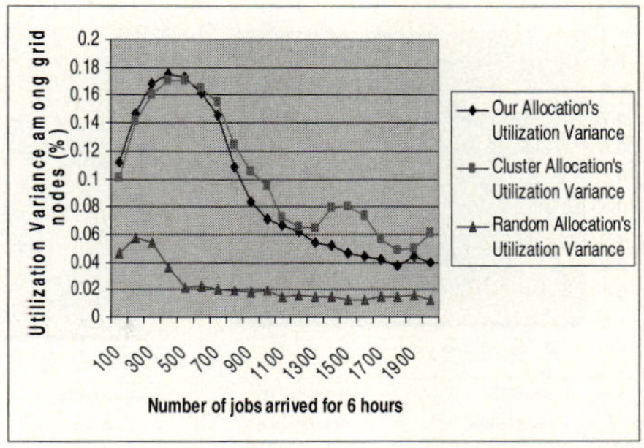

Fig. 4. Grid Nodes' Utilization Variance Results of Our Allocation, Cluster Allocation, and Random Allocation

hours from the beginning of the experiment and using Poisson distribution to distribute the arrival rate of the requests to the Grid system. The number of requests ranges from 100 to 2000. The collecting information is throughput, max waiting time, average waiting time, and resource utilization.

With our allocation, we use the functional dependency to distribute the application components whenever they are ready to be executed. For the cluster allocation, we do not consider the application components and their dependency. Therefore, we assign one request in only one Grid node. For the random allocation, we separate the application request into a component level and randomly distribute it to any suitable nodes.

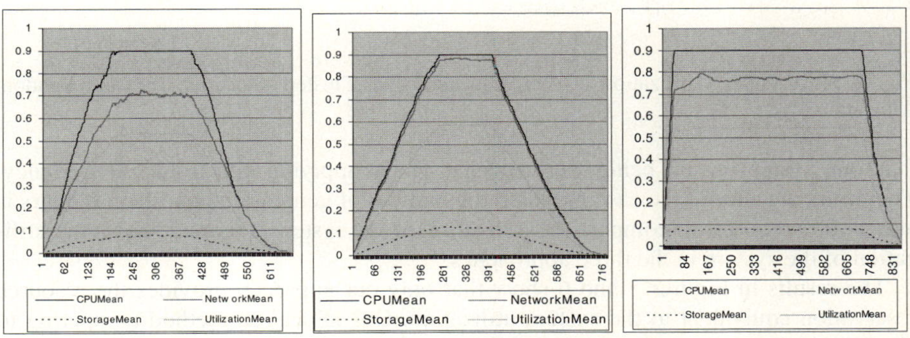

(a) (b) (c)

Fig. 5. Mean Values of Resource Reservation of Our Allocation (a); Cluster Allocation (b); and Random Allocation (c)

The results (showed in Figures 2, 3, and 4) show that our solution always has the best throughput in most of test cases. The waiting time of our allocation is also the best result. The utilization variance of our allocation is better, compared to the cluster allocation. Due to the busy waiting, the random allocation yields the lowest utilization variance, but the throughput and waiting time are the worst. These results have proved

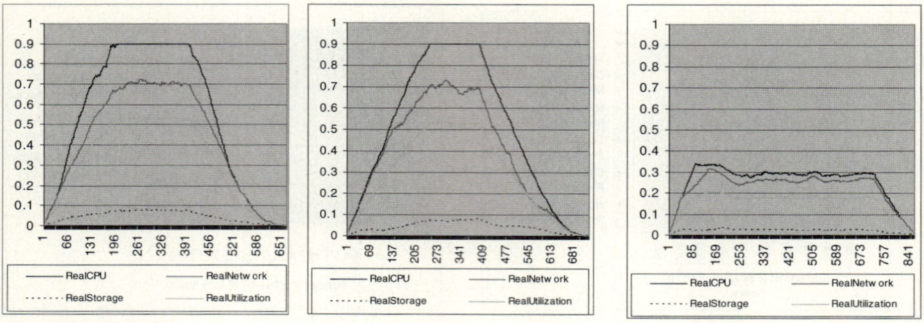

(a) (b) (c)

Fig. 6. Mean Values of Real Utilization of Our Allocation (a); Cluster Allocation (b); and Random Allocation (c)

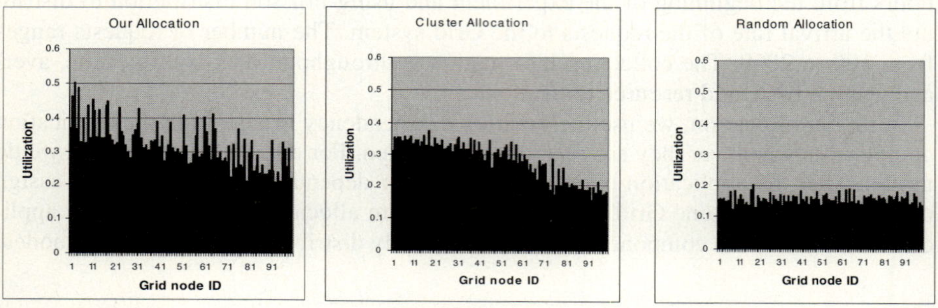

(a) (b) (c)

Fig. 7. Grid Nodes' Utilization of Our Allocation (a); Cluster Allocation (b); and Random Allocation (c)

that our system gains better performance when applying functional dependency. Therefore, we choose the case in which the number of generated requests in 6 hours is about 1000 requests to compare the utilization of the system. Figure 5 shows the utilization of the system in the three approaches.

The results in Figures 5 and 6 show that only our approach provides the resource reservation equivalent to the system utilization. Our allocation method comparing to cluster allocation method also provides better resource utilization as in Figure 6 (a) and (b). The random allocation method shows a great difference between resource reservation and resource utilization. Figure 7 also shows that our approach achieves the best utilization, compared to other approaches. Our allocation method has better distributing balance, comparing to cluster allocation method when the random approach achieves the worst utilization.

4.2 Mixing Batch Request and Composite Web Service Request Simulation

The purpose of this experiment is to demonstrate the system in the realistic workload cases in which the grid will have different type of requests submitted at different time period with different requirements. In this experiment, we collect the resource utilization of system, the maximum waiting time, the average waiting time of the composite web service requests, and the throughput of each type of requests.

The day time experiment uses the number of requests which is chosen based on the previous results. We already knew that the simulation system reaches the peak of utilization when the number of heavy web service requests is around 1000. Besides, in day time, there will be not so many batch job requests submitted to the system. Therefore, we set 1000 heavy composite web service requests and 200 light batch job requests. The heavy composite web service requests are submitted within 6 hours from the beginning of the experiment and generated with the arrival rate based on Poisson distribution.

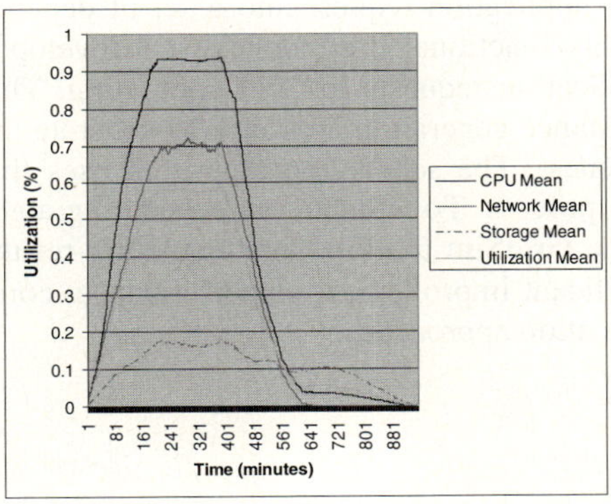

Fig. 8. Mixed Request Simulation – Day Time Utilization Results

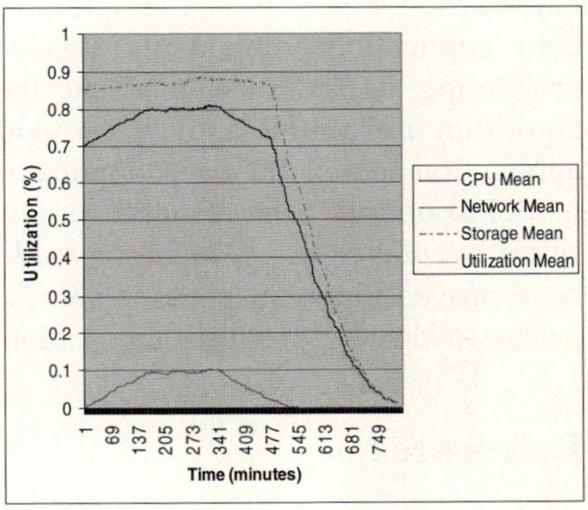

Fig. 9. Mixed Request Simulation – Night Time Utilization Results

The results show that all the composite web services have average waiting time 7 minutes (max is 29 minutes). Comparing to the 4 hour-request duration, this is an acceptable results. Besides, Figure 8 shows that the utilization of the system and the variance of grid nodes' utilization are as good as the experiment results only with composite web services. In the night time experiment, we consider that we have a list of heavy batch job requests already submitted and, during experiment time, there will be a small number of light composite web services submitted to the system. The night time results in Figure 9 show that our system can achieve high performance when scheduling for a major number of Batch job requests with a small number of composite web service requests.

Using the GridSim toolkit, we developed a simulator to experiment our new approach on grid resource management. Based on the simulator, we created different test scenarios to compare processing performance of composite web service requests of our allocation algorithm with that of standard cluster allocation algorithm and that of random allocation algorithm. The results showed that our approach always provides best utilization performance, throughput, and reasonable utilization variance between grid nodes. Our allocation approach which is based on functional dependency always provides better results comparing to standard cluster allocation approach while the random allocation approach showed the worst utilization and throughput.

For the practical of our experimentation, we consider the realistic workload cases in which the composite web service requests are processed collaterally with batch job requests. In this type of experiment, we divide into two test cases: day time experimentation and night time experimentation. All the results showed that our approach could provide high utilization performance even in the artificial real-world cases.

5 Conclusion

In this paper, we propose an online application modeling approach for grid resource management. The approach uses functional dependency in the application model. The proposed architecture of application service management, based on the functional dependency structure, can structuralize the application request into a set of dependency application components. Based on this functional dependency, we develop a scheduling algorithm to distribute the application requests in Grid computing. This algorithm uses online application model instance generation approach to generate the application model for each application request. The scheduling algorithm uses this model to optimize the resource assignment process. To validate our scheduling algorithm, we develop a simulator based on the GridSim toolkit. The simulating results have proved that our approach shows significant improvement of performance, comparing to cluster allocation and random allocation approaches.

References

1. Raman, R. and Livny, M.. (1998). "Matchmaking: Distributed Resource Management for High Throughput Computing", Proceedings of the Seventh IEEE International Symposium on High Performance Distributed Computing, Chicago, IL.
2. Henderson, R. and Tweten, D.. (1996). "Portable Batch System: External reference specification," Technical report, NASA Ames Research Center.
3. W. Allcock, J. Bester, J. Bresnahan, S. Meder, P. Plaszczak, S. Tuecke. (2003). "GridFTP: Protocol Extensions to FTP for the Grid". Global Grid ForumGFD-RP
4. G. Kar, A. Keller, and S. Calo, (2000) "Managing Application Services over Service Provider Networks: Architecture and Dependency Analysis," in Proceedings of NOMS 2000, Honolulu.
5. R. Buyya and M. Murshed, (2002) "GridSim: A Toolkit for the Modeling and Simulation of Distributed Resource Management and Scheduling for Grid Computing", CCPE, Volume 14, Issue 13-15, Wiley Press, Nov.-Dec..
6. SPEC CPU2000 Results, http://www.spec.org/cpu2000/results/cpu2000.html
7. Klaus Krauter, Rajkumar Buyya, Muthucumaru Maheswaran. (2001). "A taxonomy and survey of grid resource management systems for distributed computing", Software: Practice and Experience Volume 32, Issue 2
8. Ian Foster, Carl Kesselman, and Steven Tuecke. (2001). "The Anatomy of the Grid - Enabling Scalable Virtual Organizations", Intl. Journal of Supercomputing Applications.
9. I. Foster and C. Kesselman. (1997). "Globus: A Metacomputing Infrastructure Toolkit.". Intl Journal of Supercomputer Applications, Volume 11, No. 2.

Distributed Proximity-Aware Peer Clustering in BitTorrent-like Peer-to-Peer Networks

Bin Xiao[1], Jiadi Yu[1,2], Zili Shao[1], and Minglu Li[2]

[1] Department of Computing
The Hong Kong Polytechnic University, Hong Kong
{csbxiao, csjdyu, cszlshao}@comp.polyu.edu.hk
[2] Department of Computer Science and Engineering
Shanghai Jiao Tong University, China
{jdyu, li-ml}@cs.sjtu.edu.cn

Abstract. In this paper, we propose a hierarchical architecture for grouping peers into clusters in a large-scale BitTorrent-like underlying overlay network in such a way that clusters are evenly distributed and that the peers within are relatively close together. We achieve this by constructing the CBT (Clustered BitTorrent) system with two novel algorithms: a peer joining algorithm and a super-peer selection algorithm. Proximity and distribution are determined by the measurement of distances among peers. Performance evaluations demonstrate that the new architecture achieves better results than a randomly organized BitTorrent network, improving the system scalability and efficiency while retaining the robustness and incentives of original BitTorrent paradigm.

Keywords: Proximity-aware, Clustered BitTorrent (CBT), peer-to-peer networks, super-peer, scalability.

1 Introduction

Peer-to-Peer (P2P) applications have become popular in contexts such as Internet file sharing. P2P technology has a number of advantages over the traditional server-client content distribution model. The hardware is inexpensive, it is scalable so as to accommodate a large number of users and large amounts of content, it is fault tolerant when content is being shared by multiple sources, and has faster download time.

One of the most popular P2P file-sharing applications is BitTorrent [1], [2]. BitTorrent is not, however, unproblematic. In a BitTorrent network [3], each client peer joins a separate *torrent* to share the downloading of a specific file. A torrent contains a *tracker* and peers that are currently online, all of which are sustained by a track server. This torrent tracker collects the state of every peer in the torrent and returns a random list of peers in response to the joining request of a peer in BitTorrent. The torrent tracker and all of the peers together in a torrent form a mesh overlay network. This mesh overlay network is flat and works well when the network is small. Two problems arise, however, when the network becomes larger to the point where there are tens of thousands of

E. Sha et al. (Eds.): EUC 2006, LNCS 4096, pp. 375–384, 2006.

participating peers, which is possible in a real-world BitTorrent overlay network. The first problem is that random connections among peers in the mesh overlay network make it possible for geographically distant peers to connect, increasing file downloading time. The second problem is that a large number of peers can cause bottlenecks in the torrent tracker.

It is possible to obviate these problems by using a hierarchical architecture to construct large-scale BitTorrent overlay networks. In such an approach, the overlay network is composed of several (or tens of) clusters of peers. Each cluster behaves as a BitTorrent community and keeps the robustness and incentives scheme of file sharing of the BitTorrent system. It selects a peer to be a super-peer in a cluster and this super-peer becomes a *local tracker*. The torrent tracker supervises all of the super-peers. This hierarchical architecture prevents the torrent tracker from being overloaded. If we can group peers according to their real-world proximity, we can further reduce average latencies for packet delivery between peers and increase the network bandwidth usage.

In this paper, we present a hierarchical architecture CBT (Clustered BitTorrent) for grouping proximate peers, as may be found in BitTorrent-like P2P applications. We build the scalable hierarchy overlay network using two novel algorithms, the peer joining algorithm and the super-peer selection algorithm. These allow a peer to join the cluster in which it is closest to its super-peer among all super-peers. As a result, all peers in a cluster are proximate in the underlying network topology. The proposed peer joining algorithm is a distributed algorithm in the sense that the peer itself makes the decision as to which cluster to join when it first contacts the torrent tracker. The proposed super-peer selection algorithm identifies a super-peer by selection from regular peers as that peer which is maximally distant from all existing super-peers. This distributes peers evenly among clusters and produces a small cluster diameter. Performance evaluations show that the new CBT can achieve good performance and scalability, markedly improving file download speed and reducing the torrent tracker load.

This paper is organized as follows. In the next section, we introduce related work. Section 3 describes the proposed hierarchical CBT (Clustered BitTorrent) system to be applied in BitTorrent-like P2P networks. Section 4 presents the construction of CBT applying the peer joining algorithm and super-peer selection algorithm. Section 5 shows the simulation results, and Section 6 offers our conclusions.

2 Related Work

The research on Peer-to-Peer (P2P) file sharing [4],[5],[6],[7] has attracted much attention. The most representative and perhaps currently most popular file sharing system is BitTorrent. Previous work, such as [2], [8], [9], mainly focus on the understanding of the BitTorrent mechanisms. Not much work proposes approaches to handling a large-scale P2P overlay network to leverage the load on the tracker, and improving file sharing efficiency. The approaches could lie in the construction of hierarchy architecture in BitTorrent and the proximity-aware joining of peers into a group. This kind of hierarchical architecture-based node clustering has been applied in decentralized P2P networks, such as FastTrack [10], SODON [11], and ECSP [12].

Research has been conducted separately as well to study the grouping of nearby peers. Beaconing scheme [13] proposes a way to find nearby peers to a given peer through the contact of several beacons, and investigates the case when the number of possible peers is large. The network-aware method [14] uses the prefixes and network information in BGP (Border Gateway Protocol) routing table snapshots to identify clusters that group nearby peers. The property has been explored in [15] that proximate peers exchanging pieces of a file can improve the file sharing efficiency in the BitTorrent network. The paper proposed a scheme to build a proximity-based overlay network, which aims at returning a list containing nearby peers to a downloader. Thus, the scheme in [15] can achieve part of robustness compared with the original BitTorrent system since some peers could be hot-spots.

3 CBT System

In this section, we will present the CBT (Clustered BitTorrent) system, its architecture, the file download process of a peer and functions of system elements, such as the torrent tracker and super-peer. In a BitTorrent-like P2P network that shares content among all participants, each participating peer can upload pieces of a shared file that it holds for other peers to access while simultaneously downloading other pieces. In such a scenario there could be tens of thousands of participants or even more, creating the need for a scalable system that fully utilizes network resources, such as a hierarchically clustered system.

3.1 System Architecture

Figure 1 shows the CBT system architecture. Peers which are close by each other are grouped in individual clusters. An unspecified number of these clusters are then grouped as a Clustered BitTorrent (CBT). When a small number of peers join a torrent, the CBT may only contain a single cluster. This cluster is called as the fundamental cluster, in which the torrent tracker is the cluster head. The CBT may have several to tens of clusters to accommodate a large number of peers. This hierarchical system is composed of a torrent tracker and three types of peers: *seed*, *downloader*, and *super-peer*. The torrent tracker is responsible for collecting the state of every peer in the fundamental cluster and for returning a random list of peers in response to the request of a new arrival to be allowed to join the fundamental cluster. Of the three types of peers, the seed is a peer that shares all the pieces of a file. The downloader is a peer that simultaneously downloads and uploads pieces of a file with others. The task of the super peer is to act like a local tracker, tracking all elements in its cluster. All super-peers are connected to the torrent tracker to form a backbone overlay network.

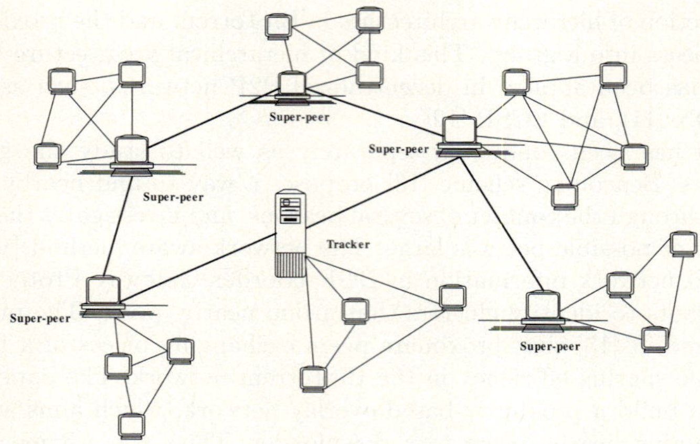

Fig. 1. A hierarchical architecture of CBT in a proximately grouped P2P overlay network

A cluster is a basic component in CBT. To improve the CBT system performance, we construct a cluster such that the included super-peer, seeds and downloaders are relatively close for file sharing. The downloader thus can get a shared file from nearby peers with a high speed and decrease the network traffic. In order to enhance the reliability and scalability of the system, each cluster selects a backup peer, which copies the entire cluster state information periodically from the super-peer. When a super-peer offlines or leaves the network, a selected backup peer takes over as the super-peer.

3.2 File Download Process

A new peer to CBT who aims at downloading a shared file needs to take two steps, the step to join a cluster and the step to exchange data with other peers in the same cluster. In the first step, a peer locally decides which cluster to join in the hierarchical P2P network. Following the same procedure as in the BitTorrent system when a user clicking on the torrent of the shared file, a peer links to the torrent tracker. In CBT, if there is only one cluster (the fundamental cluster), the peer directly joins the cluster and receives a list that contains random peers to connect from the torrent tracker. If there are more than one cluster, the peer receives a list of all super-peers (including the torrent tracker itself) from the torrent tracker. From these super-peers, the new arriving peer selects the nearest super-peer and joins its cluster.

In the second step, the downloader contacts the selected super-peer to connect with random peers in the same cluster to begin the pieces exchange process. The downloader receives the list of peers from the super-peer in the joining cluster rather than from the torrent tracker. Inside a cluster, the file downloading mechanism is exactly the same as in a BitTorrent community [3]. Each peer can apply the *choking* algorithm to provide a cooperative way of file sharing. The pieces exchanged can comply with the *rarest piece first* algorithm to assure more seeds available in the system. The random list of peers to connect with for a downloader maintains the robustness to avoid hot-spots of popular peers that may receive downloading requests from many others, and to make each peer involve in the file uploading and downloading process.

3.3 Functions of the Torrent Tracker and Super-Peers

The torrent tracker in the new proposed CBT system can perform not only the same functions as a tracker in the traditional BitTorrent system i.e., it collects registration information about each peer in the fundamental cluster. Also, the torrent tracker needs to monitor the super-peer backbone network. To get the information of super-peers, the torrent tracker must communicate with them periodically. Because the torrent tracker has much less job than in a traditional BitTorrent, supervising a small part of peers and the backbone super-peers, its overhead is reduced and a tracker server can handle more torrents.

A super-peer acts as a local cluster tracker in the CBT and provides file sharing as well. In a cluster as the cluster head, a super-peer collects and maintains state information of all peers in its cluster to provide information for their random connections. Meanwhile, super-peers exchange their states with the torrent tracker periodically for the cluster management. Super-peers are designed to reduce load on the torrent tracker and they are chosen among peers who are willing to serve as a super-peer. A super-peer can be selected from seeds that have more network resources to be a cluster tracker and are willing to provide the super-peer service. The selected super-peers should be evenly distributed in a global P2P overlay network such that the size of each cluster is similar with a super-peer at its center. Note that although a seed can be selected as a super-peer, it is not true that all seeds will become super-peers.

4 CBT Construction

When a new arrival user clicks on a torrent link to start to download a shared file from CBT, the user as a peer has to decide which cluster to join. In each cluster, a super-peer functioning as a cluster head must be decided too. In this section, we describe the peer joining algorithm for a peer to join a closer cluster, and the super-peer selection algorithm to achieve an even distribution of clusters.

4.1 Peer Joining Algorithm

In the hierarchical CBT system, a new arrival wishes to join a cluster such that the randomly connected peers are in its vicinity. If all peers are within a small distance from the cluster super-peer, which stands at the cluster center, the arriving peer may attain this goal by finding the nearby super-peer and joining its supervised cluster. We present the peer joining algorithm for a peer purposely joining a closer cluster. This is a distributed algorithm and can be applied locally in each client peer.

Before the presentation of the peer joining algorithm, we deliver notations to be used in the paper. Let $H\{p_0, p_1, ..., p_{k-1}\}$ be a set of peers in a network, where k is the number of total peers. Let $P\{sp_0, sp_1, ..., sp_{m-1}\}$ be a set of super-peers that behave as trackers in separate clusters, where m is the number of super-peers and $P \subseteq H$. Let $SP_i\{sp_i, b_0, b_1, ..., b_{n-1}\}$ ($i = 0, 1, ..., m-1$ and n is the number of peers in the cluster SP_i) be a set of peers in the ith cluster. Thus, we have $SP_i \subseteq H$ and $H = SP_0 \cup SP_1 \cup ... \cup SP_{m-1}$. Let u be an arriving peer that needs to find a closer super-peer. The peer joining algorithm returns a super-peer sp_j, such that $\forall q \in P$, $dist(u, sp_j) \leq dist(u, q)$, i.e., sp_j is the closest super-peer to the new peer u and u should join the cluster SP_j. Note that $dist(u, v)$ shows the distance between two peers u and v and it can represent either the RTT (Round-Trip-Time) value, TTL (Time-To- Live) value or the combination of them.

The Peer Joining Algorithm

Instance: The super-peer set P and $|P| = m$, clusters SP_i ($i = 0, 1, ..., m-1$), the peer u.

step 1. The new peer u measures the distance from itself to every super-peer in P, and get distance information $dist(u, sp_i)$ in terms of the RTT value ($dist_{RTT}(u, sp_i)$) and the TTL value ($dist_{TTL}(u, sp_i)$) ($i = 0, 1, ..., m-1$).

step 2. Find a super-peer sp_j from P, such that $sp_j \in P$ and $\forall q \in P$, $dist(u,sp_j) \leq dist(u, q)$, i.e., the super-peer sp_j is the closest super-peer to the peer u in the set P.

step 3. The peer u joins the cluster that contains the super-peer sp_j and $SP_j = SP_j \cup \{u\}$.

The time complexity for this algorithm is $O(m)$.

4.2 Super-Peer Selection Algorithm

A super-peer performs the local tracker functions in a cluster. Once a new cluster has been created, a super-peer must be selected and the candidate peer should show a high tendency to stay online and be a seed. We present a super-peer selection algorithm to solve which seeds will be selected as super-peers.

The super-peer selection algorithm will choose t ($t \geq 1$) seeds to be new super-peers and each new super-peer stands for a new cluster. The t newly constructed clusters together with previous clusters should have a global distribution to contain all peers in a hierarchy P2P system such that the average distance from a peer to its cluster super-peer is short. Let $S\{s_0,s_1,...,s_{r-1}\}$ be a set of current seeds where r is the number of seeds in H and $S \subseteq H$. Given a peer s and the super-peer set P, we define the distance between s and P as $Dist(s, P) = min\{dist(s, sp_0), dist(s, sp_1), ..., dist(s, sp_{m-1})\}$ where $dist(s, sp_i)$ denotes the distance between two peers s and sp_i. The super-peer selection algorithm is represented as follows.

The Super-peer Selection Algorithm

Instance: The super-peer set P and $\mid P \mid = m$, the seed set S and $\mid S \mid = l$, let t be the number of new super-peers to be selected and $t \leq l$.

step 1. Find a seed s_i from S such that $\forall q \in S$, $Dist(s_i, P) \geq Dist(q, P)$, i.e., the seed s_i is the farthest seed in S to the set P of super-peers.

step 2. Select s_i as a new super-peer and it is added to the set P, i.e., $P = P \cup \{s_i\}$ and $\mid P \mid = \mid P \mid +1$, $S = S - \{s_i\}$ and $\mid S \mid = \mid S \mid -1$.

step 3. Repeat step 1 to step 2 until the number of super-peers in the set P increases to $m + t$, i.e., $\mid P \mid = m + t$.

The super-peer selection algorithm takes $O(m + t)$ time per iteration to generate a super-peer. Totally we have t iterations and the time complexity for this algorithm is $O(t \cdot (m + t))$. The described super-peer selection algorithm always chooses a new seed that has the farthest distance to all existing super-peers. This algorithm leads to an even distribution of peers among clusters and achieve a small diameter for each cluster.

5 Performance Evaluation

In this section, we present simulation results to evaluate the original BitTorrent system and our proposed hierarchy system CBT. We designed a simulator to precisely quantify system overhead and effectiveness in terms of *download completion time* in different system sizes. The download completion time is the time required for a peer to complete downloading all pieces of a file starting from the peer joining a P2P network. We highlight that our proposed algorithms, the peer joining algorithms and the super-peer selection algorithms, show their impacts on decreasing the download completion time of peers.

In our simulations, an 8MB file, which is divided into 16 pieces and 512K per piece, was shared from seeds by variable numbers of peers concurrently. The available bandwidth between two peers for data delivery is relevant to their packet overlay distance. A wide bandwidth corresponds to a short distance and a narrow bandwidth corresponds to a long distance. Every peer can connect at most 8 other peers. The system contains 8 seeds initially and we can construct 8 clusters with those 8 seeds as super-peers.

5.1 Impact of Clustering Peers

We compared our hierarchical cluster system CBT, which applies the peer joining algorithm, with a BitTorrent-like system in the simulation environments with different number of peers involved. The average download completion time for each peer and how many peers finish the download job in an interval are two important factors to demonstrate the efficiency of a P2P system. The download performance is evaluated in terms of the percentage of peers to be seeds

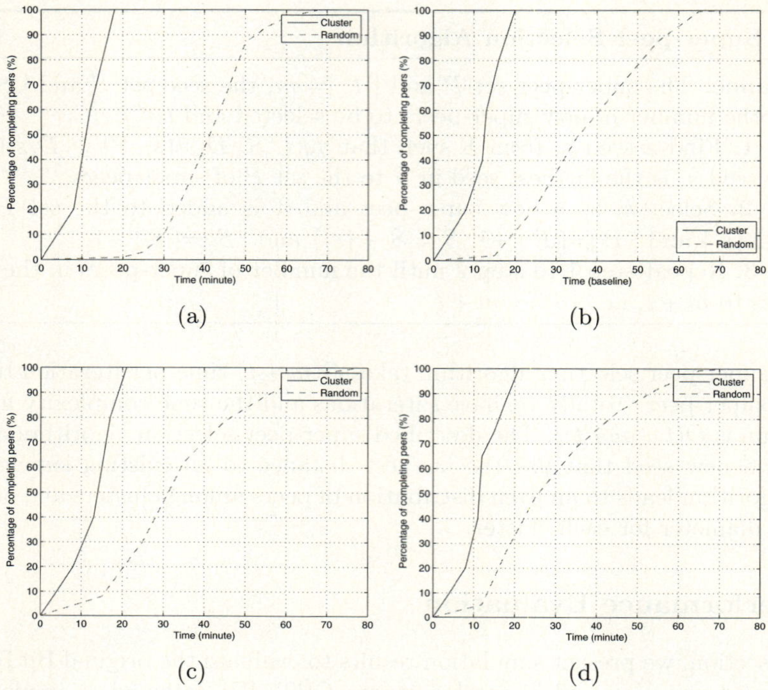

Fig. 2. Percentage of peers to be seeds in different scales in a network (a) 100 peers; (b) 500 peers; (c) 1000 peers; (d) 1500 peers

(Figure 2). The simulation results show that the cluster system (CBT) can achieve a faster download speed and higher file availability than the random-connection BitTorrent network does. In the Figure, the *Cluster* and *Random* curves represent the simulation results of the CBT system and random-connection BitTorrent network respectively.

Figure 2(a)-(d) display the percentage of peers who complete all pieces of a shared file to become seeds in networks of different scales. We chose respectively 100, 500, 1000 and 1500 concurrently running peers to evaluate two compared systems, CBT and BitTorrent. In both systems, the percentage of peers to be seeds increases gradually as the simulation time moves forward. However, the percentage of peers to be seeds in CBT is always higher than that of the random network as in BitTorrent. As denoted in Figure 2(c), the time for the last peer to complete the job is around 20 minutes in the cluster system (CBT) while it is around 80 minutes in the random network, which is 4 times slower. This means that the total download time for all peers completing their jobs is remarkably reduced in our system. In other words, the CBT system obtains a faster speed to render every peer becoming a seed than a random-connection BitTorrent network does.

5.2 Impact of Super-Peer Selection

The super-peer selection shows its impact on the file sharing efficiency in hierarchical P2P networks, like CBT. A well designed super-peer selection algorithm can evenly distribute all peers into distinct clusters. In this subsection, we show that by applying the proposed super-peer selection algorithm, all downloaders can quickly get all pieces of a file compared to the system with random super-peer selection mechanism. We show their comparison results in terms of the maximum (Figure 3(a)) and average (Figure 3(b)) download completion time.

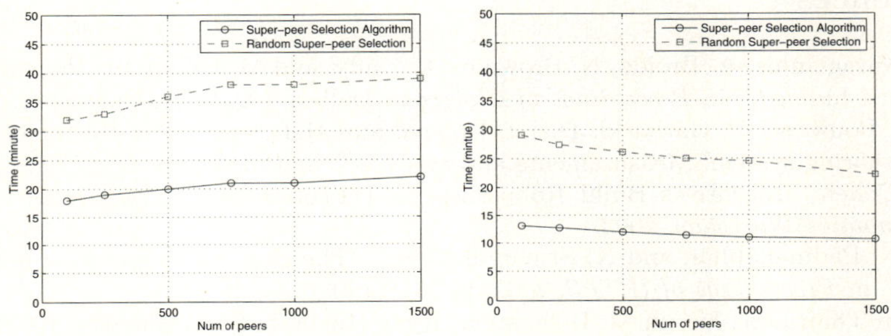

(a) (b)

Fig. 3. Download completion time (a) Maximum download completion time; (b) Average download completion time

Figure 3(a) displays the maximum download completion time in all downloaders given varied number of peers in networks with and without the super-peer selection algorithm. The maximum download completion time denotes the required time for the last peer to hold the entire file. The simulation result depicts that the system employing the super-peer selection algorithm can obtain almost half the time as in the system without such algorithm. In the testing system with 1500 peers, the maximum download completion time is less than 40 minutes in a hierarchical system, which is still less than the time required in a flat random connection network (e.g., BitTorrent) as shown in Figure 2(d).

In Figure 3(b), we plot the average download completion time for varied number of peers in networks with and without the super-peer selection algorithm. The simulation result demonstrates that, with the super-peer selection algorithm, the average download completion time is shorter than that without it. For example, a system applying the proposed super-peer selection algorithm can decrease the average download completion time up to about 50% in the network having 500 peers, and up to about 60% in the network having 1000 peers.

6 Conclusion

To build a scalable large-scale hierarchical overlay network, we propose a novel architecture in the CBT system that employs the peer joining algorithm and super-peer selection algorithm. The first algorithm addresses how to form clusters and the second algorithm determines the local tracker in each cluster. To precisely group a peer into a cluster, we can use the proximity measurements of both the RTT value and TTL value between a pair of peer and super-peer. Such measurements are practical in a real P2P overlay network environment. This paper provides simulation results to demonstrate that the distributed proximity-aware peer clustering method is able to achieve good performance and scalability, and can be used to build a large-scale BitTorrent-like P2P overlay network.

References

1. T. Karagiannis, A. Broido, N. Brownlee, kc claffy, and M. Faloutsos, "Is p2p dying or just hiding?," in *Proceedings of Globecom,* Dallas, TX, USA, November, 2004.
2. J.A. Pouwelse, P. Garbacki, D.H.J. Epema, and H.J. Sips, "The BitTorrent P2P file-sharing system: Measurements and analysis," in *Proceedings of IPTPS*, 2005.
3. B. Cohen, "Incentives Build Robustness in BitTorrent," in *Proceedings of P2P Economics Workshop*, 2003.
4. V. N. Padmanabhan and K. Sripanidkulchai, "The case for cooperative networking," in *Proceedings of IPTPS*, 2002, pp. 178-190.
5. Boon Thau Loo, Joseph M. Hellerstein, Ryan Huebsch, Scott Shenker, Ion Stoica, "Enhancing P2P File-Sharing with an Internet-Scale Query Processor," in *Proceedings of VLDB 2004*, pp.432-443.
6. Christoph Lindemann,Oliver P. Waldhorst, "A Distributed Search Service for Peer-to-Peer File Sharing in Mobile Applications," In *Proceedings of. International Conference on Peer-to-Peer Computing (P2P)*, September 2002, pp. 73-80.
7. K. P. Gummadi, R. J. Dunn, S. Saroiu, S. D. Gribble, H. M. Levy, and J. Zahorjan, "Measurement, Modeling, and Analysis of a Peer-to-Peer File-Sharing Workload," In *Proceedings of the. nineteenth ACM symposium on Operating systems*, ACM Press, 2003, pp. 314-329.
8. L. Guo, S. Chen, Z. Xiao, E. Tan, X. Ding, and X. Zhang, "Measurements, Analysis, and Modeling of BitTorrent-like Systems," in *Proceedings of Internet Measurement Conference 2005 (IMC 2005)*, New Orleans, LA, USA, October, 2005.
9. D. Qiu, and R. Srikant, "Modeling and performance analysis of BitTorrent-like peer-to-peer networks," in *Proceedings of SIGCOMM04*, Aug. 2004, pp. 367-378.
10. FastTrack website, http://www.fasttrack.nu/
11. P. Zheng and C. Wang, "SODON: A High Availability Multi-Source Content Distribution Overlay," in *Proceedings of ICCCN*, Chicago, USA, October, 2004, pp. 87-92.
12. J. Li, and S.T. Vuong, "An Efficient Clustered Architecture for P2P Networks," in *Proceedings of the 18th International Conference. on Advanced Information Networking and Applications*, 2004, pp. 278-283.
13. C. Kommareddy, N. Shankar and B. Bhattacharjee, "Finding close friends on the Internet," in *Proceedings of 9th ICNP*, 2001, pp. 301-309.
14. B. Krishnamurthy and J. Wang, "On Network-Aware Clustering of Web Clients," in *Proceedings of ACM Sigcomm*, Sweden, 2000, pp. 97-110.
15. A. Qureshi, "Exploring Proximity Based Peer Selection in BitTorrent-like Protocol," *MIT 6.824 student project*, 2004, Available at: http://pdos.csail.mit.edu/6.824-2004/reports/asfandyar.pdf.

Distributed Invocation of Composite Web Services

Chang-Sup Park[1] and Soyeon Park[2]

[1] Department of Internet Information Engineering,
University of Suwon, Korea
park@suwon.ac.kr
[2] Department of Computer Science,
University of Illinois at Urbana-Champaign
soyeon@uiuc.edu

Abstract. Web services provide a useful means to integrate heterogeneous applications distributed over the Internet based on XML and Web technologies. This paper presents an approach to execute hierarchically interacting web services efficiently. We provide a system architecture which can distribute invocations of web services over service providers by exploiting intensional XML messages embedding external web service calls. We also propose a greedy heuristic algorithm to generate an efficient strategy of executing web service calls, which can improve overall performance of distributed web service systems on the Internet.

1 Introduction

Web services are emerging as a major technology for integration of heterogeneous applications distributed over the Internet. They are self-contained, modular units of application logic which provide business functionality to other applications via Internet connections based on XML messages and Web protocols. Applications can be assembled from a set of appropriate web services and do not need to be developed from scratch. A new web service also can be composed of existing web services, which function as both clients and servers to the other web services.

Successive composition of web services builds a hierarchical structure of interactions among a large number of web services. By using *intensional* XML messages containing calls to external web services, a web service can delegate the invocation of a web service to the other one. XML-based SOAP message and protocol used for web service invocation involve clients, as well as servers, considerable performance overhead [5, 7]. Since the peer nodes have different capability and performance depending on their computing resource and workload, and communication cost between a pair of peer nodes are also different, it is desirable to select one which can execute the web service invocation most efficiently.

This paper proposes a method for executing invocation of composite web services efficiently which interact hierarchically and can return intensional results. The proposed method effectively distributes the workload on activating and completing web service calls by exploiting intensional XML data as input and output messages of web services. We provide a cost-based optimization technique to enhance overall performance of the

E. Sha et al. (Eds.): EUC 2006, LNCS 4096, pp. 385 – 393, 2006.

entire web service systems. We also utilize user agents to support various kinds of web clients with different capabilities and constraints.

The paper is organized as follows. In Section 2, previous work on web service composition and application of intensional data is provided. System architecture for composite web services exchanging intensional data is presented in Section 3, and an algorithm for generating an efficient invocation strategy for web services considering intensional data is proposed in Section 4. Section 5 draws conclusion with some future work.

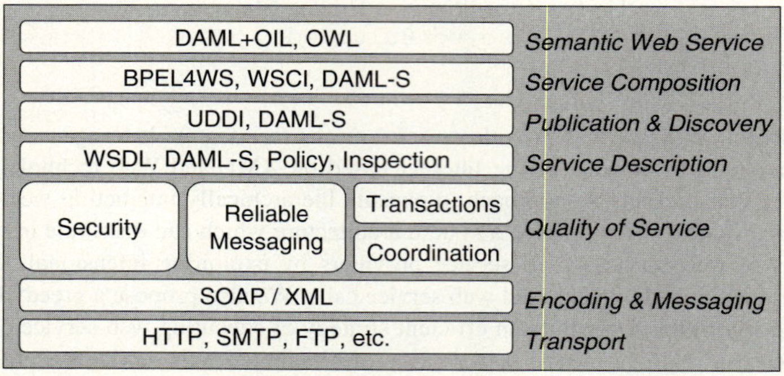

Fig. 1. Web service protocol stack

2 Backgrounds and Related Work

Deployment of web services is supported by various standards including Web Service Description Language (WSDL), Universal Description, Discovery, and Integration (UDDI), and Simple Object Access Protocol (SOAP). These standards respectively support definition of the functions and interfaces of web services, advertisement of web services to the community of potential user applications, and binding for remote invocation of web services [14]. Fig. 1 shows a set of suggested protocols and languages comprising web services technologies.

As a useful means to realize the service-oriented architecture paradigm in software development, extensive researches and developments have been done on the web services including web service composition, semantic description and discovery of web services, and improvement of quality of services [4]. While the business logic of a web service can be implemented in general procedural programming languages, special languages have been proposed in industries which make use of process models to describe web service composition effectively, such as Web Service Flow Language (WSFL), XLang, Business Process Execution Language for Web Services (BPEL4WS), and Web Service Choreography Interface (WSCI) [13]. Researches on the semantic web such as DAML-S ontology language support automated discovery, execution, composition, and interoperation of web service [10]. For enhancing quality of composite web services, L. Zeng et al. [15] proposed a general QoS model for web services and an algorithm for selecting optimal web services in composition of a new service. A. Mani and A. Nagarajan [9] specified various kinds of QoS requirements for web services and techniques for satisfying them.

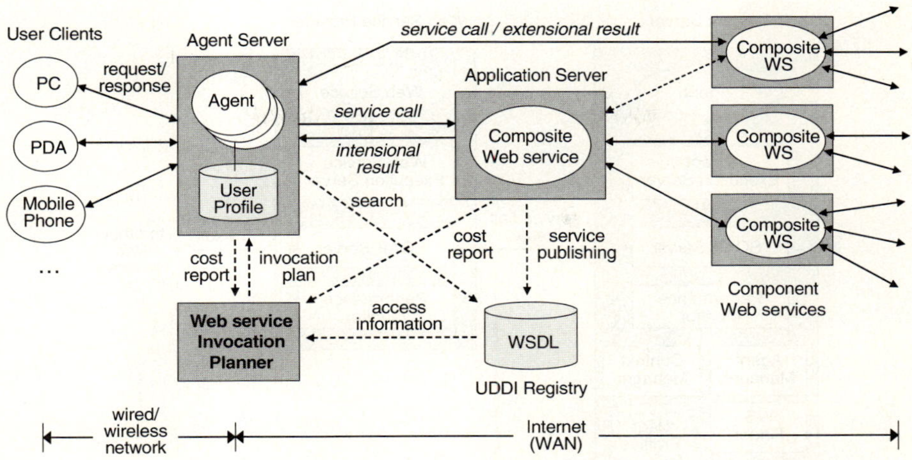

Fig. 2. System architecture

Recently, there have been proposed several approaches and applications exploiting intensional data which embeds calls to external web services [2, 3, 8]. Active XML [2] is a framework for data integration in a peer-to-peer environment which uses web services exchanging intensional data called Active XML documents. Each peer node provides Active XML services allowing clients to access the Active XML documents stored in the peer's repository. Active XML services can be specified as parameterized queries over Active XML documents which contain calls to external web services provided by other peers. Thus, they can be used to search, gather, and integrate data distributed over the peer-to-peer nodes effectively [1].

3 System Architecture

Fig. 2 shows the execution environment of composite web services considered in this paper. Composite web services interact with other web services available on the network. Web services can be accessed and invoked from various user client devices. They usually expect composite web services to complete execution and return *extensional* data as a final result whose type was defined by WSDL since they often have difficulties in materializing intensional data embedding service calls due to limitations such as computing power and security constraints. To support such user clients, we adopt software agents which execute independently of other web services and can handle intensional data instead of the clients [6]. They receive service requests from user clients, find and call appropriate web services, perform deferred invocation of web services contained in intensional results, and deliver final results to the clients. They are deployed at the location near to clients, which select and access an agent through a wired or wireless communication network.

The UDDI registry manages description and access information of published web services and provides clients with an interface to search them. The web service

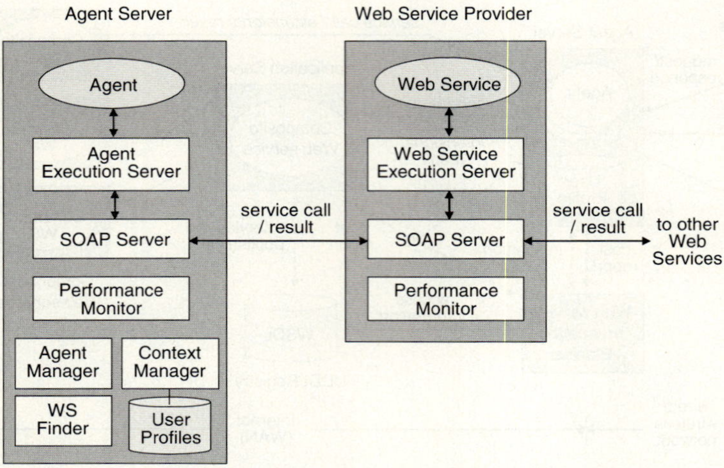

Fig. 3. Architecture of an agent server and a web service provider

invocation planner generates an efficient invocation strategy for web services using access and cost estimation information of web services which are provided by the UDDI registry and the performance monitors in web service providers, respectively. The detailed method is described in Section 4.

The architecture of the agent and web service providers is presented in Fig. 3. Functions of the common components are as follows:

- The SOAP server handles encoding and decoding of SOAP messages sent to and received from external web services.
- The web service/agent execution server performs creation and parsing of intensional XML data exchanged with other web services. It may activate calls to external web services contained in an intensional result returned from a web service and integrate all the partial results into the final extensional or intensional result. If a web service invocation plan is provided, it can be used to determine the web service calls to be activated by the execution server.
- The performance monitor continuously checks the performance and workload of a web service provider or agent server as well as communication costs with other web services in order to estimate execution cost of web services invocation. The estimated costs are delivered to the web service invocation planner and used to generate an optimized invocation plan for web services as shown in Section 4.

The agent server also has additional components:

- The context manager personalizes the use of web services by exploiting predefined user profiles and context information.

- The web services finder uses semantic information of available web services to select and bind appropriate services satisfying user requirements dynamically when they are not statically bound or provided by clients.
- The agent manager manages system resources and the life-cycle of agent instances in the agent server.

4 Web Service Invocation Strategy

In this paper, we assume that intensional XML data can be used as input parameters and output results of the operations in web services. It means that the values of input parameters or execution results can contain calls to other web services, whose caller and invocation time are dynamically determined in run-time. To support the intensional parameters and results, the methods for type definition and type checking of the web service messages need to be extended [11].

The use of intensional data makes it possible that hierarchically interacting web services are invoked and executed in many different ways. For example, a composite web service can return to its caller an intensional result containing calls to a subset of component web services, and for each deferred invocation the caller web service can either execute it by itself or send it to its caller successively. In general, different invocation plans have different execution costs since the peer nodes that can call a web service have different performance, workload, and communication cost to the target web service. Therefore, an optimization strategy is required to generate an efficient invocation plan for involved web services.

In this section, we propose a method for generating a cost-efficient invocation plan for web services to improve the overall performance of distributed execution of web services. For global optimization of web service invocation, it is assumed that access information and invocation costs of web services are available from the UDDI registry and the performance monitor in each peer node, as described in Section 3. The optimization result is offered to all the peer nodes and used to determine whether to execute a service call or transmit intensional parameters/results to other web services.

4.1 Problem Definition

For the simplicity of description, it is assumed that there is no cycle in a sequence of service calls and there exists only one invocation path between any pair of web services. If we denote the set of finite number of vertices representing web services by V_d, the set of directed arcs connecting two web services representing a service invocation by A_d, and the weighting function for an arc in A_d which gives service invocation cost by W_d, the call relations among web services can be represented by a weighted directed tree $DT=(V_d, A_d, W_d)$ which is called *the call definition tree* for web services in this paper.

Given a call definition tree DT, a directed acyclic graph $DT^*=(V_d, A_d^*, W_d^*)$, where A_d^* is the transitive closure of A_d including weighted arcs for all the pair of vertices connected by a path in DT, represents all the possible ways of invoking web services in the intensional result passing approach. Fig. 4-(a) shows an example.

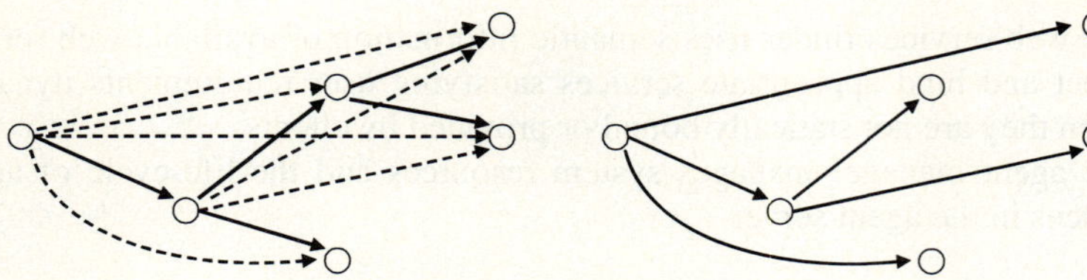

(a) Web services call definition tree DT and DT* (b) An invocation instance

Fig. 4. An example of call definition and invocation of web services

Fig. 5. An invocation plan infeasible for intensional result passing

Considering intensional result passing, we have two observations related with the invocation of web services. First, if a path exists between a pair of web services v and w in DT, an execution instance is possible in which v calls w. In other words, given a path $(s_1, s_2, \ldots, s_n)$ in DT, if an intensional result containing a call to s_n is returned from s_{n-1} to s_1 directly or indirectly, web service s_1 can invoke web service s_n. Second, in a feasible execution instance for a given DT, each web service should be called from one caller web service and the result should be returned to the caller. Specifically, if we let $ET=(V_e, A_e, W_e)$ be a tree representing an invocation plan with intensional result passing, there cannot exist two different vertices s_i and s_j such that both arcs (s_i, s_k) and (s_j, s_k) are contained in A_e for all vertices s_k in V_e. These imply that an invocation plan for web services should be a spanning tree for DT^*, as shown in Fig. 4-(b). Furthermore, we have the following theorem.

Theorem 1. Assume that web services are executed with intensional results and let $P_d(v, w) = (s_1, s_2, \ldots, s_n)$ $(s_1=v, s_n=w)$ be the path from v to w $(v \neq w)$ over the call definition tree DT. In all invocation trees representing execution instances of service invocation, $ET=(V_e, A_e, W_e)$, if $(s_i, s_j) \in A_e$ then $(s_k, s_l) \notin A_e$ for some vertices k and l such that $k < i < l < j$ or $i < k < j < l$ $(1 \leq i, j, k, l \leq n)$ □

Fig. 5 shows an infeasible instance of service invocation which is described in Theorem 1. An *optimal invocation plan* for web services returning intensional results can be defined based on the above properties. Given a call definition tree $DT= (V_d, A_d, W_d)$ for a set of web services, let Γ be a set of spanning trees for DT^* which satisfy the following condition: for all vertices v and w having a path $P_d(v, w)=(s_1, s_2, \ldots, s_n)$ $(s_1=v, s_n=w)$ in DT, if $(s_i, s_j) \in A_e$ then $(s_k, s_l) \notin A_e$ such that $i < k < j < l$ or $k < i < l < j$ $(1 \leq i, j, k, l \leq n)$. If we define

$$W(T) = \sum_{a \in A} W(a)$$

for a weighted tree $T=(V, A, W)$, a tree T_0 such that

$$W(T_0) = \underset{T' \in \Gamma}{Min}(W(T'))$$

is called the optimal invocation plan for the given web services.

On the other hand, intensional parameters containing calls to other web services can be also utilized when data dependency exists between the input and output of a pair of web services invoked from the same web service. For example, assume that a web service *A* invokes other web services *B* and *C*. If the input value of *C* depends on the result of *B*, an execution instance is possible in which *A* invokes *C* with an intensional input parameter containing a call to *B* and *C* invokes *B* on behalf of *A* before it executes its own business logic. Thus, data dependencies among component web services and service calls with intensional parameters make various ways of service invocation possible. This subsequently derives the same kind of optimization problem as the one with the intensional result passing.

4.2 The Proposed Method

A naïve solution for the optimization problem described in Section 4.1 is to search the solution space exhaustively by enumerating all the possible invocation plans and select the one with a minimum execution cost. While the method always results in the optimal solution, it requires huge amount of execution time in investigating all the possible solutions. For example, considering the vertices in the given call definition tree in the increasing order of their depth, we can generate all the invocation plans for the set of vertices whose depths are no deeper than *k* from the ones for the set of vertices whose depths are no deeper than *k*-1. This enumeration process takes exponential time in the number of web services, which means that it is not efficient enough to be applicable for a large number of web services rapidly growing over the Internet. We can use a heuristic search method such as A* algorithms [12] in order to avoid an exhaustive search by pruning an irrelevant part of the search space. However, the worst-case performance cannot be improved from the exhaustive search method.

We propose a greedy algorithm shown in Fig. 6 to produce an efficient invocation plan for the given web services in a more efficient way. To generate an invocation tree, it searches the vertices in the call definition tree in a breadth-first manner. For each vertex visited during search, it selects a vertex as its caller and inserts an arc connecting them in the current invocation tree. For a visited vertex *w*, only the ancestor vertices of *w* can be its caller, which are on the actual invocation path $P_e(r, v)$ from the root vertex *r* to the parent vertex *v* of *w* in the invocation tree. We select one of them by considering the costs of invoking the descendent web services of *w* as well as the cost of invoking *w*. Specifically, denoting the set of descendent vertices of *w* by *Desc*(*w*), we select as the caller of *w* a web service *u* in $P_e(r, v)$ which makes the value of

$$W_d^*(u,w) + \sum_{x \in Desc(w)} \underset{t \in P(r,u)}{Min}\, W_d^*(t,x)$$

minimal, as shown in Fig. 7. This requires that for the vertices in *Desc*(*w*) we should find their callers with minimum costs from a different set of ancestor vertices in $P_e(r, u)$ repetitively, which are determined by the position of the vertex *u* on the path $P_e(r, v)$. Therefore, the time complexity of finding the caller of *w* is $O(|Desc(w)| \cdot l^2)$ where *l*

Greedy Algorithm
Input: a call definition tree $DT = (V_d, A_d, W_d)$
Output: an invocation tree for DT
begin
  Let Q be a queue to store nodes in DT. $Q := \varnothing$;
  Let $ET = (V_e, A_e, W_e)$ be the result invocation tree. $ET := (\{r\}, \varnothing, \varnothing)$;
  while $Q \neq \varnothing$ **do**
    $v :=$ Dequeue(Q);
    Let $(s_1, s_2, \ldots, s_n)$ be the sequence of nodes in $P_e(r, v)$ in ET.
    for each child node w of v in DT **do**
      Find u such that $u = \underset{u' \in P_e(r,v)}{Min}\left(W_d^*((u', w)) + \sum_{x \in Desc(w)} \underset{t \in P_e(r,u')}{Min} W_d^*((t, x)) \right)$.
      $V_e := V_e \cup \{w\}$; $A_e := A_e \cup \{(u, w)\}$; $W_e := W_e \cup \{W_d^*((u, w))\}$;
      Enqueue(Q, w).
    end for;
  end while;
  return ET;
end.

Fig. 6. A greedy algorithm

is the length of $P_e(r, v)$. The algorithm can be improved to $O(|Desc(w)|\cdot l)$ by using more memory space. Specifically, we can avoid a lot of comparisons by considering the vertex u on the path $P_e(r, v)$ in the increasing order of depth, storing the selected minimum-cost callers and their costs for the descendent vertices in $Desc(w)$ for a specific position of the vertex u, and reusing the stored information in the next step with the next position of the vertex u. As a result, if we denote the number of web services by n, the overall optimization algorithm can be executed in

$$O(\textstyle\sum_{i=1}^{h} |Desc(w)| \cdot i \cdot f^{i}) = O(n \log^2 n).$$

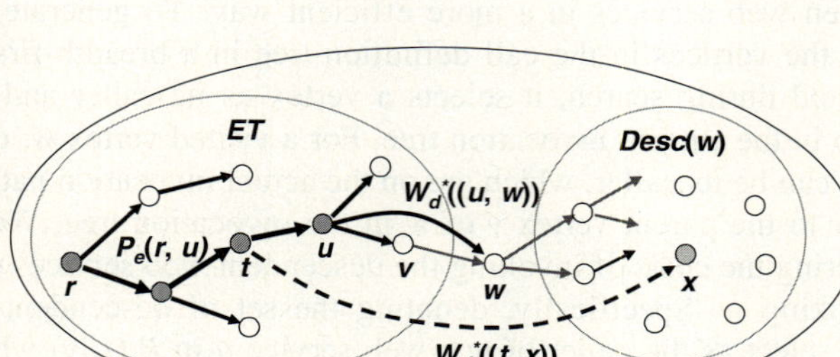

Fig. 7. Selection of the caller of w in the proposed greedy algorithm

5 Conclusion and Future Work

This paper addressed the problem of finding a cost-optimal invocation plan for hierarchically interacting composite web services which can exchange intensional data containing calls to other web services. Considering a large number of ways of invoking web services possible in such environment, we proposed a heuristic algorithm to generate an efficient invocation strategy for web services. It can enhance the overall performance of web services by distributing tasks involved in the activation and completion of the web services effectively over the participating peer nodes.

Future work includes performance evaluation of the proposed method and development of a distributed optimization algorithm for guaranteeing autonomy of the web services. We also plan to study on the efficient invocation strategies for web services exploiting both intensional parameters and results.

References

1. Abiteboule, S., Benjelloun, O. Milo, T., Manolescu, I., Weber, R.: Active XML: A Data-Centric Perspective on Web Services. Technical Report, No. 381. GEMO, INRIA Futurs (2004)
2. Active XML. http://activexml.net/
3. Apache Jelly: Executable XML. http://jakarta.apache.org/commons/jelly/
4. Curbera, F., et al.: The Next Step in Web Services. Communications of the ACM, 46(10) (2003) 29-34
5. Davis, D., Parashar, M.: Latency Performance of SOAP Implementations. Proc. of the 2nd IEEE/ACM International Symposium on Cluster Computing and the Grid (CCGrid2002) (2002) 407-412
6. Jennings, N., Wooldridge, M.: Software Agents, IEE Review, 42(1) (1996) 17-20
7. Kohlhoff, C., Steele, R.: Evaluating SOAP for High Performance Business Applications: Real-Time Trading Systems. Proc. of WWW'03 (2003)
8. Macromedia Coldfusion MX. http://www.macromedia.com/
9. Mani, A., Nagarajan, A.: Understanding Quality of Service for Web Services. IBM developerWorks (2002)
10. McIlraith, S. A., et al.: Semantic Web Services. IEEE Intelligent Systems, 16(2) (2001) 46-53
11. Milo, T., Abiteboul, S., Amann, B., Benjelloun, O., Dang Ngoc, F.: Exchanging Intensional XML Data. Proc. of ACM SIGMOD Conference (2003)
12. Nilsson, N. J.: Artificial Intelligence: A New Synthesis. Morgan Kaufmann Publishers, Inc., San Francisco, CA (1998)
13. Solanki, M., Abela, C.: The Landscape of Markup Languages for Web Service Composition. Technical Report, De Montfort Univ. (2003)
14. Tsalgatidou, A., Pilioura, T.: An Overview of Standards and Related Technology in Web Services. Distributed and Parallel Databases, 12(2) (2002) 135-162
15. Zeng, L., et al.: Quality Driven Web Services Composition. Proc. of Int'l Conf. on WWW (2003) 411-421

System Software for Flash Memory: A Survey

Tae-Sun Chung[1], Dong-Joo Park[2], Sangwon Park[3], Dong-Ho Lee[4], Sang-Won Lee[5], and Ha-Joo Song[6]

[1] College of Information Technoloty, Ajou University, Korea
tschung@ajou.ac.kr
[2] School of Computing, College of Information Science, Soongsil University, Korea
[3] Computer Science & Information Communication Engineering Division, Hankuk University of Foreign Studies, Korea
[4] Department of Computer Science and Engineering, Hanyang University, Korea
[5] School of Information and Communications Engineering, Sungkyunkwan University, Korea
[6] Division of Electronic, Computer and Telecommunication, Pukyong National University, Korea

Abstract. Recently, flash memory is widely adopted in embedded applications since it has several strong points: non-volatility, fast access speed, shock resistance, and low power consumption. However, due to its hardware characteristic, namely "erase before write", it requires a software layer called FTL (Flash Translation Layer). This paper surveys the state-of-the-art FTL software for flash memory. This paper also describes problem definitions, several algorithms proposed to solve them, and related research issues. In addition, this paper provides performance results based on our implementation of each of FTL algorithms.

Keywords: Flash memory, Embedded System, File System.

1 Introduction

Flash memory has inherently strong points compared to traditional hard disk: non-volatility, fast access speed, shock resistance, and low power consumption. Therefore, it has been widely adopted in embedded applications such as USB flash memory, CF card memory, mobile devices, and so on. However, due to its hardware characteristics, flash memory-based applications require special software operations while reading (writing) data from (to) flash memory.

One of basic hardware characteristics of flash memory is that it has an erase-before-write architecture [4]. That is, in order to update a location on a flash memory, it has to be first erased before the new data can be written to it.

Moreover, the erase unit (block) is larger than the read or write unit(sector) [4] resulting in the major performance degradation of the overall flash memory system.

Therefore, the system software called FTL (Flash Translation Layer) should be introduced [1,2,5,8,10,11]. The basic scheme for FTL is as follows. By using the logical to physical address mapping table, if a physical address location

E. Sha et al. (Eds.): EUC 2006, LNCS 4096, pp. 394–404, 2006.

mapped to a logical address is previously written, the input data is written to an empty physical location to which no data have ever been previously written and then the mapping table is updated due to newly changed logical/physical address mapping. This protects one block from being erased per overwrite.

In applying the FTL algorithm to real embedded applications, there are two major considerations: the storage performance and the SRAM memory requirement. With respect to the storage performance, as flash memory has special hardware characteristics as mentioned above, the overall system performance is mainly affected by the write performance. In particular, since the erase cost is much more expensive than the write or read cost, it is very important to minimize the erase operations. Additionally, the SRAM memory required to keep the mapping information is so valuable resource in real embedded applications that if an FTL algorithm requires large SRAM memory, it will increase the product cost of embedded applications, leading to losing the price competitiveness.

In this paper, we survey the-state-of-the-art FTL algorithms. Gal et al. [6] have also provided algorithms and data structures for flash memories. Compared to the work, our work focuses on FTL algorithms and does not discuss file system issues [9,13,7]. we describe the problem definition, the FTL algorithms proposed to solve it, and the related research issues. In addition, we provide performance results based on our implementation of each of FTL algorithms.

This paper is organized as follows. Section 2 describes problem definition. Section 3 shows how the previous FTL algorithms can be classified, and Section 4 presents performance results. Finally, Section 5 concludes the paper.

2 Problem Definition and FTL Functionalities

2.1 Problem Definition

First, we define operation units in the flash memory system as follows.

Definition 1. *A sector is the smallest amount of data which is read or written at a time. That is, a sector is the unit of read or write operations.*

Definition 2. *A block is the unit of the erase operation on flash memory. The size of a block is multiples of the size of a sector.*

Figure 1 shows the software architecture of the flash file system. We will focus on the FTL layer in Figure 1. The file system layer issues a series of read or write commands with a logical sector number each, to read data from, or write data to, specific addresses of flash memory . The logical sector number is converted to a real physical sector number of flash memory by some mapping algorithm in the FTL layer.

Thus, the problem definition of FTL is as follows. We assume that flash memory is composed of n physical sectors and the file system - the upper layer - considers a flash memory as a block-i/o device that is consisted of m logical sectors. Since a logical sector has to be mapped at least one physical sector, the number m is less than or equal to n.

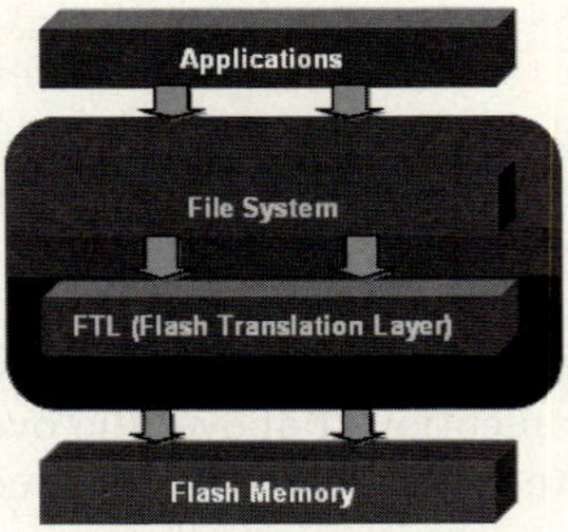

Fig. 1. Software architecture of the flash memory system

Definition 3. *Flash memory is composed of a number of blocks and each block is composed of multiple sectors. Flash memory has the following characteristics: If the physical sector location on flash memory was previously written, it has to be erased in the unit of block before the new data can be overwritten. The FTL algorithm is to produce the physical sector number in flash memory from the logical sector number given by the file system.*

2.2 FTL Functionalities

An FTL algorithm is supposed to provide the following functionalities.

- Logical to physical address mapping: The main functionality of an FTL algorithm is to convert logical addresses from the file system to physical addresses of flash memory.
- Power-off recovery: Even though a sudden power-off occurs during FTL operations, the data structures of the FTL system should be recovered and its consistency has to be maintained.
- Wear-leveling: FTL should include the wear-leveling function to wear down memory blocks as evenly as possible.

3 A Taxonomy for FTL Algorithms

In this section, we suggest a taxonomy of FTL algorithms according to features such as addressing mapping, mapping information management, and the size of the SRAM table.

3.1 Addressing Mapping

Sector Mapping. A naive and intuitive FTL algorithm is the sector mapping [1]. In sector mapping, every logical sector is mapped to a corresponding physical sector. Therefore, if there are m logical sectors seen by the file system, the row size of logical to physical mapping table is m.

For example, Figure 2 shows an example of sector mapping. In the example, we assume that a block is composed of four pages and so there are totally 16 physical pages, where each page is organized into the sector and spare areas. If we also assume that there are 16 logical sectors, the row size of the mapping table is 16. When the file system issues a command - "write some data to LSN (Logical Sector Number) 9", the FTL algorithm writes the data to PSN (Physical Sector Number) 3 according to the mapping table in case the PSN 3 has not been written before.

But, in other case, the FTL algorithm looks for an empty physical sector, writes data to it, and adjusts the mapping table. If there is no empty sector, the FTL algorithm will select a victim block from flash memory, copy back the valid data to the spare free block, and update the mapping table. Finally, it will erase the victim block, which will become the spare block.

In order to rebuild the mapping table after power outage, the FTL algorithm either stores the mapping table to flash memory or records the logical sector number in the spare area on each writes to the sector area.

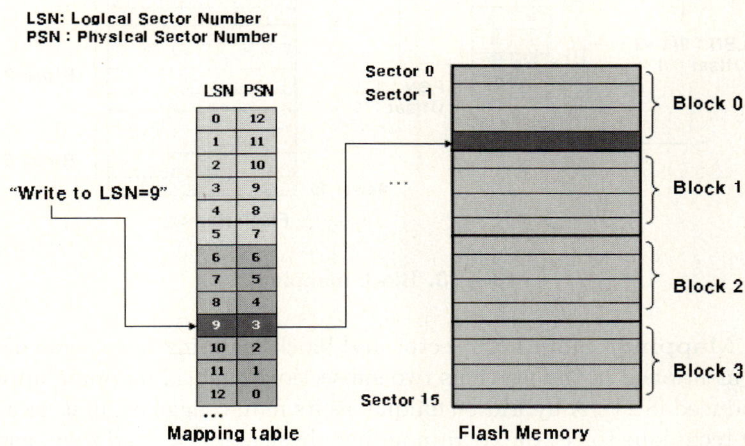

Fig. 2. Sector mapping

Block Mapping. The sector mapping algorithm requires such a large memory space (SRAM) that it is hardly feasible for small embedded systems. For this reason, the block mapping-based FTL algorithms [2,5,10] are proposed. The basic idea of the block mapping algorithms is that the logical sector offset within a logical block is identical to the physical sector offset within the physical block.

In the block mapping scheme, if there are m logical blocks seen by the file system, the row size of logical to physical mapping table is m. Figure 3 shows an example of the block mapping algorithm. Assuming that there are four logical blocks, the row size of the mapping table is four. If the file system issues the command "write some data to LSN 9", the FTL algorithm calculates the logical block number 2(=9/4) and the sector offset 1(=9%4), and then finds physical block number 1 using the mapping table. Since in the block mapping algorithm, the physical sector offset equals the logical sector offset, the physical sector location can be easily determined.

Hence the block mapping algorithm requires a small size of mapping information. However, if the file system issues writes with the same LSNs many times, the FTL algorithm has to perform the copy and erase operations frequently, leading to severe performance degradation.

For rebuilding the mapping table, the FTL algorithm records the logical block number in the spare area of the first page of the physical block.

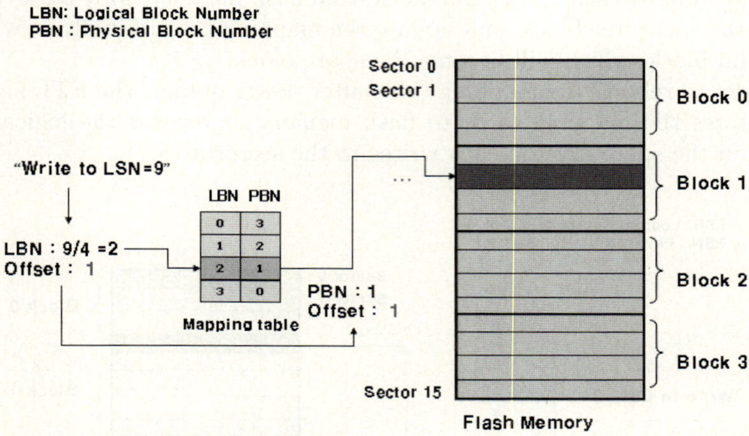

Fig. 3. Block mapping

Hybrid Mapping. Since both sector and block mapping have some disadvantages as mentioned in the previous two subsections, hybrid mapping approaches are introduced [8,11]. A hybrid technique, as its name suggests, first uses a block mapping technique to get the corresponding physical block , and then, uses a sector mapping technique to find an available empty sector within the physical block.

Figure 4 shows an example of the hybrid technique. When the file system issues the command "write some data to LSN 9", the FTL algorithm calculates the logical block number 2(=9/4) for the LSN, and then, finds the physical block number 1 from the mapping table. After getting the physical block number, the FTL algorithm allocates an empty sector for the update. In the example, since the first sector of the pysical block 1 is empty, the data is written to the first sector location. In this case, since the two logical and physical sector offsets(i.e., 2 and 1, respectively) differ from each other, the logical sector number 9 should be written to the spare area in page 1 of the physical block 1. For rebuilding the mapping table, not only this information but also the logical block numbers have to be recorded in the spare areas of the physical blocks.

When reading data from flash memory, the FTL algorithm first finds the physical block number from the mapping table using the given LSN, and then,

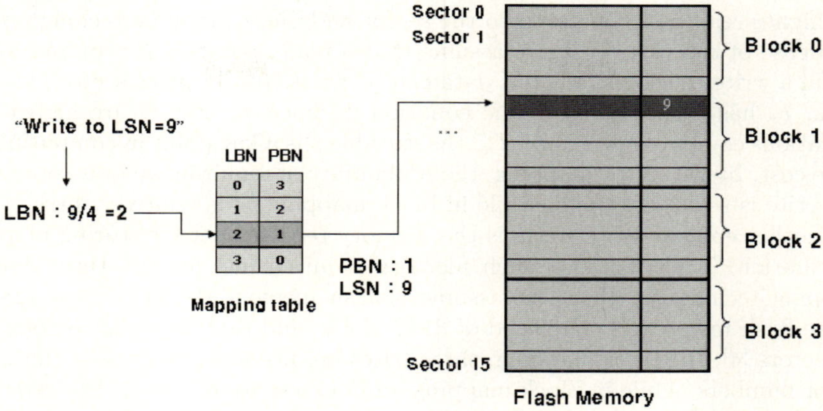

Fig. 4. Hybrid mapping

by reading the logical sector numbers from the spare areas of the physical block, it can get the most recent value for requested data.

Comparison. We compare the performance of FTL algorithms in two perspectives: file system- issued read/write performance and memory requirement for storing mapping information.

The read/write performance of an FTL algorithm can be measured by the number of flash I/O operations (read, write, and erase), since the read/write performance is I/O-bounded. We assume that the mapping table of an FTL algorithm is maintained in SRAM, and the access cost of the mapping table is zero, then the read and write costs can be computed by the following two equations, respectively.

$$C_{read} = xT_r \tag{1}$$

$$C_{write} = p(T_r + T_w) + (1 - p)(T_r + (T_e + T_w) + T_c) \tag{2}$$

C_{read} and C_{write} above are the costs of read and write issued from the file system layer, respectively, and T_r, T_w, and T_e are the costs of read, write, and erase processed in the flash memory layer. T_c is the cost of copies needed to move sectors within a block to other free block before erasing and to copy back after erasing. p is the probability that a write command does not incur any erase operation. We assume that the input logical sector within the logical block is mapped to one physical sector within a physical block.

In the sector and block mapping techniques, the variable x in the equation 1 has 1, since the sector to be read can be found directly from the mapping table. However, in the hybrid technique, the value of the variable x is in the range of $1 \leq x \leq n$, where n is the number of sectors within a block. This is because the requested data can be read only after scanning the logical sector numbers stored in the spare areas of a physical block. Thus, the hybrid mapping scheme has higher read cost compared to the sector and block mapping techniques.

In case of the write cost, we assume that a read operation is required before actual a write to see if the input data can be written to in-place sector location. Thus, T_r has to be added in the equation 2. Since T_e and T_c are higher cost operations compared to T_r and T_w, the variable p is a key point in computing the write cost. In the sector mapping, the probability of requiring an erase operation per write is relatively small, while in block mapping, it is relatively high.

Another comparison criteria is the memory requirement for storing mapping information. Table 1 shows such memory requirements for the three address mapping techniques. Here, we assume a flash memory device of size 128MB, where flash memory is composed of 8192 blocks and each block is composed of 32 sectors [4]. In sector mapping, three bytes are needed to represent the whole sector numbers, while in block mapping, only two bytes are needed to represent the whole block numbers. An hybrid mapping requires three bytes for block mapping and for sector mapping within a block, respectively. From the Table 1 block mapping requires the smallest SRAM memory as expected.

Table 1. Memory requirement for mapping information

	Bytes for addressing	Total
Sector mapping	3 Bytes	3B * 8192* 32 = 768KB
Block mapping	2 Bytes	2B *8192= 16KB
Hybrid mapping	(2+1) Bytes	2B*8192+1B*32*8192 = 272KB

3.2 Managing Address Mapping Information

The most important meta information in the FTL algorithms is the address mapping information. In order to be able to rebuild the address mapping table during a power-on process, the address mapping information should not be lost in the sudden power-offs, and therefore it has to be persistently kept somewhere in flash memory. We can classify the techniques for storing the mapping information on flash memory into two categories: map block method and per block method.

Map Block Method. A map block method stores the address mapping information into some dedicated blocks of flash memory called map blocks. If we use one map block, erase operations on the map block happens so frequently. Hence we use several map blocks in order to lessen such frequent erases.

In the case that the mapping information may be changed due to writes issued by the file system, the above recording job will be done. When performing the recording job, if there is no unused sector in the map blocks pool, erase operations on all the map blocks have to be executed to make some free map blocks. The mapping table can be cached in SRAM for fast mapping lookups. In this case, the mapping table has to be rebuild in SRAM by reading the latest sector of the latest map block from flash memory during a power-on process.

Per Block Method. The address mapping information can be stored to each physical block of flash memory. Differently from the map block method, logical block numbers are stored in the spare area of the first sector of each physical block. In addition, in order to to keep the mapping from a logical sector number to the sectors in a physical block, the logical sector numbers are recorded in each sector in the block. When rebuilding the mapping table due to power-off, both the logical block numbers and logical sector numbers in the spare areas of flash memory are used.

3.3 RAM Table

The size of RAM is very important in designing the FTL algorithm because it is a key factor in overall system cost. The smaller the RAM size, the lower the system cost. If a system has enough RAM, the performance can be improved. The FTL algorithms have their own RAM structures and we can classify the FTL algorithms according to their RAM structures. RAM is used to store following information of the FTL algorithms.

- Logical to physical mapping information: The major usage of RAM is to store the logical to physical mapping information. By accessing the RAM information, the physical flash memory location for reading or writing data can be found efficiently.
- Free memory space information: Once free memory space information in flash memory is stored in RAM, an FTL algorithm can manage the memory space without further flash memory accesses.
- Information for wear-leveling: The wear-leveling information can be stored in RAM. For example, the erase count of flash memory blocks may be stored in RAM.

4 Experimental Evaluation

For the simulation, we got various access patterns that the FAT file system [3] issues to the block device driver when it gets a file write request.

We will report performance results over two representatives of access patterns in embedded applications: Symbian [12] and Digicam. The first one is the workload of 1M byte file copy operation in Symbian operating system and the second one is the workload of digital cameras.

Figure 5-(a) shows the total elapsed time for the Digicam pattern. The x axis is the test count and the y axis is the total elapsed time in millisecond. At first, flash memory is empty, and flash memory is occupied as the iteration count increases. The result shows that the Log scheme shows the best performance. It is interesting that the Log scheme shows the better performance than the sector mapping which requires a lot of SRAM resources for mapping. We think the reason is that the workload of the Digicam is mostly composed of sequential write operations and the Log scheme operates almost ideally in the sequential write patterns.

Since the sector scheme uses a LSN-to-PSN mapping table, it has to update the mapping table each time overwrite operations are performed. This means it has to write the change in the mapping table to flash memory whenever a logical sector is overwritten, which is not happen so many times in Log scheme that uses a LBN-to-PBN mappings. In the experiment, we configured that there are 32 sectors in a block. Therefore, LSN-to-PSN mapping table have to be updated approximately 30 times often than the LBN-to-PBN mapping. Therefore, even though the sector mapping scheme incurs less erase operations (Figure 5-(b)), it has longer overall execution time than the Log scheme.

The SSR and Mitsubishi techniques show the poor performance compared to other techniques. We think the main reason is that the one logical block is mapped to only one physical block in the SSR and Mitsubishi techniques. In particular, when erasing a block in the SSR technique, since many valid sectors exist in the erased block, many copy operations are necessary and the probability that the erased block will be erased again in the future is very high. The Log scheme shows the better performance than FMAX. It is because, we think, that merging algorithm of FMAX is poor than that of the Log scheme in our workload.

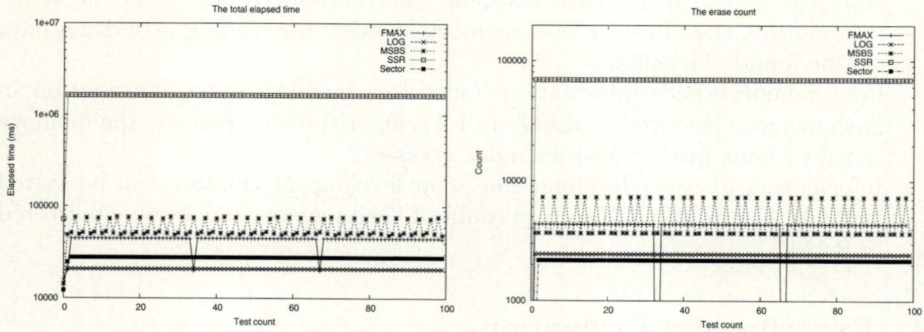

(a) The total elapsed time (b) Erase counts

Fig. 5. Digicam: The total elapsed time and erase counts

Figure 5-(b) shows the erase count. The result is similar to the result of the total elapsed time. This is because the erase count is the most dominant factor in the overall system performance. [4] says that the running time ratio of read (1 page), write (1 page), and erase (1 block) is 1:7:63 approximately. We can see that the sector mapping requires the smallest erase counts. In sector mapping scheme, a logical sector can be mapped to any free physical sector. Most of the blocks are either full of invalid blocks or full of valid blocks. Therefore merge operations between blocks with valid sectors are uncommon, causing less erase operations.

Figure 6-(a) and Figure 6-(b) show the performance result in the Symbian workload. In the Symbian workload, the sector mapping shows the best

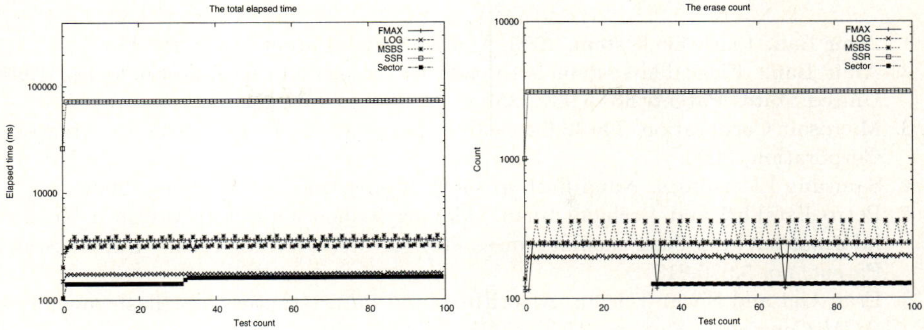

(a) The total elapsed time (b) Erase counts

Fig. 6. Symbian: The total elapsed time and erase counts

performance. This result comes from the fact that the workload of Symbian, in contrast to Digicam, has many random write operations. Thus, in the Log scheme, the erase operation occurs frequently compared to the sector mapping.

5 Conclusion

In this paper, we have surveyed the state of the art FTL algorithms. First, we classified the FTL algorithms into three categories according to the address mapping method: sector, block, and hybid. In most cases, the sector mapping method shows the best performance but it requires much memory resources. The block mapping technique requires the smallest memory resources but its performance is the worst. Thus, the hybrid technique is proposed. In addition, the meta information storage techniques are classified into two categories: per block method and map block method. Finally, various FTL techniques differ in using RAM tables. We implemented various FTL algorithms such as FMAX, sector mapping, Log scheme, SSR, and Mitsubishi, and showed the performance results. The Log scheme shows good performance in the sequential access patterns. We can see that the workload of flash memory system has great impact on the overall performance of a flash memory system. For a further study, we want to design an FTL algorithm which has best performance while requiring smallest resources by exploiting the access patterns of file systems.

Acknowledgment

This work was supported in part by MIC & IITA through IT Leading R&D Support Project (2006-S-040-01) and was supported partly by the Ministry of Information and Communication, Korea under the ITRC support program supervised by the Institute of Information Technology Assessment, IITA-2005-(C1090-0501-0019), and also supported partly by Seoul R&BD Program(10660).

References

1. Amir Ban. Flash file system, 1995. United States Patent, no. 5,404,485.
2. Amir Ban. Flash file system optimized for page-mode flash technologies, 1999. United States Patent, no. 5,937,425.
3. Microsoft Corporation. Fat32 file system specification. Technical report, Microsoft Corporation, 2000.
4. Samsung Electronics. Nand flash memory & smartmedia data book, 2004.
5. Petro Estakhri and Berhanu Iman. Moving sequential sectors within a block of information in a flash memory mass storage architecture, 1999. United States Patent, no. 5,930,815.
6. Eran Gal and Sivan Toledo. Algorithms and data structures for flash memories. *ACM Computing Surveys*, 37(2), 2005.
7. A. Kawaguchi, S. Nishioka, and H. Motoda. Flash Memory based File System. In *USENIX 1995 Winter Technical Conference*, 1995.
8. Jesung Kim, Jong Min Kim, Sam H. Noh, Sang Lyul Min, and Yookun Cho. A space-efficient flash translation layer for compactflash systems. *IEEE Transactions on Consumer Electronics*, 48(2), 2002.
9. M. Resenblum and J. Ousterhout. The Design and Implementation of a Log-structured File System. *ACM Transactions on Computer Systems*, 10(1), 1992.
10. Takayuki Shinohara. Flash memory card with block memory address arrangement, 1999. United States Patent, no. 5,905,993.
11. Bum soo Kim and Gui young Lee. Method of driving remapping in flash memory and flash memory architecture suitable therefore, 2002. United States Patent, no. 6,381,176.
12. Symbian. http://www.symbian.com, 2003.
13. M. Wu and W. Zwaenepoel. eNVy: A Non-Volatile, Main Memory Storage System. In *International Conference on Architectural Support for Programming Languages and Operating Systems*, 1994.

Loop Striping: Maximize Parallelism for Nested Loops*

Chun Xue[1], Zili Shao[2], Meilin Liu[1], Meikang Qiu[1], and Edwin H.-M. Sha[1]

[1] University of Texas at Dallas
Richardson, Texas 75083, USA
{cxx016000, mxl024000, mxq012100, edsha}@utdallas.edu
[2] Hong Kong Polytechnic University
Hung Hom, Kowloon, Hong Kong
cszlshao@comp.polyu.edu.hk

Abstract. The majority of scientific and Digital Signal Processing (DSP) applications are recursive or iterative. Transformation techniques are generally applied to increase parallelism for these nested loops. Most of the existing loop transformation techniques either can not achieve maximum parallelism, or can achieve maximum parallelism but with complicated loop bounds and loop indexes calculations. This paper proposes a new technique, *loop striping*, that can maximize parallelism while maintaining the original row-wise execution sequence with minimum overhead. Loop striping groups iterations into stripes, where a stripe is a group of iterations in which all iterations are independent and can be executed in parallel. Theorems and efficient algorithms are proposed for loop striping transformations. The experimental results show that loop striping always achieves better iteration period than software pipelining and loop unfolding, improving average iteration period by 50% and 54% respectively.

1 Introduction

Nested loops are the most critical sections in applications such as signal processing, image processing, fluid mechanics, and weather forecasting. To improve the performance on these applications, parallel architectures and systems are generally used. How to generate code for nested loops on parallel architectures is a challenging problem for compilers. This paper proposes a new technique, loop striping, that can achieve maximum parallelism and keep the original row-wise execution sequence with minimum overhead.

Existing loop transformation methods, like wavefront processing[2,8], achieve higher level of parallelism for nested loops by changing the execution sequence of the nested loops. This sequence of execution is commonly associated with a schedule vector s, also called an ordering vector, which affects the order in which

* This work is partially supported by TI University Program, NSF EIA-0103709, Texas ARP 009741-0028-2001, and NSF CCR-0309461, NSF IIS-0513669, Microsoft, USA.

E. Sha et al. (Eds.): EUC 2006, LNCS 4096, pp. 405–414, 2006.

the iterations are performed. The iterations are executed along hyperplanes defined by s.

Different methods have different means in the selection of an appropriate schedule vector. Among these type of loop transformation methods, unimodular transformation [5,13,12] is one of the major techniques. It unifies loop transformations like loop skewing [14], loop interchange [3], and loop reversal to achieve a particular goal, such as maximizing parallelism or data locality. The sequence of execution as well as the loop bounds and loop indexes are all changed as the result of unimodular transformation. Another technique, Multi-Dimensional retiming [11], restructures the loop body to achieve full parallelism within an iteration. Then the actual scheduling of the fully-parallelized iterations can be done by unimodular transformation [13]. More researches have been building on top of unimodular transformations. Anderson and Lam [4] apply unimodular transforms to loop nests to increase the granularity of parallelism, find the maximum degree of communication-free parallelism across loops, and heuristically introduce communication where necessary.

Unimodular transformation adds overhead to the transformed loops while achieving higher level of parallelism. First, non-linear index bound checking needs to be conducted on the new loop bounds to assure correctness. Second, loop indexes become more complicated compared to the original loop indexes, and additional instructions are needed to calculate each new index so that the actual array values stored in memory can be correctly referenced.

To have simple loop bounds and simple loop indexes while achieving the maximum parallelism, we propose a new loop transformation technique, *loop striping*. Loop striping selects iterations into stripes, where a stripe is a group of iterations in which all the iterations are independent and can be executed in parallel. With proper selection of iterations to be placed into the same stripe, loop striping ensures that all the iterations in the same stripe can be executed in parallel.

While both loop striping and loop unfolding group iterations to increase parallelism, loop striping is more advanced than loop unfolding [10] for nested loops. Loop unfolding only unfolds iterations within the same dimension, and it does not change the dependencies between iterations. As a result, there is a lower bound of iteration period which is the shortest average time to schedule an iteration. Unfolding can only reach this lower bound. We will show that loop striping can transform nested loops in such a way that we can always group iterations into stripes, where there is no dependency between any two iterations in the same stripe. Hence, there is no lower bound on iteration period for loop striping. We conduct experiments on a set of digital filters with two dimensional loops. The experiment results show that loop striping always achieves better iteration period than loop unfolding and software pipelining.

The remainder of this paper is organized as follows. Section 2 introduces basic concepts and definitions. The theorems and algorithms are proposed in

Section 3. Experimental results and concluding remarks are provided in Section 4 and 5, respectively.

2 Basic Concepts and Definitions

In this section, we introduce some basic concepts which will be used in the later sections. First we introduce the model and notion that we use to analyze the nested loops. Second, several related loop transformation techniques are explained.

Multi-dimensional Data Flow Graph is used to model loops and is defined as follows. A *Multi-dimensional Data Flow Graph (MDFG)* $G = \langle V, E, d, t \rangle$ is a node-weighted and edge-weighted directed graph, where V is the set of computation nodes, $E \subseteq V * V$ is the set of dependence edges, d is the multi-dimensional delays between two nodes, also known as dependence vectors, and t is the computation time of each node. We use d(e) = (d.x, d.y) as a general formulation of any delay shown in a two-dimensional DFG (2DFG).

An *iteration* is the execution of each node in V exactly once. The computation time of the longest path without delay is called the *iteration period.* Iterations are identified by a vector i, equivalent to a MD index. An iteration is associated to a static schedule. A static schedule of a loop is repeatedly executed for the loop. A static schedule must obey the precedence relations defined by the subgraph of an MDFG, consisting of edges without delays. If a node v at iteration j, depends on a node u at iteration i, then there is an edge e from u to v, such that d(e) = j - i. An edge with delay (0,0, ... , 0) represents a data dependence within the same iteration. A legal MDFG must have no zero-delay cycles.

Iterations are represented as integral points in a Cartesian space, called *iteration space* , where the coordinates are defined by the loop control indexes. Such points are identified by a vector $\widehat{i}$, equivalent to a multi-dimensional index. The components of $\widehat{i}$ are arranged from the outermost loop control index to the innermost one, always implying a row-wise execution.

A *schedule vector s* is the normal vector for a set of parallel equitemporal hyperplanes that define a sequence of execution of an iteration space. By default, a given nested loop is executed in a row-wise fashion, where the schedule vector $s = (1, 0)$.

Unfolding is also called unrolling or unwinding, is widely used in compiler design [1]. A schedule of unfolding factor f can be obtained by unfolding G f times. That is, a total of f iterations are scheduled together, and the schedule is repeated every f iterations. We say the unfolded MDFG $G_f = (V_f, E_f, d_f, t_f)$ is a MDFG obtained by unfolding G f times. Set V_f is the union of $V^0, V^1, ..., V^{f-1}$.

One cycle in G_f consists of all computation nodes in V_f. The period during which all computations in a cycle are executed is called *cycle period.* The Cycle period C(G_f) of G_f equals $\max\{t_f(p_f) \mid d_f(p_f)=0 \ \forall \ p_f \text{ in } G_f\}$. During a cycle period of G_f, f iterations of G are executed. Thus, the *iteration period* of G_f is equal to C(G_f)/f, in other words, the average computation time for each iteration in G. For the original MDFG G, the iteration period is equal to C(G). An algorithm can find C(G) for a MDFG in time $O(|E|)$[9].

The *iteration bound* is defined to be the maximum time-to-delay ratio of all cycles,
$B(G) = \max T(l)/D(l)$ for all cycle l in G
where $T(l)$ is the sum of computation time in cycle l, and $D(l)$ is the sum of delay counts in cycle l. A schedule is rate-optimal if the iteration period of this schedule equals its iteration bound. The value $B(G)$ can be found in time $O(|V||E|log|V|)$, when the total number of delays and total computation time are upper bounded by $O(|V|k)$, where k is a constant[6]. For a unit-time DFG, it takes only time $O(|V||E|)$ to compute the bound $B(G)$ [7].

When there is no resource constraint and a sufficiently large number of iterations are executed together, there is always a static schedule that can achieve the rate-optimality. For a general-time DFG, Parhi and Messerschmitt [10] showed that if the unfolding factor is the least common multiple of the delay counts of all cycles, a rate-optimum schedule can be achieved.

Unimodular is a loop transformation technique that unify all combinations of loop interchange or permutation, skewing and reversal. It can generate an optimal solution in compilation for parallel machines that which loop transformations, and in what order, should be applied to achieve a particular goal, such as maximizing parallelism or data locality [13]. The derivation of the optimal compound transformation consists of two steps. The first step puts the loops into a canonical form, namely a fully permutable loop nest. And the second step then transforms the fully permutable loop nest to exploit according to the target architecture. Specifically, to maximize the degree of fine-grain parallelism, wavefront transformation is used in the second step.

3 Loop Striping

In this section, we propose a new loop transformation technique, *loop striping*. First the basic concepts are introduced, and the property and theorems related to loop striping are discussed. Then the procedures and algorithm to transform the loops after striping are presented. In the following, theorems and algorithms are presented with two dimensional notations, which can be easily extended to multi-dimensions.

3.1 Basic Concepts

In this section, we introduce the theoretical foundations for the proposed loop transformation technique, loop striping.

Definition 1. *A stripe is a group of iterations that there is no dependency between any two of the iterations.*

We call a nested loop after loop striping transformation as a striped nested loop. To group iterations into stripes, we need to use loop striping technique defined as follows. Given an MDFG G = (V, E, d, t) representing an n-dimensional nested loop, *loop striping with vector s = (f,g)* will group iterations into stripes. Two important variables for the loop striping technique, f and g, are defined in the following.

Definition 2. *Striping factor f determine the number of iterations that will be placed into the same stripe. Striping offset g determine the direction of the loop striping, where iteration (1,0) and iteration (0,g) will be placed in the same stripe if the striping factor is 2.*

Loop Striping groups multiple iterations into one stripe to be scheduled together. With a carefully selected striping offset g, we can group the iterations where there are no dependency among them. In this way, there is no lower bound on the iteration period given no resource constraint and sufficiently large number of iterations. This is the key difference between loop striping and loop unfolding. In the following section, we will prove that we can always find such a striping offset g, so that there is no dependency among the striped iterations. Before we prove that we can always find a proper striping offset g, we will first introduce the following lemma.

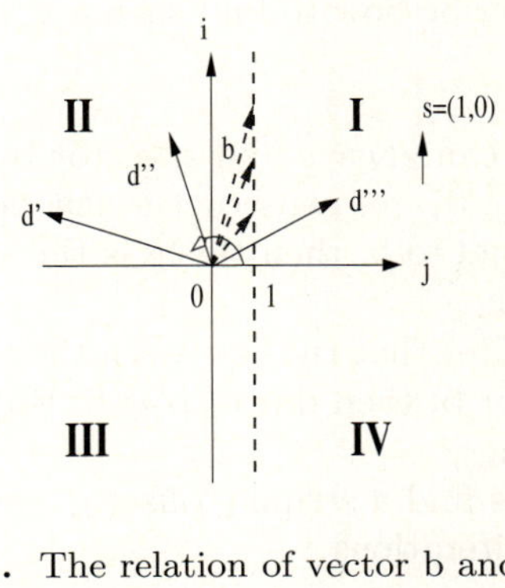

Fig. 1. The relation of vector b and d ∈ D

Lemma 1. *Given a MDFG G = (V, E, d, t) representing an n-dimensional nested loop, and set D is the set that* $\forall$ *d* $\in$ *D, d(e)* $\neq$ *(0,0). we can always find a vector b=(x,1), such that* $\forall$ *d* $\in$ *D, d* $\cdot$ *b > 0.*

Proof. We will prove by finding such a vector b(x,1). Since we are given a MDFG that represents an n-dimensional nested loop, by default, this nested loop can be executed in a row-wise fashion.
$\Rightarrow$ The schedule vector s=(1,0) is always realizable.
$\Rightarrow \forall$ d $\in$ D, d $\cdot$ s $\geq$ 0.
$\Rightarrow$ All d $\in$ D stay in region I and II only as shown in Figure 1.

With this understanding, we will find the vector b=(x,1) as following. We will first sort all d $\in$ D by its angle with j axis. Let d' be such a d $\in$ D, such that the angle between d' and j axis is the largest. We can easily find a vector b=(x,1) that can satisfy d' · b > 0, this same vector will be able to satisfy ∀ d ∈ D, d · b > 0. Here is how we find such a b=(x,1):

Let d'=(d'_i, d'_j), since b=(x,1) and d' · b > 0
$\Rightarrow d'_i \cdot x + d'_j \cdot 1 > 0 \Rightarrow d'_i \cdot x > -d'_j \Rightarrow x > -d'_j/d'_i$
since x > 0 and x is an integer,

$$x = \begin{cases} -\lceil d'_j/d'_i \rceil + 1 & d'_j < 0 \\ 1 & d'_j = 0 \\ 0 & d'_j > 0 \end{cases}$$

With this selection of x, we know that we can always find such a b=(x,1), that ∀ d ∈ D, d · b > 0.

Theorem 1. *Given an MDFG G = (V, E, d, t) representing an n-dimensional nested loop, a striping offset g can always be found so that there is no dependence between the striped iterations.*

Proof. By definition, assuming a striping factor of 2, for an striping offset g, iteration (1,0) and iteration (0,g) will be in the same stripe. To prove that we can always find such a g that iteration (1,0) and iteration (0,g) have no dependency between them, first we describe how to find such a g, and then prove that g fits our criteria.

Step 1, find g:

Following Lemma 1, we can always find a vector b=(x,1), such that d(e) · b > 0 for every d(e) ≠ (0,0,...,0), we construct a new vector c=(1,g) where g=x, so that vector c is orthogonal to b. then this g is the striping offset.

Step 2, g fits our criteria:

If there is such a delay d'(e) that runs between the iterations in a stripe, then d'(e) is orthogonal to vector b, then d'(e) · b = 0. But we know for every d(e), d(e) · b > 0. Contradiction.

Therefore, we can always find a striping offset g such that there is no dependence between the striped iterations.

After the loop striping transformation, the new program can still keep row-wise execution, which is an advantage over the loop transformation techniques that need to do wavefront execution and need to have extra instructions to calculate loop bounds and loop indexes.

3.2 The Loop Striping Technique

In this section, we present how to implement the loop striping transformation technique. An algorithm to generate the code for loop striping is presented. Based on a specific architecture, considering the resource constraints, we can find a corresponding loop striping factor and loop striping offset that can achieve the desired parallelism.

We first present some notations. Assume that the original nested loop and the loop striping transformed loop are in the following format:

Original Nested Loop:	Loop Striping transformed Loop:
for $I^1 = L_o^1$ to U_o^1	for $I^1 = L_n^1$ to U_n^1 step by S_n^1
for $I^2 = L_o^2$ to U_o^2	for $I^2 = L_n^2$ to U_n^2 step by S_n^2
...	...
$B_o(I^1, I^2, I^3, \ldots, I^i)$	$B_n(I^1, I^2, I^3, \ldots, I^i)$
...	...
end for	end for
end for	end for

where $I^1, I^2, I^3, \ldots, I^i$ are the loop indexes, $L_o^1, L_o^2, L_o^3, \ldots, L_o^i$ are the minimum values for each of the loop indexes in the original loop, $U_o^1, U_o^2, U_o^3, \ldots, U_o^i$ are the maximum values for each of the loop indexes in the original loop, and $B_o(I^1, I^2, I^3, \ldots, I^i)$ is the function that represent the loop body of the original loop with $I^1, I^2, I^3, \ldots, I^i$ as the input parameters. For the striped nested loop, we use the same notations except that subscript n replaces the subscript o.

Using these notations, the algorithm that transform the original nested loop into the new nested loop after striping is given as Algorithm 3.1.

Algorithm 3.1. The code generation for loop striping

Require: DFG $G = \langle V, E, d, t \rangle$, the striping factor f, the original loop body function $B_o(I^1, I^2, I^3, \ldots, I^i)$, the original loop bounds $L_o^1, L_o^2, \ldots, U_o^1, U_o^2, \ldots$
Ensure: the new loop body function $B_n(I^1, I^2, \ldots, I^i)$, the new loop bounds $L_n^1, L_n^2, \ldots, U_n^1, U_n^2, \ldots$, the new loop steps $S_n^1, S_n^2, \ldots$

$g \leftarrow$ find_offset(G) (shown in Algorithm 3.2);
for x = 0 to f-1 do **do**
  Append function $B_o(I^1 + x, I^2 - x * g, I^3, \ldots, I^i)$ to $B_n(I^1, I^2, I^3, \ldots, I^i)$;
end for
for y = 0 to i do **do**
  $L_n^y = L_o^y$; $U_n^y = U_o^y$; $S_n^y = 1$;
end for
$L_n^2 = g; S_n^1 = f;$

In the algorithm, we first duplicate the original loop body f times. Each time we increase the loop index I^1 by 1 and decrease the loop index I^2 by striping offset g. After the new loop body is generated, we will change the minimum value of loop index L_n^2 to be g, which means the starting point of the second level loop is offset by the striping offset g. Finally, the step variable of the outer most loop is increased by the striping factor f, which is because we are scheduling f original iterations at a time. In the algorithm, we use the function shown in Algorithm 3.2 to obtain a striping offset. This function follows the steps described in the proof of Lemma 1.

For algorithm 3.1, it takes $O(|E|)$ time to find the striping offset g, where $|E|$ is the number of edges in the original MDFG. It takes $O(f \times N)$ to complete the code generation, where f is the striping factor and N is the number of instructions in the original loop body. Hence the total time complexity for Algorithm 3.1 is $O(|E| + f \times N)$.

Algorithm 3.2. Function find_offset(G)

Require: MDFG $G = \langle V, E, d, t \rangle$
Ensure: Striping offset g
D ← $\{d | d \neq (0, 0, \ldots 0)\}$;
Find d'=(d'_i, d'_j) ∈ D that d'_j / d'_i is the minimum ;

$$g = \begin{cases} -\lceil d'_j / d'_i \rceil + 1 & d'_j < 0 \\ 1 & d'_j = 0 \\ 0 & d'_j > 0 \end{cases}$$

return g;

4 Experiments

In this section, we conduct experiments based on a set of DSP benchmarks with two dimensional loops: WDF (Wave Digital Filter), IIR (the Infinite Impulse Response Filter), 2D (the Two Dimensional filter), Floyd (Floyd-Steinberg algorithm), and DPCM (Differential Pulse-Code Modulation device).

For each benchmark, we compare the iteration periods of the initial loops, the iteration periods for the transformed loops obtained by software pipelining, the iteration periods for the transformed loops obtained by loop unfolding, and the iteration periods of the transformed loops obtained by loop striping. The results are shown in Table 1. In the Table1, columns "Initial", "S. Pipe.", "Unfolding", and "Striping", represent the iteration periods of the initial loops, the iteration periods after applied software pipelining, the iteration periods of the unfolded loops, and the iteration periods of the striped loops, respectively. Iteration periods in the table are average iteration periods. For unfolded or striped loops, the iteration periods are obtained by two steps: first calculate the cycle periods for unfolded or striped loops and then divide the cycle periods by the unfolding factor or striping factor. At the end of Table 1, row "Avg. Iter. Period" shows the average iteration period for each according column. The last row "Iter-re. Avg. Impv." is the average improvement obtained by comparing loop striping with other techniques. Compared to loop unfolding, iterational retiming reduces iteration period by 54%. Compared to software pipelining, iterational retiming reduces iteration period by 50%.

From our experiment results, we can clearly see loop striping technique can do much better in increasing parallelism and timing performance on nested loops than software pipelining and loop unfolding. While software pipelining and loop unfolding improves iteration period for single dimensional loops, loop striping technique significantly reduces iteration period further for multi-dimensional loops. As the unfolding/striping factor grows larger, the improvement becomes more and more substantial. Having a smaller iteration period means that we can complete each iteration faster. As a result, our technique can significantly improve the timing performance for applications with nested loops.

Table 1. Comparison of iteration period among list scheduling, software pipelining, loop unfolding and loop striping

Benchmark	**Iteration Period (cycles)**			
unfolding/striping factor=2				
Benchmark	Initial	S. Pipe.	Unfolding	**Striping**
IIR	5	2	4.5	**2.5**
WDF	6	1	3	**3**
FLOYD	10	8	10	**5**
2D(1)	9	1	5.5	**4.5**
2D(2)	4	4	4	**2**
DPCM	5	2	4.5	**2.5**
MDFG1	7	7	7	**3.5**
MDFG2	10	10	10	**5**
unfolding/striping factor=4				
Benchmark	Initial	S. Pipe.	Unfolding	**Striping**
IIR	5	2	3.3	**1.3**
WDF	6	1	1.5	**1.5**
FLOYD	10	8	10	**2.5**
2D(1)	9	1	3.8	**2.3**
2D(2)	4	4	4	**1.0**
DPCM	5	2	3.3	**1.3**
MDFG1	7	7	7	**1.8**
MDFG2	10	10	10	**2.5**
unfolding/striping factor=6				
Benchmark	Initial	S. Pipe.	Unfolding	**Striping**
IIR	5	2	2.8	**0.8**
WDF	6	1	1	**1**
FLOYD	10	8	10	**1.7**
2D(1)	9	1	3.2	**1.5**
2D(2)	4	4	4	**0.7**
DPCM	5	2	2.8	**0.8**
MDFG1	7	7	7	**1.2**
MDFG2	10	10	10	**1.7**
unfolding/striping factor=8				
Benchmark	Initial	S. Pipe.	Unfolding	**Striping**
IIR	5	2	2.6	**0.6**
WDF	6	1	0.8	**0.8**
FLOYD	10	8	10	**1.3**
2D(1)	9	1	2.9	**1.1**
2D(2)	4	4	4	**0.5**
DPCM	5	2	2.6	**0.6**
MDFG1	7	7	7	**0.9**
MDFG2	10	10	10	**1.3**
Avg. Iter. Period	7	4.38	4.82	2.2
Iter-re. Avg. Impv.	**68%**	**50%**	**54%**	

5 Conclusion

In this paper, we propose a new loop transformation technique, loop striping. Loop striping can achieve the maximum parallelism while maintaining the original schedule vector, namely keeping the row-wise execution sequence. In this way, loop striping simplifies the new loop bounds and loop indexes calculation and reduces overhead. We believe loop striping is a promising technique and can be applied to different fields for nested loop optimization.

References

1. A. Aiken and A. Nicolau. Optimal loop parallelization. *ACM Conference on Programming Language Design and Implementation*, pages 308–317, 1988.
2. A. Aiken and A. Nicolau. *Fine-Grain Parallelization and the Wavefront Method.* MIT Press, 1990.
3. J. R. Allen and K. Kennedy. Automatic loop interchange. *ACM SIGPLAN symposium on Compiler construction*, pages 233–246, 1984.
4. J. M. Anderson and M. S. Lam. Global optimizations for parallelism and locality on scalable parallel machines. *ACM SIGPLAN Conference on Programming Language Design and Implementations*, pages 112–125, Jun. 1993.
5. U. Banerjee. *Unimodular Transformations of Double Loops.* MIT Press, 1991.
6. K. Iwano and S. Yeh. An efficient algorithm for optimal loop parallelization. Dec. 1990.
7. R. M. Karp. A characterization of the minimum cycle mean in a digraph. *Discrete Mathematics*, 23:309–311, 1978.
8. L. Lamport. The parallel execution of do loops. *Communications of the ACM SIG-PLAN*, 17:82–93, FEB. 1991.
9. C. E. Leiserson and J. B. Saxe. Retiming synchronous circuitry. *Algorithmica*, 6:5–35, 1991.
10. K. K. Parhi and D. G. Messerschmitt. Static rate-optimal scheduling of iterative data-flow programs via optimum unfolding. *IEEE Transactions on Computers*, 40:178–195, Feb. 1991.
11. N. L. Passos and E. H.-M. Sha. Full parallelism in uniform nested loops using multi-dimensional retiming. *International Conference on Parallel Processing*, pages 130–133, Aug. 1994.
12. M. E. Wolf and M. S. Lam. A data locality optimizing algorithm. *ACM SIGPLAN conference on Programming Language Design and Implementation*, 2:30–44, June 1991.
13. M. E. Wolf and M. S. Lam. A loop transformation theory and an algorithm to maximize parallelism. *IEEE Transactions on Parallel and Distributed Systems*, 2:452–471, OCT. 1991.
14. M. Wolfe. Loop skewing: the wavefront method revisited. *International Journal of Parallel Programming*, 15(4):284–294, Aug. 1986.

Efficient Error Control for Scalable Media Transmission over 3G Broadcast Networks

Kyungtae Kang, Joonho Lee, Yongwoo Cho, and Heonshik Shin

School of Computer Science and Engineering
Seoul National University, Seoul, 151-744, Korea
{ktkang, jlee108, xtg05, shinhs}@cslab.snu.ac.kr

Abstract. Broadcast and mobile phone technologies have now combined to provide wireless multimedia services. 3GPP2 has introduced the Broadcast and Multicast Services (BCMCS) architecture in a 3G wireless network. BCMCS are capable of supplying multimedia content, which requires successive frames to arrive within a specific time interval. We analyze the execution time of Reed-Solomon decoding, which is the MAC-layer forward error correction scheme used in cdma2000 1xEV-DO BCMCS, under different air channel conditions. The results show that the time constraints of MPEG-4 cannot be guaranteed by Reed-Solomon decoding when the packet loss rate (PLR) is high, due to its long computation time on current hardware. To alleviate this problem, we propose three error control schemes. Our static scheme bypasses Reed-Solomon decoding at the mobile node to satisfy the MPEG-4 time constraint when the PLR exceeds a given boundary. Our second, dynamic scheme corrects errors in a best-effort manner within the time constraint, instead of giving up altogether when the PLR is high. The third, video-aware dynamic scheme fixes errors in a similar way to the dynamic scheme, but in a priority-driven manner which improves the quality of the final video. Extensive simulation results show the effectiveness of our schemes compared to the original FEC scheme.

Keywords: cdma2000 1xEV-DO, broadcast, error control schemes, Reed-Solomon, MPEG-4 FGS.

1 Introduction

Broadcast services are now widespread over wireless networks, making it possible to watch television on handheld devices. These broadcast and multicast services (BCMCS) [1][2] are currently being standardized by various mobile wireless standards bodies, and commercial operations have just begun. It is highly probable that multimedia broadcasting will become a 'killer application', in the wireless network environment.

Wireless networks are much more prone to errors than wired networks. In order to reduce the packet loss rate (PLR), some form of error correction mechanism is necessary to remove and restore the original information. Forward error correction (FEC) has been widely suggested for video broadcast applications,

E. Sha et al. (Eds.): EUC 2006, LNCS 4096, pp. 415–425, 2006.

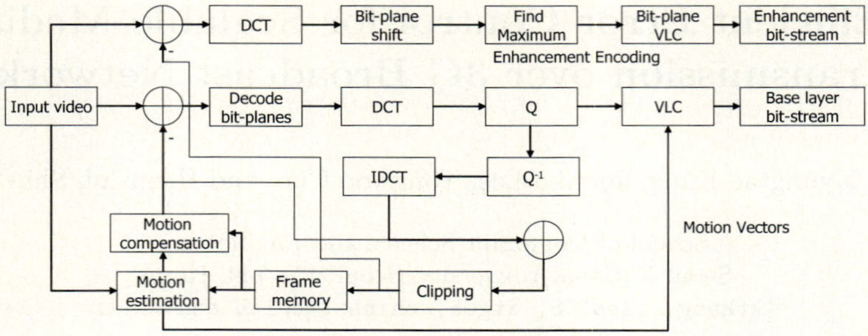

Fig. 1. FGS encoder block diagram

due to the combination of strict delay requirements and the semi-reliable nature of video streams. In current BCMCS, Reed-Solomon (RS) coding is used for FEC [3][4]. However, RS coding is designed to fix errors accurately but not efficiently, and this causes several problems in BCMCS.

In our study, MPEG-4 [5] is the target multimedia application. To ensure an uninterrupted supply of images, the MPEG-4 standard specifies a strict timing constraint, but the RS decoder takes no account of this. We propose three solutions to this problem, realized as static, dynamic and video-aware dynamic error control schemes (ECS). All of the schemes bypass RS decoding if there is not enough time to correct the errors.

2 Multimedia in BCMCS

2.1 MPEG-4 FGS Overview

To cope with the growing requirement for flexible stream transport, an MPEG working group has introduced a scalable video coding scheme called fine granularity scalability (FGS). The FGS video coding scheme in MPEG-4 not only provides an effective method of video compression, but also adapts its bit-rate flexibly to changing network conditions.

The FGS scheme encodes video frames into two layers, distinguished by the priority of the information that they contain, using bit-plane coding of discrete cosine transform (DCT) coefficients [7]. The layer containing information that is essential to the decodability of the whole video stream is called the base layer. The second layer is called the enhancement layer and includes more detailed information for improving the quality of the decoded video. The enhancement layer is obtained by bit-plane DCT coefficient coding of the differences between the original picture and the picture degraded by image transformations, as shown in Fig. 1. Because bit-plane coding considers each quantized DCT coefficient as a binary rather than a decimal number, each bit-plane of the enhancement data stream has its own level of significance, from the MSB (most significant bit) to the LSB (least significant bit). This makes it simple to truncate the enhancement layer to a reduced number of bits. After receiving the whole of the base layer, the quality of the video increases proportionally as more of the enhancement layer is received.

However, this arrangement leaves the base-layer stream very sensitive to channel errors and, if the decoder finds any errors in the base layer, the enhancement layer of the current frame is discarded, whether it is correct or not. Should they go undetected, errors in the base layer will propagate to the start of the next group of pictures and cause serious drifting problems in the enhancement layers of subsequent frames. The enhancement layer is more tolerant, as we have seen, and in any case errors in that layer cannot degrade the video quality below the lower bound provided by the base layer.

To utilize this layered approach effectively, the more important base layer should be provided with more protection against errors than the less important enhancement layer. But the error recovery scheme in the current BCMCS standard makes no allowance for the different value of the two layers, and each is equally likely to be damaged during transmission.

2.2 Real-Time Constraints Imposed by MPEG-4 Video Streams

An MPEG-4 system should have a maximum delay of 100ms from input to system decoder [5]. The corruption of this timing constraint will sequentially corrupt all the timing references and cause a system crisis, because all the rates in the system decoder will be modified. Once a system crisis has occurred, the system decoder will stop all the decoding processes, initialize every buffer and timing count, and allow itself to be re-initialized.

Guidelines for managing timing constraints and buffers in an MPEG-4 transport stream (TS) decoding process, and the rules that must be followed in order to satisfy the timing reference, are described elsewhere [9].

3 BCMCS Error Recovery Technique

3.1 Reed-Solomon Coding in BCMCS

The ECB structure is designed to allow efficient recovery from bursts of errors, by the way that such bursts are interleaved spatially within the ECB. Let M be the number of MAC packets in each row of the ECB (see Fig. 2). As M increases, the time-diversity also increases and thus a mobile node which is in a time-varying shadow environment is still able to recover a substantial amount of corrupted data. The organization of BCMCS is such that the value of M for a given ECB has to be less than or equal to 16.

In the context of MPEG-4 FGS video, the contents of an ECB are as shown in Fig. 2. Assuming the data rate of the base and enhancement layers of the video flow are b_B and b_E respectively, the number of packets allocated to each layer will be in the ratio $b_B : b_E$. The base-layer and enhancement-layer packets are segregated within the ECB in such a manner that all the MAC packets in each ECB sub-block correspond to the same layer. If the values of $(M \times b_B)/b$ and $(M \times b_E)/b$ (see Fig. 2 again) are both integers and are less than

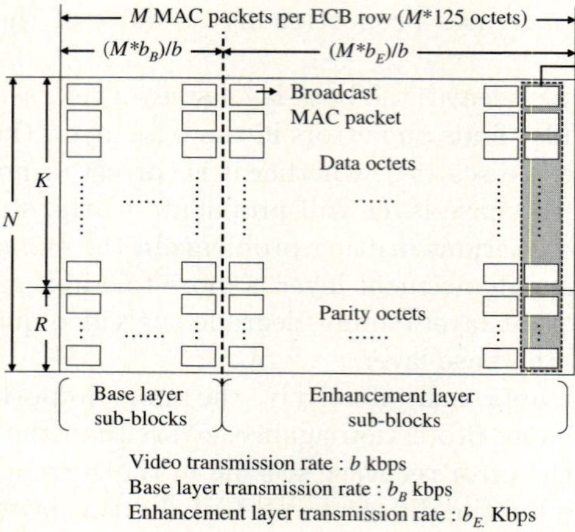

Fig. 2. Logical structure of an ECB

the value of M, then all sub-blocks can be allocated to either the base-layer or the enhancement-layer section without any overlap. This segregation helps to prioritize the recovery of base-layer packets when only limited recovery is possible due to the timing constraints of MPEG-4.

3.2 Analysis of the Current Reed-Solomon Decoding Technique

One of the most widely used chipset solutions that is able to support a cdma2000 1x system is the QUALCOMM MSM5000 Mobile Station *Modem*™ (MSM), which uses the ARM7TDMI core as its microprocessor. We therefore used an ARM7TDMI testbed.

The decoding times for different values of the packet loss rate (PLR) were measured without a cache. We found that values of PLR at the physical layer have a linear relationship with execution time, as shown in Fig. 3. In this

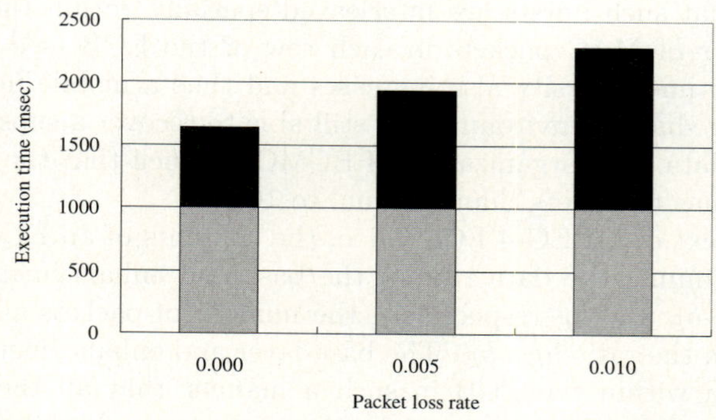

Fig. 3. Execution time of RS decoding on a cacheless system

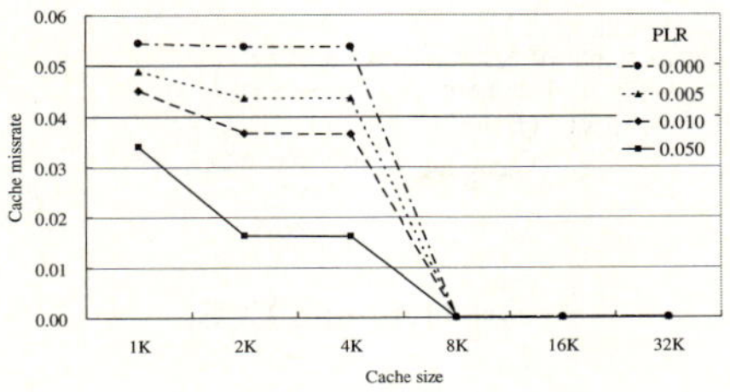

(a) I-cache

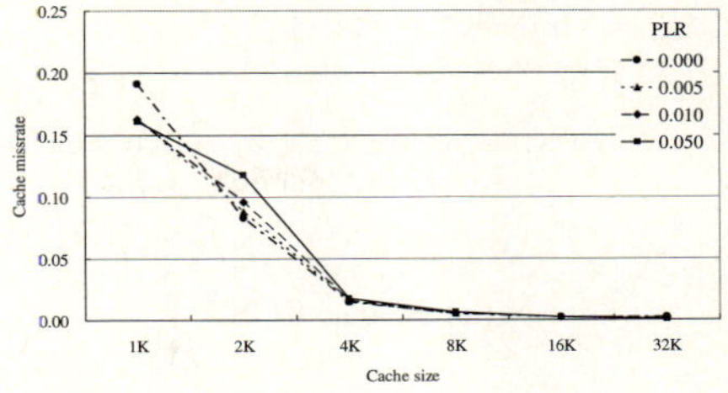

(b) D-cache

Fig. 4. Cache miss rate against cache size

figure, the gray bars show the timing deadline for processing the application layer multimedia service, and the black bars indicate the excess time required for RS decoding. ¿From this measurement, we see that RS decoding without a cache exceeds the time constraint of an MPEG-4 system, and the issue is therefore reduced to determining the best cache size.

We measured the miss rates of both the instruction and data cache while varying their size between 2k and 32k. The results shown in Figs. 4(a) and 4(b) indicate that cache size and miss rate are inversely proportional up to a cache size of 8k, but after that there is negligible improvement. The cache miss rate stabilizes if both the instruction and data cache are larger than 16k.

These two measurements suggest that, as the caches become bigger, the time required for RS decoding is reduced. We conducted an experiment to measure the execution time of RS decoding with instruction and data cache both sized at 16k, because the cache miss ratio has stabilized when both caches are this big. The results, shown in Fig. 5, indicate that PLR and execution time have a linear relationship, which we can use to decide whether RS decoding can be performed within the MPEG-4 time constraint. ¿From this graph, we can see that RS decoding can be completed on time up to a PLR of 1%, at which point decoding takes a little less than 100ms.

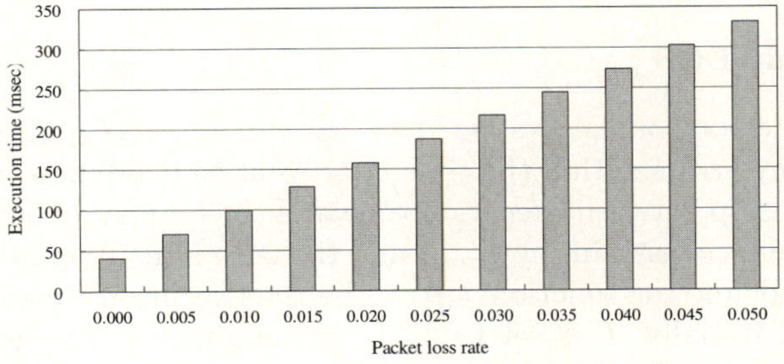

Fig. 5. RS execution time against PLR

```
Pmax = threshold_PER;
P = received_PER;
if (P < Pmax){
        while (there_is_a_sub_block) {
                do_RS_decoding();
        }
}
```

(a) Static ECS.

```
Tmax = threshold_Time;
T = Tmax
while (there_is_a_sub_block || T > f(0)) {
        n = number_of_errors;
        if (f(n) < T) {
                do_RS_decoding();
                T = T - f(n);
        }
}
```

(b) Dynamic ECS.

Fig. 6. Pseudocode of the static and dynamic ECS

4 Proposed Error Recovery Scheme

4.1 Static ECS

Timing is the main constraint on an MPEG-4 system, especially the 100ms ceiling on the PCR interval. Thus, we begin by proposing a static error control system based on the idea of anticipating whether RS decoding can be completed before this deadline, using the linear relation between PLR and execution time in a mobile node. This scheme omits RS decoding altogether if the system cannot meet the MPEG-4 timing constraint. Its pseudocode is shown in Fig. 6(a). Let P_{max} be the maximum PLR for which RS decoding can be completed in time. By the time that an ECB block arrives at the RS decoding layer, a mobile node will also have received the PLR of the physical layer. We will call the packet loss rate of data arriving at a mobile node through the physical layer the *given PLR*; and we will call the PLR after decoding the *recovered PLR*. We will denote the given PLR by P and, if it is greater than P_{max}, the node will omit RS decoding. Otherwise, it will perform RS decoding and correct the errors.

A shortcoming of this static scheme is that, when $P > P_{max}$, no use is made of the remainder of the PCB interval. The static ECS causes all the data to bypass RS decoding if the given PLR is greater than P_{max}, even though some of the errors might be fixed within the allowable time interval, and the MPEG-4 time constraint satisfied.

4.2 Dynamic ECS

Our dynamic error control system does not cut off at P_{max}. Instead, it will correct as many errors within the time constraint as it predicts as it can, based on the relationship between execution time and the number of errors. We denote the MPEG-4 time constraint by T_{max}, and the time remaining by T, as shown in Fig. 6(b). We define the function $f(n)$ to be the execution time of RS decoding with n errors. Initially, T is set to T_{max}. Whenever the RS decoder performs error correction, it will calculate $f(n)$ for the current sub-block and compare it with T. If T is less than $f(n)$, the decoder skips the current sub-block and starts on the next one. This procedure continues until it reaches the last sub-block, or insufficient time remains to fix even a single error.

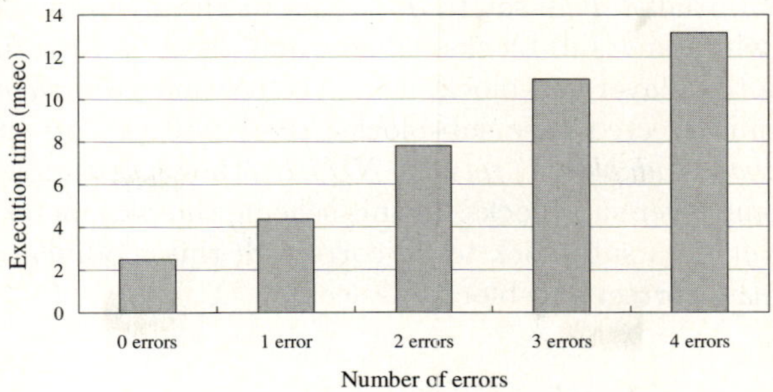

Fig. 7. Execution times for correcting a code word with different numbers of errors

To determine $f(n)$, we measured the time required to correct one sub-block of the ECB. We repeated this measurement to find a worst-case value, which provides a maximum bound on the time for RS decoding. These results, set out in Fig. 7, show that the execution time and the number of errors are linearly proportional, making $f(n)$ a linear function.

The execution time of RS decoding is dependent on the CPU and can be measured using a variety of tools. Thus, our dynamic ECS can be applied to any environment if this execution time is known.

4.3 Video-Aware Dynamic ECS

Our video-aware dynamic error control system uses same technique as the dynamic one, except that it differentiates between sub-blocks in the base and enhancement layer. In MPEG-4 FGS, there is a fixed ratio between the number of base and enhancement sub-blocks, but we know that base-layer sub-blocks are more important. In this third scheme, base-layer sub-blocks are corrected first, followed by enhancement-layer sub-blocks if time remains.

The pseudocode for this ECS is shown in Fig. 8. We will denote the sub-block to be corrected by F, with the rest of the notation following that for the

```
Tmax = threshold_Time;
T = Tmax
while (there_is_a_sub_block || T > f(0)) {
        F = find_base_sub_block();
        if (F == NULL)
                F = find_enhancement_sub_block();
        n = number_of_errors;
        if (f(n) < T) {
                do_RS_decoding(F);
                T = T - f(n);
        }
}
```

Fig. 8. Pseudocode of the video-aware dynamic ECS

dynamic ECS. Initially, T is set to T_{max}, as in the dynamic scheme. The algorithm runs while any sub-blocks remain and there is also time in hand. It looks first for a base-layer sub-block, using the routine $find\_base\_sub\_block()$. If there are any uncorrected base sub-blocks, these will be corrected first; otherwise (i.e. $find\_base\_sub\_block()$ returns $NULL$), the algorithm will begin to correct enhancement-layer sub-blocks. In this scheme the parameter of the function $do\_RS\_decoding()$ is a sub-block to be corrected; this modification is necessary to ensure that the correct sub-block is selected.

5 Performance Evaluation

5.1 Experimental Environment

We will first see how many errors can be corrected within the MPEG-4 time constraint. To do this we generated a template data-stream with errors that model those of an actual air channel, by injecting errors generated by a channel error model. In this study, we used the simple threshold model suggested by Zorzi [11][12] to simulate the behavior of data errors which arise in transmission over fading channels. Fading in the air channel is assumed to have a Rayleigh distribution.

By choosing different values for the physical-layer packet loss rate and for $f_d N_{BL} T$ (which is the Doppler frequency normalized to the data-rate with block size N_{BL}, where f_d is the Doppler frequency, equal to the mobile velocity divided by the carrier wavelength), we can model different degrees of correlation in the fading process of radio channels. The value of $f_d N_{BL} T$ determines the correlation properties, which are related to the mobile speed for a given carrier frequency. When $f_d N_{BL} T$ is small, the fading process has a strong correlation, which means long bursts of errors (slow fading). Conversely, the occurrence of errors has a weak correlation for large value of $f_d N_{BL} T$ (fast fading). In these experiments, we set the value of $f_d N_{BL} T$ to 0.02, which correspond to moderate fading.

The performance of Reed-Solomon coding was measured using the SEE (SNU Energy Explorer) [13]. In this simulation, the ARM7TDMI core and the SEC 128Mbit SDRAM array (K4S280832A) were operated at 200MHz and 100MHz respectively. The target application is assumed to be a multimedia service and the proportion of CPU time used by RS decoding is assumed to be 5%. We used a Foreman video sequence encoded with a bit-rate of 220kbps, running at 30 frames per second. The stream is handled by our reference MPEG-4 FGS codec, which is derived from the framework of the European ACTS Project Mobile Multimedia Systems (MoMuSys) [14], but modified for our experiments. The video streams consists of a base layer with a bit-rate of 110 kbps, and an enhancement layer with a bit-rate of 110 kbps. Physical packets were modulated using QPSK and transmitted at 1228.8kbps. Thus, the amount of data, N_{BL}, that can be fitted into one time slot is 256 bytes.

5.2 Experimental Results

We conducted a simulation to measure the PSNR [15] of the original Reed-Solomon scheme, which is shown in Fig. 9(a). We found the average PSNR of the original scheme to be 16.01dB. Without any ECS, the decoder performs RS error recovery for every block. This causes so much computation that the PCB time interval is eventually exceeded.

We notice from Fig. 9(a) that, once the PSNR drops, it stays at a low level for a while. This is caused by a system reset. If the arrival of the PCR is delayed, the SCF will be damaged. This leads successively to damage to the DTS and PTS and eventually causes the entire system to be re-initialized, which results in degradation of the video quality, as explained elsewhere [9].

We have measured the PSNR achieved by the three proposed schemes. Fig. 9(b) shows the results achieved by the static ECS. Compared to the original scheme, it is noticeable that, once the PSNR has dropped to around 3dB, it quickly recovers. This is because the static ECS skips RS decoding if it cannot meet the MPEG-4 time interval, which prevents re-initialization and results in instant recovery. The corrected average PSNR is 30.42dB, which is 14.41dB higher than that of the original scheme.

Fig. 9(c) shows the results achieved by the dynamic ECS, which exhibit fewer fluctuations than those of the static ECS, because the former does as much RS decoding as it can in the time available. Reduced fluctuation leads to smoother video and a higher-quality experience for a user who is watching the screen of a mobile node. Dynamic ECS achieves an improved PSNR of 32.84dB.

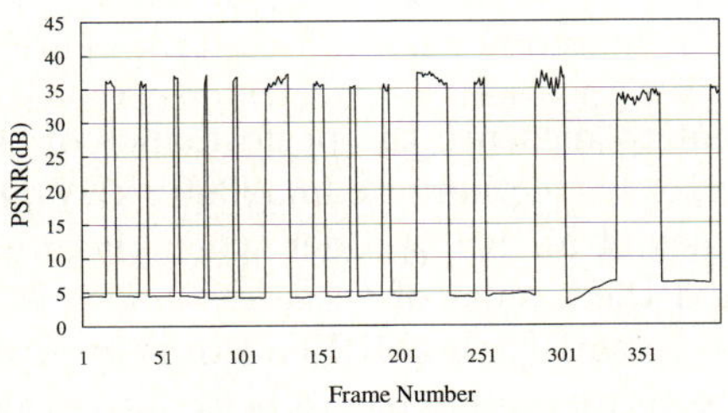

(a) Original scheme

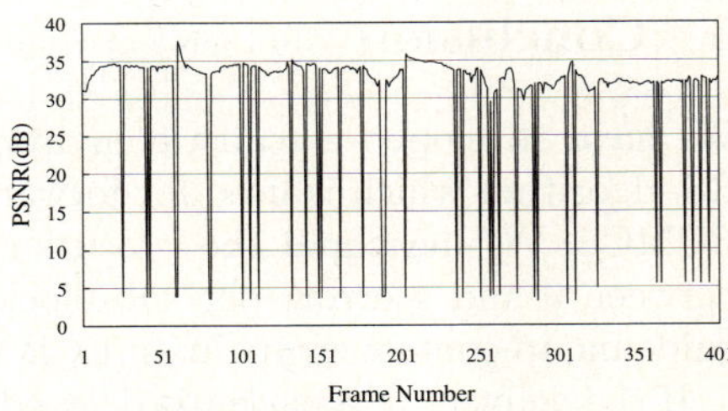

(b) Static ECS

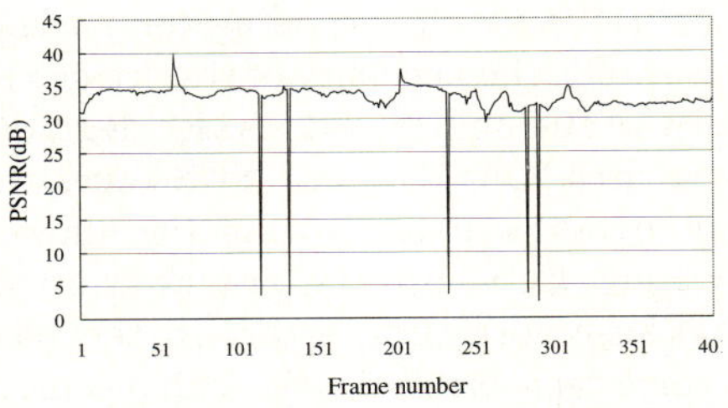

(c) Dynamic ECS

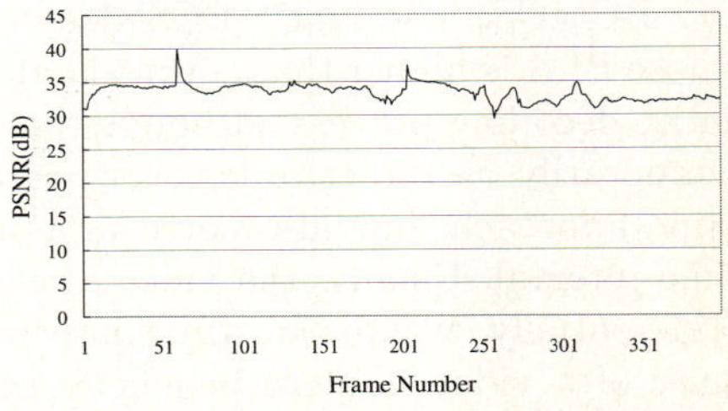

(d) Video-aware dynamic ECS

Fig. 9. PSNR of original and proposed schemes (given PLR = 5%)

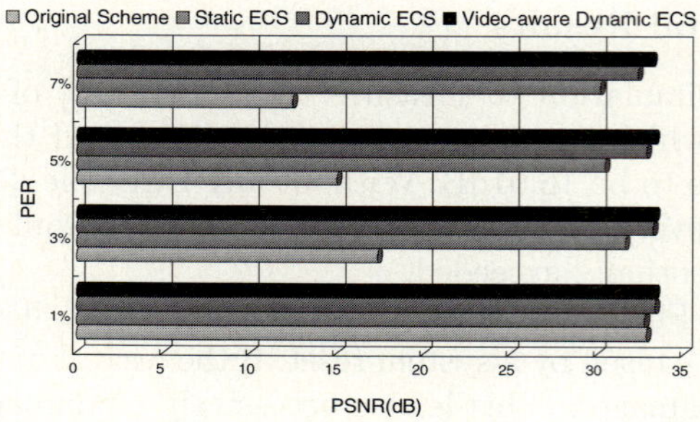

Fig. 10. Comparison of PSNR of original and proposed schemes

Fig. 9(d) shows the results for video-aware dynamic ECS, which exhibit the fewest fluctuations, with an average PSNR of 33.29dB. Fig. 10 compares the average PSNR of the original and the three new schemes. It shows that, when the given PLR is 1%, there is not much difference between the schemes: if there are few errors, all of them can usually be corrected within the MPEG-4 time interval, and so all the schemes have a similar PSNR. But, as the number of errors increases, the benefit of using one of our schemes becomes more noticeable. For all the error-rates that we tested, the relative ranking of our three error control schemes remains the same: best-effort recovery has better performance than the static scheme, but recovering higher-priority packets is best.

6 Conclusion

We have developed a realistic environment to measure the performance of the RS algorithm which is used for forward error correction in cdma2000 1xEV-DO BCMCS. We measured the execution times of an RS decoder when there are between 0 and 4 errors per sub-block, and the results of these tests suggest a guideline to control errors in an ECB so as to satisfy the MPEG-4 time interval.

If the delivery of a packet is delayed, the entire system has to be re-initialized, which dramatically degrades the quality of service. Therefore, it is critical to synchronize the timing in multimedia applications that use cdma2000 1xEV-DO BCMCS. The static ECS does this by skipping RS decoding for packets whose PLR is higher than a threshold. This avoids the necessity of restarting the entire decoding process, although the quality of the multimedia service degrades temporarily as the error recovery rate decreases. Our dynamic ECS takes the same approach, but also corrects as many errors as it can within the allowed time interval. Finally, the video-aware dynamic ECS corrects base-layer errors preferentially within the time interval, because correcting errors in the base layer of a video is more beneficial than correcting errors in the enhancement layer, and thus achieves a further quality improvement. Our simulation results show that these schemes greatly increase the PSNR compared to the original error correction scheme.

References

1. J. Wang, R. Sinnarajaj, T. Chen, Y. Wei, E. Tiedemann, and QUALCOMM, "Broadcast and multicast services in cdma2000," *IEEE Communications Magazine*, vol. 42, no. 2, pp. 76-82, February 2004.
2. 3GPP2, X.P0019 v 0.1.3, Broadcast-Multicast Services (BCMCS) Framework Draft Document, August 2003.
3. P. Agashe, R. Rezaiifar, P. Bender, and QUALCOMM, "cdma2000 high rate broadcast packet data air interface design," *IEEE Communications Magazine*, vol. 42, no. 2, pp. 83-89, February 2004.
4. 3GPP2, C.S0054 v1.0, cdma2000 High Rate Broadcast-Multicast Packet Data Air Interface Specification, February 2004.
5. ISO/IEC 14496-2, Coding of Audio-Visual Objects - Part2, May 2004.
6. W. Li, "Overview of fine granularity scalability in mpeg-4 video standard," *IEEE Transactions on Circuits and Systems for Video Technology*, vol. 11, no. 3, pp. 301-317, March 2001.
7. W. Li, F. Ling, and H. Sun, "Bitplane coding of dct coefficients," ISO/IEC JTC1/SC29/WG11, MPEG97/M2691, October 1997.
8. W. Li and Y. Chen, "Experiment result on fine granularity scalability," ISO/IEC JTC1/SC29/WG11, MPEG99/M4792, March 1999.
9. Y. Cho, K. Kang, and H. Shin, "Proactive Reed-Solomon Bypass (PRSB): A Technique for Real-Time Multimedia Processing in 3G Cellular Broadcast Networks," *Proc. 11th IEEE International Conference on Embedded and Real-Time Computing Systems and Applications*, vol. 4, pp. 532-538, September 2005.
10. R. Parry, "cdma2000 1xEV-DO [for 3G communications]," *IEEE Potentials*, vol. 21, no. 4, pp. 10-13, October-November 2002.
11. M. Zorzi and R. R. Rao, "On the statistics of block errors in bursty channels," *IEEE Transactions on Communications*, vol. 45, pp. 660-667, June 1997.
12. M. Zorzi, R. R. Rao, and L. B. Milstein, "Error statistics in data transmission over fading channels," *IEEE Transactions on Communications*, vol. 46, no. 11, pp. 1468-1477, November 1998.
13. I. Lee, Y. Choi, Y. Cho, Y. Joo, H. Lim, H. G. Lee, H. Shim, and N. Chang, "Web-based energy exploration tool for embedded systems," *IEEE Design and Test of Computers*, Vol. 21, Issue. 6, pp. 572-586, November-December, 2004.
14. A. Pearmain, A. Carvalho, A. Hamosfakidis, and J. Cosmas, "The momusys mpeg-4 mobile multimedia terminal," *Proc. 3rd ACTS Mobile Summit Conference*, pp. 224-229, June 1998.
15. R. C. Gonzalez, and R. E. Woods, *Digital Image Processing*, Addison-Wesley, 1992.

Implementation Synthesis of Embedded Software Under Operating Systems Supporting the Hybrid Scheduling Model

Zhigang Gao, Zhaohui Wu, and Hong Li

College of Computer Science, Zhejiang University
Hangzhou 310027, Zhejiang, China
{gaozhigang, wzh, lihong}@zju.edu.cn

Abstract. Implementation synthesis of embedded software has great influence on implementing embedded software's non-functional requirements, such as real-time, memory consumption, and low power, etc. In this paper, we focus on the implementation synthesis problem under a class of operating systems that supports the hybrid-scheduling model, that is, task sets have preemptable tasks and non-preemptable tasks. We propose a time analysis technology and an implementation synthesis method with the ability of design space exploration and optimization. Experimental evaluation shows our implementation synthesis method yields real-time embedded software with lower system overheads.

1 Introduction

Implementation synthesis of embedded software, as a part of embedded software integration, refers to the process from logical software design models (abbr. design models) to implementation models on specific platforms. Most non-functional requirements, such as real-time, memory consumption, and low power, are implemented and optimized during the implementation synthesis of embedded software, which makes it an important stage in the design of embedded systems.

Currently, almost all the research work [4, 7, 8] is based on the assumption that the underlying operating system (OS) uses the priority-based fully preemptive scheduling strategy. Although this kind of scheduling strategy is widely used in currently commercial real-time OS, there are also other scheduling strategies that can achieve better effects in some specific domains. Hybrid scheduling is such an example. It mixes preemptable tasks with non-preemptable ones. This kind of scheduling strategy makes sense when the execution time of a task is in the same magnitude of the time of context switches, RAM is required to use economically or the execution of a task must not be interrupted. It is one of the scheduling modes supported by the specification of OSEK/VXD [9], a wildly accepted specification in automotive electronic industries.

Under the hybrid scheduling strategy, the implementation synthesis involves not only priority assignments to tasks, but also scheduling property (preemptable or non-preemptable) assignments to tasks. In this paper, we focus on the implementation

E. Sha et al. (Eds.): EUC 2006, LNCS 4096, pp. 426 – 436, 2006.

synthesis of real-time embedded software running on uniprocessor with the goal of satisfying real-time and reducing system overheads. We propose the time analysis technology and a new implementation synthesis method, which is an extension of Gu et al.'s work [7], to address the implementation synthesis problem under OSs supporting the hybrid-scheduling model.

The rest of this paper is organized as follows. Section 2 presents the software models and implementation strategy. Section 3 describes the time analysis technology under the hybrid-scheduling model. We describe the process of implementation synthesis in section 4. The experimental evaluation results are given in section 5. Finally, we give conclusions and future work with section 6.

2 Software Models and Implementation Strategy

In terms of the model presented by Wang et al. [1, 2], a component is a logical software entity that can carry out certain functions triggered by events (we do not differentiate between the term "event" and the term "message" in the following sections, and use them interchangeably). An action is defined as the computation performed by a component when receiving an event. A transaction is a sequence of actions that are triggered by an external input event, possibly cut through one or more components. The components in a transaction communicate through buffered asynchronous messages. For simplicity, we only consider the *or* relation when more than one input event trigger the same output event, that is, a component can issue the output event once it receives any event from its input ports.

In design models, one action of a component has the worst-case execution time (WCET), and a transaction has a fixed period and a fixed deadline. In this paper, we assume the deadline of a transaction is no more than its period.

We use transaction-based runtime models. It is the counterpart of transactions in design modes, which consisting of a sequence of related tasks (the transactions in design modes and the transactions in runtime models can be differentiated according to their context). Each task has a period and an end-to-end (e2e) deadline. After being created and initialized, a task waits for events. When an event arrives, the task does the corresponding computation and sends one or more messages to other tasks. And then it goes back to wait for another event. Since tasks may use some shareable resources, it is necessary to synchronize the access to mutually exclusive resources.

During implementation synthesis, we chose *Component-Based Multi-Threading* (CBMT) strategy, where a thread consists of one or more components. It has the benefits of reasonable context-switching overheads, sufficient parallelism, optimal memory consumption, and better support for software engineering [7].

3 Time Analysis for CBMT Under the Hybrid Scheduling Model

For the time analysis of CBMT, Gu et al. [5, 7] used the modified form of the time analysis algorithm presented by Harbour, Klein, Lehoczky [10] (They call it the HKL algorithm.). The method presented by Gu et al. is suitable for the OSs supporting the priority-based preemptive scheduling model, but not suitable for the OSs supporting the hybrid scheduling model.

The task model used in HKL algorithm assumes that a task consists of one or more subtasks. For example, a task τ_i consists of n subtasks, $(\tau_{(i,1)}, \tau_{(i,2)}, \ldots, \tau_{(i,n)})$. $P_{(i,j)}$ refers to the priority of the subtask $\tau_{(i,j)}$. $P_{min(i)}$ refers to the minimum priority of all the subtasks of τ_i. When $P_{min(m)} > P_{(i,j)}$, τ_m has *multiply preemptive effect* on $\tau_{(i,j)}$. If $\exists k, (P_{(m,1)}, \cdots, P_{(m,k)} > P_{(i,j)}) \wedge (P_{(m,k+1)} < P_{(i,j)})$, τ_m has *singly preemptive effect* on $\tau_{(i,j)}$. τ_m has *blocking effect* on $\tau_{(i,j)}$ if $\exists k, l, (P_{(m,l)} < P_{(i,j)}) \wedge ((P_{(m,l+1)}, \cdots, P_{(m,k)}) > P_{(i,j)}) \wedge (P_{(m,k+1)} < P_{(i,j)})$. If the priority of several continuous subtasks of τ_m is higher than $P_{min(i)}$, they are called an H segment; If the priority of several continuous subtasks of τ_m is lower than $P_{min(i)}$, they are called an L segment.

The canonical form of a task τ_i is a task τ_i' whose subtasks maintain the same order, but with priority levels that do not decrease. Harbour et al. proved that the completion time of τ_i was equal to that of τ_i'. When we calculate the worst case response time (WCRT) of τ_i, first, transform task τ_i into its canonical form, τ_i', denoted as $(\tau_{(i,1)}', \tau_{(i,2)}', \cdots, \tau_{(i,m)}')$, then analyze each subtask's completion time in τ_i' one by one. The completion time of the last subtask of τ_i' is equal to the completion time of τ_i'.

In the HKL algorithm, $\mathbf{C_{(i,k)}}$ is the WCET of $\tau_{(i,k)}'$; $\mathbf{MP_{(i,k)}}$ is the tasks that have multiply preemptive effect (type-1 tasks) on $\tau_{(i,k)}'$; $\mathbf{SP_{(i,k)}}$ is the tasks that has singly preemptive effect (type-2 tasks) on $\tau_{(i,k)}'$; and $\mathbf{B_{(i,k)}}$ is the blocking time suffered by $\tau_{(i,k)}'$.

The HKL algorithm works well under the four assumptions given by Harbour et al. But the HKL algorithm does not consider context-switching overheads and blocking time caused by resource sharing and other factors. In the design models of this paper, the total blocking time comes from three aspects: blocking time caused by high priority task, which has been discussed in the HKL algorithm, blocking time caused by sharing resources that must be accessed serially, and blocking time caused by sharing components among multiple transactions. Gu et al. considered the influence caused by sharing components. However, the blocking time they discussed is only suitable for the situation that different input messages trigger different output messages. Moreover, context-switching overheads in Gu et al.'s work does not consider an H/L segment may include more than one tasks. In the following, we extend the HKL algorithm for performing time analysis on CBMT.

In design models, there are three typical relations: (1) One input message triggers an action sequence. The action sequence outputs messages to multiple components, as shown in Fig. 1 (a). We call this kind of sharing relation *1-M sharing*; (2) Any of multiple messages can trigger a sequence of actions, as shown in Fig. 1 (b). We call this kind of sharing relation *M-1 sharing;* and (3) Multiple different messages trigger multiple different action sequences on multiple sharing components, as shown in Fig. 1 (c). We call this kind of sharing relation *M-M sharing*. In comparison to the task model used in HKL algorithm, the time analysis for CBMT is more complex due to the above three cases. The *M-M sharing* has the same influence on the time analysis with *M-1 sharing*, thus we only research the other two component sharing relations.

In order to perform time analysis for design modes, we regard components as scheduling entities. We still use the notion of subtask to denote the tasks in

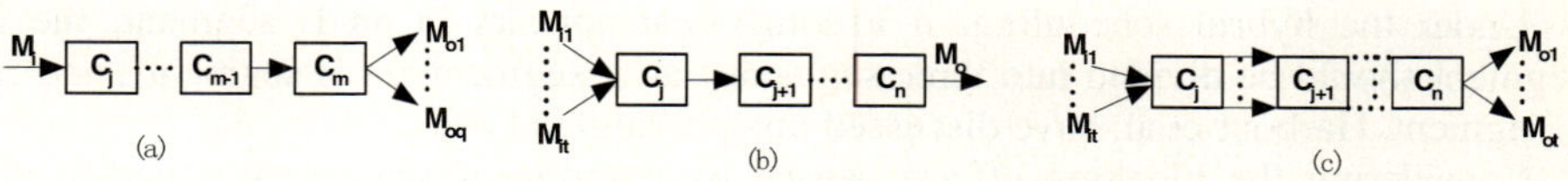

Fig. 1. Component-sharing relations (a) *1-M* sharing (m$\geq$j) (b) *M-1* sharing (n$\geq$j) (c) *M-M* sharing (n$\geq$j)

transactions. We use τ_{Ci} to denote the subtask that a component C_i belongs to, and use $CO_{\tau(i,j)}$ to denote the component that a subtask $\tau_{(i,j)}$ consists of. In Fig. 1 (a), assuming that Tr_1-Tr_q are transactions that M_{o1}-M_{oq} belong to.

1-M sharing has the following influence on the execution time of subtasks:

- Among the transactions that share multiple common components, one transaction does not preempt or block the other transactions.
- The preemption time (including multiple preemption time and single preemption time) caused by the subtasks that consist of sharing components should only be calculated in one transaction.

In the following discussion of *M-1 sharing*, we use the example shown in Fig. 1 (b), and assume Tr_1-Tr_t are transactions that M_{i1}-M_{it} belong to. For an randomly selected transaction Tr_i from Tr_1-Tr_t, its canonical form is a transaction with subtask sequence $(\tau_{(i,1)}',\cdots,\tau_{Cj}',\cdots,\tau_{Ck}'\cdots,\tau_{Cn}'\cdots)$. τ_{Ck}' is a subtask among τ_{Cj}'-τ_{Cn}'.

Under the relation of *M-1 sharing*, a subtask consisting of a shared component cannot be preempted or blocked by succeeding subtasks. For example, in Fig. 1 (b), τ_{Cj} cannot be preempted or blocked by τ_{Ck}, where $\tau_{Ck} \in \{\tau_{Cr} \mid j < r \leq n\}$. There are two cases in the calculation of the WCRT of subtasks:

- For subtasks before τ_{Cj}, their WCRT can be calculated by using the HKL algorithm.
- For subtasks τ_{Cj}'-τ_{Cn}', the preemption time and the blocking time caused by other transactions in Tr1-Trt can be calculated by using the following equation (1).

The preemption effect of a transaction only occurs once under the condition of *M-1 sharing* because multiple transactions use the same components. So we regard it as blocking effects. The blocking time suffered by $\tau_{(i,j)}'$ because of *M-1 sharing* is denoted as:

$$B_{CM1}^{(i,j)} = \sum_{Tr_p \in PE(i,j)) \wedge (CO_{\tau(p,q)} = CO_{\tau(i,j)'})} CET(PC_{(p,i,j)}) \tag{1}$$

Where $PC_{(p,i,j)}$ denotes the components before $CO_{\tau(i,j)'}$ in transaction Tr_p that exhibits preemption effects on $\tau_{(i,j)}'$, $CET(PC_{(p,i,j)})$ denotes the sum of the WCET of all components in $PC_{(p,i,j)}$. $PE_{(i,j)}$ denotes the transactions that have preemption effects (including multiple preemption effects and single preemption effects) on $\tau_{(i,j)}'$ in Tr_1-Tr_k except Tr.

Under the hybrid scheduling, if a component appears in an L segment, the L segment should be divided into three segments: an L segment, an H segments, and an L segment. Harbour et al. have discussed this problem in [10].

Considering the blocking effects caused by component sharing, we modify the $MP_{(i,j)}$ to $MP_{(i,j)}'$, $SP_{(i,j)}$ to $SP_{(i,j)}'$. They are denoted as:

$$MP_{(i,j)}' = MP_{(i,j)} - \{Tr_u \mid \exists m, CO_{\tau_{(i,j)}'} = CO_{\tau_{(u,m)}}\}$$
$$SP_{(i,j)}' = SP_{(i,j)} - \{Tr_u \mid \exists m, CO_{\tau_{(i,j)}'} = CO_{\tau_{(u,m)}}\}$$

Except the blocking time $B_{(i,j)}$ which is caused by inner H segments, the blocking time suffered by the subtask $\tau_{(i,j)}'$ consists of three aspects: the blocking time $B_{CM1}^{(i,j)}$, which is caused by *M-1 sharing*; the blocking time $B_{CMM}^{(i,j)}$, which is caused by *M-M sharing*, and can be calculated using similarly method in equation (1); and the blocking time $B_O^{(i,j)}$, which is caused by sharing resources and has been discussed by Gu et al. in [7]. It is denoted as:

$$B_{(i,j)}^* = B_O^{(i,j)} + B_{CM1}^{(i,j)} + B_{CMM}^{(i,j)}$$

The context-switching time is mainly caused by multiply preemptive tasks, so we only consider this kind of time overheads. The context-switching time suffered by $\tau_{(i,j)}'$ because of $Tr_p \in MP_{(i,j)}$ is:

$$CS_{(i,j)} = 2N_p \cdot CS_{sys}$$

Where N_p is the subtask number in Tr_p, CS_{sys} is the context-switching overheads.

If $\tau_{(i,j)}'$ is a preemptable subtask, its completion time is:

$$t_{(i,1)} = B_{(i,1)}^* + B_{(i,1)} + \sum_{Tr_p \in MP_{(i,1)}'} \left\lceil \frac{t_{(i,1)}}{T_p} \right\rceil (C_p + CS_{(i,1)}) + \sum_{Tr_p \in SP_{(i,1)}'} C_p^h + C_{(i,1)}$$
$$t_{(i,j)} = t_{(i,j-1)} + B_{(i,j)}^* + \sum_{Tr_p \in MP_{(i,j)}'} \left[\lceil t_{(i,j)} / \mathrm{T}_p \rceil - \lceil t_{(i,j-1)} / \mathrm{T}_p \rceil \right] (C_p + CS_{(i,j)})$$
$$+ \sum_{Tr_p \in SP_{(i,j)}'} \min(1, \left[\lceil t_{(i,j)} / \mathrm{T}_p \rceil - \lceil t_{(i,j-1)} / \mathrm{T}_p \rceil \right]) C_p^h + C_{(i,j)} \quad when \quad j > 1 \quad (2)$$

Where $C_{(i,j)}$ is the WCET of $\tau_{(i,j)}'$, T_p is the period of Tr_p, C_p is the WCET of Tr_p, and C^h_p is the WCET of the first H segment of Tr_p. Under the condition of *1-M sharing*, the WCET of sharing components only be calculated in one transaction.

According to algorithm proposed by Wang et al. [6], the response time of a non-preemptable task consists of waiting time $W_{(i,j)}$ and the execution time $C_{(i,j)}$. However, the algorithm reported by Wang et al is based on independent tasks. For a non-preemptable subtask $\tau_{(i,j)}'$, its completion time is:

$$
\begin{aligned}
&t_{(i,j)} = t_{(i,j-1)} + W_{(i,j)} + C_{(i,j)} \\
&W_{(i,1)} = B^*_{(i,1)} + B_{(i,j)} + \sum_{Tr_p \in MP'_{(i,1)}} \left(1 + \left\lceil \frac{W_{(i,1)}}{T_p} \right\rceil\right)(C_p + CS_{(i,1)}) + \sum_{Tr_p \in SP'_{(i,1)}} C_p^h \\
&W_{(i,j)} = B^*_{(i,j)} + \sum_{Tr_p \in MP'_{(i,j)}} \left[\left\lceil (W_{(i,j)} + WT_{(i,j-1)}) / \mathrm{T}_p \right\rceil - \left\lceil WT_{(i,j-1)} / \mathrm{T}_p \right\rceil\right] \cdot (C_p + CS_{(i,j)}) \\
&\quad + \sum_{Tr_p \in SP'_{(i,j)}} \min(1, \left[\left\lceil (W_{(i,j)} + WT_{(i,j-1)}) / \mathrm{T}_p \right\rceil - \left\lceil WT_{(i,j-1)} / \mathrm{T}_p \right\rceil\right]) C_p^h \\
&where \quad WT_{(i,j)} = \sum_{k=1}^{j} W_{(i,k)}. \quad when \quad j > 1
\end{aligned}
\tag{3}
$$

4 The Process of Implementation Synthesis

Implementation synthesis includes initialization and task generation, as shown in Fig. 2. In this paper, we choose SA to perform task generation because of its effectiveness in dealing with discrete optimization problem. Our optimization objective is to increase Critical Scaling Factor (CSF) [3] and reduce system overheads. CSF is an index that is used to evaluate time sensitivity of a task set. The bigger the CSF of a system is, the more stable a system is. The energy function is defined as:

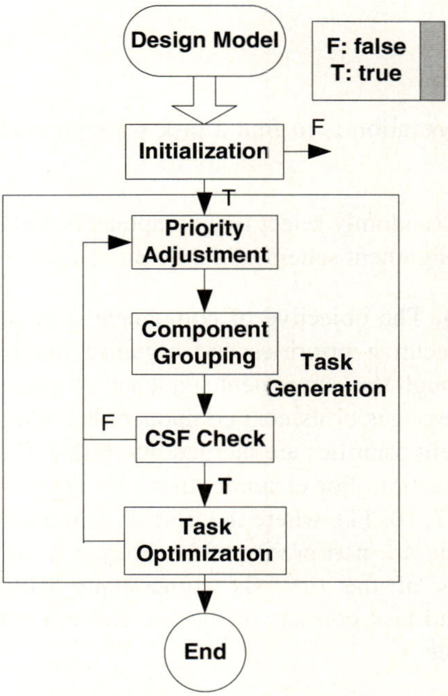

Fig. 2. The process of implementation synthesis

$$E_{(S)} = -CSF + \frac{1}{10 \cdot N_c} \cdot N_{sys}$$

Where N_c denotes the number of components in the design model, N_{sys} is the total times of context switches when each task completes its once execution. When the generated task set has the expected $E_{(s)}$ and no change occurs during some steps (we set it 1000), the SA ends successfully.

4.1 Initialization

The purpose of initialization is to abstract all transactions in a design model and assign components' initial priorities. It is include two steps:

First, transaction set generation. We use the method proposed in [4] to find transactions in the design model.

Second, assign initial priorities of components. We follow the rules: (a) In a transaction, the nearer a component is from the event source, the higher its priority is; and (b) The longer the period of a transaction is, the higher the priority levels of the components that it includes is. If two transactions have the same period, the transaction with longer execution time (the sum of WCET of all its components) is assigned the higher priorities. It should be pointed out that a component shared by multiple transactions is assigned the same priority as the shortest-period transaction using this component.

4.2 TASK Generation

The purpose of task generation is to find a task set with acceptable CSF. It includes three steps.

Priority Adjustment. Randomly select two components and exchange their priorities to find other priority assignment schemes in the search space of SA.

Component Grouping. The objective of component grouping is to merge adjacent components with consecutive priorities and organize them into tasks. It works as follows: Following through the component sequence of a transaction, if a component with multiple output messages or its next component has multiple input messages, the components with adjacent priorities are merged into tasks. Then continue to find other component in this transaction. For example, there are eight components with priority sequence (3, 5, 4, 6, 8, 7, 10, 11), where the first six components are preemptable and the last two components are non-preemptable. They can be merged into two tasks. The first task consists of the first six components with priorities 7 and it is preemptable. The second task consists of the last two components with priorities 11 and it is non-preemptable.

CSF Check. The completion time of a transaction can be obtained using the equation (2) and equation (3). From the completion time and deadlines of all transactions, the

CSF of the system can be obtained. If CSF is acceptable, we continue the next step. Otherwise, go to the step of priority adjustment.

Task Optimization. Its purpose is to reduce the number of tasks and the context-switching time by merging adjacent tasks and adjusting their preemption properties.

We use APT_{sys} denote the average times that all tasks are preempted by other tasks in transaction set, APT_i denoting the average times that a task τ_i is preempted by other tasks in transaction set.

The algorithm of task optimization is shown in **Algorithm TP.**

Algorithm TP(TS)

```
  /* TS is the set of tasks. E(s) denotes the energy of
the transaction set. CSFacc is the threshold that judges
whether CSF is acceptable. */
m = The transaction number in TS;
for ( j=0; j<m; j++){
  Tr = The j^th transaction in TS;
  n= The number of tasks in Tr;
  for (i=0; i<n; i++) {
    Ti = The i^th task in Tr;
    if (APT_i > APT_sys && Ti has preemptable property){
     Make Ti a non-preemptable task;
     Calculate the current E(s);
    if (E(s) increase || CSF < CSFacc)
      Make Ti a preemptable task;
    }
  }
  for ( j=0; j<m; j++){
     Tr = The j^th transaction in TS;
     n= The number of tasks in Tr;
    for (i=0; i<n; i++) {
      Ti= The i^th task in Ts;
      if   (Ti   and   T(i-1)   have   different   preemptive
         properties) continue;
      if (APT_i < APT_sys && APT_i-1 < APT_sys) {
        Merge Ti and T(i-1) into a tasks Ti', and use the
        higher  priority  between  Pi  and  P(i-1)  as  the
        merged task's priority;
       Calculate the current E(s);
      }
       if (E(s) increase)
         Break Ti' up into the original Ti and T(i-1);
     }
   }
}
```

Algorithm TP searches all tasks in transactions, and try to assign preemptable property to tasks that have more preempted times in order to reduce context-switching overheads. In this process, CSF should be no less than the expected value and E(s) does not increase. After that, merge adjacent tasks to reduce the number of tasks.

5 Experimental Evaluation

In order to evaluate the performance of the algorithm presented in this paper, we constructed the design model with the following parameters: transaction number: 40; the number of components in each transaction: 5-10; period of transactions: 10-2000ms; the WCET of component: 1-25ms; context-switching time: 8 microseconds. There were *1-M*, *M-M* and *M-1* sharing among components. There were sharing resources among components. All components in the design model were preemptable and left a large freedom degree for priority assignment. A fixed CSF (1.15) was chosen in the experiments. The experiments were performed on a PC running Windows XP, with 2500MHz CPU speed and 512Mb memory.

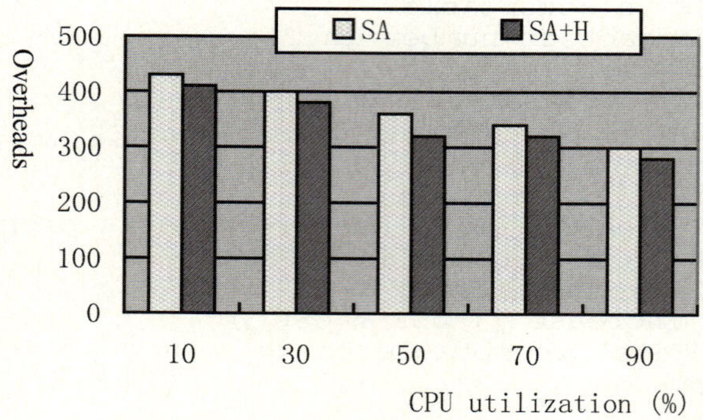

Fig. 3. The comparison of system overheads

In order to obtain the reduction of context-switching time, we compared the method proposed in this paper, named SA+H, to the method only using SA, named SA, under the same condition, but it did not assign preemption properties to tasks in SA. We counted the context-switching times when every task completed once execution. The experimental result is shown in Fig. 3. In comparison to SA, the context-switching times of SA+H are less than those of SA at different CPU utilization. The difference of context-switching times between SA and SA+H is maximal when the CPU utilization is 50 percent. This is because they are both effective when CPU utilization is low. But SA+H shows its advantage when the CPU utilization is moderate because the more accurate time analysis algorithm in section 3.1 makes non-preemptable tasks generated effectively. The difference of context-switching times between SA and SA+H becomes little as the increase of CPU utilization. It is because the non-preemptable properties of some tasks influence task merging. Non-preemptable tasks lead to a reduction of 10 percent in context-switching time in SA+H (not shown in Fig. 3). Although the non-preemptable tasks contribute a small part in total context-switching time, it is significant to assign non-preemptable properties to a task to make its execution uninterrupted in some safe-critical applications.

We investigated the distribution of the non-preemptable tasks in a task set generated with the proposed method in this paper. The experiment was performed with CPU utilization of 70%. The experimental result shows the non-preemptable tasks occur more frequently in the tasks with shorter WCET. It is because tasks with larger WCET have greater possibility to destroy the shedulability of system than tasks with smaller WCET. It also confirms the fact that hybrid-scheduling property is more suitable for tasks with smaller WCET and tasks that cannot interrupt for special reasons.

6 Conclusions and Future Work

This paper proposes a new method for the implementation synthesis of embedded software under OS that supports the hybrid-scheduling model. It is an extension of implementation synthesis method that is based on priority-based fully preemptive scheduling and enlarges the application range of implementation synthesis technology. We propose a time analysis method for CBMT and an implementation synthesis method with the design space exploration and optimization ability. This method can yield real-time implementation and has lower system overheads. The work focusing on the influence of other resource constraints, such as memory, energy, on implementation synthesis, is on the way.

Acknowledgments

This research was supported by 863 National High Technology Program under Grant No. 2005AA1Z2020 and Key Program of Science and Technology Department of Zhejiang Province under Grant No. 2004C21057.

References

1. 1 Wang, S., Merrick, J. R., and Shin, K. G.: Component allocation with multiple resource constraints for embedded real-time software design. In proc. IEEE Real-Time and Embedded Technology and Applications Symposium. (2004) 219-226
2. Wang, S., and Shin, K. G.: An architecture for embedded software integration using reusable components. In proc. International Conference on Compilers, Architecture, and Synthesis for Embedded Systems. (2000) 110-118
3. Vestal, S.: Fixed-priority sensitivity analysis for linear compute time models. IEEE Trans. Software Eng., vol. 20. (1994) 308-317
4. Kodase, S., Wang, S., and Shin, K. G.: Transforming structural model to runtime model of embedded software with real-time constraints. In Proc. Design, Automation and Test in Europe Conference . (2003) 20170-20175
5. Gu, Z., Wang, S., and. Shin, K. G.: Synthesis of real-time implementation from UML-RT models. In Proc. IEEE RTAS Workshop on Model-Driven Embedded Systems. (2004)
6. Wang, L., and Wu, Z.: Schedulability Test for Fault-Tolerant Hybrid Real-time Systems with Preemptive and Non-preemptive tasks. In Proc. the Fourth International Conference on Computer and Information Technology. (2004) 1169-1174
7. Gu, Z., and Shin, K. G.: Synthesis of Real-Time Implementations from Component-Based Software Models. In Proc. IEEE Real-Time Systems Symposium. (2005)

8. Bartolini, C., Lipari, G., and Natale, M. D.: From functional blocks to the synthesis of the architectural model in embedded real-time applications. In Proc. IEEE Real Time and Embedded Technology and Applications Symposium. (2005) 458-467
9. OSEK/VDX Operating System, Version 2.2.1, Jan. 16, 2003. [Online]. Available: http://www.osek-vdx.org/mirror/os221.pdf
10. Harbour, M., Klein, M. H., and Lehoczky, J.: Timing analysis for fixed-priority scheduling of hard real-time systems. IEEE Trans. Software Eng., vol. 20, no. 2. (1994) 13-28

Designing Dynamic Software Architecture for Home Service Robot Software*

Dongsun Kim[1] and Sooyong Park[2,**]

[1] Department of Computer Science, Sogang University, Shinsu-Dong, Mapo-Gu, Seoul, 121-742, Republic of Korea
darkrsw@sogang.ac.kr

[2] Department of Computer Science and Interdisciplinary Program of Integrated Biotechnology, Sogang University, Shinsu-Dong, Mapo-Gu, Seoul, 121-742, Republic of Korea
sypark@sogang.ac.kr

Abstract. Behavior, situations and environmental changes in embedded software, such as robot software, are hard to expect at software design time. To deal with dynamic behavior, situations and environmental changes at runtime, current software engineering practices are not adequate due to the hardness of software modification. An approach to resolve this problem could be making software really "*soft*" that enables runtime software modification. We developed a practical framework called SHAGE(Self-Healing, Adaptive, and Growing SoftwarE) to implement reconfigurable software in home service robots. SHAGE enables runtime reconfiguration of software architecture when a service robot encounters unexpected situations or new user requirements. This paper focuses on designing reconfigurable software architecture, so called, dynamic software architecture. We also conducted a case study on a home service robot to show applicability of the framework. The results of the study shows practicality and usefulness.

1 Introduction

This research issued from the intelligent service robot for the elderly project in Center for Intelligent Robotics (CIR) at KIST(Korea Institute of Science and Technology). This project was faced with 'how to satisfy and adapt changing requirements more faster at runtime'. Home service robots provides services such as 'delivering a newspaper', 'reading a book', 'making a cup of coffee', and so on. These services have its own quality attributes(e.g. speed, accuracy, safety, and etc). For example, the user gives a command to his/her robot to move with only a goal position. But situations can be diverse; a) when the user holds a party, there may be many visitors. They are unrecorded and moving objects for the robot. In this case, the robot needs to move more carefully, even though

* This research was performed for the Intelligent Robotics Development Program, one of the 21st Century Frontier R&D Programs funded by the Ministry of Commerce, Industry and Energy of Korea.

** To whom all correspondence should be addressed.

E. Sha et al. (Eds.): EUC 2006, LNCS 4096, pp. 437–448, 2006.

it may be getting slow. the robot's software architecture must be reconfigured to provide high safety a quality attribute, for example, a map-builder that uses vision, laser sensors, sonar sensors but takes a lot of time to build a map. b) when the user is home alone, there are only recorded objects. In this case, the robot can move more quickly. To satisfy this situation, the robot's software architecture must be reconfigured to provide high speed as a quality attribute, for example, a component that uses only laser sensors but takes less time to build a map.

In both cases a) and b), the robot must recognize situations of the environment and infer the user's requirements to adapt its software architecture. If there is no cost limitation, the robot can prepare all possible functionalities to satisfy all quality attributes. Unfortunately, robots have cost limitation because they are consumer products. Thus, a robot cannot have all possible software components as well as hardware components. In addition to cost limitation, robot developers cannot predict all possible interrelations between quality attributes and robot software architecture. This temporal limitation leads to new software architecture configurations for each new set of quality attributes after the robot sold.

In this paper, we focuses on dynamic software architecture that enables software architecture reconfiguration. To handle this we proposes slot-based two level software architecture working in SHAGE framework. In section 2, we explain SHAGE framework which is a basis of slot-based two level software architecture which is described in section 3. Also, we show the results of a case study conducted in a robot in section 4. Then, we draw conclusion in section 5.

2 Background

SHAGE[1]. Framework is developed to give a self-managed software capability to robot software in the project. The Framework consists of two parts which are separated by a dashed line as depicted in figure 1. The inner part is installed in each robot and consists of seven modules. The outer part provides repository services for robots to obtain new knowledge which describes 'how to adapt'. The target architecture(beneath the reconfigurator) represents the software architecture of the robot and the target of reconfiguration. This paper addresses how to design this software architecture.

Seven modules in the inner part of the framework are the Monitor, the Architecture Broker, the Component Broker, the Decision Maker, the Learner, the Reconfigurator, and the Internal Repositories. The monitor is responsible for observing the current situation of the environment(this is what observer does) and evaluating the result of adaptation that the framework does(this is what evaluator does). The architecture broker searches candidate architectures based on architecture reconfiguration strategies and composes candidate component compositions for the selected architecture by using concrete component retrieved by the component broker. The component broker finds concrete components which will be arranged into an architecture and retrieves the components from

[1] Formerly it was AlchemistJ as described in [1].

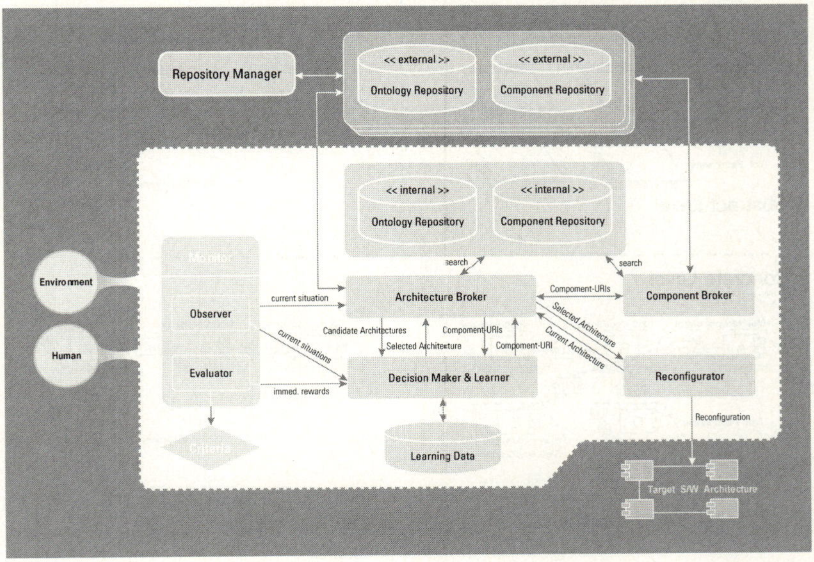

Fig. 1. SHAGE Framework consists of two parts; the inner part has seven modules: the Monitor(not in our scope yet), the Architecture Broker, the Component Broker, the Decision Maker, the Learner, the Reconfigurator, and (internal) Repositories. The outer part consists of repository servers that provide repository services.

repositories. The decision maker determines an best-so-far architecture from a set of candidate architectures that the architecture broker found and an best-so-far component composition from candidate component compositions that the architecture broker composed. The learner accumulates rewards evaluated by the evaluator in the monitor and the decision maker uses these accumulated rewards to choose the best-so-far architecture and the best-so-far component composition. The learning data is a knowledge repository for the learner. The reconfigurator manages and reconfigures the software architecture of the robot based on the best-so-far architecture and the best-so-far component composition which are selected by the decision maker. The internal repositories consists of the ontology repository and the component repository. The ontology repository contains architecture reconfiguration strategies that describes functionalities the robot must have and component ontologies that describes characteristics of a component. The component repository contains components implemented to be used in the robot software architecture.

The outer part of the framework is a set of servers containing external repositories. Each server has an ontology repository and a component repository as the inner part has. Internal repositories in the robot requests new ontologies and components when the robot cannot adapt its behavior to the current situation properly. Also External repositories broadcasts new knowledge to update robots' internal repositories globally. The repository manager is installed in each server and has tools for addition and removal of ontologies and components. From the

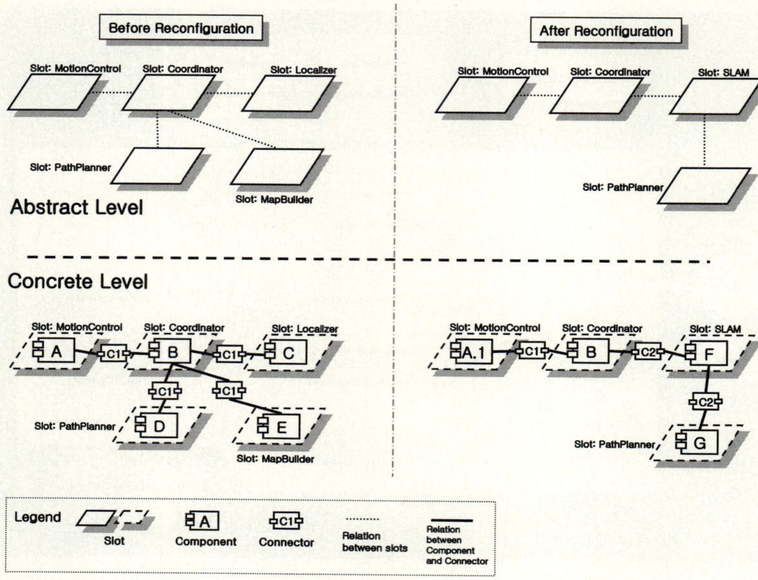

Fig. 2. The Slot-based Two Level Software Architecture Approach consists of the abstract level and the concrete level. In this approach, first, slots are reconfigured in the abstract level and then, components and connectors are placed in the concrete level.

next section, this paper proposes an architectural style to support for designing dynamic software architecture of robot systems.

3 Slot-Based Two Level Software Architecture

3.1 Overview

Dynamic software architecture enables runtime changes of software[2,3]. The slot-based two level software architecture approach provides two level adaptation mechanism; the abstract level and the concrete level(shown in figure 2). At the abstract level, there are only *slots*. A slot represents an abstract component that describes services. A service describes functionality that a slot should provide. A service does not indicates a specific method or a concrete component but describes what messages a slot can be requested and what results a slot returns.

At the concrete level, each slot is filled by one concrete component. A concrete component is an executable code, for example .class files in Java or .so files in C++, implemented by predefined component implementation rules(will be explained from section 3.2 to section 3.4). Every component in the framework must implement common interfaces which can process messages such as 'start', 'stop', and 'suspend' and specific interfaces which realize services on a slots and processes component-specific messages that the component can receive and give. These specific interfaces are described by the component description language shown in figure 3. The component description language is a XML-based language and describes required interfaces that contains messages that the component can request to other components and provided interfaces that can process messages other components requested.

When the architecture broker requests reconfiguration of the robot software architecture, the reconfigurator re-organizes the architecture based on the selected architecture reconfiguration strategy(will be explained in section 3.4) and places components based on the components the decision maker selected and then selects and places connectors between components based on the component descriptions. In detail, the mismatch indicator(will be explained in section 3.3) in the reconfigurator measures mismatches between components and finds suitable connectors. For example, two components have been deployed in two different machines, the reconfigurator selects a remote connector which enables remote communication such as RPC or RMI. After all components are connected, the reconfigurator sends a 'start' messages to every new component in the architecture and reports that reconfiguration is done to the architecture broker.

From section 3.2 to 3.4, this paper proposes an approach to design adaptable components and connectors to be used in dynamic software architecture and to author architecture reconfiguration strategies for runtime reconfiguration of the architecture.

3.2 Designing Adaptable Software Components

Constructing dynamic software architecture begins with designing adaptable software components. SHAGE Framework offers templates and guidelines for designing and implementing adaptable software components. To design software components in SHAGE Framework, first, a designer must identify services of a component. There are two types of services for each component; provided and required services.

A provided service represents what the software component provides to other software components and a required service represents what the software component needs to execute its functionalities. These services of a component is described by a component description language. SHAGE Framework also provides a language for describing a component as shown in figure 3. Each service is described by 'name', 'type' and 'msg' fields. The 'name' field represents a unique service name in a component to be used in implementation. The 'type' field describes classification of a service to check compatibility with other services. Classification is determined by service ontologies in the ontology repository(shown in figure 1). These ontologies depicts generalization relations between services; from abstract services to specific services, for example, from 'pathplanning' to 'pathplanning.laserbased', to 'pathplanning.laserbased.gradient'. The 'msg' fields represents requests that a service can push to other services in case of a required service or requests that a service can receive from other services in case of a provided service. The 'msg' fields consist of argument fields and a response field. Argument fields describe data which is needed to process a message. An argument field consists of a name field of the argument and a type field of the argument that describes syntactical and semantical type(e.g. double, float, array of double, robot pose, global map, etc). A response field is provided when the message has return values.

```xml
<?xml version="1.0" encoding="euc-kr"?>
<Component>
    <name>Navigator.Mapbuilder:LaserbasedMapbuilder</name>
    <description>Laser sensor-based mapbuilder</description>
    <thread value="false"/>
    <language value="CPP"/>
    <deployment value="MainSBC"/>
    <location URI="navigator.mapbuilder.laserbasedmapbuilder.LaserbasedMapbuilder"/>
    <provided-interfaces>
          <service type="Algorithmic.MapBuilding.LaserbasedMapBuilding"
    name="MapBuilder">
                    <msg name='ReadMap'>
                              <reponse>
                                        <arg name='Map'
    type='Primitive.double[500][500]'/>
                              </reponse>
                    </msg>
                    <msg name='UpdateMap'>
                              <arg name='dRobotPos' type='Primitive.double[3]'/>
                              <reponse>
                                        <arg name='Map'
    type='Primitive.double[500][500]'/>
                              </reponse>
                    </msg>
          </service>
    </provided-interfaces>
    <required-interfaces>
    </required-interfaces>
</Component>
```

Fig. 3. An example of a component description. The component description language is a XML-based language and describes services of components, an implementation language, a deployment location, the location of executable code, and so on.

While the component description language illustrates external part of a component, component implementation templates provides guidelines for inner structure of a component. As depicted in figure 4, inner structure of a component consists of provided/required interfaces, a service manager, and component-specific modules. A required interface encapsulates a message using data from a component-specific module through the service manage of a component and sends the message to a required port of a connector(see section 3.3). A provide interface receives an encapsulated message and elicits data from the message and calls the service manager to execute the functionality that the message indicates. A service manager has two roles; one is to select an appropriate required interface and send data to the required interface when a component-specific module requests a service in other components, and the other is to select an appropriate component-specific module and send data to the component-specific module. A set of component-specific modules is a group of objects to implement application-specific functionalities. With this structure, a component interacts with other components through connectors.

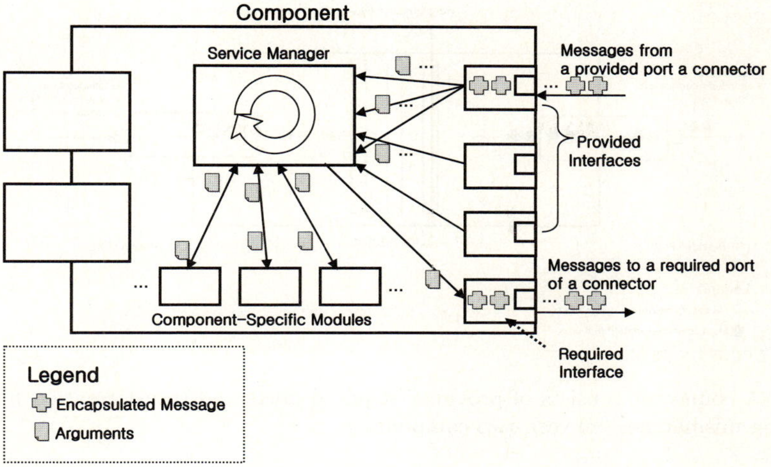

Fig. 4. A component consists of provided/required interfaces, a service manager, and component-specific modules

3.3 Designing Connectors

A connector is responsible for relaying messages between components and transforming data embedded in the messages for components to do their functionalities correctly. The project of CIR(see section 1) consists of over thirty laboratories at universities and companies. During the project we realized that most developers in laboratories had diverse backgrounds such as mechanical engineering, electrical engineering, and so on(few was computer science). This fact caused a lots of different representations for one notion. They used different data formats for maps, a robot pose, etc. For example, to represent a robot pose, one group of developers uses a column-major double array that length is three while the other group uses a row-major integer array that has same length. Another problem was that they would not unify representations because their components are not dedicated to the project and are used to other projects. Moreover, each group claimed their representation was most appropriate for the project and some groups complained that they had no time to redesign all components to follow new unified formats. To handle this situation, SHAGE framework provides guideline for implementing connectors.

In the framework, each connector is implemented based on the template depicted in figure 5. A connector consists of a provided port, a required port, and transformation filters. A required port receives messages from required interface in a component and interprets the messages to prepare transformation. A provided port encapsulates messages and sends the messages to a provided port in a component. Transformation filters are composed by the mismatch indicator in the reconfigurator. The mismatch indicator measures mismatches between two components by comparing descriptions of the components(see figure 3 and section 3.2) when software architecture is reconfigured and new components

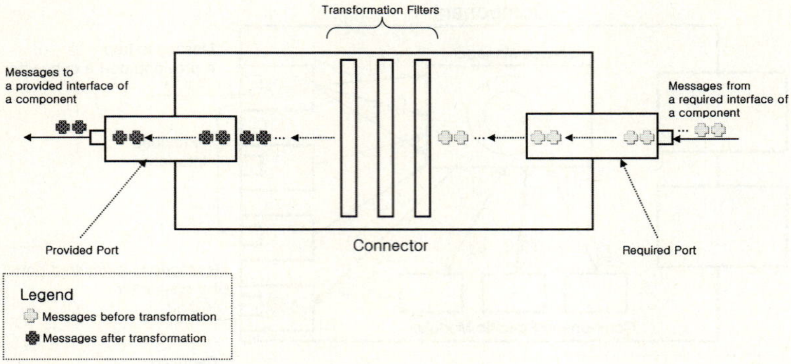

Fig. 5. A connector consists of provided/required ports and transformation filters for resolving mismatches between two components

are introduced in the architecture at runtime. Based on the measured mismatches, the mismatch indicator composes transformation filters by using pre-implemented filters in the component repository(see figure 1). A pre-implemented filter is a predefined conversion rule implemented by developers. We investigated conversion rules of data such as maps, a robot pose, and so on by interviewing developers and classified them. Eventually, mismatches in the software architecture at runtime could be resolved without modifying existing code by using connectors.

3.4 Authoring Architecture Reconfiguration Strategies

To satisfy user requirements(see section 1), software architecture of a robot should be reconfigured at runtime without suspension. Architecture reconfiguration strategies enables runtime reconfiguration of software architecture on SHAGE framework. Strategies are described by a XML-based language shown in figure 6. A strategies illustrates how the current software architecture should be reconfigured at runtime. A strategy only indicates abstract level reconfiguration, i.e. reconfiguration of slots shown in figure 2. Once abstract level architecture is reconfigured, the reconfigurator automatically places components into slots and selects connectors to link components.

Each strategy consists of 'description', 'profile', and 'configuration' fields. The 'description' field is a natural language description of a strategy. The 'profile' field describes minimum constraints that the current software architecture should have before reconfiguration to prevent failure of reconfiguration(e.g. existence of slots to prevent replacement slots). The 'configuration' field describes how slots are reconfigured. In the field, Three command are possible, i.e. 'replace', 'add', and 'remove'. To request slot-replacement or addition , services of slots should be described. These services are corresponding to the services in component descriptions described section 3.2. If a new slot is introduced in software architecture by slot-replacement or addition, the component broker in the framework(see figure 1) searches a set of candidate components that can process indicated services from the component repository. Then, the decision maker selects the most appropriate component in the set of candidate components based on learning data the learner accumulated. With the selected component, the reconfigurator reconfigures the current software architecture to a new software architecture as described in the strategy.

3.5 Related Work on Dynamic Software Architecture

Hillman's work[4,5] proposed an open framework for dynamic reconfiguration which supports component addition, removal, and replacement. This work focused only on a framework architecture and reconfiguration scripts to support reconfiguration. There was no concerns on designing components and connector and constructing software architectures. Hadas[6,7] framework provides facilities to dynamically change inner structure of a component. Hadas offers a good methodology for designing adaptable components which contains the way to reconfigure methods and data of a component by using metamethods and metainvocation mechanism. But this framework did not concerned architecture-based reconfiguration so that there was no way to design connectors and software architectural styles. Oreizy's work[8,9,2] is a famous research for architecture-based reconfiguration which provides the C2 architectural style as a reconfigurable software architecture style(which contains ways to design components and connectors), xADL as a architectural description language[2], and ArchStudio as a framework to support architecture-based adaptation of software at runtime. But C2 architectural style has restrictions such that a component can have at most two connections, upper and bottom and all connectors should be bus style connectors.

```
<?xml version="1.0" ?>
<reconfiguarationdescription name="http://sembots.icu.ac.kr/reconf#ToVisionbasedLocalization">
  <description>
    Change the current robot architecture into vision based Localizer
  </description>
  <profile>
    <required slotName="http://sembots.icu.ac.kr/service#Localizer"
              action="http://sembots.icu.ac.kr/action#Replace"/>
    <required slotName="http://sembots.icu.ac.kr/service#MapBuilder"
              action="http://sembots.icu.ac.kr/action#Remove"/>
  </profile>
  <configuration>
    <script>
      <Replace slotName="http://sembots.icu.ac.kr/service#Localizer">
        <services>
          <service name="http://sembots.icu.ac.kr/service#VisionbasedLocalization"/>
          <service name='http://sembots.icu.ac.kr/service#VisionbasedMapBuilding'/>
        </services>
      </Replace>
      <Remove slotName="http://sembots.icu.ac.kr/service#MapBuilder"/>
    </script>
  </configuration>
</reconfiguarationdescription>
```

Fig. 6. Architecture reconfiguration strategies describes abstract level reconfiguration. A strategy describes replacement, addition, and removal of slots.

[2] xADL describes a snapshot of software architecture, not a architecture reconfiguration language.

4 Experiment

The experiment was designed as follows: 1. initially the user of the robot needs 'more faster navigation', so the robot is configured mainly to use faster sensors(say, laser sensors). 2. while moving, the robot is stuck by a table because the bottom of the table is empty but the current sensors can detect only knee height objects. Then, the user asks the robot to move 'more carefully'. 3. The robot tries to reconfigure its software architecture to detect objects that the current sensors cannot detect.

We implemented a few components and configured the initial software architecture of the robot for navigation as shown in figure 7.(a). Each component can be executed independently. 'MotionControl' component controls wheels and 'Localizer' measures the current position of the robot based on encoder data which means how many degrees the wheels rotated. 'MapBuilder' makes a map around the robot based on sensor data from laser sensors. 'PathPlanner' plans a path from the current position to a goal position based on data from 'Localizer' and 'MapBuilder'. 'Coordinator' gets the goal position from the user of the robot and relays data between components. Based on these components the robot can moves without collisions except tables.

We designed a room as an experimental environment. we placed two tables; one was covered by a tablecloth and the other was not. The robot was placed at the same line on which the two tables were placed. In other words, "robot - table with a cloth - table without a cloth" on the same line in sequence. After configuring the initial architecture of the robot, The user put a goal position to 'Coordinator' and requested 'more faster maneuver'. The goal position was between two tables and the robot verified that the current architecture was suitable for the user's requirement. The robot decided the initial architecture is enough because laser sensors were very fast and precise. Then, the robot started to move and its laser sensors could detect a tablecloth, so the robot could move without collisions. This was not an abnormal situation, so the robot did not need adaptation. Then, we put the other goal position over the second table. In this case, the robot could not detect the table and rushed to the table. The user requested the robot to stop and to realize the situation and to adapt it.

When the robot was requested to adapt its behavior, the monitor in the framework detected the current situation. This situation was passed to the architecture broker. The architecture broker began the adaptation process. The situation was the current architecture could not detect all object in the room so the robot needed to find other functionalities to detect some other objects which could not be observable with the current architecture. The framework tried to apply various architectural configurations. First, the framework selected a strategy that adds a slot which have a localization service and a mapping service(figure 7.(b)). After abstract level reconfiguration, the reconfigurator successfully placed the SLAM(Simultaneous Localization And Mapping) component and appropriate connectors. A connector named 'D' represents two components around the connector are deployed in the same SBC while a connector named 'R' represents they are deployed in two different SBCs. In this case the SLAM

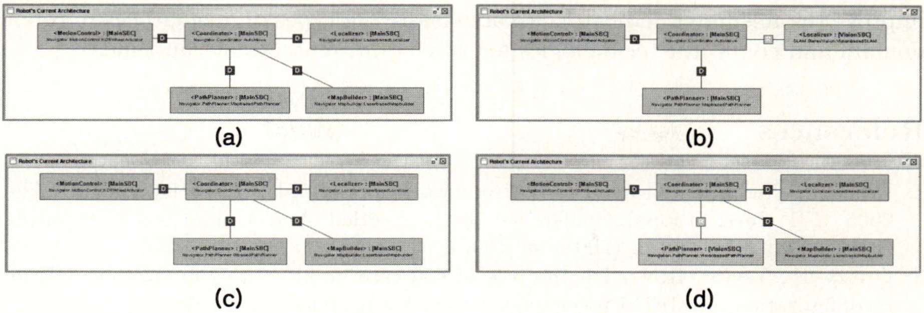

Fig. 7. Various software architectures of the robot during reconfiguration

component was deployed in 'Vision SBC', so that the connector named 'R' was placed. In detail, the SLAM component used a different format to represent a robot pose as explained in section 3.3, the mismatch indicator selected a transformation filter that convert two different format for a robot pose in 'Coordinator' and the SLAM component. The reconfigured architecture worked, but it did not satisfy user's requirements because the SLAM component also could not detect the table. In this manner the framework also tried to apply another strategy shown in figure 7.(c). But the framework realized(and learned) these was not able to solve the situation, and finally selected a strategy including a slot which had a vision-based path planning service. Then, the reconfigurator placed a path planner component that implements a vision-based path planning service(figure 7.(d)). During (a)-(d) the user did not interrupt and put more inputs.

This experiment shows the framework enables the robot to reconfigure robot software architecture successfully by applying the dynamic software architecture approach this paper proposed.

5 Conclusions

We proposed the slot-based two level software architecture as a dynamic software architecture approach for embedded systems especially in robot domain. This approach offers a method to design adaptable components and connectors and to author architecture reconfiguration strategy.

In order to verify operations of the framework, we have implemented an instance of self-adaptive robot software with 'infortainment robot' and examined the ability of adaptation of the robot from the experiment. The robot has adapted its behavior to user's feedback and the current situation.

As mentioned in section 3.3 the project consists of lots of laboratories and they have made a number of software components. These components are made based on different assumptions and platforms. Also these have different interfaces, data types, granularity, and scopes. These differences may cause lots of mismatches when the framework reconfigures the robot's software architecture. In order to improve the mismatch indicator, we are classifying types of mismatches in robot domain and connector technologies for solving mismatches at run-time.

References

1. Kim, D., Park, S.: Alchemistj: A framework for self-adaptive software. In: The 2005 IFIP International Conference on Embedded And Ubiquitous Computing (EUC'2005), LNCS3824. (2005) 98–109
2. Oreizy, P., Taylor, R.N.: On the role of software architectures in runtime system reconfiguration. In: IEE Proceedings - Software Engineering. (1998)
3. Allen, R.J., Douence, R., Garlan, D.: Specifying dynamism in software architectures. In: Proceedings of the Workshop on Foundations of Component-Based Software Engineering. (1997)
4. Hillman, J., Warren, I.: Meta-adaptation in autonomic systems. In: 10th IEEE International Workshop on Future Trends of Distributed Computing Systems. (2004)
5. Hillman, J., Warren, I.: An open framework for dynamic reconfiguration. In: 26th International Conference on Software Engineering. (2004)
6. Ben-Shaul, I., Cohen, A., Holder, O., Lavva, B.: Hadas: A network-centric framework for interoperability programming. In: Proceedings of the Second IFCIS International Conference on Cooperative Information Systems. (1997)
7. Ben-Shaul, I., Holder, O., Lavva, B.: Dynamic adaptation and deployment of distributed components in hadas. IEEE Transaction on Software Engineering **27(9)** (2001) 769–787
8. Oreizy, P., Medvidovic, N., Taylor, R.N.: Architecture-based runtime software evolution. In: Proceedings of the 20th international conference on Software engineering. (1998)
9. Oreizy, P.: Issues in the runtime modification of software architectures. Technical report, Department of Information and Computer Science, University of California, Irvine (1996)

A Processor Extension for Cycle-Accurate Real-Time Software

Nicholas Jun Hao Ip and Stephen A. Edwards*

Department of Computer Science, Columbia University

Abstract. Certain hard real-time tasks demand precise timing of events, but the usual software solution of periodic interrupts driving a scheduler only provides precision in the millisecond range. NOP-insertion can provide higher precision, but is tedious to do manually, requires predictable instruction timing, and works best with simple algorithms.

To achieve high-precision timing in software, we propose instruction-level access to cycle-accurate timers. We add an instruction that waits for a timer to expire then reloads it synchronously. Among other things, this provides a way to exactly specify the period of a loop.

To validate our approach, we implemented a simple RISC processor with our extension on an FPGA and programmed it to behave like a video controller and an asynchronous serial receiver. Both applications were much easier to write and debug than their hardware counterparts, which took roughly four times as many lines in VHDL. Simple processors with our extension brings software-style development to a class of applications that were once only possible with hardware.

1 Introduction

How do you write a piece of software that runs at a specific rate? The most primitive way—familiar to those of us who cut our teeth programming eight-bit microprocessors—is to carefully count the number of cycles taken by each instruction and insert NOPs to pad it out to achieve specific temporal behavior.

While NOP insertion provides precise control, it relies on predictable instruction timing, simple control structures, and either compiler support or a patient programmer. Dean's software thread integration [1,2,3] takes the idea farther: his compiler pads a non-real-time thread with code from a real-time thread.

Periodic timer interrupts are the usual alternative to NOP insertion. Such interrupts usually trigger a real-time scheduler that can resume threads at a particular "tick." Virtually all modern operating systems use this technique.

Precision is the main limitation of the periodic timer interrupt approach. A longer period is preferred to reduce overhead (Linux is typical: it uses a 10 ms clock) since each tick takes time away from useful tasks by requiring an interrupt and the execution of a scheduling algorithm. Some, such as Kohout et al. [4], implement the scheduler in hardware to address the overhead.

* Edwards and his group are supported by an NSF CAREER award, gifts from Intel and Altera, and grants from the SRC and New York State's NYSTAR program.

E. Sha et al. (Eds.): EUC 2006, LNCS 4096, pp. 449–458, 2006.

The precision of the periodic timer-based approach is limited by factors such as the interrupt frequency, how long interrupts are ever disabled in any piece of software, the execution time of the real-time scheduler code, and the presence of higher-priority tasks on the system. It typically only achieves a resolution in the millisecond range. Furthermore, a variety of fencepost-like pitfalls make this technique even less predictable. Labrosse [5, §2.32] discusses these issues.

We propose a processor architecture extension—an instruction that accesses timers—able to prescribe cycle-level timing. The idea is simple and powerful: to allow program to specify exactly how many cycles it will take to execute. This extension enables elegant software to have the timing precision of hardware. We realized our approach by implementing on an FPGA a processor that we programmed to generate video and receive asynchronous serial communication.

Our extension introduces an assembly-level *deadline* instruction[1] that controls a small set of cycle timers that count down to zero and wait. The operands of a *deadline* instruction are a timer and a new count for the timer. When executed, *deadline* delays until its timer has reached zero, then reloads the timer and immediately executes the next instruction. If the timer has already reached zero, which usually means that the intended deadline has already passed, the *deadline* instruction simply reloads the timer and continues.

Putting a *deadline* instruction at the beginning of a block of code that ends with another *deadline*, therefore, guarantees that the block runs in at least the amount of time given by the argument to *deadline*. Furthermore, putting a single *deadline* instruction inside a loop forces the period of the loop to be no less than the delay value. In both cases, if the code takes longer than the given number of cycles to execute, the *deadline* instruction does essentially nothing. Worst-case execution time analysis must still be performed to guarantee a given deadline will always be met, but at least such analysis is not integral to achieving a particular timing behavior, unlike NOP insertion.

Another advantage of our approach is that a program that meets all its deadlines will still run correctly (i.e., at the same rate) on a faster processor provided all *deadline* cycle counts are adjusted for the higher clock frequency.

Our technique is best for hard real-time embedded systems with tight, short deadlines; periodic interrupts work fine for systems needing less precise timing control. We intend our technique to be used for multi-core processors in embedded systems, i.e., where each real-time task has a dedicated processor. Our goal is to provide a software-style approach to implementing behavior that was previously possible only in hardware.

To validate our approach, we implemented a MIPS-like processor on an FPGA and programmed two tasks: a text-mode video controller and an asynchronous serial receiver with auto-baud-rate detection. Although hardware for such functionality has existed for years and carefully-written software has also achieved such behavior, we believe our approach is the easiest yet.

[1] Unlike our *deadline*, the common wait-for-interrupt instruction needs an external timer interrupt whose behavior must also be controlled.

2 Related Work

Previous approaches have modified the processor or a language, rarely both.

Henzinger and Kirsch's Giotto [6] language prescribes task timing. Its run-time system relies on traditional RTOS scheduling algorithms, which is both a positive—they are able to leverage the extensive work on scheduling—and a negative—it only provides coarse-grained timing control.

The synchronous languages Esterel [7] and Lustre [8] provide cycle-level control over concurrent software. Their cycles, however, are coarse, equal to the worst-case execution time of the main program loop. Roop et al. [9] propose a processor for Esterel, but their focus is performance, not predictability.

Dean's software thread integration (STI) [3] takes a different approach to achieving timing precision. STI inserts code from a high-priority foreground process into code for a best-effort background process. Programmer-supplied constraints direct the process, which increases the size of the executable between 12 and 15× (see Welch et al. [3]) because foreground loops are unrolled.

STI requires minimal hardware support (i.e., predictable instruction timing—something common in small embedded processors), but extensive compiler support, simple (predictable) control structures, and can generate very large code.

Real-time guarantees demand worst-case execution time analysis. WCET analysis always involves conservative approximations because the problem is intractable in general, and the problem is especially difficult for modern processors. For example, Ferdinand et al. [10] tackle the problem for avionics code with simple control structures, but find even this is difficult because of the shared instruction and data cache of the target Motorola ColdFire CPU.

Engblom [12] notes there are few accurate timing models for modern processors, due partially to poor documentation, but but also because the designers treat such models as treasured intellectual property. So even if the analysis of the code were flawless, the WCET may still be wrong.

WCET is necessary in our approach if we want to prove that a program will meet all its deadlines (i.e., reach each *deadline* statement before its timer has expired), but we do not need WCET to produce a working program, unlike NOP-insertion techniques such as STI.

The Virtual Simple Architecture (VISA) of Frank Mueller et al. [13,14] attacks WCET by running run real-time tasks on a slow processor with predictable timing. At the same time, they run the same real-time tasks and additional soft-real-time tasks on a faster, less-predictable processor. If the simple processor overtakes the faster one, they switch to the simpler one to meet deadlines.

A few groups have proposed alternative processor architectures for real-time systems. For example, a group of processors can run Java bytecode [15,16]. None, however, provide a scheduling mechanism any more precise than the usual periodic timer interrupt approach used on more general-purpose processors.

As discussed earlier, timer-interrupt-based scheduling introduces overhead, so some, such as Kohout et al. [4] and Xyron Semiconductor, have implemented real-time scheduling algorithms in hardware to alleviate this problem. However, such techniques do not provide the predictability of our approach.

add	Rd, Rs, Rt	Integer add	or	Rd, Rs, Rt	Logical OR
addi	Rd, Rs, imm16	Integer add immediate	ori	Rd, Rs, imm16	Logical OR immediate
and	Rd, Rs, Rt	Logical AND	sb	Rd, (Rt + Rs)	Store byte
andi	Rd, Rs, imm16	Logical AND immediate	sbi	Rd, (Rs + offset)	Store byte immediate
be	Rd, Rs, offset	Branch on equal	sll	Rd, Rs, Rt	Shift left logical
bne	Rd, Rs, offset	Branch on not equal	slli	Rd, Rs, imm16	Shift left logical immediate
j	target	Unconditional jump	srl	Rd, Rs, Rt	Shift right logical
lb	Rd, (Rt + Rs)	Load byte	srli	Rd, Rs, imm16	Shift right logical immediate
lbi	Rd, (Rs + offset)	Load byte immediate	sub	Rd, Rs, Rt	Integer subtract
mov	Rd, Rs	Move register (synonym)	subi	Rd, Rs, imm16	Integer subtract immediate
movi	Rd, imm16	Move immediate (synonym)	dead	T, Rs	Wait for timer and reload
nand	Rd, Rs, Rt	Logical NAND	deadi	T, imm16	Wait for timer immediate
nandi	Rd, Rs, imm16	Logical NAND immediate	xnor	Rd, Rs, Rt	Exclusive NOR
nop		No operation	xnori	Rd, Rs, imm16	Exclusive NOR immediate
nor	Rd, Rs, Rt	Logical NOR	xor	Rd, Rs, Rt	Exclusive OR
nori	Rd, Rs, imm16	Logical NOR immediate	xori	Rd, Rs, imm16	Exclusive OR immediate

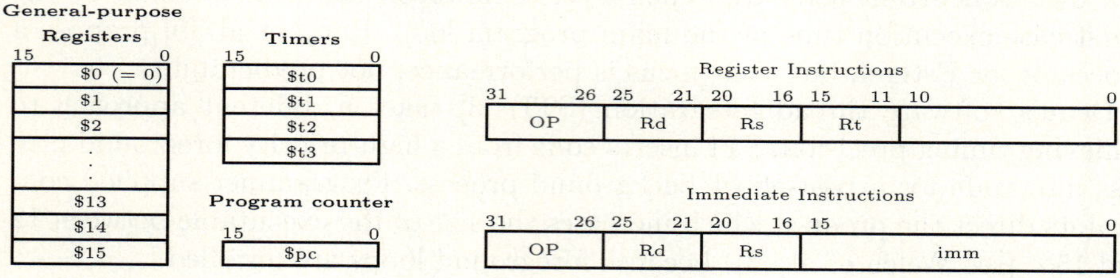

Fig. 1. Instruction set, Programmer's Model, and Instruction Encoding

3 Our Real-Time Processor

To validate our instruction-level timer extension, we implemented a 25 MHz MIPS-like processor in VHDL on a Xilinx Spartan 3 XC3S200 FPGA. Its design was deliberately simple. It executes a single instruction per cycle with no pipelining. It is centered around a sixteen-bit ALU and sixteen general-purpose registers (register zero always returns zero). Its only novelty is the group of sixteen-bit timer registers, which are controlled by the *deadline* instruction.

Figure 1 shows the instruction formats. We employed a Harvard architecture with 32-bit-wide instructions. Both program and data memory reside on chip. Our applications only required byte-wide data, so our processor only provides byte-wide load and store instructions (data is zero-extended on load).

The instruction set, Figure 1, is unremarkable. Arithmetic instructions come in three-register and two-register-with-immediate variants. It is a load/store architecture: only the LB/LBI and SB/SBI instructions transfer bytes to/from memory. The *mov* instruction is a synonym for *or* with register $0.

3.1 The Deadline Instruction

The *deadline* instruction is the main novelty in our processor. It has two formats:

dead *T*, *Rs*
deadi *T*, *imm16*

where *T* is one of the four timer registers $t0, $t1, $t2, or $t3, *Rs* is one of the sixteen general-purpose registers, and *imm16* is a 16-bit immediate data value.

Each timer register counts down one per cycle, stopping when it reaches zero. When execution reaches a *deadline* instruction, it pauses there until the given

```
deadi $t0, 8
add   $r1, $r2, $r3
deadi $t0, 10
add   $r1, $r2, $r3
```

(a)

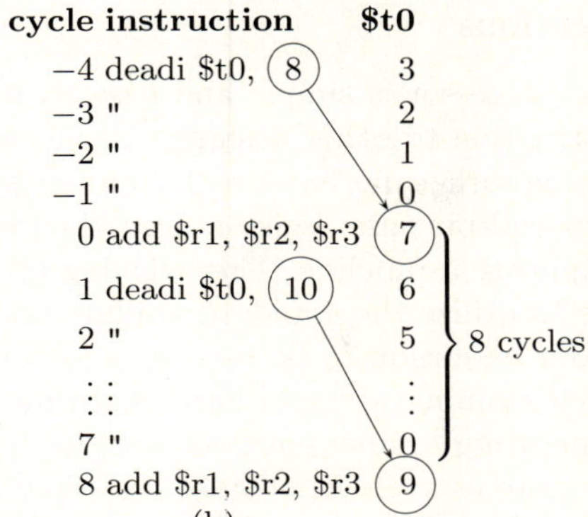

(b)

Fig. 2. (a) A code fragment with two *deadline* instructions and (b) its temporal behavior. The *deadline* instruction guarantees the two *add* instructions are executed 8 cycles apart.

timer register reaches zero. In the cycle following the one in which the timer has a zero count, the timer is reloaded with the source value, either from a register or an immediate value, and the instruction following the *deadline* executes.

Figure 2 illustrates the operation of the *deadline* instruction. Here, it is being used to ensure that exactly eight cycles occcur between the end of the first *deadline* and the end of the second. To achieve this, the second *deadline* delays for seven cycles to compensate for the single cycle *add* instruction. Assuming the timer $t0 has value 3 when the first *deadline* is executed, it waits until the timer elapses. (This is implicitly assuming the timer had been set at the beginning of an earlier block.) In the cycle following this (cycle 0 in the figure), the first *add* instruction executes, then the second *deadline* delays until cycle 8, when the second *add* instruction starts. The semantics of the *deadline* instruction therefore guarantee that the code between the two *deadlines* takes exactly eight cycles to execute, provided it does not require more.

Using *deadline* instructions is preferable to padding the program with NOPs, the usual technique for achieving such precise timing. A key advantage is that code using *deadline* does not have to know its execution time. For example, using *deadline* can deal with loops with a variable (but bounded) number of iterations; inserting NOPs would require the program, at runtime, to calculate the number of cycles the loop took and then delay for the remaining amount of time. Especially when each iteration of the loop is variable (e.g., because of conditionals), this can grow very complex.

Reduced code size is another advantage. Except where no NOP-padding is necessary, fewer *deadline* instructions are necessary to achieve the same effect.

Finally, our approach produces a sort of temporal binary compatibility. Provided the numbers loaded in the timers are corrected, a program using our technique that meets all its deadlines will behave identically (i.e., with the same timing and function) on a faster processor.

3.2 Ramifications

Our prototype processor is simple and easy to modify; we expect adding such a *deadline* instruction to other designs will be just as easy. Modern processors have pipelines and other mechanisms for hiding latency, but since *deadline* only manipulates special-purpose registers and then only rarely, it should not substantially complicate a pipeline. The delaying effect of the *deadline* instruction should be able to utilize the standard stalling ability of a pipeline.

We intend our extension to be used in a setting where there are many small processors, each running a single hard real-time task. While this is less flexible than an operating system environment, we believe such inflexibility is wise for embedded systems with strict hard real-time constraints. The move toward multi-core processors makes this all the more plausible.

We doubt the *deadline* instruction would work in a multitasking operating system setting, which strives to give processes the illusion of having the processor to themselves. An OS would save and restore timers on context switches, decrementing them when the process is running. However, a naïve scheduler would not be enough to achieve timing goals.

While running multiple hard real-time tasks on a single processor is attractive, it leads to the usual challenges of priority assignment, schedulability, etc. One simple case is when a processor is running a single hard real-time task and multiple best-effort ones. In this case, the real-time task could use the *deadline* instruction to set and achieve deadlines and the processor could run the best-effort tasks when the real-time task was waiting for a timer to expire.

4 A Text-Mode Video Display Controller

To evaluate our processor, we programmed it to behave as a text-mode video controller. A VGA (640×480) pixel clock is a little over 25 MHz—the clock frequency our processor achieved on the FPGA—so it not fast enough to do something interesting for each pixel. We made register $14 feed an eight-bit video shift register, although we could have used memory-mapped I/O.

Figure 3 shows the complete assembly code for our text-mode video controller. Lines 1–3 initializes three constants: the number of character columns (80), the total number of characters to be displayed on the screen (we display an 80 × 30 grid), and the height of each character (16 scan lines).

The code on lines 6–47 generates ten blank lines (the back porch), two lines of vertical synchronization, then thirty-three blank lines (the front porch). Each of these uses a loop over each line, and in each loop, timer $t1 is used to ensure each line is exactly 800 pixel cycles long: 96 cycles of horizontal synchronization, 48 cycles of back porch, 640 active cycles, and 16 cycles of front porch.

Lines 50–76 is a collection of three nested loops (for characters, lines, and rows) handles the active lines of video. Lines 63–69 fetches each character (line 64 and loads the pixel data for the current line of the character (line 67) into the shift register. Since each character is eight pixels across, the shift register is reloaded once every eight cycles, as dictated by the *deadline* in line 66. This code uses six

```
1  movi $11, 80   ; # columns
2  movi $12, 2400 ; = 80 × 30
3  movi $13, 16   ; lines/character
4
5  field:
6  ; Vertical front porch
7    movi $1, 0
8    movi $2, 10    ; number of lines
9  vfrontporch:
10   deadi $t1, 96   ; h. sync period
11   movi $14, VB+HS+HB
12   deadi $t1, 48   ; back porch
13   movi $14, VB+HB
14   deadi $t1, 640 ; active region
15   movi $14, VB
16   deadi $t1, 16   ; front porch
17   movi $14, VB+HB
18   addi $1, $1, 1
19   bne  $1, $2, vfrontporch
20 ; Vertical sync
21   movi $1, 0
22   movi $2, 2     ; number of lines
23 vsync:
24   deadi $t1, 96
25   movi $14, VS+VB+HS+HB
26   deadi $t1, 48
27   movi $14, VS+VB+HB
28   deadi $t1, 640
29   movi $14, VS+VB
30   deadi $t1, 16
31   movi $14, VS+VB+HB
32   addi $1, $1, 1
33   bne  $1, $2, vsync
34 ; Vertical back porch
35   movi $1, 0
36   movi $2, 33    ; number of lines
37 vbackporch:
38   deadi $t1, 96
39   movi $14, VB+HS+HB
40   deadi $t1, 48
41   movi $14, VB+HB
42   deadi $t1, 640
43   movi $14, VB
44   deadi $t1, 16
45   movi $14, VB+HB
46   addi $1, $1, 1
47   bne  $1, $2, vbackporch
48
49 ; Generate lines of active video
50   movi $2, 0              ; reset line address
51 row:
52   movi $7, 0              ; reset line in char
53 line:
54   deadi $t1, 96           ; h. sync period
55   movi $14, HS+HB
56   ori   $3, $7, FONT ; font base address
57
58   deadi $t1, 48           ; back porch period
59   movi $14, HB
60   deadi $t1, 640          ; active video period
61   mov  $1, 0              ; column number
62
63 char:
64   lb    $5, ($2+$1)       ; load character
65   shli  $5, $5, 4         ; *16 = lines/char
66   deadi $t0, 8            ; wait for next character
67   lb    $14, ($5+$3)  ; fetch and emit pixels
68   addi  $1, $1, 1         ; next column
69   bne   $1, $11, char
70
71   deadi $t1, 16           ; front porch period
72   movi $14, HB
73   addi $7, $7, 1          ; next row in char
74   bne  $7, $13, line      ; repeat until bottom
75   addi $2, $2, 80         ; next line
76   bne  $2, $12, row       ; until at end
77
78   j      field
```

Fig. 3. Assembly code for the video controller. Code on the left handles synchronization around the active text region. Code on lines 63–69 is the main display loop.

of these eight cycles; additional tricks, such as restructuring the font in memory to eliminate the *shli* in line 65, could reduce this.

The *line* loop (lines 53–74) generates sixteen scan lines—one row of characters. It begins by generating a horizontal synchronization pulse: the *deadline* on line 54 that effectively defines the length of the hsync pulse because the first instruction following it (line 55) turns on the pulse and the instruction after the next *deadline*—the *movi* of line 59—turns off the hsync signal.

The *deadline* in line 71 defines the time (16 cycles) of the front porch signal (i.e., horizontal blanking) since just after the next *deadline* that will be executed (either the beginning of the *line* loop in line 54 or in the vertical front porch code—line 10) turns on horizontal synchronization.

This example illustrates two idioms for timer programming. In one, the *deadline* statements is placed at the beginning of a block that sets some signals. The interaction between this *deadline* and the next makes the block run in the prescribed number of cycles prescribed by the first *deadline*. For example, the *deadline* in line 54 uses timer $t1 to make sure that the assertion and deassertion of hsync occur exactly ninety-six clock cycles apart. Practically, the *deadline* in line 54 sets the timer and the *deadline* in line 58 actually performs the delay.

Placing a *deadline* in a loop forces it to execute with the given period. The *deadline* in line 66 does this to ensure that a new character is displayed every eight clock cycles. The loop starts with an *lb* (line 64) that fetches the character

```
    movi $3, 0x0400     ; final bit mask (10 bits)
    movi $5, 651        ; half bit time for 9600 baud
    shli $6, $5, 1      ; calculate full bit time

 wait_for_start:
    bne  $15, $0, wait_for_start
got_start:
    wait $t1, $5        ; sample at center of bit
    movi $14, 0         ; clear received byte
    movi $2, 1          ; received bit mask
    movi $4, 0          ; clear parity
    dead $t1, $6        ; skip start bit
receive_bit:
    dead $t1, $6        ; wait until center of next bit
    mov  $1, $15        ; sample
    xor  $4, $4, $1     ; update parity
    and  $1, $1, $2     ; mask the received bit
    or   $14, $14, $1   ; accumulate result
    shli $2, $2, 1      ; advance to next bit
    bne  $2, $3, receive_bit
check_parity:
    be   $4, $0, detect_baud_rate
    andi $14, $14, 0xff  ; discard parity and stop bits
    j    wait_for_start

 detect_baud_rate:
    movi $6, 0            ; time of start bit
wait_for_start2:
    bne  $15, $0, wait_for_start2
wait_for_end_of_start:
    mov  $1, $15
    addi $6, $6, 3        ; remember end of start bit
    be   $1, $0, wait_for_end_of_start
    sri  $5, $6, 1        ; calculate half bit time
    j    got_start
```

Fig. 4. Assembly code for an asynchronous serial receiver. This reads 8-E-1-formatted data and adjusts the baud rate on a parity error.

from memory (register \$2 holds the address of the leftmost character in the line, and \$1 holds the current column number). A *shli* (line 65) multiplies the character number by sixteen to calculate its offset in the font since each character in the font is sixteen bytes long to produce an 8×16 matrix. We should have arranged the font so that the first line of each character was the first 256 bytes, the next line the next 256, etc., to avoid this shift. The *deadline* in line 66 guarantees the *lb* in line 67 that fetches data from the font (the base address for the current line in the character is in \$3—it was calculated during horizontal sync), is executed once every eight cycles, i.e., once every eight pixels—exactly the length of the pixel shift register.

This example uses two timers: \$t1 for the line (horizontal synchronization and blanking), and \$t0 for the characters. While a single timer would suffice, using two allows line timing to be separated from character timing. For example, it is possible to display only thirty-five characters across by changing the value in \$11, which is compared to the column in \$1 at the bottom of the *char* loop. This changes the execution time of the loop, but since it does not affect timer \$t1, the front porch will still come 640 cycles after the end of the back porch because of the earlier *deadline* instruction.

The simplicity of writing software compared to hardware description language was the main reason we undertook this work, and the video controller bears this out: the assembly code for the video controller is only 78 lines. Its behavior matches that of a 450-line VHDL implementation we wrote earlier.

5 An Asynchronous Serial Communication Receiver

We also coded and ran an asynchronous serial communication receiver (half a UART) with auto baud-rate detection. Its real-time constraints are far less stringent than the video controller, but it embodies a richer algorithm because it works with different baud rates. In particular, it uses computed delays to handle different baud rates.

We connected the serial input to register \$15, which returns either all 0s or all 1s depending on the serial input, and connected register \$14 to a group of LEDs that display the received character.

Figure 4 shows the code, which uses our processor's ability to load timers with non-constant values. The main loop (lines 5–24) waits for the falling edge of a start bit (line 6), delays half a bit time (the contents of \$5–line 8), then samples each incoming bit (line 15) and accumulates the result in \$14 (line 18). We hold a mask indicating the bit being received in \$2 and AND it with the state of the serial port to determine which bit to accumulate in \$14.

When a parity error occurs (the parity of the received byte is maintained in \$4), the code switches over to the *detect_baud_rate* routine (lines 26–35). This also waits for a start bit (line 29), but then looks for the next rising edge (line 33), which it assumes is the LSB of the byte being transmitted. The *wait_for_end_of_start* routine calculates how long this takes—relying on the cycle-level predictability of the processor—and uses it as the new whole-bit time. This can be fooled by bytes whose LSBs are zero.

Although a somewhat unfair comparison, a comparable receiver unit of a mini-UART coded in VHDL by Ovidiu Lupas (from opencores.org) is 154 lines long; our receiver is only 35 and includes auto baud rate detection.

6 Conclusions

We presented a processor extension—instruction-accessible timers—that provides real-time programs with cycle-accurate timing. To validate our approach, we implemented a simple MIPS-like processor that runs on a Xilinx Spartan-3 FPGA at 25 MHz and coded a text-mode video controller and a serial receiver for it. In each case, the assembly-language description was about one quarter the size of the equivalent VHDL, and vastly easier to develop and debug.

While not helpful for soft real-time tasks, our approach greatly simplifies the development of controllers that previously could only be implemented in hardware or through very careful assembly-level coding. Our contribution is to increase the number of applications that can be coded in a software style, which tends to be much more succinct and easier to get right.

We plan to make better use of the time a *deadline* instruction currently idles the processor. Hardware support to run a best-effort thread during this time is one approach. Thekkath and Eggers [17] discuss when this is wise choice for general-purpose processors, but our aims are different. Running more threads may lead to a hardware fixed-priority preemptive scheduler (Kohout et al. [4]).

We also plan to improve the quality of our processor. The MIPS-like architecture we chose was simple to implement but not the best for an FPGA.

We will provide higher-level language support, using C macros for timer control. However, we plan to leave the user responsible for specifying the timing constraints, rather than letting, say, the compiler infer them. A compiler able to perform worst-case execution time analysis, however, would be very helpful.

References

1. Dean, A.G.: Compiling for concurrency: Planning and performing software thread integration. In: Proc. Real-Time Systems Symposium, Austin, Texas (2002)
2. Dean, A.G.: Efficient real-time fine-grained concurrency on low-cost microcontrollers. IEEE Micro **24**(4) (2004) 10–22
3. Welch, B.J., Kanaujia, S.O., Seetharam, A., Thirumalai, D., Dean, A.G.: Supporting demanding hard-real-time systems with STI. IEEE Trans. on Computers **54**(10) (2005) 1188–1202
4. Kohout, P., Ganesh, B., Jacob, B.: Hardware support for real-time operating systems. In: Proceedings of the First International Conference on Hardware/Software Codesign and System Synthesis (CODES+ISSS), Newport Beach, California (2003)
5. Labrosse, J.: MicroC/OS-II. CMP Books, Lawrence, Kansas (1998)
6. Henzinger, T.A., Kirsch, C.M.: The embedded machine: Predictable, portable real-time code. In: Proceedings of the ACM SIGPLAN Conference on Program Language Design and Implementation (PLDI), Berlin, Germany (2002) 315–326
7. Berry, G., Gonthier, G.: The Esterel synchronous programming language: Design, semantics, implementation. Science Comp. Programming **19**(2) (1992) 87–152
8. Caspi, P., Pilaud, D., Halbwachs, N., Plaice, J.A.: LUSTRE: A declarative language for programming synchronous systems. In: Proceedings of the Symposium on Principles of Programming Languages (POPL), Munich, Germany (1987)
9. Roop, P.S., Salcic, Z., Dayaratne, M.W.S.: Towards direct execution of Esterel programs on reactive processors. In: Proceedings of the International Conference on Embedded Software (Emsoft), Pisa, Italy (2004)
10. Ferdinand, C., Heckmann, R., Langenbach, M., Martin, F., Schmidt, M., Theiling, H., Thesing, S., Wilhelm, R.: Reliable and precise WCET determination for a real-life processor. In: Proceedings of the International Conference on Embedded Software (Emsoft). Volume 2211 of Lecture Notes in Computer Science., North Lake Tahoe, California (2001) 469–485
11. Engblom, J.: Static properties of commercial embedded real-time programs, and their implication for worst-case execution time analysis. In: Proc. Real-Time Technology and Applications Symposium (RTAS), Vancouver, Canada (1999)
12. Engblom, J.: On hardware and hardware models for embedded real-time systems. In: Workshop on Real-Time Embedded Systems (WRTES), London, UK (2001)
13. Anantaraman, A., Seth, K., Rotenberg, E., Mueller, F.: Enforcing safety of real-time schedules on contemporary processors using a virtual simple architecture (VISA). In: Real-Time Systems Symposium (RTSS), Lisbon (2004) 114–125
14. Anantaraman, A., Seth, K., Rotenberg, E., Mueller, F.: Virtual simple architecture (VISA): Exceeding the complexity limit in safe real-time systems. In: Proc. Intl. Symp. Computer Architecture (ISCA), San Diego (2003) 350–361
15. Schoeberl, M.: Real-time scheduling on a Java processor. In: Proceedings of the 10th International Conference on Real-Time and Embedded Computing Systems and Applications (RTCSA), Gothenburg, Sweden (2004)
16. Hardin, D.S.: Real-time objects on the bare metal: An efficient hardware realization of the Java virtual machine. In: Proceedings of the Fourth International Symposium on Object-Oriented Real-Time Distributed Computing (ISORC), Magdeburg, Germany (2001) 53–59
17. Thekkath, R., Eggers, S.J.: The effectiveness of multiple hardware contexts. In: ASPLOS-VI: Proceedings of the sixth international conference on Architectural support for programming languages and operating systems. Volume 29 of ACM SIGPLAN Notices., San Jose, California (1994) 328–337

Next Generation Embedded Processor Architecture for Personal Information Devices

In-Pyo Hong, Yong-Joo Lee, and Yong-Surk Lee

The School of Electrical and Electronic Engineering, Yonsei University,
134 Shinchon-dong, Seodaemoon-gu, 120-749, Seoul, Korea
{necross, leemann}@dubiki.yonsei.ac.kr, yonglee@yonsei.ac.kr

Abstract. In this paper, we proposed a processor architecture that is suitable for next generation embedded applications, especially for personal information devices such as smart phones, PDAs, and handheld computers. Latest high performance embedded processors are developed to achieve high clock speed. Because increasing performance makes design more difficult and induces large overhead, architectural evolution in embedded processor field is necessary. Among more enhanced processor types, out-of-order superscalar cannot be a candidate for embedded applications due to its excessive complexity and relatively low performance gain compared to its overhead. Therefore, new architecture with moderate complexity must be designed. In this paper, we developed a low-cost SMT architecture model and compared its performance to other architectures including scalar, superscalar and multiprocessor. Because current personal information devices have a tendency to execute multiple tasks simultaneously, SMT or CMP can be a good choice. And our simulation result shows that the efficiency of SMT is the best among the architectures considered.

1 Introduction

Using simple RISC processors as CPUs for personal information devices such as smart phones, PDAs, and handheld computers is one of the major applications of embedded processors. The characteristics of application programs are similar to that of desktop computers and the need for high performance is getting stronger. However, the limitation in chip size and power consumption prevent the handheld computers from applying more powerful processor cores as their CPUs. The latest commercial processor, ARM11 core, adopts single-issue in-order scalar architecture which is the simplest form among current processor types. Current architectural evolutions in this kind of processors concentrate on increasing clock speed through deeper pipelines [1]. Some embedded processors employ high performance out-of-order superscalar technique that induces large chip area and design complexity. However, they are mainly used for network/communication equipments or home game machines that are neither mobile nor battery-powered. Due to their complexity, these processors cannot be used for handheld devices. Therefore, new processor architecture that boosts

E. Sha et al. (Eds.): EUC 2006, LNCS 4096, pp. 459 – 468, 2006.

architectural performance while suppressing the complexity under the affordable level is needed.

This paper is organized as follows. In section 2, previous works are described. In section 3, architecture models that we simulated are presented in detail. Section 4 shows our simulation methodology and workloads. And after we present simulation results in section 5, section 6 concludes.

2 Previous Works

Most conventional embedded processors adopt simple scalar architecture with 3 to 5 stages of pipeline. These processors can work well when applications are limited to simple personal data management and when multi-tasking is not necessary. However, because mobile internet and multimedia applications are getting popular, personal information devices are requested to cover the application domain of desktop computers. Architectural evolution in this field is concentrated on increasing clock speed while minimizing performance penalty of longer pipeline and suppressing power consumption overhead by using intelligent clock speed and voltage control [1]. Although various techniques are used to prevent negative effects, super-pipelining induces decrease in IPC and fast clock speed requires more power [2][3]. Therefore architectural enhancement that can fundamentally overcome these problems is needed.

Some researchers tried to adopt multithreading to embedded processors [4][5]. They added multiple register sets for multiple hardware contexts and made instructions from multiple threads issue-able cycle by cycle while keeping the other part of the processor unchanged. This architecture type is a kind of fine-grain multithreading. With this simple multithreading, they intended to improve response of processors to randomly triggered events because multithreading architecture does not require context switching on interrupt handling. However, the throughput of these processors is limited to 1 IPC even in ideal cases. Although they invest the largest overhead of multithreading, multiple register sets, the potential of multithreading cannot be fully exploited in the fine-grain multithreading architecture. It is mainly because issue width is restricted to one instruction while more TLP (Thread Level Parallelism) exist. As a result, previous multithreading processors improve response of the processor when multiple events are pending and make real performance closer to the ideal level by switching threads dynamically in wasted cycles.

Enhanced architectures that can improve architectural performance are superscalar and SMT (Simultaneous MultiThreading) [6]. However, it is impossible to use these gigantic processor architectures for our target application that requires tiny and simple hardware, unless it is simplified dramatically. A few researches tried to adopt the SMT technique to embedded applications. However, they are very limited to the applications that require massive parallel data processing such as network processors. In most cases, the complexity is not a matter of concern because the equipments have sufficient space and stable power supply [7][8].

3 Architecture Models

3.1 Baseline Architecture

Our baseline architecture is a reference for comparison against proposed architecture. It resembles current embedded processors which has longer pipeline and single instruction issue mechanism. The instruction set architecture (ISA) is compatible with ARM ISA version 5.

The pipeline has 7 stages and designed to achieve higher clock frequency. Fig. 1 shows the microarchitecture and the pipeline. In fetch stage, a single-ported 128-entry branch target buffer with bimodal direction prediction fields is installed. To track dependencies, a scoreboard is employed To access the scoreboard array and calculate the availability of source operands, separated issue stage is needed. The ARM ISA requires a maximum of three source registers for shifter operand feature. Increasing register read path to three ports incurs additional register read delay and the shifter that must be serially attached to ALU induces great timing overhead to the functional unit. Therefore we divided execution stage to two stages, that is, a register read stage and an execution stage. The architecture described above fetches and executes a single instruction each cycle. We call this architecture scalar architecture in the rest of this paper.

The scalar architecture can be easily extended to execute two instructions per cycle in program order. Although out-of-order scheduling of instructions is needed to maximize ILP, it induces tremendous overhead. Therefore we restrict the issue order to strict program order. First of all, the fetch and decode bandwidth is increased to two instructions. Secondly, to check dependencies successfully, the number of scoreboard array ports is doubled. To fetch the increased number of operands and execute multiple instructions, additional ports of register file and a supplementary

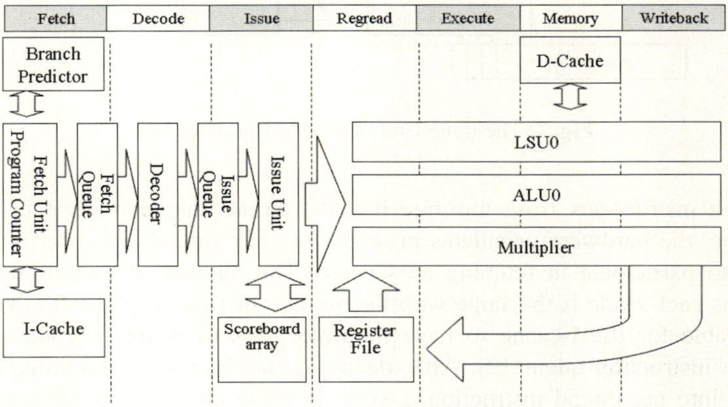

Fig. 1. The microarchitecture and pipeline structure of the baseline processor

ALU is also employed. Finally, a write port of register file is added to support write-back of two instructions in the same cycle. We call this architecture as superscalar in the rest of this paper.

3.2 Multiprocessor Architecture

Multiple scalar or superscalar processors can be organized to form a multiprocessor model. We organized two or four of our scalar and superscalar model into multiprocessor models. Each processor core has its own level-1 caches because the level-1 cache must be tightly coupled with the processor core and sharing a cache induces timing overhead. Because there is no level-2 cache in embedded processors, the cores communicate with each other through the main memory bus.

3.3 In-Order SMT Architecture

We developed an SMT architecture that executes instructions in program order. Although we used the term, SMT, the architecture does not resemble the original SMT except for the fact that multiple threads share execution resources. Our multithreading architecture is from our in-order baseline processor models.

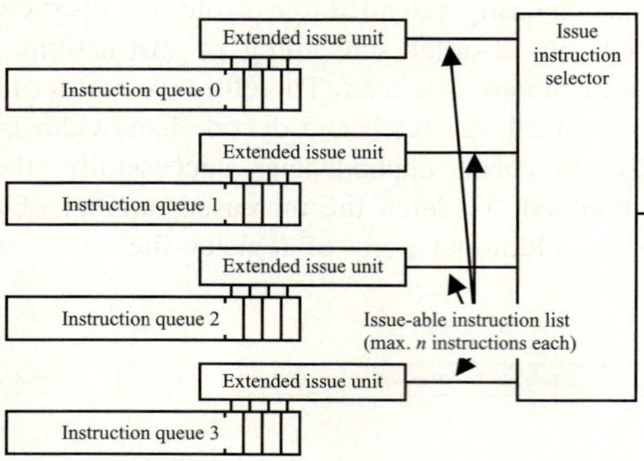

Fig. 2. The Issue Unit of the SMT architecture

To fetch instructions from multiple threads, thread selection stage is added. In select stage, the hardware calculates priorities of each thread and determines which thread is to participate in fetching next cycle. The number of threads that fetches instructions each cycle is the same with the number of I-cache ports. It is known that it is desirable for the I-cache to have multiple ports to maintain good instruction mixture in instruction queue [9]. After decoding the fetched instructions, a decoder puts them into per-thread instruction queues. In these queues, dependency checking and selection for issue take place. In scalar architecture, issue unit checks whether the oldest instruction in the queue can be issued or not using scoreboard. If the result is positive, the instruction is sent to a functional unit. Our SMT architecture extended this decision procedure. If the issue bandwidth is represented as n instructions per cycle, per-thread dependency check logic determines whether the preceding n instructions can be issued or not. After the decision is over, select logic chooses n instructions among all issue-able instructions across the threads, as shown in fig. 3.

An essential part that needs to be modified to support multithreading is the register file. Because the hardware must maintain contexts of multiple threads, register file, program counter and status registers of every thread must be duplicated. This is the largest overhead of our multithreading architecture. While the size of register file must be increased and renaming unit must be changed to accommodate the new register file in the out-of-order SMT architecture, the register file in in-order SMT is merely duplicated and multiplexed. Moreover, because the number of architectural registers is the same with that of physical registers in our SMT model, absolute complexity of our register file is much lower than that of the original SMT architecture. Another modification is in dependency tracking mechanism. Our baseline architecture adopts a dependency tracking method in which every single register needs a corresponding scoreboard entry. Therefore, each thread must have its own scoreboard array.

Our multithreading architecture models are divided into two categories. The first is a fine-grain multithreading architecture with issue bandwidth of one instruction. And the second is SMT architecture that can issue multiple instructions from any thread simultaneously. Fig. 4 shows the two architectures. In this figure, the number of supported threads is set to two and maximum two instructions can be issued per cycle in the SMT architecture model.

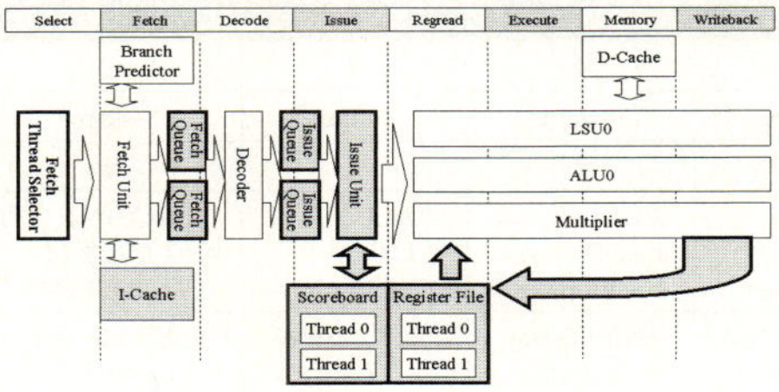

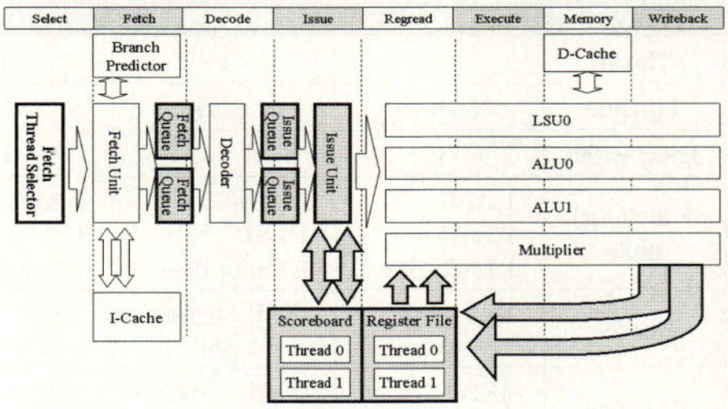

Fig. 3. Multithreading architecture models; single issue fine-grain multithreading (left), in-order SMT (right)

4 Methodology

A cycle-based execution-driven simulator is used in this research. The core part of the simulator is from our previous research [10]. ARM ELF binary loader and system call handling routine that is compatible with ARM Linux is derived from Simplescalar ARM port [11]. Multiple ARM binaries are read simultaneously and participate in the simulation on multithreading architecture. By setting the number of supported threads to one, the simulator operates as a scalar or a superscalar architecture model.

When performing simulation, we set initial options as described in table 1.

In this research, most workloads are derived from MiBench embedded benchmark suite [12] and we programmed an application that performs the IEEE 802.11 WLAN WEP (Wired Equivalent Privacy) algorithm [13]. In personal information devices, internet and streaming multimedia applications are getting as important as traditional personal data management applications that replace a pocket diary. Therefore, workloads are organized to represent the trend that requires multi-tasking of multimedia and networking applications. Detailed information about the workloads is as follows.

- Web browsing: While the processor is receiving packets from a secured WLAN channel, it decodes a html text and a jpeg image.
- Streaming audio and e-book: While the processor is decoding a streaming MP3 audio sequence via WLAN channel, it searches a specific word in an e-book text.
- Smart phone (Voice phone call): While encoding a raw voice data into ADPCM signals and decoding reversely, the processor handles a GSM communication channel.
- Smart phone (Web browsing via GSM channel): While receiving data from a GSM channel, the processor decodes an html text and a jpeg image.
- Secured file transmission: The processor encrypts a plain text file into AES encrypted text and transmits it through a WLAN channel with enabled WEP.

Table 1. Brief descriptions about simulated architecture models

	Scalar	Superscalar	FGMT	SMT_sm	SMT_lg	CMP_is*N*_pr*M*
Thread	1	1	4	4	4	*M*
Pipeline	7-stage	7-stage	8-stage	8-stage	8-stage	7-stage
Issue width	1	2	1	2	4	*N*
Functional units	1 ALU 1 LSU 1 Multiplier	2 ALU 1 LSU 1 Multiplier	1 ALU 1 LSU 1 Multiplier	2 ALU 1 LSU 1 Multiplier	4 ALU 2 LSU 1 Multiplier	(N ALU)**M* (*N*/2 LSU)**M* (1 Multiplier)**M*
I cache	8KB / 8-way 1 port	8KB / 8-way 1 port	8KB / 8-way 2 ports	8KB / 8-way 2 ports	8KB / 8-way 2 ports	(8KB / 8-way 1 port)**M*
D cache	8KB / 8-way 1 port	8KB / 8-way 1 port	8KB / 8-way 1 port	8KB / 8-way 1 port	8KB / 8-way 2 ports	(8KB / 8-way 1 port)**M*
BTB	128	128	128	128	128	128**M*

5 Simulation Results and Optimization

5.1 Overall Performance Comparison

We have simulated eight architecture variations. In Fig. 5, the performance evaluation results are shown. Because in-order instruction scheduling is employed, superscalar architecture cannot increase performance dramatically. It shows only 19% of speedup which is not sufficient for next-generation processors. On the other side, architectures that utilize thread-level parallelism raise performance greatly. Even the simplest single-issue FGMT achieves 51% increased performance. Two-issue processor models, SMT_sm and CMP_is1_pr2, nearly double the performance. The largest four-issue processor models, SMT_lg, CMP_is2_pr2 and CMP_is1_pr4, increase performance by the ratio of 120% to 280%. In the absolute performance aspect, CMP with four individual scalar cores is the best. However, it means that four individual processors with their own caches on a chip are needed. While threads in SMT architecture share many hardware resources, such as caches, branch predictors, TLBs, and functional units, the CMP must have those individually. Because most part of the chip area is devoted to memory blocks including cache memory and MMU, sharing capability of the SMT has great influence on overhead. Therefore, cost-performance efficiency of the SMT is better than that of the CMP. Moreover, the CMP_is1_pr4 shows the same performance with the scalar architecture when there is only one thread to execute. On the other side, the SMT can execute the thread as fast as the superscalar architecture, that is, 19% faster than the CMP.

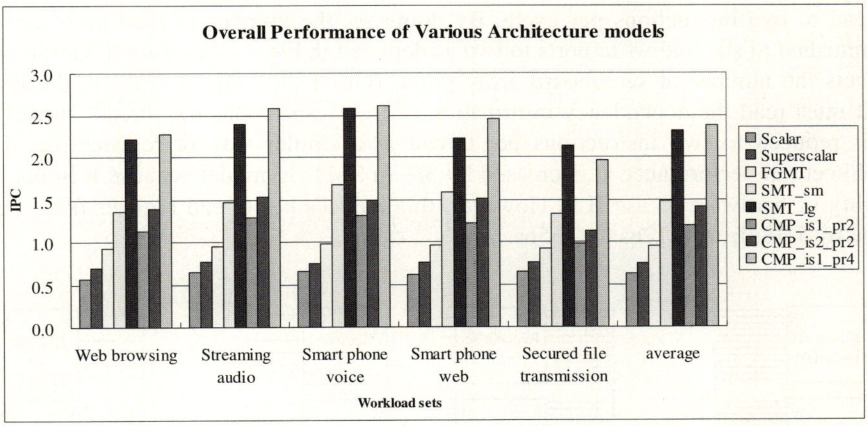

Fig. 4. Performance evaluation results of various architecture models

5.2 More Practical SMT Architecture

To exploit TLP (Thread Level Parallelism) well, instructions from multiple threads must be fairly distributed across the per-thread instruction queues. For this reason, fetching instructions from multiple threads every cycle has positive effect on performance. Therefore, our multithreading architecture also has multiple instruction cache ports, one port for two threads. In our simulation, limiting the number of I-cache ports to one induces average 14.8% of performance penalty in four-thread SMT_lg architecture when thread selection algorithm is round-robin. However, it can be recovered by changing the thread selection algorithm to a more intelligent one. We adopted a selection algorithm which calculates the number of total instructions in instruction queues separately according to threads and selects the thread that has the smallest number of instructions in the queues. By doing so, the simulation result with one I-cache port can be the same as that with two I-cache ports in the SMT_lg architecture model. We used ECACTI model to estimate the effect of the number of cache ports [14]. In a cache memory with 8KB of capacity, 32-byte of line size and 8-way set associative configuration, reducing two read ports to a single port decreases access time from 1.28ns to 0.96ns when 0.10um fabrication process is supposed. Total area is diminished by about 41%, in detail, from 0.017cm^2 to 0.010cm^2. We can achieve 33% of increase in clock speed by simplifying the I-cache and employing the intelligent thread selection algorithm.

Another impractical part is in the register file. In our SMT architecture, a maximum of four instructions from a thread can be issued every cycle. This incurs serious overhead in register file. As stated before, ARM ISA requires maximum three source operands per instruction and four instructions uses maximum 12 read ports and four write ports in worst case. This means that each per-thread register set must have 12 read ports and four write ports to supply source operands of four issued instructions successfully. This excessive number of register file ports is a problem. To mitigate this overhead, we restrict the maximum number of issue-able instructions per thread to two instructions per cycle. By doing so, the number of read ports can be diminished to six, and write ports to two as depicted in Fig. 6. This simplification also affects the number of scoreboard array ports. Before the issue restriction, the issue unit must read the dependency information of four instructions per thread. However, it is reduced to two instructions per thread in a similar way of register file. The architectural performance is decreased by 3% in SMT_lg model because it limits the ability of hardware to use ILP. However, this reduces per-thread register file access time by 41%, from 1.12ns to 0.65ns.

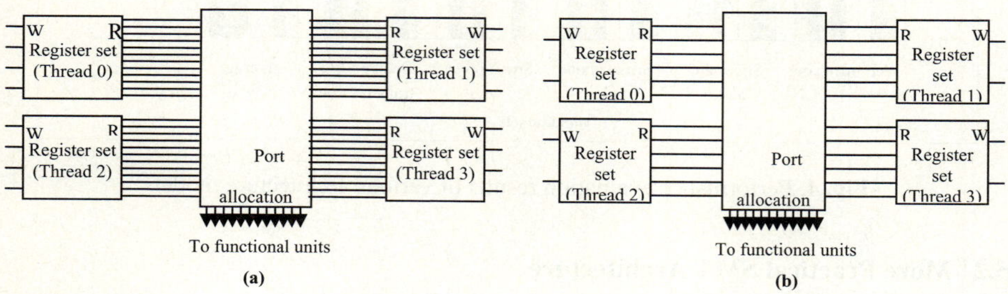

Fig. 5. Reducing the number of register file ports (a) before limiting issue width (b) after limiting issue width to two instructions per thread

5.3 Rough Estimation on Complexity

To evaluate cost-performance relations, we estimated gate counts of all the architectures simulated. Instead of designing all processor models into hardware, we manipulate the approximated area overhead based on the gate count of real ARM9 processor hardware. Total gate counts of a new architecture can be estimated by manipulating gate counts of individual sub-blocks. Though it is not accurate, it can be used as data for comparison. Therefore, meaningful data is not absolute gate counts but relative size. The result is summarized in table 2. To compare the architectures, the unit of IPC per million gates (IPC/area field in the table) is used in the table. Although IPC values of SMT_lg and CMP_is1_pr4 are the best, cost-performance of SMT_sm and SMT_lg is better. Therefore, the in-order SMT architecture can be a strong candidate of next generation processors for personal information devices.

Table 2. Estimated area overhead and cost-performance

	Scalar (ARM9)	Super-scalar	FGMT	SMT_sm	SMT_lg	CMP is*1*_pr*4*
ALU	8.1	16.2	8.1	16.2	32.4	8.1*4
Multiplier	9.8	9.8	9.8	9.8	9.8	9.8*4
Register file	22	44	88	176	176	22*4
Control	4.2	6.3	6.3	6.3	8.4	4.2*4
Decode	2	4	2	4	8	2*4
Forwarding	2	4	2	4	8	2*4
MMU	87	87	87	87	87	87*4
BUS i/f	12	12	12	12	12	12*4
Cache	278	278	278	278	278	278*4
Total area	425.1	461.3	493.2	593.3	619.6	1748.4
Area overhead	-	8.52%	16.02%	39.57%	45.75%	311.29%
IPC/area	1.49	1.62	1.92	2.50	3.73	1.36

6 Conclusions

In this paper, a new processor architecture that is suitable for the CPU of personal information devices is proposed. Simple architectures that are focused on using TLP rather than ILP can achieve high performance without complex out-of-order scheduling of instructions. It is due to the application characteristics of latest personal information devices. Current applications of personal computing machines are getting more network and multimedia oriented than ever while traditional applications merely managing personal information that consists of text data. This inclination requires the processor core to perform multi-tasking.

Under the assumption above, we set up several workload sets that represent applications of the personal information devices, and various processor architectures that have complexity within affordable level are simulated by using the workloads. To avoid excessive overhead, all processor models employ in-order instruction scheduling policy. And some optimizations that reduce hardware overhead of in-order SMT model is proposed. Because the processor cannot exploit ILP well in in-order issue mechanism, superscalar shows the speedup under 20%. On the other hand, SMT and CMP architectures that uses TLP as their performance source outperforms superscalar model with large gap. Although IPC values of the two architectures in case of multithreaded workloads are similar, SMT occupies less area and complexity. Moreover, the SMT can achieve similar performance with superscalar when executing single-threaded workload while the CMP cannot. As a result, proposed simple SMT shows the best cost-performance efficiency.

Acknowledgements

The work presented in this paper is supported by Korea Sanhak Foundation.

References

1. David Cormie, *The ARM11™ Microarchitecture*, ARM Ltd, 2002
2. V. Agarwal, M. S. Hrishikesh, S. W. Keckler and D. Burger,"Clock Rate versus IPC: The End of the Road for Conventional Microarchitectures", Proc. of the 27th Annual International Symposium on Computer Architectures, pp. 248 - 259, 2000
3. Claasen, "High speed: not the only way to exploit the intrinsic computational power of silicon," Digest of Technical Papers, Solid-state Circuits Conference, pp.22~25, 1999
4. U. Brinkschulte , C. Krakowski , J. Kreuzinger , Th. Ungerer, "A Multithreaded Java Microcontroller for Thread-Oriented Real-Time Event Handling," Proceedings of the 1999 International Conference on Parallel Architectures and Compilation Techniques, p.34, October 12-16, 1999
5. J. Kreuzinger, A. Schulz, M. Pfeffer, T. Ungerer, U. Brinkschulte, C. Krakowski. "Real-time scheduling on multithreaded processors," the proceedings of seventh international conference on Real-Time Systems and Applications, pp. 155, 2000
6. Dean M. Tullsen, Susan J. Eggers, and Henry M. Levy, "Simultaenous Multithreading: Maximizing On-Chip Parallelism," Proceedings of 22nd Annual International Symposium on Computer Architecture, pp. 392-403, Santa Margherita Ligure, Italy, May 1995
7. Patrick Crowley, Marc E. Fiuczynski Jean_Loup Baer, and Brian N. Bershad, "Characterizing Processor Architectures for Programmable Network Interfaces," Proceedings of the 2000 International Conference on Supercomputing, May 2000.
8. Peter N. Glaskowsky, "Networking Gets XStream," Microprocessor Report, November 13, 2000
9. Dean M. Tullsen, Susan J. Eggers, Joel S. Emer, and Henry M. Levy, "Exploiting Choice: Instruction Fetch and Issue on an Implementable Simultaneous Multithreading Processor," Proceedings of 23rd Annual International Symposium on Computer Architecture, pp. 191-202, Philadelphia, Pennsylvania, May 1996
10. Byung In Moon, Moon Gyung Kim, In Pyo Hong, Ki Chang Kim, and Yong Surk Lee, "Study of an In-order SMT Architecture and Grouping Schemes," International Journal of Control, Automation, and Systems, Volume 1, Number 3, pp.339~350, September 2003
11. *SimpleScalar Version 4.0 Test Releases*, SimpleScalarLLC, http://www.simplescalar.com/v4test.html
12. Matthew R. Guthaus, Jeffrey S. Ringenberg, Dan Ernst, Todd M. Austin, Trevor Mudge, Richard B. Brown, "MiBench: A free, commercially representative embedded benchmark suite," IEEE 4th Annual Workshop on Workload Characterization, Austin, Texas, December 2001
13. ANSI/IEEE Std 802.11-1999, Wireless LAN Medium Access Control (MAC) and Physical Layer (PHY) Specifications
14. Mahesh Mamidipaka and Nikil Dutt, "eCACTI: An Enhanced Power Estimation Model for On-chip Caches," Center for Embedded Computer Systems (CECS) Technical Report TR-04-28, Sept. 2004

A Secret Image Sharing Scheme Based on Vector Quantization Mechanism

Chin-Chen Chang [1,2], Chi-Shiang Chan[1], and Yi-Hsuan Fan[1]

[1] Department of Computer Science and Information Engineering, National Chung Cheng University, Chiayi, Taiwan 621
{ccc, cch, fyh93}@cs.ccu.edu.tw

[2] Department of Information Engineering and Computer Science, Feng Chia University, Taichung, Taiwan 40724
ccc@cs.ccu.edu.tw

Abstract. In this paper, we proposed an image sharing method adopting (*t*, *n*) threshold scheme. The secret image goes through Vector Quantization (VQ) scheme and permutes the locations of indices to obtain permuted indexed secret image. We select *t* indices to form a (*t*-1)-degree polynomial by taking *t* indices as its coefficients. Then, the values of blocks' indices in cover image are fed into the (*t*-1)-degree polynomial to get the output values. After embedding the output values back to the pixels in block, we can obtain meaningful shadow images. Any *t* out of *n* shadow images can reconstruct the permuted indexed secret image. By inversing permutation and decoding VQ indices, we can finally reconstruct the secret image. Experimental results show that our method can get high image quality for the resultant shadow images and reconstruct secret images as well.

Keywords: Image sharing, (*t*, *n*) threshold scheme, vector quantization.

1 Introduction

As the rapid growth of communication, texts and images are often digitized in order to be processed, stored, and transmitted on the wide Internet easily. For these exposed data, security is the most important concern anywise. To protect a secret file, the simplest way is to encrypt it with a secret key. However, there are two drawbacks for such a system. If illegal people can obtain the secret key to decrypt the secret file, the file might be likely stolen. Besides, the secret file cannot be revealed completely if the secret key is lost or destroyed accidentally. To solve the safekeeping and distribution problems, it is necessary to design a secret key management to protect the secret key on multi-party secure protocols [4, 5, 6, 8]. Secret sharing method is one formal strategy of the possible solutions.

The first secret sharing scheme called (*t*, *n*) threshold scheme was proposed by Shamir [11] and Blakley [1] independently. It can distribute and share secret information among *n* participants in such a way and no one can obtain any useful information from the shared data. Referring to security, any *t* qualified participants of

E. Sha et al. (Eds.): EUC 2006, LNCS 4096, pp. 469 – 478, 2006.

n can reconstruct the secret completely, but any t-1 have no information about the secret absolutely. The concept of secret sharing has been used widely in many commercial or military applications, such as launching a missile, opening a bank vault or a safety deposit box, etc. In addition, there are lots of researches and studies that have already been proposed, which focus on improving the security of the system [2, 3, 12].

Furthermore, secret sharing schemes have been applied to secret images sharing. The secret data are by far secret images in the application. However, directly using the (t, n) threshold scheme requires large memory space. To improve this drawback, Thien and Lin proposed a secret image sharing method derived from the original (t, n) threshold scheme in [9]. Thien and Lin's method generates a (t-1)-degree polynomial for each t gray value and set the t gray values as the coefficients. Here, we must label a fixed number for each shadow and take this number as a parameter input to feed into the (t-1)-degree polynomial to get result values. Consisting of those result values, then we can recover the shadow image.

Nevertheless, in Thien and Lin's method [13], we can see nothing else but some random gray level pixels. Moreover, each shadow image must be labeled a fixed number. Once the labeled number is lost unfortunately, this shadow image will be invalid. Another drawback of Thien and Lin's method is that any gray pixels, whose values are larger than 250 in a secret image, must be truncated to 250.

To improve those drawbacks, we shall propose a novel secret image sharing method in this paper. In our method, we do not need to label each shadow image. Instead, the parameter of each shadow image is set according to the VQ-index of each block. Furthermore, we embed sharing data into cover images so that the shadow images can be meaningful images to achieve the secret date transmission, rather than random-dot images.

The rest of this paper is organized as follows. To begin with, we shall review the related works in Section 2. Then, we will continue to present our method in Section 3. In Section 4, we shall offer our experimental results to demonstrate the effectiveness of our new method. Finally, the conclusions will be given in Section 5.

2 Related Works

Shamir first proposed the (t, n) threshold scheme that uses a polynomial to process the secret sharing. The final purpose is to split a secret data S into n shadows, and any t shadows can be used to reconstruct the secret data. If the number of shadows is less than t, the secret data cannot be revealed. To achieve this purpose, we first choose a prime number p and t-1 random numbers, $a_1, a_2, \ldots, a_{t-1}$. Then, we build a ($t$-1)-degree polynomial with filling a_0 , $a_1, \ldots, a_{t-1}$ into this polynomial, where a_0 is the secret data S. The (t-1)-degree polynomial is shown below.

$$f(x) = (a_0 + a_1 x + a_2 x^2 + \ldots + a_{t-1} x^{t-1}) \bmod p. \quad (1)$$

Once we have a (t-1)-degree polynomial, we can choose n random numbers $y_0, y_1, \ldots, y_{n-1}$ and calculate n values $d_0 = f(y_0)$, $d_1 = f(y_1)$, $\ldots, d_{n-1} = f(y_{n-1})$. Those n shadows are (y_0, d_0), (y_1, d_1), $\ldots (y_{n-1}, d_{n-1})$. If we get any t shadows, we can reconstruct the (t-1)-degree polynomial by using Largrange's interpolation. It goes without saying that the secret data S can be obtained through the reconstructed the $(t\text{-}1)$-degree polynomial.

In 2002, Thien and Lin applied (t, n) threshold scheme to process the image sharing. The main idea of Thien and Lin's method is to fill t gray pixel values of the secret image into a $(t\text{-}1)$-degree polynomial as its coefficients. The scheme then calculates $f(1), f(2), \ldots, f(n)$. The value $f(1)$ is taken as the gray pixel value of the first shadow image, and $f(2)$ is taken as the gray pixel value of the second shadow image, and likewise. Finally, we can obtain n shadow images. Having any t shadow images, we can successfully recover the original secret image. Note that the number which shadow image belongs to must be kept in mind.

One more step must been performed before applying (t, n) threshold scheme to gray level images. That is, gray pixels, whose values are larger than 250, must be adjusted to 250. The reason is described below. The range of a pixel value is from 0 to 255 and the prime number p of the $(t\text{-}1)$-degree polynomial must be within this range. In Thien and Lin's method, they chose 251 as the prime number p, which is the greatest prime number no larger than 255. Once we set 251 as prime number p, the reconstructed values of $a_0, a_1, \ldots, a_{t\text{-}1}$ are also in the range from 0 to 250. Therefore, we must truncate all pixels of values from 251 to 255 in secret images to 250.

We now describe Thien and Lin's method step by step as below.

```
Step 1. Adjust the gray pixels whose values are larger
        than 250 to 250.
Step 2. Permute the locations of the pixels in the
        secret image.
Step 3. Pick up t non-taken pixels in the permuted
        image.
Step 4. Form a (t-1)-degree polynomial by using t non-
        taken pixels as its coefficients.
Step 5. Calculate f(1), f(2), …, f(n).  Put the value
        f(1) to the first shadow image, f(2) to the
        second shadow image, and likewise.
Step 6. Mark t non-taken pixels as taken pixels. Go
        back to Step 3 until all pixels are marked as
        taken pixels.
```

We here give a simple example to illustrate Thien and Lin's method. The flowchart is shown as Fig. 1. Assume that the values of t and n are 2 and 3, respectively. Because the first two values of non-taken pixels are 4 and 7, the polynomial is $f(x) = 4+7x$. We label the first shadow image, the shadow image A, as number 1, label the second shadow image, the shadow image B, as number 2, and likewise. The values of $f(1)$, $f(2)$ and $f(3)$ are 11, 18 and 25, respectively, which are the first pixel values of the shadow image A, shadow image B and shadow image C, respectively. Repeating the same procedure, we can obtain three shadow images.

When reconstructing the permuted secret image, we can pick any two from these three shadow images to do our job. For example, we here have the shadow images A and C. Because the label number of these two images are 1 and 3, respectively, we can reconstruct the polynomial $f(x) = 4+7x$ by using (1, 11) and (3, 25). The first and second pixel values of the permuted secret image are thus 4 and 7, respectively. Therefore, we can follow the same procedure to reconstruct the whole pixel values in

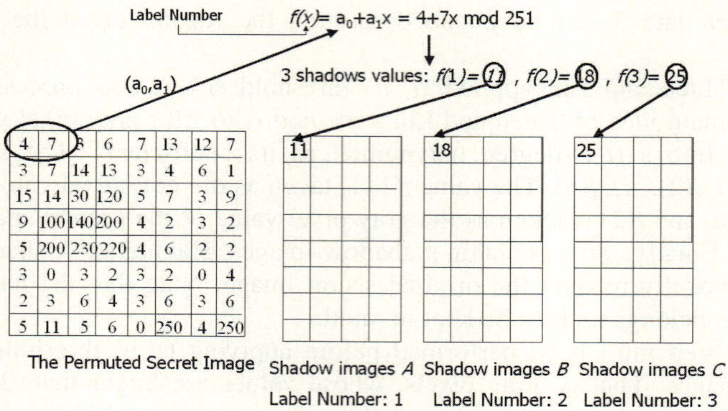

Fig. 1. An example of Thien and Lin's method

the permuted secret image. Adopting the inverse-permutation operation, the secret image can be revealed finally.

3 The Proposed Method

First of all, as we mentioned in Section 2, the results of Thien and Lin's method are n shadow images and those shadow images are only some random gray level pixels. This might catch the notice of grabbers. In order to enlarge the hidden quantity and make the shadow images meaningful, we encode the secret image using Vector Quantization (VQ) and embed the sharing data into cover images.

Second, in Thien and Lin's method, each shadow image must be labeled a fixed number and all these numbers must be kept in mind. If we forget any labeled number of a shadow image, this shadow image will become invalid. For instance, if we forget which label number the shadow image *A* belongs to in Fig. 1, that means we will lose one parameter to reconstruct the $(t\text{-}1)$-degree polynomial. To solve this problem, the parameter of each shadow image is set according to the VQ-index.

Third, Thien and Lin's method chose 251 as the prime number p. Those gray pixels, whose values are larger than 250 in a secret image, must be truncated to 250. In our proposed method, we chose 257 as the prime number p, so that we do not need to truncate any VQ-index value of a secret image. However, the value of $f(x)$ might be larger than 255, that is, 256. In this case, we can adjust x to make $f(x)$ in the range from 0 to 255. The details will be explained in the following paragraphs.

We now briefly introduce Vector Quantization (VQ) technique first. VQ technique is an image-compression technique. In this VQ mechanism, the codebook plays an important role, which consists of elements called codewords. Each codeword has its corresponding index that can be used to reach the codeword. All codewords are obtained from training several candidate blocks in the images using the LBG algorithm [10]. In the encoding phase, the original image is divided into non-overlapping blocks as codewords, each of which is of the same size. Therefore, we can find the most similar codewords for a sequence of non-overlapping blocks. By only recording the corresponding indices for codewords, the image then could be compressed using VQ technique. In the decoding phase, because of holding a sequence of indices, we can reconstruct the image by looking up codewords in the codebook according to the indices. The flowchart of VQ technique is drawn as Fig. 2.

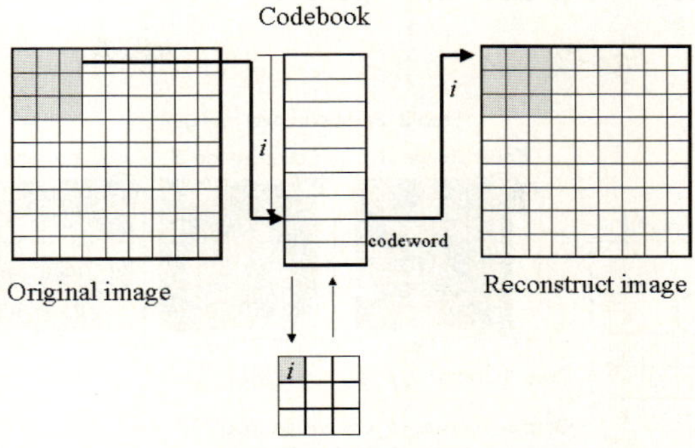

Fig. 2. The flowchart of the *VQ* method

Now, we introduce our secret image sharing scheme based on Vector Quantization (VQ). There exist two phases in our proposed method. One is sharing phase and the other is revealing phase.

Step 1. Transform a secret image into VQ indices using Vector Quantization (VQ) technique. Permute the locations of the indices of the secret image.

Step 2. Set the one least significant bit of all pixels in cover images as 0. Partition all cover images into non-overlapping blocks and use Vector Quantization (VQ) to find out indices of those non-overlapping blocks.

Step 3. Pick up t non-taken indices in the permuted indexed image and form a (t-1)-degree polynomial by taking t non-taken indices as its coefficients, where the value of prime number P is 257.

Step 4. Pick a block that has capacity to hide data from each cover image. Assume their indices are $I_1, I_2, \ldots, I_n$.

Step 5. Check whether there exist two picked indices whose values are the same. If there is so, randomly select one block from those two, and replace this block with another similar block in the codebook and store this similar block back to cover images. Repeat this step until all picked blocks have different indices.

Step 6. Calculate $f(I_1)$, $f(I_2)$, …, $f(I_n)$. Check whether there exists any result valued 256. If so, replace this block with another similar one in the codebook and store this similar block back into cover images. Then, go back to Step 5.

Step 7. Embed the result value $f(I_1)$ to the one least

significant bit of all pixels in the picked block in the first shadow image, embed $f(I_2)$ in the second shadow image, and likewise.

Step 8. Mark t non-taken pixels as taken pixels. Go back to Step 3 until all pixels are marked as taken pixels.

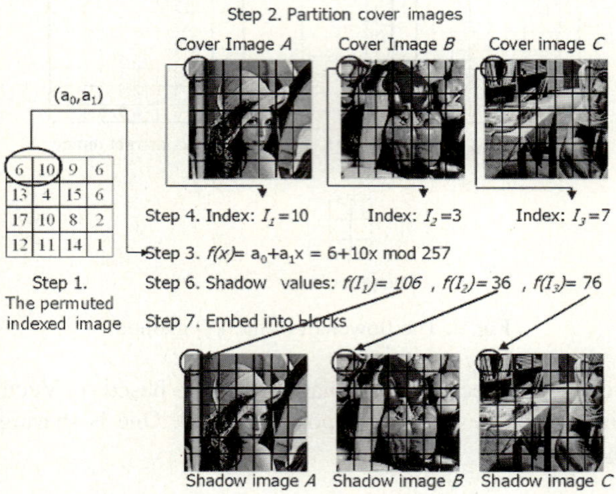

Fig. 3. The flowchart of our proposed method

We give a simple example with a flowchart Fig. 3 to illustrate our proposed method in the following. Assume that the values of t and n are 2 and 3, respectively.

The first two values of non-taken indices are 6 and 10, and the polynomial is $f(x) = 6+10x$. As for cover images, they are partitioned into 4×4 non-overlapping blocks, that is totally, there are 16 pixels in each block. As shown in Fig. 3, the index value of the first block in cover image A is $I_1 = 10$, the index value of the first block in cover image B is $I_2 = 3$, the index value of third block in cover image C is $I_3 = 7$, and the values of $f(I_1)$, $f(I_2)$ and $f(I_3)$ are 106, 36 and 76, respectively. We directly substitute one least significant bit of pixels with these result values. To be more precise, the 8-bit representation of 106 is $(01101010)_2$. And because the bit value of first bit is 0, we replace the least significant bit of first pixel in the first block of cover image A with 0. The bit value of the second bit is 1, so we replace the least significant bit of second pixel in first block of cover image A with 1, and likewise.

Note that there exist 16 pixels in each block, which means the total number of bits that can be hidden in one block is 16. However, we only embed 8 bits into a block. There still have 8 bits that can be used to hide data. Therefore, we carry out the same procedure to produce another polynomial $f(x) = 9+6x$ from another two non-taken indices. Then, we calculate the values of $f(I_1)$, $f(I_2)$ and $f(I_3)$ and they are 69, 27 and 51, respectively. The value 69 is embedded into another non-embedded 8 bits of the

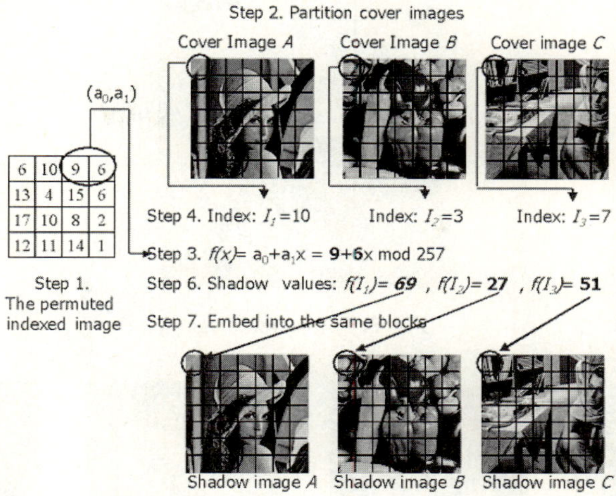

Fig. 4. The flowchart of our proposed method

same block in the cover image *A*. After going through the same procedure, we can obtain three shadow images.

In the revealing phase, if we have any two shadow images, we can reconstruct the permuted indexed secret image. Here, we pick up the shadow images *A* and *C*. We first partition these two images into 4×4 non-overlapping blocks. For the first block, we can find out its corresponding index 10 for shadow image *A* and index 7 for shadow image *C*. After that, we extract 8 bits from least significant bit of 8 pixels in first block. The extracted value from the shadow image *A* is 106 and that from the shadow image *C* is 76. Through two points (10, 106) and (7, 76), the polynomial $f(x)=6+10x$ can be reconstructed. Therefore, the first and second pixel values of the permuted indexed secret image are 6 and 10, respectively. We can use the same procedure to reconstruct the whole pixel values in the permuted indexed secret image. Performing the inverse-permutation operation, the secret indexed image can finally be revealed entirely.

4 Experimental Results

In this section, we will demonstrate our experimental results and show the image quality of our method. Our secret image F-16 is shown in Fig. 5, of size 512 × 512 pixels, and cover images are named Lena, Pepper, Barb and Baboon, the size of which is 256 × 256, as shown in Fig. 6.

In our first experiment, (2, 3) threshold secret sharing scheme is performed, and the secret image is shared by three shadow images. Any two shadow images can be chosen to reveal the original secret image. The experimental results are shown in Figs. 7 and 8.

Fig. 5. The secret image

(a) Lena (b) Pepper (c) Barb (d) Baboon

Fig. 6. The grayscale cover images

(a) A secret image (b) The VQ-compressed image of (a) (c) The reconstructed secret image

Fig. 7. The experimental results for the secret image with size 512 × 512 pixels

(a) (b) (c)

Fig. 8. Three meaningful shadow images with size 256 × 256 pixels

In our second experiment, (2, 4) threshold secret sharing scheme is carried out, and the secret image is shared by four shadow images. Similarly, any two shadow images can reveal the original secret image. The experimental results are shown in Figs. 9 and 10.

(a) A secret image (b) The VQ-compressed image of (a) (c) The reconstructed secret image

Fig. 9. The experimental results for the secret image with size 512 × 512 pixels

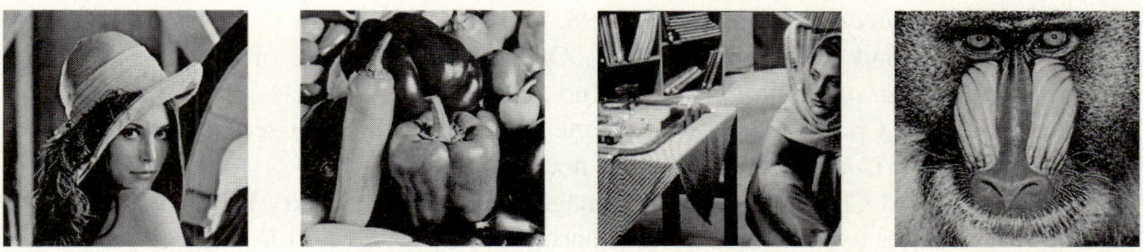

(a) (b) (c) (d)

Fig. 10. Four meaningful shadow images with size 256 × 256

The quality of three shadow images in (2, 3) threshold secret sharing scheme and four shadow images in (2, 4) threshold secret sharing scheme are shown in Table 1 and Table 2, respectively

Table 1. The *PSNR*'s adopting (2, 3) threshold secret sharing scheme

Image Types	Images	*PSNR* (in dB)
Shadow images	Lena	48.0931
	Pepper	46.2767
	Barb	43.4503
Reconstructed image	F-16	30.5798

Table 2. The *PSNR*'s adopting (2, 4) threshold secret sharing scheme

Image Types	Images	*PSNR* (in dB)
Shadow images	Lena	48.0931
	Pepper	46.2630
	Barb	43.4483
	Baboon	39.6525
Reconstructed image	F-16	30.5798

5 Conclusions

The (*t*, *n*) threshold scheme was proposed to process secret sharing. In 2002, Thien and Lin proposed a (*t*, *n*) threshold scheme to deal with secret image sharing. Although it works, there exist some drawbacks. In this paper, we proposed an improved method to solve those drawbacks. Moreover, Vector Quantization (VQ) is employed to further increase the hiding capacity. According to our experimental results, shadow images and the secret image can still have high quality. In a word, our new scheme, as a whole, is quite a practical method to process image sharing.

References

1. Blakley, G.. R., "Safeguarding Cryptographic Keys," *Proceedings AFIPS 1979 National Computer Conference*, vol. 48, New York, USA, no. 4-7, 1979, pp. 313-317.
2. Beimel, A. and Chor, B., "Universally Ideal Secret-sharing Schemes," *IEEE Transactions on Information Theory*, vol. 40, no. 3, 1994, pp. 786-794.
3. Beimel, A. and Chor, B., "Secret Sharing with Public Reconstruction," *IEEE Transactions on Information Theory*, vol. 44, no. 5, 1998, pp.1887-1896.
4. Brickell, E. F. and Davenport, D. M., "On the Classification of Ideal Secret Sharing Schemes," *Journal of Cryptology*, vol. 4, no. 73, 1991, pp. 123-134.
5. Chan, C. C. and Chang, C. C., "A Scheme for Threshold Multi-secret Sharing," *Applied Mathematics and Computation*, vol. 166, no. 1, 2005, pp. 1-14.
6. Chang, C. C. and Chuang, J. C., "An Image Intellectual Property Protection Scheme for Gray-level Images using Visual Secret Sharing Strategy," *Pattern Recognition Letters*, vol. 23, no. 8, 2002, pp. 931-941.
7. Gray, R. M., "Vector Quantization," *IEEE ASSP Magazine*, 1984, pp. 4-29.
8. Hwang, K. F. and Chang, C. C., "Recent Development of Visual Cryptography," *Intelligent Watermarking Techniques*, World Scientific Publishing Company, chapter 16, 2004, pp. 459-480.
9. Kamin, E. D., Greene, J. W., and Hellman, M. E., "On Secret Sharing Systems," *IEEE Transaction on Information Theory*, vol. IT-29, no. 1, 1983, pp. 35-41.
10. Linde, Y., Buzo, A., and Gray, R. M., " An Algorithm for Vector Quantizer Design, " *IEEE Transactions on Communications*, vol. 28, 1980, pp. 84-95.
11. Shamir, A., "How to Share a Secret," *Communication of the ACM,* vol. 22, no. 11, 1979, pp. 612-613.
12. Stinson, D. R., "Decomposition Constructions for Secret-sharing Schemes," *IEEE Transaction on Information Theory*, vol. 40, no. 1, 1994, pp. 118-124.
13. Thien, C. C. and Lin, J. C., " Secret Image Sharing, " *Computer & Graphics*, vol. 26, 2002, pp. 765-770.

A Framework for Managing the Solution Life Cycle of Event-Driven Pervasive Applications

Johnathan M. Reason[1], Han Chen[1], ChangWoo Jung[2], SunWoo Lee[2], Danny Wong[1], Andrew Kim[2], SooYeon Kim[2], JiHye Rhim[2], Paul B. Chou[1], and KangYoon Lee[2]

[1] IBM T.J. Watson Research Center, 19 Skyline Drive, Hawthorne, NY 10532
{reason, chenhan, dcwong, pchou}@us.ibm.com

[2] IBM Ubiquitous Computing Laboratory, The MMAA Building, 467-12 Dogok-dong, Gangnam-gu, Seoul 135-700
{jungcw, samlee, akhkim, sooyeon.kim, jhrhim, keylee}@kr.ibm.com

Abstract. Event-driven, embedded applications that embody the composition of many disparate components are emerging as an important class of pervasive applications. For such applications, realizing solutions often requires a breadth of expertise. Consequently, managing the solution life cycle can be a very complex, time-intensive process. In this paper, we present a framework that eases the complexity of managing the life cycle of event-driven, pervasive solutions. We call this framework Rapid Integrated Solution Enablement or RISE. Component composition and software reuse are two central concepts of RISE, where solutions are graphically composed from reusable components using a visual editor. We describe the RISE architecture and discuss an initial prototype implementation that leverages open source technologies, such as Eclipse. Additionally, we illustrate the efficacy of RISE with an example solution for RFID supply chain logistics.

1 Introduction

Pervasive applications are becoming prevalent in our society, especially ones with embedded solutions that are driven by events originating from various sensor modalities. The apparatus comprising an embedded solution is often assembled from disparate components, including hardware devices (e.g., sensors, actuators, programmable logic controllers, and displays) and software components (e.g., device adapters, agents, and event correlators). Thus, realizing an embedded solution can be a very complex process that requires a high-degree of expertise across many specialty domains, such as embedded programming, networking, device adapter programming, wireless communications, and user interface design.

These specialties are often performed across solution partners, including device OEMs, solution integrators, solution developers, and the customers. Solution integrators must integrate the hardware devices and software components into the apparatus, solution developers must write application code for specific customer requirements, solution developers must test and validate the solution, and

E. Sha et al. (Eds.): EUC 2006, LNCS 4096, pp. 479–488, 2006.

IT staff must incorporate the solution into the IT infrastructure. This approach often leads to one-off solutions that are not flexible enough to accommodate new requirements.

RISE is a graphical, actor-oriented software framework for managing the life cycle of event-driven, embedded solutions. Through greater reuse of component-based, customizable software, RISE can lower the total cost of ownership, facilitate rapid development, deployment, and management, and improve flexibility of solutions through dynamic configuration. RISE exploits the concepts of component composition, software reuse, and heterogeneous models of computation to provide the tooling and runtime support.

This paper is organized as follows. Sect. 2 describes the foundational background, Sect. 3 describes the RISE architecture, Sect. 4 describes our initial prototype implementation, Sect. 5 discusses a use case example, and we conclude with some comments about ongoing work in Sect. 6.

2 Background

In this section, we discuss the core concepts that form the basis of RISE and introduce the terminology used throughout the remainder of this paper.

2.1 Related Work

RISE gets its motivation from other tools that provide a graphical block diagram methodology for actor-oriented modeling. To name a few, Simulink from The Mathworks®, LabVIEW® from National Instruments, and Ptolemy II from the The Ptolemy Project of the University of California at Berkeley are examples of actor-oriented design environments. While all of these tools (and others) have their strengths and weaknesses, we found all of them lacking a unified framework for deployment and management of embedded environments. Nevertheless, we find instruction in their theoretical underpinnings and leverage some specific results from Ptolemy II.

Actor-Oriented Design. In actor-oriented modeling, components are called actors and can communicate and execute with other actors in a model, where a model is the composition of one or more actors. Hewitt first introduced the term actor to describe the concept of autonomous reasoning agents [1], and later Agha refined the term to describe a formalized model of concurrency [2,3,4]. The Ptolemy Project has further refined the term to embody more models of concurrency and support actors that do not necessarily have their own thread of control [5,6].

All actors have an external component interface that abstracts its internal state and behavior. An actors interface is defined by its port/parameter specification, where ports represent points of communication for an actor and parameters affect the behavior of an actor. Parameter values can be static or dynamic during execution of a model.

Connections between ports are called channels, and actors communicate over channels via some method of messaging. Thus, actors do not interact directly with other actors, only through channels. This differs from object-oriented design, where components communicate through method calls.

A model can also have an external interface, which represents a hierarchical notion of abstraction. A model's interface also consists of ports and parameters, which can be connected by channels to other ports of the model or to the ports of the model's internal actors. Similarly, a model's parameters can be used to determine the parameter values of its internal actors.

Model of Computation. The concepts above describe the abstract syntax of actor-oriented modeling. However, the semantics are governed by its model of computation (MoC).

An MoC defines the semantics of inter-component communications and the runtime execution semantics of a model. One might think of a model of computation as the rules governing component interaction and execution. These rules govern when and how a component invokes its internal computation, updates its state, and communicates through its ports.

There are many well know models of computation, too many to enumerate here. One key result coming from The Ptolemy Project is its comprehensive study of concurrent MoCs, and Ptolemy II provides open source, Java implementations for a full list of MoCs [7]. The initial RISE prototype leverages MoC implementations from Ptolemy II (see Sect. 4.3).

2.2 RISE Terminology

We mostly adopt the actor-oriented terminology described in Sect. 2.1, with a few extensions and differences. We define two general types of actors: atomic and composite. Atomic actors represent the most primitive of actors and are typically implemented in a high-level programming language, such as Java. In contrast, composite actors are hierarchical actors that are constructed by graphically connecting atomic actors and other composite actors. We reserve the term model to represent a composite actor that is a deployable application, and we use connection instead of channel.

Additionally, an atomic actor can be behavior-polymorphic, which we define as an atomic actor that has a generic external interface (i.e., ports and parameters), but defines an abstract interface for its internal implementation. Thus, behavior-polymorphic actors can have multiple concrete internal implementations. We use behavior-polymorphic actors to model actors that have similar attributes, such as a device adapter for a particular family of devices. Behavior-polymorphism complements the notions of data- and domain-polymorphism found in Ptolemy II [8,9,10].

3 Architecture

The RISE software architecture is comprised of three platforms: RISE Development Platform (RDP), RISE Runtime Platform (RRP), and RISE Library Server

Platform (RLP). RDP provides the tooling for developers to build, deploy, and manage RISE-based solutions. RRP provides the software that supports execution of RISE-based solutions. While, RLP provides the means by which RISE runtimes can dynamically discover the actors that comprise a solution.

3.1 Development Platform

Fig. 1 illustrates the software architecture for RDP. The underlying computing framework for RDP is a Java virtual machine (JVM) running on a hardware device (e.g., Java 2 Standard Edition on a personal computer). The middleware layer provides the software that serves as the building blocks for the tooling and the artifacts created by the tooling. The tools layer provides all the functions that comprise the integrated development environment (IDE).

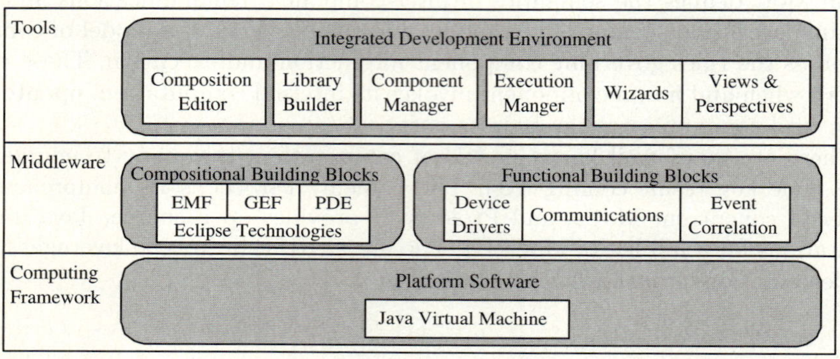

Fig. 1. RDP contains three layers: computing framework, middleware, and tooling

Integrated Development Environment. RDP's IDE provides a graphical user interface for a user to construct actors, models, and libraries. The tools that comprise the IDE are a composition editor, a component manager, a library builder, and a model execution manager. The composition editor presents a user with a canvas to edit an actors structural elements and to drag-n-drop actors from the component manager to the model diagram.

The component manager maintains the persistent storage of reusable components available from the local environment. The library builder is a utility that packages one or more actors or models into a deployable library and installs the library to an appropriate library server. The execution manager is a utility that provides the user interface and protocol to load models in the runtime, retrieve a model from the runtime, and display execution events. The IDE also supports a number of wizards, views, and perspectives to provide an intuitive design flow. One important view of the IDE is the library view, which provides four different means to access reusable actors (see Sect. 4.4).

Compositional Building Blocks. Eclipse technologies provide the compositional building blocks of RDP's IDE (see Sect. 4.2).

Functional Building Blocks. The devices that produce the event and data streams for a solution and comprise a solutions apparatus are central to most event-driven applications. Thus,the device adapters that provide the application-level software interface to devices are an important category. RDP supports building device adapters on top of manufacturer-specific device drivers or using generic device drivers (e.g., serial port). In addition, RDP provides the framework for porting other device adapters to the RISE device adapter abstraction via Eclipse plug-in technology.

Distributed communications where one instance of a solution might need to communicate to other remote entities, such as an enterprise server, is another important category. Using polymorphic components, RDP provides the framework for developing reusable communications components that can support different implementations of well know communications paradigms, such as HTTP client/servlet, publish/subscribe, and UDP/TCP.

Event correlation is the general terminology given to middleware technology that can identify patterns in one or more data sources, define events as the occurrence of one or more patterns, and then use the detected events to trigger some action. A user usually configures the patterns and events through a set of rules, which are specified by a rule language and executed by a correlation engine. RDP provides the framework for developing solutions with event correlation components.

3.2 Runtime Platform

Fig. 2 illustrates the software architecture for RRP, which contains two layers: computing framework and runtime. The underlying computing framework for RRP is the Open Services Gateway Initiative (OSGi) Service Platform Release 3 specification [11]. The runtime layer provides the runtime libraries and the runtime execution services.

OSGi Service Platform Release 3. OSGi defines a framework on which multiple applications can run on a single JVM. Using the OSGi framework, application developers partition applications into services, and then package these services into application bundles. Bundles can register services with the framework that other bundles can use; thereby, facilitating the sharing of services at the package level. In RISE, we package all RISE-specific technologies into OSGi bundles, including the RISE runtime libraries and runtime execution services.

Runtime Libraries. A RISE runtime library is an OSGi bundle that contains the class definitions for one or more RISE actors and/or models. Because RISE libraries are OSGi bundles, they derive all the benefits provided by the framework, including dynamic installation, automatic resolution of dependencies, and import/export of services and packages. These benefits provide a convenient means for supporting a dynamic, distributed method for resolving the composition of model during runtime. In particular, the child actors of a model need not be loaded from the same library, nor do all the libraries have to reside on the same library server.

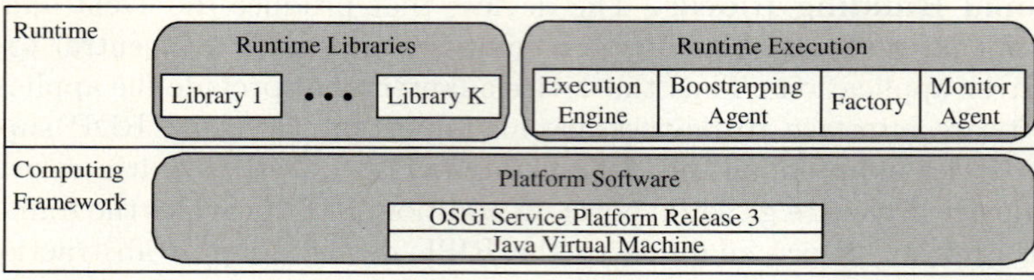

Fig. 2. The primary services of RRP are the bootstrapping agent, the factory, the execution engine, and the monitor agent. These services provide loading and unloading of a model, instantiation of the actors, execution of a model, and execution monitoring.

Runtime Execution. The execution engine specializes a model to a particular MoC. The engine also supports execution of models with a heterogeneous mixture of MoCs, which is a concept we borrow from the Ptolemy Project. For our application domain, we exploit this concept primarily by augmented discrete event or data flow semantics with control flow.

The bootstrapping agent loads a model into the execution engine, passing along any necessary parameters. The bootstrapping agent provides a server interface for clients to connect to it. Clients can load fully executable models or load by reference. In the latter case, the composition of a model must be resolved and its child actors instantiated. For this purpose, the agent defers to the factory.

The factory services the bootstrapping agents requests to instantiate a RISE model, and it maintains inventory of all RISE actors available to the runtime. A RISE library contributes its actors to the factory through a factory contributor interface. The RISE factory exports its factory contributor interface via normal OSGi protocol. This function allows the runtime to add new libraries dynamically, thereby facilitating remote deployment and service discovery.

The monitor agent is the runtime service that allows clients, such as an RDP, to monitor execution flow of an RRP. This agent is primarily used for debugging during development.

3.3 Library Server Platform

The software architecture for RLP contains two layers: computing framework and library server. The underlying computing framework for RLP is also OSGi. The library server layer provides a reusable library repository, a library manager, and a deployment protocol, which interacts with the bootstrap agent in RRP for deploying libraries on demand.

The library manager supervises the storage and deployment of libraries in a heterogeneous network of devices. Through a deployment protocol, the library server delivers a library to an RRP in response to a request coming from the factory in an RRP. The library manager also provides an interface that allows an

RDP to present a library browser view. Additionally, RLP provides the means of binding a generic polymorphic actor with its concrete implementation.

4 Implementation

4.1 OSGi Implementation

For our particular implementation of OSGi, we use Service Management Framework (SMF) 3.7, which comes with WebSphere Studio Device Developer (WSDD) 5.7.1. WSDD is built on Eclipse 2.11 technology. SMF facilitates deployment and it provides a standardized framework for RRP and RLP.

4.2 RDP Implementation

RDP is implemented on top of WSDD in the form of Eclipse plug-ins. The persistent state of all actors and models constructed using RDP is captured by the data model, which was designed using Eclipse Modeling Framework (EMF). Solutions created with the composition editor are persisted in XMI format, which is converted to Java code using a code generator. The generated Java code utilizes base classes defined in the runtime package.

The GUI for the IDE is built using Graphical Editor Framework (GEF), which provides the visual layout of all the graphical objects displayed in a model diagram.

A library view plug-in provides four different means to access reusable actors. First, there is a workspace folder containing all the RISE libraries under development in the current workspace. Second, there is a list of all available library servers, each of which contains a list of libraries of reusable actors. Third, there is a base library folder, which contains libraries of some pre-packaged actors available to the local environment. Lastly, there is an anonymous folder that lists the contained component classes of the composite actor currently being edited by the developer. This plug-in interacts with the component manager and any number of library servers.

A set of resource management plug-ins provide the wizards for creating RISE projects and libraries. A set of runtime management plug-ins provide the execution manager functionality. Additionally, RDP provides a local RRP and RLP, which enable rapid testing of solutions.

4.3 RRP Implementation

We implement the RISE runtime execution services as SMF bundles, and we deploy them on an SMF runtime. To date, we have tested RRP on a windows platform and on an embedded Linux platform (Arcom Viper®). For the embedded RRP, SMF runs on J9.

Our execution engine leverages the Discrete Event, Finite State Machine, and Synchronous Data Flow implementations from Ptolemy II. Since RISE execution services are SMF bundles, they also benefit from dynamic updates. As new services become available, for example a new MoC, RRP can discover the service and update the execution engine upon loading a model that uses the new MoC.

4.4 RLP Implementation

We implement the RISE deployable libraries as SMF bundles and install them in an SMF bundle server, using the tools provided by RDP. Currently, the RISE actor libraries include implementations of components relevant to the RFID application domain. We have implementations of various device adapters (e.g., motion sensors, RFID readers, and LED actuators), communications protocols (e.g., HTTP and publish/subscribe messaging), custom controllers and agents, and basic logic actors. For event correlation, we have an implementation for Application Level Event (ALE).

5 RFID Dock Door Receiving Use Case

The dock door receiving use case is an RFID application of supply chain management. In this section, we describe our experience in building a RISE solution to support this use case.

Referring to Fig. 3, while goods are being physically moved through the dock door, the RFID reader will read the goods' pallet and case RFID tags. The tag data is sent to the store's backend system, which will then check the data against the database to determine if the tags just read should be accepted or rejected. The accept/reject status is reported back to a controller at the dock door, then the controller's logic triggers a status indication on the light stack.

Fig. 4 illustrates what might be the initial step of building the solution, testing the RFID reader. The model was constructed via drag-n-drop from the library server view. The reader as a polling device whose poling frequency is optionally driven by an external clock. During the duty cycle of the polling period, the reader activates its antennas and starts reading tags in its field-of-view. Since an RFID reader can detect multiple tags in one read, the reader device packages multiple reads in the form of a map. Thus, a transform actor is needed to split the

Fig. 3. The demo apparatus contains a delivery vehicle (1), a warehouse dock door (2), a ranging sensor (3), an embedded controller (4), an RFID reader (5), and a light stack (6)

Fig. 4. Snapshot of the editing canvas illustrating an example model for testing an RFID reader

Fig. 5. RISE model for eliminating duplicate reads from RFID reader

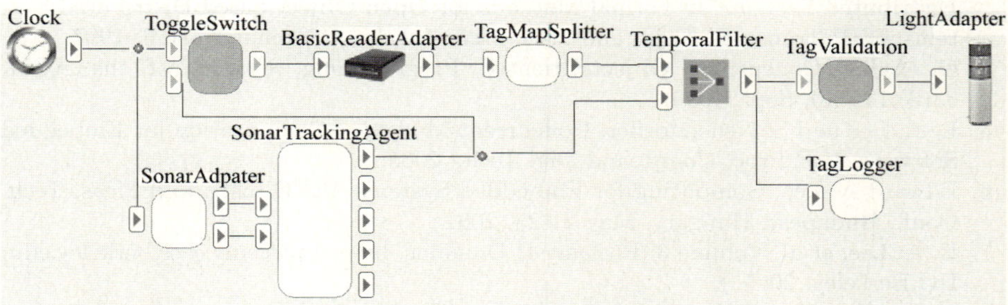

Fig. 6. Complete RISE model for the example dock door receiving use case

map into its individual RFID tag data objects. The output of the map splitter is simply sent to a tag logger, which writes the RFID tag ID to a stream.

Fig. 5 illustrates the ease with which a developer can modify an existing solution. Since the RFID reader adapter is designed to report any tag that it detects during a poll, redundant RFID tag reads are often observed. Thus, we can improve our model with a temporal filter to eliminate duplicate tag reads.

Fig. 6 shows the complete RISE model that implements the dock door receiving use case, which is an extension of the previous examples. Major additions include a sonar range sensor, a tracking agent, a light adapter, and tag validation. Like the reader, the sonar device is a polling device whose period is driven by a clock. The sonar device's output is processed by the tracking agent, which determines whether an object is in proximity to the dock door. The tag validation component communicates to the backend system and controls the light stack.

While some base knowledge of RFID systems is required for constructing useful scenarios, this example illustrates how changing the behavior of an existing solution is quite simple.

6 Future Work

This paper represents results from the first phase of the RISE project. The prototype developed provides a platform for us to evaluate the methodology. We plan to conduct user studies involving naïve users and practitioners. We are also addressing scale and management issues by adding capability to support solutions involving multiple, distributed computing nodes.

References

1. C. Hewitt, Viewing Control Structures as Patterns of Passing Messages, Jour. of Art. Intel., 8(3):323363, June 1977.
2. G. Agha, Actors: A Model of Concurrent Computation in Distributed Systems, MIT Press, Cambridge, MA, 1986.
3. G. Agha, Abstracting Interaction Patterns: A Programming Paradigm for Open Distributed Systems, in Formal Methods for Open Object-based Distributed Systems, IFIP Trans., E. Najm and J.-B. Stefani, Eds., Chapman & Hall, 1997.
4. G. Agha, Concurrent Object-Oriented Programming, Comm. of the ACM, 33(9):125140, Sept. 1990.
5. E. A. Lee and S. Neuendorffer, Concurrent Models of Computation for Embedded Software, IEE Proc. Comp. and Dig. Tech., 2005.
6. Edward A. Lee, Computing for Embedded Systems, IEEE Instr. and Meas. Tech. Conf., Budapest, Hungary, May 21-23, 2001.
7. E. A. Lee, et al, Volume 3: Ptolemy II Domains, http://ptolemy.eecs.berkeley.edu, UC Berkeley, 2005.
8. L. de Alfaro and T. A. Henzinger, Interface Theories for Component-Based Design, Proc. of EMSOFT 2001, Tahoe City, CA, LNCS 2211, Springer-Verlag, Oct 2001.
9. E. A. Lee and Y. Xiong, A Behavioral Type System and Its Application in Ptolemy II, Formal Aspects of Computing Journal, special issue on Semantic Foundations of Engineering Design Languages, Volume 16, Number 3, August 2004.
10. R. Milner, A Theory of Type Polymorphism in Programming, Jour. of Comp. and Sys. Sci., 17, pp. 375-384, 1978.
11. OSGi Alliance, OSGi Service Platform, Release 3 Specification, http://www.osgi.org, March 27, 2003.

A Fast Instruction Set Evaluation Method for ASIP Designs

Angela Yun Zhu[1], Xi Li[1], Laurence T. Yang[2], and Jun Yang[1]

[1] Department of Computer Science
University of Science and Technology of China
Hefei, Anhui 230027, P.R. China
{yukiyun, stuart}@mail.ustc.edu.cn, llxx@ustc.edu.cn
[2] Department of Computer Science
St. Francis Xavier University
P.O. Box 5000, Antigonish, B2G 2W5, NS, Canada

Abstract. ASIPs are designed specifically for a particular application or a set of applications. Their instruction sets must be carefully tailored to provide high performance as well as to meet non-functional constraints such as silicon area and power consumption. Traditionally, evaluation of different candidate instruction sets is all carried out through simulation. However, the growing design complexity and time-to-market pressure have rendered simulation increasingly infeasible. In this paper, we present an instruction level modeling method that can rapidly evaluates several important aspects of a selected instruction set. Experimental results show that we can prune a large number of candidate instruction sets with the model, accelerate design space exploration and alleviate the pressure on simulation.

1 Introduction

Application Specific Instruction set Processors (ASIPs) are in between custom architectures such as Application Specific Integrated Circuits (ASICs) and commercial programmable processors such as General Purpose Processors (GPPs). ASIPs typically consist of a configurable base processor core and a base instruction set, plus the capability to extend the instruction set. The goal of ASIP design is to optimize performance for an application domain while minimizing the area and energy costs.

One of ASIP design approaches is language-driven design space exploration, based on Architecture Description Languages (ADLs) [2] [3][4]. An ADL specification is used to generate a software toolkit including compilers, simulators, assemblers, etc.. Design space exploration is then performed with these tools. During the instruction set design of an ASIP, first, some pre-designed extensible instructions are chosen as candidates from a provided library. Then, instruction set tailoring and extension according to a specific application domain is conducted with the help of the toolkit generated. Research done on the instruction set design for ASIPs include [8][9][10].

E. Sha et al. (Eds.): EUC 2006, LNCS 4096, pp. 489–498, 2006.

Traditionally, simulation approach is used throughout the ASIP designs, including the process to optimize hardware parameters, instruction matching to meet the functional requirements of the specific applications, and estimating the non-functional constraints such as size and power for the ultimate synthesizable instruction set. However, the long simulation time often gets in the way of the time-to-market, rendering the design-simulate-analyze methodology not feasible. Our method aims at reducing simulation when evaluating the instruction set, meanwhile keeping the concern on non-functional parameters such as power and size.

The remainder of this article is organized as follows: In Section 2, we outline our technical approach. Section 3 introduces our basic data structures and Section 4 elaborates on our method. In Section 5, we present our preliminary experimental results and analysis. Section 6 concludes our work.

2 Technique Outline

Fig. 1 shows the process of instruction selection and instruction set extension. The following is a corresponding explanation:

1. Application specifications in a high-level language (e.g. C, C++) and the pre-designed extensible instruction library in HDL are translated into an intermediate representation (IR) respectively. This is called the *translation phase*. We use *Data Flow Graph (DFG)* as our intermediate representation.
2. During the *instruction matching phase*, we try to cover the DAGs representing the dataflow of each basic block in an application by DFGs representing the dataflow of instructions selected from the instruction template library. This results in covered basic blocks and a candidate instruction set.
3. Construct the *Instruction Parameter Table (IPT)*, which reflects the estimated parameters of each single instruction.
4. Construct the *Instruction set Evaluation Model (IEM)*, with which we are able to rapidly evaluate overall cost of the *candidate instruction set*.
5. Evaluate the instruction set using *IEM*, under system design constraints.
6. Use *IEM* to help the instruction set optimization (instruction clustering). Instruction extensions are specified with the architecture description language *xpADL* [16], and corresponding items are added to *IPT*. Reconstruct *IEM* and repeat *5*, *6*, until the evaluation results are fair.

Representing dataflow of basic blocks and template instructions with DFGs is trivial. And we adopt the instruction matching algorithm described in [6] to do the initial DFG covering of basic blocks. In the following sections, we will focus on our methods according to step 3 through step 6 stated above.

3 Instruction Parameter Table *IPT*

In this section, we introduce a static resource model called the *Instruction Parameter Table (IPT)*, which specifies the execution and design parameters of every

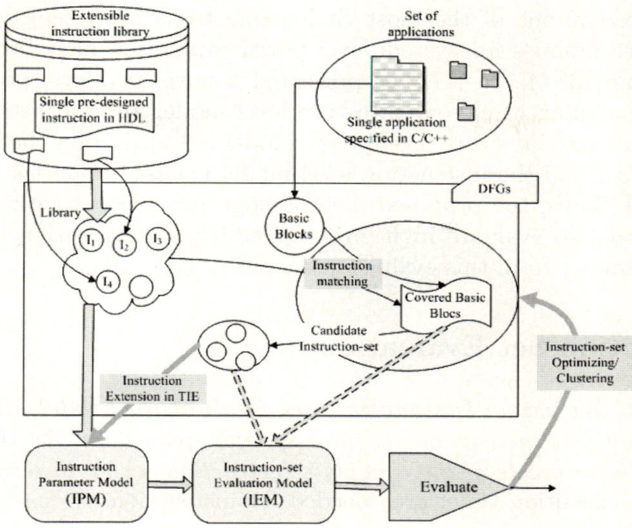

Fig. 1. Instruction set design for an ASIP

individual instruction. The table will be further used to construct the *Instruction set Evaluation Model (IEM)*, which aims to evaluate several aspects of a selected instruction set.

Definition 1. *An* ***Instruction Parameter Table (IPT)*** *is a table to describe the evaluated cost of a single instruction execution, where*

- $\mathcal{I}$ *is a set of* instructions,
- *for each* $I \in \mathcal{I}$,
  - cc (I) *is the clock cycle needed to execute instruction* I *on given hardware;*
  - area (I) *is the lut number* [1] *of units to implement an extended instruction* I*;*
  - power (I) *is the evaluated power consumption for the execution of instruction* I*;*

Values of the first two parameters can be obtained with some tools. We generate Verilog code for each instruction and put the codes through the Synplicity tools [1] for the timing (clock cycle) and area (lut number) numbers. Our ASIP design is based on a pre-fabricated processor core, thus the pre-designed instructions will not cause additional area on our chip. That is, the area size constraint is only relevant when we need to generate a new instruction. This is indicated in our *Instruction set Evaluation Model* later.

Instruction level power evaluation techniques are used to get the third parameter in the table. With the popularization of embedded systems, low power

[1] We use the *lut* number because our experiment environment is based on FPGA. The *gate* number would be used **if synthesize to ASIC.**

design has become one of the most challenging tasks in system development. A lot of the techniques for system-level power evaluation have been proposed in the past [12][13][14]. In [17], we presented a novel two-level power estimation model, including a microarchitecture level model and an instruction level model. The microarchitecture level power model is based upon the structure of the components, and the instruction level model is based upon the microarchitecture model. Thus, the proposed methodology provides us with an accurate and rapid model to evaluate high level embedded system design. We get our *power(I)* parameter from this evaluation model.

4 Instruction Set Evaluation

Definition 2. *We use an* ***Instruction set Evaluation Model (IEM)*** *to fast evaluate a candidate instruction set for a specific application. An* IEM *includes four estimation formulae of the candidate instruction set* $\mathcal{W}$ *in terms of* power consumption, execution time, area needed for instruction extension, *and* code size, *formularized as:*

$$Area(\mathcal{W}) = \sum_{I \in \mathcal{W}} area(I); \tag{1}$$

$$Size(\mathcal{W}) = length(I) \times |T_W|; \tag{2}$$

$$Time(\mathcal{W}) = SPN_{delay}(transform(W)); \tag{3}$$

$$Energy(\mathcal{W}) = \sum_{I \in \mathcal{W}} power(I) \times t(I) \times count(I). \tag{4}$$

Here, *t(I)* in formula (4) is execution time needed to execute an instruction I. It can be got directly from *cc(I)*, which is defined in IPT together with *area(I)* and *power(I)*. Note that $area(I) = 0$ if I is a pre-designed instruction, so the total area cost is the number of luts we needed for adding some new kinds of instructions in an instruction set. *count(I)* is the number of times instruction I appeared in the instruction flow of the application execution. It will be explained a little later.

Fig. 2(a) shows the data flow of a basic block, which is covered by instructions selected. Take each instruction as a node we get a DAG (Directed Acyclic Graph) W in Fig. 2(b). The node number of W, $|T_W|$, shows the number of instructions in a compiled application code segment. $length(I)$ is the length of instructions for a pre-decided instruction set architecture, which is always an invariable. Thus, formula (2) tells that the code size is decided by both the length of every instruction and the number of instructions in a compiled application code segment.

4.1 Execution Time Estimation

In our fast evaluation model, we use the DAG (Fig. 2(b)) to evaluate the relevant performance of execution time. Two problems must be considered first. One is

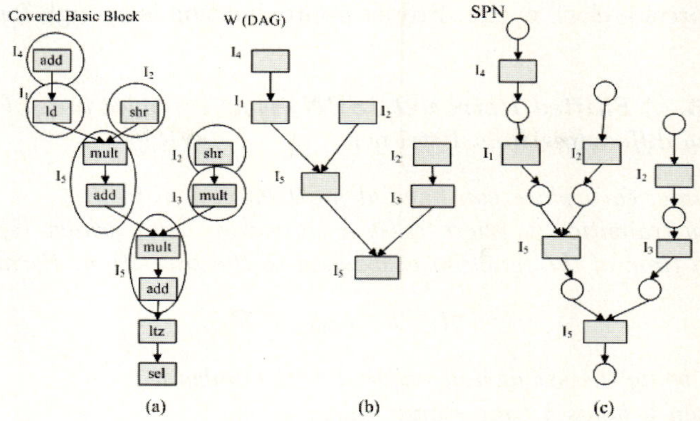

Fig. 2. An example

the iteration times of each basic block. The other one is how the structure of the graph, those concurrency and dependency, affect the pipelining of the actual instruction flow.

We use two vectors to help illustrate our evaluation method, one is θ, the other is φ. For each node t in DAG W, if $t \in B$, B is a basic block, then $\theta(t) = \theta(B)$ is the iteration times of B, and $\varphi(t) = \varphi(B)$ is the parallelability of B, which means the execution time of t can be reduced to $\frac{t}{\varphi(t)}$ by pipelining. So the whole execution time can be expressed as:

$$\sum_{B \in W} \frac{\sum_{t \in B} t_{delay}}{\varphi(B)} \times \theta(B) = \sum_{t \in W} \frac{t_{delay} \times \theta(t)}{\varphi(t)}. \tag{5}$$

For $\theta(B)$ in formula (5), we use executive without compiling optimization of the application as the input to an instruction set simulator *ISAsim* [2], and get the execution frequency θ of basic blocks with the profiling module of *ISAsim*. Although the profiling of this vector parameter based on a simulation technique, our evaluation method can still be helpful and faster because we only need the same θ when evaluating among different instruction set with the same application.

Another problem is to get the actual execution time of each basic block. This is complex due to the pipeline behavior. However, the greatest parallelism we can get from pipelining will be constrained by the dependency in the DAG (flow graph). We approximate the actual pipelined execution time of the basic block with timed Petri net. This is reasonable for two sakes: First, architecture relative optimization can't be performed before instruction set is decided and our methods just consider the maximum possibility of parallelism; Second, we just want to compare between different instruction selections, thus we don't

[2] *ISAsim* is part of *xpSIM* generated by our *xpADL*, we will briefly introduce them later.

need actual precise clock cycles, Proper approximation is enough for evaluating preference.

Definition 3. *A* ***Shifted Petri net (SPN)*** *is an extended timed Petri net[15] with following differences from* Petri net*:*

- *At any time, each place can have at most one token in it.*
- *For every transition* t*, there exist a transition delay which represents the execution time of the function associated to the transition. Formally,*

$$\forall t \in T, \exists t_{delay} \in \mathcal{R}_0^+,$$

with $\mathcal{R}_0^+$ *being the set of non-negative real numbers.*
- *Each token* k *holds a time stamp* k_{time}*.*
- *When a transition* t *is fired, the marking* M *will generally change by removing all the tokens from the pre-set* $^\circ t$ *and depositing one token into each element of the post-set* t°*, and*

$$k_{time} = \max_{j \in J}\{j_{time}\} + t_{delay}, \forall k \in K,$$

where J *is the set of tokens in* $^\circ t$*, and* K *is the set of tokens in* t°

Algorithm 1: *TRANSFORM*

Input: DAG $W = (T_{TG}, E_{TG})$; IPT.
Output: $SPN = (P, T; F, M_0)$.
for each $t' \in T_{TG}$
  $count(I) = count(I) + \theta(t')$;
  $t = new_t$; $t = t'$;
  $t_{delay} = \theta(t') \times lookup_{IPT}(t', cc)$;
  put t into T;
  if $^\circ t' = \emptyset$ {
    $p = new_p$; put p into inP;
    $f = new_f$; put $f = (p, t)$ into F; }
  else if $t'^\circ = \emptyset$ {
    $p = new_p$; put p into $outP$;
    $f = new_f$; put $f = (t, p)$ into F; }
end for
for each $e = (t'_1, t'_2) \in E_{TG}$
  $p = new_p$; put p into P;
  $f = new_f$; put $f = (p, t)$ into F;
  $f = new_f$; put $f = (t, p)$ into F;
end for
$P = P \bigcup inP \bigcup ourP$;
$M_0 = P \rightarrow 0$
return $SPN = (P, T; F, M_0)$;

Algorithm 2: ***GET*** SPN_{delay}

Input: $SPN = (P, T; F)$.
Output:
execution time of the SPN SPN_{delay}
for each $p \in inP$
  $k = new_{token}$; $k_{time} = 0$;
  put k into p; $M_0(p) = 1$;
end for
while ($\exists t \in T$, t is *enabled*), do
  $fire(t)$;
end while
$SPN_{delay} = \max_{p \in outP}\{k_{time}(p)\}$;
return SPN_{delay};

Formula (3) according to Algorithm 1 and Algorithm 2 is based on this approximation. Algorithm 1 describes how to transform a DAG into a Shifted Petri Net.

Vector θ is bound to each t in line 4 and 6. So line 4 keeps the accumulation for the instruction frequency $count(I)$, which is used in our power evaluation; and line 6 takes the block frequency into consideration of whole execution time as the numerator on the right of formula 5. Algorithm 2 uses firing rules of timed Petri net to evaluate the execution time with instruction level parallelism to incarnate the parallelability $\varphi(t)$ on the right of formula 5.

4.2 Power Consumption

Formula 4 uses *count(I)* get from Algorithm 1 and simply adds all the power consumption estimation value of each instruction used in the application to get the total power consumption of application implementation with the candidate instruction set. From the view of pipeline, this is not correct since power consumption of a single instruction are different between being *stall* and being *normal*, i.e., in pipeline, power consumption of an instruction is related to its previous instructions executed, deploy policy, even related to the memory system of the CPU. Thus, estimating the running power consumption of an application is difficult. However, the instruction level power consumption parameters we get from [17] is an average normal running values, which dissipates the power consumption of *stall* in to every instruction in the power model. The experiment in [17] also shows that the relevant error compared to the result of *SimplePower*[5] is less than 10%.

4.3 xpADL Driven Develop Environment

Our fast evaluation method is part of our system-level develop platform for ASIP. We have explored a design environment driven by an architectural description language called *xpADL* [16]. It can generate a tool kit used for DSE including rechargeable simulators and compilers. In the method of this paper, two tools are used. One is the simulator *xpSIM* mentioned in block frequency profiling. Another tool we used from *xpADL* is *xpSYN*. During instruction set optimization, extended instructions are specified in *xpADL*, and relies on the synthesizer *xpSYN* to generate an efficient hardware implementation, often with the Verilog code. The codes will be further put through the Synplicity tools [1] to obtain instruction information such as timing and area. We add these information into our *Instruction Parameter Table (IPT)*.

5 Experimental Results and Analysis

5.1 Experimental Setup

We conduct a case study to demonstrate the effectiveness of our approach in the following steps:

First, use *PISA* [7] instruction set as pre-designed instruction library. Describe it using xpADL, and generate a simulator *xpSIM* as reference. Then, *IPT* construct is done by using *xpPower* in [17] with $2.5V$, $50MHz$ to get instruction-level power evaluation, and by using *Synplify Pro* map to *Xilinx xc2s200* to get instruction clock cycle (and we also use it later to get the luts number of extended instructions). Add different instructions to the original instruction set $\mathcal{W}$, get candidate instruction sets and evaluate them using *IEM*. Take *susan_smooth* program for example, after some profiling, we get three candidate instruction set $\mathcal{W}1$, $\mathcal{W}2$, and $\mathcal{W}3$ by adding fabricated instructions $a * b + c$, $a + b + c$, and $a * b + c * d$ respectively. Some evaluation parameter values are shown in Table 1. Lastly, the above steps are iterated for different instruction set extensions.

5.2 Results and Analysis

We apply our fast evaluation method on several different instruction set extension, then analyze the rationality of our evaluation results, also compare the time evaluation to our *xpSIM* generated from xpADL. We find that time evaluation results differ a lot from simulation. However, the trend of which instruction set can make application faster is almost the same. For other evaluation factors, there is no exercised comparative standard, however, they are consisted to the system designers' empiricism. (e.g. Fig. 3 for *susan_smooth* from Table 1).

$$E_{\mathcal{W}} = \frac{1}{Power(\mathcal{W})^{\beta_P} \times Size(\mathcal{W})^{\beta_S} \times \left(C + Area(\mathcal{W})^{\beta_A}\right) \times Time(\mathcal{W})^{\beta_T}}. \quad (6)$$

Formula (6) combines the evaluation parameters in IEM and indicates when an instruction set is more superior. Fig. 4 is $E_{\mathcal{W}}$ of four code segment on four instruction-set respectively, with β all set to 1. It indicates that instruction set

Table 1.

IS	Area (luts)	Size (bytes)	Time (cc)	Energy	Total Instr_count
$\mathcal{W}$	0	184160	42241680	326697097	61533089
$\mathcal{W}1$	543	173184	41592513	317305112	57666965
$\mathcal{W}2$	62	179584	42221870	325052831	59864311
$\mathcal{W}3$	1054	184128	42231774	326584738	61525951

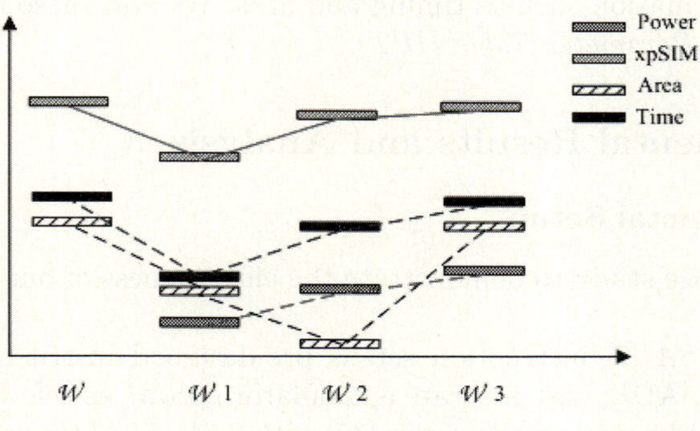

Fig. 3. Compared evaluation results

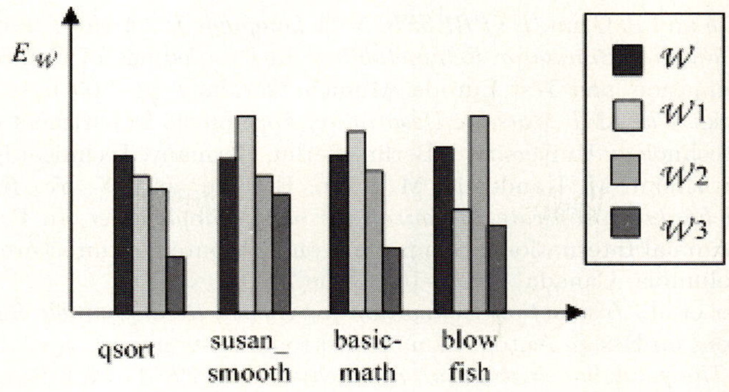

Fig. 4. Efficiency of different instruction sets

$\mathcal{W}1$ might be the best choice for *susan_smooth*. Actually, we noticed that, the instruction $mult + mflo$ appeared with a frequency about 6.283% in the final execute flow, while $addiu + addu$ appeared with about 2.712% and instructions in the form of $a * b + c * d$ appeared with about 0.0116%. On the other hand, instruction extension with form $a * b + c$ is not suitable for *blowfish*. This is because there is not *mult* instruction in *flowfish*.

6 Conclusions

In this paper we propose a method for fast evaluating the instruction set targeted towards a certain application, with several design constraints. We use the Instruction level Parameter Table and an Instruction set Evaluation Model to compare different candidate instruction sets concerning their power consumption, code size, chip area and execution time. Our model is not as precise as the simulation techniques, but it has three important advantages. First, when handling a large number of candidate instruction sets, our method fast pre-prunes most of them, reducing the dependence on simulation (which is always the bottleneck in the design space exploration). Second, while simulators only focus on performance, our evaluation method also provides an overall view of the instruction set design. Lastly, we use Petri net in our model to get time evaluation. The flow graph representation of Petri net eases the application profiling since loops and concurrency are explicitly illustrated. This is much better than analyzing the instruction flow provided by a simulator.

For future work, we try to make our model more precise and applicable to a broader range of instruction set architectures.

References

1. *http://www.synplicity.com/ (Synplify and Synplify Pro Reference Manual).*
2. V. Zivojnovic, S. Pees, and H. Meyr. *LISA - Machine Description Language and Generic Machine Model for HW/SWCo-Design.* In Proceedings of the IEEE Workshop on VLSI Signal Processing. San Francisco, CA, USA. pp.127-136. October 1996.

3. A. Halambi and P. Grun. *EXPRESSION: A Language for Architecture Exploration through Compiler/Simulator Retargetability.* In Proceedings of Conference of Design, Automation, and Test Europe. Munich, Germany. pp. 100-104. March 1999.
4. M. Freericks. *The nML Machine Description Formalism.* Department of Computer Science, Technology University of Berlin, Berlin, Germany, Technical Report. 1991.
5. N. Vijaykrishnan, M. Kandemir, M. Irwin, H. Kim, and W. Ye. *Energy driven integrated hardware-software optimizations using simplepower.* In Proceedings of the 27th Annual International Symposium on Computer Architecture. Vancouver, British Columbia, Canada. pp. 95-106. June 2000.
6. R. Kastner et al.. *Instruction Generation for Hybrid Reconfigurable Systems.* ACM Transactions on Design Automation of Electronic Systems, vol. 7, no. 4. Apr. 2002.
7. C. Vieri. *The pendulum instruction set architecture (PISA)* MIT Reversible Computing Project Internal Memo., May 1996.
8. J. Van Praet, G. Goossens, D. Lanneer, and H. De Man. *Instruction set definition and instruction selection for ASIPs.* In Proceedings of the 7th International Symposium on High-Level Synthesis. Ontario, Canada. pp. 11-16. May 1994.
9. M. Arnold and H. Corporaal.. *Designing domain specific processors.* In Proceedings of the 9th International Workshop on Hardware/Software Codesign. Copenhagen, Denmark. pp. 61-66. April 2001.
10. P. Faraboschi, G. Brown, J. A. Fisher, G. Desoli, and F. Homewood. *Lx: A technology platform for customizable VLIW embedded processing.* In Proceedings of the 27th Annual International Symposium on Computer Architecture (ISCA-00). Vancouver, Canada. pp. 203-213. June 2000.
11. C. Brandolese, W. Fornaciari, F. Salice, and D. Sciuto, *An instruction-level functionality-based energy estimation model for 32-bits microprocessors.* In Proceedings of the Annual ACM/IEEE Design Automation Conference (DAC-00). Asia and South Pacific. pp. 346-351. June 2000.
12. M. Barocci, L. Benini, A. Bogliolo, B. Ricco, and G. De Micheli. *Lookup table power macro-models for behavioral library components.* In Proceedings of the Design, Automation and Test of Europe, Paris, France. pp. 173-181. February 1998.
13. E. Macii, M. Pedram, and F. Somenzi. *High-level power modeling, evaluation, and optimization.* IEEE Transactions on CAD of Intergrated Circuits and Systems. vol. 17, pp. 1061-1079. November 1998.
14. J. Luo, L. Zhong et al. *Register binding based RTL power management for control-flow intensive designs.* IEEE Transactions on CAD of Intergrated Circuits and Systems. vol 23, No. 8, pp. 1175-1183. Augest 2004.
15. T. Murata. *Petri Nets: Properties, Analysis and Applications.* Proceedings of the IEEE. 77(4), pp. 541-580. 1989.
16. X. Li, X.H. Zhou, et al. *xp-ADL: A key issue in software and hardware codesign.* In Proceedings of 2002 Conference of Open Distributed and Parallel Computing Symposium (DPCS-02). Wuhan, China. pp. 100-104. 2002.
17. X. Li, Z.G. Wang, et al. *Study on system-level power model for low power optimization.* Acta Electronica Sinica. vol 32, no. 2, pp. 205-208. February, 2004.

An ARM-Based Embedded System Design for Speech-to-Speech Translation

Shun-Chieh Lin, Jhing-Fa Wang, Jia-Ching Wang, and Hsueh-Wei Yang

Department of Electrical Engineering, National Cheng Kung University,
No.1, Dasyue Rd., East District, Tainan City, 70101, Taiwan, R.O.C.
{jason, wangjf, wjc, thyndo}@icwang.ee.ncku.edu.tw

Abstract. Previous research shows that there are two architectures for speech-to-speech translation (S2ST) system implementation. One is client-server based systems that should be built on the server computer but not available anytime or anywhere. The other is to build portable stand-alone devices but lacks the real-time performance. Therefore, this work presents an embedded system design for portable S2ST applications. This system is characterized by small size, low cost, real-time operation, and high portability. For realization of the proposed S2ST system, this work designs the ARM-based SoPC architecture, the speech translation intellectual property, and software procedures of the proposed SoPC. The entire design was implemented on ALTERA EPXA10. The English-to-Mandarin translation process can be completed within 0.5 second at a 40 MHz clock frequency with 1,200 translation patterns. The maximum frequency is 46.22 MHz, and the usage of logic elements is 19,318 (50% of the total logic elements of the EPXA10 device).

1 Introduction

Speech-to-speech translation (S2ST) has made significant advances over the past decade, with several high-visibility projects (JANUS [1], Verbmobil [2], EUTRANS [4], MATRIX [5], and others [3], [6], [7]) significantly advancing the state-of-the-art. Table 1 shows a comparison among the related S2ST systems. There are two architectures for speech-to-speech translation system implementation – server-client based systems and stand-alone handheld devices. For server-client based systems, a system is available on a central S2ST server and client access of the S2ST server is made possible by using digital cellular phones and internet. For S2ST handheld devices, they enable foreign tourists and business travelers to talk to locals through them for face-to-face communication.

Nevertheless, a critical shortcoming of server-client based S2ST systems is that they should be built on the server computer. In other words, while taking face-to-face cross-language communication to locals, it is not available anytime or anywhere. An obvious solution would be to build portable stand-alone S2ST devices. However, previous works show that real-time S2ST with a resource-limited device is still a problem. Moreover, both of these two architectures are platform-dependent S2ST applications, i.e., they need some kinds of operation systems. This limitation would

E. Sha et al. (Eds.): EUC 2006, LNCS 4096, pp. 499 – 508, 2006.

Table 1. A Comparison among Related Spoken Language Translation Systems

System	Vocabulary Size	Response time	Specification
JANUS [1]	3,000~5,000	≤ 2 times real-time	PC-based platform (server-client)
Verbmobil [2]	≥10,000	4 times real-time	PC-based platform (server-client)
EUTRANS [4]	1,701(English) 2,459(Italian)	≤ 3 times real-time	PC-based platform (server-client)
MATRIX [5]	13,000	0.1 sec for TDMT	PC-based platform (server-client)
Isotani *et al.* [7]	20,000(English) 50,000(Japan)	Slower than V_R5500 processor	Pocket PC PDA (206 MHz StrongARM/64 MB RAM)
Speechalator [8]	–	≥2~3 sec	Pocket PC PDA (400 MHz StrongARM/64 MB RAM)

Therefore, an embedded system design solution is proposed by realizing the entire S2ST system within a single chip. This chip only requires a few peripheral components for complete operation, and is characterized by small size, low cost, real-time operation, high productivity and embedability for any information appliance (IA). The entire proposed S2ST system is implemented with ARM-based system-on-a-programmable-chip (SoPC) platform –Altera™ Excalibur™ EPXA10 development board. The rest of this paper is organized as follows. Section 2 gives the framework of the proposed S2ST embedded system. Section 3 discusses the ARM-based hardware/software co-design of the SoPC architecture. The implementation result is given in Section 4. Finally, conclusions and future works are provided in Section 5.

2 Framework of the Proposed Embedded System

2.1 The Proposed S2ST Process

The proposed speech-to-speech translation is based on a two-layer translation template retrieval method, a kind of integration of speech analysis and language translation [8]. The adopted template retrieval approach is directly from speech to speech without language models like other automatic speech recognition (ASR) approaches. With identifying speech features based on one-stage algorithm [9], translation primarily stays in the speech modality and does not go through a textual modality. The adopted method not only retrieves the optimal translation template, but also extracts the appropriate target patterns.

To formulate the template retrieval between input speech (X_1^L) and the v-th translation template (r_v), we use the following notations: l represents the frame index within X_1^L, $1 \le l \le L$, j represents the translation pair $\langle s_j^v, t_j^v \rangle$ index within r_v, $1 \le j \le J$, and k represents the frame index within the j-th source speech pattern s_j^v and its mapped target speech pattern denoted by t_j^v, $1 \le k \le K_j$. Then for each input frame, the one-stage based accumulated distortion $d_A(l, k, j)$ is defined by:

$$d_A(l,k,j) = d(l,k,j) + \min_{k-2\le m\le k}\left(d_A(l-1,m,j)\right), \tag{1}$$

for $2 \le k \le K_j$, $1 \le j \le J$, where $d(l,k,j)$ is the local distortion between the l-th frame of X_1^L and the k-th frame of the source speech pattern s_j^v. The recursion in (1) is carried out for the internal frames (i.e., $k \ge 2$) of each source pattern. At the pattern boundary, i.e., when $k = 1$, the recursion can be calculated as:

$$d_A(l,1,j) = d(l,1,j) + \min\left[\min_{1\le m\le J}\left(d_A(l-1,K_m,m)\right), d_A(l-1,1,j)\right]. \tag{2}$$

And the best path is determined by

$$d_G^v = \min_{1\le j\le J}\left[d_A\left(L,K_j,j\right)\right]. \tag{3}$$

In this work, the retrieved template is decided by

$$\hat{v} = \arg\min_{1\le v\le V}\left[d_G^v\right]. \tag{4}$$

According to the decided $\hat{v}$-th template from (4), the target speech patterns $\{t_j^{\hat{v}}\}_{j=1}^J$ can be obtained from $\{s_j^{\hat{v}}\}_{j=1}^J$, where $s_j^{\hat{v}}$ is identified and extracted. With the determined speech patterns, these waveforms are reordered and rearranged with adequate overlapping portions to generate speech with the waveform similarity overlap and add (WSOLA) algorithm [10]. In general, while inputting a source speech, the speech is adjusted by a signal pre-processing and used to extract speech features. The extracted features of the source speech are imported to identify speech input for each template features in template retrieval. A hypothesized template is then selected using a ranking process and the identified source patterns are extracted from it. According to the waveform translation database, the target patterns are obtained from the identified source patterns. The hypothesized target patterns are used to produce speech output via the corresponding speech generation template by waveform replacement based on the WSOLA method.

2.2 The Proposed SoPC Architecture

According to the computation complexity analysis of the S2ST system, the highest computational load comes from the template retrieval. Furthermore, while template size increases, more computational load raises for template retrieval. Therefore, the template retrieval procedure needs to be partitioned into hardware implementation. The remainder procedures of the proposed S2ST system is implemented by ARM assembler or C language and executed by ARM-based processor.

The timing scheduling diagram after the partitioning is illustrated in Fig. 1. While the system receives enough speech data from speech recording process, the feature extraction procedure is loaded after speech pre-processing and the extracted features are used to process template retrieval for each template and extract the identified

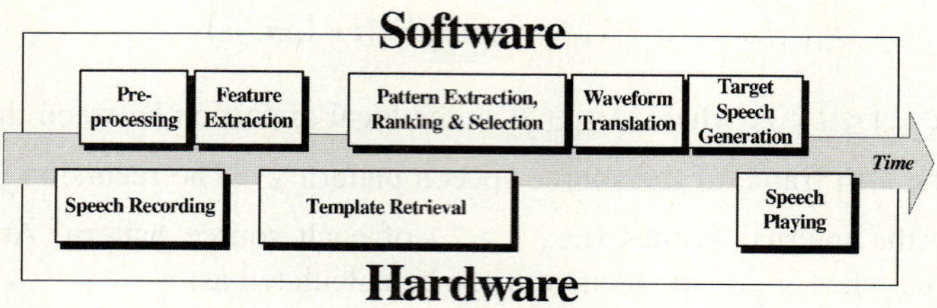

Fig. 1. Hardware/software scheduling after partitioning

patterns. After ranking for selecting a hypothesized template, the identified source-patterns are used to translate into target waveform patterns for target speech generation and the generated target speech is outputted for users by speech playing process.

According to the prior HW/SW partition results, besides the ARM-based processor, which is used for system control and software process, two specific intellectual properties (IPs) are designed for template retrieval and the controller of ADC/DAC circuit board. Figure 2 shows an overall block diagram of the SoPC architecture for the proposed S2ST system. The on-chip bus architecture of the proposed SoPC is based on the advanced microcontroller bus architecture (AMBA™). The proposed architecture contains the advanced high-performance bus (AHB) and the advanced peripheral bus (APB). ARM-based processor stripe is the only master of the AHB. The template retrieval IP and the AHB-APB Bridge are both AHB-compliant slave IP, and the controller for the converter board is an APB-compliant slave IP. Three major databases are stored in a FLASH memory. Software instruction codes and temporary data for ARM-based processor and template retrieval IP are stored in on-chip single-port SRAM and dual-port SRAM.

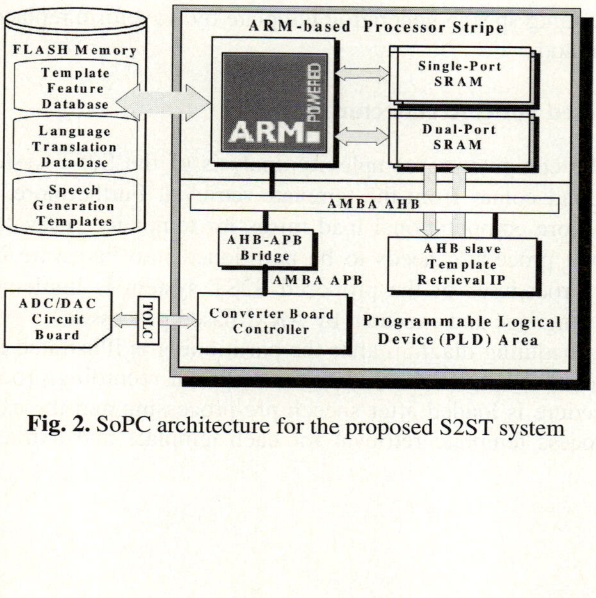

Fig. 2. SoPC architecture for the proposed S2ST system

3 ARM-Based Hardware/Software Co-design

3.1 AHB Slave IP Design of Template Retrieval

There are four on-chip RAMs are used by the IP, as listed in Table 2. The template header RAM and the test feature RAM are wrapped in the AHB slave. ARM-based processor must write the speech input features and template header information to input feature RAM and template header RAM, respectively, via the AHB bus before validating template retrieval IP. The core of template retrieval IP is divided into two parts, the controller and the body. The function of controller is used to handle the operation of template retrieval IP by referring to the information which stored in the template header RAM. The AHB slave interface of template retrieval IP supports single and incrementing burst AHB transfers without read transfer.

Table 2. Description of RAMs for AHB-Compliant Template Retrieval IP

RAM	Memory Type	Size
Test feature RAM	Dual-port RAM built in PLD	8 Kbytes
Template header RAM	Dual-port RAM built in PLD	2 Kbytes
Template feature RAM	Dual-port SRAM 0 in ARM stripe	64 Kbytes
Decision RAM	Dual-port SRAM 1 in ARM stripe	64 Kbytes

Dependence Graph Projection of Template Retrieval. To exemplify our design concept, Figs. 3(a) and 3(b) display two dependence graphs (DGs) of the template retrieval. These dependence graphs are constructed according to (1) and (2), and can be regarded as the template retrieval space.

The DG shown in Fig. 3(a) describes the case with 12 frames in the input speech. There are three source patterns in this template, and the frame number of them is 7, 8, and 6, respectively. The DG shown in Fig. 3(b) has 8 frames in the input speech and 2 patterns in the template. The frame number of the two patterns in this template is 6 and 7, respectively. The different frame numbers within different input speeches cause the variation along the horizontal axis in the template retrieval space. The different pattern numbers within different templates and the different frame numbers within different patterns are responsible for the variation along the vertical axis in the template retrieval space. The architecture design for coping with the variation of the structure of the template retrieval space is described as follows. First, horizontal projection is performed in the original DGs (Fig. 3(a)) and the result is shown in Fig. 3(c). This projection reduces the two-dimensional (2-D) template retrieval space into a one-dimensional (1-D) one and eliminates the variation resulting from different frame numbers within different input speeches. Each node in Fig. 3(c) requires a register to store the computational results for the distortion accumulation of the next frame. The nodes within one column are divided into different blocks according to the patterns they belong to. Thus the DG in Fig. 3(c) consists of three blocks corresponding to three different patterns.

To further reduce the size of the DG, a vertical projection is performed in Fig. 3(c). This projection transforms the three-block DG into a one-block DG (see Fig. 3(e)).

Because the frame numbers for the blocks are different, the largest frame number is taken as the frame number for the new one-block DG. To deal with the discrepancy of having different frame numbers within different patterns, we added some multiplexers. In addition, two extra registers are added in front of each node to replace the two eliminated blocks. Figure 3(e) is then modified as Fig. 3(g) to have a regular wire connection. Figures 3(b), 3(d), 3(f) and 3(h) provide another example of the use of horizontal and vertical projections. One can find that the frame number and the register number for a certain node between the DGs in Figs. 3(g) and 3(h) are different. To combine the two DGs into a single one, the largest frame number and the largest register number between them are chosen, see Fig. 3(i). The added multiplexers in front of each node provide the selectivity among the one-block DGs.

Hardware Design of Template Retrieval

Distortion Unit Design. Each node in the template retrieval DG associates with a local distortion. The local distortion between a frame of the template and a frame of the input speech is defined by

$$\sum_{i=0}^{P} |R_i - U_i|, \tag{5}$$

where R_i and U_i denote the i-th cepstral coefficient in the R-th frame of the template and the U-th frame of the input speech, respectively, and P is the cepstrum order.

SIPO Unit Design. The serial-in parallel-out unit acts as an interface between the distortion unit and all the PEs. The local distortions obtained from the distortion unit are serially fed into the SIPO unit. After all local distortions for a block have been put into the SIPO register, they are sent to all the PEs in parallel.

PE Unit Design. Each node in the DGs shown in Fig. 3(i) is implemented as a processing element. After receiving all the accumulated distortions from the registers, the PE selects the minimum accumulated distortion, and then adds it to the local distortion $d(l,k,j)$. The result is the new accumulated distortion $d_A(l,k,j)$ associated with the current node. In addition to the accumulation process, the PE also generates the decision information that indicates the source node in a path transition.

Integrated Architecture. According to the situation of a general conversation, the architecture of Fig. 3 has been modified to accommodate 16 patterns for each template and 31 frames for each pattern. Assume that the template number of the proposed S2ST system is 100, the average amount of pattern for each template is 12, and the average frame number for each pattern is 25. A user input a series of speech signal for 3 seconds with 8 KHz sampling rate i.e. the input contains about 126 frames. The required clock cycles for the process of template retrieval IP is 18.9 M $(126\times12\times25\times100\times10\div2)$. If the clock frequency is 40 MHz(i.e. clock cycle = 25ns), the processing time is 0.4725 second $(18.9\times10^6\times25\times10^{-9})$, which meets real-time constrains by comparing with Table 1.

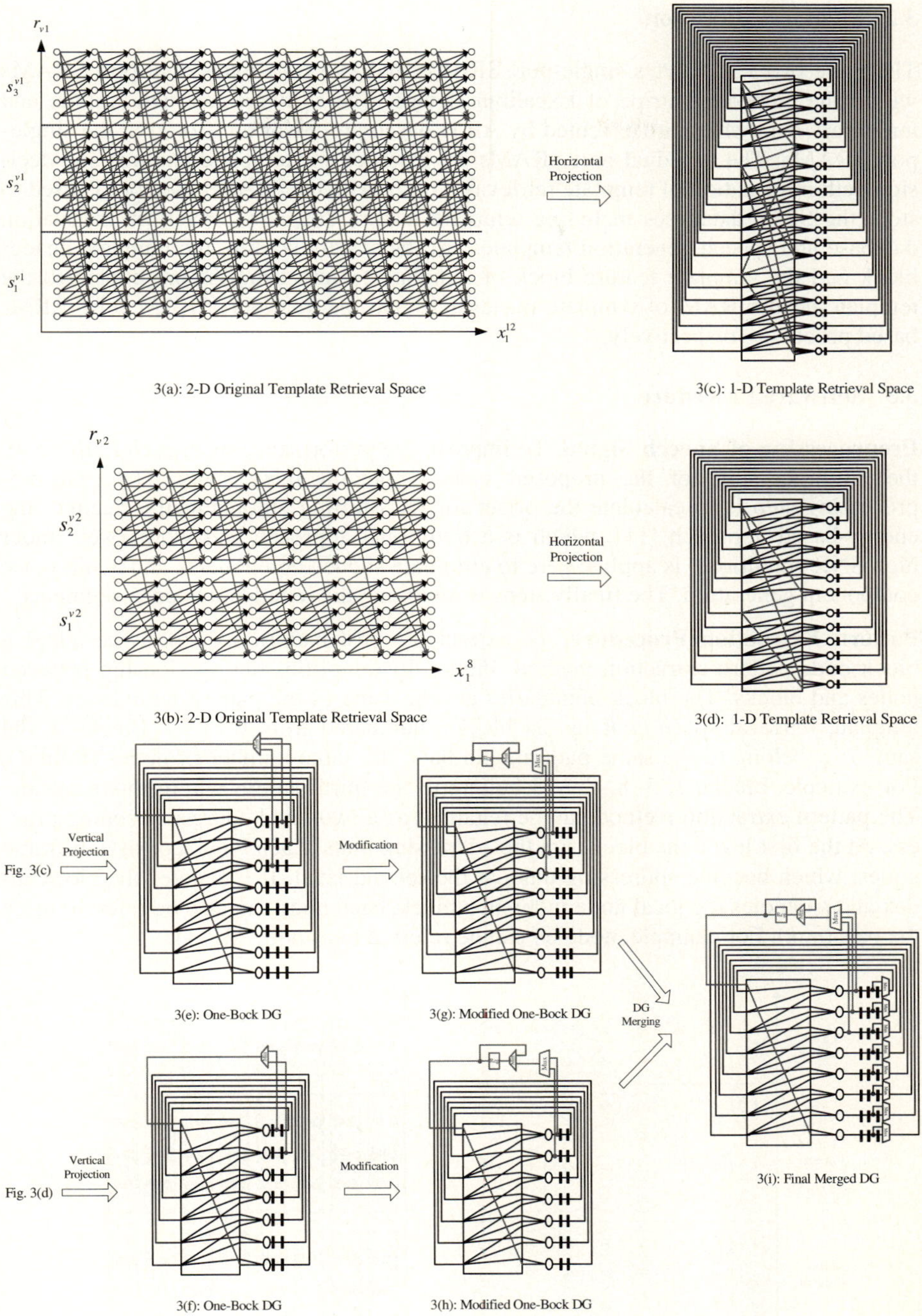

Fig. 3. Architecture inference of the template retrieval based on DG

3.2 Memory Allocation

There are two 128 Kbytes single-port SRAMs and two 64 Kbytes dual-port SRAMs within the embedded stripe of Excalibur device. The software instruction code and temporary data which are executed by ARM-based processor are stored in the single-port SRAMs. The two dual-port SRAMs are reserved for template features and decision path information of template retrieval. The 16 Mbytes FLASH memory is used to store the S2ST databases including template feature database, waveform translation database and speech generation templates. At the system startup, the template header block and the template feature block of template feature database are copied to the template header RAM of template retrieval IP and the dual-port SRAM 0 by ARM-based processor, respectively.

3.3 Software Procedure

Preprocessing of Speech Signal. To improve the performance on speech translation, the pre-processing for the proposed system contains three steps. The first pre-processing step is to calculate the offset for DC shifting automatically. Second, the energy-based approach [11], which is a traditional approach and works well under high SNR conditions, is applied here to eliminate silence components and avoid noise component generation. The finally steps is removing the redundant silence segments.

Pattern Extraction Procedure. To extract the best pattern sequence, we adopt a block-node pattern extraction method. Figure 4 exemplifies the relationship between nodes and blocks. The block boundaries are the same as the pattern boundaries. This template retrieval space contains 24 blocks, numbered from 0 to 23. Blocks in the same row belong to the same pattern, and have the same number of nodes (frames). For example, blocks 2, 5, 8, ..., 23 belong to the third pattern within this template. The pattern extraction method can be regarded as a two-level address decoding process. At the first level, the blocks are the addressing units. Each block consists of frame nodes, which become addressing units at the second level. If b denotes the block index and k denotes the local node index in a block, each node can also be referred to by the pair (b, k). For example, node 64 can be referred to as node (21, 1).

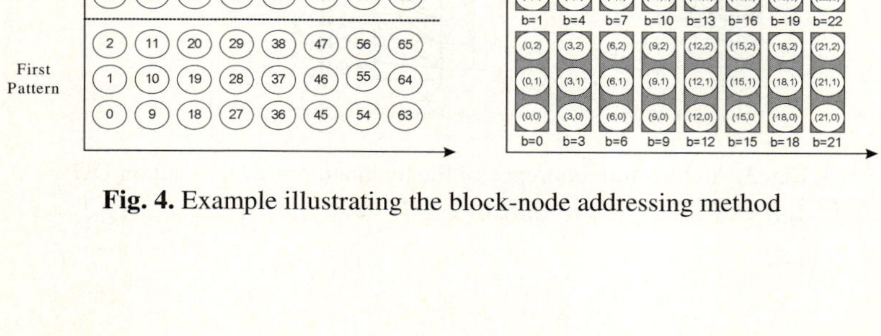

Fig. 4. Example illustrating the block-node addressing method

The decision word is generated for each block, and is denoted by $D \equiv \{d_0, d_1, d_2, \cdots, d_{K-1}, e\}$, where K is the largest number among all the block node ones, e is the pattern decision information from the first node of a block, and d_k, $0 \le k \le K-1$, is the decision information from the k-th node of a block. We use e to indicate the source pattern for an external (between-patterns) transition, and d_k to indicate the source node for an internal (within-patterns) transition. Assume that K_j denotes the number of nodes in the j-th pattern. Table 3 lists the transition information described by the decision word (K = 31 and *max_pattern_number* = 16, in the proposed S2ST system).

Table 3. Transition Information and Bit Allocation of a Decision Word

Decision information	Transition information	Bit allocation
d_0	d_0= 0: internal transition, i.e. $(l\text{-}1, k, j) \rightarrow (l, k, j)$; d_0= 1: external transition, referred to e	1 bit
d_1	d_1= 0: $(l\text{-}1, k, j) \rightarrow (l, k, j)$; d_1= 1: $(l\text{-}1, k\text{-}1, j) \rightarrow (l, k, j)$;	1 bit
$d_2, \cdots, d_k, \cdots, d_{K-1}$	d_k = 0: $(l\text{-}1, k, j) \rightarrow (l, k, j)$; d_k = 1: $(l\text{-}1, k\text{-}1, j) \rightarrow (l, k, j)$; d_k = 2: $(l\text{-}1, k\text{-}2, j) \rightarrow (l, k, j)$;	2 bits
e	$(l\text{-}1, K_e\text{-}1, e) \rightarrow (l, k, j)$;	$\lceil \log_2 max\_pattern\_number \rceil$ bits

4 Implementation Results

The user-interfaces on EPXA10 are four push-button switches, eight LEDs and a bit of DIP switch. The four push-button switches and the bit of DIP switch connect to the five individual interrupt signals to the ARM-based processor. Resource summary of

Table 4. Summary of Resource Usage on EPXA10

Resource	Usage
Device	EPXA10F1020C2
Logic cells	19318 / 38400 (50 %)
Registers	9480/ 42658 (22 %)
I/O pins	79 / 715 (10 %)
Global signals	5
ESBs	40 / 160 (25 %)
Macrocells	0 / 2560 (0 %)
ESB pterm / CAM bits used	0 / 327680 (0 %)
Total memory bits	81920 / 327680 (25 %)
FastRow interconnects	0 / 120 (0 %)
PLLs	0 / 4 (0 %)
LVDS transmitters & LVDS receivers	0 / 16 (0 %)
Maximum fan-out node	hclock
Maximum fan-out	9509
Total fan-out	77777
Average fan-out	4

the proposed system on EPXA10 are listed in Table 4. The maximum frequency is 46.22 MHz, and the usage of logic elements is 19,318 (50% of the total logic elements of the EPXA10).

5 Conclusions and Future Works

For a portable and real-time speech-to-speech translation embedded system, this work proposes the system-on-a-programmable chip (SoPC) realization. The system design is implemented with ARM-based Altera EPXA10 SoPC development board. The speech translation process can be completed within 0.5 second at a 40 MHz clock rate with 1,200 translation patterns while the number of templates is 100. The prototype chip was tested and found to be capable of performing within the expected specifications of real time. In the future, with various design of software or firmware, the proposed SoPC architecture would be used for different applications of pattern recognition. In addition, the AMBA-based architecture of the proposed S2ST SoPC would effortlessly integrate with other AMBA-compliant hardware devices for embedding and providing the function of speech translation on them.

References

1. Lavie, A., Waibel, A., Levin, L., Finke, M., Gates, D., Gavaldá, M., Zeppenfeld, T., Zhan, P.: JANUS III: Speech-to-Speech Translation in Multiple Languages. Proc. IEEE Int. Conf. Acous., Speech, & Sig. Processing (1997) 99–102
2. Wahlster, W. (ed.): Verbmobil: Foundations of Speech-to-Speech Translation. Springer-Verlag, Berlin Heidelberg New York (2000)
3. Ney, H., Nießen, S., F. Och, J., Sawaf, H., Tillmann, C., Vogel, S.: Algorithms for Statistical Translation of Spoken Language. IEEE Trans. Speech Audio Processing 8 (2000) 24–36
4. Casacuberta, F., Llorens, D., Martnez, C., Molau, S., Nevado, F., Ney, H., Pastor, M.. Pico, D., Sanchis, A., Vidal, E., Vilar, J. M.: Speech-to-Speech Translation based on Finite-State Transducers. Proc. IEEE Int. Conf. Acous., Speech, & Sig. Processing (2001) 613–616
5. Sugaya, F., Takezawa, T., Yokoo, A., Yamamoto, S.: End-to-End Evaluation in ATR-MATRIX: Speech Translation System between English and Japanese. Proc. Eur. Conf. Speech Comm. Tech. (1999) 2431–2434
6. Isotani, R., Yamabana, K., Ando, S., Hanazawa, K., Ishikawa, S., Emori, T., Hattori, H., Okumura, A., Watanabe, T.: An Automatic Speech Translation System on PDAs for Travel Conversation. Proc. IEEE Int. Conf. Multimodal Interfaces (2002) 211–216
7. Waibel, A., Badran, A., Black, A. W., Frederking, R., Gates, D., Lavie, A., Levin, L., Lenzo, K., Tomokiyo, L. M., Reichert, J., Schultz, T., Wallace, D., Woszczyna, M., Zhang, J.: Speechalator: Two-Way Speech-to-Speech Translation on a Consumer PDA. Proc. Eur. Conf. Speech Comm. Tech. (2003) 369–372
8. Wang, J. F., Lin, S. C., Yang, H. W.: A New Two-Layer Approach for Speech-to-Speech Translation. Proc. Int. Sym. Chinese Spoken Language Processing (2004) 321–324
9. Rabiner, L. R., Juang, B. H. (ed.): Fundamentals of Speech Recognition. Prentice-Hall (1993)
10. Verhelst, W., Roelands, M.: An Overlap-Add Technique based on Waveform Similarity (WSOLA) for High Quality Time-Scale Modification of Speech. Proc. IEEE Int. Conf. Acous., Speech, & Sig. Processing (1993) 554–557
11. Rabiner, L. R., Sambru, M. R.: An Algorithm for Determining the Endpoints of Isolated Utterances. The Bell System Technical Journal 54 2 (1975) 297–315

Human Computer Interaction for the Accelerometer-Based Mobile Game

Jonghun Baek[1], Ik-Jin Jang[2], KeeHyun Park[3], Hyun-Soo Kang[4], and Byoung-Ju Yun[5]

[1] Dept. of Information and Communications, Kyungpook National University, Daegu, 702-701, South Korea
[2] Samsung Electro-Mechanics
[3] College of Information and Communication, Keimyung University, Daegu, 704-701, South Korea
[4] School of ECE, Chungbuk National University, Chungju, 361-763, South Korea
[5] School of Electrical Engineering and Computer Science, Kyungpook National University, Daegu, 702-701, South Korea
bjisyun@ee.knu.ac.kr

Abstract. As a result of growth of sensor-enabled mobile devices such as PDA, cellular phone and other computing devices, in recent years, users can utilize the diverse digital contents everywhere and anytime. However, the interfaces of mobile applications are often unnatural due to limited resources and miniaturized input/output. Especially, users may feel this problem in some applications such as the mobile game. Therefore, novel interaction forms have been developed in order to complement the poor user interface of the mobile device and to increase the interest for the mobile game. In this paper, we describe the demonstration of the gesture and posture input supported by an accelerometer. The application example we created are AM-Fishing game on the mobile device that employs the accelerometer as the main interaction modality. The demos show the usability for the gesture and posture interaction.

1 Introduction

Advances in mobile computing and micro electro mechanical systems (MEMS) enable the development of games which lead about user's interest on the mobile phone, PDA, and other portable devices. Presently, mobile devices have been made popular to everyone, and users always carry with them. In this sense, the mobile game is becoming more popular, especially with the recent release of the portable devices such as Sony's PlayStation Portable or Samsung's SCH-G100/SPH-1000. It shows that this area has huge potential for growth.

Traditional desktop-based user interfaces have been developed on the basis that user's activities are static states. User interface design for desktop devices can use all of its visual resources. The representative desktop-based interaction mechanisms are keyboard, mouse and joystick. In general, these are very graphical and still more detailed for desktop-based applications. In contrast, interaction mechanisms of the mobile devices can not utilize all or any of their visual resources by reasons not only that activities of users are dynamic states [1] but also the mobile devices have the

E. Sha et al. (Eds.): EUC 2006, LNCS 4096, pp. 509 – 518, 2006.

limited resource and the small LCD display. Games on the mobile devices rely on key-pad, stylus-pen and input-panel. When using these mechanisms to manipulate mobile devices, it may lead to the time delay and the difficult operation because the small button may be manipulated repeatedly. So, it may make the users to lose their interests in the games [2].

There have been various studies about new input/output methods to solve this problem; voice recognition and gesture recognition are representative cases [1]-[4]. Voice recognition comes hard to apply to it because it is unsuitable for the user interface of the mobile game. The other way to design user interface is to recognize the gesture of the user. The user's gesture-based input by interaction between human and computer enable user to approach easily more than desktop PC. The gesture recognition needs additional devices that can detect user's gesture and must be able to embed in mobile devices. The trend of this field is much using the embedded camera [5]. The camera-based user interface may be uncomfortable for use because user's gesture must be transmitted to the mobile device under condition that user carries it in hand. Plus, the camera is comparative high cost. Therefore, it needs new method that can detect user's gesture easier and faster in mobile environment. In other words, proper sensors are necessary to detect actions or to recognize gestures of the user in the case of mobile and portable devices, and the processing capacity and mobile convenience should be considered before applying sensors. MEMS accelerometers are suitable sensors that coincide in this purpose. There have been various studies about using acceleration in recognizing gestures [6]-[8]. To use the gesture as input/output interface of the mobile devices, each gesture should be definitely discriminated each other. Otherwise, useless situation or inappropriate gestures can cause malfunction. Therefore, we sort context information in context-aware computing.

In this paper, to supplement lacking the user interface of the mobile devices, we propose the novel user interface that recognizes user's gestures such as swing and tilt, and estimates the user's posture. The application example we created is a fishing game. To improve efficiency that is expected by applying the accelerometer, with considering many restriction elements such as processing capacity, we propose the structure of the system that embedded in the accelerometer and the algorithm of the signal processing of the accelerometer for the mobile devices, which is the motion-based interaction technology and context-aware computing technology.

2 Context Information

Unlike designing user interface for traditional desktop applications, mobile devices can sort complex context information. Therefore many kinds of context information in context-aware computing environment are sorted [3][9].

Traditional desktop applications wait until user inputs data through the keyboard or mouse before execute especial action. Context-aware applications with sensors, however, can offer or require information even through non-conscious input of user by estimating motion of user at specific time and in particular place. Context-aware computing analyzes changing contexts in ubiquitous computing environment, and discriminates whether the information is valid or not, and then it generates the control event that requests or delivers information to execute the application.

In this paper, we detect context information called the "gesture" and "behavior", and calculate displacement amount of computer from the acceleration in order to gesture recognition and posture estimation. These user's gestures and behaviors are very important factors in ubiquitous computing environment. For examples, pull & push can be used to control the TV (e.g zoom in and out the display, etc.), a tilt can be used to control the TV (e.g. volume and channel control, etc.) and scroll the display of the mobile device, a snatch can be used to control the bell of the cellular phone and to converter the windows of the PDA, etc., and a posture can be used to automatically turn on the mobile devices or receive any information from the object that attached RFID tag when user puts the mobile devices toward their chest in ubiquitous computing environment. Especially, the user's posture estimation technology can correct the various postures of the user such as walking, running and sitting in daily life as well as be applied to the sports science by the fusion of the sensors.

3 System Description

User interface for the mobile devices is designed by a general-structure that is available to the sensor's output at the same time in diverse control interface to increase the expected efficiency by applying the sensor, because the mobile devices have many restriction elements such as processing capability, limited resources (e.g. memory, battery). Fig. 1 is our system that is designed to use the accelerometer by a general-purpose in mobile device.

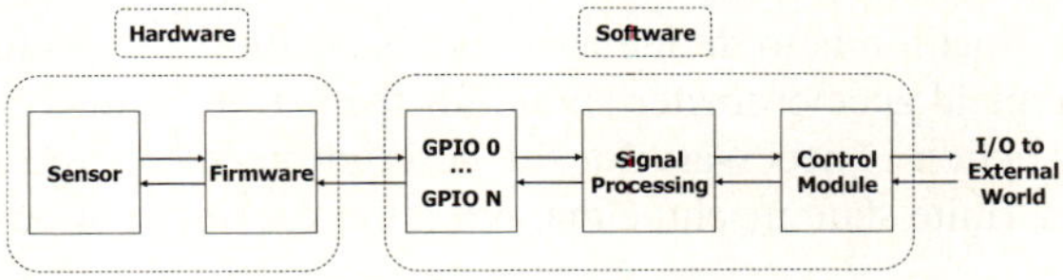

Fig. 1. An architecture of the mobile device that embedded the accelerometer

Fig. 2 shows that the system generates the control event by processing the signal detected from the accelerometer in software structure of the mobile devices with the RTOS (real time operation system) environment. The accelerometer's output is passed through a dispatcher that asks the GPIO for the signal of the accelerometer and passes through two parallel filters; a lowpass filter for a static acceleration such as tilt and gravity and a highpass filter for a dynamic acceleration such as vibration, shock, and impulse. The lowpass and highpass filtered output then goes to a signal processing for each application and then it generates a gesture-based control event and controls or executes the applications. To decrease overheads that are generated by attaching the accelerometer to the mobile device, we designed the structure that control events do not pass to the control module but to a task module.

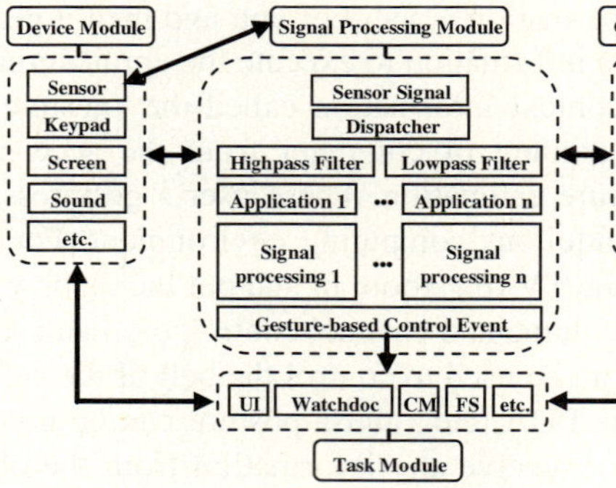

Fig. 2. A block diagram of the mobile device with the RTOS environment

4 Accelerometer Signal Processing for the Mobile Game

In the game of the existing mobile devices, control of the direction and action of a character is done by using the key-pad. In our hand gesture- and posture-based mobile interaction technique, we show the usability for the use of the accelerometer that is embedded in the mobile device and the effect of the input.

In the process of the user's motion recognition, actually, there are several cases that the acceleration signal for the user's action often misrecognized. For examples, there are malfunction by the user's hand tremble, the non-necessary gesture, and misrecognition. In addition, in the case that several gestures are occurred almost at the same time in one action, how we can distinguish each gesture. To resolve these limitations and problems, we proposed that the signal processing method for the gesture recognition and posture estimation is to define each user's posture and gesture stage by stage as considering a typical accelerometer signal for the action. Namely, a representation scheme for user's action is necessary for the description of each posture and gesture. Therefore we use a finite state machine that has a finite number of possible stages.

4.1 The Scenario for the Fishing Game

We assume that the action for fishing game consists of the nine stages as followings:

- In the initial stage, the position of the mobile device is assumed that user is gripping the mobile device in an attention state (see Fig. 3(a) and section A in the Fig. 5(b)).
- First, in the beginning stage, the user takes the mobile device toward their chest (see Fig. 3(b) and section B in the Fig. 5(b)). It informs the beginning of the game by the estimating of the user's posture.
- Second, in the ready stage, the mobile device (fishing rod) is located above the user's shoulder before throwing the fishing rod. It informs the throwing gesture by estimating of the user's posture (see Fig. 3(c) and section C in the Fig. 5(b)).
- Third, in the throwing stage, we determine the movement distance, velocity, power, and path-direction of the fishing rod for the user's action (see Fig. 3(d) and section D in the Fig. 5(b)).

- Fourth, in the waiting stage, at the time, the user takes the mobile device toward their chest and then waits a bite of the fishes (see Fig. 3(e) and section E in the Fig. 5(b)).
- Fifth, in the snatching stage, snatching motion that user tried to land it immediately when the fish are on the feed (see Fig. 3(f) and section F in the Fig. 5(b)).
- Sixth, in the pull & push stage, pulling & pushing gesture indicate that user pulls the fishing rod toward user's chest like user reels in fish in real fishing to consume the power of the fish, and then user watches the mobile phone to check the state of the fish (ex. power of the fish) (see Fig. 3(g) and section G in the Fig. 5(b).
- Seventh, in the right and left tilting stage, tilting gesture indicate that user tilts the fishing rod to take the fish by their chest direction and to consume the power of the fish (see Fig. 3(h) and section H in the Fig. 5(b)).
- Finally, in the finishing stage, the user takes the mobile device toward their chest again and then user verifies the experimental result (see Fig. 3(i) and section I in the Fig. 5(b)).

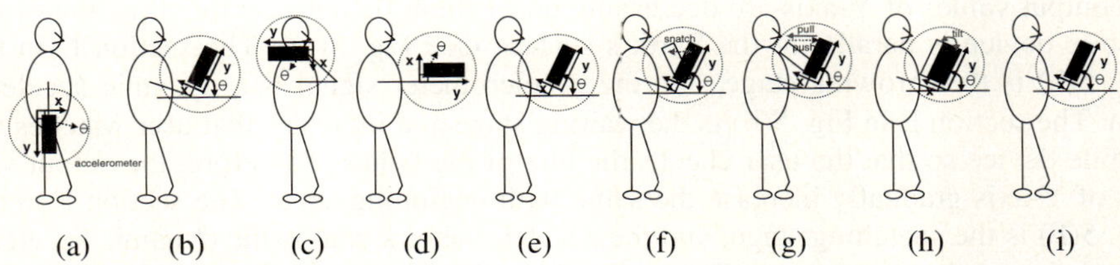

Fig. 3. Examples of the fishing action and the location of the accelerometer in the each stage; (a) initial stage, (b) beginning stage, (c) ready stage, (d) throwing stage, (e) waiting for a bite stage, (f) snatching stage, (g) pull & push stage, (h) tilting stage, and (i) finishing stage. A θ is the angle between the mobile device and the ground.

4.2 Accelerometer Signal Analysis for the Fishing Action

An experiment was conducted to assess the usability of the accelerometer as interaction technique for the mobile games. Thirty subjects (27 males and 3 females, ages 23 to 33, all were colleagues who volunteered for the study) participated in this study. First, we observed the output patterns of the accelerometer for the fishing action as the above scenario (see Fig. 4).

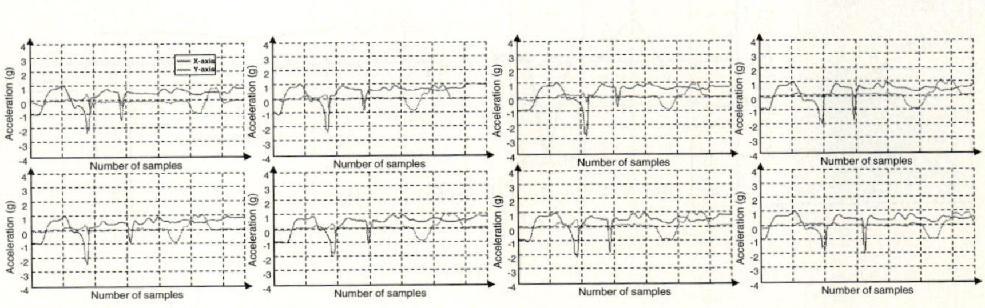

Fig. 4. Signal patterns of the eight participants for the fishing game

Fig. 4 was the result of the experiment for the representative eight subjects among of the thirty subjects. Though the amplitudes are different each other for their action, the all output patterns are almost similar in all the experiments. To analysis the acceleration signal of the gestures for the fishing action, we considered the typical signal type for the fishing action (see Fig. 5(b)).

In the Fig. 5, the direction of the mobile device is parallel to the Earth's surface, and X- and Y-axis are pointing the right and forward direction, respectively (see Fig. 5(a)). Therefore, the output values of the X- and Y-axis are both 0g. The section A in the Fig. 5(b) indicates that the user's posture is "attention". The direction of the mobile device of this case is that X- and Y-axis are pointing the right and the Earth's gravitational field, respectively, and the output values are 0g (0°) and -1g (-90°), respectively. The section B in the Fig. 5(b) indicates that user's posture changed from "attention" to beginning stage. In this case, the output values of Y-axis gradually increase because the Y-axis is changed from direction of the Earth's gravitational field to its reverse. And X-axis nearly remains the same. The section C in the Fig. 5(b) indicates that user's posture changed from beginning stage to ready stage. In this case, the output values of Y-axis are decreasing up to about 0g because the direction of the mobile device is parallel to the Earth's surface (see Fig. 3(c)). The section D in the Fig. 5(b) is the throwing stage, and the accelerometer signal is a dynamic acceleration. The section E in Fig. 5(b) is the waiting stage and indicates that user watches the mobile device so that the user checks the bite of the fishes. Therefore, the output values of Y-axis gradually increase the same with beginning stage. The section F in the Fig. 5(F) is the snatching stage, and the accelerometer signal is the dynamic acceleration the same throwing stage. The section G in the Fig. 5(g) is the pull & push stage, and the output values of the accelerometer gradually decrease and then increase. The section H in the Fig. 5(b) is the tilting stage, and the output values of the accelerometer decrease to -1g when user tilt to the right and increase to +1g when user tilt to the left. Finally, the section I in the Fig. 5(b) is the finishing stage that user ascertains the practice result, and the user's posture is the same with beginning stage about the output of the accelerometer.

Generally, the output acceleration of this accelerometer has been converted to the acceleration that varies between ±1g. However, in the fishing action, the acceleration having over ±1g is detected because the dynamic acceleration such as throwing and

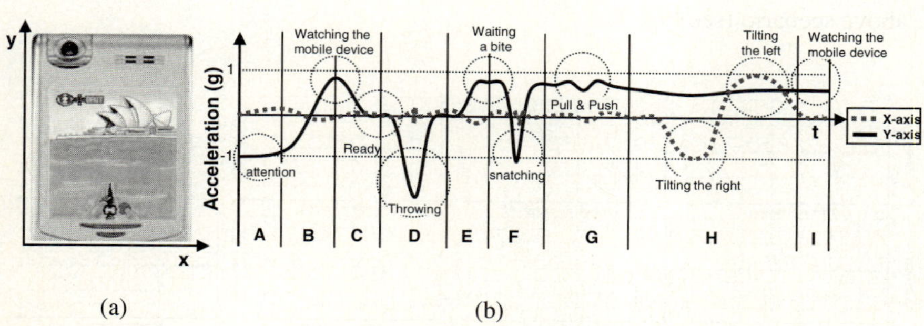

Fig. 5. (a) the direction of the accelerometer that is embedded to the mobile device, (b) the typical user's action in fishing game

snatching exists. Namely, in the fishing action, all of the gesture and posture are a static acceleration except for the throwing and snatching gestures (see Fig. 5(b)).

4.3 Posture Estimation

To estimate user's posture carrying the mobile device, we calculate θ for each state as shown in Fig. 3. The accelerometer uses the force of gravity as an input vector to determine orientation of an object in space. The X- and Y-axis of the accelerometer are pointing the right and forward direction, respectively. If the accelerometer is ideal state, the accelerometer's digital outputs (X- and Y-axis) are 0g when it is parallel to the earth's surface and a scale factor is 12.5% duty cycle change per g. However, the accelerometer may not always be level when the applications using the accelerometer are executed on the mobile device, and calibration is recommended by the manufacturer. The method to do a more accurate calibration is to slowly rotate the accelerometer 360° and to make measurements at ±90°. The following table 1 shows the calibration results with the changes in the X- and Y-axis as the accelerometer that embedded in the mobile device is tilted ±90° through gravity. These experimental results were recorded at each Y-axis orientation to horizon. If the accelerometer is ideal state, the duty cycle is changed 62.5% into 37.5% both X- and Y-axis when angle is changed ±90°. However, in this experiment, the duty cycles of the X- and Y-axis are (66.2-40.6)/2=12.8%/g and (60.1-36.4)/2=11.9%/g, respectively [9].

Table 1. Output of X- and Y-axis respond to changes in tilt

Y-axis	X output		Y output	
Orientation to horizon	PWM (%)	Acceleration (g)	PWM (%)	Acceleration (g)
90	53.40	0.000	60.10	1.000
75	50.43	-0.232	59.69	0.961
60	47.41	-0.468	58.56	0.866
45	44.80	-0.672	56.73	0.713
30	42.77	-0.831	54.31	0.509
15	41.51	-0.929	51.54	0.276
0	40.60	-1.000	48.25	0.000
-15	41.36	-0.941	45.39	-0.240
-30	42.55	-0.848	42.58	-0.476
-45	44.72	-0.678	40.02	-0.692
-60	47.25	-0.481	38.17	-0.847
-75	50.19	-0.251	36.98	-0.947
-90	53.40	-0.000	36.40	-1.000

To determine a range of the θ for the user's posture, with the various postures of the thirty participants, we collected data a two-dimensional time series for about three seconds at the sampling rate of the 140 samples/s from the outputs of the accelerometer (ADXL202EB). We examined the optimal threshold value to determine the convergence of the user's posture. Here, the convergence of the user posture was determined using the threshold valued and following form,

$$\mu - z \times \frac{\sigma}{\sqrt{n}} < \text{Threshold value} < \mu - z \times \frac{\sigma}{\sqrt{n}} \qquad (1)$$

where, μ is mean of the population which is output of the accelerometer, z is normal distribution, σ is variance for the population, and n is number of samples. The 90% (z=1.65) of the total samples is used for the confidence interval. The following table 2 shows the result of the confidence interval.

Through the experiment mentioned above (Table 1), the angle of the mobile device for each user's posture is estimated: it is about -90° for attention, about 39.5° ~ 46.8° for watching the mobile device, about -16° ~ 7° for ready, about 35.5° ~ 54° for waiting the bite, and about 37.6° ~ 40° for watching the mobile device after tilting gesture.

Table 2. Threshold value for estimating user posture; min, max, mean and standard deviation values of Y-axis for each posture

Posture	Min	Max	Mean	Standard deviation	T(Threshold value)
Attention	-1.0000	-0.9730	-0.9852	0.0040	-0.9918 < T < -0.9786
Watching the mobile device	0.6260	0.7580	0.6853	0.0282	0.6388 < T < 0.7318
Ready	-0.3540	0.1620	-0.0703	0.1168	-0.2631 < T < 0.1225
Waiting the bite	0.5840	0.8520	0.6724	0.0784	0.5840 < T < 0.8017
Watching after tilting	0.5960	0.6500	0.6290	0.0098	0.6127 < T < 0.6452

4.4 Implementation

The gestures used in the fishing game are the throwing, snatching, and tilt; the throwing gesture is expressed as the movement distance and the velocity of the fishing rod by measuring the acceleration for the user's throwing gesture, the path-direction of the fishing rod is expressed by X-axis of the accelerometer when user throw the fishing rod. We consider the range of the power and the tilt in the throwing stage in order to determine the movement distance, the velocity, and the path-direction of the fishing rod. Because it is difficult to distinguish between the dynamic acceleration like the

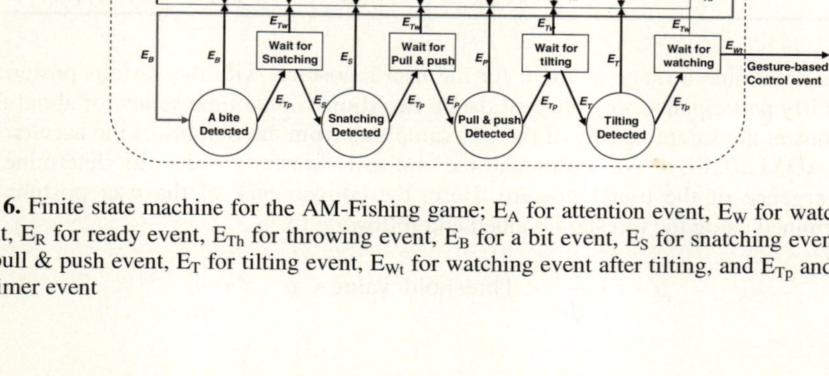

Fig. 6. Finite state machine for the AM-Fishing game; E_A for attention event, E_W for watching event, E_R for ready event, E_{Th} for throwing event, E_B for a bit event, E_S for snatching event, E_P for pull & push event, E_T for tilting event, E_{Wt} for watching event after tilting, and E_{Tp} and E_{Tw} for timer event

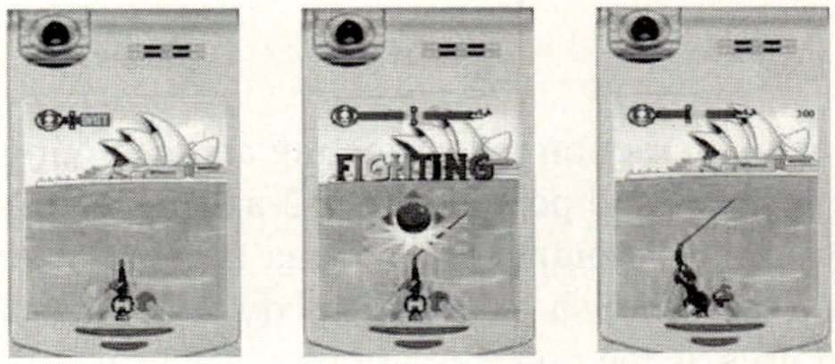

(a) (b) (c)

Fig. 7. AM-Fishing game; (a) throwing mode, (b) snatching mode, and (c) tilting mode on the mobile device

throwing and the static acceleration like the posture, and the noises as the unnecessary user's action and hand tremble have to be removed, the state machine is needed. The state machine for the mobile fishing game recognizes and processes the user's action by the designed scenario by treating only valid gesture or posture in each state. The input of the state machine is the accelerometer signal by lowpass filter and the output is gesture-based control event. Fig. 6 is structure of the state machine.

To demonstrate our application in games we have developed the mobile game called AM-Fishing game (see Fig. 7). In the game the user has to throwing the mobile device with his real arm into a virtual fishing site.

5 Experimental Results

We measured the recognition rate of the gesture and posture for the performance evaluation. The sampling rate is set 20Hz. We define practiced man and non-practiced man as the participant and the malfunction includes non-function, mis-recognition, and overtime. The table 3 shows the recognition rate for each gesture and posture. This result is useful in terms of the gesture- and posture-based control interface and technique for inducing the interest and realism for the mobile game as well as providing the convenience of the control. For example, in the AM-Fishing game, we can improve the realism by using the gesture and posture in the control interface. Also, this enables to induce extra-interest through the dynamic motion for the control of the game. This is because that the interface for controlling the motion of game characters enables user to feel higher realism as we prefer to use joystick instead of keyboard in the personnel computer-based game.

Table 3. Recognition rate of the gesture and posture in the AM-Fishing game

User	Number of plays	Number of functions	Number of mal-functions	Recognition rate (%)
Practiced man	75	71	4	94.7%
Non-practiced man	75	68	7	90.7%

6 Conclusion

We implemented the new interaction by estimating and detecting the context information as user's various gestures and postures with 2-axis accelerometer. We considered the typical fishing action by the output type of the accelerometer for 30 participants. Because it is difficult to distinguish between the dynamic acceleration and the static acceleration, and the noises as the unnecessary user's action and hand tremble have to be removed, the state machine is needed. The state machine for the mobile fishing game recognizes and processes the user's action by the designed scenario by treating only valid gesture or posture in each state. As a result, this will enhance not only the convenience to use but also the interest and realism for the mobile game.

Acknowledgement. This work was supported by the Ministry of Education, Korea, under the BK21 project.

References

[1] M. Ehreumann, T. Lutticke and R. Dillmann, Dynamic Gestures as an Input Device for Direction a Mobile Platform, IEEE International Conference on Robotics and Automation, vol. 3, pp. 2596-2601, 2001.

[2] V. Paelke, C. Reimann and D. Stichling, Foot-based mobile Interaction with Games, ACM SIGCHI International Conference on Advances in Computer Entertainment Technology, pp. 321-324, 2004.

[3] P. Indrajit, S. Togesh, O. Ercan and S. Rajeev, Toward Natural Gesture/Speech HCI: A Case Study of Weather Narration, Workshop on Perceptual User Interfaces, pp. 1-6, 1998.

[4] B. N. Schilit, N. Adams, and R. Want, Context-Aware Computing Applications, In Proceedings of the 1st International Workshop on Mobile Computing Systems and Applications, pp. 85-90, 1994.

[5] L. Gupta and S. Ma, Gesture-Based interaction and Communication: Automated Classification of Hand Gesture Contours, IEEE Transactions on Systems, Man, and Cybernetics, vol. 31, No. 1, pp. 114-120, 2001.

[6] S. Sotiropoulos, K. Papademetriou and A. Dollas, Adaptation of a Low Cost Motion Recognition System for Custom Operation from Shrink-Wrapped Hardware, Proceedings of the 2003 ACM SIGMM workshop on Biometrics methods and applications, pp. 107-114, 2003.

[7] A Wilson and S. Shafer, "XWand: UI for Intelligent Spaces, In Proc. CHI, pp. 545-552, 2003.

[8] K. Partrige, S. Chatterjee, V. Sazawal, G. Borriello and R. Want, TiltType: Accelerometer-Supported Text Entry for Very Small Devices, In UIST02: In Proceedings of the 15th annual ACM Symposium on User Interface Software and Technology, pp. 201-204, 2002.

[9] G. D. Abowd, A. K. Dey, P. J. Brown, N. Davies, M. Smith and P. Steggles, Towards a Better Understanding of Context and Context-Awareness, In HUC'99: In Proceeding of 1st International Symposium on Handheld Ubiquitous Computing, pp. 304-307, 1999.

[10] Low-cost ±2g/±10g Dual Axis iMEMS Accelerometers with Digital Output ADXL202/ADXL210 Data Sheet, Analog Devices Corporation, 1999.

Using Automatic Facial Expression Classification for Contents Indexing Based on the Emotional Component

Uwe Kowalik, Terumasa Aoki, and Hiroshi Yasuda

Research Center of Advanced Science and Technology
The University of Tokyo,
4-6-1 Komaba Bldg.#3, Meguro-ku Tokyo, 153-8904 Japan
{uwe, aoki, yasuda}@mpeg.rcast.u-tokyo.ac.jp

Abstract. Within the last decade the development of new technologies in the multimedia sector has advanced with stunning pace. Due to the availability of high-capacity mass storage devices at low cost private multimedia libraries containing digital video and audio items have recently gained popularity. Although attached meta-data like title, actor's/actress' name and creation time eases the task of finding preferred contents, it is still difficult to find a specific part within a movie one enjoyed before by remembering the time code. In this paper we introduce the BROAFERENCE system that provides a solution for the above problem. We propose meta-data creation based on recorded user experience derived from facial expressions containing joy, sadness and anger events as well as interest focus data. In the following the system layout, functionality and conducted experiments for system verification will be introduced to the reader.

Keywords: Facial expression, emotion, video retrieval.

1 Introduction

Facial expressions are playing an important role in human communication. They convey information of emotional states of joy, anger, fear, disgust or surprise [1]. In [2] it is proposed, that this basic emotions have corresponding prototypic facial expressions. P. Ekman developed the 'Facial Action Coding System' (FACS). 'FACS' is a systematic approach of defining a general, atomic set of facial action units (AU) based on visually perceived muscle movements in human faces. Any possible facial expression can be described by a combination of multiple AUs [2] [3]. Although the process of FACS-coding is still a manual task for certified FACS-coders, several automatic approaches have been presented lately [4]. In front of this background we have developed the BROAFERENCE system. BROAFERENCE provides a platform for delivering interactive multimedia applications over IP based networks. One or more terminals may be connected to the system. Each terminal is equipped with a module for tracking, analyzing and recording facial expressions of the user in front of the terminal's screen. Our approach for indexing multi media contents is based on the temporal correlation between emotional triggers caused by a screen event at a certain media time and the related facial expression. The expression can be automatically perceived in the user's face taken by a video camera connected to the BROAFERENCE terminal. The facial expression parameters will be synchronously stored along

E. Sha et al. (Eds.): EUC 2006, LNCS 4096, pp. 519 – 528, 2006.

with the media time, while the user is watching e.g. a movie. This data form a set of meta-information that is associated with the contents. Due to the synchronization between media time and occurrence time of a certain facial action event it is possible to find a specific part of a movie later by looking for e.g. the highest intensity of a 'smile' expression in order to identify funny parts in the movie. A gaze detection module estimates the screen area visited by the user's eye. This information can be used to perform an analysis of user's focus of interest during the contents consumption. In the following we will first describe the system layout and functionality of the modules. In order to verify the systems performance we conducted user experiments with the specific goal to prove the reliability of the real-time smile detection module. The experimental setup, execution and results will be explained later. Finally we will summarize the paper and give an outlook to the future work.

2 Related Works

In [7] news video archives are indexed with a lexicon of 100 semantic concepts, e.g. sports, people, etc. Users may query by concepts or combinations of them and access the resulted video on a semantic level. In [8] video documents are automatically indexed with 17 specific concept detectors for speech and noise analysis [9]. Keywords are automatically derived from the speech recognition result. The keywords forming a 400 dimensional vector after a PCA has been applied. The keyword vector represents a conceptual description for each video document. In addition a low-level color histogram based indexing is performed on the key frames. Above works are using a contents based indexing approach. In [10] it is suggested to take the user behavior while watching a video from a private video data base into account. The user actions, e.g. *pause*, *stop*, *fast forward*, etc. are stored in a log-file for later examination. Different behavioral types are defined and a specific user's type is derived from the log-file of his/her watching behavior. Whereas the approaches of contents indexing presented in [7] [8] are contents oriented, the approach in [10] is more near to our approach i.e. user oriented. In this paper we present our idea of exploiting emotion data derived from facial expressions for video indexing in large private video data bases. With our approach a user can find specific contents based on how much oneself (or others) enjoyed the contents previously.

3 System Overview

In Fig. 1 the general network structure of the BROAFERENCE system is shown. A video server (broadcast station) sends the movie or TV program to an IP multicast address that is known to the clients (participants). Using IP broadcasting ensures that the timestamps of the media stream packets received by a client terminal are consistent through all clients. The advantage by doing so lies in the fact, that the recorded meta-data sets for a certain transmission are comparable between different users later. The BROAFERENCE system also supports connections between different client terminals, which allow the establishment of individual video chat sessions while the user is watching the program.

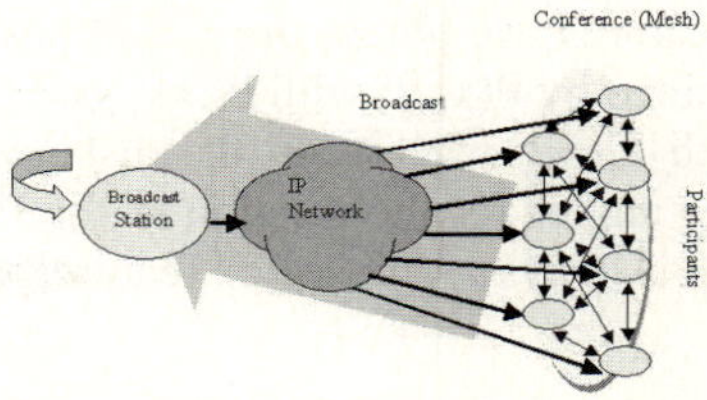

Fig. 1. Network structure of the BROAFERENCE system

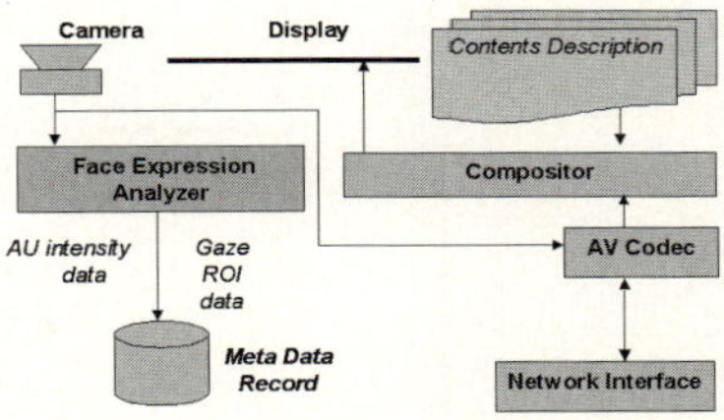

Fig. 2. Terminal block diagram

Fig. 2 shows the block diagram of a terminal. The BROAFERENCE system facilitates a flexible scene composition paradigm. A compositor module is responsible for assembling the final screen presentation based on the given contents description. The description will be loaded at start up from either a local or remote location. The scene description defines a tree structure of 2D, 3D, AV and interactive objects. The description format is text-based and similar to the VRML97 markup language. This approach is widely used and provides a high level of flexibility to build multimedia applications.

AV streams received/sent via the RTP network interface will be decoded/encoded by appropriate codecs. A face expression analyzer is connected to a local camera. This module automatically derives the intensity values of facial expressions from a set of tracked face feature points and stores them along with the media time of the received TV program building an index file that is used later for identifying parts of the contents that the user e.g. enjoyed.

3.1 Face Expression Analyzer

A commercial, vision based face tracker provided by 'NVision' is used to track the user's face and to extract relevant feature points. Video images taken from a video camera are fed into the face tracker module, which detects the face by searching deformation invariant features in a gray level image, derived from the current video frame. The output is a set of 22 feature points, i.e. a vector of 44 elements consisting of the x- and y-components of the features (Fig. 3).

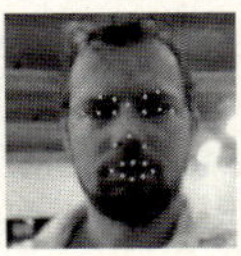

Fig. 3. Face tracker output: 22 feature points

In addition to the facial features, we obtain the global position of the face' projection in the image plane determined by P(x, y) with 0<=x, y<=1.0 independent of the image size. A scale factor z with z ~ d, where d is the distance of the face to the camera plane, as well as the Euler-angles for the rotation of the face around the x-, y- and z-axis are provided as well. Always a sub-set of feature points is involved to form a specific facial expression.

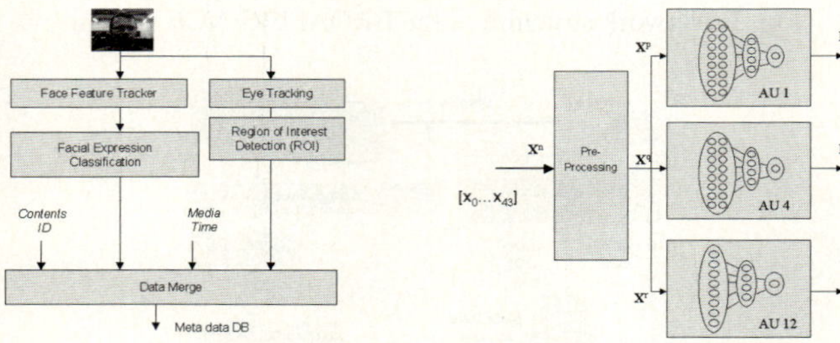

Fig. 4. Facial expression analyzer (left) and expression classifiers with preprocessing

The *facial expression classification module* (Fig. 4) exploits this correlation in order to perform the expression classification. The left part of Fig. 4 shows the block diagram of the facial expression analyzer. It consists of the *expression classifier module* and the *gaze detection module*. The *gaze detection module* will be described later. Currently tree classifiers for facial expressions have been implemented (AU1, AU12 and AU4). The intensity of the AU1 classifier output refers to the activity of the 'inner brow raiser' muscle. The activity of the 'zygmaticus major' muscle is measured by the intensity of the AU12 classifier output. The 'inner eye brow lowerer' muscle's contraction level is expressed by the AU4. The AU1 activity is related to the occurrence of sadness events experienced by a human. Activity of AU12 can be perceived when a person smiles. The 'inner eyebrow lowerer' muscle is incorporated in angry facial expressions. The feature vector will be preprocessed before passing it to the classifier. The preprocessing step reduces the dimension of the input vector from 44 parameters (all features) to the appropriate number of parameters used by the specific classifier. A subset of eight feature points is involved in our approach of smile-detection (AU12). The preprocessing step performs a selection of the features defining the mouth shape. For the classification of AU1 we are using the three features describing the position of nose root, left and right inner eyebrow corner. The AU4 intensity is calculated based on the same features as AU1, whereas the training data are different. A compensation of head translation, rotation and scale (z-component) is performed for all data before applying a neural network classifier to the feature vector. Due to the real-time constraints of the system simple Artificial Neural Network structures (ANN) have been designed in order to reduce the processing time. The ANN consists of three layers. The input layer has a number of neurons that fits the number of elements of the feature vector. A hidden layer consisting of four neurons has been found to perform well. The output of each classifier is a single neuron that provides the intensity value for each classifier. For training the networks the 'Resilient Propagation' method (*Rprop*) was used. A detailed description can be found in [6].

Compensation of Head Movement and Rotation

The goal of the compensation step is to separate feature movements caused by head motion from those caused by facial expression changes. The exploited tracker provides head center position, scale and rotation (Euler angles around x-, y- and z-axis) parameters. The compensation is done in two steps. First, translation, scale and in-plane rotation around the z-axis are compensated by simply applying the inverse transform to the feature point positions. The result is still not stable against out-of-plane head rotations. The impact of out-of-plane head rotations on the feature positions can be approximated by Eq.1 provided the angles around x-axis and y-axis (α, β) are known and assuming parallel projection. Than an adaptive depth map estimation algorithm is applied to each feature in order to compensate displacement errors caused by a feature depth Z_0>0

$$X' = X \cdot \cos\beta + Z \cdot \sin\beta$$
$$Y' = Y \cdot \cos\alpha - Z \cdot \sin\alpha \qquad \text{Eq. 1}$$

The adaptive depth map estimation for compensating out-of-plane head rotations works as follows.

1. Capture a reference shape S_0 of feature points at $\alpha = \beta = 0$
2. Calculate expected X'_0, Y'_0 in subsequent frames assuming a rigid planar face model where Z=0 for each feature point and $\alpha, \beta > 0$ using Eq.1
3. Calculate the displacement $dx = X' - X'_0$, $dy = Y' - Y'_0$
4. Calculate and store a compensation term z via Eq.1 assuming dx and dy are caused by unknown $Z_0 \neq 0$
5. Calculate dz in subsequent frames until $dx, dy < \varepsilon$ where ε is the maximum allowed displacement error.
6. Finish z-estimation, if $dx, dy < \varepsilon$ for all features

Fig. 5 shows a result of the compensated feature position (x-component) over frame number for the nose tip (left) and a depth map example.

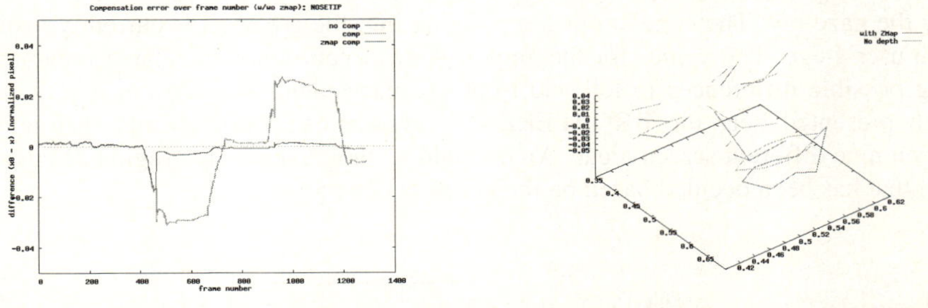

Fig. 5. Displacement error with/with out depth map estimation (left) and depth map example

3.2 Video Database for Classifier Training

A video database has been created for deriving the training data for the AU classifiers. It consists of assembled video sequences each about 2 minutes of length. Each sequence shows maximum (or minimum respectively) expressions taken from six different people. In order to get real (not posed) facial expressions, the people have been ask to perform different tasks while filming there face. Comedy strips have been presented to the persons for getting data for AU12 (smile intensity). The 'angry face' expression data (AU1) and data for AU4 have been extracted from a video taken while people were playing an online computer game. The final video data for extracting the training data set have been created by frame-based inspection and assembling of appropriate parts.

3.3 Gaze Estimation Module

The gaze estimation module was developed in order to gain information about the user's focus of interest while watching the TV program or movie. We define the focus of interest as the time that a user's gaze spends on a certain screen area. The gaze direction will be estimated based on the eye pose of the person in front of the screen. The gaze tracker incorporates a 3D head/eye model to simulate the physics of real head and eye movement (Fig. 6). The geometric parameters provided by the face tracker module are used to estimate the resulting view angle taking into account the connection of 3D transforms between head and eye rotation. While the head rotation parameters provided by the tracker module are used to transform the head model, the estimated eye rotation is applied to the 3D eye models. Fig. 7 shows a screen shot of the gaze estimation output.

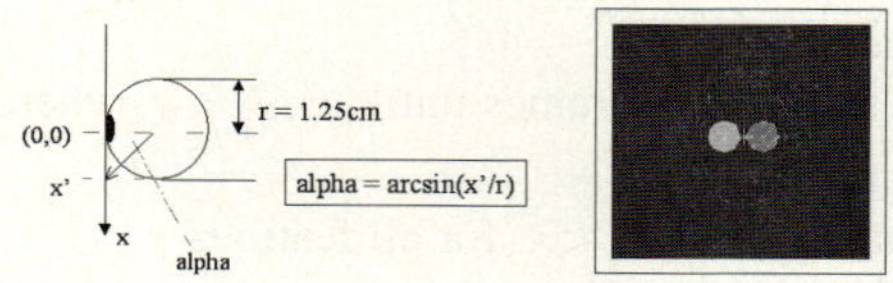

Fig. 6. 3D eye model used for gaze estimation

Two cone geometries reaching from the eyes to the screen's image plate are simulating the gaze ray. The cone's tops are pointing into the area that is currently visited by the user's eye. The values for the angles of eye rotation are calculated separately, taking possible differences in left and right eye movement into account. By the approach presented here the BROAFERENCE system can automatically distinguish between nine different screen areas. An overlaid rectangle marks the region of interest (ROI) that has been decided based on the pointing cone tops.

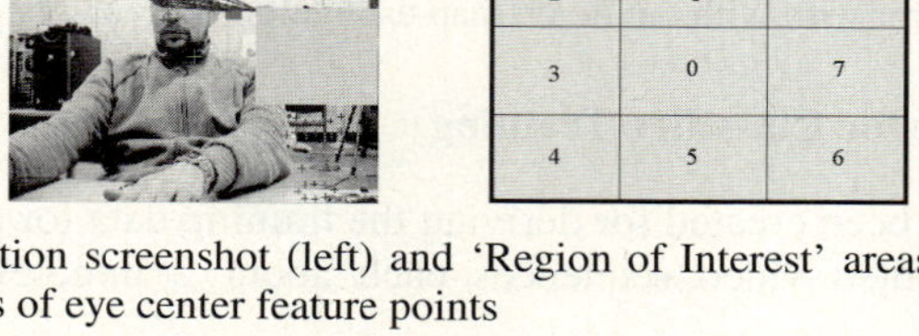

Fig. 7. Gaze estimation screenshot (left) and 'Region of Interest' areas on the screen derived from 2D coordinates of eye center feature points

3.4 Index Data File Format

A simple proprietary file format has been developed to store the intensity values of AU1, AU4, AU12 and the region code of the estimated region of interest along with the media time. The file format is packet oriented. Each packet contains the indexing information related to a specific media time stamp. The beginning of a packet is indicated by a packet start code followed by the media time. This allows fast and random access to the index data. The ROI code is stored as an 8 bit integer value. The intensity values, indicating the *joy*, *anger* or *sadness* factor, are stored as 32bit floating-point values subsequently. The packet structure would allow a streamed distribution of the meta-data, which could be interesting in the context of media research in a future ubiquitous network environment for e.g. collecting online user feedback on delivered multimedia contents.

4 Experiments and Discussion of the Results

In order to validate the function of the BROAFERENCE system approach for indexing of digital video contents delivered over IP network experiments have been carried out. We describe the experiments for all three classifiers in the following.

4.1 AU1 and AU4 Classifier

The performance tests for AU1 and AU4 have been carried out on video data that have been recorded for the classifier training, whereas this data where not part of the training set. A simple test application has been written in order to browse the created indexing data manually (Fig. 8)

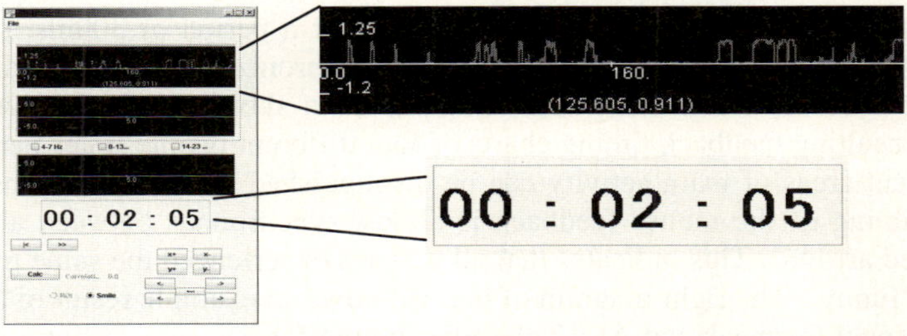

Fig. 8. Media time browser application

The black area displays the recorded intensity values along with the media time. The time of occurrence of a high intensity for AU1 and AU4 has been selected manually by pointing to the peak with the mouse pointer. The application translates the mouse position to the appropriate media time of the movie that shows the facial action of the test person. It has been found that the AU4 classifiers for anger detection performed quite well. We achieved 83% correct classification results for angry faces from the untrained video data base. In contrast the classification result of the AU1 classifier showed a lower reliability (high intensity, but actually no sadness event has recognized by a human observer). We achieved a correct classification of sad face expressions of 68%. This is due to the fact that the displacement of inner eyebrow feature is very small. It seems to be not sufficient to rely only on the inner eyebrow feature points for classification of AU1. An incorporation of texture properties of the area above the inner eyebrow features may lead to more stable results.

4.2 AU12 Classifier

For evaluation of the AU12 classifier performance participants have been asked to watch comedy scenes by using the BROAFERENCE system. A direct feedback method was used to evaluate the automatically derived intensity values of facial expression of smile against the true user experience. The evaluation setup is shown in Fig. 9.

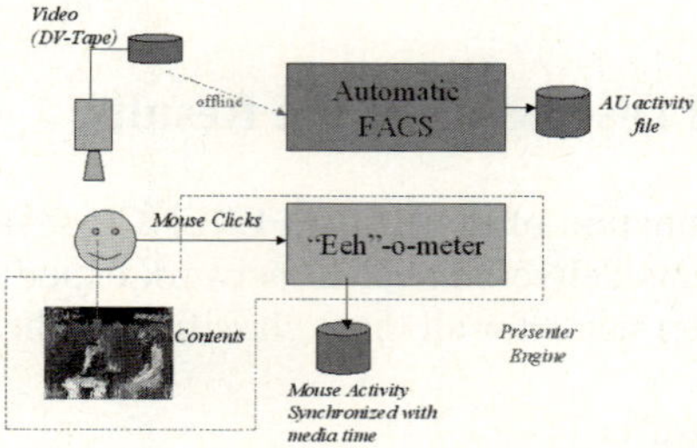

Fig. 9. Setup of the direct feedback evaluation method

A camera records the user's face while watching comedy scenes with the BROAFERENCE system. The recorded video data where used to derive intensity data of AU12 offline. Users have been asked to give feedback by clicking a mouse button in the case they see some funny part of the content. The so called "Eeh-o-meter" module in Fig. 9 integrates the number of mouse clicks over a period of 300ms. Each click restarts the timer interval. The click time was synchronized with the media time of the presented content. The same contents have been shown to all subjects. Fig. 10 shows the resulting feedback timing charts of four different people (inter-person, left). Four different areas of main activity can be distinguished (dotted lines). Inside these areas the timing of the mouse feedback is almost synchronous between all subjects (closed lined arrows). This indicates that all persons experienced the same parts of the content as 'funny'. The right diagram of Fig. 10 shows an example result of the timing between manual feedback and AU12 classifier output for one subject (intra-person). It can be seen that the manual feedback starts after the smile-onset (onset=time from minimum to next first maximum of intensity) and lies completely inside the range of maximum occurrence of AU12. This interestingly applies for about 90% of the recorded data. The reason is that the subjects seem to be completely immersed into the contents during this time and do not control their environment. The onset-time has been measured and lies between 0.5 to 1.5 seconds in the recorded data. This value differs usually amongst people. Due to the above results, the AU12 intensity output was perfectly applicable to identify funny parts over the content timeline. The same application as the one used for AU1/AU4 verification was taken to map intensity peaks to media time.

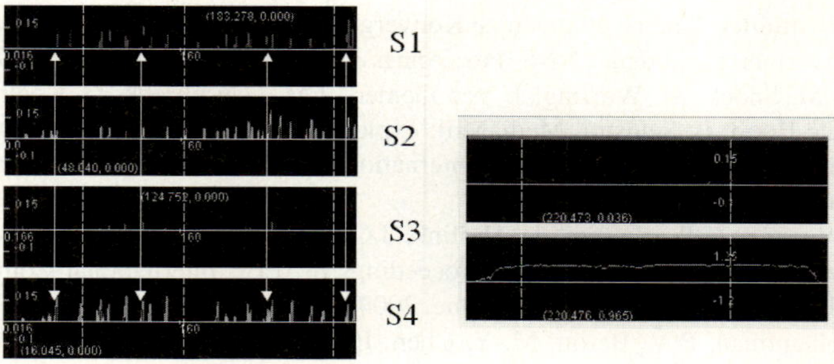

Fig. 10. Inter-person feedback timing (left) and intra-person AU12 intensity vs. feedback timing

5 Conclusion and Future Work

In this paper we have presented a new approach of indexing digital contents based on emotional events that normally occur while watching it. The idea is to exploit facial expressions since they are cues for 'how much' a person is riveted on the contents. The intensity of those facial expressions is automatically measured based on the position of tracked facial feature points. Currently three descriptors referring to the action units AU1, AU4 and AU12 in the Facial Action Coding System have been implemented. While AU12 is related to the smile intensity (*joy* emotion), the intensity of AU1 indicates the emotional state of *sadness*. AU4 indicates the experience of *anger* events. Each descriptor's output is an intensity value accordingly to its AU. The intensity values are recorded during watching the contents and a search engine may access this data in order to extract media time stamps that are related to the user's previous *joy* or *sadness* experience. The results of conducted user experiments have shown, that automatically derived intensity values for AU12 expressions are reliable enough to serve as indexing hints for identifying contents based on the emotional component of *joy* experience. Future work will concentrate on the reliability improvement for the AU1 classifier. Further interest lies in analyzing dynamics of more complex facial expressions based on the here presented automatic approach.

References

1. P. Ekman, Facial Expressions, in T. Dalgleish, M. Power (eds.), Handbook of Cognition and Emotion, New York, John Willey&Sons Ltd., 1999
2. P. Ekman, Facial expression and emotion, AmericanPsychologist,48, 384-392
3. Paul Ekman, Wallace V. Friesen, and Joseph C. Hager: The new (2002) Facial Action Coding System (FACS)
4. Gwen Littlewort, Marian Stewart Bartlett, Ian Fasel, Joshua Susskind, Javier Movellan. "Dynamics of Facial Expression Extracted Automatically from Video," *cvprw*, p. 80, Conference on Computer Vision and Pattern Recognition Workshop (CVPRW'04) Volume 5, 2004.
5. FACSAID, http://face-and-emotion.com

6. M Riedmiller. Untersuchungen zu Konvergenz und Generalisierungsverhalten überwachter Lernverfahren mit dem SNNS. Proceedings of the SNNS 1993 workshop, 1993
7. C.G.M. Snoek, M. Worring, J. Van Gemert, J.M. Geusebroek, D. Koelma, G.P. Nguyen, O. De Rooij, F. Seinstra, MediaMill: exploring news video archives based on learned semantics. Proc. of the 13th ACM international conference on Multimedia, Singapore, November 2005
8. M.Worring, G.P. Nguyen, L. Hollink, J.C. Gemert, D.C. Koelma, Accessing video archives using interactive search, Proceedings of IEEE International Conference on Multimedia and Expo, IEEE, Taiwan, June, 2004.
9. A. Hauptman, R.V. Baron, M.-Y. Chen, Informedia at TRECVID 2003 : Analyzing and Searching Broadcast News Video
10. S. Mongy, F. Boulali, C. Djeraba, Analyzing user's behavior on a video database, Proc. of Workshop on Multimedia Data Mining. Chicago, IL, USA, 2005

A Framework for Data Management and Transfer in Grid Environments*

Haojie Zhou[1,2], Xingwu Liu[1], Liqiang Cao[1], and Li Zha[1]

[1] Research Center for Grid and Service Computing, Institute of Computing Technology, Chinese Academy of Sciences, Beijing 100080, China
[2] Graduate School of the Chinese Academy of Sciences, Beijing 100080, China
{Zhouhaojie, xlw, caolq, char}@software.ict.ac.cn

Abstract. The main obstacles to grid file management come from the fact that grid file resources are typically stored in heterogeneous and distributed environment and accessed through various protocols. In this paper, we propose a grid file management system called Vega [1][2] Hotfile2 for data-intensive application in widely distributed systems and grid environments. Widely distributed and heterogeneous storage resource can converge into a single uniform storage resource using virtualization techniques in Hotfile2. It is a grid middleware provides a uniform file resources view and a high level interface to access widely distributed and heterogeneous data resources. Presented here are two services that we believe are fundamental to any grid file management system: high-performance, secure transport and metadata management. In this paper, we discuss many aspects of our design and implementation in Hotfile2, present the file system interface designed to support distributed applications such as batch job. Experiments are done to illustrate its performance, extensibility, and various other features.

Keywords: VEGA, GOS , Hotfile2, distributed file management, data grid.

1 Introduction

Grid computing applications require the efficient management and transfer of terabytes or petabytes of data in wide area, distributed computing environments. Hence, many grid file systems and grid file management tools have been developed, among which are Grid FTP [3], GASS [4] and the Storage Resource Broker (SRB) [5] and so on.

Unfortunately, these grid file systems typically use incompatible and unpublished protocols for accessing data and therefore each requires a private client. Secondly these grid file systems can not be dynamically deployed to or undeployed, so they dissatisfy the requirement of managing and using the file resource in grid environment. Thirdly, to avoid unauthorized access, most network firewalls block all

* This work is supported in part by the China Ministry of Science and Technology 863 Program (Grant No. 2005AA119010), the National Natural Science Foundation of China (Grant No. 69925205), and the China National 973 Program (Grant No. 2003CB317000 and No. 2005CB321807), and Chinese Academy of Sciences Distinguished Scholars Fund (Grant No. 20014010).

E. Sha et al. (Eds.): EUC 2006, LNCS 4096, pp. 529 – 538, 2006.

but HTTP socket ports. But the existing grid file management systems need special socket port which may bring security problem. We design and implement a grid middle ware Hotfile2 to cover these problems.

The China National Grid aims to construct a grid environment and illustrate the function of grid environments. The Vega GOS V2[1] [2] and its the associated utilities have been implemented based on J2SE and Apache Tomcat/axis to validate the Vega Grid architecture and core techniques, such as agora, grip, and the EVP grid resource space model. Most core services of the Vega GOS has been heavily debugged and integrated into a package which is called Vega GOS V2 and has been released and deployed on the China National Grid. The Hotfile2 is the system level software in the integrated grid environment provides data service for GOS and its applications deployed in Vega GOS V2 such as batch service. It also offers the grid users a separated file space.

Based on Web service technology and HTTP protocol, this paper address the design and implementation of a three-layer file system framework and develops a web-service based grid file transfer protocol. The Hotfile2 system has been integrated into China National Grid Project and applied to many research projects (e.g. Biologic Gene Test and Navigation Simulation).Listed below are some features:

- Hotfile2 can be dynamically deployed, maintained and used, so it is extensible for user's demand on storage resources.
- Hotfile2 is a protocol between services and file naming in Hotfile2 is based on service name and service address.
- Control channel and data channel in Hotfile2 is HTTP based, provides security and generic performance file transfer only using HTTP socket.

The rest of this paper is organized as follows: section 2 presents our file system framework names Grid File Address Space Model, naming, file transfer protocol and security in Hotfile2; section 3 discusses the Hotfile2 deployment in GOS environment; section 4 presents how to using Hotfile2 to access files resource to support batch developed for GOS; section 5 discusses the performance of Hotfile2 contrasting to GridFTP and GASS; section 6 introduces some related works; section 7 concludes this paper, with further work briefly discussed..

2 System Architecture

2.1 Grid File Address Space Model

The Vega Grid Team developed a grid address space model called the EVP Grid Resource Space Model[2]. The model stratifies a grid into three layers: effective layer, virtual layer and physical layer. Native resources and services located at individual grid nodes are called physical resources (P). These resources and services are abstracted into location-independent virtual resources (V) at the grid operating system layer. The grid end users can presented with effective resources (E) views, e.g. through GOS V2 Portal. This hierarchical mechanism greatly facilitates solving such problems in Grid Systems as single resource image, uniformly resource access, and convexity of information [6].

According to the EVP Grid Resource Space Model for Grids, we developed a Grid file storage resource space model. Grid file storage resource space is composed of three layers.

Physical storage space: the collection of storage resources at grid nodes. Storage resource here means the file system on grid nodes. Note that grid nodes may be distributed and heterogeneous and the file system may be different.

Virtual storage space: the abstraction of physical storage resources provides uniform accessing interface. From the view of virtual storage space, storage resources are still distributed.

Effective storage space: provide a convenient interface for programmers or end-users, and resolves authentication, authorization and access control problems in grid systems.

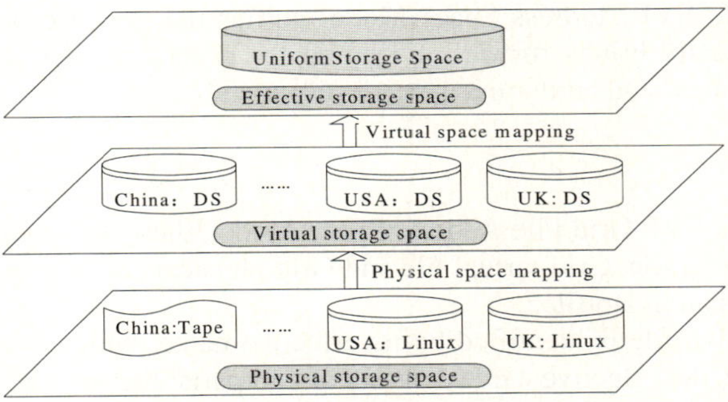

Fig. 1. The process of constructing a storage resource space

Figure 1 describes a bottom up process to construct a storage resource space model. Physical storage space is composed of distributed, heterogeneous storage resources. The physical storage space can be transformed into distributed but homogeneous virtual storage resources through storage resource space mapping which is located in agoras (an implementation of VO in GOS V2). In virtual storage space, the heterogeneity of storage resource is eliminated but still distributed. The Grid effective storage space is composed of Grid users' storage space and can be transformed into virtual resource space in agoras through storage resource space mapping. In effective storage space, the distributed, heterogeneous storage resources can be viewed as a single storage space.

Since the storage resource space model is divided into effective storage space, virtual storage resource and physical storage space, files in our Hotfile2 system are divided into grid effective file, grid virtual file and grid physical file, and we construct a top-down EVP Grid File Address Space Model based on EVP Storage resource model.

Grid effective file: the file which is visible and operable by end-users and grid applications. The effective file name is exclusive in users' file space.

Grid virtual file: the exclusive identifier of grid file in whole file management system, which is similar to the file handle in Unix file system or the public file handle in NFS. The grid virtual file unifies the interface for accessing virtual file resource and the right expression for current user. It is a self-contained data structure for accessing physical storage resource rather than an abstraction of file. Grid virtual file is dynamic and created while file operation.

Grid physical file: grid physical file is the files stored at physical storage resource(e.g. NTFS file system on Windows or EXT3 file system on Linux) which may be distributed and heterogeneous.

A grid effective file is visible to grid user and grid applications. Through name mapping, an effective file in user space can be mapped into virtual file which is exclusive in the whole grid system including self-contained information for accessing physical file. A grid virtual file can be mapped into a grid physical file through virtual storage resource selection. While grid user or grid application accessing files in Hotfile2, where the file is stored and what kind the target file system is of is transparent.

The Grid File EVP Address Space Model unifies the grid user's file space. This section theoretically brings forward a method fro accessing files in heterogeneous, dynamic, distributed and autonomic storage resources.

2.2 Naming

According to the EVP Grid File Address Space Model, there are three kinds of files in grid: Grid effective file, Grid virtual file and Grid physical file. Presented below is the naming mechanism in Hotfile2.

A grid effective file is identified by its effective name, which is exclusive in grid user's file space. An effective name consists of two parts: the first part is the identifier of transfer protocol , with "efile://" indicating accessing file through HTTP and "efiles://" indicating transfer file through SSL(Security Socket Layer); the second part is the file path and the file in grid user's file space.

Example of effective file name in Hotfile2

```
efile://Gos/HelloWord.txt
means using TCP/IP to access file: /Gos/HelloWord.txt
efiles://Gos/HelloWord.txt
means using SSL to access file: /Gos/HelloWord.txt
```

Virtual file name and physical file name is transparent to end users. A virtual file name is composed of three parts: the first part is the transfer protocol "vfile"; the second is the data service address which only can be understood by Vega Router[15]; the third part is the file path including user information; the forth part is a exclusive identifier in the appointed data service.

Example of virtual file name in Hotfile2

```
vres://data service address %User Info%local identifier
```

Physical file name information dose not actually exist in Hotfile2 system and it is stored physical storage node. The virtual file name includes a file identifier which can be translated into physical file name on physical storage grid node. The format of physical file name is the same as a file name in traditional file system.

Effective file name, virtual file name and other metadata is stored in metadata service. Before grid user accessing a file in Hotfil2, metadata service should be invoked first to do naming mapping and access control and so on.

2.3 File Transfer Protocol

Control channel and data transfer channel in Hotfile2 transfer protocol are also based on HTTP. Hotfile2 transfer protocol includes server side and client side. The server side provides file operation interface based on SOAP which can work in grid independently. But using web service directly increases complexity in application programming. To resolve this problem, we provide file transfer protocol client. We provide file transfer client API for programmers.

File transfer protocol server side in GOS V2 is a Web Service runs on GOS Server composed of three modules: file transfer control module; file transfer model and local file system at the server node.

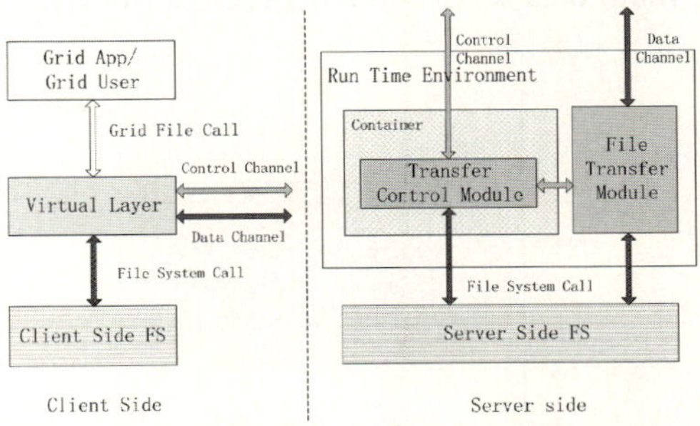

Fig. 2. The structure of Hotfile2 transfer protocol

There are three layers on the client side: Grid Application/ Grid User, virtual layer and client side local file system. Grid Applications and Grid Users operate files using file transfer client API. The Virtual layer hides the local or remote file operation. Upon receiving a local file request, the virtual layer using system call at client side local file system. if a remote file request is received, the virtual layer redirect the request to the control channel or data channel on the destination server.

2.4 Security

User authentication is not addressed in Hotfile2, it is solved in GOS V2. Under development is a community service provides authorization service which facilitates community-based access control implemented in GOS V2. To access Hotfile2 system, the grid user should be authorized to access metadata service and data service of Hotfile2 in community service.

Access control in Hotfile2 using ACL which is stored in metadata service. To share files in Hotfile2 file management system, we provides grant and revoke mechanism. Files and directories can be grant accessing permission or revoke accessing permission to another user or a group in local community by the owner. More flexible file sharing mechanism will be provided soon.

Meta data in Hotfile2 is secure while metadata service using GOS V2 security mechanism [16] which is WS-Security compatible using Handler chains mechanism and GOS context. Data can be secured while in transit by using SSL protocol, but it is stored using plain test in physical storage node and data can be illegal accessed and modified by the node administrator.

HTTP based Hotfile2 system is unsecured but has better performance in data transfer. HTTPS based Hotfile2 provides the same secure rank compares to GridFTP and GASS.

3 Deployment

The Hotfile2 server side is composed of two modules: metadata service module managing all metadata information in Hotfile2 and data service providing physical file storage and file transfer service. Currently, the Hotfile2 system integrates a single metadata service and multi data service to compose the Hotfile2.

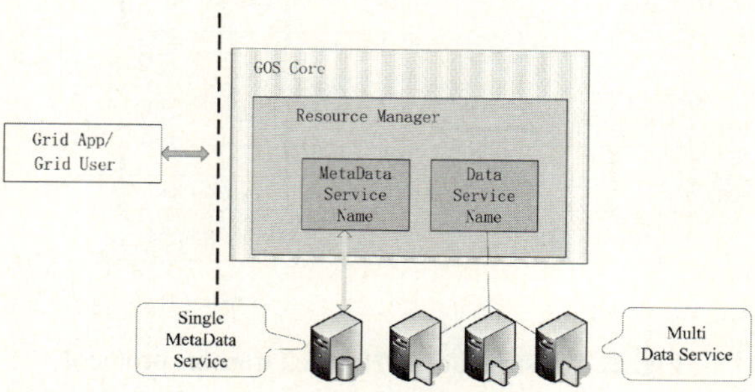

Fig. 3. Deploy structure of Hotfile2 in GOS

Metadata service and data service should be registered into Resource Manager System in GOS V2. Metadata service name and data service name constituted the effective storage space mentioned in Grid file address space model and the physical distributed metadata service and data service constituted the physical storage space. Data service name can be mapped to multi physical data service and physical data service can be dynamically registered into GOS System consequently. So Hotfile2 system provides a extensible storage space for user's dynamic demands.

Physical data service may be distributed and heterogeneous. It's unnecessary for grid applications and grid users to know the physical node position and the operation system running on the nodes, and where and how a file is stored. These are all transparent to end users.

4 Applications

We use batch service to show how Hotfile2 is used in grid applications.

In GOS V2, a batch is encapsulated as a web services. Batch Service is deployed on grid nodes and can be dynamically registered into GOS System. If a batch job is submitted a batch work through GOS Portal, GOS core will select an appropriate physical batch service to process the batch request according to the resource selection policy. There are two problems in processing a batch request:

- How to stagein file during submitting a batch while the processing node is unsure.
- How to stageout file after the batch is end.

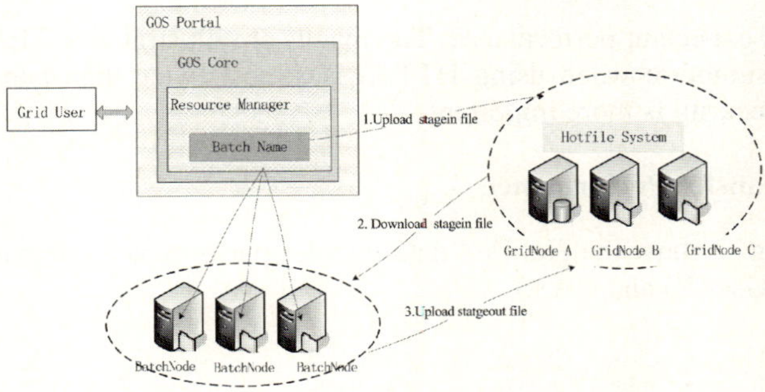

Fig. 4. Example of batch example using Hotfile2 in GOS V2

These problems can be solved using Hotfile2 system. When a user submits a batch job to grid system, the stagein file is uploaded to Hotfile2 (see phase 1 in Fig. 4.). After selecting a physical Batch service to processes the batch request, the stagein file is downloaded from Hotfile2 to the appointed node (phase 2 in Fig. 4.). While the processing is end, the stageout file will be upload to Hotfile2 again (phase 3 in Fig. 4.).As a result, grid users can view and download the stageout file in his own file space using tools or through the Hotfile2 user portal.

5 Performance Evaluation

Experiments are done to evaluate the performance of our Hotfile2. We deployed Data services on computers with 2 xeon 2.4G CPUs, 1GB memory and 36GB utltra3 SCSI hard disk running red hat Linux 7.3 and JVM 1.4.2. The Client is PC with PIII 1G CPU, 512M memory and 60GB ATA-100 hard disk running WinXP and JVM 1.4.2. The Server and Client are connected by 100M fast Ethernet.

5.1 Meta Data Performance

While testing the performance of metadata service running on GOS, each metadata operation such as Create Dir and Create File is tested 10 times, and the average time

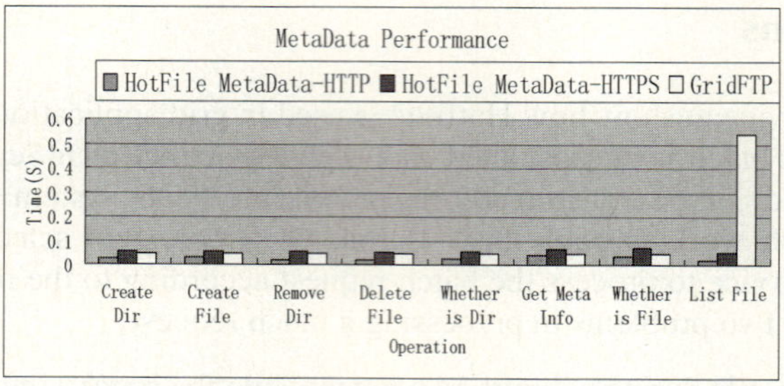

Fig. 5. Meta Service performance in Hotfile2

is taken as its expectant performance. The results are illustrated in Figure 5. Note that the time consumption when using HTTPS is almost twice that using HTTP, but it pays if high security is more important.

5.2 Data Transfer Performance

Fig. 6 and Fig. 7 show the Hotfile2 data transfer performance compared to GridFTP (deployed in GT3.2) and GASS.

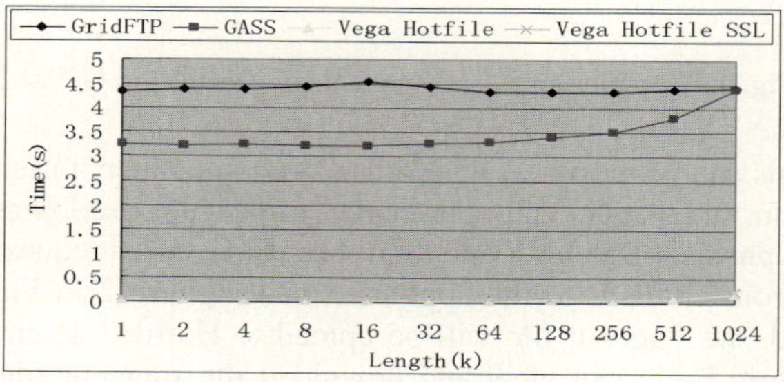

Fig. 6. Performance of three protocol while transfer files smaller than 1 megabyte

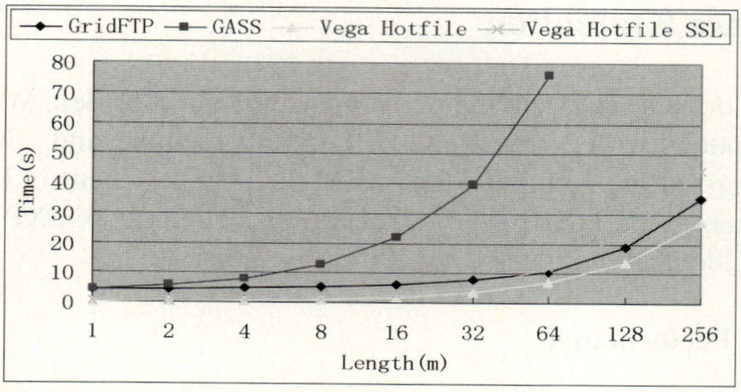

Fig. 7. Performance of three protocols while transfer files between 1megabyte and 256

GridFTP and GASS are significantly slower than Hotfile2 while transfer small files(smaller than 1 megabyte). Spending immovable time in constructing security data channel accounts for the low performance of GridFTP.

While transferring files ranging from 1 megabyte to 256 megabyte, GASS is the slowest protocol. Hotfile based on HTTP is the fastest because there is no encoding and decoding overhead in data transfer. Hotfile based on HTTPS is faster than GridFTP if the transferred files are smaller than 64 megabyte.

6 Related Work

GridFTP is an extensions of standard FTP protocol that create a universal grid-wide transport protocol which is an important part of Globus Toolkit[8] . It provides not only secure, high throughput data transfer even on high-speed wide area networks, but also third party transfers which allow the source, destination, or both to be striped, with arbitrary and potentially different topologies or even file access mechanisms. GridFTP is the foundation module in many data grid project.

GASS[4] (Global Access to Secondary Storage) is an regularly used data management and access protocol in Globus project. GASS defines a global name space via Uniform Resource Locators and allows applications to access remote files via standard I/O interfaces. High performance is achieved by incorporating default data movement strategies that are specialized for I/O patterns common in wide area applications and by providing support for programmer management of data movement.

The first edition of Hotfile[10,]implemented in VEGA GOS V1 is based on GridFTP and GASS. It wraps GridFTP and GASS or any other file transfer protocol compatible with Hotfile structure into a unified vegafile protocol providing a user level grid file systems with low overhead and high usability.

7 Conclusion and Future Work

In this paper we have presented our design and implementation of Hotfile2. Hotile2 provides a uniform file resources view and a high level interface to access distributed, heterogeneous storage resources. It can be dynamically deployed and undeployed in GOS V2 environment hence providing an extensible storage resource space to meet the grid application requirements. Based on GSI, HTTPS and other security mechanism, it provides secure communication and transport in grid environments.

Based on HTTP, control channel and data transfer channel in Hotfile2 solve the firewall problem, and our protocol achieves better performance in transferring small and middle files comparing to GridFTP and GASS,.

Further improvement of Hotfile2 is now under way. For example, to implement reliable and third party file transfer, to ensure consistency in file replica and replica selection, and to define a set of file access interfaces which is compatible with the POSIX file interface.

References

1. Li Zha, Wei Li, Haiyan Yu, Jiping Cai "Service Oriented VEGA Grid System Software Design adn Evaluation" Chinese Journel of Computers Vol.28 No.4 April 2005 495~504
2. Zhiwei Xu, Wei Li, Li Zha, Haiyan Yu, Donghua Liu, Vega: A Computer Systems Approach to Grid Computing, Journal of Grid Computing, 2004, Vol.2, Issue 2□109~120
3. H Stockinger, A Samar, B Allcock, I Foster, K Holtman, and B Tierney. File and Object Replication in Data Grids. Journal of Cluster Computing, 2002, 5(3)305-314
4. 4. Joseph Bester, Ian Foster, Carl Kesselman. GASS: A Data Movement and Access Service for wide Area Computing System. In: Proceedings of the Sixth Workshop on Input/Output in Parallel and Distributed Systems. ACM Press New York, NY, USA May, 1999
5. R Moore, A Rajasekar, and M Wan. The SDSC Storage Resource Broker. In: Procs. of CASCON'98, Toronto, 1998
6. Z.Xu A Model of Grid Address Space with Applications, VGSD- 2, (2002)
7. I. Foster, C. Kesselman, G. Tsudik, and S. Tuecke. A security architecture for computational grids. In ACM Conference on Computers and Security, pages 83~91. ACM Press, 1998.
8. I. Foster and C. Kesselman. The Globus Project: A Status Report. In Proceedings of the HeterogeneousComputing Workshop, pages 4–18. IEEE Press, 1998.
9. Berners-Lee, T., Masinter, L. and M. McCahill, "Uniform Resource Locators (URL)," RFC1738 prop, (1994)
10. Liqiang Cao ,Jie Qiu, Li Zha, Haiyan Yu, Wei Li"Design and Implementation of Grid File Management System Hotfile" Grid and Cooperative Computing - GCC 2004: Third International Conference pp 129-136
11. The POSIX standards: http://www.opengroup.org/onlinepubs/007904975/toc.htm.
12. B. White, A. Grimshaw, and A. Nguyen-Tuong, "Grid-based File Access: the Legion I/O
13. Model" , in Proc. 9th IEEE Int. Symp. on High Performance Distributed Computing (HPDC), pp 165-173, (2000)
14. J.Kubiatowicz et al., "OceanStore: An Architecture for Global-Scale Persistent Storage",Proceedings of the Ninth international Conference on Architectural Support forProgramming Languages and Operating Systems (ASPLOS), (2000)
15. I.Foster, C. Kesselman, J. Nick, S. Tuecke; The Physiology of the Grid: An Open GridServices Architecture for Distributed Systems Integration, Open Grid Service Infrastructure WG, Global Grid Forum, (2002)
16. Hai Mo, Zha Li, Liu Haozhi, A Scalable Resource Locating Service in Vega Grid , Proceedings of the Fourth International Workshop on Grid and Cooperative Computing (GCC2005), Dec. 2005, Beijing, China pp 597-608.
17. Efficient and Loosely Coupled Security Mechanism in Vega Grid Honglei Dai, Shuoying Chen, Li Zha, Zhiwei Xu pp.714-720 Semantics, Knowledge and Grid SKG2005

MMSDS: Ubiquitous Computing and WWW-Based Multi-Modal Sentential Dialog System

Jung-Hyun Kim and Kwang-Seok Hong

School of Information and Communication Engineering, Sungkyunkwan University, 300, Chunchun-dong, Jangan-gu, Suwon, KyungKi-do, 440-746, Korea
kjh0328@skku.edu, kshong@skku.ac.kr
http://hci.skku.ac.kr

Abstract. In this study, we suggest and implement Multi-Modal Sentential Dialog System (MMSDS) integrating 2 sensory channels with speech and haptic information based on ubiquitous computing and WWW for clear communication. The importance and necessity of MMSDS for HCI as following: 1) it can allow more interactive and natural communication functions between the hearing-impaired and hearing person without special learning and education, 2) according as it recognizes a sentential Korean Standard Sign Language (KSSL) which is represented with speech and haptics and then translates recognition results into a synthetic speech and visual illustration in real-time, it may provide a wider range of personalized and differentiated information more effectively to them, and 3) above all things, a user need not be constrained by the limitations of a particular interaction mode at any given moment because it can guarantee mobility of WPS (Wearable Personal Station for the post PC) with a built-in sentential sign language recognizer. In experiment results, while an average recognition rate of uni-modal recognizer using KSSL only is 93.1% and speech only is 95.5%, advanced MMSDS deduced an average recognition rate of 96.1% for 32 sentential KSSL recognition models.

1 Introduction

The multi-modal interfaces integrating various sensory channels such as speech, vision and haptic can increase the bandwidth and application of human-computer interaction and it may improve the interactive properties and functions of the system. The functionality of a multi-modal interface can be fairly extensive, and it may find their applications in a number of fields. To name only a few examples, they proved to be a viable aid for visually impaired users, an alternative to WIMP (Windows, Icon, Menu, and Pointer based interfaces) interfaces in mobile computing, an entertaining extension of computer games [1]. In recent years, there have been a lot of innovations and evolutions in the areas of human-computer interaction, multi-modal interface and speech and sign language recognition as a part of natural language understanding. As a case study on a multi-modal interaction and sign language, we can find and introduce the following examples. Siska Fitrianie et al. described a computer model for a multi-modal communication system based on the famous Eliza question-answering

E. Sha et al. (Eds.): EUC 2006, LNCS 4096, pp. 539 – 548, 2006.

system [2], Wu jiangqin et al. implemented 26 word-level sign language recognition system using neural network and HMM hybrid method [3] and a multi-agent modal language for concurrency with non-communicating agents is introduced by Stefano Borgo [4]. Also, Silvia Berti and Fabio Paternò developed multi-modal interfaces for different platforms starting with logical user interface descriptions in multi-device Environments [5] and Mark Barnard et.al introduced on multi-modal audio-visual event recognition for analysis of football games [6]. However generally, according as most of traditional studies like this keep the accent on an implementation of uni-modal recognition and translation system that recognizes and represents one of various natural components based on wire communications net and a vision technology, they have not only several restrictions such as limitation of representation, conditionality on the space and limitation of the motion, but also some problems such as uncertainty of measurement and a necessity of complex computational algorithms. Nevertheless, users can issue requests using speech, gesture and so on, or dynamic fusions of the two based on ubiquitous computing.

Consequently, we suggest and implement advanced MMSDS integrating speech and KSSL gestures based on the VXML for WWW-based speech recognition (and synthesis) and ubiquitous computing-oriented WPS with a built-in KSSL recognizer. The advantages of our study are as following: 1) it improves efficiency of KSSL input module according to the wireless communication net and user need not be constrained by the limitations of a particular interaction mode at any given moment, 2) our study that allows dialog and communication functions between the hearing-impaired and hearing person is very important and essential, and 3) it recognizes and represents continuous KSSL with flexibility in real time and can provide a wider range of personalized and differentiated information more effectively.

In section 2, we describe an implementation of WPS-based embedded KSSL recognizer. Also, a synopsis of WWW-based VXML module and integration architecture of speech and KSSL for MMSDS are given in section 3. In section 4, we evaluate a performance of the system with recognition experiment results for sentential KSSL recognition models. Finally, this study is summarized in section 5 together with an outline of challenges and future directions.

2 Wearable Personal Station-Based Embedded KSSL Recognizer

2.1 Regulation and Components of the KSSL

Sign language is a language which uses manual communication instead of sound to convey meaning - simultaneously combining hand shapes, orientation and movement of the hands, arms or body, and facial expressions to fluidly express a speaker's thoughts [7]. However, not only a absolute natural learning and interpretation of such KSSL very difficult and takes a long time to represent and translate it fluently in hearing person, but also understanding and learning of spoken language in the hearing-impaired is impossible and uncertain. In other words, because the KSSL is very complicated and is consisted of considerable numerous gestures, motions and so on, it are impossible that recognize all dialog components which are represented by the hearing-impaired. Therefore, we prescribe that this paper is a fundamental study for perfect dialog and communication between the hearing-impaired and hearing person, and selected 25 basic KSSL gestures connected with a travel information scenario according to the "Korean Standard Sign Language Tutor (KSSLT)[8]". And necessary 23 hand gestures for travel information - KSSL gestures are classified as hand's shapes, pitch and roll degree. Consequently, we constructed 32 sentential KSSL recognition models according to associability and presentation of hand gestures and basic KSSL.

2.2 Improved KSSL Input Module Using Wireless Haptic Devices

For an improved KSSL input module, we adopted blue-tooth module for wireless sensor network, 5DT company's wireless data (sensor) gloves and fastrak® which are one of popular input devices in the haptic application field. Wireless data gloves are basic gesture recognition equipment that can acquires and capture various haptic information (e.g. hand or finger's stooping degree, direction) using fiber-optic flex sensor. The structural motion information of each finger in data glove are captured by f1=thumb, f2=index, f3=middle, f4=ring and f5=little in regular sequence. Each flexure value has a decimal range of 0 to 255, with a low value indicating an inflexed finger, and a high value indicating a flexed finger. Also, the fastrak® is electromagnetic motion tracking system, a 3D digitizer and a quad receiver motion tracker. And it provides dynamic, real-time measurements of six degrees of freedom; position (X, Y, and Z Cartesian coordinates) and orientation (azimuth, elevation, and roll) [9], [10]. The architecture and composition of KSSL input module is shown in Fig. 1.

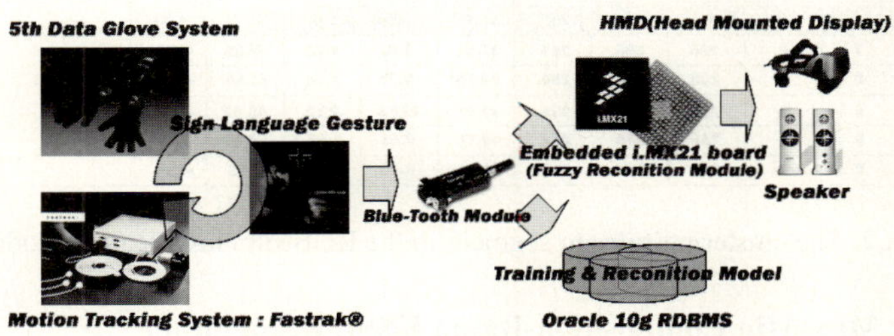

Fig. 1. The architecture and composition of KSSL input module

2.3 Feature Extraction and Recognition Models Using RDBMS

A statistical classification algorithms such as K-means clustering based on attributes into k partitions, QT (Quality Threshold) clustering that is an alternative method of partitioning data, fuzzy c-means clustering algorithm and Self-Organizing Map (SOM) based on a grid of artificial neurons whose weights are adapted to match input vectors in a training set had been applied universally in a traditional pattern recognition systems with unsupervised training, including machine training, data mining, pattern recognition, image analysis and bioinformatics [11], [12], [13]. However, such classification algorithms have some restrictions and problems such as the necessity of complicated mathematical computation according to multidimensional features, the difficulty of application in a distributed processing system, relativity of computation costs by patterns (data) size, minimization of memory swapping and assignment. Accordingly, for a clustering method for efficient feature extraction and a construction of training / recognition models based on a distributed computing, we suggest and introduce improved RDBMS (Relational Data-Base Management System) clustering module to resolve such a restrictions and problems. The RDBMS is database management system that maintains data records and indices in tables and their relationships may be created and maintained across and among the data and tables. Also, it has the capability to recombine the data items from different files, providing powerful tools for data usage [14]. The RDBMS-based analytic functions for substantial pattern clustering and segmentation are designed to address such problems as "calculate a running total", "find percentages within a group", "top-N queries", " compute a moving average" and many more [15]. A clustering rule to segment valid gesture record set and invalid record set in the RDBMS classification module is shown in Fig. 2.

1. Difference Between Preceding Average(preceding 3 and 1) and Current Row Value
2. Decide validity : Preceding Average - Current Value = 52-17 = 35

Average Between 3 Preceding and 1 Preceding from Current Row : 52

1. Difference between Preceding Average and Current Row Value > 5
2. 'X'(Invalidity Record) check

SerialNO	F1THUMB	F1INDEX	F1MIDDLE	F1RING	F1LITTLE	F1X-POSI.	F1Y-POSI.	F1Z-POSI.	F1_Px	F1_Py	GESTURE DATA...	VALIDITY
22	73	86	255	255	255	50.90	-14.53	-4.74	55.42	-5.71		X
23	51	48	255	255	255	52.05	-11.97	-2.13	53.29	-4.95		X
24	32	15	255	255	255	53.99	- 9.50	0.01	50.02	-4.75		X
25	17	0	255	255	255	51.03	- 10.60	-1.05	51.11	-4.83	Omission...	X
26	7	0	255	255	255	52.01	- 9.85	-1.02	49.85	-5.23		
27	0	0	255	254	255	52.78	- 8.77	-1.75	51.85	-6.02		
28	0	0	253	254	255	49.87	- 10.18	-2.12	48.97	-5.27		
29	0	0	255	255	254	48.71	- 9.43	-1.92	52.85	-4.89		
30	0	0	255	255	255	51.09	- 8.75	-1.75	47.93	-4.94		

Fig. 2. The clustering rules to segment in the RDBMS classification module.

2.4 Fuzzy Max-Min Composition-Based KSSL Recognition

Fuzzification and Membership Function. For a design of membership function, many types of curves can be used, but triangular or trapezoidal shaped membership functions are the most common because they are easier to represent in embedded-controllers [18]. So, we applied trapezoidal shaped membership functions for representation of fuzzy numbers-sets, and this shape is originated from the fact that there are several points whose membership degree is maximum. The proposed the fuzzy membership functions are shown in Fig. 3.

Fuzzy Logic: Max-Min Composition of Fuzzy Relation. In this paper, we utilized the fuzzy max-min composition to extend a crisp relation concept to relation concept

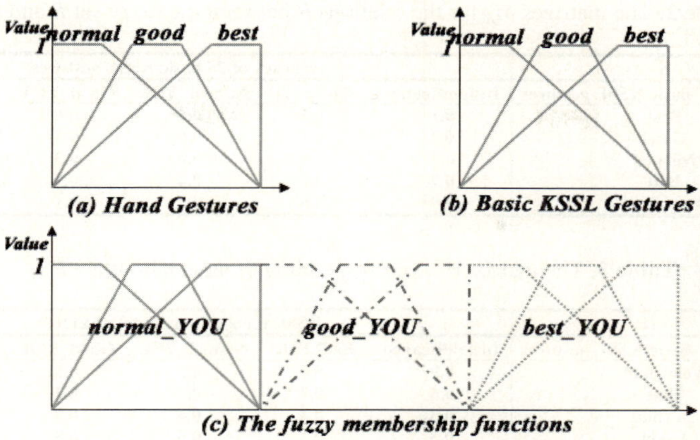

Fig. 3. The fuzzy membership functions for KSSL recognition. Because fuzzy numbers-sets according to KSSL recognition models are very various and so many, we represent membership functions partially: "YOU" in KSSL).

with fuzzy proposition and to reason approximate conclusion by composition arithmetic of fuzzy relation. Two fuzzy relations *R* and *S* are defined on sets *A*, *B* and *C* (we prescribed the accuracy of hand gestures and basic KSSL gestures, object KSSL recognition models as the sets of events that are happened in KSSL recognition with the sets *A*, *B* and *C*). That is, $R \subseteq A \times B$, $S \subseteq B \times C$. The composition $S \bullet R = SR$ of two relations *R* and *S* is expressed by the relation from *A* to *C*, and this composition is defined in equation (2) [17].

$$\text{For } (x, y) \in A \times B,\ (y, z) \in B \times C,$$
$$\mu_{S \bullet R}(x, z) = \underset{y}{Max}\ [Min\ (\mu_R(x, y), \mu_S(y, z))] \tag{2}$$

$S \bullet R$ from this elaboration is a subset of $A \times C$. That is, $S \bullet R \subseteq A \times C$. If the relations *R* and *S* are represented by matrices M_R and M_S, the matrix $M_{S \bullet R}$ corresponding to $S \bullet R$ is obtained from the product of M_R and M_S; $M_{S \bullet R} = M_R \bullet M_S$. That is, we can see the possibility of occurrence of B after A, and by S, that of C after B in Table 1, 2. For example, by matrices M_R, the possibility of "Best" $\in B$ after "Best" $\in A$ is 0.9.

Table 1. The matrices M_R for the relations *R* between the fuzzy set *A* and *B*

R	Accuracy of basic KSSL gestures				
Accuracy of hand gestures	Best	Good	Normal	Bad	Very_bad
Very_bad	0.0	0.1	0.2	0.6	0.9
Bad	0.0	0.2	0.3	0.8	0.6
Normal	0.2	0.3	0.6	0.4	0.3
Good	0.7	0.9	0.5	0.3	0.2
Best	0.9	0.7	0.5	0.2	0.1

Table 2. The matrices M_R for the relations R between the fuzzy set B and C

S	Accuracy of 25 basic KSSL gestures				
Accuracy of basic KSSL gestures	**Insignificance**	**Bad_YOU**	**Normal_YOU**	**Good_YOU**	**Best_YOU**
Best	0.1	0.2	0.4	0.6	0.9
Good	0.2	0.3	0.5	0.8	0.7
Normal	0.3	0.4	0.6	0.3	0.2
Bad	0.7	0.8	0.4	0.2	0.1
Very_bad	0.9	0.6	0.3	0.1	0.0

Table 3. The matrix $M_{S \bullet R}$ corresponding to the relations $S \bullet R$

S • R	KSSL recognition model : "YOU"				
Accuracy of basic KSSL gestures	**Insignificance**	**Bad_YOU**	**Normal_YOU**	**Good_YOU**	**Best_YOU**
Very_bad	0.9	0.6	0.3	0.2	0.1
Bad	0.6	0.7	0.4	0.2	0.2
Normal	0.3	0.4	0.4	0.3	0.3
Good	0.3	0.3	0.5	0.8	0.7
Best	0.2	0.3	0.4	0.6	0.9

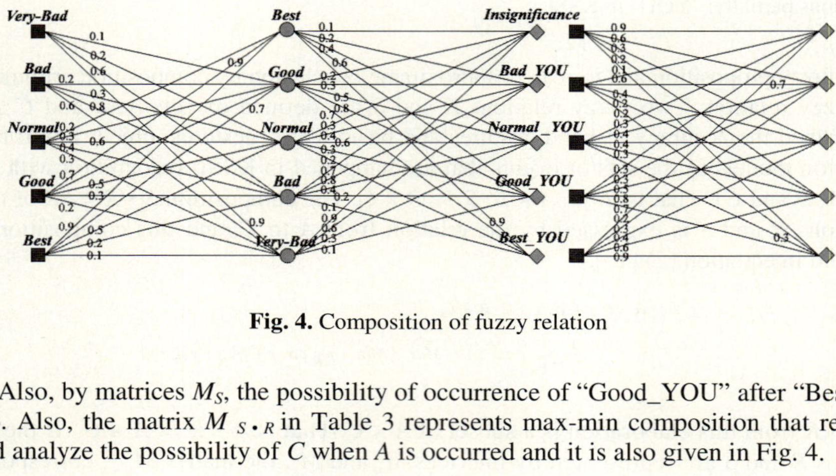

Fig. 4. Composition of fuzzy relation

Also, by matrices M_S, the possibility of occurrence of "Good_YOU" after "Best" is 0.6. Also, the matrix $M_{S \bullet R}$ in Table 3 represents max-min composition that reason and analyze the possibility of C when A is occurred and it is also given in Fig. 4.

3 Voice-XML for WWW-Based Speech Recognition and Synthesis

3.1 Components and Architecture of Voice-XML

VXML is the W3C's standard XML format for specifying interactive voice dialogues between a human and a computer [18]. A document server (e.g. a Web server) processes requests from a client application, the VXML Interpreter, through the VXML interpreter context. The server produces VXML documents in reply, which are processed by the VXML interpreter. The VXML interpreter context may monitor user inputs in parallel with the VXML interpreter. For example, one VXML interpreter context may always listen for a special escape phrase that takes the user to a high-level personal assistant, and another may listen for escape phrases that alter user preferences like volume or text-to-speech characteristics.

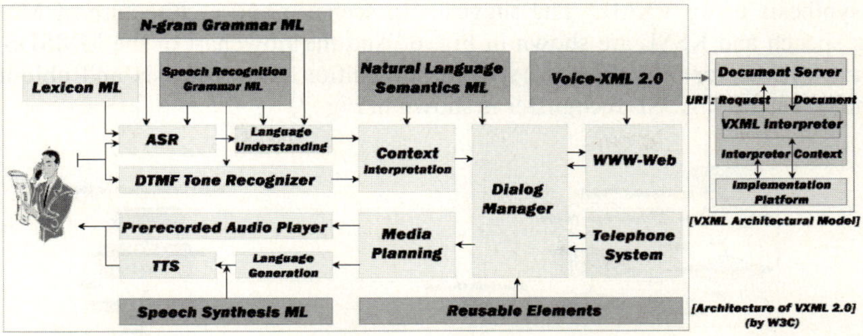

Fig. 5. The components of architectural model and architecture of W3C's VXML 2.0

The implementation platform is controlled by the VXML interpreter context and by the VXML interpreter. The components of architectural model and architecture of VXML 2.0 by W3C are shown in Fig. 5.

3.2 Integration of Speech and KSSL for MMSDS

The user connects to VXML server through internet and PSTN using WPS based on wireless networks (middleware) and telephone terminal, and input prescribed speech and KSSL. The user's sentential speech data which is inputted into telephone terminal transmits to ASR-engine (we used 'HUVOIS-TTS' that is speech recognition and synthesis S/W for visually-impaired people and developed by KT Corp. in Korea), and saves sentential ASR results to MMI database. Also, user's KSSL data which is inputted into embedded WPS is recognized by sentential KSSL recognizer, transmits and saves sentential recognition results to VXML server using TCP/IP protocol based on middleware and wireless sensor networks. Sentential ASR and KSSL recognition results execute comparison arithmetic by internal SQL logic, and transmit arithmetic results to MMSDS. These arithmetic results are definite intention that user presents. Finally, user's intention is provided to user through speech (TTS) and visualization. The KSSL recognition processes of MMSDS synchronize with the speech recognition

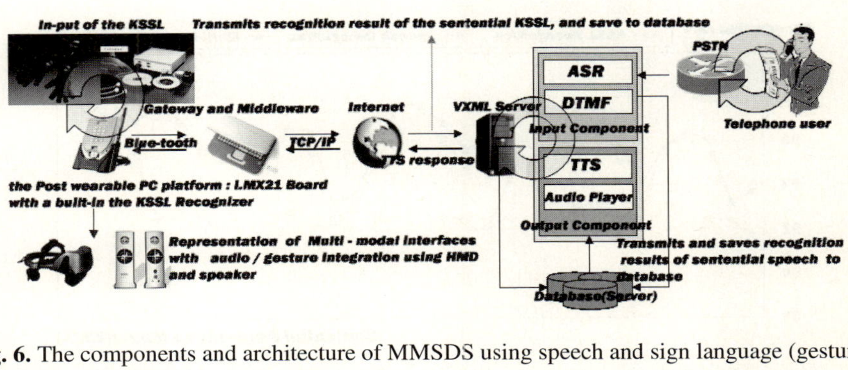

Fig. 6. The components and architecture of MMSDS using speech and sign language (gestures)

and synthesis using VXML. The suggested a scenario and architecture of MMSDS using speech and KSSL are shown in Fig. 6. And the flowchart of the MMSDS integrating VXML for WWW-based speech recognition and synthesis and ubiquitous-oriented sentential KSSL recognizer is shown in Fig. 7.

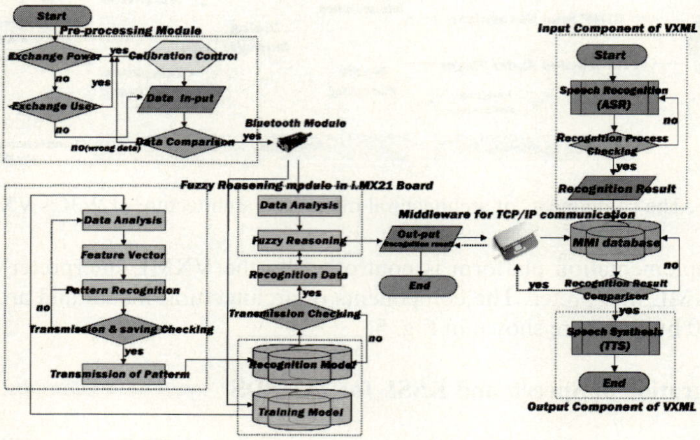

Fig. 7. The flowchart of the MMSDS integrating VXML and KSSL Recognizer

4 Experiments and Results

The distance between the KSSL input module and embedded WPS for processing of the KSSL recognition composed in about radius 10M's ellipse form. When user inputs the KSSL and speech, we move data gloves and receivers of motion tracker to prescribed position. For every 20 reagents, we repeat this action 15 times. While user inputs the KSSL using data gloves and motion tracker, speak using blue-tooth headset of telephone terminal. Experimental results, the uni-modal and MMSDS recognition rate for 32 sentential recognition models are shown in Table 4. Also, the comparison charts are given in Fig.8 respectively.

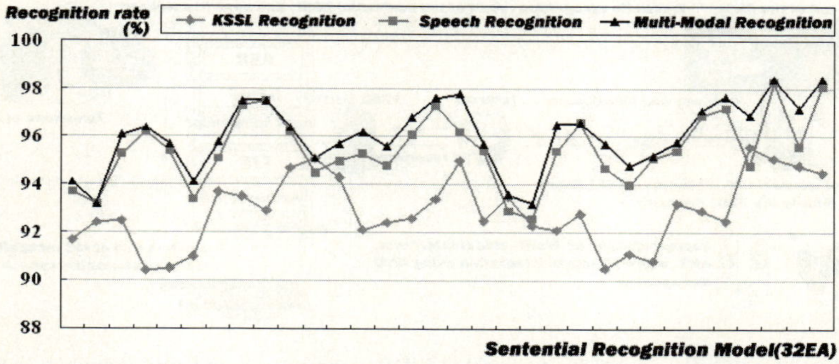

Fig. 8. An average recognition rate of the uni-modal and MMSDS

Table 4. An uni-modal and MMSDS recognition rate about 32 sentential recognition models

Sentential Recognition Model			Uni-modal recognition rate		MMSDS recognition rate
			The KSSL (%)	Speech (%)	The KSSL + Speech (%)
I	go	to museum	92.7	93.7	94.2
		to airport	92.4	93.7	93.9
		to station	92.5	95.8	96.1
	come	from museum	90.4	96.2	96.4
		from airport	92.5	95.4	95.7
		from station	92.4	93.4	94.1
	arrive	at museum	93.7	95.1	95.8
		at airport	94.5	96.9	97.4
		at station	92.9	96.5	96.5
	love	you	94.7	96.2	96.4
	lost	my passport	95.3	94.5	95.1
	am	sorry	94.3	95.0	95.7
		fine	92.1	95.3	96.2
		a Korean	92.4	94.8	95.6
		from Korea	92.6	96.1	96.8
	want	to Seoul	93.4	97.3	97.6
-	thank	you	95.0	96.2	97.8
Are	you	ok?	92.7	95.4	95.7
You	are	welcome	93.5	93.1	93.6
We	go	to museum	92.3	93.6	93.7
		to airport	93.1	95.4	96.5
		to station	92.8	96.6	96.6
	come	from museum	90.5	94.7	95.7
		from airport	92.3	95.1	95.2
		from station	90.8	95.1	95.2
	arrive	at museum	93.2	95.4	95.8
		at airport	92.9	96.9	97.1
		at station	92.5	97.2	97.2
-	good	morning	95.6	94.8	96.1
		afternoon	95.1	98.3	98.4
		evening	94.8	95.6	97.2
		night	94.5	98.1	98.4
An average recognition rate			93.1	95.5	96.1

5 Conclusions

Ubiquitous and wearable computing is an active topic of study, with areas of study including multi-modal user interface design, augmented reality, pattern recognition, using of wearable for specific applications or disabilities. As preliminary study for recognition and representation of KSSL, our researchers implemented hand gesture recognition system that recognize 19 hand gestures according to a shape and stoop degree of hand. Accordingly, with this preliminary study, we implemented WPS-based sentential MMSDS integrating VXML module (speech) and sentential KSSL recognizer (gesture). In experiment results, the MMSDS is more efficient and powerful than uni-modal recognition system that uses one in the KSSL (gesture) or speech. Especially, while the average recognition rate of uni-modal recognition system that use KSSL (gesture) only is 93.1%, the MMSDS deduced an average recognition rate of 96.1% and showed difference of an average recognition rate as much as about 3.0%. In conclusion, we clarify that this study is fundamental study for implementation of advanced multi modal recognizer integrating the human's five senses such as sight, hearing, touch, smell, and taste to take the place of traditional uni-modal for recognizer in natural and sign language processing.

Acknowledgement

This research was supported by the MIC (Ministry of Information and Communication), Korea, under the ITRC (Information Technology Research Center) support program supervised by the IITA (Institute of Information Technology Assessment)" (IITA-2005- C1090-0501-0019) and this work was supported by the Brain Korea 21 Project in 2006.

References

1. M. Fuchs, P. et al.: Architecture of Multi-modal Dialogue System. TSD2000. Lecture Notes in Artificial Intelligence, Vol. 1902. Springer-Verlag, Berlin Heidelberg New York (2000) 433–438
2. Siska Fitrianie. et al.: A Multi-modal Eliza Using Natural Language Processing and Emotion Recognition. TSD 2003. Lecture Notes in Artificial Intelligence, Vol. 2807. Springer-Verlag, Berlin Heidelberg New York (2003) 394-399
3. Wu jiangqin. et al.: A Simple Sign Language Recognition System Based on Data Glove.. ICSP98, IEEE International Conference Proceedings (1998) 1257-1260
4. Stefano Borg.: A Multi-agent Modal Language for Concurrency with Non-communicating Agents. CEEMAS 2003. Lecture Notes in Artificial Intelligence, Vol. 2691. Springer-Verlag, Berlin Heidelberg New York (2003) 40-50
5. Silvia Berti and Fabio Paternò.: Development of Multi-modal Interfaces in Multi-device Environments. INTERACT 2005. Lecture Notes in Computer Science, Vol. 3585. Springer-Verlag, Berlin Heidelberg New York (2005) 1067-1070
6. Mark Barnard. et al.: Multi-Modal Audio-Visual Event Recognition for Football Analysis. IEEE XI11 Workshop on Neural Networks for Signal Processing, IEEE Workshop Proceedings (2003) 469-478
7. Use of Signs in Hearing Communities.: http://en.wikipedia.org/wiki/Sign_language
8. S.-G.Kim.: Korean Standard Sign Language Tutor, 1st, Osung Publishing Company, Seoul (2000)
9. J.-H.Kim. et al.: Hand Gesture Recognition System using Fuzzy Algorithm and RDBMS for Post PC. FSKD2005. Lecture Notes in Artificial Intelligence, Vol. 3614. Springer-Verlag, Berlin Heidelberg New York (2005) 170-175
10. 5DT Data Glove 5 Manual and FASTRAK® Data Sheet.: http://www.5dt.com
11. Richard O. Duda, Peter E. Hart, David G. Stork.: Pattern Classification, 2nd, Wiley, New York (2001)
12. Dietrich Paulus and Joachim Hornegger.: Applied Pattern Recognition, 2nd, Vieweg (1998)
13. J. Schuermann.: Pattern Classification: A Unified View of Statistical and Neural Approaches, Wiley&Sons (1996)
14. Relational DataBase Management System.: http://www.auditmypc.com/acronym/RDBMS.asp
15. Oracle 10g DW Guide.: http://www.oracle.com
16. W. B. Vasantha kandasamy.: Smaranda Fuzzy Algebra. American Research Press, Seattle (2003)
17. Scott McGlashan et al.: Voice Extensible Markup Language (VoiceXML) Version 2.0. W3C Recommendation, http://www.w3.org (1992)

A Speech and Character Combined Recognition Engine for Mobile Devices

Min-Joung Kim[1], Soo-Young Suk[2], Ho-Youl Jung[3], and Hyun-Yeol Chung[3]

[1] School of EECS, Yeungnam University
214-1, Dae-Dong, Gyung-San, Gyungbuk, Republic of Korea
manjuk@paran.com
[2] Information Technology Research Institute, AIST
AIST Tsukuba Central 2, 1-1-1 Umezono, Tsukuba, Ibaraki 305-8568, Japan
sy.suk@aist.go.jp
[3] School of EECS, Yeungnam University
214-1, Dae-Dong, Gyung-San, Gyungbuk, Republic of Korea
{hoyoul, hychung}@yu.ac.kr

Abstract. A Speech and Character Combined Recognition Engine (SCCRE) is developed for working on Personal Digital Assistants (PDA) or on mobile devices. In SCCRE, feature extraction from speech and character is carried out separately, but recognition is performed in an engine. The recognition engine employs essentially CHMM (Continuous Hidden Markov Model) structure and this CHMM consists of variable parameter topology in order to minimize the number of model parameters and reduce recognition time. This model also adopts our proposed SSMS (Successive State and Mixture Splitting) for generating context independent model. SSMS optimizes the number of mixtures through splitting in mixture domain and the number of states through splitting in time domain. When we applied our developed engine which adopts SSMS to speech recognition for mobile devices, SSMS can reduce total number of Gaussian up to 40.0% compared with the fixed parameter models at the same recognition performance. This leads that SSMS can reduce the size of memory for models to 65% and that for processing to 82%. Moreover, recognition time decreases 17% with SSMS model but still maintains the recognition rate.

Keywords: Speech, Character, Recognition, SSS, Embedded.

1 Introduction

There has been much interest in intelligent multimodal interfaces with the growth of mobile information devices. This is primarily motivated by a need for providing convenient user interface to small size of mobile devices such as PDA. In some customized PDAs, speech recognition and character recognition modalities have already offered, so as to maximize convenient user interfaces [1]. Such small mobile devices have employed two different engines for speech and character recognition so far. However, this recognition structure is not desirable for small size of mobile devices in

E. Sha et al. (Eds.): EUC 2006, LNCS 4096, pp. 549 – 559, 2006.

terms of memory management and cost. One solution is to use of a unified processor for both speech and character recognition modalities. In this paper, our interest is focused on the SCCRE.

Hidden Markov Model (HMM) is the most widely technique used in speech recognition and it has been successfully applied in the recognition of Korean on-line handwritings [2]. Therefore, our SCCRE employs HMM as a basic model structure for construction of both speech and character recognition units, so as to be effectively applied to memory limited low cost devices. Especially, context independent CHMM of phoneme or grapheme (Korean character phone) is used as a basic recognition unit in SCCRE. The following conditions should be satisfied for CHMM based SCCRE to be effectively applied to customize mobile devices; 1) Combined recognition engine has to maintain recognition accuracy as in each individual system. 2) Real time processing should be achieved. For these reason, the size of CHMM should be minimized for real time processing.

Usual CHMM has a fixed parameter model topology (i.e. a fixed number of states and a fixed number of mixtures). But this topology can not represent wide variety of distinctive features sufficiently in an individual recognition unit. In case of on-line character recognition, it is more effective to have a different number of states for the different units, for example "ㄱ(g)" and "ㄹㅂ(rb)" have 2 and 6 states respectively[2]. For speech recognition, there have been similar trials. Several approaches such as parameter histogram, AIC (AKAIKE Information Criterion)[3], and BIC (Bayesian Information Criterion)[4] [10] have been proposed to reduce the number of parameters with the smallest error rate. These approaches have variable parameter model which consists of variable number of states and variable number of mixtures. However, these approaches determine the number of states and mixtures for a recognition unit (phoneme or grapheme) without considering those of other units. This can lead to decrease the recognition rate. As these approaches have the same number of mixtures for all recognition units, a recognition unit that has a compact distribution must also have a complicated structure and this can cause real time processing difficult.

Therefore, our main interest is focused on developing a method that selects a suitable number of states and a suitable number of mixtures in each individual recognition unit. In this work, a splitting algorithm of GOPDD (Gaussian Output Probability Density Distribution) is employed to decide model topology automatically. This algorithm is similar to SSS (Successive State Splitting)[5], which is often used in tied states context dependent models. But, our method is different from the SSS, as it splits the GOPDD in mixture domain not in context domain.

This paper is organized as follows. The following section gives a brief review of SCCRE architecture with the preprocessing of speech and on-line character recognition. Section 3 presents the previous variable parameters models. Section 4 describes the proposed splitting method of GOPDD. Recognition results for SCCRE are given in Section 5. Finally, some conclusions are presented in Section 6.

2 Speech and Character Combined Recognition Engine

2.1 System Architecture

Fig. 1 shows combined recognition system architecture for working on PDA or on mobile devices. In this system, we assume that the character (cursive script) and speech inputs are taken through touch screen and microphone, respectively. The preprocessing and the feature extraction are carried out on each modality, but provide the parameter observations to CHMM based combined recognition engine. Total 115 M-mixture CHMM models are trained through labeling. The combined CHMM models consist of 48 phone-like units for speech and 67 graphemes for character. The recognition is performed by using OPDP (One Pass Dynamic Programming) algorithm [7].

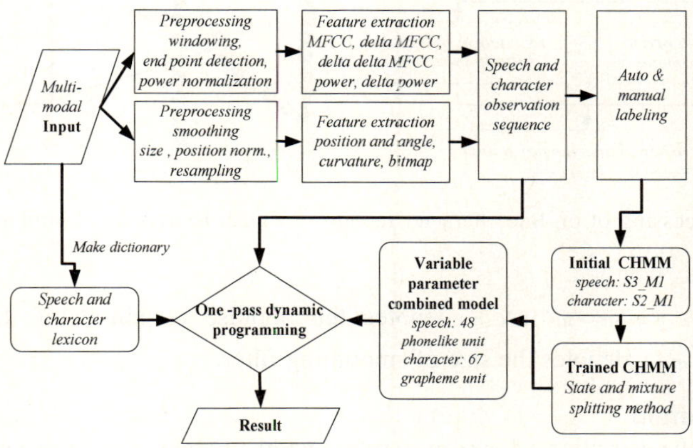

Fig. 1. System architecture

2.2 Preprocessing

39-order of MFCC (Mel Frequency Cepstral Coefficient) is extracted for speech recognition, where CMN (Cepstral Mean Normalization) is applied for taking account into environmental noise. The features for character recognition consist of 6-order of position parameters and 9-order of bitmap parameters. In the rest of this sub-section, we describe about preprocessing of Korean character briefly.

Fig.2 shows the preprocessing steps of on-line character recognition. Assume that the handwriting inputs are obtained through touch screen and the sampling rate is set to higher than 100 sample per second for different devices. In order to make users freely in writing style and writing position, the preprocessing step is given as follows:

A) Smoothing

Smoothing is carried out on the pen trajectory of the input character to reduce noises from input device. A smoothed point $\hat{x}_i$ is obtained by convolution, as given by

$$\hat{x}_i = C_{-n} \cdot x_{i-n} + \ldots + C_0 \cdot x_i + \ldots + C_m \cdot x_{i+m} \tag{1}$$

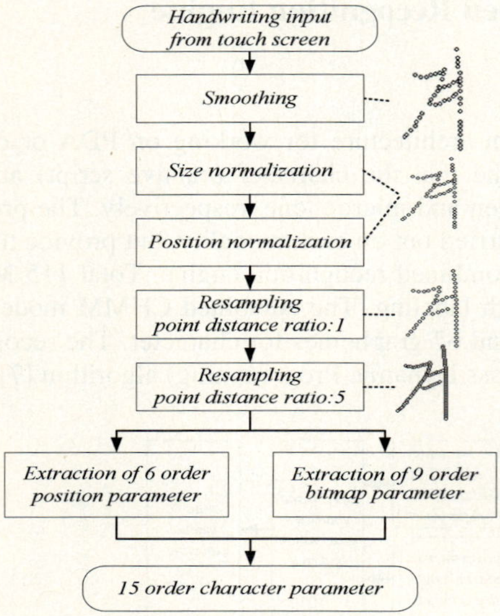

Fig. 2. Preprocessing of on-line character recognition

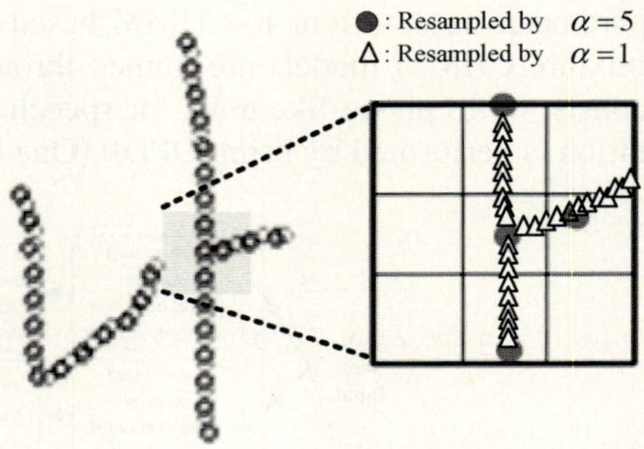

Fig. 3. Extraction of bitmap parameter

Where C_j, $for\ j = -n, -(n-1), \Lambda, m$ denotes the impulse responses of the smoothing filter, and $n+m+1$ denotes the size of smoothing filter.

B) Normalization

To rule out the variation of writing styles, width, height, and starting positions of input words should be normalized to the reference geometry. In word-based recognition system, the pre-determined height for all input words is used for the normalization of width and height. In other words, the height of input words are scaled to the reference height and width of the words are adjusted with the same scaling factor used in the height normalization. The starting position is also adjusted into the fixed position to remove the variations of each input words.

C) Re-sampling

Sampled data are re-sampled to yield a new sequence of data having equidistant in space to compensate different sampling rate and different writing speed. The following equidistant re-sampling procedure is applied. The coordinate of a new sample (px_j, py_i) is obtained by bi-linear interpolation as follows.

$$px_i = \alpha \frac{(px_j - px_{j-1})}{\sqrt{(px_{j-1} - x_j)^2 + (py_{j-1} - y_j)^2}} + px_{j-1}$$
$$py_i = \alpha \frac{(py_j - py_{j-1})}{\sqrt{(px_{j-1} - x_j)^2 + (py_{j-1} - y_j)^2}} + py_{j-1} \qquad (2)$$

Where α denotes the desirable distance in spaces.

D) Feature Extraction

For each data point of the re-sampled sequence, a 15 dimensional feature vector is calculated, which consists of 2 local information features for absolute x and y positions, 2 local angle parameters, 2 curvature parameters, and 9 bitmap based global information features [8]. Fig. 3 shows an example of bitmap parameter extraction. The circles and the triangles denote the re-sampled sequences in case of $\alpha=5$ and $\alpha=1$. Distribution of points (re-sampled with $\alpha=1$) within 3×3 window is used for extracting bitmap parameter as show in this figure.

3 Conventional Variable Parameter Model

This chapter gives brief reviews of general variable parameter model topology selection methods with more details of ML and BIC algorithms.

3.1 Variable Parameter Model Selection Topology

In general, model selection is done by choosing the topology $\hat{T}$ such that.

$$\hat{T} = \arg\max_T P(T \mid X) = \arg\max_T p(T)P(X \mid T) \tag{3}$$

A common practice in Bayesian model selection is to ignore the prior over the structure $P(T)$ (that is, assuming equal prior across all topologies) and using the evidence $P(X \mid T)$ as the sole criterion for model selection such that.

$$\begin{aligned} P(X \mid T) &= \int p(X \mid T, \theta) p(\theta \mid T) d\theta \\ &\approx \log p(X \mid \theta_{ML}) - C(k, N) \end{aligned} \tag{4}$$

Where θ_{ML} is estimated model of θ using MLE (Maximum Likelihood Estimate). Note that (4) is written as the likelihood term and the penalty term $C(k,N)$ which depend number of training data N and number of parameter k [4].

3.2 ML Topology Selection Method

ML topology selection method is to find the model, θ^*, that maximizes the log likelihood, so as to determine a suitable number of state and number of mixtures at each recognition unit.

$$\theta^* = \max_{\hat{\theta}_i}\{\sum_{n=1}^{N} \log P(X_n \mid \hat{\theta}_i)\} \tag{5}$$

Where $\hat{\theta}_i$ is i-th model trained by the maximum likelihood estimate, and X_n is n-th data, N is the size of data set. Fig. 4 shows an example of log likelihood. The maximum values are circled. In case of Korean phoneme "aa", 5 states and 4 mixtures model, denoted as S5_M4, shows the maximum likelihood over the interval of 3 ~ 6 states and 1 ~ 4 mixtures.

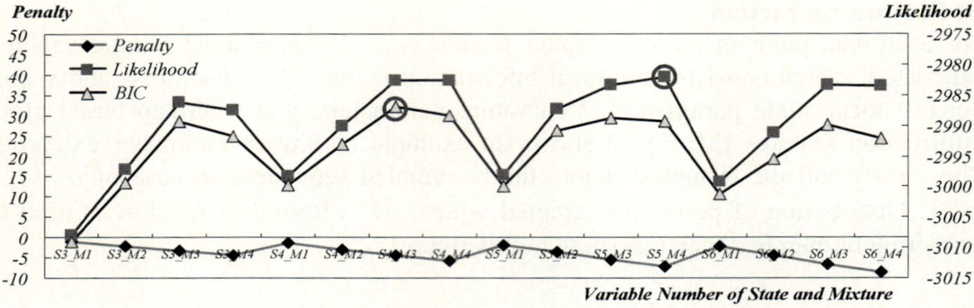

Fig. 4. Log likelihood, penalty and BIC of Korean phoneme "aa"

3.3 BIC Topology Selection Method

BIC is defined as the sum of log likelihood and a penalty term. The penalty term depends on the number of model parameters and the size of data set. BIC topology selection method is to find the model, θ^{**} , that maximizes BIC, so as to determine a suitable number of state and number of mixtures at each recognition unit.

$$\theta^{**} = \max_{\hat{\theta}_i}\{\sum_{n=1}^{N} \log P(X_n \mid \hat{\theta}_i) - \frac{k_i}{2}\log N\} \quad (6)$$

Where k_i is the number of i-th model parameter and N is the size of the data set. Fig. 4 also shows that the S4_M3 model has the maximum BIC (sum of maximum likelihood and the penalty term).

4 Successive State and Mixture Splitting

The acoustical characteristics of phonemes are greatly influenced by phoneme context, speaker characteristics, and the speaking rate of utterance. Many algorithms such as SSS-FREE, ML-SSS[10], DT(Decision Tree)-SSS[6] have been proposed for constructing context dependent models. Generally, it is known that the context dependent models perform better than the context independent models, but require much more memory for processing. Taking account into low cost, memory limited mobile device, context independent model is applied to SCCRE in this paper.

Here, we propose a splitting algorithm, called SSMS (Successive State and Mixture Splitting), which splits the GOPDD for variable parameter context independent model.

Unlike the SSS algorithm generating context dependent model, the SSMS constructs context independent models with suitable number of states and mixtures for each recognition units by splitting GOPDD. The SSS is done in time and context domains, while the SSMS splits the GOPDD in time and mixture domain. The outline of the SSMS is illustrated in Fig. 5. The algorithm consists of three steps as follows.

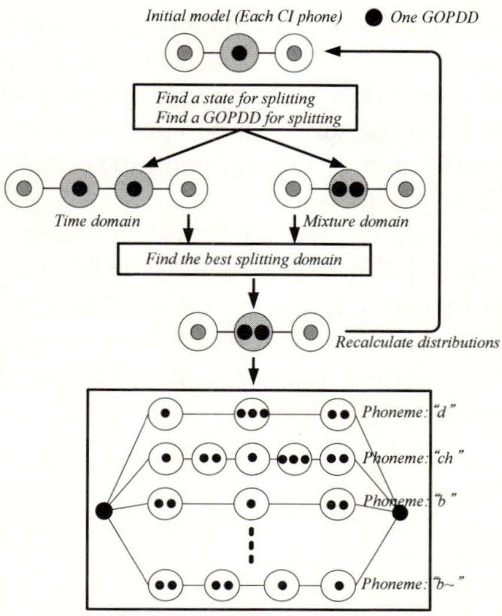

Fig. 5. Generation of a SSMS model

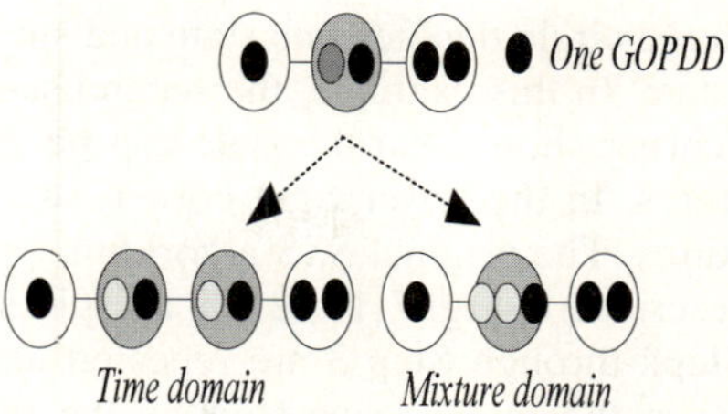

Fig. 6. The splitting examples in time and mixture domain

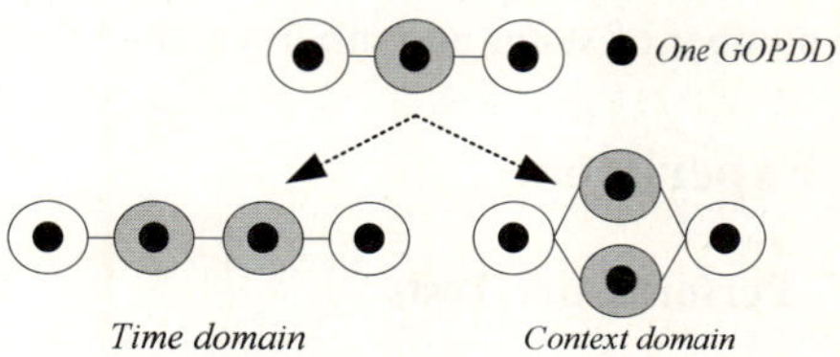

Fig. 7. The splitting examples in time and context domain

Step 1: Train initial models
Two different initial models should be constructed for speech and handwritten character, respectively. For speech, HMM with context-independent three states and one mixture is used as the initial model and context-independent two states and one mixture is used for character, so as to well represent up to the simple grapheme with the shortest length.

Step 2: Find GOPDD for splitting
For each state S(i) with M-mixture GOPDD, the normalized distribution size d_i is calculated. S(m) will be the state to split which gives the maximum d_i among all samples.

$$d_i = \sum_{k}^{K} \frac{\sigma_{ik}^{\ 2}}{\sigma_{Tk}^{\ 2}} \cdot \sqrt{n_i}$$
$$\sigma_{ik}^{\ 2} = \sum_{m}^{M} \lambda_{im} \sigma^2{}_{imk} + \sum_{m}^{M} \sum_{m'=m+1}^{M-1} \lambda_{im} \lambda_{im'} (\mu_{imk} - \mu_{im'k})^2 \tag{7}$$

Where, k denotes the dimension of the feature vector, $\lambda_{im}\lambda_{im'}$ represent weight coefficients, n_i denotes the number of training sample assigned to the state, $\sigma_{ik}^{\ 2}$ denotes the k-th variance of all samples.

Step 3: Split the GOPDD
The selected state in step 2 is then split in time and mixture domain respectively. The Baum-Welch algorithm is applied to the split states in each domain in order to find maximum likelihood path. Fig. 6 shows a simple splitting example of SSMS. Where

the large circle denotes one state and small circle denotes one GOPDD in corresponding state. In this example, the second state on upper line is split by SSMS. The lower left corner shows that the state can be split into two states with the same number of mixtures. In the lower right corner, two mixtures in the state can be split into three mixtures. The original SSS algorithm split the states in both context and time domain as described in Fig. 7. Note that all split states have one mixture.

Step2 through Step 3 are repeated until M-mixture reaches the specified number. Because the model generated by the three steps of SSMS has suitable number of states and each state has appropriate number of mixtures, the proposed algorithm can be regarded as to be more general for generating variable context independent model. In addition, this algorithm allows more effective memory managements, in terms of the number of states and mixtures, than the fixed parameter model.

5 Experiments

5.1 Performance Tests

452 KPBWs (Korean Phoneme Balanced Words) uttered by 38 male are used for constructing SI (speaker independent) model in speech recognition, and on-line cursive handwritten characters by 10 writers for character recognition. Table 1 shows the analysis conditions of SCCRE.

To show the effectiveness of variable parameter model using SSMS, we compare it with conventional fixed parameter model and DT-SSS HM-Nets (Hidden Markov Network)[6]. SI word recognition rate with fixed parameter model and variable parameter model using SSMS is shown in Fig. 8. As the figure indicates, the recognition accuracy increases as the number of GOPDD increases. The dotted line indicates the recognition performance by SSMS model, and straight-line indicates the recognition performance by fixed parameter models having number of states from 3 to 6. The recognition rate by SSMS model increases faster than other fixed models to the maximum recognition rate of 98.2%.

Table 1. Analysis conditions for speech/character data

	Speech	Character
Preprocessing	8kHz sampling, 16bits 16ms hamming window 5ms frame shift	100 samples/sec smoothing size/position normalization distance re-sampling
Feature	12 MFCCs 12 delta MFCCs 12 delta delta MFCCs 1 power, 1 delta power	2 absolute X,Y positions 2 angles 2 curvatures 9 modified bitmaps
DB	KLE Korean words	KAIST Korean written characters
Model	M mixture variable parameter CHMM	

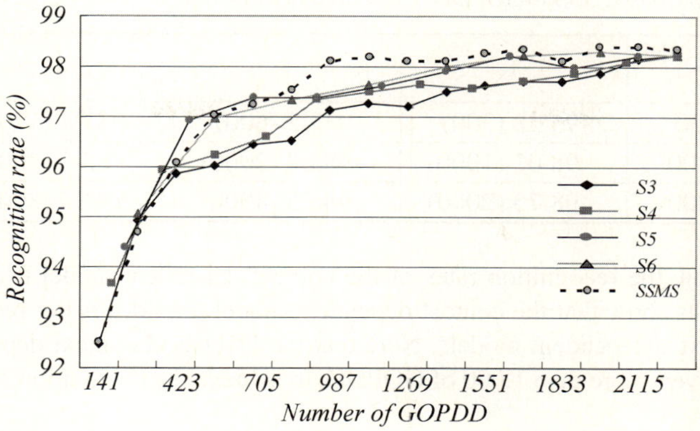

Fig. 8. Comparison of recognition rates between SI fixed parameter models from 3 states(*S3*) to 6 states(*S6*) and SI variable parameter model by SSMS(Where, no. of GOPDD= no. of phones *x* no. of states *x* no. of mixtures)

Table 2. Number of GOPDD of each model reaching to the maximum recognition accuracy of 98.2%

Model	S3	S4	S5	S6	SSMS
#GOPDD	2115	2256	1645	1692	987

Table 2 shows the number of GOPDD of each model that reaches to the maximum recognition accuracy of 98.2%. In this table, we can find that the number of GOPDD is 1,692 for the fixed parameter model and 987 for SSMS model to reach 98.2% of recognition rate. Therefore, SSMS models have 40% fewer parameters than the fixed model. For running in PDA, fixed parameter model has size of 630Kbyte and requires a memory of 3.42Mbyte; SSMS model has size of 410Kbyte and requires a memory of 2.81Mbyte, leading that SSMS can reduce the size of memory for models to 65% and that for processing to 82%. Moreover, recognition time decreases 17% with SSMS model but still maintains the recognition rate.. Moreover, recognition time decrease 17% with SSMS model but still maintain the recognition rate. Table 3 shows examples of model topology by SSMS that achieves maximum recognition results. In case of phoneme "g", the number of state is 5 and the first state has 4 mixtures, the second four, the third 7…etc.

Table 3. Examples of model topology by SSMS Model

Phone	# Total state	1	2	3	4	5	6
G	5	4	4	7	5	6	-
gg	6	7	4	4	3	3	2
aa	3	3	7	8	-	-	-
ih	3	4	9	11	-	-	-

Table 4. DT based SSS (#GOPDD) (#M: number of Mixture, #S: number of State)

#S \ #M	1	2	4
300	95.28 (300)	97.42 (600)	98.08 (1200)
1000	98.01 (1000)	98.67 (2000)	98.97 (4000)
2000	98.75 (2000)	98.75 (4000)	99.19 (8000)

Table 4 show the recognition rates of the context dependent model using DT based SSS. The results show that the context dependent model provides better recognition rate than the context independent models. Note that the DT based context dependent model requires, however, more than 1,000 of GOPDD, to achieve the recognition rate of 98.2%.

6 Conclusions

This paper describes an on-line SCCRE working on PDA or on mobile devices. In the SCCRE, feature extraction for speech and for character is carried out separately, but recognition is performed in an engine.

Usual CHMM has a fixed parameter model topology (i.e. a fixed number of states and a fixed number of mixture models), but can not represent wide variety of distinctive feature parameters sufficiently in an individual recognition unit. Therefore, it would be better if variable parameter model is used to reduce the number of parameters while maintaining the recognition rate.

SSMS method was proposed for generating the variable parameter model automatically. The proposed allows reducing effectively the number of mixtures through splitting in mixture domain instead of in context domain. The experimental results indicate that the proposed model have the same recognition rate of the best fixed parameter model, with only 60% parameters of the fixed model. This leads that SSMS can reduce the size of memory for models to 65% and that for processing to 82%. Moreover, recognition time decreases 17% with SSMS model but still maintains the recognition rate. This means that the proposed SSMS is suitable for applying in compact mobile devices such as PDA.

Acknowledgement

This research was supported by the MIC(Ministry of Information and Communication), Korea, under the ITRC(Information Technology Research Center) support program supervised by the IITA(Institute of Information Technology Assessment).

References

1. Suk, S.Y., Kim, M.J. and Chung, H.Y.: An on-line speech and character combined recognition system for multimodal interfaces, EALPIIT Proc., (2002) 89-92
2. Sin, B. K. and Kim, J.: A Statistical Approach with HMMs for On-line Cursive Hangul(Korean Script) Recognition, Second International Conference on Document Analysis and Recognition Proc., Zuchuba, Japan (1993) 147-150

3. Tong, H.: Determination of the order of a markov chain by Akaike`s information criterion, Journal of Applied Probability, 12, (1975) 488-497
4. Li, D., Biem, A. and Subrahmonia, J.: Hmm topology optimization for handwriting recognition, ICASSP Proc. (2001)
5. Takami, J. and Sagayama, S.: A successive state splitting algorithm for efficient allophone modeling, ICASSP-92 Proc., Vol. 1. (1992) 573-576
6. Takaki, H., Mashahru, K., Akinori, I. and Masaki, K.: A Study on HM-Nets using Decision Tree-based Successive Splitting, ICSP-97 Proc. (1997) 383-387
7. Nakagawa, S.: A connected spoken word recognition method by O(n) dynamic programming pattern matching algorithm, ICASSP Proc. (1983) 296-299
8. Ralph, G., Stefan, M. and Alex, W.: Run-on recognition in an on-line handwriting recognition system, Carnegie Mellon Univ. Press. (1997)
9. Biem, A., Ha, J.Y. and Subrahmonia, J.: A Bayesian model selection criterion For HMM Topology Optimization, ICASSP Proc. (2002) 989-992
10. Jitsuhiro, T., Nakamura, S.: Automatic generation of non-uniform HMM structures based on variational Bayesian approach, ICASSP Proc., Vol. 1. (2004) 805-808
11. Li Deng.: Distributed speech processing in MiPad's multimodal user interface, IEEE Trans. Speech and Audio., Vol. 10, No. 8. (2002) 605-619

Scalable Fingerprinting Scheme Using Statistically Secure Anti-Collusion Code for Large Scale Contents Distribution

Jae-Min Seol and Seong-Whan Kim

Department of Computer Science,
University of Seoul, Jeon-Nong-Dong, Seoul, Korea.
{seoleda@hotmail.com, swkim7@uos.ac.kr}

Abstract. Fingerprinting schemes use digital watermarks to determine originators of unauthorized/pirated copies. Multiple users may collude and collectively escape identification by creating an average or median of their individually watermarked copies. Previous fingerprint code design including ACC (anti-collusion code) cannot support large number of users, which is a common situation in ubiquitous contents distribution environment. We propose a practical scalability solution, which extends previous ACC codebook generation scheme. We design a scalable ACC scheme using a Gaussian distributed random variable to increase the robustness over average and median attack. We implemented our scheme using human visual system based watermarking scheme, and the fingerprinted copy of standard test images show good perceptual quality. The result shows good collusion detection performance over average and median collusion attacks for large scale user population.

Keywords: Scalable, anti-collusion code, digital fingerprinting.

1 Introduction

A digital watermark or watermark is an invisible mark inserted in digital media, and fingerprinting uses digital watermark to determine originators of unauthorized/pirated copies. Multiple users may collude and collectively escape identification by creating an average or median of their individually watermarked copies. An early work on designing collusion-resistant binary fingerprint codes for generic data was based on marking assumption, which states that undetectable marks cannot be arbitrarily changed without rendering the object useless. However, multimedia data have very different characteristics from generic data, and we can embed different marks or fingerprints in overall images, which biased strict marking assumption. Recently, an improvement was to merge the low level code (primitive code) with the direct sequence spread spectrum embedding for multimedia and extend the marking assumption to allow for random jamming [1]. Min Wu presented the design of collusion-resistant fingerprints using code modulation. They proposed a (k-1) collusion-resistant fingerprints scheme, and the (k-1) resilient ACC is derived from (v, k, 1) balanced incomplete block design (BIBD) [2]. The resulting (k-1) resilient

E. Sha et al. (Eds.): EUC 2006, LNCS 4096, pp. 560 – 569, 2006.

ACC code vectors are v-dimensional, and can represent n = $(v^2 - v) / (k^2 - k)$ users with these v basis vectors.

We present a scalable ACC fingerprinting design scheme, which extends ACC for large number of user support. Simply replicating ACC codebook does not work, because there are ambiguous cases for determining who colluders are. We extend the ACC (anti-collusion code) scheme using a Gaussian distributed random variable for medium attack robustness. We evaluate our scheme with standard test images, and show good collusion detection performance over two powerful attacks: average and median collusion attacks.

2 Related Works

An early work on designing collusion-resistant binary fingerprint codes was presented by Boneh and Shaw in 1995 [3], which primarily considered the problem of fingerprinting generic data that satisfy an underlying principle referred to as the marking assumption. The marking assumption states that undetectable marks cannot be arbitrarily changed without rendering the object useless; however, it is considered possible for the colluding set to change a detectable mark to any state (collusion framework). Under the collusion framework, Boneh and Shaw show that it is not possible to design totally c-secure codes, which are fingerprint codes that are capable of tracing at least one colluder out of a coalition of at most c colluders. Instead, they used hierarchical design and randomization techniques to construct c-secure codes that are able to capture one colluder out of a coalition of up to c colluders with high probability.

Fingerprint codes (e.g. c-secure codes) for generic data was intended for objects that satisfy the marking assumption, multimedia data have very different characteristics from generic data, and a few fundamental aspects of the marking assumption may not always hold when fingerprinting multimedia data. For example, different marks or fingerprints can be embedded in overall images through spread spectrum techniques, thereby it makes impossible for attackers to manipulate individual marks at will. As shown in Equation (1), Min Wu presented the design of collusion-resistant fingerprints using code modulation [2]. The fingerprint signal wj for the j-th user is constructed using a linear combination of a total of v orthogonal basis signals $\{\mathbf{u}_i\}$, multiplied by the coefficients $\{b_{ij}\}$, representing the fingerprint codes from $\{\pm 1\}$.

$$w_j = \sum_{i=1}^{v} b_{ij} \mathbf{u}_i. \tag{1}$$

An anti-collusion code (ACC) is a family of code vectors for which the bits shared between code vectors uniquely identifies groups of colluding users. ACC codes have the property that the composition of any subset of K or fewer code vectors is unique. This property allows for the identification of up to K colluders. It has been shown that binary-valued ACC can be constructed using balanced incomplete block design (BIBD) [4]. The definition of (v, k, λ) BIBD code is a set of k-element subsets (blocks) of a v-element set χ, such that each pair of elements of χ occur together in exactly λ blocks. The (v, k, λ) BIBD has a total of n = $(v^2 -v)/(k^2 -k)$ blocks, and we can represent (v, k, λ) BIBD code using an v x n incidence matrix M, where M(i, j) is set to 1 when the i-th element belongs to the j-th block, and set to 0 otherwise. The corresponding (k – 1)-resilient ACC code vectors are assigned as the bit complements (finally represented using -1 and 1 for the 0 and 1, respectively) of the columns of the incidence matrix of a (v, k, 1) BIBD. The resulting (k-1) resilient ACC code vectors are v-dimensional, and can represent n = $(v^2 -v) / (k^2 -k)$ users with these v basis vectors.

3 Scalable and Robust Fingerprint Scheme

Min Wu's fingerprinting scheme cannot easily extend to support large number of users because it is based on (v, k, λ) BIBD code design. Because we should have more overhead for bigger BIBD code, we designed a scalable fingerprint scheme, which can make large number of fingerprints from small BIBD code.

3.1 Codebook Design

In our scheme, we construct each user's fingerprint as the composition of ACC (w_i) and a Gaussian distributed random signal λ as shown in Figure 1. The dimension of code vectors (M) can be increased to fit the size of fingerprinting users.

We can view our scheme as a two level spreading: direct sequence spreading and frequency hopping. We used same spreading (direct sequence spreading) as ACC and we spread the ACC over M image blocks (frequency hopped), thereby we can increase the number of fingerprint codes. This scheme has strong advantages that we can control the number of fingerprint codes easily.

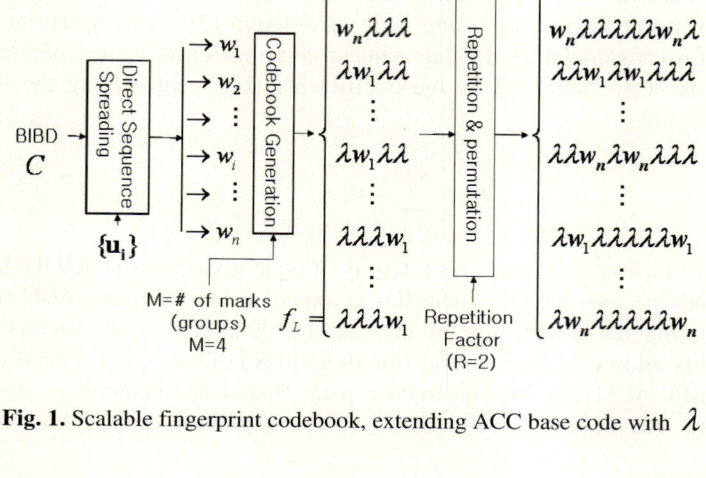

Fig. 1. Scalable fingerprint codebook, extending ACC base code with λ

3.2 Fingerprint Embedding and Detection

Once we generated the code vectors, we embed the fingerprint codes over M x R selected regions as shown in Figure 2. Fingerprinting regions (blocks) are chosen based on the model of NVF (Noise Visibility Function) [5]. Each user l's fingerprint f_l is constructed by repetition and permutation like Dan Boneh's fingerprinting scheme. For example, $w_1\lambda\lambda\lambda$ (M = 4 case) is enlarged 2 (R = 2 case) times ($w_1w_1\lambda\lambda\lambda\lambda\lambda\lambda$) and shuffled ($w_1\lambda\lambda\lambda\lambda\lambda w_1\lambda$). The permutation sequence is unique to all users, but unknown to attackers. Repetition and permutation prevent interleaving collusion attack. $f_l(i)$ is inserted signal into i-th block, each $f_l(i)$ can be ACC or λ signal, and is embedded in the M×R selected image blocks (there are R ACC signals and (M-1)× R λ signals.

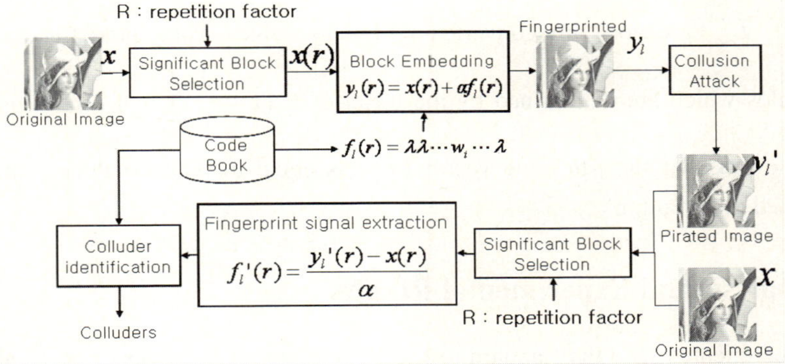

Fig. 2. Scalable fingerprint embedding / extraction of fingerprint f_l for user l

To embed ACC (w_i) signal in a specified block y_i, we use the following Equation (2). To increase the fingerprint robustness, we inserted ACC signal over R image blocks. All the ACC (w_i) are the same, however, the resulting watermark will be different, depending on $1-NVF$, which considers the local HVS masking characteristics [6].

$$y_i = x + (1-NVF)w_i, \qquad w_i = \sum_{j=1}^{v} c_{ij}\mathbf{u_i}. \tag{2}$$

$$NVF(i,j) = \frac{1}{1+\sigma_x^2(i,j)}$$

Likewise, λ signal embedding uses the following Equation (3). To un-correlate the λ signal, we use the random variable for λ signal, instead of simply choosing zero vectors. σ is used to increase median attack robustness. If we increase σ, we can increase the median attack robustness because there is little difference between λ signals and w_i ; however, we can risk the decrease of detection precision.

$$y_i = x + (1 - NVF)\lambda, \quad \lambda \sim N(0, \sigma^2) \tag{3}$$

We used non-blind scheme for fingerprint detection. To detect collusion, we used the collusion detection vector T, which can be computed using the same Equation (4) as Min Wu's as follows [2].

$$T_{mark\ i} = \{t_1, t_2, \cdots, t_v\} \quad = \frac{1}{R} \sum_{r=1+R\times(i-1)}^{R} \frac{f_l'(r) \cdot \{u_1, u_2, \cdots, u_v\}}{\sqrt{|f_l'(r)|^2 \times |u_i|^2}} \tag{4}$$

Next, $T_{mark\, i}$ vectors are converted to binary values using predefined adaptive thresholds which are determined by the mean of t_i ($\bar{t} = \frac{1}{v}\sum_{i=1}^{v} t_i$). Checking binary vector over C, if the j-th code vector ($c_{\cdot i}$) is equal to binary values, j-th user is suspected to be traitor.

4 Analysis and Experimental Results

We experimented with the standard test images. Figure 3 shows test images and their enlarged fingerprints. After fingerprint embedding, the average PSNR is over 41 dB with good subjective quality.

We tested our scalable fingerprinting code for various collusion attacks (average, median, min, max, min-max, modified negative, randomized negatives) for the test images. Average collusion is widely used collusion attack [8], because it is efficient to attack fingerprints, and also it makes better image quality after collusion (usually it increases 4-5 dB). Figure 4 shows a collusion example, when six colluders make pirated copies from their fingerprinted copies. Figure 4 shows original images, and the colluded (average, median collusion) copies.

We used N (0, 16) for λ signal, and we chose σ^2 as 16.0 experimentally to tradeoff between median attack robustness and false positive error rate. We can compute the probability of false positive (there is no collusion, but the λ signal makes similar results as collusion occurs) error as Equation (5). If any marks are purely linear combination of λ, their $\bar{t}$ (the mean of t_i) will be zero. Using Equation (5), we can correctly differentiate linear combination of λ and others. We use the student's T test for the mean of one normal sample [9]. For example, if $w_1\lambda\lambda\lambda$ and

Fig. 3. Fingerprinted images, and their fingerprints (Enlarged), the number of Marks (M) =10, Repetition factor (R) =16, Block size = 32x32: (top) Baboon (PSNR: 40.69 dB), (second) Lena (PSNR: 44.07 dB), (third) Boat (PSNR: 45.45 dB), (bottom) Barbara (PSNR: 42.72 dB)

$\lambda w_3 \lambda\lambda$ collude using average attack, we can extract signals $(w_1+\lambda)/2$, $(\lambda+w_3)/2$, $(\lambda+\lambda)/2$ and $(\lambda+\lambda)/2$ at each mark, and we can distinguish mark 1,2 and mark 3,4 using Equation (5).

$$P(\tau|H_0)=G(\tau),\ \ where\ \tau=\frac{\overline{t}-0}{S/\sqrt{v}},\ \ \overline{t}=\frac{1}{v}\sum_{i=1}^{v}t_i,\ \ S=\frac{1}{v-1}\sum_{i=1}^{v}(t_i-\overline{t})^2 \tag{5}$$

$$G(\tau) = \int_{\tau}^{\infty} \frac{\Gamma([r+1/2])}{\sqrt{\pi r}\Gamma(r/2)} (1+w^2/r)^{-(r+1)/2} dw, \text{ where } r = v - 1$$

Original Image | Attacked Image (Average) PSNR: 51.74 dB | Attacked Image (Median) PSNR: 50.67dB

Fig. 4. Original, average, and median attacked images

To increase both the detection precision and median attack robustness, we can increase the R in embedding step. If we use the average of signal over R blocks, we can correctly differentiate the linear combination of λ and others with high probability, because the variance of τ gets smaller (σ^2/R) than the variance of original signal (σ^2). Figure 5 and Figure 6 show the fingerprint detection result (T vectors) after average and median collusion attacks with detection threshold mean of t_i set. (Because as colluders are increase, the amplitude of t_i are decreased) We used the same detection procedure as average collusion attack, and show the same colluder identification. Median attack is a powerful attack; however, our approach shows good performance. Setting the significant level of H_0 to 0.05, we will suspect the users in mark 1, 3, and 7.

Decoding mark 1, mark 3and mark 7, we can compute T vectors {0000 0000 0011 1111}, {0111 1111 1100 0000}.and {1011 10111 110 1011}, as shown in Figure 5 and Figure 6. Checking T vectors over (16, 4, 1) BIBD code matrix as shown in Figure 7, we can suspect {w_1, w_2, w_3} in mark 1 {w_4,w_5} in mark 3 and {w_7} in mark 7 as colluders. Using codebook design rule, we can know that colluders are users with fingerprint code C = {w_1λλλλλλλλλ, w_2λλλλλλλλλ, w_3λλλλλλλλλ, λλw_4λλλλλλλ, λλw_5λλλλλλλ, λλλλλλ w_7λλλ}

We analyzed the average number of fingerprinted images to erase fingerprints (successful collusion). Figure 8 shows that colluders should have 40 fingerprinted images (or 40 colluding members) on average case, to erase the fingerprints for our scalable fingerprinting scheme with (16, 4, 1) BIBD and scalability m = 40. If we use the larger BIBID codes (e.g. (61, 5, 1) BIBD code), we can get much bigger collusion robustness.

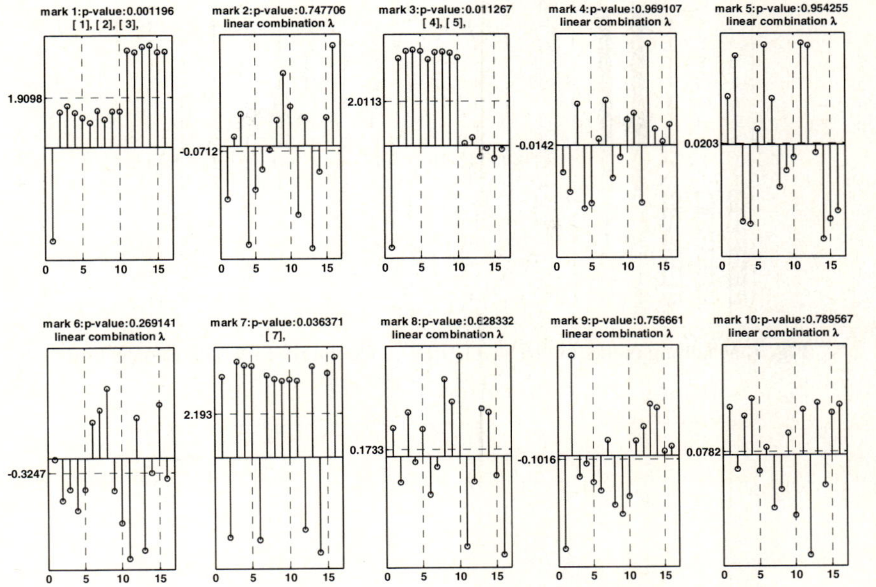

Fig. 5. Detection result after average attack

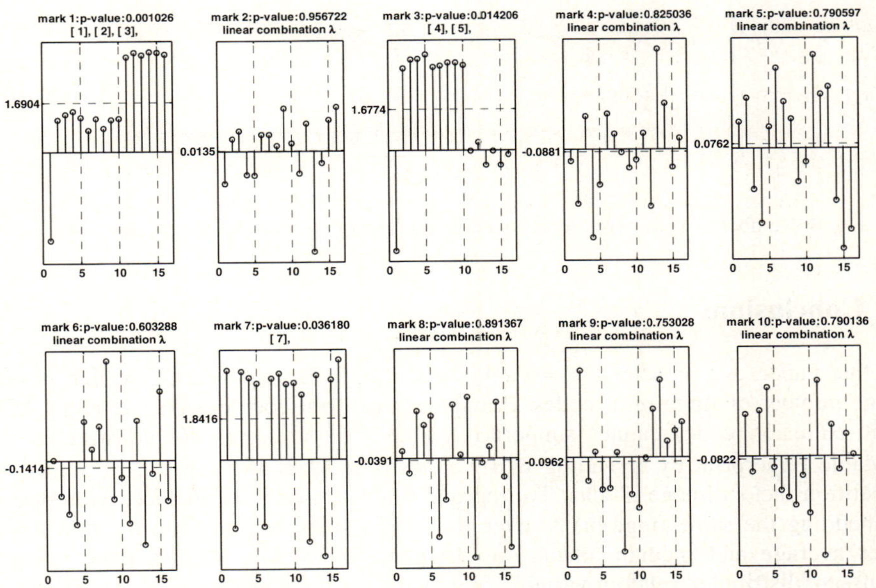

Fig. 6. Detection result after median attack

$$\mathbf{C}=\begin{pmatrix}
-1 & -1 & -1 & -1 & -1 & 1 & 1 & 1 & 1 & 1 & 1 & 1 & 1 & 1 & 1 & 1 & 1 & 1 & 1 & 1 \\
-1 & 1 & 1 & 1 & 1 & -1 & -1 & -1 & -1 & 1 & 1 & 1 & 1 & 1 & 1 & 1 & 1 & 1 & 1 & 1 \\
-1 & 1 & 1 & 1 & 1 & 1 & 1 & 1 & 1 & -1 & -1 & -1 & -1 & 1 & 1 & 1 & 1 & 1 & 1 & 1 \\
-1 & 1 & 1 & 1 & 1 & 1 & 1 & 1 & 1 & 1 & 1 & 1 & 1 & -1 & -1 & -1 & -1 & 1 & 1 & 1 \\
1 & -1 & 1 & 1 & 1 & -1 & 1 & 1 & 1 & -1 & 1 & 1 & 1 & -1 & 1 & 1 & 1 & -1 & 1 & 1 \\
1 & -1 & 1 & 1 & 1 & 1 & -1 & 1 & 1 & 1 & -1 & 1 & 1 & 1 & -1 & 1 & 1 & 1 & -1 & 1 \\
1 & -1 & 1 & 1 & 1 & 1 & 1 & -1 & 1 & 1 & 1 & -1 & 1 & 1 & 1 & -1 & 1 & 1 & 1 & -1 \\
1 & 1 & -1 & 1 & 1 & -1 & 1 & 1 & 1 & 1 & -1 & 1 & 1 & 1 & 1 & 1 & -1 & 1 & 1 & -1 \\
1 & 1 & -1 & 1 & 1 & 1 & 1 & -1 & 1 & 1 & 1 & 1 & -1 & 1 & -1 & 1 & 1 & -1 & 1 & 1 \\
1 & 1 & -1 & 1 & 1 & 1 & 1 & 1 & -1 & 1 & 1 & -1 & 1 & -1 & 1 & 1 & 1 & 1 & -1 & 1 \\
1 & 1 & 1 & -1 & 1 & -1 & 1 & 1 & 1 & 1 & 1 & 1 & -1 & 1 & 1 & -1 & 1 & 1 & -1 & 1 \\
1 & 1 & 1 & -1 & 1 & 1 & -1 & 1 & 1 & 1 & 1 & -1 & 1 & 1 & 1 & 1 & -1 & -1 & 1 & 1 \\
1 & 1 & 1 & -1 & 1 & 1 & 1 & 1 & -1 & -1 & 1 & 1 & 1 & 1 & -1 & 1 & 1 & 1 & 1 & -1 \\
1 & 1 & 1 & 1 & -1 & 1 & -1 & 1 & 1 & 1 & 1 & 1 & -1 & -1 & 1 & 1 & 1 & 1 & 1 & -1 \\
1 & 1 & 1 & 1 & -1 & 1 & 1 & -1 & 1 & -1 & 1 & 1 & 1 & 1 & 1 & 1 & -1 & 1 & -1 & 1 \\
1 & 1 & 1 & 1 & -1 & 1 & 1 & 1 & -1 & 1 & -1 & 1 & 1 & 1 & 1 & -1 & 1 & -1 & 1 & 1
\end{pmatrix}$$

Fig. 7. Matching marks in (16, 4, 1)-BIBD code matrix for colluder detection

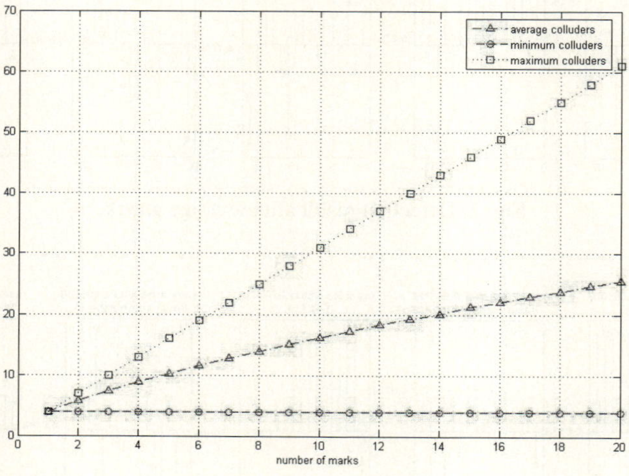

Fig. 8. Number of marks (m) versus average number of colluder for successful collusion

5 Conclusions

In this paper, we presented a scalable ACC fingerprinting scheme, which covers large number of fingerprint codes. Previous fingerprint code design including ACC (anti-collusion code) cannot support large number of users. We constructed the scalable fingerprint by spreading BIBD codes over M×R (M: number of marks; R: repetition factor) image blocks. To improve the detection performance, we repeated embedding the same fingerprints over R image blocks. To increase the robustness over average and median attack, we designed a scalable ACC scheme using a Gaussian distributed random variable. We evaluated our fingerprints on standard test images, and showed good collusion detection performance over average and median collusion attacks.

References

1. Yacobi, Y.: Improved Boneh-Shaw content fingerprinting. in Proc. CTRSA2001 (2001) 378–91
2. Trappe, W., Wu, M., Wangm Z. J., Liu, K. J. R.,: Anti-collusion fingerprinting for multimedia. IEEE Trans. Signal Proc. vol. 51, Apr. (2003) 1069-1087
3. Boneh, D., Shaw, J.: Collusion-secure fingerprinting for digital data. IEEE Trans. Inform. Theory, vol. 44, Sept. (1998) 1897–1905
4. Colbourn, C. J., Dinitz, J. H.: The CRC Handbook of Combinatorial Design. Boca Raton, FL: CRC Press (1996)
5. Voloshynovskiy, S., Herrige, A., Baumgaertner, N., Pun, T.: A stochastic approach to content adaptive digital image watermarking. Lecture Notes in Computer Science: 3rd Int. Workshop on Information Hiding, vol. 1768, Sept. (1999) 211-236
6. Watson, A. B., Borthwick, R., Taylor, M.: Image quality and Conf. Human Vision, Visual Processing, and Digital Display VI (1997)
7. Kim, S.W., Suthaharan, S., Lee, H.K., Rao, K.R.: An image watermarking scheme using visual model and BN distribution. IEE Elect. Letter, vol. 35 (3), Feb. (1999)
8. Zhao, H., Wu, M., Wang, J., Ray Liu, K. J.: Nonlinear collusion attacks on independent Fingerprints for multimedia. ICASSP. vol. 5, Apr. (2003) 664-667
9. V. K. Rohatgi, “An Introduction to Probability Theory and Mathematical Statistics”, John Wiley & Sons, Inc. (1976)

Broadcasting Group Information to Ensure Consistency and Correctness in Mobile Computing Environments*

Daein Kim and Buhyun Hwang

Department of Computer Science Chonnam National University,
300 Yongbong-dong, Gwang-ju, Korea
{dikim, bhhwang}@chonnam.ac.kr

Abstract. Recent advances in wireless communication technology and popularity of portable computers have rendered the mobile computing environments that users access the information via wireless channel, regardless of the situation or the location. In this environments, a mobile host have a cache to avoid the bandwidth usage and improve the response time of transactions. However, the cache mechanism does not guarantee the serializable execution of mobile transactions. In this paper, we propose the BGI-MT method that mobile hosts can make a commit decision by using the group information. Also our method can improve the cache efficiency in the case that the disconnection of mobile hosts is longer than the broadcast interval of the window report.

1 Introduction

In wireless mobile network, the server may exchange the data items and the control information with mobile hosts using broadcast strategies, but frequent broadcast technique requires high communication costs and causes a bottleneck due to the limited channel[1]. Therefore, caching technique is especially important to use the bandwidth efficiently and improve the response time of transactions in mobile computing environments which are characterized by narrow bandwidth, limited battery, host's mobility, and frequent disconnection from the server[3,7]. In this strategy, a server broadcasts an invalidation report to ensure the cache consistency. However, it becomes difficult for the mobile hosts to know whether their cached data items are still valid or not before the arrival of an invalidation report. Thus, this method defers the commit decision of mobile transactions to ensure theirs serializable execution until the invalidation report is arrived[5]. In this paper, we find out the problems of cache invalidation methods and propose the method to solve them while ensuring the serializable execution of mobile transactions. Our method makes a commit decision by using the group information before receiving an invalidation report, and avoids discarding the entire cache in the case that the disconnection of mobile hosts is longer than the broadcast interval of an invalidation report.

* This work was supported by KOrea Science and Engineering Foundation(KOSEF R05-2003-000-10532-0).

E. Sha et al. (Eds.): EUC 2006, LNCS 4096, pp. 570–579, 2006.

2 Related Work

In [1], three strategies that use invalidation reports to fulfill the obligations has been suggested. In these methods, a server periodically broadcasts update information to ensure the cache consistency of a mobile host. But, these methods have a problem that the response time of mobile transactions can be long since mobile transactions is answered after receiving the next report[1].

In [4], UFO(Update First Order) detects inconsistency between cached data items in mobile hosts and the updated data items in the server. UFO protocol checks whether there is any overlap between the broadcast data set and the write set of update transactions during the current data broadcast period. If there is an overlap, the server knows that any conflicting data items have been existed and rebroadcasts the overlapped data items. But, this protocol may require additional cost since the broadcast schedule of conflicting data items should be reconstructed at the server. Also, if all conflicting data items are not rebroadcasted in one broadcast period, the similar conflict can be happened.

In [5], OCC-UTS^2(Optimistic Concurrency Control with Update TimeStamp Span) method is devised to guarantee the serializability of mobile transactions. In OCC-UTS^2 method, mobile hosts locally ensure the serializable execution of mobile transactions without server's intervention. Also a server does not handle the commit requests for mobile transactions issued by mobile hosts and thus the uplink traffic does not affect overall performance seriously. But, this method can make an incorrect commit decision of mobile transactions, as shown in Fig.1.

3 Problem Statement

Fig.1 shows the example that a mobile transaction reads inconsistent data items by uncontrolled data broadcast.

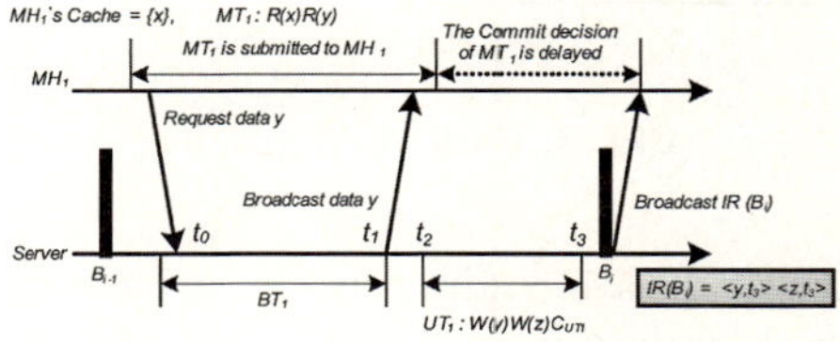

Fig. 1. Incorrect abort decision of a mobile transaction

In Fig.1, the mobile transaction MT_1 wants to read x and y, is submitted to the mobile host MH_1. As MH_1 has only data x in its cache, it sends the request message for y to execute MT_1. In the server, the broadcast transaction BT_1 is executed between t_0 and t_1, and makes the data broadcast schedule containing y. The server broadcasts y at time t_1 and the update transaction UT_1 which updates

y and z is executed between t_2 and t_3. Therefore the execution of MT_1 is serializable since MT_1 reads y which is not updated in this broadcast period. However, in the previous methods, the commit decision of MT_1 is deferred until received an invalidation report from the server. At time B_i, MT_1 receives the invalidation report and makes an abort decision since MT_1 accesses y which is involved in the invalidation report. But, it is an incorrect abort decision.

The biggest problem of invalidation report broadcast methods is that mobile transactions can read data items from theirs cache at any time, even if the data is being updated at the server. But mobile hosts do not know the update occurrence until receiving the invalidation report from the server. Therefore, the execution of mobile transactions have a potential possibility that mobile transactions access the different timing data, namely inconsistent data. In this paper, we propose the BGI-MT(Broadcast Group Information-for Mobile Transaction) method. In our method, a broadcast transaction is executed several times during an invalidation report broadcast period to improve the response time of mobile transactions. Also, a mobile host uses the group information to make a commit decision before receiving the invalidation report.

4 BGI-MT Algorithm

4.1 Discussion on Grouping

In [9], there are many issues that concern data grouping, namely, how data items should be grouped and the size of each group or the number of groups, and so on. In [9], entire database is basically grouped into four categories according to the update rate and the demand rate as shown in Fig.2.

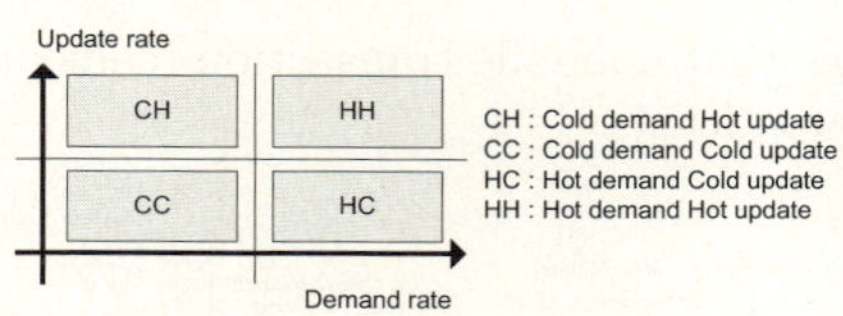

Fig. 2. Basic data group

In Fig.2, the validity of data including in Hot update group, e. g. CH group and HH group is lower than data including in other groups since it is frequently updated. Also, the cache hit ratio of data including in Hot demand group, e. g. HC group and HH group is higher than data including in other groups. Similar to [9], we assume that entire database is basically grouped according to the update rate and the demand rate. Relatively, to improve the cache efficiency of our scheme, data items including in lower update rate group or higher demand rate group are divided into a number of groups. That is to say, the number of groups including HC category is the most, but the number of groups including CH category is the least. Also, additional data groups can be achieved by analyzing information about the past usage patterns with data mining techniques, e. g. association rule[2].

4.2 BGI-MT Method

In BGI-MT, a server broadcasts four types of reports, e. g. the invalidation report, the window report, the data report, and the group report. A server broadcasts the invalidation report $IR(B_i)$ to maintain the cache consistency of mobile hosts where B_i is a time point when the report is broadcast. The invalidation report $IR(B_i)$ is defined as follows.

Definition 1. *Invalidation Report $IR(B_i)$,*

$$IR(B_i) = \{[j, TS(j)] \,|j \in D, and\ B_i - L < TS(j) < B_i\}$$

D is a set of data items in the database, j is an identifier of data item that has been updated in the server during a broadcast period L, and $TS(j)$ is the most recent update timestamp of data j.

A server maintains the update information of data items to prepare for the disconnection of mobile hosts. This update information of data items is defined as the window report. If the window report broadcast interval is N times of the invalidation report interval L, the window report includes the update information of data items during $N \times L$. The window report $WR(B_i)$ is defined as follows.

Definition 2. *Window Report $WR(B_i)$,*

$$WR(B_i) = \{[j, TS(j)] \,|j \in D, and\ B_i - W < TS(j) < B_i\}$$

D is a set of data items in the database, j is an identifier of data item that has been updated in the server during a broadcast period W, and $TS(j)$ is the most recent update timestamp of data j.

In a server, a broadcast transaction collects the data information requested by mobile hosts, and makes a schedule for the next data broadcast. A server broadcasts the data report $DR(B_i)$ where B_i is a time point when data are broadcast. The data report $DR(B_i)$ is defined as follows.

Definition 3. *Data Report $DR(B_i)$,*

$$DR(B_{di}) = \{[j, TS(j)] \,|j \in D\}$$

D is a set of data items in the database, j is a data item that has been requested by mobile hosts during the execution of a broadcast transaction, and $TS(j)$ is the most recent update timestamp of data j.

In our scheme, data items of database are grouped according to the update rate, access rate, and update pattern, and so on. The group report $GR(B_i)$ is defined as follows.

Definition 4. *Group Report $GR(B_i)$,*

$$GR(B_i) = \{[k, TS_l(k)]\,|k \in G\}$$

G is a set of data groups, k is a group identifier of data items that have been updated in the server, and $TS_l(k)$ is the most recent update timestamp about data items of group k.

In our scheme, if the current available bandwidth is sufficient, a server broadcasts the group report with the data report to improve the response time of a mobile transaction. Also, the group report is broadcast with the window report that is composed the most recent update timestamp of entire group to prevent the entire cache dropping. Also, a mobile host MT keeps its read data set $ReadSet(MT)$ as follows, to decide a immediate commit decision of MT.

Definition 5. *$ReadSet(MT)$,*

$$ReadSet(MT) = \{d_1, d_2, ..., d_i \in D(1 \leq i \leq n)\}$$

MT is the mobile host identifier, D is a set of data items in the database, and $d_i(1 \leq i \leq n)$ is the identifier of data items accessed by MT.

If one of the following three types of condition is satisfied, our algorithm makes a commit decision and a mobile host commits its mobile transaction immediately. We assume that B_{IL} is the last broadcast time of an invalidation report and G_{MT} is the list of group including $ReadSet(MT)$.

Immediate Commit Decision Condition
Type 1.All data items in $ReadSet(MT)$ have a equal timestamp.
Type 2.The Timestamps of all data items in $ReadSet(MT)$ are less than B_{IL}.
Type 3.The Timestamps of all data items in $ReadSet(MT)$ are greater than $MAX\{TS_l(j), j \in G_{MT}\}$ or not involved in the group report.

If all data items accessed by a mobile transaction MT have a single timestamp TS_c, it has accessed the snapshot of database at time TS_c. We think that a snapshot of database is consistent. Thus, in the case of Type 1, MT can be immediately committed. In the case of Type 2, MT sees the snapshot of database at time B_{IL}. This means that one of the $ReadSet(MT)$ is cached in the current invalidation report broadcast period, but it is not updated in this period. Thus, in the case of Type 2, MT can be immediately committed. In the case of Type 3, MT sees the latest snapshot of data items. That is to say, MT cached the data items after update transactions have been completed. If each data item in $ReadSet(MT)$ has been cached after the commit of the most recent update transaction, its cache timestamp is bigger than the $MAX\{TS_l(j), j \in G_L\}$.

```
Input:   B_IL : The last broadcast time of an invalidation report
         ReadSet(MT) : The read set of a mobile transaction MT
         G_MT : List of groups including ReadSet(MT)
         TSc(x) : Timestamp of data x in mobile host

Output:  Commit decision of MT

begin
  Step 1: MT executes its all operations
  if ReadSet(MT) has a single timestamp then
     Commit MT;
  else
     Delay the commit decision of MT until receiving the group report;
  endif
  Step 2: MT received the group report from the server
  if G_MT is not included in the group report then
   Commit MT;
  else if TSc(x) of every data x in ReadSet(MT) < B_IL then
     Commit MT;
  else if TSc(x) of every data x in ReadSet(MT) > MAX{[TS_l(G_MT)]} then
     Commit MT;
  else
     Delay the commit decision of MT until receiving an invalidation report;
  endif
end
```

Fig. 3. Commit decision algorithm of BGI-MT

Thus, if Type 3 condition is satisfied, MT sees a consistent snapshot of a database. In BGI-MT, the commit decision of a mobile transaction is shown in Fig.3.

If the execution of a mobile transaction does not satisfy at least one of three types of condition, the commit decision of a mobile transaction is delayed until receiving the invalidation report from the server. Assume that a mobile host MH only has a data item x included group j in its cache. If MH is disconnected and reconnected, MH waits for listening a window report from its server to verify the consistency of cache content. When MH receives a window report, it compares its disconnection period with the broadcast period of the window report. In [1,5], if the disconnection period of MH is greater than the broadcast period of a window report W, MH drops the all cache contents. However, in BGI-MT, if the data timestamp of included group j is bigger than the timestamp $TS_l(j)$ of group report, we can ensure the validity of data items included group j since $TS_l(j)$ means the last update time of data items of included group j. Fig.4 shows an example that the disconnection period of a mobile host is longer than the broadcast period of a window report, but a mobile host avoids discarding the entire cache contents in our scheme.

We assume that data x and y are included in group G_1 and G_2, respectively. Also All update timestamps of G_1 and G_2, e. g. $TS_l(G_1)$ and $TS_l(G_2)$ are t_0 initially. In Fig.4, a mobile host MH_1 sends the request message of data x and y and the server broadcasts the data report containing data x and y at time t_1 and t_2, respectively. Thus, timestamps of x and y in MH_1's cache are all t_0 which is the initial timestamp in a server. Suppose MH_1 disconnects at time t_3 and

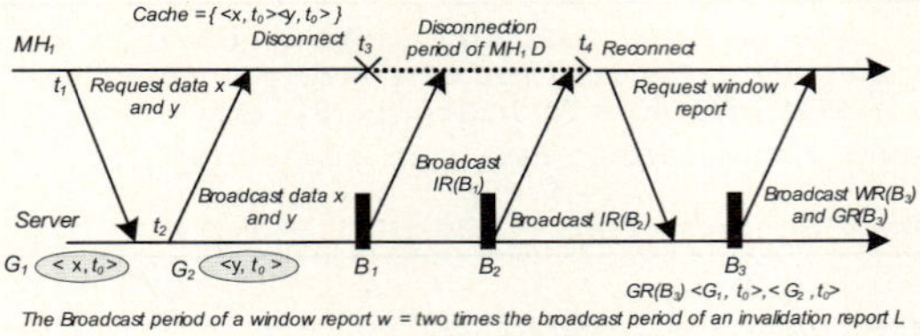

Fig. 4. After disconnection, cache management example

reconnects at time t_4. Also, a server broadcast the invalidation report $IR(B_1)$ and $IR(B_2)$ at time B_1 and B_2(where $t_3 < B_1 < B_2 < t_4$) during disconnection of MH_1(between t_3 and t_4), respectively. Let the period of a window report W is two times the period of an invalidation report L. After reconnection time t_4, MH_1 requests the window report to verify the its cache contents. In our scheme, a server broadcasts the window report $WR(B_3)$ and $GR(B_3)$ at time B_3, and MH_1 verifies its cache validation In BGI-MT, timestamp $TS_l(G_{id})$ of group report means the last update time of data items included group G_{id}. In Fig.4, if data items of group G_1 and G_2 are not updated in the disconnection of MH_1, update timestamps of G_1 and G_2 are t_0. Thus, even if the disconnection period of MH_1 D exceeds the period of a window report W, MH_1 does not drop x and y since their timestamps are equal to the timestamps of group report $TS_l(G_1)$ and $TS_l(G_2)(t_0 = t_0)$, respectively.

5 Analytical Model

In this section, we analyze the response time and the bandwidth usage of mobile transactions. As a comparison baseline, we choose UFO method and OCC-UTS^2 method since two methods ensure the serializable execution of mobile transactions and maintain the cache consistency by receiving the invalidation report and they are similar to our method. Similar to [1,5], we begin by stating some assumptions of our model:

. The server broadcasts an invalidation report per every L seconds.
. Each mobile transaction accesses to n data items in average.
. The access rate of each data item is λ(follow an exponential distribution).
. The update rate of each data item is μ(follow an exponential distribution).
. P_{OCC} and P_{BGI} are the probability that the execution of a mobile transaction meets the immediate commit condition in OCC-UTS^2 and BGI-MT, respectively.
. The average data caching time $MT_{caching}$ for a mobile transaction accessing n data items can be computed with the following equation, is $n \times (1-h) \times (data\ transfer\ time)$.

5.1 Average Response Time of a Mobile Transaction

If the invalidation report is broadcast per every L seconds, the average delay time of a mobile transaction is $\frac{L}{2}$ seconds. In UFO method, the average response time of mobile transactions RT_{UFO} is computed as:

$$RT_{UFO} = MT_{caching} + \frac{L}{2} \tag{1}$$

In OCC-UTS^2 method, we can compute the probability that a mobile transaction leads to a successful commit by immediate validation. In order for a mobile transaction to be committed by immediate validation, data items accessed by a mobile transaction should not be updated, even if cached in current invalidation report period. In OCC-UTS^2 method, the average response time of mobile transactions RT_{OCC} is computed as:

$$RT_{OCC} = MT_{caching} + \frac{L}{2} \times (1 - P_{OCC}) \tag{2}$$

In BGI-MT method, if the execution of a mobile transaction MT meets at least one of the three types of condition, MT is committed immediately. Suppose data items of groups including $ReadSet(MT)$ are not updated at least E_1 seconds or E_2 seconds such as Fig.5.

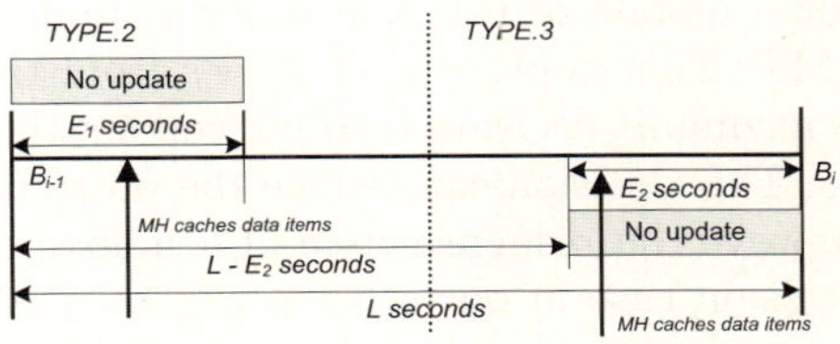

Fig. 5. The reason for response time in BGI-MT

In BGI-MT method, immediate commit condition Type 1 is equal to the immediate commit condition of OCC-UTS^2 method. Fig.5 shows the case that the execution of a mobile transaction meets the immediate commit condition Type 2 or Type 3. In order for a mobile transaction to meet condition Type 2 or Type 3, a mobile transaction should cache data items during E_1 seconds or E_2 seconds, respectively. Assume that cached data items are not updated during E_1 seconds or E_2 seconds, respectively. Thus, we can compute the average response time of mobile transactions in BGI-MT method, RT_{BGI} is computed as:

$$RT_{BGI} = MT_{caching} + \frac{L}{2} \times (1 - P_{BGI}) \tag{3}$$

Based on these analysis, we compute the response time and the commit rate of mobile transactions on various methods. Similar to the parameter setting of [1,5], our analysis is performed based on the scenarios as follows.

Scenario.1
A mobile client access the information, such as weather, stock, location, or traffic information at the rate of $0.1(\lambda = 0.1)$ and this information is changed at the rate of $0.005(\mu = 0.005)$.

Scenario.2
A mobile client access the information at the rate of $0.01(\lambda = 0.01)$ and a mobile transaction access to three data items.

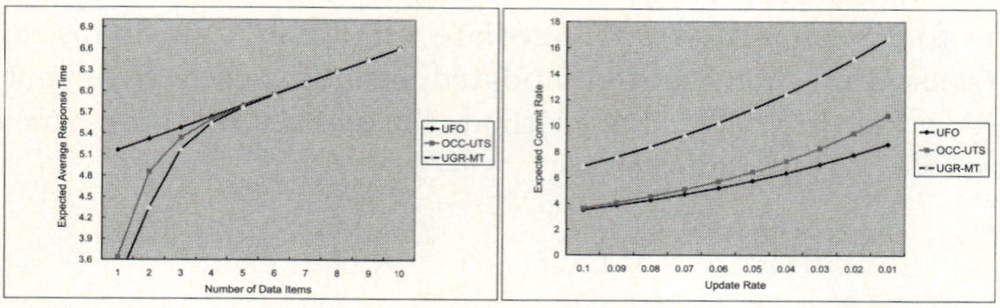

(a) The response time of a mobile transaction (b) The commit rate of a mobile transaction

Fig. 6. The response time and the commit rate on various schemes

From the results shown in Fig.6, we observe that the smaller the number of data items accessed by a mobile transaction n or the update rate μ, the better performance of BGI-MT. This improvement comes from the two points. First, our scheme can make a commit decision before receiving the invalidation report against other schemes. This decision can reduce the possibility of false invalidation and may well improve the response time of a mobile transaction. Second, immediate commit decision case in our scheme will be a great opportunity for transaction waited its verification to reduce the possibility of the incorrect abort decision, such as Fig.1. Incorrect abort decision is a cause that the restart of mobile transactions and limited bandwidth usage are increased and system performance is lower.

5.2 Bandwidth Usage of Our Scheme

In our scheme, a server will broadcast the additional control information e.g. the group report to improve the response time of mobile transactions and the cache efficiency of mobile hosts, against other schemes. This control information may cause the bottleneck of wireless network by increasing the limited bandwidth usage. However, in our scheme, this information is selectively transmitted from the server to mobile hosts if only the current available bandwidth is sufficient. Also, if the size of group report is large, a server will broadcast partially the control information which is particular group-centered e.g. the group of HC category. Thus, the overhead of additional broadcast will not be crucial to the system performance since it is optional control information. Also, our scheme can reduce the false invalidation caused by the disconnection of a mobile host.

In previous schemes, these drawbacks lead to transmit the additional data and increase bandwidth usage, one the other hand our scheme can minimize these problems.

6 Conclusion and Future Work

In this paper, we have proposed a new method for guaranteeing the serializable execution of mobile transactions, called BGI-MT, using the data group information. BGI-MT method for improving the response time of mobile transactions makes a commit decision by using the group information of data items before receiving an invalidation report from the server. Also, our scheme can prevent the entire cache dropping, even though the disconnection of a mobile host is longer than the broadcast interval of a window report. Through the analytical model, we have shown that our method is superior to other methods, in terms of the average response time and the commit rate of mobile transactions. For the future work, we have to study a data grouping method which is an important issue in our scheme, particularly to improve the response time of mobile transactions and to reduce the communication.

References

1. D. Barbara and T. Imielinski, "Sleepers and Workaholics: Caching Strategies in Mobile Environments(Extended Version)," VLDB Journal Vol.4, No.4, pp.567-602, 1995.
2. J. Han, J. Pei, and Y. Yin, "Mining Frequent Patterns without Candidate Generation," In Proc. ACM SIGMOD Conference on Management of Data, pp.1-12, May 2000.
3. S. Kim, S. Yang and S. Lee, "Maintaining Mobile Transactional Consistency in Hybrid Broadcast Environments," ACTA Information Vol.41 pp.65-81, Aug. 2004.
4. K. Lam, M. Au and E. Chan, "Broadcasting Consistent Data to Read-Only Transactions from Mobile Clients," The Computer Journal, Vol.45, No.2, pp.129-146, 2002.
5. S. Lee, "Caching and Concurrency Control in a Wireless Mobile Computing Environments," IEICE Transaction on Information System, Vol.E85-D, No.8, pp.1284-1296, Aug. 2002.
6. J. B. Lim and A. R. Hurson, "Transaction Processing in Mobile, Heterogeneous Database Systems," IEEE Transactions on Knowledge and Data Engineering, Vol.14, No.6, pp.1330-1346, Nov. 2002.
7. C. Lin, H. Hu, and D. Lee, "Adaptive Data Delivery in Wireless Communication Environment," Wireless Networks, Vol.10, pp.103-120, March 2004.
8. N. Prabhu, V. Kumar, I. Ray and G. Yang, "Concurrency Control in Mobile Database Systems," Proc. AINA2004 18th International Conference, Vol.2 pp.83-86, March 2004.
9. K. L. Tan and J. Cai, "Broadcast-Based Group Invalidation : An Energy-Efficient Cache Invalidation Strategy," Information Sciences, Vol.100, pp.229-253, Aug. 1997.

A Fuzzy-Based Service Adaptation Middleware for Context-Aware Computing*

Ronnie Cheung, Jiannong Cao, Gang Yao, and Alvin Chan

Department of Computing, Hong Kong Polytechnic University
{csronnie, csjcao, csgyao, cstschan}@comp.polyu.edu.hk

Abstract. In a mobile environment, it is desirable for mobile applications to adapt their behaviors to the changing context. However, adaptation mechanism may emphasize more on overall system performance, while neglecting the needs of individual. We present a generalized Adaptive Middleware Infrastructure (AMI) to cater for individual needs in a fair manner, while maintaining optimal system performance. Furthermore, due to the vagueness in context nature and uncertainty in context aggregation for adaptation, we propose a Fuzzy-based Service Adaptation Model (FSAM) to achieve generality and improve the effectiveness of service adaptation. By fuzzification of the context and measuring the fitness degree between the current context and the optimal situation, FSAM adopts the most appropriate service. We have evaluated the FSAM inference engine within the middleware AMI by an application Campus Assistant. The performance is analyzed and compared with a conventional threshold-based approach.

Keywords: Middleware infrastructure, fuzzy theory, context-aware, service adaptation, mobile computing.

1 Introduction

In a mobile environment, the variations and constraints of communication and computing resources introduced by the dynamical nature of wireless transmission call for adaptive context-aware applications that can adapt their behaviors to the contexts. In this paper, we present an Adaptive Middleware Infrastructure (AMI), which sits between applications and the operating system [1] [[3]. The fairness among applications and between the high-level applications and the low-level operating system both are taken into account. AMI provides applications with the most suitable service based on predefined policies so as to achieve adaptability to the changing context. It consists of well-defined modules in support of middleware functionalities to improve the generality.

The area of context-aware middleware has attracted many researchers [9]. In system CARISMA [4], the context-aware middleware compares the application

* This project is supported by RGC research grants under Project Ref. No. PolyU 5200/04E and also partially supported by Hong Kong Polytechnic University under the ICRG grant G-YD63.

E. Sha et al. (Eds.): EUC 2006, LNCS 4096, pp. 580–590, 2006.

profile and the current context to evaluate which policy to be adopted. In [5], the functionality of a service code module is adapted on the basis of the estimation of resource usage. However, these systems are problem-specific or focus on software realization while AMI emphasizes a generic reference infrastructure.

The effectiveness of service adaptation to the current context is a another challenge in context-aware computing, due to the vagueness of the context nature from the perspective of human, and the uncertainty in context aggregation when making adaptation decision under the circumstance of multi-dimensional context. Introducing fuzzy techniques is one of promising approaches to deal with these problems.

We formalize a context-aware service adaptation framework and propose a Fuzzy-based Service Adaptation Model (FSAM) [2]. We employ the linguistic variables and membership degrees to carry out the fuzzification of the context situation, so that the vagueness of context can be quantified. The fitness function is developed to produce an overall fitness degree of the current context, corresponding to each predefined policy, in order to adopt the most suitable one for service selection and delivery. The fitness degree is obtained by measuring the distances between the current context and the predefined reference context situation.

Much research has been done on fuzzy-based adaptation. In [6], the authors offer a survey on applying fuzzy theory to adapting QoS requirements in communication networks. In [7], the fuzzy control theory is used for QoS adaptation in distributed multimedia applications. Again, the approaches are usually developed for a specific domain and not targeted at a generic service adaptation model, while FASM deals with application-independent service adaptation.

We implement the AMI along with the FSAM as the inference engine in the Campus Assistant application. The application offers different quality level of chat and email services adaptive to continuously-varying context. The variations of context are simulated to trigger service adaptation. Based on the experiment results, the performance of the fuzzy-based solution is analyzed and compared with the conventional threshold-based context aggregation approach for context-aware adaptation.

2 Adaptive Middleware Infrastructure (AMI)

The Adaptive Middleware Infrastructure (AMI), which allows generic applications to exercise context-awareness [1] [3], aims at the integration of all relevant features and the synergy achieved by a well-established and unified baseline architecture in order to promote the development of context-aware computing.

All the relevant features that AMI integrates include context collection, context composition, context reference engine, context delivery, adaptive middleware services, ToS and QoS enforcement, etc. As shown in Figure 1, the features are embodied in the four major modules in our system:

The first module is the Context Space. It contains Context Detectors, Context Composers and Fuzzy Context Composers that detect and compose low-level contexts into higher level representations. Examples of context detectors could be the wrappers for OS event, an application's computing activities. The fuzzy context composers composite low-level context information, marshalling the dynamic and uncertainty of the environment, and presents the current context in a generic form. For example, a fuzzy context composer could be monitoring all network-related detectors and determine the quality of network connection with the membership degree.

The second module is the Middleware Service Space. This is the execution environment for both Public Middleware Services (one set of services that are sharedamong all applications) and Application Specific Middleware Services (each mobile application has its own set of services). These adaptive middleware services are provided to individual applications under the control of the Fuzzy Inference engine.

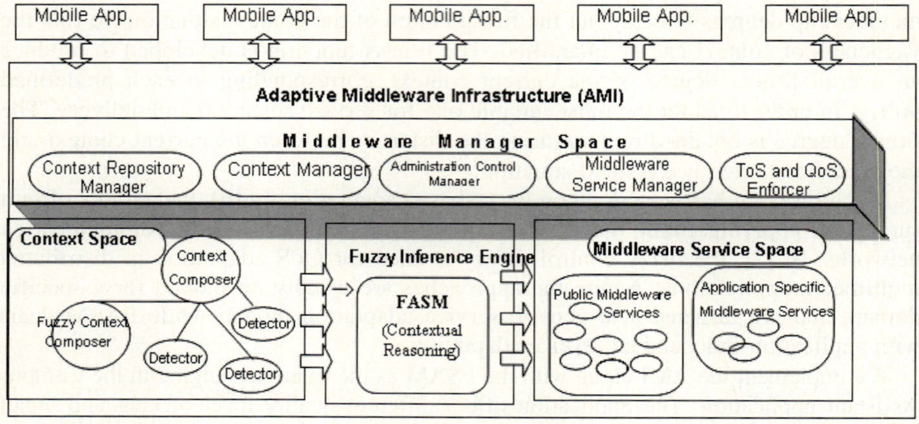

Fig. 1. Adaptive Middleware Infrastructure

The third module is the Fuzzy Inference Engine, which determines the middleware services according to the current context and the requirement of application-specific ToS and QoS. In order to control the middleware services, the fuzzy inference engine is aware of the programmable properties of the middleware service. To adjust quantitative parameters for the middleware services, the fuzzy inference engine calls the corresponding adjustment functions. To switch among the middleware services, the inference engine stops exporting certain services while activate others.

The fourth module is the Middleware Manager Space. The middleware manager space contains five system managers, which coordinates all management operations within the AMI. The Administration Control Manager component manages the admission of mobile applications that subscribe the services of the middleware. The Context Manager controls the runtime environment for the context objects, including the low level context detectors and high level context composers. The Context Repository Manager stores the records on all contextual information, such that queries on context history are possible. The Middleware Service Manager coordinates with admission control. It also allocates and controls the resources for newly subscribed services. The ToS and QoS Enforcer are used for monitoring the ToS and QoS levels for each connected application.

3 Fuzzy-Based Service Adaptation Model (FSAM)

The core component of the AMI is the fuzzy inference engine, which determines service adaptation according to the context derived from the context space. We have developed the Fuzzy-based Service Adaptation Model (FSAM) as the inference engine [2]. FSAM takes the context information and other policy definitions as the input. The output of FSAM is the adaptation decision, which will be used by the middleware service manger to reconfigure services. In this section, first we define the concepts and terminology used in FSAM. Then we introduce the fitness function base on the definitions. Finally, the procedure of decision-making in FSAM is illustrated using the following formulas:

Service: A service is a functionality provided in the application. The service can be delivered at different quality level or with different resource constraints. Let S= $\{s_1, s_2, s_3, \ldots, s_q\}$ $(1 \leq q)$, represent the service set, where s_i $(1 \leq i \leq q)$ represents the *i*-th service.

Policy: A policy is a rule which determines which quality level of service to be delivered based on the context. Let $P_i = \{p_i^1, p_i^2, \ldots, p_i^{mi} \mid i \in [1, q]\}$ be a set of policies, where p_i^j $(1 \leq j \leq m)$ represents the *j*-th policy corresponding to the *i*-th service s_i. m_i is the number of the policy corresponding to s_i.

Context: A context is one of conditions to determine a policy for service selection. Let $C=\{c_1, c_2, \ldots, c_n\}$ be a set of context, where c_i $(1 \leq i \leq n)$ represents the *i*-th context information, *n* is the number of all context.

Context Situation: A Context Situation is the composite context information to represent the context at any given time *t*. It is denoted by a set of 3-element tuples:

$$\mathrm{SI}(t) = \{(c_i, lv_b, \mu_{c_i\, lv_b}(\mathrm{value\_of}(c_i, t)) \mid c_i \in C, i \in [1,n], b \in [1,k]\} \tag{1}$$

where, $c_i (1 \leq i \leq n)$ is a context, $lv_b (1 \leq b \leq k)$ is a linguistic value, $\mu_{c_i\, lv_b}(x) \in [0,1]$ is the predefined membership function for "c_i is lv_b", $value\_of(c_i,t)$ represents the value of context c_i at time *t*.

Standard Reference Depositary: Given a service s_i, with respect to each policy p_i^j $(1 \leq j \leq m)$, we assume that there must exist a specific Context Situation associated with p_i^j. On the basis of the Context Situation, the policy p_i^j is the most suitable policy for service s_i and has to be adopted. Intrinsically, the most suitable policy means a tradeoff between resource constraints in certain context and the service to be delivered. A most suitable Context Situation is referred to Standard Reference Context Situation. We call the aggregation of $\{\mathrm{SR}(p_i^1), \mathrm{SR}(p_i^2), \ldots, \mathrm{SR}(p_i^{mi})\}$, $p_i^j \in P_i$, as the Standard Reference Depositary of P_i and denote it by $\mathrm{SRD}(P_i)$.

$$\mathrm{SR}(p_i^j) = \{(c_i, lv_b, \mu_{c_i\, lv_b}(best\_value\_of(c_i)) \mid c_i \in C, i \in [1,n], lv_b \in LV, b \in [1,k]\} \tag{2}$$

Fitness Function: In practice, a Context Situation at time *t* usually is at certain distance away from any $\mathrm{SR}(p_i^j)$, so we define the Fitness Function to evaluate the Fitness Degree of the Context Situation at time *t* against Standard Reference Context

Situation SR(p_i^j). Given a service s_i, the Fitness Function is the mapping from the Context Situation at time t and Standard Reference Context Situation SR(p_i^j) to the Fitness Degree of policy p_i^j : (FF): SI(t)*SR(p_i^j) $\rightarrow$ FD(p_i^j),

$$\mathrm{FF}(\mathrm{SI}(t), \mathrm{SR}(p_i^j)) = \frac{1}{\sum_{i=1}^{size\_of(SR(p_i^j))} \left|\mu(best\_value\_of(c_i)) - \mu(value\_of(c_i,t))\right|^{l_i}} \tag{3}$$

where $size\_of(SR(p_i^j))$ represents the number of tuples in SR(p_i^j), $\mu(x)$ is the membership function appears in i-th vector, l_i is a natural number.

In function (3), the denominators are for the calculation of the distance between SI(t) and SP(p_i^j). After obtaining the fuzzy distance, we calculate the reciprocal to obtain the Fitness Degree. When $l_i=1$, the function uses Hamming Distance; when $l_i=2$, the function uses Euclidean Distance, both are classical methods for calculating fuzzy distance between two statuses [8]. When $l_i=3$, we regard l_i as a weight value for a context, which can be adjusted by individual application to affect policy choice.

4 Implementation and Evaluation

In this section, we implement the FSAM model as the contextual inference engine within the AMI in a hypothetic application Campus Assistant.

4.1 Application Campus Assistant

The Campus Assistant is a mobile context-aware application running on mobile platforms. Through the wireless network, the Campus Assistant enables the user to communicate with each other in real time, or retrieve and send emails by offering Chat and Email services. Due to the spatial and temporal variations of wireless communication and computing resources, the Campus Assistant tries to detect the changing context and deliver the different quality level of service, in order to maintain an acceptable level of perception when the resources available become inadequate.

Such adaptation is predefined by certain rules, i.e. policies in the system. The Chat service has three policies: textChat, voiceChat and videoChat. The Email service has five policies: headMail, fullMail, encryptedMail, bigMail and encryptedBigMail. Each policy is corresponding to a certain quality level of service. The context can have many aspects due to the multidimensional characteristics, including communication, computing, geographical, organizational, etc. To simplify the context analysis, only Network_maxRate, CPU_clockRate, Network_delay, RAM_freeSpace are taken in account in our case. The characteristics of vagueness and subjectivity in context are handled by the aforementioned fuzzy-based inference engine FSAM.

4.2 FSAM Configuration and Procedures

Corresponding to FSAM theoretic framework, we assume that the inference engine with the following configurations in the application.

Service: S = {chat, email}, i.e. S_1=chat and S_2= email

Policies: P_1 = {textChat, voiceChat, videoChat},

P_2 = {headMail, fullMail, encryptedMail, bigMail, encryptedBigMail}

Context: C={Network_maxRate,CPU_clockRate,Network_delay,RAM_freeSpace}

Context Situation: 4-element tuples

SI(t)={(Network_maxRate, high, $\mu_{\text{Network\_maxRate high}}$ (value_of(Network_maxRate, t))),
(CPU_clockRate, high, $\mu_{\text{CPU\_clockRate high}}$ (value_of (CPU_clockRate, t))),
(Network_delay, low, $\mu_{\text{Network\_delay low}}$ (value_of (Network_delay, t))),
(RAM_freeSpace, high, $\mu_{\text{RAM\_freeSpace high}}$ (value_of (RAM_freeSpace, t)))}

Membership Functions: context c_i ($i=1,2,3,4$), application-specific and produced from releateddomains

$$C_1=\begin{cases} 0 & B<1\text{Kbps} \\ \dfrac{\log_{10} B/1k}{5} & 1k\leq B\leq 100\text{Mbps} \\ 1 & B>100\text{Mbps} \end{cases} \quad (4)$$

Fig. 2. Network_maxRate high membership function

$$C_3=\begin{cases} 0 & T>1000\text{ms} \\ 1-\dfrac{\log_{10} T/0.1}{4} & 0.1\leq T\leq 1000\text{ms} \\ 1 & T<0.1\text{ms} \end{cases} \quad (5)$$

Fig. 3. Network_delay low membership function

$$C_2=\begin{cases} 0 & F<2\text{MHz} \\ \dfrac{\log_{10} F/2M}{3} & 2M\leq F\leq 2\text{GHz} \\ 1 & F>2\text{GHz} \end{cases} \quad (6)$$

Fig. 4. CPU_clockRate high membership function

$$C_4=\begin{cases} 0 & R<50\text{KB} \\ \dfrac{\log_{10} R/50k}{4} & 50k\leq R\leq 500\text{MB} \\ 1 & R>500\text{MB} \end{cases} \quad (7)$$

Fig. 5. RAM_freeSpace high membership function

Standard Reference Context Situation: As in Table 1, the most suitable values of context corresponding to each policy is predefined.

Table 1. Standard Reference Context Situation

	Network_max Rate(kbps)	CPU_clock Rate(MHz)	Network_ delay(ms)	RAM_free Space(KB)
textChat (p_1^1)	4	20	500	0.2
voiceChat (p_1^2)	200	300	10	4
videoChat (p_1^3)	10000	1000	0.2	200
headMail (p_2^1)	2	4	n/a	0.2
fullMail (p_2^2)	10	10	n/a	0.4
encryptedMail (p_2^3)	10	100	n/a	10
bigMail (p_2^4)	500	50	n/a	2
encryptedBigMail (p_2^5)	500	1000	n/a	100

Standard Reference Depository: Based on Table 1 and membership functions, the SRD(P$_1$') and SRD(P$_2$') are determined as in Table 2.

Table 2. SRD(P'$_1$)and SRD(P'$_2$)

		Network_max Rate High	CPU_clock Rate High	Network_ delay Low	RAM_free Space High
SRD(P'$_1$)	SR(p_1^1)	0.12	0.33	0.08	0.15
	SR(p_1^2)	0.46	0.72	0.50	0.48
	SR(p_1^3)	0.80	0.90	0.92	0.90
SRD(P'$_2$)	SR(p_2^1)	0.06	0.10	n/a	0.15
	SR(p_2^2)	0.20	0.23	n/a	0.23
	SR(p_2^3)	0.20	0.57	n/a	0.58
	SR(p_2^4)	0.54	0.47	n/a	0.40
	SR(p_2^5)	0.54	0.90	n/a	0.83

With the configuration, we initiate the reasoning and decision-making procedures in FSAM. First we use the membership functions to map the current context into the Context Situation. Then, by substiting the values of the current context SRD(P_1) and SRD(P_2) into the Fitness Function formula (3) to compute the fitness degrees. E.g.

$$FF(SI(t),SR(P_1^1)=1/((0.12-\mu_{\text{Network\_maxRate } high}(\text{value\_of(Network\_maxRate, t)})^3$$
$$+ (0.33 - \mu_{\text{CPU\_clockRate high}}(\text{value\_of(CPU\_clockRate, t)})^3$$
$$+ (0.8- \mu_{\text{Network\_delay low}}(\text{value\_of(Network\_delay, t)})^3$$
$$+ (0.15- \mu_{\text{RAM\_freeSpace low}}(\text{value\_of(RAM\_freeSpace, t)})^3)$$

Finally, regarding each service, the policy $P_{suitable}$ which has the maximum fitness degree will be the most suitable one to be adopted. For chat service: $P_{suitable}$=Max {FF(SI(t), SR(P_1^1)), FF(SI(t), SR(P_1^2)), FF(SI(t), SR(P_1^3))}; For email service: $P_{suitable}$=Max {FF(SI(t), SR(P_2^1)), FF(SI(t),SR(P_2^2)), FF(SI(t),SR(P_2^3)), FF(SI(t),SR(P_2^4)), FF(SI(t),SR(P_2^5)).

4.3 Evaluation

We simulate the variations of the changing context by means of generating multiple sets of 4-element tuples (Network_maxRate, CPU_clockRate, Network_delay, RAM_freeSpace). The 4-element tuples are fed into the FASM inference engine in a time-series manner. Since the network bandwidth and network delay play a significant role in affectomg the performance of applications hosted in a mobile device, we produce two segments of changing network bandwidth and delays to simulate the varying of wireless communication to trigger the adaptation in a severely fluctuating manner. As in Figure 6 and Figure 7, 160 sets of tuples are generated.

For the purpose of evaluation, a conventional threshold-based context aggregation and service adaptation approach is also implemented in the Campus Assistant application as the inference engine. Similar to the VDS system by Cristian Koliver et al in [6], a formula of QoS parameter aggregation is offered and addressed. Since the QoS parameters constitute a subset of context, so we apply the formula to the field of context-aware service adaptation.

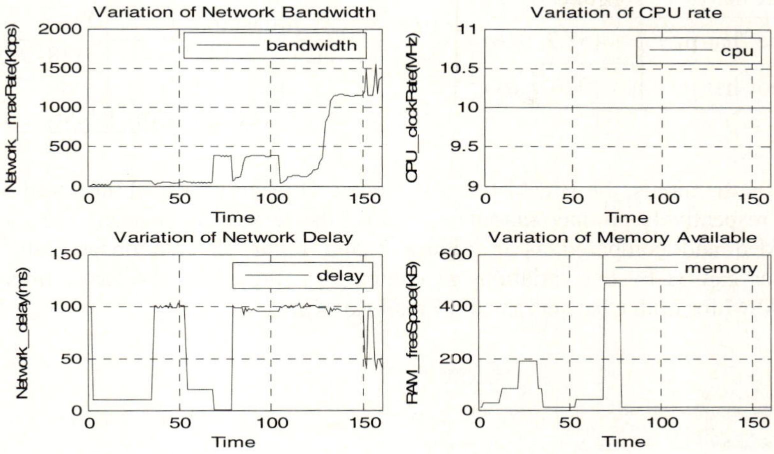

Fig. 6. Variation of contexts

A service adaptation mode M is defined by the formula: $M = (f_1 w_1 + f_2 w_2 +\ldots+ f_i w_i)$, where f_i denotes the adaptation factor of each context. w_i represents the weight for each context, where $i=\{1,2,3,4\}$, and is employed to adjust the influence on adaptation of each context. It alleviates the compensation between different contexts as well. According to the predefined association between mode M and policy, the right policy will be adopted to deliver the suitable service based on the context at a given time t. When mapping context c_i to its adaptation factor: $f_{i,}=s_i c_i$, where $c_i \in C_i$, $i=\{1,2,3,4\}$ s_i is the scaling factor to scale $f_{i,}$ to a normalized range. C_i = [min, max] determines a valid range for each context, where min is the lower bound and max is the upper bound. If the context is beyond the range of $C_{i,}$ it will be rejected and ignored. In our implementation, the specific values are congfigured as follows:

Context: c_i={Network_maxRate,CPU_clockRate,Network_delay,RAM_freeSpace}
Weight: w_i=1, to match the FSAM setting; Scaling Factor: s_i=1;
Adaptation Factor: $f_i=c_{i,}$ where $i=\{1,2,3,4\}$;

For chat service: $M=c_1/c_3+c_2+c_4$, since the context Network_maxRate and Network_delay are relevant; For email service: $M=c_1+c_2+c_4$, since each context are independent; For either chat or email service, the thresholds are heuristic and produced in the following Table 3 and Table 4. Similar to the fuzzy-based FASM, the threshold-based inference engine produces the adaptation mode M. The policy corresponding to M will be adopted as the current adaptation strategy.

Table 3. Thresholds of adaptation mode for Chat service

Chat Policies	M
textChat(p_1^1)	[*min*, 53.2)
voiceChat(p_1^2)	[53.2, 926)
videoChat(p_1^3)	[926, *max*)

Table 4. Thresholds of adaptation mode for Email service

Email Policies	M
headMail (p_2^1)	[*min*, 15.2)
fullMail (p_2^2)	[15.2, 38)
encryptedMail (p_2^3)	[38, 98)
bigMail (p_2^4)	[98, 496)
encryptedBigMail(p_2^5)	[496, *max*)

Based on the inputs, the FASM fuzzy engine and the conventional threshold-based approach respectively produce outputs to control the service adaptation. The outputs are recorded and compared as in Figure 7 and Figure 8. We observe that the fluctuations caused by the variations of context are filtered by the fuzzy inference engine FASM for both Chat service and Email service.

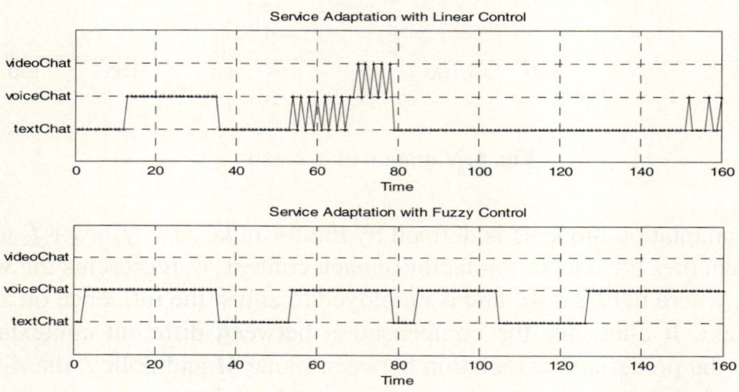

Fig. 7. Chat service adaptation

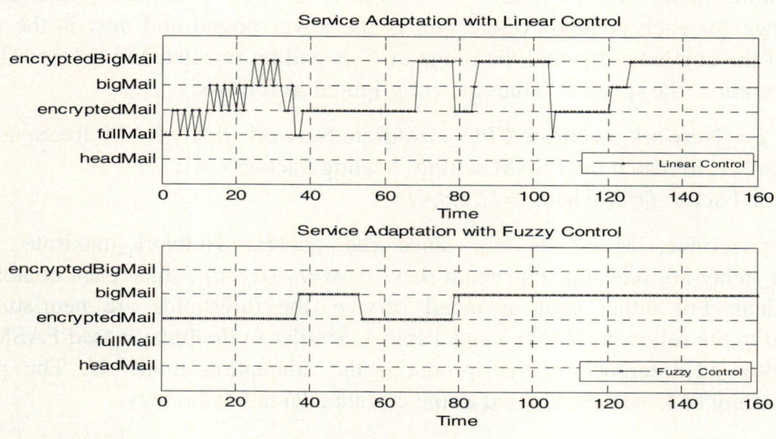

Fig. 8. Email service adaptation

In contrast, the threshold-based inference engine appears to be transparent to the variations. Particularly, regarding to the latter, in the situation of severely fluctuations of context changing, the service adaptation becomes unstable and keep changing accordingly. This phenomenon is called jitter and the jitters may lead to unbearable deterioration of service quality no matter the policy adopted is suitable to the context or not. From the perspective of microeconomics, it would not be difficult to observe that the adaptation curves by FASM are relatively smoother than those by threshold-based approach. This means the fuzzy-based solution has a better tolerance to the variations of context, which leads to the improvement of effectiveness of the service adaptation

As in Figure 9, it would not be difficult to conclude that the complexity of the approach majorly depends on the membership functions defined in FASM according to the procedures described earlier. Nevertheless, the membership functions are application-specific and relevant to particular scenarios. In our implementation, the computational cost of FASM inference engine and the conventional threshold-based approach are calculated in terms of running time. Due to the limits of the timer accuracy of the soft clock in the Windows operating system, we record the computation time in the unit of 20 service adaptations rather than once. As in Figure 9, the conventional threshold-based approach occupies very low machine time because of its linear characteristics. The computation time of the FASM engine varies, but the maximum is below 150 milliseconds. This is acceptable for most applications even in real-time scenarios.

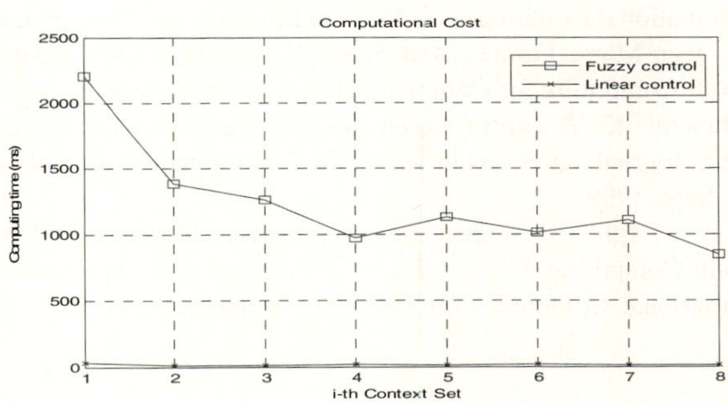

Fig. 9. Computational cost

5 Conclusion and Future Work

In this paper, we introduce a generic middleware infrastructure AMI. A fuzzy-based service adaptation model FSAM is developed as inference engine within AMI. We formalize a framework by fuzzification of the context and measuring the fitness degree of the current context. The policy with the maxium degree will be adopted. We verify the effectiveness of FSAM compared to a conventional threshold-based approach based on the simulation results.

Since the Context Repository module in AMI maintains a historic record of context, the service adaptation can be not only reflective to the current context, but also be adaptive to the predictable future context. We consider the context prediction as the extension of the context-awareness in the time domain. The incorporation of context prediction would efficiently increase the effectiveness and reduce the response time.

References

1. Ronnie Cheung, "An Adaptive Middleware Infrastructure for Mobile Computing", Proceedings of 14th WWW2005 Conference, pp. 996-997, ACM Press, 2005
2. Jiannong Cao, Na Xing, Alvin T.S Chan, Yulin Feng, Beihong Jin, "rvice Adaptation Using Fuzzy Theory in Context-aware Mobile Computing Middleware", Proceedings of the 11th IEEE International Conference on Embedded and Real-Time Computing Systems and Applications, pp. 496-501, 2005
3. Ronnie Cheung, "An Adaptive Middleware Infrastructure Incorporating Fuzzy Logic for Mobile Computing", in Proceedings of the International Conference on Next Generation Web Services Practices, IEEE Computer Society Press, pp 449-451 Korea, 2005
4. Capra, L., Emmerich, W., Mascolo, C.,"CARISMA: context-aware reflective middleware system for mobile applications", IEEE Transactions on Software Engineering, Volume: 29, Issue: 10, pp.929 – 945, Oct. 2003
5. Vivien Wai-Man Kwan, Francis Chi-Moon Lau, Cho-Li Wang, "Functionality adaptation: a context-aware service code adaptation for pervasive computing environments", Proceedings of IEEE/WIC International Conference on Web Intelligence, pp.358 – 364, Oct. 2003
6. Cristian Koliver, Jean-Marie Farines, and Klara Nahrstedt, "QoS Adaptation Based on Fuzzy Theory" Soft Computing for Communications, Springer-Verlag, pp. 245–267, 2004
7. Baochun Li, Nahrstedt, K.,"A control-based middleware framework for quality-of-service adaptations" IEEE Journal on Selected Areas in Communications, Volume: 17, Issue: 9 pp. 1632 – 1650, Sept. 1999
8. Constantin A. "Fuzzy Logic and Neuro-Fuzzy Applications Explained", Prentice Hall, 1995
9. Capra, L., "Mobile Computing Middleware for Context-Aware Applications" Proceedings of the 24th International Conference on Software Engineering, pp.723 – 724, 19-25 May 2002

Next Generation Mobile Service Environment and Evolution of Context Aware Services

JungSook Bae[1], Jae Yong Lee[2], Byung Chul Kim[2], and Seungwan Ryu[3]

[1] Mobile Telecommunications Research Division, ETRI 161 Gajong-Dong, Yusung-Gu, Taejon 305-350, Korea
[2] Department of Information and Communications Engineering, ChungNam National University, Korea
[3] Department of Information Systems, Chung-Ang University, Korea
jsbae@etri.re.kr, {jyl, byckim}@cnu.ac.kr, rush2384@cau.ac.kr

Abstract. Context aware service which provides best suitable services for a user by analyzing user's needs and situational information, will be one of the promising next generation (NG) mobile services. In this paper, we propose the NG mobile service environment based on the NG mobile service platform and evolutional phases of context aware services in the NG mobile service environment. We then introduce the Context Aware Follow-me (CAF) service developed as a prototype of promising NG context aware mobile service followed by introduction of testbed system developed to investigate feasibility of the CAF service.

Keywords: Next Generation Mobile Service, Next Generation Mobile Service platform, Context Aware Service.

1 Introduction

The next generation (NG) mobile communication aims at the support of high speed data rate and the convergence of various networks such as 2G and 3G wireless, WLAN, WPAN, DAB and DVB[1,2]. Also, the vision of NG mobile telecommunications has a thread of connection to the concept of ubiquitous computing networks where anyone is able to circulate all kinds of information or contents without restrictions on time, location, device, and data rate [3,4]. Therefore, in the NG mobile communications it will be possible to make a communication community having no restriction on time and location, and thus context awareness will be realized using various sensors and devices and related technologies under such ubiquitous NG mobile communications environment. By such context awareness, context aware service which provides best suitable services for a user by analyzing user's needs and situational information will be one of the promising NG mobile services [5].

In contrast to existing mobile services provided mainly by network operators, NG mobile services are expected to be provided by many mobile service providers, called the third party service providers, other than network operators. Under such NG

E. Sha et al. (Eds.): EUC 2006, LNCS 4096, pp. 591 – 600, 2006.

mobile service environment, the mobile service platform offers various means of connecting users and service providers will play a very important role in supporting various future mobile services not only for service providers to provide services effectively but also for users to use services easily.

In this paper, we propose the architecture and functions of the NG mobile service platform and evolutional phases of context aware services in the NG mobile service environment. We classify evolutional phases based on ranges of context information and evolutional trend of telecommunication technologies and networking environment in the NG mobile communication environment. Then, we propose the Context Aware Follow-me (CAF) service as a prototype context aware service that will be provided in NG mobile communication environment. The CAF service is designed to support seamless mobility of user service by domain federation and provides optimized service based on various context information such as user's location and preference, capability of devices located around a user, and characteristics of services in use.

This paper is organized as follows. In next section, the NG mobile service environment is described with the focus on the NG service platform. In section 3, four evolutional phases of context aware services are proposed. In section 4, design concept, scenario, an overall system architecture, a prototype test-bed system and example service flow of CAF service are presented. Finally, we conclude this paper in section 5.

2 Next Generation Mobile Service Environment

In the next generation (NG) mobile service environment, the mobile service platform will play a very important role in supporting various future mobile services not only for service providers to provide services effectively but also for users to use services easily. Figure 1 describes architecture and functions of the NG mobile service platform.

In order to provide NG mobile services, a mobile service platform should have various functionalities such as service provisioning function *(SPF)*, context processing function *(CPF)*, service session management function *(SSMF)*, and security function *(SF)*. *SPF* is responsible for registration and management of various context aware services. In addition, based on context information provided from CPF, SPF provides the best suitable context aware service to a user through service generation procedure where candidate services for a user are found, composed and adapted to the service environment existing around the user. *CPF* stores crude context information collected by various context collectors in a standard format and infers useful context service information that can be directly used for service provisioning. *SSMF* is responsible for establishment of a session for service between a user and a service provider as well as service mobility for seamless service provisioning regardless of user's location and movement. *SF* is responsible for authentication and admission of services and other security related tasks during service provision period.

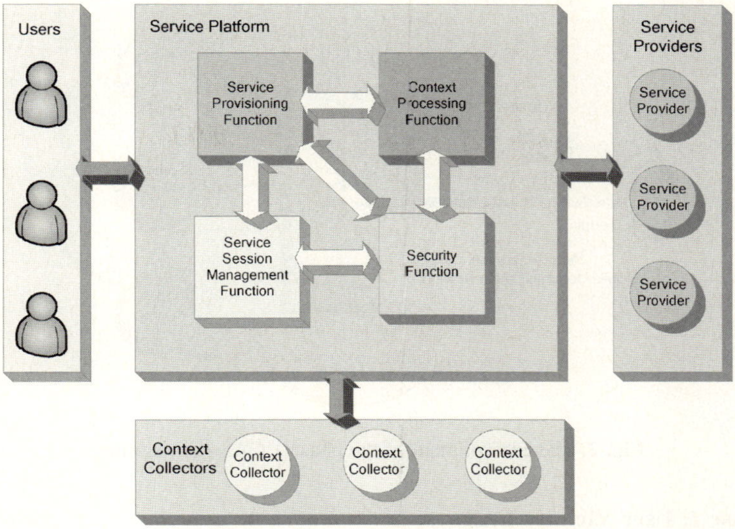

Fig. 1. A NG mobile service platform

3 Evolutional Phases of Context Aware Service

We classify the provision of context aware service (CAS) into four evolutional phases based on ranges of context information and evolutional trend of telecommunication technologies and networking environment in the next generation (NG) mobile service environment.

3.1 Phase 1: User Input Based CAS

The phase 1 *user input based CAS* uses context information inputted by a user through intelligent mobile terminals or generated in mobile terminals or mobile communication system during service provisioning. Context information used in this phase is time, schedule information, user status, user information such as the phone number and address, user activities such as meeting, eating and resting, caller information, and network information.

Figure 2 shows environment and traffic flows for the phase 1 CAS provisioning. The phase 1 CAS is provided by following procedure. A user requests services based on available service list offered by wide area service platform via mobile communication network. At this moment, context information collected by the mobile terminal is transferred to the wide area service platform with the service request. Then the service platform selects a suitable service provider based on registration information of the user and the received context information, and supports service traffic delivery between a user and the selected service provider.

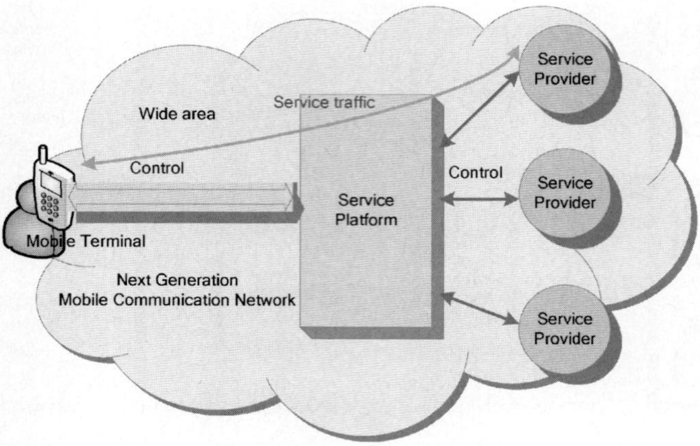

Fig. 2. The environment of the phase 1 CAS provisioning

3.2 Phase 2: User Vicinity CAS

Due to development of sensor technologies, various sensors are embedded in an intelligent mobile terminal and ambience context information such as physical, location, and environmental information around a user is collected. The phase 2 *user vicinity CAS* is provided by combining such ambient information with context information obtained for phase 1 services.

Figure 3 shows environment and traffic flows for the phase 2 CAS provisioning.

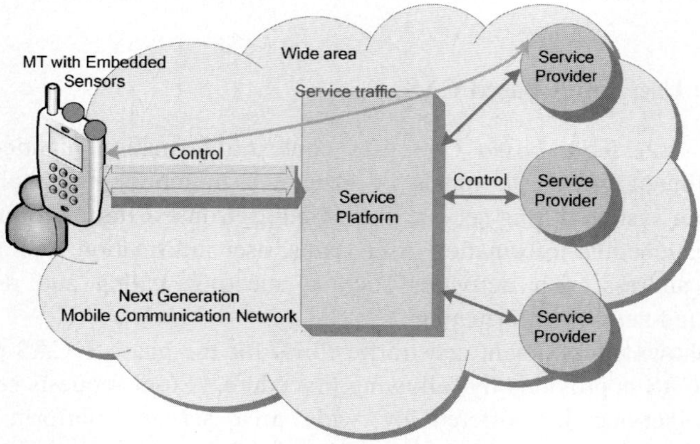

Fig. 3. The environment of the phase 2 CAS provisioning

The phase 2 CAS provisioning procedure is almost same as that of phase 1 except the fact that range of context information is expanded to measured user context information and ambient information.

3.3 Phase 3: Intra-domain CAS

In phase 3 *Intra-domain CAS*, with advent of short range communication technologies, introduction of sensor networking, and penetration of intelligent appliance devices having communication and computing ability, range of context-awareness will be expanded. And, specific services provided within a local area where a user is located will be appeared. In addition, since CAS will be provided via not only the user's mobile terminal but also other best suitable devices based on user's preference, service mobility will be accomplished.

Figure 4 shows environment and traffic flows for the phase 3 CAS provisioning.

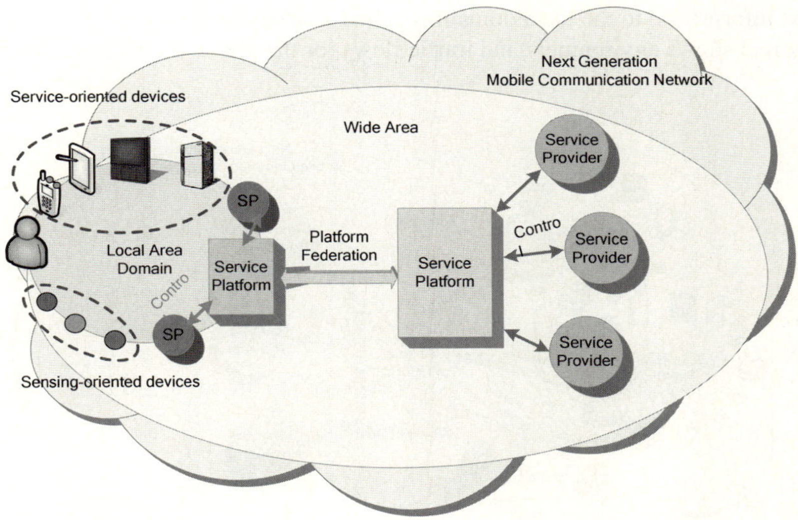

Fig. 4. The environment of the phase 3 CAS provisioning

In phase 3 CAS, it will be used that context information collected by sensing-oriented and service-oriented devices located in close proximity of the user in addition to other collected context information defined in phase 1 and 2. Sensing-oriented devices collect ambience information of a specific area, body status information of human and animals, and necessary physical characteristics for living, whereas service-oriented devices like information appliances collect device information such as device availability and device capability and other context information obtained while serving. A service platform located within a local domain, called a *local service platform (LSP)*, stores and manages context information collected from sensing and service oriented devices. The LSP also manages information about services provided within a domain. In this phase, when a user selects a CAS, one of two possible types of CASs, a local domain CAS and a wide area CAS, is provided according to user's selection of service and its coverage. If the selected service can be supported by using context information stored and managed at a LSP, a local domain CAS will be provided. Conversely, if it is required to provide a wide area CAS, related context information stored and managed at a LSP is transferred to the *wide area service platform (WSP)* so that the WSP can provide suitable CAS by means of federation between the LSP and the WSP.

3.4 Phase 4: Global CAS

In the phase 4 *Global CAS*, the range of context-awareness will be expanded to all domains based on all IP networking environment of NG mobile communication and standardized context information transmission method between service platforms. In this paper, for the convenience, the domain where the user is located is called the *local domain*, and other domain where the user is not located but transmits various context information to the local domain is called *remote domains*.

Figure 5 shows environment and traffic flows for the phase 4 CAS provisioning.

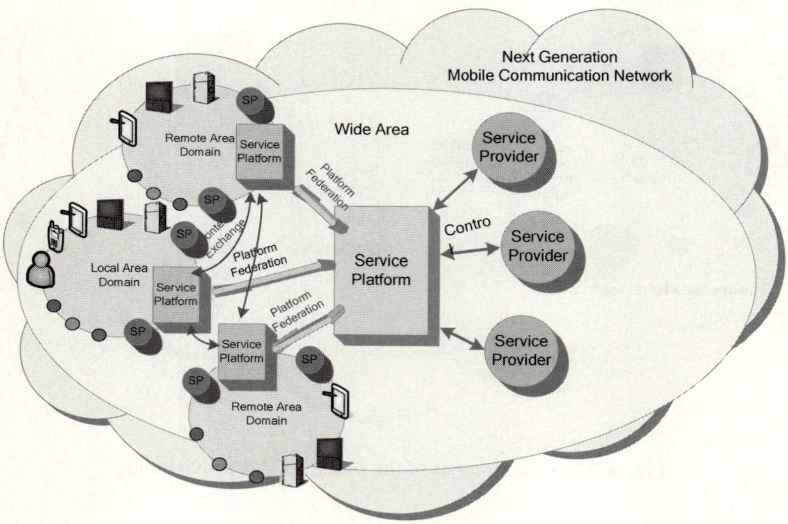

Fig. 5. The environment of the phase 4 CAS provisioning

Under such environment, a user can control a remote domain or get various information about emergency, urgency, or concerning information from remote domains. In addition, a user can get an efficient and customized CAS by means of federation with other services provided in remote domains. Context information is directly exchanged between local domains with assistant of the wide area service platform for interconnection, federation and control of such inter-domain activities. In other words, a user can search information of remote domains authorized to use and selects a remote domain among them to get service and context information from it. Then the wide area service platform gives the selected remote domain an order to send required service and context information the local domain where the user is located. Finally, the local domain gets required information from the remote domain.

4 The Context Aware Follow-Me Service

4.1 Concepts and Scenario

In this paper, we propose the *Context Aware Follow-me (CAF)* service developed as a prototype next generation (NG) context aware mobile service. CAF service is designed for providing optimal services using best suitable devices based on user's location and preference, capability of available devices and characteristics of services in use. CAF service provides service features such as context awareness, service mobility, service personalization, service adaptation.

A possible service scenario of the CAF service is given below.

- Tom is driving a car on the way home. He takes French lesson using the mobile foreign language lesson service. Since he is driving, he takes lesson only in audio sound mode. After arriving home, Tom gets out of the car, but the lesson is continued via his mobile terminal with giving audio and video mode services simultaneously. As soon as he enters living room the lesson service is shifted to a TV. After finishing French lesson, Tom begins taking a bath. When he is in bath room, Jain calls him, and the call is forwarded to a smart mirror equipped in bath room only with voice mode. When the bath is over, the call is shifted to his mobile terminal with giving voice and video mode simultaneously.

4.2 System Architecture

The system for the CAF service is divided into the indoor domains and the outdoor service area.

Each domain is consisting of several elements such as a service platform, a location server, location management systems, a media adaptation server and smart devices.

Functions of each system element are as follows.

- A service platform manages service information within its domain area, identifies and authorizes a user, collects context information about users and service devices, and provides optimized services via best suitable devices by controlling session and mobility.
- A location management system detects the user's current location.
- A location server identifies user's current location.
- A media adaptation server trans-codes media to be suitable to the selected intelligent device and, vise versa.
- A smart device has communication capability with system elements in domain and multimedia service support capability.
- A mobile terminal can support multi radio access technologies such as CDMA, WLAN and WPAN.

4.3 The Test-Bed System for CAF Service

In order to investigate feasibility of the CAF service, we developed a test-bed system. As shown in Figure 6, the test-bed system consists of two domains such as a car

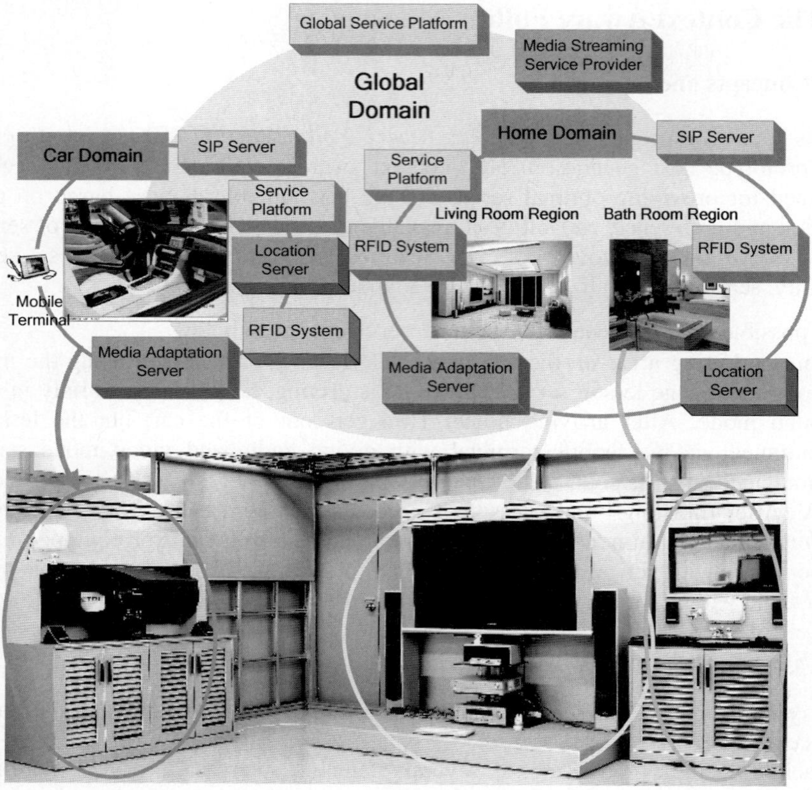

Fig. 6. Test-bed system for the CAF service

domain, and a home domain, and outdoor area in addition to a mobile terminal that can roam those domains. In each domain, location systems are based on RFID.

4.4 Service Flow in Test-Bed System

Figure 7 presents a sample CAF service flow for a specific situation when a user enters home from outdoors domain while using the VOD service via his mobile terminal and show how the CAF service is provided in this situation. We describe message flows among service elements such as the mobile terminal (MT), the outdoor service platform, the home domain service platform, the location server (LS), the media adaptation server (MAS), the smart home theater system (SHTS), the smart mirror (SM) and the VOD service provider.

The home domain service platform collects device related context information such as the device location, the device capability and the availability from service devices exist in the home domain. When Tom and his MT are recognized, the home domain service platform transfers service platform information to the MT with executing authorization procedure for Tom. If the authorization is succeeded, the MT reports the

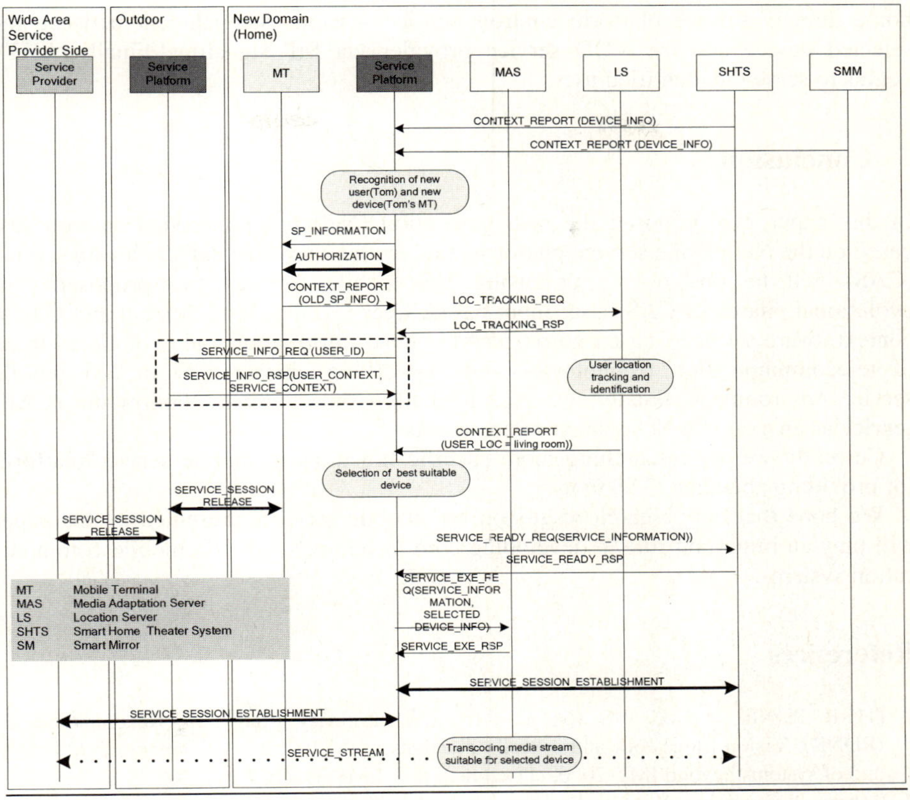

Fig. 7. The CAF service flow in test-bed system

context information such as information of the latest connected service platform (outdoor service platform). The home domain service platform requests context information of the identified user stored in the outdoor service platform. Upon receiving such request from the home domain service platform, the outdoor service platform delivers context information such as services in use, user profile and preferences, and other context information and controls service session release between the MT and the VOD service provider. At the same time, the home domain service platform requests location tracking information of Tom to the LS. Since the LS detects that Tom enters living room, it informs the current location and location tracking information of Tom to the home domain service platform. Then, based on collected context information such as user's current location, user's profile and preference, device information and service information, the home domain service platform selects the SHTS as the best suitable service device. Then, the home domain service platform delivers service information to the SHTS to make it ready for service. At the same time, the home domain service platform delivers information about service and selected device as well as requests for streaming media code transformation to the MAS to give the SHTS optimal service environment. Then, the home domain service platform controls service session establishment between the selected device and the VOD service provider via SIP signaling. Finally, SHTS begins to serve the identified user.

5 Conclusion

In this paper, we proposed the next generation (NG) mobile service environment based on the NG mobile service platform. And, with a view that context aware service (CAS) will be one of the promising NG mobile services, we proposed four evolutional phases of CAS, User input based, User vicinity, Intra-domain and Global context aware services, based on ranges of context information and evolutional trend of telecommunication technologies and networking environment in NG mobile service environment. Finally, we presented the Context Aware Follow-me (CAF) service as an example NG context aware service.

Currently we are researching more specific functions of mobile service platform for providing abundant CAS to user.

We hope that our research results on NG mobile services presented in this paper will play an important role in developing core technologies of NG mobile communication systems.

References

1. ITU-R PDNR M.[IMT-VIS (641-E R15)], "Preliminary draft new Recommendation (PDNR): Vision framework and overall objectives of the future development of IMT-2000 and of systems beyond IMT-2000," Document 8F/TEMP/316-E, 4 Jun. 2002.
2. Robert Berezdivin, Robert Breinig, and Randy Topp, "Next-Generation Wireless Communications Concepts and Technologies," IEEE Communicaions Magazine, 40(3), pp. 108-116, March, 2002.
3. S. Ryu and D. Oh and G. Shin and K. Han and S. Hwang and S. Park: "Research Activities on the Next Generation Mobile Communications and Services in Korea," IEEE Communicaions Magazine, 43(9), pp. 122–131, September, 2005.
4. S. Arbanowski and P. Ballon and K. David and O. Droegehorn and H. Eertink and W. Kellerer and H. Kranenburg and K. Raatikainen and R. Popescu-Zeletin: "I-centric Communications: Personalization, Ambient Awareness, and Adaptability for Future Mobile Services," IEEE Communicaions Magazine, 42(10), pp. 63–69, September, 2004.
5. J. Bae and J. Ha and S. Yoon and S. Kim: "A Ubiquitous Health Care Service Based on Multi-Agent Technology: Art Therapy Service," Proceedings of World Telecommunications Congress, October, 2004.

Efficient Routing Protocol Using Virtual Connection and Load Balancing for Network Mobility

SungHo Kim and Sunshin An

Computer Network Lab., Dep. Of Electronics Engineering, Korea University
Sungbuk-gu, Anam-dong 5ga 1, Seoul, Korea, Post Code: 136-701,
Phone: +82-2-925-5377; Fax: +82-2-3290-3674
{shkim, sunshin}@dsys.korea.ac.kr

Abstract. Internet users are increasingly becoming more and more demanding, expecting Internet access anytime, anywhere, making ubiquitous, next generation networks a requirement. Uninterrupted connection, even in the case of moving networks, is expected. It is important for a vehicle network to reduce signaling traffic in wireless channels and have fast handover. To achieve these requirements, in this paper, a MRP based rouging scheme for network mobility, is proposed. In order to achieve fast handover, a candidate FA if found, which a mobile network is attached to, making an initial virtual connection to a Mobile Router (MR). In addition, the throughput of a wireless channel is upgraded, by reducing signaling traffic through load balancing. The performance of the proposed scheme is evaluated through a series of simulations using Network Simulator (ns-2).

Keywords: FA(Foreign Agent), HA(Home Agent), MNN(Mobile Network Node) and MR(Mobile Router).

1 Introduction

Wireless networks are evolving towards all-IP-based infrastructures, allowing seamless integration between wired and wireless networks [1]. In addition, the number of passengers, with a laptop, mobile phone or mobile notebook, demanding the use of the Internet at any location, is increasing. Even though these users may be in vehicles such, as a train and aircraft, continuous Internet use when using these devices is desired. In recent years, the IETF has developed protocols such as MIPv4(Mobile IPv4) and MIPv6(Mobile IPv6), for supporting seamless connectivity with mobile hosts[2][3]. However, MIPv4 and MIPv6 suffer from the problem that is difficult to support a moving mobile network. In order to cope with this problem, the IETF NEMO(NEtwork MObility) working group has proposed a NEMO Basic protocol, based on the Mobile Router (MR) for Network mobility. A MR acts on behalf of the nodes within its mobile network, performing routing operation and Home Agent function for Mobile Network [10]. The reasons of supporting a MR base for network mobility are as follows. First Mobile Network Nodes (MNNs) in mobile networks can reduce transmission power because the radio transmission distance from

E. Sha et al. (Eds.): EUC 2006, LNCS 4096, pp. 601 – 609, 2006.

an on-board device to the MR is much shorter than to another Access Router on the Internet. Secondly, after MNNs establishment with MR, when the Mobile Network(MN) is moving, handover frequency MNNs can be reduced, as the MR only operates handover. In addition, once MNNs join the MN, they do not need to maintain their Internet address [4].

The NEMO Basic protocol, provides uninterrupted connectivity for MNNs, but, does not consider routing optimization. A routing scheme based on NEMO, uses MIPv6 for routing optimization and allows a MR to transmit a binding update message to each Correspondence Node (CN). This results in binding update implosion in large network, towards the MR .

To cope with this problem, the Ernst proposed Prefix Scope Binding Update(PSBU) method, was proposed. In this method, a MR obtains a Care of Address (CoA) from its attachment using MIPv6. The MR transmits this CoA to All CNs using PSBU. In this scheme, the MR overloads when transmitting a binding update message periodically to all CNs. Currently most schemes that provide network mobility are not sufficient in supporting fast handover. In addition, the MR suffers from overload, when performing a binding update and routing function. To cope with these problems, the proposed scheme is provided as follows. First, fast handover is provided, by using a candidate Foreign Agent (FA) for virtual connection. Second, a Mobile Router Proxy (MRP) for a MR is created. The MRP performs a binding update for each CNs as a substitute for the MR. Therefore, the MRP enables load balancing, to reduce the MR overload and upgrade performance of the mobile network, reducing traffic in the wireless zone between the MR and Access Router (AR).

The subsequent sections of this paper are organized as follows. Section 2 provides related work. Then the MRP based routing scheme is described in Section 3. The evaluation of the proposed scheme is presented in Section 4, and some concluding remarks are provided in Section 5.

2 Related Work

In this section, various schemes regarding most recent network mobility developments are introduced, and their characteristics are discussed. In the case of using MIPv4 for network mobility, the MR acts as a FA, it provides MNNs with CoA. The packets, destined for MNNs within a MN, are transmitted through the HA. For global connectivity of fixed nodes within a MN, the MR permanently registers the Home of Address (HoA) of the MR to the Home Agent (HA), as a CoA of the MR. MIPv4 supports MNNs within a MN as a single mobile node for network mobility. Whenever network mobility occurs, each MNN obtains a CoA from the MR and then performs a binding update to HA. Therefore this scheme makes it difficult for a MNN to maintain an address, as well as resulting in binding update implosion of the MR. In this case, using MIPv6 for network mobility, the MR must operate a binding update to CNs.

NEMO was designed to provide uninterrupted connectivity for MNNs within MN, without considering routing optimization. The MR in NEMO acts on behalf of MNNs within MN. That is, the MIPv4/v6 performs a binding update only for the MR but NEMO performs it for all mobile networks to the HA. The follow details NEMO Basic protocol operation principles. When a mobile network is moving, the MR registers the mobile network prefix to the HA. This prefix is used by the HA, which intercepts packets destined to MNNs and forwards them to the MR. The MR decapsulates the packets in turn, and then transmits them to the MNNs. In the case where the packets destined to egress, the HA decapsulates the packets and forwards them to the CNs.

The scheme using MIPv6 routing optimization for network mobility has binding update implosions because the MR performs a binding update for all CNs. To solve these problems, the PSBU method, together with the Optimized Route Cache (ORC) Management protocol, exists.

The PSBU uses MIPv6 extension to broadcast the mobile network prefix to the HA and all CNs. When the PSBU performs a binding update, it initially registers all mobile networks to the HA. At this point, the MR uses MIPv6, obtaining the CoA from its attachment point. This CoA is transmitted to all CNs in the mobile network using PSBU. The PSBU performs binding, and this binding relates to the mobile network prefix CoA of the MR. Before transmitting packets, the CN verifies accordance with the destination prefix and mobile network prefix in the binding cache. If it is matched, the packets are transmitted through the CoA of the MR, using a routing extension header. Therefore the PSBU provides optimal routing between CNs and MNNs.

However, the MR has overload when processing everything. In addition, when there are lots of CNs, the MR has a problem of transmitting periodic PSBU to all CNs.

3 Efficient Routing Protocol(ERP)

3.1 Preliminaries

The following scenarios must be considered for network mobility. Network mobility moves pre-defined low & high speeds, and stops at pre-defined stations, MNNs within MNs can move randomly. Currently, most routing schemes for network mobility have problems as follows.

(1) No routing optimization: NEMO has a problem that All packets of a MN can communicate to CNs only via the HA

(2) The MR's binding update implosion: when providing routing optimization using MIPv4/v6, the MR has a problem that MR transmits periodic binding update messages to a number of CNs

(3) Signaling overload: high error rate and bursty errors in a wireless channel zone between MR and AR(like a FA) exist. Therefore, it is import for this network to reduce signaling overload.

In order to solve the above problems, the ERP based routing scheme is proposed as follows.

(4) Fast Handover: Since the MR makes temporary tunneling using a candidate, prior to the FA mechanism, when the MR reaches a foreign network, it can minimize registration delay time.

(5) MR's Load Balancing: Since the MRP performs binding a update function for the CN, the MRP can reduce the overload of the MR, as well as signal the traffic of a wireless channel zone.

New concepts regarding candidate FA and MRP are defined, for the proposed scheme

Definition 1: The candidate FA is set of foreign agents which the mobile network will move into. The candidate FA provides a minimizing registration delay time, in order to support fast handover when a MN moves. That is, the candidate FA is registered, prior to temporary tunneling to the HA. The current FA or HA searches the candidate FA, based on $P_t(x_t, y_t)$, in Section 3.3.1, using a predicted traveling distance.

Definition 2: The MRP(Mobile Router Proxy) performs proxy function of the MR. The *MRP on behalf of the MR operates a binding update to the CNs for the MNNs within the MN.* The MRP is the root router in one domain and its function can add a traditional router easily.

3.2 ERP Architecture

In this section, the search method of the candidate FA using predicted traveling distance, and how it forms an establishment between MR and MRP, is presented.

3.2.1 MRP Establishment

The following represents the process of MRP establishment

(1) Handover Initialization
When the MN is a home network, the MR registers its own home address and mobile network prefix to the HA and then the MR transmits its own speed periodically, together with location information to the HA. Like Fig 1, the HA calculates the $P_t(x_t, y_t)$ in 3.3.1

(2) After the MN searches the FA, which the MN moves into, the HA transmits the network prefix of the MN to the FA of AS2.

(3) Temporary tunneling setup
The FA creates temporary tunneling with the HA, which is the MR-CoA uses to assign to the MR. At that time the FA creates an initial connection descriptor for the session.

(4) Mobile network moving
Mobile network is attached into the FA of AS2.

(5) HA Registration
After the MR receives the connection descriptor, the MR connects the session using the connection descriptor, to the FA. The MR transmits the binding update message to the HA.

(6) MRP establishment
The MR selects the domain root router in the new foreign network as the MRP. The MR transmits information, which is the address of the CNs for the MNNs within the MN, to the MRP1 using IPv6 address extension.

(7) CN updating
On behalf of the MR, the MRP1transmits a periodic binding update message to each of the CNs. After each of the CNs receives this message, They transmit packets destined to the MNN to MRP1. Packets destined to the MRP1 are transmitted to the FA, and then to the MR, then the MR transmits the packet MNNs within the MN. The MRP1 transmits a periodic binding update message to indicate the lifetime of the binding cache to the CNs.

3.2.2 Handover Processing

Followings are procedures about virtual connection for L3, handover process for L2.

Virtual connection for L3 Handover

(1) The oFA requests periodically a MR's velocity & location information to the MR.
(2) The MR responses with current velocity & location information to oFA
(3) The oFA calculates the MR's predicted traveling distance based on formula (5)
(4) The oFA requests MR's handover with MR's HoA, oFA's IP addr, MNP(Mobile Network Prefix), estimated time to handover.
(5) If there are candidate FAs (1 or more FA), which can satisfy the condition of Step 4, go to next step. Otherwise this operation is finished.
(6) The candidate FA responses the oFA for handover confirmation
(7) The oFA sends candidate FA's IP address to the MR.
(8) The candidate FA requests virtual connection to HA.
(9) The HA responses to the candidate FA
(10) The candidate FA sends connection descriptor to the MR.
(11) Setups virtual connection for the MR

Handover procedure for L2

(1) The MR is moving into new FA.
(2) The MR performs scanning procedure.
(3) The MR sends MR's connection descriptor to new FA.
(4) If nFA had MR's connection descriptor, response confirmation message to the MR. Otherwise this operatifson is closed here for virtual connection and MR performs general L3 Handover procedure.
(5) Setups complete tunneling between L2 and L3

4 Performance Evaluation

The performance evaluation of the proposed scheme has been tested and evaluated using temporary tunneling, through simulations of CMU's wireless extensions for Network Simulator (ns-2). Also we developed MR and candidate FA by modifying MobiWan[12]. For load balancing, we modified function of MIPv6 at domain root router to perform binding update for CNs among function of MR. Also we added this function of virtual connection to FA. The nodes use an 802.11 radio and MAC model provided by CMU extensions. The radio propagation range for each node is 100 meters. The wired network capacity is 10/50/100Mbps(Base station, Site Router, Border Router, respectively) and mobile node's speed is 2M/s. The simulation time is 100sec and the mobility model is GNMM. In simulation, we simulated that domain are 2, sites are 8, total number of wired-nodes are 28 and MR is 1.

4.1 Network Mobility Model

The design for mobility is important in correcting the evaluation of the routing algorithm. The Random Waypoint Mobility Model(RWMM) and Gauss-Markov Mobility Model(GNMM) is used as independent mobility for each node.

Proposed routing scheme is a group mobility model, in which mobile nodes move together. In this paper, the Group Network Mobility Model(GNMM) is developed, to evaluate the proposed routing scheme. The Reference Point Group Mobility Model(RPGM), is used widely, to express the random motion of each mobile node within a group, in addition to the random motion of one group[11]. The RPGM demonstrates that group movement is based on the path traveled by the logical center for the group. The motion of the group center completely characterizes the movement of its corresponding group of mobile nodes, including their direction and speed. The individual mobile nodes randomly move around their pre-defined reference points, with movements depending on the group movement.

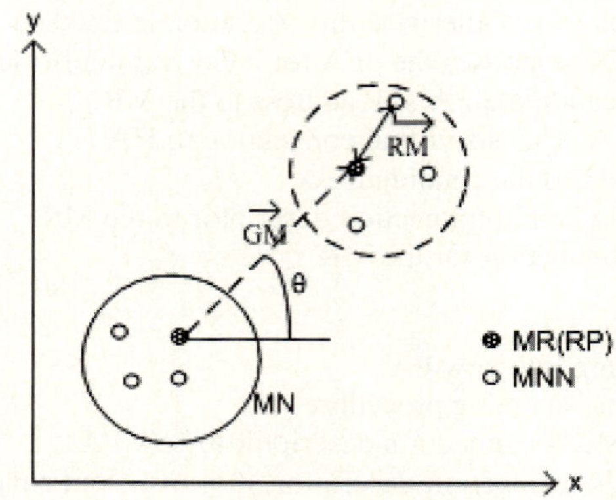

Fig. 1. Network Mobility using the GNMM model

Fig 1 presents the MN motion composed of one MR and three MNNs, using the GNMM Model, which is modified by the RPGM.

At time t, the MR acts as a Reference Point((RP_{t-1})) for three MNNs. The GNMM uses Group motion vector $\overrightarrow{GM}$, in order to calculate Reference Point RP_t at time instant t. $\overrightarrow{GM}$ is composed of velocity vector V_t = (v, θ) and position $P_t(x_t, y_t)$ of the MN. Therefore candidate FA can be found using $\overrightarrow{GM}$. Velocity vector and position can be written, following at time instant t.

$$V_t = \min[\max(V_{t-1} + \overline{V}, 0), V^{\max}] \tag{1}$$

$$\theta_t = \theta_{t-1} + \overline{\theta} \tag{2}$$

Here $\overline{V}$, is the variation of speed, uniformly distributed at $[-S_t^{\max} * \overline{V}, S_t^{\max} * \overline{V}]$. $S_t^{\max}$ represents maximum acceleration. In addition, $V^{\max}$ is the maximum speed of the MN. In formula (2), $\overline{\theta}$ is the variation of direction, and is uniformly distributed at $[-\gamma * \overline{V}, \gamma * \overline{V}]$. γ is the maximum angular, as a MN motion.

$$x_t = x_{t-1} + V_t * \cos\theta_t \quad (3)$$

$$y_t = y_{t-1} + V_t * \sin\theta_t \quad (4)$$

The new position of each MNN is calculated by summing the random motion vectors $\overrightarrow{RM}$ and RP_t.

At RP_t, distance of $\overrightarrow{RM}$, the distance between MNNs and MR, is uniformly distributed within a predefined radius center. Each MNN within MN is implemented using the Random Waypoint Mobility Model. Based on formula (3), (4)

$$P_t(x_t, y_t) \quad (5)$$

(5) is New position of Network Mobility.

4.2 MR's Load Balancing

We simulate to know how many MR generates binding update messages for CNs and Simulation is increasing the number of CNs. Binding updates are composed of HA and CN at MR. In real world, MR performs binding update to CNs for MNNs within MN. In this simulation, one MR means one mobile network. What it is increasing CNs means that MNNs within MN send and receive packets with CNs. Therefore, it is significant to measure the number of binding update to evaluate overload of MR owing to binding update according to increasing CNs. We generate traffics between CNs and MR to measure this. The traffic is generated ping per second. When MR receives new CoA, MR sends binding update CNs per seconds and per 10 seconds to refresh binding cache of CNs. We find influence on wireless channel between MR and AR(Access Router, like a FA) through simulation.

MR performs many and frequently binding update according to increasing the number of CNs. Like fig 2, the number of binding update of MR is increased rapidly according to increasing CNs.

In proposed scheme, the number of binding update of MR is increased linearly according to increasing CNs. We find that MRP can reduce overload of MR as MRP performs binding update for CN instead of MR and MRP upgrade mobile network efficiency as it reduce signaling traffic over wireless channel zone.

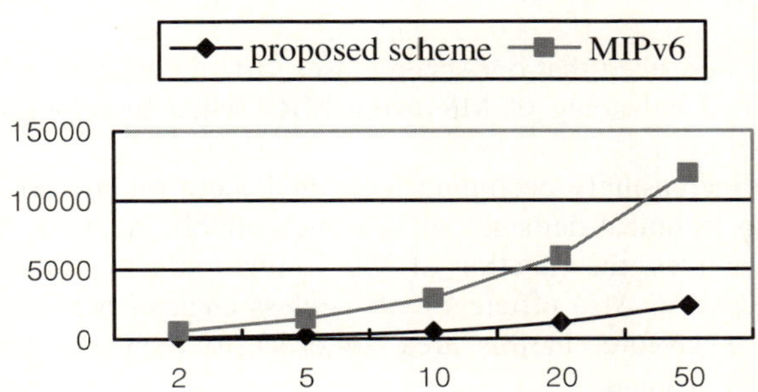

Fig. 2. MR's # of Binding Update

In Fig 2, X axis is the number of CNs and Y axis is all Binding update of MR. The number of Binding Update is that MR performs binding updates for HA and CNs. As you see like a Fig 2, the number of Binding update of proposed scheme is smaller than MIPv6. Fig 2 illustrates that proposed scheme uses efficiently bandwidth in wireless channel because MR does not send signaling messages. Also in MIPv6, we find that Binding Update is increasing rapidly according to increasing the number of CNs. Which presents that overload of MR is increasing rapidly according to increasing the number of CNs of MNNs within MN.

4.3 Fast Handover

Fig 3 shows handover latency time according to speed variation of MR. X axis is speed of MR, Y axis is handover latency time. Also we have tested that the number of CNs is set 10. We assumed that moving path of mobile network moves pre-defined path. Proposed scheme can minimize handover latency time because the current FA or HA searches the candidate FA using a predicted traveling distance and the candidate FA is registered, prior to temporary tunneling to the HA.

Fig 3 illustrates that proposed scheme can maintain small & regular handover latency time and it can support seamless handover.

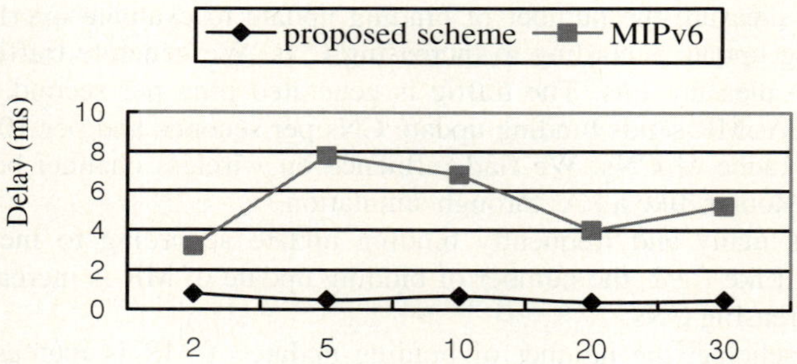

Fig. 3. Handover latency time

5 Concluding Remarks

In this paper, we described that our scheme uses virtual connection for fast handover and it develop load balancing of MR using MRP when In-vehicle mobile network moves.

According to increasingly becoming more and more mobile communication, we expect increasing technical demands of in-vehicle mobile network. When in-vehicle mobile network moves, the function of MR is important to use internet for nodes within mobile network. Also efficiency of wireless channel between MR and AR is very important. Therefore, in this area, in order to reduce signaling traffic, we proposed MRP mechanism.

Like simulation, as the MRP on behalf of the MR operates a binding update to the CNs for the MNNs within the MN, even increasing the number of CNs, proposed scheme can maximize efficiency of bandwidth and provide load balancing of MR as reducing signaling traffics in wireless channels. Also when mobile network moves, proposed scheme can minimize handover latency time because the current FA or HA searches the candidate FA using a predicted traveling distance and the candidate FA is registered, prior to temporary tunneling to the HA. In this simulation, we find that how many binding update for CNs has influence on wireless channels and if reduction of signaling traffic in wireless channels has influence on all mobile network.

Acknowledgments. This research was supported by the MIC(Ministry of Information and Communication), Korea, under the ITRC(Information Technology Research Center) support program supervised by the IITA(Institute of Information Technology Assessment).

References

1. Campbell, J. Gomez, " IP Micro-Mobility Protocols", ACM SIGMOBILE Mobile Computing and Communications Review, Vol. 4, October 2000, pp. 45-53.
2. Perkins, Ed., "IP Mobility support for IPv4", IETF RFC 3344, August 2002. Jonson D., Perkins C., "Mobility Support in IPv6",(draft-ietf-mobile-ipv6-24.txt), Internet Draft, IETF, June 30 2003, Work in Progress
3. Eranga Perera, Vijay Sivaraman, Aruna Senevirantne, " Survey on network mobility Support", Mobile Computing and Communication Review,Volume 8, Number 2 April 2004.
4. A. Valko, "Cellular IP: A New Approach to Internet Host Mobility", ACM Computer Communication Review, January 1999.
5. R. Ramjee, T. La Porta, Salgarelli, S. Thuel, K. Varadhan, "IP-Based Access Network Infrastructure for Next-Generation Wireless Data Networks", IEEE Personal Communications, August 2000, pp. 34-41.
6. E. Gustafsson, A. Jonsson, C. Perkins, "Mobile IPv4 Regional Registration", ftp://ftp.ietf.org/internet-drafts/draft-ietf-mobileip-reg-tunnel-07.txt, October 2002.
7. Liesbeth Peters, Ingrid Moerman, Bart Dhoedt, Piet Demeester, "Micro-Mobility Support for Random Access Network Topologies", WCNC 2004, IEEE Communications Society.
8. IAN F. Akyildiz, Jiang Xie, and Shantidev Mohanty, " A survey of mobility management in next-generation All-IP-based wireless systems", IEEE Wireless Communications, August 2004.
9. Devarapalli V., Wakikawa R., Pertrescu A., Thubert P. "NEMO Basic Support Protocol" (draft-ietf-nemo-bsic-support-02.txt), Internet Draft, IETF, December 2003, Work in Progress
10. X.Hong, M.Gerla, G.Pei, and C.Chang. A group mobility model for adhoc wireless networks. In Proceedings of the ACM International Workshop on modeling and simulation of wireless and mobile systems , Agust 1999.
11. MobiWan: NS-2 extensions to study mobility in Wide-Area IPv6 Networks, http://www.inrialpes.fr/planete/pub/mobiwan/
12. T.Ernst and K.Uehara, "Connecting automobiles to the Internet", ITST Workshop, pp.257-262, Nov.2002

Network Mobility in MIPv6 Considering Arrival Time

Sun Ok Yang[1] and SungSuk Kim[2,*]

[1] Dept. of Computer Science & Engineering, Korea University, Seoul, S. Korea
soyang@disys.korea.ac.kr
[2] Dept. of E-Businees, SeoKyeong University, Seoul, S. Korea
sskim03@skuniv.ac.kr

Abstract. Mobile IPv6 represents a global solution, providing mobility management for a wide variety of radio technologies, devices, and applications. In particular, Network Mobility basic support protocol is the one of fundamental solutions in MIPv6 which reduces the number of binding update messages issued from mobile network nodes except mobile routers. That is, it never reduces the number of binding update messages which mobile router issues. Significant research results relating to Network Mobility have been reported over last several years. However, practical and common issues exist within the technology; specification of Binding Update Lifetime has a substantial impact the system performance. The binding update message should be delivered periodically for the purpose of user location notification and binding authorization. If the lifetime is too short, the traffic load resulting from the messages may be significant. In addition, issues related to authorization can be problematic. In this paper, therefore, Network Mobility considering arrival time is devised to solve the binding update explosion of mobile routers without security problem in Network Mobility.

Keywords: network mobility, binding update, mobility type, kcredit, arrival time, mean resident time.

1 Introduction

Mobile IP[1, 2] is recognized to be a promising solution for mobile communications including cellular backbone. In Mobile IP, *home agent (HA)* located in the home network manages mobile's location and forwards packets destined to the mobile in the visited network. IETF has commissioned *NEMO (NEtwork MObility)* working group[3] to extend the existing protocols or develop new ones to support network mobility in an IPv6 network[4]. Among several kinds of issues in NEMO, we take an interest in a *binding update* message *(BU)* management which *Mobile Router (MR)* transmits to its HA and relevant *correspondent nodes (CNs)*. A MR sends BU message to its HA and CNs each time it changes its point-of-attachment. Figure 1 shows BU explosion of mobile network. *Local Fixed Node (LFN)* is permanently located in a mobile network and *mobile network node (MNN)* can be attached to mobile network [4, 5]. MR is a border router of a mobile network and CNs are all nodes

* Corresponding author.

E. Sha et al. (Eds.): EUC 2006, LNCS 4096, pp. 610 – 619, 2006.

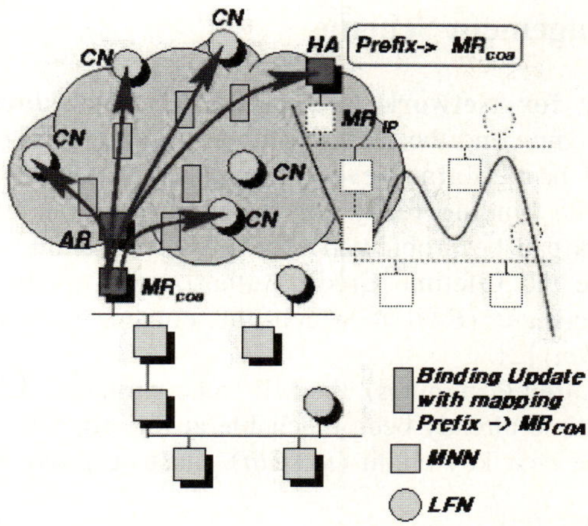

Fig. 1. Binding Update explosion

communicating with MR, LFNs and MNNs. If the lifetime of BU is set too short , HA quickly detects that the MR is disconnected from the network. It, however, needs a lot of BU messages transmission over, which overburden processing overload on HA and deteriorates wireless bandwidth utilization. In addition, transmission of BUs from MR to a large number of CNs would cause a BU explosion. To suppress those BUs, only multicast delivery BUs has been proposed. Like this, multicast delivery of BUs for large mobile networks an innovative trend. However, MR should still send multicast delivery BU frequently to the number of CNs. Conversely, when BU message with long lifetime is received, HA and CNs keep it in a binding cache until the lifetime expires. Therefore, the number of BUs decreases and overhead for the messages is also reduced. However, issues relating to authorization can be problematic in terms of the current *return routability for network prefix* mechanism. The binding record will eventually occupy more space in both data structures-the *Binding Cache* and *Binding Update List*-of MRs [2]. As a result, a scheme is required to obtain the proper lifetime value, considering both the cases.

The authors in [6] propose a secure and lightweight extension of return routability in *Mobile IPv6 (MIPv6)*. The lifetime value can be long (upper bound is 8 hours). Thus, signaling can be reduced and the MN is not required to wake up as frequently. However, it is assumed that MN is a stable node, which may become an issue. If some information containing each MR's mobility pattern is known in advance in NEMO, an unreasonable assumption can be removed. Thus, we consider some kinds of vehicle (e.g. bus, train, airport etc.), which have uniform movement pattern for some networks. If the information related with each vehicle's past movements is maintained locally and is available, we can guess the current resident time considering arrival time and thus the proper MR's BU lifetime can be given whenever the vehicle enters a network. To do so, a MR records a kind of log whenever it leaves a network. It periodically computes the binding lifetime values for all its visited networks and maintains them in its profile. When the MR moves into any network after forming the profile, if there is any record for the network in it, an adaptive lifetime is applied to the BU lifetime.

2 Binding Management Scheme

Return Routability for Network Prefix (RRNP) Procedure: NEMO requires periodic RRNP procedure and the reestablishment of the binding at the CN [7]. This authorization should be performed every 7 minutes. It can represent a burden for MRs, which have the binding ready for a possible packet but are not currently communicating. This can be problematic for a MR in standby mode. To solve the problem, we include the Lifetime Credit Authorization option [6] in the BU and *Binding Acknowledgement (BA)* of which the content is based on the binding management key (*Kbm*) [2].

Instead of a fixed limit (7 minutes), the MR can continue to use an existing address test longer than the time already been reachable at this address. To authorize this, a keyed hash using the next key credit (*Kcredit*), must be provided and calculated as follows:

$$\boldsymbol{Kcredit = hash(Kbm_N \mid hash(Kbm_{N-1} \mid hash(Kbm_{N-2} \mid \dots Kbm_1)))}$$

here | denotes concatenation and Kbm_1 through Kbm_N are used to calculate the Binding Authorization Data option in the BU and all subsequent BUs. The next *Kcredit* is calculated based on the previous *Kcredit* and the latest *Kbm*. The MR and CNs should both hold some state in the binding cache entries, related to the credit authorization. The following conceptual information must be kept: The total time of binding for MR's home address, the current *Kcredit* value and the number of *Kbm* values is included in the *Kcredit* value.

Binding Update Messages: A binding for a MR is all fours that contain the home address, CoA, network prefixes and the binding lifetime. In this paper, three kinds of BU messages are used according to the lifetime.

(1) $\boldsymbol{BU_\alpha}$ has a default lifetime (LT_α) of BU, which is the same value as one used in existing MIPv6 [2]. After switching to new domain, a MR should send BU_α to its HA and CNs, asking it to direct all incoming packets to new CoA.
(2) $\boldsymbol{BU_\beta}$ has an adaptive lifetime (LT_β) and *Kcredit* value of BU, which is computed based on local profile. A MR has to transmit it to its CNs. This value is the total time which will keep the current binding for MR's home address. The number of *Kbm* is the result that this value is divided by 3.5 minutes [2]. *Kcredit* value is calculated by using these values.
(3) $\boldsymbol{BU_0}$ contains zero lifetime value (LT_0) of BU. When a MR migrates to a network in another domain before BU_β has expired, it will be used to notify CNs that the cached data about BU_β has become stale and thus they have to remove the data.
That is, BU_α and BU_0 are originally used in MIPv6 but BU_β is newly devised in this paper. BU_β will be used only where the guessed resident time is longer than a threshold value.

Proposed Scheme: Vehicles (train, bus and airport, etc) have uniform movement path in some networks. When a MR in them leaves a network, information (*moving log*) regarding the visit, is recorded. The log contains an ordered pair (*l, AT, DT*), which means network identifier, arrival time and departure time, respectively.

```
// Whenever a MR moves out a network.
// Count_b:Threshold of Count
If(MR have visited network m){t=DT_n-AT_n
If(t >ρ*LTα){Record moving log
                  Count_m = Count_m + 1
                  Sum_m  = Sum_m +  t_n    }    }
```

```
//Periodic calculation
//LT:lifetime
Mean=Sum_m/Count_m
For(all moving logs to network m){Calculate Var_m}
                                                //equation (1)
If(Count_m<Count_b)LT=LTα
Else{If(Mean_m<=ρ*LTα or 'mobility type I')LT=LTα
        Else{LTβ=Mean_m*V
      LT = LTβ      }         }
```

Fig. 2. Lifetime calculation algorithm

The average resident time and the frequency of logs in network are considered when the adaptive lifetime (LT_β) is calculated. When the MR moves from network m to another, it adds current information to a moving log. The average resident time for all visited networks is periodically calculated and the algorithm is described in Fig. 2. At first, the resident time (t_n) for n^{th} visit to network m is computed by just subtracting the AT from the DT. The comparison of t_n and $\rho{*}LT_\alpha$ is used to exclude the moving log where the resident time is small (that is, the case where a MR recently passed by the network for a moment while migrating to a specific destination). It is assumed that t_n is compared with ρ (≥ 1) times as long as LT_α. Sum_m and $Count_m$ mean total resident time and total visit number to network m respectively. During the calculation, if the number of visits to network m is less than a constant value ($Count_b$), BU_α will be used since poor (or no) regularity is found in network m. The variance as well as the average resident time in this case is considered. To begin with, the movement patterns for all networks in the profile are divided into ***mobility type R*** and ***I*** to present the degree of accuracy the profile. To quantify the difference, the variance is calculated for all networks as Eq. (1):

$$Var_m = \frac{1}{n}\sum_{i=1}^{n}(t_i - Mean_m)^2 \tag{1}$$

If Var_m is smaller than constant δ, network m is classified as *mobility type R* (the reliable network). Otherwise, the network belongs to ***mobility type I*** where the profile cannot give reliable information. The lifetime value for the next BU is calculated by multiplying the mean resident time by the constant V. The calculated value, LT_β, will be used as the lifetime for BU_β when the MR visits network m after creating the profile.

The resident time for some networks often depends on the arrival time. In this way, we devise a scheme which considers the time region of the arrival time to enhance the accuracy of the profile.

During periodic calculations, the mean resident time per (*network ID, arrival time region*) pair must be considered, not simply the network. To do so, a scheme to determine the arrival time regions from moving logs is required. Five different cases are considered as shown in Fig. 3. The following information is also maintained in the profile per arrival time region:

- AT_{mn}^{high}: the highest (or latest) arrival time
- DT_{mn}^{low}: the lowest (or earliest) departure time
- $Count_{mn}$: the number of visits included in the nth arrival time region
- $TotalCount_{mn}$: the total number of visits considered in the nth arrival time region

where subscriptions n and m represent n^{th} arrival time region to network m. Since the arrival time region is considered as well as the visiting network, each arrival time region maintains its visiting number ($TotalCount_{mn}$, $Count_{mn}$) separately.

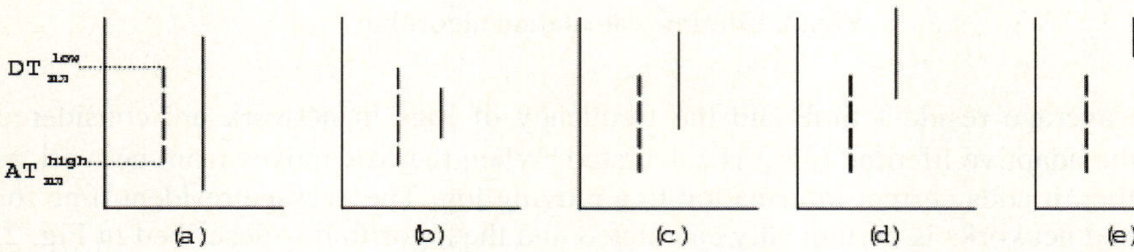

Fig. 3. Various Cases of Visiting Time

In the figure, the vertical dotted line represents the time interval ($Interval_{mn}=DT_{mn}^{low}- AT_{mn}^{high}$) that one arrival time region calculated. The solid line presents the current visiting time. In the case of Fig. 3-(e), it is natural to exclude a new visit from the arrival time region. Visit in Fig. 3-(a) or (b) requires to verification of the MR resides too long or too short in the network. If the resident time is longer than $3/2\times Interval_{mn}$ or shorter than $1/2\times Interval_{mn}$, the difference between both grows too long and thus, the current visiting log cannot provide reliable information. That is, the log is completely excluded; the log is not too long, the log is also used in periodic calculations. Not only the length of resident time but also the time that a MR has arrived must be considered. Figure 3-(c) and (d) initially appear to be similar cases. However, if both are considered, the arrival time region does not provide useful information. Thus, the following process is required for an accurate determination.

middle = $Interval_{mn}$ /2
if (middle ≥ arrival time of current visit)
the current log includes the nth arrival time region
else the current log is excluded

Then, if the current log is included into n^{th} arrival time region of network m, $Count_{mn}$ and $TotalCount_{mn}$ both increase by 1. Otherwise, only $TotalCount_{mn}$ increases by 1 (Fig. 3-(a) and (b)) since this variable will be used to determine the accuracy of the profile. If the arrival time in the current visit is earlier than AT_{mn}^{high}, it is enough to be considered contrary to the cases shown in Fig. 3-(c), (d), and (e). The moving log excluded from the above algorithm will be used to form another arrival time region, except the regions described in Fig. 3-(a) and (b). After arrival time regions are determined using this method, both comparisons between ratio $Count_{mn}$ and $TotalCount_{mn}$ and Var_m are required to evaluate the usefulness of the information regarding the arrival time region. That is, if Var_m is smaller than δ and $Count_{mn}/TotalCount_{mn}$ is larger than γ, the arrival time region to network m is regarded as ***regular mobility type***. In the other cases, it is considered that without regularity (***irregular mobility type***).

3 Performance Analysis

Simulation Model: The simulation model for the scheme is depicted in Fig. 4. Each MR collects log data that contain (l, AT_n, DT_n) whenever it leaves a visited network. It is assumed that the resident time at any network follows Gamma distribution [8] with shape parameter α. As it is generally known, Gamma distribution is selected because it can be shaped to represent various distributions as well as measured data that cannot be characterized by a particular distribution.

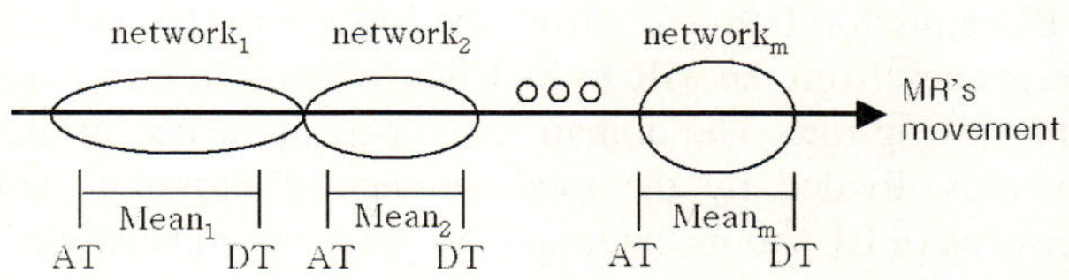

Fig. 4. Simulation Model

Equations (2), (3), and (4) describe the density function for resident time, the mean resident time at a visited network and the variance for the resident time distribution, respectively, where t is the resident time at each visited network.

$$f(t) = \frac{\lambda^\alpha}{\Gamma(\alpha)}(\lambda t)^{\alpha-1}e^{-\lambda t}, t \geq 0 \tag{2}$$

$$E(t) = \frac{\alpha}{\lambda} \tag{3}$$

$$V(t) = \frac{\alpha}{\lambda^2} \tag{4}$$

It is important to note, however, that the resident time follows an exponential distribution where parameter $\alpha=1$, $\lambda=1/E(t)$ in Gamma distribution. The results are shown as the amount of bandwidth allocated by those messages.

All parameters of our experiments are presented in table 1. The constant parameters defined in previous section are first described in the table where ρ and $Count_b$ are used to check whether to consider the current movement log or not, and δ and γ to defermine mobility type of the network. The values are selected from various experiment settings however they will not affect the overall performance since both scheme and NEMO treat diconnection in the same manner. *V* mean the weight value for the calculated lifetime of *regualr mobility type*.

Table 1. Parameter Settings

Parameter	Value	Meaning
ρ	2	
$Count_b$	10	Threshold of Count
δ	10	Constant value to determine regular mobility type
γ	0.8	Constant value of $Count_{mn}/TotalCount_{mn}$ for regular mobility type
V	1.0	V value for regular type
κ	0.3	Intra-domain moving rate

The Results: In Eq. (5) and (6), BW_{NEMO} and BW_{PRO} mean the amounts of the allocated bandwidth for BUs in NEMO and the proposed scheme, respectively. $Size_{BU}$ is defined as the size of a BU (88bytes = IPv6 header (40bytes) + Binding Update Extension Header (28bytes) + Mobile Network Prefix Option (20bytes)) [4, 7]. f_{HA} is denoted as the BU emission frequency from the MR to its HA and f_{CN} is the average BU emission frequency from the MR to its CNs. When a MR migrates, κ represents the intra-domain moving rate. The domain-crossing rate is 1-κ, meaning the number of crossing domains divided by the total number of crossing subnets. The MR transmits *M* consecutive BUs to its external CNs, and transmits another BU to its HA, receiving a BA from HA.

In Eq. (5), *#CN* is the number of the current CNs which are not on the MR's home network. When a MR migrates along networks, it transmits a BU to each CN and to its HA equal to f_{CN} and f_{HA}. In Eq. (6), if the profile information proposed in this paper can be used, the refreshment frequency may be reduced to f_{PRO}.

$$BW_{NEMO} = Size_{BU} \times \{\kappa \times (f_{CN} \times (\#CN+1)+f_{HA})+(1-\kappa) \times (M \times \#CN+2)\} \tag{5}$$

$$BW_{PRO} = Size_{BU} \times \{\kappa \times (f_{PRO} \times (\#CN+1)+f_{HA})+(1-\kappa) \times (M \times \#CN+2)\} \tag{6}$$

$$BW_{NEMO\_multi} = Size_{BU} \times f_{NEMO\_multi} \tag{7}$$

$$BW_{PRO\_multi} = Size_{BU} \times f_{PRO\_multi} \tag{8}$$

In Eq. (7) and (8), BW_{NEMO_multi} and BW_{PRO_multi} show the amounts of the allocated bandwidth for multicast delivery BUs in NEMO and the proposed scheme, respectively. $Size_{BU}$ is the same as one described above. f_{NEMO_multi} and f_{PRO_multi} are the multicast refreshment frequency in NEMO and the proposed scheme, respectively.

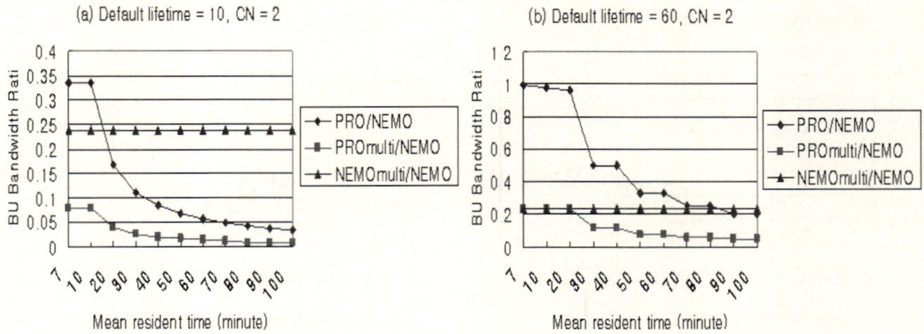

Fig. 5. The comparison of BU bandwidth in Gamma distribution in case of CN=2

Figure 5, 6, 7 and 8 represent the comparison between the proposed schemes(*PRO, PROmulti*) and NEMO(*NEMO, NEMOmulti*) in Gamma and an exponential where the mean resident time varies from 7 to 100 minutes and variance is set to 0.01. When It is assumed that a MR migrates as *regular mobility type* in 30% of the all networks recorded in the profile, *irregular mobility type* in the remaining 70%. As mentioned in Section 2, the networks recorded as *regular mobility type* provide reliable information for their subsequent visits than those with *irregular mobility type*. BU bandwidth depends on *#CN*, f_{HA}, f_{CN}, $f_{PRO,}$ f_{NEMO_multi} and f_{PRO_multi}. The behaviors of the BU bandwidth are almost identical, when variance is 0.01 and 0.1. Figure 5 and 6 represent only results where variance is 0.01. In the figure, the Y-axis value is a relative value comparing the schemes. That is, if the value is smaller than 1.0, the proposed schemes save more bandwidth than the other schemes. At first, it is known that variance has little influence on overall performance. The reason is as follows: Vehicles have irregular movement patterns and variance is one of the factors that affect irregularity. Thus, the profile is used to capture reliable information unaffected by the factors, i.e., variance.

From Fig. 5-(a), ratio of PRO to NEMO decreases as mean resident time increases. In case where mean resident time=50, only 10% of messages are required with PRO compared with NEMO. Ratio NEMOmulti to NEMO shows a fixed value as the mean resident time increases since both are never benefited from the profile. However, ratio PROmulti to NEMO decreases near to 0 as mean resident time increases.

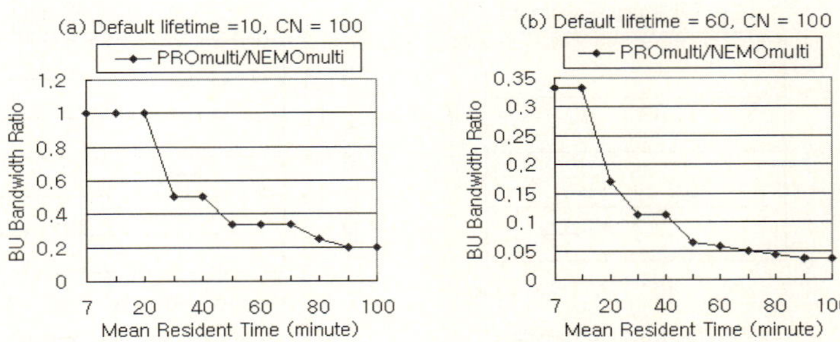

Fig. 6. The comparison of BU bandwidth in Gamma distribution in case of CN=100

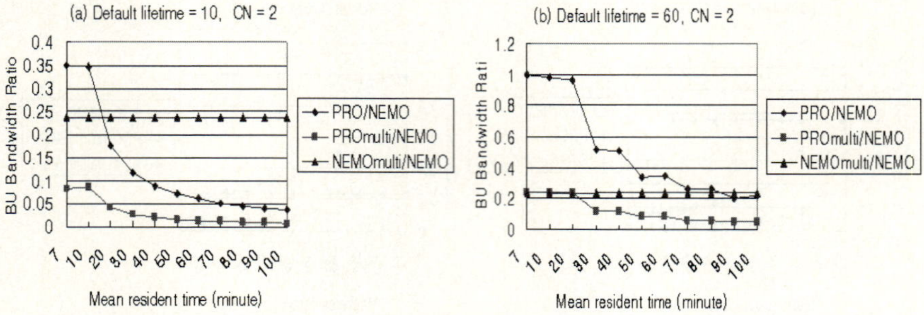

Fig. 7. The comparison of BU bandwidth in an exponential distribution in case of CN=2

Figure 5-(b) shows the results when LT_α is set to 60 seconds. In the figure, ratio of *PRO* to *NEMO* decreases less than that in Fig. 5-(a). This indicates that the BU bandwidth ratio is affected by the longer LT_α. Namely, the amount of BU for all schemes generated much less than that in Fig.5-(a). Thus, we come to know that bandwidth usage in the *PRO* is the more efficient than the NEMO from Fig. 5. In addition, the *PROmulti* is also the more efficient than the *NEMOmulti*.

In Fig. 6, it is described ratio of *PROmulti* to *NEMOmulti* when #CN =100. As the number of CN increases, multicast BU frequency in *PROmulti* and *NEMOmulti* is not affected by the number of CN. However, both are affected by the lifetime. Where mean resident time is 40 minutes, *PROmulti* requires 50% of messages in Fig 6-(a) and only 12% of messages in Fig 6-(b), compared with *NEMOmulti*.

The reason is that *NEMOmulti* BUs are transmitted to its HA and CNs when the MR is roaming but the *PROmulti* only transmits the BUs to refresh time is also lengthened if a long resident time is computed for the current location from the profile. There may be differences between the computed lifetime and real resident time. In spite of this, the level of reduced bandwidth is substantial, in networks where MRs are determined as consisting mainly of *regular mobility type*. In particular, when a MR does not migrate across domains frequently, most of the signaling load is generated by the refreshing BUs. The central improvements proposed in this paper, are achieved by decreasing

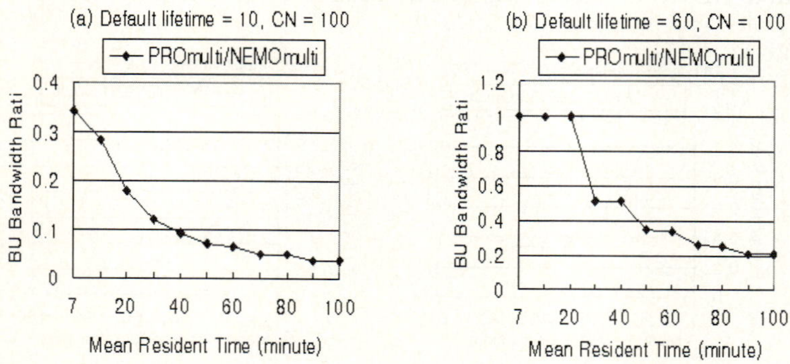

Fig. 8. The comparison of BU bandwidth in Exponential distribution in case of CN=100

the number of periodic refreshing BUs. Figure 7 and 8 represent the comparison between the proposed schemes(*PRO, PROmulti*) and NEMO(*NEMO, NEMOmulti*) in an exponential distribution where the mean resident time varies from 7 to 100 minutes. The behaviors of BU bandwidth ratio in Fig. 7 and 8 are almost identical with those in Fig. 5 and 6. That is, the function of the resident time distribution rarely has an influence on the overall performance.

As a result, in case of the MR has a *regular mobility type*, it is important to note he re that the mean resident time can be much longer than LT_α in reality. The MRs, therefore, will only transmit a small number of messages. Although the MR migrates regular, the default mechanism in NEMO will be used and thus there is little additional overhead. Thus, the efficiency of the proposed schemes can improve over the results presented in this paper.

4 Conclusion

In this paper, network mobility considering arrival time is proposed in MIPv6. The overhead incurred by frequent BUs is reduced, by capturing some regularity in movement patterns of each MR. That is, from the MR's arrival time as well as average resident time in visited networks, the adaptive lifetime is computed and applied dynamically. The main contributions in this paper, are allowing limited wireless bandwidth to be utilized effectively, and greatly improving the efficiency in the MR, by reducing the amount of BU messages. However, the correctness of the profile is required for more in depth analysis, to ascertain the effects of each parameter through data mining algorithms since the proposed schemes are based on local profiles.

References

1. C. Perkins, *IP mobility support for IPv4*, RFC 3344, Aug. 2002.
2. B. Johnson, C. Perkins and J. Arkko, *Mobility Support in IPv6*, RFC 3775, June, 2004.
3. http://www.ietf.org/html.charters/nemo-charter.html
4. V. Devarapalli, R. Wakikawa, A. Petrescu and P. Thubert, *Network Mobility (NEMO) Basic Support Protocol*, RFC 3963, IETF, Jan. 2005.
5. T. Inoue, N. Takahashi, and T. Miyazaki, "Hierarchical Location Management Scheme Based on Collaboration of Mobile Nodes", *IEICE Trans. Commn.*, Vol. E87-B, No.3, pp.470-479, Mar. 2004.
6. Arkko, J. and Vogt, C., Credit-Based Authorization for Binding Lifetime Extension, draft-arkko-mipv6-binding-lifetime-extension-00, 2004.
7. C. Ng and J. Hirano, "Extending Return Routability Procedure for Network Prefix (RRNP)," *Internet Draft*, draft-ng-nemo-rrnp-00.txt, Oct. 2004.
8. Y. B. Lin, W. R. Lai and R. J. Chen, "Performance Analysis for Dual Band PCS Networks", *IEEE Journal on Trans. on Computers*, Vol. 49, No.2, Feb. 2000, pp 148-159.

Service-Oriented Device Anycasting Using Quality First Search in Wireless Personal Area Network

Chien-Chung Su[1], Kuo-Shiang Lu[1], Mong-Fong Horng[2], Chao-Lieh Chen[3], Yau-Hwang Kuo[1], Jang-Pong Hsu[4], and Wen-Hsin Cheng[4]

[1] Center for Research of E-life Digital Technology, Department of Computer Science and Information Engineering, National Cheng Kung University, Tainan, Taiwan
{succ, liugs, kuoyh}@ismp.csie.ncku.edu.tw

[2] Department of Computer Science and Information Engineering, Shu-Te University, Kaohsiung, Taiwan
mfhorng@mail.stu.edu.tw

[3] Department of Electronics Engineering, Kun-Shan University, Tainan, Taiwan
frederic@ieee.org

[4] Advanced Multimedia Internet Technology Incorporation, Tainan Hsien, Taiwan
{jp, vincent}@amit.com.tw

Abstract. Service-oriented device anycasting using quality first search (DA-QFS) approach is proposed to coordinate various portable devices for providing wireless personal area network (WPAN) services[1]. We adopt a cross-layer design standing on not only the lower (network and data link) layer's point of view but also higher (application) layer's point of view to provide quality WPAN services. In DA-QFS the service profile (SP) of a WPAN service is well-represented by the proposed characterized task graph (CTG). The proposed weighted device anycasting (WDA) process then takes connectivity, implicit distance, work degree, and mobility as the criteria to select the most quality device according to the information embedded in CTG. The simulation results on energy consumption, packet loss rate, average delay, and re-start time show that DA-QFS is an efficient approach, especially in the environment with highly mobile devices and multiple users.

1 Introduction

In smart space, a user request can be accomplished by coordinating multiple devices around [1][2]. Consequently, automatically organizing various devices to provide wireless personal area network (WPAN) services is an important issue in smart space. There are significant previous results which principally focused on data link and network layers [3][4]. However, it is a challenge to provide a quality WPAN service only from lower layer's point of view. Therefore, a cross-layer

[1] This paper is based partially on work supported by the National Science Council, Taiwan under Grant NCS-94-2213-E-006-081.

E. Sha et al. (Eds.): EUC 2006, LNCS 4096, pp. 620–629, 2006.

design [5] is indispensable to bridge the gap of quality issues between higher and lower layers. For instance, Basu et al [6] published task-based device anycasting using breadth first search (DA-BFS) approach. In DA-BFS the required device classes and their associations of a WPAN service are denoted by nodes and edges in a task graph (TG), respectively. According to the BFS tree derived from TG, the required devices classes are instantiated from root node (user device) to leaf nodes (leaf device classes). Distance is the explicit factor which affects network performance and is the only criterion to select a device by DA-BFS. However, more implicit factors should be involved for determining the quality device in the environment with highly mobile devices and multiple users.

In proposed service-oriented device anycasting using quality first search (DA-QFS) approach, we embed detailed information of a WAPN service in the proposed characterized task graph (CTG). The proposed weighted device anycasting (WDA) process then takes four weighted factors, connectivity, implicit distance, work degree, and mobility to be the selection criteria according to the information embedded in CTG. By adjusting the weights of factors, DA-QFS is certainly applied to the WPAN services with different quality requirements in diverse environments. The simulation results on energy consumption, packet loss rate, and packet delay show that DA-QFS is efficient even in the environment with highly mobile devices and multiple users.

The rest of this paper is organized as follows. In Section 2, the problem statement and related issues are introduced. The proposed approach is described in Section 3. Then, we show the simulation setup and results to evaluate the proposed approach in Section 4. Finally, the conclusion and future work follows.

2 Related Work

A service profile (SP) describing the requirements of a WPAN service can be represented by a task graph (TG). In this paper, TG is denoted by (N_{TG}, E_{TG}) indicating the device classes needed to provide the WPAN service and the necessary associations between these device classes, respectively. A real network (RN) is denoted by (N_{RN}, E_{RN}). Each node in RN indicates a portable device. Each edge in RN indicates that two end nodes are in the mutual transmission range. The set of all candidate devices in RN of a device class $n_* \in N_{TG}$ is denoted by $\widetilde{N}_* \subset N_{RN}$. The instantiated device of n_* is denoted by $\overline{n}_* \in N_{RN}$ which is most quality one among all $\widetilde{n}_*^i \in \widetilde{N}_*$. For instance, the device class A is denoted by n_A as show in Fig. 1(a). $\widetilde{N}_A = \{\widetilde{n}_A^1, \widetilde{n}_A^2\}$ is the set of all candidate devices of n_A as show in Fig. 1(b). $\widetilde{n}_A^1$ is regarded as the instantiated device, $\overline{n}_A$, of n_A as shown in Fig. 1(c).

In order to provide the WPAN service, a device anycasting (DA) process is required to discover a quality pair of mappings, $\varphi_N : N_{TG} \to N_{RN}$ and $\varphi_E : E_{TG} \to P_{RN}$ where P_{RN} is the set of paths between all instantiated devices in RN. The following issues should be considered in DA process:

1) The location of the instantiated device. If a device class is instantiated only by its instantiated parent device in BFS tree, then the location of this

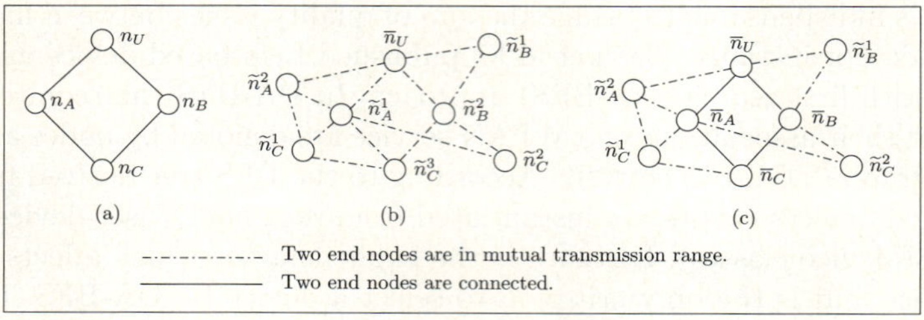

Fig. 1. (a) Service profile of a WPAN service. (b) A real network. (c) A pair of mapping from (a) to (b).

instantiated device is not necessarily the most quality one. For instance, we assume that $\overline{n}_A$ is the instantiated parent device of n_C in BFS tree in Fig. 1. Although the distance between $\widetilde{n}_C^1$ and $\overline{n}_A$ is the shortest, $\widetilde{n}_C^1$ is not the quality device because it is unable to directly communicate with $\overline{n}_B$. Therefore, $\widetilde{n}_C^2$ and $\widetilde{n}_C^3$ are more quality since they are in the transmission range of $\overline{n}_A$ and $\overline{n}_B$. In addition, if (n_A, n_C) is a data flow with high traffic load and (n_B, n_C) is a control flow with low traffic load, $\widetilde{n}_C^3$ is more quality than $\widetilde{n}_C^2$ because $\widetilde{n}_C^3$ is much closer to $\overline{n}_A$.

2) The work load of the instantiated device. The "hot device" problem means that the system loads of the devices with the same functionalities are imbalanced. The packet loss rate and packet delay of the WPAN service may become higher because the high-loaded devices are selected. The problem is obvious in the environment with multiple users. In addition, φ_N is not necessarily a one-to-one mapping. The performance is improved if the task on a device class is distributed among multiple instantiated devices.

3) The mobility of the instantiated device. If an instantiated device is highly mobile, then the corresponding device class likely needs to be frequently re-instantiated.

According to above issues, four implicit factors are regarded as the criteria for instantiating a device class in the proposed approach. First, factor of connectivity is the number of instantiated parent devices in the transmission range of a candidate device. Second, the traffic load is embedded in the factor of implicit distance. Third, the factor of work degree is involved to balance the system load of devices. Finally, the factor of mobility is also involved to prevent the WPAN service from being interrupted due to the movement of the instantiated devices.

3 The Proposed Approach

The service-oriented device anycasting using quality first search (DA-QFS) approach is proposed to automatically organize the portable devices for providing quality WPAN services. DA-QFS consists of a service profile (SP) represented by characterized task graph (CTG) and a device anycasting (DA) process named weighted device anycasting (WDA). In this paper, the status of a device is assumed to be discovered by service discovery protocols [7][8].

3.1 Characterized Task Graph

An example of characterized task graph (CTG) for the WPAN service described in Fig. 1(a) is shown in Fig. 2. Two new features are added in CTG. First, the relative ratio of expected traffic load on each association between two device classes is specified according to the behavior of the WPAN service. The relative ratio of expected traffic load on (n_M, n_N) is denoted by $\epsilon_{(n_M,n_N)}$ in CTG. It is important to specify the expected traffic loads for instantiating a device class because energy consumption is direct proportion to the amount of transmitted data according to the general energy model in wireless networks [9]. For example, both n_A and n_B have associations with n_C as shown in Fig. 2. If the expected traffic load on (n_B, n_C) is higher than the expected traffic load on (n_A, n_C) (i.e. $\epsilon_{(n_B,n_C)} > \epsilon_{(n_A,n_C)}$), then the candidate device, $\widetilde{n}_C^i$, with smallest value of $\epsilon_{(n_B,n_C)} \times dist\left(\overline{n}_B, \widetilde{n}_C^i\right) + \epsilon_{(n_A,n_C)} \times dist\left(\overline{n}_A, \widetilde{n}_C^i\right)$ has priority to be regarded as $\overline{n}_C$ where $dist\left(\overline{n}_B, \widetilde{n}_C^i\right)$ and $dist\left(\overline{n}_A, \widetilde{n}_C^i\right)$ are the distances from $\widetilde{n}_C^i$ to $\overline{n}_B$ and $\overline{n}_A$, respectively. Second, since the requirement of multiple instantiated devices for a device class is critical to several distributed WPAN services, the maximum number of instantiated devices of each device class is specified in CTG. The notation, $n_*[k]$, means that at most k instantiated devices can be selected for n_* where $n_*[1]$ is also represent by n_* for short. For example, at most x and y instances could be selected for n_B and n_C in Fig. 2, respectively.

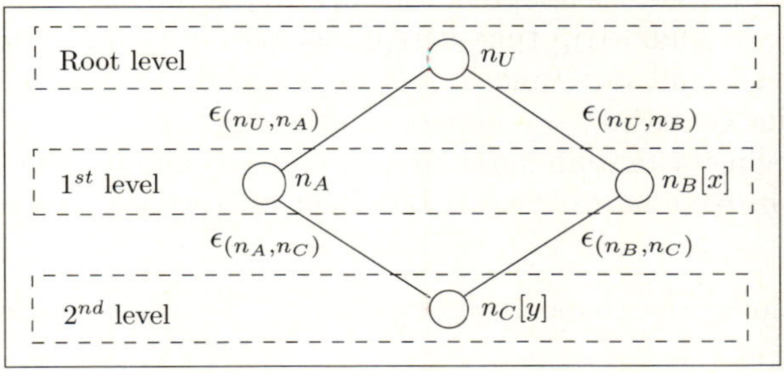

Fig. 2. An example of CTG

3.2 Weighted Device Anycasting

In order to select the quality instantiated devices, the weighted linear combination of four implicit factors: connectivity, implicit distance, work degree, and mobility is regarded as the criterion for instantiating a device class. The weights in the weighted linear combination are specified according to the requirements of WPAN service and current environment. The proposed weighted device anycasting (WDA) process in DA-QFS is similar to WCA [10]. WCA is proposed to choose the cluster heads for cluster-based routing protocol (CRP) in mobile ad-hoc network. The optimal solution for selecting devices for WPAN service and selecting cluster heads for CRP is proved as an NP-hard problem [11]. Hence, existing solutions to this problem are based on distributed approaches. However, if the device classes are not carefully instantiated in real network (RN), then the overhead to maintain the existing connections is increased due to the topology change [10]. Therefore, WDA is a semi-distributed approach. The status of all candidate devices are collected locally and the decision of instantiated device is made centrally. Before we introduce the WDA, some notations are defined as follows:

- n_t is the device class being instantiated in CTG.
- $\widetilde{N}_t$ is the set of all candidate devices of n_t in RN.
- $\widetilde{n}_t^i$ is a candidate device with index i in RN ($\widetilde{n}_t^i \in \widetilde{N}_t$).
- P_{n_t} is the set of n_t's parents in CTG. For example, P_{n_A}, P_{n_B}, and P_{n_C} are $\{n_U\}$, $\{n_U\}$, and $\{n_A, n_B\}$, respectively.
- $\overline{P}_{\widetilde{n}_t^i}$ is the set of instantiated parent devices of n_t's parents in CTG which are in the transmission range of $\widetilde{n}_t^i$. If $\overline{n}_P$ belongs to $\overline{P}_{\widetilde{n}_t^i}$, then n_P belongs to P_{n_t}. However, although n_P belongs to P_{n_t}, it is not true that $\overline{n}_P$ belongs to $\overline{P}_{\widetilde{n}_t^i}$.
- $dist(M, N)$ is the distance between device M and device N.
- $dist_{max}$ is the maximum distance which two nodes are can directly communicate with each other.

Two typical definitions of $dist(M, N)$ are Euclidian distance and round trip time [12]. If Euclidian distance is adopted, then $dist_{max}$ is the maximum transmission range. However, if round trip time is regarded as the distance, then $dist_{max}$ is the threshold of round trip time. A device is unable to directly communicate with another device without a response in $dist_{max}$.

When n_t is being instantiated, the weighted linear combination of four implicit factors for each candidate device is obtained by the user device in WDA as follows:

Step 1) Obtaining the connectivity for all $\widetilde{n}_t^i \in \widetilde{N}_t$. The connectivity of $\widetilde{n}_t^i$ is given by

$$C_{\widetilde{n}_t^i} = \frac{|P_{n_t}| - |\overline{P}_{\widetilde{n}_t^i}|}{|P_{n_t}|} \tag{1}$$

where $|P_{n_t}|$ and $|\overline{P}_{\widetilde{n}_t^i}|$ are the degrees of P_{n_t} and $\overline{P}_{\widetilde{n}_t^i}$, respectively.

Step 2) Obtaining the implicit distance for all $\widetilde{n}_t^i \in \widetilde{N}_t$. The implicit distance of $\widetilde{n}_t^i$ is given by

$$D_{\widetilde{n}_t^i} = \sum_{\forall \overline{n}_P, \overline{n}_P \in \overline{P}_{\widetilde{n}_t^i}} \alpha(n_P, n_t) \frac{dist(\overline{n}_P, \widetilde{n}_t^i)}{dist_{max}} \tag{2}$$

where $\alpha(n_P, n_t)$ is the normalized traffic load on (n_P, n_t). $\alpha(n_P, n_t)$ is given by

$$\alpha(n_P, n_t) = \frac{\epsilon(n_P, n_t)}{\sum_{\forall n_n, n_n \in P_{n_t}} \epsilon(n_n, n_t)} \tag{3}$$

where ϵ is the relative ratio of expected traffic load specified in CTG.
Step 3) Obtaining the work degree for all $\widetilde{n}_t^i \in \widetilde{N}_t$. The work degree of $\widetilde{n}_t^i$ is given by

$$L_{\widetilde{n}_t^i} = \frac{I_{\widetilde{n}_t^i}}{\lambda_{\widetilde{n}_t^i}} \tag{4}$$

where $I_{\widetilde{n}_t^i}$ is the number of users using $\widetilde{n}_t^i$, and $\lambda_{\widetilde{n}_t^i}$ is the maximum number of users who can use $\widetilde{n}_t^i$. The value of $\lambda_{\widetilde{n}_t^i}$ depends on the computation power of $\widetilde{n}_t^i$.
Step 4) Obtaining the mobility for all $\widetilde{n}_t^i \in \widetilde{N}_t$. In our paper, the mobility of $\widetilde{n}_t^i$ is defined as the difference of observed distances. Assume that $k+1$ samples of observed distance at $t_0, t_1, t_2, ..., t_{k-1}, t_k$ and the mobility of $\widetilde{n}_t^i$ is given by

$$M_{\widetilde{n}_t^i} = \frac{1}{|\overline{P}_{\widetilde{n}_t^i}|} \frac{1}{k} \sum_{\forall \overline{n}_p, \overline{n}_p \in \overline{P}_{\widetilde{n}_t^i}} \sum_{j=1}^{k} \frac{|dist(\overline{n}_P, \widetilde{n}_t^i)_{t_j} - dist(\overline{n}_P, \widetilde{n}_t^i)_{t_{j-1}}|}{dist_{max}} \tag{5}$$

where $dist(\overline{n}_P, \widetilde{n}_t^i)_{t_j}$ is the observed distance at t_j.
Step 5) Obtaining the weighted linear combination for all $\widetilde{n}_t^i \in \widetilde{N}_t$. The weighted linear combination of $\widetilde{n}_t^i$ is given by

$$W_{\widetilde{n}_t^i} = w_C C_{\widetilde{n}_t^i} + w_D D_{\widetilde{n}_t^i} + w_L L_{\widetilde{n}_t^i} + w_M M_{\widetilde{n}_t^i} \tag{6}$$

where w_C, w_D, w_L, and w_M are the weights of four implicit factors and $w_C + w_D + w_L + w_M = 1$. The weights of four implicit factors are specified according to the requirements of the WPAN service and current environment. For multimedia services w_L and w_M are set to high to avoid selecting a high-loaded device and a highly mobile one which results in long packet delay. In the other hand, if the energy consumption is a critical concern, then w_C and w_D are set to high to reflect the importance of energy conservation.
Step 6) The candidate device with the smallest value of weighted linear combination is regarded as the instantiated device of n_t.
Step 7) Step 2-6 are repeated to instantiate remaining device classes until all device classes are instantiated.

The number of additional control packets sent to collect the status of all candidate devices in DA-QFS is given by $\sum_{i=1}^{n}(p_i + k_i \times l_i)$ where n, p_i, k_i, and l_i are the number of device classes required to provide the WPAN service, the number of instantiated parent devices of n_i, the number of candidate devices of n_i, and the level of n_i in CTG, respectively. Therefore, the number of additional control packets depends on the size and the structure of CTG (i.e. the service profile of WPAN service). Typically, n is small for a WPAN service. The functionalities provided by multiple simple device classes can be provided by a complex device class to further reduce n. On the other hand, p_i and l_i vary on the structure of CTG. This is an issue to design the best service profile for a given WPAN service.

In DA-QFS the weighted linear combination of four implicit factors on all instantiated devices are updated periodically by user device to maintain the performance of the WPAN service and to prevent the WPAN service being interrupted. Therefore, a device class needs to be re-instantiated when the weighted linear combination of current instantiated device drops by δ percent. The value of δ is determined according to the sensitivity to the performance of the WPAN service.

4 Simulation Result

4.1 Service Profile in Simulation

All simulation is accomplished with ns-2. The TG and CTG of the given WPAN service are depicted in Fig. 3(a) and Fig. 3(b), respectively. The parameters in our simulation are shown in Table 1. The Euclidian distance is adopted. In DA-BFS the HELLO timer is set to 7 seconds for detecting a failed device [6]. In DA-QFS if the weighted linear combination of an instantiated device drops by 10 percent, then the corresponding device class needs to be re-instantiated.

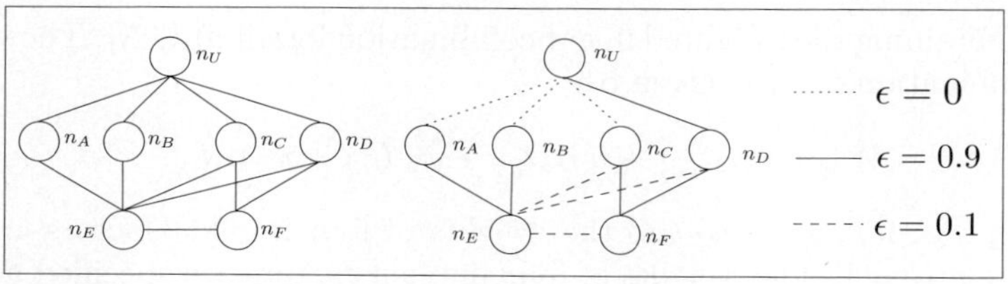

Fig. 3. (a) The TG and (b) The CTG of the given WPAN service

Table 1. Simulation Parameters

Number of device classes	6
Number of physical devices	60 (10 per device class) + n (number of users)
Number of user devices	1, 10
Relative traffic load ratio	Data flow: 0.9, Control flow: 0.1
Initial energy	1000 joules
(w_C, w_D, w_L, w_M)	(0.1, 0.35, 0.1, 0.45)
Simulation area	100 x 100 (m2)
Transmission range	30 (m)
Mobility model	Random Waypoint
MAC protocol	IEEE 802.15.4
Routing protocol	AODV
Simulation period	110 (sec)
Maximum speed	1, 5, 10, 15, 20 (m/s)

4.2 Performance Comparison

The performance metrics on energy consumption, packet loss, packet delay, and re-start time are evaluated. Two scenarios: (a) 1 user and (b) 10 users are simulated when the devices move with various maximum speeds. All experiment result is the mean value of 10 runs for each simulation.

1) Energy Consumption. In wireless network, the energy consumption is dominated by distance and the number of transmitted bits. Therefore, if a device with small implicit distance is regarded as the instantiated device for each device class, then the energy of each instantiated is efficiently conserved. The energy consumption for 1 user and 10 users are shown in Fig. 4(a) and Fig. 4(b), respectively. Because the implicit distance is a criterion in DA-QFS, the accumulated energy consumption of DA-BFS is smaller than the accumulated energy consumption of DA-BF. The difference is obvious when the maximum speed is from 10m/s to 20m/s. This is because the number of device classes needed to be re-instantiated is larger when the devices are highly mobile. Therefore, the energy is consumed to re-instantiate the failed device classes and to transmit the lost packets in DA-BFS is more than the energy consumed in DA-QFS.

2) Packet Loss Rate. The observed average packet loss rate is also reduced as show in Fig. 4(c) and Fig. 4(d). However, the difference between the scenario with 1 user and the scenario with 10 users is unobvious because the factor of work degree is less concerned in our simulation.

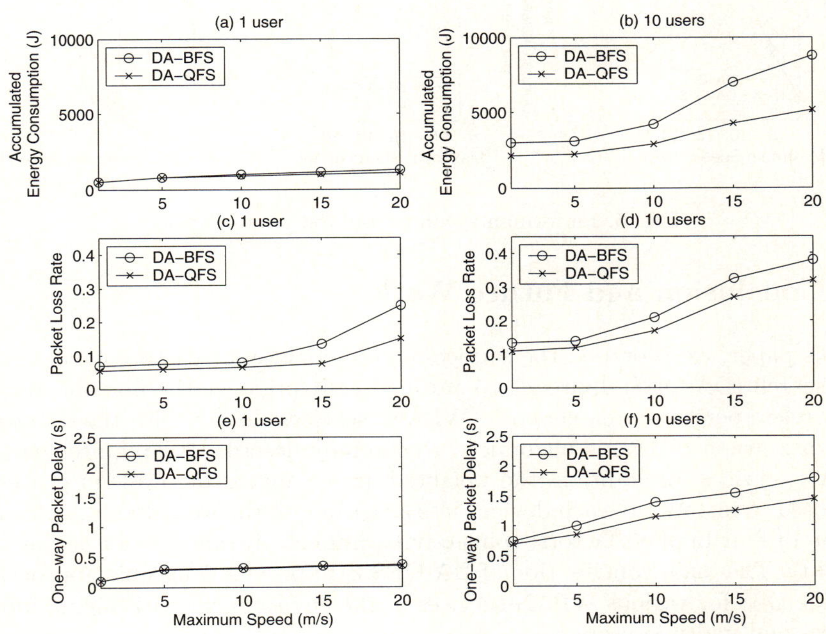

Fig. 4. Performance comparison on energy consumption, packet loss, and packet delay

3) Packet Delay. Because the packet delay depends on the distance between the sender and the receiver, the one-way packet is low when the devices with small implicit distance are selected. The results depicted in Fig. 4(e) and Fig. 4(f) show that DA-QFS is suitable for the environment with multiple users because the observed one-way packet delay is obviously improved with the increased number of users.

4) Re-start Time. Finally, the re-start time spent on re-starting an interrupted WPAN service is observed. The re-start time is the product of the average number of interruption events, the average number of device classes needed to be re-instantiated per interruption event, and the average time spent on reinstantiating a device class. In our simulation the average time spent on re-instantiating a device class is 0.05 seconds for DA-BFS and is around 0.1 for DA-QFS. However, the number of interruption events and the number of device classes needed to be re-instantiated per interruption event are both reduced in DA-QFS as shown in Fig. 5(a) and Fig. 5(b), respectively. Thus, although the time spent on re-instantiating a device class in DA-QFS is higher than the time spent in DA-BFS, DA-QFS still perform well on re-start time as shown in Fig. 5(c).

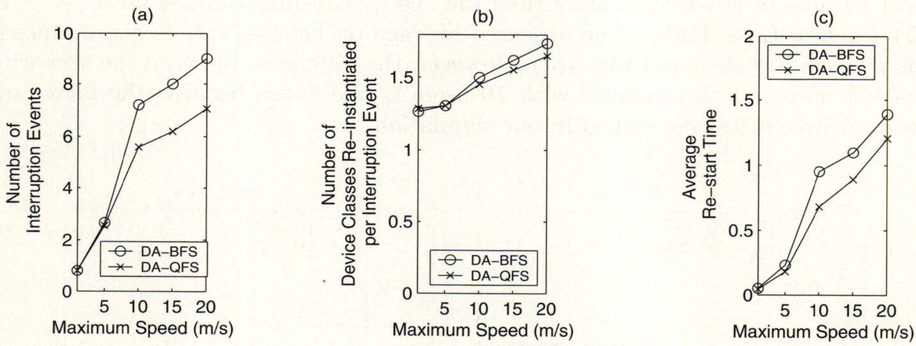

Fig. 5. Performance comparison on re-start time

5 Conclusion and Future Work

In this paper, we proposed the service-oriented device anycasting using quality first search (DA-QFS) approach to automatically organize the portable devices for wireless personal area network (WPAN) services. In DA-QFS the characterized task graph (CTG) is introduced to carefully describe the requirements for WPAN services. In addition, the weighted device anycasting (WDA) process is proposed to instantiate each device class according to the weighted linear combination of four implicit factors: connectivity, implicit distance, work degree, and mobility. The main contribution of DA-QFS is to provide a feasible approach to provide QoS for various WPAN services in the environment with highly mobile devices and multiple users.

An CTG generator creating a tree-based service profile (SP) will help us to reduce the overhead introduced by DA-QFS in the proactive manner. In addition, an adaptive WDA is another work in the future. There are two issues in an adaptive WDA. First, an algorithm takes SP as input and returns the weights in weighted linear combination of four implicit factors. Second, a feedback mechanism takes the status of the WPAN service as input and returns the adjusted weights in weighted linear combination of four implicit factors. Therefore, a better performance of the WPAN service can be expected.

References

1. M. Bohlen, J. Fabian, D. Pfeifer, and J.T. Rinker: Prototypes in pervasive computing. IEEE Pervasive Computing, **4(4)** (2005) 78–80
2. R. Banerjee: From research to classroom a course in pervasive computing. IEEE Pervasive Computing, **4(3)** (2005) 83–86
3. C. L. Chen, K. R. Lee, R. S. Wang, and Y. H. Kuo: An Energy-proportional Routing Algorithm for Lifetime Extension of Clustering-based Wireless Sensor Networks. In Proc. of Workshop on Wireless, Ad Hoc, and Sensor Networks, (2005)
4. R. F. Heile et al: IEEE Standard Part 15.3: Wireless Media Access Control (MAC) and Physical Layer (PHY) Specifications for High Rate Wireless Personal Area Networks (WPANs). IEEE, (2003)
5. V. Srivastava and M. Motani: Cross-layer design: a survey and the road ahead. IEEE Communications Magazine, **43(12)** (2005) 112–119
6. P. Basu, W. Ke, and T. D. C. Little: Dynamic Task-Based Anycasting in Mobile Ad Hoc Networks. Mobile Networks and Applications, **8(5)** (2003) 593–612
7. A. Joshi, D. Chakraborty, and Y. Yesha: An Integrated Service Discovery and Routing Protocol for Ad Hoc Networks. Technical Report, TR-CS-0323, University of Maryland, Baltimore County, (2003)
8. S. Helal, N. Desai, and C. Lee: Konark-A Service Discovery and Delivery Protocol for Ad-Hoc Networks. In Proc. of Third IEEE Conf. Wireless Comm. Networks, (2003)
9. K. Pahlavan and P. Krishnamurthy: Principles of Wireless Networks: A Unified Approach. Prentice Hall, (2001)
10. M. Chatterjee, S. K. Das, and D. Turgut: WCA: A Weighted Clustering Algorithm for Mobile Ad Hoc Networks. J. Cluster Computing, **5(2)** (2002) 193–204
11. S. Basagni, I. Chlamtac and A. Farago: A generalized clustering algorithm for peer-to-peer network. In Proc. of Workshop on Algorithmic Aspects of Communication, (1997).
12. E. Wu, J. Tsai, and M. Gerla: The effect of radio propagation on multimedia, mobile, multiho networks: models and countermeasures. In: Proc. of IEEE Singapore International Conference on Networks, (1997) 411–425

BaseStation Assisted TCP: A Simple Way to Improve Wireless TCP

Shaoen Wu, Saâd Biaz, Yiming Ji, and Bing Qi

Dept. of Computer Science and Software Engineering
Auburn University
107 Dunstan Hall, Auburn University,
AL, 36849-5347, USA
{wushaoe, sbiaz, jiyimin, qibing1}@auburn.edu

Abstract. In recent years, extensive research effort has been devoted to TCP congestion control in hybrid wired-wireless networks. A general agreement is that the TCP sender should respond differently to wireless losses and disconnection, i.e., not slow down as drastically as for congestion losses. Thus, research focus for wireless TCP congestion control is the discrimination between the wireless inherent packet losses and the network congestion packet losses in wired network. In addition, researchers attempt to detect temporary or lengthy wireless disconnection. This paper proposes a simple but novel strategy, dubbed *BSA-TCP* (Base Station Assisted TCP), (1) to accurately discriminate wireless losses from wired network congestion losses and (2) to detect and notify a TCP sender about wireless disconnections. The key distinctive feature of the proposed scheme is its general use for most issues at stake for TCP over wireless: loss discrimination, wireless disconnection and handoffs. It also circumvents the asymmetric problem that acknowledgements might follow different paths from those of data packets. Such asymmetry problem is common to mechanisms that buffer and retransmit wireless lost data packets locally at the base station. The proposed method also addresses energy efficiency.

Keywords: wireless TCP, energy efficiency, loss discrimination.

1 Introduction

With wireless network evolving popularly to access Internet, enormous research effort has been dedicated to TCP congestion control over hybrid networks. Extensive efforts include [1,2,3,4,5,6,7,8,9,10]. In conventional wired networks, TCP congestion control assumes that the packet loss is due to network congestion. If a packet loss occurs, a TCP sender will throttle its sending rate by reducing its congestion window size [11]. If network congestion is severe, the TCP sender will time out and start from slow-start phase for packet transmission. Therefore the network load is reduced at the cost of throughput. When a wireless link is involved, there are mainly two cases defeating the TCP congestion control. The first case is packet drop due to data bits error or packet loss through existing poorly connected wireless link, which is severely prone to interference. The wireless packet loss misleads TCP sender as congestion loss. The second case results

E. Sha et al. (Eds.): EUC 2006, LNCS 4096, pp. 630–641, 2006.

from temporary or lengthy wireless disconnection due to some physical factor, such as handoff, location obstacles or weather [12]. The disconnection can improperly trigger timeouts at the TCP sender. Thus, for packet loss and packet drop under poor wireless channel conditions, a key is loss discrimination, so that the TCP sender reacts appropriately to each type of loss: throttle as usual for congestion losses, but keep up for other losses. However, as for the wireless disconnection, some explicit or implicit feedback is needed to notify TCP sender not to invoke slow-start [11]. As a result, the throughput can be largely improved for those TCP applications, like Web browsing or FTP, through the wireless link. Several innovative solutions were proposed to address these problems and difficulties in wireless TCP congestion control. Some of them can discriminate the wireless loss with some probability, such as [1]. And, others, like [2], [7], [8], [10], proposed mechanisms with local buffering and retransmission of lost wireless packet with the help of some intermediate network components, like the base station or the access point.

Proposed BSA-TCP tries to cover all these problems with simple but efficient techniques. We assume that TCP data packets flow from host in wired network to wireless terminal. This assumption is reasonable because most TCP application servers are wired connection. In the proposed strategy, the base station or wireless access point identifies the congestion loss from packet sequence number gap between two successive arriving packets on wired path between the fixed host (TCP sender) and the base station. Then the base station notifies the mobile host (TCP receiver) of the congestion loss by setting a flag in the header of out of order packets. This flag means for the mobile host that the packet loss is due to congestion. If there is no flag set in packet header, it assumes the loss occurred on the wireless link. The mobile receiver can then notify the loss diagnosis with a flag on the acknowledgment (duplicate acknowledgment in fact) to fixed host (TCP sender). Thus, the sender fixed host can appropriately responds to different packet losses. In addition, the basestation detects wireless disconnection and feeds it back to the fixed host by keeping a *copy* of the last acknowledgment sent from mobile host to fixed host. If the wireless connection is cut off or handoff happens, the base station detects this with cooperation from lower layers and send the acknowledgment copy with a *zero receive window*. This trick exploits the TCP ZWA (Zero Window Advertisement) to force the sender into persist mode [13]. Thus the sender does not suffer from the wireless disconnection.

Comparably, since no data packet buffering is required at the base station, the proposed technique eliminates partial work load at the base station and totally maintains the end-to-end semantic. The proposed scheme discriminates packet loss with absolute precision and feeds back wireless disconnections with the cooperation from lower layers. In addition, it doesn't suffer from the asymmetric path problem. For the implementation considered, this mechanism requires limited processing and can coexist with regular TCP.

The remaining of this paper is organized as follows: In Section 2, the related progress and achievement similar to the proposed work strategy is briefly surveyed. Section 3 describes the proposed schema and its advantages and disadvantages. Section 4 discusses the simulation. Finally, Section 5 concludes this paper.

2 Related Research

To discriminate the wireless loss and notify the sender about wireless disconnection, researchers have proposed innovative mechanisms to address these issues in different location of a hybrid wired/wireless path. Generally, these proposals can be characterized into two first-level categories: end-to-end and non-end-to-end.

End-to-end: In this category, the TCP connection retains the end-to-end semantic. Most of the proposals fall into this category because the end-to-end semantic is very important and basic to end-to-end transport protocols and it should be preserved in any technique enhancement. In the end-to-end category, some proposals still require the cooperation of intermediary nodes, like routers, on the wired network. Some involve the base station. And exceptionally, Freeze-TCP [4] is a genuine end-to-end mechanism that does not require any intermediate node's cooperation.

Router involved: In this sub-category, the queue management is expected to help discriminate wireless losses. Since these routers are located before the wireless hop, this type of mechanism still works even if acknowledgments follow different paths from data packets path. The proposal "de-randomize packet loss" [1] is such an innovative mechanism. When congestion happens, the router deliberately, **not randomly**, drops some specific pre-marked packets. Then the mobile receiver can discriminate packet losses with high probability. The receiver notifies the fixed host sender about the nature of the packet loss. This mechanism is very promising in packet loss discrimination because it doesn't split the TCP connection. However, it's difficult to detect wireless disconnections, which cannot be neglected in the wireless environment.

Base station as a gateway: The base station acts as a proxy or gateway to bridge wired path and wireless connection. With cross-layer cooperation or connection splitting, the base station help discriminate packet losses or notify the sender about the wireless disconnections. When the base station buffers data packets and retransmits lost packets (on wireless link), the sender in general is "shielded" from wireless losses: it does not detect them. Since losses are locally recovered, this speeds up the recovery of wireless lost packets.

Snoop [2] is an innovative model typically in this subcategory with a link layer that is TCP-aware. It buffers data packets at the basestation, and examines each acknowledgement to detect wireless packet losses. It locally retransmits wireless lost packets and blocks duplicate acknowledgments related to wireless losses. Snoop improves the throughput by hiding wireless losses from the fixed host (sender) and locally retransmitting wireless losses. However, Snoop requires buffering data packets for each TCP connection. Also, Snoop has no mechanism to cope with wireless disconnections. Another creative idea is **M-TCP** [7]. M-TCP splits the TCP connection into two connections at the *Supervisor Node* (it could be the base station): One TCP connection from sender to BaseStation, and a second TCP connection from BaseStation to mobile host. The BaseStation acknowledges data for the first TCP connection only when the mobile host acknowledges data on the second TCP connection. Note that the BaseStation holds the last acknowledgment from mobile host to fixed host (sender). If no acknowledgment is received by the BaseStation over some period, it infers that wireless disconnection happens. In order to inform the sender, the BaseStation modifies the last acknowledgement with zero window and sends it back to force the sender into persist mode. New acknowledgments from the mobile host will exit the sender out of the persist mode. M-TCP mainly handles the disconnection and low-bandwidth situations adn it is not concerned with packet losses due to packet error. Obviously, M-TCP mechanism requires a precise timing scheme to ensure that the last acknowledgment be sent before the sender times out.

Despite many advantages, generally, the above strategies in this subcategory have the following limitations:

- Local retransmissions at the BaseStation may result in high cost buffering of TCP flows. Because the number of transiting TCP flows is hard to estimate, buffer dimensioning becomes a key issue. Besides, large buffers will require considerable processing when inserting or retrieving packets. This problem is more severe with high-speed wireless links because it needs to buffer more outstanding packets.
- In addition, schemes in this category often face a common problem named *asymmetric path problem* when acknowledgments passes through a reverse path different from that of the data packets. This case is possible, for example in handoff.

No intermediate node involved: Besides above proposals, there is a mechanism named **Freeze-TCP** [4], which doesn't involve any intermediate node. The mobile host detects the impending disconnection to BaseStation with some kind of trigger (for example, from layer-two). Before the disconnection, such as the handoff, occurs, the mobile host freezes the sender with a Zero Window Advertisement (ZWA) in advance. When the connection is restored, the mobile host will re-open the congestion window at the sender with normal acknowledgments. Freeze-TCP is especially efficient for wireless disconnections during handover. However, it does not discriminate wireless losses from congestion losses. Also, it does not handle well unplanned wireless disconnections: some wireless disconnection cannot be predicted due to, for example, an obstacle while roaming. Other similar work in this category includes **TCP-Real** [14] and **TCP-Westwood** [15].

Non end-to-end: Proposals in this category split the connection between the fixed host and mobile host into two TCP connections: these two TCP connections work independently without preserving end-to-end semantic. **I-TCP** [10] is such a strategy. It splits the TCP connection at the BaseStation. The first one is the usual TCP connection from fixed host to base station. The second one from base station to mobile host spans the wireless hop. The base station buffers all data packets and acknowledges receipt to the fixed host. So, the first TCP connection in general deals only with congestion losses and is unaware of losses over the wireless hop: the base station locally retransmits packets lost over the wireless link. Therefore, one major problem is that, even if the wireless connection is fairly poor and the receiver doesn't receive many packets, the original sender (fixed host) will assume that all transmissions are successful . This is the key weakness of I-TCP.

In summary, here are the desirable characteristics that a scheme should fulfill to improve TCP over hybrid wired-wireless networks:

1. The mechanism should be able to discriminate wireless losses and identify a wireless disconnection. These two issues are related to some degree. For example, although some innovative mechanism can discriminate packet losses very well, the

receiver may not be able to send any discrimination feedback if the wireless disconnection lasts too long, leading TCP sender to timeout. This greatly degrades the performance. At the same time, only the base station can accurately diagnose the nature of a packet loss.
2. The end-to-end semantic of TCP should be preserved in the new proposal because it's the core of a transport layer protocol.
3. When a base station is involved, the proposed scheme should take into account the problem of different forward and reverse path problem.
4. When a wireless disconnection occurs, the re-transmission in the wireless connection should be minimized to maximize energy efficiency for power sensitive mobile terminals [6].
5. The last desired characteristic is that the implementation of the new scheme should be simple and compatible with the existing regular TCP.

Some of the above proposals solve the problem of packet loss discrimination while others address the problem of wireless disconnection. A few address the simplicity issue. The proposed BSA-TCP can efficiently address these issues.

3 Basestation Assisted TCP

In this section, we firstly explain how Basestation Assisted TCP **BSA-TCP** works in detail. Then a brief analysis is sketched followed by a discussion regarding implementation concerns.

3.1 BSA-TCP Mechanism

Basically, this proposal is a kind of end-to-end mechanism involving the BaseStation as a gateway. But there is no split of the TCP connection and no buffering of data packets. The proposed scheme addresses all issues discussed above. At the same time, it should be easy to implement in practice. Table 1 summarizes the characteristics of different proposals involving a BaseStation. The table includes only those schemes similar or related to the proposed scheme.

BSA-TCP retains the end-to-end semantic and efficiently addresses the problems wireless TCP faces up, such as loss discrimination and detection of disconnection. With the cooperation from the BaseStation, the wireless loss can be discriminated and the disconnection can be detected and fed back to the sender. In this proposal, we assume that

Table 1. Wireless TCP Mechanisms Comparision

Mechanism	I-TCP	M-TCP	Freeze-TCP	BSA-TCP
End-to-end	no	yes	yes	yes
Loss discrimination	yes	no	no	yes
Wireless disconnection	no	yes	yes	yes
Light buffering at BaseStation	no	no	yes	yes
Asymmetic path problem	yes	yes	yes	no
IPSec problem	yes	yes	no	yes

local retransmissions at wireless link layer work well. This assumption is reasonable because almost all popular wireless link layer protocols, such as link layer of IEEE802.11 and 3G network [16,17,18], include the local link layer retransmission, like ARQ, with tighter timing constraints than TCP at transportation layer. We also assume that the base station can detect the wireless disconnection from link layer signalling. For instance, when link layer infers that the wireless link is disconnected, it signals to upper layers. In the following, we discuss how BSA-TCP works and solves each problem confronted by wireless TCP.

BSA-TCP requires the cooperation of the sender, the BaseStation and the receiver. Packet discrimination can be signaled using an unused bit on the TCP header or using a new option field. The BaseStation is the best place where (1) to accurately discriminate packet losses and (2) to feed back a wireless disconnection to sender because an acknowledgment message from the mobile host cannot be sent through during a wireless disconnection. Thus, the BaseStation is a key element to the solution. The following explains in detail how different components operate collaboratively and procedurally in this strategy.

Fixed Host (TCP sender): The functionality at the sender is pretty simple. The fixed host must appropriately react to packet losses. It checks the discrimination flag in the acknowledgement: If set, the fixed host infers that the packet loss is a wireless loss and does not trigger any congestion control mechanism to throttle the sending rate: The TCP sender just retransmits the lost packet. All other actions and parameters are the same as in traditional TCP without packet loss. Otherwise, if the discrimination flag is not set, the sender infers that this is a congestion loss and regular TCP congestion control algorithms are invoked. In case of wireless disconnection, the TCP sender gets an implicit feedback with the acknowledgment of zero flow control receive window from BaseStation. Therefore, the TCP sender enters into persistent mode [13], in which it freezes all the parameters and waits for a fresh acknowledgment.

Mobile Host (TCP receiver): In this strategy, the mobile host requires only a slight modification to check whether to set the loss discrimination flag in the acknowledgment (based on the loss notification flag in data packet). When the mobile host receives a data packet, it checks whether a loss discrimination flag is set or not. If the flag is set, it infers that the packet sequence gap is due to the congestion losses. Then the mobile host does not set the wireless loss flag in the acknowledgement so that congestion control is invoked at the sender. If loss discrimination flag is not set in data packet, the mobile host knows that the sequence gap is due to wireless packet drops or loss in the wireless connection. Then it sets the wireless loss flag in all following duplicate acknowledgments so that the TCP sender fixed host identifies the loss as not related to congestion. Then the TCP sender doesn't reduce the congestion window and just retransmits the lost packet. Note that the flag is set in all following duplicate acknowledgments (DACK) in case the first DACK with the flag set is lost on the wireless link.

BaseStation: In this strategy, the BaseStation performs significant tasks: It accurately discriminates packet losses and detects the wireless disconnection.

Loss discrimination: the BaseStation monitors the sequence number of every data packet passing through it towards the mobile host. If there is sequence gap between two successive data packets, it accurately infers that the packet loss or out of order is due to network congestion ahead of wireless link. If that case, the BaseStation sets a flag in the out of order packet header to notify the mobile host that the sequence gap is NOT due to a wireless loss. Or, the BaseStation will keep data packets unchanged. This notification cooperates with above work of Fixed Host and Mobile Host to achieve the wireless discrimination.

Disconnection detection: The wireless disconnection from BaseStation to mobile host can be detected by the local link layer retransmission with timer mechanism. As we mentioned above, most of the wireless link layer protocols today are integrated with the retransmission capability. And normally the timer value for this link layer retransmission is contingent than that of timer for the TCP packet loss.

We assume our agent at the BaseStation will get a notification or trigger from the link layer when link layer retransmission times out. This is a reasonable assumption because the IEEE802.21 organization is working on a standard concerning such notifying triggers [19]. The BaseStation can then infer the wireless link is unavailable to mobile host.

In good wireless channel condition, when the BaseStation relays the acknowledgement back to the TCP sender, it retains one *copy* of the last acknowledgement. If it detects wireless disconnection, it resets the receive windows in the copy of the acknowledgement to 0 and resends this acknowledgement back to the TCP sender fixed host. Because the receive window is different from the previous acknowledgement, this acknowledgement will not be thought as a Duplicate Acknowledgement at the TCP sender. The receive window 0 in the acknowledgement forces the TCP sender into persist mode, in which the TCP sender freezes all parameters in congestion control and waits for the update acknowledgement to reactivate. This is different from M-TCP [7]. In M-TCP, the BaseStation holds the last acknowledgement **itself**, not the *copy* of it. Thus, M-TCP requires a delicate timing mechanism to make sure the absence of that last acknowledgement will not cause TCP sender to time out. Since our proposal doesn't hold the acknowledgement itself, just a copy of it, no timing mechanism is required with the proposed solution. When the wireless connection is restored, the BaseStation gets notification from the link layer and re-sends the copy of the last acknowledgement with the receiving window unchanged (original non null receive window) back to TCP sender. Or it relays back a new acknowledgement from mobile host. Then this non-zero receive window acknowledgement activates the TCP sender to normal transmission status with the congestion window restored. It's obvious that this reopened congestion window is far more aggressive and thus the throughput should improve significantly.

Asymmetric Path: In this strategy, there is no TCP connection split at the BaseStation. The BaseStation doesn't buffer data packets. Therefore it avoids the problem of acknowledgements transmitted on different path from that of data packets: For example, after a handoff, the acknowledgement might go through a new BaseStation. When the TCP sender receives the acknowledgement, it need not know where the acknowledgement passed through and just responds as end-to-end.

From the above discussion, we can conclude that the BSA-TCP has the following advantages:

- It does not split a TCP connection. Thus, it retains the end-to-end semantic.
- At the same time, because no packet is buffered at BaseStation, this strategy does not require the monitoring of acknowledgements from the mobile host and therefore avoids the asymmetric acknowledgement path issue.
- Since the BaseStation is the bridge between wired and wireless links, it accurately discriminates the wireless loss.
- The ability to detect wireless disconnections can efficiently reduce spurious retransmissions. Thus this proposal is energy efficient to some degree.
- Furthermore, precise wireless packet loss discrimination and feedback of wireless disconnection efficiently eliminates TCP timeouts resulting from wireless link, and thus avoids the low-efficient slow-start phase.
- Additionally, it's compatible with the regular TCP. If the TCP sender does not "understand" the loss discrimination setting, it will ignore this setting and will respond conservatively as the regular TCP sender. And if the receiver mobile host has no such implementation, it will not discriminate the loss flag from the BaseStation and just act as the regular TCP receiver. Thus there is almost no influence on the regular TCP as the bottom line operation.

Note also that, although there is a little implementation needed for wireless discrimination at the sender, as for detecting wireless disconnection, this functionality runs at the BaseStation, and there is no extra implementation needed at the sender. The reason is that, even with the regular TCP, the 0 window acknowledgement from BaseStation will force TCP sender to work for wireless disconnection.

However, the BSA-TCP confronts one common problem for all mechanisms that involve monitoring TCP header packets in intermediate nodes such as a BaseStation. If IPSec is used, intermediate nodes, including the BaseStation, cannot read the TCP header [3] and extract information such as sequence numbers. Another disadvantage is to work cross layer, which is supposed to be a trend as to complex wireless network in the future.

3.2 BSA-TCP Performance and Implementation Brief Analysis

In [1], the authors derived the enhanced formula to estimate the TCP connection throughput with the wireless link. Consider a discriminator with accuracies A_c and A_w is used for congestion loss and wireless loss with TCP (A_c represents the ratio of congestion losses correctly diagnosed. A_w is similarly defined for losses not related to congestion). p_c and p_w respectively represent the congestion packet loss rate and wireless packet loss rate. The throughput can be expressed as:

$$Thrg_w = \frac{1}{RTT\sqrt{\frac{2bp_{cN}}{3}} + T_0 min(1, 3\sqrt{\frac{3bp_{cw}}{8}})p_{cw}(1+32p_{cw}^2)} \tag{1}$$

where $p_{cN} = A_c p_c + (1 - A_w)p_w$ and $p_{cw} = p_c + p_w$. Without discrimination, the traditional TCP throughput should take $p_{cN} = p_c + p_w$ and $p_{cw} = p_c + p_w$ with $A_c = 1$ and $A_w = 0$. Since BSA-TCP accurately discriminates all types of losses, then $A_c = 1$ and $A_w = 1$. Moreover, timeouts at TCP sender are eliminated for the wireless losses.

Therefore, the value p_{cw} in above equation reduces to p_c. As a result, the throughput for BSA-TCP can be expressed as:

$$Thrg_{BSA} = \frac{1}{RTT\sqrt{\frac{2bp_c}{3}} + T_0 min(1, 3\sqrt{\frac{3bp_c}{8}})p_c(1+32p_c^2)} \tag{2}$$

In other words, the throughput is the same as on strictly wired network. Thus the theoretical throughput can be achieved through the BSA-TCP, without considering wireless disconnection, should be

$$\frac{Thrg_{BSA} - Thrg_w}{Thrg_w} \tag{3}$$

In practical implementation, as for the loss flag presented in currently TCP packet header, two possible ways are available. One is to use an unused or reserved bit in one field of TCP header. The other method is to use options of the TCP header.

4 Simulation and Analysis

We evaluate the performance improvement with network simulator *ns-2* [20]. Mainly, the performance improvement is due to two contributions: one from the packet loss discrimination and the other from the wireless disconnection detection. Since our strategy in detecting wireless link disconnection is essentially similar to that of M-TCP [7], it is reasonable to expect the same improvement. Thus, this paper only focuses on evaluating throughput improvement resulting from the sole contribution of packet loss discrimination.

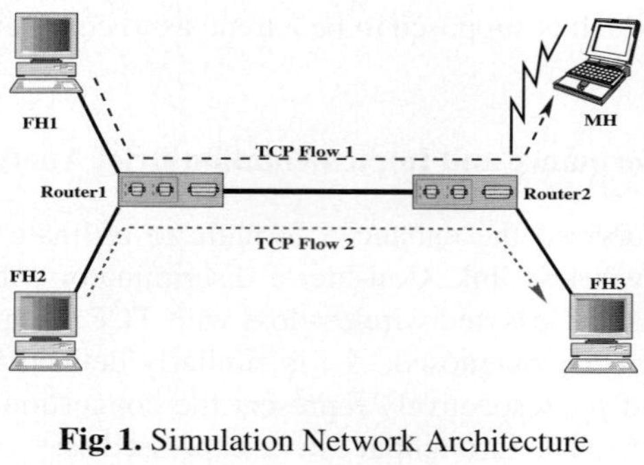

Fig. 1. Simulation Network Architecture

Based on the popular IEEE802.11, wireless link bandwidth is chosen from 10 Mbps through 100 Mbps in our experiments, with the concern that current WLAN normally covers data rate from 11 Mbps to 108 Mbps (in recently IEEE802.11g). The propagation delay varies from 2ms to 8ms for wireless link. Two-state Markov wireless loss is taken as the error model in target wireless connection, in which the link good state and bad state probability are respectively 0.7 and 0.3. When link is in bad state, the wireless packet error rate $L_{BadStateLossRate}$ ranges from 0.001 to 0.1, and 0.0001 to 0.01

for $L_{GoodStateLossRate}$ in good state. Thus the overall loss rate in the wireless link in experiment should be:

$$L = 0.7L_{GoodStateLossRate} + 0.3L_{BadStateLossRate} \tag{4}$$

We evaluate the performance improvement for TCP-Newreno and TCP-Sack. The basic configuration is in Figure 1. Because of the space limitations, we just include part of the results here.

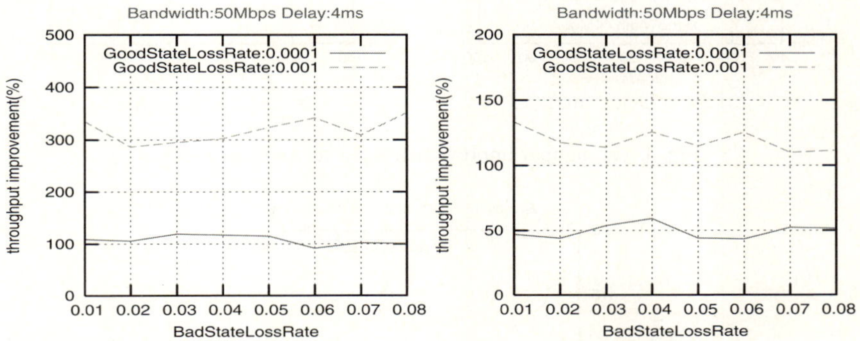

(a) TCP-Sack (b) TCP-Newreno

Fig. 2. Throughput Improvement in different TCP flavors

In Figure 2(a), and Figure 2(b), the x-axis represents the wireless packet loss rate in bad state, which ranges from 0.01 to 0.08. The y-axis represents the BSA-TCP throughput improvement in percentage over the regular TCP (no wireless loss discrimination). The short one hop delay used in these two experiments stands for the delay at the last hop (wireless access) in WLAN network. These figures show that TCP-Newreno and TCP-Sack exhibit a significant performance improvement even when the good state packet loss rate is very low. The improvement is more dramatic when the good state packet loss is higher. In general, the throughput improvement is over 50% for TCP-NewReno, 100% for TCP-Sack.

Overall, the throughput improvement is more significant for TCP-Sack than for TCP-Newreno. TCP-Sack exploits better the discrimination of losses and is more efficient in avoiding spurious retransmissions.

Figure 3(a) illustrates the impact of bandwidth (at the bottleneck) and large propagation delay on throughput improvement. Figure 3(a) plots three curves for bandwidths 30 Mpbs, 60 Mpbs, and 90 Mbps. The y-axis is the improvement compared to regular TCP and x-axis is the propagation delay value of the wireless lossy link. This figure illustrates that wireless bandwidth doesn't have much effect on improvement. Higher round trip time results in better throughput improvement when loss discrimination is used. Without loss discrimination, regular TCP takes more time to recover from halving the congestion window. As the round trip time increases, regular TCP gets more penalized by halving the congestion window when losses occur. Loss discrimination eliminates this penalty for wireless losses. But, as shown in Figure 3(b), when the propagation delay is too large, the improvement decreases drastically. This is because long

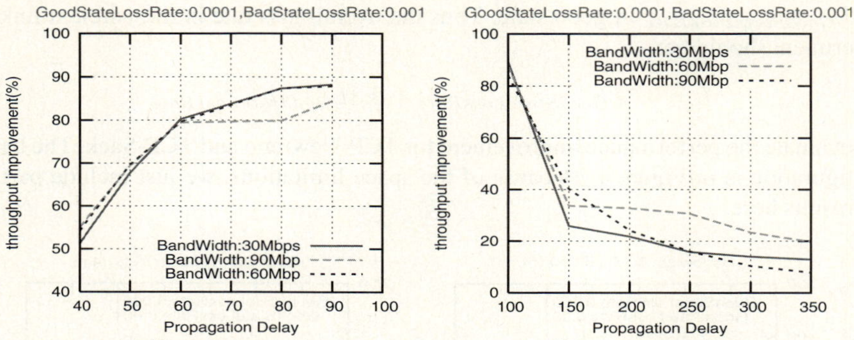

(a) Short Delay (ms) (b) Large Delay (ms)

Fig. 3. Throughput Improvement in different Bandwidth

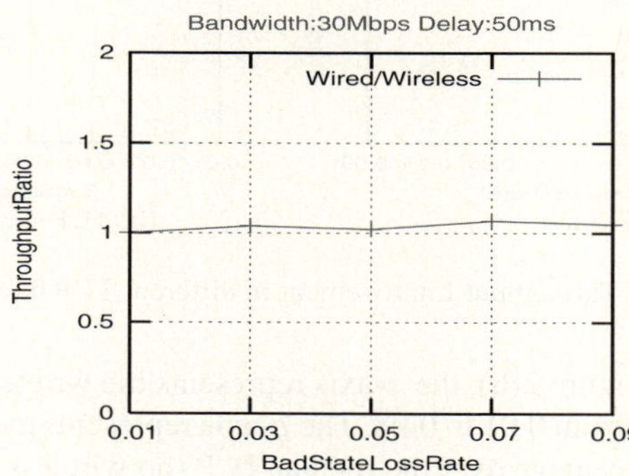

Fig. 4. BSA-TCP Fairness on Throughput

propagation delay results in less packets lost in wireless link and thus less "room" for improvement.

Fairness is also evaluated when BSA-TCP is introduced. As shown in Figure 1, two different TCP flows pass through the same backbone. One is from a fixed host to another fixed host connected to network through wired links. The other is from a fixed host to mobile host with BSA-TCP. The result demonstrated in Figure 4 reports the fairness. Here, the x-axis is the wireless packet loss rate in bad state. The y-axis, $ThroughputRatio$, represents the throughput of TCP flow 1 through wireless link with BSA-TCP over that of the TCP flow 2 in the wired regular TCP connection. It's observed that the ratio varies around 1, which justifies the fairness.

As stated above, since the M-TCP [7] has exhaustedly explored wireless disconnections, this work does not replicate such simulation efforts.

5 Conclusion

This paper introduces a novel strategy, dubbed BSA-TCP, for wireless TCP congestion control. With the BaseStation helping in packet loss discrimination and feeding back the disconnection notification, BSA-TCP efficiently addresses the wireless disconnection detection, loss discrimination and asymmetric path issues common in wireless TCP. We also find that the BaseStation is necessary in the wireless TCP when the disconnection is considered and if we want to discriminate the loss precisely and deterministically. With consideration of the easy implementation in practice and the wireless TCP problems it can solve, this strategy is pretty efficient.

References

1. Biaz, S., Vaidya, N.: "De-Randomizing" Congestion Losses to Improve TCP Performance Over Wired-Wireless Networks. IEEE/ACM Transactions on Networking **13** (2005) 596–608
2. H. Balakrishnan, S. Seshan, E.A., Katz, R.: Improving TCP/IP Performance over Wireless Networks. In: the 1st ACM Intl' Conf. On Mobile Computing and Networking (Mobicom). (1995)
3. V.Tsaoussidis, I.Matta: Open Issues on TCP for Mobile Computing. In: Wireless Communications and Mobile Computing. Volume 2. (2002)
4. Goff, T., Moronski, J., Phatak, D.: Freeze-TCP: A True End-to-End Enhancement Mechanism or Mobile Environ Environments. In: INFOCOM. (2000)
5. Bakshi, B., Krishna, P., Vaidya, N., Pradhan, D.: Improving Performance of TCP over Wireless Networks. In: the IEEE 17th ICDCS'97. (1997) 365–373
6. Balakrishnan, H., Padmanabhan, V., Seshan, S., Katz, R.: A Comparison of Mechanisms for Improving TCP Performance over Wireless Links. ACM/IEEE Transactions on Networking **5** (1997) 756–769
7. Brown, K., Singh, S.: M-TCP: TCP for Mobile Cellular Networks. In: the ACM SIGCOMM Computer Communication Review. (1997) 19–43
8. Haas, Z., Agrawal, P.: Mobile-TCP: An Asymmetric Transport Protocol Design for Mobile Systems. In: the IEEE International Conference on Communications (ICC'97). (1997)
9. Bhagwat, P., Bhattacharya, P., Krishna, A., Tripathi, S.K.: Enchancing Throughput over Wireless LANs using Channel State Dependent Packet Scheduling. In: INFOCOM. (1996) 1133–40
10. Bakre, A., Badrinath, B.: I-TCP: Indirect TCP for Mobile Hosts. In: Proceedings of the IEEE ICDCS'95. (1995)
11. Jacobson, V.: Congestion avoidance and control. In: Symposium proceedings on Communications architectures and protocols. (1988) 314–329
12. Tanenbaum, A.S.: Computer Networks. Prentice Hall (2002)
13. Richard, S.: TCP/IP Illustrated, Volume 2: The Implementation. Addison-Wesley (1994)
14. Tsaoussidis, V., Zhang, C.: Tcp-real: Receiver-oriented congestion control. Computer Networks **40** (2002) 477–497
15. C. Casetti, M. Gerla, S.M.M.Y.S., Wang, R.: Tcp westwood: Bandwidth estimation for enhanced transport over wireless links. In: In Proceedings of ACM Mobicom. (2001) pp 287–297
16. IEEE802.11: http://standards.ieee.org/getieee802/download/802.11-1999.pdf. (1999)
17. 3GPP: TSG, RAN Physical layer procedures (FDD), version 5.3.0 (2002)
18. Bender, P., Black, P., Grob, M., Padovani, R., Sindhushayana, N., Viterbi, A.: CDMA/HDR: A Bandwidth-Efficient High-Speed Wireless Data Service for Nomadic Users. In: IEEE Communications Magazine. (2000) 70–77
19. IEEE802.21: http://www.ieee802.org/21/archived_docs/Documents/ fmip_and_l2trigger.pdf. (2005)
20. ISI: (http://www.isi.edu/nsnam/ns/)

Modeling Asymmetric Slot Allocation for Mobile Multimedia Services in Microcell TDD Employing FDD Uplink as Macrocell

Dong-Hoi Kim

Department of Electronic and Communication Engineering,
College of IT, Kangwon National University,
Chuncheon, Kangwon-do, Republic of Korea, 200-701
donghk@kangwon.ac.kr

Abstract. This paper introduces an analytical approach which is provided to calculate the downlink and uplink capacities of the time division duplex (TDD) system utilizing the underused frequency division duplex (FDD) uplink which shares the same frequency band. Then the ratio of downlink and uplink slots in one frame is adjusted, so as to prevent the radio resource waste due to asymmetric traffic characteristic in mobile multimedia services. The computer simulation shows that the resource waste problem can be considerably solved through the asymmetric slot allocation. Thus, this paper can be useful as a guideline in the course of planning a two-layer hierarchical cell structure (HCS) employing the TDD system as a microcell and FDD system as a macrocell as well as a mean to increase the performance of such a system.

1 Introduction

The next wireless communication systems will provide multimedia services including the voice of IP (VoIP) and video streaming, Internet access, and broadcast service [1]. Unlike the VoIP service, asymmetric characteristics of many services (e.g., Internet access and broadcast service) bring about serious radio resource wastes. Thus, as the traffic unbalance between two links may incur an unacceptable resource waste, problems related to it have been studied [2] [3] [4]. The time division duplex (TDD) scheme has been proposed to accommodate asymmetric communications between uplink and downlink. In a TDD communication system, since the uplink has unused surplus channels due to an asymmetric traffic characteristic, it is necessary to adjust the ratio of slots between uplink and downlink in one frame so as to obtain a minimum resource waste. Consequently, such a slot allocation can play an important role in wireless multimedia communication services which require the optimum radio resource utilization.

In this paper, it is assumed that both the frequency division duplex (FDD) and TDD systems can be combined in a single hierarchical structure. The aforementioned systems may be divided into two cases. In one case, they have different frequency bands, and in the other case, they have the same frequency band. This paper deals with the latter case when they share the same frequency band,

E. Sha et al. (Eds.): EUC 2006, LNCS 4096, pp. 642–651, 2006.

and further considers a two-layer environment with the microcell employing the TDD system and the macrocell employing the FDD system [5]. The uplink and downlink capacities of the TDD system by considering the interferences in both links in the microcell TDD and an uplink in the macrocell FDD are calculated. Recently, the 3rd generation partnership project (3GPP) has generated necessary information about the 2.6 GHz FDD system, as detailed below [7]:

- 2500 $\sim$ 2570 MHz: Uplink (UE transmit, Node B receive)
- 2620 $\sim$ 2690 MHz: Downlink (base station (BS) transmit, mobile station (MS) receive)
- The co-existence with IMT2000 technology within 2500 $\sim$ 2690 MHz shall be considered.
- Assigned blocks shall be in multiple of 5.0 MHz.

As a reference, the FDD system is based on the wideband code division multiple access (W-CDMA) system parameters as specified in the 3GPP [6]. This paper is organized as follows. In Section 2, the system model is introduced. In Section 3, the TDD system capacity is analyzed. Section 4 shows that the traffic unbalance problem is evaluated and solved by adjusting the number of slots between uplink and downlink in the TDD cell as a microcell for the cases of sharing the FDD uplink band as a macrocell. The conclusion is given in Section 5.

2 System Model

In general, three different duplexing schemes are used in the wireless communication system design: frequency division duplex (FDD), time division duplex (TDD), and space division duplex (SDD). The FDD is one of the most common duplex schemes in the cellular system. In a TDD system, uplink and downlink transmissions occur at different times and usually share the same frequency. In a FDD system, uplink and downlink channels are located on separate frequencies and occur at the same time. There is a notable savings in power from the TDD architecture which is a direct result of turning the receiver off while in transmission mode and vice versa. However, a disadvantage exists. There is a reduction of the global capacity since there can be no transmission of data while in receiving mode unlike the FDD system. In essence, the TDD system must handle fewer users in a given area than in the FDD system.

All cases which can be considered in a two-layer hierarchical cell structure (HCS) employing the TDD as a microcell and the FDD as a macrocell can be categorized into four different cases in terms of sharing frequency bands and applied direction of links as follows. In the case of a TDD system utilizing an underused FDD uplink, both forward and reverse links have to be taken into account assuming an ideal power control. Case 1: The interference between the FDD uplink as a macrocell and the TDD uplink as a microcell. Case 2: The interference between the FDD uplink as a macrocell and the TDD downlink as a

Table 1. All cases in a two-layer HCS employing the TDD as a microcell and the FDD as a macrocell

	FDD	TDD
case 1	Uplink	Uplink
case 2	Uplink	Downlink
case 3	downlink	Uplink
case 4	downlink	Downlink

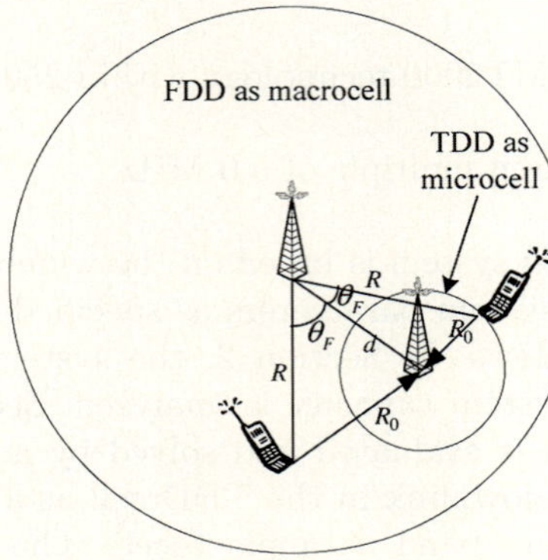

Fig. 1. The interference between the FDD uplink as a macrocell and the TDD uplink as a microcell (case 1)

microcell. Furthermore, in the case of a TDD system utilizing an underused FDD downlink, the following two cases need to be considered. Case 3: The interference between the FDD downlink as a macrocell and the TDD uplink as a microcell. Case 4: The interference between the FDD downlink as a macrocell and the TDD downlink as a microcell.

For all four different cases, the calculation of the other-cell interference and the same-cell interference are calulated as follows. Interferences of case 1 are pictured as in Fig. 1. The other-cell interference which all MSs in the FDD have influence on a BS in the TDD can be calculated. Also, the same-cell interference that other MSs except its own MS in a TDD have an effect on a BS in the TDD system can be calculated. Interferences of case 2 are explained in Fig. 2. The other-cell interference of case 2 can be obtained as follows. Firstly, the interference which all MSs in the FDD have an effect only on a MS in TDD is calculated. Because all MSs in the TDD are assumed to be distributed uniformly, the interferences of other MSs in the TDD can be easily calculated. Similarly, in order to get the same-cell interference in Fig. 2, this paper firstly calculates the interference on a MS in the TDD by a BS in the TDD and then the interference on other MSs in the TDD from the BS in the TDD. Effects of transmission power in a BS in the FDD are represented in Fig. 3 (case 3). The other-cell interference which a BS in the FDD has an effect on a BS in the TDD is calculated. The same-cell interference that all MSs except its own MS in the TDD have effects on a BS in

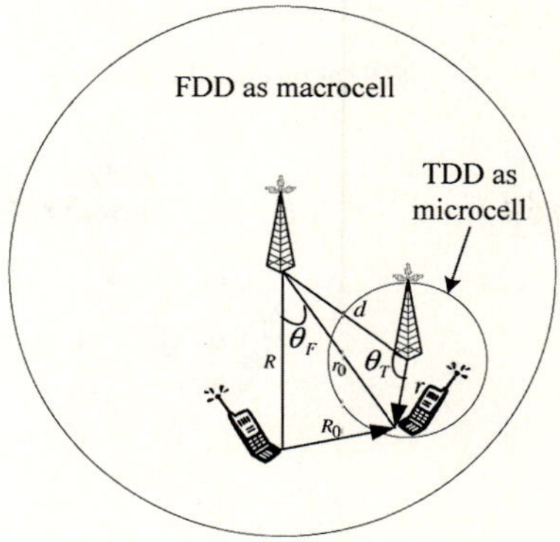

Fig. 2. The interference between the FDD uplink as a macrocell and the TDD downlink as a microcell (case 2)

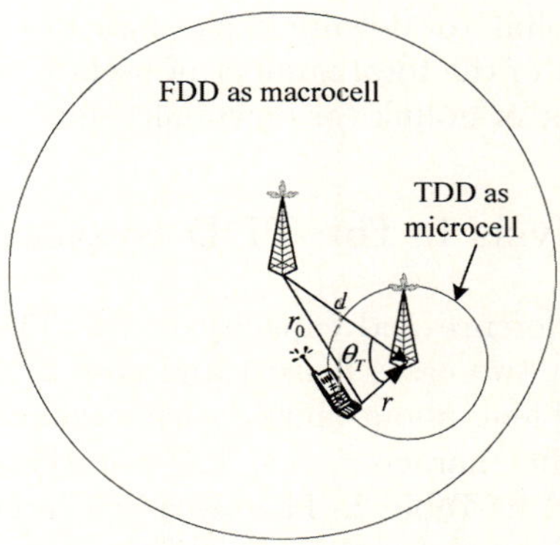

Fig. 3. The interference between the FDD downlink as a macrocell and the TDD uplink as a microcell (case 3)

the TDD for uplink can be calculated, as in Fig. 1. Finally, Fig. 4 represents all the interferences of case 4. The other-cell interference which a BS in the FDD has influence on all MSs in the TDD in Fig. 4 is calculated, with the following method. The interference which can be calculated as a BS in the FDD has an effect on only a MS in the TDD, and then the interference which other MSs receive from a BS in the FDD can be estimated. The same-cell interference in Fig. 4 can be calculated as the same method as that in Fig. 2.

All calculated interferences can be put into the capacity estimation in the TDD system. This paper considers the uplink and downlink capacity of TDD system utilizing the underused FDD uplink which shares the same-frequency band (case 1 and case 2). It is known that, in the TDD cell, the interference in the uplink slot can be calculated without any concern with the one in the downlink slot, because they are used at different instances of time. It is also assumed that users are evenly distributed over slots in each frame, so that the

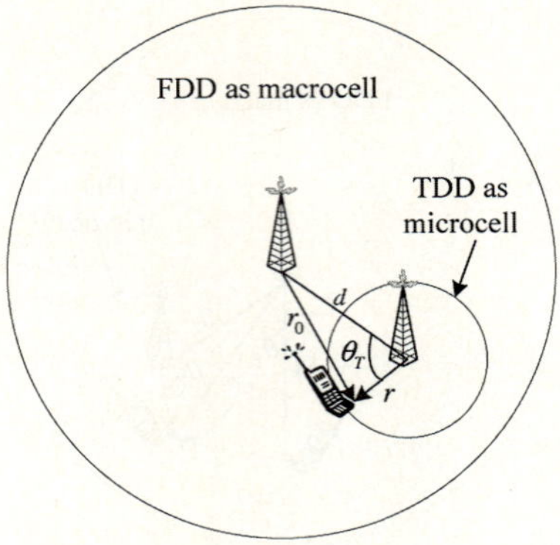

Fig. 4. The interference between the FDD downlink as a macrocell and the TDD downlink as a microcell (case 4)

number of users in an uplink (or downlink) slot may be equal to the value that is obtained by the division of the total number of users in all uplink (or downlink) slots to the total number of uplink (or downlink) slots.

3 Capacity Analysis in the TDD System

In calculating the interference and capacity in the TDD system [3] [8], this paper considers the first two cases (case 1 and case 2) among all four cases in Table 1 to deal with problems about unused surplus channels, usually the uplink, due to asymmetric traffic characteristics. The notations used in the following analysis are summarized in Table 2. The other-cell interference and the same-cell interference are calulated for the two different cases as discussed above. Fig. 1 shows the interference in the TDD uplink of case 1. In order to calculate the uplink capacity of the TDD system in Fig. 1, the other-cell interference on the BS in the TDD system caused by the MSs in the FDD system must be determined. The same-cell interference on the BS in the TDD system caused by other MSs except its own MS must also be determined. Assuming an ideal power control, the bit energy-to-noise density ratio $(E_b/N_0)_{TDD}^{up-up}$ in the TDD uplink of case 1 can be modelled as (1).

$$(E_b/N_0)_{TDD}^{up-up} = \frac{P_{TDD}}{P_{TDD}(\frac{M_{TDD}^{up-up}}{N_{up}} - 1)\frac{R_{TDD}^{up}}{B} + I_{FDDtoTDD}^{up-up}\frac{R_{TDD}^{up}}{B}} \quad (1)$$

where R_{TDD}^{up} is the uplink data rate for a TDD cell and B denotes the spreading bandwidth (thus, $\frac{B}{R_{TDD}^{up}}$ is the spreading factor). This paper has also assumed that every slot is equally and symmetrically loaded in one frame. Note, however, that this paper ignores the background noise and the shadowing effect to simplify (1), and since the activity factor belongs to the data, it is set as 1. The second

Table 2. The notations used in this paper

Notation	Description
$(E_b/N_0)_{TDD}^{up-up(down)}$	Bit energy-to-noise in the TDD when FDD is uplink and TDD is uplink (downlink)
$(C/I)_{TDD}^{up-up(down)}$	Carrier-to-interference ratio in the TDD when FDD is uplink and TDD is uplink (downlink)
$M_{TDD}^{up-up(down)}$	Total number of users in the TDD when FDD is uplink and TDD is uplink (downlink)
$I_{FDDtoTDD}^{up-up(down)}$	Interference from the FDD cell BS to the TDD cell BS when FDD is uplink and TDD is uplink (downlink)
M_{FDD}^{up}	Total number of users in the FDD uplink
$R_{FDD}(R_{TDD})$	Radius of macrocell (microcell)
$\theta_{FDD}(\theta_{TDD})$	Degrees of an angle of macrocell (microcell)
$P_{FDD}(P_{TDD})$	Required received power at uplink in the FDD (TDD) BS
$P_{TDD,max}$	Downlink transmission power in the TDD BS
$N_{up}(N_{down})$	Number of uplink (downlink) slots in one frame
γ	Ratio of traffic channels to total Tx channels
$1-\gamma$	Ratio of control channels to total Tx channels
$\gamma\phi_i$	Power of traffic channel i in the TDD
h	Orthogonal factor
L_i	Path loss of ith mobile in the TDD mode
d	Distance between FDD BS and TDD BS

term of the denominator in (1) corresponds to the other-cell interference, which can be expressed as (2).

$$I_{FDDtoTDD}^{up-up} = \frac{M_{FDD}^{up} P_{FDD}}{(\pi R_{FDD}^2 - \pi R_{TDD}^2)} \Big(\int_0^{2\pi} \int_0^{R_{FDD}} (\frac{R}{R_0})^4 R dR d\theta_{FDD} - \int_{-\cos^{-1}(\frac{R^2+d^2-R_{TDD}}{2Rd})}^{\cos^{-1}(\frac{R^2+d^2-R_{TDD}}{2Rd})} \int_{d-R_{TDD}}^{d+R_{TDD}} (\frac{R}{R_0})^4 R dR d\theta_{FDD} \Big) \tag{2}$$

where

$$R_0 = \sqrt{R^2 + d^2 - 2Rd\cos\theta_{FDD}} \tag{3}$$

The carrier-to-interference ratio $(C/I)_{TDD}^{up-up}$ is obtained by dividing (1) by the spreading factor, which is given as (4).

$$(C/I)_{TDD}^{up-up} = \frac{P_{TDD}}{P_{TDD}(\frac{M_{TDD}^{up-up}}{N_{up}} - 1) + I_{FDDtoTDD}^{up-up}} \tag{4}$$

Thus, if (4) is expressed as a function of M_{TDD}^{up-up}, the capacity in the TDD uplink of case 1 can be (5).

$$M_{TDD}^{up-up} = N_{up}\Big(\frac{1}{(C/I)_{TDD}^{up-up}} + 1 - \frac{M_{FDD}^{up} I_{FDDtoTDD}^{up-up}}{P_{TDD}}\Big) \tag{5}$$

Fig. 2 shows the interference in the TDD downlink of case 2. The calculation of the other-cell interference in Fig. 2 is similar to that of the other-cell interference in Fig. 1. As it is assumed that all MSs in the TDD have a uniform distribution, the same-cell interference in Fig. 2 using the following method can be calculated.

This paper firstly calculates the interference on a MS in the TDD by a BS in the TDD and then the interference on other MSs in the TDD from the BS in the TDD. The bit energy-to-noise density ratio $(E_b/N_0)_T^{up-down}$ in the TDD downlink of case 2 can be (6).

$$(E_b/N_0)_{TDD}^{up-down} = \frac{\gamma \phi_i L_i}{(1-\gamma\phi_i)hL_i \frac{R_{TDD}^{down}}{B} + I_{FDDtoTDD}^{up-down} \frac{R_{TDD}^{down}}{B}} \tag{6}$$

where R_{TDD}^{down} is the downlink data rate for a TDD cell. r_0 and R_0 in Fig. 2 is (7) and (8).

$$r_0 = \sqrt{r^2 + d^2 - 2rd\cos\theta_{TDD}} \tag{7}$$

$$R_0 = \sqrt{R^2 + r_0{}^2 - 2Rr_0\cos\theta_{FDD}} \tag{8}$$

The other-cell interference can be (9).

$$\begin{aligned} I_{FDDtoTDD}^{up-down} = & \frac{M_{FDD}^{up} P_{FDD}}{(\pi R_{FDD}^2 - \pi R_{TDD}^2)} \Big(\int_0^{2\pi} \int_0^{R_{FDD}} (\frac{R}{R_0})^4 R dr d\theta_{FDD} \\ & - \int_{-\cos^{-1}(\frac{R^2+d^2-RTDD}{2Rd})}^{\cos^{-1}(\frac{R^2+d^2-R_{TDD}}{2Rd})} \int_{d-R_{TDD}}^{d+R_{TDD}} (\frac{R}{R_0})^4 R dr d\theta_{FDD} \Big) \end{aligned} \tag{9}$$

Therefore, if (6) is expressed as a function of $M_{TDD}^{up-down}$, the capacity in the TDD downlink of case 2 can be (10).

$$M_{TDD}^{up-down} = \frac{\gamma}{(C/I)_{TDD}^{up-down}(h + \frac{1}{\pi R_{TDD}{}^2}\int_0^{2\pi}\int_0^{R_{TDD}} (\frac{I_{FDDtoTDD}^{up-down}}{L_i}) r dr d\theta_{TDD})} \tag{10}$$

4 Result and Discussion

In this section, this paper calculates the capacities for uplink and downlink of the TDD system using the equations illustrated in section 3. The simulation parameters used are summarized in Table 3. The values of P_{FDD}, P_{TDD}, and $P_{TDD,max}$ are determined from a simulation. In Fig. 5, let us examine the situation, where the ratio of slots is the same between uplink and downlink; that is, the uplink slot number (N_{up}) is 7 and the downlink slot number (N_{down}) is also 7 among all 14 slots for data in one frame. This paper performs the following simulation with the values of parameters in Table 3. Therefore, the result of the simulation with these conditions can be discussed in this paper. To compare the

Table 3. Fixed parameters for simulation

Parameter	Value	Unit
R_{FDD}	1000	m
R_{TDD}	50	m
P_{FDD}	-132.3	dB
P_{TDD}	-122.5	dB
$P_{TDD,max}$	-33.0	dB
$(C/I)_{TDD}$	-8.5	dB
h	0.2	
γ	0.9	
d	300	m
Bandwidth	5	MHz

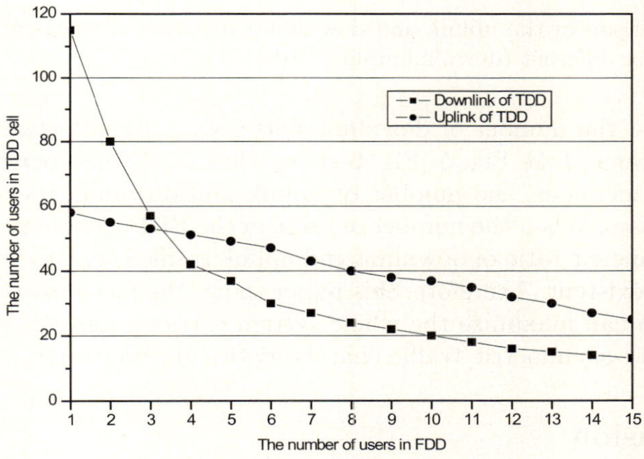

Fig. 5. Comparison of the uplink and downlink capacities of the TDD system where the ratio of slots is the same (downlink : uplink = 7 : 7)

capacities of downlink and uplink in the TDD cell, the number of users in the TDD cell is examined, as the number of users in the FDD cell increases. In Fig. 5, as the number of users in the FDD uplink increases, the number of users in each of the TDD uplink and downlink is decreased. For instance, as the number of users in the FDD uplink increases by a range of 4 to 12, the number of users in the TDD uplink decreases by a range of 50 to 30. In the case of the TDD downlink, similar results are acquired. When the number of the FDD users is smaller than 4, the TDD cell capacity is limited by the uplink. On the contrary, it can be noted that, with these results, the capacity of the downlink is limited when the number of users in the FDD ranges from 4 to 15. This result shows that, in the case of asymmetric traffic, as a great number of resource wastes occur, the number of downlink slots in one frame for the TDD cell should be increased.

In Fig. 6, this paper considers the other situation, where the ratio of slots are asymmetric between uplink and downlink; that is, the number of uplink slots

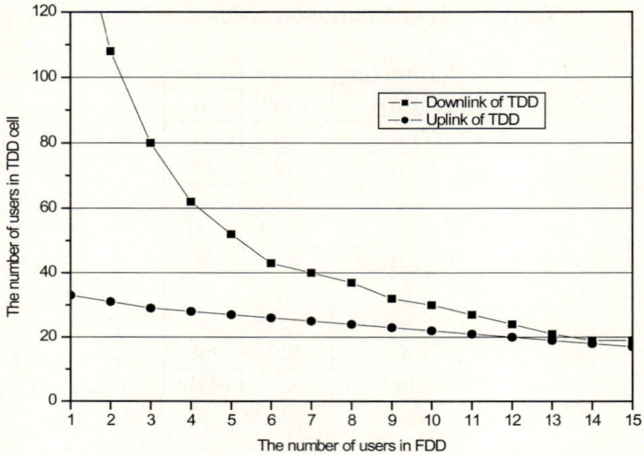

Fig. 6. Comparison of the uplink and downlink capacities of TDD system where the ratio of slots are different (downlink:uplink=10:4)

(N_{up}) is 4 and the number of downlink slots (N_{down}) is 10 among 14 slots for data in one frame. Like Fig. 5, Fig. 6 shows that as the number of users in the FDD system increases, the number of uplink and downlink users in the TDD system decreases. When the number of users in the FDD system ranges from 4 to 7, if the asymmetric ratio of downlink and uplink traffic is 2:1, the resource waste is nearly non-existent. Therefore, this paper shows the fact that the asymmetric slot allocation can maximize the whole system capacity and the resource waste problem due to asymmetric traffic characteristics are improved.

5 Conclusion

The proposed modeling can be adopted for the situation in which the service is asymmetric between uplink and downlink. The coverage of the TDD system will be smaller for low and medium data rate services than the comparable FDD service. To avoid interference, furthermore, the smaller cells are better choices. Therefore, the TDD system is most suitable for small cells with high data rate services. In this paper, considering the other-cell interference from the FDD uplink and the same-cell interference in the TDD cell from a standpoint of the TDD cell, the capacities of uplink and downlink which belong to the TDD cell are investigated. The results indicate that the capacity of the TDD system may be limited by any link of the TDD cell as a microcell in the case of sharing the FDD uplink band as a macrocell.

In many services of the next generation mobile communication system, it is obvious that asymmetric traffic characteristics will exist between uplink and downlink. The overall capacity will be maximized in the TDD cell as long as the ratio of the number of slots used by the frame in the TDD cell is controlled to maximally apply the asymmetry between uplink and downlink in line with the characteristics of the service used in the TDD cell. According to the results, it has to be pointed out that the asymmetric slot allocation between uplink and downlink in the TDD cell utilizing the underused FDD uplink which shares the same frequency band plays an important role in planning of the hierarchical cell structures.

References

1. 3GPP TSG-Radio Access Network Meeting #13 RP-010660, Beijing, $18^{th} - 21^{st}$, September 2001.
2. L. L. Wang, S. X. Wang, and X. Y. Sun, "Dynamic Resource Allocation for Multimedia CDMA Wireless System with Downlink Beamforming and Power Control," Proceedings of Wireless and Optical Communications (WOC 2003), July, 2003.
3. A. De Hoz and C. Cordier, "W-CDMA Downlink Performance Analysis," IEEE VTC'99-Fall, Amsterdam, The Netherland, Vol. 2, pp.968∼972, 1999.
4. Yunjian Jia, Yoshitaka Hara, and Shinsuke Hara, "Performance of TDD-SDMA/TDMA System with Multi-Slot Assignment in Asymmetric Traffic Wireless Network," PIMRC 2002, September, $15^{th} - 18^{th}$, 2002.
5. H. Haas and G. J. R. Povey, "A Capacity Investigation on UTRA-TDD Utilising Underused UTRA-FDD Uplink Resources," UMTS Terminals and Software Radio (Ref. No. 1999/055), IEE Colloquium on, pp.7/1∼7/6, 1999.
6. H. Holma and A. Toskala, WCDMA for UMTS, John Wiley & Sons, Ltd., 2001.
7. 3GPP TSG-Radio Access Network Work Item Description Sheet after meeting #26 Active WIs, January, 2005.
8. J. S. Lee and L. E. Miller, CDMA Systems Engineering Handbook, Artech House Publisher, 1998.

Dynamic Clustering for Coverage-Time Maximization in Two-Tiered Hierarchical Sensor Network Architectures*

Joongheon Kim[1], Wonjun Lee[2,**], Dongshin Kim[2], Eunkyo Kim[3], Hyeokman Kim[4], and Sanghyun Ahn[5]

[1] Digital Media Research Lab., LG Electronics, Seoul, Korea
[2] Department of Computer Science and Engineering, Korea University, Seoul, Korea
wlee@korea.ac.kr
[3] LG Electronics Institute of Technology, LG Electronics, Seoul, Korea
[4] School of Computer Science, Kookmin University, Seoul, Korea
[5] Department of Computer Science and Statistics, University of Seoul, Seoul, Korea

Abstract. This paper proposes dynamic clustering for coverage-time maximization (DC-CTM) in sensor networks. The coverage-time is defined as the time until one of cluster heads (CHs) runs out of energy in clustering-based sensor networks. DC-CTM regulates cluster radii for balanced energy consumption among CHs for coverage-time maximization. By using DC-CTM, three advantages can be achieved. The first one is balanced energy consumption among CHs. The second one is minimized energy consumption in each CH. The last one is the consideration of mobility on CHs. The novelty of proposed scheme, DC-CTM scheme, is shown by various simulation-based performance analyses.

1 Introduction

In recent years, many research efforts on sensor networks have become one of the most active research topics in wireless networking technologies [1]. Due to the limited power source of sensor nodes, energy consumption has been concerned as the most critical factor when designing sensor network protocols. Facing these challenges, several schemes, i.e., clustering-based topology control, have been investigated [2]- [7]. In topology control schemes of wireless sensor networks, clustering-based topology control schemes are widely used. By the advantages of clustering-based topology control, many clustering-based sensor networks protocols are proposed. In this paper, we consider the non-homogeneous clustering-based sensor networks as a reference network model. In non-homogeneous clustering-based sensor networks [2] [5] [6], different types of sensor nodes are used in the aspect of computing power, energy status, and

* This work was jointly supported by grant No. R01-2005-000-10267-0 from the Korea Science and Engineering Foundation (KOSEF) in the Ministry of Science and Technology and grant No. 10016756 from the Growth Power Technology Development Project, funded by the Ministry of Commerce.

** Corresponding author.

E. Sha et al. (Eds.): EUC 2006, LNCS 4096, pp. 652–661, 2006.

Table 1. Parameters used for modeling of energy consumption

Parameters	Descriptions
E_{CH_k}	The energy consumed in a CH named k
$E_{communicate_k}$	The energy consumption of data communication in a CH named k
$E_{process_k}$	The energy consumption of data processing in a CH named k
α_{t_k}	The energy/bit consumed by transmitter electronics in a CH named k
α_{r_k}	The energy/bit consumed by receiver electronics in a CH named k
α_{amp_k}	The energy/bit consumed in the transmit op-amp in a CH named k
d	The distance that the message traverses. i.e., distance between two CHs
E_{tx_k}	The energy consumed to send b bits in the node named k
E_{rx_k}	The energy consumed to receive b bits in the node named k

etc. In two-tiered hierarchical sensor network architecture, we use the concept of coverage-time as a measurement index of network lifetime. The coverage-time is defined as the time until one of CHs runs out of energy, resulting in an incomplete coverage of the sensing region [7]. In this paper, a dynamic clustering for coverage-time maximization scheme (DC-CTM) is proposed. DC-CTM scheme can achieve balanced energy consumption among CHs by regulating cluster region. Also for more adaptability in practical applications, the consideration of mobility on CHs is required. Therefore DC-CTM scheme is designed under the consideration of a CH is a mobile device. The remainder of this paper is organized as follows. In Section 2, we investigate the energy model of mobile device. Section 3 describes the proposed dynamic clustering scheme for coverage-time maximization. Section 4 shows the simulation-based performance evaluation of the proposed scheme. In section 5, we show the related work. Finally, section 6 concludes this paper.

2 Energy Model of a Cluster Head

A CH has a circuit for signal conditioning and conversion, digital signal processor, and wireless radio link [8]. Therefore the energy consumption of a CH is summation of the energy consumption on data communication ($E_{communicate_k}$) and the energy consumption on data processing ($E_{process_k}$). That is,

$$E_{CH_k} = E_{communicate_k} + E_{process_k} \tag{1}$$

All parameters used in this section are explained in Table 1.

1) Energy consumption on data communicating: The energy consumption on data communicating is as follows:

$$E_{tx_k} = (\alpha_{t_k} + \alpha_{amp_k} \times d^2) \times b \tag{2}$$

$$E_{rx_k} = \alpha_{r_k} \times b \tag{3}$$

Therefore, the total energy consumption on data communication in a CH named k is as follows:

$$E_{communicate_k} = E_{tx_k} + E_{rx_k} \tag{4}$$

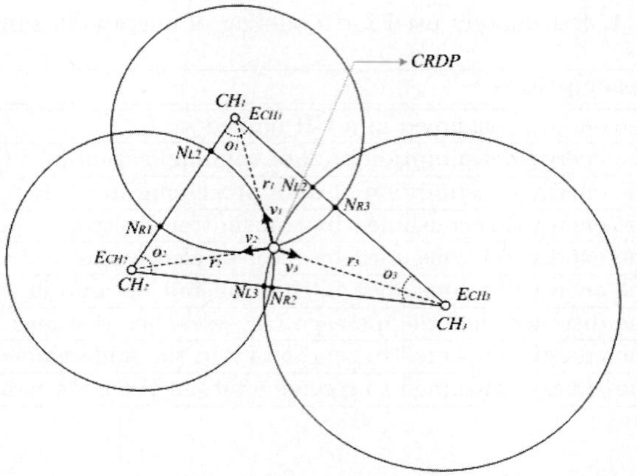

Fig. 1. System model for upper tier in two-tiered hierarchical sensor network architecture

2) Energy consumption on data processing: The model depends on the cycles in the program. In general, the energy consumption on data processing is significantly smaller than data communication.
3) Concluding remarks: By from Eq. (1) to Eq. (4), the energy model of a CH can be derived as follows:

$$E_{CH_k} = E_{communicate_k} + E_{process_k} \cong (\alpha_{t_k} + \alpha_{r_k} + \alpha_{amp_k} \times d^2) \times b \quad (5)$$

3 Dynamic Clustering for Coverage-Time Maximization (DC-CTM) Scheme

A DC-CTM scheme aims to cover the entire network with the balanced energy consumption of each CH by regulating the cluster range. DC-CTM scheme consists of two phases and one iteration policy. In this algorithm, we assume that a sink node knows the position of each CH.

3.1 Initial Phase

In initial phase, the CHs deployed at random to construct a triangle for determining 'Cluster Radius Decision Points (CRDPs)' that can lead balanced energy consumption among CHs and minimize energy consumptions of CHs while covering the entire network field as shown in Fig. 1. Delaunay triangulation [9], which guarantees the construction of an approximate equilateral triangle, is used for constructing a triangle.

3.2 Dynamic Cluster Control (DCC) Phase

After initial phase is over, DC-CTM scheme goes to 'dynamic cluster control (DCC) phase'. The design rationale of DCC phase is as shown follows: The cluster radii of three CHs including the construction of a triangle can be dynamically

Table 2. Parameters Used For Description of DC-CTM Scheme

Parameters	Descriptions
CH_k	Cluster head, named k
S_{CH_k}	The area of in a CH named k
$\|CH_k\|$	The number of cluster head
$CRDP$	Cluster Radius Decision Point
v_k	Vector from $CRDP$ to CH_k
θ_k	The angle between neighbor cluster heads
r_k	The distance between $CRDP$ and CH_k
ϕ_k	Weight factor of CH_k
m	The number of weight functions

controlled by using a CRDP as a pivot. The each distance between each CH and CRDP becomes radius of

each cluster. As shown in Fig. 1, the triangle which is composed by three CHs. To find the optimal CRDP, we make two scenarios. One scenario is for the all CHs have same functionality. The other scenario is for the all CHs have different functionality.

1) DCC phase for homogeneous CHs: The DCC phase of DC-CTM scheme in all CHs are same functionality is described in this subsection. The size of overlapping area, the solution of objective function which is proposed in this section, can be obtained by extracting the size of triangle from the summation of three sectors in Fig. 1. By this basic concept, we can derive the objective function to find the CRDP for minimizing the overlapping areas of each sector. Because main purpose of this phase is minimized energy consumption, if we can consider energy status in this phase, more efficient result can be derived. As considering energy factor, two kinds of approach are possible. First one is nonlinear programming based approach (NLP-based approach) and the other one is vector computation based approach (VC-based approach). The objective function of NLP-based approach is as shown follows:

$$\textbf{minimize: } f(r_1, r_2, r_3, \theta_1, \theta_2, \theta_3, E_{CH_1}, E_{CH_2}, E_{CH_3})$$

$$= \frac{1}{2}\sum_{i=1}^{3} \theta_i \cdot r_i^2 \frac{E_{CH_i}}{\frac{1}{3}\sum_{j=1}^{3} E_{CH_j}} - S_{triangle} \tag{6}$$

$$\textbf{s.t. } r_i^2 = (x_{CRDP} - x_i)^2 + (y_{CRDP} - y_i)^2$$

The notations used in Eq. (6) is shown in Table II. By using energy factors as a weight factors in Eq. (6), we can find the position of CRDPs under the consideration of energy status of CHs. By applying Eq. (5) into Eq. (6),

$$\textbf{minimize: } f_{Homo\_NLP}(r_1, r_2, r_3, \theta_1, \theta_2, \theta_3, E_{CH_1}, E_{CH_2}, E_{CH_3})$$

$$= \frac{1}{2}\sum_{i=1}^{3} \theta_i \cdot r_i^2 \frac{(\alpha_{t_i} + \alpha_{r_i} + \alpha_{amp_i} \times d^2)}{\frac{1}{3}\sum_{j=1}^{3}(\alpha_{t_j} + \alpha_{r_j} + \alpha_{amp_j} \times d^2)} - S_{triangle} \quad (7)$$

$$\textbf{s.t. } r_i^2 = (x_{CRDP} - x_i)^2 + (y_{CRDP} - y_i)^2$$

In NLP-based approach, it may generate additional computation overheads due to an iterative NLP method. We thus consider another method based on vector computation (VC-based approach) to reduce computation overheads. In VC-based approach, the objective function does not consider energy factor as shown in Eq. (8). The energy factor is considered in iterative vector calculus as shown in Eq. (9).

$$\textbf{minimize: } f_{VC}(r_1, r_2, r_3, \theta_1, \theta_2, \theta_3)$$

$$= \frac{1}{2}\sum_{i=1}^{3} \theta_i \cdot r_i^2 - S_{triangle} \quad (8)$$

$$\textbf{s.t. } r_i^2 = (x_{CRDP} - x_i)^2 + (y_{CRDP} - y_i)^2$$

To consider the energy status in iterative calculus, we compute the following equation iteratively.

$$CRDP^{n+1} = CRDP^n$$

$$- \sum_{i=1}^{3} \theta_i \cdot r_i^2 \frac{(\alpha_{t_i} + \alpha_{r_i} + \alpha_{amp_i} \times d^2)}{\frac{1}{3}\sum_{j=1}^{3}(\alpha_{t_j} + \alpha_{r_j} + \alpha_{amp_j} \times d^2)} \times \frac{CRDP^n - CH_i}{||CRDP^n - CH_i||} \quad (9)$$

$$\textbf{s.t. } CRDP^n = (x_{CRDP}, y_{CRDP})$$

$$CH_i = (x_{CH_i}, y_{CH_i})$$

In VC-based approach, we just have to update the coordination of CRDP in previous step. Therefore, the repeated vector computation is much simpler than NLP computation at the aspect of algorithm complexity.

2) DCC phase for heterogeneous CHs: In previous subsection, we consider that all CHs have same functionality and hardware constraint. However if any CHs have more computing power and the CHs takes more member nodes than assigned, the coverage-time can be extended. Therefore the objective functions can be re-designed as follows. The descriptions of notations are in Table 2.

$$\textbf{minimize: } f(r_1, r_2, r_3, \theta_1, \theta_2, \theta_3, \phi_{CH_1}, \phi_{CH_2}, \phi_{CH_3})$$

$$= \frac{1}{2}\sum_{i=1}^{3} \theta_i \cdot r_i^2 \frac{\phi_{CH_i}}{\frac{1}{3}\sum_{j=1}^{3}\phi_{CH_j}} - S_{triangle} \quad (10)$$

$$\textbf{s.t. } r_i^2 = (x_{CRDP} - x_i)^2 + (y_{CRDP} - y_i)^2$$

Eq. (11) is the modified CRDP repositioning formula for heterogeneous CHs by VC-based approach.

$$CRDP^{n+1} = CRDP^{n} - \sum_{i=1}^{3} \theta_i \cdot r_i^2 \frac{\phi_{CH_i}}{\frac{1}{3}\sum_{j=1}^{3}\phi_{CH_j}} \times \frac{CRDP^n - CH_i}{||CRDP^n - CH_i||} \quad (11)$$

$$\textbf{s.t. } CRDP^n = (x_{CRDP}, y_{CRDP})$$
$$CH_i = (x_{CH_i}, y_{CH_i})$$

3.3 Iteration Policy

When event frequently occur in some specific areas where a certain CH consumes its energy a lot. In this situation, the CHs in the target region will consume more energy and the operation will be relatively more important than the other CHs in the other area of the network of lower tier. Then a sink has to change the radius of clusters to balance energy consumption of each CH and to preserve the energy of the CH which has higher priority than the other CHs.

4 Performance Evaluation

The novelty of DC-CTM scheme is shown by performance evaluation. Based on the predefined simulation environment, the evaluation of DC-CTM scheme is performed.

4.1 Simulation Environment

In this section, the simulation environment for performance evaluation of DC-CTM scheme is described. There are two types of DC-CTM scheme in this simulation evaluation. The first one is 'DC-CTM: homo' and the second one is 'DC-CTM: hetero'. The 'DC-CTM: homo' is a scheme where all CHs have same functionalities and system architecture. On the other hand, 'DC-CTM: hetero' considers the difference of functionalities and system architecture in each CH. We compare DC-CTM scheme against the method that has a fixed cluster radius. The cluster radius is fixed, but it has to be extended to the distance to allow communication among all CHs. We define such a method as Fixed Radius (FR).

4.2 The Accumulated Number of Collide Packets

The accumulated number of collided packets is a very important measurement index in designing high-performance protocols. As shown in Fig. 2, we measured number of collided packets. 'DC-CTM: homo' and 'DC-CTM: hetero' have similar performance. Because the weight functions assigned to each CH are not related to the clustering area. The number of collided packets depends on the clustering area. Therefore the weight factors that not related to the clustering area have no effects. Therefore the performance between 'DC-CTM: homo' and 'DC-CTM: hetero' is almost same, but DC-CTM: homo' has a slightly better performance than 'DC-CTM: hetero'. The reason is that the energy factor which is considered in 'DC-CTM: homo' is related to the clustering area.

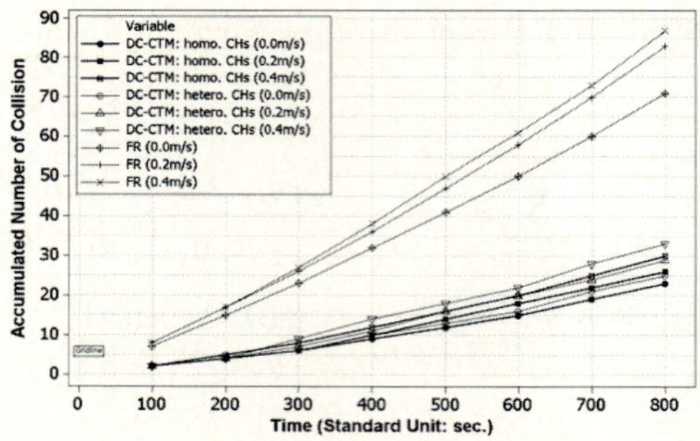

Fig. 2. Accumulated Number of Packets

4.3 Coverage-Time

The coverage-time is defined as the time until one of cluster heads (CHs) runs out of energy resulting in an incomplete coverage of the sensing region as mentioned in previous section [7]. Therefore the coverage-time is a critical factor when measuring network lifetime of clustering-based networks. Fig. 3 shows the coverage-time when all CHs are same. Fig. 4 shows the coverage-time when CHs do not have the same functionalities and system architecture. In this case, it is important for heterogeneous CHs to consider the characteristics of network environment. As shown in Fig. 4, 'DC-CTM: hetero' has longer coverage-time than 'DC-CTM: homo' and FR because of the consideration of the characteristics of network environment. As described in Fig. 3 and Fig. 4, as the velocity of mobile CHs increases, the coverage-time becomes increasingly smaller. Therefore, high mobility on CHs can lead to less coverage-time.

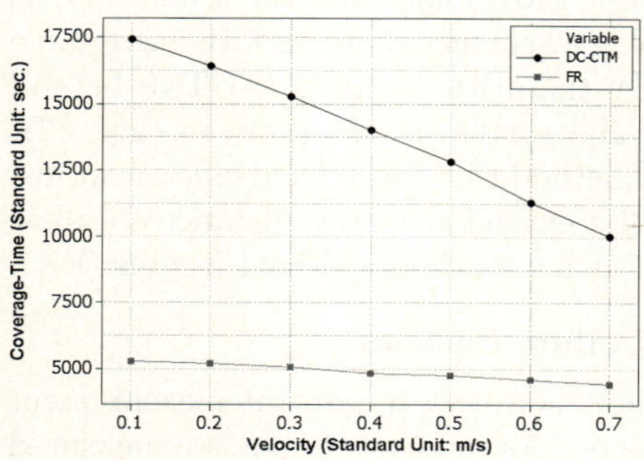

Fig. 3. Coverage-Time: Homogeneous CHs

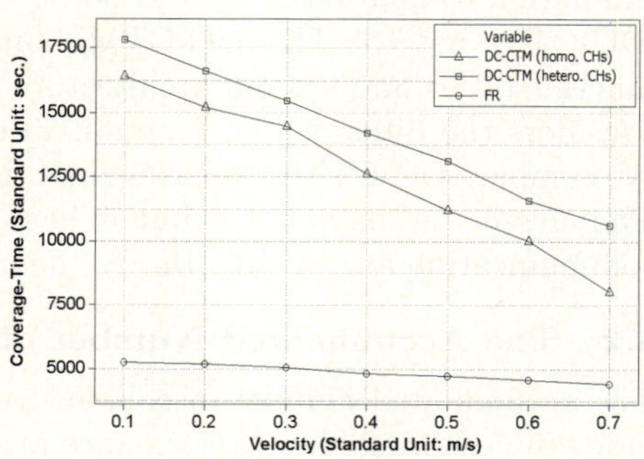

Fig. 4. Coverage-Time: Heterogeneous CHs

4.4 The Standard Deviation of Residual Energy on Each CH

CH Under the definition of coverage-time, the balanced energy consumption of each CH is important to maximize network lifetime. To show balanced energy

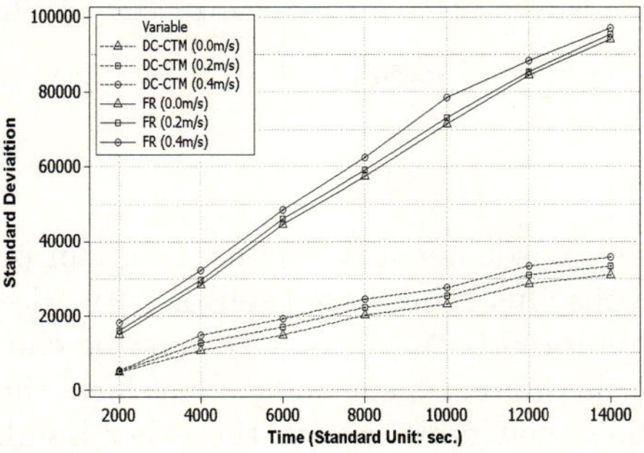

Fig. 5. Std. Dev. of Residual Energy of Each CH: Homogeneous CHs

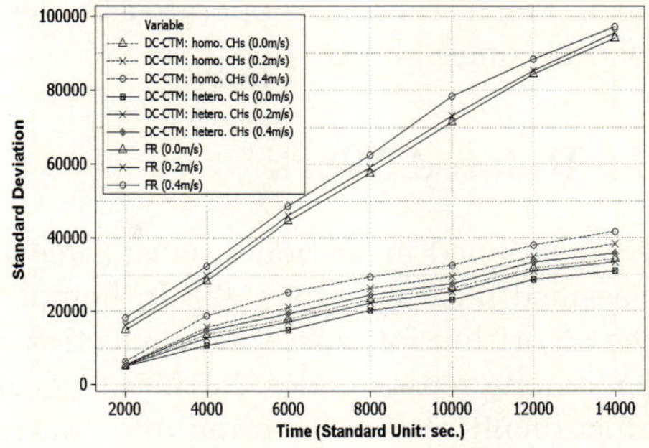

Fig. 6. Std. Dev. of Residual Energy of Each CH: Heterogeneous CHs

consumption in each CH, we measure and show the standard deviation of residual energy in CHs. For more detailed performance evaluation, Fig. 5 shows results when all CHs have the same functionalities and Fig. 6 shows the results when each CH has different functionalities. As shown in Fig. 5, DC-CTM takes balanced energy consumption. Also when we measure the performance of DC-CTM, we consider the mobility of CHs. Since a higher mobility leads to an unstable network topology, when mobility becomes higher, the performance of DC-CTM becomes lower. Fig. 6 shows the standard deviation of residual energy of each CH. Also in Fig. 6, we show the novelty of the DC-CTM.

4.5 The Tolerance Against Traffic Load

If one CH takes too much data from sensor nodes in lower tier, the traffic load from the sensor nodes becomes larger. If balanced data processing cannot be achieved, one CH can have enlarged ability for processing data from the lower tier. This phenomenon leads to the early energy exhaustion of the CH. In Fig. 7, we can observe that 'DC-CTM: hetero' takes the highest tolerance against traffic

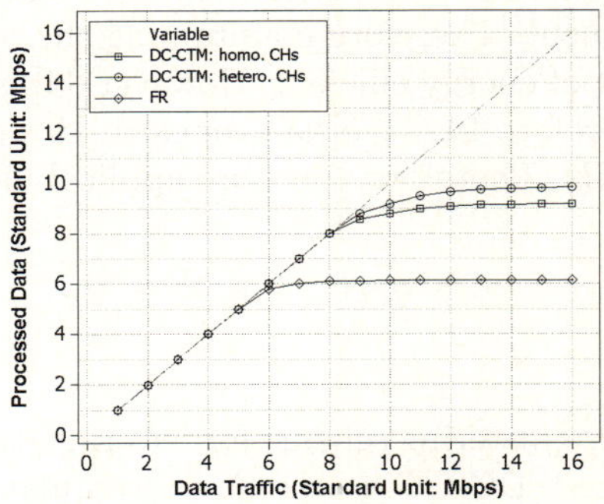

Fig. 7. Processed Data per Data Traffic

load. The CH which is operated by 'DC-CTM: hetero' can take until the traffic load becomes almost 10 Mbps.

5 Related Work

As mentioned in section 1, clustering-based sensor network architecture can be classified into two types [2]. In homogeneous clustering-based sensor networks, the algorithm for cluster head election is required because the CH must be chosen among sensor nodes. In this structure, therefore, sensor nodes must have the functionalities for clustering and controlling their clusters. On the other hand, in non-homogeneous clustering-based sensor networks [2] [5] [6]. In this structure, CHs have more computing power, less energy constraint, and less hardware constraint than a sensor node. In homogeneous clustering-based sensor networks [3], all the sensor nodes are identical in terms of battery energy and hardware constraint. Therefore, the cluster head selection algorithm is required. There are many clustering-based topology control schemes in homogeneous clustering-based sensor networks. Among the schemes, LEACH [3] is the notable clustering schemes. LEACH constructs its clusters with a distance-based approach. A distance-based scheme, however, cannot consider the energy status of each CH. The property can lead energy inefficiency in power-constrained sensor nodes. For more efficiency, therefore, hierarchical network architecture is required. Then, the sensor nodes can save their energy and make more energy efficient network architecture than homogeneous clustering-based sensor networks. There are numerous topology control algorithms for non-homogeneous clustering-based sensor networks [2] [4]- [6]. In [5], base on the operation which has the concept of balanced energy consumption. However [5] must totally share information to operate proposed algorithm. Maintaining global information to operate proposed algorithm can be a burden to CHs. Therefore decentralized scheme is required. The proposed scheme in [4] has a two-tiered sensor network architecture. By using this hierarchical clustering-based sensor networks, the proposed scheme in [4] can achieve more energy efficiency. In [4], however, the radii of clusters are fixed. In this system, the performance of scheme depends on each radius of the cluster. That is to say, it can be a waste of energy when a cluster has a larger radius than its requirement. Therefore maintaining the optimal cluster radius is important in the aspect of energy efficient. However [4] is impossible to regulate the cluster radius. Therefore LLC [6] is proposed. However in LLC we cannot consider mobility on CHs. Therefore, for more applicability, we design DC-CTM scheme.

6 Conclusion

In this paper, a dynamic clustering scheme for coverage-time maximization (DC-CTM) has been proposed. DC-CTM scheme can regulate the cluster radius for balanced energy consumption for coverage-time maximization while the entire lower sensor network field is still being covered totally by clusters. Low-Energy

Localized Clustering (LLC) in [6] makes the first trial in this approach. However LLC did not consider the mobility on CHs. To accomplish these objectives, DC-CTM scheme dynamically regulates the radius of each cluster. There exist three kinds of main contributions in DC-CTM proposed in this paper. The first one and the second one are balanced energy consumption for coverage-time maximization and minimized energy consumption in each CH. We show 'balanced energy consumption among CHs' and 'minimized energy consumption among CHs' by simulation based performance evaluation. The last one is the consideration of mobility on CHs. By basic design rationale of DC-CTM scheme, the mobility on CHs can be shown. Our ongoing work includes the exploration of the applicability of DC-CTM to practical network environments such as RFID networks [10] was one of preliminary products of such efforts.

References

1. D. Estrin, R. Govindan, J. Heidemann, and S. Kumar, "Next Century Challenges: Scalable Coordination in Sensor Networks," in Proc. of ACM MobiCom, Seattle, WA, USA, Aug. 1999.
2. J. Kim, J. Choi, and W. Lee, "Energy-Aware Distributed Topology Control for Coverage-Time Optimization in Clustering-Based Heterogeneous Sensor Networks," in Proc. IEEE VTC, Melbourne, Australia, May 2006.
3. W. Heinzelman, A. Chandrakasan, and H. Balakrishnan, "Energy-Efficient Communication Protocol for Wireless Microsensor Networks,"' in Proc. of HICSS, Hawaii, USA, Jan. 2000.
4. J. Pan, Y. T. Hou, L. Cai, Y. Shi, and S. X. Shen, "Topology Control for Wireless Sensor Networks," in Proc. of ACM MobiCom, San Diego, CA, USA, Sep. 2003.
5. G. Gupta and M. Younis, "Load-Balanced Clustering of Wireless Sensor Networks," in Proc. IEEE ICC, Achnorage, AK, USA, May 2003.
6. J. Kim, E. Kim, S. Kim, D. Kim, and W. Lee, "Low-Energy Localized Clustering: An Adaptive Cluster Radius Configuration Scheme for Topology Control in Wireless Sensor Networks," in Proc. of IEEE VTC, Stockholm, Sweden, May 2005.
7. T. Shu, M. Krunz, and S. Vruhula, "Power Balanced Coverage-Time Optimization for Clustering-based Wireless Sensor Networks," in Proc. of ACM MobiHoc, IL, USA, May 2005.
8. R. Min, M. Bhardwaj, S.-H. Cho, A. Sinha, E. Shih, A. Wang, and A. Chandrakasan, "An Architecture for a Power-Aware Distributed Microsensor Node," in Proc. of IEEE SiPS, Lafayette, LA, USA, Oct. 2000.
9. F. Aurenhammer, "Voronoi Diagrams - A Survey of a Fundamental Geometric Data Structure," ACM Computing Surveys, 23(3):345-405, Sep. 1991.
10. J. Kim, W. Lee, J. Yu, J. Myung, E. Kim, and C. Lee, "Effect of Localized Optimal Clustering for Reader Anti-Collision in RFID Networks: Fairness Aspect to the Readers," in Proc. of IEEE ICCCN, San Diego, CA, USA, Oct. 2005.

An Enhanced Hybrid Rerouting Scheme for Handoff in Wireless ATM Networks

Bih-Hwang Lee[1], Su-Shun Huang[1], and Hsin-Pei Chen[2]

[1] Department of Electrical Engineering
National Taiwan University of Science and Technology, Taiwan
{lee, sshuang}@ccg.ee.ntust.edu.tw
[2] Department of Computer Science and Information Engineering
Ching Yun University, Taiwan
hpchen@cyu.edu.tw

Abstract. For handoff in wireless ATM networks, a call might be rerouted because ATM basically provides connection-oriented service. We propose an enhanced hybrid rerouting scheme (EHRS) for handoff in wireless ATM networks, which combines the concepts of multicast rerouting, anchor rerouting, path extension and dynamic rerouting methods to effectively reduce handoff call dropping ratio, new call blocking ratio, and handoff delay. An analytical model and simulation experiments obtain performance measurements. According to the results, EHRS performs better than the different schemes.

Keywords: wireless ATM network, handoff, rerouting, dropping ratio, blocking ratio.

1 Introduction

Asynchronous transfer mode (ATM) network has several advantages, such as high transmission rate, large bandwidth, low delay, low cell loss rate (CLR), low bit error rate (BER) [1]. ATM network can dynamically allocate bandwidth and provide the quality of service (QoS) for different services; hence it is widely used as network backbone. Wireless ATM (WATM) emerges the advantages of the wired ATM [2] and the characteristics of wireless transmission to offer mobility and convenient communication.

Handoff mechanism is very important in mobile communications [3–5]. Lack of a good handoff mechanism may cause a call dropped when a mobile terminal (MT) is leaving a base station (BS) for a new BS. Because ATM basically provides connection-oriented service, a new route must first be found before setting up a new connection when handoff occurs, which is called rerouting. Some rerouting methods are proposed, such as connection reestablishment [6], path extension [7], anchor rerouting [8], dynamic rerouting [9], multicast based rerouting [10], hybrid rerouting, etc.

A new path may be an optimal route if it is setup by connection reestablishment method, but the setup time is longer and it does not used the original route. Path extension method can effectively reduce handoff delay and need not change the original route at all, but the required bandwidth may hugely increase if handoff frequently occurs. Anchor rerouting method changes the original path only from

E. Sha et al. (Eds.): EUC 2006, LNCS 4096, pp. 662 – 671, 2006.

anchor switch to old BS and keeps the other parts, but the required bandwidth may hugely increase similar to path extension method. Dynamic rerouting method is more complicated, but its new path may be close to the optimal; it can effectively reduce the required bandwidth and the disruption delay, but it relatively takes longer while looking for the crossover switch (COS) and causes longer handoff delay. According to multicast rerouting method, an old BS first multicasts the information of the setup path to its neighboring BSs when handoff occurs. After an MT is moving to a new BS, it similarly sets up a new path to its neighboring BSs and remove the path disjoint to the new BS. Although this method is the fastest, the required bandwidth may be very huge. Hybrid rerouting mostly combines the above-mentioned methods; it generally combines two or more methods to satisfy different applications or environments, e.g., the idea of combining path extension and dynamic rerouting may yields a good rerouting method [10].

There are some factors to be considered while designing a rerouting method in wireless ATM network, such as the complexity of the protocol to send signals, the optimal path, and handoff delay. We propose an enhanced hybrid rerouting scheme (EHRS) for handoff in wireless ATM networks, which combines the concepts of multicast rerouting, anchor rerouting, path extension and dynamic rerouting methods to effectively meet the above-mentioned requirements.

2 The Enhanced Hybrid Rerouting Scheme (EHRS)

2.1 System Architecture

A WATM network includes three important components: ATM switch, base station (BS), and mobile terminal (MT) as shown in Fig. 1. The wired ATM network acts as a transmission backbone and operates with the cellular network; it can then connect to the other networks. BS provides an interface between the wired and wireless networks. MT is the moving device at the user end, such as notebook, cellular phone and so on. It is necessary to perform handoff procedure when MT moves from the coverage of a BS to the coverage of a new BS.

Generally in WATM network infrastructure, several BSs are grouped into a cluster administered by an ATM switch. Handoff may occur in two ways: intracluster and intercluster handoffs. It is simpler to process intracluster handoff, because the rerouting scheme does not need to process the intervention of a switch in the backbone network. Conversely, intercluster handoff procedure needs to process the intervention of a switch because it needs to find a proper COS in the backbone ATM network. Generally, the probability of intracluster handoffs is greater than that of intercluster handoff; it is cited if a cluster contains more than three rings [11]. However, the loading of an ATM switch may be too heavy if a cluster contains too many BSs. Therefore we adopt a cluster with three rings (i.e., 19 cells in a cluster) for further analysis.

2.2 The Enhanced Hybrid Rerouting Scheme (EHRS)

EHRS combines the concepts of multicast rerouting, anchor rerouting, path extension and dynamic rerouting methods. The following steps show how EHRS works, while the related flowchart is shown in Fig.2.

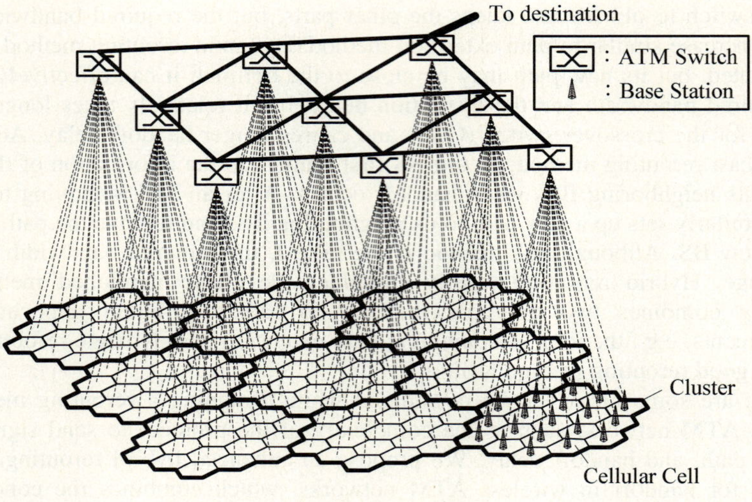

Fig. 1. An example of WATM network infrastructure

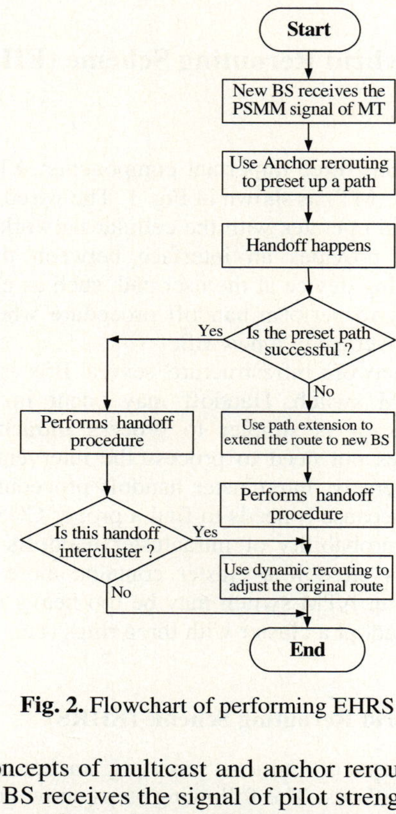

Fig. 2. Flowchart of performing EHRS

(1) Preset paths: The concepts of multicast and anchor rerouting methods are used to preset routes. When BS receives the signal of pilot strength measurement message (PSMM), the BS adopts the anchor rerouting method to build a route in advance.

If the cell contains the preset route and MT belongs to the same cluster, the route is built directly from anchor switch to this cell, otherwise the route is built from anchor switch to COS and then from COS to this cell.

(2) Perform handoff procedure: MT can quickly finish handoff procedure if the cell of handoff region has already had a preset route; or the path extension method is used to set up the route.

(3) Adopt path extension: When the preset route fails, this route is directly extended to the entering cell of MT to save handoff time.

(4) Adjust path dynamically: When this handoff is intercluster handoff or adopts path extension to set up the route, dynamical adjustment is needed by choosing the switch closest to COS to get the optimal path to reduce bandwidth.

3 Analysis of the Handoff Signaling Messages Using EHRS

EHRS combines suitable handoff procedures and dynamical path adjustments to obtain better performance. Handoff may succeed or fail and occur in either intracluster or intercluster, hence EHRS considers four different situations, i.e., the successful or failure preset path for intracluster and intercluster handoffs. Different handoff procedures may need different handoff signaling messages and processing time. However, by the limited paper length, we only show the analysis of the successful preset path for intracluster handoff in this paper.

3.1 Analysis of the Successful Preset Path for Intracluster Handoff

In order to successfully preset path for intracluster handoff, the related handoff procedure may need eighteen steps as shown in Fig. 3, while Tables 1 and 2 collect

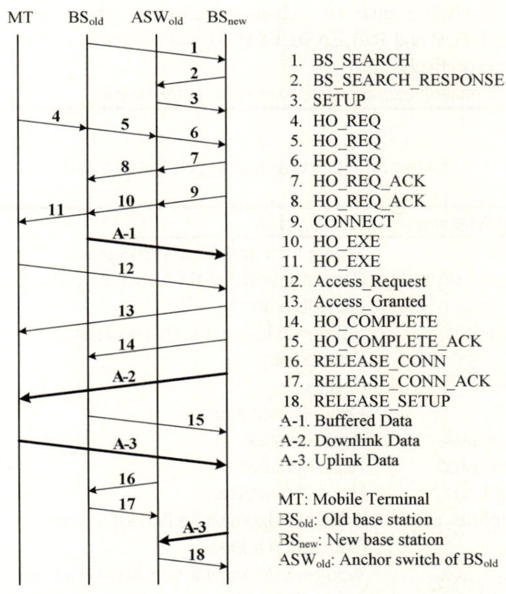

Fig. 3. The timing sequence for the successful preset path for intracluster handoff

Table 1. Message transmission times

Parameters	Message Type	Transmitted on	Value
T_w	Signaling	Wireless links	$S_s / BW_s + T_{PW}$
T_{sw}	Signaling	Switch-to-switch links	$S_s / BW_s + TP_{SW}$
$T_{d(w)}$	Data	Wireless links	$S_d / BW_d + T_{PW}$
$T_{d(sw)}$	Data	Switch-to-switch links	$S_d / BW_d + T_{PSW}$

Table 2. Input parameters

Parameters	Description	Value
S_s	Signaling message size	56 bytes
S_d	Data packet size	8 k bytes
BW_s	Signaling channel bandwidth	450 kbps
BW_d	Data channel bandwidth	9 Mbps
T_{Pw}	Propagation delay on the wireless link	50 μs
T_{PSW}	Propagation delay on the inter-switch link	50 μs
T_{PBS}	Propagation delay on the BS-to-BS link	20 μs
T_{STP}	Processing time in nodes only Signal Transfer Point (STP) function required	0.3 ms
T_{PSS} T_{PSB}	Processing time of SETUP message in a switch or a BS, respectively	8 ms 16 ms
T_{COS}	Processing time of signaling message that execute COS discovery function in a switch	4 ms
T_{SWr} T_{BSr}	Processing time of RELEASE_CONN and RELEASE SETUP messages in a switch or a BS, respectively	4 ms 8 ms
T_{PS} T_{PB}	Processing times for switching an ATM cell in a switch or a BS, respectively	10 μs 20 μs
T_{ASW} T_{BS}	Processing time of signaling messages (other than SETUP and RELEASE_CONN) in a switch or a BS, respectively	3 ms 6 ms
T_{SM}	Signaling message processing time at the mobile	5 ms

Table 3. Signaling messages for handoff

Signaling Messages	Description
BS_search	Search for a new BS to preset path
BS_ search _reply	Response from the BS having the preset path
HO_req	Handoff request
HO_req_ack	Acknowledgement for handoff request
SETUP	Setup a path
CONNECT	Connect
HO_exe	Handoff execution
Access_request	Access request
Access_granted	Access granted
HO_complete	Handoff complete
HO_complete_ack	Acknowledgement for handoff complete
CONN_rel	Connection release
CONN_rel_ack	Acknowledgement for connection release
SETUP_rel	Release the path

some parameters for performance analysis [12] and Table 3 shows the meanings of the signaling messages [13].

The signaling procedure in Fig. 3 is explained and summarized in Table 4.

Table 4. Meanings of the signaling messages in Fig. 3

Steps	Meaning of signaling messages	Time for the step
1	Initially MT locates at the coverage of the old base station BS_{old}. According to the moving direction of MT, BS_{old} looks for three new base stations (BS_{new}) most possibly for the MT to handoff, then it presets the new path to BS_{new} by sending the message BS_search.	T_{S1}
2	BS_{new} notices anchor switch (ASW_{old}) to preset the route by sending the BS_search_reply message.	T_{S2}
3	ASW_{old} sets up a path to BS_{new}.	T_{S3}
4	MT asks BS_{new} for handoff but it first sends the handoff request to BS_{old}.	T_{S4}
5	BS_{old} forwards the handoff request to ASW_{old}.	T_{S5}
6	ASW_{old} forwards the handoff request to BS_{new}.	T_{S6}
7	BS_{new} replies the acknowledgement through ASW_{old} first after receiving the handoff request message.	T_{S7}
8	ASW_{old} forwards the acknowledgement of the handoff request to BS_{old}.	T_{S8}
9	BS_{new} asks to connect to ASW_{old} by sending the CONNECT message.	T_{S9}
10	ASW_{old} notices MT to execute handoff procedure, but this message will be sent to BS_{old} first.	T_{S10}
11	ASW_{old} forwards the acknowledgement of the handoff request to indicate MT.	T_{S11}
12	MT begins the handoff procedure and sends the Access_request message to BS_{new} to request the wireless channel.	T_{S12}
13	BS_{new} sends the Access_granted message to MT and provides MT enough bandwidth, because a connection has been successfully setup.	T_{S13}
14	BS_{new} will notice BS_{old} that the handoff procedure has been completed, but this message will send to ASW_{old} first, then to the BS_{old}.	T_{S14}
15	BS_{old} sends the acknowledge message to ASW_{old} and BS_{new}.	T_{S15}
16	ASW_{old} sends the message to releases the BS_{old}'s connection after ASW_{old} knows that BS_{old} has sent the HO_complete_ack message to BS_{new}.	T_{S16}
17	BS_{old} sends the acknowledgement message to ASW_{old}.	T_{S17}
18	ASW_{old} releases the other two preset paths.	T_{S18}

$$T_{S1} = T_{PBS} + T_{BS} \tag{1}$$

$$T_{S2} = T_{SW} + T_{ASW} \tag{2}$$

$$T_{S3} = T_{SW} + T_{PSB} \tag{3}$$

$$T_{S4} = T_{PW} + T_{BS} \tag{4}$$

Similarly, the times for the other steps can be easily obtained.

3.2 Analysis of Dynamic Path Adjustment

Before performing the dynamic path adjustment, we need to find a new COS on the original path, where the COS is closest to the switch connecting to the new BS. If two or more switches satisfy the above-mentioned condition, the farther COS from the old BS is chosen. The procedure of dynamic path adjustment completes, if the new COS has set up a new route to the new BS.

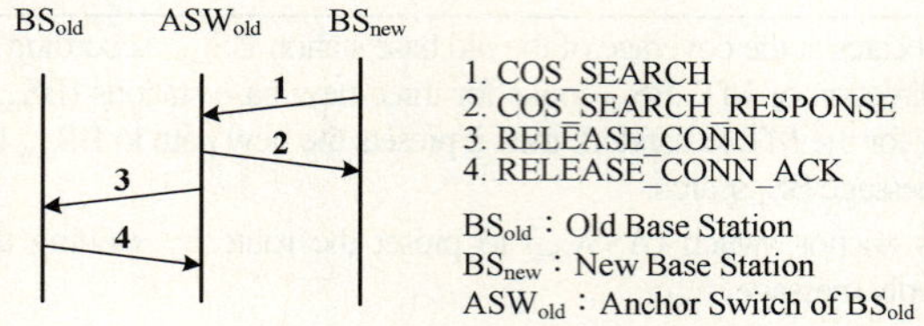

Fig. 4. The signaling procedure of dynamic path adjustment after intracluster handoff

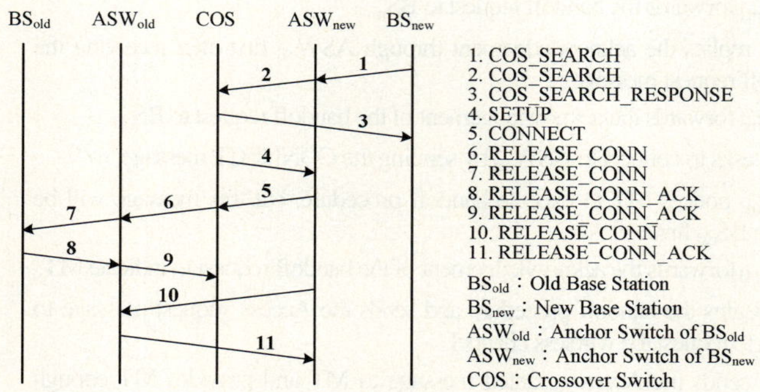

Fig. 5. The signaling procedure of dynamic path adjustment after intercluster handoff

Figure 4 shows the signaling procedure of dynamic path adjustment when path reservation fails for intracluster handoff. Figure 5 shows the signaling procedure of dynamic path adjustment for intercluster handoff, which consists of 11 steps and are needed whatever path reservation succeeds or not.

3.3 Performance Measurements

In order to analyze the proposed method, the performance measurements, such as handoff call dropping ratio, new call blocking ratio, and handoff delay, are defined and shown as follows.

(1) Handoff call dropping ratio (R_{hd})

$$R_{hd} = \frac{N_{hd}}{N_h} \times 100\ \% \tag{5}$$

Where N_{hd} is the total number of handoff calls being dropped, while N_h is the total number of handoff calls in the total observation time.

(2) New call blocking ratio (R_{nb})

$$R_{nb} = \frac{N_{nb}}{N_n} \times 100\ \% \tag{6}$$

Where N_{nb} is the total number of new calls being blocked, while N_n is the total number of new calls in the total observation time.

(3) Handoff delay

The handoff delay T_{HD} is the time interval between when an MT sends a handoff request message (HO_REQ) and when the MT receives a handoff execution message (HO_EXE). Therefore, T_{HD} can be obtained by summing the times of all signaling messages between HO_REQ and HO_EXE. The handoff delay for the Intracluster handoff with successful preset path is shown in (7).

$$T_{HD} = T_{S4} + T_{S5} + T_{S6} + T_{S7} + T_{S8} + T_{S9} + T_{S10} + T_{S11} \tag{7}$$

4 Simulation Results

4.1 The Parameters of the Simulated System

Without loss generality, we assume that the simulated system consists 9 clusters, where a cluster has 19 cells and is managed by an ATM switch; a cell has a radius of 500 m. A BS and a switch have the maximum transmission rates of 9 Mbps and 622 Mbps, respectively. We also assume that the network traffic mainly includes voice, video, and data flows with the percentages of 19%, 4%, and 77%, respectively. For voice and video traffics, we assume that the call holding times are exponentially distributed with the means of 3 and 10 minutes, respectively [14], while the transmission rate of data is also exponentially distributed with a mean of 128kbps [15]. The related parameters are listed in Table 5 [14], [15].

Table 5. Numerical values for the different traffic models

Traffic Type	CBR (voice)	VBR (video)	ABR (data)
Percentage	19 %	4 %	77 %
Minimum Transmission Rate	64 kbps	64 kbps	64 kbps
Mean Transmission Rate	64 kbps	256 kbps	128 kbps
Maximum Transmission Rate	64 kbps	512 kbps	512 kbps
Mean Holding Time	3 min	10 min	-
Mean Data Size	-	-	3 Mbytes

4.2 Simulation Results

In this section, the performance of EHRS is evaluated and compared with the path extension, anchor rerouting, and dynamic rerouting by simulation.

Figure 6(a) shows for handoff call dropping ratio that EHRS is the best and the path extension scheme is the worst, while the other two schemes perform little better.

The path extension scheme simply extends the original connection to the switch connecting the new BS. The original BS will not release the bandwidth after handoff procedure until the connection finishes, hence the path extension scheme occupies more bandwidth and results in greatest handoff call dropping ratio. EHRS presets path and reserves bandwidth for MT in advance, and dynamically adjusts the path to make it optimal after handoff procedure, hence it has least handoff call dropping ratio. Similarly for the new call blocking ratio, EHRS still is the best and the path extension scheme is the worst, while the other two schemes perform little better as shown in Fig. 6(b). The path extension scheme occupies too much bandwidth during handoff and causes new calls having less bandwidth, but the others do not waste so much bandwidth especially for EHRS.

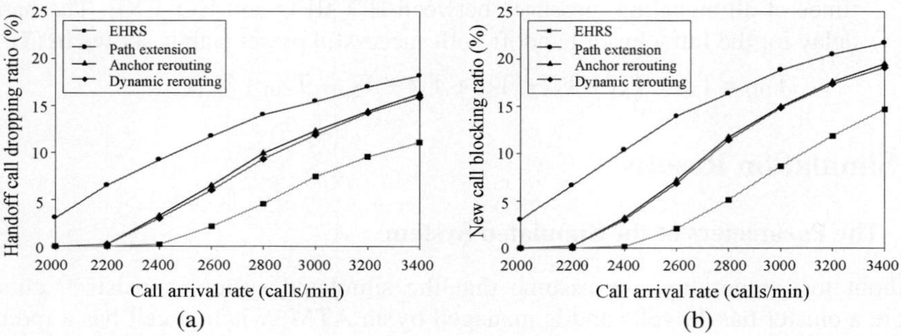

Fig. 6. (a) Handoff call dropping ratio versus call arrival rate. (b) New call blocking ratio versus call arrival rate.

Figure 7 shows for handoff delay that EHRS is the best; the anchor rerouting and path extension schemes are the next, but the dynamic rerouting scheme is the worst. The dynamic rerouting scheme has the longest handoff delay, because it has to find out a COS before setting up the path and spends a lot of searching time. EHRS may achieves fast handoff, because EHRS performs the COS discovery and path setup procedures in advance and the new BS simply allocates the required bandwidth for the MT.

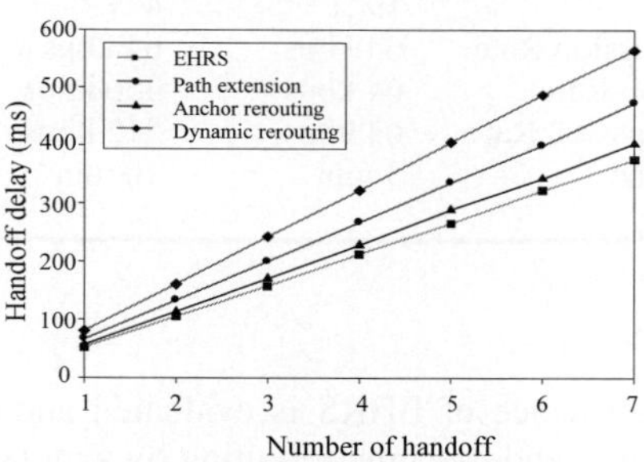

Fig. 7. Handoff delay versus number of handoff

5 Conclusion

In this paper, an enhanced hybrid rerouting scheme (EHRS) is proposed for handoff in wireless ATM networks, which combines the concepts of multicast based rerouting, anchor rerouting, path extension and dynamic rerouting. Basically EHRS uses path reservation before handoff and dynamically adjusts the path to make it optimal after handoff. According to the previous shown results, EHRS has the best performance in handoff call dropping ratio, new call blocking ratio, and handoff delay. Actually, EHRS still is good in other performance issues. In other words, EHRS achieves low handoff call dropping ratio, new call blocking ratio, and handoff delay.

References

1. The ATM Forum Technical Committee: Traffic Management Specification Version 4.0. Apr. (1996)
2. Kubbar, O., Mouftah, H.T.: Multiple Access Control Protocols for Wireless ATM: Problems Definition and Design Objectives. IEEE Commun. Mag., vol.35, no.11, 93–99, Nov. (1997)
3. Marichamy, P., Chakrabarti, S., Maskara, S.L.,: Overview of handoff schemes in cellular mobile networks and their comparative performance evaluation. In: Proceedings IEEE VTC'99, vol.3, pp.1486–1490, Sep. (1999)
4. Tripathi, N.D., Reed, J.H., VanLandinoham, H.F.: Handoff in cellular systems. IEEE Commun. Mag., vol.5, no.6, pp.26–37, Dec. (1998)
5. Marsan, M.A., Chiasserini, C.F., Cigno, R.L., Munafo, M., Fumagalli, A.: Local and global handovers for mobility management in wireless ATM networks. IEEE Commun. Mag., vol.4, no.5, pp.16–24, Oct. (1997)
6. Keeton, K., et al.: Providing connection oriented network services to mobile hosts. In: Proceedings USENIX Symp. Mobile and Location Independent Computing, pp.83–102, (1993)
7. Chan, S., Chan, K.S., Ko, K.T., Yeung, K.L., Wong, E.W.M. : A combined path-extension and rerouting handoff scheme for wireless ATM networks. In: Proceedings IEEE GLOBECOM'98, vol.3, pp.1396–1401, Nov. (1998)
8. Cheng, M., Rajagopalan, S., Chang, L.F., Pollini, G.P., Barton, M.: PCS Mobility Support over Fixed ATM Networks. IEEE Commun. Mag., vol.35, no.11, pp.82–92, Nov. (1997)
9. Toh, C.K.: Performance evaluation of crossover switch discovery algorithms for wireless ATM LAN's. In: Proceedings IEEE INFOCOM 96, pp.1380–1387, (1996)
10. Varshney, U.: Two Connection Re-Routing Schemes for Wireless ATM Environment. In: Proceedings IEEE Int. Conf. Univ. Personal Commun.(ICUPC'97), vol.2, pp.733-737, (1997)
11. Toh, C.K.: The design and implementation of hybrid handover protocol for multi-media wireless LANs. In: Proceedings MobiCOM' 95, pp.49–61, (1995)
12. Banh, B. A. J., Anido, G. J., Dutkiewicz, E.: Handover re-routing schemes for connection oriented services in mobile ATM networks. In: Proceedings INFOCOM '98, vol.3, pp.1139–1146, (1998)
13. Kim, T.S., Kim, S.: A fast rerouting scheme using reservation in wireless ATM. IEEE Trans. Veh. Technol., vol.52, no.4, pp.1125–1142, July (2003)
14. Akyildiz, I.F., Levine, D.A., Joe, I.: A Slotted CDMA Protocol with BER Scheduling for Wireless Multimedia Networks. IEEE/ACM Trans. Netw., vol.7, no.2, pp.146–158, Apr. (1999)
15. Ramanathan, P., Sivalingam K.M., Agrawal D.P., Kishore S.: Dynamic resource allocation schemes during handoff for mobile multimedia wireless networks. IEEE J. Sel. Areas in Commun., vol.17, no.7, pp.1270–1283, July (1999)

Bridging Nodes Density: A Connection Stability Heuristic for Dynamic Ad-Hoc Networks

Stefan Penz and Martin Wenig

RWTH Aachen University, Informatik 4,
52056 Aachen, Germany
{penz, wenig}@cs.rwth-aachen.de

Abstract. Wireless ad-hoc networks are commonly supposed to be a key technology for future ubiquitous computing environments. The dynamic nature of such networks demands mechanisms that allow the users to assess the availability of given network connections. In this paper we present a novel connection stability heuristic based on neighborhood information of intermediary network nodes. This heuristic identifies nodes that are able to bridge broken network links and thus improve connection stability. Extensive simulation experiments are presented that show the applicability of the heuristic, even though it does not require any special hardware equipment or exact signal strength measurements. Moreover, it imposes only negligible additional effort for the nodes and for the network.

Keywords: Bridging Nodes, Connection Stability, Quality Assessment, Mobile Ad-hoc Networks, Provider Selection.

1 Introduction

Ubiquitous computing environments exhibit a far more decentralized and dynamic structure than traditional computer networks. In order to facilitate ubiquitous network access even in infrastructureless areas, mobile nodes have to form multi-hop ad-hoc networks. Such networks require specialized middleware mechanisms for discovery and selection of suitable providers for needed network services such as internet gateways or peripheral devices.

Due to inevitable radio transmission effects, the Quality-of-Service (QoS) properties of wireless network connections (e.g. available bandwidth or transmission delay) are far more heterogeneous than in fixed networks and should thus be considered for the selection of alternative service providers. Still, existing service discovery systems for dynamic ad-hoc networks (e.g. [1,2]) do not consider connection properties.

Many popular network services require long-term accessibility of a selected provider. This QoS property is hard to achieve in dynamic ad-hoc networks that generally suffer from instable network connections. However, the authors are unaware of any service discovery or provider selection system that considers connection stability as QoS property. Therefore, a capable connection stability prediction system is needed that reflects the future accessibility of a given service

E. Sha et al. (Eds.): EUC 2006, LNCS 4096, pp. 672–681, 2006.

provider. This prediction system can then be integrated into existing service discovery systems to enable stability-aware provider selection.

In this paper, we propose a simple heuristic for the stability prediction of network connections. The heuristic is fairly accurate to support provider selection. The real-world applicability of the corresponding assessment mechanisms was a major design goal. Virtually any mobile node should be able to conduct the assessment procedure independent of its hardware equipment. Moreover, since the bandwidth capacity of multi-hop ad-hoc networks is significantly lower than in wireless infrastructure networks [3,4], the assessment procedure for the heuristic has been designed to minimize the load it imposes to the network.

The rest of the paper is organized as follows. Section 2 takes a look at existing stability prediction systems and their limitations. In Sect. 3 a path-independent connection stability metric is defined and Sect. 4 presents the actual bridging node heuristic. Section 5 describes an efficient assessment procedure for this heuristic and Sect. 6 demonstrates the applicability for provider selection by simulation of a typical use case. The paper closes with a conclusion and an outlook on future research activities in Sect. 7.

2 Related Works

Over the past years, the stability of network and communication structures in mobile networks has been subject to several research activities. The systems proposed in literature primarily differ in the kind of information they use to assess the stability. In [5] an *affinity* parameter is proposed that tries to predict the lifetime of a communication link, i.e. the direct radio connection between two neighboring hosts, by measuring the corresponding radio signal strength and its variation over time. A strong and relatively constant radio signal indicates a high stability of the link. The stability of a multi-hop communication path is determined by the weakest link of the path, i.e. the link with the smallest affinity. A similar approach is presented and analyzed in [6].

The accuracy of such signal strength measurements suffers inevitably from enormous link quality fluctuations due to transient physical layer effects [7]. These phenomenons are not addressed by the proposed systems and may adulterate the predicted lifetime significantly. The same holds true for the statistical analysis of link and path availability in [8,9].

In [10] the expiration time of a given link is predicted by the node's location and velocity data. A more sophisticated method for assessing path availability from predicted movement data is presented in [11] (revised in [12]). These approaches circumvent the inaccuracy of signal strength measurements, but assume each node to be equipped with a geolocation system, e.g. a GPS receiver. Although more and more mobile devices have integrated GPS subsystems, especially low-cost devices will most probably miss that feature for the foreseeable future. Besides that, satellite-based geolocation systems tend to fail in indoor environments. Therefore we think that GPS receivers or similar equipment should not be mandatory for stability prediction.

All approaches mentioned above try to estimate the residual time that a given link or routing path will exist. However, if such a path breaks, all relevant routing protocols (e.g. DSR [13] or AODV [14]) for multi-hop ad-hoc networks are able to reestablish the connection over an alternative path – if one is available. Therefore, an instable routing path does not necessarily imply that the communication connection to the destination node is instable as well. Therefore, we distinguish between *path stability*, i.e. the duration that a particular routing path persists uninterruptedly, and *connection stability* which refers to the existence of *any* routing path between two nodes. From the user's or application's point of view the connection stability is obviously far more important than the path stability.

3 Connection Stability Metric

In order to design and evaluate stability prediction procedures, an appropriate metric is needed that reflects the stability of a network connection independent of the actual paths that were used to keep the connection. Figure 1 shows the timeline of a measurement interval starting at t_s and ending at t_e. During this time interval we distinguish between active connection periods where transmissions can take place (marked bold) and passive periods where no route can be established between source and destination. We denote the active period durations by $\Delta t_1, \ldots, \Delta t_k$ for k distinct periods during the measurement interval.

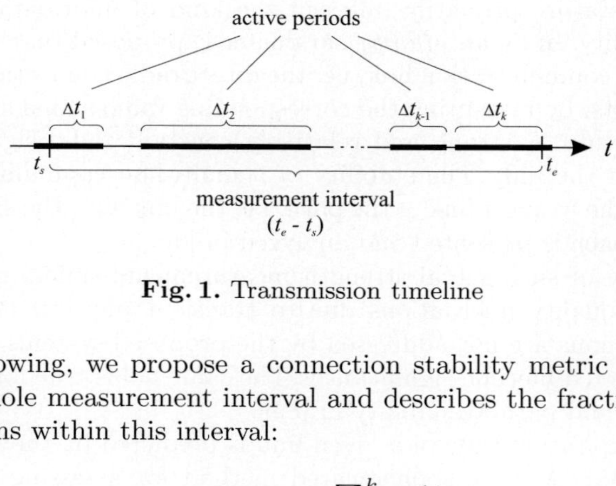

Fig. 1. Transmission timeline

For the following, we propose a connection stability metric $S_c(n_1, n_2)$ that regards the whole measurement interval and describes the fraction of all active period durations within this interval:

$$S_c(n_1, n_2) = \frac{\sum_{i=1}^{k} \Delta t_i}{t_e - t_s} \tag{1}$$

This metric reflects the availability of any communication path between source and destination. The longer a connection can be active during a fixed transmission interval, the more stable is the network connection. Note that the significance of the metric depends on the length of the measurement interval. Too short intervals may result in imprecise stability assessment results. Therefore, we chose a rather long measurement interval of 100 seconds for our simulations.

4 Connection Stability Prediction

In the following, two heuristics will be presented that both allow for efficient and applicable connection stability prediction. They rely on topology information that is available at the nodes of a pre-established network path. The path itself can be determined by an arbitrary routing protocol. This restriction allows for collecting all necessary data by the transmission of a single packet[1] via this path.

4.1 Shortest Path Heuristic

Apparently, the stability of a connection depends significantly on the distance between source and destination. A long distance requires a large number of network nodes to traverse, each of which increases the probability for a – possibly unrepairable – connection failure. We analyzed this interrelationship by simulation of different scenarios with the network simulator *ns-2* [15].

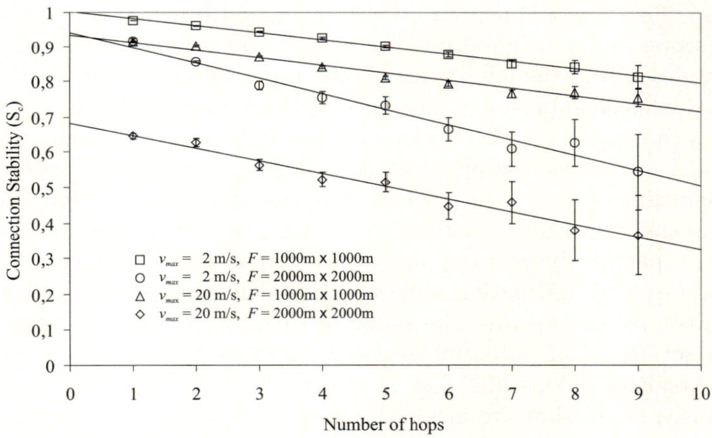

Fig. 2. Impact of path length

For each of the 100.000 simulation runs, 30 nodes were placed randomly on a square area of size F and two of those were picked randomly as source and destination. All nodes move according to the random waypoint mobility model with a maximum speed v_{max} during movement periods and stand still for a maximum pause time of 60s in between. After a movement initialization phase a connection is established between source and destination by the DSR routing protocol [13] and the number of hops is counted for the current routing path. In the following 100s, the source node periodically sends packets to the destination node in order to check path availability. Subsequently, the connection stability metric S_c is computed.

[1] In general, the source node initiates the measurement process and retrieves the result. Therefore, a round trip with two end-to-end transmissions is necessary, but the actual information can be collected by only one of these transmissions.

Figure 2 shows the simulation results for four scenarios with an area size of either $F = 1000m \times 1000m$ (dense scenarios) or $F = 2000m \times 2000m$ (sparse scenarios) and a node maximum speed of either $v_{max} = 2m/s$ (pedestrian scenarios) or $v_{max} = 20m/s$ (vehicular scenarios). The error indicators mark the 95% confidence intervals. The connection stability apparently decreases linearly with the number of hops. Hence, the path length heuristic seems to be a viable way to assess connection stability by a single measurement transmission that counts the number of hops between source and destination.

4.2 Bridging Node Density Heuristic

The shortest path heuristic solely relies on direct path information and disregards valuable stability factors that are available at the path nodes. Therefore, we propose a novel *Bridging Node Density Heuristic* which achieves better results throughout all examined simulation scenarios. However, the assessment procedure can still be conducted by a single transmission between source and destination. This reasonable restriction to a single transmission focusses the assessment scope to the neighborhood of the current routing path, i.e. the set of network nodes within the joint transmission range of all nodes the path consists of. However, this neighborhood information allows inference about potential fallback nodes that can fix broken links and thus influence connection stability.

We model a wireless network with N nodes $n_1, \ldots, n_N$ by a set of potential bidirectional links $\{n_i, n_j\}$ for each pair of nodes n_i and n_j that are in each other's transmission range. Without loss of generality we assume the current transmission path to be $p = (n_1, n_2, \ldots, n_P)$ for a path of length $(P-1)$ with source node n_1 and destination node n_P. In order to assess the connection stability between n_1 and n_P, we take a look at each link $\{n_i, n_{i+1}\}$ of the path and identify a set $B_{i,i+1}$ of potential *bridging nodes* that are destined to bridge a potential breakage of this link. Let L_i denote the set of link neighbors of node n_i. Obviously, nodes that are inside the link neighborhood set of both nodes n_i and n_{i+1} are prominent candidates for bridging, so we set $B_{i,i+1} := L_i \cap L_{i+1}$.

Figure 3(a) depicts an active link $\{n_i, n_{i+1}\}$ of a current connection being assessed. The intersection of both transmission areas contains three other nodes including n_b. The node n_b is able to establish links to both n_i and n_{i+1} and is thus a potential bridging node, i.e. $n_b \in B_{i,i+1}$. If n_i and n_{i+1} leave the mutual transmission area (Fig. 3(b)), the link n_i, n_{i+1} breaks, but dynamic routing mechanisms can bridge the resulting gap by replacing it with the links $\{n_i, n_b\}$ and $\{n_b, n_{i+1}\}$. Thus, the bridging node n_b confirms the connection stability.

The more potential bridging nodes exist, the higher is the probability that a link breakage can be fixed. Hence, the density of potential bridging nodes over the path p is presumably a proper connection stability heuristic:

$$D(p) = \frac{1}{P-1} \sum_{i=1}^{P-1} |B_{i,i+1}| = \frac{1}{P-1} \sum_{i=1}^{P-1} |L_i \cap L_{i+1}| \tag{2}$$

Note that the density is normalized to the path length $P-1$. This ignores the fact that longer paths are less stable than short path as analyzed in Sect. 4.1.

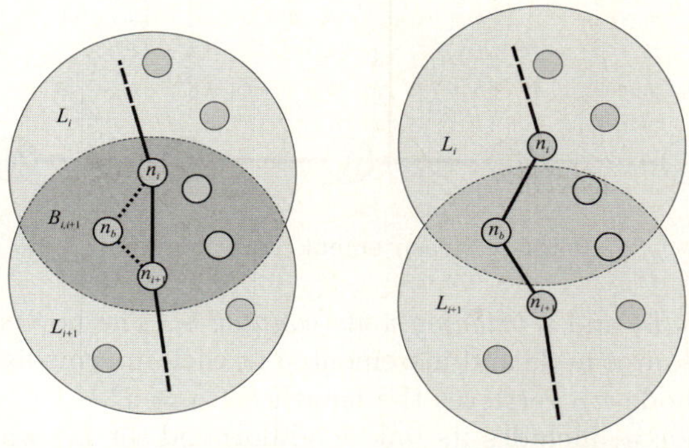

(a) n_b bridging node for link (n_i,n_{i+1}) (b) n_b bridges interrupted link

Fig. 3. Bridging of link interruptions

Thus, in order to improve the accuracy of our connection stability heuristic we finally factor in this linear correlation by weighting $D(p)$ with the reciprocal of the path length:

$$D'(p) = \frac{1}{P-1} D(p) = \frac{1}{(P-1)^2} \sum_{i=1}^{P-1} |B_{i,i+1}| \tag{3}$$

The bridging node density heuristic considers the path length as well as the density of potential bridging nodes as stability criterion.

5 Assessment Procedure

As mentioned before, one major design goal was the efficient real-world applicability of the heuristic. For the computation of $D'(p)$, only the path length and the link neighbor sets L_i of all path nodes are needed. The path length can be retrieved by including a counter into the measurement packet and incrementing it at each node of the path. The only information that an intermediary node has to maintain is the link neighbor set. Many routing protocols inherently keep this information for route selection purposes. If the routing protocol does not offer this information, nodes can normally retrieve this information by passively monitoring the network traffic in its vicinity.

As a matter of course, this information has to be propagated to the destination node. If every single link neighbor set is collected and transmitted by the measurement packet, each intermediary node would increase the size of the packet. This might strain network resources significantly – especially for long paths in dense networks. Therefore, we propose to calculate the bridging node density iteratively at each path node, so that only the transmission of a single link neighbor set is necessary.

The procedure is illustrated in Fig. 4. Each path node n_i includes three information entities into the measurement packet: a *hop counter* h_i, the link

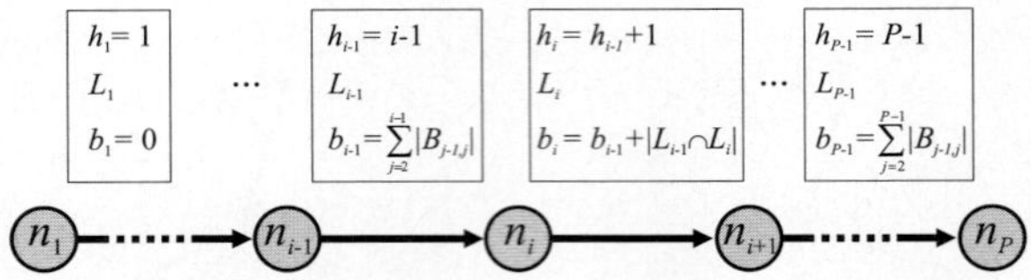

Fig. 4. Measurement Transmission

neighborhood set L_i and a *bridging node counter* b_i. The hop counter is initialized to 1 by the source node and incremented at each intermediary node, so that the destination node n_P retrieves the length $h_{P-1} = P - 1$ of the path. Additionally, each node n_i includes its link neighborhood set L_i, which is needed to calculate the bridging node counter. This counter sums up the number of bridging nodes for all path links. Therefore, n_1 initializes $b_1 = 0$. Each intermediary node n_i adds the number of potential bridging nodes $|B_{i-1,i}| = |L_{i-1} \cap L_i|$ for the previous link to the current counter value b_{i-1}. The destination node finally adds $b_P = b_{P-1} + |B_{P-1,P}|$ and is thus able to determine the bridging node density

$$D'(p) = \frac{1}{(P-1)^2} \sum_{i=1}^{P-1} |B_{i,i+1}| = \frac{b_P}{h_{P-1}^2}. \tag{4}$$

The amount of additional data transferred over single links essentially depends on the size of the link neighborhood set of the sending node. This would be a problem only in extremely dense networks which normally do not suffer from stability problems.

6 Performance Analysis

In order to quantify the benefit of the novel stability parameter, we set up a typical use case and analyzed it under different scenarios with the network simulator *ns-2* [15]. The use case is characterized by a user who wants to chose one of ten otherwise identical service providers by the predicted stability of the corresponding connection. Therefore, the user conducts the assessment with each provider and naturally chooses the one with the highest predicted stability. Independently of this choice, we measure the actual stability S_c (c.f. Sect. 3) for all ten connections during an interval of 100 seconds and compare the heuristic's choice to the average stability of the paths.

The general setup of the simulation equals the scenario described in Sect. 4.1, i.e. for each simulation run, 30 nodes with a transmission range of 250m were randomly placed on a square area either of size $F = 1000m \times 1000m$ (dense scenarios) or $F = 2000m \times 2000m$ (sparse scenarios) and were moved according to one of four movement profiles. In detail, we defined a pedestrian scenario (avg. speed $v_{avg} \approx 1m/s$) and a vehicular scenario ($v_{avg} \approx 10m/s$) for the mobility models *random waypoint (RW)* and *manhattan grid (MG)*.

For each simulation run, ten provider nodes and a user node n_u are randomly chosen. After each simulation run, we calculate the actual stability $S_c(n_u, n_i)$

for the connections between n_u and each of the service providers n_i. Let R be the set of providers that are reachable at all during the measurement period and $\hat{n} \in R$ be the provider with the highest predicted stability. Then we can define the gain G of the prediction system for a single simulation run by

$$G := \frac{S_c(n_u, \hat{n}) - (\frac{1}{|R|} \sum_{n_i \in R} S_c(n_u, n_i))}{\frac{1}{|R|} \sum_{n_i \in R} S_c(n_u, n_i)} = \frac{|R| S_c(n_u, \hat{n})}{\sum_{n_i \in R} S_c(n_u, n_i)} - 1. \quad (5)$$

In order to rank the performance of the bridging node heuristic, we compared its gain to the gain of a system that selects a provider simply by random and a system that solely utilizes the shortest path heuristic (c.f. Sect. 4.1). Furthermore, we calculated the maximum possible gain by considering also a optimal prediction system. This hypothetical system always selects the provider which later proves to offer the most stable connection.

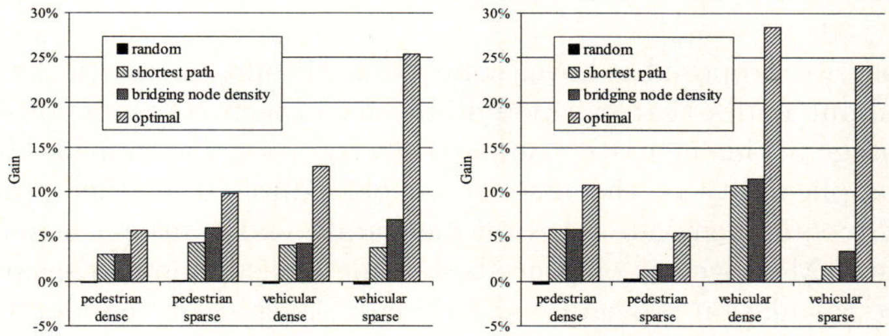

(a) Random Waypoint (b) Manhattan Grid

Fig. 5. Connection stability gains

Figure 5 shows the simulation results. Unsurprisingly, the random provider selection attains virtually no gain compared to the average S_c stability for any setup. The shortest path heuristic and the bridging node heuristic achieve moderate gains of up to 11.5%. However, the bridging node heuristic achieves about 36% to 61% of the maximum achievable gain for pedestrian networks and 14% to 40% for vehicular networks.

For dense networks, the bridging node heuristic appears to have no noteworthy advantage compared to the shortest path heuristic. Though in sparse networks it significantly increases the gain of the shortest path heuristic by 38% (RW) respectively 58% (MG) for pedestrian scenarios and even by 83% (RW) respectively 96% (MG) for vehicular scenarios. Apparently, the bridging node heuristic reveals its advantages primarily in sparse networks with fast moving nodes, i.e. in highly dynamic networks with very unstable connections. In fact, these are the networks that essentially require a stability prediction system.

The gain of the optimal prediction system varies significantly for different scenarios. The vehicular scenarios apparently allow a higher maximum gain than pedestrian scenarios. The low velocity in pedestrian networks leads to comparatively stable connections: nearly 40% of all connections are available for more than 90% of the interval. Therefore, a stability prediction system has just a small margin for the gain. In contrast, vehicular scenarios exhibit a more instable behavior which allows the prediction systems to achieve higher gains.

Generally, the stability behavior of a connection depends on the mobility profile. For instance, gains increase with the node density in our Manhattan Grid networks, but interestingly decrease with the density in Random Waypoint networks. Anyway, movement scenarios that were used for the analysis distribute the nodes more or less evenly over the specified area. In reality, ad-hoc networks are supposed to exhibit a far more heterogeneous distribution with very dense areas (e.g. crowded city streets) and significantly sparser areas (e.g. backyards). The bridging nodes heuristic obviously prefers stable connections through dense areas. Therefore we can assume that the bridging node heuristic will perform even better in such real-life networks.

7 Conclusions and Outlook

In this paper we proposed a novel connection stability heuristic based on information about nodes that can potentially fix broken transmission links. The main advantage of this heuristic compared to traditional systems is the efficient real-world applicability of the assessment procedure. It neither requires special hardware equipment nor relies on inaccurate and transient signal strength measurements. Moreover, it only needs a single measurement transmission and the iterative calculation procedure additionally saves sparse communication resources.

Simulation experiments demonstrated the applicability of the heuristic for QoS-aware provider selection. Apparently, the bridging node heuristic gives a fair improvement for connection stability in comparison to random provider selection. Especially in sparse networks with fast moving nodes and instable connections, the bridging node heuristic outperforms the path length heuristic and legitimates the marginal overhead.

The bridging nodes heuristic inevitably requires information from intermediary nodes. Since transport and application layer protocols generally have no access to intermediary node information, routing layer support is needed. Therefore, future work will include the practical integration of the assessment procedure into existing ad-hoc routing protocols and the approvement of accuracy by the consideration of spatial and temporal density fluctuations.

References

1. Lee, C., Helal, A., Desai, N., Verma, V., Arslan, B.: Konark: A System and Protocols for Device Independent, Peer-to-Peer Discovery and Delivery of Mobile Services. IEEE Transactions on Systems, Man, and Cybernetics, Part A **33** (2003)
2. Klein, M., König-Ries, B., Obreiter, P.: Lanes – A Lightweight Overlay for Service Discovery in Mobile Ad Hoc Network. In: Proceedings of the 3rd Workshop on Applications and Services in Wireless Networks, Berne, Switzerland (2003)

3. Li, J., Blake, C., De Couto, D.S.J., Lee, H.I., Morris, R.: Capacity of Ad Hoc Wireless Networks. In: Proceedings of the 7th ACM International Conference on Mobile Computing and Networking, Rome, Italy (2001) 61–69
4. Sun, T., Yang, G., Chen, L.J., Sanadidi, M.Y., Gerla, M.: A Measurement Study of Path Capacity in 802.11b Based Wireless Networks. In: Proceedings of the Wireless Traffic Measurements and Modeling Workshop, Seattle, WA, USA (2005)
5. Paul, K., Bandyopadhyay, S., Mukherjee, A., Saha, D.: Communication Aware Mobile Hosts in Ad-Hoc Wireless Network. In: Proceedings of the IEEE International Conference on Personal Wireless Communications, Jaipur, India (1999)
6. Lim, G., Shin, K., Lee, S., Yoon, H., Ma, J.S.: Link Stability and Route Lifetime in Ad-hoc Wireless Networks. In: Proceedings of the 31st International Conference on Parallel Processing Workshops, Vancouver, Canada (2002) 116–123
7. Turau, V., Renner, C., Venzke, M., Waschik, S., Weyer, C., Witt, M.: The Heathland Experiment: Results And Experiences. In: Proceedings of the REALWSN'05 Workshop on Real-World Wireless Sensor Networks, Stockholm, Sweden (2005)
8. Yu, D., Li, H., Gruber, I.: Path Availablilty in Ad Hoc Networks. In: Proceedings of the 10th International Conference on Telecommunications (ICT'2003), Tahiti, French Polynesia (2003)
9. Tseng, Y.C., Li, Y.F., Chang, Y.C.: On Route Lifetime in Multihop Mobile Ad Hoc Networks. IEEE Transactions on Mobile Computing **2** (2003) 366–376
10. Su, W., Lee, S.J., Gerla, M.: Mobility prediction and routing in ad hoc wireless networks. International Journal of Network Management **11** (2001) 3–30
11. Jiang, S., He, D., Rao, J.: A Prediction-based Link Availability Estimation for Mobile Ad Hoc Networks. In: Proceedings of the IEEE INFOCOM 2001, Anchorage, AK, USA (2001) 1745–1752
12. Jiang, S.: An Enhanced Prediction-Based Link Availability Estimation for MANETs. IEEE Transactions on Communications **52** (2004) 183–186
13. Johnson, D.B., Maltz, D.A.: Dynamic Source Routing in Ad Hoc Wireless Networks. In Imielinski, T., Korth, H., eds.: Mobile Computing. Volume 353. Kluwer Academic Publishers (1996) 153–181
14. Perkins, C., Belding-Royer, E., Das, S.: Ad hoc On-Demand Distance Vector (AODV) Routing. RFC 3561 (Experimental) (2003)
15. Fall, K., Varadhan, K.: The ns Manual (formerly ns Notes and Documentation). The VINT Project. (2005) http://www.isi.edu/nsnam/ns/ns-documentation.html.

A Base Station Centralized Simple Clustering Protocol for Sensor Networks

Giljae Lee, Minsun Lee, Woojin Seok, Junguk Kong, and Okhwan Byeon

Korea Institute of Science and Technology Information,
52, Eoeun-dong, Yuseong, Daejeon, Korea
{giljael, mleeoh, wjseok, kju, ohbyeon}@kisti.re.kr

Abstract. Sensor nodes in wireless sensor network are severely energy-constrained. This has been a key factor to limit its performance. So far, many energy-efficient routing protocols have been proposed. Cluster-based routing protocols have been paid much attention because of their advantages. However, the cluster-based routing protocols require information on the locations of the sensor nodes in the network to construct clusters. Due to cost, it is not feasible to know the locations of all sensor nodes in the network. In this paper, we propose *a base station centralized simple clustering protocol* (BCSP) which requires no location information of the sensor nodes. Instead, BCSP utilizes information on the remaining energy of each sensor node and the number of cluster heads which is changed depending on the circumstance of the sensor network. From performance experiments, BCSP shows better performance than *low-energy adaptive clustering hierarchy* (LEACH).

1 Introduction

Recent advances in wireless communication and electronics have enabled developing low cost, low power, and multi-functional sensor nodes, which are small and can communicate with neighbor nodes within short distances. *Wireless sensor network* (WSN) usually consists of a base station and many sensor nodes. The sensor nodes are randomly distributed in the sensor network field and monitor temperature, air pressure, motion, and so on. After sensing, the sensor nodes send the sensing data to the base station. Here, the base station acts as a gateway to deliver the data from the sensor nodes to users who need it. In WSN, the number of the sensor nodes can be tens of thousands. Therefore, it could be difficult to initialize the sensor nodes and to manage the sensor network. This is why self-configuring the sensor nodes and saving energy via an efficient routing protocol [1] are desirable in WSN.

Conventionally two protocols have been used in WSN. One is direct communication protocol and the other is multi-hop communication protocol such as the *Minimum Transmission Energy* (MTE) routing protocol. In the direct communication protocol, the distant sensor nodes from the base station dissipate their energy faster than others because they send their data to the base station directly. In the MTE routing protocol, each node acts as a router for other sensor nodes. Therefore, energy is consumed faster if more sensor nodes are adjacent

E. Sha et al. (Eds.): EUC 2006, LNCS 4096, pp. 682–691, 2006.

to the base station [4]. To overcome the problems in the conventional protocols, data centric protocols such as *the Sensor Protocols for Information via Negotiation* (SPIN) [5] and *the directed diffusion* (DD) [6] have been proposed. As far as data transmission and data collection are concerned, the data centric protocols are more efficient than the conventional transmission methods. However, the data centric protocols require many control messages and thus cause long latency to set routing paths. On the other hand, cluster-based routing protocols involve reduced control messages. In addition, the cluster-based routing protocols have bandwidth reusability, enhanced resource allocation, and improved power control. One disadvantage in the cluster-based routing protocols is that cluster heads are fixed, carry out more energy-intensive processes, and therefore their energy consumption is greater than non-cluster head nodes. As a result, network lifetime is short.

In this paper, we propose *a base station centralized simple clustering protocol* (BCSP) for sensor networks which is energy-efficient. Some related works on cluster-based routing protocols for sensor networks will be presented in Section 2. In Section 3, we explain BCSP in detail. In Section 4, we present performance results of BCSP and comparison with original LEACH and LEACH-C protocol. Finally, we conclude with some conclusions and future works.

2 Related Works

Low-energy adaptive clustering hierarchy(LEACH) was proposed to solve the prob-ems in the cluster-based protocols. LEACH is based on hierarchical clustering structure model. In order to increase the lifetime of the sensor network, LEACH changes cluster heads periodically. LEACH involves two main steps; the setup phase and the steady state phase. The setup phase involves cluster head selection part and cluster construction part. After cluster heads are chosen from sensor nodes, the cluster head sensor nodes broadcast advertisement message. The message contains cluster head ID which is the sensor node ID. Based on the advertisement message, non-cluster head sensor nodes know which nodes are new cluster heads in the sensor network. The new cluster head nodes use *the carrier-sense multiple access* (CSMA) *medium access control* (MAC) protocol to transmit it. Non-cluster head sensor nodes then select most relevant cluster head node according to the signal strength of the advertisement message from the cluster head nodes and send join request message back to the selected cluster head node for registration. Once the selected cluster head node receives join message, the cluster head nodes make *a time division multiple-access* (TDMA) schedule to exchange data with non-cluster sensor nodes without collision. The cluster head node broadcasts the schedule to its member nodes, and then the member sensor nodes start sending their data to the base station through their cluster head node during the steady state phase.

In LEACH, a cluster head node is selected according to sensor nodes probability value. As far as optimal energy consumption is concerned, it is not desirable to select a cluster head node randomly and construct clusters. However, repeating round can improve total energy dissipation and performance in the sensor network. In spite of these advantages, LEACH has some shortcomings: remaining energy of sensor nodes is not considered to construct clusters, and LEACH protocol fixes the number of cluster head nodes in the sensor network which is a parameter used in the setup phase. Therefore, it is difficult to increase and decrease the size of the sensor network. Moreover, LEACH does not guarantee the number of cluster head nodes and their distribution because the cluster head nodes are selected stochastically by the value of probability [4]. To overcome the shortcomings in LEACH, various cluster-based protocols such as *LEACH-centralized* (LEACH-C) and *Base-Station Controlled Dynamic Clustering Protocol* (BCDCP) have been proposed. In these protocols, cluster head nodes are selected by the base station in the sensor network.

LEACH-C is the extended version of LEACH. It is the same as LEACH except the setup phase. In cluster construction step, all sensor nodes in the sensor network send their information, which includes their ID, remaining energy level, and position information to the base station. Then, the base station calculates average energy of the sensor network and chooses a candidate set of cluster head nodes that have more energy than the average in the sensor network. Here, the base station executes *annealing algorithm* to find the most optimized and energy-efficient number of clusters with the candidate set of cluster head nodes. After clusters are constructed, the base station transmits information about cluster head nodes, their members, and their TDMA schedule to all sensor nodes. Then, non-cluster head sensor nodes decide own TDMA slot and come in sleep state until their own data transmission turn [3].

In BCDCP, the base station randomly changes cluster head nodes as in LEACH, constructs *cluster-to-cluster* (CH-to-CH) routing paths, and carries out other energy-intensive tasks such as data aggregation, compression, and fusion. BCDCP constructs balanced clusters where each cluster head has approximately equal number of member nodes to avoid overload, and cluster head nodes are uniformly distributed in the sensor field. It uses CH-to-CH routing to transfer data to the base station. Similar to LEACH-C, energy information sent by all sensor nodes is used to construct clusters in the setup phase. The base station uses *balanced clustering technique* for distributing load of cluster head nodes, and *iterative cluster splitting algorithm* to find optimal number of clusters. After this setup phase, the base station makes a multiple CH-to-CH routing paths, creates a schedule for each cluster, and then broadcasts schedule in-formation to the sensor network. In the data communication phase, the cluster head nodes transfer data from sensor nodes to the base station through the CH-to-CH routing paths [7].

3 Proposed Protocol

In this section, we explain the proposed protocol, BCSP in detail. LEACH-C and BCDCP use the base station and location information of the sensor nodes to increase lifetime of the sensor network. As mentioned previously, it is however difficult to know locations of all sensor nodes due to cost. There are also network overhead for all sensor nodes to send their information to the base station at the same time every setup phase due to the number of sensor nodes involved in the sensor network.

In BCSP, the base station uses the remaining energy of each sensor node and the number of sensor nodes alive in the sensor network. Therefore, the protocol does not need location information of the sensor nodes. In addition, the base station can select cluster head nodes with desirable number depending on sensor network and use this information in constructing clusters. The base station selects cluster head nodes by considering the remaining energy of sensor nodes, and broadcasts the list of the new cluster head nodes to the sensor network in the cluster construction phase. In the data communication phase, sensor nodes transmit their energy information together with their own sensing data. Therefore, BCSP can keep away from overhead originated by directly sending setup information of sensor nodes to the base station during the cluster construction phase.

3.1 Network Model

In this paper, we assume a sensor network model, similar to those used in LEACH, with the following properties.

- Sensor nodes are energy-constrained.
- The base station is supplied by power outside, and has enough memory and computing capability for energy intensive tasks.
- Each sensor node always has data to transmit it to the base station at a fixed rate.
- Each sensor node can directly communicate with other sensor nodes by varying their transmission power in the sensor network.
- The location of each sensor node is fixed.
- System lifetime is defined as the time when last sensor node dies in the senor net-work.

BCSP is composed of a base station and 100 sensor nodes and has following char-acteristics.

- The base station can change the desirable number of cluster head nodes regarding the variation of the sensor network size.
- The base station decides cluster head nodes based on the amount of remaining energy of both each sensor node and the sensor network. It also reflects the number of cluster head nodes changed by the sensor network size.
- Sensor nodes transmit energy information to the base station in the data communication phase together with their own sensing data.

3.2 Energy Model

Energy model of BCSP is based on energy model of LEACH [3]. Energy consumption can be mainly divided into two parts: receiving and transmitting message.

In transmission, it needs additional energy to amplify signal depending on the distance to the destination. In this paper, we suppose that power attenuation depends on distance between a transmission node and a reception node. The propagation loss is assumed to be inversely proportional to d^2 while it is assumed to be inversely proportional to d^4 at long distances. To transmit a k-bit message a distance d, the radio expends the following energy:

$$\begin{aligned} E_{T_x}(k,d) &= E_{T_{x-elec}}(k) + E_{T_{x-amp}}(k,d) \\ &= \begin{cases} E_{elec} \times k + \epsilon_{friss-amp} \times k \times d^2 & \text{if } d < d_{crossover} \\ E_{elec} \times k + \epsilon_{two-way-amp} \times k \times d^4 & \text{if } d \geq d_{crossover} \end{cases} . \end{aligned} \quad (1)$$

At reception, exhausted energy is given by

$$E_{R_x}(k,d) = E_{R_{x-elec}}(k) = E_{elec} \times k. \quad (2)$$

Here, E_{elec}, $\epsilon_{friss-amp}$ and $\epsilon_{two-way-amp}$ are identical to those of LEACH.

3.3 Cluster Construction Phase

In the cluster construction phase, the base station broadcasts advertisement message, which includes a list of new cluster head nodes selected by the base station according to the amount of remaining energy of each sensor node (BS_ADV). At first cluster construction phase, however, the base station sends cluster information as zero, because the base station cannot recognize energy level of each sensor node and the number of sensor nodes in the sensor network.

If a sensor node is found to be a new cluster head node according to the advertisement message, the sensor node broadcasts new advertisement message that includes its own information (CH_ADV). Otherwise, non-cluster head nodes discard advertisement message from the base station and wait new advertisement message from new cluster head nodes. When non-cluster head nodes receive messages from cluster head nodes, the non-cluster head nodes choose their own cluster head node using the strength of signal, and then send join message to the cluster head node (JOIN).

In the first cluster construction phase, since the advertisement message from the base station includes just null value, sensor nodes carry out cluster head selection algorithm (3) of LEACH. Otherwise, sensor nodes carry out the operations explained above. The other operations in the cluster construction phase are identical to those of LEACH. As the cluster construction ends, cluster head nodes make a schedule for their own sensor nodes and broadcast it to their own sensor nodes (CH_SCHE). N is the number of sensor nodes in the sensor network, and k is the desirable number of cluster head nodes. The $P_i(t)$ represents the probability that a sensor node i is a cluster head node. It is identical to the formation of LEACH.

$$P_i(t) = \begin{cases} \frac{k}{N - k \times (r \bmod \frac{N}{k})} & C_i(t) = 1 \\ 0 & C_i(t) = 0 \end{cases} . \quad (3)$$

3.4 Data Communication Phase

In the data communication phase, each sensor node transmits sensing data to its own cluster head node according to communication schedule (SN_DATA). Cluster head nodes gather data sent by sensor nodes and do aggregation, fusion and compression. After that, cluster head nodes transmit processed data that include remaining energy level of each sensor node to the base station (CH_DATA).

The base station passes raw data through the Internet or other networks, and it stores information of remaining energy of each sensor node for the next cluster construction phase. Now, the base station can know the amount of energy of each sensor node and the number of sensor nodes in the sensor network. The base station can use various kinds of algorithms to calculate the suitable number of cluster heads considering size of the sensor network as well as the number of sensor nodes. In this paper, we use 5 percent of the number of sensor nodes as the optimum number of cluster head nodes that was found from the experiment in LEACH. Therefore, the base station decides 5 percent of sensor nodes as new cluster head nodes in descendant order of the amount of remaining energy every cluster construction phase.

Figure 1 shows the flow of the cluster construction phase and the data communication phase, as we explained above.

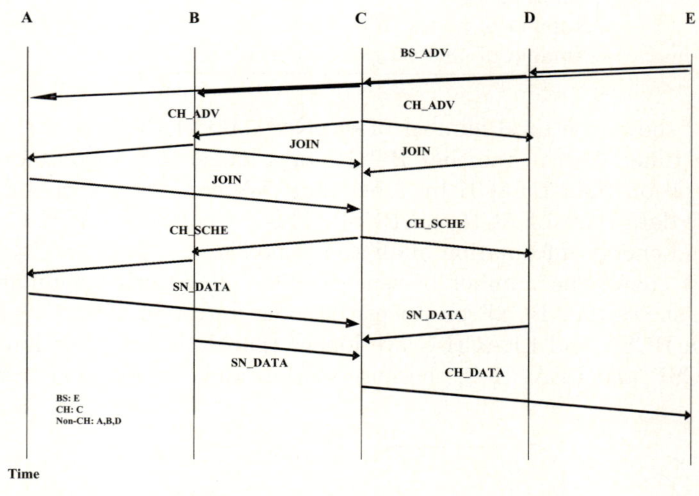

Fig. 1. The message flow of the construction phase and the data communication phase in BCSP

4 Performance Evaluation

In this section, we show performance evaluation of BCSP. We simulated with ns-2 leach extension [8] and implementation [9]. Simulation environment is equal to those of LEACH and Table 1 shows simulation parameters. We assume that sensor nodes initially have equal initial energy, $0.5J$. The area of the sensor network was set to $100m \times 100m$. The base station is located at $(50m, 50m)$ inside the sensor network. In simulation, we define system lifetime as the time when no sensor nodes send data to the base station. Performance was measured by total messages successfully delivered to the base station, system lifetime, the number of cluster head nodes per round, and average consumed energy in each simulation time. Then, we compared the simulation results with LEACH and LEACH-C.

Table 1. Parameters for simulation

Parameter	Value
Network Grid	$(0, 0) \times (100, 100)$
BS	(50, 50)
$d_{crossover}$	$87m$
ϵ_{elec}	$50nJ/bit$
$\epsilon_{friss-amp}$	$10pJ/bit/m^2$
$\epsilon_{two-way-amp}$	$0.0013pJ/bit/m^4$
$\epsilon_{aggregation}$	$5nJ/bit$
Data packet size	$500bytes$
Packet header size	$25bytes$
Initial energy	$0.5J$
Number of nodes (N)	100
Number of clusters (k)	5 (5% of N)

Figure 2 shows the total number of received data at the base station during simulation time. We can see that BCSP stays longer and sends more data to the base station than LEACH by 7 percents. We can also see that LEACH-C sends more data than LEACH and BCSP. This is because LEACH-C uses both location and energy information of all sensor nodes.

Figure 3 shows the number of sensor nodes alive during simulation time. The figure shows that BCSP produces the longest system lifetime. The system lifetimes in BCSP and LEACH-C are longer than LEACH. This is the reason that in BCSP and LEACH-C, the base station knows remaining energy of all

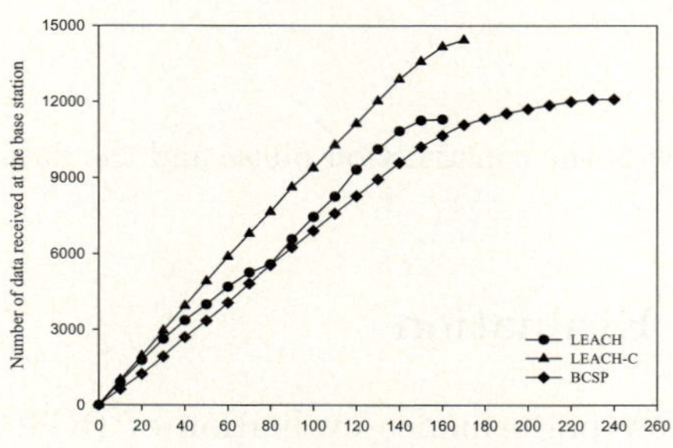

Fig. 2. Number of data received at the base station during simulation time

sensor nodes in the sensor network, and it uses the information on selecting cluster head nodes and constructing clusters. Besides, BCSP has system lifetime much longer than LEACH-C by, changing the number of cluster head nodes according to the number of the sensor nodes in the sensor network. In result, BCSP exceeds the system lifetime of LEACH by no less than 50 percent and the one of LEACH-C by 41 percent.

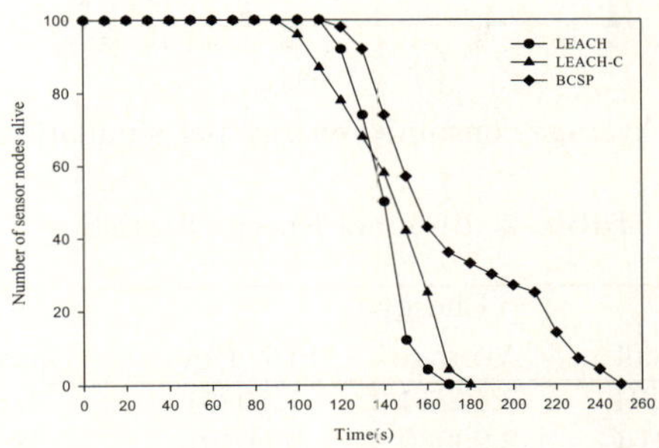

Fig. 3. Number of sensor nodes alive per simulation time

In Figure 4, we can see the change in the number of the cluster head nodes per simulation round. In LEACH, each sensor node uses equation 3 as a selection criterion. LEACH chooses cluster head nodes randomly regardless of the amount of energy of each sensor node. On the other hand, LEACH-C has the fixed number of the cluster head nodes by making use of the location and energy information of each sensor nodes in the sensor network. This is the reason why BCSP has system lifetime much longer than LEACH-C.

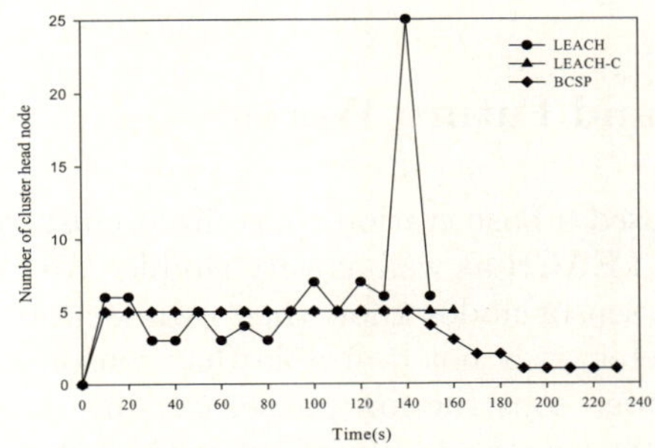

Fig. 4. Number of cluster head nodes per simulation time

Figure 5 shows the average consumed energy per each simulation time. We can see that the number of the cluster head nodes is followed by consumed energy linearly. Table 2 shows residual energy statistics. LEACH dissipates more energy than others, but its average data, sent to the base station, per $1J$ is the smallest, for much of consumed energy of each sensor node is used to cluster constructing and communicating with cluster head nodes. The biggest standard deviation of

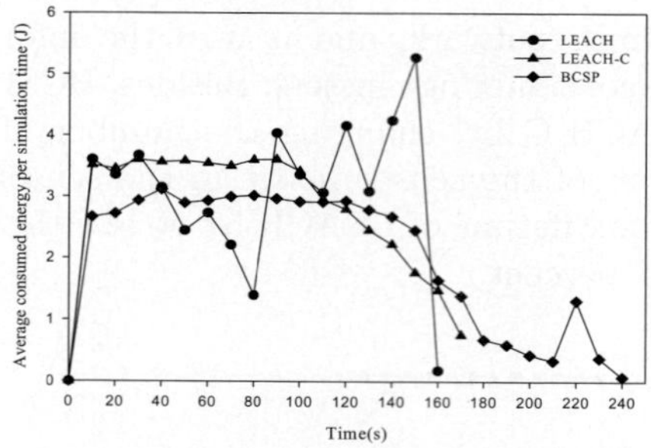

Fig. 5. Average consumed energy per simulation time

Table 2. Residual Energy Statistics

Protocol	Energy J Average	Std. Dev.	Ave. Data (Data/J)
LEACH	3.12314	1.19851	226.01
LEACH-C	2.93060	0.89101	289.64
BCSP	2.07222	1.09602	243.11

the average consumed energy shows the reason. The LEACH-C makes it appear that it is the most efficient among three protocols when it comes to average consumed energy and average data per $1J$.

Throughout the simulations, we can see that BCSP is better than LEACH in all simulation metrics. In that simulation, LEACH-C is a bit better than BCSP. On the other hand, BCSP is superior to LEACH-C in terms of system lifetime, since BCSP changes the number of the cluster head nodes every cluster construction phase.

5 Conclusions and Future Works

In summary, we proposed a base station centralized clustering protocol for sensor networks modified LEACH as well as very simple. We focus on the fact that it is expensive that all sensor nodes know their own location information. Moreover, to construct cluster, it is not desirable that sensor nodes send their own information every cluster construction phase, causing overhead unnecessarily. BCSP carries out cluster construction without inefficient sensor-node-broadcast to notify the base station of their information because sensor nodes send their information, necessary to construct optimal clusters, together sensing data. In addition, BCSP can change the desirable number of cluster head nodes with the sensor network size. Simulation showed that BCSP improves in all simulation metrics compared with LEACH. However, BCSP only surpasses LEACH-C in system lifetime. As we mentioned above, this is because BCSP is just concentrated in solving the problem that the number of cluster head nodes is decided irregularly.

BCSP does not still guarantee uniform distribution of cluster head nodes and the number of their member nodes. Therefore, we are now considering a better cluster based routing protocol than BCSP, which distributes cluster head nodes more uniformly and constructs similar-sized clusters without location information. When these problems are solved, it is without location information of each sensor node that our proposed protocol might have performance as good as LEACH-C or other related protocols.

References

1. I. F. Akyildiz et al., Wireless Sensor Networks: A Survey, Elsevier Sci. B. V. Comp. Networks, vol. 38, no. 4, 2002, pp. 393-422.
2. J. N. Al-Karaki and A. E. Kamal, Routing Techniques in Wireless Sensor Networks: A Survey, IEEE Wireless Communications, vol. 11, no. 6, 2004, pp. 6-28.
3. W. B. Heinzelman, A. P. Chandrakasan, and H. Balakrishnan, An Application-Specific Protocol Architecture for Wireless Microsensor Networks, IEEE Wireless Communication, vol. 1, no. 4, 2002, pp. 660-670.
4. W. R. Heinzelman, A. P. Chandrakasan, and H. Balakrishnan, Energy-Efficient Communication Protocol for Wireless Microsensor Networks, Proc. 33rd Hawaii International Conf. System Sciences, 2000.
5. W. R. Heinzelman, J. Kulik, and H. Balakrishnan, Adaptive Protocols for Information Dissemination in Wireless Sensor Networks, Proc. 5th Annual international Conf. Mobile Computing and Networking, 1999, pp. 174-185.
6. C. Intanagonwiwat, R. Govindan, and D. Estrin, Directed Diffusion: A Scalable and Robust Communication Paradigm for Sensor Networks, Proc. 6th Annual International Conf. Mobile Computing and Networking, 2000, pp. 56-67.
7. S. D. Muruganathan, D. C. F. Ma, R. I. Bhasin, and A. O. Fapojuwo, A Centralized Energy-Efficient Routing Protocol for Wireless Sensor Networks, IEEE Communication Magazine, vol. 43, no. 3, 2005, pp. S8-S13.
8. The MIT uAMPS ns Code Extensions Version 1.0, http://www-mtl.mit.edu/research/icsystems/uamps/research/leach/leach_code.shtml.
9. J. A. Pamplin, NS2 Leach Implementation, http://www.internetworkflow.com/resources/ns2_leach.pdf

Simulation Cost Reduction Strategies for Behavioral Model Verification in Bayesian Based Stopping Rule

Kang Chul Kim[1], Chang-Gyoon Lim[1], Jae Hung Yoo[1], and Seok Bung Han[2]

[1] Department of Computer Engineering, Chonnam National University,
San 96-1, Dunduck-Dong, Yeosu, Chonnam, Korea
kkc@chonnam.ac.kr
[2] Department of Electronic Engineering, Gyeongsang National University,
Gajwa-Dong, Jinju, Gyeongnam, Korea
hsb@nongae.gsnu.ac.kr

Abstract. This paper presents two additional strategies to reduce simulation time for Bayesian based stopping rules in VHDL model verification. The first is that a semi-random variable is defined and the data staying in the semi-random variable range are skipped when stopping rule is running, and a turning point that can partition a random variable into a semi-random and a genuine random variable is chosen. The second is that the old values of parameters are kept when phases of stopping rule change. 12 VHDL models are examined, and the simulation results demonstrate that more than approximately 25% of clock cycles are reduced when using the two proposed strategies with 0.6% branch coverage rate loss.

Keywords: Verification, behavioral VHDL model, stopping rule, branch coverage, semi-random variable.

1 Introduction

As VLSI fabrication technology has rapidly developed, it is possible to implement SoC(System on Chip) which comprises CPU, memory controller, bus controller, and so on. However, the technologies for the design and the verification of complicated chips have not developed rapidly, therefore, design verification of behavioral models is becoming difficult and has become a critical and time-consuming process in hardware design. Approximately 70% of the design effort in SoC, IP, ASIC, etc., has been consumed in the verification process, and design and verification engineers work together from the beginning of IC design [1,2,3].

It is impossible to know that the design being verified is indeed functionally correct with 100% certainty. That is the reason code coverage is required to be used. Many different types of coverage criteria have been defined including statement, branch, block, expression, and path coverage[4,5,6]. Among these criteria, branch coverage has been chosen as a good metric to verify hardware designs.

A large number of clock cycles should be consumed to verify a design by using coverage metrics because random test patterns have been used in complex VHDL models. Several examples demonstrate that 5 billion instruction simulation cycles can

E. Sha et al. (Eds.): EUC 2006, LNCS 4096, pp. 692 – 701, 2006.

be run to ensure fault-free chip before tapeout[7,8,9]. Therefore, techniques that can seek the optimal stopping point should be developed and it is necessary to take productive stopping rules and strategies to reduce verification time and cost in a verification process.

This paper presents two additional strategies to reduce clock cycles for the Bayesian based stopping rule in VHDL model verification. In the first strategy, a semi-random variable is defined and the data located in the semi-random variable range are skipped when the stopping rule is running. A turning point partitioning the given random variable into a semi-random and a genuine random variable is chosen. In the second, the old values of parameters are kept when the phases of stopping rule change. More than approximately 25% of clock cycles are reduced using the two proposed strategies with few losses of branch coverage.

In section Ⅱ, previous work is introduced, and proposed strategies are explained in section Ⅲ. Section Ⅳ presents simulation results and discussions of the results. Finally, conclusion of this paper is presented in section Ⅴ.

2 Bayesian Based Stopping Rules

Many methods for testing software program have been developed[10,11,12]. Recently, Poisson distribution and Bayesian estimation based stopping rules were introduced by [10] and [13].

[10] suggested a compounded counting process using empirical Bayesian princeples and introduced the stopping rule in verification of VHDL programs. The key idea is to combine two probability distributions, that is, the number and the size of interruption. The parameters of probability distributions are assumed random variables by using Bayesian estimation.

[13] observed the outcome of branch coverage at every testing clock cycle and predicted the number of branches to be covered at time t. In this method, the number to be covered is expressed by branch coverage random process X_t. X_t is divided into two probabilities, interruption N_t, where one or more new branches are covered at time t, and the size of the interruptions W_t. The conditional distribution functions of the interruption occurrences, D_t, is defined. Next, a PMF(Probability Mass Function) extraction experiments are conducted in order to estimate the best fitted distribution function at every discrete time t, and Poisson probability distribution function is chosen. Then W_t is defined to be a random process distributed as a Poisson process with β_t as

$$W_t \sim e^{-\beta_t} \frac{\beta_t^{\,w-1}}{(w-1)!} . \tag{1}$$

Here, β_t is a random variable representing the parameter of the Poisson distribution that should be estimated from the simulation history and is defined as $\beta_t = \beta g(t)$ for constant β and a decreasing function g(t) and $G(t) = \sum_{j:d_j=1} g(j)$.

The probability of having an interruption during the testing process, p(t), is estimated for every discrete time t. This p(t) is decomposed into a shape function f(t) and an amplitude value ς_t, p(t)= ς_t f(t), where the ς_t values can be determined statically or dynamically based on the history of testing the behavioral model. The gamma function of β is given by

$$\Gamma(\beta;\gamma,r)=\frac{\gamma^r}{\Gamma(r)}e^{-\gamma\beta}\beta^{r-1}. \tag{2}$$

Then, the statistical model for the branch coverage increase for a given history of verification is derived. And Bayesian analysis is achieved by calculating the likelihood function of the Bayesian parameter, β_t, and given the verification history, the coverage is expected at time t>T as

$$\hat{\beta}=\frac{r+x_t-n_t}{\gamma+G(t)}, \tag{3}$$

$$E\{W_t \mid \vec{x}\}=1+\frac{r+x_t-n_t}{\gamma+G(t)}g(t). \tag{4}$$

Finally, the total number of branches to be covered at future time t>T is predicted as

$$E\{X_t \mid \vec{x}\}=x_T+\sum_{j=T+1}^{t}(1+\frac{r+x_t-n_t}{\gamma+G(t)}g(j))\varsigma f(j). \tag{5}$$

In some papers[14,15], a new test pattern is generated at every simulation cycle and fed into a model, however [14] represents a new verification strategy. When data bits have to be fixed for certain times, a pattern for a certain number of clock cycles is used, that is, 1, 2, 4, 6 clock cycles are remained for each phase stage. The mixed strategy of random testing improves branch coverage[16].

The methods of above papers have improved behavioral model verification. If a few additional strategies are introduced, it is suggested that the verification cost can be reduced much further. A numerical result of an experiment can be a random variable when the value of it is not exactly expected. But the random variable used in [13] has a predictable value for some clock cycles from the beginning point. It is suggested that this random variable can be divided into two regions, that is, semi-random and genuine random variables. If the data in the semi-random variable range are skipped, the simulation time can be considerably reduced.

[16] did not use the previous simulation results when simulation phase changed. Bayesian estimation expects the future event by using the event estimated from the history of previous simulations, so it is reasonable to make use of the previous results in a current simulation.

In addition, [13] and [16] have the constraint that stops simulation when branch coverage is zero for first 30 consecutive clock cycles in every phase, but sometimes this can become a problem because the constraint can be of greater significance than stopping rules, and ultimately make the simulation stop.

3 Proposed Strategies for Reducing Simulation Cost

The overall expected value of X_t is the sum of all the expected sizes of interrupts after time T as showed in (5). X_t and W_t have been assumed to be random variables for all clock cycles. If x_T is large in (5), the expected value of X_t is large, that is, the larger the sum of all coverage before time T, the longer the stopping point. Therefore the sum of coverage before time T should be low in order to reduce the stopping point in the time axis.

Table 1. Cumulative branch coverage vs. clock cycle

	B C(Branch Coverage)											
S# t	S1	S2	S3	S4	S5	S6	S7	S8	S9	S10	S11	S12
1	35	35	58	47	47	69	58	47	35	58	49	93
2	53	92	111	94	94	153	111	94	92	111	92	166
3	54	95	123	102	102	156	123	102	95	123	127	218
4	58	111	123	133	133	178	123	133	111	123	129	228
5	68	140	126	145	145	210	126	145	140	126	132	231
6	68	143	139	146	146	214	139	146	143	139	136	238
7	68	148	142	146	146	216	142	146	148	142	139	239
8	68	151	170	146	146	222	170	146	151	170	139	239
9	68	151	172	154	154	222	172	154	151	172	144	244
10	68	152	182	159	159	222	182	159	152	182	148	249

Table 2. Branch coverage for 10 test patterns at the first two clock cycles

	B C																							
S#	S1		S2		S3		S4		S5		S6		S7		S8		S9		S10		S11		S12	
t TP	t=1	t=2	t=1	t=2	t=1	t=2	t=1	t=2	t=1	t=2	t=1	t=2	t=1	t=2	t=1	t=2	t=1	t=2	t=1	t=2	t=1	t=2	t=1	t=2
1	35	16	35	57	58	53	47	47	47	47	69	84	58	53	47	47	35	57	58	53	49	42	93	73
2	35	17	35	60	58	49	47	44	47	44	69	77	58	49	47	44	35	60	58	49	49	41	93	93
3	35	18	35	59	58	55	47	43	47	43	69	76	58	55	47	43	35	59	58	55	49	59	93	92
4	35	14	35	59	58	51	47	46	47	46	69	76	58	51	47	46	35	59	58	51	49	58	93	90
5	35	15	35	56	58	46	47	44	47	44	69	83	58	46	47	44	35	56	58	46	49	47	93	83
6	35	16	35	56	58	48	47	45	47	45	69	83	58	48	47	45	35	56	58	48	49	46	93	66
7	35	15	35	56	58	53	47	45	47	45	69	83	58	53	47	45	35	56	58	53	49	51	93	83
8	35	11	35	57	58	47	47	45	47	45	69	84	58	47	47	45	35	57	58	47	49	44	93	73
9	35	17	35	60	58	56	47	44	47	44	69	77	58	56	47	44	35	60	58	56	49	56	93	84
10	35	12	35	60	58	53	47	44	47	44	69	77	58	53	47	44	35	60	58	53	49	42	93	76

The values of random variables are not known with certainty, that is, only a set of possible time and probability of the random variables are known. In this paper, a semi-random variable is defined as a variable of which value is certainly not known, but all values of the variable are greater than the reference value. Table 1 presents cumulative branch coverage for ten simulation clock cycles from the starting point for 12 sample VHDL models. Every branch coverage for a few clock cycles from t=1 is comparatively large.

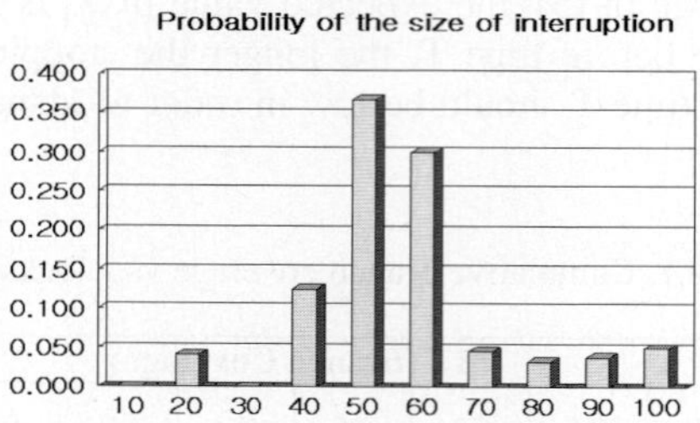

Fig. 1. Histogram of branch coverage for first and second clock cycles

Table 2 presents that the number of branch coverage with 10 test patterns is comparatively high for first and second simulation clock cycles. Fig. 1 presents the histogram of branch coverage in table 2. The probability that the size of interruption is less than 10 is 0, and all the branch coverage is higher than 10 for the two consecutive clock cycles.

Table 3 presents branch coverage at each cycle for 10 clock cycles with the same test pattern. For example, if the reference value has been chosen as 6, branch coverage is 35 and 18 at t=1 and t=2 respectively for sample S1, so the branch coverage in the time range between t=1 and t=2 defines a semi-random variable, and the branch coverage in the time range for t>2 defines a genuine random variable.

Table 3. Branch coverage for each clock cycle

CC	BC											
	S1	S2	S3	S4	S5	S6	S7	S8	S9	S10	S11	S12
1	35	35	58	47	47	69	58	47	35	58	49	93
2	18	57	53	47	47	84	53	47	57	53	43	73
3	1	3	12	8	8	3	12	8	3	12	35	52
4	4	16	0	31	31	22	0	31	16	0	2	10
5	0	29	3	12	12	32	3	12	29	3	3	3
6	0	3	13	1	1	4	13	1	3	13	4	7
7	0	5	3	0	0	2	3	0	5	3	3	1
8	0	3	28	0	0	6	28	0	3	28	0	0
9	0	0	2	8	8	0	2	8	0	2	5	5
10	0	1	10	5	5	0	10	5	1	10	4	5

The time is partitioned into two regions, TS and TR. TS is defined as TS={t_1, …,t_k }, where W_t (t_i)≥V_r for all i=1,2,..,k. and the next W_t (t_{k+1})<V_r, where V_r is a reference value. Then the interval TR is defined as TR={t_{k+1}, …,∞}, where W_t (t_i) can take non-negative value for all i=k+1,…, ∞.

It is important to note that values of the size of interruption W_t s are comparatively large for a few clock cycles from the beginning point even though the exact values of W_t s can not be predicted. W_t can be divided into two regions, that is, W_{ts} is a semi-random variable in the first region of a random variable and W_{tr} is a random variable in the other region as

$$W_t = W_{ts} \,\|\, W_{tr} \,. \tag{6}$$

W_{ts} in the first part of a random variable is so large that the data in the semi-random variable range can be skipped when the stopping rule is running because W_t s are not predicted by the Poisson's distribution function. The semi-random variable is extremely important because the cumulative branch coverage in the semi-random variable nearly reaches half the total coverage though the first region has a few clock cycles. Therefore it is very important to make a reasonable choice for the turning point at a random variable because it has a great effect on the stopping point.

The dark dashed line presents the probability of W_t for S7 in Fig. 2[13]. If the value of W_t is greater than 6, the probability of N_t is quite low. It can be recognized that the probability that the values of W_t are greater than 6 is very small in the genuine random variable range, but the probability in the semi-random variable is always 1. The reference or turning point is decided to be the first value of W_t having the frequency more than 1% at first from the beginning point. In Fig.2, W_t of which branch coverage is less than 6 at first is chosen as a turning point, which divides a random variable into a semi-random and a genuine random variable. Depending on behavioral models and test patterns, the branch coverage is randomly varied as the number of clock cycle increases, therefore the position of the reference value can not be fixed in time region. Instead, this is dynamically decided while simulation is running.

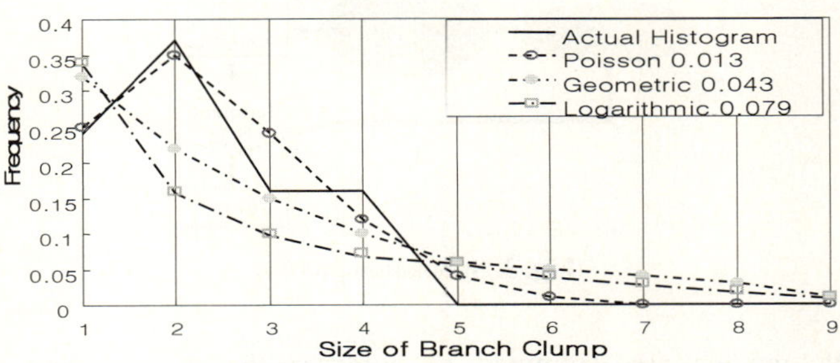

Fig. 2. Histogram fitting example of W_t for S7

The first additional strategy is proposed as follows. The branch coverage in the semi-random variable range W_{ts} defined in (6) is skipped while the stopping rule is running, then stopping point will become short because x_T becomes lower in (5). As the stopping point is shorter, the problem that total branch coverage becomes low must be considered. But random test patterns are used in most behavioral model verifications before testing a chip, and the increase in branch coverage rate abruptly drops as the number of random test pattern increases beyond the turning point, therefore it can be predicted that total branch coverage does not rapidly decrease when the data in the semi-random region W_{ts} is skipped.

The values of parameters obtained at the previous phases in (5) until time T are reset when a new phase starts in [13]. But the Bayesian model predicts the expected branch coverage using the previous branch coverage. The overall expected value of X_t at any time t>T given the verification history up to time T is the sum of all the expected sizes of interruptions after time T. Thus the second additional strategy is proposed, where the old data obtained in the previous phase can be used as initial values in the next phase.

Applying the new verification strategies to the stopping rule of the Bayesian model can reduce clock cycles and improve performance of behavioral model verification.

4 Simulation Results and Discussions

In order to inspect the proposed algorithm, QuickVHDL simulator of Mentor Graphics is used. Fig. 3 explains the overall simulation process. The random test patterns are generated and the phase of test pattern is chosen, then simulation is conducted with the VHDL sample program and input files. The branch coverage is calculated during simulation, and the simulator decides whether the simulation continues or quitting by branch coverage and the proposed strategies.

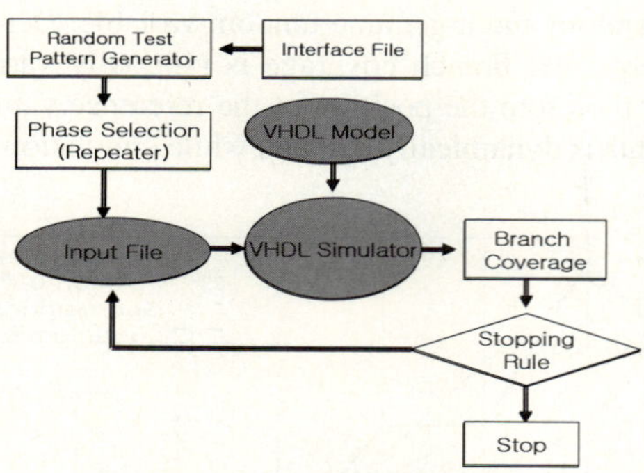

Fig. 3. Simulation process

12 VHDL models are examined to compare the effectiveness of proposed strategies with stopping rule of [14]. Table 4 presents the information of sample VHDL models.

Table 5 presents 3 kinds of simulation results obtained while the proposed stopping rule is run with branch coverage of each clock cycle. In Table 5, SB is the result for static Bayesian estimator in [13]. SBF is the result for the proposed estimator, which is identical to SB except for two differences. The first is that the data of branch coverage that is greater than 6 from the beginning time are not used for the simulation because they stay in the semi-random variable range, and the second is that the result

Table 4. Sample VHDL programs used in simulation

Sample	Description	# of code line	#of branch
S1	16 megabit byte-wide top boot 150ns	1880	373
S2	CMOS syncBIFIFO 256x36x2	4657	251
S3	SyncFIFO with bus-matching 1024x36	5015	302
S4	SyncFIFO 2048x36	4667	225
S5	SyncFIFO 2048x36	4710	225
S6	CMOS syncBIFIFO 1024x36x2	4949	296
S7	SyncFIFO with bus-matching 1024x36	4963	302
S8	SyncFIFO 2048x36	4777	225
S9	CMOS syncBIFIFO 512x36x2	4752	251
S10	SyncFIFO with bus-matching 512x36	4973	302
S11	SyncBIFIFO with bus-matching 512x36x2	5498	399
S12	SyncBIFIFO with bus-matching 1024x36x2	5770	470

of previous phase in (5) has been used in the next phase simulation whenever phases change under the same condition of SB. Estimator SB30 is same to SBF except that the constraint that makes the simulation stop in a current phase is added to SBF whenever each branch coverage for 30 consecutive test patterns from an arbitrarily starting point is zero.

Compared to SB, clock cycles are reduced to 24.6% and 59.1% and branch coverage are reduced to 0.6% and 1.5% for SBF and SB30, respectively. Most branches are detected in the semi-random variable range and the coverage rate decreases as the number of clock cycles increases and the increase in coverage rate becomes very slow after the turning point. SB30 and SBF have 3 and 2 additional constraints compared to SB respectively as discussed in section Ⅲ, but obtain much better results than SB.

Table 5. Simulation results of SB, SB30 and SBF

Sample	SB[13]		SB30		SBF	
	CC	BC	CC	BC	CC	BC
S1	1854	128	530	128	1460	128
S2	631	199	493	204	1461	206
S3	808	232	495	231	485	231
S4	673	192	485	192	482	192
S5	789	195	485	195	482	195
S6	2249	273	490	247	489	249
S7	809	232	495	231	496	231
S8	2181	208	649	203	1456	208
S9	631	199	493	204	1461	206
S10	808	232	495	231	496	231
S11	1982	245	596	245	1460	247
S12	2080	364	628	348	1462	360
SUM	15,495	2,699	6,334	2,659	11,690	2,684

Estimator SB1 is the same as SBF, but the simulation does not stop even though the branch coverage is zero for 30 successive clock cycles from the starting point of phase Φ1, Φ2, Φ3, 4Φ. Simulation results of SB and SB1 for 4 phase stages are presented in table 6. Here, the branch coverage of Φ0 are results obtained before the turning point, that is, they are in a semi-random variable region, therefore the branch coverage is skipped while the stopping rule is operating. Let 30ZBC be zero branch coverage for 30 consecutive clock cycles from the beginning point. The numbers in CC column of SB are ones of clock cycles consumed for each phase, but the numbers in CC column of SB1 means cumulative clock cycles for each phase including Φ0. The total clock cycles of SB are much less than one of SB1 in S9 because the simulation of S9 under SB stops by 30ZBC constraints in phase Φ2, Φ4, but SB suffers from a drawback that the cumulative branch coverage is relatively low. The cumulative clock cycles of SB in S1 and S12 is much larger because they are not affected by 30ZBC constraint. SB1 in S1, S9, and S12 has no 30ZBC constraint, but the cumulative clock cycles are 1462 on average with good branch coverage. It can be concluded that the stopping points are decided by the proposed strategies.

Table 6. Comparison of SB and SB 1 for S1,S9, and S12

PH	S1				S9				S12			
	SB		SB1		SB		SB1		SB		SB1	
	CC	BC	CC	BC	CC	BC	CC	BC	CC	BC	CC	BC
Φ0			2	53			2	92			4	228
Φ1	94	121	88	121	99	183	88	177	112	336	90	336
Φ2	188	1	161	122	60	0	161	182	60	0	163	336
Φ3	120	0	306	122	292	16	308	192	324	10	308	346
Φ4	1452	6	1460	128	180	0	1461	206	1584	18	1462	360
TOT	1854	128	1460	128	631	199	1461	206	2080	364	1462	360

It is difficult to obtain 100% branch coverage because random test patterns are applied to the simulator. The effect of semi-random variable is hidden because some simulation results have 30ZBC so that the simulation stops by 30ZBC constraints. Simulation results of Table 5 that do not have 30ZBC in phase Φ4 are selected and represented in Table 7 again to consider the effect of the proposed strategies. The simulation results of SBF reduce 2259 clock cycles with losses of 2 branch coverage because SBF skips the branch coverage detected in the W_{ts} region.

Table 7. Comparisons of SB and SBF without constraint of 30ZBC

Sample	SB		SBF	
	CC	BC	CC	BC
S1	1854	128	1460	128
S8	2181	208	1456	208
S11	1982	245	1460	247
S12	2080	364	1462	360
SUM	8097	945	5838	943

5 Conclusion

This paper proposes strategies that can be used to reduce clock cycles in behavioral model verification. The techniques are applied to 12 sample programs and the simulation results demonstrate that a large number of clock cycles are reduced with a few losses in branch coverage. In the future, finding the trade-off of branch coverage vs. consumption of clock cycle and an efficient turning point that can further reduce the number of simulation clock will be studied.

References

1. Frank Vahid, Tony Givargis. : EMBEDDED SYSTEM DESIGN : A Unified Hardware/ Software Introduction. John Wiley & Sons, Inc. (2002)
2. Samiha Mourad, Yervant Zorian. : Principles of Testing Electronic Systems. John Wiley & Sons, Inc. (2000)
3. Janick Bergerson.: Writing testbenches : functional verification of HDL model. Kluwer Academic (2003)
4. Jjm Lipman.: Covering your HDL chip-design bets. EDN, (Oct. 22, 1998) 65-70
5. Brian Barrera, "Code coverage analysis-essential to a safe design," Electronic Engineering, (Nov. 1998) 41-43
6. Kevin Skahill, "A designer's guide to VHDL design and verification," Engineering Software, (Feb. 1996) 149-158
7. A. Von Mayrhauser, et. Al., "On choosing test criteria for behavioral level hardware design verification", IEEE International Hign Level Design Validation and Test Workshop, Berkeley, CA, (2000)
8. A. Hajjar, Chen T, Improving the efficiency and quality of simulation-based model verification using dynamic Bayesian criteria, Quality Electronic Design, Proceedings International Symposium, (March 2002) 304-309
9. J. Gately, "Verifying a million gate processor", Integrated System Design, (1997) 19-24
10. M. Sahinoglu, A. Von Mayrhauser, A. Hajjar, T. Chen, C. Anderson, " On the efficiency of a compound Poisson stopping rule for mixed strategy testing", IEEE Aerospace conference, Track 7, (Mar. 1997)
11. W. Howden, " Confidence-based reliability and statistical coverage estimation", Proceedings on the international symposium on software reliability engineering, (Nov. 1997) 283-291.
12. S. Chen, S. Mills, "A binary markov process model for random testing", IEEE transactions on software engineering, v22, n3, (Mar. 1996) 218-223
13. Amjad Fuad A. Hajjar, "Bayesian Based Stoping Rules for Behavioral VHDL Verification", Ph. D Dissertation, Fall 2000.
14. R. Ramchandani, D. Thomas, "Behavioral test generation using mixed integer nonlinear programming", International test conference, (1994) 958-967
15. G. Hayek, C. Robach, "From specification validation to hardware testing: a unified method", International Test conference, (1996) 885-893
16. T. Chen, M. Sahinoglu, A. Mayrhauser, A. Hajjar, A. Anderson, "Achieving the quality for behavioral models with minimum effort", 1st international symposium on quality in electronic design, (Mar. 2000)

Low Power Hardware-Software Partitioning Algorithm for Heterogeneous Distributed Embedded Systems

Tianyi Ma, Jun Yang, and Xinglan Wang

Computer and Information Engineering of College
Harbin University of Commerce 150001, Harbin, China
ma_tian_yi@163.com

Abstract. Hardware-software partitioning is one of the most crucial steps in the design of embedded systems, which is the process of partitioning an embedded system specification into hardware and software modules to meet performance and cost goals. A majority of former work focuses on the problem of meeting timing constraints under minimizing the amount of hardware or minimizing time under hardware area constraints. The trends towards energy-efficient design of distributed embedded systems indicate the need for low power hardware-software partitioning algorithms, which are not enough emphasized so far. In this paper, we design tabu search on a chaotic neural network to solve the low power hardware-software partitioning problem. By introducing chaotic dynamics and utilizing the refractory effects of neurons as the tabu effects, the realized tabu search gets partitioning result with lower energy consumption, when compared with genetic algorithm.

Keywords: Hardware-software co-design, hardware-software partitioning, tabu search, chaotic neural network, low power.

1 Introduction and Related Work

Embedded systems have become omnipresent in wide variety of applications, such as telecommunication systems, consumer electronics, and other mass products. Modern embedded systems are often implemented as heterogeneous distributed systems. For completing complex embedded system under rigorous time and cost constraints, the hardware-software co-design of these, mostly, mixed software and hardware systems is an inevitable necessity [1]. One of the most crucial steps in the hardware-software co-design of embedded systems is hardware-software partitioning, that is, deciding which components of the systems should be realized in hardware and which ones in software [2]. Partitioning system specification into hardware and software, system designers have to take into account conflicting requirements on performance, power, cost, chip size, etc., and try to archive an optimal tradeoff. Hardware-software partitioning lies at one of the highest level of abstraction for the design of embedded systems, and drastically impacts the cost and performance of the whole system [3], so a good system partitioning is essential for the overall quality of embedded systems. It is also known that higher level of the design hierarchy where power is tackled, higher is the power reduction possible [4]. So low power hardware-software partitioning will consumedly reduce system power consumption.

E. Sha et al. (Eds.): EUC 2006, LNCS 4096, pp. 702 – 711, 2006.

Minimizing power consumption of embedded systems is a crucial task of modern embedded systems, but low power hardware-software partitioning algorithms, which are not enough emphasized in the past. However, the recent development of the portable-application market has intensified the interest in system-level design techniques for energy-efficient embedded systems.

Dave et al. proposed the first approach that targeted the reduction of power dissipation throughout the co-synthesis process [5]. They used a constructive algorithm to solve the classical multi-rate distributed system co-synthesis problem. This work was extended to target low power embedded systems, hence low power partitioning is only byproduct of their work.

Dick and Jha [6] reported a multi-objective genetic algorithm based co-synthesis approach. This framework simultaneously partitions and schedules task graphs for embedded systems. Their approach tries to obtain tradeoffs of different objectives, and power consumption is also one of these optimized objectives.

In [7], Henkel introduces a low-power hardware/software partitioning approach for core-based systems. Their approach is based on the idea of mapping clusters of operations/instructions to a core that yields a high utilization rate of the involved resources and thus minimizing power consumption. Their approach is low power hardware-software partitioning of embedded core-based systems, however, our work is low power partitioning problem of distributed embedded systems. And moreover, theirs is based on a fine-grained (instruction/operation-level), whereas, our approach is coarse-grained (task/procedure-level).

Peter et al. [8] proposed a simplified hardware-software partitioning formal model. Software implementation of a task is only associated with a software cost, which may be the running time, and hardware implementation of a task is associated with a hardware cost, which can be for instance area, energy consumption etc. The authors try to abandon details of the partitioning problem so as to solve the partitioning problem of large systems. They first took into account the partitioning problem of cost-constrained systems using integer linear programming, and subsequently dealt with the same problem using genetic algorithm. However the model is too simplified, so it may be difficult to be used for solving actual partitioning problem. In our work, we propose the applied formal model of partitioning problem under enlightening of their model, and use tabu search to look for the energy consumption minimum of hardware-software partitioning problem under system execution time constraint, hardware components' area constraints and software processors' memory constraints. By introducing chaotic dynamics and utilizing the refractory effects of neurons as the tabu effects, we realize the tabu search on a chaotic neural network. It can be seen from results of experiments that through reasonably designing the producing methods of candidate solutions, our algorithm is clearly superior to genetic algorithms.

2 Problem Formalization

2.1 Preliminary Definitions

An embedded system application is specified as a set of communicating tasks, represented by a task graph $G_s(V, EG)$. V is the set of graph vertices where vertex $v_i \in V$, $i \in [1,n]$, is the tasks of the systems that will be partitioned. Each vertex of task graph represents a function or a process, an atomic unit of functionality to be executed. EG is the set of graph edges where each edge $eg_{ij} \in EG$ represents communication between vertex v_i and v_j.

The target architecture on which system tasks can be executed or implemented is captured using an architecture graph $G_a(PE, CL)$, where nodes set PE consists of processing components and edges set CL is composed of communication links. Every component $PE_p \in PE$, $p \in [1,k]$, is processing elements which are probably heterogeneous, like general-purpose processors, ASIPs, FPGAs, and ASICs. For distinguishing software processors from hardware components, we define $PE = PE_s \cup PE_h$, $PE_s = \{s_1, s_2, ..., s_a\}$ denotes software processors set, consisting of different types and numbers of general-purpose processors or ASIPs; $PE_h = \{h_1, h_2, ..., h_b\}$ denotes hardware components set, including different types and numbers of FPGAs or ASICs, and $k = a + b$.

An infrastructure of communication links, $CL = \{c_1, c_2, ..., c_w\}$, consisting of buses and point-to-point connections, connects these components.

Each task of the system specification might have multiple implementations, and therefore it can be potentially mapped to several components able to execute this task. In the task graph $G_s(V, EG)$, each vertex $v_i \in V$, $i \in [1,n]$, is assigned to six aspects properties set, $\{\{e_i^{s_m}\}, \{e_i^{h_n}\}, \{t_i^{s_m}\}, \{t_i^{h_n}\}, \{m_i^{s_m}\}, \{a_i^{h_n}\}, i \in [1,n]\}$. $e_i^{s_m}$ and $t_i^{s_m}$ respectively represents the software energy consumption and execution time for a given vertex v_i on a specified processor s_m, $m \in [1,a]$. $e_i^{h_n}$ and $t_i^{h_n}$ respectively represents the hardware energy consumption and execution time for a given vertex v_i on a specified hardware unit h_n, $n \in [1,b]$. Similarly, the software implementation of the function requires memory $m_i^{s_m}$ on the processor s_m and the hardware implementation requires area $a_i^{h_n}$ on the hardware unit h_n.

Each edge $eg_{ij} \in EG$ is associated with two aspects properties set, $\{\{e_{ij}^{c_l}\}, \{t_{ij}^{c_l}\}\}$. $t_{ij}^{c_l}$ denotes the time taken to transfer data through bus c_l, $l \in [1,w]$, if v_i and v_j are mapped to different processing elements which communicate by bus c_l, and $e_{ij}^{c_l}$ represents energy consumption for completing the data transfer. For each possible task partitioning, all these attribute values are given in a technology library. These values are either based on previous design experience or on estimation techniques.

2.2 Hardware-Software Partitioning Model

Hardware-software partitioning P can be defined as: $V : P = \{V_{s_1}, ..., V_{s_a}, V_{h_1}, ..., V_{h_b}\}$, where $V_{s_1} \cup ... \cup V_{s_a} \cup V_{h_1} \cup ... \cup V_{h_b} = V$ and $V_{s_1} \cap ... \cap V_{s_a} \cap V_{h_1} \cap ... \cap V_{h_b} = \Phi$; the partitioning of graph edges are $EG : P = \{EG_{c_1}, ..., EG_{c_w}\}$, where $EG_{c_1} \cup ... \cup EG_{c_w} \subseteq EG$ and $EG_{c_1} \cap ... \cap EG_{c_w} = \Phi$.

The energy consumption model E_P of partition P:

$$E_P = \sum_{s_m \in PE_s} \sum_{v_i \in V_{s_m}} e_i^{s_m} + \sum_{h_n \in PE_h} \sum_{v_i \in V_{h_n}} e_i^{h_n} + \sum_{c_l \in CL} \sum_{eg_{ij} \in EG_{c_l}} e_{ij}^{c_l} \qquad (1)$$

The energy consumption model E_P is presented as the sum of three portions, the energy dissipation of executing tasks partitioned to all software processors, the energy dissipation of executing tasks implemented on all hardware components and that of all communications involved on all buses or point to point links, respectively.

The time dissipation model T_P of partition P may be similarly constituted, so

$$T_P = \sum_{s_m \in PE_s} \sum_{v_i \in V_{s_m}} t_i^{s_m} + \sum_{h_n \in PE_h} \sum_{v_i \in V_{h_n}} t_i^{h_n} + \sum_{c_l \in CL} \sum_{eg_{ij} \in EG_{c_l}} t_{ij}^{c_l} \quad (2)$$

The memory usage model $M_P^{s_m}$ of processor s_m, $m \in [1,a]$:

$$M_P^{s_m} = \sum_{v_i \in V_{s_m}} m_i^{s_m}, m \in [1,a] \quad (3)$$

In the specified partition P, $M_P^{s_m}$ is the sum of memory request of all tasks mapped to the processor s_m.

The used hardware area model $A_P^{h_n}$ of hardware unit h_n, $n \in [1,b]$:

$$A_P^{h_n} = \sum_{v_i \in V_{h_n}} a_i^{h_n}, n \in [1,b] \quad (4)$$

In the specified partition P, $A_P^{h_n}$ is the sum of area usage of all tasks mapped to the hardware component h_n.

2.3 Low Power Hardware-Software Partitioning Problem

Based on the above hardware-software partitioning model, the low power hardware-software partitioning problem can be defined as:

$$Min(E_P), \text{ and } T_P \le T_0,\ M_P^{s_m} \le M_0^{s_m}, m \in [1,a],\ A_P^{h_n} \le A_0^{h_n}, n \in [1,b]$$

T_0 is the time constraint of embedded system application which is taken from the interval $[0, \sum_{v_i \in V} \min(t_i^{s_1}, t_i^{s_2}, ..., t_i^{s_m})]$, and $M_0^{s_m}$ is memory amount dedicated by processor $s_m, m \in [1,a]$, similarly, $A_0^{h_n}$ is hardware area amount of hardware component $h_n, n \in [1,b]$.

For getting valid and low power hardware-software partitioning result, our hardware-software partitioning heuristic algorithm is guided by the following cost function, which minimizes energy consumption while simultaneously satisfying all cost constraints. It takes the following form:

$$\begin{aligned} \min f = E_P + \sum_{s_m \in PE_s} P_{s_m} \max(0, M_P^{s_m} - M_0^{s_m}) + \\ \sum_{h_n \in PE_h} P_{h_n} \max(0, A_P^{h_n} - A_0^{h_n}) + P_t \max(0, T_P - T_0) \end{aligned} \quad (5)$$

Where $P_{s_m}, m \in [1,a]$, $P_{h_n}, n \in [1,b]$ and P_t are adjusted coefficients, respectively corresponding to every processor memory constraint, every hardware component area constraint, and system execution time constraint.

Theorem 1. The low power hardware-software partitioning problem is *NP-hard*.

The problem is not in NP, since a given solution for the problem cannot be verified in polynomial time to be the minimal power consumption. For specifying the NP-hardness of our problem, we reference the complexity result of problem dealt with in paper [8]. Arato etc., define the hardware-software partitioning problem, which minimizes the system execution time under hardware cost constraint, and they prove that the problem is NP-hard. Comparing with their problem, we define low power hardware-software partitioning problem, which minimizes the system power consumption under system execution time constraint, memory constraint of every processor and area constraint of every hardware component. Thus, the proved *NP-hard* problem in paper [8] is a special case of our problem, and hence, the problem in our definition is also *NP-hard*.

3 Proposed Algorithm

We realize the tabu search on chaotic neural network (TS_CNN) by introducing chaotic dynamics and utilizing the refractory effects of neurons as the tabu effects. In the following, we use symbol $i, i=1,\Lambda,n$ to denote task v_i , $i\in[1,n]$ and use symbol $j, j=1,\Lambda,k$ to denote processing element $PE_j \in PE$, $j\in[1,k]$. In the tabu search, we produce candidate solutions for each current solution by changing the assignments of tasks of specified number and keeping the others unchanged. The different number of tasks to be re-assigned leads to the different size of the candidate solutions. In this paper, we specify that the number of candidate solutions equals to $n\times k$ for any size of tasks to be re-assigned. For the detail, we assume that the size of tasks to be re-assigned equals to $S+1$ ($0\le S\le n-1$), and then we obtain $n\times k$ candidate solutions for every current solution.

3.1 Realizing Tabu Search by Chaotic Neural Network

Corresponding to the above $n\times k$ candidate solutions, we construct neural network by creating $n\times k$ neurons to realize the tabu search. Our approach includes both the tabu effect and chaotic dynamics, and it is realized by the following equations with an asynchronous updating:

$$\xi_{ij}(t+1)=\beta\Delta_{ij}(t) \tag{6}$$

$$\eta_{ij}(t+1)=-W\sum_{a=1,a\neq i}^{n}\sum_{b=1,b\neq j}^{k}x_{ab}(t)+W \tag{7}$$

$$\zeta_{ij}^{1}(t+1)=-\alpha\sum_{d=0}^{t}k_r^d\{x_{p_1q_1}(t-d)+z_{p_1q_1}(t-d)\}+\theta\ ,\ \ldots\ldots, \tag{8}$$

$$\zeta_{ij}^{S}(t+1)=-\alpha\sum_{d=0}^{t}k_r^d\{x_{p_Sq_S}(t-d)+z_{p_Sq_S}(t-d)\}+\theta \qquad 0\le S\le n-1 \tag{9}$$

$$\gamma_{ij}(t+1)=-\alpha\sum_{d=0}^{t}k_r^d\{x_{ij}(t-d)+z_{ij}(t-d)\}+\theta \tag{10}$$

$$x_{ij}(t+1)=g\{\xi_{ij}(t+1)+\eta_{ij}(t+1)+\zeta_{ij}^{1}(t+1)+\zeta_{ij}^{S}(t+1)+\gamma_{ij}(t+1)\} \tag{11}$$

$$g(y)=1/(1+e^{-y/\varepsilon}) \tag{12}$$

When we produce candidate solutions by only changing the assignment of one task, namely, $S=0$, variables $\zeta_{ij}^{1},\Lambda,\zeta_{ij}^{S}$ will be eliminated. Where β is the scaling parameter for the gain effect; K_r is the decay parameter of the tabu effect; α is the scaling parameter of the tabu effect; $\Delta_{ij}(t)$ is the gain of the objective function value and $\Delta_{ij}(t)=f_0(t)-f_{ij}(t)$; $f_0(t)$ is the objective value of the current solution at time t and $f_{ij}(t)$ is the value of the candidate solution at time t which is produced by assigning task i to component j, p_1 to q_1,... and p_S to q_S; $x_{ij}(t)$ is the output of the $(i,j)^{th}$ neuron at time t, $\xi_{ij}(t)$, $\eta_{ij}(t)$, $\zeta_{ij}^{1}(t)$,..., $\zeta_{ij}^{S}(t)$ and $\gamma_{ij}(t)$ are the internal state of the $(i,j)^{th}$ neuron at time t corresponding to the gain effect, the value of mutual inhibitory connections, the tabu effect of the assignment of p_1 to q_1, ... that of p_S to q_S and that of i to j, respectively. W is the connection weights, and θ is the positive bias.

If $x_{ij}(t+1)>0.5$, the $(i,j)^{th}$ neuron fires and the task i is assigned to component j, p_1 to q_1, ..., and p_S to q_S, respectively. Because many tasks are required to re-assign to new components in one updating, all these assignments should be memorized as tabu effect to avoid the same assignment to be carried out in the range of tabu list size. Then, the tabu list consists of assignments of (i,j), (p_1,q_1), ... and (p_S,q_S). Aiming at actual application, we introduce accumulated variables $z_{ij}(t)$ ($i,i=1,\Lambda,n$, $j,j=1,\Lambda,k$) corresponding to assignments of i to j, which are executed with firing of other neurons than the $(i,j)^{th}$ neuron even though the corresponding $(i,j)^{th}$ neuron does not fire. And then $z_{p_lq_l}(t)$ should also be prepared for memorizing the assignment of (p_l,q_l) which does not correspond to the label of a firing neuron, $l=1,\Lambda,S$. In the case of the new updating iteration t+1, all variables $z_{ij}(t+1)$ are reset to 0. For memorizing the assignment of p_l to q_l until next updating of the $(p_l,q_l)^{th}$ neuron, the output of the $(i,j)^{th}$ neuron is added to the accumulated output of the $(p_l,q_l)^{th}$ neuron. This procedure is realized as follows: after the updating of the $(i,j)^{th}$ neuron, if the $(p_l,q_l)^{th}$ neuron is already updated on this iteration t, $x_{ij}(t+1)$ is added to $z_{p_lq_l}(t+1)$. Otherwise, $x_{ij}(t+1)$ is added to $z_{p_lq_l}(t)$, $l=1,\Lambda,S$.

For numerical calculation, Eq. (8), (9) and (10) can be reduced as follows:

$$\zeta_{ij}^{1}(t+1)=k_r\gamma_{p_1q_1}(t)-\alpha\{x_{p_1q_1}(t)+z_{p_1q_1}(t)\}+R \tag{13}$$

$$\zeta_{ij}^{S}(t+1)=k_r\gamma_{p_Sq_S}(t)-\alpha\{x_{p_Sq_S}(t)+z_{p_Sq_S}(t)\}+R \tag{14}$$

$$\gamma_{ij}(t+1)=k_r\gamma_{ij}(t)-\alpha\{x_{ij}(t)+z_{ij}(t)\}+R \tag{15}$$

Where $R=\theta(1-k_r)$.

4 Experiment Results

The algorithm has been implemented in C, and tested on a Pentium IV 3.0GHz PC with 256MHz memory. Since TS_CNN is a heuristic rather than an exact algorithm, we had to determine both its performance and the quality of the solutions, empirically.

For this purpose, we compared it with genetic algorithm (GA) [8], which is universal for hardware-software partitioning and may be used for solving low power partitioning problem. And then the approach [8] is based on heterogeneous distributed embed systems as same as ours.

For general partitioning problem, there does not exist a widely accepted benchmark. We use a real-world GSM encoder task graph to test our approach, which consists of 53 tasks and 81 edges and is taken from [9].

The mapped target architecture in our experiments consists of one general processor and two ASICs, and these processing elements are connected through a bus, forming a heterogeneous distributed embedded system. The properties of these processing elements are listed in Table 1.

Table 1. Target architecture description

General Processor	Frequency (KHz)	Memory (byte)
	25000	2575860
HW-Component	Frequency (KHz)	Area (mm^2)
ASIC0	2500	18374
ASIC1	2500	50000
Bus	Frequency (KHz)	Average Power (μw)
	66000	4881.648
	Package Size (b)	Package Overhead (b)
	8	33

For detecting the influence for system power consumption when simultaneously change several tasks mapping schemes for producing candidate solutions of current solutions, we select 9 different values of parameter S, $S=1$, $S=2$, ..., $S=9$ for experiments and compare the results. According to the producing way of candidate solutions given in above section, we can obtain 53×3 candidate solutions of each current solution in the every iteration of applying tabu search. For comparing with GA on the same condition, we set the population size of genetic algorithm equal to 159. The crossover possibility and mutation possibility are set to 0.9 and 0.5, respectively.

Through initial extensive experiments, we select a group of tabu search algorithm parameters, which are reasonable and can be combined to produce preferable solutions. The final parameters we select are the following: $k_r = 0.8$, $\alpha = 1$, $\beta = 2, \varepsilon = 0.001, W = 0.0001, R = 0.001$. The system time constraint is taken from the interval $[0, \sum_{v_i \in V} \min(t_i^{s_1}, t_i^{s_2}, ..., t_i^{s_m})]$, we select $0.5 \times \sum_{v_i \in V} \min(t_i^{s_1}, t_i^{s_2}, ..., t_i^{s_m})]$ as the system execution time constraints.

Based on initial experiments, we respectively run TS_CNN 100 times according to different parameter S. For impartially comparing the influence of different parameter S, the above each experiment is run on the basis of same initial values and same iteration size 200. For reviewing the performance of our approach, we also execute genetic algorithm 100 times according to above population pool size and parameters.

We compute the mean of 100 times experiments of every S, for thoroughly comparing the influence of different parameter S for objective function value. Then, we also compute the mean of 100 times random experiments of GA. As a whole, we not only compare the influence of different parameter S for TS_CNN approach, but also we compare TS_CNN with GA for detecting the performance of our approach.

Mean of energy function value for different methods are list in Figure 1. We found that when $S = 6$, that is to say, the number of tasks to be re-assigned for producing candidate solutions equals to 7, the obtained mean of energy function value is the lowest, and that becomes larger with the movement of the parameter S towards the two opposite directions. From Figure 1, it can also be seen that the mean obtained by genetic algorithm is far worse than that by the tabu search with $4 \le S \le 9$, which indicates that tabu search on chaotic neural network can find average lower power consumption solution than GA.

The distributions of energy function value when $S = 6$ are given in Figure 2, accompanying with the power consumption distribution from GA. Distribution curves display the number of solutions whose energy values f belong to the following eight open intervals, respectively, $f<6$, $6<f<7$, $7<f<8$, $8<f<9$, $9<f<10$, $10<f<20$, $20<f<30$ and $f>30$. As shown in Figure 2, the distribution of energy values with TS_CNN all concentrates on the former five intervals, and there are no solutions belonging to $f > 10$, whereas, there are 11 solutions of belonging to $f > 10$ with GA. The distribution characteristic illustrates that all the solutions produced by TS_CNN more approach global optimization than GA, which accord with the result obtained from mean curve. Even if in the former part of the figure 2, there are more solutions to fall in the intervals $f < 6$ and $6 < f < 7$ with TS_CNN of $S = 6$ than those of GA, which further proves that we can obtain more solutions of lower energy function values by tabu search with $S = 6$.

The performance enhancement of our approach should owe to the complex dynamics of chaotic neural network, which avoid search to be trapped in undesirable local minima. In addition, the fact that TS_CNN can produce average better solution than GA also illuminates that the tabu effect implemented by refractory effect of neurons is effective.

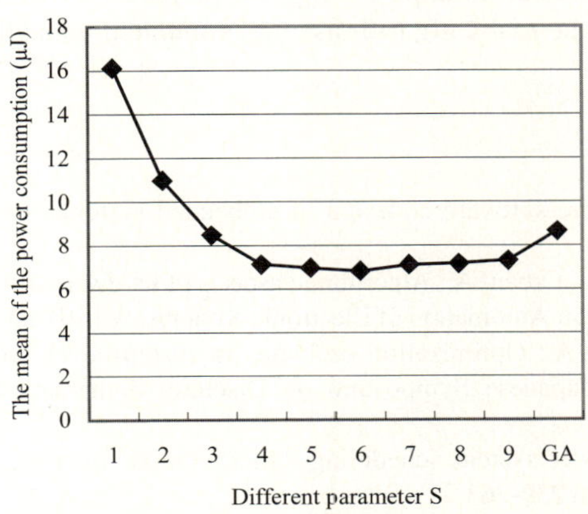

Fig. 1. The mean value of random 100 time experiments of different parameter S

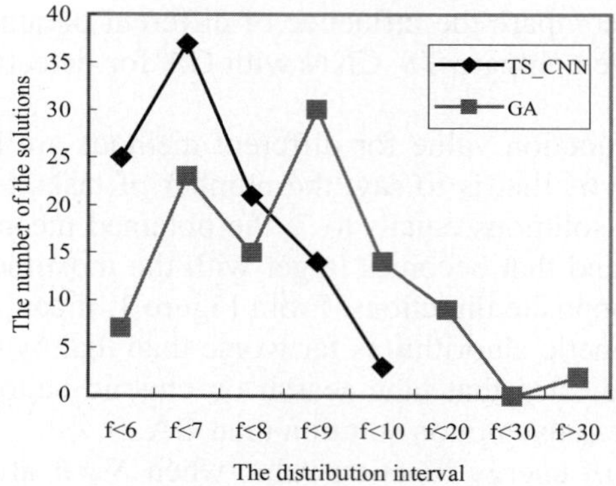

Fig. 2. Solutions distribution comparison of GA and TS_CNN with $S = 6$

5 Conclusions and Future Work

In this paper, we have introduced a new formal model for the low power hardware-software partitioning problem. This model has made it possible to investigate the optimization objective and constraints of the problem formally. Moreover, we have presented a tabu search on a chaotic neural network, which is a novel approach for the low power hardware-software partitioning of heterogeneous distributed embedded systems. In our empirical tests on a task graph of real-world GSM encoder, we find that the algorithm obviously outperforms genetic algorithm by properly producing candidate solutions of current solutions. For the specified example, when the number of tasks to be re-assigned equals to 7, the obtained mean of energy function value is the lowest. We attribute the better low power partitioning result to these facts that our formal model is valid, and the novel idea of designing tabu search on a chaotic neural network is fit to solve the problem.

Our future plans include more tests of the algorithm using other real-world examples and hypothetical examples. And we prepare to extend the algorithm and compare it with other heuristic algorithms, e.g., simulated annealing.

References

1. Wayne, W.: Hardware-software codesign of embedded systems. Proceedings of the IEEE, vol. 82, no. 7 (1994)
2. Arató, P., Mann, Z.A., Orbán, A.: Algorithmic aspects of hardware/software partitioning. ACM Transactions on Design Automation of Electronic Systems, vol. 10, no. 1, (2005) 136-156
3. Mann, Z.A., Orbán, A.: Optimization problems in system-level synthesis. Proceedings of the 3rd Hungarian-Japanese Symposium on Discrete Mathematics and Its Applications, Tokyo (Japan)(2003)
4. Jha, N.K.: Low power system scheduling and synthesis. In: Proc. Int. Conf. Computer-Aided Design, (2001) 259-263

5. Dave, B. P., Lakshminarayana, G., Jha, N. K.: COSYN: Hardware-software co-synthesis of heterogeneous distributed embedded systems. IEEE Trans. On VLSI Systems, vol. 7, 1999(92–104)
6. Dick, R. P., Jha, N. K.: MOGAC: A multiobjective genetic algorithm for the hardware-software co-synthesis of distributed embedded systems. IEEE Trans. Computer-Aided Design, vol. 17 (1998)
7. Henkel, J.: A Low Power Hardware/Software Partitioning Approach for Core-Based Embedded Systems. In: Proceedings of the 36th ACM/IEEE conference on Design automation conference, (1999) 122-127
8. Arato, P., Juhasz, S., Mann, Z.A., Orban, A., Papp, D.: Hardware/software partitioning in embedded system design. In: Proceedings of the IEEE International Symposium on Intelligent Signal Processing (2003)
9. Schmitz, M.T.: Energy Minimisation Techniques for Distributed Embedded Systems. Ph.D.dissertation, University of Southampton University, United Kingdom (2003)

Refactoring-Based Stepwise Refinement in Abstract System-Level Design

Ryosuke Yamasaki[1], Kazutaka Kobayashi[1], Nurul Azma Zakaria[1], Shuji Narazaki[2], and Norihiko Yoshida[1]

[1] Saitama University, 255 Shimo-Ohkubo, Sakura-ku, Saitama, Japan
{ryosuke, kazutaka, azma, yoshida}@ss.ics.saitama-u.ac.jp
[2] Nagasaki University, Bunkyo 1-14, Nagasaki, Japan
narazaki@cs.cis.nagasaki-u.ac.jp

Abstract. Stepwise refinement in system-level design corresponds to restructuring an internal structure of a system while preserving functions of the system. We are aiming to build the restructuring process based on refactoring techniques. In this paper, we describe a restructuring procedure to obtain a concrete specification description from an abstract one. Moreover, we describe some existing refactorings used in restructuring steps and a new refactoring for system-level design. We designed a simple internet-router as an example. As a result, we obtained a specification model defined in the SpecC methodology from an abstract one. Moreover, our proposal shows that our research opens a new application field of refactoring, refactoring can be applied sufficiently to system-level design, and the refactoring can be the basis of stepwise refinement.

1 Introduction

System-level design methodology, which is aiming to derive interactively and cooperatively a cycle-accurate hardware implementation and software implementation from an abstract specification where hardware and software are not distinguished and concept of time is abstracted, obtains remarkable results to improve design productivity of system-LSI/System-on-Chip. Some programming languages, called system-level description languages, are proposed in order to realize the design methodology. SystemC [1] and SpecC [2] have a concept of object-orientation. As a methodology, the SpecC design methodology [2] based on SpecC is well-defined and systematized.

Recently, not only languages but also design methodologies based on object-orientation are being researched actively. When designers represent the first system specification in object-oriented modeling languages such as UML, designers must satisfy some description constraints of models defined in a methodology.

For example, a specification model in the SpecC methodology has some description constraints; such as (1) a series of related functions are grouped as a behavior; (2) channels, ports, and global variables are used to connect behaviors; and (3) behaviors access to own ports to communicate each other. However,

E. Sha et al. (Eds.): EUC 2006, LNCS 4096, pp. 712–721, 2006.

in a modeling method in object-oriented design, a function is grouped by data and procedures related to the data. Moreover, to separate a computation and a communication by (2) and (3) is enabled after (1).

There are two ways to bridge the gaps between a specification model and a model of object-oriented design; (a) representing a specification model in UML directly, or (b) transforming a system specification in UML to a specification model. In case of (a), designers must consider a structure of functions when describing the first specification. In case of (b), it is necessary to establish a concrete transformation procedure preserving the functions of the system.

Restructuring method of a system structure while preserving its functions have been researched in program semantics and software engineering. Program transformation and refactoring have been established.

We are aiming to systematize stepwise refinement steps based on refactoring in order to realize (b). Preliminary result is shown in [3], it focused on obtaining a concrete system description in SpecC from an abstract one in Java. In this paper, we focus on the earlier phase than a creation phase of a specification model in SpecC methodology. Moreover, we describe concrete procedures based on refactoring in order to derive the specification model in SpecC from an executable specification that is created from a system specification in UML.

The remainder of this paper is organized as follows. In section 2, we describe system restructuring techniques, particularly the refactoring. In section 3, we describe our restructure procedures and a new refactoring for system-level design. In section 4, we describe an example design and its result. In section 5, we introduce related works, and section 6 describes the conclusions.

2 System Restructuring Techniques

There are two methods to restructure a system description to another one by rewriting the internal structure of the system, while preserving the external behavior/functions of the system, program transformation and refactoring. However, compilation and optimization in compiling are not included in the two restructuring methods because the description form is preserved.

2.1 Program Transformation

Program transformation is based on logic and mathematic, and it is a theoretical method that rewrites a program following transformation rules whose validity are guaranteed strictly. Therefore, this method enables to restructure an internal structure of a system preserving strictly its external behavior. Partial evaluation and meta-programming might be included. This method is studied for program customization, derivation, efficiency improvement, and so on. However, there are few application experiences to a large/complex program because transformation rules, procedures, and system specification are described as logical/mathematical expressions.

2.2 Refactoring

High reusability is one of the most important advantages of object-oriented design. However, it is actually too difficult to draw it to its maximum from the first design. Then, refactoring is systematized as a method that improves maintainability, readability, reusability, and modularity in later design phase by restructuring a system.

Refactoring is a collection of program rewriting rules for each situation and purpose. The collection is systematized on the purposes of rewriting and program structures. For example, *Extract Class*, *Form Template Method*, and *Move Method* are refactoring names, and a program code of *Extract Method* in Java is shown in Fig. 1. *Extract Method* is used to reduce repeat codes by aggregating fragments of the code, and to improve modularity and readability by decomposing too longer method. In Fig. 1(a), console output statements in `for` block (line 4–5) are extracted as a method `multiDisp` shown in Fig. 1(b), line 4–7. As a result, readability of the method `display`, reusability of the method `multiDisp`, and modularity of the whole system are improved. Details of other rewriting rules cited later by its name are shown in reference [4].

Refactoring is a practical method, and a theoretical strictness is not guaranteed completely. Instead, it is easier than program transformation to apply rewriting-rules to restructure a real-world system. For the above-mentioned reasons, we adopt refactoring.

```
1:void display(int t){
2: int i;
3: printHeader();
4: for(i=0;i<t;i++){
5:  System.out.print(i);}}
```

(a) Original.

```
1:void display(int t){
2: printHeader();
3: multiDisp(t);}
4:void multiDisp(int t){
5: int i;
6: for(i=0;i<t;i++){
7:  System.out.print(i);}}
```

(b) Method extracted.

Fig. 1. Example: Extract method

3 Outline of Proposed Methodology

A restructuring of system descriptions consists of four steps; (1) representing a system specification, (2) generating an executable specification from (1), (3) re-grouping, and (4) replacing behavior-method call to channel-method call and adding channel-port. Fig. 2 shows changes of a system structure in proposal method. In Fig. 2(c), it assumes that a grouping policy is shared-memory communication. In Fig. 2, a rectangle is an object or a behavior, an oval is a method, an arrow is a method call, a broken line is an access to a variable, and a black rectangle is a port.

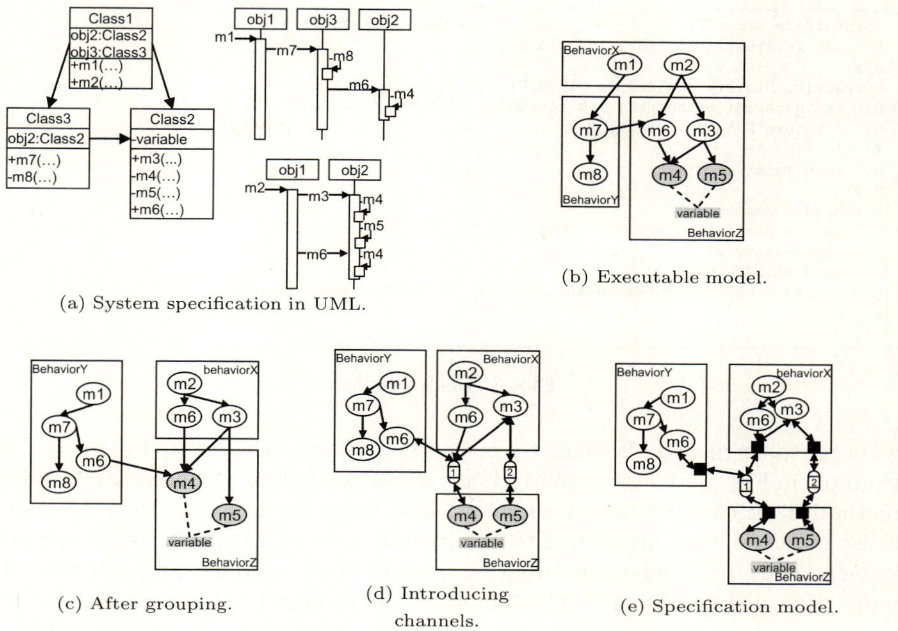

(a) System specification in UML.

(b) Executable model.

(c) After grouping.

(d) Introducing channels.

(e) Specification model.

Fig. 2. Outline of design flow

3.1 Restructuring Flow

1. Specification Representation. Designers represent a system specification in UML (Fig. 2(a)). At this abstract level, computation and communication are not separated. Following the concept of object-oriented design, a grouping unit is the collection of the data and the procedures related to the data.

2. Executable Specification Description. Designers describe an executable specification in SpecC by relating an object and a behavior. All methods that should be public are defined in `interface` referring class diagrams or sequence diagrams. For example, the `BehaviorZ` implements `m3` and `m6`. All behaviors can communicate each other by method call. We call such public method "behavior-method". Behavior-methods are defined in `interface`, and we call such interface "behavior-interface". For example, in Fig. 3 shown later, the line 1–3 are behavior-interface, and line 5–7 are behavior-method. The behavior `Master` can access to behavior-method directly (line 14 in Fig. 3).

At this abstraction level, designers verify through simulation and test that required functions are satisfied. After that, to simplify a latter restructuring, all behaviors are applied *Self Encapsulate Field*. By this refactoring, all methods that access to internal variables are limited to accessor (getter/setter method). In Fig. 2(b), the method `m4` and `m5` are accessors.

3. Re-grouping. Related functions are grouped by each start method of a method call chain. A method called by other methods can belong to all behaviors

```
interface SlaveIF{                            //behavior-interface
  int getArea(int height, int width);
};
behavior Slave() implements SlaveIF{
  int getArea(int height, int width){      //behavior-method
    return height * width;
  }
  void main(void){}
};
behavior Master() {
  int height = 3, width = 5, area = 0;
  Slave slave();
  void main(void){
    area = slave.getArea(height, width); // behavior-method call
  }
};
```

Fig. 3. Before replace

where a caller method belongs to, or can belong to a new created behavior. For example in Fig. 2(b), the method `m1`, `m6`, `m7` and `m8` belong to `BehaviorY`, and the method `m2`, `m3` and `m6` belong to `BehaviorX`. First, by applying *Move Method* to those methods, they are moved to `BehaviorX` and/or `BehavorY`. Next, behavior-interfaces are re-defined according to changes after applying *Move Method.* Finally, three groups, `BehaviorX`, `BehaviorY` and `BehaviorZ` are created.

4. Introduce Channel and Add Channel-Port. Designers must replace behavior-method call to channel-method call. "Channel-method" becomes public by implementing interfaces, and we call a calling to it "channel-method call".

First, designers classify behavior-method calls. For example in Fig. 2(c), they are classified into two, `m4` and `m5`. Second, designers check up sent/received data by the method call, and define channel according to the data. Third, designers rewrite a code calling a behavior-method to a channel-method call. After that, designers remove an `implements` code. As a result, designers obtain an executable specification shown in Fig. 2(d). Continuously, designers add ports to behaviors, and rewrite a channel-method call to a channel-port access.

From the above restructuring, designers obtain a rewritten description shown in Fig. 2(e). Channel definition, rewriting to channel-method call, and adding channel-port are described in 3.2.

3.2 Replace Behavior-Method Call to Channel-Method Call

Here, we describe a new refactoring for system-level design, *Replace Behavior-method call to Channel-method call.* In a specification model in SpecC methodology, behaviors communicate data by using channels, ports, and global variables. Moreover, it is necessary to specify the input/output of data.

To satisfy those description constraints, first, channels are defined according to parameters, arguments and returned value. Next, designers replace behavior-method call to channel-method call. The replacing procedures are described below with Fig. 3, Fig. 4 and program code.

Designers subdivide a behavior-method call into four methods, send argument, receive argument, send result, and receive result (line 3–6 in Fig. 4 respectively).

```
 1:#define INVALID -99999
 2:interface GetAreaIF{                                      //channel-interface
 3:  void reqSend(int height, int width);
 4:  void reqRecv(int *height, int *width);
 5:  void ackSend(int area);
 6:  void ackRecv(int *area);};
 7:channel GetAreaCh() implements GetAreaIF{
 8:  int height=INVALID, width=INVALID, area=INVALID;
 9:  event req1, req2, ack1, ack2;
10:  bool lock=false; event release;                        // for concurrent access control
11:  void reqSend(int arg1, int arg2){                      //channel-method
12:    while(lock){wait(release);} lock=true;               // for concurrent access control
13:    height=arg1; width=arg2; notify(req1); wait(req2);}
14:  void reqRecv(int *arg1, int *arg2){                    //channel-method
15:    while(height == INVALID){wait(req1);}
16:    (*arg1)=height; (*arg2)=width;
17:    notify(req2); height=INVALID; width=INVALID;}
18:  void ackSend(int arg){                                 //channel-method
19:    area=arg; notify(ack1); wait(ack2);}
20:  void ackRecv(int *arg){                                //channel-method
21:    while(area==INVALID){wait(ack1);}
22:    (*arg)=area; notify(ack2); area=INVALID;
23:    lock=false; notify(release);}};                      //for concurrent access control
24:behavior Slave(GetAreaIF getAreaCh){
25:  int getArea(int height, int width){return height * width;}
26:  void main(void){
27:    int height = 0, width = 0, area = 0;
28:    getAreaCh.reqRecv(&height, &width);                  //receive argument
29:    area = getArea(height, width);                       //original processing
30:    getAreaCh.ackSend(area);}};                          //send result
31:behavior Master(GetAreaIF getAreaCh) {
32:  int height=3, width=5, area=0;
33:  void main(void){
34:    getAreaCh.reqSend(height, width);                    //send argument
35:    getAreaCh.ackRecv(&area);}};                         //receive result
```

Fig. 4. After replace

Second, a new channel implementing them is defined (line 7–23 in Fig. 4). Third, designers add a channel-port by applying *Add Parameter* to a calling/called behavior (line 24 and 31 in Fig. 4). A code of behavior-method call in the calling behavior (line 14 in Fig. 3) is rewritten to "send argument" and "receive result" (line 34 and 35 in Fig. 4 respectively). Also, codes of "receive arguments", "original processing", and "send result" are added to `main` method (line 28–30 in Fig. 4 respectively). In case of Fig. 4, to realize exclusive access, designers insert line 10, 12, and 23 in Fig. 4 to channels.

4 Example Design and Result

As an example design, we adopted internet-router. We designed three kinds of router, "distance vector", "link state", and "path vector". In addition, the specification is limited to only basic functions because the purpose of this experiment is not designing routers. In this paper, we explain the distance-vector router.

We used UML to represent the first specification with Pattern Weaver 1.0 [5], and SpecC languages to describe executable specifications with VisualSpec 3.5 [6]. To simplify, we prohibited dynamic instantiation, instance transference, and recursion call.

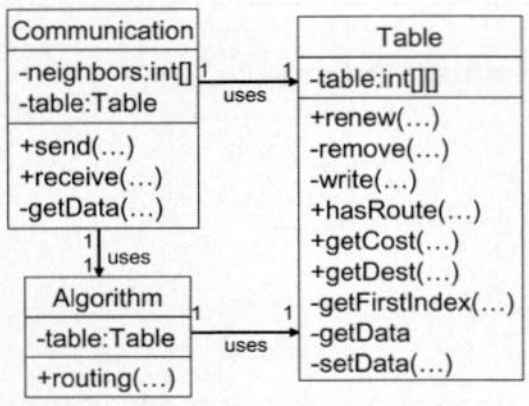

Fig. 5. System specification in a class diagram

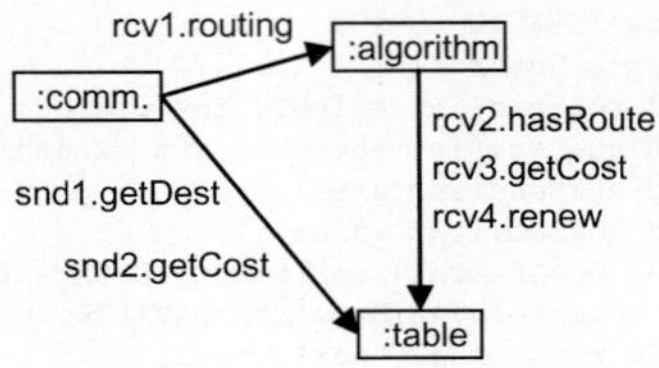

Fig. 6. System specification in a communication diagram

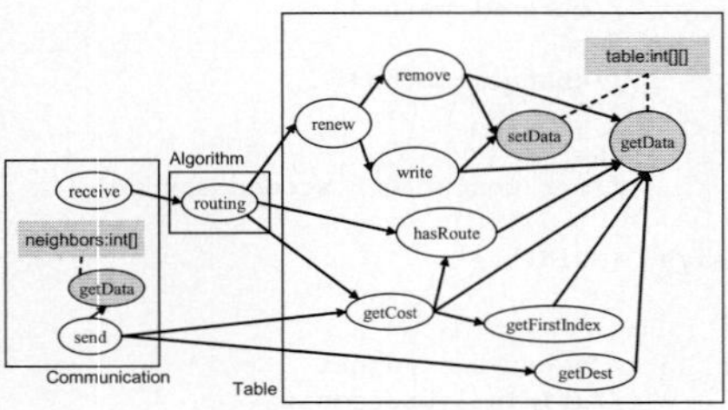

Fig. 7. Executable model

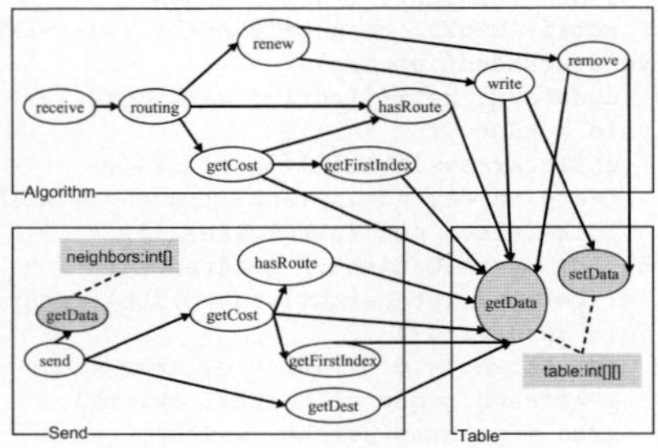

Fig. 8. After grouping

4.1 Design Flow

1. Behavior of Router. From use case analysis, we obtained three basic functions, exchanging route information, route exploration, and management of a route table. Moreover, we defined three classes, Communication, Algorithm, and Table. We described not only class diagram, usecase description, and usecase diagram but also sequence diagram, communication diagram, and so on. In this paper, only class diagram and communication diagram are illustrated in Fig. 5 and 6 respectively.

The router behaves according to the below procedures, `rcv1`, `rcv2`, `rcv3` and `rcv4` in Fig. 6, when the router receives a route information. And the router behaves according to the below procedures, `snd1` and `snd2` in Fig. 6, when the router sends own route information to neighbors.

2. Executable Specification Description. We described an executable specification in SpecC according to the previous specification. By relating a class to a behavior, we defined three behaviors, "Communication", "Algorithm", and "Table". The executable specification is illustrated in Fig. 7. Oval, rectangle, arrow, and a broken line represent method, behavior, method-call, and an access to variables respectively.

3. Re-grouping. Each start method, `receive` and `send`, and other methods relating to the start method belong to two behaviors. These two behaviors,

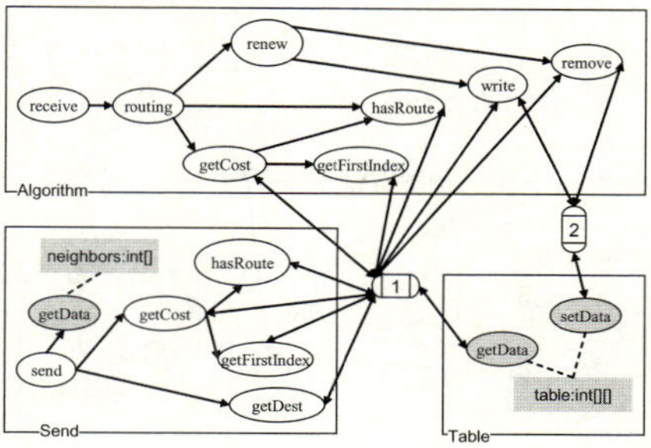

Fig. 9. Introducing channels

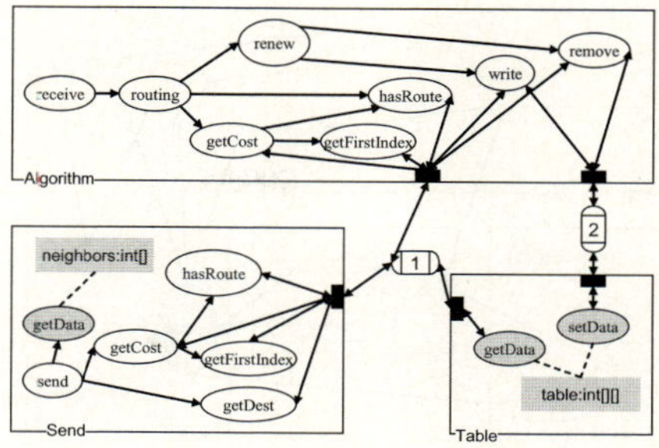

Fig. 10. Specification model

Rreceive and Send, are created by dividing Communication. The internal variable table in Table and accessors are left in Table. In addition, the internal variable neighbors in Communication belongs to Send.

The behavior Receive is created by applying *Extract Class* to the method receive in Communication. After applying, only send and accessor are left in Communication. To rename Communication to Send, *Rename* is applied to the behavior Communication because the main function of Communication is only to send route information. There are eight methods belong to the behavior Receive and six methods belong to the behavior Send. To move those methods to each behavior, *Move Method* is applied to each method. To rename Receive to Algorithm, *Rename* is applied to the behavior Receive because the main function of Receive is execution of routing algorithm.

As a result of the above restructuring, we obtained a re-grouped description shown in Fig. 8.

4. Introduce Channel and Add Channel-Port. In Fig. 8, there are two behavior-method calls, getData and setData. Therefore, we defined eight channel-methods and two channels according to the behavior-method by applying 3.2. From these restructuring, we obtained the executable specification shown in Fig. 9. Next, we added channel-ports to behaviors Algorithm, Send, and Table by applying 3.2. From these restructuring, we obtained an executable specification which can satisfy description constraints of the specification (Fig. 10).

4.2 Experimental Results and Discussions

It was confirmed that the specification model (Fig. 10) behaved just same as the first executable specification (Fig. 7) by the simulation. Moreover, the bug was not mixed by rewriting at all, and there was not returning to previous steps in this experiment either.

The policy of grouping the relating function is various. For example, the method getCost and other related methods can be grouped together as a behavior GetCost illustrated in Fig. 11 and Fig. 12. As a result, the behavior Algorithm must wait until the behavior GetCost is released, and vice versa.

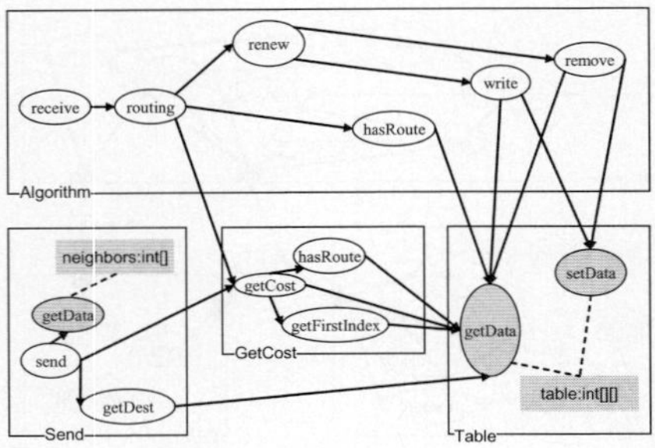

Fig. 11. Executable model, sharing the behavior `GetCost`

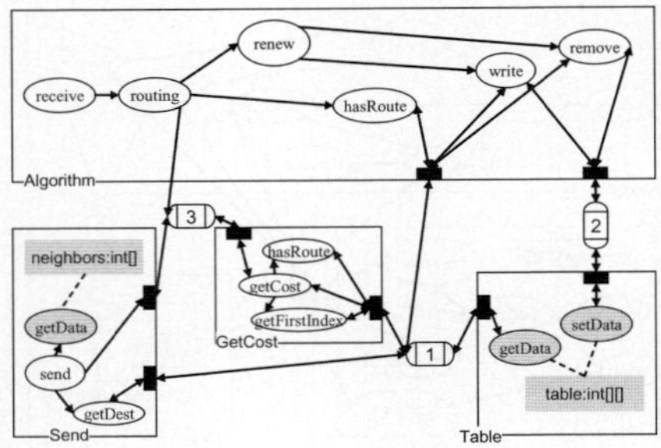

Fig. 12. Specification model, sharing the behavior `GetCost`

Designers can restructure a system description to various structures by using refactoring, while considering the trade-off such as processing time.

5 Related Works

[7] and [8] use to describe a system specification in UML and SystemC. [7] enables to generate SystemC codes from a system specification in UML using UML-profile. However, designers need to consider the structure and connection relation of function modules when describing a system specification. [8] also generates SystemC codes from a system specification in UML using Rational Rose RT tool. In this research, some descriptions in UML are limited to represent connection and communication between modules. These two researches belong to the approach (a) explained in section 1.

There are some researches applying MDA [9] to SoC design such as [10] and [11]. However, it is difficult to confirm through simulation whether behaviors of a system are correct or not. In our method, designers can trace and control any refinement steps, and any anytime the specification is executable.

Program derivation of a systolic array from a mathematical specification [12] is an application of program transformation to system-level design. This brings the completely validated implementation formally because based on program transformation. However, the application example to the real-world design is few because same reason. In our method, it is easier than program transformation to apply to a real-world design because our method based on refactoring.

6 Summary and Conclusions

In this paper, we described an application of existing refactoring to system-level design, and proposed a new refactoring for system-level design. Additionally, we described concrete refinement steps that refine an executable specification based on refactoring. Designers can restructure a system specification in safely, because the external behaviors (or functions) are preserved. Proposal restructuring steps enable designers to describe a system specification at higher level.

The most important of future works is an automation of whole restructuring flow. Some simple refactoring are automated in some integrated development environments (IDE). We aim to realize a design automation based on our proposal, referring those tools.

References

1. T. Grötker, S. Liao, G. Martin, and S. Swan, "System Design with SystemC", Kluwer Academic Publishers, 2002.
2. Daniel D.Gajski, J. Zhu, R. Dömer, A. Gerstlauer, and S. Zhao, "SpecC: Specification Language and Methodology", Kluwer Academic Publishers, 2000.
3. R. Yamasaki, K. Kobayashi, N. Yoshida, and S. Narazaki, "Application of Refactoring Techniques to Abstract System Level Design", IEICE/IPSJ Information Technology Letters, Vol.4, September 2005.
4. M. Fowler, K. Beck, J. Brant, W. Opdyke, and D. Roberts. "Refactoring", Addison-Wesley, 1999.
5. Pattern Weaver 1.0, Technologic Arts Inc., url: http://pw.tech-arts.co.jp/pw/index.html
6. VisualSpec 3.5, InterDesign Technologies Inc., url: http://www.interdesigntech.co.jp/english/
7. E. Riccobene, P. Scandurra and A. Rosti, "A SoC Design Methodology Involving a UML 2.0 Profile for SystemC", Proc. of the Design, Automation and Test in Europe (DATE'05), Vol. 2, pp.704–709, March, 2005.
8. W.H. Tan, P.S. Thiaggarajan, W.F. Wong, Y. Zhu and S.K. Pialakkat, "Synthesizable SystemC Code from UML Models", 41th Design Automation Conference (workshop UML for SoC Design), 2004.
9. MDA, url: http://www.omg.org/mda/
10. P. Boulet, J.-L. Dekeyser, C. Dumoulin, and P. Marquent, "MDA for SoC Embedded Systems Design, Intensive Signal Processing Experiment", SIVOES-MDA workshop at UML2003, pp.20–24, October, 2003.
11. Stephen J. Mellor, John R. Wolfe, Campbell McCausland, "Why System-on-Chip Needs More UML like a Hole in the Head", Proc. of the Design, Automation, and Test in Europe (DATE'05), Vol. 2, pp.834–835, 2005.
12. N. Yoshida, "Transformational Derivation of Highly Parallel Programs", Proc. 3rd Int'l Conf. Supercomputing, Vol.3, pp.445–454, Boston, 1988.

Custom Instruction Generation Using Temporal Partitioning Techniques for a Reconfigurable Functional Unit

Farhad Mehdipour[1], Hamid Noori[2], Morteza Saheb Zamani[1], Kazuaki Murakami[2], Koji Inoue[2], and Mehdi Sedighi[1]

[1] Computer and IT Engineering Department, Amirkabir University of Technology, Tehran, Iran
{mehdipur, szamani, msedighi}@aut.ac.ir
[2] Department of Informatics, Graduate School of Information Science and Electrical Engineering, Kyushu University, Japan
noori@c.csce.kyushu-u.ac.jp, {murakami, inoue}@i.kyushu-u.ac.jp

Abstract. Extracting appropriate custom instructions is an important phase for implementing an application on an extensible processor with a reconfigurable functional unit (RFU). Custom instructions (CIs) are usually extracted from critical portions of applications. It may not be possible to meet all of the RFU constraints when CIs are generated. This paper addresses the generation of mappable CIs on an RFU. In this paper, our proposed RFU architecture for an adaptive dynamic extensible processor is described. Then, an integrated framework for temporal partitioning and mapping is presented to partition and map the CIs on RFU. In this framework, two mapping aware temporal partitioning algorithms are used to generate CIs. Temporal partitioning iterates and modifies partitions incrementally to generate CIs. Using this framework brings about more speedup for the extensible processor.

1 Introduction

An extensible processor with a reconfigurable functional unit (RFU) can be an alternative to General Purpose Processors (GPPs), Application-Specific Integrated Circuits (ASICs) and Application-Specific Instruction set Processors (ASIPs) to achieve enhanced performance in embedded systems. ASICs are not flexible and have an expensive and time consuming design process. On the other hand, GPPs are very flexible but may not offer the necessary performance. ASIPs are more flexible than ASICs and have more potential to meet the high-performance demands of embedded applications, compared to GPPs but the synthesis of ASIPs traditionally involved the generation of a complete instruction set architecture for the targeted application. This full-custom solution is too expensive and has long design turnaround times.

Another method for providing enhanced performance is application-specific instruction set extension. By creating application-specific extensions to an instruction set, the critical portions of an application's dataflow graph (DFG) can be accelerated by using custom functional units. The nodes of these DFGs are the instructions of critical potion of applications and the edges of DFGs represent the dependency

E. Sha et al. (Eds.): EUC 2006, LNCS 4096, pp. 722 – 731, 2006.

between instructions. In our method, custom instruction is a sequence of instructions that are extracted from hot basic blocks (HBBs). HBBs are basic blocks which are executed more than a predefined number of times. A basic block is a sequence of instructions that is terminated by a control instruction. Instruction set extension improves performance and reduces energy consumption of processors but not as effective as ASICs. Instruction set extension also maintains a degree of system programmability, which enables them to be utilized with more flexibility. Using an extensible processor with a reconfigurable functional unit proposes favorable tradeoff between efficiency and flexibility, while keeping design turnaround time much shorter. The reconfigurable part of an extensible processor executes critical portions of an application to gain higher performance. It can be coarse grain or fine grain. The latter is more flexible but it is slower comparing with the coarse grain one. Extracting CIs from applications is an important stage in accelerating application execution. Some generated CIs cannot be mapped on reconfigurable hardware because some RFU constraints, like physical constraints, cannot be considered at the CI generation phase. We call this kind of CIs *rejected CIs*.

Identifying optimal set of custom instruction to improve the computational efficiency of applications has received significant attention recently. Research in reconfigurable computing is often more in line with our goal. Some papers in reconfigurable computing investigate the identification of application sections that are mapped to a reconfigurable fabric. In [7], the authors combine template matching and generation based on the occurrence of patterns which usually led to small templates. Methods presented in [5] and [8] impose further constraints by allowing multiple input-single output patterns. Arnold et al. [1] avoid the exponentially increase of these patterns by using an iterative technique that detects 2-operator patterns, replace their occurrences in the DFG and repeats the process. Atasu et al. [2] search a full binary tree and decide at each step whether or not to include a particular instruction in a pattern, but they do not take into account the underlying hardware architecture. Clark et al. [4] search possibly good patterns by starting with small patterns and expanding them considering the input, output and convexity constraints [16].

In this paper, we propose a novel framework for generating CIs. Our main goal is proposing a framework for generating CIs for AMBER, an adaptive dynamic extensible processor presented in [11]. However, this framework can be used for CI generation as a general methodology. AMBER uses a coarse grain reconfigurable functional unit with fixed resources. Initial CIs are generated by a CI generation tool and some of them might be rejected because of violating RFU constraints. Rejection of CIs decreases the speedup. We do not use any pruning algorithm for making smaller CIs from rejected CIs because obviously, by using bigger CIs, more speedup can be obtained. We use a mapping-aware *temporal partitioning* algorithm to generate CIs.

Temporal partitioning can be stated as partitioning a data flow graph into a number of partitions such that each partition can fit into the target hardware and also, dependencies among the graph nodes are not violated [3, 6]. Different algorithms have been presented for temporal partitioning. Karthikeya et al. [6] proposed algorithms for temporal partitioning and scheduling of large designs on area constrained reconfigurable hardware. *SPARCS* [12] is an integrated partitioning and synthesis framework, which has a temporal partitioning tool to temporally divide and schedule the DFGs on a reconfigurable system. Tanougust et al. [15] attempted to find the minimum area while meeting timing constraints during temporal partitioning. In [14], Spillane and Owen focused on finding a sequence of conditions for an optimized scheduling of configurations to achieve the desired trade-offs among reconfiguration time, operation speed and area. In [9], a design flow was proposed for the compilation of data flow graphs for a reconfigurable system. In this paper, we propose a modified version of this framework for generating appropriate CIs for the RFU of AMBER. In this framework, temporal partitioning is done iteratively and gets feedbacks from mapping to modify partitions and map them onto the RFU. Also, it takes advantages of the basic design flow of [9] to generate CIs and improve target extensible processor speedup.

In Section 2, the architecture of RFU proposed for AMBER is described. Section 3 discusses the design flow proposed for generating CIs and details of temporal partitioning algorithms and their incremental versions. In Section 4, experimental results are presented and finally, Section 5 concludes the paper.

2 AMBER RFU Architecture

In [11] an adaptive extensible processor (AMBER) was presented which has the capability of tuning its extended instructions to the running application. AMBER uses a RISC processor as the base processor. In the first stage of this work, a coarse grain reconfigurable functional unit (RFU) was designed for AMBER using a quantitative approach [4]. The presented RFU architecture is an array of functional units (FUs) (Fig. 1). FUs support all fixed point instructions of the base processor except multiplication, division and load. Twenty-two applications from Mibench [17] were used to provide quantitative analysis. In addition, a mapping tool was developed to map CIs on the RFU. The details of RFU design is out of scope of this paper, and therefore we describe the specification of the final architecture. According to the obtained results, eight inputs, six outputs and 16 FUs brought about a reasonable CI rejection rate. Rejection rate represents the percentage of CIs that cannot be mapped on the RFU according to its defined constraints. In the proposed architecture, there are left to right connections in the 4th row and right to left connections in the 3rd row. The outputs of FUs in each row are fully connected to the inputs of FUs in the subsequent row. Moreover, there are extra vertical connections, as in Fig. 1, between non-subsequent rows to keep the CI rejection rate low.

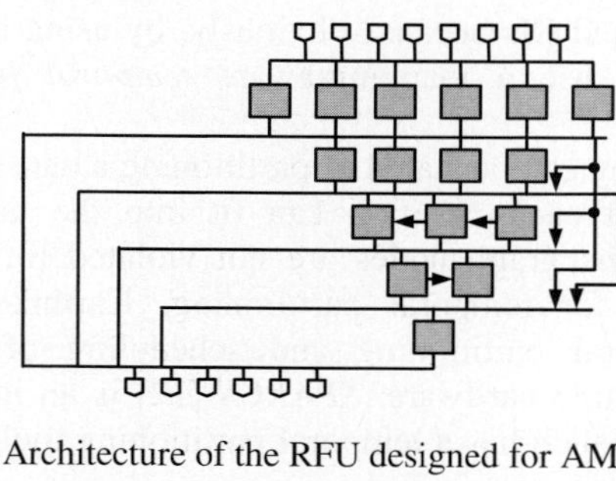

Fig. 1. Architecture of the RFU designed for AMBER

3 Integrated Temporal Partitioning and Mapping

As mentioned in Section 1, in this paper, our main focus is on a method for CI generation. In the following sections, we explain the details of the approaches used for generating CIs.

3.1 Overview

Initial CIs were extracted from hot basic blocks of applications according to the algorithm presented in [11]. Two different approaches for generating appropriate CIs are presented. Appropriate CI set means the set of CIs which satisfy the RFU primary constraints and may have the capability of being mapped successfully on the RFU. RFU *primary constraints* are the architectural constraints including the number of inputs, outputs and nodes. In the first approach (*CIGen*) (Fig. 2(a)), appropriate CIs are generated for each application considering the RFU primary constraints by using the CI generation tool. For rejected CIs, *CIGen* follows a conservative method to generate appropriate CIs. One important drawback of this CI extraction procedure is that it cannot consider all of the constraints such as routing resources constraints. Therefore, some of these CIs may not be mapped to the RFU and should be executed on the base processor.

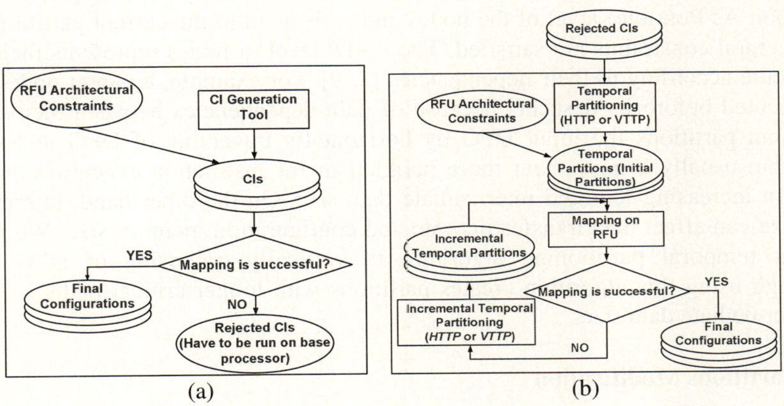

Fig. 2. Design flows for *CIGen* (a) and the *Integrated Framework* (b)

Integrated Framework is the second CI generation approach that performs an integrated temporal partitioning and mapping process to generate mappable CIs. The proposed design flow for *Integrated Framework* is shown in Fig. 2(b). This design flow takes rejected CIs and attempts to partition them to appropriate CIs with the capability of being mapped on the RFU. In our methodology, a DFG corresponds to a CI and partitions obtained from the integrated temporal partitioning process are the same appropriate CIs which are mappable on the RFU. In the first stage, RFU primary constraints are considered to generate initial CIs. Then for each CI generated in the first step, the mapping process is done and the generated CIs are accepted and finalized if they can be mapped on the RFU. Otherwise, an incremental temporal partitioning algorithm modifies the CI (partition) by moving some of the nodes to the subsequent CI (partition). Mapping algorithm attempts to reduce total connection length between the nodes and satisfy the RFU architectural constraints simultaneously. In the next step, the mapping process is repeated. This process is done iteratively until all partitions are mapped successfully on RFU. This framework gains the following advantages:

1. Reducing the number of rejected CIs that can affect the overall performance by partitioning the rejected CIs to appropriate CIs which can be mapped on the RFU.
2. Using a mapping-aware temporal partitioning process to prohibit the rejection of CIs by modifying CIs according to the feedbacks obtained from the mapping process.

In the *Integrated Framework,* two algorithms were developed for temporal partitioning which are described in the following section.

3.2 Horizontal and Vertical Traversing Temporal Partitioning (*HTTP* and *VTTP*)

HTTP [9] is used as the first temporal partitioning algorithm in the *Integrated Framework*. This algorithm traverses DFG nodes horizontally according to the *ASAP* (As Soon As Possible) level of the nodes and adds them to the current partition while architectural constraints are satisfied. The *ASAP* level of nodes represents their order to execute according to their dependencies [2, 9]. For example, a parent node should be executed before its descents because of data dependencies between them. *HTTP* algorithm partitions the input DFG by horizontally traversing of DFG nodes. This algorithm usually brings about more parallelism for instruction execution that may result in increasing required intermediate data size. On the other hand, intermediate data size can affect data transferring rate and configuration memory size. We present another temporal partitioning algorithm to vertically traversing of DFG nodes. Although using this algorithm creates partitions with longer critical paths it reduces the intermediate data size.

3.3 Partitions Modification

In *Integrated Framework*, each partition which does not satisfy RFU constraints, is modified by selecting and moving proper nodes to the subsequent partition and then a new iteration starts. For *HTTP* and *VTTP* algorithms, two different strategies are used as incremental algorithms for partition modification.

Incremental HTTP. This complementary algorithm selects a node and moves it to the ext partition. A new partition is created and the number of partitions is increased by f there is no more partition. The best choice for moving nodes are the nodes with est *ASAP* level. All nodes in a partition are sorted according to their *ASAP* level e node with the highest *ASAP* level is selected to move to the subsequent . In Fig. 3(a), the nodes 15, 13, 11, 9, 14, 12, 10, 8, 3, 7 are selected in order d to the next partition.

Incremental VTPP. This algorithm chooses another strategy for selecting and moving the nodes. The most important characteristic of *VTTP* is extracting long paths by in-depth traversing of DFG nodes. Therefore, selecting nodes from a partition should be done according to this property; otherwise the results of the modification process will converge to those of the *HTTP* algorithm. Our experiments justify this statement. In the first attempt, a node with the highest *ASAP* level is selected and moved to the next partition. In other attempts for modifying the same partition, the nodes are selected from the path where the previous moved node had been located. A node with the highest *ASAP* level from another path is selected if there is still any node belonging to the current partition on the processing path. In Fig. 3(b), the nodes 15, 14, 6, 13, 12, 5, 11, 10, 4, 7 are selected in-order and moved to the next partition during the incremental *VTTP*.

3.4 Mapping Procedure

In our *Integrated Framework*, the mapping process is the same as the well-known placement problem [13]. Mapping process can be defined as the placement of the DFG nodes on a fixed architecture RFU, to determine the appropriate positions for DFG nodes on the RFU. Minimizing the connection length, area and the longest wire are usually the main goals in this process [13]. Assigning CI instructions or DFG nodes to FUs is done based on the priority of the nodes. We calculated *slack* of nodes [10] to determine their priority for partitioning. Slack of each node represents its criticality. For example, slack equal to *0* means that it is on the critical path of DFG and should be scheduled with the highest priority. *ASAP* level of nodes determines the order of partitioning for the nodes with equal slack value.

The nodes with lower value of *ASAP* level should be scheduled according to their execution order in the DFG. Therefore, in the first step, *ASAP, ALAP* (As Late As Possible) and *slack* values of each node in the DFG are determined [9, 10]. Assigning a position for each selected node starts by determining an appropriate row for that node. Row number is set to the last row if the selected node is on a critical path with the length more than or equal to the RFU depth. Otherwise, row number is selected according to *slack* and *ALAP* of the selected node and the number of unoccupied cells available in the RFU rows. For the nodes which do not belong to any critical path longer than the RFU depth, their starting row is set to *ALAP- slack -1*. This means that we reserve FUs of the lower rows for the nodes belonging to the critical path. Therefore, spiral shaped mapping of nodes are possible for long critical paths. After determining the row number, an appropriate column is determined for the selected node. Column number is determined according to the minimum connection length criterion. All unoccupied cells of the RFU in the determined row are checked to find an FU which gives the minimum connection length. For each row, a maximum capacity is considered to prohibit gathering many nodes in a row. Capacity of rows is determined with respect to the longest critical path and the number of critical paths in the DFG. Referring to the RFU architecture in Fig. 1 and its routing resources, though the RFU depth is equal to 5, our mapping algorithm can map CIs whose critical path length are at most equal to 8. Fig. 3 show examples of mapping of CIs on the RFU. Corresponding CI of the first partition in Fig. 3(b) has been mapped on RFU in a spiral shaped path because of its long length.

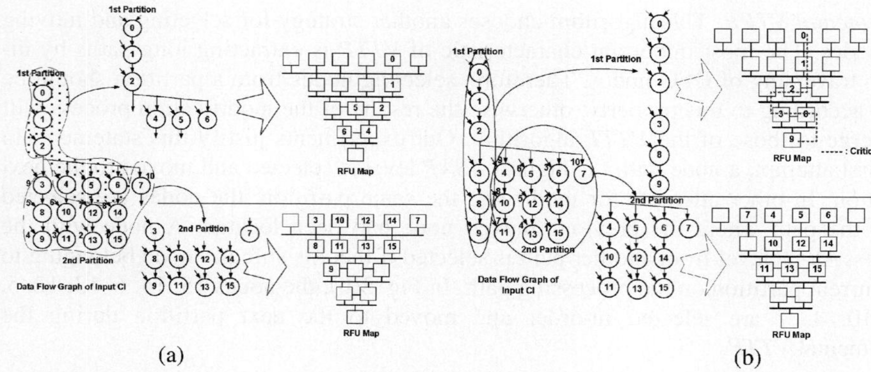

Fig. 3. Examples of *HTTP* (a) and *VTTP* (b) and their related incremental versions

4 Experimental Results

SimpleScalar tool set (PISA configuration)[18] and 22 applications of Mibench [17] were used for doing experiments. Initial CIs were generated according to the method proposed in [11]. CI rejection rate with respect to RFU architectural constraints was about 10%. Table 1 shows the minimum and maximum length of initial CIs. Also it shows the minimum length of rejected CIs which are applied to *Integrated Framework*. Application names include rejected CIs are shown in bold face. Last column of Table 1 depicts in 9 of the 22 applications, there was not any rejected CI, which means that all CIs in these applications were mapped on the RFU successfully. Also, for 13 of the 22 applications that include rejected CIs, CI rejection percentage is at least 1.9% for *sha* and at most 43.2% for *blowfish* and *blowfish(dec)*.

The base line processor was a 4-way in-order RISC processor with a 32KB L1 data cache (1 clock cycle latency); a 32KB L1 instruction cache (1 clock cycle latency) and a 1MB unified L2 cache (6 clock cycles latency). On the other hand, it was assumed that the RFU has a variable latency based on the length of the longest critical path [11]. It was presumed that the first row of the RFU takes one clock cycle and the other rows take 0.5 clock cycles for execution. For generating appropriate CIs, as mentioned in Section 3, we used two different approaches. First, we used *CIGen* to generate CIs with respect to RFU constraints. For these CIs, the mapping process was done and some of them were rejected again at the mapping stage because of the RFU routing resource constraints. Experiments show that 10 of 13 applications already have some rejected CIs using the *CIGen*.

In the second approach, we used the *Integrated Framework* to partition the rejected CIs and generate appropriate CIs, which are successfully mapped on the RFU. We compared two *HTTP* and *VTTP* algorithms with respect to critical path length of generated CIs, intermediate data size and speedup. Fig. 4(a) compares two algorithms with respect to intermediate data size. For 6 of 13 applications, intermediate data size is smaller using *VTTP*. For 7 remaining applications intermediate data size is the

Table 1. CIs length for Mibench applications

Application Name	Min. CI length	Max. CI length	Min. Rejected CI length	CI Rejection %
adpcm(enc)	5	7	-	0
adpcm(dec)	5	7	-	0
bitcounts	**4**	**20**	**20**	**14.3**
blowfish	**5**	**16**	**15**	**66.7**
blowfish (dec)	**5**	**16**	**15**	**66.7**
basicmath	3	11	-	0
cjpeg	**5**	**59**	**11**	**20.7**
crc	5	5	-	0
dijkstra	4	9	-	0
djpeg	**4**	**48**	**8**	**23.8**
fft	**3**	**16**	**16**	**8.3**
fft (inv)	**3**	**16**	**16**	**8.3**
gsm (dec)	**5**	**14**	**14**	**6.3**
gsm (enc)	**4**	**26**	**13**	**9.5**
lame	**3**	**13**	**7**	**8.3**
patricia	3	6	-	0
qsort	5	7	-	0
rijndael (enc)	**5**	**16**	**10**	**46.3**
rijndael (dec)	**5**	**18**	**10**	**57.1**
sha	**5**	**18**	**7**	**18.5**
stringsearch	5	9	-	0
susan	6	10	-	0

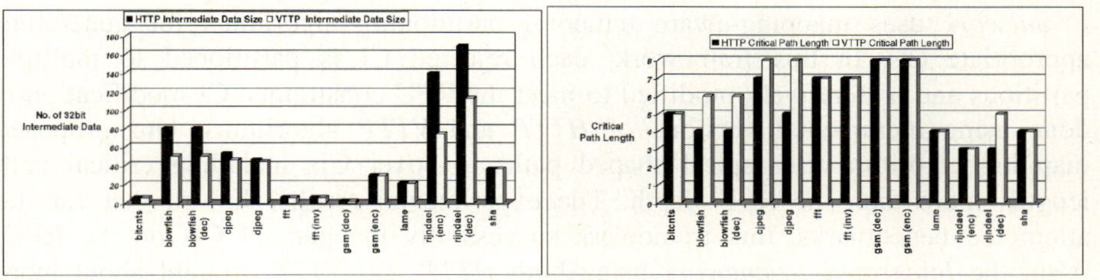

(a) (b)

Fig. 4. Intermediate data size (a) maximum critical path length for CIs (b)

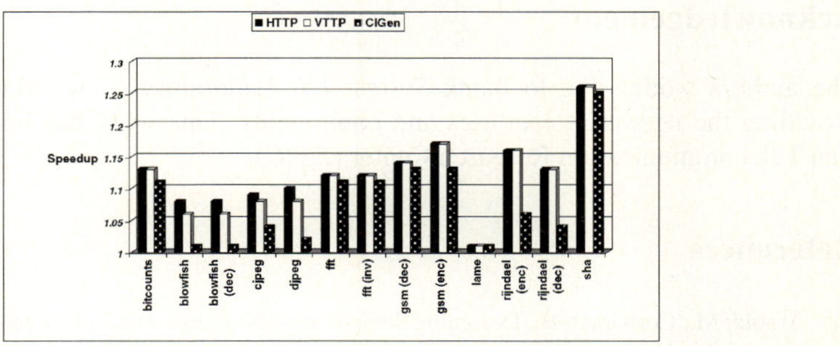

Fig. 5. Speedup comparison between *HTTP, VTTP* and *CIGen*

same. Another comparison was done with respect to critical path length. Fig. 4(b) shows that *VTTP* generated CIs with critical length equal to or more than *HTTP* because it traverses DFG nodes in depth, whereas *HTTP* traverses them horizontally. Finally, we compared both algorithms regarding the speedup obtained from the extensible processor. Fig. 5 depicts the comparison of speedup achieved using *HTTP* and *VTTP*. Using both of these algorithms, all CIs were mapped successfully on the RFU but *HTTP* resulted in better speedup, since it benefits from parallelism more in the instruction execution. In other words, critical path length is less using *HTTP*, and therefore, RFU execution latency was smaller. In addition, according to Fig. 5, both *HTTP* and *VTTP* offer better speedup compared to *CIGen*.

5 Conclusion

In this paper, an integrated framework was presented to address generating appropriate custom instructions and mapping them on the RFU of an adaptive extensible processor.

First, an RFU was presented for AMBER, a dynamic adaptive extensible processor. Generating appropriate CIs by applying the RFU constraints to the CI generation tool may still cause some generated CIs to be rejected. This approach does not have the capability of considering constraints such as routing resource constraints before mapping. *Integrated Framework* is the second approach we used to generate CIs. This framework can be used as a general approach for generating CIs. *Integrated Framework* uses mapping-aware temporal partitioning algorithms for generating appropriate CIs. In this framework, each rejected CI is partitioned to multiple partitions and is iteratively modified to meet the RFU constraints. CI modification is done using incremental versions of *HTTP* and *VTTP* algorithms. Our proposed mapping algorithm uses spiral shaped paths to cover CIs including critical path lengths more than the RFU depth. The experimental results showed that for the attempted benchmarks, this framework successfully mapped all CIs on the RFU. Also, the *Integrated Framework* using both *HTTP* and *VTTP* brought about more speedup enhancement compared to *CIGen*. In addition, *HTTP* gained higher performance in comparison with *VTTP* because of more instruction parallelism.

Acknowledgement

The authors would like to thank *System LSI* Laboratory of Kyushu University for providing the necessary facilities and equipments. This work has been supported by Iran Telecommunication Research Center *(ITRC)*.

References

1. Arnold, M., Corporaal, H., Designing domain-specific processors. In Proceedings of the Design, Automation and Test in Europe Conf, 2001, pp. 61-66.
2. Atasu, K., Pozzi, L., Lenne, P., Automatic application-specific instruction-set extensions under microarchitectural constraints, 40th Design Automation Conference, 2003.
3. Bobda, C., Synthesis of dataflow graphs for reconfigurable systems using temporal partitioning and temporal placement, Ph.D thesis, Faculty of Computer Science, Electrical Engineering and Mathematics, University of Paderborn, 2003.

4. Clark, N., Kudlur, M., Park, H., Mahlke, S., Flautner, K., Application-Specific Processing on a General-Purpose Core via Transparent Instruction Set Customization, In Proceedings of the 37th annual IEEE/ACM International Symposium on Microarchitecture, 2004.
5. Halfhill, T.R., MIPS embraces configurable technology, Microprocessor Report, 3 March 2003.
6. Karthikeya, M., Gajjala, P., Dinesh, B., Temporal partitioning and scheduling data flow graphs for reconfigurable computer, IEEE Transactions on Computers, vol. 48, no. 6, 1999, pp. 579–590.
7. Kastner, R. Kaplan, A., Ogrenci Memik, S., Bozorgzadeh, E., Instruction generation for hybrid reconfigurable systems, ACM TODAES, vol. 7, no. 4, 2002, pp. 605-627.
8. Lee, C., Potkonjak, M., Mangione-Smith, W.H., MediaBench: A tool for evaluating and synthesizing multimedia and communications systems, In Proceedings of the 30-th Annual Intl. Symp. On Microarchitecture, 1997, pp 330-335.
9. Mehdipour, F., Saheb Zamani, M., Sedighi, M., An integrated temporal partitioning and physical design framework for static compilation of reconfigurable computing system, International Journal of Microprocessors and Microsystems, Elsevier, vol. 30, no. 1, Feb 2006, pp. 52-62.
10. Micheli, G.D., Synthesis and optimization of digital circuits, McGraw-Hill, 1994.
11. Noori, H., Murakami, K., Inoue, K., General Overview of an Adaptive Dynamic Extensible Processor Architecture, Workshop on Introspective Architecture (WISA'2006) , 2006.
12. Ouaiss, I., Govindarajan, S., Srinivasan, V., Kaul M., Vemuri R., An integrated partitioning and synthesis system for dynamically reconfigurable multi-FPGA architectures, In Proceedings of the Reconfigurable Architecture Workshop, 1998, pp. 31-36.
13. Sherwani N, Algorithms for VLSI physical design automation, Kluwer-Academic Publishers, 1999.
14. Spillane, J., Owen, H., Temporal partitioning for partially reconfigurable field programmable gate arrays, IPPS/SPDP Workshops, 1998, pp. 37-42.
15. Tanougast, C., Berviller, Y., Brunet, P., Weber, S., Rabah, H., Temporal partitioning methodology optimizing FPGA resources for dynamically reconfigurable embedded real-time system, International Journal of Microprocessors and Microsystems, vol. 27, 2003, pp. 115-130.
16. Yu, P., Mitra, T., Characterizing embedded applications for instruction-set extensible processors, In Proceedings of Design and Automation Conference, 2004, pp. 723- 728.
17. http://www.eecs.umich.edu/mibench.
18. http://www.simplescalar.com.

Scheduling of Transactions Based on Extended Scheduling Timed Petri Nets for SoC System-Level Test-Case Generation

JinShan Yu, Tun Li, Yang Guo, and QingPing Tan

School of Computer Science
National University of Defense Technology
Changsha 410073, P.R. China
yujinshan@yeah.net

Abstract. The effective scheduling of transactions has a great potential for SoC functional verification. Petri nets have proven to be a promising technique for solving scheduling problem. This paper aims at presenting a Petri-net based approach to the scheduling of transactions generated by a test-case generator. Firstly, an extended scheduling timed Petri nets (ESTPN) model is given to support transaction scheduling. Secondly, the short term of 'scheduling of transactions problem' is formulated by means of an ESTPN which can accommodate various scheduling policies. Finally, transactions scheduling schemes and scheduling algorithm based on ESTPN are given and cases are studied.

1 Introduction

It is well known that verification today constitutes about 70% to 80% of the total design effort for SoC. Due to SoC's increasing complexities, SoC and multi-chip system developers can no longer rely on traditional simulation tools, testbenches, and methodologies, but must augment new verification methodology. The industry has raise the verification bar to the next level of abstraction -- transactions -- to ensure that designers and verification engineers have the tools and methodologies that give them a higher degree of confidence in their designs. Transaction-Based Verification (TBV) [1] enables the use of transactions at each phase of the verification cycle. A transaction is a single conceptual transfer of high-level data or control. It is defined by its begin time, end time, and all the relevant information associated with the transaction. For example, the relevant information (or attributes) of a Read transaction includes address and data. Transactions can be as simple as a memory Read/Write or as complex as the transfer of an entire structured data packet through a communication channel. The transaction level is the level at which the intended functionality of the design is specified and, therefore, the level at which the design can be verified in a most effective way. Raising the level of abstraction from signals to transactions facilitates the creation of tests, the debugging process, and the measurement of functional coverage. Therefore, there is a growing interest for the TBV methodology, techniques, tools and coverage analysis method.

E. Sha et al. (Eds.): EUC 2006, LNCS 4096, pp. 732–741, 2006.

In this paper, we're interested in how to schedule transactions based on extended scheduling timed Petri net (ESTPN) to generate certain SoC system-level test cases. The advantage of ESTPN-based method is: Firstly, Petri-net based approach can graphically and concisely represent timing constraints of transactions in a single coherent formulation, which is very helpful for the designers to better understand and formulate the transactions scheduling problems. Secondly, it can support sequent, concurrent, weight-based, random, while scheduling schemes and these basic scheduling schemes can be composed to generate the more complex schemes. Thirdly, changes in the markings in an ESTPN model completely describe the evolution of different transactions scheduling policies, and use timed Petri nets analysis tools to check their schedulability.

The rest of the paper is organized as follows. Section 2 outlines the related works. Section 3 presents the formal definition for our extended scheduling timed Petri net. Section 4 presents how to map transactions scheduling problem into ESTPN. Section 5 lists the transaction scheduling schemes and scheduling algorithm. Cases studies are given in section 6. Finally section 7 provides some concluding remarks.

2 Related Works

For SoC, characterized by the integration of several interacting components ('cores'), cores act in parallel - as a result, logic bugs in systems and SoCs are often related to scenarios which are timing dependent. Some bugs in the design may only show up when test occur in a specific ordering, are separated by a specific time interval, or are executed concurrently. Flexible transaction scheduling is necessary to show up the design bugs and reduce test cost. In [8], R. Emek proposed a transaction scheduling language which has been implemented in the random test-case generator: X-Gen [9]. Harrod demonstrated the use of the AMBA-bus dedicated for test purpose [2].

Research has been going on in developing techniques for test scheduling, test access mechanism (TAM) and testability analysis. Recently, there are three major methods to solve the test scheduling problem: 1) graph-based techniques [11-14], 2) bin-packing methods [15-19], and 3) ILP/MILP approaches [20-25]. A survey of test scheduling methods is presented in [10]. Moreover, much research has been done simultaneously on Petri nets and scheduling problems during the last two decade. The general discuss for schedule problem based on Petri net is shown in [26]. Using Petri nets for the modeling of scheduling problems is not a new idea. However, according to our knowledge, there is no report in literatures on transaction scheduling based on Petri net. In this paper, we present a transaction scheduling method based on extended scheduling timed Petri nets (ESTPN's) for SoC system-level test case generation. ESTPN's are more like the graphical representation of the scheduling language described in [8]. However, ESTPN's are more systematic and visualizable because they utilize existing concepts and techniques of Petri nets along with additional representation of timing. In our model, time constraint is associated with place, transition and places denote the scheduled transactions. Weight is associated with arc. Its formal definition will be given in section 3.

3 Extended Scheduling Timed Petri Net

The scheduling timed Petri net (Scheduling-TPNs) was introduced in [27]. For the works of schedulability analysis by Scheduling-TPNs, we refer the reader to Jeffreay J.P. Tsai [27, Li Huifang [28] and Roux [29]. We extend Scheduling-TPNs by adding weight to arc, and achieve extended timed constraint Petri net (ESTPN). Its formal definition is:

Definition 1. A (Scheduling) *Extended Timed constraint Petri net* is a tuple, $ESTPN = (P,T,F,C,D,W,P,M,M_0)$, where:

1. $P = \{p_1, p_2,..., p_m\}$ is a finite set of places, denoting the scheduled transactions.

2 $T = \{t_1, t_2,..., t_n\}$ is a finite set of *transitions* such that $T \cap P = \varnothing$. For transaction scheduling, we include three kinds of transitions: basic transition, random transition, weight-based transition.

3. $F \subset (P\times T)\mathrm{Y}(T\times P)$ is a set of *arcs(flow relation)*.

4. C is a set of integer pairs, $(T_{\min}(pt_j), T_{\max}(pt_j))$ where pt_j is either a place or a transition.

5. D is a set of transaction processing time $[F_{dur}(p_j)]$, where p_j is a place.

6. $W : F \rightarrow \{1,2,....\}$ is a weight function.

7. $P : p_j \rightarrow \{1,2,\mathrm{K}\}$ is a priority function, assigning a priority to place p_j.

9. M is a set of marking with $m - vector$, $\{M_{(p_1)},\Lambda, M(p_j),\Lambda, M(p_m)\}$, where $M_{(p_j)}$ denotes the numbers of token in place p_j.

10. $M_0 : P \rightarrow \{1,2,...\}$ is the initial marking.

Figure 1 shows an ESTPN sample. The state of an ESTPN is given by the distribution of tokens over the places and the corresponding timestamps. Firing a transition results in a new state. This way we can generate a sequence of states s_0, s_1, Λ, s_n, corresponding to a transaction scheduling sequence, such that s_0 is the initial state and s_{i+1} is the state reachable from s_i by firing a transition.

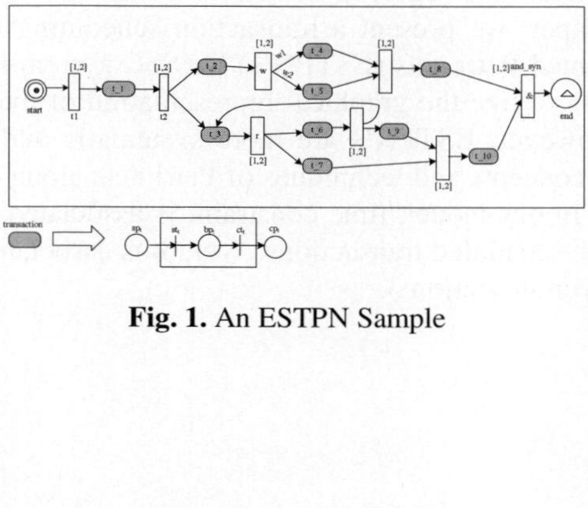

Fig. 1. An ESTPN Sample

Several basic definitions for ESTPN's schuedulability analysis are:

Definition 2. A transition t_i with a time pair, it is said to be enabled if each of its input places has at least one token.

Definition 3. A transition t_i, which is enabled at time $T0$, is said to be *firable* during the time period form $T0+TC_{\max}(t_j)$ in which $TC_{\max}(t_j)\geq TC_{\min}(t_j)$.

A friable transition can fire but there is no guarantee that the firing will complete successfully because the firing of a transition takes a period of time $F_{dur}(t_j)$. All the tokens (denotes as $TK's$) used for enabling a transition t_j will be preserved during the $t_j's$ firing, and $TK's$ can be used to enable other transitions if t_j fails to complete their firing. If all the transitions enabled by $TK's$ fail to complete their firing, $TK's$ will be trapped in their corresponding places.

Definition 4. A transition is said to be schedulable if it is friable and can complete its firing successfully, i.e., $(TC_{\max}(t_j)-TC_{\min}(t_j))\geq FIRE_{dur}(t_j)$.

Definition 5. A marking M_n is said to be reachable in $PN's$ modeling if there is a firing sequence, $\sigma=(M_0 t_0 M_1 \Lambda\ M_j t_j \Lambda\ t_n M_n)$.

The set of all possible markings reachable from M_0 is denoted by $R(M_0)$, and the set of all possible firing sequences from $L(M_0)$. With the considering of timing constraints, in ESTPN's modeling, a marking M_n is said to be reachable if and only if all transitions in σ are proved to be schedulable with respect to the timing constraints, i.e. , $(TC_{\max}(t_j)-TC_{\min}(t_j))\geq F_{dur}(t_j)$.

4 Mapping Transaction Scheduling Problems into ESTPN

To show that ESTPN can be used to model and analyse transaction scheduling problems, we provide a translation from transaction scheduling problem to a 'suitable' extended timed constraint Petri net. A transaction t is defined by its begin time, end time, and all the relevant information. So we can identify three stages for transaction t: (1) t is waiting to be processed, (2) t is being processed and (3) t has been processed. Basically, Figure 2 shows how we model a transaction t in terms of an ESTPN. Transitions st_t and ct_t represent the beginning and termination of transaction t respectively. The place sp_t, bp_t and cp_t correspond to the stages just mentioned.

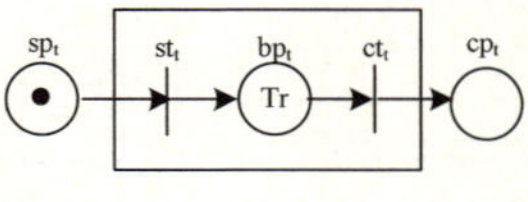

Fig. 2. Mapping Transaction Scheduling into ESTPN

Now transaction scheduling problem can be easily formulated by the following procedures:

Step1: For transaction $trans_i$, each scheduling activity is represented by two transitions st_t, ct_t and one place bp_t.

Step2: In terms of transaction partial order, all the transactions involved in a test case are linked, and modeled as an EPTPN model.

Step3: All the scheduled transactions are interconnected, and a complete EPTPN model for the scheduling of transactions is created.

5 Transaction Scheduling Schemes and Scheduling Algorithm

5.1 Transaction Scheduling Schemes

Base transaction scheduling schemes in ESTPN include sequent, concurrent, while, weight-based, random. These scheduling schemes can be composed to generate more complex scheduling sequence, named composed scheduling scheme.

(1) Sequent Scheduling Scheme

In sequent scheduling scheme, transaction t' is scheduled after transaction t has been accomplished, i.e. bus write transaction preceding bus read transaction. It is modeled by adding extra places. Figure 3 shows the situation where transaction t precedes transaction t', i.e. the execution of transaction t has to be completed before the execution of transaction t'. Place $pre < t, t' >$ prevents $st_{t'}$ form firing until ct_t fires. Notes that places are used to model the stages of a transaction.

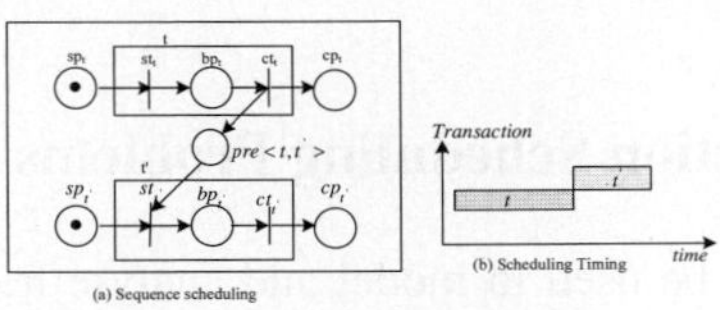

Fig. 3. Sequent Scheduling Scheme and Scheduling Timing

(2) Concurrent Scheduling Scheme

Concurrent scheduling scheme is modeled as shown in Figure 4. Transaction t and t' are scheduled concurrently.

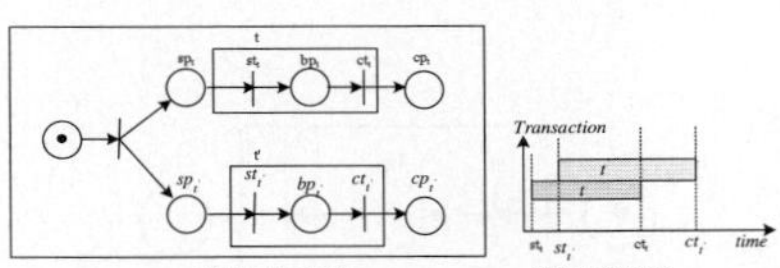

Fig. 4. Concurrent Scheduling Scheme and Scheduling Timing

(3) While Scheduling Scheme

In while scheduling scheme, transaction can be scheduled many times. While scheduling scheme can be used to generate burst mode transactions. Figure 5 shows this case.

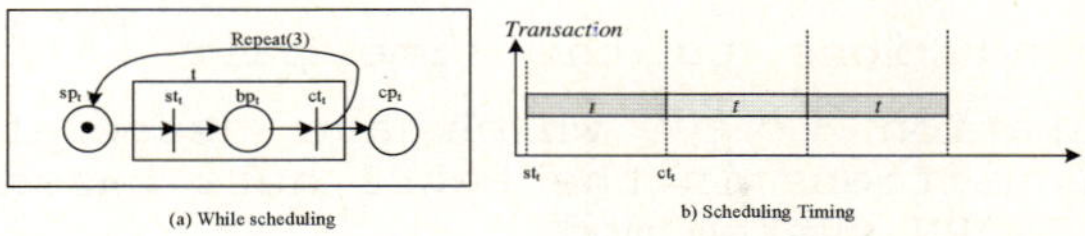

Fig. 5. While Scheduling Scheme and Scheduling Timing

(4) Weight-Based Scheduling Scheme

In weight-based scheduling scheme, scheduler first evaluates the weights on output arcs from weight transition, and schedules the transaction with greatest weight. Figure 6 shows this case.

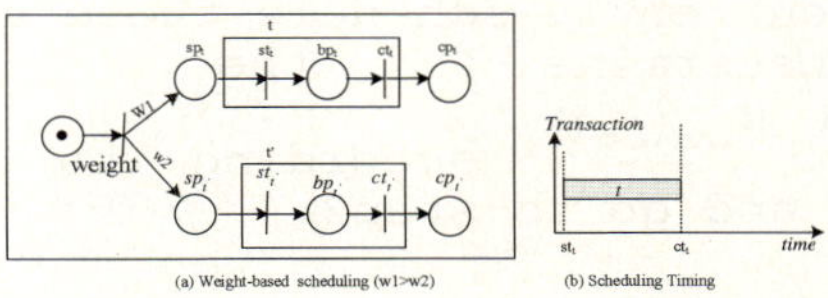

Fig. 6. Weight-based Scheduling Scheme and Scheduling Timing

(5) Random Scheduling Scheme

In random scheduling scheme, random transition is used to randomly schedule one transaction. Figure 7 shows this case.

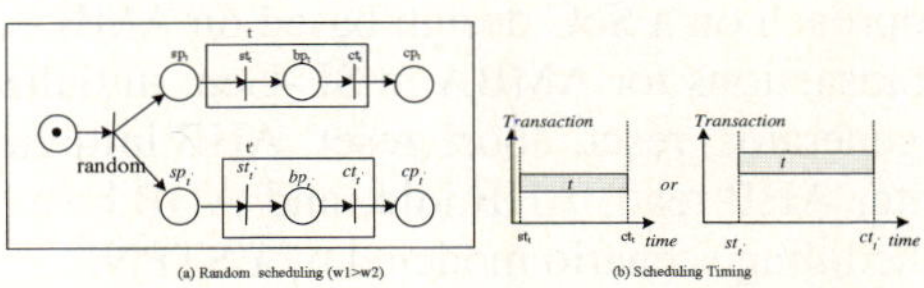

Fig. 7. Random Scheduling Scheme and Scheduling timing

(6) Composed Scheduling Scheme

Above five basic scheduling schemes can be composed to generate more complex scheduling scheme, named composed scheduling scheme.

5.2 Scheduling Algorithm

Based on extended scheduling timed Petri net model, we present the following transactions scheduling algorithm:

Step1 Model transaction scheduling problem and the imposed time constraints using ESTPN:

Step1.1 Model the transaction scheduling problem as a Petri net based model.

Step1.2 Mapping the time constraints for the transactions and conditions to the time pair $[T_{\min}(pt_j), T_{\max}(pt_j)]$ and the time duration $[F_{dur}(p_j)]$ which are associated with the places or transitions in the Petri nets based model. Then prepare the ESTPN system model.

Step1.3 Determine the initial marking M_0 and its arrival time $T_{Arr}(M_0)$.

Step2 Determine all friable transitions in marking M_k (if k=0, then $M_k = M_0$) and find the number J of all friable transitions. If the friable transition is the start transition of one transaction and timing constraints is met, scheduling transaction. If there are several such transitions, concurrently schedule these transactions.

Step3 Determine the next mark $\{M_{next(p_1)}, \Lambda, M_{next}(p_j), \Lambda, M_{next}(p_m)\}$ according to the Petri net transition rule, and go to step2.

Step 4 Stop.

6 Case Studies

We have implemented this scheduling methodology in our SoC system-level functional verification prototype system: SL-Gen. SL-Gen provides interfaces to time Petri nets analysis tools (Remeo [30], TINA [31]) to simulate and analysis transaction scheduling Petri nets model.

We illustrate our approach on a SoC design based on AMBA 2.0 Specification. We create the following transactions for AMBA in SL-Gen: initialize_amba, HCLK_generator, abort_HCLK_generator, reset, abort_reset, AHB.initialize_ahb_master, AHB.write, AHB.abort_write, AHB.read, AHB.idle, and AHB.busy. Figure 8 shows one AMBA transaction scheduling scenario modeled by ESTPN.

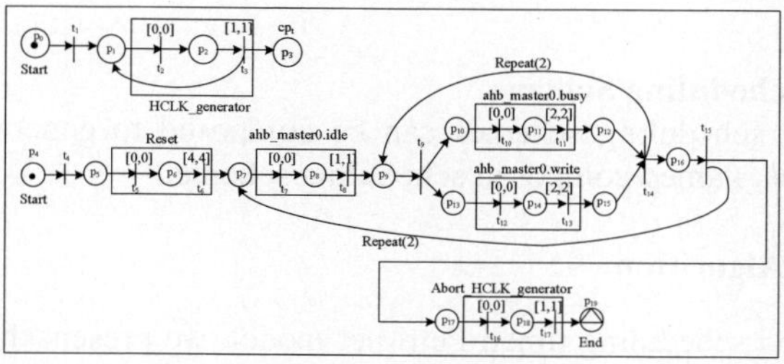

Fig. 8. AMBA Transaction Scheduling Scenario

SL-Gen automatically generates the following system-level testbench:

```
Initial
   integer burstLength;
    $timeformat(-9,3,"ns",7);
// $Initialize
  tb_initialize_amba;
// Apply transaction scheduling
  HCLK_generator_looping;
reset;
   repeat (2) // number of bursts to perform
    begin
        ahb_master0.idle;
        writedata.randomize;
        repeat (2)
            begin
               ahb_master0.  busy   (writedata.addr,  1,
writedata.size, writedata.burst);
               ahb_master0.   write     (writedata.trans,
writedata.addr,
 writedata.data, writedata.size, writedata.burst);
     writedata.addr  =  writedata.addr  +  (1  <<  write-
data.size);
     writedata.randomize_data;
            end
    end
Abort_HCLK_generator;
 end
```

In SL-Gen, we can get the following simulation timing, shown in Figure 9.

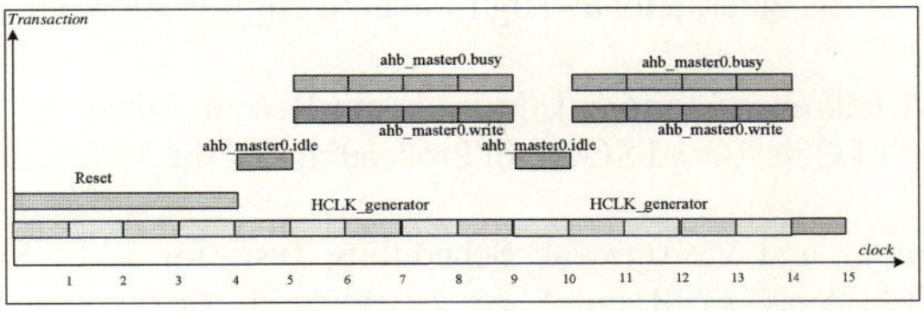

Fig. 9. AMBA Transaction Scheduling Timing

7 Conclusions

An extended scheduling timed Petri net (ESTPN) formulation for the scheduling of transactions has been proposed. Changes in the markings in an ESTPN model completely describe the evolution of different transactions scheduling problem. The great benefit of the Petri-net based approach is graphically and concisely represent timing constraints of transactions in a single coherent formulation, which is very helpful for the designers to better understand and formulate the transactions scheduling problems. Moreover, it is understood from this research that the Petri-net based approach has a great potential for solving a variety of complicated scheduling problems in transaction based test case generation. In this regard, further research is also being undertaken to accommodate complicated constraints such as resource, power, TAM and to implement the integrated design of the supervisory control and scheduling of transactions for SoC functional verification.

Acknowledgments

This work was supported by National Natural Science Foundation of China under Grant No. 60403048 and No. 60573173.

References

1. Cadence Berkeley Labs: The Transaction-Based Verification Methodology. Technical Report # CDNL-TR-2000-0825, August 2000.
2. http://www.synopsys.com/
3. http://www.verisity.com/html/specmanelite.html
4. http://www.chronology.com/
5. http://www.testbuilder.net
6. http://www.systemc.org
7. Rohit Jindal and Kshitiz Jain: Verification of Transaction-Level SystemC models using RTL Testbenches. In Proceedings of the First ACM and IEEE International Conference on Formal Methods and Models for Co-Design (2003)199-204
8. R. Emek and Y. Naveh: Scheduling of Transactions for System-Level Test-Case Generation. In Proceedings of the Eighth IEEE International High-Level Design Validation and Test Workshop (2003) 149-154
9. R.Emek, I.Jaeger, Y.Naveh, G.Bergman, G.Aloni, Y.Katz, M.Farkash, I.Dozoretz and A.Goldin: X-Gen: A Random Test-Case Generator for Systems and SoCs. In Proceedings of the Seventh IEEE International High-Level Design Validation and Test Workshop (2002) 145–150
10. V. Iyengar, K. Chakrabarty, and E.J. Marinissen: Recent Advances in Test Planning for Modular Testing of Core-Based SOCs. In Proceedings of the 11th Asian Test Symp (2002) 320-325
11. R. Chou, K. Saluja, and V. Agrawal: Scheduling Tests for VLSI Systems under Power Constraints. IEEE Trans. VLSI, vol. 5, no. 2 (1997)175-185
12. P. Rosinger, B. Al-Hashimi, and N. Nicolici: Power Profile Manipulation: A New Approach for Reducing Test Application Time under Power Constraints. IEEE Trans. Computer-Aided Design of Integrated Circuits and Systems, vol. 21, no. 10 (2002)1217-1225
13. D. Zhao and S. Upadhyaya: Adaptive Test Scheduling in SoC's by Dynamic Partitioning. In Proceedings of the 17th IEEE Int'l Symp. Defect and Fault Tolerance in VLSI Systems (2002) 334-342
14. D. Zhao and S. Upadhyaya: Power Constrained Test Scheduling with Dynamically Varied TAM. In Proceedings of the 21st VLSI Test Symp (2003) 273-278
15. E.G. Coffman Jr., M.R. Garey, D.S. Johnson, and R.E. Tarjan: Performance Bounds for Level-Oriented Two-Dimensional Packing Algorithm. SIAM J. Computing, vol. 9 (1980) 809-826
16. Y. Huang, W.-T. Cheng, C.-C. Tsai, N. Mukherjee, O. Samman, Y.Zaidan, and S.M. Reddy: Resource Allocation and Test Scheduling for Concurrent Test of Core-Based SoC Design. In Proceedings of IEEE Asian Test Symposium (ATS) (2001) 265-270

17. Y. Huang, W.-T. Cheng, C.-C. Tsai, N. Mukherjee, O. Samman, Y.Zaidan, and S.M. Reddy: On Concurrent Test of Core-Based SoC Design. J. Electronic Testing: Theory and Applications, vol. 18(2002) 401–414
18. V. Iyengar, K. Chakrabarty, and E.J. Marinissen: Wrapper/TAM Co-Optimization, Constraint-Driven Test Scheduling, and Tester Data Volume Reduction for SOCs. Proc. 39th Design Automation Conf (2002) 685-690
19. Y. Huang, S.M. Reddy, W.-T. Cheng, P. Reuter, N. Mukherjee,C.-C. Tsai, O. Samman, and Y. Zaidan: Optimal Core Wrapper Width Selection and SOC Test Scheduling Based on 3D Bin Packing Algorithm. In Proceedings of ITC 2002 (2002)74-82
20. Y. Huang, W.-T. Cheng, C.-C. Tsai, N. Mukherjee, and S.M.Reddy: Static Pin Mapping and SOC Test Scheduling for Cores with Multiple Test Sets. In Proceedings of the Fourth International Symposium on Quality Electronic Design (2003) 99- 104
21. M. Nourani and C. Papachristou: An ILP Formulation to Optimize Test Access Mechanism in SoC Testing. In Proceedings of ITC 2000 (2000)902-910
22. K. Chakrabarty: Test Scheduling for Core-Based Systems Using Mixed Integer Linear Programming. IEEE Trans. Computer-Aided Design, vol. 19(2000)1163-1174
23. V. Iyengar and K. Chakrabarty: Precedence-Based, Preemptive, and Power-Constrained Test Scheduling for System-on-a-Chip. In Proceedings of the 19th IEEE VLSI Test Symposium (2001) 368-374
24. M. Nourani and J. Chin: Power-Time Trade-Off in Test Scheduling for SoCs. In Proceedings of IEEE International Conference on Computer Design(ICCD '03)(2003) 548-553
25. James Chin and Mehrdad. Nourani: FITS: An Integrated ILP-Based Test Scheduling Environment. IEEE Trans. on computer, VOL. 54, NO. 12(2005) 1598- 1613
26. W.M.P. van der Aalst: Petri net based scheduling. Computing Science Reports 95/23, Eindhoven University of Technology, Eindhoven (1995)
27. Jeffrey J.P.Tsai, Steve Jennhwa Yang and Yao-Hsiung Chang: Timing Constraints Petri Net and Their Application to Schedulability Analysis for Real-Time System Specification. IEEE Transaction on Software Engineering, VOL. 21. NO. 1(1995)
28. Li Huifang and FAN Yushun: Schedulability analysis method for Timing Constraint Petri Nets. Tsinghua Science and Technology, Vol.7, No.6(2002) 596-601
29. Roux, O.H., Deplanche, A.M: A t-time Petri net extension for real time-task scheduling modeling. European Journal of Automation (JESA) 36 (2002) 973-987
30. 20. Guillaume Gardey, Didier Lime, Morgan Magnin, and Olivier (H.) Roux. Romeo: A Tool for Analyzing Time Petri Nets. CAV 2005, LNCS 3576 (2005) 418-423
31. B. Berthomieu, P-O. Ribet, and F. Vernadat. The tool TINA: Construction of abstract state. spaces for Petri nets and time Petri nets. International Journal of Production Research, V42, N14(2004)

Automatic Generation of Hardware/Software Interface with Product-Specific Debugging Tools*

Jeong-Han Yun[1], Gunwoo Kim[1], Choonho Son[2], and Taisook Han[1]

[1] Dept. of Computer Science, Korea Advanced Institute of Science and Technology
[2] Network Technology Laboratory, Korea Telecom
{dolgam, reshout}@pllab.kaist.ac.kr, choonho@kt.co.kr, han@cs.kaist.ac.kr

Abstract. Software programmers want to manage pure software, not hardware-software entanglements. Unfortunately, traditional development methodologies cannot clearly separate hardware and software in embedded system development process. We propose a *Hardware/software INterface GEnerator*; we call it HINGE. After receiving device specifications including device usage rules for each device, HINGE automatically generates device API, device driver, and device controller for each device. In addition, HINGE equips device APIs to check the device usage rules at run-time. Consequently, HINGE gives support to not only fast prototyping but also device usage rule-debugging in embedded software.

1 Introduction

Traditional embedded system development process repeats requirement analysis, separated hardware/software design, implementation, and test. This process raises three controversial arguments. First, this process needs many implementation-iterations caused by information miscommunication or requirement changes. Any of them impacts the entire development team. Second, hardware/software interface(Figure 1) implementation and integration are tedious and error-prone; 40% of product development time is spent for system integration, and more 60% of operating system's errors are born from here[1]. Finally, system debugging and requirement check are too hard. Equivocal error messages from device drivers do not tell the exact cause of errors.

To overcome these problems, we propose a *Hardware/software INterface GEnerator*; we call it HINGE. After receiving an *interface specification* for each device from system designers, HINGE generates the hardware/software interface for each device.

Moreover, HINGE generates rule-checking codes based on device usage rules in API specification, and inserts them into device APIs. The inserted codes

* This research was supported by the MIC(Ministry of Information and Communication), Korea, under the ITRC(Information Technology Research Center) support program supervised by the IITA(Institute of Information Technology Assessment) (IITA-2005-C1090-0502-0031).

E. Sha et al. (Eds.): EUC 2006, LNCS 4096, pp. 742–753, 2006.

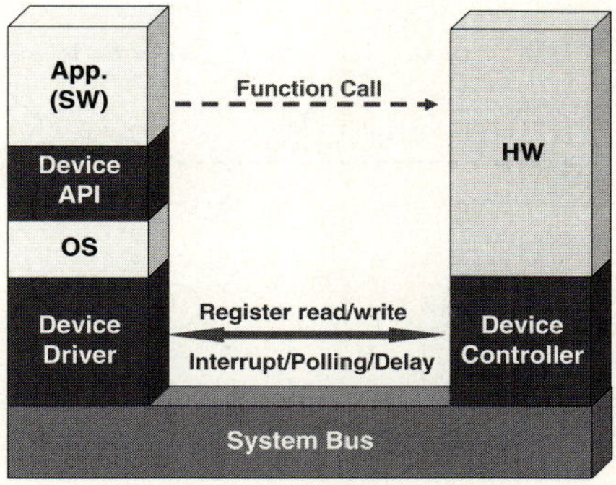

Fig. 1. Hardware/Software Interface: device API, device driver, and device controller

notice wrong usages of devices using return values of device APIs[1]. With the generated device APIs, software-development groups can easily detect device usage errors by the return values of the device APIs at run-time. Therefore, all of the generated device APIs is suitable for a good rule-debugging tool or a device exception handler.

This paper is organized as follows. Section 2 defines the interface specification as HINGE's input. Section 3 explains the automatic generation of hardware/software interface. The case study of HINGE is in Section 4. Section 5 summaries the related work about hardware/software interface. Section 6 concludes the paper.

2 Interface Specification

Interface specification is our representation of hardware/software interface information as HINGE's input. It is divided into four categories as follows:

API Specification: declaration of interface relations
Driver Specification: definition of communication events[2]
Controller Specification: memory assignment of hardware
System Specification: information of a target machine

Each specification is written in XML format.

2.1 API Specification

Push-Pull interface has been used to show who is a major actor between sender and receiver. We apply Push-Pull interface to *API specification.*

---

[1] Alarms with special return values generally apply to software libraries; for example, the return value 0 of `malloc` function in C libraries means the failure of dynamic memory allocation.

[2] The events can be interpreted as variables in software, and as signals in hardware.

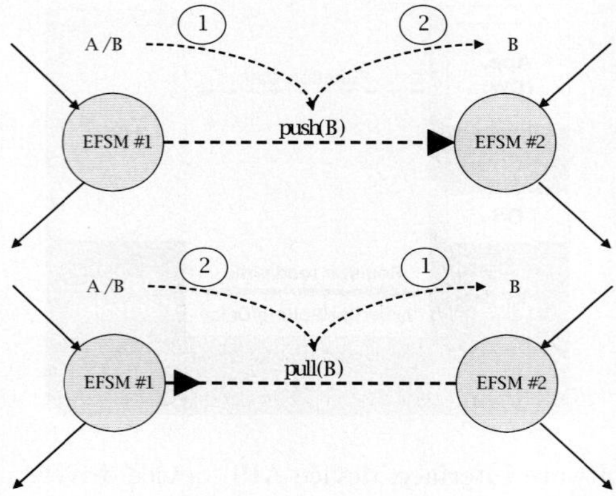

Fig. 2. Push interface and Pull interface: our graphic notation

Push-Pull Interface. We can represent communications between two EFSMs[6] by Push-Pull interface. Push interface means that a receiver always detects[3] events as soon as a sender emits[4] it. On the other hand, Pull interface means that a receiver detects events when it wants. Using these two interfaces, we can represent delivery/processing order of communication events exactly.

Both Push interface and Pull interface in Figure 2 are delivering an output event B from EFSM #1 as an input event to EFSM #2, but the behaviors between EFSM #1 and EFSM #2 are different.

From API specification, When an event is occurred, EFSM #1 sends the event into EFSM #2 by Push mechanism. That is, EFSM #1 is an active sender, and EFSM #2 is a passive receiver. Therefore, the sender controls the synchronization timing of two EFSMs in Push interface. Push interface can be manipulated by interrupt or polling mechanism.

However, EFSM #2 decides the timing or receiving events in Pull interface, even if the event is occurred in the EFSM #1. That is, EFSM #1 is a passive sender, and EFSM #2 is an active receiver. Therefore, the receiver controls the synchronization timing of two EFSMs in Pull interface.

API Specification. API specification consists of three parts

1. Function type of each device API
2. Interface definition using Push-Pull interface
3. Automata for describing device usage rules: the execution order among device APIs or permitted range of parameters

HINGE generates device API from API specification. Whenever the device API is called, it checks the device usage rules. That is, it returns positive value

[3] Detecting events can be considered as reading the data of variables with regard to software and as receiving signals with regard to hardware.

[4] Emitting events can be interpreted as writing the data of variables in respect of software and as sending signals in respect of hardware.

```
<Driver>
  <event name='adder'>
    <sw2hw sw_var='uint8 a' hw_port='A [7:0]' />
    <sw2hw sw_var='uint8 b' hw_port='B [7:0]' />
    <hw2sw sw_var='uint8 c' hw_port='C [7:0]' />
    <interrupt pin_name='27' hw_name='ready' />
  </event>

  <event_layout id='adder' virtual_address='0xf1810000'>
    <offset id='0' sw='a' map='[7:0]' to='A [7:0]'/>
    <offset id='1' sw='b' map='[7:0]' to='B [7:0]'/>
    <offset id='2' sw='c' map='[7:0]' from='C [7:0]'/>
  </event_layout>
</Driver>
```

Fig. 3. An example of driver specification

that indicates the current state number on device usage rule automata. If embedded software breaks an device usage rule, the device API returns negative one of the current state number. We will show an example in Section 4.

2.2 Driver Specification

Driver specification is used by HINGE to generate device drivers. Figure 3 is an example. Driver specification is composed of two parts:

1. communication event : the connection between the device driver's arguments and hardware ports
2. communication event layout : the mapping to virtual address

HINGE uses memory mapped I/O for hardware/software communication[5]. So all events must be mapped to their own fixed virtual addresses in kernel memory.

2.3 Controller Specification

Controller specification contains low-level information such as system bus and the memory space of hardware. Figure 4 is an example of controller specification. Using these information, HINGE generates device controller: a composition of address decoder and data decoder.

2.4 System Specification

System specification has the information about CPU and operating system. Figure 5 shows the abstract grammar of system specification.

[5] In our experimental environment, devices are implemented on FPGA for prototyping. FPGA module has physically continuous address space. This address space is used for kernel memory.

```
<Controller>
  <AddrDecoder>
    <addr id='CX_A' width='[21:1]'/>
    <chip_select id='NPX_CS5' type='active low'/>
    <write from='0' to='1'/>
    <read from='2' to='2'/>
  </AddrDecoder>
  <DataDecoder>
    <data id='CX_D' width='[15:0]'/>
    <write_enable id='NPX_PWE' type='active high'/>
    <read_enable id='GPIO27' type='active low'/>
  </DataDecoder>
</Controller>
```

Fig. 4. An example of controller specification

$$
\begin{aligned}
SYSTEM &::= CPU \;\; OS \\
CPU &::= CPUTYPE \;\; ENDIAN \\
CPUTYPE &::= \mathit{xscale} \mid \mathit{x86} \\
ENDIAN &::= \mathit{little} \mid \mathit{big} \\
OS &::= LINUX \\
LINUX &::= KERNEL \;\; DRIVER \\
KERNEL &::= \mathit{2.4} \mid \mathit{2.6} \\
DRIVER &::= -\mathit{1} \mid \mathit{PositiveInteger}
\end{aligned}
$$

Fig. 5. The abstract grammar for system specification

Now HINGE supports Linux operating system with Intel Xscale architecture. The kernel version of Linux is one of 2.4 or 2.6, which are the major versions of the Linux kernel. The `DRIVER` specifies a major number of hardware devices. If the specified number is a positive integer, the device is statically allocated by that number. Otherwise, the device is dynamically allocated by the operating system.

3 Hardware/Software Interface

From the interface specification, HINGE automatically generates hardware/ software interface: device API, device driver, and device controller. Figure 6 is our target board architecture.

3.1 Device API

Device API is a high-level encapsulation of device drivers; embedded software can access devices like software libraries through device API.

Especially, device API generated by HINGE provides debugging faculties which can detect wrong usages of device APIs with the following procedure:

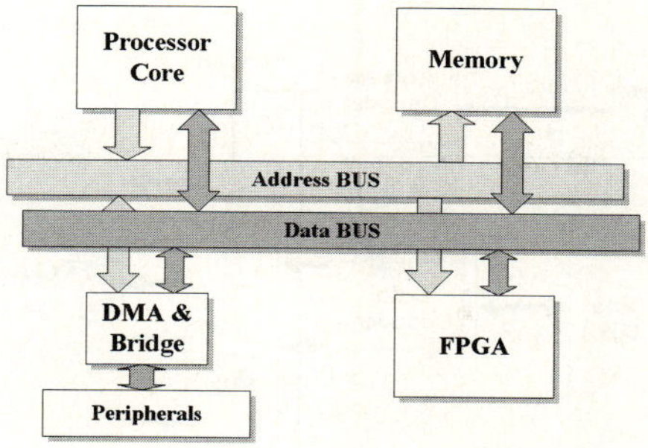

Fig. 6. Our target board architecture

1. Each device API memorizes the device's current state in its device usage rule automata.
2. If device API is called in a wrong way, it returns the negative value of the current state number.
3. If device API is called in a right way, it moves to the next state by this usage and returns the positive value of the state number.

After checking above conditions, the device API transfers hardware/software communication events using the device drivers.

3.2 Device Driver

HINGE generates character device drivers for target operating systems. Fundamental functions are `open`, `close`, `read`, `write`, and `llseek`.

In Linux environment, each function of device driver has common model. HINGE generates device drivers through these common device driver models.

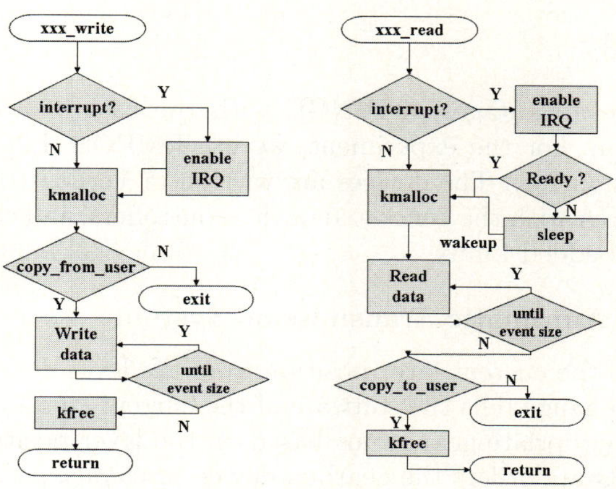

Fig. 7. The models of `write` and `read` functions

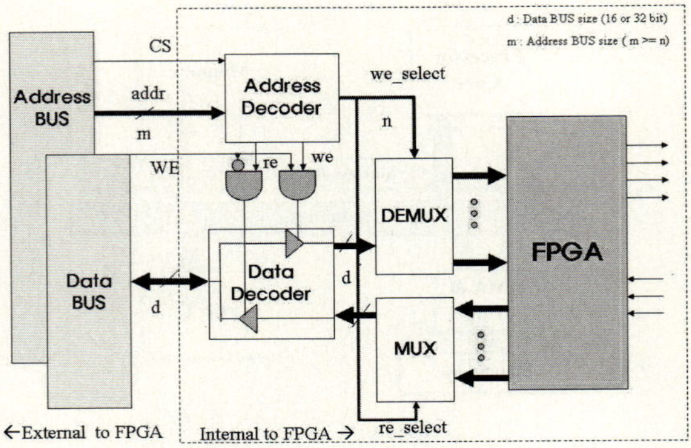

Fig. 8. Schematic diagram of the read/write module

These models can be applied to any device driver. Figure 7 shows the models of `write` and `read` functions.

Like `write` and `read` functions, HINGE automatically generates other device driver functions based on the common driver models.

3.3 Device Controller

The device controller consists of an address decoder and a data decoder. The address decoder gets a physical address from the address bus, and emits control signals for the data decoder. The data decoder reads or writes data according to control signals emitted by the address decoder.

A device can be classified into three functional models by behaviors of the data decoder: read module, write module, and read/write module. Among of them, Figure 8 shows the schematic diagram of the read/write module. HINGE generates Verilog codes based on that schematic diagram.

4 Case Study

We will show the advantages of HINGE with the case of a simplified automatic transmission. For the experiment, we use EMPOS II[2] with embedded Linux(kernel version 2.4). The devices are written in Verilog HDL. The devices are loaded on FPGA with the generated device controllers, and the device drivers are loaded on embedded Linux.

4.1 Design of Automatic Transmission System

The software gets the current lever position from the lever device by Pull interface, and the rpm gauge tells the software of the current rpm by Push interface. After deciding appropriate gear ratios based on the lever position and the current rpm, the software orders the gearbox device to change gear ratios by Push interface. Figure 9 is the informal representation of the entire system using our graphic notation for Push-Pull interface.

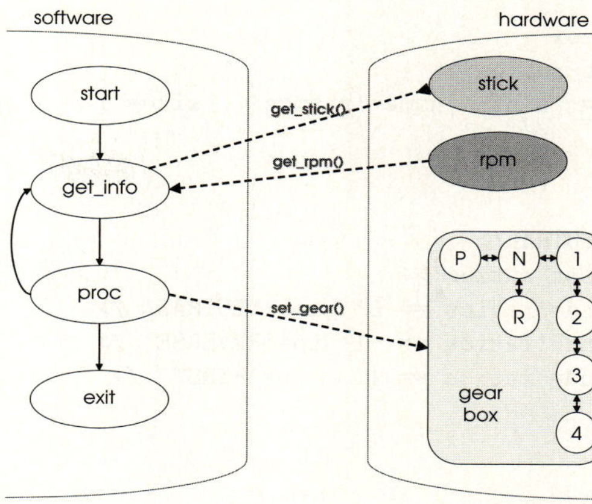

Fig. 9. Push-Pull Interface of simplified automatic transmission

4.2 The Use of HINGE

To check whether the software uses devices correctly, we should express device usage rules by state automata in API specification. In case of the gearbox device, it has several states corresponding to ratios. Its API specification is shown in Figure 10. A ratio -1 denotes the reverse gear, and a ratio 100 does the parking gear; others are omitted.

The experimental results of simplified automatic transmission are depicted in Table 1 and Table 2.

By using generated device APIs instead of kernel functions, software can check or handle error cases at run-time. For example, when the current gear ratio is

Table 1. Automatic_transmission's interface specification(lines of code)

	API	Driver	Controller	System	Total
`stick`	14	8	12	9	43
`rpm`	14	9	12	9	44
`gearbox`	56	8	12	9	85
`Total`	84	25	36	27	172

Table 2. Generated codes from the interface specification in Table 1(lines of code)

	API (C)	Driver (C)	Controller (Verilog)	Makefile	Total
`stick`	33	87	74	15	209
`rpm`	33	94	74	15	216
`gearbox`	68	88	92	15	263
`Total`	134	269	240	45	688

```
<API>
  <device id='gearbox'>
    <func name='set_ratios'>
      <param type = 'uint8' name='ratios'   size='1'    op='write' />
    </func>
  </device>
  <automata>
    <state name='NEUTRAL'>
      <func name='set_ratios'>
        <action cond='ratios == 0'  to='NEUTRAL' />
        <action cond='ratios == -1' to='REVERSE' />
        <action cond='ratios == 1'   to='FIRST' />
      </func>
    </state>
    ...
    <state name='SECOND'>
      <func name='set_ratios'>
        <action cond='ratios == 1' to='FIRST' />
        <action cond='ratios == 3' to='THIRD' />
      <func>
    </state>
    ...
    <state name='PARKING'>
      <func name='set_ratios'>
        <action cond='ratios == 0'   to='NEUTRAL' />
        <action cond='ratios == 100' to='PARKING' />
      </func>
    </state>
  </automata>
</API>
```

Fig. 10. A portion of the API specification of the hardware component gearbox

set to 'second gear', if the software orders the gearbox device to set gear ratio 'neutral gear', `set_ratios` returns '-SECOND'; '-SECOND' indicates the error occurrence on the device state 'SECOND' in the device usage rules(Figure 11). Each state name automatically defines a constant in generated device APIs.

5 Related Work

Codesign Tools. The major difference between HINGE and interface generators of other codesign systems is the device API to check the device usage rules at run-time. To the best of our knowledge, none of codesign frameworks service the debugging interface like that.

Approaches to automatic interface generation including CHINOOK[5] and POLIS[6] describe a system with a set of codesign finite state machines(CFSMs) which use FIFO queues. Since these codesign environments keep all of target architecture information, development groups using these environments do not

```
void auto_transmission() {
  int chk, lever, rpm;
  ...
  while(1) {
    chk = get_lever(&lever);
    if (chk < 0) {
      printf("get_lever error : error_code=%d\n", chk);
      exit(1);
    }
    chk = get_rpm(&rpm);
    if (chk < 0) {
      printf("get_rpm error : error_code=%d\n", chk);
      exit(1);
    }
    if (lever==0) {
      chk = set_ratios(0);
      if (chk== -SECOND) { // if current gear ratio is second
        if (rpm < 1500) {
          chk = set_ratio(1);
        }
      }
      else if (chk < 0) {
        printf("set_ratios error : error_code=%d\n", chk);
        exit(1);
      }
    }
    ...
  }
}
```

Fig. 11. Software `auto_transmission` using device APIs

write the hardware/software interface specification. This is why these environments are not flexible for architecture modification.

COSMOS[7], COSYMA[8], and CoWare[9] use concurrently-running processes using remote procedure calls(RPCs) for communications. This mechanism is more complicate than shared memory and may cause inefficiency. COSMOS and CoWare are now commercially available from AREXSYS[10] and CoWare[11].

Interface Generation. Traditionally, device drivers have been written in C due to its efficiency and flexibility. Unfortunately, sophisticated device interaction protocols and C's lack of type safety make driver code complex and prone to failure. Device drivers account for 70–90% of bugs in the Linux kernel and have error rates up to three to seven times higher than the rest of the kernel[12]. So various approaches have been suggested to improve the reliability of low-level software, device driver software, and device controller in many researches[1,4,13,14,15,16,17,18,19].

These tools support device interfaces well. Nevertheless, bugs of embedded software may be born from wrong device usages as well as device interfaces implementation itself. Some of them provide fundamental but simple debugging interfaces[1,4,9,19]. However, our tool generates device APIs that can alarm wrong device usages based on API specification. This helps embedded software debugging and exception handling for wrong device usages.

6 Conclusion

Our ultimate goal is the separation of hardware- and software-development process. For that purpose, we propose interface specification as hardware/software interface description methodology and implement the hardware/software interface generator HINGE. Our approach makes four contributions to embedded software development.

First, API specification using Push-Pull interface can show the more realistic interfacing mechanisms than other interface description methodologies.

Second, interface specification can be used for a common specification document between hardware- and software-development groups. Especially, software development groups can learn the device usage rules for product requirements.

Third, HINGE automatically generates all of hardware/software interfaces for target devices. Automatic hardware/software interface generation can significantly reduce the burdens of embedded system development.

Finally, generated device APIs return negative values when embedded software violates the device usage rules. So, the device APIs generated by HINGE can help requirement-, function- or rule-level tests; software programmers can omit additional work just like rule-check function programming.

References

1. QuickDriver, http://www.etri.re.kr/www_05/search/view_03.php?fclass=01&idx=1247
2. Hanback Electronics CO.LTD, http://www.hanback.co.kr/
3. A. Rajawat, M.Balakrishnan, and A. Kumar, "Interface Synthesis : Issues and Approaches", *Proceedings of the 13th International Conference on VLSI Design*, pp.92–97, 2000.
4. WindRiver, http://www.windriver.com/
5. P. Chou, R. Ortega, and G. Borriello, "Interface co-synthesis techniques for embedded systems", *Proceedings of the IEEE/ACM International Conference on CAD (ICCAD)*, pp.280–287, 1995.
6. F. Balarin, A. Jurecska, and H. Hsieh et al, *Hardware-Software Co-Design of Embedded System: The Polis Approach*, Kluwer Academic Press, Boston, 1997.
7. T. B. Ismail, M. Abid and A. Jerraya, "COSMOS: A codesign approah for communicating systems", *Proceedings of the 3rd International workshop on Hardware/software Co-Design*, pp.17–24, Grenoble, France, 1994.
8. R. Ernst, J. Henkel, T. Benner, W. Ye, U. Holtmann, D. Hermann, and M. Trawny, "COSYMA environment for hardware/software cosynthesis of small embedded systems", *Microprocessors and Microsystems*, Vol.20, pp.159–166, 1996.
9. D. Verkest, K. Van Rompaey, and I. Boolsens, *Co-Ware - A Design Environment for Heterogeneous Hardware/Software Systems*, 1, Nov. 1996.

10. Arexsys. http://www.arexsys.org/
11. CoWare. http://www.coware.com/
12. A. Chou, J. Yang, B. Chelf, S. Hallem, and D. R. Engler, "An empirical study of operating system errors", *Proceedings of the 18th ACM Symposium on Operating Systems Principles*, volume 35 of *Operating System Review*, pp 73–88, Banff, Alberta, Canada, October 2001.
13. F. Hessel, P. Coste, P. Lemarrec, N. Zergainoh, J. M. Daveau, and A. A. Jerraya, "Communication and Interface Synthesis on a Rapid Prototyping Hardware/Software Codesign System", *IEEE International Workshop on Rapid System Prototyping*, 1998.
14. M. Eisenring and J. Teich, "Domain-Specific Interface Generation from Dataflow Specifications", *Proceedings of the 6th International Workshop on Hardware Software Codesign*, pp. 43–47, 1998.
15. L. Palopoli II, G. Lipari, L. Abeni, M. D. Natale, P. Ancilotti, and F. Conticelli, "A Tool for Simulation and Fast Prototyping of Embedded Control Systems", *Languages, Compilers, and Tools for Embedded Systems*, pp. 73–81, 2001.
16. F. Merillon, L. Reveillere, C. Consel, R. Marlet, and G. Muller, "Devil: An IDL for Hardware Programming", *Proceedings of the 4th USENIX Symposium on Operating System Design and Implementation*, pp. 17-30, San Diego, California, October 2000.
17. S. Wang and S. Malik, "Synthesizing Operating System Based Device Drivers in Embedded Systems", *Proceedings of the First International Conference on Hardware/Software Codesign and System Synthesis(CODES+ISSS)*, Newport Beach, CA, October 2003.
18. S. A. Edwards, "SHIM: A language for Hardware/Software Integration", *Synchronous Languages, Applications, and Programming*, 2005.
19. C. L. Conway, and S. A. Edwards, "NDL: A Domain-Specific Language for Device Drivers", *Languages, Compilers, and Tools for Embedded Systems*, pp. 30–36, Washington, DC, June 2004.

Fault-Tolerant VLIW Processor Design and Error Coverage Analysis

Yung-Yuan Chen, Kuen-Long Leu, and Chao-Sung Yeh

Department of Computer Science and Information Engineering
Chung-Hua University, Hsin-Chu, Taiwan
chenyy@chu.edu.tw

Abstract. In this paper, a general fault-tolerant framework adopting a more rigid fault model for VLIW data paths is proposed. The basic idea used to protect the data paths is that the execution result of each instruction is checked immediately and if errors are discovered, the instruction retry is performed at once to overcome the faults. An experimental architecture is developed and implemented in VHDL to analyze the impacts of our technique on hardware overhead and performance degradation. We also develop a comprehensive fault tolerance verification platform to facilitate the assessment of error coverage for the proposed mechanism. A paramount finding observed from the experiments is that our system is still extremely robust even in a very serious fault scenario. As a result, the proposed fault-tolerant VLIW core is quite suitable for the highly dependable real-time embedded applications.

1 Introduction

In recent years, VLIW processor has become a major architectural approach for high-performance embedded computing systems. Several notable examples of VLIW are Intel and HP IA-64 [1], TI TMS320C62x/67x DSP devices and Fujitsu FR500. As processor chips become more and more complicated, and contain a large number of transistors, the processors have a limited operational reliability due to the increased likelihood of faults or radiation-induced soft errors especially when the chip fabrication enters the deep submicron technology [2]. Also indicated specifically in [3], it is expected that the bit error rate in a processor will be about ten times higher than in a memory chip due to the higher complexity of the processor. And a processor may encounter a bit flip once every 10 hours. Thus, it is essential to employ the fault-tolerant techniques in the design of high-performance superscalar or VLIW processors to guarantee a high operational reliability in critical applications. Recently, the reliability issue in high-end processors is getting more and more attention [3-9].

The previous researches in reliable microprocessor design are mainly based on the concept of time redundancy approach [3-9] that uses the instruction replication and recomputation to detect the errors by comparing the results of regular and duplicate instructions. The instruction replication, recomputation schedule and result comparison of regular and duplicate instructions can be accomplished either in software level – source code compilation phase to generate redundant code for fault detection [4], [7], [8] or in hardware level [3], [5], [6], [9]. In [7], [8], the authors adopted software

E. Sha et al. (Eds.): EUC 2006, LNCS 4096, pp. 754–765, 2006.

techniques for detecting the errors in superscalar and VLIW processors respectively. The compiler-based software redundancy schemes have the advantage of no hardware modifications required, but the performance degradation and code growth increase significantly as pointed out in [3], [5]. The hardware redundancy approach requires extra hardware and architectural modification to manage the instruction replication, recomputation and comparison to detect the errors.

The deficiencies in previous studies are summarized as follows. First, most of the studies in the literature focus only on the aspect of error detection and neglect the issue of error recovery; thereby, those designs are incomplete so that we have difficulty in investigating the effectiveness of the error detection scheme without considering the error recovery jointly. Second, they lack the precise evaluation of the hardware overhead caused by the incorporation of fault tolerance; therefore, it is hard to justify the soundness of the approaches. Thirdly, the performance degradation due to the error detection and error recovery is significant during program execution. Moreover, the performance analysis only takes the performance degradation resulting from the fault detection into account. They are short of the analysis of error recovery time demanded to overcome the transient faults. The error recovery time mainly depends on the error-detection latency, which can be calculated from the time of regular instruction execution to the time of duplicate instruction recomputation. Owing to variable latency, the analysis of latency effect on performance is quite involved, and therefore, it complicates the analysis of the impact of error recovery on performance. Further, the latency may be unacceptably long. If an error cannot be detected in a short time, it will increase the error recovery time as well as program execution time. Such a lengthy recovery may be detrimental to the real-time applications. Last but not least, the previous studies rarely perform the quantitative evaluation of error coverage and the probability of common-mode failures [10] for the systems in various fault environments. Thus, it is hard to validate the fault tolerance ability of the schemes due to lack of the measures of error coverage.

This work is going to address the issues stated above. In Section 2, a fault-tolerant approach concentrating on the dependable data path design of VLIW processors is proposed. The approach proposed is quite comprehensive in that it comprises the error detection and error recovery. Hardware architecture and the measurements of hardware overhead and performance degradation are presented in Section 3. In Section 4, a thorough error coverage analysis is conducted to validate our scheme. The conclusions appear in Section 5.

2 Fault-Tolerant Data Path Design

Two types of faults described below are addressed in the error detection and error recovery: 1. Correlated transient faults [11] (e.g., a burst of electromagnetic radiation) which could cause multiple module failures. 2. Near-coincident faults [12] – recovery can be affected by this kind of faults. It is evident that the adopted fault model in this study is more rigid and complete compared to the single-fault assumption commonly applied before. Besides the concern of the fault model, an important goal for the design of error-recovery process is to simplify its complexity and meanwhile achieve the time efficiency to recover the errors. Overall, the design concern here is to propose a fault-tolerant VLIW core for the highly dependable real-time embedded applications. However, we note that due to the more rigid fault model and severe fault situations considered, it requires developing a more powerful fault-tolerant scheme to raise the system reliability to a sound level.

A VLIW processor core may possess several different types of functional modules in the data paths, such as integer ALU and load/store units. A couple of identical modules are provided for a specific functional type. We assume that the register file is protected by an error-correcting code. In the following, we present the main ideas employed in our scheme to detect and recover errors occurring in the data paths and then use three identical modules to demonstrate our fault-tolerant approach.

2.1 Concurrent Error Detection and Real-Time Error Recovery

We note that the length of error recovery time mainly depends on the error-detection latency. Hence, the error-detection scheme has a significant impact on the efficiency of the error recovery. Most of the previous studies may suffer the lengthy error recovery because the execution results of each instruction cannot be checked immediately. Therefore, to achieve the real-time error recovery, the execution results of each instruction must be examined immediately and if errors are found, the erroneous instruction is retried at once to overcome the errors. So, the error-detection problem can be formalized as how to verify the execution results instantly for each instruction, i.e. how to achieve no error-detection latency. We develop a simple concurrent error-detection (CED) scheme, which combines the duplication with comparison, henceforth referred to as comparison, and majority voting methodologies to solve the above error-detection problem.

CED Scheme. The following notations are developed

- n : Number of identical modules for a specific functional type (we call it type x). n is also the maximum number of instructions that can be executed concurrently in the modules of type x;
- s : Number of spare modules added to the type x, $s \geq 0$;
- m : Number of instructions in an execution packet for type x, $m \leq n$.

An execution packet is defined as the instructions in the same packet can be executed in parallel. There are $n+s$ modules for type x. As we know, if $m \times 2 > n+s$ then it is clear that the system won't have the enough resources to check the instructions of an execution packet concurrently. Under the circumstances, the current execution packet needs to be partitioned into several packets that will be executed sequentially. Given an execution packet, there are three cases to consider:

Case 1: $m \times 2 = n+s$. In this case, each instruction can be checked by the comparison scheme.

Case 2: $m \times 2 < n+s$. We can divide the instructions into two groups: G(1) and G(2). There are $m1$ instructions and $m2$ instructions in G(1) and G(2) respectively, where $m1+m2=m$, $m1, m2 \geq 0$. Each instruction in G(1) and G(2) can be examined by the

triple modular redundancy (TMR) scheme and duplication with comparison, henceforth referred to as comparison, scheme respectively. It is worth noting that to deal with the correlated transient faults, which may cause the multiple module failures, the TMR scheme is enhanced to have the ability to detect the multiple module errors. The following equations and criterion are used to decide $m1$ and $m2$. The equations are $m1\times3+m2\times2\leq n+s$; $m1+m2=m$; $m1,m2\geq0$. There may have several solutions derived from the equations. Since TMR can tolerate and locate one faulty module compared to the comparison, the criterion employed is to choose a solution which has the maximal value of m_1 among the feasible solutions. In other words, TMR has the benefit to avoid activating the procedure of error recovery while only one faulty module occurs. In contrast to TMR, comparison scheme needs to spend time for error recovery. The concern here is again the consideration of real-time applications.
Case 3: $m\times2>n+s$. Due to limited resources, m instructions cannot be all checked at the same cycle by TMR and/or comparison schemes. Therefore, we need to partition m instructions into several sequential execution packets such that the instructions in each packet can be examined concurrently. However, some extra cycles are required to guarantee that each instruction can be verified while it is executed. This implies that the performance of program execution will be degraded. The degree of performance degradation depends on the occurring frequency of the Case 3 during the program execution. The compromise between hardware overhead and performance degradation can be accomplished by choosing a proper s.

In general, the performance degradation for program execution in our dependable VLIW processor stems mainly from two sources: first is the extra cycles demanded for detecting the errors; second is the time for error recovery in order to overcome the effect of errors in the system. The error-recovery scheme is presented next.

Error-Recovery Scheme. Since each instruction is executed and verified at the same time, the instruction retry can be adopted to overcome the errors in an effective manner. When control unit of data paths receives the abnormal signals from the detection circuits, the procedure of error recovery will be activated immediately to recover the erroneous instructions. The following notations are used to explain the proposed error-recovery scheme:

- $m_x(i)$: The *ith* module of type x, where $1\leq i\leq n+s$;
- TMR($m_x(i)$, $m_x(j)$, $m_x(k)$): TMR using $m_x(i)$, $m_x(j)$, $m_x(k)$, where $i\neq j\neq k$. In the following, the term of TMR($m_x(i)$, $m_x(j)$, $m_x(k)$) is abbreviated to TMR_x(*i*, *j*, *k*);
- *r_no*: Number of retries permitted for an incorrect instruction, where $r\_no>0$.

During the error recovery, each erroneous instruction is retried individually with the TMR scheme. We allow performing *r_no* retries for an instruction to conquer the errors before declaring fail-safe. Since TMR scheme represented as TMR_x(*i*, *j*, *k*) is employed for the instruction retry, an issue arises as how to determine the (*i*, *j*, *k*) for each retry. As we know, there are $\binom{n+s}{3}$ combinations of (*i*, *j*, *k*). Let S_TMR be a set that contains $\binom{n+s}{3}$ combinations of TMR_x(*i*, *j*, *k*). Hence, S_TMR can be represented as {TMR_x(1, 2, 3), …, TMR_x(1, 2, $n+s$), …, TMR_x(1, $n+s-1$, $n+s$), TMR_x(2, 3, 4), …, TMR_x(2, $n+s-1$, $n+s$), …, TMR_x($n+s-2$, $n+s-1$, $n+s$)}, where $n+s \geq 3$. It is clear that selecting the TMR_x(1, 2, 3) constantly for each retry, for example, is the simplest approach, which has the advantage of simple implementation but can only tolerate one faulty module during the recovery process. In contrast to that, selecting elements one by one based on the element sequence in S_TMR for the retries is the highly complicated approach. Such an approach suffers from the high implementation cost, but on the other hand it can tolerate $n+s-2$ faulty modules if we set $r\_no \geq \binom{n+s}{3}$. The remaining question in the design of selection policy for TMR retry is how to compromise between the implementation complexity and the number of faulty modules being tolerated. A sound selection policy for TMR retry is presented next.

Selection Policy. On the basis of the above discussion, a set named SS_TMR, a subset of S_TMR, is created to guide the instruction-retry process. SS_TMR is given below: SS_TMR= {TMR_x(i, $i+1$, $i+2$), where $1 \leq i \leq n+s-2$ }. As seen from SS_TMR, the proposed retry process possesses a high regularity in its selection policy. So, it is easy to implement the SS_TMR policy compared to the S_TMR.

After the analyses for some values of n and s, we decide to adopt the SS_TMR selection policy due to the following reasons: first, we note that the probability of three or more modules failed concurrently should be low; second, most of the faults are transient type, which may disappear during the recovery process; and last one is the low implementation complexity compared to the S_TMR policy. From the first two reasons, we can infer that both selection policies have the similar fault tolerance capabilities. It is evident that the SS_TMR selection policy can utilize the module resources efficiently so as to recover the errors in a short time. Thus, the program execution can continue without lengthy error-recovery process. In summary, our error-recovery scheme can provide the capability of real-time error recovery, which is particularly important for the applications demanding the reliable computing as well as real-time concern.

2.2 Reliable Data Path Design: Case Study

In the following illustration, without loss of generality, we assume only one type of functional module, namely ALU, in the data paths. In this case study, the original VLIW core contains three ALUs ($n=3$) and therefore, three ALU instructions can be issued at most per cycle. A spare ALU ($s=1$) is added to prevent the severe performance degradation as explained below. From CED scheme described in Section 2.1, we note that if no spare is added then $m=2$ or 3 execution packets will fall into Case 3. Consequently, the performance may be degraded significantly. Hence, the cost of a spare is paid to lower the performance degradation. Clearly, adding three spares in order to eliminate the performance degradation completely is not a feasible choice.

According to CED scheme with $n=3$ and $s=1$, $m=1$ falls into Case 2. The ($m1,m2$) can be (1, 0) or (0, 1). Clearly, (1, 0) is selected as the final solution. So, if an execution packet contains only one ALU instruction then it will be checked by TMR scheme. For $m=2$, it is Case 1. Each instruction will be checked by comparison scheme. For $m=3$, it is Case 3. The three concurrent ALU instructions need to be scheduled to two sequential execution packets where one packet contains two instructions and the other holds the rest one; and therefore, one extra ALU cycle is required to complete the execution of three concurrent ALU instructions for error-detection purpose.

CED Process. Given $n=3$ and $s=1$, the notation CMP_ALU(*i*, *j*) is used to denote an instruction executed with the comparison scheme using the *ith* and *jth* ALUs.

```
while (not end of program)
  {switch (m)
    {case '1':
         TMR_ALU(1, 2, 3); if (TMR_ALU detects more than one
         ALU failure) then the "Error-recovery process" is
         activated to recover the failed instruction.
     case '2':
         the execution packet contains two instructions: I1
         and I2.
         I1: CMP_ALU(1, 2);   I2: CMP_ALU(3, 4);
         if (I1 fails) then the "Error-recovery process" is
         activated to recover I1.
         if (I2 fails) then the "Error-recovery process" is
         activated to recover I2.
     case '3':
         the packet is divided to two packets and executed
         sequentially.
     }}
```

Error-recovery process:

```
    i ← 1;
    While (r_no > 0)
     {TMR_ALU(i, i+1, i+2);
      if (TMR_ALU succeeds) then the error recovery succeeds
      → exit;
      else { r_no ← r_no − 1;  i ← i+1;  if (i ≥ 3) then
    i ← 1;}}
    recovery failure and the system enters the fail-safe
    state.
```

3 Hardware Implementation and Performance Evaluation

To validate the proposed approach, an experimental fault-tolerant VLIW architecture based on the scheme presented in Section 2.2 is developed. Figure 1 illustrates the architecture implementation, where $n=3$, and $s=1$ for ALUs. The features of this 32-bit VLIW processor are stated as follows: • the instruction set is composed of twenty-five 32-bit instructions; • each ALU includes a 32x32 multiplier. For simplicity of demonstration, the proposed approach does not apply to the load/store units; • a register file containing thirty-two 32-bit registers with 12 read and 6 write ports is shared with modules and designed to have bypass multiplexors that bypass written data to the read ports when a simultaneous read and write to the same entry is commanded; • data memory is 1K x 32 bits. The structure consists of five pipeline stages: 'instruction fetch and dispatch', 'decode and operand fetch from register file', 'execution', 'data memory reference' and 'write back into register file' stages. This experimental architecture can issue at most three ALU and three load/store instructions per cycle. Note that the 'Error Analysis' block in execution stage, which was created only to facilitate the measurement of the error coverage during the fault injection campaign, is not a component for the VLIW processor displayed in Figure 1.

A fault-tolerant VLIW processor based on the architecture of Figure 1 and the features mentioned previously was realized in VHDL. The implementation data by UMC 0.18μm process are shown in Table 1. The area does not include the instruction memory as well as the 'Error Analysis' block. For performance consideration, we require that the clock frequency of the fault-tolerant VLIW processor must retain the same as that of non fault-tolerant one. It is worth noting that the overhead of 'ALU_Control' unit is only 0.26 percent compared to the area of the non fault-tolerant VLIW core. This implies that the control task of our scheme is simple and easy to implement. The performance degradation caused from the CED demand is between 0.6% and 34.3% for eight benchmark programs, including heapsort, quicksort, FFT, 5×5 matrix multiplication and IDCT (8×8) etc..

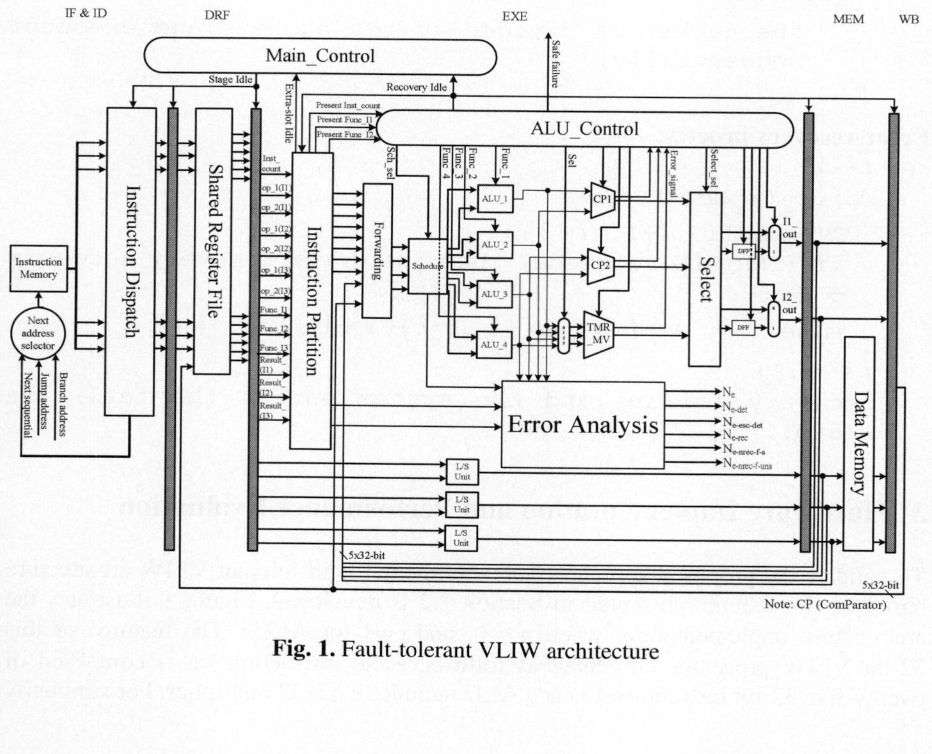

Fig. 1. Fault-tolerant VLIW architecture

Table 1. Comparing our approach with non fault-tolerant VLIW core

	Area (μm^2)	Overhead	ALU_Control(μm^2)	System clock (MHz)
Non fault-tolerant VLIW	9319666			128
Our approach	10708296	14.9%	24215	128

4 Error Coverage Analysis

In this section, the error coverage analysis based on the fault injection [13] is conducted to validate our scheme. A comprehensive fault tolerance verification platform comprising a simulated fault injection tool, ModelSim VHDL simulator and data analyzer has been built. It offers the capability to effectively handle the operations of fault injection, simulation and error coverage analysis. The core of the verification platform is the fault injection tool that can inject the transient and permanent faults into VHDL models of digital systems at chip, RTL and gate levels during the design phase. The tool adopts the built-in commands of VHDL simulators to inject the faults into VHDL simulation models. Injection tool can inject the following classes of faults: '0' and '1' stuck-at faults, 'Z': high-impedance and 'X': unknown faults. Weibull fault distribution is employed to decide the time instant of fault injection.

Our tool supports a fault injection analysis, which can provide us the useful statistics for each injection campaign. The statistical data for each injection campaign represents a fault scenario. We can exploit the injection tool to produce a variety of fault scenarios such that the fault-tolerant systems can be thoroughly validated. The injection tool can assist us in creating the proper fault environments that can be used to effectively validate the capability of a fault-tolerant system and examine the strength of a fault-tolerant system under various fault scenarios. Therefore, the proposed verification platform helps us raise the efficiency and validity of dependability analysis.

4.1 Fault-Tolerant Design Metrics

Figure 2 illustrates the error handling process in our fault-tolerant system. CED scheme uses the comparison and TMR to detect the errors. Hence, the following types of errors will escape being detected and such detection defects will result in the unsafe failures (or called common-mode failures [10]): one is the two ALUs produce the same, erroneous results to comparator; another is two or three of ALUs produce the identical, erroneous results to TMR. Once errors are detected and need to be recovered, the error-recovery process is activated. Three possible outcomes could happen for each instruction retry using TMR scheme. One possibility is that the recovery is successful; another is retry fails and the system enters the fail-safe state; the last possibility is two or three of ALUs produce the identical, erroneous results to TMR such that the system encounters the fail-unsafe hazard. From Figure 2, if errors happen, the system could enter one of the following states: 'successful recovery and restore the normal operation', 'fail-safe' and 'fail-unsafe' states.

The design metrics as described below are exploited to justify our approach:

- $Pf-uns$: Probability of system entering the fail-unsafe state;
- $Ce-\det$: Error-detection coverage, i.e. probability of errors detected;
- $Ce-rec$: Error-recovery coverage, i.e. probability of errors recovered given errors detected;
- Ce : Error coverage, i.e. probability of errors detected and recovered;
- $Pf-s$: Probability of system entering the fail- safe state;
- $Pt-\det-f-s$: State transition probability from 'detected' state to 'fail-safe' state.
- $Pt-\det-f-uns$: State transition probability from 'detected' state to 'fail-unsafe' state.
- $Pf-uns-\det$: Probability of system entering the fail-unsafe state due to the detection defects stated earlier;
- $Pf-uns-rec$: Probability of system entering the fail-unsafe state due to the recovery defects stated earlier;

The parameters Ne , $Ne-\det$, $Ne-esc-\det$, $Ne-rec$, $Ne-nrec-f-s$ and $Ne-nrec-f-uns$ (called the error-related parameters) represent the total number of errors occurred, the number of errors detected, the number of errors escape being detected, the number of errors recovered, the number of errors not recovered and system enters the 'fail-safe' state and the number of errors not recovered and system enters the 'fail-unsafe' state, respectively. The design metrics can be expressed as follows

$$Pf-uns-\det=\frac{Ne-esc-\det}{Ne};Ce-\det=\frac{Ne-\det}{Ne}=1-Pf-uns-\det;Ce-rec=\frac{Ne-rec}{Ne-\det}. \quad (1)$$

$$Pt-\det-f-s=\frac{Ne-nrec-f-s}{Ne-\det};Pt-\det-f-uns=\frac{Ne-nrec-f-uns}{Ne-\det}; \quad (2)$$
$$Pf-uns-rec=Ce-\det\times Pt-\det-f-uns.$$

$$Pf-s=Ce-\det\times Pt-\det-f-s;Pf-uns=Pf-uns-\det+Pf-uns-rec;$$
$$Ce=Ce-\det\times Ce-rec;Ne=Ne-\det+Ne-esc-\det; \quad (3)$$
$$Ne-\det=Ne-rec+Ne-nrec-f-s+Ne-nrec-f-uns.$$

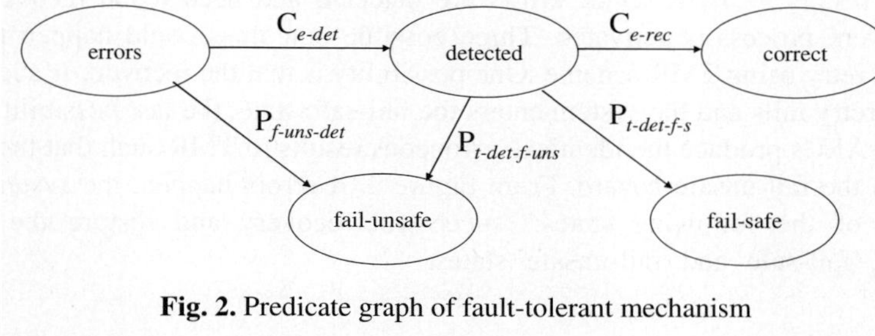

Fig. 2. Predicate graph of fault-tolerant mechanism

4.2 Simulation Results and Discussion

We have conducted a huge amount of fault injection campaigns to validate the proposed fault-tolerant VLIW scheme under various fault situations. We performed a comprehensive experiment to explore a particular fault-related parameter, namely fault-occurring frequency, to see its impact on the fault-tolerant metrics. By adjusting the fault-occurring frequency, we can create a variety of fault scenarios, which can be used to measure how robust can our fault-tolerant system reach under the different fault environments? The common rules of fault injection campaigns are: 1) value of a fault is selected randomly from the s-a-1 and s-a-0; 2) injection targets cover the entire 'EXE' stage as shown in Figure 1. The common data of fault injection parameters are: $\alpha=1$ (useful-life), failure rate (λ) = 0.001, probability of permanent fault occurrence = 0, fault duration = 5 clock cycles. In addition, the number of retries *r_no* is set to four. Next, we discuss the outcomes obtained from the experiments.

Fault-Occurring Frequency. The goal of this experiment is to observe the effect of the fault-occurring frequency on the design metrics depicted in Section 4.1. In this experiment, we copy each of the following benchmark programs: '*N! (N=10)*', '*5×5 matrix multiplication*', '$2\sum_{i=1}^{5} A_i \times B_i$', four times and then the twelve programs are combined in random sequence to form a workload for the fault simulation. The length of workload is equal to 4384 (clocks) ×30 (ns/clock).

Note that if workload and fault duration are constant, the quantity of faults injected, i.e. fault-occurring frequency, will influence the degree of fault overlap. For instance, while the quantity of faults injected increases, the degree of fault overlap will become more serious. In other words, the various fault-occurring frequencies will lead to the different fault environments. Hence, in order to investigate the effect of the fault-occurring frequency on error coverage, we conduct five fault injection campaigns with various numbers of faults injected. The statistical analysis of an injection campaign is able to disclose the fault activity within the simulation. Clearly, the larger the number of faults injected (i.e. higher fault-occurring frequency), the worse of fault environment will be due to a higher occurring frequency of multiple faults including correlated, mutually independent and near-coincident transient faults. Therefore, the statistical analysis helps designers choose a set of desired fault scenarios to test the ability of fault-tolerant systems. As a result, the proposed fault-tolerant verification platform can furnish more comprehensive and solid error coverage measurements.

Figure 3 characterizes the effect of fault-occurring frequency on the fault-tolerant design metrics. The experimental results obtained have 95% confidence interval of ±0.138% to ±0.983%. The outcomes shown in Figure 3 reveal the fault tolerance capability of our scheme in the various fault environments. It is evident that the error coverage decreases with the increase of fault-occurring frequency. Meanwhile, the system has a higher chance to enter the fail-safe and fail-unsafe states when the probability of occurrence of multiple faults rises. The safe failure occurs once the error-recovery process cannot overcome the errors due to a serious fault situation. Overall, the results presented in Figure 3 are quite positive and sound those declare the effectiveness of our fault-tolerant scheme even in a very bad fault environment.

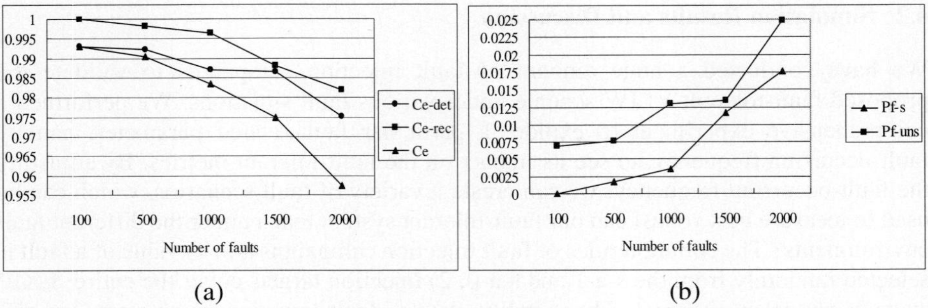

Fig. 3. Fault-tolerant metric analysis. (a) coverage. (b) probabilities of fail-safe and fail-unsafe.

5 Conclusions

This paper presents a new fault-tolerant framework for VLIW processors that focuses mainly on the reliable data path design. Based on a more rigid fault model, a CED and real-time error recovery scheme is proposed to enhance the reliability of the data paths. Our approach provides the design compromise between hardware overhead, performance degradation and fault tolerance capability. This framework is quite useful in that it can give the designers an opportunity to choose an appropriate solution to meet their need. Several significant contributions of this study are: 1. Integrate the error detection and error recovery into VLIW cores with reasonable hardware overhead and performance degradation. It is worth noting that the proposed fault-tolerant framework can achieve no error-detection latency and real-time error recovery. Consequently, our scheme is suitable for the real-time computing applications that demand the stringent dependability. 2. Conduct a thorough fault injection campaigns to assess the fault-tolerant design metrics under a variety of fault environments. Importantly, we provide not only the error-detection and error-recovery coverage, but also the fail-safe and fail-unsafe probabilities. Acquiring the fail-unsafe probability is crucial for us to understand how much possibility the system could fail without notice once the errors occur. Moreover, a couple of fault environments, which represent the various degrees of fault's severity, were constructed to validate our scheme so as to realize the capability of our scheme in different fault scenarios. So, such experiments can give us more realistic and comprehensive simulation results. The effectiveness of our mechanism even in a very severe fault environment is justified from the experimental results.

Acknowledgments. The authors acknowledge the support of the National Science Council, Republic of China, under Contract No. NSC 92-2213-E-216-005 and NSC 93-2213-E-216-019.

References

1. Huck, J. et al.: Introducing the IA-64 Architecture. *IEEE Micro*, Vol. 20, issue: 5, pp. 12-23, Sep.-Oct. 2000.
2. Karnik, T., Hazucha, P., Patel, J.: Characterization of Soft Errors Caused by Single Event Upsets in CMOS Processes. *IEEE Trans. on Dependable and Secure Computing*, Vol. 1, issue: 2, pp. 128-143, April-June 2004.

3. Nickle, J. B., Somani, A. K.: REESE: A Method of Soft Error Detection in Microprocessors. *DSN'01*, pp. 401-410, 2001.
4. Holm, J. G., Banerjee, P.: Low Cost Concurrent Error Detection in A VLIW Architecture Using Replicated Instructions. *Intl. Conf. on Parallel Processing*, pp. 192-195, 1992.
5. Franklin, M.: A Study of Time Redundant Fault Tolerance Techniques for Superscalar Processors. *IEEE Intl. Workshop on Defect and Fault Tolerance in VLSI Systems (DFT'95)*, pp. 207-215, 1995.
6. Kim, S., Somani, A. K.: SSD: An Affordable Fault Tolerant Architecture for Superscalar Processors. *Pacific Rim Intl. Symposium. On Dependable Computing*, pp. 27-34, 2001.
7. Oh, N., Shirvani, P. P., McCluskey, E. J.: Error Detection by Duplicated Instructions in Super-Scalar Processors. *IEEE Trans. on Reliability*, Vol. 51, (1), pp. 63-75, March 2002.
8. Bolchini, C.: A Software Methodology for Detecting Hardware Faults in VLIW Data Paths. *IEEE Trans. on Reliability*, Vol. 52, (4), pp. 458-468, December 2003.
9. Qureshi, M. K., Mutlu, O., Patt, Y. N.: Microarchitecture-Based Introspection: A Technique for Transient-Fault Tolerance in Microprocessors. *DSN'05*, pp. 434 – 443, June-July 2005.
10. Mitra, S., Saxena, N. R., McCluskey, E. J.: Common-Mode Failures in Redundant VLSI Systems: A Survey. *IEEE Trans. on Reliability,* Vol. 49, (3), pp. 285 – 295, Sept. 2000.
11. Avizienis, A., Laprie, J.-C., Randell, B., Landwehr, C.: Basic Concepts and Taxonomy of Dependable and Secure Computing. *IEEE Trans. on Dependable and Secure Computing*, Vol. 1, issue: 1, pp. 11-33, Jan.-March 2004.
12. Dugan, J. B., Trivedi, K. S.: Coverage Modeling for Dependability Analysis of Fault-Tolerant Systems. *IEEE Trans. on Computers*, Vol. 38, (6), pp. 775-787, June 1989.
13. Clark, J., Pradhan, D.: Fault Injection: A Method for Validating Computer-System Dependability. *IEEE Computer*, 28(6), pp. 47-56, June 1995.

Interconnect Estimation for Mesh-Based Reconfigurable Computing

Haibin Shen, Rongquan You, Yier Jin, and Aiming Ji

Institute of VLSI Design, Zhejiang University,
Hangzhou, P.R. China
{shb, yourq, jinye, jiam}@vlsi.zju.edu.cn

Abstract. The paper presents a new stochastic model for mesh-based reconfigurable computing. Under the conditions of several statistical assumptions, closed formulae of probability and mathematical expectation are derived for each type of connections. Both the theoretical deduction and simulation results are given to verify our approach. The elementary research can be applied to implement and optimize the interconnect resource of mesh-based reconfigurable computing.

Keywords: Interconnect, reconfigurable computing, mesh-based, probability.

1 Introduction

Reconfigurable computing is emerging as the new paradigm for satisfying the simultaneous demand for application performance and flexibility [8]. Thus, Many applications have been mapped onto reconfigurable architectures [2,9,10,11,12]. These applications include object recognition, image filtering, fingerprint matching, image compression, and stereo vision, and many applications have been demonstrated to have superior performance on reconfigurable architectures compared to other existing architectures [8].

A very attractive interconnection scheme is the mesh-connected computer because of its simplicity, regularity, and the fact that the interconnections occupy only a fixed fraction of the area no matter how large the chip [3,6]. Mesh-based reconfigurable computing (MBRC) is realized by a processing element (PE) array, and the design of PE includes operators and interconnections. Although rich interconnect resource can provide high flexible interconnect ability, it increases the area and power of the array. Formerly, the interconnect space exploration of reconfigurable computing is mostly accomplished by analyzing and comparing, which is not precise enough [6]. In related research, a typical estimation for the interconnections in gate arrays has been presented in [5], and following research has worked out more precise results, which can estimate the channel width, the routablity and the wire length [3, 7, 14]. Because the interconnections of MBRC are different from those of gate array, the models for the latter one are not suitable for the former one. In this paper, elementary research on interconnect estimation of MBRC is presented.

E. Sha et al. (Eds.): EUC 2006, LNCS 4096, pp. 766–775, 2006.

The organization of this paper is as follows. In Section 2, we define the interconnect resource. Section 3 provides an overview of the stochastic model and proposes the main statistical assumptions. The task of estimating the probabilities of interconnections and their mathematical expectations is the subject of Section 4. The comparison of theoretical estimation and simulation results is given in Section 5. Section 6 serves as the conclusion.

2 Interconnect Resource

The interconnect resource of mesh-based reconfigurable computing belongs to PEs, and many PEs constitute a PE array as Fig. 1.

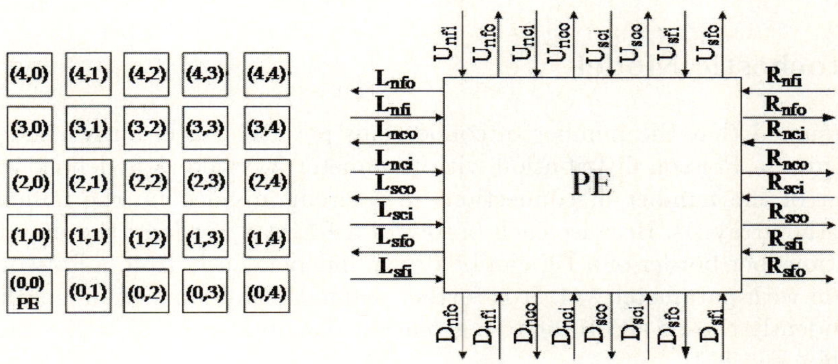

Fig. 1. Interconnect model of reconfigurable processing element array

In Fig. 1, the interconnect resource of a PE includes four borders of it, which are denoted as U, D, L and R, and the types of connections are classified as follows:

(1) Connections among PEs. "*i*" , "*o*", "*n*" and "*s*" denote "input", "output", "nearest neighbour" and "hop neighbour" respectively, in which "nearest neighbour" means the connection can only be connected to the nearest PE with the length of 1 unit (e.g. the connection length between PE(0, 0) and PE(0, 1) is 1 unit), and "hop neighbour" means the connection can only be connected to the PE which is at the same row or column with the length of w units.

(2) Connections in PEs. "f" and "c" denote "function connections" and "channel connections", in which the former ones mean the connections are connected

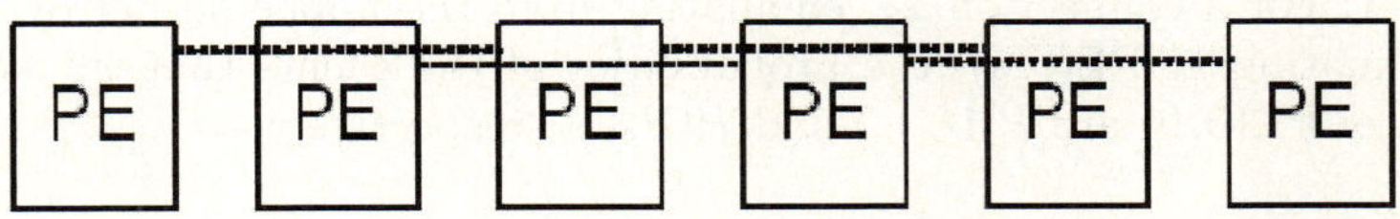

Fig. 2. Hop neighbour connections with $w = 2$

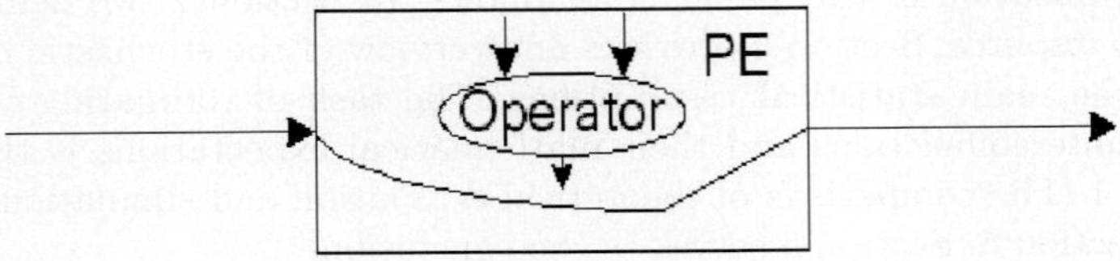

Fig. 3. Function connections and channel connections in a PE

to the operators in PEs, serving as the inputs or outputs of the operators, and the latter ones mean the connections are not connected to the operators, but traverse from one border to another of a PE. Function connections and channel connections are implemented by using multiplexors in PEs.

3 Stochastic Model

It is assumed that the number of connections per PE can be drawn independently from a Poisson distribution with parameter λ, where λ is defined as the quotient of the number of connections in a circuit divided by the number of PEs in the array [1]. Because each border of a PE is equivalent, the number of connections per border of a PE can be drawn independently from a Poisson distribution with parameter $\lambda/4$. It is further assumed that connection length L is independently chosen according to a geometric distribution $G(L) = (1-\varepsilon)\varepsilon^{L-1}$, where $0 < \varepsilon < 1$ [1].

Different from other networks, the connections of PEs are directional. Assume x_1 is a connection starting from PE(a, b) and ending at PE(u, v), our stochastic model always chooses the path with the minimal Manhattan distance $L = |u - a| + |v - b|$, and chooses hop neighbour connection if possible. Thus, there are $C_L^{|u-a|} (= C_L^{|v-b|})$ possible paths from PE(a, b) to PE(u, v). When PE(u, v) is at the same row or column with PE(a, b), x_1 can only choose one border of PE(u, v), otherwise x_1 can choose two borders of it. On the other hand, a connection x_2 drawn from PE(a, b) with length L, can end at $4L$ possible PEs. Therefore, x_2 can end at $(8L - 4)$ possible borders in the PE array. Assume that x_2 chooses one border out of the $(8L - 4)$ possible borders with the same probability, the probability of choosing each border is $q(L) = \frac{1}{8L-4}$.

4 Probabilities of Connections

Lemma 1. For a connection x_3, emanating from the upper border of PE$(0, 0)$ and terminating at PE(r, s), the probabilities of the events that x_3 uses U_{nfo} and U_{sfo} of PE$(0, 0)$ are $P(U_{nfo})$ and $P(U_{sfo})$, respectively:

$$P(U_{nfo}) = \sum_{L=1}^{\infty} G(L) \frac{\sum_{s=-L+1}^{L-1} C_{L-1}^{|s|}}{\sum_{s=-L+1}^{L-1} C_{L-1}^{|s|} + \sum_{s=-L+w}^{L-w} C_{L-w}^{|s|}} \quad (1)$$

$$P(U_{sfo}) = \sum_{L=1}^{\infty} G(L) \frac{\sum_{s=-L+w}^{L-w} C_{L-w}^{|s|}}{\sum_{s=-L+1}^{L-1} C_{L-1}^{|s|} + \sum_{s=-L+w}^{L-w} C_{L-w}^{|s|}} \qquad (2)$$

where, $L = |r| + |s|$, the length of hop neighbour connection $w > 1$, and $C_0^0 = 1$. When $L < w$, $C_{L-w}^{|s|} = 0$

Proof. As Fig. 1, if x_3 uses U_{nfo} of PE(0, 0), it will pass through PE(1, 0), and there are $C_{L-1}^{|s|}$ possible paths from PE(1, 0) to PE(r, s). Because our stochastic model always chooses the path with the minimal Manhattan distance, PE(r, s) should be above the dash in Fig. 4. Thus, there are $\sum_{s=-L+1}^{L-1} C_{L-1}^{|s|}$ possible paths for x_3 with length L. Similarly, if x_3 uses U_{sfo} of PE(0, 0), it will pass through PE(w, 0), and then PE(r, s) should be above the dashdot in Fig. 4. Thereby, there are $C_{L-w}^{|s|}$ possible paths from PE(r, s) to PE(w, 0), and there are $\sum_{s=-L+w}^{L-w} C_{L-w}^{|s|}$ possible paths for x_3 with length L.

Among the connections starting from the upper border of PE(0, 0) with length L, the proportion of using U_{nfo} is $\frac{\sum_{s=-L+1}^{L-1} C_{L-1}^{|s|}}{\sum_{s=-L+1}^{L-1} C_{L-1}^{|s|} + \sum_{s=-L+w}^{L-w} C_{L-w}^{|s|}}$. Furthermore, according to the assumption that connection length L is independently chosen from a geometric distribution $G(L)$ in Section 3, we have Equation (1). For the same reason, we have Equation (2).

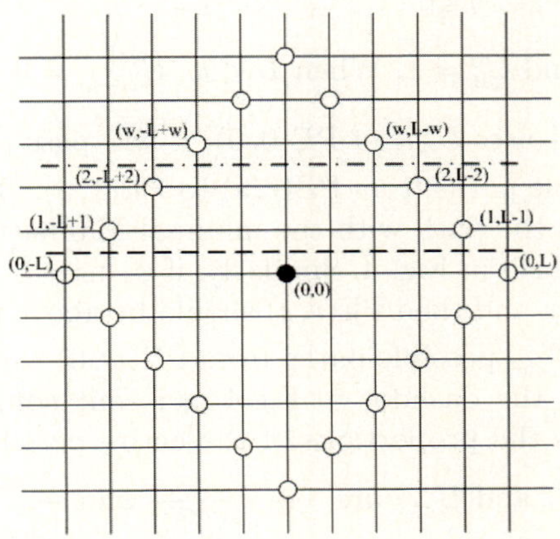

Fig. 4. All the $4L$ endpoints of the connections emanating from or terminating at PE(0, 0) with the length of $L = 5$ and the length of hop neighbour connection $w = 3$

Lemma 2. Let $X(U_{nfo})$ and $X(U_{sfo})$ be the number of connections emanating from U_{nfo} and U_{sfo} of PE(0, 0). Then, $X(U_{nfo})$ and $X(U_{sfo})$ are independent and Poisson distributed with parameters $P(U_{nfo})\lambda/4$ and $P(U_{sfo})\lambda/4$, respectively.

Proof. $G(L)\frac{\sum_{s=-L+1}^{L-1} C_{L-1}^{|s|}}{\sum_{s=-L+1}^{L-1} C_{L-1}^{|s|}+\sum_{s=-L+w}^{L-w} C_{L-w}^{|s|}} < G(L) < \varepsilon^{L-1}$.When $|\varepsilon| < 1$, geometric progression $\sum_{L=1}^{\infty} \varepsilon^{L-1}$ is convergent, so according to comparison principle, progression $\sum_{L=1}^{\infty} G(L)\frac{\sum_{s=-L+1}^{L-1} C_{L-1}^{|s|}}{\sum_{s=-L+1}^{L-1} C_{L-1}^{|s|}+\sum_{s=-L+w}^{L-w} C_{L-w}^{|s|}}$ is convergent too, which means that $P(U_{nfo})$ is a constant. It is known that the product of a constant and a random variable which is Poisson distributed is also Poisson distributed. Since the number of connections emanating from the upper border of PE(0, 0), $X(U)$ is independent and Poisson distributed with parameter $\lambda/4$, $X(U_{nfo}) = P(U_{nfo})X(U)$ is Poisson distributed with parameter $P(U_{nfo})\lambda/4$. For the same reason, $X(U_{sfo})$ is Poisson distributed with parameter $P(U_{sfo})\lambda/4$.

Lemma 3. For a connection x_4, terminating at the upper border of PE(0, 0) and emanating from PE(r, s), the probabilities of the events that x_4 uses U_{nfi} and U_{sfi} of PE(0, 0) are $P(U_{nfi})$ and $P(U_{sfi})$, respectively. Let $X(U_{nfi})$ and $X(U_{sfi})$ be the number of connections terminating at U_{nfi} and U_{sfi} of PE(0, 0). Then, $X(U_{nfi})$ and $X(U_{sfi})$ are independent and Poisson distributed with parameters $P(U_{nfi})\lambda$ and $P(U_{sfi})\lambda$, respectively, where

$$P(U_{nfi}) = \sum_{L=1}^{\infty} G(L)q(L) \sum_{s=-L+1}^{L-1} \frac{C_{L-1}^{|s|}}{C_{L-1}^{|s|} + C_{L-w}^{|s|}} \tag{3}$$

$$P(U_{sfi}) = \sum_{L=1}^{\infty} G(L)q(L) \sum_{s=-L+1}^{L-1} \frac{C_{L-w}^{|s|}}{C_{L-1}^{|s|} + C_{L-w}^{|s|}} \tag{4}$$

where $L = |r| + |s|$, and $C_0^0 = 1$. When $L < w$, $C_{L-w}^{|s|} = 0$.

Proof. As Fig. 1, if x_4 uses U_{nfi} of PE(0, 0), it will pass through PE(1, 0), and there are $C_{L-1}^{|s|}$ possible paths from PE(r, s) to PE(1, 0). Because our stochastic model always chooses the path with the minimal Manhattan distance, PE(r, s) should be above the dash in Fig. 4. Similarly, if x_4 uses U_{sfo} of PE(0, 0), it will pass through PE$(w, 0)$, and then PE(r, s) should be above the dashdot in Fig. 4. Thereby, there are $C_{L-w}^{|s|}$ possible paths from PE$(w, 0)$ to PE(r, s).

All the PEs above the dashdot in Fig.4 can emit connections to U_{nfi} and U_{sfi} of PE(0, 0), thus the proportions of the entire possible paths with length L terminating at U_{nfi} and U_{sfi} are $\frac{C_{L-1}^{|s|}}{C_{L-1}^{|s|}+C_{L-w}^{|s|}}$ and $\frac{C_{L-w}^{|s|}}{C_{L-1}^{|s|}+C_{L-w}^{|s|}}$, respectively. Besides, all the PEs between the dash and dashdot in Fig. 4 can only emit connections to U_{nfi} of PE(0, 0), and the number of such PEs is $2(w - 1)$.

Based on the assumptions that connection length L is independently chosen from a geometric distribution $G(L)$ and the probability of choosing one border of the endpoints is $q(L)$ in Section 3, we have Equation (3). As Lemma 2, $G(L)q(L)\sum_{s=-L+1}^{L-1} \frac{C_{L-1}^{|s|}}{C_{L-1}^{|s|}+C_{L-w}^{|s|}} < G(L)\frac{1}{8L-4}(2L-1) < \frac{1}{4}\varepsilon^{L-1}$, so $P(U_{nfi})$ is a constant. According to another assumption that the number of connections per PE can be drawn independently from a Poisson distribution with parameter λ in Section 3, $X(U_{nfi})$ is Poisson distributed with parameter $P(U_{nfi})\lambda$. For the same reason, we have Equation (4) and $X(U_{sfi})$ is Poisson distributed with parameter $P(U_{sfi})\lambda$.

Lemma 4. For a connection x_5, emanating from PE(r,s) and terminating at PE$(-t+|h|,-h)$, where $t>0$, $h=-t,-t+1,\cdots,t-1,t$ and $hs\geq 0$, the probabilities of the events that x_5 uses U_{nci} and U_{sci} of PE$(0,0)$ are $P(U_{nci})$ and $P(U_{sci})$, respectively:

$$P(U_{nci})=\sum_{L=2}^{\infty}G(L)\sum_{t=1}^{L-1}\sum_{s=-(L-t-1)}^{L-t-1}\sum_{h=-t}^{t}\frac{C_{L-t-1}^{|s|}C_t^{|h|}}{C_L^{|s|+|h|}}q'(L,s,h,t) \quad (5)$$

$$P(U_{sci})=\sum_{L=w+1}^{\infty}G(L)\sum_{t=1}^{L-w}\sum_{s=-(L-t-w)}^{L-t-w}\sum_{h=-t}^{t}\frac{C_{L-t-w}^{|s|}C_t^{|h|}}{C_L^{|s|+|h|}}q'(L,s,h,t) \quad (6)$$

where, $L=|r|+|s|+t$, $C_0^0=1$ and

$$q'(L,s,h,t)=\begin{cases}0,\ hs<0\\ q(L),\ hs\geq 0 \text{ and } (h=0 \text{ or } h=\pm t)\\ 2q(L),\ \text{others}\end{cases}$$

Proof. If x_5 uses U_{nci} of PE$(0,0)$, it will pass through PE$(1,0)$. For each t, x_5 is divided into three segments: the first is from PE(r,s) to PE$(1,0)$ with length $L-t-1$, the second is from PE$(1,0)$ to PE$(0,0)$ with length 1, and the third is from PE$(0,0)$ to PE$(-t+|h|,-h)$ with length t. Thus, there is $C_{L-t-1}^{|s|}C_t^{|h|}$ possible paths form PE(r,s) to PE$(-t+|h|,-h)$ if x_5 uses U_{nci} of PE$(0,0)$. Since there are $C_L^{|s|+|h|}$ possible paths from PE(r,s) to PE$(-t+|h|,-h)$, taking into account the assumption that the probability of choosing one border of the endpoints is $q(L)$, the probability of using U_{nci} is $\frac{C_{L-t-1}^{|s|}C_t^{|h|}}{C_L^{|s|+|h|}}q(L)$.

As Fig. 5, when the length of x_5 is L, there are $2(L-t-1)+1$ starting points and $2t+1$ endpoints for each t. Not each of the starting points and endpoints can constitute a point-pair which denotes a possible path of x_5 because they have to satisfy that $hs\geq 0$. In addition, when $h=0$ or $h=\pm t$, x_5 can only terminate at one border of the endpoint, otherwise x_5 can end at two borders of it. Calculating the sum of the probabilities for all point-pairs, we have the probability of using U_{nci} with length L is $\sum_{t=1}^{L-1}\sum_{s=-(L-t-1)}^{L-t-1}\sum_{h=-t}^{t}\frac{C_{L-t-1}^{|s|}C_t^{|h|}}{C_L^{|s|+|h|}}q'(L,s,h,t)$. With the assumption that connection length L is independently chosen from a geometric distribution $G(L)$, we have Equation (5). Because

$$\begin{aligned}G(L)\sum_{t=1}^{L-1}\sum_{s=-(L-t-1)}^{L-t-1}\sum_{h=-t}^{t}\frac{C_{L-t-1}^{|s|}C_t^{|h|}}{C_L^{|s|+|h|}}q'(L,s,h,t)&<G(L)\sum_{t=1}^{L-1}\sum_{s=-(L-t-1)}^{L-t-1}\sum_{h=-t}^{t}1\cdot 2q(L)\\ &=G(L)\sum_{t=1}^{L-1}\frac{1}{4L-2}[2(L-t)-1](2t+1)<G(L)\sum_{t=1}^{L-1}\frac{1}{4L-2}\cdot 2L\cdot 3t\\ &=(1-\varepsilon)\varepsilon^{L-1}\frac{3L}{2L-1}\frac{L(L-1)}{2}<\varepsilon^{L-1}\frac{3L}{L}\frac{L^2}{2}=\frac{3}{2}\varepsilon^{L-1}L^2=u(L)\end{aligned}$$

and $\lim_{L\to\infty}\frac{u(L+1)}{u(L)} = \lim_{L\to\infty}\varepsilon(1+\frac{1}{L})^2 = \varepsilon < 1$, according to D Alembert discriminance, progression $\sum_{L=1}^{\infty}u(L)$ is convergent. Thereupon, according to comparison principle, progression

$$\sum_{L=2}^{\infty}G(L)\sum_{t=1}^{L-1}\sum_{s=-(L-t-1)}^{L-t-1}\sum_{h=-t}^{t}\frac{C_{L-t-1}^{|s|}C_t^{|h|}}{C_L^{|s|+|h|}}q'(L,s,h,t)$$

is convergent too, which means that $P(U_{nci})$ is a constant.

For the same reason, if x_5 uses U_{sci} of PE(0,0), it will pass through PE$(w,0)$. Then, we have Equation (6) and $P(U_{sci})$ is a constant too.

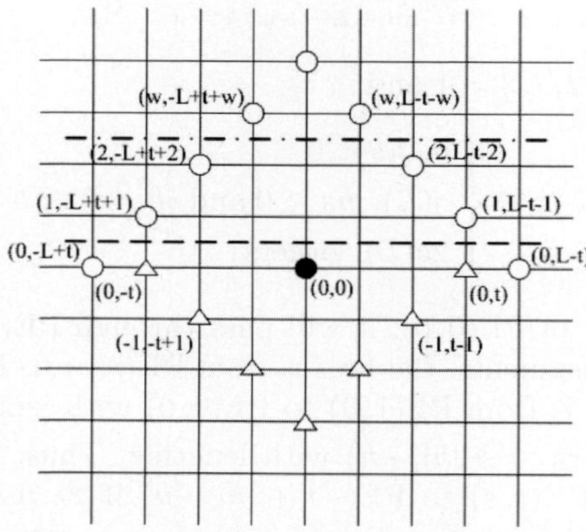

Fig. 5. All the starting points (denoted as circles) and endpoints (denoted as triangles) of the connections traversing PE(0,0) with $L = 7$, $w = 3$, and $t = 3$

Lemma 5. For a connection x_6, emanating from PE(r,s) and terminating at PE$(t-|h|,-h)$, where $t > 0$, $h = -t, -t+1, \cdots, t-1, t$ and $hs \geq 0$, the probabilities of the events that x_6 uses U_{nco} and U_{sco} of PE(0,0) are $P(U_{nco})$ and $P(U_{sco})$, respectively:

$$P(U_{nco}) = \sum_{L=2}^{\infty}G(L)\sum_{t=1}^{L-1}\sum_{s=-(L-t)}^{L-t}\sum_{h=-(t-1)}^{t-1}\frac{C_{L-t}^{|s|}C_{t-1}^{|h|}}{C_L^{|s|+|h|}}q''(L,s,h,t), \quad (7)$$

$$P(U_{sco}) = \sum_{L=w+1}^{\infty}G(L)\sum_{t=w}^{L-1}\sum_{s=-(L-t)}^{L-t}\sum_{h=-(t-w)}^{t-w}\frac{C_{L-t}^{|s|}C_{t-w}^{|h|}}{C_L^{|s|+|h|}}q'''(L,s,h,t), \quad (8)$$

where $L = |r| + |s| + t$,

$$q''(L,s,h,t) = \begin{cases} 0, & hs < 0 \\ q(L), & hs \geq 0 \text{ and } (h = 0 \text{ or } h = \pm(t-1)) \\ 2q(L), & \text{others} \end{cases}$$

and

$$q'''(L,s,h,t) = \begin{cases} 0, & hs < 0 \\ q(L), & hs \geq 0 \text{ and } (h = 0 \text{ or } h = \pm(t-w)) \\ 2q(L), & \text{others} \end{cases}$$

Proof. As Lemma 4.

Lemma 6. Let $X(U_{nci})$, $X(U_{sci})$, $X(U_{nco})$ and $X(U_{sco})$ be the number of connections traversing U_{nci}, U_{sci}, U_{nco} and U_{sco} of PE(0,0), respectively. Their mathematical expectations are:

$$E[X(U_{nci})] = \frac{P(U_{nci})}{P(U_{nci}) + P(U_{sci})} E[X(U_{ci})]$$

$$E[X(U_{sci})] = \frac{P(U_{sci})}{P(U_{nci}) + P(U_{sci})} E[X(U_{ci})]$$

$$E[X(U_{nco})] = \frac{P(U_{nco})}{P(U_{nco}) + P(U_{sco})} E[X(U_{co})]$$

$$E[X(U_{sco})] = \frac{P(U_{sco})}{P(U_{nco}) + P(U_{sco})} E[X(U_{co})],$$

where $X(U_{ci}) = X(U_{nci}) + X(U_{sci})$, $X(U_{co}) = X(U_{nco}) + X(U_{sco})$ and $E[X(U_{ci})] = E[X(U_{co})] = \frac{\lambda}{4}\frac{\varepsilon}{1-\varepsilon}$.

Proof. The number of PEs that a connection traverses with length L is $X(L) = L-1$. With the assumption that connection length L is independently chosen from a geometric distribution $G(L) = (1-\varepsilon)\varepsilon^{L-1}$, the mathematical expectation of $X(L)$ is $E[X(L)] = \sum_{L=1}^{\infty} G(L)(L-1) = \frac{\varepsilon}{1-\varepsilon}$. Let n and m be the number of connections in a circuit and the number of PEs in the array, respectively. Thus, the mathematical expectation of the number of connections traversing per PE is $\frac{n}{m}\frac{\varepsilon}{1-\varepsilon} = \lambda\frac{\varepsilon}{1-\varepsilon}$. Since four borders of a PE are chosen with the same probability, we have $E[X(U_{ci})] = E[X(U_{co})] = \frac{\lambda}{4}\frac{\varepsilon}{1-\varepsilon}$.

From Lemma 4, the probabilities of the events that x_5 uses U_{nci} and U_{sci} of PE(0,0) are $P(U_{nci})$ and $P(U_{sci})$, respectively, so the proportion of using U_{nci} is $\frac{P(U_{nci})}{P(U_{nci})+P(U_{sci})}$, and $E[X(U_{nci})] = \frac{P(U_{nci})}{P(U_{nci})+P(U_{sci})} E[X(U_{ci})]$. For the same reason, we have $E[X(U_{sci})]$, $E[X(U_{nco})]$ and $E[X(U_{sco})]$.

5 Estimation and Simulation

It is known that the mathematical expectation of a random variable which is Poisson distributed with parameter λ is λ. Thus, we are able to have $E[X(U_{nfi})]$, $E[X(U_{sfi})]$, $E[X(U_{nfo})]$, $E[X(U_{sfo})]$, $E[X(U_{nci})]$, $E[X(U_{sci})]$, $E[X(U_{nco})]$ and $E[X(U_{sco})]$ from Lemmas 1-6.

Using Lemmas 1 and 2, we have $E[X(U_{nfo}) + X(U_{sfo})] = \frac{\lambda}{4}$. On the other side, we have $E[X(U_{nfi}) + X(U_{sfi})] = \frac{\lambda}{4}$ from Lemma 3. Therefore, the mathematical expectation of the number of connections emanating from the upper border of PE(0, 0) is equal to that of the number of connections terminating at the upper border of it. Additionally, from Lemmas 4 and 5, we have $E[X(U_{nci})] = E[X(U_{nco})]$ and $E[X(U_{sci})] = E[X(U_{sco})]$.

A simulation program is exploited to verify our approach. With the assumptions that the number of connections per PE can be drawn independently from a Poisson distribution with parameter λ, connection length L is independently chosen from a geometric distribution $G(L) = (1 - \varepsilon)\varepsilon^{L-1}$, where $\varepsilon \in (0, 1)$, and the probability of choosing one border of the endpoints is $q(L)$, the program routes all the connections with the minimal Manhattan distance and calculates the average number of connections using U_{nfo}, U_{sfo} and so on, such as $\overline{X(U_{nfo})}$ and $\overline{X(U_{sfo})}$. The inputs of the simulation program are n, m, w and ε, where n is the number of connections in the circuit, m is the number of PEs in the array, w is the length of hop neighbour connection, and ε is the parameter of geometric distribution $G(L)$. Table 1 is the results of the simulation program with $w = 2$ and $\varepsilon = 0.3$ [7], and Table 2 is the theoretical estimation using Lemmas 1-6.

Table 1. Simulation results

n	m	$\overline{X(U_{nfo})}$	$\overline{X(U_{sfo})}$	$\overline{X(U_{nfi})}$	$\overline{X(U_{sfi})}$	$\overline{X(U_{nco})}$	$\overline{X(U_{sco})}$	$\overline{X(U_{nci})}$	$\overline{X(U_{sci})}$
251	16	3.53	0.39	3.50	0.42	1.20	0.20	1.23	0.17
319	16	4.34	0.64	4.44	0.55	2.06	0.30	1.97	0.39
479	25	4.21	0.58	4.22	0.57	1.89	0.33	1.88	0.34
688	25	6.15	0.73	6.18	0.70	2.31	0.37	2.28	0.40

Table 2. Theoretical estimation

n	m	$E[X(U_{nfo})]$	$E[X(U_{sfo})]$	$E[X(U_{nfi})]$	$E[X(U_{sfi})]$	$E[X(U_{nco})]$	$E[X(U_{sco})]$	$E[X(U_{nci})]$	$E[X(U_{sci})]$
251	16	3.61	0.31	3.70	0.22	1.41	0.27	1.41	0.27
319	16	4.58	0.40	4.70	0.28	1.79	0.34	1.79	0.34
479	25	4.41	0.38	4.52	0.27	1.72	0.33	1.72	0.33
688	25	6.33	0.55	6.49	0.39	2.47	0.48	2.47	0.48

6 Conclusion

We presented a new stochastic model for mesh-based reconfigurable computing based on the statistical distributions. The average number of each type of connections is estimated, and the simulation results demonstrate the effectiveness of our approach. With our elementary research, designers can estimate the required interconnection resource quickly and optimize their design of PE array accordingly. Incorporating more knowledge from the actual design process, the further research is directed to developing an estimation of other interconnect design parameters such as area occupancy, signal delay, power dissipation, etc.

References

1. A. El Gamal, "Two-dimensional stochastic model for interconnections in master slice integrated circuits," *IEEE Trans. Computer-Aided Design*, Vol. CAD-1, 1981.
2. C. Bobda, and A. Ahmadinia, "Dynamic interconnection of reconfigurable modules on reconfigurable devices," *Design & Test of Computers, IEEE*, Vol. 22, Issue 5, pp. 443 - 451, 2005.
3. R. Miller, V.K. Prasanna-Kumar, D.I. Reisis, and Q.F. Stout, "Parallel computations on reconfigurable meshes," *IEEE Transactions on Computers*, Vol. 42, Issue 6, pp. 678 - 692, 1993.
4. J. Cong, and Z. Pan, "Interconnect performance estimation models for design planning," *IEEE Transactions on Computer-Aided Design of Integrated Circuits and Systems*, Vol. 20, Issue 6, pp. 739-752, 2001.
5. S.D. Brown, J. Rose, and Z.G. Vranesic, "A stochastic model to predict the routability of field-programmable gate arrays," *IEEE Transactions on Computer-Aided Design of Integrated Circuits and Systems*, Vol. 12, Issue 12, pp. 1827 - 1838, 1993.
6. M. Maresca, and P. Baglietto, "A programming model for reconfigurable mesh based parallel computers," *Programming Models for Massively Parallel Computers*, pp. 124-133, 1993.
7. X. Song, Q. Tang, D. Zhou, and Y. Wang, "Wire space estimation and routability analysis," *IEEE Transactions on Computer-Aided Design of Integrated Circuits and Systems*, Vol. 19, Issue 5, pp. 624 - 628, 2000.
8. K. Bondalapati, and V.K. Prasanna, "Reconfigurable computing systems," Proceedings of IEEE, pp. 356 -359, 2002.
9. D.A. Buell, J.M. Arnold, and W. J. Kleinfelder, "FPGAs in a Custom Computing Machine," IEEE Computer Society Press, 1996.
10. J. Vuillemin, P. Bertin, D. Roncin, M. Shand, H. Touati, and P. Boucard, "Programmable Active Memories: Reconfigurable Systems Come of Age," *IEEE Transactions on VLSI Systems*, Vol. 4, No. 1, pp. 56-69, 1996.
11. P. Athanas and A. Abbott, "Real-Time Image Processing on a Custom Computing Platform," *IEEE Computer*, pp. 16-24, 1995.
12. J. Woodfill and B. Von Herzen, "Real-Time Stereo Vision on the PARTS Reconfigurable Computer," *IEEE Symposium on FPGAs for Custom Computing Machines*, 1997.
13. C. Philip , and S. Dirk, "The interpretation and application of Rent's rule," *IEEE Transactions on Very Large Scale Integration (VLSI) Systems*, Vol. 8, No. 6, pp. 639-648, 2000.
14. Z. Dai, and D.K. Banerji, "Routability prediction for Field Programmable Gate Arrays with a routing hierarchy," *VLSI Design*, pp. 85-90, 2003.

Efficient Logic Circuit for Network Intrusion Detection*

Huang-Chun Roan[1], Chien-Min Ou[2], Wen-Jyi Hwang[1,**], and Chia-Tien Dan Lo[3]

[1] Graduate Institute of Computer Science and Information Engineering, National Taiwan Normal University, Taipei, 117, Taiwan
[2] Department of Electronics Engineering, Ching Yun University, Chungli, 320, Taiwan
[3] Department of Computer Science, University of Texas at San Antonio, San Antonio, TX 78249, USA

Abstract. A novel architecture for a hardware-based network intrusion detection system (NIDS) is presented in this paper. The system adopts an FPGA-based signature match co-processor as a core for the NIDS. The signature matcher is based on an algorithm that employs simple shift registers, or-gates, and ROMs in which patterns are stored. As compared with related work, experimental results show that the proposed work achieves higher throughput and less hardware resource in the FPGA implementations of network intrusion detection.

1 Introduction

A network intrusion detection system (NIDS) monitors network traffic for suspicious data patterns and activities. It informs system administrators when malicious traffic is detected so that proper actions may be taken. Many NIDSs such as SNORT [1] prevent computer networks from attacks using pattern-matching rules. The computational complexity of NIDSs therefore may be high because of the requirement of the string matching during their detection processes.

The SNORT system running on general purpose processors may only achieve up to 60 Mbps [2] throughput because of the high computational complexity. Since these systems do not operate at line speed, some malicious traffic can be dropped and thus may not be detected. To accelerate the speed for intrusion detection, several FPGA-based approaches have been proposed [2,3,4,5,6]. Because the NIDS rules do not change frequently, the cost for FPGA implementations may not be high as compared with their software-based counterparts. Moreover, the hardware implementation can exploit parallelism for string matching so that the throughput of NIDSs can be increased.

One popular way for FPGA implementation is based on regular expressions [4,7], which results in designs with low area cost and moderate throughput

* This project is partially supported by the Center for Infrastructure Assurance and Security at UTSA and US Air Force under grant #26-0200-62.

** To whom all correspondence should be sent.

E. Sha et al. (Eds.): EUC 2006, LNCS 4096, pp. 776–784, 2006.

acceleration. In this approach, a regular expression is generated for every pattern. Each regular expression is then implemented by a nondeterministic finite automata (NFA) or deterministic finite automata (DFA). In the finite automata implementations, efficient exploitation of parallelism is difficult because the input stream is scanned one character at a time. Another alternative for FPGA implementation is to use the content addressable memory (CAM) [3,6]. By the employment of multiple comparators in the CAM, the processing of multiple input characters per cycle is possible. This may effectively increase the throughput at the expense of higher area cost.

The objective of this paper is to present a novel FPGA implementation approach for NIDSs achieving both high throughput and low area cost. The proposed architecture is based on the shift-or algorithm for exact string matching [8]. The shift-or algorithm is an effective software approach for pattern matching because of its simplicity and flexibility. However, it may not perform well when the pattern size is larger than the computer word size, which is the case for many SNORT patterns. Accordingly, the software implementation of shift-or algorithm may not be suited for SNORT systems.

On the other hand, the hardware implementation of shift-or algorithm imposes no limitation on the pattern size. In our architecture, each SNORT pattern is only associated with a ROM and a shift register for pattern comparison, which are designed in accordance with the pattern size. Because of its simplicity, the architecture may operate at a higher clock rate as compared with other implementations. In addition, the number of logic elements (LEs) for the circuit implementation is reduced significantly when the ROM is realized by the embedded RAM blocks of the FPGA. The area cost therefore may be lower than the existing designs [3,6]. Moreover, although the proposed architecture in its simplest form only processes one character at a time, the architecture can be extended to further enhance the throughput of the circuit. Multiple characters can be scanned and processed in one cycle at the expense of slight increase in area cost.

The proposed architecture has been prototyped and simulated by the Altera Stratix FPGA. Experimental results reveal that the circuit attains the throughput up to 5.14 Gbits/sec with area cost of 1.09 LE per character. The proposed architecture therefore is an effective solution to high throughput and low area cost NIDS hardware design.

2 Preliminaries

This section briefly describes the shift-or algorithm for exact string matching. Suppose we are searching for a *pattern* $P = p_1 p_2 ... p_m$ inside a large *text* (or *source*) $T = t_1 t_2 ... t_n$, where $n \gg m$. Every character of P and T belongs to the same alphabet $\Sigma = \{s_1, ..., s_{|\Sigma|}\}$.

Let R_j be a bit vector containing information about all matches of the prefixes of P that end at j. The vector contains $m+1$ elements $R_j[i], i = 0, ..., m$, where $R_j[i] = 0$ if the first i characters of the pattern P match exactly the last i

	s_k	a	b	c
S_k	$i=1$	0	1	1
	$i=2$	0	1	1
	$i=3$	1	0	1

(a)

j	0	1		2		3		4		5	
	R_j	S_c	R_j	S_c	R_j	S_c	R_j	S_c	R_j	S_c	R_j
i = 0	0		0		0		0		0		0
1	1	0	0	1	1	0	0	0	0	1	1
2	1	0	1	1	1	0	1	0	0	1	1
3	1	1	1	1	1	1	1	1	1	0	(0)

(b)

Fig. 1. An example of shift-or algorithm with pattern $P = aab$ and text $T = acaab$, (a) The bit vector S_k associated with each symbol $s_k \in \Sigma = \{a, b, c\}$ for the pattern P, (b) The bit vector R_j for the text T, where one occurrence of P is found (encircled)

characters up to j in the text (i.e., $p_1p_2...p_i = t_{j-i+1}t_{j-i+2}...t_j$). The transition from R_j to R_{j+1} is performed by the recurrence:

$$R_{j+1}[i] = \begin{cases} 0, \text{ if } R_j[i-1] = 0 \text{ and } p_i = t_{j+1}, \\ 1, \text{ otherwise}, \end{cases} \tag{1}$$

where the initial conditions for the recurrence are given by $R_0[i] = 1, i = 1, ..., m$, and $R_j[0] = 0, j = 0, ..., m$. The recurrence can be implemented by the simple shift and OR operations. To see this fact, we first associate each symbol $s_k \in \Sigma$ a bit vector S_k containing m elements, where the i-th element $S_k[i]$ is given by

$$S_k[i] = \begin{cases} 0, \text{ if } s_k = p_i, \\ 1, \text{ otherwise}. \end{cases} \tag{2}$$

Assume $t_{j+1} = s_c$. Based on eq.(2), the recurrence shown in eq.(1) can then be rewritten as

$$R_{j+1}[i] = R_j[i-1] \; OR \; S_c[i], i = 1, ..., m. \tag{3}$$

We can clearly see now the transition from R_j to R_{j+1} involves to no more than a shift of R_j and an OR operation with S_c, where $t_{j+1} = s_c$. Figure 1 shows an example of the exact string matching based on the shift-or algorithm, where $P = aab$ and $\Sigma = \{a, b, c\}$. The bit vector S_k associated with each $s_k \in \Sigma$, which is determined by eq.(2), is given in Figure 1.(a). In this example, $T = acaab$. Therefore, $s_c = a, c, a, a$ and b for $j = 1, 2, 3, 4$ and 5, respectively. The S_c associated with s_c for each j can be found from the table shown in Figure 1.(a). Given S_c and R_{j-1}, the R_j can be computed by eq.(3), as shown in Figure 1.(b). Note that, when $j = 5$, it can be found from Figure 1.(b) that $R_j[3] = 0$. Therefore, one occurrence of P is found when $j = 5$.

3 The Architecture

The proposed architecture for SNORT pattern matching is shown in Figure 2. The architecture contains M modules, where M is the number of SNORT rules for intrusion detection. The incoming source is first broadcasted to all the modules. Each module is responsible for the pattern matching of a single rule. The

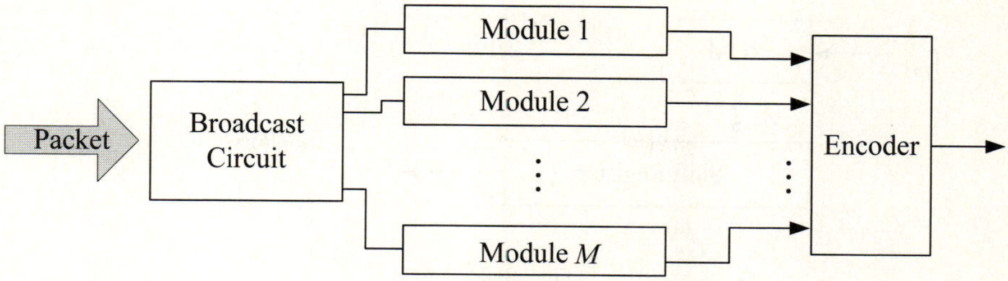

Fig. 2. The basic structure of the proposed circuit, where M is the number of rules implemented by the circuit

encoder in the architecture receives the intrusion alarms issued by the modules detecting matched strings, and transfers the alarms to the administrators for proper actions.

3.1 Basic Module Circuit

The module operates by scanning the source string one character at a time. Therefore, *after* the clock cycle j, the circuit completes the string matching process up to t_j. Moreover, the character t_{j+1} is the input character to the module during the clock cycle $(j+1)$. Assume $t_{j+1} = s_c$. The input character t_{j+1} is first delivered to the ROM for the retrieval of S_c to the OR gates. Each OR gate i has two inputs: one is from the i-th output bit of the ROM (i.e., $S_c[i]$), and the other is from the output of FF $(i-1)$, which contains $R_j[i-1]$ during the clock cycle $j+1$. From eq.(3), it follows that the OR gate i produces $R_{j+1}[i]$, which is then used as the input to the FF i. The $R_{j+1}[i]$ therefore will become the output of FF i during the clock $j+2$ for the subsequent operations.

Note that, during the clock cycle $j+1$, the m-th OR gate produces $R_{j+1}[m]$, which is identical to 0 when $p_1p_2...p_i = t_{j-i}t_{j-i+1}...t_{j+1}$. In this case, the module will issue an intrusion alarm to the encoder of the NIDS. Therefore, the output of the OR gate m is the check point of exact string matching with pattern size m.

For the FPGA devices with embedded memories, the ROM may be implemented solely by the memory bits. Hence, the LEs are required only for the implementation of the shift register. The circuit therefore may have low area cost (in terms of the number of LEs) for the FPGA implementation of SNORT rules.

To implement the ROM, we first note that each ASCII character in a SNORT rule contains 8 bits. Therefore, $|\Sigma| = 256$ and the ROM contains 256 entries for pattern matching. The ROM size can be reduced by observing the fact that some symbols s_k in the alphabet Σ may not appear in the pattern P. Accordingly, they have the same bit vectors $S_k = \mathbf{1}$. These symbols then can share the same entry in the ROM for storage size reduction. One simple way to accomplish this is to augment a new symbol s_0 (with $S_0 = \mathbf{1}$) in the alphabet Σ. All the symbols s_k having $S_k = \mathbf{1}$ are then mapped to s_0 by a symbol encoder as shown in Figure 4. These symols then share the same entry associated with s_0 in the ROM.

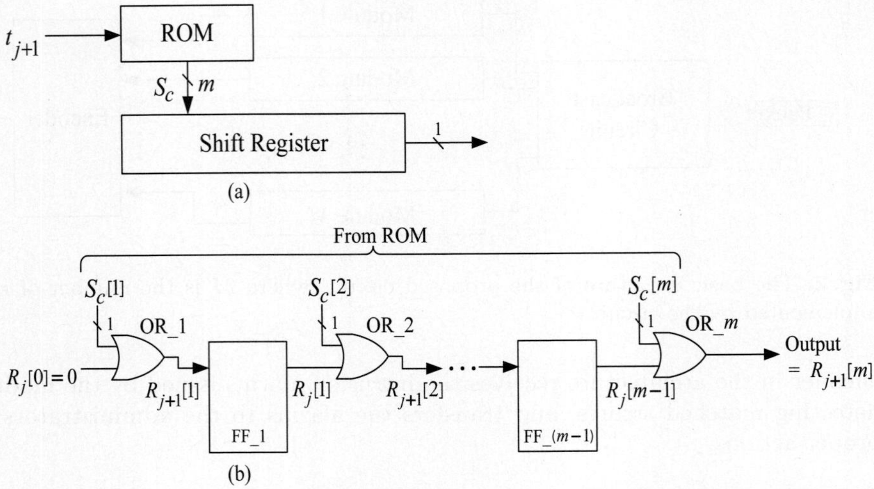

Fig. 3. The basic circuit of each module for exact pattern matching, (a) The block diagram of the circuit, (b) The shift register circuit during clock cycle $j + 1$

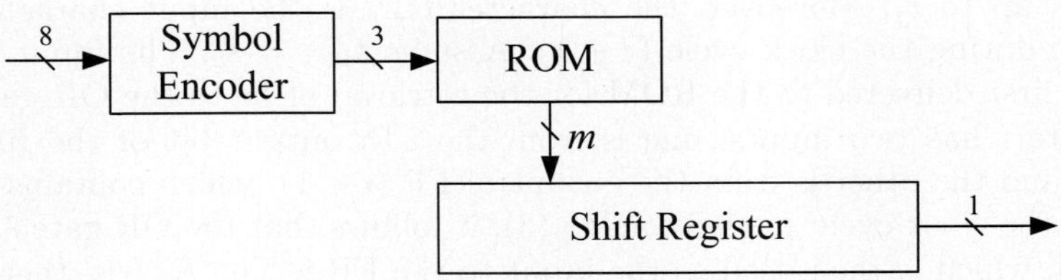

Fig. 4. The augment of a symbol encoder for reducing the ROM size. In this example, each input character is assumed to be an ASCII code (8 bits). We also assume the SNORT rule uses only 7 symbols in the alphabet. The output of the symbol encoder therefore is 3 bits.

Since the LEs are required for the implementation of the symbol encoders, the area cost may be high if each module has its own symbol encoder. We can lower the area cost by first dividing the SNORT rules into several groups, where the rules in each group use the same set of symbols. Therefore, all the rules in the same group can share the same symbol encoder, as shown in Figure 5. The overhead for the realization of symbol encoders then can be reduced.

3.2 High Throughput Module Circuit

The basic module circuit shown in Figure 3 only process one character per cycle. The throughput of the NIDS can be improved further by processing q characters at a time. This can be accomplished by grouping q consecutive characters in the source into a single symbol. Without loss of generality, we consider $q = 2$. Let

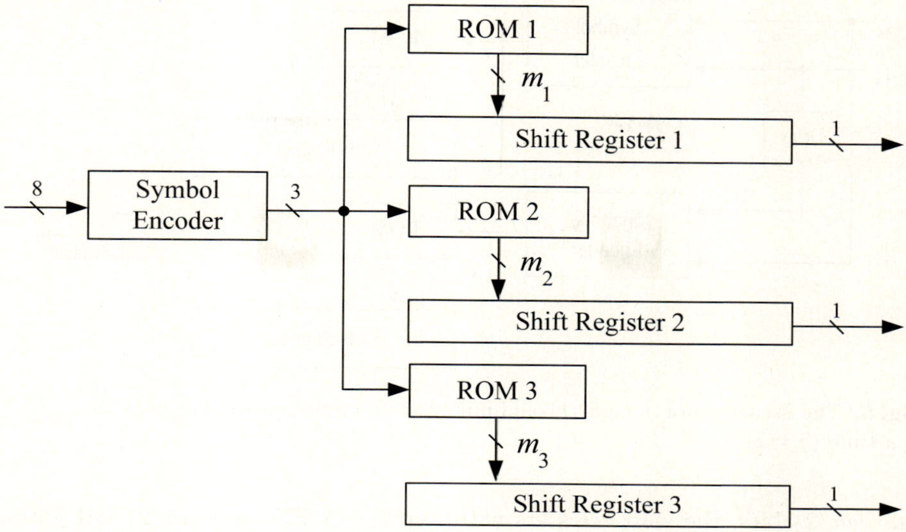

Fig. 5. The sharing of the same symbol encoder by three different SNORT rules. Each character is also assumed to be an ASCII code. All the SNORT rules use the same alphabet consisting of 7 symbols.

$\Omega = \{x_1, ..., x_{|\Omega|}\}$ be the alphabet for the new symbols, where $x_i = (y_1, y_2)$, and $y_1, y_2 \in \Sigma$.

Based on Ω, a pattern P can be rewritten as $P = u_1 u_2 ... u_{\lceil m/2 \rceil}$, where $u_i = (p_{2i-1}, p_{2i})$. Note that $u_{\lceil m/2 \rceil} = (p_{m-1}, p_m)$ when m is even. However, when m is odd, $u_{\lceil m/2 \rceil} = (p_m, \phi)$, where ϕ denotes "don't care," and can be any character in Σ. We can then associate a bit vector X_k containing $\lceil m/2 \rceil$ elements for each symbol $x_k \in \Omega$, where the i-th element of X_k is given by

$$X_k[i] = \begin{cases} 0, \text{ if } x_k = u_i, \\ 1, \text{ otherwise.} \end{cases} \tag{4}$$

A ROM containing $X_1, ..., X_{|\Omega|}$ can then be constructed for shift-or operations. In this case, the ROM contain $|\Omega| = |\Sigma|^2$ entries, where each entry has $\lceil m/2 \rceil$ bits. It is therefore necessary to employ a larger ROM for a module with higher throughput. A symbol encoder similar to that shown in Figure 4 can be employed to reduce the ROM size. In this case we augment a new symbol x_0 (with $X_0 = \mathbf{1}$) in the alphabet Ω. All the symbols x_k having $X_k = \mathbf{1}$ are then mapped to x_0 by the symbol encoder.

Note that the string matching operations ending at j over the alphabet Ω are equivalent to the operations ending at either $2j$ or $2j + 1$ (but not both) over the alphabet Σ. It is necessary to perform the matching process ending at every location of the source over the alphabet Σ. Therefore, we employ two shift registers in the module as shown in Figure 6, where one is for even locations, and the other is for odd locations. Moreover, since each entry of the ROM contains

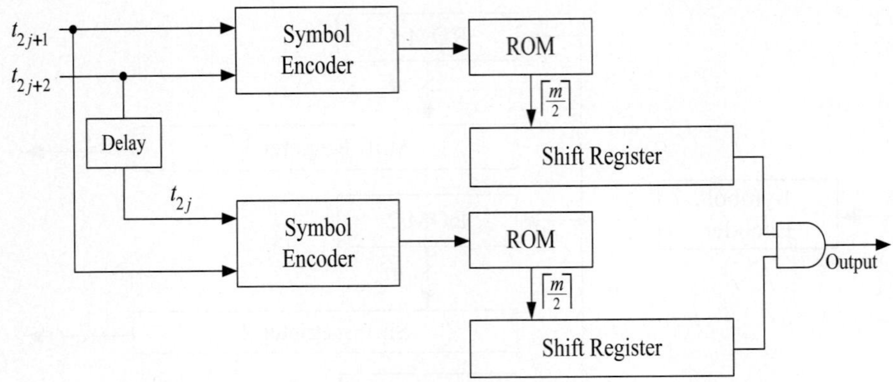

Fig. 6. The structure of a high throughput module circuit processing two characters at a time ($q = 2$)

only $\lceil m/2 \rceil$ bits, the shift registers with $\lceil m/2 \rceil - 1$ FFs and $\lceil m/2 \rceil$ OR gates are sufficient for the operations. When m is even, the total number of FFs and OR gates in the high throughput circuit is identical to those in the basic circuit presented in the previous subsection.

To perform the string matching operations ending at the *even* locations of the source over Σ, we convert the source T to the sequence $T_e = e_1e_2...$ over alphabet Ω, where $e_j = (t_{2j-1}, t_{2j})$. During the clock cycle $j+1$, symbol e_{j+1} is fetched to the ROM. This is equivalent to the scanning of two characters t_{2j+1} and t_{2j+2} simultaneously for shift-or operations.

The shift-or operations at the *odd* locations of the source can be performed in the similar manner, except that the source T is extracted as $T_o = o_1o_2...$, where $o_j = (t_{2j}, t_{2j+1})$. During the clock cycle $j+1$, we scan the symbol o_j. From Figure 6, we observe that o_j can be obtained from e_j and e_{j+1} via delaying and broadcasting operations. Therefore, the shift-or operations at even and odd locations share the same input as shown in the figure.

4 Experimental Results and Comparisons

This section presents experimental results of the proposed architecture. Table 1 compares the throughput, the number of LEs per character, total number of memory bits and operating frequency of the proposed circuits with and without the symbol encoder. The throughput indicates the maximum number of bits per second the circuit can process. For the sake of simplicity, only the circuits processing one character at a time (i.e., $q = 1$) are considered in the table. Moreover, for the circuit with symbol encoders, the rules using the same set of symbols will share the same symbol encoder, as shown in Figure 5. We use the Altera Quartus II as the tool for circuit synthesization. The target FPGA device is Stratix EP1S80.

Table 1. Comparisons of the proposed architecture with and without symbol encoder, where the number of characters available for pattern matching is 1568 characters

Design	Throughput (Gb/s)	Logic cells /char	Memory bits	Operating Frequency (MHz)
Without symbol encoder	2.57	0.97	387,584	321.03
With symbol encoder	2.57	0.99	25,738	321.03

Table 2 shows the throughput, the number of LEs per character, the memory bits and operating frequency of our circuits with $q = 1$ and $q = 2$ realized by the FPGA device Stratix EP1S80. As shown in Table 2, because the circuit with $q = 2$ processes two characters for each clock cycle, it has higher throughput than that of the cuicuit with $q = 1$, which processes one character per cycle only. On the other hand, it can also be observed from Table 2 that the circuit with $q = 2$ has slightly higher number of LEs per character. This is because the circuit has more complex address encoders for reducing the storage size in ROM. In addition, for $q = 2$, the string matching operations for each rule requires two independent ROMs as shown in Figure 6. Therefore, the number of memory bits used by the circuit with $q = 2$ is higher than that of the circuit with $q = 1$.

Table 3 compares the FPGA implementations of the proposed architecture with those of the existing related works. Note that the exact comparisons of these circuits may be difficult because they use different distance measures, and are realized by different FPGA devices. However, it can still be observed from the

Table 2. Comparisons of the proposed architecture with $q = 1$ and $q = 2$, where the number of characters available for pattern matching is 1568 characters

Design	Throughput (Gb/s)	Logic cells /char	Memory bits	Operating Frequency (MHz)
$q = 1$	2.57	0.99	25,738	321.03
$q = 2$	5.14	1.09	40,768	321.03

Table 3. Comparisons of various string matching FPGA designs

Design	Device	Throughput (Gb/s)	Chars	Logic cells /char
Proposed architecture ($q = 1$)	Altera Stratix EP1S40	2.25	5004	0.96
Proposed architecture ($q = 2$)	Altera Stratix EP1S40	5.14	1568	1.09
Gokhale et al. [3]	Xilinx VirtexE-1000	2.2	640	15.2
Hutchings et al. [4]	Xilinx Vertix-1000	0.248	8003	2.57
Singaraju et al. [5]	Xilinx Virtex2VP30-7	6.41	1021	2.2
Sourdis-Pnevmatikatos [6]	Xilinx Spartan33-5000	4.91	18000	3.69
Moscola et al. [7]	Xilinx VirtexE-2000	1.18	420	19.4

table that our circuits have effective throughput-area performance as compared with existing work. This is because our design is based on the simple shift-or algorithm. The simplicity of circuit allows the string matching operations to be performed at high clock rate with small hardware area. In particular, when $q = 2$, our circuit attains the throughput of 5.14 Gbits/sec while requiring only the area cost of 1.09 LEs per character. These facts demonstrate the effectiveness of our design.

5 Conclusion

A novel FPGA implementation of network intrusion detection based on shift-or algorithm is presented in this paper. The proposed algorithm in the basic form processes one character at a time, and contains only a ROM and a simple shift register for each pattern matching. The throughput can be further enhanced by processing multiple characters in parallel. Both the basic form and two-character at a time of the proposed algorithm are implemented in our experiments. Comparisons with exsiting work reveal that our design is one of the cost-effective solutions to the FPGA implementations of the network intrusion detection.

References

1. SNORT official web site `http://www.snort.org`.
2. Ramirez, T., Lo, C.D.: Rule set decomposition for hardware network intrusion detection. in the 2004 International Computer Symposium (ICS 2004) (2004)
3. Gokhale, M., Dubois, D., Dubois, A., Boorman, M., Poole, S., Hogsett, V.: Granidt: towards gigabit rate network intrusion detection technology. Proceedings of the International Conference on Field Programmable Logic and Application (2002) 404–413
4. Hutchings, B.L., Franklin, R., Carver, D.: Assisting network intrusion detection with reconfigurable hardware. Proceedings of the IEEE Symposium on Field-Programmable Custom Computing Machines (2002) 111–120
5. Singaraju, J., Bu, L., Chandy, J.A.: A signature match processor architecture for network intrusion detection. Proceedings of the IEEE Symposium on Field-Programmable Custom Computing Machines (2005) 235–242
6. Sourdis, I., Pnevmatikatos, D.N.: Pre-decoded cams for efficient and high-speed nids pattern matching. Proceedings of the IEEE Symposium on Field-Programmable Custom Computing Machines (2004) 258–267
7. Moscola, J., Lockwood, J.W., Loui, R.P., Pachos, M.: Implementation of a content-scanning module for an internet firewall. Proceedings of the IEEE Symposium on Field-Programmable Custom Computing Machines (2003) 31–38
8. Baeza-Tates, R., Gonnet, G.: A new approach to text searching. Communications of the ACM **35** (1992) 74–82

A Multi-protocol Baseband Modem Processor for a Mobile RFID Reader

Seok Joong Hwang[1], Joon Goo Lee[1], Seon Wook Kim[1], Sunshin Ahn[1], Si-Gyung Koo[2], Jihun Koo[2], Kyung Ho Park[2], and Woo Shik Kang[2]

[1] Compiler and Embedded System Laboratory
Department of Electronics and Computer Engineering
Korea University, Seoul, Korea
{nzthing, nextia9, seon, sunshin}@korea.ac.kr
[2] Communication and Network Laboratory
Samsung Advanced Institute of Technology, Korea
{sg.koo, jihun.koo, pkh5247, wskang}@samsung.com

Abstract. In RFID (Radio Frequency IDentification) systems, a tag reader communicates with tags, reads their identification codes, and accesses their related database through network infrastructure. There are many research activities in RFID systems for industrial applications such as delivery, manufacturing, and so on, but there is few on mobile devices such as cellular phones and PDAs. This paper presents architecutre of a multi-protocol RFID reader on mobile devices. We have considered several design parameters, such as low power consumption, cost effectiveness and flexibility. We prototyped our system on the ARM-based Excalibur FPGA with iPAQ PDA, and also a chip with 0.18um technology for verification of our architecture.

Keywords: RFID, Mobile, WIPI, HAL, Multi-protocol, Baseband Modem.

1 Introduction

Nowadays we are thinking about assigning a unique identification and its associated information to an object for a ubiquitous computing environment. To realize a ubiquitous world (u-world) which completes the ubiquitous computing and networking environment, we need to prepare for smart networking infrastructures and instinctive information capturing systems. In the u-world, huge amounts of connected computing devices provide a convenience environment to us. There are lots of activities to support network infrastructures to offer for convenience to people by using many computing devices seamlessly.

One of the potential and attractive ideas to support the u-world is to use RFID (Radio Frequency IDentification) systems. In RFID systems, we attach a tag onto an object where a unique identification code is stored in the tag. A tag reader communicates with the tag by a radio frequency signal, reads the code from the tag, and accesses its related database through network infrastructure

E. Sha et al. (Eds.): EUC 2006, LNCS 4096, pp. 785–794, 2006.

for getting more information. Figure 1 shows the environment especially for mobile-based RFID systems. the RFID tag is attached to a statue as an object and the tag's information is read by RFID readers on mobile devices. We can get the detailed information (name, description, and so on) about the statue by accessing Internet.

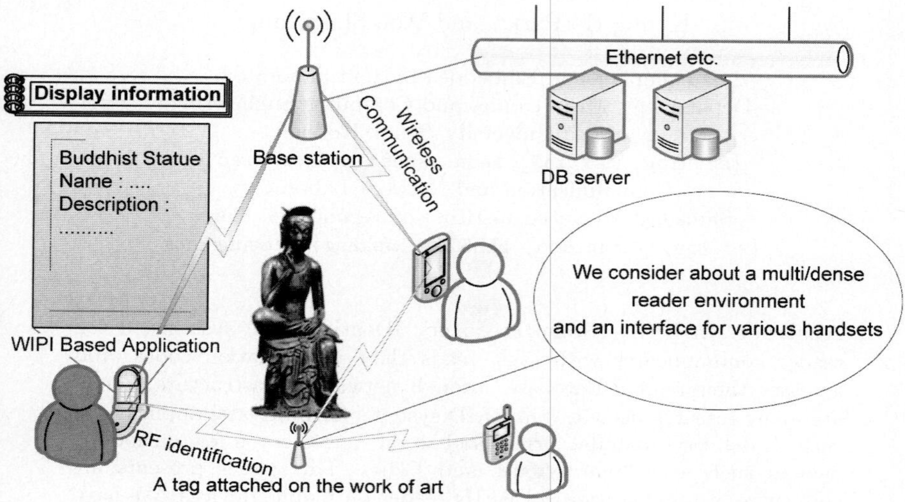

Fig. 1. Example of a mobile RFID environment

In general, an industrial reader system is widely available in delivery and manufacturing services. The whole system is highly optimized for accuracy and speed performance by locating each reader at fixed and optimized location. Also, the size of the industrial reader is large, since there is no resource constraint such as power consumption and area. The RFID system in the mobile environment has some different scenarios from the industrial one. Because the reader is carried anywhere and anytime, We should consider several design parameters, such as low power consumption, cost effectiveness and flexibility. The resource optimization is very important in the mobile environment, and flexibility is required for supporting the wide scope of mobile devices and their applications.

In this paper, we present architecture of a multi-protocol RFID reader on mobile devices such as mobile phones and PDAs. We have prototyped our system on the ARM-based Excalibur FPGA [1] with iPAQ PDA, and also we have fabricated a chip with 0.18um technology for verification of our architecture.

The paper consists of the followings: In Section 2, we present an overview of our multi-protocol RFID readers architecture. We present the hardware architecture in Section 3 in detail. The experimental design is discussed in Section 4, and finally the conclusion is made in Section 5.

2 Architecture Overview

Figure 2 shows an overall software and hardware organization of a multi-protocol RFID reader for our system. The RFID reader consists of tightly integrated four parts, a RF circuit, baseband hardware logics, RFID software components, and a handset.

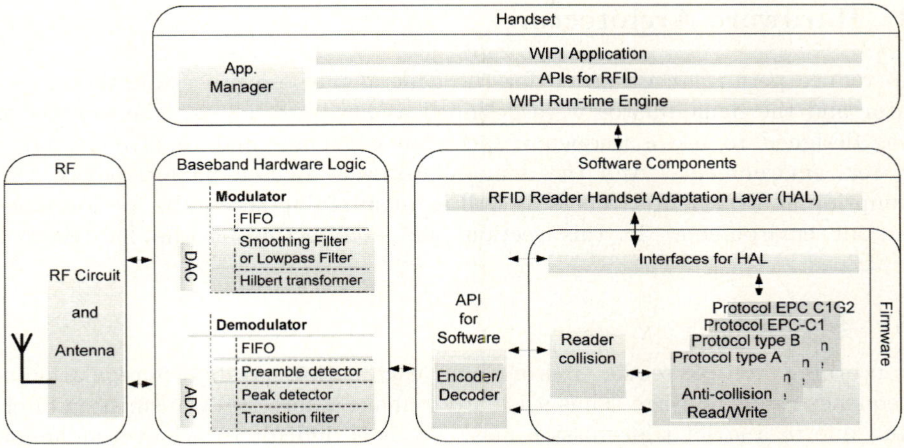

Fig. 2. Software and hardware organization of our mobile RFID reader

In a physical layer of RFID systems, ASK modulation is common to all the passive RFID protocols [2, 3, 4, 5], because it is easy to implement ASK modulation in a passive tag which has cost and power concerns. But, ASK signal is poor at performance than other modulation schemes. Thus our modulator and demodulator were carefully designed to manipulate this signal efficiently. And they were implemented in hardware logics as they requires higher performance than other workloads, moreover there is hard real-time constraint. As a result , we were able to implement most of other functionalities of a RFID reader in software to support multi-protocols and the next coming standards easily at lower operating frequency.

The RFID software components consist of baseband modem APIs, a firmware, HAL interfaces, and WIPI-based applications. And these components are running on a general purpose processor (ARM9) . The baseband modem APIs provide interfaces to access baseband modem hardware logics and RF circuits for controlling modem hardware. The firmware includes anti-collision algorithms, reader collision algorithms, interfaces with handset adaptation layer (HAL), and so on. The HAL is an abstract layer to provide hardware independence to an application. WIPI (Wireless Internet Platform for Interoperability) [6] is the common platform envisioned by the Korean Ministry of Information and Communication for running mobile applications on any handset independent to vendors. WIPI serves as a backbone for content providers to develop applications that run seamlessly on any mobile platform. Any WIPI-based application can access and control a RFID reader through HAL interfaces in a uniform manner. A thorough description of the detail software architecture is provided by Lee et al [7].

In the following section, we will present the hardware architectures in detail.

3 Hardware Architecture

To reduce performance burden for the general purpose processor, the modulator and the demodulator were designed as hardware logics. The modulator was designed to use a frequency spectrum efficiently and to give flexibility in real environments. And the demodulator was focused on low power consumption and cost effectiveness as well as maintaining acceptable performance on our environment. In this section, the architecture of the hardware is explained.

3.1 Modulator

Concerning multiple reader environments, each nation has its own regulation of frequency resource usage. Thus it is hard to make a universal transmission filter. And due to a strict transmission mask [5], it is difficult to achieve maximum transmission speed which is specified in each RFID standard.

In order to resolve the problem, our modulation filters were designed to support SSB (Single Side Band) transmission to use frequency spectrum efficiently in addition to DSB (Double Side Band) transmission, and all filters were design to be programmable for easy adaptation in real environments. The transmitted data on a forward link are written into FIFO. They are converted to rectangular pulses by a pulse generator, and then filtered by a 16-tap FIR pulse shaping filter. In the DSB transmission, the pulse shaped signal is transmitted to I channel and Q channel, which is tied to zero. In the SSB transmission, I and Q channel signals are generated by the Hilbert transformer, which was implemented with a 31-tap FIR filter, from the pulse shaped signal.

Table 1 shows the maximum transmission speeds of each standard with our filter, and each filter configuration satisfies with the Korean RFID regulation. Resulting signal spectrum satisfies with transmission mask for the first neighbor

Table 1. Filter configurations for each standard

Standards	Forward link		Filter configurations			
	Bit rate	Link frequency	Type	Sampling frequency	Passband frequency	Stopband frequency
EPC C1	15 Kbps	120 kHz	SSB	1200 kHz	120 kHz	180 kHz
ISO Type B	40 Kbps	40 kHz	DSB	400 kHz	80 kHz	100 kHz
EPC C1G2	80 Kbps	80 kHz	DSB	400 kHz	80 kHz	100 kHz
	80 Kbps	80 kHz	SSB	800 kHz	80 kHz	110 kHz

channel where 20dB attenuation is occurred in 200 kHz channel bandwidth which is allowed in the Korean regulation.

3.2 Demodulator

The acquisition of a signal in the mobile-RFID system introduces several design difficulties. First, since a mobile system requires low power consumption and cost effective design, we chose a direct conversion and single antenna architecture. While the direct conversion architecture has a merit for reduction system cost compared to devices with IF-based architectures, it brings about various inter-modulations and spurious signals on account of local oscillator and self-mixing interference leakage [8,9,10,11]. These are sources of DC offset fluctuation which is difficult to be eliminated, and these sources degrade overall system performance. Moreover, as both a forward link and a return link use the same frequency band with a shared single antenna, leakage power of the transmission signal is about 30dB larger than power of the receiving signal in our system. Thus the situation is deteriorated. There are several kinds of compensation techniques which are complex or expensive.

Second, the oscillator frequency of a passive tag is inaccurate. According to the protocol in [5], the reader should be working to a tolerance ±22% in a receiving link frequency. Conventional receivers estimate the signal by using a matched filter (MF). It has advantages that it results in a correlation gain by integrating the received signal over the symbol period T while averaging out the zero-mean AWGN. It is known as an optimal receiver which maximizes SNR as described in Equation (1) [12]. But it is effective when there is only AWGN in noise components. With considering other noise components such as DC offset fluctuation, we can express the SNR as Equation (2).

$$SNR_{max} = \frac{2E}{N_0} \tag{1}$$

$$(\frac{S}{N})_T = \frac{|\int_{-\infty}^{\infty} H(f)S(f)e^{j2\pi fT}df|^2}{\frac{N_0}{2\int_{-\infty}^{\infty}|H(f)|^2df} + |\int_{-\infty}^{\infty} H(f)N_{Drift}(f)e^{j2\pi fT}df|^2} \tag{2}$$

If we constraint the numerator to be 1, the problem of maximizing SNR is reduced to minimizing the denominator. The second component of the denominator can be amplified if there is correlation gain between an impulse response of the MF and one of DC offset fluctuation. It means that the maximum performance of the receiver cannot be obtained by the MF if there is no additional DC offset compensation technique.

There are three kinds of solutions. One is to suppress the leakages using bandpass filtering in a carrier frequency level. It has a limitation since the frequencies are same between expected received signal and leakage components. Another technique [8, 10, 11] is to compensate the DC offset fluctuation by tracking and estimating it, or by bandpass filtering in a baseband level. This approach requires exquisite control with additional system resources or it maybe impractical for ASK signal. The third technique is to use efficient coding rules which have closely zero correlation gain with DC offset fluctuation ("dc-free" coding rule). But it cannot be adopted in the RFID system, because most standards do not establish coding rules which provide such a property.

Thus we developed a cost effective receiver architecture with good immunity from DC offset fluctuation as well as good feasibility. This architecture is called *a transition trigger*. The transition trigger architecture focuses on providing robust performance in presence of DC offset fluctuation and supporting every coding rule in the RFID standards. While a conventional MF recovers a symbol by estimating a maximum likelihood level of a symbol, the transition trigger recovers a symbol by triggering transitions caused by the symbol. The transition trigger consists of three major components which are a transition filter, a peak detector and a bit slicer.

The transition filter is an alternative of the conventional MF. It estimates a transition component of a received signal. By using the estimation, we can determine whether transition occurred or not. While impulse and frequency responses of the conventional MF are expressed as Equation (3), (4) [12], responses of the transition filter are defined as Equation (5), (6).

$$h(t) = u(t) - u(t - T) \quad for\ 0 \leq t \leq T \tag{3}$$

$$H(f) = Tsinc(fT)e^{-j\pi fT} \tag{4}$$

$$h(t) = u(t) - 2u(t - T) + u(t - 2T) \quad for\ 0 \leq t \leq 2T \tag{5}$$

$$H(f) = Tsinc(fT)(e^{-j\pi fT} - e^{-3j\pi fT}) \tag{6}$$

Figure 3 shows the frequency response of the filter which suppresses the DC offset fluctuation and maximizes the transition component of a source signal efficiently. Conceptually, we can recover a symbol using this filter if the timing of a received signal is known already. In this case, we can use a simple comparator to determine symbol values. When the output of the transition filter is greater than a certain threshold at the switching point between symbols, the output of the comparator is inverted. If not, the output is kept. To evaluate the immunity of the transition filter compared to the conventional MF, we simulated BER performance of both filters with the DC offset fluctuation in addition to AWGN. The fluctuation is modeled simply as a low frequency continuous wave. Figure 4 shows the simulation data. The 1000 bits FM0 coded tag responses were received 100 times. The link frequency of responses was 80 kHz, a sampling frequency was 640 kHz and the amplitude of the fluctuation was equal to symbol signals. In Figure 4 (a), the BER of the MF is more excellent than the transition filter in absence of the fluctuation. Because the MF is best able to average out the AWGN. But the performance of the transition filter is acceptable since we do not need extreme performance in our target environment. The required receiver sensitivity is -96dBm. In this case, the output SNR of our RF circuit including ADC is 12.9dB. Thus our design targets on BER 10^{-3} in SNR 12.9dB. Besides the immunity of the fluctuation is more important factor. As shown in (b)$\sim$(d) of Figure 4, while performance of the MF is degraded severely, the transition filter shows good immunity. It is important that it is done without any additional

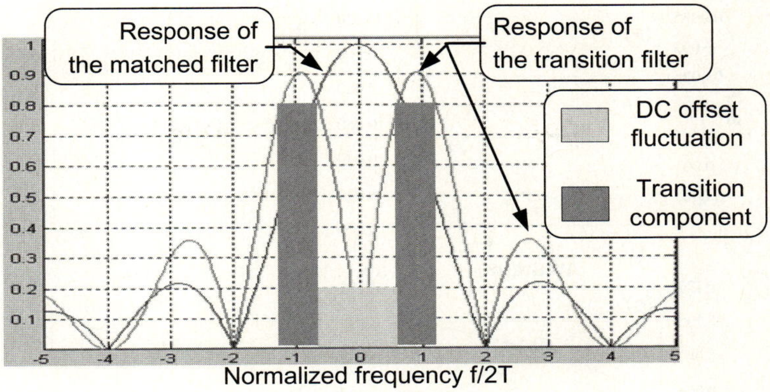

Fig. 3. Spectrum of the transition filter

processing such as a bandpass filtering. Thus our design is cost effective as well as acceptable in a term of performance.

The peak detector finds points at which transition is occurred by tracking the output of the transition filter. Basically, it detects peaks by comparing a signal to the threshold which is adjusted dynamically and has two strategies. First, it recognizes a peak when a signal crosses zero level after it went across the threshold.

Second, even if a signal does not cross the threshold, the detector recognizes a peak when it goes across the opposite threshold level after zero-crossing. After recognizing a peak, the detector determines the peak point which has maximum correlation gain between a present point and a previous recognized point. And the detector updates the threshold to be half of the current peak value.

Using the information of peak positions, a bit slicer recovers symbols. Basically it determines symbols using peak polarities and distance between peak positions. For example, assuming a symbol has a period T, the slicer determines whether there is one symbol when peak-to-peak distance is closed to T or not. However, it is a problem that the receiver does not know the period T exactly. As previously mentioned, the oscillator frequency of a passive tag is inaccurate and the reader should be working to a tolerance ±22% in a receiving link frequency. It means that we cannot recover symbols using just a peak-to-peak distance. Thus we buffers the distances to obtain an actual link frequency. Our receiver has 7 bit-slicers which has different periods each other. Each slicer is connected with preamble detection buffers which detect a preamble from the received signal. If the preamble is detected from any preamble detection buffer, a bit-slicer selector determines one bit-slicer which is used for symbol recovery by calculating actual receiving link frequency using buffered peak distances.

Using the transition trigger architecture, we achieved the receiver performance as shown in Table 2. It was obtained from a simulation that received 160 bit tag responses of EPC class-1 Gen2 1000 times. As a result, our receiver is working to a tolerance ±22% at a receiving link frequency.

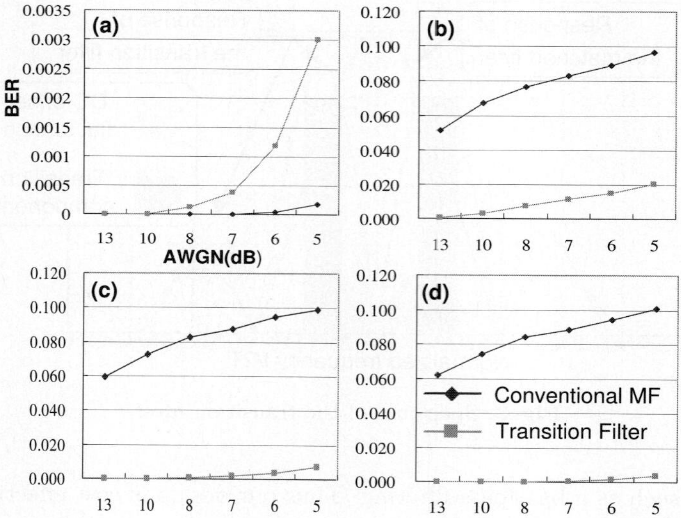

Fig. 4. BER performance in the DC offset fluctuation. DC offset fluctuation frequency: (a) No fluctuation (b) 16kHz (c) 8kHz (d) 4kHz.

Table 2. Receiver performance in AWGN

Timing Error		SNR				
		12.9dB	10dB	9dB	8dB	6dB
-22%	BER (Bit Error Rate)	0.0	0.0	0.023	0.0131	0.1181
	PER (Packet Error Rate)	0.0	0.0	1.1%	3.8%	35.8%
0%	BER	0.0	0.0	0.0071	0.0045	0.0733
	PER	0.0	0.0	0.3%	1.6%	23.5%
+22%	BER	0.0	0.0	0.001	0.0047	0.0802
	PER	0.0	0.0	0.3%	2.6%	32.6%

Until now, we present our hardware architecture. It has signal processing features to reduce performance burden for a general purpose processor. And it is focused on low power consumption and cost effectiveness as well as maintaining acceptable performance on our environment. In the following section, we present the experimental design for verification of our architecture.

4 Experimental Design

We implemented our prototyped baseband modem logic on the ARM-based Excalibur FPGA, ultra high frequency (UHF) RF circuit with filters, direct conversion up/down mixers, a PLL, a power amplifier and a palm sized antenna. The baseband modulator and the demodulator were implemented in FPGA. And the RFID firmware is running on an ARM9 processor on the Excalibur.

The baseband modem APIs allow us to control forward/return link frequencies, transmitting/receiving bit streams, PLL, TX/RX gains, and turn on/off each RF part. Our firmware has functions of inventory using anti-collision algorithms, and also has read/write functions if a protocol supports. Also special functionalities for security such as kill or lock at EPC protocols are accomplished.

A HAL application was coded on a personal digital assistants (PDA) using a graphic user interface (GUI) based on PocketPC 2002. Using a universal asynchronous receiver/transmitter (UART), the HAL application on PDA and the RFID baseband modem were connected. When a user chooses a HAL command on GUI, the HAL application sends a message to UART with predefined format and waits for a response from the firmware. The firmware of the baseband modem receives this message from the HAL application and decodes the message. After decoding the message, the firmware calls and executes a suitable function in an algorithmic part or a baseband modem API. If the firmware executes the function successfully, it sends back a response message, also a predefined format, to the HAL application. The HAL application displays proper information according to the responded message.

Finally, we fabricated the chip version of the reader with 0.18 um technology. Figure 5 shows this chip which is implemented with about 80k gate baseband logic, ARM9 processor, ADC, DAC and SRAM. Die size of the chip is 5mm by 5.27mm. And the power consumption of the baseband logic is estimated to 21.705mW with 25MHz clock frequency, 30% Flip-flop ratio and 10% switching activity. It can be more reduced, because the necessary clock frequency is just about 4 MHz actually. But we use unified 25MHz clock frequency for the MCU and the baseband logic to eliminate an additional PLL. At last, we demonstrated our chip embedding to a PDA phone at 2005 USN/RFID Conference & Exhibition which was held in Korea.

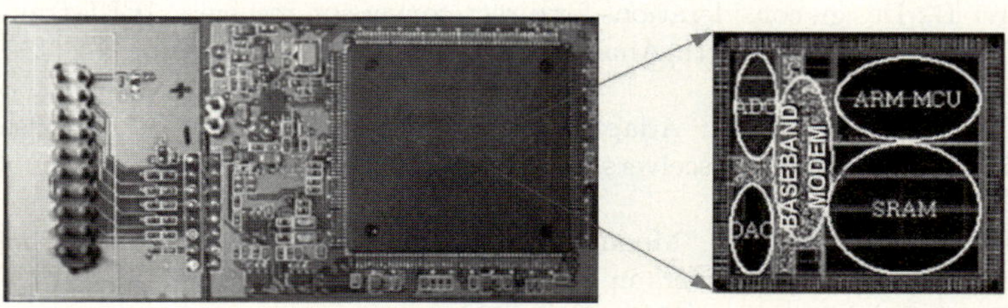

Fig. 5. Chip version of the multi-protocol RFID reader for mobile devices

5 Conclusion

In this paper, we presented architecture and implementation of a multi-protocol RFID reader on mobile devices such as mobile phones and PDAs. There are many research activities in industrial RFID systems, but there is few on mobile devices. We focused on low power consumption, cost effectiveness and flexibility.

Also, our firmware interacts with Handset Adaptation Layer (HAL) in order to support WIPI (Wireless Internet Platform for Interoperability) architecture on mobile devices. Any WIPI application can use our RFID reader's functionalities to query tags' information from Internet through HAL interfaces. We prototyped our system on the ARM-based Excalibur FPGA with iPAQ PDA, and also we fabricated a chip with 0.18um technology for verification of our architecture.

We have ported our implementation onto only software implementation written in Java. We have implemented our own Java core called TalusCore which can accelerate the Java applications in real time. It will support more flexibility and portability with extreme low power consumption.

References

1. Altera Corperation: Excalibur devices. (http://www.altera.com/)
2. International Organization for Standardization: ISO/IEC FDIS 18000-6, ISO standard document. (http://www.iso.org)
3. EPCglobal Inc: EPC class 0, EPC global standard documents. (http://www.epcglobalinc.org/ standards_technology/specification.html)
4. EPCglobal Inc: EPC class 1, EPC global standard documents. (http://www.epcglobalinc.org/standards_technology/specification.html)
5. EPCglobal Inc: EPC class 1 gen 2, EPC global standard documents. (http://www.epcglobalinc.org/standards_technology/specification.html)
6. The Korean Ministry of Information and Communication: Wireless Internet Platform for Interoperability (WIPI). (http://wipi.or.kr)
7. Lee, J.G., Hwang, S.J., Kim, S.W., Ahn, S., Park, K., Koo, J.H., Kang, W.S.: Software architecture for a multi-protocol rfid reader on mobile devices. In: Second International Conference on Embedded Software and Systems. (2005) 81–88
8. Abidi, A.A.: Direct-conversion radio transceivers for digital communications. IEEE journal of solid-state circuits **30** (1995) 1399–1410
9. Razavi, B.: Design considerations for direct-conversion receivers. IEEE transactions on Circuits and Systems II: Analog and Digital Signal Processing **44** (1997) 428–435
10. Cavers, J.K., Liao, M.W.: Adaptive compensation for imbalance and offset losses in direct conversion transceivers. IEEE transactions on vehicular technology **42** (1993) 581–588
11. Lehne, M., Stonick, J.T., Moon, U.: An adaptive offset cancellation mixer for direct conversion transceivers in 2.4ghz cmos. In: IEEE International Symposium on Circuits and Systems. (2000) I319–I322
12. Sklar, B.: Digital Communications Fundamentals and Applications, 2nd Edition. Prentice-Hall, Englewood Cliff, NJ (2001)

Write Back Routine for JFFS2 Efficient I/O

Seung-Ho Lim[1], Sung-Hoon Baek[1], Joo-Young Hwang[2], and Kyu-Ho Park[1]

[1] Computer Engineering Research Laboratory,
Department of Electrical Engineering and Computer Science,
Korea Advanced Institute of Science and Technology
{shlim, shbaek}@core.kaist.ac.kr, kpark@ee.kaist.ac.kr
[2] Embedded OS Lab.
Samsung Electronics
jooyoung.hwang@samsung.com

Abstract. When flash memory is used as a storage in embedded systems, block level translation layer is required between conventional filesystem and flash memory chips due to its physical characteristics. A far more efficient use of it is the design of a filesystem itself without no extra layer of translation. However, since flash filesystem does not use block device layer, it cannot utilize deferred I/O although deferred I/O enhances write latency by delaying the flushing jobs. Linux operating system generally uses the write back routine for deferred I/O using kernel thread, which writes back dirty pages and buffers through the block device layer. In this paper, we design and implement efficient I/O for JFFS2 flash filesystem based on flash memory. For this, we first analyze the write procedure of JFFS2 filesystem in detail, and derive the drawback and overhead. Then, we design the flash write back routine for deferred I/O. We apply it to the Linux JFFS2 by implementing *fflush* and *flash_writeback* kernel thread. The designed flash write back routine can reduce average write latency when the kernel buffers are enough to get the users data.

1 Introduction

Flash memory has become an increasingly important component as a nonvolatile storage media because of its small size, shock resistance, and low power consumption[1]. In nonvolatile memories, NOR flash memory provides fast random access speed, but high cost and low density, compared with NAND flash memory. NAND Flash has advantages in large storage capacity and relatively high performance for large read/write in contrast to NOR flash. Recently, the capacity of NAND flash memory for one chip becomes 2GB, and this will be increased quickly. Based on the NAND flash chip, solid state disk was developed and this could be used as a storage system in labtop computer[3]. Therefore, NAND flash is widely used as data storage in embedded systems and also likely to be used for PC based systems in the near future. Specifically, NAND Flash memory chips are arranged into blocks, and each block has a fixed number of pages, which is the unit of read or write. A page is further divided into a data region for storing data and a spare region for storing the status of the data region. In first generation, the typical page size was 512 bytes, the additional spare

E. Sha et al. (Eds.): EUC 2006, LNCS 4096, pp. 795–804, 2006.

region was 16 bytes, and the block size was 16 KB, which was composed of 32 pages. As its capacity grew, the page size of the next generation became 2 KB with an additional 64 bytes spare region, and the block size became 128 KB.

Due to the flash memory characteristics, form of Electrically Erasable Read Only Memory (EEPROM), no in-place update is allowed. This means that when data is modified, new data must be written to an available free page in another position, and this page is considered as a live page. The page which contains old data is considered as a dead page. As time passes, a large portion of flash memory is composed of dead pages, and the system should reclaim the available free pages for write operations. The erase operation makes free pages available. However, because the unit of an erase operation is a block, which is much larger than a write unit, this mismatch causes an additional copy operation of live pages in erasing the block somewhere else. This process is called garbage collection. To address these problems, a flash translation layer has been introduced between the conventional filesystem and flash memory[5]. This block level layer redirects the location of updated data from one page to another page and manages current physical location of each data in the mapping table. The mapping between the logical location and physical location can be maintained either at the page level (FTL)[2] or at the block level (NFTL)[6]. However, the use of an conventional filesystem has many performance restrictions when using on the flash memory because conventional filesystems are designed for disk based storage system.

A far more efficient use of flash memory as storage would be possible through the use of a filesystem designed specifically for use on such devices, with no extra layer of translation in between. One such design is Journaling Flash File System 2[9]. The JFFS2 is a log-structured filesystem which stores nodes containing data and metadata to every free region in flash chip, sequentially. This sequential write is performed for each flash block. One of the most serious problem in JFFS2 is very poor read/write response time at users feeling. When writing new user's data, JFFS2 makes new node which contains both inode information and data, writes to the flash medium using flash driver interface directly. Then, node tree structure is managed and maintained in the main memory using the specific data structures such as jffs2 inode cache and node fragment lists. Whenever the write is performed from users, it is not returned from kernel until all the data are written out to flash memory. There are two reasons that JFFS2 uses synchronous I/O scheme for write operation. First, JFFS2 does not use block device layer, so it cannot use the buffer cache mechanism. Although JFFS2 maintains the compatible interface with the virtual file system(VFS) layer and uses the page cache from the VFS, the deferred I/O mechanism in Linux operating system should use both page cache and buffer cache. Second, flash memory should preserve the write sequentiality for each flash block, which is from the inherent characteristics of flash memory. JFFS2 should preserve the write sequentiality of the node to be written. This write transaction mechanism which is implemented in JFFS2 gives much latency and response time to users and degrades the overall system read/write performance.

In this paper, we design and implement the write back routine for JFFS2 filesystem on the flash memory storage. Linux OS generally use the write back routine for deferred I/O using *pdflush* and *kupdate* kernel thread, which writes back the dirty memory pages and buffers to the real storage medium through the block device layer. For this, we first analyze the write procedure of the JFFS2 filesystem in detail, and derive the drawback and overhead. Then, we design the flash write back routine for the flash filesystem deferred I/O whose method is similar to the Linux *pdflush* and *kupdate* operation for dirty buffers. We implement the flash flush operation and apply to the JFFS2 flash filesystem. The remainder of the paper is organized as follows: Section 2 describes the background of Linux deferred I/O mechanism. Section 3 explain the designed write back routine for JFFS2, and Section 4 describe the performance evaluation of write back routine. Finally, we conclude in Section 5.

2 Background

In this section, we describe the write procedure in Linux kernel internals[11]. The overall procedure is described in Figure 1. The *write*() system call involves moving data from the user mode address space of the calling process into the kernel data structures, and then to storage. There are two important data structures in implementing filesystem, the one is file_operations and the other is address_space_operations. The write method of the file_operations object permits each filesystem type to define a specialized write operation. It is the a procedure that basically identifies the blocks involved in the write operation, copies the data from user mode address space into some pages belonging to the page cache, and marks the buffers in those pages as dirty. Generally, filesystems implement the write method of the file object, which is inherited by the file_operations, by means of the *generic_file_write*() function. The prepare_write and commit_write methods of the address_space_operations object specialize the generic write operation implemented by *generic_file_write*() for files. Both of them are invoked once for every page of the file that is affected by the write operation. Each block based filesystem implements simply a wrapper for common function. For example, EXT2 filesystem[7] implements the prepare_write function by means of the following function:

```
int ext2_prepare_write(struct file *file,
                       struct page *page, unsigned from, unsigned to) {
    return block_prepare_write(page,from,to,ext2_get_block)
}
```

The *ext2_get_block*() function translates the block number relative to the file into a logical block number, which represents the position of the data on the physical block device. The *block_prepare_write*() function takes care of preparing the buffers and the buffer heads of the file's page. Once the prepare_write function returns, the *generic_file_write*() function updates the page with the data stored in the user mode address space using *copy_from_user*() macro. Next,

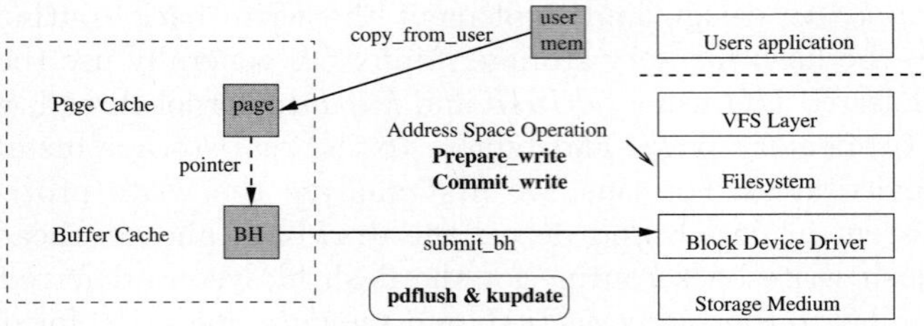

Fig. 1. Write Procedure and data structures in Linux Kernel

the *generic_file_write*() function invokes the commit_write function of the address_space_operations. The commit_write function can be also implemented by a wrapper for the common function, *block_commit_write*(). It considers all buffers in the page that are affected by the write operation; for each of them, it sets the BH_Uptodate and BH_Dirty flags and inserts the buffer head in the BUF_DIRTY list and in the list of dirty buffers of the inode. After the commit_write function returns, the *generic_file_write*() function does the same job until every page is updated by the prepare_write and commit_write methods.

The dirtied pages and buffers are not sent to the block layer and flushed to the storage medium immediately. Linux allow the deferred writes of dirty buffers into block devices, since this noticeably improves system performance. At the system's aspect, I/O bandwidth is increased and at the users aspect, the write response time is reduced. A dirty buffer might stay in main memory until the last possible moment. However, when the system failure occurs, the updated data are lost if the dirty buffers are not flushed to permanent storage. Also, the size of main memory would have to huge at least as big as the size of the accessed block devices. Therefore, the dirty buffers are flush to storage under the following conditions; The buffer cache gets too full and more buffers are need, too much time has elapsed since a buffer has stayed dirty, or *sync*() system call is invoked. Among these conditions, first two conditions are occurred by the system's request. To perform flushing the dirty buffers, Linux runs kernel thread called *pdflush* and *kupdate* in Linux kernel 2.6. While the *pdflush* kernel thread is activated when there are too many dirty buffers or when more buffers are needed, the *kupdate* kernel thread is introduced to flush the older dirty buffers. Therefore, the *kupdate* thread is a periodic timeout function that flush the dirty buffers to the real storage medium.

3 Write Back Routine for JFFS2

In this section, we explain the implementation of JFFS2 write back routine. Since the read/write operation of flash filesystem is strongly related to the filesystem architecture, our implementation of write back routine is only dedicated to JFFS2 filesystem. However, the design concept can be generalized to all of the flash memory based file system. Actually, it is our future work.

There are some implementing issues in applying the write back routine in flash filesystem. First, like the *pdflush* kernel thread and *kupdate* function, the kernel thread and writeback function are required whose roles are transferring the deferred data to the lower layer for real flushing, similar to previous ones. Second, another data structure is required that contains the information to be deferred data just like a buffer_head in general system, since JFFS2 cannot utilize buffer_head data structure. Lastly, the connecting code should be implemented between JFFS2 write code and writeback kernel thread code. The jffs2_prepare_write and jffs2_commit_write method of the JFFS2 address_space object do the jobs. The Figure 2 shows the overall implementation of JFFS2 write back routine.

```
struct jffs2_flash_bh \{
    struct list\_head queue\_list;
    unsigned short type;
    struct page *page;
    unsigned start;
    unsigned end;
    unsigned size;
}
```

The defined structure jffs2_flash_bh is shown in above. It should have variables that jffs2 prepare_write and commit_write function can deliver the important parameters. In the structure, queue_list represents the jffs2_flash_bh list that is to be scheduled for real flushing, and the type represents JFFS2 node type. The page, start, end and size means page pointer, page start address, page end address, and written size, respectively. These are the arguments from generic_file_write function. When $jffs2\_prepare\_write()$ function is called, the jffs2_flash_bh is allocated for node and the member variable, *page, in jffs_flash_bh is is set to the value from the $generic\_file\_write()$. However, there is no data write and only node contains metadata in the $jffs2\_prepare\_write()$, the variables, start and end, have null values. Jffs2_flash_bh is inserted into the flash_bh list for deferred write. The flash_bh list, in here, contains all the deferred jffs2_flash_bh structure objects. It is generated when write back kernel thread is initialized. which is done using the queue_list and Linux list_head macros. Then jffs2_prepare_write returns. The $jffs2\_commit\_write()$ does the similar job, which also allocates one jffs2_flash_bh, and so on. In addition, the start, end and size is set for the data writing, then the constructed structure is inserted into the flash_bh list. After that, the VFS related inode information is updated such as update time and inode size. Since original JFFS2 writes page data to flash memory immediately, pages are not set to anything in JFFS2 address_space operations. We should prolong the page lifetime until the data in pages are written to flash memory by the write back routine. It is done by setting pages appropriate flags and not releasing page memory. Then, $jffs2\_commit\_write()$ returns.

JFFS2 write back routine is composed of $fflush$ kernel thread, and a timer function called $flash\_writeback$. The $fflush$ kernel thread is created during system initialization. It executes $fflush()$ function, that gets the argument function,

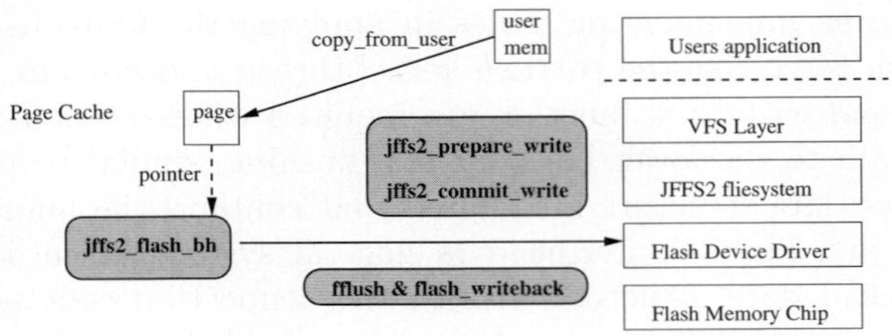

Fig. 2. Write Back Routine of JFFS2 in Flash Memory based Storage

called *wb_flash*(), which selects some nodes from flash_bh list and forces an update of corresponding flash memory pages and blocks. This argument function is transferred from the flash_writeback timer function. The flash_writeback timer function is created by the Linux timer interface, *mod_timer*(), that sets the timer interval and the function to be executed when the timer is expired. When it is created, list_head for the list management of jffs2_flash_bh, called flash_bh, is generated. In *mod_timer*() setting, we set the *wb_flash*() to be executed, later it is executed when *fflush* thread has scheduled. The *wb_flash*() function is key function that actually schedule the jffs2_flash_bh elements in list which are gatherd from *jffs2_prepare_write*() and *jffs2_commit_write*(). In wb_flash, it checks whether the flash_bh contains any list element or not. If it is, it gets one element from the list and tries to write it to flash memory. It makes appropriate type of JFFS2 node, fills node variables with metadata and data, and sends it to lower layer by calling *jffs2_write_dnode*() function. If the write is done with success, the element is eliminated from the list. The *wb_flash*() function iterates the same job until timer function is expired or threshold number of elements that is written in this time becomes over. The list scheduling and merging can be considered while dealing the elements. Each data size and offset in the element is likely to align with the Linux page size and offset since address_space operation in Linux is performed with page aligned. Therefore, the offset alignment of elements in the list is likely to be continuous order, which can be merged. This operation is done until the element cannot be merged into previous ones. Or, the merging should be stopped when merged data size is exceed the size of flash block because JFFS2 node should not be exceed the size of flash memory block. The JFFS2 node can be generated with the merged element, and flushed into flash memory. Since flash memory should ensure the sequential write order for each flash block, the merged node should be written immediately. Merging the elements reduce the number of JFFS2 nodes, thus it can reduce the system overhead not only managing the node fragments list but also flash memory storage itself.

Finally, special treatments are required for special filesystem operations. When *fsync*() system call is called, the file should be flushed into flash memory immediately. In this case, jffs2_fsync method in file object tries to write jffs2_flash_bh elements which are related to the file by finding them in the flash_bh list, making

JFFS2 nodes and programming to flash memory. When filesystem is unmounted, all the list elements should be written to flash memory.

4 Performance Evaluation

We have experimented JFFS2 write performance with our implementation of write back routine for JFFS2 deferred I/O. For the experiments, we use the embedded system which is composed of ARM CPU based system with ARM9 192MHz clock frequency and 32MB main memory[12]. The used NAND flash memory is newly designed memory chip, OneNAND[4]. OneNAND has NOR interface, however, the memory sell is composed of NAND array. It can be connected to the memory system bus, and used for storage. Therefore, there is no problem the performance test to see the flash memory based flash filesystem. The developed and experimented software platform is Linux 2.6.9. In the Linux kernel, we have modified and implemented the JFFS2 write back routine. The experimental environments are summarized in Table 1. The test program we use is the tiobench[13] benchmark program, which is designed to test I/O performance with multiple running threads. The tiobench generates multiple threads that do the read/write operations with specific file size. When they call read/write system call, the write unit, called block size, can be set. In our experiments, we set three types of block size 4KB, 64KB, and 128KB to evaluate the performance for various request size distributions.

We compare the designed method with the EXT2 and JFFS2 original version. The EXT2 is set upon the linux mtdblock ftl layer, and JFFS2 original version means that is constructed without our writeback method. Figure 3 shows the overall experimental results. The latency means the time of read or write for one block. In the Figures, both in EXT2 and JFFS2, the write back method represents very low average write latencies until the file size becomes 16MB. When the file size is over 16MB, average write latencies of them increase dramatically. This threshold value suggests available main memory size for buffering. When the buffers are sufficient to copy users data, these two methods copy file from user address to kernel buffers, but real flushing are not done immediately. However, if buffers are not enough, Linux should flush the dirty buffers immediately to make free buffers. On the other hand, the original JFFS2 shows steady average write latency while varying the file size, since JFFS2 flushes the requests immediately. The reason that EXT2 and JFFS2 write back has higher latencies than that of JFFS2 when file size becomes 16MB is very large peak of maximum latency for some written blocks, which is due to the OS scheduling effect and CPU utilization of bulk flushing. The flushing overhead is realized from the Table 2, which represents the write latency distribution for 4KB block size, for each filesystem. When system feels lack of free memory, more kernel flush threads occupy cpu utilization to make more free memory by reducing the timer wakeup intervals. Also in wb_flash, as pending requests are increased, number of flushed requests are also increased. Therefore, the maximum latency is thousands of average latency when the file size is large, as shown in Table 2. However, this phenomenon rarely occurs. As block size is increased, experiments give similar results, which

Table 1. Experimantal Platform Environment and NAND Flash Memory Characteristics

Experimental Platform	NAND Flash Memory Characteristic.
Platform : OMAP 5912 OSK	Part Number : KFG1G16U2M
Memory : SDRAM 32MB	Block Size : (128K+4K)Bytes
CPU : ARM9 168MHz	Page Size : (2K+64)Bytes
Flash Memory : OneNAND 128MB	Page Read Time : 30us
OS : Linux 2.6.9	Page Program Time : 220us
MTD Snapshot Ver. : 2005/10/22	Block Erase Time : 2ms

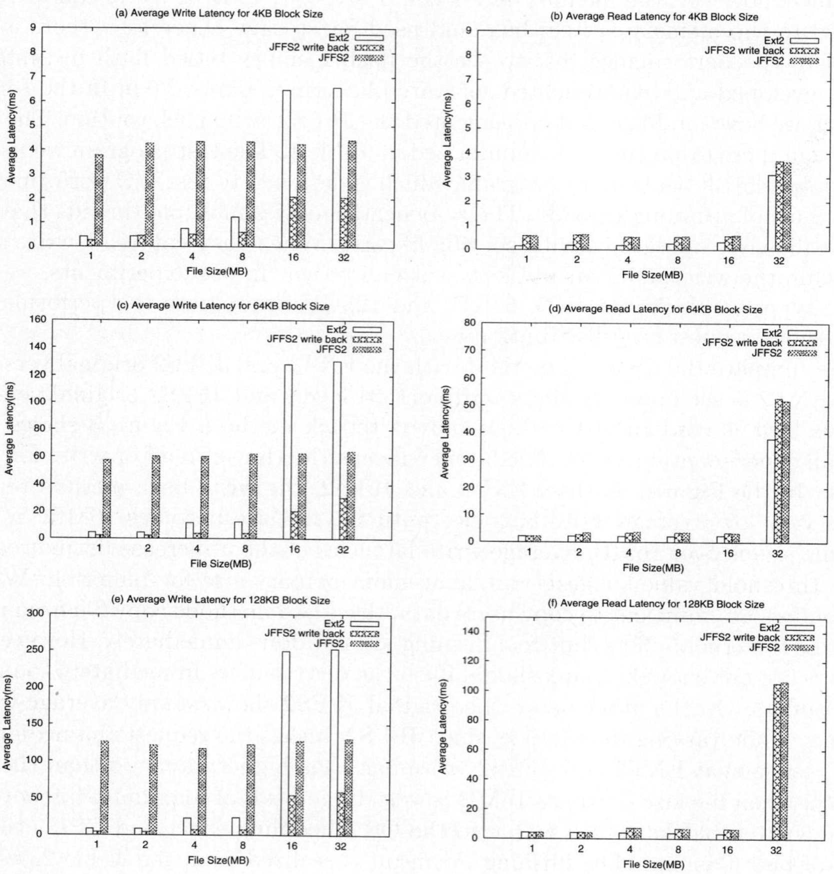

Fig. 3. Experimental Results for Tio Benchmark Program with different file sizes

increase average latency as block size increases. The read latency similar results of that of write except the average latency of JFFS2 original version. It is from the caching effect of written file.

Table 2. Experimental Results for Tio Benchmark Program, which represents write latency distribution for each 4KB block write

Filesystem	size \ time	<0.4	0.4<	0.5<	1<	10<	100<	10000<
Ext2	1MB	28	211	15				
	2MB	27	443	41				
	4MB	30	899	94				
	8MB	27	1811	197	12			
	16MB	81	3584	405	9	2	14	1
	32MB	89	7315	673	74	7	31	2
	size \ time	1.9<x<2	2<	3<	4<	5<	10<	100<
JFFS2	1MB	185	56		13	1		
	2MB	372	110		28	1		
	4MB	726	235	1	56	4	2	
	8MB	1435	403	12	113	44	5	35
	16MB	2791	828	37	261	92	7	79
	32MB	5505	1697	90	488	249	15	147
	size \ time	0.2<	0.3<	0.5<	1<	10<	100<	10000<
JFFS2 WB	1MB	243	12					
	2MB	495	15				1	
	4MB	988	32				3	
	8MB	1971	70				6	
	16MB	3926	154	2	3		9	1
	32MB	7786	315	13	55	2	18	2

5 Conclusion

In this paper, we design and implement the efficient I/O mechanism for JFFS2 filesystem based on the flash memory storage. Linux OS generally uses the write back routine for deferred I/O using *pdflush* and *kupdate* kernel thread, which writes back the dirty memory pages and buffers to the real storage medium through the block device layer. However, flash memory based filesystem, JFFS2, does not use block device layer, so they cannot utilize Linux deferred I/O. When writing new user's data, JFFS2 makes new node which contains both inode information and data, writes to the flash medium using flash driver interface directly. Whenever the write is performed from users, it is not returned from kernel until all the data are written out to flash memory. This write transaction mechanism gives much latency and response time to users and degraded the overall system read/write performance. Therefore, we implement the deferring mechanism of write requests to enhance write latency. For this, we first analyze the write procedure of the JFFS2 filesystem in detail, and derive the drawback and overhead. Then, we design the flash write back routine for deferred I/O whose method is similar to the Linux deferred I/O mechanism. We apply to the JFFS2 flash filesystem by implementing *fflush* kernel daemon and *flash_writeback* routine in Linux kernel. The designed flash write back routine can reduce average latency of write operations when the buffers are enough to get the users data.

References

1. F. Douglis, R. Caceres, F. Kaashoek, K. Li, B. Marsh, and J. A. Tauber, "Storage alternatives for mobile computers", *In Proc. of the 1st Symposium on Operating Systems Design and Implementation(OSDI)*, 1994, pp 25-37

2. Intel Corporation, "Understanding the flash translation layer(FTL) specification", http://developer.intel.com/.
3. Samsung Electronics Co., "NAND Flash Memory & SmartMedia Data Book", 2002.
4. Samsung Electronics Co., "OneNAND Specification", 2005.
5. "Memory Technology Device (MTD) subsystem for Linux.", http://www.linux-mtd.infradead.org.
6. A. Ban, "Flash file system,", *United States Patent, no. 5,404,485*, April 1995.
7. Card R, Ts'o T, Tweedie S., "Design and Implementation of the Second Extended Filesystem.", *The HyperNews Linux KHG Discussion*, http://www.linuxdoc.org, 1999.
8. A. Kawaguchi, S. Nishioka, and H. Motoda, "A Flash-Memory Based File System", *Usenix Technical Conference*, 1995.
9. D. Woodhouse, "JFFS: The Journalling Flash File System", *Ottawa Linux Symposium*, 2001.
10. Mendel Rosenblum and John K. Ousterhout, "The Design and Implementation of a Log-Structured File System". *ACM Transactions on Computer Systems*, 10(1), 1992.
11. Daniel P. Bovet and Marco Cesati, "Understanding the Linux Kernel",. O'reilly
12. Texas Instruments Co., "OMAP 5912 Startker Kit(OSK)", http://focus.ti.com/omap/docs/omaphomepage.tsp.
13. Threaded I/O bench for Linux http://sourceforge.net/projects/tiobench/

Register Array Structure for Effective Edge Filtering Operation of Deblocking Filter

Jongwoo Bae[1], Neungsoo Park[2,*], and Seong-Won Lee[3]

[1] System LSI Division, Samsung Electronics, Co. Ltd., Suwon, Korea
jwp.bae@samsung.com
[2] Dept. of Computer Engineering, Konkuk University, Korea
neungsoo@konkuk.ac.kr
[3] Dept. of Computer Engineering, Kwangwoon University, Korea
swlee@kw.ac.kr

Abstract. In this paper we propose a novel deblocking filter architecture using register array structure for standard video codec hardware. The proposed register array consists of multiple sub-macroblocks for a single macroblock and several sub-macroblock registers for the up and left neighboring macroblocks. The operation procedure of the register array is also presented. The proposed register array achieves fast operating speed and small circuit size at the same time.

1 Introduction

Most modern image processing systems use compressed image data that are generated by standard video codec. Widely used standard codecs are MPEG-1, MPEG-2, and MPEG-4 of International Telecommunication Union (ITU) and Motion Picture Experts Group (MPEG) recommendations. Recently new standard of MPEG-4 AVC (H.264) [1] has great attention because of its higher compression ratio. Research and standardization of H.264 are actively performed worldwide to achieve even higher compression ratio [2,3].

A video decoder system consists of a processor, multiple hardware modules to decode the compressed image data, memory, and peripherals such as DMA and PCI. The decoding hardware modules are Parser, Entropy Decoder, Inverse Transformer, Predictor, and Deblocking Filter. The compressed image data are restored to the original image sequence by sequential processing of the hardware modules.

During the compression process, image data are divided into "macroblocks" that are the basic unit of compression. Due to the individual processing of each macroblock, the restored image data has blocking effect which indicates the distortion of data discontinuity at the macroblock boundary. Since the blocking effect is appeared as a lattice in which the size of a square matches the size of a macroblock, the distortion is highly perceptual and seriously degrades subjective image quality. Deblocking is a process to reduce the blocking effect and deblocking filter [4] is the hardware module that performs deblocking. The detail algorithm of deblocking is presented in the H.264 documentation [1].

---

* Corresponding author.

E. Sha et al. (Eds.): EUC 2006, LNCS 4096, pp. 805 – 813, 2006.

In this paper, we present register array structure of deblocking filter to reduce calculation time of filtering operations. The proposed register array structure effectively reduces vertical filtering operation time. The efficient operation procedure for the proposed register array structure is also proposed.

Section 2 describes general operation of deblocking filter. The structure and operation of the proposed deblocking filter are presented in Section 3. In the Section 4 we analyze the performance of the proposed deblocking filter. Finally, we conclude the paper in Section 5.

2 Background Information

Deblocking filter operates on the uncompressed image data that is the largest data in the H.264 decoder system. Thus many researchers have studied efficient operation of the deblocking filter. Sima et al. proposed the pipelined deblocking filter [5]. In the pipelined deblocking filter, steps of the deblocking filtering are pipelined to improve processing performance. Li et al. propose the parallelized deblocking filter [6]. In addition to pipelining of the deblocking filter, they rearrange processing elements to improve the parallelism of the deblocking filter. Huang et al. proposed a small register array structure [7]. However, the Huang's register array does not have enough performance to process full size HDTV.

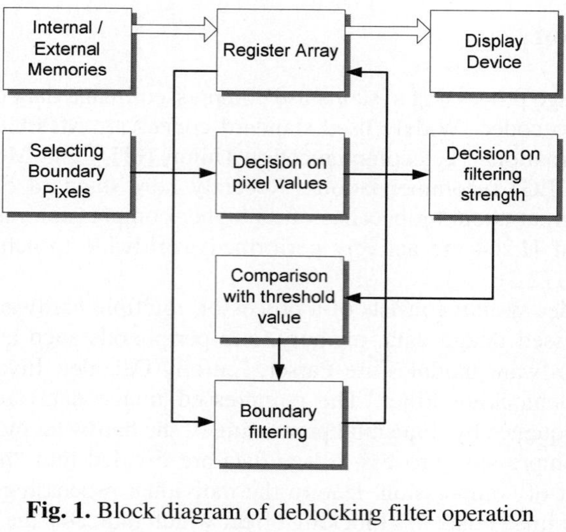

Fig. 1. Block diagram of deblocking filter operation

Fig. 1 shows general operations of a deblocking filter. In the figure the deblocking filter first selects boundaries to perform filtering, then reads corresponding pixel data from memory to a register array. Filtering strength is decided to prevent excessive filtering on real edges. Threshold value is compared to check if the filtering operation is performed or not. Once filtering operation is decided to perform, pixels in the register array is processed with the deblocking filter and output to the display device.

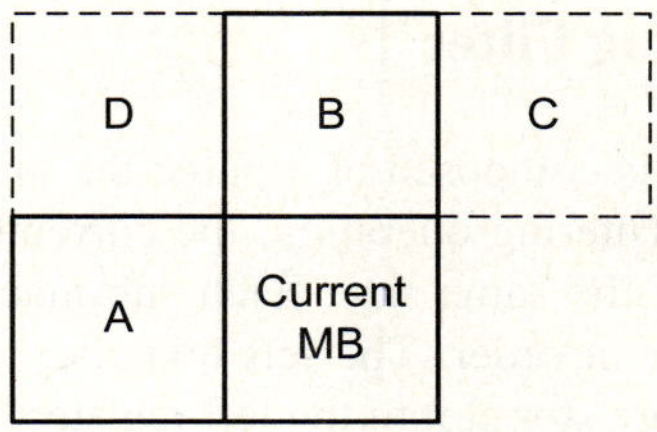

Fig. 2. A macroblock (MB) and its neighboring macroblocks for the deblocking filter

Since the individual compression of macroblocks cause blocking effect, the deblocking filter also individually operates on macroblocks. Fig. 2 shows that a macroblock to be processed and its neighboring macroblocks (A and B) that is necessary to the deblocking filgering.

Filtering operation on a single macroblock respectively performs on a Luminance component and two Chrominance components. A macroblock consists of 16×16 pixels. The 16×16 of a macroblock is divided into 16 sub-macroblocks of 4×4 pixels. The deblocking filtering also removes blocking effect at the boundaries of the sub-macroblocks.

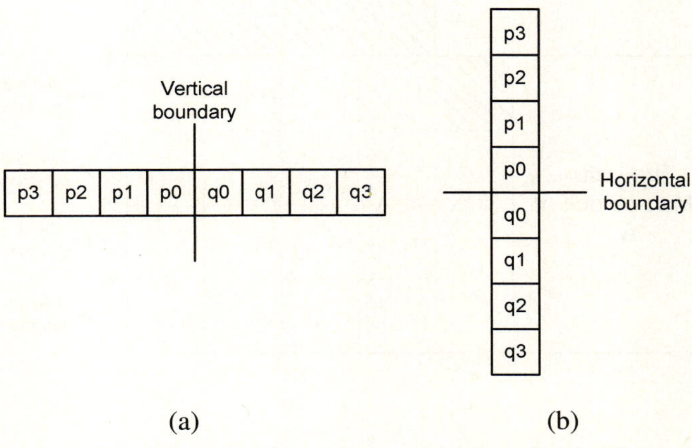

Fig. 3. Pixels used in deblocking filtering (a) Pixels in vertical filtering (b) Pixels in horizontal filtering

Fig. 3(a) shows pixels used in vertical deblocking filter and Fig. 3(b) shows pixels in horizontal deblocking filter. As shown in Fig. 3, 8 consecutive pixels are necessary to the deblocking filter. Thus, the conventional deblocking filtering, especially vertical filtering, using 8 vertical consecutive pixels for a single filtering operation is accompanied 8 memory accesses. As to a single macroblock, the total required memory access cycle is 768. This long latency cause serious problems to real-time processing of high resolution videos such as HDTV programs.

3 Proposed Deblocking Filter

In this paper, register array is composed of 3 parts: the main register, the left register, the upper register. For the filtering operation, the current macroblock is divided into several sub-macroblocks of the same size. Each sub-macroblock are stored into and read from the main register in order. The left boundary data of the sub-macroblock stored in the main register are stored into the left register. The upper boundary data of the sub-macroblock stored in the main register are stored into the upper register. In the upper register, the initial data for the current macroblock comes from the upper macroblock, and then the data coming out from the main register after the sub-macroblock computation is stored.

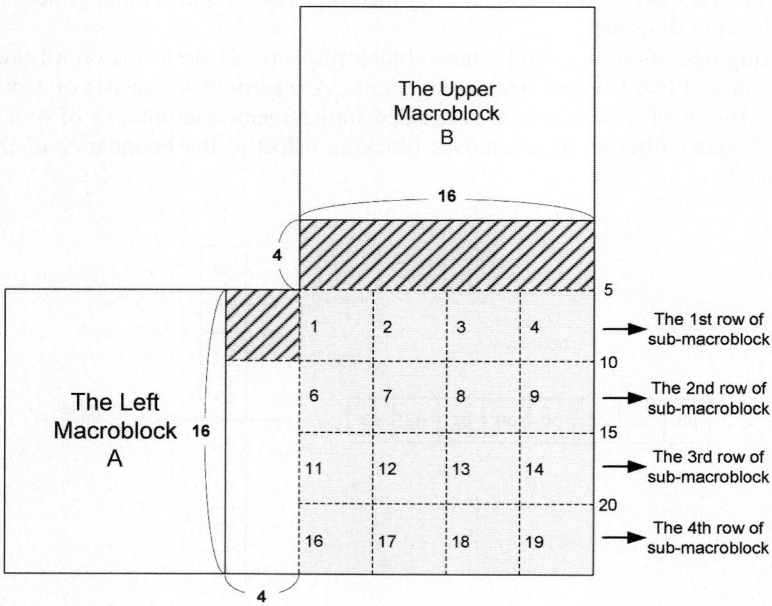

Fig. 4. The order of filtering operation for a macroblock

3.1 Implementation of Deblocking Filtering

Fig. 4 shows the order of filtering operation for a macroblock. The dotted line is the horizontal and vertical boundary for filtering operations. As shown in Fig. 4, the current macroblock is divided into 4 rows of sub-macroblocks. The size of a row is 16×4. For the 1st row of sub-macroblocks, horizontal filtering operation is performed sequentially, and then the vertical filtering operation is performed. These filtering operations are applied to the 2nd, 3rd, and 4th row of sub-macroblocks.

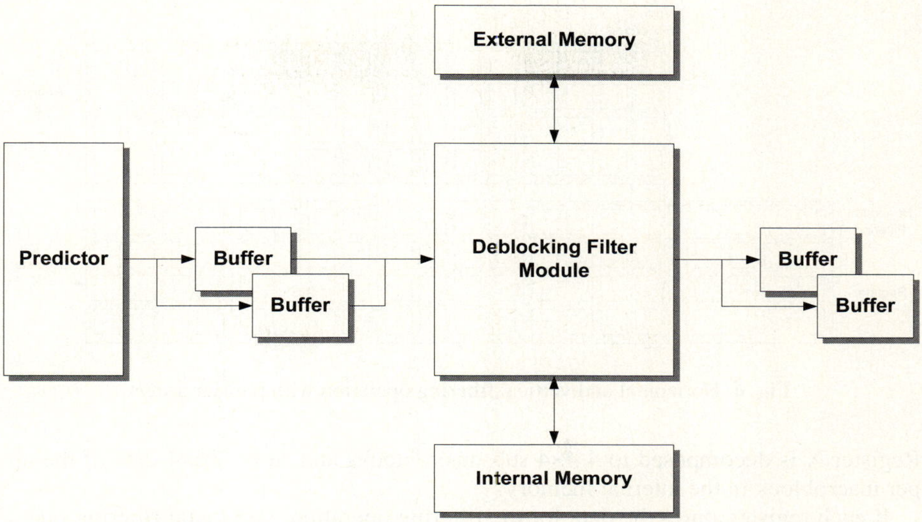

Fig. 5. The block diagram of the deblocking filter module for filtering operation

As shown in Fig. 5, the prediction results are stored into the dual buffer. The luminance and chrominance component of the current macroblock read from the dual buffers are stored into internal register arrays of the deblocking filter module. The left macroblock A and the upper macroblock B adjacent to the current macroblock as shown in Fig. 4 are read from the external memory, stored into the internal memory, and then re-stored into the register arrays.

As discussed in Fig. 4, the current macroblock is divided into 4 rows of sub-macroblocks and then filter operations are performed. The data of the 1st row of the sub-macroblocks are stored into register arrays. From the upper macroblock B, the 16×4 data adjacent to the 1st row of sub-macroblocks are read from the external memory, stored into the internal memory, and then re-stored into register arrays. From the left macroblock A, the 4×16 data adjacent to the current macroblock are stored into the internal memory and then the only upper 4×4 data block are re-stored into register arrays. Therefore, the 4×16 data from the macroblock A and the 16×4 data from the macroblock B are stored into the internal memory. The deblocking filter module performs the filter operation with the data in register arrays and then stores the result into the dual buffer.

3.2 Implementation of the Proposed Register Array

As shown in Fig. 6, the register arrays is composed of 16×4 Register **X**, 4×4 Register **A**, and 4×16 Register **B**. The Register X is decomposed of 4 4×4 sub-macroblocks. It stores the 1st row of sub-macroblocks of the current macroblock which are read from the dual buffer storing the prediction results. Register A stores the upper 4×4 sub-macroblock of the left macroblock in the internal memory. Register B as same as

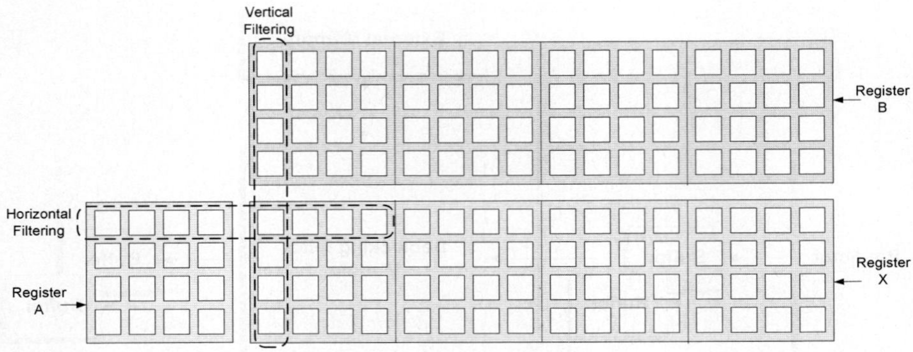

Fig. 6. Horizontal and vertical filtering operation with register arrays

Register X is decomposed to 4 4×4 sub-macroblocks and stores 16×4 data of the upper macroblock in the internal memory.

If each register stores the data for the filtering operation, horizontal filtering operations for the current row of sub-macroblocks in the Register X are performed with the data in Register A. And then, vertical filtering operations are performed with data in Register B.

At first, the horizontal filter operation with the sub-macroblock in Register X takes the data in Register A and the 4 leftmost data in Register X. It performs on the vertical boundary data between 4-pixel data.

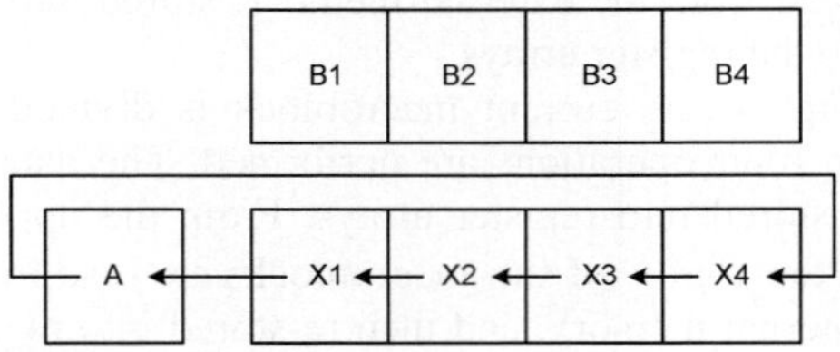

Fig. 7. Shift operation of the register array for horizontal filtering

As shown in Fig. 7, if the filtering operation with the sub-macroblock X1 is completed, the data in each register are shifted left by 4×4. So, the data in X1 sub-macroblock are moved to register A, X2 to X1, X3 to X2, X4 to X3, and then the data in Register A(A1) to X4. After that, the same procedure (filtering → shifting) is repeated until the horizontal filtering operations are completed with the data in Register X. After 4 times shift operation, the data in Register A is moved to the X1 position. Therefore, the data is moved to the initial position by one more left shift operation.

The vertical filtering operation is performed with the row data of sub-macroblocks in Register X. This vertical operation takes the data in Register B. There is one horizontal boundary between data in Register X and Register B. The vertical filtering operation is performed to 16 pixels on this horizontal boundary.

If these horizontal and vertical filtering operations are completed with a 16×4 row of sub-macroblock, the next row of sub-macroblocks are filled into the Register X. The previous data in Register X are moved to the Register B, and the new 4×4 data in Register A are read from the internal memory. The first data in Register A and Register B are sent to the external memory. This overall procedure is repeated with an entire macroblock. Therefore, the movement between the new sub-macroblock data and sub-macroblock data after filtering operation and output from Register A and B are concurrently performed.

3.3 Implementation of Register I/O

Fig.8 shows the I/O operation of the register array. As shown in Fig. 8(a), the leftmost sub-macroblock in the 2nd row are stored into register X1 and the next sub-macroblock (a2) of macroblock A in the internal memory is stored into Register A. The previous data (x1) in register X1 is shifted into register B1 and the previous data (b1) in register B1 is sent out the external memory.

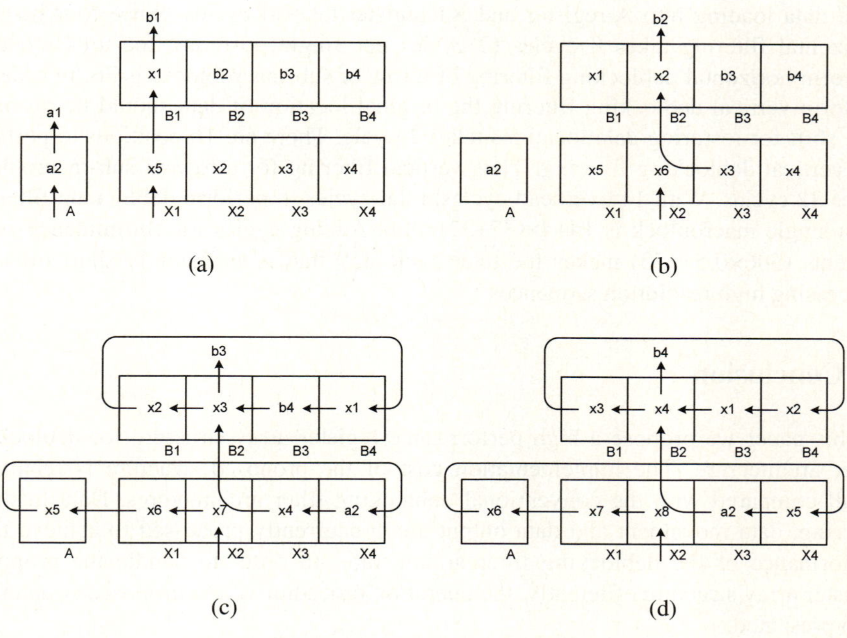

Fig. 8. The I/O operation of register array

As shown in Fig. 8(b), the next sub-macroblock (x6) in the 2nd row are inputted into register X2. The previous data (x2) in register X1 are shifted into register B2 and the previous data (b2) in the register B2 are sent out. At the same time, the horizontal filtering operations are performed on data (a2 and x5) in register A and X1. After filtering operation for register X1, data in each Register A and X are shifted left by 4×4 as shown in Fig. 8(c). The data in Register B is also shifted by 4×4. After the shift operation, the horizontal filtering operation is performed on the x6 and x5 in Register X1 and A, respectively. Concurrently, the 3rd sub-macroblock in the 2nd row is stored into the register X2 and the previous 3rd sub-macroblock (x3) in the 1st row is shifted into register B2. The previous data (b3) in register B2 is sent out.

After fourth sub-macroblock data (x8) of the 2nd row of sub-macroblocks is loaded into register X2, the rest of filtering operation is performed as shown in Fig. 8(d). Once horizontal deblocking filtering of a row of sub-macroblocks is completed, data is shifted to go back their original position. Then vertical deblocking filtering is performed on the data of X-register.

The procedures are repeated with the other rows of sub-macroblocks until processing of the entire macroblock is finished. It should be noticed that data is loaded into X1-register at the initial state. For all other case, data is loaded into X2-register.

4 Performance Analysis

The proposed deblocking filtering can process a single macroblock as followings: First data loading into A-register and X1-register takes 4 cycles. Since four lines of horizontal filtering takes 8 cycles (2 cycles per single position), the total cycle to perform horizontal deblocking filtering of a row of sub-macroblocks is 36. In order to perform vertical deblocking filtering the original location of data should be restored. The shift for restoring data locations takes 1 cycle. There are 16 positions to perform the vertical deblocking filtering. Thus vertical filtering for a row of sub-macroblock takes 32 cycles. With 14 overhead cycles, total cycles to perform deblocking filtering on a single macroblock is 14+4×(37+32)=306. Adding cycles for chrominance components (306×0.5=153) makes the total cycle 459 that is sufficiently short time for processing high resolution sequences.

5 Conclusion

In this paper we propose a high performance register array structure for deblocking filter architecture. The implementation cost of the proposed structure is relatively small compared with the conventional deblocking filter architectures. Data loading, filtering, data movement and data output are concurrently processed to achieve high performance of the deblocking filter architecture. In order to handle the proposed register array structure efficiently, the operation procedure of the proposed structure is also presented.

Acknowledgement

This work is partly supported by Samsung Electronics Co. Ltd. under Blue Architecture Project and partly supported by the Ministry of Information and Communication, Korea, under the ITRC program supervised by the IITA.

References

1. Draft ITU-T recommendation and final draft international standard of joint video specification (ITU-T) Rec. H.264/ISO/IEC 14 496-10 AVC. Document JVTG050. Joint Video Team (JVT) of ISO/IEC MPEG and ITU-T VCEG (2003)
2. Wiegand, T., Sullivan, G., Bjntegaard, G., Luthra, A.: Overview of the H.264/AVC video coding standard. IEEE Trans. Circuits Syst. Video Technol. 13 (2003) 560-576
3. Ostermann, J., Bormans, J., List, P., Marpe, D., Narroschke, M., Pereira, F., Stockhammer, T., Wedi, T.: Video coding with H.264/AVC: Tools, performance, and complexity. IEEE Mag. Circuits and Syst. 4 (2004) 7-28
4. P. List, A. Joch, J.L.G.B., Karczewicz, M.: Adaptive deblocking filter. IEEE Trans. Circuits Syst. Video Technol. 13 (2003) 614-619
5. M. Sima, Y.Z., Zhang, W.: An efficient architecture for adaptive deblocking filter of h.264/AVC video coding. IEEE Trans. Consum. Electron. 50 (2004) 292-296
6. Li, L., Goto, S., Ikenaga, T.: A highly parallel architecture for deblocking filter in H.264/AVC. IEICE Trans. Inf. & Syst. E88-D (2005) 1623-1629
7. Huang, Y.W., Chen, T.W., Hsieh, B.Y., Wang, T.C., Chang, T.H., Chen, L.G.: Architecture design for deblocking filter in H.264/JVT/AVC. In: IEEE Proc. Int. Conf. Multimedia and Expo 2003. Volume 1. (2003) 693-696

Quantitative Service Differentiation: A Square-Root Proportional Model

Xiaobo Zhou[1] and Cheng-Zhong Xu[2]

[1] Department of Computer Science, University of Colorado at Colorado Springs, 1420 Austin Bluffs Parkway, Colorado Springs, CO 80918, USA
zbo@cs.uccs.edu

[2] Department of Electrical & Computer Engineering, Wayne State University, 5050 Anthony Wayne Drive, Detroit, MI 48202, USA
czxu@wayne.edu

Abstract. Due to the open and dynamics nature of ubiquitous computing environments and services, quantitative service differentiation is needed to provide controllable quality of service (QoS) levels to meet changing system configuration and resource availability and to satisfy different requirements of applications and users. A proportional differentiation model was proposed in the DiffServ context, which states that QoS factors of certain classes of aggregated traffic be proportional to their differentiation weights. While it provides compelling proportionality fairness to clients, it lacks of the support of a server-side QoS optimization with respect to the resource allocation. In this paper, we propose and promote a square-root proportional differentiation model for delay-sensitive Internet services. Interestingly, both popular QoS factors with respect to delay, queueing delay and slowdown, are reciprocally proportional to the allocated resource usages. We formulate the problem of quantitative service differentiation as a resource allocation optimization towards the minimization of *system delay*, defined as the sum of weighted responsiveness of client request classes. We prove that the optimization-based resource allocation scheme essentially provides square-root proportional service differentiation to clients. We then propose a generalized rate-based resource allocation approach. Simulation results demonstrate that the approach provides quantitative service differentiation at a minimum cost of system delay.

1 Introduction

Popular Internet services must be scalable to support a large number of concurrent client requests reliably, responsively, and economically [3]. These scalability and availability requirements pose great challenge on both processing power and networking capacity. Meanwhile, clients of Internet services are diverse with respect to service expectations and access devices. To meet changing system configuration and resource availability and to satisfy different application and client requirements, there is an increasing demand for provisioning of different

E. Sha et al. (Eds.): EUC 2006, LNCS 4096, pp. 814–823, 2006.

levels of quality of service (QoS) [2,4,7,10,12]. Service differentiation is to provide a certain level of QoS guarantee to a class of aggregate requests based on predefined service level agreements with the clients. It can provide degraded levels of QoS to client requests when a server is heavily loaded, but also adapt the service quality to meet the variety of client preferences and devices. By adjusting the level of QoS, service differentiation techniques are able to postpone the occurrence of request rejection as the server load increases. They achieve the scalability in terms of cost-effectiveness. In addition, service differentiation can also provide an incentive for different charging policies for most of today's QoS-sensitive Internet services.

The service differentiation architecture is also demanded in ubiquitous computing and communications. By blending computers into the ubiquitous networking infrastructure, ubiquitous computing provides people with a most wide range of communication and information access services. The services are ensured to be accessible anytime, anywhere on any device. Provisioning of such services is a challenge because of the diversity of access devices and access networks. Their capabilities to receive, process, store and display media-rich content vary greatly. A user who accesses streaming services on a cellular phone must expect different service qualities from users on a highend workstation with high bandwidth networking capacities. A service differentiation architecture supports such heterogeneous QoS requirements and preferences by adapting the stream quality to various devices and access patterns.

To provide quantitative QoS differentiation, the proportional differentiation model [4] was proposed which states that QoS metrics of certain classes of aggregated requests should be proportional to their differentiation parameters, independent of their workloads. It is accepted as an important relative differentiation model and is applied in the proportional delay and loss rate differentiation in packet forwarding and dropping [4]. It is also adopted for server-side service differentiation [7,11]. While the proportional model provides compelling proportionality fairness to clients, it lacks of the support of a server-side QoS optimization with respect to the resource allocation. This is due to the fact that from the server's perspective, the QoS factor offered to a client is usually not proportional to the resource usage allocated.

In this paper, we propose and promote a square-root proportional differentiation model for delay-sensitive Internet services, in which delay is the key QoS metric. We find that both popular delay factors, queueing delay and slowdown, are reciprocally proportional to the allocated resource usages according to the foundations of queueing theory. Note that slowdown measures the ratio of a request's queueing delay to its service time. It is known that clients are more likely to anticipate short delays for "small" requests and more willing to tolerate long delays for "large" requests [5]. The slowdown metric characterizes the relative queueing delay. We formulate the problem of quantitative service differentiation as a resource allocation optimization towards the minimization of system delay, defined as the sum of weighted delay of client request classes. We prove that the optimization-based resource allocation scheme essentially provides square-root proportional differentiation to clients. We then propose a generalized rate-based resource allocation approach. Simulation results demonstrate that the approach provides quantitative service differentiation at a minimum system delay.

The structure of the paper is as follows. Section 2 reviews related work. Section 3 gives the square-root proportional differentiation model with a generalized resource allocation approach. Section 4 focuses on the performance evaluation. Section 5 concludes the paper with remarks on the implementation issues.

2 Related Work

The concept of service differentiation is not new. It was first invented for QoS-aware packet scheduling in the network core. The proportional differentiation model has been extensively studied in packet scheduling with respect to packet delay, packet loss, and connection bandwidth; see [4] for a representative approach. The work in [7] demonstrated that some approaches developed for proportional delay differentiation on networks can be tailored for its provisioning on Internet servers. While the model is compelling and important for Internet services due to its inherent proportional fairness and predictability properties, it lacks of the resource allocation optimization from the server's perspective.

On the basis of request classification, the objective of service differentiation on servers can be realized in five aspects: admission control, feedback control, content adaptation, resource allocation, and request scheduling. Admission control can provide QoS guarantees on delivered services, such as response time and bandwidth, to different classes. The work in [8] developed an admission control mechanism to provide differentiated bandwidth allocation to multiple service classes in a Web server. Feedback control operates by responding to measured deviations from the desired performance. The work in [9] proposed to integrate a queueing model with proportional integral control for relative request delay guarantees in Web servers. Multimedia objects are becoming a prevalent part of Web content. Content adaptation techniques are often used to deliver the media-rich objects in different formats, resolutions, sizes, color depths, and other quality control options for service differentiation purposes [12].

Priority-based request scheduling and rate-based resource allocation are general resource management approaches to ensuring the QoS of requests or preserving the quality spacings between two classes. There are efforts on priority-based request scheduling with admission control for response time differentiation [2]. Incoming requests were categorized into the appropriate queues and executed according to their priority levels [2]. The approach was shown to be effective for service differentiation in terms of queueing delays between lower and higher priority classes of traffic, but with no guarantee of quality spacings. In this paper, we propose and promote a square-root proportional differentiation model, which essentially provides the resource allocation optimization and proportionality fairness at the same time. We adopt a rate-based resource allocation approach in the simulations and performance evaluation.

3 A Square-Root Proportional Model

Predictability and controllability are two basic requirements of quantitative service differentiation. Predictability requires that higher priority classes receive better or no worse service quality than lower priority classes. Controllability requires that a scheduler contain a number of controllable parameters that are adjustable for the control of quality spacings between classes. An additional requirement is fairness. Fairness is a quantitative extension of the predictability, which describes how much better QoS received by a class compared with that received by another class.

Proportional fair-sharing is compelling and important for various Internet services due to its inherent proportional fairness and predictability properties. Assuming incoming requests are classified into N contending classes, the proportional differentiation model aims to ensure the quality spacing between class i and class j to be proportional to certain pre-specified differentiation parameters δ_i and δ_j [4]. We consider delay as the key QoS factor in delay-sensitive Internet services. The quality factor of a request class is then represented by the inverse of its delay. That is,

$$\frac{q_i}{q_j} = \frac{\delta_j}{\delta_i} \qquad 1 \leq i, j \leq N,$$

where q_i and q_j are the delay factors of class i and class j, respectively. The model essentially considers the proportional fairness to the clients. From the viewpoint of the server, however, it lacks the support of a system-wide QoS optimization with respect to the resource allocation.

In the following, we formulate a general resource allocation problem that aims to optimize a system-wide QoS to the server. We will prove that the derived allocation scheme also provides proportional service differentiation, in square root, to the clients. The basic idea of QoS provisioning is to divide the resource allocation procedure into a sequence of short intervals. In each interval, based on the measured resource utilization and the predicted workload, the available resource usages of the server are differently allocated to N task servers handling traffic classes. We assume the processing rate of a server can be proportionally allocated to the task servers. Each task server presents a processing unit that handles requests from the same class in a FCFS manner. The objective of the optimization is to minimize the system delay. Based on the delay factor (q_i) for individual request classes, the system delay is naturally defined as $\mathcal{G} = \sum_{i=1}^{N} \delta_i q_i$, the weighted delay of all request classes. We introduce the system delay as the system-wide QoS of a delay-sensitive Internet server. We formulate the resource allocation for quantitative service differentiation as the following optimization problem:

$$\text{Minimize} \quad \mathcal{G} = \sum_{i=1}^{N} \delta_i q_i \tag{1}$$

$$\text{subject to} \quad q_i = f(c_i, l_i), \tag{2}$$

$$\sum_{i=1}^{N} c_i < C. \tag{3}$$

(1) defines the objective function of the quantitative service differentiation. It is to minimize the system delay of the server. It implies that requests from higher classes get lower delay (higher QoS). The rationale is its feasibility, differentiation predictability and controllability. (2) gives the definition of q_i with the allocated resource usage (c_i) and the workload (l_i) of class i. We assume that the server has a single processing resource bottleneck. Although processing a request often needs to consume resources of different types, resource management usually focuses on the allocation of the most critical resource [2,5]. (3) gives the constraint of the resource allocation, where C is the resource available during the current resource allocation interval, which is the server's processing capacity minus the overhead of resource usage collection and allocation in each interval. A processing rate allocation scheme is needed to determine the amount of the resource usages allocated to the task servers for handling requests so that the resource utilization is maximized.

For quantitatively predictable and controllable differentiation, we need to have a closed form expression of quality factor(s) with respect to resource allocation. We find that both popular delay factors, queueing delay and slowdown, are reciprocally proportional to the allocated resource usage (processing rate). We consider a general workload model on each task server. Let m_1, m_{-1}, and m_2 be the first moment (mean), the moment of its inverse, and the second moment of the service time distribution, respectively. According to Pollaczek-Khinchin formula [6], we have

Lemma 1. *Given an $M/G/1$ FCFS queue on a task server i, where the arrival process has workload l_i. Then, the delay factor q_i is reciprocally proportional to the allocated resource usage to server i (c_i). That is,*

$$q_i = f(c_i, l_i) = \frac{\propto l_i}{2(c_i - l_i)}, \tag{4}$$

where $\propto$ is a value determined by the service time distribution of the traffic workload.

Proof. Let d_i and s_i be the queueing delay and slowdown of a job on the task server i, respectively. Let λ_i denote the arrival process of request class i. We have $l_i = m_1\lambda_i$. According to Pollaczek-Khinchin formula [6], we have

$$d_i = \frac{\lambda_i m_2}{2(c_i - \lambda_i m_1)} = \frac{m_2/m_1 l_i}{2(c_i - l_i)} = \frac{\propto l_i}{2(c_i - l_i)}, \qquad \propto = m_2/m_1. \tag{5}$$

$$s_i = d_i m_{-1} = \frac{m_2 m_{-1}/m_1 l_i}{2(c_i - l_i)} = \frac{\propto l_i}{2(c_i - l_i)}, \qquad \propto = m_2 m_{-1}/m_1. \tag{6}$$

It concludes the proof.

Theorem 1. *The optimal resource allocation scheme to (1) essentially provides square-root proportional QoS differentiation. That is,*

$$\frac{q_i}{q_j} = g(l_i, l_j)\sqrt{\frac{\delta_j}{\delta_i}}, \tag{7}$$

where function $g(l_i, l_j)$ describes the workload relationship of two classes.

Proof. The optimization of (1) $\sim$ (3) is essentially a continuous convex separable resource allocation problem. According to foundations of resource allocation theory, its optimal solution occurs when the first order derivatives of the objective function over variables c_i are equivalent. Specifically, the optimal solution to (1) occurs when

$$-\frac{\propto \delta_i l_i}{(2(c_i - l_i))^2} = -\frac{\propto \delta_j l_j}{(2(c_j - l_j))^2} \qquad 1 \le i, j \le N. \tag{8}$$

It follows that

$$\frac{c_i - l_i}{c_1 - l_1} = \sqrt{\frac{\delta_i l_i}{\delta_1 l_1}}, \quad 1 \le i \le N. \tag{9}$$

Together with the constraint (3), the set of equations (9) leads to a linear equation system. It follows the generalized rate-based resource allocation approach as

$$c_i = l_i + \frac{(C - \sum_{j=1}^{N} l_j)\sqrt{\delta_i l_i}}{\sum_{j=1}^{N}\sqrt{\delta_j l_j}}. \tag{10}$$

The first term of (9) ensures that the task server will not be overloaded. The second term means that the remaining capacity of the server is proportionally allocated to different classes according to their scaled arrival rates and differentiation parameters.

Accordingly, the delay factor of a request class is calculated as

$$q_i = \frac{\propto l_i \sum_{j=1}^{N}\sqrt{\delta_j l_j}}{2(C - \sum_{j=1}^{N} l_j)\sqrt{\delta_i l_i}}. \tag{11}$$

It follows that

$$\frac{q_i}{q_j} = \sqrt{\frac{l_i}{l_j}}\sqrt{\frac{\delta_j}{\delta_i}}. \tag{12}$$

(12) shows that the allocation approach has the property of square-root proportional fairness as well, where $g(l_i, l_j) = \sqrt{l_i/l_j}$. It concludes the proof.

Thus, this square-root proportional allocation scheme meets a two-fold objective: one is the (square-root) proportional service differentiation provisioning; the other is the optimization of the resource allocation with respect to the system-wide QoS metric.

Remark. Recall that $l_i = m_1\lambda_i$. According to (12), the predictability of service differentiation holds if and only if $\sqrt{\lambda_i/\lambda_j} \le \sqrt{\delta_i/\delta_j}$ for $1 \le j < i \le N$. Otherwise, the predictability, that is, $q_i \le q_j$ if and only if $i > j$, will be violated. One solution is temporary weight promotion in [13]. When it is applied in this context, based on the current session arrival rates and the number of visits to a state in sessions, the scheduler temporarily increases weight δ_i in the current resource allocation interval so that the predictability of the relative service differentiation holds. In this context, the allocation scheme becomes heuristic.

4 Performance Evaluation

To evaluate the rate-based resource allocation approach on quantitative service differentiation, we built a simulator. The processing rate allocation can be implemented by the use of many different mechanisms, as we are going to discuss in Section 5. In this work, we built a simulator because that without being affected by the methods of implementations, simulation can effectively evaluate the performance of the rate allocation schemes by itself. The simulator consists of a number of request generators, waiting queues, a load estimator, a processing rate allocator, and a number of task servers. We conducted the simulations with requests generated by using GNU scientific library. We consider *Bounded Pareto* distribution, a typical heavy-tailed distribution, for the service time distribution of workloads. Given a distribution, the first moment m_1, the moment of its inverse m_{-1}, and the second moment m_2 can be represented in closed forms [11]. Due to the space limitation, we show the results of slowdown differentiation only, while the results of queueing delay differentiation are similar. Each result reported is an average of 100 runs, unless otherwise specified.

4.1 Impact of Square-Root Proportional Model on System QoS

Fig. 1 shows the results of system slowdown with the increase of server load by the use of the square-root rate allocation approach proposed in this paper and the proportional rate allocation scheme proposed in [11]. The predefined differentiation weight ratio of high priority class to low priority class ($\delta_1 : \delta_2$) is 4:1. The workload ratio of the two classes ($l_1 : l_2$) is 1:4.

Fig. 1(a) illustrates the effectiveness of the generalized rate allocation approaches by comparing the achieved system slowdown with the calculated slowdown. We found that simulation results closely agree with the expected results under various load conditions, before the server is heavily loaded ($\leq 70\%$). The gap between the simulated results and the expected results increases as the server load increases. This is due to the variance of both inter-arrival time distributions and the heavy-tailed service size distributions. When the workload is above 80%, the server observes more backlogged jobs. Slowdown of some backlogged jobs could be very large, which increases the variance of the simulation results. Second, we find that the square-root proportional rate allocation approach can reduce system slowodown significantly compared to that received by the proportional approach. The improvement is shown in Fig. 1(b) with both predicted and simulated values. We also want to note that when two classes have the equal workload, the proportional approach indeed achieved the same system slowdown as a non-differentiation approach did (the results are not shown due to

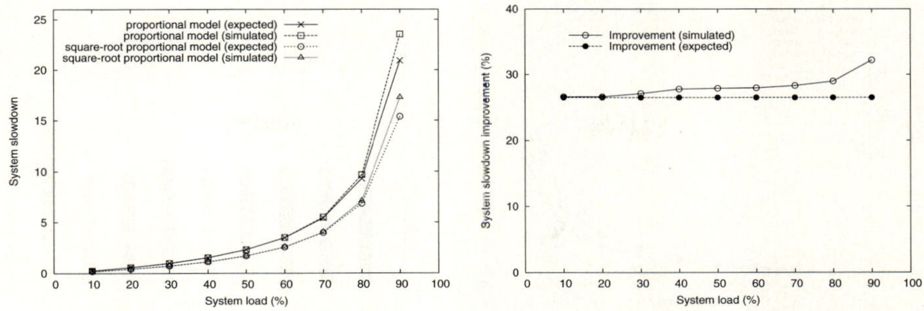

(a) System slowdown values (b) System slowdown improvement

Fig. 1. System slowodown and its improvement due to different differentiation schemes

the space limitation). The results demonstrate the superiority of the square-root proportional model in optimizing resource allocation for minimizing the system slowdown. Also, we note that the improvement degree of system slowdown is dependent on the workload ratio and differentiation weight ratio of the classes.

4.2 Differentiation Properties of Square-Root Proportional Model

We then show the differentiation predictability and controllability of the rate allocation approaches. The predefined differentiation weight ratio of two classes ($\delta_1 : \delta_2$) is set to 2:1. The workload ratio of two classes ($l_1 : l_2$) is set to 1:1.

Fig. 2 shows the quantitative slowdown differentiation when the server workload changes from 10% to 90%. The results were due to the square-root proportional rate allocation approach. Fig. 2(a) shows a per-class view of request slowdown. It shows that the expected results closely agree with the simulated results when the workload is moderate. This is due to the fact that the rate allocation approach is guided by the predictive queueing model. When the system load is close to system capacity, say at 90%, the rate allocation approach generates poor predictability. This can be explained by the fact that as the system load is close to its capacity, the impact of the variance of inter-arrival times on slowdown dominates. This mitigates the controllability of the queueing-theoretical rate allocation approach. Fig. 2(b) shows the achieved slowdown ratio of two classes with the 95% confidence interval measured with 20 runs. As the workload is close to the server capacity, the predictability is not desirable.

We then show the differentiation results by the use of the proportional rate allocation approach. Fig. 3 depicts the achieved per-class request slowdown with the 95% confidence interval measured with 20 runs at different system workload conditions. It has the basic similar shape as Fig. 2. Results show that the rate allocation approach is able to achieve the proportional differentiation as well. From these results, we find that the generalized rate allocation approaches can achieve the objective of providing quantitative service differentiation to classes with different differentiation parameters under various system load conditions in long timescales.

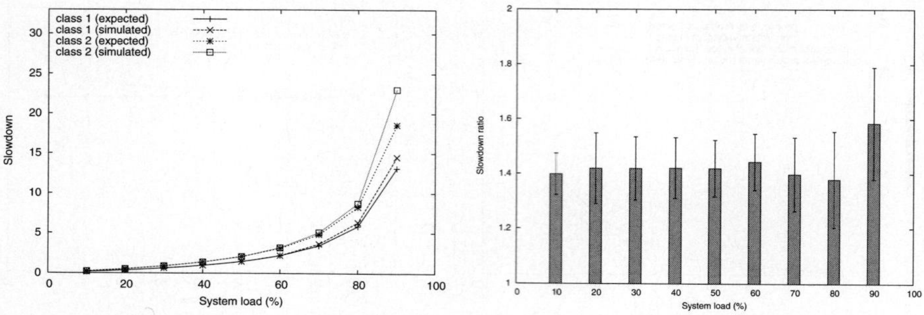

(a) Average slowdown (b) Slowdown ratios

Fig. 2. Two-class differentiation due to the square-root proportional model

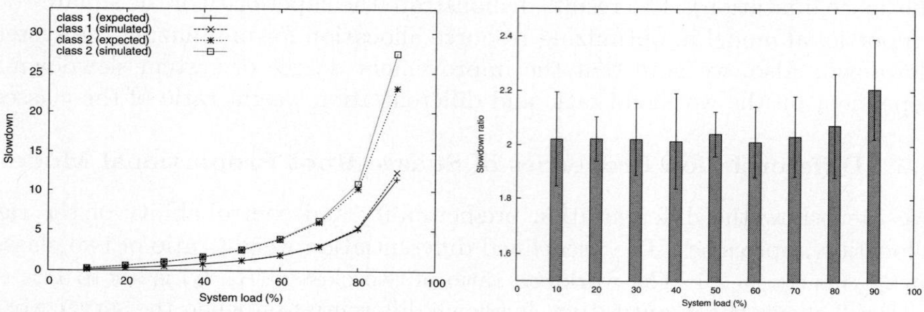

(a) Average slowdown (b) Slowdown ratios

Fig. 3. Two-class differentiation due to the proportional model

We conducted a wide ranger of sensitivity analysis. We varied the number of request classes, the arrival rate ratios of the classes, and the differentiation weight ratios of the classes. While we do not have space to present all of the results, note that we did not reach any significantly different conclusion regarding to the quantitative service differentiation achieved by two models.

5 Conclusion and Future Work

In this paper, we proposed a square-root proportional service differentiation model for ubiquitous computing environments and services. It was derived from the resource allocation optimization towards minimizing the system slowdown of an Internet server. We proved that the optimization-based allocation scheme essentially provides square-root proportional fairness to clients. Simulation results demonstrated that the derived rate allocation approach can provide quantitative service differentiation at a minimum of system delay.

A challenging issue left is how to allocate resources to meet an allocation of processing rate. In the theoretical analysis, we adopted the concept of task server to represent the processing rate that can be allocated to a traffic class. In practice, it can be a process on an individual Web server, a thread on a multi-thread server, a processor in a parallel machine, and a node in a server cluster. Process abstraction serves both as a protection domain and as a resource principal in current general-purpose operating systems. However, because an application does not have the control over the consumption of resources that the kernel consumes on behalf of the application, resource principals do not always coincide with processes. There are efforts on OS support for service differentiation, as exemplified by resource containers [1]. The implementation of the rate allocation schemes on servers deserves further study and evaluation.

Acknowledgement. This research was supported in part by an award from the Committee on Research and Creative Works (CRCW) of the University of Colorado at Colorado Springs.

References

1. G. Banga, P. Druschel, and J. Mogul. Resource containers: A new facility for resource management in server systems. In *Proc. USENIX OSDI*, 1999.
2. X. Chen and P. Mohapatra. Performance evaluation of service differentiating Internet servers. *IEEE Trans. on Computers*, 51(11):1,368–1,375, 2002.
3. C.-Z. Xu. Scalable and Secure Internet Services and Architecture. Chapman & Hall/CRC Press, ISBN 1-58488-377-4, 2005.
4. C. Dovrolis, D. Stiliadis, and P. Ramanathan. Proportional differentiated services: Delay differentiation and packet scheduling. In *Proc. ACM SIGCOMM*, pages 109–120, 1999.
5. M. Harchol-Balter. Task assignment with unknown duration. *Journal of ACM*, 29(2):260–288, 2002.
6. L. Kleinrock. *Queueing Systems, Volume II.* John Wiley and Sons, 1976.
7. S. C. M. Lee, J. C. S. Lui, and D. K. Y. Yau. A proportional-delay diffserv-enabled Web server: admission control and dynamic adaptation. *IEEE Trans. on Parallel and Distributed Systems*, 15(5):385–400, 2004.
8. K. Li and S. Jamin. A measurement-based admission-controlled Web server. In *Proc. IEEE INFOCOM*, pages 544–551, 2000.
9. C. Lu, X. Wang, and X. Koutsoukos. Feedback utilization control in distributed real-time systems with end-to-end tasks. *IEEE Trans. on Parallel and Distributed Systems*, 16(6):550–561, 2004.
10. M. M. Rashid, A. S. Alfa, E. Hossain, and M. Maheswaran. An analytical approach to providing controllable differentiated quality of service in web servers. *IEEE Trans. on Parallel and Distributed Systems*, 16(11):1022–1033, 2005.
11. X. Zhou, J. Wei, and C.-Z. Xu. Processing rate allocation for proportional slowdown differentiation on Internet servers. In *Proc. IEEE IPDPS*, pages 88–97, 2004.
12. X. Zhou and C.-Z. Xu. Harmonic proportional bandwidth allocation and scheduling for service differentiation on streaming servers. *IEEE Trans. on Parallel and Distributed Systems*, 15(9):835–848, 2004.
13. H. Zhu, H. Tang, and T. Yang. Demand-driven service differentiation for cluster-based network servers. In *Proc. IEEE INFOCOM*, pages 679–688, 2001.

Power-Efficient Route Discovery (PERDP) for ODMA Systems

Ray-Guang Cheng, Jia-Yang Hung, and Yao-Yuan Liu

Department of Electronic Engineering,
National Taiwan University of Science and Technology,
Taipei 106, Taiwan, R.O.C.
{crg, M9202217, D9402404}@mail.ntust.edu.tw

Abstract. This work presents a power-efficient route discovery protocol (PERDP) to reduce signaling overhead of the power-efficient routing (PER) mechanism for Opportunity Driven Multiple Access (ODMA) networks. An analytical method was proposed to derive the control parameters to achieve a given connectivity probability. Simulation results demonstrate the accuracy of the analysis and the superiority of the proposed PERDP. It is found that the signaling overhead of the proposed PERDP is 12.03% and 24.85% lower than that of dynamic source routing (DSR) and PER mechanism, respectively, under 90% connectivity probability in a high UE-density environment.

1 Introduction

Opportunity Driven Multiple Access (ODMA) [1] is a cellular multihop relaying protocol that has been considered by the third-generation partnership project (3GPP) working group but finally dropped due to the concerns over implementation complexity, battery life of users on standby, and signalling overhead issues [2]. Most of these implementation issues are highly related to the chosen routing mechanism in ODMA. In ODMA, user data is exchanged between a sending mobile station (also known as user equipment (UE) in UMTS) and the base station (called Node B in UMTS) by being relayed through other intermediate UEs. The sending UE should establish a path through the intermediate UEs to Node B prior to data exchange, which introduces additional signaling overhead, and thus results in extra power consumption for certain UEs. Hence, a good routing mechanism with low signaling overhead would be essential while realizing ODMA.

The functions of ODMA closely resemble those of mobile ad-hoc networks (MANET) [3]. However, they differ mainly in that Node B is located in a well-known fixed position in ODMA; however, both communication parties are mobile in MANET. Several power-aware routing methods [4]-[9] have been proposed for MANET and ODMA cellular networks. Most of the proposed methods are evolved from dynamic source routing (DSR) protocol [10] and ad-hoc on-demand distance-vector (AODV) routing protocol [11]. Two significant assumptions are made in the aforementioned approaches. The first assumption is that each node

E. Sha et al. (Eds.): EUC 2006, LNCS 4096, pp. 824–833, 2006.

retains the up-to-date location information and/or power metrics of the other nodes. This assumption may be effective in MANET but is not suitable for mobile cellular networks. Because each UE in a mobile cellular network does not have up-to-date information of other UEs due to the discontinuous reception (DRX) function. This assumption can be relieved by employing reactive-routing approaches [12]. However, existing reactive-routing approaches can only obtain the information of other UEs after executing route discovery; hence, some routing control messages are wasted on processing non-attainable ODMA requests (i.e., those requests whose power or latency requirements cannot be attained by utilizing the ODMA technology). The second assumption is that the extra power used by RREQ signaling is ignored. Because the RREQ in MANET is always flooded among all UEs with the UE's maximum transmission power and without hop-count limitation. Consequently, the UE's transmission power can be up to several Watts in a mobile cellular network and cannot be neglected.

In [13], we proposed a reactive-based routing mechanism, named power-efficient routing (PER), to solve the implementation problems of ODMA. Similar to existing reactive routing protocols, PER utilize flooding to delivers the route request (RREQ) to the destination (i.e., BS). Although flooding is necessary for discovering routes, it introduces extra radio interference to existing communications. Hence, it is beneficial to eliminate unnecessary flooding such that the interference can be minimized. However, the reduced flooding may result in a potential risk. That is, no route could be found if BS fails to receive any RREQ. Therefore, one of the implementation challenges in ODMA is to remove unnecessary flooding while diffusing RREQs to BS with a high probability.

This paper presents a power-efficient route discovery protocol (PERDP) to reduce unnecessary flooding of PER in ODMA networks. The unnecessary flooding is prevented by reducing the the number of RREQ forwarding participants. PERDP utilizes the received power-strength, instead of connectivity or overheard information, to select valid forwarding participants. Hence, extra interference can be prevented. The rest of this paper is organized as follows. Before going into details, the background of PER mechanism is first introduced in Section 2. The proposed PERDP is described in Section 3, and its key parameters and their effect on the system performance are discussed. Section 4 presents an investigation of the proposed PERDP's performance via numerical analysis and simulation. Conclusions are finally drawn in Section 5.

2 PER Mechanism

A TDD-ODMA network comprising a Node B and several non-mobile ODMA-enabled UEs, which are identified by their user-specific identities (ODMA_IDs), is considered herein. To simplify the description, "UE" is used to denote an ODMA-enable UE in the rest of this paper. In an ODMA transmission, the UEs are categorized in three types: *SendingUE*, *BackerUE*, and *RelayUE*. A *SendingUE* originates the ODMA transmission. The other UEs that act as forwarding participants in the ODMA route discovery within the cell are *BackerUE*s. Among these

BackerUEs, some will be identified as *RelayUEs*, which are responsible for relaying data packets between the *SendingUE* and Node B. Note that UEs that do not have sufficient residual-power may optionally disable some ODMA functionalities (e.g., RREQ flooding) to reduce unnecessary power consumption.

The PER mechanism is used by a *SendingUE* to identify a minimum-power path to Node B. Prior to the route discovery, PER mechanism utilizes a co-linear model to estimate the optimal number of *RelayUE*, denoted by N_{opt}, required by the minimum-power path. It was shown in *Lemma 1* of [13] that the lower bound of the total power consumption for an ODMA link is achieved if the distances between any two adjacent relay nodes are all equal to d_{opt}, where $d_{opt}= d/(N_{opt}+1)$ and d is the distance between *SendingUE* and Node B. It suggests that a *SendingUE* can flood RREQ with transmission radius d_{opt} to discover the *RelayUEs* to achieve the lower bound in a co-linear network topology with sufficiently high UE-density. For normal or low UE-density, the lower bound may not be achieved, however, one can still discover *RelayUEs* in the vicinity of the expected equal-distance locations to identify a minimum-power path from all possible routes to Node B. As a result, the transmission radius of each *BackerUE* should be increased by an amount of Δd to discover those *RelayUEs*, as demonstrated in Fig. 1(a). In Fig. 1(a), UE_1 is *SendingUE* and $N_{opt}=1$ is assumed; d_{max} is the maximum transmission radius of Node B and each UE, and the expected location predicted by *Lemma 1* is marked by 'X'. As demonstrated in 1(a), *BackerUEs* located in the region where the two circles overlap (i.e., UE_5, UE_7, and UE_8) could be possible *RelayUE* candidates. Hence, in PER, only these *BackerUEs*, rather than all *BackerUEs* in the entire cell, should forward RREQ during route discovery, which reduces the number of forwarding participants.

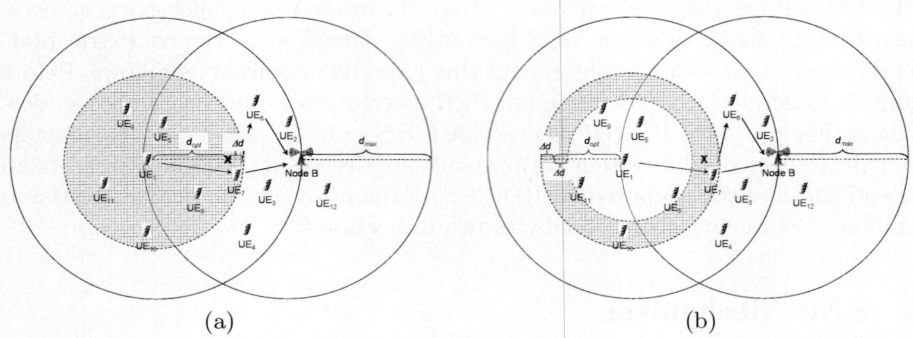

Fig. 1. (a) A network topology illustrates the PER mechanism. (b)The basic concept of the PERDP mechanism.

The procedure of PER consists of three phases: access phase, path discovery phase, and path setup phase. In access phase, the *SendingUE* adjusts its transmission power to P_{ini} and sends an ODMA service request carrying P_{ini} to Node B. Node B can predict P_{opt} and N_{opt} from P_{ini}. By using these predicted P_{opt}

and N_{opt}, Node B can check whether the ODMA request is attainable or not. For non-attainable ODMA requests, Node B simply terminates the procedure by replying the *SendingUE* with a rejection message. For attainable ODMA requests, Node B further derives P_{TX_RDP} and N_{opt}, and sends a confirmation message carrying P_{TX_RDP} and N_{opt} to the *SendingUE*. In path discovery phase, similar to DSR [10], the *SendingUE* broadcasts an RREQ through the ith paths to the Node B to collect $P_{total,i}$. In this phase, each *BackerUE* floods the RREQ with transmission power P_{TX_RDP} and discards the RREQ that exceeds the hop-count limitation N_{opt} . Based on the collected $P_{total,i}$, Node B can identify the minimum-power path. Finally, Node B sends an RREP packet back to the *RelayUEs* along the identified path in path setup phase. The derivation of P_{ini}, P_{TX_RDP}, and N_{opt} can be found in [13].

3 Power-Efficient Route Discovery Protocol

In this section, a power-efficient route discovery protocol (PERDP) is proposed to reduce the number of flooded RREQs in PER while maintaining an acceptable connectivity probability. In this section, the basic concept of PERDP is first described and the analytical method used to derive the control parameters is then elaborated. Finally, the procedure required to adopt PERDP to the PER mechanism is illustrated.

The basic concept of PERDP is illustrated in Fig. 1(b). It can be found that the flooded RREQs during the access phase of PER can be further reduced by selecting only *BackerUEs* located in the shaded ring region (which is bounded by an outer circle and an inner circle with radius $d_{opt} + \Delta d_+$ and $d_{opt} - \Delta d_-$, respectively) as forwarding participants. In this example, only UE_7 is selected as the *BackerUE* that is allowed to forward RREQ to its neighbors.

In PERDP, the transmission radius of RREQ flooded by *SendingUE* and *BackerUEs* is fixed and is set to be $d_{opt} + \Delta d_+$. In each flooding, only *BackerUEs* located in the ring region bounded the two circles with radius $d_{opt} + \Delta d_+$ and $d_{opt} - \Delta d_-$ are allowed to forward the RREQ. The flooding repeats until the RREQ reaches Node B or the RREQ has been forwarded by N_{opt} *BackerUEs*. The setting of Δd_+ and Δd_- depends on the UE-density and a target connectivity probability P_s. The target connectivity probability is the minimum probability that a *SendingUE* can find a path, to Node B through exactly N_{opt} *RelayUEs*. One may increase P_s by enlarging Δd, but it also increases the number of flooded RREQs as well as the radio interference. Hence, there is a tradeoff between P_s and the flooding efficiency. In the following, an analytical model is proposed to determine P_s as a function of Δd and UE-density for the case of N_{opt}. Before going into details, the parameters used in the following analysis is summarized below:

- A: the area of the cell under investigation.
- m: the total number of UEs in the cell. Note that the UE-density is equal to m/A.
- N_{opt}: the optimal number of *RelayUE* estimated by PER.

d: the distance between the *SendingUE* and Node B.

P_s: the connectivity probability, which is the probability that a *SendingUE* UE_0 can establish a path through N_{opt} *RelayUEs* to Node B. P_s is set by the network operator.

Δd_+: the outer distance offset used by PERDP.

Δd_-: the inner distance offset used by PERDP.

R: $R \triangleq d_{opt} + \Delta d_+$ is the radius of the outer circle. Note that R is also the maximum transmission range of each flooded RREQ.

r: $r \triangleq d_{opt} - \Delta d_-$ is the radius of the inner circle.

d_S: the distance between a given *RelayUE* and the *SendingUE*.

d_N: the distance between a given *RelayUE* and Node B.

Note that d_{opt}, Δd_+, Δd_-, d_s, and d_N can be estimated from the corresponding received power by applying the Friis free space equation as demonstrated in [13].

Figures 2(a) and (b) show a geometry model used to determine P_s for $N_{opt} = 1$. Two conditions are considered in deriving P_s: $\Delta d_+ \leq \Delta d_-$ and $\Delta d_+ > \Delta d_-$. In both cases, a *SendingUE* can find a route to Node B if there are at least one *BackerUE* located in the area A_0. Hence, the connectivity probability can be derived as

$$P_s = 1 - Pr\{\text{No } BackerUE \text{ is located in } A_0\} = 1 - (1 - \frac{A_0}{A})^m. \quad (1)$$

In Fig. 2(a), the case of $\Delta d_+ \leq \Delta d_-$ is depicted. Let x be the distance from a point in the shaded region to Node B. From the figure, it can be found that x falls in the range of $[d - R, R]$ and the length of the arc corresponding to radius x is $2x\theta$. Hence, the area of A_0 can be calculated by integrating the arcs for different x. That is,

$$A_0 = \int_{d-R}^{R} 2x\theta dx = 2\int_{d-R}^{R} x \cdot cos^{-1}(\frac{x^2 + d^2 - R^2}{2xd})dx \quad (2)$$

The case of $\Delta d_+ > \Delta d_-$ is depicted in Fig. 2(b). Similarly, A_0 can be obtained by

$$\begin{aligned} A_0 &= \int_{d-R}^{R} 2x\theta dx - \int_{d-r}^{R} 2x\phi dx \\ &= 2[\int_{d-R}^{R} x \cdot cos^{-1}(\frac{x^2 + d^2 - R^2}{2xd})dx - \int_{d-r}^{R} x \cdot cos^{-1}(\frac{x^2 + d^2 - r^2}{2xd})dx] \quad (3) \end{aligned}$$

For given values of P_s, A, m, and d, R and r can be obtained by solving Eqs. (1) and (2) (or (3)).

For the easy of demonstration, the results of $\Delta d_+ = \Delta d_- \triangleq \Delta d$ is presented herein. Figure 3 shows the message flows employed to demonstrate a scenario of PERDP using the example shown in Fig. 1(b). In this scenario, UE_1 is the *SendingUE*; UE_j, for j=2 to 12, are *BackerUEs*; and, $N_{opt} = 1$ is assumed. With PERDP, the access phase of the PER mechanism is modified as follows.

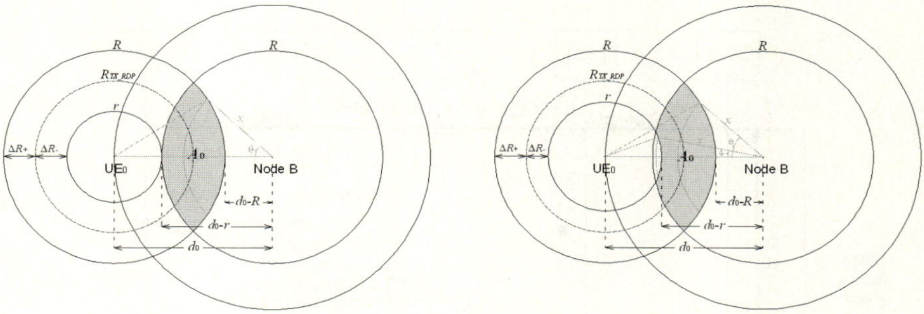

(a) (b)

Fig. 2. A single-hop example: (a) $\Delta d_+ \leq \Delta d_-$ (b) $\Delta d_+ > \Delta d_-$

Access Phase

Step 1. Prior to communicating with Node B, the *SendingUE* UE_1 measures P_{avg} , adjusts its transmission power to P_{ini} , and then sends an RRC_Connection_Req [14] carrying P_{ini} to Node B.

Step 2. The UEs that receive the RRC_Connection_Req message can detect the received power of the message then get the distance, d_S .

Step 3. Upon receiving the RRC_Connection_Req message, Node B adjusts its transmission power to P_{ini} and acknowledges an ODMA_Relay_Prepare carrying P_{TX_RDP} and N_{opt} to UE_1 .

Step 4. The UEs that receive the ODMA_Relay_Prepare message can detect the received power of the message then get the distance, d_N .

Step 5. After the UEs receive two messages, they will implement the *BackerUE* decision as illustrated in Fig. 4 . Note that each BackerUE can estimate d_S and d_N via open-loop power control.

Step 6. The UEs can resolve their state if they are the *BackerUE* and in operation mode. If the UEs which just receive one of two above messages before timeout period, they will transfer operation mode to sleep (SLP) mode.

4 Numerical Results

Simulations were conducted on ns2 simulator to verify the effectiveness of the proposed PERDP. The load balancing capability of ODMA was not investigated herein. Hence, a single cell with 20 to 100 UEs was considered. All UEs were assumed to be uniformly distributed within a square area with dimensions 1km×1km. The following parameters were used in the simulation, $d = 600$ m, $R_{TX\_RDP} = 150$ to 200 (m) and $N_{opt} = 1$. In all case, ΔP is adjusted to guarantee a 90% successful connectivity probability (i.e., $P_{S\_min} = 0.9$)

Fig. 5 illustrates the accuracy of the numerical analysis for $N_{opt} = 1$. In this figure, the numerical analysis is indicated by a solid line and the simulation result is marked by a dotted line. It can be found the accuracy of the numerical analysis, where the simulation results always fall within the 95% confidence interval of

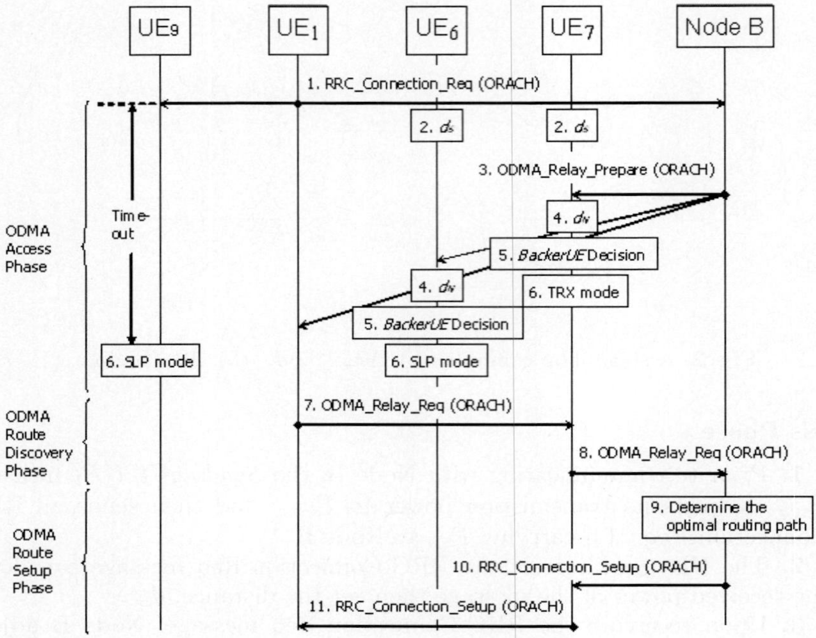

Fig. 3. Message flow of the PER with PERDP

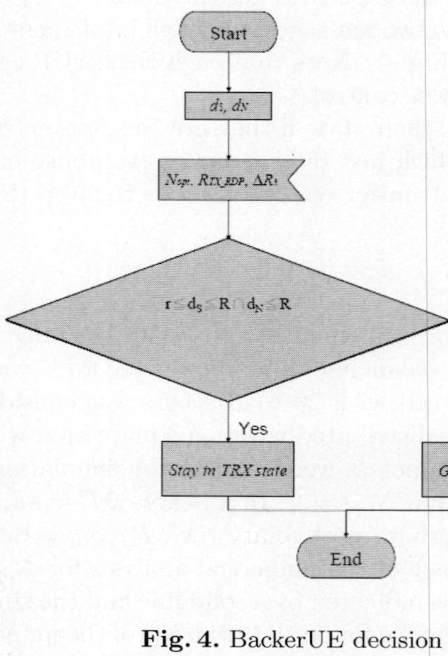

Fig. 4. BackerUE decision flow

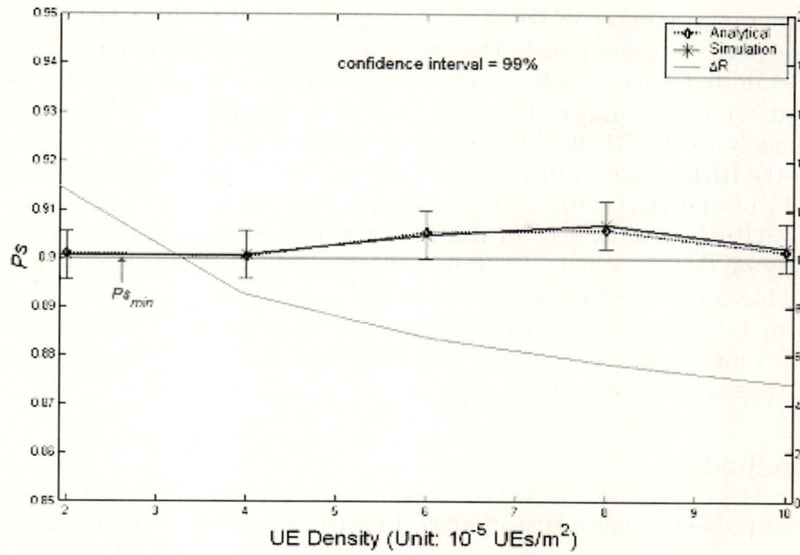

Fig. 5. Accuracy of the numerical analysis:1-hop

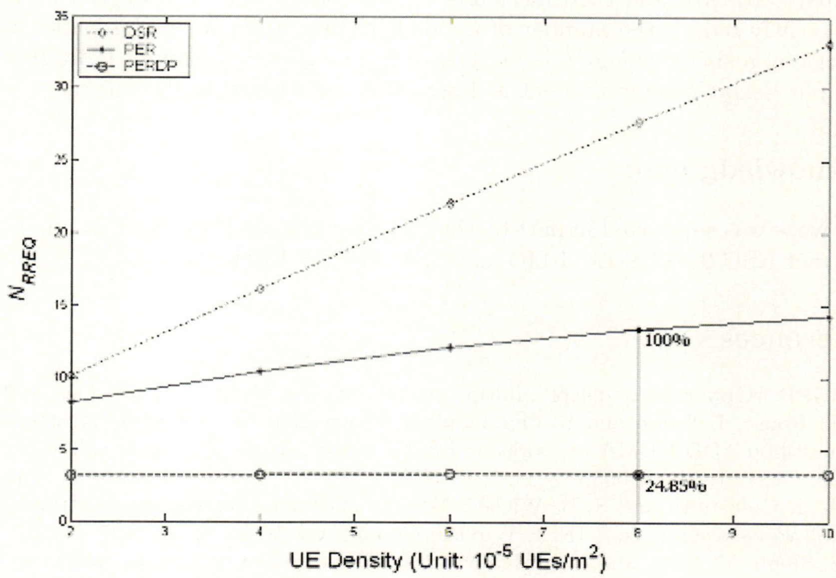

Fig. 6. The analysis of total number of RREQs:1-hop

the numerical analysis. The red solid line is used to indicate $P_{S\_min} = 0.9$. Fig. 6 demonstrates the performance improvement of the proposed PERDP algorithm compared to DSR and PER methods. In Fig. 6, three lines are used to illustrate the required total number of RREQs, N_{RREQ} , for establishing a ODMA path during the path discovery phase. The performance of DSR, PER and PERDP is marked by dotted squares, solid stars and dotted circles, respectively. It can be found that the total number of RREQs flooded by the *BackerUEs* is increased proportionally to the UE density. It is because that, in DSR, each UE always forwards the RREQ, and in PER, the number of the UEs that located in shaded area could be the *BackerUE* is still too much. The higher the UE density is, the more RREQs are flooded. In contrast, for a given successful connectivity probability of $P_{S\_min} = 0.9$, PERDP reduces ΔP as the increase of the UE density. Therefore, it approximates the optimal condition predicted by the PER mechanism. It is found that signaling overhead of the proposed PERDP is 12.03% and 24.85% lower than that in DSR and PER respectively for $P_{S\_min} = 0.9$ in high UE density environment.

5 Conclusion

This paper presents a mechanism, named PERDP, to reduce unnecessary flooding of reactive routing protocols in ODMA networks. An analytical method was proposed to derive the control parameters required to discover a route for a given connectivity probability. The accuracy of the analysis is verified by simulation. Compared to DSR and PER mechanisms, it is found that the proposed PERDP may greatly reduce the number of flooded RREQs in PER. In this paper, only the case of a single *RelayUE* is investigated. The generalization of PERDP to a multiple *RelayUEs* environment is deserved to be studied in the future.

Acknowledgment

This work was supported in part by the National Science Council, Taiwan, under Contract NSC 94-2219-E011-005 and NSC 94-2218-E011-011.

References

1. 3GPP, "Opportunity driven multiple access,"3G TR 25.924, v. 1.0.0, Dec. 1999.
2. T. Rouse, I. Band, and S. McLaughlin, "Congestion-based routing strategies in multihop TDD-CDMA networks," *IEEE J. Select. Areas Commun.*, vol. 23, no. 3, pp. 668–681, Mar. 2005.
3. A. J. Goldsmith and S. B. Wicker, "Design challenges for energy-constrained ad hoc wireless networks," IEEE Wireless Comm., vol. 9, no. 4, pp. 8-27, 2002.
4. S. Singh, M. Woo, and C.S. Mghavendra, "Power-aware routing in mobile ad hoc networks," Proc. of ACM/IEEE MobiCOM, pp. 181-190, 1998.
5. A. Michail and A. Epremides, "Energy efficient routing for connection-oriented traffic in wireless ad hoc networks," Wireless Networks, vol. 8, pp. 517V533, 2003.
6. J. H. Chang and L. Tassiulas, "Energy conserving routing in wireless ad-hoc networks," Proc. of IEEE INFOCOM, pp. 22-31, 2000.
7. V. Rodoplu and T. H. Meng, "Minimum energy mobile wireless networks," IEEE J. Selected Areas in Communications, vol. 17, no. 8, pp. 1333V1344, August 1999.

8. R. Wattenhofer, L. Li, P. Bahl, and Y. M. Wang, "Distributed topology control for power efficient operation in multihop wireless ad hoc networks," Proc. of IEEE INFOCOM, April 2001.
9. Vodafone Group, "ODMA routing with procedures for mobile originated calls, mobile terminated calls, and location update," Tdoc TSGR2#2(99) 179, 3GPP RAN WG2, March 1999.
10. D. Johnson, and D. Maltz, "Dynamic source routing in ad hoc wireless etworks," Mobile Computing, pp. 153-181, 1996.
11. C. E. Perkins, E. M. Belding-Royer, and I. Chakeres, "Ad hoc on demand distance vector (AODV) routing," IETF Internet draft, Oct 2003,
12. A. Safwat, H. S. Hassanein, and H. T. Mouftah, "Structured proactive and reactive routing for wireless mobile ad hoc networks," The Handbook of Ad Hoc Wireless Networks, CRC Press, 2002.
13. Ray-Guang Cheng, Shin-Ming Cheng, and Phone Lin, "Power-efficient routing (PER) mechanism for ODMA systems," IEEE Transaction on Vehicular Technology, vol. 55, no. 4, July 2006.
14. H. Karl (Editor), "An overview of energy-efficiency techniques for mobile communication systems," Report of AG Mobikom WG7, Oct. 2003.

Energy Efficient Routing for Wireless Sensor Networks with Grid Topology

Hock Guan Goh[1], Moh Lim Sim[2], and Hong Tat Ewe[1]

[1] Faculty of Information Technology
[2] Faculty of Engineering,
Multimedia University, Jalan Multimedia,
63100 Cyberjaya, Selangor, Malaysia
{hggoh, mlsim, htewe}@mmu.edu.my

Abstract. Agricultural monitoring using wireless sensor networks has gained much popularity recently. In this paper, we review five existing flat-tree routing algorithms and proposed a new algorithm suitable for applications such as paddy field monitoring using wireless sensor network. One of the popular data collection methods is the data aggregation approach, where sensor readings of several nodes are gathered and combined into a single packet at intermediate relay nodes. This approach decreases the number of packets flowing and minimizes the overall energy consumption of the sensor network. However, most studies in the past do not consider the network delay in this context, which is an essential performance measure in real-time interactive agricultural monitoring through Internet and cellular network. We propose an algorithm called Information Selection Branch Grow Algorithm (ISBG), which aims to optimize the network in achieving higher network lifetime and shortening the end-to-end network delay. The performance of this algorithm is assessed by computer simulation and is compared with the existing algorithms used for data aggregation routing in wireless sensor networks.

Keywords: WSN, routing algorithm, energy efficient routing, grid topology.

1 Introduction

Recent technological advancement in micro-electro-mechanical systems (MEMS) has enabled small and inexpensive wireless communication nodes comprising of transducers, transceivers, and micro-controllers to be deployed on a large scale. These devices are able to communicate with each other and form a self-organized network called Wireless Sensor Network (WSN). WSN represents a new generation of real-time embedded system with wireless networking capability. Albeit it has significant energy storage constraint as compared to the traditional wireless networks meant for human or computer communications, WSN has great potential benefits when deployed in the many areas.

For paddy field monitoring, the sensor nodes are often deployed in a grid topology. The main important issues for WSN monitoring application are to maximize the network lifetime and minimize the end-to-end network delay. A node that ran out of the energy will cause data loss in the corresponding sensing area. This will also affect

E. Sha et al. (Eds.): EUC 2006, LNCS 4096, pp. 834 – 843, 2006.

the routing performance of the intermediate nodes. Critical event such as sudden flooding could happen in the paddy field especially after a heavy rain. Such sensor readings are very critical and need to be sent to the user as fast as possible. Any delay in taking the right action will cause the owner of the farm a huge loss. However, most studies [1] in the past do not focus much on the network delay, which is an essential performance measure in real-time interactive agricultural monitoring through Internet and cellular network. Our work aims to optimize the network in achieving higher network lifetime and shortening the end-to-end network delay.

2 System Model

2.1 Grid Topology

From the example of application deployment as shown in Fig. 1, the network topology is modeled as a 2D network with $n \times n$ fixed nodes. For illustration, a 2D grid topology with 4×4 fixed nodes as shown in Fig. 2 is considered. Distances between the two adjacent wireless nodes are the same and equal to *d*. Each node is denoted by an index. Communications can only occur between nodes that are linked neighbours with a separation distance of *d*. The base station is defined as a sensor node that is connected to a gateway (data sink) with a wired cable. Any of the nodes can be selected as a base station. Once it is deployed, it will not be moved. The base station is assumed to have an unlimited supply of power and possesses a superior computational capability.

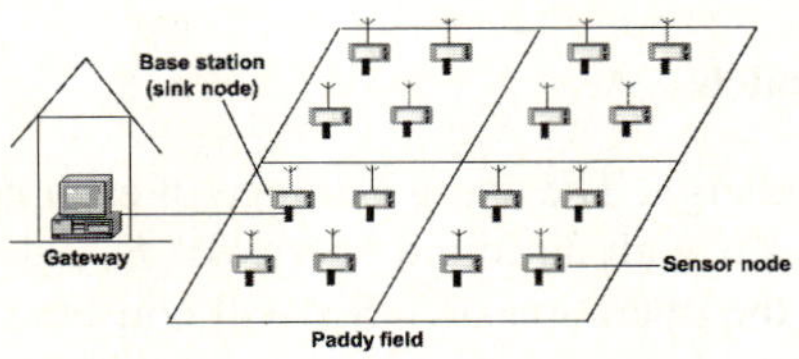

Fig. 1. Example of a grid topology deployment in a paddy field

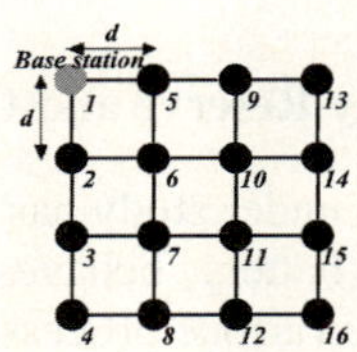

Fig. 2. Example of 2D grid topology and the base station is placed at the corner

2.2 Data Aggregation Approach

Several technical limitations of WSNs [2] have called for a need of alternative data collection approach which is more energy-efficient than the traditional approaches. One of the methods proposed for data collection in WSN is data aggregation [3], [4]. The general idea of data aggregation is to combine the data coming from multiple sources, process them into a single packet, and forward it toward the destination, namely the base station. The process will be repeated until the aggregated data reach the base station. This will eliminate redundancy, minimize the number of transmissions, and thus save the energy resource. Two approaches of data aggregation for data collection in WSNs are considered here:

Intermediate Processed Data Aggregation (IPDA): All sensor readings will be aggregated by processing and consolidating the information into a single packet at the intermediate relay nodes. Sensor data originating from each node has a fixed length of 30 bytes.

Cascaded Data Aggregation (CDA): All sensor readings will be aggregated by cascading the contents from different sources at the intermediate relay nodes without any analysis or further processing. This process will be repeated at all intermediate relay nodes before the data finally reach the base station. Sensor data originating from each node is 16 bytes long, which consists of 2 bytes of node ID and 14 bytes of actual sensor data.

2.3 Packet Format

Two kinds of packet format for data aggregation are considered here: packet format for IPDA as shown in Fig. 3 and CDA as shown in Fig. 4.

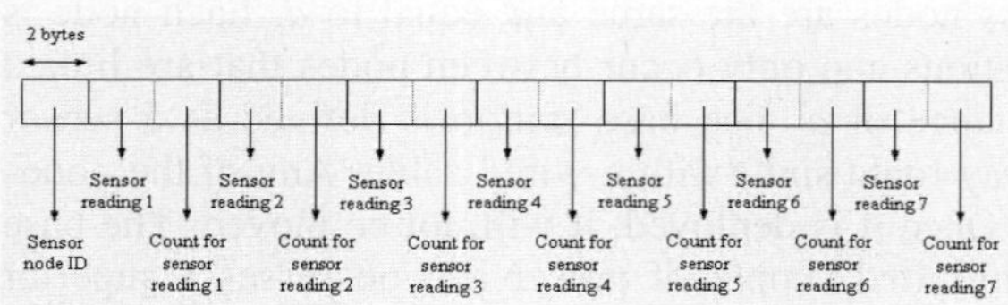

Fig. 3. Packet format for IPDA

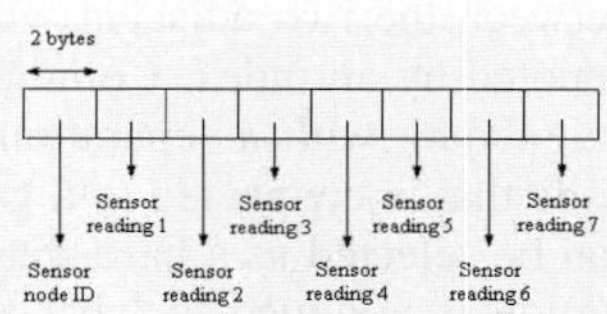

Fig. 4. Packet format for CDA

2.4 Energy Reserve and Consumption Models

The system under study has finite reserve of energy. The energy storage of each node, namely the battery, behaves like a leaky bucket with an initial energy of E_{total} Joule. Meanwhile, various processes carried out in the operation of WSN will consume and drain out the energy reserve. In this study, we model the energy consumption due to packet transmission and packet reception, i.e., the processes that mainly consume the energy [5]. A popular radio model called the first-order radio model as discussed in [5] is used to estimate the energy cost of transmitting and receiving data. In this simple radio model, it is assumed that the energy dissipated to run the transmitter circuitry, $E_{Tx\text{-}elec}$ is the same as the receiver circuitry, $E_{Rx\text{-}elec}$ where $E_{Tx\text{-}elec} = E_{Rx\text{-}elec} = E_{elec}$. The equation used to calculate the cost of transmitting a k-bit data packet across a distance d is defined as follows:

$$E_{Tx}(k, d) = E_{Tx\text{-}elec}(k) + E_{Tx\text{-}amp}(k, d) = E_{elec} \times k + E_{amp} \times k \times d^2, \quad (1)$$

where E_{amp} is the energy dissipated by transmitter amplifier to achieve an acceptable signal-to-noise ratio. The receiving cost for a k-bit data packet is given by:

$$E_{Rx}(k) = E_{Rx\text{-}elec}(k) = E_{elec} \times k \quad (2)$$

The amount of energy consumed by a node is given by $E_{consume} = E_{Tx} + E_{Rx}$. A node is considered dead when it has run out of the energy.

2.5 Communication Delay Model – Point-to-Point Delay and End-to-End Network Delay

Four kinds of delay contribute to point-to-point node delay. These are processing delay, queuing delay, transmission delay, and propagation delay. In the simulation, the transmission delay and propagation delay are assumed to be fixed for every node and queuing delay is considered to be negligible. The end-to-end packet delay, which is the time it takes for a packet to be transferred from a transmitter to a receiver, is given as:

$$T_i = T_{frame,\, i} + T_{propagation,\, i}\,, \tag{3}$$

where $T_{frame,\, i}$ = data packet size / channel transmission rate, $T_{propagation,\, i}$ = link length / signal propagation speed, and subscript i denotes the i-th link. It should be noted that any delays due to processing, queuing, acknowledgement, or negative acknowledgement are not taken into consideration. End-to-end delay of a network is defined as the total amount of time for all the aggregated data to be sent back to the base station. In our simulation model, we consider the following equation for the time it takes for all the data to be aggregated back to the base station.

$$\text{End-to-end network delay,} \qquad T_{total} = \max_{1 \le j \le b} \left\{ \left[\sum_{i=1}^{L} (T_i) \right]_j \right\}, \tag{4}$$

where L is the total number of links in a branch of the base station, T_i is the maximum end-to-end packet delay of the i-th link from the base station, subscript j denotes the j-th branch, and b the total number of branches of the base station.

3 Existing Routing Algorithms

3.1 Stream-Based Routing Algorithm

In the stream-based routing algorithm [6], sequential data aggregation approach is used for data collection. Data packets are passed and aggregated sequentially from all other nodes to the base station. The disadvantage of stream-based routing is that a longer time will be needed to collect data from the entire network.

3.2 Row-to-Column Routing Algorithm

In the row-to-column routing algorithm [6], shortest path data aggregation approach is adopted for data collection. Each sensor node is organized into an n^2 grid and information is passed row-by-row towards the row of the base station. For the row where the base station is located, the information is passed in the column-by-column fashion to the base station node. In such a routing scheme, the information takes the shortest path from the source node to the base station in terms of number of hops.

3.3 Cluster-Based Routing Algorithm

One of the disadvantages of row-to-column routing is that nodes that share the same row with the base station are particularly burdened. An improvement to this is the cluster-based routing scheme [6], where grouping of nodes before data aggregation is considered. Each neighbouring node is the cluster head of a group of the nodes and the information from group nodes takes the shortest path to the head. The purpose of this method is to distribute the energy dissipation in each node more equally.

3.4 Tree-Based Routing Algorithm

Tree-based routing algorithm [7] uses a set of rules (phase 1: node searching, phase 2: parent node selection, and phase 3: link establishment) to establish the links between two nodes starting from the base station. The algorithm uses random parent selection method, where a node will randomly choose its parent node when it receives more than one message. This process of links establishment will continue until all the nodes in the network are connected.

3.5 Node-Centric Load Balancing Routing Algorithm

Construction of a balanced topology in terms of fair distribution of nodes among the branches of a network will help to increase the network performance [8]. In this case, neighbouring information plays an important role in the construction of network topology. In Node-Centric Load Balancing (NCLB) routing algorithm [8], it constructs a load-balanced tree in sensor networks of asymmetric architecture. Neighbouring information is needed to grow the routing tree by periodically broadcast the nodes existence. The algorithm consists of a basic algorithm and an adjustment algorithm. The basic algorithm constructs the routing tree by selecting the lightest most restricted branch and following by the selection from the heaviest border node with most growth space. Spiral adjustment is proposed to use for the adjustment algorithm. The adjustment algorithm will either push neighbours from the heavily loaded branches to the lighter ones or pull neighbours to the lightly loaded branches from the heavier ones.

4 Newly Proposed Routing Algorithm – ISBG Routing Algorithm

An improved algorithm may be designed by utilizing the information of the neighbouring information to construct a better balanced topology. In this paper, we propose an algorithm, which is a modification of the Tree-Based routing algorithm, called Information Selection Branch Grow (ISBG) algorithm for energy-efficient data aggregation routing in wireless sensor networks. It is clear that any node that consumes the highest energy will be the first node to run out of energy. By minimizing the energy consumption of the highest energy consumption node, the network lifetime can be prolonged. In tree topology, with balanced nodes distribution among all branches, all child nodes attached to a parent node will handle approximately the same amount of network traffic thus consume approximately the same amount of energy. The idea of minimizing end-to-end network delay is by developing branches where leaf nodes have minimum number of hops from the base station. Our proposed ISBG algorithm consists of a basic algorithm as shown in Fig. 5 and a two-stage adjustment algorithm as shown in Fig. 6 and Fig. 7. The following terminologies are defined:

- Unmarked nodes: nodes that do not have a parent node.
- Weight: the number of unmarked nodes found at the immediate neighbouring nodes.
- Degree of Freedom or "growth space" of a node: the sum of weights of the unmarked neighbouring nodes.
- Unit factor: number of children nodes and itself.
- Total aggregated unit: the sum of the unit factors along the path starting from the base station until the node.
- Balance criteria: when all branches of a base station have equal number of child nodes.

4.1 Basic Algorithm of ISBG

For the ISBG basic algorithm, it iteratively grows a balanced tree outwards from the base station root. All nodes in the topology will periodically broadcast their existence and its neighbouring nodes' information. At each step, the algorithm will first select a potential branch to grow. The step will be followed by selection of a potential node to be grown. Finally, the algorithm will update the topology information. The whole process will repeat until all the unmarked nodes have been found.

To select the potential branch to grow, this is done by considering the descending priority order in a series of Potential Branch Consideration (PBC): i) the lightest weight, ii) the smallest number of child nodes of a base station's branch, iii) minimum degree of freedom, iv) the smallest total aggregated unit, and lastly v) random selection. The next step is to select a potential node to be grown. The potential node is selected based on descending priority order in a series of Potential Node Consideration (PNC): i) the heaviest weight, ii) the maximum degree of freedom, and iii) random selection. Once the potential branch and potential node are found, a link will be established between them. Finally, the algorithm will update the topology information. The whole process will be repeated until all the unmarked nodes are found.

4.2 Adjustment Algorithm

The topology that is formed after the ISBG basic algorithm may not be able to achieve balanced distribution for a large topology, such as 10×10 grid topology. Thus, adjustment algorithms are needed to achieve better balance distribution and enhance the network lifetime after the construction of network topology using the basic algorithm. In this case, two types of adjustment algorithms can be considered: i) inter-branch adjustment and ii) intra-branch adjustment. Inter-branch adjustment is done through pushing the neighbouring branch nodes from the heavier branch to the lighter branch or pulling the neighbouring

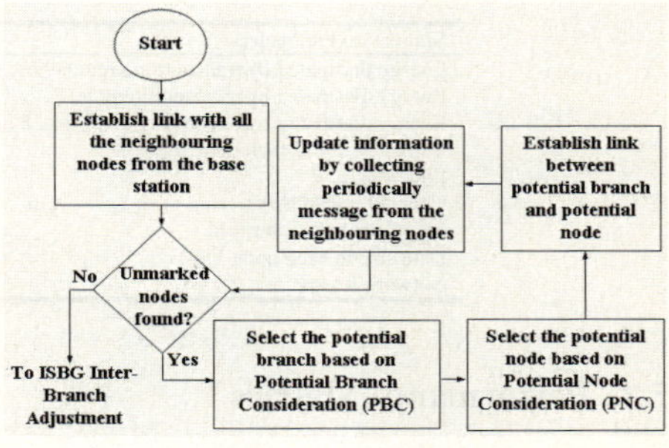

Fig. 5. Flow chart of ISBG Basic Algorithm

branch nodes from the heavier branch to the lighter branch. Further analysis shows that the network lifetime and the end-to-end network delay may increase after the inter-branch adjustment. Thus, intra-branch adjustment is needed to reduce the end-to-end network delay. Intra-branch adjustment is done by moving a node attached to a higher total-aggregated-unit parent node to a lower total-aggregated-unit parent node of the same branch from the base station.

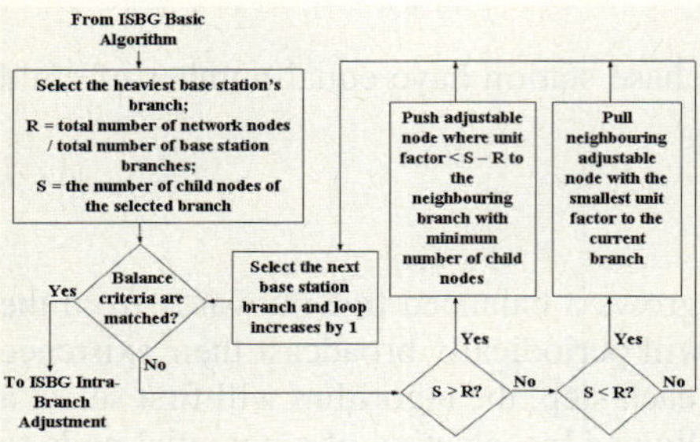

Fig. 6. Flow chart of ISBG Inter-Branch Adjustment Algorithm

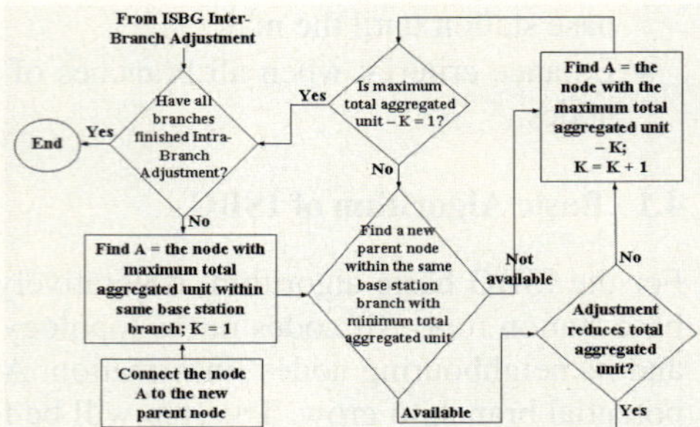

Fig. 7. Flow chart of ISBG Intra-Branch Adjustment Algorithm

5 Simulation and Performance Analysis

For performance analysis, a discrete event based simulator has been developed using C procedural programming language. The simulation parameters (in Table 1) are used in the simulation of this study. Several comparisons have been done for the ISBG routing algorithm with the Stream-Based [6], the Row-To-Column-Based [6], the Cluster-Based [6], the Tree-Based [7], and the NCLB [8] routing algorithms through IPDA and CDA approaches. The simulation is carried out for 10×10 grid topology by selecting the base station at every location of the grid once at a time. For each location where the base station is being selected, the simulation is run for 1000 times.

Table 1. Simulation Parameters

Simulation Parameters	IPDA	CDA
Energy dissipated by transmitter circuitry, $E_{Tx\text{-}elec}$	50 nJ/bit	50 nJ/bit
Energy dissipated by receiver circuitry, $E_{Rx\text{-}elec}$	50 nJ/bit	50 nJ/bit
Energy dissipated by transmitter amplifier, E_{amp}	100 pJ/bit/m^2	100 pJ/bit/m^2
Initial energy in each node, E_{total}	1.0 J	1.0 J
Link length, d	10 m	10 m
Channel transmission rate	10 kbps	10 kbps
Signal propagation speed	3.0×10^8 m/s	3.0×10^8 m/s
Data size in each node	30 bytes	16 bytes
Network losses	None	None

5.1 Performance Metrics

Two important performance metrics are discussed in this article: the network lifetime and the end-to-end network delay.

Network Lifetime: Energy consumption determines the lifetime of a sensor network. Communicating wirelessly consumes more power at the nodes compared with any other activities such as processing and sensing. Hence, the performance analysis does not consider energy dissipation for computation, sensing, listening for incoming packets, and other tasks. Network lifetime is defined as the time between the moment the network operates and the moment the first node runs out of its energy.

End-to-End Network Delay: End-to-end network delay is measured from the time where all the sensor readings are collected back to the base station. It is calculated starting from the time when the sensor data are sent from the leaf nodes to the intermediate nodes until all the sensor data reach the base station. Delays due to processing, queuing, acknowledgement, or negative acknowledgement are ignored.

5.2 Performance Results

Fig. 8 shows the average network lifetime for six routing algorithms. Among all the algorithms, the Stream-Based routing algorithm performs well and achieves a good network lifetime for IPDA. While for the ISBG routing algorithm, its performance is comparable to other algorithms. For IPDA, the packet sent to the neighbouring nodes each time would be the same. Therefore, the node that receives packets from or sends packets to the minimum neighbouring nodes will consume less energy. The Row-To-Column-Based, the Cluster-Based, the Tree-Based, the NCLB, and the ISBG routing algorithms have more than one child node in the intermediate nodes, so the energy consumption of the neighbouring nodes next to the base station will be higher than the Stream-Based routing algorithm. Fig. 9 shows the average end-to-end network delay for six routing algorithms using IPDA. Although the Stream-Based routing algorithm performs well in terms of network lifetime but it causes a long delay. This is because the packet needs to be forwarded sequentially and this will cause longer time to collect all the sensor readings back to the base station. The Row-To-Column-Based, the Cluster-Based, and the Tree-Based routing algorithms have shown comparable performances with the shortest end-to-end network delay as compared to others. This is because those algorithms are using the shortest path collection to the base station.

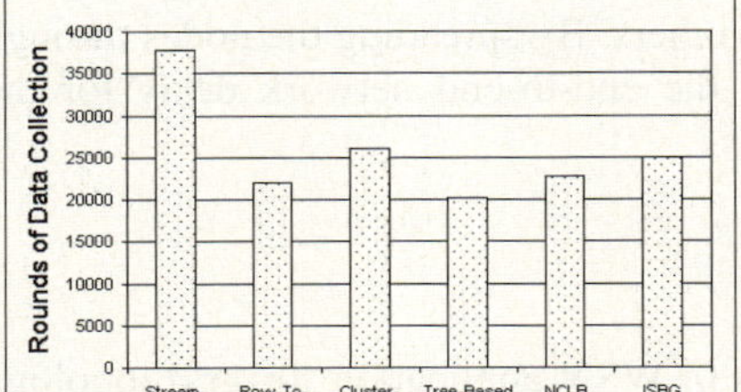

Fig. 8. Average network lifetime comparison using IPDA

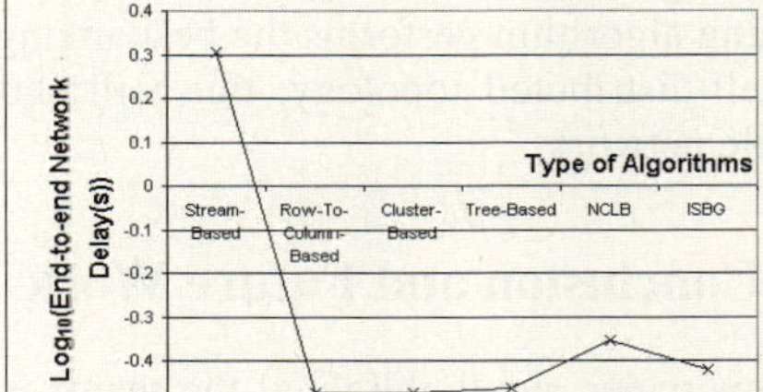

Fig. 9. Average end-to-end network delay comparison using IPDA

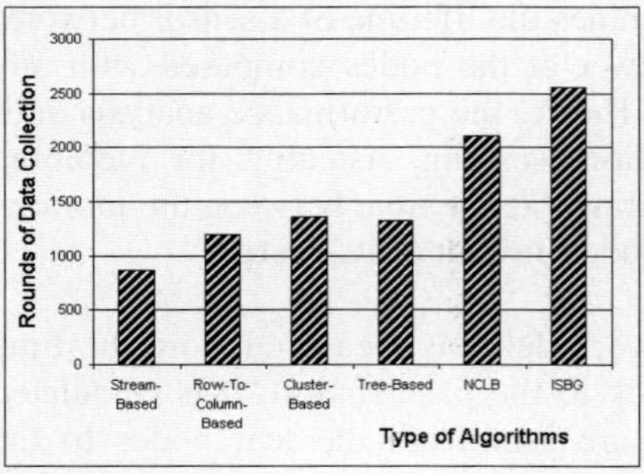

Fig. 10. Average network lifetime comparison using CDA

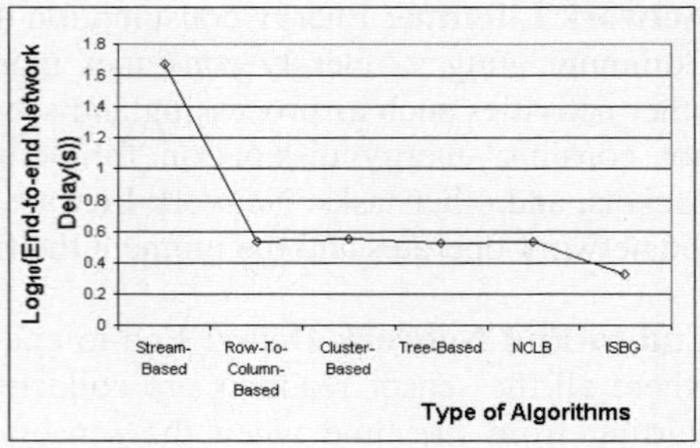

Fig. 11. Average end-to-end network delay comparison using CDA

The ISBG routing algorithm performs moderately because partial of the sensor data may not be aggregated back to the base station using the shortest path. It causes longer delay as compared with the Row-To-Column-Based, the Cluster-Based, and the Tree-Based routing algorithms.

Fig. 10 shows the average network lifetime for six routing algorithms using CDA. For CDA, the ISBG routing algorithm performs the best among the others. The ISBG routing algorithm is able to distribute the nodes more evenly over all possible branches and thus able to achieve longer network lifetime. CDA will cause the packet length longer when the packet is closer to the base station. So, methods with sequential collection of the sensor readings, such as the Stream-Based routing algorithm will highly suffer from poor network lifetime. Fig. 11 shows the average end-to-end network delay for six routing algorithms using CDA. Sequentially in aggregation such as the Stream-Based routing algorithm performs poor for end-to-end network delay due to the packet needs to be forwarded node-by-node in a single direction. This kind of routing will cause longer time to collect all the sensor readings back to the base station. The Row-To-Column-Based, the Cluster-Based, and the Tree-Based routing algorithms have shown comparable performances with the shortest end-to-end network delay as compared to others for IPDA. This is because those algorithms are using the shortest path collection to the base station. The ISBG routing algorithm performs the best among the others. By spreading the nodes through a well-distributed topology, this will shorten the end-to-end network delay for the whole network.

6 Conclusion and Future Work

In this paper, we highlighted the major issues in WSN application for grid topology such as in the paddy field monitoring. We carried out a study on the existing flat-tree routing algorithms for end-to-end data collection. Due to the challenges in end-to-end data collection for real-time paddy field monitoring, we proposed a new algorithm called Information Selection Branch Grow (ISBG) routing algorithm, which perform reasonably well in terms of network lifetime and network delay. Although the Intermediate Processed Data Aggregation (IPDA) is able to give an overview of the conditions (maximum, minimum, or average of sensor readings) in the field, Cascaded Data Aggregation (CDA) is more appropriate to be used for precise paddy field monitoring, where all the sensor data are needed to be collected to the base station for detailed data analysis. The results show that the ISBG routing algorithm is the best selection for end-to-end data collection using CDA. This algorithm can be extended to other kinds of monitoring applications for wireless sensor networks.

References

1. Al-Karaki, J.N., Kamal, A.E.: Routing Techniques in Wireless Sensor Networks: A Survey, IEEE Wireless Communications, Vol. 11, No. 6, (2004) 6-28
2. Chong, C.-Y., Kumar, S.P.: Sensor Networks: Evolution, Opportunities, and Challenges, Proceedings of the IEEE, Vol. 91, No. 8, (2003) 1247-1256
3. Krishnamachari, L., Estrin, D., Wicker, S.: The Impact of Data Aggregation in Wireless Sensor Networks, Proceedings of the 22nd International Conference on Distributed Computer Systems Workshops, (2002) 575-578
4. Heidemann, J., Silva, F., Intanagonwiwat, C., Govindan, R., Estrin, D., Ganesan, D.: Building Efficient Wireless Sensor Networks with Low-level Naming, Proceedings of the ACM Symposium on Operating Systems Principles, Banff, Canada, (2001)
5. Heinzelman, W., Chandrakasan, A., Balakrishnan, H.: Energy-Efficient Communication Protocol for Wireless Microsensor Networks, Proceedings of the International Conference on System Science, Hawaii, (2000)
6. Zhang, J., Shi, H.: Energy-Efficient Routing for 2D Grid Wireless Sensor Networks, Proceedings of the IEEE International Conference on Information Technology: Research and Education (ITRE'03), (2003) 311-315
7. Goh, H.G., Sim, M.L., Ewe, H.T.: Performance Study of Tree-Based Routing Algorithm for 2D Grid Wireless Sensor Networks, Proceedings of the 12th IEEE International Conference on Networks (ICON'04), (2004) 530-534
8. Dai, H., Han, R.: A Node-Centric Load Balancing Algorithm for Wireless Sensor Networks, Proceedings of the IEEE Global Telecommunications Conference (GLOBECOM'03), Vol. 1, (2003) 548-552

Performance Evaluation of Mobile IP Agents' Auto-reconfiguration Mechanisms in MANET

Cláudia J. Barenco Abbas[1], Georges Amvame-Nze[2], and L. Javier García Villalba[3]

[1] Departamento de Computación y Tecnología de la Información
Universidad Simón Bolívar - USB
Oficina MYS 213-B, Apartado Postal 89.000
Caracas, 1080 Venezuela
barenco@ldc.usb.ve

[2] Faculty of Technology, Electrical Engineering School
University of Brasilia – UnB
Brasília, 70900 Brazil
georges@labcom.unb.br

[3] Grupo de Análisis, Seguridad y Sistemas (GASS)
Departamento de Sistemas Informáticos y Programación (DSIP)
Facultad de Informática, Despacho 431
Universidad Complutense de Madrid - UCM
C/ Profesor José García Santesmases s/n, Ciudad Universitaria
28040 Madrid, Spain
javiergv@sip.ucm.es

Abstract. This paper presents a Dynamic Reconfiguration of Mobile IP Agents (DRMIPA) and failure free architecture integrated in Mobile Ad hoc Networks (MANETs). The proposal is due to the fact that: actual infra-structured networks do not implement the Mobile IP (MIP) protocol, all MIP agents are static and the cost of having redundancy for MIP agents' failure is often high. As MANETs are created temporarily at any location, we propose a solution that would allow the integration of MIP with MANET. Doing so, groups of MIP nodes in MANETs would enjoy the IP mobility at any foreign or local network that doesn't implement MIP. New algorithms and messages are proposed for the new Dynamic Reconfiguration and fault tolerant Mobile IP Agents in MANET. A simulation performance analysis using the Network Simulator (NS2) is presented.

Keywords: DRMIPA, MIP, AODV, MANET, Fault Tolerance.

1 Introduction

The Ad hoc network nodes have great flexibility and responsiveness after being implemented [1]. Nonetheless, there might be a need for those nodes in the new network to be able to use an internet connection and still be reached by their Home Network from a fixed or another distant Ad hoc network area. For such matter, the Mobile IP group foresaw the need for a mobile node attached to its Home Network to

E. Sha et al. (Eds.): EUC 2006, LNCS 4096, pp. 844 – 853, 2006.

be able to move to other networks (called Foreign Networks) keeping its Home Address (its logical address obtain at the Home Network) throughout the path to the next destination and, having the possibility to keep track of local services it had at the home network [2]. For this reason, two IP addresses have to be assigned to the Mobile node so it would be reached in the Home Network by a fixed and permanent IP address and at the Foreign Address by the so called Care-Of Address (COA), which would represent its new point of attachment away from home, Figure 1 (a).

The current work proposes a solution to integrate both architecture, MIP and MANET. The new scenario would not depend of an infrastructure network with or without MIP Gateways. The new approach would make groups of MIP nodes, in MANETs; enjoy Internet access and IP mobility at any foreign or local network.

This approach is different from related works because MIPv4's Foreign Agent (FA) and Home Agent (HA) are now mobile and part of a mobile ad hoc network [4], [5], [6] and [13], Figure 1 (b). In [8], [9] and [10], an Efficient Fault-Tolerant Protocol for Mobility Agents in Mobile IP is proposed, but the issue takes place in an infrastructure network.

We believe that there is a need in having an independent MIPv4 architecture, from the one studied in [4], [5] and [6], to attend this kind of situation. So why not making all agents mobile and having total freedom from networks that have no MIP. As these agents are now mobile there would also be a need to turn them failure free.

For that reason, we propose new Mobile IP agents by naming them Active and Passive Agents where the active agent would be the one in service and the passive agent the one in idle, the system will be known as DRMIPA (*Dynamic Reconfiguration of Mobile IP Agent*) [14]. The contributions of the present work are as follow:

- The challenge of having a Home and Foreign Agent inside the Ad hoc network. Therefore, we would have to maintain the Mobile IP Agent's functionalities from the fixed Network into MANET.
- A DRMIPA node can operate as a MIPv4 node. The algorithm ensures session continuity for all nodes in MANET, even as the mobile agents' shutdown or move to another IP network.
- The new DRMIPA network can be created temporarily at any foreign or local network to allow nodes in having Internet and IP mobility. Access of their Home Network would be available anytime, anywhere.
- The election of a passive agent HA (FA) to provide a fault tolerance mechanism if the active agent HA (FA) leaves or ceases its participation in the network. This would support MN users with continuous network connections while at the Home or Foreign Network.
- The solution proposes a bidirectional tunnel between DRMIPA nodes and their HA (FA) agents. So, all traffic between nodes passes through the home and/or foreign agent. The AODV protocol is used for all routing purposes.

In all the above cases, we agree on the need of a foreign network implementing a gateway having two interfaces for this scenario to work: one to access the Internet and the other one to access any MANET network.

2 Dynamic MIP Agent in MANET

2.1 Mobile IP in Ad Hoc Network

The current MIP proposal is to support IP mobility in different environments. The HA, being a router located at the Home Network, provides information regarding the service location to the Mobile Node (MN) when away from home and serves as one of the end tunnels to be built during a data transaction, [3]. Located at its Home Network, the MN uses its home address to receive and exchange data with other nodes in the area such as the correspondent host (CH). When moving to another network (a Foreign Network) it receives a Care-Of Address (COA) in that location and will be able to maintain its communication data when roaming, Figure 1 (a). To facilitate the transaction of data between the HA and the MN, a FA is used as the other end tunnel during the registration's request, reply and data exchange. The routing protocol used in this work is the Ad hoc On demand Distance Vector (AODV) for being more reliable and scales better than DSDR. This is a reactive protocol that uses Route Request (RREQ) and Route Reply (RREP) for route discoveries between Ad hoc nodes, which are maintained active upon discovery, [7].

In the Ad hoc Network there is no infrastructure that can allow a greater control of MNs. When they move from one IP area to another, their current services should be available as needed at the foreign Ad hoc Network, similar to what occurs with Mobile IP in an infrastructure network. To that extent, the MANET and MIP should be combined to allow the registry of any mobile nodes entering and leaving its IP area of propagation and forcing all MANETs to implement a Mobile Home and Foreign Agents (named in this work as MHA and MFA), for further node connectivity.

Figure 1 (b) shows the suggested system having a virtual path between the origin and destination nodes (the represented destination MN in *DRMIPA2* is originally from *DRMIPA1*). The data leaves its origin passing thru the active MHA and MFA; both will always serve as end tunnels up to the desired destination node. When away from home network, all MNs data transaction has to be between active agents so that MIP mechanisms behave as before when they were part of the WLAN topology. The routing process is supported by AODV along both MANETs' path.

2.2 Issues Facing Agent Mobility

As we expect any MHA (MFA) to be shutdown, leave its IP area or move to another Ad hoc Network at anytime, the proposed DRMIPA algorithms have to be installed in all MNs to maintain dynamic reconfiguration and fault tolerance. In such conditions, the associated services to mobility of a visiting MN, previously registered at the foreign MFA, need to be preserved outside its MANET Home Network. Therefore, each new Mobile Agent (MA $\Leftrightarrow$ {MFA or MHA}) should be duplicated, one serving as an active agent and the other as a passive agent. This technique helps to maintain a fault tolerance mechanism for these mobile agents. By this mean, it is assured that in case a MA is being deactivated or leaves its functionality of MFA (MHA), it will be replaced by a previously preconfigured passive MFA (MHA), which would then exercise its activities as a new active MFA (MHA) and in turn elects the next passive MFA (MHA).

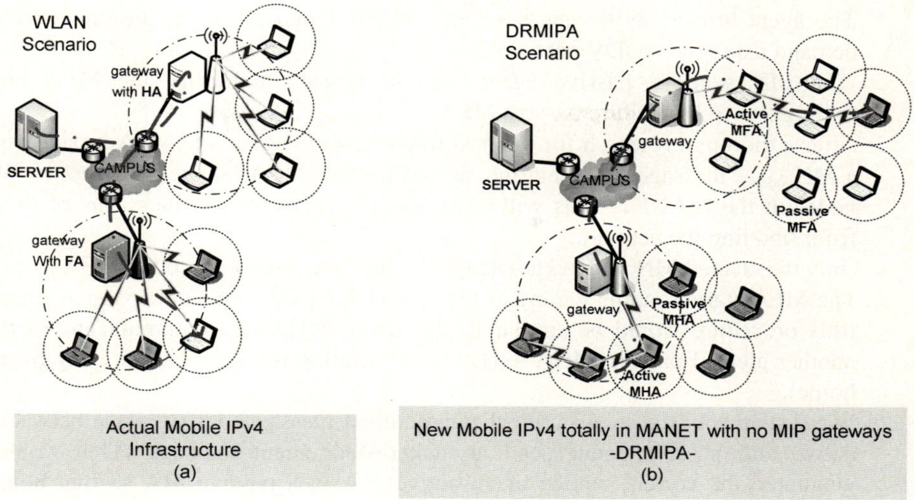

Fig. 1. MIPv4 in WLAN (a) and the proposed MIPv4 in MANET with WLAN access: DRMIPA (b)

3 Proposed Algorithm

The following steps exemplify a passive agent election and binding signaling from an active MFA to a MN in the same network. The active agent uses actual MIP agent advertisement with the existence of a new 2-bit *A*-flag, Figure 2. If a MN has only the MIP algorithm implemented and not DRMIPA, the *A*-flag would not be an issue but this MN would not participate at the election process, as described below:

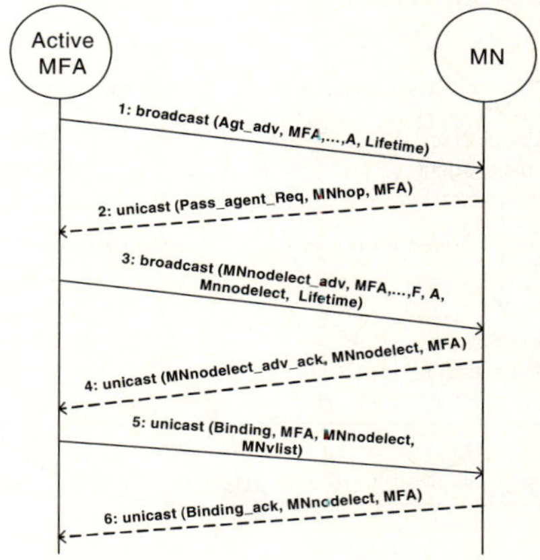

Fig. 2. Passive agent election and binding signaling

1: The agent broadcasts the message into MANET and all routes are created on demand using the AODV protocol.
2: The MN sends a passive agent request message to notify the MFA his willingness to be a future passive MFA.
3: After a thorough research for the best future passive agent, the MFA broadcasts a $MN_{nodelect}$ message including the elected passive MFAs' logical address to all nodes in the MANET. This will cease passive agent request messages of MN from flooding the network.
4: Only the elected MN will acknowledge the previous broadcast to the MFA.
5: The MFA starts sending a copy of his MN visiting list to the new passive agent (this procedure would be similar to the active MHA that communicates with another elected passive MHA except when sending the list of MNs away from home).
6: For system robustness, all critical transactional messages taking place between active and passive agent need an acknowledgement message. This would guarantee the correct replica of an active MA in a passive MA so that node workload redirection is softer in case of failure.

All MN implementing DRMIPA would have their state as shown in Figure 3. The EXIT state would occur if an algorithm failure is detected. At the LISTEN state, all messages from the network are analyzed.

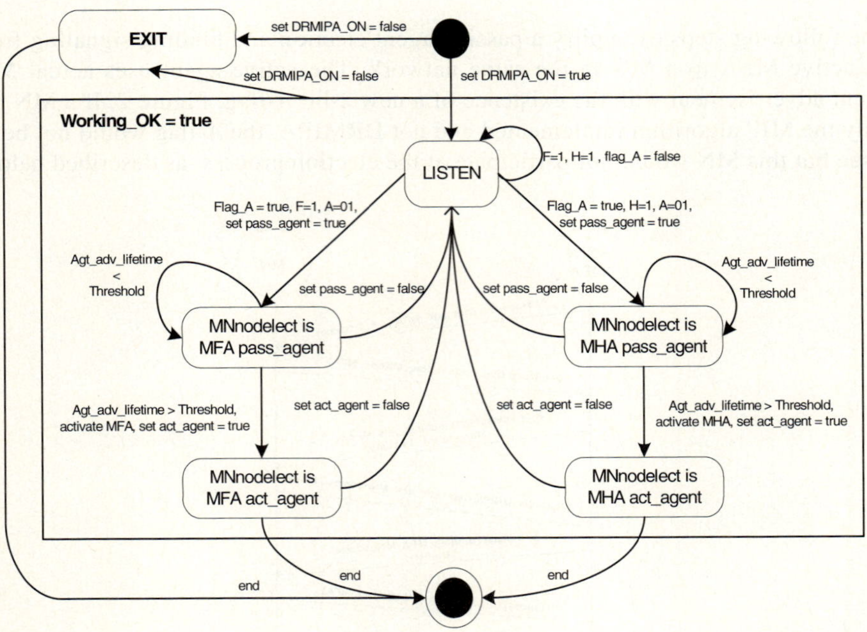

Fig. 3. MNnodelect basic state diagram

If no *A*-flag appears in the advertisement, it means that the MN is in a normal MIP network. This would guarantee a transparent MIP functionality and no DRMIPA process will take place. If a MIP agent advertisement contains the *A*-flag, one of two things can take place for the message to be process as coming from a MFA (having the *F*-flag set) or MHA (having the *H*-flag set). The elected MN, known as MNnodelect would be in a MFA (MHA) passive agent state. While agent advertisements lifetime are less than a certain threshold time, the MNnodelect will monitor any eventual active MFA (MHA) failure. Meanwhile, the MFA (MHA) synchronizes their MN list to the new MNnodelect.

If the agent advertisements' lifetime exceeds the threshold time, the node goes to a MFA (MHA) active agent state and the previously obtained lists would be included in the new MFA (MHA) list. At this point the other active agent should cease operations. And by doing so, the new active agent would be aware of previously registered MN at the old active agent. Now the active agent algorithm is working and an auto configuration mechanism begins for passive agent election. If any MNnodelect leaves the network or ceases operation as active (passive) agent, it must return to its original LISTEN state. The present work emphasizes the fact that a node can be an active or passive agent as long as it maintains its normal MIP functionalities as a simple MN. And this is due to the fact that: if a MN has an undergoing data transmission with another MN and is elected as passive agent, it must not cease its operations as a normal MIP node.

If after a certain period of time the active MFA does not send any agent advertisement, the passive agent assumes his functionalities as new active agent. The active agent's activation algorithm is as fallowed:

```
Gratuitous_exit := true
pass_agent := true
receive(Gratuitous_exit, MHA/MFA, MNnodelect ) message
from MHA/MFA;
    if Gratuitous_exit ∧ pass_agent then begin
unicast (Gratuitous_exit_ack, MNnodelect, MHA/MFA)
message to MHA/MFA;
    activate MFA/MHA algorithm;
set Flag-A=11 ∧ broadcast (Agt_adv,MHA/MFA,…, A,
Lifetime) message to Network{MFA ∧ MHA} nodes;
    set pass_agent := false;
    set act_agent := true;
    end
      else if (Adv_lifetime > Threshold) ∧ pass_agent
  then activate MFA/MHA algorithm;
set    Flag-A=11    ∧    broadcast(Agt_adv,MHA/MFA,…,A,
Lifetime) message to Network{MFA ∧ MHA} nodes;
          set pass_agent := false;
          set act_agent := true;
  end
```

4 Implementation

The DRMIPA is implemented on the HUT Dynamics' MIP software in conformance to RFC 2002, [3] and [12], for real world scenario. For the purpose of tracing the new DRMIPA messages, *ethereal version-0.10.12's* source code has been modified. The initial configuration of the system requires a manual setup of the MHA (MFA) for all further processes explained previously, in session 3, to be implemented. The present work does not allow more than one active and passive agents running in the network at the same time. We assume that all MANETs' MN implements the DRMIPA algorithm. Meanwhile, a performance analysis has being done under NS2 as we shall see in session 5. Between all messages, one is used for all MNs in the network, implementing DRMIPA, to cease their requests as candidates for passive agent (this is a way to stop flooding inside the network), as seen in Figure 4. This message is a MNnodelect Advertisement. A 32 bits field is used for MNs to know which one has being elected by the active agent and start behaving as a passive agent. The new elected passive agent is now a redundant active agent in idle. We have defined the type this advertisement with the decimal value 82, and an *A=01* flag. This *01* flag means that the message is coming from the active agent.

```
 0                   1                   2                   3
 0 1 2 3 4 5 6 7 8 9 0 1 2 3 4 5 6 7 8 9 0 1 2 3 4 5 6 7 8 9 0 1
-+-+-+-+-+-+-+-+-+-+-+-+-+-+-+-+-+-+-+-+-+-+-+-+-+-+-+-+-+-+-+-+
|     Type      |    DRMIPA     | A |           Lifetime         |
+-+-+-+-+-+-+-+-+-+-+-+-+-+-+-+-+-+-+-+-+-+-+-+-+-+-+-+-+-+-+-+-+-
|          Active Mobile Foreign/Home Agent Address             |
+-+-+-+-+-+-+-+-+-+-+-+-+-+-+-+-+-+-+-+-+-+-+-+-+-+-+-+-+-+-+-+-+-
|            Elected Passive Agent Mobile Address               |
+-+-+-+-+-+-+-+-+-+-+-+-+-+-+-+-+-+-+-+-+-+-+-+-+-+-+-+-+-+-+-+-+-
```

Fig. 4. MNnodelect Advertisement (*Type = 82, A=01*)

5 Simulation Analysis

The DRMIPA protocol has being implemented under NS2 version 2-27 [11]. The original CMU-Trace file was partially modified such that MIP and DRMIPA traces could appear at the NS2 trace file interpreter. The simulation scenario has 10 static mobile nodes using a Two-Ray channel characteristic in a 670x670 flat grid size. This would help in a better way for understanding the delay and bandwidth utilization between the MHA (MFA) and elected passive agent when compared to receiving and transmitting MIP and DRMIPA messages at the same time. From (1), the percentage of bandwidth utilization between active and passive agents can be obtained making *data_sent = data_recv = 54bytes*. Due to overhead messages used in the wireless scenarios, a bandwidth of 5,5 Mbps is used instead of 11Mbps. The average latency of DRMIPA messages was *0,011s* according to DRMIPAs' trace file. The above numbers in (1) give us a bandwidth utilization of *1,4%*. This value shows us how small the occupation of such messages is during the simulation.

$$\%Utilization = \frac{(data\_sent + data\_recv) * 8}{(bandwith * time)} 100 \quad (1)$$

The delay in Table 1 was measured using a one way mean delay scenario. The purpose of doing so is for a better comparison of MIP and DRMIPA messages. Equation (2) for delay calculation is:

$$\begin{aligned} Delay = & Act\_Agt(created\_and\_sent\_msg) \\ & + Pass\_Agt(processed\_msg) \\ & + Pass\_Agt(created\_and\_sent\_msg) \end{aligned} \quad (2)$$

The *Act_Agt (created_and_sent_msg)* reflects the time at which a message leaves the active agent network interface after being created. The *Pass_Agt (processed_msg)* is the time used by the passive agent to process a message coming from the active agent. The *Pass_Agent (created_and_sent_msg)* is the time a passive agent uses for creating and sending a message to respond at the previous received message from the active agent. DRMIPA messages in Table 1 are in bold characters. As MIP and DRMIPA agent advertisements have the same size and include an *A*-Flag for DRMIPA message differentiation, no changes in delay should be noticeable during simulation as can be seen in Table 1.

Table 1. MIP and DRMIPA Messages Performance Comparison

	Flags	Mean Delay (ms)	From - To
MIP_Agt_adv	H=1/F=1	1,89	
DRMIPA_Agt_adv	A=11	**1,89**	Active MFA (MHA) - MN
Reg_Request	-	2,11	
Pass_agent_Req	A=00	**2,11**	MN - Active MFA (MHA)
Reg_Reply	-	2,16	
MNnodelect_adv	A=01	**4,31**	Active MFA (MHA) - Passive MFA (MHA)
MNnodelect_adv_ack	A=10	**2,64**	Passive MFA (MHA) - Active MFA (MHA)

One way end to end delay results show that the election mechanisms are fast enough compared to the current MIP registration messages. All data where taken during a 30s simulation time. Figure 5 shows that the *MNnodelect_ADV* have the highest overhead in transmissions due to the fact that all nodes should be aware of the elected IP node's address. Once elected, the passive agent sends small *MNnodelect_ACK* messages to the active agent. That explains its small overhead compared to the rest. With this unicast approach, the passive agent will only send his acknowledgement to the MHA (MFA). The *DRMIPA_pass_REQ* stays between both messages in overhead transmissions because each node has to send a unicast message to the active agent. This method seems to be better for the current implementation as not all nodes in MANET would be DRMIPA nodes. The present scenario can also have MIP, DRMIPA and MANET nodes at the same time. So, making the *DRMIPA_pass_REQ* a unicast message would prevent other non DRMIPA nodes to receive the message and flood the network.

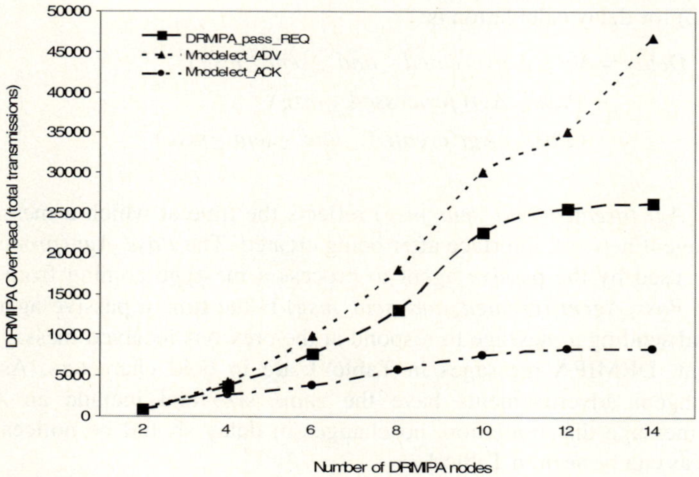

Fig. 5. DRMIPA messages overhead

In Figure 6, the simulation time taken for the passive agent election is shown. The node's positions were set randomly during simulation. The elected nodes are chosen from a passive agent list maintained in the MFA (MHA). When the simulation had 2 DRMIPA nodes it took about *0.82s* for the elected node to receive the message. This value is higher than the ones appearing in other scenarios, because the MHA was too far away from the MN during simulation. In other cases, the actual passive agent is sometimes less than 30 meter away from active agent which would explain small delay times when sending the election message.

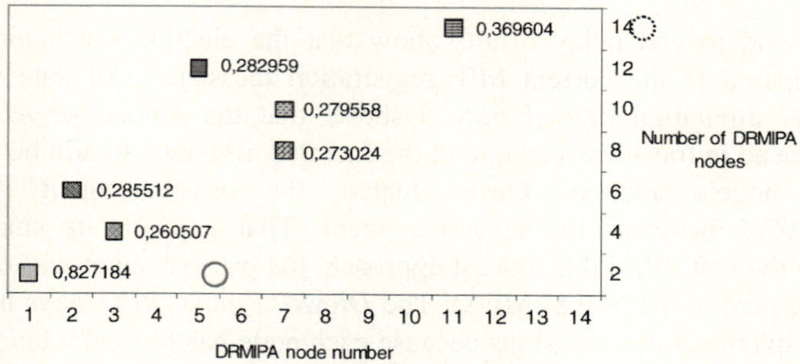

Fig. 6. Time taken for DRMIPA's Passive Agent election (in seconds)

6 Conclusions

In this article, we propose new algorithms and messages for a Dynamic Reconfiguration of Mobile IP Agents in MANET (DRMIPA) using the on demand AODV routing protocol. DRMIPA's solution can help in the integration and mobility of Mobile IP Agents and Hosts between several MANET-Internet-MANET networks. We believe that the principal gain is to maintain the interworking of multiple MIP and MANETs using MFA (MHA) in a failure free architecture. It means a total freedom in using any wireless infra-structured network where MIP doesn't exist. Now it would be possible for groups of MIP nodes in MANETs to enjoy their Internet access and IP mobility at any foreign or local network that doesn't implement MIP.

Acknowledgements

The authors thank the CNPQ (*Conselho Nacional de Desenvolvimento Científico e Tecnológico*), MEC (Ministerio de Educación y Ciencia, Spain, under Project TSI2005-00986) and MITyC (Ministerio de Industria, Turismo y Comercio, Spain, under Project FIT 360000-2005-65) for their financial support.

References

1. C. E. Perkins and E. M. Royer: Ad-hoc On Demand Distance Vector Routing. Proceedings of the 2nd IEEE Workshop on Mobile Computing Systems and Applications, (1999) 90-100
2. C. Perkins: Mobile IP Support, Technical Report IETF RFC 3220 (2002)
3. IEEE P802.11: The Working Group for Wireless LANs.
4. At: http://grouper.ieee.org/groups/802/11/
5. U. Jonsson, F. Alroksson, T. Larson, P. Johansson, G. Q. Mauire Jr.: MIPMANET-Mobile IP for Mobile Ad Hoc Networks. In: Proceedings of MOBIHOC, (2000) 75-85
6. Y. Sun, E. M. Belding-Royer, C. E. Perkins: Internet Connectivity for Ad Hoc Mobile Networks, International Journal of Wireless Information Networks special issue on "Mobile Ad hoc Networks (MANETs): Standards, Research, Applications
7. C. Ahlund, A. Zaslavsky: Integration of Ad hoc Network and IP Network Capabilities for Mobile Hosts. In: Proceeding of IEEE, (2003)
8. RFC-3561, Ad hoc On demand Distance Vector (AODV) Routing, (2003)
9. R. Ghosh and G. Varghese: Fault-Tolerant Mobile IP, Technical Report WUCS-98-11, Washington Univ., (1998)
10. J. H Ahn and C.S. Hwang: Efficient Fault-Tolerant Protocol for Mobility Agents in Mobile IP," Proc. 15th Int'l Parallel and Distributed Processing Symp, (2001) 1273-1280
11. Jenn-Wei Lin, Joseph Arul: An Efficient Fault-Tolerant Approach for Mobile IP in Wireless Systems, IEEE Transaction on Mobile Computing, Vol.2. no.3, 207-220
12. NS-2. At: http://www.isi.edu/nsnam/ns
13. HUT Dynamics Mobile IP. At: http://dynamics.sourceforge.net/
14. RFC-3963, NEMO Basic Support Protocol, at: http://www.mobilenetworks.org/nemo/
15. G. Amvame, C. Abbas and L. Villalba: Novel Dynamic Reconfiguration of Mobile IPv4 Agents Fully Integrated in MANET. In: Proceedings of the 4th International Information and Telecommunication Technologies Symposium - I2TS, IEEE R9, (2005) 46-51

Formulas and Protocols for Broadcasting in Mobile Ad Hoc Networks

Chang Wu Yu and Cheng Yao Tseng

Department of Computer Science and Information Engineering
Chung Hua University, Hsin Chu, Taiwan, ROC
cwyu@chu.edu.tw

Abstract. An operation is called *broadcasting* if a node sends a packet to all other nodes in an ad hoc network. Broadcasting is an elementary operation to support many applications in ad hoc networks. Thus, many schemes have been proposed for reducing the number of re-broadcasting packets. However, to the best of our knowledge, few papers discuss the bound of necessary broadcasting packets. In the work, we derive formulas for estimating the number of required broadcasting packets by taking three different approaches. In addition, we also propose two protocols: the cluster-head-early method and the connected-dominating-set method to reduce the redundant rebroadcast packets without exploiting the mechanisms of hello messages or cluster formation.

1 Introduction

An ad hoc network consists of a collection of mobile nodes without centralized administration and infrastructure. Each node moves arbitrarily and therefore the network topology may change frequently. Nodes of these network act as routers that discover and maintain routes to other nodes. Applications of this type of network include emergency search-and-rescue operations, meetings in which persons want to share information, and data acquisition operations inhospitable terrain [11].

An operation is called *broadcasting* if a node sends a packet to all other nodes in a network. Broadcasting is an elementary operation to support many applications in ad hoc or sensor networks. For example, AODV uses broadcasting to find a main route [9]. Flooding is the most straightforward method for broadcasting. However, flooding results in two problems:

(1) Redundant rebroadcasts: When a node receives the broadcast packet at the first time, it will rebroadcast the packet to all its neighboring nodes immediately. Such blind flooding results in lots of redundant rebroadcasts. In Figure 1, for example, node *S* initiates a broadcast, and then the neighboring nodes {1, 2, 4, 6, 7} of *S* receives the packet and rebroadcast it in turn. The rebroadcasts of node 3, node 5, and node 8 are redundant, since their neighboring node sets {12, 13}, {15, 16}, and {19, 20} have received the same packet in the broadcasting.

(2) Heavy contention: When many neighboring nodes intend to broadcast messages at the same time, they will contend for network bandwidths with each other.

E. Sha et al. (Eds.): EUC 2006, LNCS 4096, pp. 854 – 863, 2006.

Therefore, the time for the broadcasting will thus be seriously lengthened and the performance of the system will be degraded significantly.

A traditional graph technique can be used to model the desired problem. In a graph G, a set $S \subseteq V(G)$ is a *dominating set* if every vertex set not in S has a neighbor in S. A *connected dominating set* if S is a dominating set in G and the induced subgraph G_S is also connected. Theoretically, the problem to find the minimum number of rebroadcast is equivalent to finding a minimum connected dominating set containing a given vertex. However the above problem is NP-hard and seem exist no efficient algorithm so far [2].

Therefore, many heuristics have been proposed for reducing the number of re-broadcasting packets [6, 7, 10, 12, 14]. Some of them wait for a period of time to collect local connectivity information (and thus defer the completion time of the broadcasting) [6, 10, 12]. Other schemes pay high costs for maintaining cluster formation.

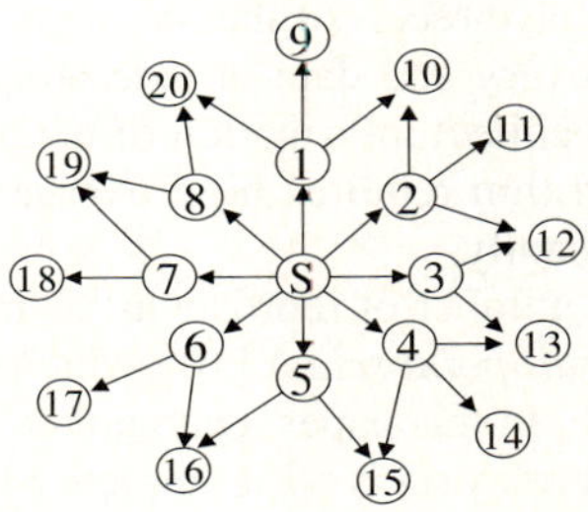

Fig. 1. Flooding results in lots of redundant rebroadcasts

To the best of our knowledge, few papers discuss the bound of necessary broadcasting packets. The bound can be used to evaluate the performance of new broadcasting protocols. In the work, we attempt to derive formulas for estimating the number of required broadcasting packets by taking three different approaches. In addition, we also propose two protocols: the cluster-head-early method and the connected-dominating-set method to reduce the redundant rebroadcast packets without exploiting the mechanisms of hello messages or cluster formation.

The rest of the paper is organized as follows. We survey related work in the next section. Section 3 shows three formulas and their derivations. In Section 4, two proposed schemes are described. Finally, Section 5 concludes the paper.

2 Related Work

In recent years, many approaches have been proposed to reduce the number of rebroadcast nodes [6, 7, 10, 12]. These can be classified into two groups: the *cluster schemes* and the *non-cluster schemes*. In the cluster scheme, the whole network consists of many clusters, and the cluster head manages the members of each cluster. Other nodes called *gateways* connect one cluster to another. In this scheme, only cluster heads and gateways can forward broadcasting packets. On the other hand, in the non-cluster scheme, every node in the network decides whether to rebroadcast a packet or not in a distributed mode.

Obviously, flooding is the most straightforward approach for this kind of broadcasting problem. Every node in flooding forwards the received packet straightly and immediately. As expected, flooding results in serious redundancy, contention, and collision.

In [6], Ni *et al.* proposed the counter-based scheme to alleviate the broadcast storm problem. When first receiving the broadcast packet, a node waits for a random number of time slots to hear the same packet from other re-broadcasting nodes. Each node is associated with a counter c to track the number of times of the same broadcast message received. Whenever $c \geq K$, the node is forbidden to rebroadcast, where K is a chosen counter threshold. They analyzed the counter threshold and the extra area that can be benefited from a rebroadcast node, and found that when $K \geq 4$ the expected additional coverage is below 0.05%.

The main idea of the proposed algorithm in [7] is that a node need not rebroadcast a message if all its neighbors have received the message. The algorithm consists of two phases: local neighbor discovery and data broadcasting. Each node in the algorithm waits for a period of time to collect information of neighboring nodes and rebroadcast nodes. As a result, the algorithm requires high overheads and defers the completion time of the broadcast significantly.

A technique restricts the number of rebroadcast as much as possible by selecting a subset of neighbors, called *multipoint relays* [10], which cover the same network region as the complete neighbors do. In this paper, Qayyum *et al.* also showed the problem of finding a minimal multipoint relay set is NP-complete by reducing from the dominating set problem. Therefore, they proposed a heuristic algorithm to compute a multipoint relay set of cardinality at most log n times the optimal multipoint relay number, where n is the number of nodes in the network. Since the information needed to compute the multipoint relays is the set of one-hop and two-hop neighbors, which are collected by sending hello messages periodically, multipoint relays requires high overheads.

3 Deriving Bounds on the Size of Required Re-broadcast Nodes for Broadcasting

In this section, the size of required re-broadcast nodes in mobile ad hoc networks is estimated by using different techniques. Throughout this article, we define n to be the number of nodes deployed randomly in the network, and r the communication radius of each mobile node.

3.1 The First Formula

An ad hoc network can be modeled as a geometry graph. A *geometric graph* $G=(V, r)$ with nodes placed in 2-dimension space R^2 and edge set $E=\{(i, j) \mid d(i, j) \leq r$, where $i, j \in V$ and function $d(i, j)$ denotes the Euclidian distance between node i and node $j\}$. Theoretically, the required rebroadcast nodes can be represented by a minimum connected dominating set. Let γ_c be the size of the minimum connected dominating set, and γ the size of the minimum dominating set. Since a connected dominating set is also a dominating set, we have that $\gamma \leq \gamma_c$. A subset S of V is called an *independent set* of $G=(V, E)$ is no two vertices of S are adjacent. We also let α denote the maximum size of independent set in a graph.

It seems difficult to obtain the exact size of the minimum connected set even we collect the overall topology of interested ad hoc networks in a snapshot. However, the degree information of the corresponding graph would help to estimate the size of required broadcast nodes due to the following theorems.

Theorem 1 [1]. For any connected graph, $\gamma_c \leq 3\gamma - 2$.

Theorem 2 [13]. Every n-vertex graph with minimum degree σ has a dominating set of size at most $n \times \frac{1+\ln(\sigma+1)}{\sigma+1}$; thus we have $\gamma \leq n \times \frac{1+\ln(\sigma+1)}{\sigma+1}$.

Combining Theorem 1 and 2, we have the following theorem.

Theorem 3. Every n-vertex graph with minimum degree σ, we have $\gamma_c \leq 3 \times (n \times \frac{1+\ln(\sigma+1)}{\sigma+1}) - 2$.

Sometime, the minimum degree σ is still difficult to know; however, when n mobile nodes are regularly distributed inside a square of length l units as shown in Figure 2, we may use the average degree of a vertex in the corresponding geometry graph to estimate the minimum degree σ.

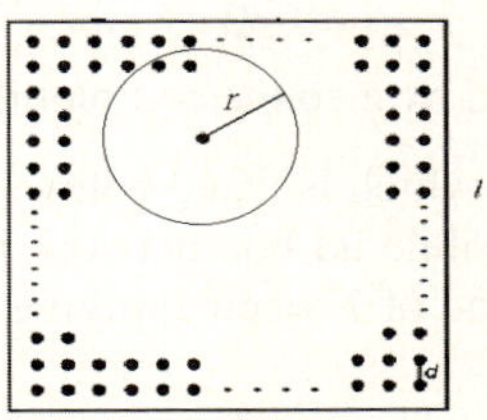

Fig. 2. Arrange n nodes in $l \times l$ region

The average degree of a vertex in the geometry graph is the number of points covered by the node's communication range r (i.e., the number of points covered by a circle with radius r). To exactly compute the number of covered points, we need to tackle an unsolved problem in number theory [3]. Therefore, we adopt a different approach. The distance d between two points in Figure 2 is $d = \frac{l}{\sqrt{n}+1}$. Then the number of points in the dash-line triangle is $1+2+3+\left(\left\lfloor \frac{r}{d} \right\rfloor+1\right) = \left(\left\lfloor \frac{r}{d} \right\rfloor+1\right) \times \left(\left\lfloor \frac{r}{d} \right\rfloor+2\right) / 2$. Consequently, the estimated number of points in the quarter of a circle (as shown in Figure 3) is

$\left(\left\lfloor \frac{r}{d} \right\rfloor+1\right)\left(\left\lfloor \frac{r}{d} \right\rfloor+2\right)/2\times\frac{1/4\pi r^2}{1/2r^2} = \left(\left\lfloor \frac{r}{d} \right\rfloor+1\right)\times\left(\left\lfloor \frac{r}{d} \right\rfloor+2\right)\times\frac{\pi}{4}$. Therefore, the estimated number of points in a circle is $\left(\left\lfloor \frac{r}{d} \right\rfloor+1\right)\times\left(\left\lfloor \frac{r}{d} \right\rfloor+2\right)\times\pi$.

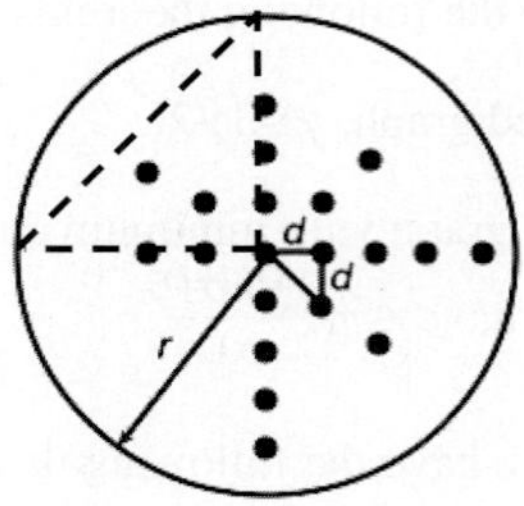

Fig. 3. The expected number of nodes covered by a node

Finally, we obtain the first upper bound of the minimum number of required re-broadcast nodes by the help of Theorem 3.

Formula 1. We probably require at most $n\times\frac{1+\ln(T+1)}{T+1}$ nodes with communication range r to rebroadcast packets where $T=\left(\left\lfloor \frac{r}{d} \right\rfloor+1\right)\times\left(\left\lfloor \frac{r}{d} \right\rfloor+2\right)\times\pi$ and $d=\frac{l}{\sqrt{n}+1}$, when the $l\times l$ deployed area is fully covered by a connected mobile network.

Another precise formula, which is listed below, for estimating the average number of neighboring nodes in a mobile ad hoc network has been proposed by Yen and Yu [15]. We also can use it instead of T when applying Formula 1.

Theorem 4. The average (expected) neighbors of a node in an ad hoc network is $(n\text{-}1)\times(\frac{\frac{1}{2}r^4-\frac{4}{3}lr^3-\frac{4}{3}mr^3+\pi r^2 ml}{m^2l^2})$, here A is a $l\times m$ rectangle deployed space and r is the communication radius of each mobile node.

3.2 The Second Formula

In this subsection, we try to derive another formula by estimating an upper bound of the maximum size of independent set. When the $l\times l$ deployed area is fully covered by a connected mobile network, the maximum size of independent set (α) is equivalent to the maximum number of circles each of which does not cover the center of any other circle. First, we deploy k circles in each of k rows where $k=\lfloor l/2r\rfloor$ (totaling k^2 circles). Moreover, we can also add a circle in the middle of every two neighboring circles (Figure 4) (totaling $2\times k(k\text{-}1)$ circles) and one circle in the center of four neighboring

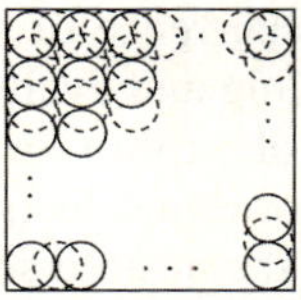

Fig. 4. The maximum size of independent set

circles (totaling $(k\text{-}1)^2$ circles). Thus we can easily obtain that $\alpha \le k^2+2\times k(k\text{-}1)+(k\text{-}1)^2=(2k\text{-}1)^2=(2\times\lfloor l/2r\rfloor\text{-}1)^2$.

By Theorem 5 and above discussion, we can obtain the second upper bound.

Theorem 5[1]. For any connected graph, $\gamma_c \le 2\alpha\text{-}1$.

Formula 2. We require at most $2\times(2\times\lfloor l/2r\rfloor\text{-}1)^2$ nodes with communication range r to rebroadcast packets when the $l\times l$ deployed area is fully covered by a connected mobile network.

3.3 The Third Formula

Another different approach is introduced in the section. Let $X_n=\{x_1, x_2, \ldots, x_n\}$ be a set of independently and uniformly distributed random points. We use $\Psi(X_n, r, A)$ to denote the *random geometric graph* (RGG) of n nodes on X_n with radius r and placed in area A. RGGs consider geometric graphs on random point configurations. Applications of RGGs include communications networks, classification, spatial statistics, epidemiology, astrophysics and neural networks [8].

A RGG $\Psi(X_n, r, A)$ is suitable to model an ad hoc network $N=(n, r, A)$ consisting of n mobile devices with a transmission radius of r unit length that are independently and uniformly distributed at random in an area A. When each vertex in $\Psi(X_n, r, A)$ represents a mobile device, each edge connecting two vertices represents a possible communication link because they are within the transmission range of each other. A geometric graph and its representing network are shown in Figure 5. In the example, area A is a rectangle that is used to model the deployed area such as a meeting room. Area A, however, can be a circle, other different shapes, or even infinite space.

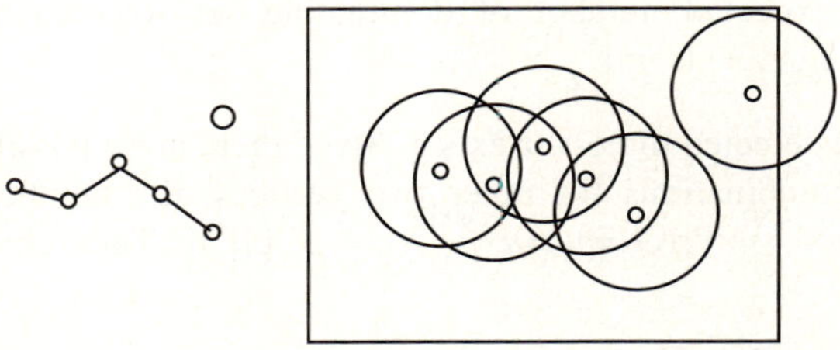

Fig. 5. A random geometric graph G with its representing network $N=(6, r, A)$, where A is a rectangle

Computing the probability of occurrence of specific subgraphs of a given RGG becomes important issues for modeling and evaluating the fundamental properties of wireless ad hoc networks. A simple algorithm for selecting a dominating set has been proposed Wu and Li [14]. Their algorithm selects the center of the induced path with length 2 (that is p_2) as a member of the desired set.

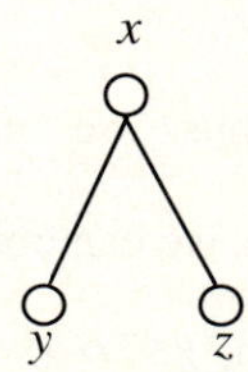

Fig. 6. The subgraphs of p_2

We can estimate the number of dominating set produced in their algorithm.

Theorem 6[16]. For arbitrary three distinct edges $e_i=(u, v)$, $e_j=(u, w)$, and $e_k=(v, w)$ in a $\Psi(X_n, r, A)$, the probability of these three edges form p_2 is $\left(\frac{3\sqrt{3}}{4}\right)\pi r^4/|A|^2$, where $u \neq v \neq w$.

With the help of Theorem 6, we can obtain the number of p_2, denoted by $N(p_2)$.

Theorem 7. The $N(p_2)$ in a $\Psi(X_n, r, A)$ is $3\times\binom{n}{3}\left(\frac{3\sqrt{3}}{4}\right)\pi r^4/|A^2|$.

Proof. First, we compute the number of hidden-terminal pairs in any RGG. Since each hidden-terminal pair consists of three distinct labeled vertices, we set S to be the selected three-vertex set. Since there are $\binom{n}{3}$ different combinations for selecting three from n vertices and three different settings for labeling one from three as the center of the hidden-terminal pairs (*i.e.* the internal node of the induced path with length 2), we have the number of hidden-terminal pairs is $3\times\binom{n}{3}\times\Pr(G_S=p_2)=3\times\binom{n}{3}\left(\frac{3\sqrt{3}}{4}\right)\pi r^4/|A|^2$ by Theorem 6. ■

Then we can obtain the third formula listed as follows.

Formula 3: The expected number of dominating set selected by Wu and Li's algorithm in a $\Psi(X_n, r, A)$ is $n\times\binom{n-1}{2}\times\left(\frac{3\sqrt{3}}{4}\right)\pi r^4/|A|^2$.

Proof. Let S be the selected three-vertex set. Since there are n possible centers in the system and $\binom{n-1}{2}$ combinations for other two vertices, the number of the desired dominating set is $n\times\binom{n-1}{2}\times\Pr(G_S=p_2)=n\times\binom{n-1}{2}\times\left(\frac{3\sqrt{3}}{4}\right)\pi r^4/|A|^2$ by Theorem 7. ■

4 Two Broadcasting Protocols

In the section, we design two protocols: the cluster-head-early method and the connected-dominating-set method for broadcasting in ad hoc networks.

4.1 The Cluster-Head-Early Method

The first approach is called the *cluster-head-early method* (CHEM) because it tries to make cluster-head nodes carry rebroadcasts early. It is helpful to first introduce a technique called the *simple clustering method* (SCM) that has been used for designing algorithms for the maximal independent set problem [4] and for devising the adaptive clustering for mobile wireless networks [5]. SCM associates each node with a distinct integer randomly selected from the set {1, 2, 3, …, *n*}, where *n* is a fairly large integer (See Figure 7). For convenience, we name each node the assigned integer from now on.

According to their assigned numbers, SCM partition nodes of the network into three kinds of sets. A *cluster head* is a node whose assigned integer is the largest as comparing to its neighboring nodes. Note that a cluster head cannot be a neighbor of another cluster head. A *cluster member* is a node that at least one of its neighbors (not itself) is a cluster head. An independent node is a node that is neither a cluster head nor a cluster member. Figure 7 shows an example. The cluster head set, the cluster member set, and the independent node set are {48, 65, 84, 96}, {2, 20, 35, 40, 54, 87}, and {44} respectively.

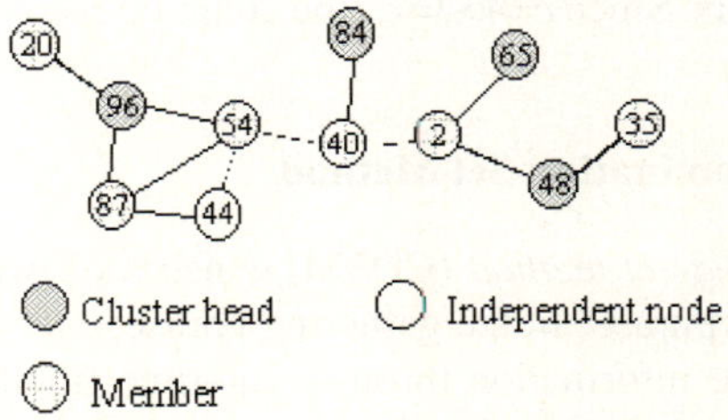

Fig. 7. Partition network nodes into three sets

However, CHEM is different from SCM. The intuitive idea of CHEM is described as follows. The rebroadcasts of cluster members would be redundant, provided cluster heads have already re-broadcasted the same packet. Cluster heads in our protocol are therefore planned to receive and rebroadcast the packet early. On the contrary, cluster members and independent nodes are required to wait for a period of time after receiving the first broadcast packet.

Note that SCM will select nodes with large weights as cluster heads. Suppose node *B* (with assigned integer *IntB*) receives the first packet from node *A* (with assigned integer *IntA*). If *IntB*>*IntA* then node *B* in CHEM forwards the packet to its neighbors without hesitation. Otherwise, node *B* will wait for t=(1-(*IntA*/*IntA*+*IntB*))×T time to receive the same packet from other nodes, where T is a predefined constant. Note that the value of t is designed intentionally to inversely proportional to the value of *IntA*.

We also associate each node with a counter c (this concept is borrowed from the counter-based scheme [6, 12]) to record the number of packets received. A counter threshold C is also chosen. Whenever $c \geq C$ in the period of t time, the node is forbidden to rebroadcast. An example is shown in the following figure.

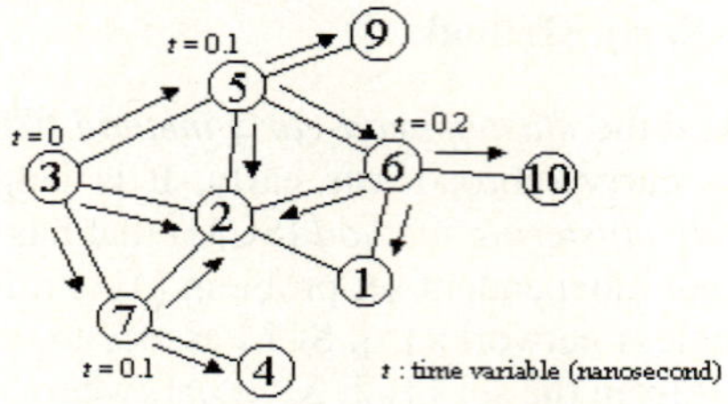

Fig. 8. An example for CHEM

Suppose that each single hop communication takes 0.1 seconds, and the count threshold C=3 and the selected constant T=1 second. In Figure 8, node 3 (the initial node) starts to broadcast a packet at t=0. Node 5, node 2, and node 7 receives the packet from node 3 at t=0.1. Since we have 5>3 (and 7>3), node 5 (and node 7) rebroadcasts the packet immediately. On the other hand, node 2 is scheduled to wait for 0.4 (=1-(3/(3+2))=2/5) seconds due to 2<3. Similarly, node 6 (at t=0.2) receives the packet and rebroadcast the packet immediately because 6>5. When t=0.3, node 2 receives four packets from its neighbors. Since c=4>3=C (the count threshold), node 2 is forbidden to rebroadcast the packet.

4.2 The Connected-Dominating-Set Method

The *connected-dominated-set method* (CDSM) consists of two phrases: the gathering phrase and the selection phrase. In the gathering phrase, every node in CDSM tries to collect neighboring node information through one-time flooding. So that the desired rebroadcast nodes can be determined and its size can also be reduced in the selection phrase. In a word, CDSM is devised for finding a small set of nodes as a connected dominating (CD) set (in graph term) which carry broadcast. We name these nodes *dominating nodes*.

Suppose that each node x is allocated with a variable *nblist* (initialized to be empty), which denote the set of collected neighboring nodes of x. In the beginning of the selection phrase, the *nblist* of a broadcasting node will be sent to all its neighbors accompanied with the subsequent broadcasting message. Then the following three rules are applied to select suitable nodes into the CD set, each of which takes responsibility for hereafter broadcasting. A dominating node must satisfy the following three rules:

Rule 1. A dominating node received the first *nblist* and its *nblist* is not covered by sender's *nblist*.

Rule 2. A dominating node must have two neighboring nodes x and y such that node x is not a neighbor of y.

Rule 3. If a dominating node receives another node's *nblist* again, the dominating node will check whether its *nblist* is included in the union of the two collected *nblists*. If the answer is not, it will still be the dominating node. Otherwise, it is not a dominating node anymore.

5 Conclusion

In this work, we have derived three formulas for estimating the number of required broadcasting packets by taking different approaches. We also proposed two broadcasting protocols without exploiting the mechanisms of hello messages or cluster formation. We have conducted extensive simulations by using ns-2 and demonstrated that our protocols outperform the counter-based scheme and flooding in rebroadcast node and latency. Owing to page limit, however, this work excludes simulation results intentionally.

References

1. P. Duchet and H. Meyniel, "On Hadwiger's number and stability number," *Ann. Discrete Math.*, vol. 13, pp. 71-74, 1982.
2. M. R. Garey and D. S. Johnson, *Computers and Intractability: A guide to the Theory of NP-completeness*, Freeman, San Francisco, 1978.
3. Peter Hall, *Introduction to the Theory of Coverage Process*, John Wiley and Sons, New York, 1988.
4. Michael Luby, "A simple parallel algorithm for the maximal independent set Problem," *SIAM Journal on Computing*, vol.15, pp. 1036-1053, 1986.
5. C.R. Lin and M. Gerla, "Adaptive clustering for mobile wireless networks," *IEEE Journal on Selected Areas in Communications*, vol.15, pp. 1265-1275, 1997.
6. Sze-Yao Ni, Yu-Chee Tseng, Yuh-Shyan Chen, and Jang-Ping Shen, "The broadcast storm problem in a mobile ad hoc network," *Mobicom'99*, pp. 151-162.
7. Wei Peng and Xi-Cheng Lu, "On the reduction of broadcast redundancy in mobile ad hoc networks," *MobiHoc*, 2000, pp. 129 -130.
8. Mathew D. Penrose, *Random Geometric Graphs*, Oxford University Press, 2003.
9. C.E. Perkins and E.M. Royer, "Ad-hoc On-demand Distance Vector routing, " *Proceedings of the 2nd IEEE Workshop on Mobile Computing Systems and Applications*, 1999, pp. 99-100.
10. Amir Qayyum, Laurent Viennot, and Anis Laouiti, "Multipoint relaying: An efficient technique for flooding in mobile wireless networks," *INRIA, Tech. Rep.*, RR-3898, 2000.
11. E. M. Royer and C.-K. Toh, "A review of current routing protocols for ad hoc mobile wireless networks," *IEEE Personal Communication*, pp. 46-55, 1999.
12. Yu-Chee Tseng, Sze-Yao Ni, and En-Yu Shih, "Adaptive approaches to relieving broadcast storms in a wireless multi-hop mobile ad hoc network," *International Conference on Distributed Computing Systems*, 2001, pp. 207-216.
13. D. B. West, *Introduction to Graph Theory*, Prentice Hall, 2001.
14. Jie Wu and Hailan Li, "Domination and Its Applications in Ad Hoc Wireless Network with Unidirectional Links," *International Conference on Parallel Processing*, 2000, pp. 189 –197.
15. L.-H. Yen and C. W. Yu, "Link Probability, Network Coverage, and Related Properties of Wireless Ad Hoc Networks," *The 1st IEEE International Conference on Mobile Ad-hoc and Sensor Systems*, 2004, pp.525-527.
16. C. W. Yu and Li-Hsing Yen, "Computing subgraph probability of random geometric graphs: Quantitative analyses of wireless ad hoc networks," *Springer-Verlag Lecture Note in Computer Science*, vol. 3731, pp. 458-472, 2005.

Traffic Adaptive IEEE 802.15.4 MAC for Wireless Sensor Networks

Younggoo Kwon and Yohan Chae

Konkuk University, 1 Hwayang-dong, Kwangjin-gu, Seoul, 143-701, Korea
{ygkwon, ychae}@konkuk.ac.kr

Abstract. IEEE 802.15.4 is a new standard uniquely designed for low rate wireless sensor networks(WSNs). It targets low data rate, low power consumption and low cost wireless networking, and offers device level wireless connectivity. In this paper, the general coordinated sleeping algorithm and the traffic-adaptive algorithm are combined in IEEE 802.15.4 MAC protocol to achieve high energy efficiency and high performance at the same time. By observing that the sporadic traffic characteristic of WSNs, we propose the traffic-adaptive IEEE 802.15.4 MAC with coordinated sleeping algorithm. Through the various performance studies, the proposed algorithm shows significant performance improvements in wireless sensor networks[1].

1 Introduction

Wireless sensor networks will be widely deployed in the future because they can monitor and control the physical environment from remote locations. These sensors are operated with limited battery power, and energy is not always renewable. The traffic inherent to WSNs is highly sporadic and does not necessarily follow any specific traffic pattern. IEEE 802.15.4 [1]-[3] is a new standard uniquely designed for low rate wireless sensor networks. It targets low data rate, low power consumption and low cost wireless networking and offers device level wireless connectivity. In this paper, we introduce an energy efficient MAC protocol that adapts with traffic situations in sensor network applications. We focus on two main attributes. At first, we use the general coordinated sleeping algorithm to achieve the energy efficiency. By considering the sporadic traffic pattern of WSNs, the actual duty cycle of each station is pretty small, which needs energy for operations. Therefore, by using a simple coordinated sleeping algorithm, we can improve the energy efficiency significantly in WSNs. Secondly, traffic information can be determined by checking the queue status of each sensor station which explicitly specify its traffic characteristics. Depending on the application at hand, traffic adaptive mechanism can be relatively simple. According to the traffic information, we dynamically change the length of the active and sleep period to support the traffic adaptive mechanism. IEEE 802.15.4 distinguishes

[1] This work was supported by the faculty research fund of Konkuk University in 2006.

E. Sha et al. (Eds.): EUC 2006, LNCS 4096, pp. 864–873, 2006.

itself from other wireless standards such as IEEE 802.11 [4] and Bluetooth [5] by some unique features for wireless personal area networks. IEEE 802.15.4 has been designed as a flexible protocol in which a set of parameters can be configured to meet different requirements. In this paper, we will investigate the operational characteristic of the IEEE 802.15.4 MAC protocol, and induce the energy efficient, traffic adaptive MAC algorithm that provides significantly high performance for WSNs.

In the next section, we explain related research works. Then, we present the newly proposed algorithm in Section 3. The performance evaluations is given in Section 4. In the final section, we present the conclusions.

2 Related Works

2.1 Power Saving Mechanisms for WSN

Many MAC protocols to save power consumption in WSNs have been proposed. Though reservation based MAC protocols have some advantages, in this paper, we focus on MAC protocols based on random access considering sensor networks' applications. One of the main approaches to MAC for WSNs, comes from its counterpart for ad hoc networks, the IEEE 802.11 standard [4]. The IEEE 802.11 standard is a CSMA/CA based protocol which is widely used in wireless LANs. Using plain 802.11 MAC for WSNs has many drawbacks. In particular, the energy consumption due to overhearing and idle-listening, is a major chunk of wasteful energy consumption. The reason for using the energy consumption model with CSMA based MACs is that they perform quite well under most circumstances and the implementation is not complex. Therefore, many researchers have worked to develop efficient CSMA based MAC protocols for WSNs. The PAMAS [12] protocol was one of the first attempts to reduce unnecessary power consumption by turning overhearing stations to sleep. The protocol, however, needs a separate control channel for coordination and avoiding overhearing. It also does not take into account idle listening, which accounts for a large portion of energy consumption. Ye et. al [6][7] proposed the S-MAC protocol that combines scheduling and contention with the aim of improving collision avoidance and scalability. The power saving is based on scheduling sleep/listen cycles between the neighbor stations. After the initial scheduling, synchronization packets are used to maintain the inter-station synchronization. When a station wants to use the channel, it has to contend for the medium. The scheme is very similar to 802.11 with physical and virtual carrier sense and RTS/CTS exchange to handle the hidden station problem. The overhearing control is achieved by putting to sleep all immediate neighbors of the sender and the receiver after receiving an RTS or CTS packet. The S-MAC operation and frame is divided into two periods; the active period and the sleep period. During the sleep period all stations that share the same schedule sleep and save energy. The sleep period is usually several times longer than the active period. Stations listen for a SYNC packet in every frame and the SYNC packet is transmitted by a device infrequently to achieve and maintain virtual clustering.

2.2 Traffic-Adaptive Mechanisms for WSN

Although S-MAC [6][7] can reduce the idle listening time, it is not optimal due to a fixed interval of listening mode. Under the network traffic is very light, i.e., no stations have data traffic to send during the active listen period, all stations still have to be awake and waste their energies. If the traffic is very heavy with fixed active period, all stations can not handle properly the traffic because they have to sleep regardless the network traffic situations. This observation leads many researchers to propose new energy efficient sensor MAC protocols that allow the stations to go to active and sleep status considering the traffic information. The Traffic-Adaptive Medium Access (TRAMA) protocol is one of the proposals to implement energy-aware schedule-based medium access with traffic information. TRAMA addresses energy efficiency by having stations going into sleep mode if they are not selected to transmit and are not the intended receivers of traffic during a particular time slot. TRAMA uses traffic information to establish transmission schedules which are propagated to one-hop neighbors. This information is then used to define when stations need to be in receive mode and when they can switch to low-power sleep mode. Besides its energy efficiency benefits, the use of traffic information also makes TRAMA adaptive to the sensor network applications. Though many algorithms are proposed in traffic-adaptive WSNs, most proposed algorithms have the complexity for announcing traffic information. Complex schedule-based protocols exhibit inherently higher delivery delays when compared to contention-based approaches, and they are not desirable considering the implementation aspect of view in wireless channels.

2.3 802.15.4 MAC

The IEEE 802.15.4 standard [1]-[3] defines the specification of physical (PHY) and medium access control (MAC) sublayer for low data rate and low power wireless devices that typically operate in short ranges. IEEE 802.15.4 MAC supports a simple one-hop star networking and, a multi-hop tree or mesh networkings too. Wireless link under 802.15.4 operates in three different frequency bands - 2.4GHz, 915MHz, and 868MHz with the max data rate of 250kbps, 40kbps and 20kbps respectively. The primary devices targeted by the IEEE 802.15.4 MAC include various kinds of wireless sensors and wireless tag or barcode readers. Since they often operate in remote locations with limited battery capacity, their life cycle is more critical aspect than the network performance, such as data throughput or latency. For those power limited devices, we can trade off network performance with power efficiency by utilizing power saving mechanism that comes with IEEE 802.15.4. The IEEE 802.15.4 standard defines beacon enabled mode and superframe structure for power saving purposes. It can operate in either beacon enabled mode or beacon disabled mode. In beacon enabled mode, a network coordinator periodically broadcasts beacons so that other nodes in the network hear the beacons to synchronize to the superframe structure suggested by the coordinator. In beacon disabled mode, however, a network coordinator does not broadcast beacons except when other nodes request beacons for scanning or association purpose. In beacon enabled networks, a coordinator broadcasts beacons with superframe structure information recorded in the beacon. When other nodes in the network receive the beacon, they obtain the superframe information and start to synchronize to the coordinator's superframe structure. A superframe structure is defined by the network beacons. A network beacon marks the start of a superframe, while it also marks the end of previous superframe at the same time. A superframe generally consists of two parts - an active part and an inactive part. The length of a superframe (beacon interval, BI) and its active part (superframe duration, SD) are determined by beacon order (BO) and superframe order (SO), respectively. The length of inactive part can be determined by subtracting superframe duration from beacon interval. The active part is divided into 16 equally sized slots and has two periods - a contention access period (CAP) and an optional contention free period (CFP). During the CAP, IEEE 802.15.4 MAC utilizes slotted carrier sense multiple access with collision avoidance (CSMA-CA) mechanism for channel access. Following the CAP, CFP can be assigned for low latency applications or applications requiring specific data bandwidth. CFP may accommodate up to seven guaranteed time slots (GTSs), each of which may occupy one or more slots.

3 Traffic Adaptive IEEE 802.15.4 MAC Protocol

Energy consumption is the primary focus of our traffic adaptive MAC algorithm. Because it is important to analyze the various sources of energy waste, we have identified the following wasting sources.

- **Control packet overheads.** Most protocols need to exchange control packets for management purposes. Because these packets do not contain any application data, they are considered as overheads.
- **Collision.** If more than two nodes transmit data at the same time, their radio signals can be jumbled due to packet collisions. Then each node has to retransmit same data which consumes more energy.
- **Overhearing.** Because IEEE 802.15.4 MAC shares the medium, any node can hear others in the transmission range. For example, when nodes A, B, and C are in the same transmission range and node A wants to send data to node B, node C picks up the signal because it does not know whether the data is destined for itself or not, until the data is received. Thus, node C wasted energy in receiving an unwanted packet.
- **Idle listening.** This is the most evident source of energy waste in most wireless networks. Nodes in wireless networks must always keep their receiver turn on because they have no idea when the data will be received. In applications that send or receive packets infrequently, energy waste in idle listening is significant and must be avoided.

In most cases, the energy waste caused by overheads, collision, and overhearing is relatively small compared to that of idle listening. Control packet overheads of

IEEE 802.15.4 MAC are MAC commands, beacons, and acknowledgements. Because we measured power consumption after the network had fully established, MAC commands for scanning and association were ignored. Only network beacons and acknowledgements were taken into account for measuring energy consumption. Regarding the collision, the efficient CSMA-CA is used. Additional collisions from hidden terminal problem are ignored due to lack of support for Request-to-send (RTS) and Clear-to-send (CTS) mechanism [4]. Thus, we designed our traffic adaptive IEEE 802.15.4 MAC with focusing on the energy waste in idle listening to be minimized. As stated above, beacon enabled IEEE 802.15.4 network uses the superframe structure to save energy consumption. Determining the superframe order is important because it has a direct relationship to the amount of energy consumed.

3.1 Traffic Adaptive Scheme

The IEEE 802.15.4 network supports broad range of applications. This means that traffics generated from these applications also vary greatly in amount. Even in the same application, traffic loads can change at the need of the application. Consider a wireless temperature sensor network that measures temperature upon the demand of an application. If the application is up to scientific purposes which need a great degree of accuracy, the temperature sampling cycle is short, like several times in a second, generating large number of packets to be transmitted. In some applications, on the other hand, such as room temperature sensors for air conditioner or heater, temperature sampling happens occasionally, several minutes or even hours, generating fewer packets than applications with short cycles. We designed traffic adaptive MAC protocol based on IEEE 802.15.4 MAC with these various circumstances under considerations. In high traffic situations, the duty cycle of the medium increases by extending the active part in the superframe to deliver packets efficiently. Likewise, the duty cycle decreases in low traffic situations by reducing the active part, thereby increasing the inactive part for power saving.

3.2 Protocol Design Overview

We should know the amount of traffic generated by the application in order to adjust the duration of the active part. One way to do this is to monitor the transmission (TX) queue of the nodes. When the traffic is high enough, a transmitter of the node will be unable to process all the packets generated. In this case, the node has to buffer the incoming packets in its own TX queue until they get processed and sent. Therefore, we can assume the traffic loads at a given moment by monitoring the TX queue status. Queue monitoring happens every time when a node wants to send packets to one of its neighboring nodes. When IEEE 802.15.4 MAC receives a packet from an application, it first buffers the packet in its TX queue. Following the packet buffering, it checks the queue status to see how many queue slots were used for packet buffering. If 80% or more of the queue slots are occupied, the node reports its current queue status by sending a special packet called Queue Status Indicator (QSI) to the coordinator for requesting modification to current superframe configuration. QSI packet is a control packet with unique identifier set into the reserved bits of IEEE 802.15.4 MAC frame control field. It must be sent right away upon request, so that a network coordinator receives it and makes changes to its superframe configuration to better deal with the high traffic situations. The problem is that the general queue puts the QSI packet at the end of the TX queue because it considers the QSI packet just as other data packets. Then the QSI packet has to wait until all of the previous 80% of packets are processed and sent. Therefore, we moved the QSI packet to the very first slot of the TX queue. This makes QSI packets be sent as soon as it enters the queue. When a network coordinator receives the QSI packet, it immediately maximizes the active period (100% duty cycle) at the next superframe by setting the superframe order equal to beacon order. This allows the node which sent the QSI packet to flush its TX queue by taking advantage of the maximized active period. If the coordinator receives more QSI packets even if it maximized the active period, it waits until when there is no more QSI packets arriving. If the coordinator receives no further QSI packets for at least n consecutive superframes (application dependant) after receiving the last QSI packet, it resets superframe order to *previous superframe order* + 1. If the superframe order was 2 before receiving the QSI packet, *previous superframe order* has the value of 2. We added 1 to this value because *previous superframe order* might not suffice the current traffic load of the network. Setting superframe order to *previous superframe order* is meaningless because nodes possibly generate another QSI packet if the traffic load at hand is still high. On the other hand, if the coordinator receives no QSI packets during m consecutive superframes (application dependant), it decreases the superframe order by 1. This enables network coordinators and nodes to deal with low traffic situations where there is no need for a long active period. The smallest number possible for the superframe order is 2 in our traffic adaptive IEEE 802.15.4 MAC.

4 Protocol Implementation

We have implemented our traffic adaptive IEEE 802.15.4 MAC to show the effectiveness of our design compared to that of general IEEE 802.15.4 MAC. We used Chipcon CC2420 Demonstration Board [9] as our development platform. The board contains Atmel 128L microcontroller [11] with built in 128 KB flash memory for programming and debugging, 32 KB external SRAM for data storage, and CC2420 RF transceiver [10]. There are two different modes that we can choose from when compiling software layer - Full Function Device (FFD) mode and Reduced Function Device (RFD) mode. We only used FFD mode for implementation.

We have carried out experiments for three different IEEE 802.15.4 MAC schemes - 10% duty cycle, 100% duty cycle, and traffic adaptive MAC. Results are given and compared to each other in the following subsections.

4.1 Experiment Environment and Parameters

The total of eight Chipcon CC2420 DBs was used for our experiments. One of them took a role as a network coordinator and remaining seven operated as network nodes. We used IEEE 802.15.4 association MAC commands to make each node join the network. Node 0 through node 6 are children of the coordinator and each node has address information on its neighboring nodes. Therefore, node 0 can send packets directly to node 1, node 1 can send packets directly to node 0 or node 2, and so on, without routing the packets to the coordinator. Node 0 is a sink for packets generated by node 6 (the source node). Packets generated by the source travels through the intermediate nodes (node 1 through node 5) to reach the destination. Parameters related to our experiments can be found on Table 1. The meaning of the variables m and n is defined in section 3. Regarding the traffic for the network, we generated 200 data packets (113 bytes each including MAC packet header) to be passed from their sources to their sinks for energy measurements. We changed the traffic load by varying the inter-arrival period of packets for checking the network throughput. In our experiments, the packet inter-arrival period varied from 0.1 to 3s. For the low rate wireless network, we also experimented with other inter-arrival periods longer than 3s.

4.2 Performance Results

We provide two experiment results in this paper - energy consumption and, aggregated throughput. We carried out the same experiment several times and average the results from each experiment to get the final results. To measure the energy consumption, we have identified three sources - transmitting and receiving of the packets, idle listening, and sleeping. To calculate the energy consumed from packet transmission and reception, we count the total number of packets transmitted and received by all nodes in each experiment. Packets include beacons, data frames, acknowledgements, and QSIs. From the length of each packet, we can calculate how many bytes were transmitted and received. Once the total bytes are known, we can also calculate the total symbol time spent in transmitting and receiving by multiplying total byte count with 2 because IEEE 802.15.4 takes two symbols to transmit single byte. From the fact that one symbol time

Table 1. Parameters for experiments

Beacon order	6
Superframe order	2 to 6
Duty cycle	6% to 100%
Address mode	16 bit short
m	4
n	2

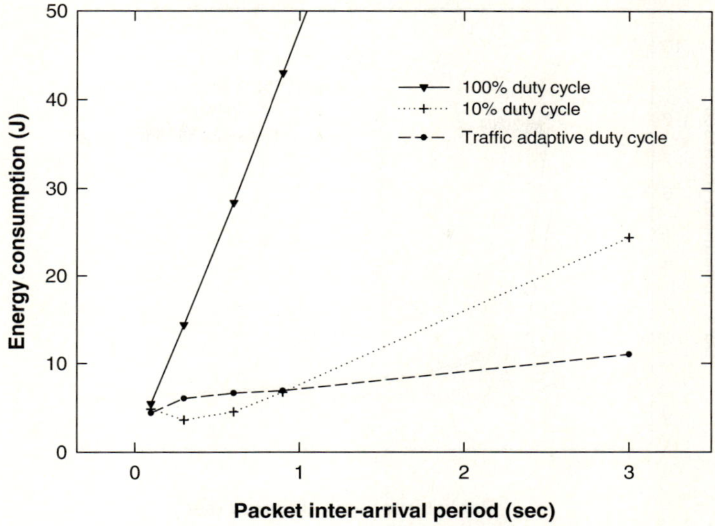

Fig. 1. Total energy consumption of the nodes

corresponds to 16 us, we can calculate the total time spent in seconds. Idle listening time can be calculated by subtracting time spent in transmitting and receiving packets from the duration of the active period. Finally, sleeping time is equal to the duration of the inactive period. Then, we can calculate the energy consumption by multiplying the time with the required power. Figure 1 shows the measured total energy consumption over the seven nodes in the network. As expected, IEEE 802.15.4 MAC with 100% duty cycle consumed far more energy than 10% duty cycle and traffic adaptive MACs. It is interesting to note that IEEE 802.15.4 MAC with 10% duty cycle generally consumed less energy than traffic adaptive 802.15.4 MAC in packet inter-arrival periods from 0.1s to 1s. This is because the duty cycle of traffic adaptive IEEE 802.15.4 MAC can go as low as 6% meaning that each node has less time to send packets from source to destination than IEEE 802.15.4 MAC with 10% duty cycle. Packets may have to be buffered waiting for the active period of the next superframe. This requires higher number of superframes (more energy) and more time (more delay and fewer throughputs) for packets to be delivered, thereby causing more energy consumption. However, traffic adaptive IEEE 802.15.4 MAC performed better as the inter-arrival period gets longer. As in Figure 1, when the inter-arrival period was longer than 1s, traffic adaptive IEEE 802.15.4 MAC consumed less energy than 802.15.4 MAC with 10% duty cycle. The power consumption at 3 inter-arrival period of IEEE 802.15.4 MAC with 100% duty cycle is over 140J, so, it is not shown in Figure 1. For much longer inter-arrival periods like 10s or more, the traffic adaptive IEEE 802.15.4 MAC outperformed the other two MACs by saving huge energy consumptions.

Figure 2 shows data throughput of the network. As expected, IEEE 802.15.4 with 100% duty cycle performed better than the other two MACs by fully

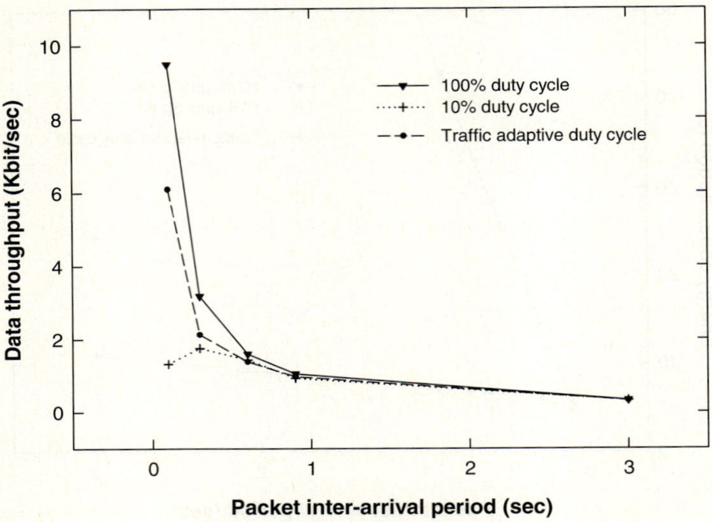

Fig. 2. Aggregated throughput

utilizing the available resource. When the inter-arrival period was less than 0.6s, traffic adaptive IEEE 802.15.4 MAC showed better performance than IEEE 802.15.4 MAC with 10% duty cycle because traffic adaptive MAC adjusted superframe order accordingly depending on the traffic situation. On the other hand, when the inter-arrival period was longer than 0.9s, all of the three MACs performed almost equally. This means that the traffic was light enough to be handled by 10% duty cycle MAC without increasing superframe order. From Figure 1, it is clear that, for inter-arrival periods longer than 0.9s, each MAC showed a different level of energy consumption, while the data throughput of the three MACs was almost the same. It shows that the traffic adaptive IEEE 802.15.4 MAC was energy efficient while achieving the same throughput performance. The IEEE 802.15.4 MAC with 100% duty cycle was the worst energy efficient MAC. When the inter-arrival period was 3s, IEEE 802.15.4 MAC with 10% duty cycle consumed energy more than twice than that of traffic adaptive IEEE 802.15.4 MAC. From Figure 1 and 2, we can see that the energy consumption difference between 10% duty cycle and traffic adaptive MAC will be larger as the inter-arrival period increases, while the data throughput of the three MACs will remain the same.

5 Conclusions

This paper proposed the traffic adaptive IEEE 802.15.4 MAC protocol specially designed for low data rate wireless sensor network applications. Energy efficiency is our primary concern in designing the whole MAC protocol. In this paper, we suggested traffic adaptive MAC protocol with high power efficient scheme in low traffic conditions as well as high traffic conditions. To achieve this, our traffic adaptive MAC algorithm increases the active duty cycle in high traffic conditions for higher throughput and reliable packet delivery, while it decreases the active duty cycle in low traffic conditions to save more energy. Traffic adaptive MAC has been implemented using CC2420 demonstration board from Chipcon and based on the IEEE 802.15.4 standard. We compared our traffic adaptive MAC to other fixed duty cycle MACs and showed that the proposed MAC achieved high energy efficiency especially in low traffic conditions, while preserving high throughput performance and easy implementation structures.

References

1. IEEE Std. 802.15.4-REVb-2005 edition, Wireless LAN Medium Access Control (MAC) and Physical Layer (PHY) Specification for Low-Rate Wireless Personal Area Networks.
2. Zheng, J., Lee, M. J.: A comprehensive performance study of IEEE 802.15.4. IEEE Press Book (2004)
3. Zheng, J., Lee, M. J.: "Will IEEE 802.15.4 make ubiquitous networking a reality? A discussion on a potential low power, low bit rate standard," Communications Magazine, IEEE **42** (2004) 140-146
4. IEEE Std. 802.11-1999 edition, Wireless LAN Medium Access Control (MAC) and Physical Layer (PHY) Specification
5. Specification of the Bluetooth System. Available online: http://www.bluetooth.org/
6. Ye, W., Heidemann, J., Estrin, D.: An energy-efficient mac protocol for wireless sensor networks. IEEE INFOCOM, New York, NY (2002) 1567-1576
7. Ye, W., Heidemann, J., Estrin, D.: Medium Access Control With Coordinated Adaptive Sleeping for Wireless Sensor Networks. IEEE/ACM Trans. on Networking **12** (2004) 493-506
8. Tijs van Dam, Koen Langendoen: An Adaptive Energy-Efficient MAC Protocol for Wireless Sensor Networks in Proc. of 1st international conf. on Embeded networked sensor systems, Los Angeles, CA, USA (2003) 171-180
9. Chipcon CC2420 Demonstration Board Kit User Manual. Chipcon Corp., Oslo, Norway. Available online: http://www.chipcon.com/
10. Chipcon CC2420 RF Transceiver Data Sheet. Chipcon Corp., Oslo, Norway. Available online: http://www.chipcon.com/
11. AVR Microcontroller ATmega128L Reference Manual. Atmel Corp., San Jose, CA. Available online: http://www.atmel.com/
12. Singh, S., Raghavendra, C. S.: "PAMAS: Power aware multi-access protocol with signalling for ad hoc networks," ACM Comput. Commun. Rev. **28** (1998) 5-26

An Efficient Relay Sensors Placing Algorithm for Connectivity in Wireless Sensor Networks*

Jyh-Huei Chang** and Rong-Hong Jan

Department of Computer and Information Science
National Chiao Tung University, Hsinchu, 30050, Taiwan
Fax: 886-3-5721490
jhchang@cis.nctu.edu.tw

Abstract. Randomly deployed sensor networks often make initial communication gaps inside the deployed area even in an extremely high-density network. How to add relay sensors such that the underlying graph is connected and the number of relay sensors added is minimized is an important problem in wireless sensor networks. This paper presents an Efficient Relay Sensors Placing Algorithm (ERSPA) for solving such a problem. Compared with minimum spanning tree algorithm and greedy algorithm, ERSPA achieves a better performance in terms of number of relay sensors added. Simulation results show that the average number of relay sensors added by minimal spanning tree algorithm is approximately up to two times than ERSPA algorithm.

1 Introduction

Randomly deployed networks often make initial communication gaps inside the deployed area even in an extremely high-density networks. In the random sensor network topology, the sensors may be sparsely located and the connectivity is no guaranteed. Therefore, finding an efficient algorithm for improving connectivity in wireless sensor networks and minimizing the number of relay sensors added is an important topic of researches.

In a finite domain, the connectivity of random network depends only on the probability distribution of critical transmission range. Many studies try to find efficient algorithms for determining the critical transmission range for connectivity [1-3]. The asymptotic distribution of the critical transmission radius for k-connectivity is derived in [1]. This study proved the critical transmission range in the unit-area square is $r_n = \sqrt{\frac{\log n+(2k-1)\log\log n+\xi}{\pi n}}$ where n is the number of network nodes and ξ is a constant. The critical transmitting range for connectivity in mobile ad hoc networks is proved in [2]. The author showed the critical

* This research was supported in part by the National Science Council, Taiwan, ROC, under grant NSC 94-2219-E-009-005 and NSC94-2752-E-009-005-PAE and in part by the Intel.

** Corresponding author.

E. Sha et al. (Eds.): EUC 2006, LNCS 4096, pp. 874–883, 2006.

transmission range (CTR) for a mobility model M is $r_M = c\sqrt{\frac{\ln n}{\pi n}}$ for some constant $c \geq 1$ where n is the number of nodes in the network. The mobility model M is assumed to be obstacle free and nodes are allowed to move only within a certain bounded area. In addition, many researches focus on maintaining sensing coverage and connectivity in wireless sensor networks [4-7]. The transmission range (R_t) must be at least twice of the sensing range (R_s) is the sufficient condition to ensure that complete coverage preservation implies connectivity among active nodes [4]. Another study [5] enhanced the work in [4] to prove that the sufficient condition for complete coverage implies connectivity is $R_t = 2R_s$. In [7], a coverage configuration protocol is proposed to achieve guaranteed degrees of coverage and connectivity. This work provided different degrees of coverage requested by applications. To measure the coverage, the work divides the sensing area into $1m \times 1m$ patches. The coverage degree of a patch is approximately by measuring the number of active nodes that cover the center of the patch.

Note that the above studies [1-7] do not discuss how to place relay sensors to improve connectivity for a disconnected ad hoc network. Thus, there are many papers proposed for finding the optimal location to place the additional nodes to achieve network connectivity [8-11]. This problem can be reduced to a minimal Steiner tree problem. In [8], a relay sensor placement algorithm to maintain connectivity is proposed. They formulated this problem into a network optimization problem, named Steiner Minimum Tree with Minimum Number of Steiner Points (SMT-MSP). This study restricts transmission power of each sensor to a small value and adds relay sensor to guarantee connectivity. Simulation results show that their method can achieve better performance in terms of total consumed power and maximum degree, especially for sparse network topology. However, their algorithm runs a time complexity in $O(N^3)$. Some heuristic algorithms for the bounded edge-length Steiner tree problem with a good approximate ratio are proposed in [9-11]. Nevertheless, these heuristic algorithms do not consider the heterogeneous transmission ranges of terminal nodes and relay nodes.

Many researches focus on finding efficient heuristic algorithms to solve the minimal additional nodes placing problems and prolong the network lifetime [12-14]. A heuristic algorithm for energy preserving problem is proposed in [12]. This algorithm transforms the mixed-integer nonlinear problem into a linear programming problem. This study provides additional energy on the existing nodes and deploys relay nodes into the network to prolong network lifetime. In [13], three heuristic algorithms are proposed for achieving connectivity of a randomly deployed ad hoc wireless networks. This work connects the network with a minimum number of additional nodes and maximize utility from a given number of additional nodes for the disconnected network. The time complexity of the greedy algorithms is $O(N^2)$ in a two dimension space where N is the number of terminal nodes.

Our motivation is to find an efficient relay sensors placing algorithm to construct a connected communication graph for connectivity and minimize total relay sensors. Assume that all terminal and relay sensors have the same transmission range and all sensors are location aware. Simulation results show that

ERSPA algorithm gives better performance in terms of the average number of relay sensors with respect to minimal spanning tree algorithm and greedy algorithm [13]. The average number of relay sensors in minimum spanning tree algorithm is approximately up to two times than ERSPA algorithm. This is because the ERSPA places relay sensors in optimal location to connect the maximal number of initial connected sub-graphs.

The remainder of this paper is organized as follows. In section 2, we describe problem formulation and network model. Section 3 illustrates the details of ERSPA algorithm. The simulation results and performance analysis are shown in section 4. Finally, the conclusions are given in section 5.

2 Problem Formulation and Network Model

Consider a wireless sensor network. We assume that the sensing area is in a two dimension space which is a bounded convex subset R of the Euclidean space. In this sensing area, the initially deploy sensors, called as terminal nodes, have been placed and a set of relay sensors are available to be added for connectivity. All terminal nodes and relay nodes are location aware such that the location information can be collected. The set of the terminal nodes is denoted as $N_t = \{N_{t1}, N_{t2}, ..., N_{tn}\}$. The transmission range of each terminal node is adjustable. Initially, the terminal nodes can adjust their transmission range to convey their location information to base station, then limit their transmission range in a bounded value R_t for energy efficient. The set of the locations of n terminal nodes denoted as $L_t = \{p_i \in R \mid i = 1, .., n\}$. The set of the initial network topology is in the form of undirected graph denoted as $G(N_t, E(L_t, R_t))$. Where $E(L_t, R_t) = \{(l_i, l_j) \mid l_i, l_j \in L_t, i \neq j, \| l_i - l_j \| \leq R_t\}$. In order to construct the connected communication graph, we can add the relay sensors to connect the initial separated sub-graphs. A solution is a set of locations to place relay sensors, $L_r = \{q_i \in R \mid i = 1, .., r\}$. The set of the relay sensors denoted as $N_r = \{N_{r1}, N_{r2}, ..., N_{rm}\}$. We formulate our problem as follows: A randomly deployed sensor network with $nR_t \times nR_t$ sensing area in the two dimension space. Given N_t and R_t, find the L_r for minimum relay sensor set N_r to make the graph $G(N_t \bigcup N_r, E(L_t \cup L_r, R_t))$ connected.

3 The Details of ERSPA Algorithm

The ERSPA algorithm includes the following three phases: 1) Find the initial graph $G(N_t, E(L_t, R_t))$; 2) Construct Delaunay; and 3) Add relay nodes. The details of the algorithm are given as follows.

Phase 1: Find the initial graph $G(N_t, E(L_t, R_t))$

Initially, divide the sensing area into $n \times n$ grids. The grid width is equal to the transmission range R_t. Connect all sensor nodes within the transmission range to construct initial connected sub-graphs by grid range searching method (see Figure 1). The details are described as follows.

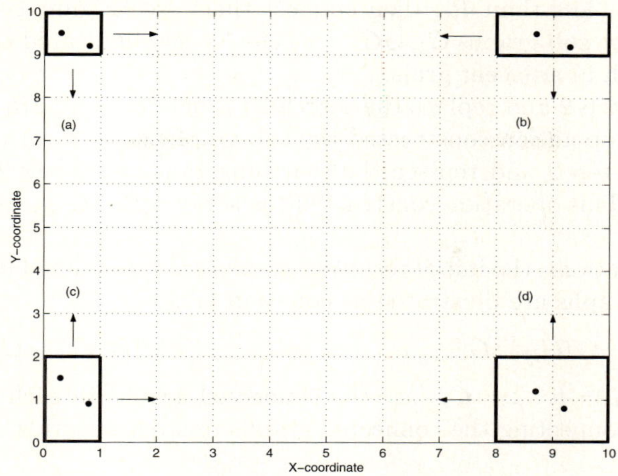

Fig. 1. An example of grid range searching method. (a) Searching range is $R_t \times R_t$. (b) Searching range is $R_t \times 2R_t$. (c) Searching range is $2R_t \times R_t$. (d) Searching range is $2R_t \times 2R_t$.

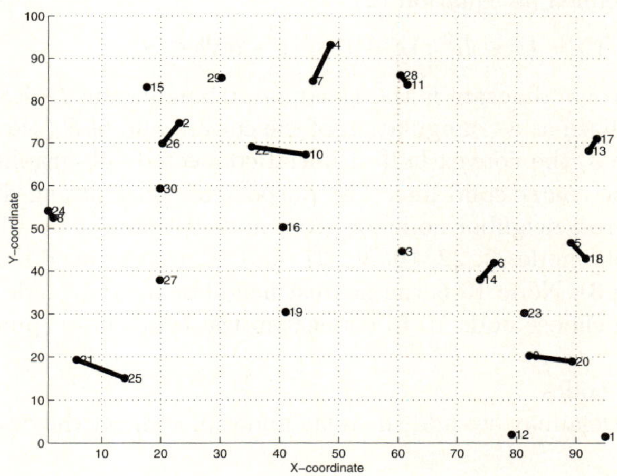

Fig. 2. The initial connected sub-graphs for a randomly deployed network with 30 sensors. The transmission range is 10 percentage of the side of the square sensing field. The initial disconnected terminal nodes indicated by the '•'-sign. The initial connected sub-graphs indicated by the coarse solid line.

Step 1: Search each grid using $R_t \times R_t$ searching range (see Figure 1-(a)). The area of $R_t \times R_t$ is equal to the area of each grid. If there exists any pair of nodes within this range, then connect them. This operation formed the sub-graphs G_{ij} where $i = 1, ..., n, j = 1, ..., n$. G_{ij} are the connected graphs in each grid.

Step 2: Search the sensing area from left to right and from top to down using $R_t \times 2R_t$ searching range. If the distance between any disconnected pair of nodes is equal or less than R_t, then connect them (see Figure 1-(b)). This operation formed the sub-graphs $G_{ij} \cup G_{i,j+1}$. The '∪'-sign indicated connecting the connected graph in adjacent grids.

Step 3: Repeat step 2 and replace the searching range by using $2R_t \times R_t$ (see Figure 1-(c)). This operation constructed the sub-graphs $G_{ij} \cup G_{i+1,j}$.

Step 4: Repeat step 2 and replace the searching range by using $2R_t \times 2R_t$ (see Figure 1-(d)). This operation constructed the sub-graphs $(G_{ij} \cup G_{i+1,j+1}) \cup (G_{i,j+1} \cup G_{i+1,j})$.

After above operations, the initial resulting graphs are constructed (see Figure 2). The resulting graphs are illustrated as equation (1).

$$G = (G_{ij} \cup G_{i,j+1}) \cup (G_{ij} \cup G_{i+1,j}) \cup (G_{ij} \cup G_{i+1,j+1}) \cup (G_{i,j+1} \cup G_{i+1,j}) \quad (1)$$

where $i = 1, ..., n, j = 1, ..., n$. G_{ij} are the connected graphs in each grid. The '∪'-sign indicated connecting the connected graphs in adjacent grids.

Phase 2: Construct Delaunay

Construct the Delaunay by using terminal nodes [15]. The construction of Delaunay is illustrated as follows. Let S be a set of points in a two dimension space. The Voronoi diagram of S, denoted as $Vol(S)$ which is decomposed into Voronoi cells $\{V_a : a \in S\}$ defined as equation (2).

$$V_a = \{x \in R^2 : |x - a| \leq |x - b| \forall b \in S\} \quad (2)$$

The dual of the Voronoi diagram is the Delaunay triangulation $Del(S)$. $Del(S)$ is geometrically realized as a triangulation of the convex hull of S (see Figure 3). As shown in Figure 3, the convex hull of initial connected sub-graphs in phase 1 is indicated by the coarse solid line. The purpose of constructing delaunay is used to find the nearest neighbor node for given node to connect by adding relay node(s). For example, nodes 3, 22, 10, 30, 27, and 19 are the neighbor nodes of node 16 (see Figure 3). Node 10 is the nearest neighbor node of node 16. Thus, for node 16, we can choose node 10 to connect in the next phase (phase 3).

Phase 3: Add relay nodes

After constructing Delaunay, we add the relay nodes to connect the disconnected sub-graphs.

Step 1: We only search the triangle including three points on its apexes and the three points are belong to three different sub-graphs. The triangles inside the convex hull of initial connected sub-graphs are not required to search. Then add a node on the circumcenter of the triangle and check whether the node can connect three sub-graphs or not. The circumcenter is the intersection of the perpendicular bisectors of the sides of the triangle. For example, triangle $(30, 26, 22)$ includes three points on its apexes that are belong to three different sub-graphs (see Figure 4). R_1 is the circumcenter of the triangle (30, 26, 22). If the distance from $R1$ to each apex of the triangle is less than transmission range R_t, then add this relay node. The relay sensors indicated by the '$*$'-sign. The '•'-sign represented initial disconnected terminal nodes and the initial connected sub-graphs represented by the coarse solid line.

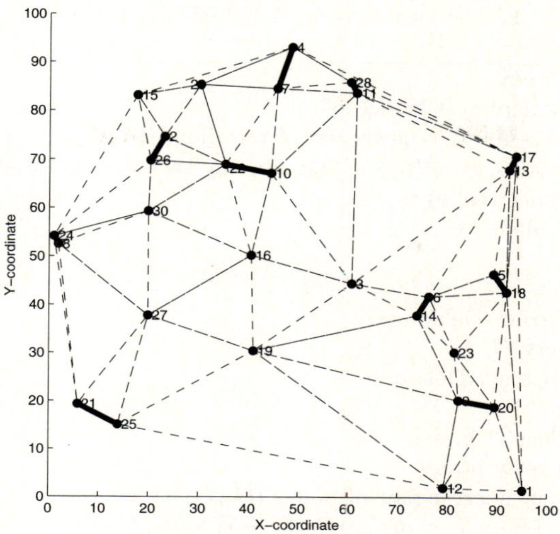

Fig. 3. An example of constructing Delaunay using 30 terminal nodes. The dash lines represented the edges of Delaunay triangulation that are not connected. The initial disconnected terminal nodes indicated by the '•'-sign. The initial connected sub-graphs indicated by the coarse solid line.

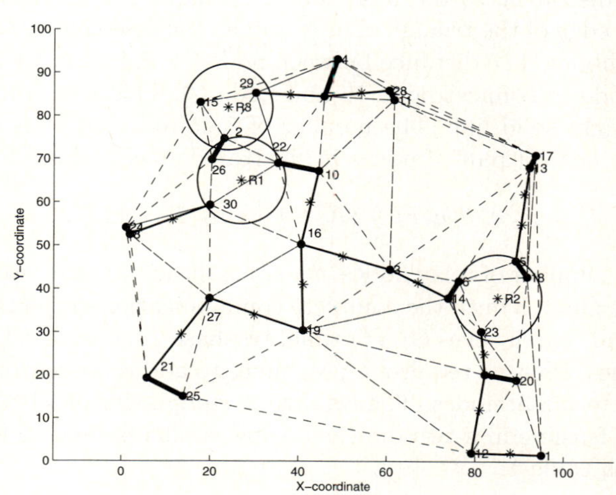

Fig. 4. An example of adding relay sensors with 30 terminal nodes. Place one relay node to connect three nodes is indicated by the circle centered at R_1. The relay sensors indicated by the '$*$'-sign. The initial disconnected terminal nodes indicated by the '•'-sign. The coarse solid line represented initial connected sub-graphs. The dash line represented the edge of Delaunay triangulation that are not connected.After adding relay node, the edge becomes connected that is indicated by slight solid line.

Table 1. The pseudo code of ERSPA algorithm

```
begin Connect
  Randomly deploy N nodes
    for (every N_t) //N_t is the set of terminal nodes
      while (d(u,v) < R_t ) // u,v are any two terminal nodes
        Connect (u,v)
      end while
    end for
end Connect
begin Construct Delaunay
    for ( every N_t )
        Construct Delaunay
    end for
end Construct Delaunay
begin Add relay nodes
    for ( every nearest pair of nodes (G_i, G_j) )
      while (K × R_t < d(u,v) ≤ (K+1) × R_t, K = 0,1,...,n)
        Add K relay nodes //K is the number of relay nodes
      end while
    end for
end Add relay nodes
```

Step 2: The disconnected terminal node only require to connect to its nearest node along the edge of the triangle. For example, the disconnected terminal node 16 has six neighbors. The distance between node 16 and node 10 is the smallest. Add a relay node to connect node 16 and node 10. This new connected edge is indicated by slight solid line. The number of required relay sensors to add into the edge of the nearest pair of nodes is illustrated as equation (3).

$$K \times R_t < d(u,v) \leq (K+1) \times R_t, K = 0, 1, ..., n \tag{3}$$

Where K is the number of relay nodes. $d(u,v)$ is the distance between node u and node v. Repeat phase 3 until the complete communication graph is connected. In phase 1, the grid search takes $O(N^2)$ time. In phase 2, construct Delaunay takes $O(NlogN)$ times. Phase 3 requires $O(N)$ times to add relay sensors. Where N is the number of terminal nodes. The total time complexity of ERSPA algorithms is $O(N^2)$. It is feasible in a two dimension space. The pseudo code of ERSPA is illustrated as in table 1.

4 Simulation Results

4.1 Performance Metrics and Environment Setup

This section presents the performance analysis of the ERSPA algorithm. The metrics for performance are given as follows.

1) Average number of relay sensors: The average number of relay sensors is defined as the required minimal average number of additional sensors to make the network connected.
2) Time complexity: Time complexity is defined as the time to run the algorithm.

The environment setup of simulation is described as follows. There are different number of terminal sensors that randomly deployed in a 100×100 two-dimensional sensing area. The maximum transmission range is 10 percentage of the side of the square sensing field. The network can convey location information of terminal nodes to base station, then limit the transmission range to a bounded value R_t for energy efficient.

4.2 Numerical Results

Comparisons of the two performance metrics were made for three schemes: ERSPA algorithm, Minimum Spanning Tree (MST) algorithm and greedy algorithm [13]. The MST algorithm has two steps. First, generates a minimum spanning tree to connect the terminal nodes. Then, place the relay nodes on the edges of the minimal spanning tree that are longer than the transmission range R_t. The MST algorithm takes $O(NlogN)$ times.

The performance metrics includes the total number of relay sensors and the time complexity. The details will illustrate as follows.

1) Average number of relay sensors: Figure 5 shows that the average number of relay nodes of ERSPA is smaller than minimum spanning tree algorithm and greedy algorithm when the the number of terminal nodes are 50 and 90. Figure 6 shows that the average number of relay nodes of ERSPA is smaller

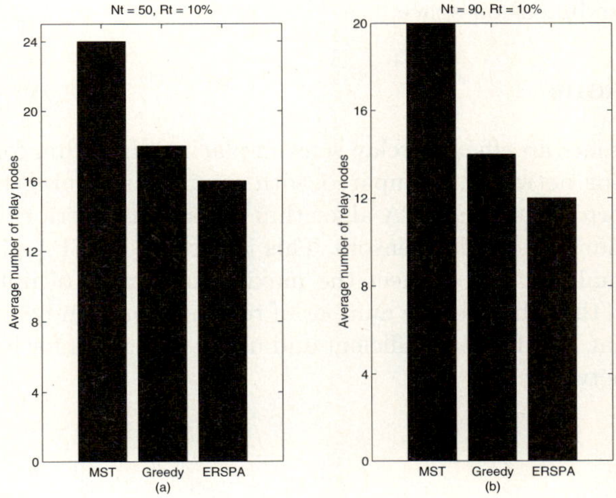

Fig. 5. (a)The average number of relay nodes for connectivity with 50 terminal nodes. (b)The average number of relay nodes for connectivity with 90 terminal nodes. The transmission range is 10 percentage of the side of the square sensing field.

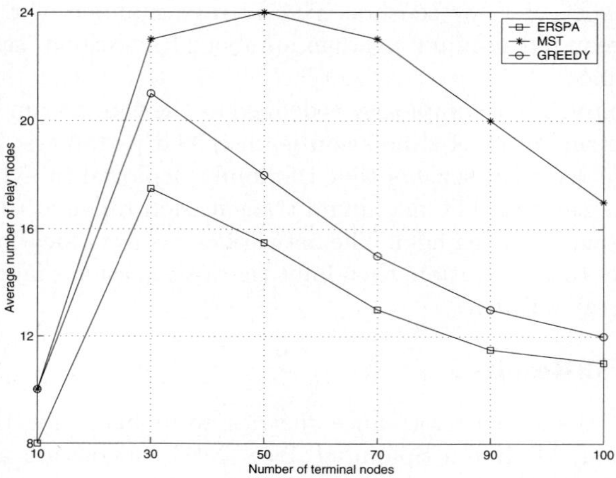

Fig. 6. The average number of relay nodes for connectivity under different terminal nodes. The transmission range is 10 percentage of the side of the square sensing field.

than minimum spanning tree algorithm and greedy algorithm under different terminal nodes. The average number of relay sensors in MST is approximately up to two times than ERSPA algorithm. This is because ERSPA find the optimal location to place relay sensors and connected the maximal number of disconnected sub-graphs.

2) Time complexity: The time complexity of ERSPA algorithm is $O(N^2)$. The minimum spanning tree takes $O(NlogN)$ times. Greedy algorithm takes $O(N^2)$ times. N is the number of terminal nodes. The time complexity of ERSPA is feasible in a two dimension space.

5 Conclusions

This paper presents an efficient relay sensors placing algorithm for connectivity in wireless sensor networks. Compared with minimal spanning tree algorithm and greedy algorithm, our ERSPA algorithm gives better performance in terms of the average number of relay sensors. This is because ERSPA places the relay sensors in optimal place to connect the maximum number of initial connected sub-graphs such that the average number of relay sensors can be minimized. We are confident that ERSPA is an efficient and useful algorithm for further wireless ad hoc sensor networks.

References

[1] R.-J Wan and C.-W. Yi: Asymptotic Critical Transmission Radius and Critical Neighbor Number for K-connectivity in Wireless Ad Hoc Networks. Proceedings of the 5th ACM international symposium on mobile ad hoc networking and computing. (2004) 1-8

[2] P. Santi: The Critical Transmitting Range for Connectivity in Mobile Ad Hoc Networks. IEEE Transaction on Mobile Computing. (2005) 310-317
[3] H. Koskinen: A Simulation-based Method for Predicting Connectivity in Wireless Multihop Networks. Telecommunicatin Systems. (2004) 321-338
[4] H. Zhang and J. C. Hou: Maintain Sensing Coverage and Connectivity in Largen Sensor Networks. Ad Hoc and Sensor Networks. (2005) 89-124
[5] D. Tian and N. D. Georganas: Connectivity Maintence and Coverage Preservation in Wireless Sensor Networks. Ad Hoc Networks. (2005) 744-761
[6] H. Gupta, S. R. Das, and Q. Gu: Connected Sensor Cover: Self-Organization of Sensor Networks for Efficient Query Execution. Prcoeedings of MobiHoc'03.
[7] X. Wang, G. Xing, Y. Zhang, C. Lu, R. Pless, and C. Gill: Integrated Coverage and Connectivity Confuration in Wireless Sensor Networks. ACM SENSYS'03.
[8] X. Cheng, D.-Z. Du, L. Wang, and B. Xu: Relay Sensor Placement in Wireless Sensor Networks. IEEE Transaction on Computers. (2001)
[9] H. Koskinen, J. Karvo, and O. Apilo: On Improving Connectivity of Static Ad-Hoc Networks by Adding Nodes. Proceedings of the 6th ACM International Symposium on Low Power Electronics and Design (ISLPED'03). (2003) 251-254
[10] I. Mandoiu and A. Zelikovsky: A Note on the MST Heuristic for Bounded Edge-length Steiner Trees with Minimum Number of Steiner Points. Information Processing Letters. (2000)
[11] D. Chen, D.-Z. Du, X. Xu, G.-H. Lin, L. Wan, and G. Xue: Approximations for Steiner Trees with Minimum Number of Steiner Points. Journal of Global Optimization. (2000)
[12] Y. T. Hou, Y. Shi, H. D. Sherali, and S.F. Midkiff: On Energy Provisioning and Relay Node Placement for Wireless Sensor Networks. IEEE Transactions on Wireless Communications. (2005) 2579-2590
[13] H. Koskinen, J. Karvo, and O. Apilo: On Improving Connectivity of Static Ad-Hoc Networks by Adding Nodes. Med-Hoc-Net. (2005)
[14] D. Ganesan, R. Christescu, and B. B. Lozano: Power-Efficient Sensor Placement and Transmission Structure for Data Gathering under Distortion Constrain. ACM Transcactin on Sensor Networks. (2005)
[15] K. Mulmuley: Computational Geometry, Prentice Hall (1994)

Performance Analysis of IEEE 802.15.4 with Non-beacon-enabled CSMA/CA in Non-saturated Condition*

Tae Ok Kim[1], Hongjoong Kim[1], Junsoo Lee[2], Jin Soo Park[3], and Bong Dae Choi[1]

[1] Department of Mathematics and Telecommunication Mathematics Research Center, Korea University, Seoul, Korea
{violetgl, hongjoong, queue}@korea.ac.kr

[2] Department of Computer Science, Sookmyung Women's University, Seoul, Korea
jslee@sookmyung.ac.kr

[3] USN Service Division, KT, Seoul, Korea
vtjinsoo@paran.com

Abstract. This paper proposes an analytical model of IEEE 802.15.4, which is a standard toward low complexity, low power consumption and low data rate wireless data connectivity. In this paper, we concentrate on the MAC performance of the IEEE 802.15.4 LR-WPAN in a star topology with unslotted CSMA/CA channel access mechanism under non-saturated modes. Our approach is to model stochastic behavior of one device as a discrete time Markov chain model. We believe that many WSN applications would benefit from our analytical model because many applications in WSN generate traffic in non-saturated mode. We obtain five performance measures : throughput, packet delay, number of backoff, energy consumption and packet loss probability. Our results are used to find optimal number of devices satisfying some QoS requirements.

1 Introduction

Recently, there has been a significant increase in research of wireless sensor networks (WSN). Network communication requirement of WSN is different from that of the traditional network because the traditional performance criteria of network are throughput, latency, and fairness, whereas in WSN, energy efficiency becomes more important. Making a system energy efficient in WSN is a challenging research topic and researchers have developed many algorithms [1,2,3].

Many researchers have concentrated on the Medium Access Layer (MAC) in WSN since traditional wireless MAC such as IEEE 802.11 is not energy efficient. However, developing mathematical model of energy efficient MAC has not been thoroughly studied. This is important because we can analyze and expect system behavior by simply applying various parameters into applications in WSN.

* This research is supported by the MIC, under the ITRC support program supervised by the IITA.

E. Sha et al. (Eds.): EUC 2006, LNCS 4096, pp. 884–893, 2006.

In this paper, we propose an analytical model of IEEE 802.15.4 which is standardized toward low complexity, low power consumption and low data rate wireless data connectivity. This standard allows two network topologies: star and peer-to-peer. In a star topology, every sensors must communicate through PAN coordinator. In a peer-to-peer topology all devices can communicate each other if both devices are within a physical range. In a star topology, network uses two types of network channel access mechanism. One is based on the slotted CSMA/CA in which slots are aligned with the beacon enabled. Another access mechanism is based on the unslotted CSMA/CA without beacon frame.

This paper concentrates on the MAC performance of the IEEE 802.15.4 network with star shaped non-beacon mode and unslotted CSMA/CA channel access mechanism under non-saturated modes. We believe that many WSN applications such as [4] would benefit from this analytical model. Our approach is to model the stochastic behavior of one device as a discrete time Markov chain model. Our Markov chain model of IEEE 802.15.4 is different from one of IEEE 802.11 [5], since no freezing of backoff counter operates during transmission of other devices and two CCA are needed in IEEE 802.15.4. Park et al. [6] also proposed analysis on 802.15.4 but they focused on saturated mode where devices have always packets to send.

In this paper, we investigate MAC performance of the IEEE 802.15.4 in non-saturated mode, where the arrival process of packets to device follows Bernoulli process with low rate, so device does not have packets to send quite often. In fact, most of real applications of LR-WPAN operate in non-saturated mode so that our analytical model will be applicable to wide range of WSN. We obtain five performance measures : throughput, packet delay, number of backoff, energy consumption and packet loss probability. Our results are used to find optimal number of devices with some constraints on these measures.

This paper is organized as follows. Section 2 proposes our analytical model of 802.15.4 in a non-saturated mode. Section 3 obtains performance measures developed from our analysis. In Section 4, parameters of non-saturated modes are explained. Section 4.1 presents numerical results of the heavy case and section 4.2 presents the light case. Section 5 concludes the paper and suggests future work.

2 Analytical Model

In order to analyze MAC performance of the IEEE 802.15.4 LR-WPAN with non-beacon mode and unslotted CSMA/CA channel access mechanism, we introduce a discrete time Markov chain model for activity of a sensor device under non-saturation modes, as shown in Fig. 1. Let n sensor devices be associated with the network coordinator. We assume that a sensor device can have only one packet at a time so that if the sensor device has a packet to transmit then no other packet is created. This assumption is reasonable because a packet's arrival occurs infrequently and the service time is rather short in the practical applications. We assume that the arrival of each packet in idle state follows a Bernoulli process with probability P_{idle}. We assume that the length of a packet measured in slots

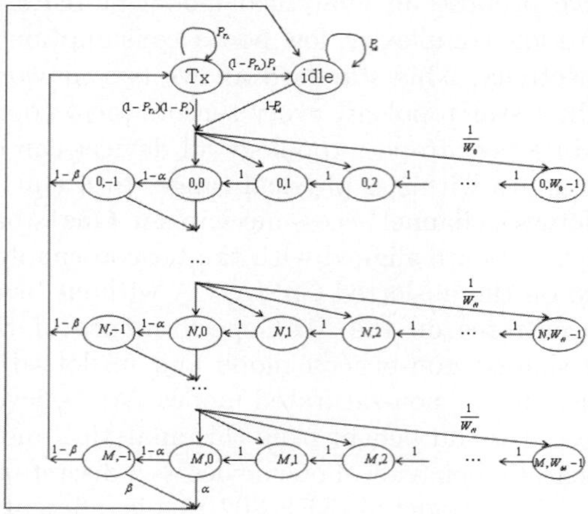

Fig. 1. Diagram of one-step transition probabilities

is geometrically distributed with mean $\frac{1}{1-P_{\mathrm{Tx}}}$ and the MAC sublayer will retry the transmission of the packet until positive acknowledgment is received.

Let $s(t)$ represent the number of backoff (NB) at time t (In contrast to models for IEEE 802.11 WLAN, t corresponds directly to system time.); $0 \leq s(t) \leq M$ where M is $macMaxCSMABackoffs - 1$. Let $b(t)$ be the backoff counter or transmission counter of the sensor device. Let us adopt the notation $W_j = 2^j W_0$ for $j \leq N$ and $W_j = W_N$ for $j > N$, where $W_0 = 2^{BE_{min}}$. The backoff counter is decremented to zero and then two CCA's are performed. The value $b(t) = -1$ corresponds to the situation that the channel is idle at the first CCA. The **Tx** state represents the state of packet transmission which includes the duration for waiting and receiving ACK. The **idle** state represents the state in which the sensor device does not have any packet to transmit. Define $X(t)$ by

$$X(t) = \begin{cases} (s(t), b(t)), & \text{when a device is in the process of backoff steps} \\ \mathbf{Tx}, & \text{when a device is in the process of packet transmission} \\ \mathbf{idle}, & \text{when a device is in the idle state} \end{cases}$$

at t. Then $X(t)$ is a discrete Markov chain with one-step transition probabilities described in Fig. 1. Let $\pi_{i,j}$, π_{Tx} and π_{idle} be the steady-state probabilities for this Markov chain. The key assumption for this Markov chain model is that the busy probabilities of the channel at the first CCA(CCA^1) and the second CCA(CCA^2) are α and β, respectively, regardless of the stages.

Next we will express the probabilities α and β and the successful transmission probability P_s in terms of $\pi_{i,j}$, π_{Tx} and π_{idle}. Since the idle probability $1-\alpha$ of the channel at CCA^1 of the given device is equal to the probability that all other $n-1$ sensor devices are in the states except the transmission state **Tx**, α can be given by :

$$\alpha = 1 - (1 - \pi_{\mathrm{Tx}})^{n-1} \tag{1}$$

To determine β we observe that the preceding slot must be idle. So β is the probability that the medium is busy when the tagged device does its CCA^2, given that the medium was idle during its CCA^1,

$$\begin{aligned}\beta &= P\{\text{the channel is busy at CCA}^2 \mid \text{the channel is idle at CCA}^1\} \\ &= \frac{P\{\text{the channel is idle at CCA}^1\text{, the channel is busy at CCA}^2\}}{P\{\text{the channel is idle at CCA}^1\}} \\ &= \frac{(1-\pi_{\mathrm{Tx}})^{n-1} - (1 - \pi_{\mathrm{Tx}} - \sum_{i=0}^{M} \pi_{i,-1})^{n-1}}{1-\alpha}\end{aligned} \tag{2}$$

The successful transmission probability, P_s, is calculated by

$$\begin{aligned}P_s &= P\{\text{successful transmission} \mid \text{the channel is idle at CCA}^1 \text{ and CCA}^2\} \\ &= \frac{\{1 - \pi_{\mathrm{Tx}} - \sum_{i=0}^{M}(\pi_{i,0} + \pi_{i,-1})\}^{n-1}}{(1 - \pi_{\mathrm{Tx}} - \sum_{i=0}^{M} \pi_{i,-1})^{n-1}}\end{aligned} \tag{3}$$

The steady-state probabilities for the Markov chain, $\pi_{i,j}$, π_{Tx} and π_{idle}, are represented as follows.

$$\begin{cases}\pi_{i,0} = (\alpha + \beta - \alpha\beta)^i \pi_{0,0} \quad \text{if } 1 \le i \le M \\ \pi_{i,-1} = (1-\alpha)\pi_{i,0} \quad \text{if } 0 \le i \le M \\ \pi_{0,j} = \pi_{0,0} - \{(1 - P_{\mathrm{Tx}})(1 - P_s)\pi_{\mathrm{Tx}} + (1 - P_{\mathrm{idle}}\pi_{\mathrm{idle}})\} \quad \text{if } 1 \le j \le W_0 - 1 \\ \pi_{i,j} = \pi_{i,0} - \frac{j}{W_i}(\alpha\pi_{i-1,0} + \beta\pi_{i-1,-1}) \quad \text{if } 1 \le i \le M,\ 1 \le j \le W_i - 1 \\ \pi_{\mathrm{Tx}} = \frac{1-\beta}{1-P_{\mathrm{Tx}}} \sum_{i=0}^{M} \pi_{i,-1} \\ \pi_{\mathrm{idle}} = \frac{1}{1-P_{\mathrm{idle}}}\{\alpha\pi_{M,0} + \beta\pi_{M,-1} + (1 - P_{\mathrm{Tx}})P_s\pi_{\mathrm{Tx}}\}\end{cases} \tag{4}$$

All steady-state probabilities for this Markov chain can be represented in terms of $\pi_{0,0}$. Since expressions for α and β in (1) and (2) require the knowledge of steady-state probabilities, $\pi_{0,0}$ can be determined by solving a nonlinear coupled system of (1), (2) and the normalization condition from (4).

3 Performance Measures

In this section, we obtain several performance measures to evaluate WSN such as throughput, delay, number of backoff, energy consumption and loss probability.

1. **Throughput:** the normalized system throughput S, defined as the fraction of time the channel is used to successfully transmit, is

$$S = \frac{n}{1 - P_{\mathrm{Tx}}} \sum_{i=0}^{M} \pi_{i,0}(1-\alpha)(1-\beta)P_s \tag{5}$$

2. **Delay:** we calculate the average delay $\mathrm{E}(D)$ for a packet, where delay is the duration from the moment of packet arrival at device to service completion point.

$$\mathrm{E}(D) = \sum_{v=0}^{M}\sum_{r=0}^{v} {}_v\mathrm{C}_r\alpha^r\{(1-\alpha)\beta\}^{v-r}(1-\alpha)(1-\beta)P_s\left(\sum_{i=0}^{v}\frac{W_i-1}{2}+2v-r\right.$$
$$\left.+\frac{1}{1-P_{\mathrm{Tx}}}\right)+\sum_{v=0}^{M}\sum_{r=0}^{v} {}_v\mathrm{C}_r\alpha^r\{(1-\alpha)\beta\}^{v-r}(1-\alpha)(1-\beta)(1-P_s)$$
$$\times\left(\sum_{i=0}^{v}\frac{W_i-1}{2}+2v-r+\frac{1}{1-P_{\mathrm{Tx}}}+\mathrm{E}(D)\right)+\sum_{r=0}^{M} {}_M\mathrm{C}_r\alpha^r\{(1-\alpha)\beta\}^{M-r}$$
$$\times\left\{\alpha\left(\sum_{i=0}^{M}\frac{W_i-1}{2}+2M-r-2\right)+(1-\alpha)\beta\left(\sum_{i=0}^{M}\frac{W_i-1}{2}+2M-r-1\right)\right\} \tag{6}$$

The first term and second term of the equation (6) describe the cases of successfully transmission and collision in first transmission, respectively. The last term of the equation (6) describes the case that the device can not attempt transmission because the channel is continuously sensed due to busy condition in CCA. After solving the system (4), we can obtain the average delay for a packet.

3. **Number of backoff:** the average number $\mathrm{E}(N_{\mathrm{backoff}})$ of backoff stages which a packet experience is

$$\mathrm{E}(N_{\mathrm{backoff}}) = \sum_{v=0}^{M}\sum_{r=0}^{v} {}_v\mathrm{C}_r\alpha^r\{(1-\alpha)\beta\}^{v-r}(1-\alpha)(1-\beta)P_s(v+1)$$
$$+\sum_{v=0}^{M}\sum_{r=0}^{v} {}_v\mathrm{C}_r\alpha^r\{(1-\alpha)\beta\}^{v-r}(1-\alpha)(1-\beta)(1-P_s)(v+1+\mathrm{E}(N_{\mathrm{backoff}}))$$
$$+\sum_{r=0}^{M} {}_M\mathrm{C}_r\alpha^r\{(1-\alpha)\beta\}^{M-r}(M+1) \tag{7}$$

4. **Energy consumption:** since power is quite critical in a sensor network, energy consumption is the most important performance measure. To obtain the total lifetime of a battery, we need a concept of average energy consumption. Park et al. [6] and Pollin et al. [7] define the normalized energy consumption as the average energy consumption to transmit one slot amount of payload. Their definition has good explanation in saturation mode. However, in non-saturation mode, their definition mismatches with our intuition, as they [7] mentioned that the energy consumption increases as the arrival rate decreases, or equivalently idle period increases. See Fig. 9 in [7]. So, we define the average energy consumption per one slot(mJ/slot), E^{slot} as total energy consumption during one cycle divided by the total number of

slots in one cycle. One cycle begins from the moment of beginning idle to the moment when the transmission of a packet is completed. Let $E_{\rm Tx}$, $E_{\rm Rx}$, $E_{\rm CCA}$ and $E_{\rm idle}$ be the energy consumption for transmission slot, receiving slot, CCA slot and idle slot. Then $E^{\rm slot}$ can be computed by

$$E^{\rm slot} = \{1 - \sum_{i=0}^{M}(\pi_{i,0} + \pi_{i,-1}) - \pi_{\rm Tx}\}E_{\rm idle} + \sum_{i=0}^{M}(\pi_{i,0} + \pi_{i,-1})E_{\rm CCA} \quad (8)$$
$$+\pi_{\rm Tx}\{(\frac{1}{1-P_{\rm Tx}} - T_{\rm wait-T_{ACK}})E_{\rm Tx} + (T_{\rm wait} + T_{\rm ACK})E_{\rm Rx}\}(1 - P_{\rm Tx})$$

where $T_{\rm wait}$ and $T_{\rm ACK}$ are the time durations measured in slots waiting ACK and sending ACK, respectively. Our definition of $E^{\rm slot}$ matches with our intuition as shown in Section 4. It is easy to find lifetime of a battery as in (9). Let $E^{\rm battery}$ be the amount of energy for battery. Then the life time of battery, $L^{battary}$ is

$$L^{battary} = \frac{E^{\rm battery}}{E^{\rm slot}} \times \sigma \ , \quad (9)$$

where σ is the length of a slot and $\sigma = 0.32$ms in case of 250 Mbps, 2.4 GHz.

5. **Loss probability:** the packet loss probability $P_{\rm loss}$ is computed by

$$P_{\rm loss} = \sum_{v=0}^{M}\sum_{r=0}^{v} {}_v{\rm C}_r\alpha^r\{(1-\alpha)\beta\}^{v-r}(1-\alpha)(1-\beta)(1-P_s)P_{\rm loss}$$
$$+\sum_{r=0}^{M} {}_M{\rm C}_r\alpha^r\{(1-\alpha)\beta\}^{M-r}\{\alpha + (1-\alpha)\beta\} \quad (10)$$

4 Numerical Examples

In the sensor network, arrivals occur quite rare and we divide non-saturated mode into three cases : heavy if $P_{\rm idle} \leq 0.9$, moderate if $0.9 < P_{\rm idle} \leq 0.99$, and light if $0.99 < P_{\rm idle} \leq 1$. P_{T_x} is set to $\frac{9}{10}$ so that the average length of a packet is 6. N and M are 2 and 4, respectively. W_0 is set to $2^3 = 8$ in our experiment. Section 4.1 presents numerical results of the heavy case and Section 4.2 presents the light case.

4.1 Heavy Case ($P_{\rm Idle} \leq 0.9$)

First, let us vary $P_{\rm idle}$ from 0.1 to 0.9 to observe overall changes of performances. Fig. 2 depicts values of parameters α, β, and P_s. Both α and β increase as the number of devices increases, while P_s decreases as we expected. Note that β is bounded by $\frac{1}{2}$ as asserted in ([7]).

Fig. 3 shows the energy consumption $E^{\rm slot}$, packet loss probability $P_{\rm loss}$, the delay E(D) and the average number E($N_{\rm backoff}$) of backoff stages needed to transmit the packet, when $P_{\rm idle}$ ranges from 0.1 to 0.9. The energy consumptions

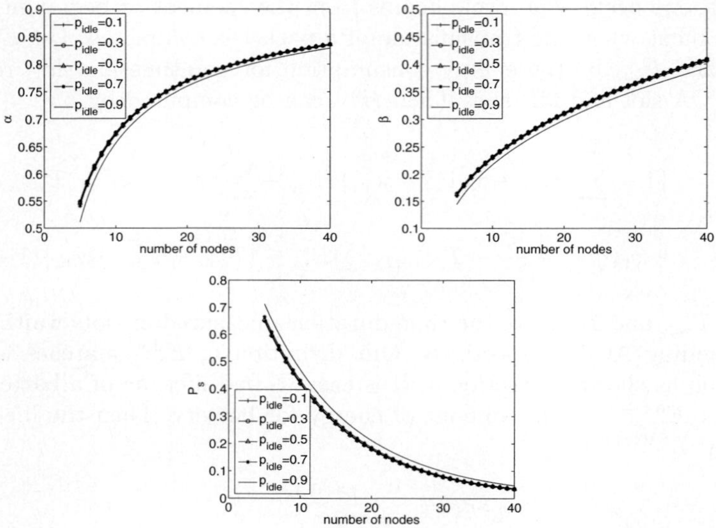

Fig. 2. Parameters for networks when P_{idle} ranges from 0.1 to 0.9

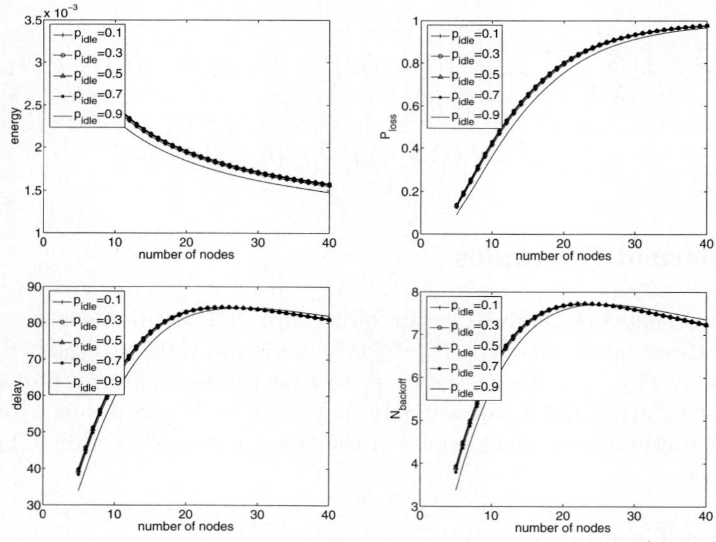

Fig. 3. Results for networks when P_{idle} ranges from 0.1 to 0.9

at T_x, R_x, and CCA states are 0.0100224mJ, 0.0113472mJ and 0.0113472mJ, respectively, [6]. A device consumes 0.000056736mJ during idle state. Both T_{wait} and T_{ACK} are set to 2. As the number of devices increases, devices will compete more with other devices to transfer, which is validated by decrease of throughput and increase of delay as illustrated in Fig. 3. As the number of devices increases,

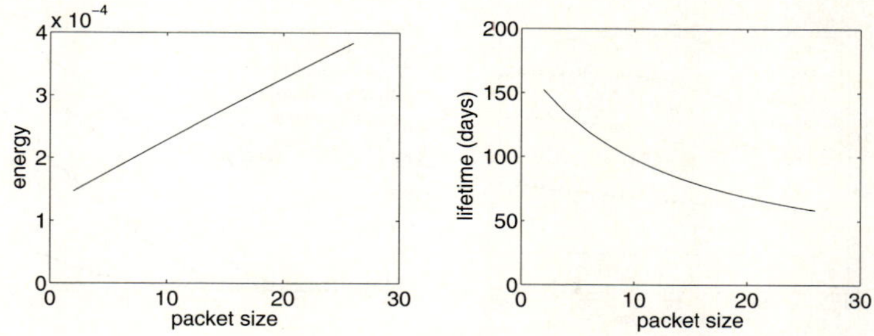

Fig. 4. Energy consumption and lifetime when the packet size increases from 2 to 26

more devices find the channel busy and go to higher backoff stages so that the energy consumption decreases and P_{loss} increases. Note that when the number of devices exceeds 20, lots of packets are dropped (large P_{loss}) and the delay is slightly reduced.

Figure 4 shows the energy consumption of a node (Left) and the lifetime (Right) when the packet size increases from 2 to 26. We assumed that a battery used in each device has a capacity of 560 mAh at 3.0V. As the packet size increases, the energy consumption increases and the lifetime decreases, which is consistent with the intuition. Similar results are observed in [4].

4.2 Light Case ($P_{\text{Idle}} \geq 0.99$)

Now let us consider a very light traffic whose P_{idle} values are greater than 0.99. In fact, packet arrivals are quite rare in many applications of the sensor network

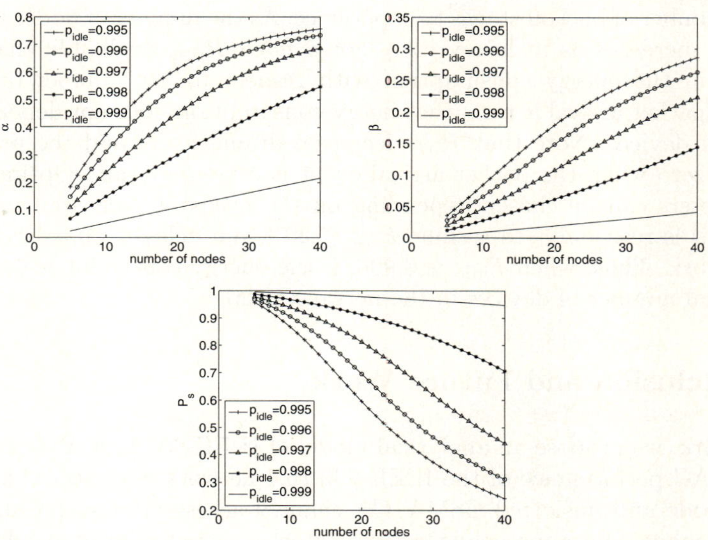

Fig. 5. Parameters for non-saturated networks when P_{idle} is near 1

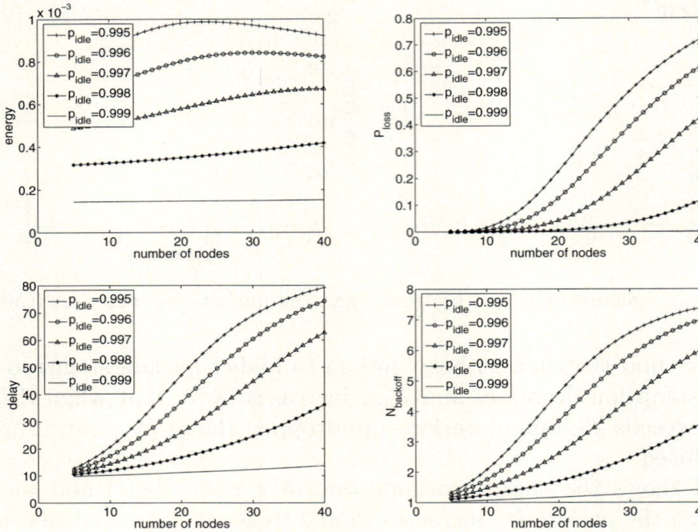

Fig. 6. Results for non-saturated networks when P_{idle} is near 1

such as body area networks. Thus, it is quite reasonable to consider light traffic sensor network. P_{idle} in this simulation changes from 0.995 to 0.999. Fig. 5 depicts values of α, β, and P_s. α and β increase and P_s decreases as the number of nodes increases.

Fig. 6 depicts the energy consumption, the packet loss probability, the delay and the number of backoff stages to experience. As the number of nodes increases, the delay increases as in heavy case. For a fixed P_{idle}, negligible changes are observed in the energy consumption with respect to the number of devices. Since the packet arrival is rare, the energy consumption does not depend on the number of devices. Note that P_{loss} decreases dramatically and the probability is almost zero when the packet arrival event is extremely rare. Optimal values of parameters can be chosen depending on the needs of each application. For example, it is reasonable to assume $P_{\mathrm{loss}} \leq 20\%$ and delay $\leq 50ms$ in the body area network. Thus, when P_{idle} is 0.996, if the energy constraint is 0.8×10^{-3}, the optimal number of devices in the network is 20.

5 Conclusion and Future Work

In this work, we propose an analytical model of IEEE 802.15.4. We concentrate on the MAC performance of the IEEE 802.15.4 network with star shaped non-beacon mode and unslotted CSMA/CA channel access mechanism under non-saturated mode. Our approach is to model stochastic behavior of one device as a discrete time Markov chain model and we believe that many WSN applications would benefit from our analytical model because many applications in WSN generate traffic in non-saturated mode. We obtain five performance measures: throughput, packet delay, number of backoff, energy consumption and packet loss probability. Our results are used to find optimal number of devices with some constraints on these measures. For example, in a body area network, with the constraint of $P_{\text{loss}} \leq 20\%$ and delay $\leq$ 50ms, when P_{idle} is 0.996 and the energy constraint is 0.8×10^{-3}, the optimal number of devices in the network is 20. Our study in this paper is limited to upload traffic. The performance analysis considering download traffic as well as upload traffic and validation with ns-2 are in progress.

References

1. Rajendran, V., Obraczka, K., Garcia-Luna-Aceves, J.J.: Energy-efficient collision-free medium access control for wireless sensor networks. In: SenSys. (2003) 181–192
2. Ye, W., Heidemann, J.S., Estrin, D.: Medium access control with coordinated adaptive sleeping for wireless sensor networks. IEEE/ACM Trans. Netw. **12**(3) (2004) 493–506
3. Polastre, J., Hill, J., Culler, D.E.: Versatile low power media access for wireless sensor networks. In: SynSys. (2004) 95–107
4. Timmons, N.F., Scanlon, W.G.: Analysis of the performance of ieee 802.15.4 for medical sensor body area networking. In: Proc. of IEEE SECON 2004. (2004)
5. Bianchi, G.: Performance analysis of the ieee 802.11 disributed coordination function. IEEE Journal on Selected Areas in Communications **18**(3) (2000) 535–547
6. Park, T., Kim, T., J.Y.Choi, Choi, S., Kwon, W.: Throughput and energy consumption analysis of ieee 802.15.4 slotted csma/ca. Electronics Letters **41**(18) (2005)
7. Pollin, S., Ergen, M., Ergen, S.C., Bougard, B., der Perre, L.V., Catthoor, F., Moerman, I., Bahai, A., Varaiya, P.: Performance analysis of slotted ieee 802.15.4 medium access layer. draft-jwl-tcp-fast-01.txt (2005)

Cross-Layer Duty Cycle Scheduling with Data Aggregation Routing in Wireless Sensor Networks

Yean-Fu Wen[1,2] and Frank Yeong-Sung Lin[1]

[1] National Taiwan University, Taiwan(R.O.C.)
[2] China University of Technology, Taiwan(R.O.C.)
{d89002, yslin}@im.ntu.edu.tw

Abstract. Well-scheduled communications, in conjunction with the aggregation of data reduce the energy waste on idle listening and redundant transmissions. In addition, the adjustable radii and the number of retransmissions are considered to reduce the energy consumption. Thus, to see that the total energy consumption is minimized, we propose a mathematical model that constructs a data aggregation tree and schedules the activities of all sensors under adjustable radii and collision avoidance conditions. As the data aggregation tree has been proven to be a NP-complete problem, we adopt a LR method to determine a near-optimal solution and furthermore verify whether the proposed LR-based algorithm, LRA, achieves energy efficiency and ensures the latency within a reasonable range. The experiments show the proposed algorithm outperforms other general routing algorithms, such as SPT, CNS, and GIT algorithms. It improves energy conservation, which it does up to 9.1% over GIT. More specifically, it also improves energy conservation up to 65% over scheduling algorithms, such as S-MAC and T-MAC.

1 Introduction

The network lifetime of a wireless sensor network (WSN), the time before communication of the environmental information is interrupted because of depleted batteries is dependent on battery capacity and energy consumption efficiency, and has become an essential issue, as we can read in [2] [4] [7] [11] [12] [13] [14] [16] [22]. Therefore, we seek to prolong network lifetime from the physical layer up to application layer, and do so with a focus on (i) the data aggregation routing; (ii) duty cycle scheduling; (iii) adjustable radii; and (iv) collision avoidance.

The data aggregation capability has been put forward as a particularly useful function for routing in terms of energy consumption in WSNs. Some literature [2] [11] [12] [13] [22] has been shown the in-network processing can save much energy. The construction of this type of data aggregation tree (i.e., a kind of reverse-multicast tree which is also a Steiner tree) has been proven to be NP-complete [10], which signifies that general algorithms cannot provide optimal solution to the problem. Krishnamachari *et al.* [12] devised three aggregation heuristics,

E. Sha et al. (Eds.): EUC 2006, LNCS 4096, pp. 894–903, 2006.

namely, the Shortest Paths Tree (SPT), Center at Nearest Source (CNS), and the Greedy Incremental Tree (GIT) to sub-optimally solve the problem. In our experimental results, we will compare the performance with these heuristics.

In addition to data aggregation, conservation of energy is accomplished by duty cycle, the reduction of idle listening that is also the most energy wasteful process in MAC protocol. Some researchers [8] [15] [16] [21] have proposed algorithms, such as S-MAC, T-MAC, and D-MAC, that schedule the activities of all sensors in order to reduce the energy consumption. This paper bridges the gap, addressing in conjunction both data aggregation and an optimal duty cycle schedule, denotes as O-MAC, that centralized determines, for each sensor, when it wakes up and when it sleeps.

The third important energy consumption saving factor is dynamic power range. Carle *et al.* [6] discuss the tradeoff between power consumption and coverage of relay node. The power consumption of transmitting data is measured as $e_u(r_u) = r_u^\alpha + c$, where α is a signal attenuation constant (between 2 to 4) [13] [20] [22], r_u is power range of the node u. Thus, the shorter range is used, the energy consumption is decreased.

The fourth factor is collisions avoidance that plays important roles in packet retransmissions as well as decreasing energy consumption. To reflect energy consumption by the number of retransmissions, the pure ALOHA approximation method [19], the extended Bianchi's model [5], and another previous work [13], based on the analysis in [18], were adopted to derive the expected number of retransmissions of a sender. In this paper, we include the equation in [13] as the node-to-node retransmission constraint.

In order to optimally solve the problem as we have stated it, we have formulated a mathematical model by which a data aggregation tree is constructed and the activities of all sensors are scheduled with adjustable radii and collision avoidance so as to minimize the total energy consumption. The solution to our mathematical formulation, where the objective function minimizes the total energy consumption of all sensors, subject to data aggregation, duty cycle scheduling, adjustable radii and the number of retransmissions constraints, is based on Lagrangian Relaxation (LR) in conjunction with optimization-based heuristics [9].

The remainder of this paper is organized as follows. In Section 2, a mixed integer nonlinear programming problem formulation of data aggregation routing problem with schedule assignment is proposed. In Section 3, LR-based approaches are presented. In Section 4, the heuristics for calculating good primal feasible solutions to these problems are developed. In Section 5, the computational results are reported. Finally, in Section 6 we present our conclusions.

2 Problem Formulation

A WSN is modeled as a graph of connected nodes, $G(V, L)$, where V represents the nodes distributed on a two-dimensional plane (X_AXIS,Y_AXIS) and $(u, v) \in L$ denotes links such that node v can receive transmissions signal from node u. The problem is formulated as the followings.

The objective function (1) is an expression of total energy consumption, including all facets of consumption within the network that take place when data is received or sent, or when nodes are idle. Note that rates E_r of energy consumption are similar, whether receiving data or idle [17].

$$Z_{IP} = min \sum_{u \in V} [(m_u - n_u)E_r + (t_{data} + RTS \sum_{v \in V} c_{uv})e_u(r_u)] \tag{1}$$

where E_r denotes as energy consumption rate of a receiving or idle node; E_s denotes as energy consumption rate of a transmission node; and t_{data} denotes as transmission time for transmitting a data packet, subject to:

- Path constraints: Constraint (2) shows the decision variable $x_p = 1$ denoting that path $p \in P_s$, where s belong to the set of source nodes S and P_s is the set of candidate paths from source s to the sink node κ; otherwise, if $x_p = 0$, no path p is used. In order to realize constraints that determine the tree, original/destination (OD) pairs must on only one path. Thus, the equation is shown as (3).

$$x_p = 0 \; or \; 1, \;\; \forall p \in P_s \;\; s \in S \tag{2}$$

$$\sum_{p \in P_s} x_p \leq 1, \;\; \forall s \in S \tag{3}$$

  Once the path, p, is selected and the link (u, v) is on the path, then the decision variable y_{uv} must be set to 1. This constraint is described by (4).

$$\sum_{p \in P_s} x_p \delta_{p(uv)} \leq y_{uv}, \;\; \forall s \in S \;\; u, v \in V \tag{4}$$

  where $\delta_{p(uv)}$ is the indicator function: equal to 1 if link (u, v) is on path p; equal to 0 otherwise. Thus, when the path p is selected and link (u, v) is on the path, the value of $x_p \delta_{p(uv)}$ is 1 and y_{uv} must be set to 1.
- Link constraints: Since this problem is to find a reversed multicast tree, five link constraints, Constraints (5)-(9), to requisite to describing structure of the tree.
  1. Decision variable $y_{uv} = 1$ denotes link (u, v) is selected, whereas $y_{uv} = 0$, link (u, v) is not selected, shown as (5). The source node s must select one node to send its message to, meaning that the number of out-degree links must be 1, shown as (6).

$$y_{uv} = 0 \; or \; 1, \;\; \forall u, v \in V \tag{5}$$

$$\sum_{v \in V} y_{sv} = 1, \;\; \forall s \in S \tag{6}$$

  2. The number of out-degree links of each node can be no greater than 1, shown as (7).

$$\sum_{v \in V} y_{uv} \leq 1, \;\; \forall v \in V \tag{7}$$

3. At least one relay node must be able to provide coverage to the sink node κ for the message to be delivered, so the summation of in-degree links is at least 1, shown as (8).

$$\sum_{u \in V} y_{u\kappa} \geq 1 \tag{8}$$

4. The total number of links on the multicast tree must be at least the number of hops H or the number of nodes in set $|S|$, whichever is greater [22], shown as (9).

$$\sum_{u \in V} \sum_{v \in V} y_{uv} \geq max\{H, |S|\} \tag{9}$$

– Node-to-node communication time constraints: Equation (10), which refers to [18], denotes the time l_{uv} needed to transmit a packet from node u to node v by CSMA/CA protocol [3].

$$l_{uv} = \frac{(e^{-\lambda \sum_{j \in V} z_{ju}(DIFS)}(RTS+SIFS+CTS+\overline{B})+DIFS+\overline{N})}{e^{-\lambda \sum_{j \in V} z_{ju}(DIFS)} e^{-(RTS+SIFS+2\theta)\sum_{j \in V} z_{jv}}} - \overline{N}, \quad \forall u, v \in V \tag{10}$$

where the bound of the delay of each link is described as (11).

$$RTS + SIFS + CTS + \overline{B} + DIFS \leq l_{uv} \leq M_5, \quad \forall u, v \in V \tag{11}$$

Note that M_5 denotes as the maximum node-to-node successful transmission time; λ denotes as the arrival rate of an event occurrence; θ denotes as the propagation time to send a packet;$\overline{B}$ denotes as average random backoff time; $\overline{N}$ denotes as average Network Allocation Vector (NAV) time; $DIFS$ denotes as Distributed Inter-Frame Space; $SIFS$ denotes as Short Inter-Frame Space; RTS denotes as RTS transmission time; and CTS denotes as CTS transmission time.

The decision variable, z_{uv}, is a 0-1 variable, shown as (12). It is equal to 1 when node v is within the transmission range of node u and link (u, v) is selected, shown as (13). However, z_{uv} must be equal to 0 as node u does not need to transmission any data, shown as (14); otherwise the equation is violated.

$$z_{uv} = 0 \ or \ 1, \quad \forall u, v \in V \tag{12}$$

$$\frac{r_u - d_{uv}}{M_1} + (1 - y_{uv}) \leq z_{uv}, \quad \forall u, v \in V \tag{13}$$

$$z_{uv} d_{uv} \leq r_u, \quad \forall u, v \in V \tag{14}$$

where d_{uv} denotes as Euclidean distance between the node u and the node v.

– The number of retransmissions: As described in Section 1, the number of retransmissions is calculated by (15) and (16), which the right hand side of (15) is referred to [18] to calculate the expected retransmissions, c_{uv}, and then set the value to be an integer.

$$c_{uv} \geq \frac{e^{-(1-y_{uv})M}}{e^{-\lambda(RTS+SIFS+2\theta)\sum_{j\in V} z_{jv}}}, \quad \forall u, v \in V \tag{15}$$

$$c_{uv} \in \{0, 1, 2, ..., T\}, \quad \forall u, v \in V \tag{16}$$

– Scheduling constraints: Constraint (17) puts limits on the time at which all incoming flow from nodes to a node u must be aggregated, denotes as m_u. Note that M_3, which is the longest end-to-end delay of the network, denotes the upper bound of m_u, which described as (18).

$$(m_v + l_{uv} + \varepsilon) - M_3(1 - y_{vu}) \leq m_u, \quad \forall u, v \in V \tag{17}$$

where ε is estimation error value, which is used for time synchronized error.

$$0 \leq m_u \leq M_3, \quad \forall u \in V \tag{18}$$

A node u involved in an aggregation tree is subject to (19). The wake up time of node u must be earlier than the aggregation time of nodes that receive from it, denotes as n_u. Note that M_4, which is the longest end-to-end delay of the network, denotes the upper bound of n_u, which described as (20).

$$n_u \leq m_u + M_4(1 - y_{vu}), \quad \forall u, v \in V \tag{19}$$

$$0 \leq n_u \leq M_4, \quad \forall u \in V \tag{20}$$

3 Solution Approach

The LR-based approach [9] is a flexible solution strategy that permits us to exploit the fundamental structure of possible optimization problems by relaxing complicated constraints into the objective function with Lagrangian multipliers [1] [9]. Before executing the LR procedures, Constraint (10) is transformed to be approximated function with the error is estimated less than 5%. The natural logarithm of either side renders this function solvable as:

$$\begin{aligned} ln(l_{uv}) = & \, ln(RTS + SIFS + CTS + 330) + 0.115 + \\ & 0.017 \textstyle\sum_{j\in V} z_{jv} + \lambda(RTS + SIFS + 2\theta) \textstyle\sum_{j\in V} z_{jv} \end{aligned} \tag{21}$$

For Constraint (15), we also take natural logarithm on both sides and get:

$$ln(c_{uv}) \geq \lambda(RTS + SIFS + 2\theta) \sum_{j\in V} z_{jv} - M_5(1 - y_{uv}) \tag{22}$$

Accordingly, the primal optimization problem is transformed into a Lagrangian dual problem. The relaxation of (4), (13), (14), (17), (19), (21), and (22) transforms the objective function (1) into a Lagrangian dual problem with a vector of non-negative Lagrangian multipliers (i.e.,$\mu^1_{suv}, \mu^2_{uv}, \mu^3_{uv}, \mu^4_{uv}, \mu^5_{uv}, \mu^6_{vu}$ and μ^7_{uv}).

$$\begin{aligned}
&Z_{LR}(\mu^1_{suv}, \mu^2_{uv}, \mu^3_{uv}, \mu^4_{uv}, \mu^5_{uv}, \mu^6_{vu}, \mu^7_{uv}) = \\
&min \sum_{u\in V}[(m_u - n_u)E_r + (t_{data} + RTS\sum_{v\in V} c_{uv})e_u(r_u)]+ \\
&\sum_{s\in S}\sum_{u\in V}\sum_{v\in V} \mu^1_{suv}\left(\sum_{p\in P_s} x_p\delta_{p(uv)} - y_{uv}\right)+ \\
&\sum_{u\in V}\sum_{v\in V} \mu^2_{uv}\left(\frac{r_u - d_{uv}}{M_1} + (1 - y_{uv}) - z_{uv}\right)+ \\
&\sum_{u\in V}\sum_{v\in V} \mu^3_{uv}(z_{uv}d_{uv} - r_u)+ \\
&\sum_{u\in V}\sum_{v\in V} \mu^4_{uv}\left(\lambda(RTS + SIFS + 2\theta)\sum_{j\in V} z_{jv} - M_5(1 - y_{uv}) - \ln(c_{uv})\right)+ \\
&\sum_{u\in V}\sum_{v\in V} \mu^5_{uv}\left(\begin{array}{l}\ln(RTS + SIFS + CTS + 330) + 0.115 + 0.017\sum_{j\in V} z_{ju} \\ +\lambda(RTS + SIFS + 2\theta)\sum_{j\in V} z_{jv} - \ln(l_{uv})\end{array}\right)+ \\
&\sum_{v\in V}\sum_{u\in V} \mu^6_{vu}(m_v + l_{vu} + \varepsilon - M_3(1 - y_{vu}) - m_u)+ \\
&\sum_{u\in V}\sum_{v\in V} \mu^7_{uv}(n_u - m_v - M_4(1 - y_{uv}))
\end{aligned} \qquad (23)$$

subject to: (2), (3), (5), (6), (7), (8), (9), (11), (12), (16), (18) and (20).

Accordingly, the (LR) is decomposed into seven independent and solvable subproblems, (SUB1), (SUB2), (SUB3), (SUB4), (SUB5), (SUB6), and (SUB7). Based on the weak Lagrangian duality theorem, which holds that for any given set of nonnegative multipliers, the LR approach finds the lower bound of the value of the primal objective value [1], in this case, Z_D is a lower bound on Z_{IP}.[1]

4 Primal Feasible Solution

To construct a reversed multicast tree, the decision variable x_p is our choice for finding primal feasible solutions, in view of the fact that once x_p is determined, the other decision variables are also determined. We have developed a heuristic for routing policy adjustment based on x_p. First, to ensure that each OD pair perceives the same link weight for the same link, we make adjustments to $c_{uv} = (\sum_{s\in S} \mu^1_{suv} + \mu^2_{uv} + \mu^3_{uv} + \mu^4_{uv} + \mu^6_{vu} + \mu^7_{uv})d^2_{uv}$. The transmission graph will be a reversed multicast tree, meeting the requirements of (2)-(9). Next, the solution set of x_p is generated by the proposed LR-based heuristic. The procedures are shown as follows for obtaining a primal feasible solution (*Primal_Heuristic_Algorithm*()) that solves the problem. Accordingly, the LR-based algorithm for solving primal problem is used according to the procedures in [1] or [9].

---

[1] For more information, please contact with the correspondence author.

Step 1. Initially, $c_{uv} = (\sum_{s\in S} \mu^1_{suv} + \mu^2_{uv} + \mu^3_{uv} + \mu^4_{uv} + \mu^6_{vu} + \mu^7_{uv})d^2_{uv}$; pseudo links connect the source nodes to the pseudo source; and a pseudo link between the sink node and pseudo destination are also set. The weights of these pseudo links are 0.

Step 2. The Dijkstra's algorithm is used to find the shortest path from the pseudo source O to the pseudo destination D.

Step 3. Once the path has been determined, the nodes on the path are marked and pseudo links with weight 0 are added between these marked nodes and the pseudo destination. The weight of pseudo link, which is on the path between pseudo source and its next hop, is set to a infinite.

Step 4. Steps 2-3 are repeated until all source nodes are marked.

Step 5. Now we have a reversed multicast tree after cyclic path has been checked. Once the $\{x_p\}$ is determined, $\{y_{uv}\}$ is also determined. According to the selected link set $\{y_{uv}\}$, the power range r_u, the number of nodes within the node u's transmission area z_{uv}, and link transmission time l_{uv} to successful transmission are calculated.

Step 6. The earliest wake up time and latest aggregated time are calculated along the DFS (Depth First Search) traced nodes. Once m_u and n_u are determined, the duty cycle schedule of each sensor node u is determined. The total energy consumption per cycle is calculated.

Figure 1 shows an example of the proposed routing algorithm. The pseudo source O, pseudo destination D, and pseudo links $O1$, $D5$, $D6$, $D7$, and $D8$ with weight 0 are initialized. In first iteration, we find the path $O-7-4-2-1-D$ from O to D. The nodes on the paper are marked in the tree set T. Then the pseudo links $D2$, $D4$, and $D7$ with weight 0 are added. But the weight of pseudo

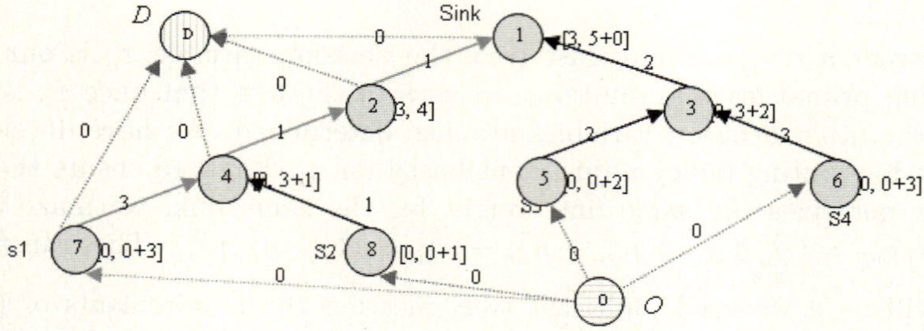

Fig. 1. The pseudo source O and pseudo destination D are added. The pseudo links are added to connect source nodes and sink node, respectively. The value on the link signifies the delay to successfully send data to next node; the $[n_u, m_u + l_{uv}]$ of each node denotes the earliest wake up time and the complete aggregated time for successful transmission.

link $O7$ is set to be infinite. Iteration by iteration, additions to the reversed multicast tree are made until all source nodes in the network have been marked in the tree.

5 Evaluation and Experimental Results

The experimental networks were comprised of N sensor nodes, with 150 nodes in the example given in Figs. 4 and network with various numbers of nodes, up to 250, in Figs. 2 and 3 randomly placed in a $10 * 10$ square unit area. The relative experimental parameter settings are referred to [3] and [13]. To evaluate the solution quality of our proposed algorithm, we compared it with three existing data aggregation routing algorithms: the GIT, SPT, and CNS algorithms are proposed in [12]. We also compared it with exist schedule strategies, such as S-MAC and T-MAC. The experimental results are shown in Fig. 4.

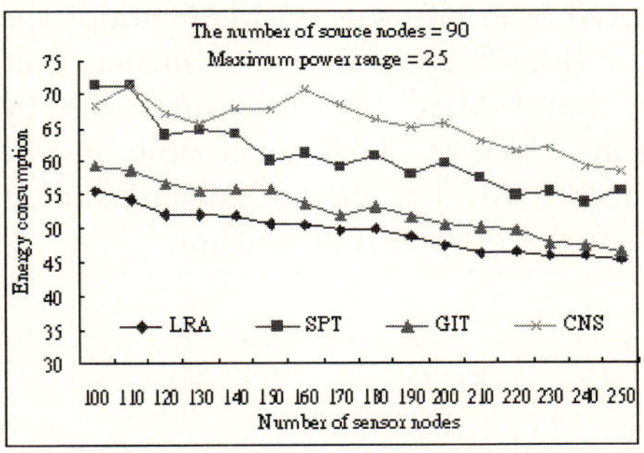

Fig. 2. Network sizes experimental results

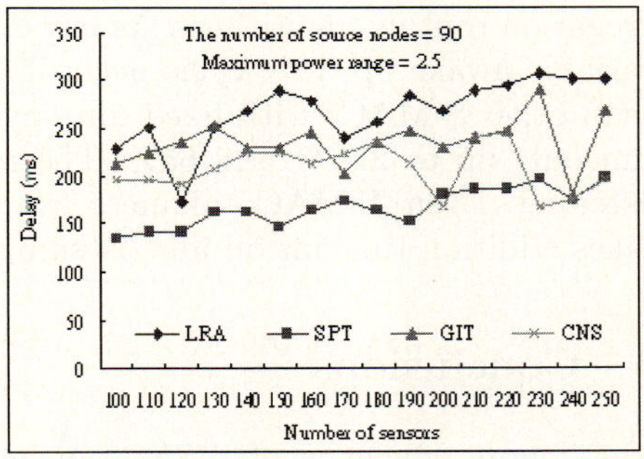

Fig. 3. Maximum end-to-end delay experimental results

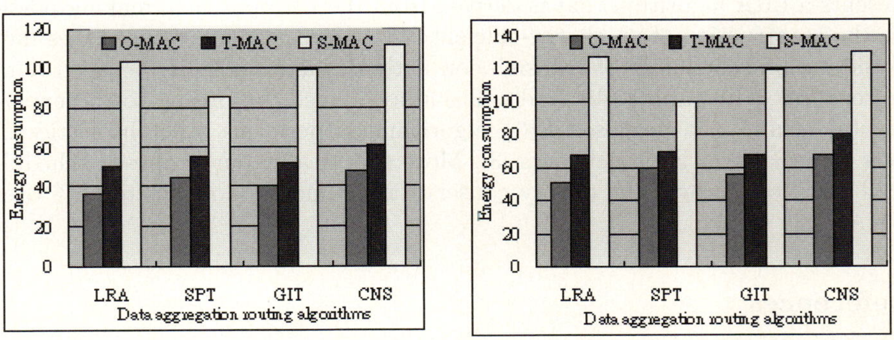

(a) the number of sources node is 90 (b) the number of sources node is 50

Fig. 4. The total energy consumption by combining data aggregation routing heuristics and scheduling heuristics

Figure 2 depicts the experimental results by which we assess the quality of each heuristics as used in networks of differing sizes, each with a fixed number of sources but a adjustable radii. The consumption decreases with the shorter radius when energy consumption evaluated by exponential distance. Thus, when there is increased network sizes, the density of sensor nodes in the fixed deployment area is higher, and overall energy consumption decreases. The effect of this on our proposed algorithm is minimal, so the solution quality of the LRA algorithm is superior to the other heuristics by up to 28.8%.

However, a longer delay does arise with the proposed algorithm than that from other algorithms, shown as Fig. 3. This additional delay, the cost of reducing duplicate transmissions, arises due to the time necessary to aggregate data before forwarding it. Other algorithms, such as SPT, do receive the most up-to-date information from the sensor nodes by adopting a single pair and a shortest path heuristic, but it must be said that the energy consumption of a network that implements one of these other algorithms is significantly higher than that achieved by the proposed algorithm.

Figure 4 shows the scheduling algorithms combine with the above data aggregation routing algorithms. As our exceptive, the proposed O-MAC adopt the variable awake up duty cycle according the data aggregation tree outperforms than other S-MAC (with fixed duty cycle) and T-MAC (variable duty cycle by timeout) up to 27.6% and 65%. The reason is S-MAC take much time on idle listening. Even T-MAC enhances from the S-MAC by timeout mechanism, it takes addition timeout on idle listening than the proposed algorithm.

6 Conclusions

The energy efficiency of WSNs can be improved by data aggregation routing, the reduction of idle listening, adjustable radii, and collision avoidance. To address these considerations, we propose a mixed integer nonlinear mathematical formulation of duty cycle scheduling with data-aggregation routing. This paper presents a LRA algorithm that is derived from the LR approach, making possible the construction of an energy-efficient data aggregation tree that takes into consideration scheduling of transmission activities and tradeoffs between data aggregation, adjustable radii, and collision avoidance. According to the experimental results, the proposed LRA algorithm outperforms other heuristics in tests, especially in large networks [3]. More specifically, our proposed scheduling heuristic improves the energy conservation, which it does up to 65% over S-MAC.

References

1. Ahuja, R.K., Magnanti, T.L., and Orlin, J.B.: Network Flows: Theory, Algorithms, and Applications. Ch. 16 Prentice-Hall (1993)
2. Akyildiz, I.F., Su, W., Sankarasubramaniam, Y., Cayirci E.: A Survey on Sensor Networks. IEEE Communications Magazine **40(8)** (2002) 102-114

3. ANSI/IEEE: 802.11: Wireless LAN Medium Access Control (MAC) and Physical Layer (PHY) Specifications. IEEE Standard 802.11 (2000)
4. Bhardwaj, M., Chandrakasan, A.P.: Bounding the Lifetime of Sensor Networks via Optimal Role Assignments. Proc. IEEE INFOCOM, New York NY (2002) 1587-1596
5. Bianchi, G.: Performance Analysis of the IEEE 802.11 Distributed Coordination Function. IEEE Journal on Selected Areas in Communications **18(2)** (2000) 535-547
6. Carle, J., Simplot, D.: Energy Efficient Area Monitoring by Sensor Networks. IEEE Computer **37(2)** (2004) 40-46
7. Chang, J.H., Tassiulas, L.: Maximum Lifetime Routing in Wireless Sensor Networks. IEEE/ACM Transactions on Networking (TON) **12(4)** (2004) 609-619
8. Dam, T.V., Langendoen K.: An Adaptive Energy-Efficient MAC Protocol for Wireless Sensor Networks. Proc. ACM SenSys Los Angeles (2003) 171-180
9. Fisher M.L.: The Lagrangian Relaxation Method for Solving Integer Programming Problems. Management Science **27(1)** (1981) 1-18
10. Garey, M.R., Johnson, D.S.: Computers and Intractability: A Guide to the Theory of NP-completeness Freeman San Francisco (1979)
11. Kalpakis, K., Dasgupta, K. Namjoshi, P.: Efficient Algorithms for Maximum Lifetime Data Gathering and Aggregation in Wireless Sensor Networks. Computer Networks Journal **42(6)** (2003) 697-716
12. Krishnamachari, B., Estrin, D., Wicker, S.: Modeling Data-Centric Routing in Wireless Sensor Networks. USC Computer Engineering Technical Report CENG (2002)
13. Lin, F.Y.S., Yen, H.H. Lin, S.P.: MAC Aware Energy-Efficient Data-Centric Routing in Wireless Sensor Networks. Proc. IEEE ICC Istanbul Turkey (2006)
14. Liu, H., Wan, P.J., Yi, C.W., Jia, X., Makki, S., Pissinou, N.: Maximal Lifetime Scheduling in Sensor Surveillance Networks. Proc. INFOCOM Miami (2005) 2482-2491
15. Lu, G., Krishnamachari, B., Raghavendra, C.: An Adaptive Energy-Efficient and Low-Latency MAC for Data Gathering in Sensor Networks. Proc. WMAN (2004)
16. Lu, G., Sadagopan, N., Krishnamachari, B., and Goel, A.: Delay Efficient Sleep Scheduling In Wireless Sensor Network. Proc. INFOCOM Miami Florida USA (2005) 2470-2481
17. Stemm, M., Katz, R.H., Measuring and Reducing Energy Consumption of Network Interfaces in Hand-held Devices. IEICE Transactions on Communications **E80-B(8)** (1997) 1125-1131
18. Sheu, S.T., Tsai, T.H. Chen, J.H.: MR2RP: The Multi-Rate and Multi-Range Routing Protocol for IEEE 802.11 Wireless Ad Hoc Networks. ACM/Kluwer Wireless Networks **9(8)** (2003) 165-177
19. Shiou, C.W., Lin, F.Y.S., Cheng, H.C., Wen, Y.F.: Optimal Energy-Efficient Routing for Wireless Sensor Networks. Proc. IEEE AINA Taipei Taiwan (2005) 325-330
20. Wieselthier, J.E., Nguyen, G.D., Ephremides, and A.: Energy-Efficient Broadcast and. Multicast Trees in Wireless Networks. Mobile Networks and Applications (MONET) **7(2)** (2002) 481-492
21. Ye, W., Heidemann, J., Estrin, D.: An Energy-efficient MAC Protocol for Wireless Sensor Networks. Proc. IEEE INFOCOM New York, NY (2002) 1567-1576
22. Yen, H.H., Lin, F.Y.S. and Lin, S.P.: Energy-Efficient Data-Centric Routing in Wireless Sensor Networks. IEICE Trans. on Communications **E88-B(16)** (2005) 4470-4480

A Link Stability Model and Stable Routing for Mobile Ad-Hoc Networks*

Min-Gu Lee and Sunggu Lee

Electrical and Computer Engineering Division
Pohang Univ. of Science and Technology (POSTECH), Pohang, S. Korea
{bluehope, slee}@postech.ac.kr

Abstract. When using shortest-distance routing for mobile ad-hoc networks (MANETs), the physical distances of links that constitute such paths tend to be very long since this leads to fewer hops between source and destination nodes. However, if the physical distance of a wireless link becomes so long that it approaches its transmission range, packet transmission error rates can increase drastically, resulting in an unstable link. Furthermore, packets are more likely to be lost due to external environment factors such as white noise and wireless interference if the signal strength is not strong enough. Therefore, it would be desirable for routing algorithms for MANETs to be able to select paths that are more likely to be stable. With this objective in mind, we propose an enhanced stability model (ESM) to estimate link stability based on signal strength. A routing algorithm based on this new model is also proposed. Simulations of the proposed ESM and previous link estimation models validate the superiority of the proposed approach. Simulations also show that the proposed routing algorithm performs particularly well when there are unreliable links.

1 Introduction

A routing algorithm for mobile ad-hoc networks (MANETs) should not only route using short-distance paths, but should also be adaptable to highly dynamic changes in network topology since the network topology can change frequently and wireless communication channels are inherently unreliable. Given a routing algorithm targeted toward finding optimal (in terms of distance) paths, the physical distance between two neighboring nodes within a path tends to be very long since this results in fewer hops. Such distances may even be close to the effective transmission range between nodes as shown in [1]. In this case, a small movement of any of the nodes involved may cause packet loss due to link disconnection. Furthermore, packets can be lost due to noise or interference in the wireless channel if the signal strength is very weak. Therefore, a MANET routing algorithm should not only seek to find short-distance paths, it should

* This work was supported by Korea Research Foundation Grant (KRF-2004-041-D00586).

E. Sha et al. (Eds.): EUC 2006, LNCS 4096, pp. 904–913, 2006.

also strive to find stable paths that take into account the mobility of nodes, low signal power and interference in the wireless channel.

In this paper, we propose a new link stability estimation model and a routing algorithm based on this new model. Section 2 reviews previously proposed routing methods that take into account link stability. Section 3 discusses various link stability estimation models and the proposed link stability model. Section 4 discusses routing algorithms that are able to support stable routing, and Section 5 shows simulation results for various link stability models on top of the target routing algorithm. Finally, conclusions are presented in Section 6.

2 Related Works

Signal stability-based adaptive routing(SSA)[2] estimates link stability based on signal strength. Each node measures signal strengths from other nodes. If a node receives a strong signal from a neighbor, which typically results if two nodes are close to each other, the link is considered as stable. If possible, SSA tries to find a path using only stable links. If it fails to find a stable path, then it tries to find a path using all possible links, resulting in an ordinary path. When a failed link is detected, an intermediate node sends an error message to the source node to notify it that the path is broken. Then the source reinitiates another path search process in order to find a new path – this causes undue overhead and is thus undesirable.

Associativity-based routing(ABR)[3] tries to find long-lived paths to destinations using estimations of link stability based on beacon messages. ABR searches all possible paths to find a path with strong links. Therefore, a path is selected for each destination based on link stability. However, the link stability model that ABR uses is not accurate for some mobility patterns.

Link life based routing protocol(LBR)[4] is another stability-based routing protocol. LBR converts signal strength into distance using a free space propagation model assumption. Based on estimated distance and maximum speed of nodes, LBR estimates link lifetime. When the source node initiates a route request, each intermediate node attaches its estimated link lifetime to the route request message. When the destination receives a route request message, it can calculate the path lifetime for that path based on the estimated link lifetimes in the path. Therefore, the destination can select a path that is expected to have the longest lifetime. In order to react to path breakage, proactive and reactive maintenance is proposed in LBR. In reactive maintenance, the source node needs to reinitiate a route request to the destination, which results in increased delay and control overhead. In proactive maintenance, a backup path is found prior to path breakage. However, the estimated path lifetime is not valid when a path is broken. Therefore, the backup path may be unstable.

The approaches discussed above require the delivery of an error message to the source node followed by reinitiation of route discovery when path breakage is detected. However, reinitiating route discovery is a very costly operation that may not be acceptable for time critical applications such as those requiring QoS routing. Furthermore, the stable routing algorithms discussed above attempt mainly to reduce routing overhead. Even if a stable path is selected when the path is initially discovered, the probability of successful packet delivery (packet delivery ratio) can decrease because the signal strength of links in the path can weaken. The purpose of stable routing should be not only reducing routing overhead but also increasing packet delivery ratio. Therefore, we propose a new stable routing algorithm that is aimed at increasing packet delivery ratio.

3 Link Stability Models

In order to support stable routing, proper estimation of link stability is required. In [5], link stability is modeled in a statistical manner based on node movement models. However, statistical approaches are not adequate for general applications because the mobility patterns of nodes cannot be known a priori. In [3], a link stability estimation model is proposed using periodic beacon signals. In order to estimate link stability, every node sends beacon messages periodically. If the number of continuous received beacon messages are beyond a certain threshold from its neighbor, then the link is considered as stable since ABR is based on the idea that nodes that have been stationary for a threshold period are less likely to move. However, this idea is not so accurate because not all nodes follow the mobility patterns that ABR assumes. The other approaches are based on signal strength. The basic idea is that signal strength weakens if the distance between two nodes grows farther apart. A path composed of weak links can easily become broken. Therefore, a signal strength-based estimation model marks a link as stable if the signal strength of the link is greater than a certain threshold.

Let us use the following notation in discussing link stability models. v_i represents a node with a unique identifier i and $e_{i,j}$ is the link between node v_i and v_j. SS_j is the signal strength of a packet received from node v_j and $SScum_j$ is the cumulative signal strength of packets received from v_j. DSS_j is the differentiated signal strength (i.e., the change in signal strength from the value measured during the previous measurement period) of neighbor v_j. ρ is an weight factor of $SScum_j$ that defines how much previous signal strength affects current $SScum_j$. Finally, Thr is the signal strength threshold above which a signal is considered to be stable.

3.1 Signal Strength-Based Link Stability Estimation Model(SBM)

SBM, proposed in [2], estimates link stability using signal strengths. Each node monitors signals from its neighboring nodes. If the signal strength of a received packet is higher than a certain threshold, the link to that neighbor is considered stable. Figure 1(a) shows the pseudocode for the procedure followed by SBM when v_i receives a packet from v_j.

Figure 1(b) shows estimation results for link stability when SBM is used. The circle with 45 degree slash marks (the stable zone) is the area where the signal strength is greater than Thr. Only nodes in the slashed area can be considered as

```
SScum_j = ρSScum_j + (1 − ρ)SS_j
if(SScum_j > Thr) {
    e_{i,j} is stable.
} else {
    e_{i,j} is unstable.
}
```

(a) Pseudocodes

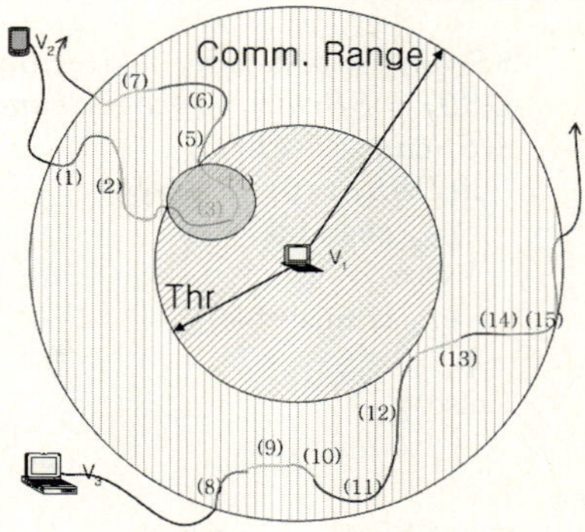

(b) Estimation results

Fig. 1. Pseudocodes and estimation results of SBM

nodes connected by stable links. The vertically slashed circle area (outer circle) is the maximum communication range of v_1. When mobile nodes are inside the small ovals, the link between those nodes and v_1 can be considered as stable. Link $e_{1,2}$ when v_2 is on path segments (1), (2), (5), (6) and (7) is considered as unstable because the signal strength received from v_1 is less than Thr. However the link $e_{1,2}$ is considered as a stable link when v_2 is on path segments (3) and (4) because the signal strength received is greater than Thr. Link $e_{1,3}$ is always considered as unstable because the signal strength received by v_3 is less than the threshold Thr throughout its journey.

3.2 Advanced Signal Strength-Based Link Stability Estimation Model(ASBM)

ASBM, proposed in [1], takes differentiated signal strength (DSS) values into account when estimating the direction of node movement. DSS indicates whether the signal strength is getting stronger or weaker. If the signal strength is getting stronger, this means that the two nodes are getting closer together and the link is getting stronger. Therefore links with increasing signal strengths are considered as stable. If the signal strength is getting weaker, this means that the two nodes are getting farther apart and the link may become disconnected. In addition, a very weak initial signal strength between two nodes also indicates a weak link. Thus, a link in which the signal strength is getting progressively weaker or is less than a threshold is considered as unstable. Since ASBM takes DSS into account, it can detect movements of nodes that can weaken link stability. Therefore, the threshold for ASBM can be set lower than the threshold for SBM, which means that the stable area is larger than with SBM. Figure 2(a) shows the pseudocode for ASBM.

Figure 2(b) shows estimated results for link stability when ASBM is used. Note that the area of the stable zone for ASBM is larger than that for SBM because Thr of ASBM is less than Thr of SBM. When v_2 is on path segments

```
SScum_j = ρSScum_j + (1 − ρ)SS_j
DSS_j = SScum_j − prevSScum_j
if(SScum_j > Thr) {
   if(DSS_j > 0) {
     e_{i,j} is stable.
   } else {
     e_{i,j} is unstable.
   }
} else {
   e_{i,j} is unstable.
}
prevSScum_j = SScum_j
```

(a) Pseudocodes

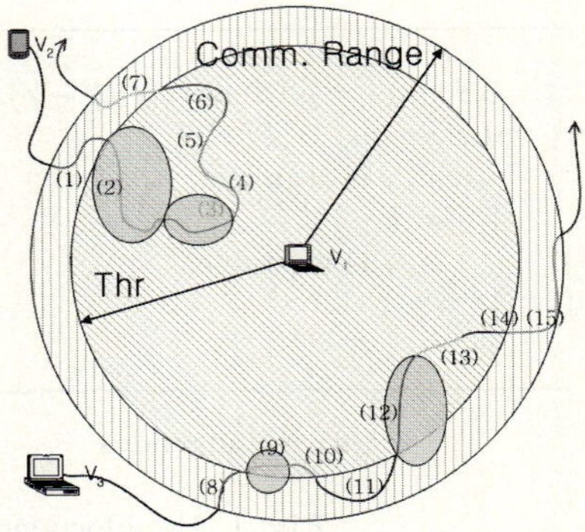

(b) Estimation results

Fig. 2. Pseudocodes and estimation results of ASBM

(2), (3), (4), (5) and (6), v_2 is inside the stable zone. DSS_2 is positive when v_2 is on path segments (2) and (3) because v_2 and v_1 are getting closer. Therefore, the link $e_{1,2}$ is considered as stable when v_2 is on path segments (2) and (3). However, DSS_2 is negative when v_2 is on path segments (4), (5) and (6) because v_2 and v_1 are getting farther apart. Therefore, link $e_{1,2}$ is considered as unstable when v_2 is on path segments (4), (5) and (6). Note that when v_2 is on a path segment (4), the distance between v_1 and v_2 is very close. Even if v_2 starts to move out immediately, it can be considered as stable because it may need a lot of time to move out of the communication range of v_1. Therefore, ASBM may result in fewer stable links than SBM. Based on similar reasoning, link $e_{1,3}$ is considered as stable when v_3 is on path segments (9) and (12).

3.3 Enhanced Stability Model (ESM)

A major shortcoming of ASBM is that it considers the link $e_{1,2}$ as unstable when v_2 is on a path segment (4) in Fig. 2(b). In order to overcome this shortcoming of ASBM, we propose a new link stability estimation model, termed the Enhanced Stability Model (ESM), that uses two thresholds. In ESM, a link is considered as stable when two nodes are located very close to each other. ESM uses two threshold Thr_1 and Thr_2 with the property $Thr_1 > Thr_2$. If the signal strength is greater than Thr_1, then the link is always considered as stable because the distance between the two nodes is very small. However, if the signal strength is less than Thr_1 but greater than Thr_2, then DSS is used to estimate link stability as in ASBM. In addition, due to external environment factors like obstacles, interference and white noise, signal strength can decrease even when the locations of both nodes are fixed. Suppose that signal strength is slightly decreased by

$SScum_j = \rho SScum_j + (1-\rho)SS_j$
$DSS_j = SScum_j - prevSScum_j$
if($SSCum_j > Thr_1$) {
  $e_{i,j}$ is stable.
} else if($SScum_j > Thr_2$) {
  if($DSS_j > \mu$) {
    $e_{i,j}$ is stable.
  } else {
    $e_{i,j}$ is unstable.
  }
} else {
  $e_{i,j}$ is unstable.
}
$prevSScum_j = SScum_j$

(a) Pseudocodes

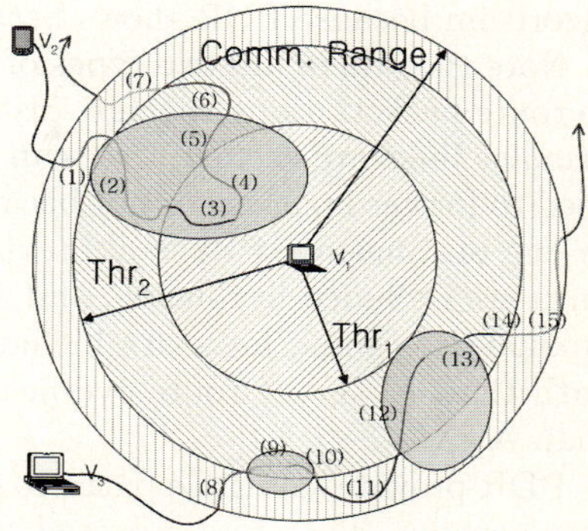

(b) Estimation results

Fig. 3. Pseudocodes and estimation results of ESM

external environment factors. In this case, ASBM considers the link as unstable because DSS becomes negative even though the actual link may still be stable. Therefore, we add a parameter μ where $\mu < 0$ to address this problem. A link is considered as unstable in ESM only when $DSS < \mu$. Figure 3(a) shows the pseudocode for ESM.

Figure 3(b) shows the estimated results for ESM. Path segments (2) and (3) are considered as stable because the signal strength is greater than Thr_2 and $DSS_2 > 0$. However, a path segment (4), which was considered as an unstable link in ASBM, is considered as a stable link in ESM because the signal strength for v_2 is greater than Thr_1 even two nodes are getting farther apart. In addition, a path segment (5) is also considered as stable in ESM because $DSS_2 > \mu$ even though v_2 is moving toward the outside of the communication range of v_1. However, a path segment (6) is considered as unstable because $DSS_2 < \mu$. Path segments (9) and (10) are considered as stable because $SScum_3 > Thr_2$ and $DSS_3 > \mu$ even though v_3 is moving toward the outside of the transmission range of v_1 when v_3 is on a path segment (10). Furthermore, path segments (12) and (13) are also considered as stable for the same reason.

4 Stable Pseudo-distance Routing (S-PDR) Algorithm

Since link stability continually changes in a MANET, a routing algorithm for such a network should be able to dynamically adapt to link stability changes in selecting a path to each destination. However, most previous algorithms provide only a single path to each destination. Thus, once a path has been selected, new link stability information cannot be used to change the path to the destination. Unlike such rigid algorithms, TORA[6] and PDR[7] provide multiple paths, and a path to each destination can be selected on a hop-by-hop basis. The most recent link stability information for each link can be used in making hop-by-hop routing decisions. Of these two algorithms, PDR is chosen as our base routing algorithm because PDR shows better performance than TORA [7].

Note that there are two types of links in PDR. Primary links are mainly used to route packets along shortest-distance paths. Auxiliary links are used when all primary links are broken. User can select whether auxiliary outgoing link can be used to forward packets or not because auxiliary outgoing links tend to be detour to the destination. PRI is abbreviation of primary only routing that auxiliary links are excluded in routing, and AUX is abbreviation of auxiliary routing that auxiliary outgoing links are included in routing. Note that PRI shows shorter path than AUX but route overhead in terms of control messages are increased than AUX.

PDR provides multiple paths to destination, but it does not take link stability into account. Therefore, we need to modify the PDR algorithm to select stable links. This modified algorithm is referred to as the stable pseudo-distance routing (S-PDR) algorithm. Since S-PDR already requires each node to store information for each of its neighbors, we can simply add a variable that represents stability into this neighbor information table. The "estimated" stability of a link $e_{i,j}$ is updated whenever a node receives packets from its neighbors using one of the estimation models discussed in Section 3. When a node selects its next hop, S-PDR selects a neighbor with the minimum height from among the nodes connected by stable links. If there are no stable outgoing links, S-PDR simply selects a minimum-height neighbor in order to reduce the path length as in PDR. Note that S-PDR can be divided into PRI and AUX parts as same as PDR.

5 Simulation Results

Simulations were conducted to evaluate the performance of the various stability models considered and to evaluate the benefits of routing using stable links. The simulation tool used was ns-2[8], which is a discrete event simulator commonly used in networking research. In order to model wireless connections accurately, the distributed coordination function (DCF) of the IEEE 802.11 standard for wireless LANs was used for the MAC and PHY layers. The data rate was set to 11 Mbps as this is a rate supported by the most common IEEE 802.11b devices.

The simulation scenarios used were based on the following setup. The simulation space was a 500m × 300m area, and the communication range of each node was set to 130m. The mobility of the nodes was controlled by a mobility generator function in ns-2 that uses a random destination model[5] with 5m/s maximum speed. Finally, the simulation time was set to 130 seconds. A source sends 256 bytes of UDP packet data to its randomly chosen destination every 1 second from 10 seconds after the simulation starts to 125 seconds. Data were collected for ten different simulation scenarios.

5.1 Error Model Used in Simulation

The error model used is a modification of the basic ns-2 error model. Basically, all packets in ns-2 are successfully received if the signal power is greater than the receiving threshold. In ns-2, each node that receives a packet calculates its receiving signal strength $RxPr$ using a propagation model based on a free-space, two-ray ground reflection or shadowing model. If the calculated $RxPr$ is greater than $RXThresh\_$, the threshold of the receiving packet, then the packet is successfully received. However, a packet received with a weak signal strength can easily be corrupted or lost due to various external environment factors such as white noise, wireless interference and other circumstances in actual wireless networks. Therefore, the ns-2 error model was modified to simulate a more reasonable error model. In our implementation, we update the receiving signal strength as $RxPr = RxPr - [0, RXThresh\_ \times MASS]$, where $MASS$ is a floating-point value in [0, 1]that represents the maximum attenuation of the signal strength. If the signal power $RxPr$ is greater than $(1 + MASS) \times RXThresh\_$, the packet is always successfully received. Otherwise, the packet can be lost with a random probability factor. Note that as $MASS$ is increased, the probability of packet loss also increases.

5.2 Performance of Primary Routing (PRI)

For the simulation, Thr of SBM is set as $1.5 \times RXThresh\_$ and Thr of ASBM is set as $1.2 \times RXThresh\_$. In ESM, Thr_1 is set as $1.5 \times RXThresh\_$, Thr_2 is set as $1.2 \times RXThresh\_$ and μ is set as $-0.3 \times RXThresh\_ \times Thr_2$.

Figure 4(a) shows packet delivery ratio versus $MASS$. The plot for PRI-NONE shows the results for PRI without a stability estimation model, and the PRI-SBM plot shows the results for PRI with the stability estimation model used in SBM. The PRI-ASBM plot shows the results for PRI with the estimation model of ASBM, and the PRI-ESM plot shows the performance of PRI with the estimation model of ESM.

As expected from Section 5.1, the packet delivery ratio is decreased if $MASS$ is increased and vice versa. Because PRI-NONE does not take link stability

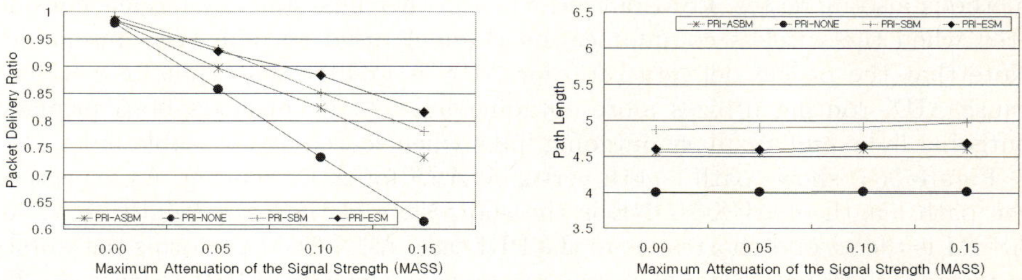

(a) Packet delivery ratio (b) Path length

Fig. 4. Performance comparison of PRI routing using various link stability models into account, it shows the worst performance in terms of packet delivery ratio. However, since PRI-NONE selects next-hop nodes from among minimum-height neighbors, path lengths produced by PRI-NONE should be the shortest. PRI-ASBM shows the worst performance, in terms of packet delivery ratio, among the stable routing algorithms. Note that the number of stable links are fewer than with other methods because, even if two nodes are very close, ASBM excludes links from the stable link list when $DSS < 0$. The result is that ASBM usually selects its next hop node from among minimum-distance-path neighbors as in PRI-NONE, thereby producing poor performance in terms of packet delivery ratio. However, the performance of ASBM in terms of path length is good. PRI-ESM shows the best performance as $MASS$ is increased because the link stability estimation method used by ESM is very accurate.

Figure 4(b) shows path length versus $MASS$. PRI-NONE shows better performance than all other algorithms because PRI-NONE only selects minimum-distance-path neighbors. As expected, PRI-ASBM shows the best performance among the S-PDR variants in terms of path length because PRI-ASBM tends to select its next hop using unstable links (selecting a minimum-distance-path using those links) because the number of stable links are fewer than with the other methods. Path lengths for PRI-ASBM and PRI-ESM are greater than PRI-NONE because these former algorithms select stable paths even if detours are necessary. PRI-SBM shows the worst performance in terms of path length because the next stable-hop-node is located relatively closer than with other methods. Note that the stable areas for PRI-ASBM and PRI-ESM are larger than for PRI-SBM.

5.3 Performance of Auxiliary Routing (AUX)

Figure 5(a) shows packet delivery ratio versus $MASS$. AUX-NONE performs worst in terms of packet delivery ratio because AUX-NONE does not take link stability into account (like PRI-NONE). AUX-ASBM also performs worst in terms of packet delivery ratio among the stable routing algorithms because the number of stable links is fewer than other methods (like PRI-ASBM). As shown in the figure, AUX-ESM performs best in terms of packet delivery ratio as expected. As $MASS$ is increased, the performance gap between ESM and other methods also increases. ESM outperform all other link stability models considered when the wireless communication channels used become very unreliable. Note that the packet delivery ratio for AUX is greater than that for PRI because AUX routing utilizes more outgoing links — it considers both primary outgoing links *and* auxiliary outgoing links when searching for stable links.

Figure 5(b) shows path length versus $MASS$ for AUX routing. As expected, the path length of AUX-NONE is the shortest, and the path length of AUX-ASBM is the second-shortest as in the PRI case. AUX-SBM performs the worst, in terms of path length, for the same reason as in the case of PRI routing. AUX-ESM performs worse than AUX-ASBM in terms of path length. Nevetheless, the difference in packet delivery ratio, which is our main concern in this paper, favors the AUX-ESM method.

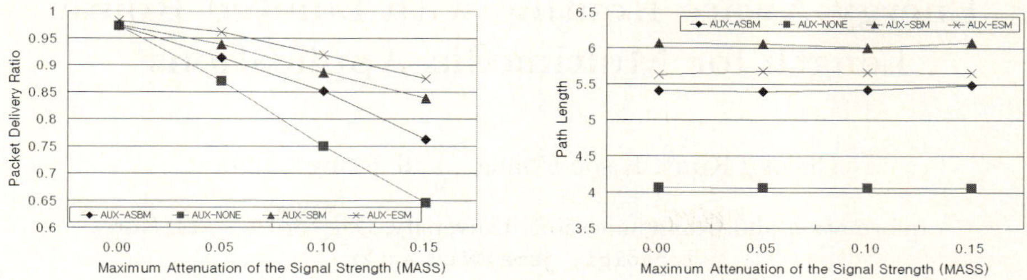

(a) Packet delivery ratio (b) Path length

Fig. 5. Performance comparison of AUX routing using various link stability models

6 Conclusion

In this paper, we propose a new link stability estimation model, termed enhanced stability model (ESM), that can be used to estimate the stability of communication links in MANETs. Analysis of example cases and simulation results show that ESM-based routing tends to perform better than routing using previous link stability estimation models in terms of the ratio of packets successfully delivered to their destinations (packet delivery ratio). Furthermore, as the reliability of the channel gets worse, the relative benefit of ESM-based routing becomes more pronounced.

References

1. G. Lim, K. Shin, S. Lee, H. Yoon and J.S. Ma, "Link Stability and Route Lifetime in Ad-hoc Wireless Networks", *Proc. IEEE ICPPW'02*, pp. 116–123, Aug. 2002.
2. R. Dube, C.D. Rais, K.-Y. Wang and S.K. Tripathi, "Signal Stability based Adaptive Routing (SSA) for Ad-Hoc Mobile Networks", *IEEE Personal Communications*, pp. 36–45, Feb. 1997.
3. C.-K. Toh, "A Novel Distributed Routing Protocol To Support Ad-Hoc Mobile Computing", *Proc. IEEE Phoenix Conf. Computer and Communications*, pp. 480–486, Mar. 1996.
4. B.S. Manoj, R. Ananthapadmanabha and C. Siva Ram Murthy, "Link life Based Routing Protocol for Ad hoc Wireless Networks", *Proc. IEEE Conf. on Computer Communications*, pp. 573–576, Oct. 2001.
5. I. Rubin and Y,-C. Liu, "Link Stability Models for QoS Ad Hoc Routing Algorithms", *Proc. IEEE VTC2003 Fall* pp. 3084–3088, Oct. 2003.
6. V. D. Park and M. S. Corson, "A Highly Adaptive Distributed Routing Algorithm for Mobile Wireless Networks", *Proc. IEEE INFOCOM*, pp. 1405–1413, 1997.
7. M.-G. Lee and S. Lee, "A Pseudo-Distance Routing(PDR) Algorithm for Mobile Ad-hoc Networks", *IEICE Trans. Fundamentals*, Vol.E89-A, No. 6, pp. 1647–1656 2006.
8. VINT Group: http://www.isi.edu/nsnam/ns.

Energy-Aware Routing with Limited Route Length for Multimedia Applications*

Cheolgi Kim[1], Kisoo Chang[2], and Joongsoo Ma[1]

[1] Information and Communications University, Daejeon 305-732, Korea
{cheolgi, jsma}@icu.ac.kr

[2] Samsung Advanced Institute of Technology, Suwon 449-712, Korea
kschang@samsung.com

Abstract. In ad hoc networks, energy preservation on communications is crucial because most of nodes are battery-powered. On the other hand, communication delay is an important factor of real-time communications. Since energy-aware routes commonly have long route lengths, which commonly result long communication delays, a trade-off has to be made on route setup between energy preservation and communication delay. Moreover, long route length also incurs high packet drop rate, which causes low reliability and high retransmission cost. We propose energy-aware route search algorithms with limited route length (EAR-LRL). We show that the computational complexities of the centralized version of our algorithms are polynomial. The simulation results show that EAR-LRL generates routes with limited route length with resonably low total transmission power.

1 Introduction

In ad hoc networks, power consumption is a critical issue because most of the participating nodes are supposed to be battery-powered. Even though the energy optimization algorithms in centralized networks have been widely investigated, most of them cannot be directly adapted to ad hoc networks. In centralized networks, base stations are exploited for energy saving of subscriber stations in many aspects, while ad hoc networks hardly have a device which is able to sacrifice itself for other nodes' energy preservation. Thus, the collaborating methods are investigated for energy saving in ad hoc networks.

One of the mostly considered approaches is transmission power control in ad hoc networks. 802.11 specifications are based on fixed power transmission because of the limitation of conventional CSMA/CA. The receiving power is given by

$$P_R = \frac{\zeta P_T}{d^K} \tag{1}$$

where ζ is a shadowing coefficient, P_T is transmission power level, d is the distance between the nodes and K is a path loss coefficient, usually larger than 2

* This research was supported by the MIC(Ministry of Information and Communication), Korea, under the ITRC(Information Technology Research Center) support program supervised by the IITA(Institute of Information Technology Assessment).

E. Sha et al. (Eds.): EUC 2006, LNCS 4096, pp. 914–923, 2006.

[1]. Given BER, transmission power is a function of the distance between the source and the destination when transmission power control is adopted. As a result of Eq. 1, the transmission power commonly decreases to a quarter when a distance between a couple of nodes decreases to a half.

To maximize the effect of power control, a lot of approaches exploit intermediate nodes as much as possible to relay the packets from source to destination while conventional routing algorithm is commonly looking for shortest hop routes. Suppose that N nodes are distributed in a line having equal distance between nearby nodes, and the leftmost node is the source and the rightmost one is the destination. The transmission power when the source delivers a packet directly to the destination, must be at least N times higher than total transmission power when all deployed nodes participate the packet relay with transmission power control by Eq. 1. As long as appropriate power control MAC is exploitable, the power efficiency with N relay nodes is up to N times better than direct transmission due to Eq. 1. We call the routing algorithm exploiting intermediate node to relay a packet for energy preservation, as *energy-aware routing*.

There are two problems in energy-aware routing: high error rate, and long end-to-end delay. If a network builds a route optimizing the total transmission power, the number of hops inherently becomes large. If the packet error rate per hop is assumed to be same per each hop, the total error rate is destined to be linearly increased when the number of hops is increased. Moreover, the end-to-end delay will basically increase as well not only because of longer route length but also because of high error rate. Some work [1,2] has shown that the higher error rate affects the power consumption as well. As a result, the energy per route is expected to increase with route length from some point of route length, due to the increasing error rate.

These problems are amplified in VoIP and multimedia streaming applications. In VoIP as well as multimedia applications, the packet becomes useless if the delivery of a packet exceeds the deadline. VoIP is a killer application in military ad hoc communication system, which is usually urgent and time-critical. Moreover, the proportion of multimedia applications is becoming crucial in ad hoc networks.

To cope with the problems, we propose power-aware routing protocols with limited route length. We strictly bound the route length to guarantee the packet delivery time or better power property. We show that the computational complexities of the centralized algorithms are polynomial, and extend to the distributed versions.

2 Related Work

There have been challenges to overcome fixed transmission power MAC. Power control MAC has been adopted to networks in different situations [3,4,5] and S. Agarwal et al. proposed and evaluated power control loop MAC in group mobility environment [3], S. Wu et al. extended the transmission power control to multi-channel ad-hoc networks [4]. T. A. ElBatt et al. proposed TDMA-based distributed packet scheduling algorithm with power control to reduce the interference and power consumption in ad hoc networks [5].

Some authors addressed the relationship between the transmission power control and RTS/CTS mechanism. RTS/CTS packets must be transmitted with highest power to announce the data packet transmission to all neighborhoods while data packet would have adjusted transmission power. E.-S. Jung et al. addressed that the nodes in the carrier sensing range and not in the transmission range will only sense RTS/CTS but data packets so they can try transmission during data packet exchange [6]. They proposed periodic power control to minimize such a problem. A. Muqattash et al. proposed POWMAC, which enhances the network capacity by allowing simultaneous transmissions from the neighbor nodes as long as the incurred interference is endurable [7]. RTS/CTS/DTS messages, replacing conventional RTS/CTS messages, have power information of following data transmission so that other nodes overhear them and decide if they communicate generating endurable interference. Their proposal significantly outperforms original 802.11 in clustered environment.

The energy-aware routing proposals to minimize the transmission power consumption have been proposed, as well [8,9,10,11,12,13]. Some work has been devoted to estimate the total transmission power in a distributed way [11,14,12]. C. Gentile et al. addressed high mobility environment by kinetic minimum-power routing in [12] while others cope with stationary environment. They have exploited the velocity of a node for the future position estimation. Clustering has been considered as a candidate to reduce the management cost by exploiting locality of the participating nodes because energy-aware routing algorithms need to manage a lot of information changing frequently [8,13]. C.-K. Toh presented a routing algorithm having low total transmission power and long battery life together by max-min approach in [10].

T. A. ElBatt et al. investigated the effect of transmission power control. They influenced the performance varies with the transmission power due to the interference range, retransmission ratio, cluster isolation and the number of hops [1]. S. Banerjee et al. also argued analytically that the route with many relay nodes do not always perform better with the proper metric including the packet error recovery efforts in [2]. They showed there is optimal number of relay nodes when we adapt *end-to-end retransmission model*. A few relay nodes do not exploit the potential reduction in the transmission energy, while a number of relay nodes cause the overhead of retransmissions to dominate the total energy budget.

3 Problem Statement

The goal of EAR-LRL is to minimize the total transmission power cost not to exceed a given route length. The reason why our approaches limit the number of hops is two folds: (1) When we add more relay nodes in the middle of the route, the end-to-end retransmission cost increases, while the total transmission cost, regardless retransmission, commonly decreases. The transmission cost and the retransmission cost make a kind of trade-off relationship with respect to the route length. S. Banerjee analyzed and showed that there exists an optimal route length in terms of the total transmission cost including retransmission cost with the given parameters in [2]. By limiting the route length to the analyzed optimal value, we can decrease the complexity of the algorithm. (2) Moreover, some real-time applications need to limit the end-to-end delay for the quality of service. Even though the end-to-end delay is not represented as a function of route length, it is highly correlated with the route length. Therefore, the delay requirement can be fairly achieved by the limit of the route length. We describe and formalize the problems in the following subsections.

Optimal route length regarding retransmission cost. A couple of transmission energy models are considered in our proposals: *typical energy model* and *retransmission-aware energy model*. Typical energy model assumes that there is no packet drop during packet delivery, so does not consider the retransmission cost, while retransmission-aware energy model considers the cost incurred by packet losses and retransmissions.

Suppose that $G = (V, E)$ represents a graph with a set of nodes, V and a set of communication links, E. In a *typical energy model*, the total expected transmission power of a route is given by

$$E_{\text{typ}}(X) = \sum_{i=1}^{n} E(x_{i-1}, x_i) = \alpha \sum_{i=1}^{n} d^K_{x_{i-1},x_i} \tag{2}$$

where $E(\cdot)$ is energy consumed in a link or a route, X is a route $[x_0, x_1, ..., x_N]$ from node x_0 to node x_N, $d_{i,j}$ is a distance between node i and j, and α is a coefficient in simplified energy equation in one hop, $E(i,j) = \alpha d^K_{i,j}$ derived from Eq. 1 given BER or receiving power. In the typical energy model, route with relay nodes, which has longer route length with short individual links, may have smaller expected energy as discussed in Sect. 1.

In *retransmission-aware energy model*, which considers the cost of packet losses and retransmissions, the total expected energy required in the reliable transmission of a single packet is given by

$$E_{\text{ret}}(X) = \frac{\sum_{i=1}^{N} \alpha d^K_{x_{i-1},x_i}}{(1 - p_l)^N} \tag{3}$$

where p_l is the packet error rate in each hop. S. Banerjee simplified the problem by adopting the line topology, [2]. In the topology, the total expected energy is simplified by

$$E_{\text{ret}} = \frac{\alpha D^K}{N^{K-1} \cdot (1 - p_l)^N}. \tag{4}$$

From Eq. 4, the optimal route length is given by

$$N_{\text{opt}} = \frac{K - 1}{-\log(1 - p_l)}. \tag{5}$$

Note that the optimal route length depends only on K and p_l, not on D. Thus, the nodes can easily derive the optimal route length with K and p_l, which can be obtained from the communication environment and link status.

Multimedia application case. Most of multimedia applications have delay constraints due to the real-time and interactive properties. We suppose that the end-to-end delay is proportional to the route length. S.-T. Sheu et al. have insisted that longer route length does not directly mean longer delay [15]. The reason is two folds: (1) longer link will have lower SINR with a fixed transmission power MAC (2) and the link with longer distance will contend with more nodes due to the larger interference area. The first fold can be ignored in our work because we assume that nodes control their transmission powers. The second one can be significant in the high contention environment. However, Most of ad-hoc network protocols have QoS-aware MACs, which provide higher priority to the time-critical applications. For example, applications with high priority can have shorter inter frame spacing time, or have reserved slot for communications. Thus, we suppose that the one-hop delay would hardly depend on the link distance for the multimedia application. However, route length inherently affects the communication delay. With this assumption, we can easily derive the maximum route length in terms of the time constraints of a certain application.

4 Energy-Aware Ad Hoc Route Search Algorithms with Limited Route Length

In this section, we show that the computational complexity of the EAR-LRL for one source node to all other nodes as destinations based on typical energy model is $O(nhk)$ where n is the number of nodes, h is the maximum route length and k is the maximum communication link degree of a node. Moreover, we also show that the complexity of the EAR-LRL algorithm from one source node to all other nodes as destinations based on retransmission-aware energy model is $O(nh^2k)$. Notice that operation $[a; b]$ makes a new sequence of nodes concatenating a and b where each a and b can be either a single node or a sequence of nodes. A sequence of nodes and a route are identical.

4.1 Route Search Algorithm Based on Typical Energy Model

Lemma 1. *The minimum energy route based on the typical energy model with route length limited to h between node u and v, $\bar{R}_h(u,v)$ is given by*

$$\bar{R}_h(u,v) = [\bar{R}_{h-1}(u,w); v] \tag{6}$$

such that w minimizes $E_{typ}([\bar{R}_{h-1}(u,w)); v])$ and $(w,v) \in E$

Proof. Let us represent $\bar{R}_h(u,v)$ as $[\hat{R}(u,w); v]$. Then, the second last node of the route is w. For a contradiction, we assume that $\hat{R}(u,w) \neq \bar{R}_{h-1}(u,w)$. Now, we have

$$E_{\text{typ}}(\bar{R}_{h-1}(u,w)) > E_{\text{typ}}(\hat{R}(u,w)). \tag{7}$$

However, $\bar{R}_{h-1}(u,w)$ is the minimum energy route from u to w with limited route length $(h-1)$. As $\hat{R}(u,w)$ must have a route length at most $h-1$, Eq. 7 conflicts with the definition of $\bar{R}_{h-1}(u,w)$. □

Lemma 1 is used for EAR-LRL based on typical energy model. As long as the communication environment is good enough so MAC protocol like ARQ guarantees sufficiently high probability of hop-by-hop delivery, we can use typical energy model because retransmission probability is supposed to be negligible. EAR-LRL based on typical energy model is simpler than that based on retransmission-aware energy model. Fig. 1 shows the centralized EAR-LRL algorithm from node u to all other nodes based on typical energy model.

```
function ROUTE ← EAR_LRL_TYP(u, h)
    if h = 0 then
        ROUTE ← [u]; return;
    end

    ROUTE ← ∅
    ROUTE' ← EAR_LRL_TYP(u, h − 1)
    V' ← {v ∈ V|[u; ··· ; v] ∈ ROUTE'}
        %% V' is set of reachable nodes in (h − 1) hops from u
    V'' ← V' ∪ {w ∈ V|(v, w) ∈ E for ∀v ∈ V'}
        %% V'' is set of reachable nodes in h hops from u

    foreach v ∈ V''
        R ← {r ∈ ROUTE'|r = [u; ··· ; w] and (w, v) ∈ E}
        find one min_r ∈ R s.t. E_typ([min_r; v]) = min_{r∈R} E_typ([r; v])
        ROUTE ← ROUTE ∪{[min_r; v]}
    end
```

Fig. 1. EAR-LRL algorithm based on typical energy model

Note that the EAR-LRL algorithm from one source node to all destinations is $O(nhr)$ where n is number of nodes, h is the route length limit, and r is maximum link degree per node.

4.2 EAR-LRL Algorithm Based on Retransmission-Aware Energy Model

EAR-LRL algorithm based on the typical energy model cannot be directly used on the retransmission-aware algorithm because the cost function is more complicate (see Eq. 4).

Lemma 2. *The minimum energy route based on the retransmission-aware energy model with route length limited to h between node u and v, $R_h(u,v)$ is given by*

$$R_h(u,v) = [R'; v] \text{ where } R' \in \bigcup_{(w,v)\in E \text{ and } 0\leq i<h} R_i(u,w) \quad (8)$$

such that R' minimizes the total energy cost $E_{ret}([R'; v])$.

Proof. Assume that $R_h(u,v) = [R';v]$ and $R' \notin \bigcup_{(w,v)\in E \text{ and } 0\le i<h} R_i(u,w)$. Moreover, suppose that j is the route length of R' and R' is represented as $[u;\cdots;w]$, so let w be the destination of R'. The assumption can be simplified as $R' \neq R_j(u,w)$ with the definition of j and w. The total energy consumption based on retransmission-aware energy model of R' and $R_j(u,w')$ is given by

$$E_{\text{ret}}([R';v]) = \frac{E_{\text{ret}}(R')}{1-p_l} + \frac{\alpha d^K_{w',v}}{(1-p_l)^j}$$

$$E_{\text{ret}}([R_j(u,w');v]) = \frac{E_{\text{ret}}(R_j(u,w'))}{1-p_l} + \frac{\alpha d^K_{w',v}}{(1-p_l)^j}$$

respectively. The assumption declares that $E_{\text{ret}}([R';v])$ must be smaller than $E_{\text{ret}}([R_j(u,w');v])$. However, it conflicts with $E_{\text{ret}}(R') > E_{\text{ret}}(R_j(u,w'))$ by the definition of $R_j(\cdot)$. □

Lemma 2 is used for EAR-LRL algorithm based on the retransmission-aware energy model. Fig. 2 shows the algorithm.

```
function ROUTE(0···h) ← EAR_LRL_RET(u, h)
    if h = 0 then
        ROUTE ← [u]; return;
    end

    ROUTE(h) ← ∅
    ROUTE(0...h − 1) ← EAR_LRL_RET(u, h − 1)
    V' ← {v ∈ V|[u, ..., v] ∈ ROUTE(h − 1)}
        %% V' is set of reachable nodes in (h − 1) hops from u
    V'' ← V' ∪ {w ∈ V|(v, w) ∈ E for ∀v ∈ V'
        %% V'' is set of reachable nodes in h hops from u

    foreach v ∈ V''
        R ← {r ∈ ⋃_{0≤i<h} ROUTE(i)|r = [u; ··· ; w] and (w, v) ∈ E}
        find min_r ∈ R s.t. E_ret([min_r; v]) = min_{r∈R} E_ret([r; v])
        ROUTE(h) ← ROUTE(h) ∪ {[min_r; v]}
    end
```

Fig. 2. EAR-LRL algorithm based on typical energy model

Note that the complexity of EAR-LRL algorithm based on retransmission-aware energy model is $O(nh^2r)$ because it has to search one dimension more than that based on typical energy model. However, the energy gain is expected to be very small as long as p_l is sufficiently small value. We can use the algorithm based on typical model for the approximation of that based on retransmission-aware model with smaller computational complexity.

5 Performance Evaluation

We simulated the centralized EAR-LRL on typical energy model. Our simulator was developed on MATLAB 7.1. 200 nodes were deployed in 800 m × 800 m 2-D square. The communication range of each node is assumed to be 200 m. Mobility and fading effects other than path-loss were not considered. The routes were assumed to be built based on the location information of the participating nodes and all possible pair of source and destination nodes were equally measured.

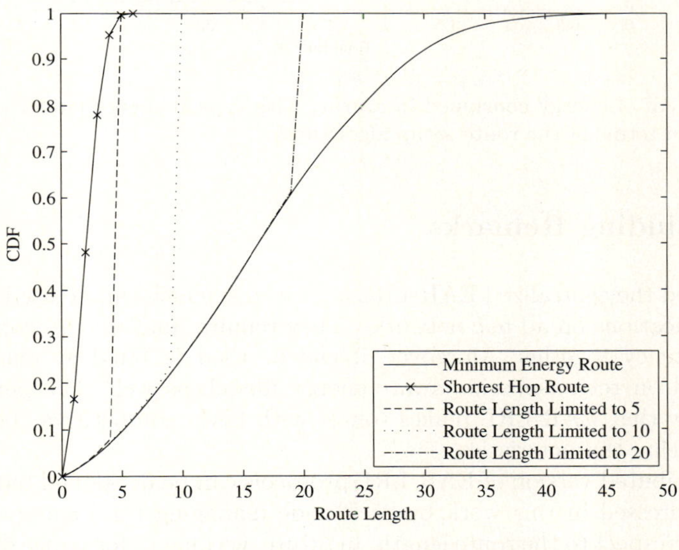

Fig. 3. The cdf of route length in terms of the route setup algorithms

As shown in Fig. 3, the minimum energy route lengths grow up to 48 hops in the simulation environment. However, routes built by EAR-LRL are shown to have strictly limited route. Our approach is expected to have good delay bound property for multimedia applications.

Fig. 4 presents the total energy consumed per route in communication with typical energy model when $\alpha = 1$ and $K = 4$. As shown, the route with limited route length of 20 is near optimal, even though its maximum route length is less than a half of that of minimum energy route. Moreover, the consumed energy with limited route length of 10 is also competent with significantly shorter route length.

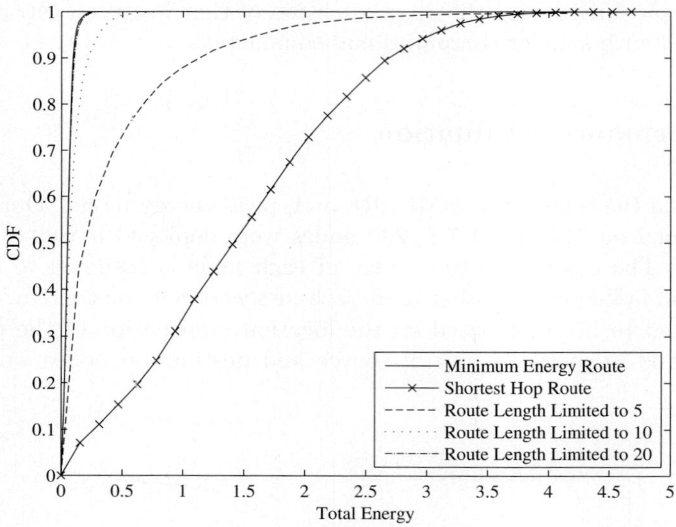

Fig. 4. The cdf of energy consumed in routing with typical energy model when $\alpha = 1$ and $K = 4$ in terms of the route setup algorithms

6 Concluding Remarks

We proposed the centralized EAR-LRL algorithms, which can be used for multimedia applications on ad hoc networks. They require small energy consumption and low latency together. Moreover, it can be used to build an energy-aware route based on retransmission-aware energy model, as well. The performance results show that EAR-LRL makes routes with fairly competitive energy costs and good delay characteristics.

The distributed version of EAR-LRL protocols can be developed based on the lemmas addressed in this work by each node managing total energy vector of routes with respect to the route length. In future, we plan to formalize distributed EAR-LRL protocols and evaluate them. Moreover, we will investigate the effect of mobility. We hopefully wish that the energy estimation on communication would help the accuracy of the energy cost estimation.

References

1. ElBatt, T.A., Krishnamurthy, S.V., Connors, D., Dao, S.: Power Management for Throughput Enhancement in Wireless Ad-Hoc Networks. In: Proc. of IEEE ICC 2000. (2000)
2. Banerjee, S., Misra, A.: Minimum Energy Paths for Reliable Communication in Multi-hop Wireless Networks. In: Proc. of the 3rd ACM Int'l Symp. on MobiHoc. (2002)

3. Agarwal, S., Krishnamurthy, S.V., Katz, R.H., Dao, S.K.: Distributed Power Control in Ad-hoc Wireless Networks. In: Proc. of the 12th IEEE Int'l Symp. on PIMRC. (2001)
4. Wu, S.L., Tseng, Y.C., Lin, C.Y., Sheu, J.P.: A Multi-Channel MAC Protocol with Power Control for Multi-Hop Mobile Ad Hoc Networks. The Computer Journal **45** (2002) 101–110
5. ElBatt, T., Ephremides, A.: Joint Scheduling and Power Control for Wireless Ad Hoc Networks. IEEE Transactions on Wireless Communications **3** (2004) 74–85
6. Jung, E.S., Vaidya, N.H.: A Power Control MAC Protocol for Ad Hoc Networks. Wireless Networks **11** (2005)
7. Muqattash, A., Krunz, M.: A Single-Channel Solution for Transmission Power Control in Wireless Ad Hoc Networks. In: Proc. of the 5th ACM Int'l Symp. on MobiHoc. (2004)
8. Kwon, T.J., Gerla, M.: Clustering with Power Control. In: Proc. of the 18th IEEE MILCOM. (1999)
9. Gomez, J., Campbell, A.T., Naghshineh, M., Bisdikian, C.: Conserving Transmission Power in Wireless Ad Hoc Networks. In: Proc. of the 9th IEEE ICNP. (2001)
10. Toh, C.K.: Maximum Battery Life Routing to Support Ubiquitous Mobile Computing in Wireless Ad Hoc Networks. IEEE communications Magazine (2001)
11. Nardis, L.D., Giancola, G., Benedetto, M.G.D.: A Power-efficient Routing Metric for UWB Wireless Mobile Networks. In: Proc. of IEEE 58th VTC 2003-fall. Volume 5. (2003) 3105–3109
12. Gentile, C., Dyck, R.E.V.: Kinetic Spanning Trees for Minimum-Power Routing in MANETS. In: Proc. of IEEE 55th VTC 2002-spring. Volume 3. (2002)
13. Gentile, C., Haerri, J., Dyck, R.E.V.: Kinetic Minimum-Power Routing and Clustering in Mobile Ad-Hoc Networks. In: Proc. of IEEE 56th VTC 2002-fall. Volume 3. (2002) 1328–1832
14. Lee, S.H., Choi, E., Cho, D.H.: Timer-Based Broadcasting for Power-Aware Routing in Power-Controlled Wireless Ad Hoc Networks. IEEE Communications Letters **9** (2005) 222–224
15. Sheu, S.T., Chen, J.: A Novel Delay-Oriented Shortest Path Routing Protocol for Mobile Ad Hoc Networks. In: Proc. of IEEE ICC 2001. (2001)

Iterative Decoding-Based Phase Estimation for OFDM Systems at Low Operating SNR*

A. Sh. Fayziyev and Kwonhue Choi

Dept. of Information and Communication Engineering, Graduates school, Yeungnam University 214-1, Dae-Dong, Gyeongsan-Si, Gyeongbuk, 712-749, Korea
fayziyev@mail.ru, gonew@yu.ac.kr

Abstract. This paper proposes a new phase estimation algorithm for turbo-coded OFDM systems at low SNR. In the proposed algorithm, phase estimation process is implemented jointly with iterative decoding process. This algorithm uses extrinsic information at each decoding iteration to estimate OFDM carrier phase rotations instead of using pilots. The proposed algorithm iteratively estimates phase rotation at each OFDM carrier by averaging soft decision extrinsic information carrier by carrier. The algorithm significantly reduces pilot insertion and thus, it is suitable for low operating SNR systems. Simulation results show that the proposed algorithm achieves significantly improved phase estimation compared to the conventional pilot assisted phase estimation and it converges to perfect phase estimation case.

1 Introduction

OFDM signaling is an efficient way to overcome multipath fading channel effects. However, OFDM systems are very sensitive to carrier frequency and phase offset. Therefore, frequency and phase synchronization are most important problems in OFDM based systems.

In the presence of frequency selective channels, each carrier of OFDM signal will have different phase offset. The problem is how to estimate the carrier phase offset from the received signal, and how to implement it relatively in short time. So far, comparatively big attention is given to development of carrier phase recovery technique. Therefore, a number of methods and algorithms of carrier phase synchronization had been developed. Nowadays, pilot assisted carrier phase synchronization method [1] is widely being used. The basic idea is to use additional high power pilot signals with less sensitivity to noise, for carriers phase estimation. This method has simple realization, but due to addition of redundant signals, data transmission rate is considerably decreased. Moreover, the method is considered as not suitable for the low operating SNR systems, due to using high power pilot signals.

* This research was supported by the MIC (Ministry of Information and Communication), Korea, under the ITRC (Information Technology Research Center) support program supervised by the IITA (Institute of Information Technology Assessment), IITA-2005- C1090-0501-0018, and in part by the Ministry of Education of Korea through its second stage of BK21 program.

E. Sha et al. (Eds.): EUC 2006, LNCS 4096, pp. 924 – 934, 2006.

The same is true for [2], where performance of the conventional pilot assisted estimation algorithm increased by using the iterative property of turbo decoders. The algorithm proposed in [2] uses soft bit estimates together with the already known pilot symbols. Such kind of operations can increase the performance of conventional pilot signal assisted phase estimation algorithm, but it still has redundancy in terms of time and power. To alleviate this problem, we should propose carrier phase estimation algorithm without pilot signals. In [3] and [4], [5] carrier phase compensation is implemented jointly with turbo decoding process. Algorithms proposed in those papers are free from the redundancy caused by additional pilot signals, but they are designed only for single carrier systems, not for multicarrier systems. Furthermore, these algorithms are designed not for channel estimation in a fading channel, but for recovering phase rotations caused by imperfect synchronization. Different method is implemented in [7], where phase estimation is achieved by applying modifications into forward and backward recursions of the SISO detection/decoding scheme. The algorithm proposed in [7] is not free from the redundancy, due to using additional pilot signals at each frame. As far as carrier phase estimation concerned, [8] gives an example of very low-complexity algorithm. However, there is no consideration about application to multicarrier systems like OFDM.

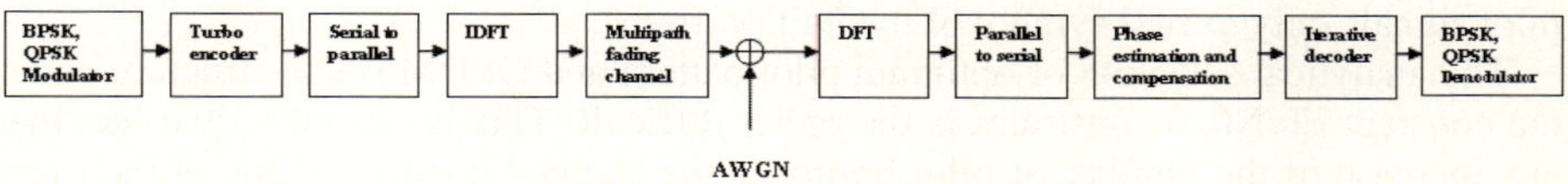

Fig. 1. Turbo coded OFDM transmission system

The main objective of this paper is to investigate new, relatively simple iterative carrier phase estimation algorithm for OFDM based systems. The proposed carrier phase estimation algorithm is based on Maximum-Likelihood approach, and compensates the carrier phase rotations iteratively, i.e., decoding process, phase estimation and correction processes are executed jointly. It makes use of the extrinsic information provided by the SISO decoder to compensate phase error. Iteratively implementing phase estimation at each iteration cycle increases the likelihood of the estimated phase, which gives the high reliable estimation of carrier phase in the end of the iterations.

In comparison with conventional pilot assisted phase estimation, the proposed algorithm does not demand redundant energy at each OFDM frame. In this paper, we investigated the BER performance of the conventional pilot assisted phase estimation algorithm in the presence of frequency selective fading channel. We considered that the frequency offset is already compensated and we showed the performance in comparison with pilot assisted phase estimation.

Simulation results show that the performance improvement of the proposed iterative phase estimation algorithm over conventional pilot assisted phase estimation is significant.

More specifically, in section 2, we described conventional pilot assisted phase estimation algorithm. In section 3, the general architecture of OFDM turbo-coded transmission system is shown. In section 4, we described the channel model used for simulations. Section 5 devoted to describing the technique of proposed iterative phase estimation algorithm. Section 6 contains simulation results, and last section has conclusions of this paper.

2 Conventional Pilot Assisted Phase Estimation

As opposed to single carrier systems, most of the OFDM systems use pilot assisted phase estimation algorithm with uniformly position of their pilot symbols in the frequency domain and equalize the channel by using simple multiplication after the FFT.

In OFDM modulation, pilots have to be inserted both in time and frequency domains. The spacing between pilot symbols in the time and frequency domains is chosen according to the sampling theorem. For our simulations, we assumed that the channel parameters are constant during the one OFDM frame, therefore spacing between pilot symbols in a time domain equal to OFDM frame duration

As we consider sufficiently short OFDM frame, we can safely assume that the channel parameters are constant within the one frame. Therefore, it does not matter how we distribute pilots in a frame. We consider the simple realization and inserted pilot signals only to first symbol of the OFDM frame.

The analytical selection of optimum pilot pattern and OFDM frame structure under the constant Eb/N0 is constraint is the rather difficult. This is caused by the fact that any increase of the number of pilot improves the channel estimation but, at the same time reduces the available energy for code transmission. In Fig. 2 has depicted the BER performance dependence of the conventional pilot assisted phase estimation from the number of pilot signal bits. Simulation results have gotten for 16 carriers, information bits in OFDM frame 1024, code rate ½.

In order to derive a channel estimate let us denote the received faded signal as *r(n)*, and pilot symbols in the received *r(n)* signal as *p(m)*.

$$r_k(n) = A_k s_k(n) e^{j\phi_k} + w(n) \tag{1}$$

where A_k and ϕ_k , amplitude fluctuation and phase rotations at k-th carrier.

If the total number of subcarriers is *K* and their durations in time domain is *M*, the estimation of the phase offset can be implemented as follows:

$$S_k = \sum_{m=1}^{M} p_k(m) \tag{2}$$

where $p_k(m)$ - is the already known *m-th* pilot symbol corresponding to the *k-th* OFDM carrier.

In this case the phase offset ϕ_k at k-th OFDM carrier is:

$$\bar{\phi}_k = \arg(S_k) \tag{3}$$

The channel estimation implemented in conventional pilot assisted phase estimation algorithm inserts pilot symbols to each OFDM frame and then applies a linear algorithm to interpolate the resultant channel estimates (see Fig. 5). The

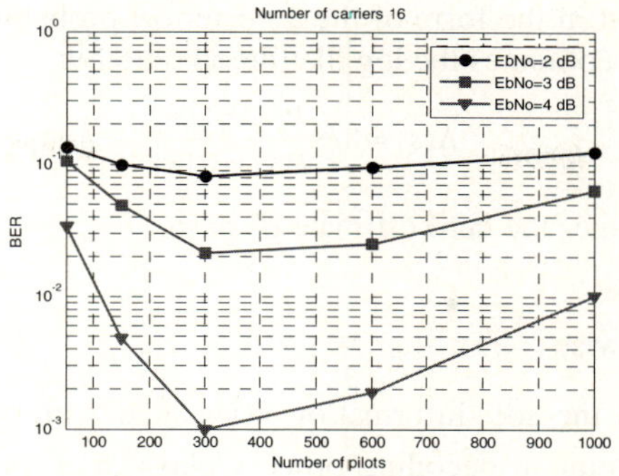

Fig. 2. BER performances vs. Number of Pilot signal bits

performance of the pilot assisted phase estimation algorithm depends on the number of pilot signals used in an OFDM frame.

3 Turbo-coded OFDM System Model

The Baseband architecture of the Turbo coded OFDM system is shown in Fig. 1. The binary information data bits are modulated by baseband modulator, which are then fed into r-rate turbo encoder. Turbo encoder consists of two RSC encoders [6]. The parity bits, outgoing from two encoders are punctured to reduce the overhead.

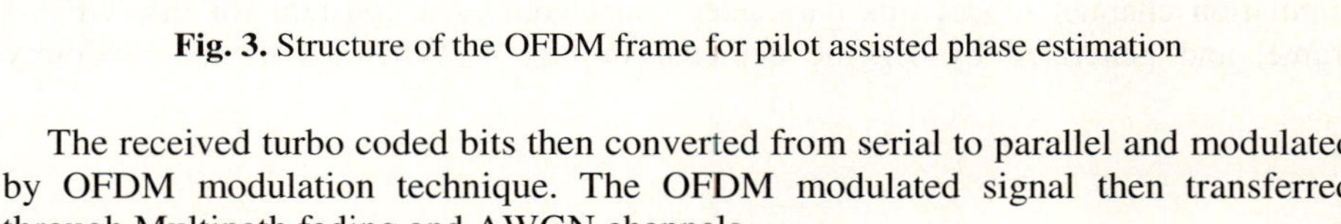

Fig. 3. Structure of the OFDM frame for pilot assisted phase estimation

The received turbo coded bits then converted from serial to parallel and modulated by OFDM modulation technique. The OFDM modulated signal then transferred through Multipath fading and AWGN channels.

Assuming that the symbol timing and frequency offset has already known and compensated the complex envelope of the t-th OFDM frame can be expressed as:

$$r^k(t) = A_k s^k(t) e^{j\phi_k} + n^k(t) \tag{4}$$

where k- carrier number, A_k -amplitude degradation at k-th carrier, ϕ_k - phase offset at k-th carrier, and finally $n^k(t)$ - is complex valued zero mean white Gaussian noise.

For decoding these received symbols MAP-algorithm which minimizes the symbol error probability is used. For each transmitted symbol, algorithm generates its hard estimate and soft output in the form of the a posteriori probability on the basis of the received sequence *r***.** It computes the log likelihood ratio by:

$$\Lambda(s) = \log \frac{P_r\{s = 1 \mid r\}}{P_r\{s = 0 \mid r\}} \tag{5}$$

The decoder determines the hard estimate of s as:

$s = 1$ if $\Lambda(s) \geq 0$

and $s = 0$ otherwise

Value $\Lambda(s)$ represents the soft information associated with the hard estimate of s. The key role in this iterative decoding process plays extrinsic information received from SISO decoders. Each decoder updates extrinsic information and transfers it to another one as *a priory* information. Such kind of operations improves the bit reliability iteration by iteration. The process is stopped after some iteration, and the hard decisions of the last received $\Lambda(s)$ are output.

4 Channel Model

The effect of the fading channel can be different. For simulations, frequency selective Rayleigh fading channel is used. In general, the faded signal in a multipath fading channel can be expressed as a summation of the reflected paths:

$$r(t) = \sum_{n=1}^{N_m} \alpha_n(t) s(t - \tau_n(t)) + n(t) \tag{6}$$

where *Nm*- number of paths, *s(t)*- is the transmitted signal, $\tau_n(t)$ - is the time variant delay for *n-th* path, $\alpha_n(t)$ -is the time variant multiplicative factor which represents signal fluctuations for *n-th* path, and finally *n(t)* is the time variant additive white Gaussian noise.

The effect of the fading channel can be represented by the $\alpha_n(t)$ parameter. In our simulation channel model this parameter considered as a constant for one OFDM frame, and generated by scheme depicted in Fig. 4. Where β -is the randomly

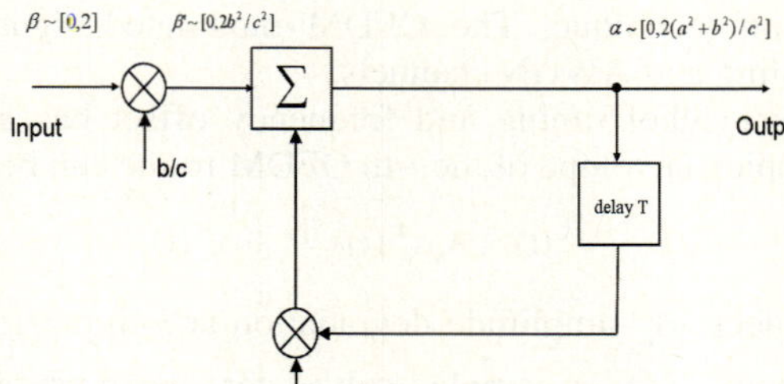

Fig. 4. Time variant multiplicative factor generator at each path

generated complex variable with mean equal to 0 and variance equal to 2. The output is the multiplicative factor α . α is the complex valued variable and can be expressed as:

$$\alpha = Ae^{j\phi} \tag{7}$$

where A , ϕ - amplitude fluctuation and phase rotations of the path.

In this proposed channel model each next generated multiplicative factor depends on previous one. The multiplicative factor is generated for each transmitted OFDM frame. In practical case, the effect of the fading channel changes with some correlation. Parameters *a, b* and *c* used to make correlation between previous and current generated values of the multiplicative factor.

Each next value of the α parameter is summation of the previous one and randomly generated variable. How high the value of the *a,* so slow the fading rate. The values of *a* and *b* should be chosen by taking into account conditions, which are needed to correlative change of the generated multiplicative factor α :

$$\begin{cases} a + b = c \\ a > b \end{cases} \tag{8}$$

The output of the proposed channel is the multiplicative factor with mean equal to 0, and variance $\frac{2(a^2+b^2)}{c^2}$.

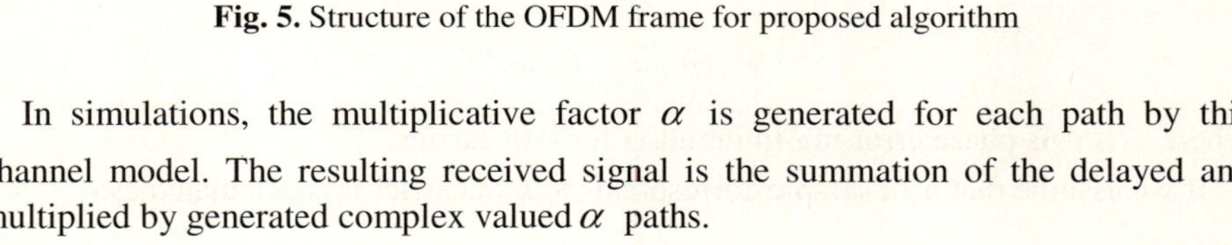

Fig. 5. Structure of the OFDM frame for proposed algorithm

In simulations, the multiplicative factor α is generated for each path by this channel model. The resulting received signal is the summation of the delayed and multiplied by generated complex valued α paths.

5 Proposed Iterative Carrier Phase Estimation Algorithm

The main idea of this paper is to provide an efficient phase estimation algorithm for Turbo-coded OFDM systems. In this section we described the iterative phase estimation algorithm which gives such kind of efficiency.

In proposed algorithm phase estimation is implemented iteration by iteration and jointly with decoding process. We assumed that the phase offset during the frame is constant and absolute value of phase offset difference between two frames is smaller than $\pi/2$. In first iteration of the decoding process, the received code samples are delivered into turbo decoder as conventional decoding process. From the second iteration, we recursively update the received samples and compensate the phase error based on the *a priory* information. Which means, we replace the received codeword sample, which has been used in previous iteration, with more reliable updated codeword symbol prior to current iteration. Therefore, as iteration process goes on, the phase estimation becomes more reliable and in the end gives more reliable estimation.

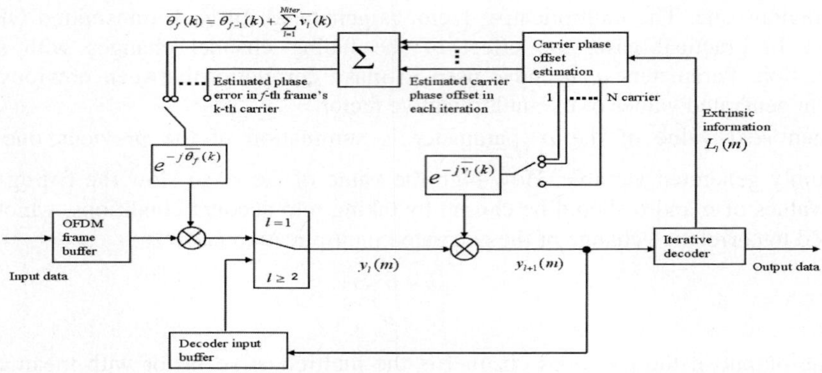

Fig. 6. Block diagram of proposed iterative phase recovery algorithm.

As the frame has a K carriers, and each of them has a different phase offset, we use parameter k to define which carrier the given m-th symbol is concerns. So, we can express that $y_l^k(m)$ denotes the sample for m-th codeword symbol used in the l-th iteration. In this case, the phase error in $y_l^k(m)$ is iteratively estimated and compensated as follows:

$$y_1^k(m) = r^k(m)$$

$$y_{l+1}^k(m) = y_l^k(m) e^{-j\bar{v}_l(k)} \tag{9}$$

where $\bar{v}_l(k)$ - is phase error in l-th iteration for k-th carrier.

If we assume that h-th sample corresponds to k-th carrier it is calculated as:

$$\bar{v}_l(k) = \angle\left[\sum_h y_l^k(h) \cdot \alpha_l^k(h)\right] \tag{10}$$

Where we average compensated soft decision received samples carrier by carrier to get more reliable phase estimation.

For BPSK modulation α_l^k is given as follows [3]:

$$\alpha_l^k(m) = \tanh \frac{L_{l,i}^k(m)}{2} \tag{11}$$

where $L_l^k(m)$ is an extrinsic information of the m-th codeword bit at the l-th iteration.

For QPSK modulation case α_l^k is given as follows [3]:

$$\alpha_l^k(m) = \tanh\frac{L_{l,i}^k(m)}{2} + j\tanh\frac{L_{l,q}^k(m)}{2} \tag{12}$$

The estimated phase error for current frame can be expressed as the sum of the phase errors at each iteration:

$$\overline{\theta}_f(k) = \overline{\theta}_{f-1}(k) + \sum_{l=1}^{L} \overline{v}_l(k) \tag{13}$$

where L-denotes number of iterations, f-frame number

For each next frame we use the estimated phase at previous frame. In this case for each next frame $r^k(m)$ is compensated with estimated phase error $\overline{\theta}(k)$ (see Fig. 6) of previous frame before delivering turbo-decoder. If consider that the phase offset for first frame estimated accurately, and the absolute value of phase offset difference between neighbor frames is smaller than $\pi/2$, the process gives high-accurate phase error estimation, which was proved by simulation results.

The main weakness of using currently estimated phase error for the next frame is that, if the estimation for some frame is incorrect all the next frames can be erroneous. To avoid such kind of propagation errors, we should periodically estimate the phase by pilots (Fig. 5). Period of pilot insertion depends on SNR value. Increasing the pilot insertion period decreases the redundant power used for pilot signals, at the same time increasing the probability of propagation errors.

6 Simulation Results

Following table shows system parameters used for simulations:

In figures Fig. 7 (a) and (b) the phase errors in OFDM carriers before and after compensation are depicted. In a fading channel, the number of reflected paths can be changed. In figures below (see Fig 8 (a) and (b)) there are shown the simulation results, for fading channels with number of paths equal to 4 and 6 respectively. In order to get these results we used channel model described in section 4. We assumed that there is a line-of-sight signal component in the channel. The results show that any increase of number of paths causes BER performance degradations in low-SNR.

Also we should take into account that the performance of the pilot assisted and proposed iterative phase estimation algorithms depends on number of carriers. Due to increasing number of carriers, information bits at each carrier decrease, which means algorithm uses fewer bits to estimate the carrier phase offset (see Fig 10, Fig 8 (a)). Increasing the number of bits in OFDM frame can avoid this degradation. In figure (Fig. 10) we also depicted BER performance of the non optimized pilot assisted case.

Table 1. System parameters used for simulation

Parameters	Value
Information bits in OFDM frame	1024
RSC generator	$[1 \ \frac{D^2+D+1}{D^2+1}]$
Number of bits in OFDM frame	2048
Number of carriers	16,32,64
Code rate	½
Number of iterations	5
Modulation type	BPSK
Bit rate, (Mbps)	0.32,0.64, 1.28
Number of paths	4,6
Max. Doppler frequency	70,120 Hz
Maximum time delay	0.1 μsec
Number of information bits per carrier	64, 32, 16
Number of Pilots (optimized)	300
Number of Pilots (non optimized)	200

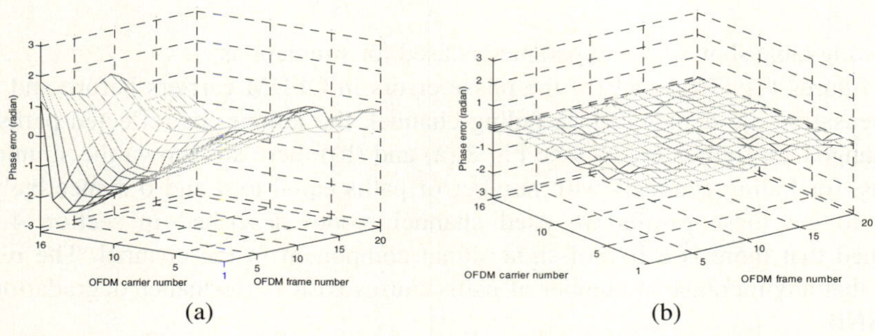

Fig. 7. Phase error in one OFDM carrier (in radian) for EbN0=3dB, Maximum Doppler frequency $f_d = 70Hz$ before (a) and after (b) compensation

One of other most important parameters of the fading channel is the Doppler frequency. Doppler frequency shows how fast the channel is changes. The higher the Maximum Doppler frequency, the worse the performance of the algorithms, which proved by simulations (Fig. 9).

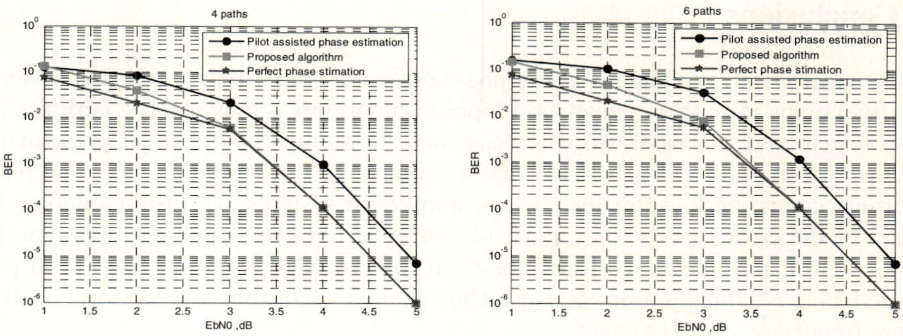

(a) (b)

Fig. 8. BER performances for 4 and 6 paths respectively (16 carriers, Max. Doppler frequency $f_d = 70Hz$)

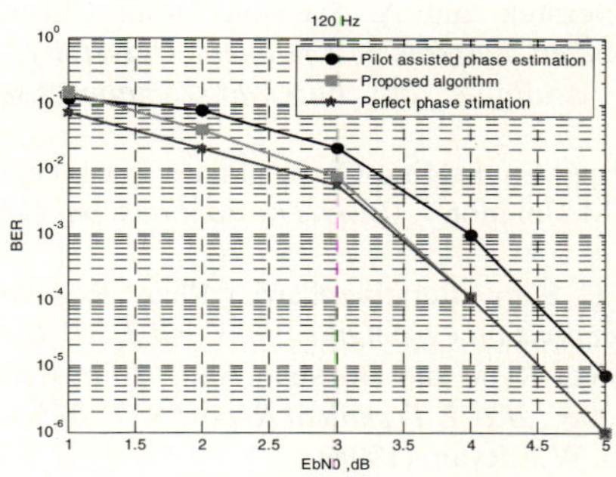

Fig. 9. BER performance for channel with Maximum Doppler frequency 120 Hz and 16 carriers (number of paths 4)

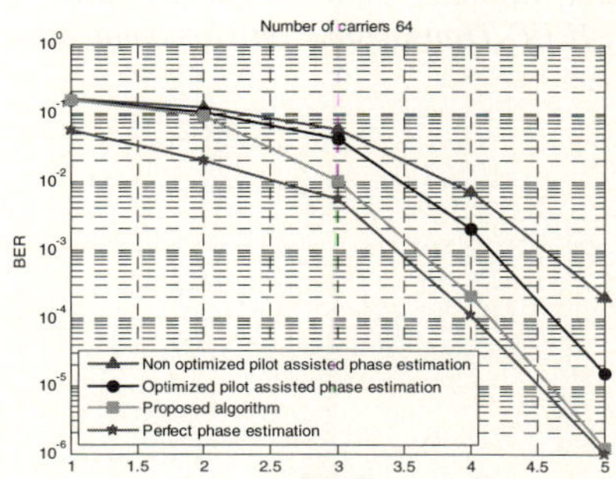

Fig. 10 BER performances for number of carriers 64 (Max. Doppler frequency $f_d = 70Hz$, number of paths 4)

7 Conclusions

In this paper we proposed new carrier phase estimation algorithm for OFDM systems. By simulations it is shown that the proposed algorithm achieves BER performance very close to perfect phase estimation case and shows much more better performance in comparison with pilot assisted phase compensation algorithm. The proposed algorithm can be very useful for low operating SNR systems, because it significantly decreases the power redundancy caused by inserted pilot signals. Proposed algorithm shows significantly better performance even for low SNR in comparison with pilot assisted phase compensation. Results showed that algorithm can perform well in severe frequency selective channels.

References

[1] F. Tufvesson, Tmaseng, "Pilot assisted channel estimation for OFDM in mobile cellular systems" *VTC 97,* pp. 1639-1643, Phoenix, Arizona, 1997

[2] M. Flament, B. Mielczarek and A. Svenson "Joint Channel Estimation and Turbo decoding for OFDM-based Systems" . *Chalmers University of Technology, SE-412 96 Gotheburg, Sweden, available at: http://db.s2.chalmers.se/download /publications/ flament_1109.pdf*

[3] V. Lottici and M. Luise "Embedding Carrier Phase Recovery Into Iterative Decoding of Turbo-Coded Linear Modulation" *IEEE Transactions on Communications*, vol.52, pp. 661-669, April 2004.

[4] Li Zhang and Alister G. Burr "Iterative Carrier Phase Recovery Suited to Turbo-Coded Systems" *IEEE Transactions on Communications, vol.3, N0. 6, November 2004.*

[5] Kwonhue Choi, Sun-Heui Ryoo and Do-Seob Ahn, "Joint Iterative Frequency and Phase Recovery for Turbo Code", *IEICE Technical Report SAT2005-41(2005-10).*

[6] A Turbo Code Tutorial, W.E.Ryan. (1998).

[7] *http://www.eecis.udel.edu/~fu/images/tc_tutorial.pdf*

[8] A. Anastasopoulos, K.M. Chugg, "Adaptive iterative detection for phase tracking in turbo-coded systems", *IEEE Transactions on Communications*, vol.49,pp. 2135-2144, Dec. 2001.

[9] C. Morlet, M.L.Boucheret, I.Buret, "Low-complexity carrier –phase estimator suited on-board implementation", *IEEE Transactions on Communications*, vol. 48, pp. 1451-1454, Sept. 2000

Semi-lock: An Efficient Cheat-Proof Synchronization Mechanism for Peer-to-Peer Game Systems

Huaping Shen[1], Sajal K. Das[2], Mohan Kumar[2], and Zhijun Wang[3]

[1] Ask Jeeves Inc., Piscataway, NJ, 08854, USA
hshen@ask.com
[2] Dept of Computer Science and Engineering,
University of Texas at Arlington, Arlington, TX 76019, USA
{das, kumar@cse.uta.edu}
[3] The Dept of Computing, Hong Kong Polytechnic University, Hong Kong
cszjwang@comp.polyu.edu.hk

Abstract. With more and more online game players having access to broadband Internet connections and high performance computers, peer-to-peer architecture offers an attractive solution for online multiplayer game design. However, message synchronization and cheat proof are two major challenges in implementing a fully distributed peer-to-peer game system. In this paper, a novel scheme, called *Semi-Lock*, is proposed to support message synchronization and prevent protocol level cheats for such systems. In Semi-Lock, peers encrypt each message by using cryptographically secure one-way hash function. A two-step validation is applied at destination peers to verify the integrity and correctness of the received messages. Trace driven simulations are conducted to verify the performance of our proposed scheme. Simulation results show that it significantly outperforms existing algorithms in terms of message latency and message synchronization ratio, with only little extra computational overhead on each peer.

1 Introduction

Real-time multiplayer online games are becoming increasingly popular due to the advancement of game design and the availability of broadband Internet access to the end users. As predicted in [8], the revenue of worldwide online gaming will grow to 5.2 billion dollars by 2006.

Existing online multiplayer games typically use a client-server architecture. Players send messages to a central server and the server broadcasts the update messages to all players. This architecture has advantages that a single authoritative server orders messages, acts as a central repository for data, and is easy to secure. However, the centralized client-server architecture also has several disadvantages. First, since every command must go from client to server and then be re-sent by the server to other clients. This adds additional latency over the minimum cost of sending commands directly to other clients. Second, the

E. Sha et al. (Eds.): EUC 2006, LNCS 4096, pp. 935–944, 2006.

server becomes a single point of failure in the game, and traffic at the server increases with the number of players which may result in localized congestion. Last, this architecture is limited by the computational power of the server. Although, scalability can be achieved by employing server clusters or computing grid, this solution incurs significant cost.

Recently, a fully distributed peer-to-peer architecture is introduced to address the above problems [4][5]. Unlike the client-server architecture, in which a single authoritative copy of the game state is kept at the server, in this peer-to-peer game architecture, each client keeps a copy of the entire game state. Each peer is allowed to send messages directly to other peers, which reduces the latency of message and eliminates localized congestion and single point failure. In order to support massively multiplayer online games, all peers are divided into different peer groups according to the locality interest in the virtual world [5], so that the event in one group will not affect other groups of the game, and players in one group form a peer-to-peer network in order to exchange event messages. A peer can be elected as the leader of one group to handle the message exchanges with other multiple groups [4].

In a peer-to-peer game architecture, each peer may experience different network delays in receiving messages from different peers. Messages from a peer further away or from one with congested link may take longer time to arrive at destination peer than that from a nearby peer or one with better network condition. Thus, to support the fairness of a peer-to-peer game, a synchronization mechanism is required at each peer to ensure the fairness of the messaging among the peers and to guarantee the consistency of the game state at each peer. Another challenge lying in the peer-to-peer game architecture is to prevent game cheats. As the definition given in [4], a game cheat is any action by a player that gives her an unfair advantage over another player. Instead of using an authoritative game server to maintain the game state, each peer keeps a copy of the game state. Thus, the peer-to-peer game architecture increases the opportunities of game cheating than the client-server architecture.

In this paper, we focus on the message synchronization and cheat-proof in the peer-to-peer game architecture. A novel mechanism, called Semi-Lock, is proposed to support message synchronization and prevent protocol level cheats while providing low message latency in such systems. In order to prevent protocol level cheats, when a peer initializes an action message, the message is encrypted by using cryptographically secure one-way hash function and is sent to other peers. After waiting a period of D_{max}, where D_{max} is a tuning parameter based on the network condition, the peer resend the plain-text message to other peers. After receiving a plain-text message, a two-step validation is applied to verify the integrity and correctness of the received message. In Semi-Lock, the game time is divided into equal frame intervals (FI). At each peer, valid messages received in one FI are executed according the rule of game application, and the game state is updated and saved at the end of each FI. Rollback operation is conducted to correct the game state if late messages are received. By adjusting the FI and D_{max} parameters, we show that Semi-Lock can meet different requirements of game designs. Trace driven simulations are conducted to verify the performance of our proposed scheme. Simulation results show that it significantly outperforms existing algorithms in terms of message latency and message synchronization ratio, with only little extra computational overhead on each peer.

The rest of this paper is organized as follows. Section 2 proposes the Semi-Lock algorithm. Implementation issues of the proposed algorithm are discussed in Section 3. Section 4 presents performance evaluation of Semi-Lock and compares it with existing approaches. Section 5 concludes the paper and discusses future research.

2 Proposed Semi-lock Scheme

As defined in [4], game cheats can be classified by layer in which they occur, such as application level cheats, protocol level cheats, and network level cheats. Application level cheats happen when cheaters modify the code of game or the operating system to gain unfair benefit. Network level cheats happens when cheaters use inherent properties of network layer. A denial of service (DoS) attack is an example of a network level cheat. On the other hand, protocol level cheats happen when cheaters read, modify or blocks the packets of game protocol to gain unfair benefit. One typical protocol level cheats is *timestamp cheat.* In peer-to-peer games, since each peer maintains its own game state, each game message must be timestamped when generated so that they can be executed at the same relative time by each peer. In timestamp cheat, after receiving a message from peer 1, peer 2 issues a message whose timestamp is before peer 1's and sends out to all peers. Thus, if peer 1 wants to attack peer 2 in his message, peer 2 can dodge the attack by cheating.

Semi-Lock focuses on the prevention of protocol level cheats, while providing low latency messaging synchronization for the peer-to-peer game architecture. In order to simplify the discussion, let P_i denote peer i in a game session and F_k denote the kth game frame interval (FI). m_{i,t_s} is a message that is generated by P_i at time t_s. We use $S_{i,F_k}^{t_k}$ to denote the game state that is generated by P_i at frame interval F_k and t_k is the commit time of last message executed in F_k. $P = \{P_1, P_2, ..., P_n\}$ is the set of peers participating in the game session. Let $D_{i,j}$ denote the network delay between P_i and P_j. We define a system parameter D_{max} as the maximal link delay among all peers in terms of number of FIs, which is given as follows:

$$D_{max} = \lceil \frac{\max\{D_{i,j} | \forall P_i, P_j \in P\}}{FI} \rceil \times FI \tag{1}$$

2.1 Semi-lock Algorithm

In Semi-Lock, all peers in one game session are assumed to have a synchronized clock by using Network Time Protocol (NTP). Network delay measurement algorithms [1] are used to acquire delay information $D_{i,j}$ between peers. When a peer, say P_i generates a game message m_{i,t_s}, the timestamp t_s is included into the message. At the same time, P_i sends out hash of message, $H(m_{i,t_s})$, to other peers in the game session. After waiting for a time period of D_{max}, the peer P_i sends out the plain-text message m_{i,t_s} to other peers. Since Semi-Lock commits the hashed message instantly after message generation, we call t_s as the *commit time* of message m_{i,t_s}, and call the time when P_i sends out the plain-text message m_{i,t_s} as the *reveal time* of this message. When a peer, say P_j, receives a hashed message $H(m_{i,t_s})$, P_j keeps $H(m_{i,t_s})$ in a hash message list L_j^H. The plain-text messages are kept in a list L_i^m, which is sorted by commit time of each message.

Semi-Lock uses a hybrid approach to synchronize game messages at each peer. The game time is broken into equal frame intervals (FI). Different from existing game protocols, in Semi-Lock, a peer is allowed to send multiple messages in an FI. At the end of each FI, all plain-text messages received in this interval are sequentially executed according to their timestamps. Before each execution, each plain-text message needs to be validated to prevent cheats as two steps as follows: *(i), the hash value of plain-text message is compared to the hash message in the hash message list to check the integrity of plain-text message; (ii), the difference between message commit time and current time should be less than $2D_{max}$ and more than D_{max}.* After the execution of all messages in a frame interval, the current game state is updated and saved in a list, called *state list* L_i^s. Each peer maintains a state list which is sorted by the generation time of each state. In one execution, if the commit time of a message is earlier than the commit time of a message in the previous saved game state, a rollback operation is conducted to correct all out-of-order messages, and the states after out-of-order message are replaced by correct game states. In order to reduce memory requirement, the game states whose commit time of last message is D_{max} earlier than current time, are removed from the game state list. The detailed description of Semi-Lock algorithm is given in Figure 1.

Figure 2 illustrates the Semi-Lock scheme. At time t_1, peer P_1 issues a game message m_{1,t_1} and commits the hash of message $H(m_{1,t_1})$ to the game session. (For clarity purpose, only game states of P_2 is illustrated and we omit the message exchange between P_1 and P_3.) Next, at time t_2, peer P_3 issues a message m_{3,t_2} and commits the hash of message $H(m_{3,t_2})$. After time period of D_{max} ($D_{max} = 4FI$) from their commit time, both P_1 and P_3 send out their plain-text messages. The delay between P_3 and P_2 is less than that between P_1 and P_2. Although, P_1 sends m_{1,t_1} before P_3 sending m_{3,t_2}, the message m_{3,t_2} arrives P_2 before m_{1,t_1}'s arrival. P_2 executes m_{3,t_2} in the frame interval after state S_2 and generates new state S_1. When m_{1,t_1} arrives at P_2 in the frame interval after state S_1, the game state rollbacks to S_2, and S_1 is recalculated by re-executing m_{3,t_2}. Finally, new state S_0 is generated and saved in the state list.

Theorem 1. *The Semi-Lock algorithm is safe: For any message m, no message that is generated after m's reveal time will be executed before m at any game instance of peers.*

For the limited space, the proof of the safety of Semi-Lock algorithm is skipped in the paper.

Begin Sender Procedure{}
  At time t_s, peer i (i.e., P_i) issues a game message m_{i,t_s}
  P_i sends out hash message $H(m_{i,t_s})$ to other peers
  Wait for D_{max} period
  P_i sends out plain-text message m_{i,t_s} to other peers
End
Begin Receiver Procedure{}
  If P_i receives a hashed message $H(m_{j,t_s})$
    Keep $H(m_{j,t_s})$ in list L_i^H
  If P_i receives a plain-text message m_{j,t_s}
    Keep m_{j,t_s} in list L_i^m sorted by t_s
End
Begin Frame Generation Procedure{}
  At frame interval F_k, when P_i generates a game frame
  Two-step validation for each message in the list L_i^m
  $M_r = \{m_{j,t_s} | \forall m_{j,t_s} \in L_i^m,\ t_s < t_{k-1} | S_{i,F_{k-1}}^{t_{k-1}} \in L_i^s\}$
  $M_c = L_i^m - M_r$
  If $M_r \neq null$
   The latest state $S_{i,F_q}^{t_q}$ whose $t_q < \min\{t_s | \forall m_{j,t_s} \in M_r\}$
    Rollback and correct all states $S_{i,F_e}^{t_e} |\ q < e < k$
  Execute all messages in M_c
  Save state $S_{i,F_k}^{t_k}$ where $t_k = \max\{t_s | \forall m_{j,t_s} \in M_c\}$
End

Fig. 1. Semi-Lock Algorithm

2.2 Optimized Semi-lock Algorithm

The basic Semi-Lock algorithm reduces the response time of each message by allowing peers to optimistically advance their game without waiting to receive all message from other peers. This leads to a better performance of responsiveness for Semi-Lock than the Lockstep protocol. However, since each peer still needs to wait for a period of D_{max} to reveal its plain-text message, Semi-Lock still suffers from poor responsiveness if there exists a peer with bad connection in the game session. In the following, we discuss two methods for optimizing the performance of Semi-Lock while still maintaining the same level security as the basic Semi-Lock algorithm.

In Semi-Lock scheme, unicast, multicast, or structured peer-to-peer overlay could be used to send messages among peers. Message transmission between any two different peers P_i and P_j requires time $D_{i,j} > 0$. According to Theorem 1, if we guarantee that after receiving plain-text message m, no peer can issue a message that will be executed before m, the safety of algorithm is not compromised. Thus, for any peer P_i, the waiting period D_{max} between commit time and reveal time can be reduced by D_{min}^i, which is P_i's minimal delay to other peers, i.e., $D_{min}^i = \min\{D_{i,j} | \forall j \neq i, P_j \in P\}$.

Furthermore, if peer-to-peer games use unicast to exchange messages among peers, optimized Semi-Lock can further reduce the waiting period of each

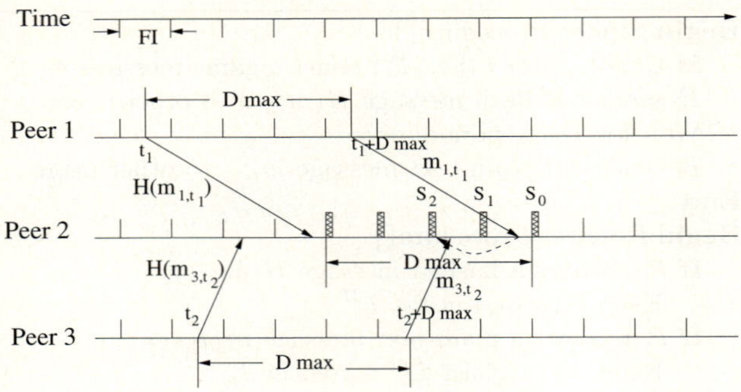

Fig. 2. Illustration of Semi-Lock

message while still maintaining the same level security as the basic Semi-Lock algorithm. With unicast communication, after commit time of a message m, P_i will wait for time period of $D_{max} - D_{i,j}$ before sending plain-text message m to P_j, where $D_{i,j}$ is the link delay between P_i and P_j. If the link delay estimation is accurate, the plain-text message m will arrive P_j late than D_{max} after message's commit time, so that after receiving plain-text m no peer can issue a message that can be executed before m.

Since each message will arrive its destination peer D_{max} time later than its commit time, all messages will be sequentially executed according to their commit time. Therefore, no rollback operation is required for optimized Semi-Lock algorithm under unicast communication when delay estimation is accurate. In later performance evaluation section, we show that optimized Semi-Lock can also achieve zero rollback performance under multicast communication when the game session uses only one multicast group to disseminate messages.

3 Implementation Issues

In order to use Semi-Lock in real peer-to-peer game systems, there are several issues that need to be addressed. In this section, we address two critical implementation issues of Semi-Lock in real network environments.

3.1 Handling Message Loss

In above section, we assume there exist reliable communication channels among peers and messages never get lost. However, in real networks, loss of packets always happens. We need to consider three different cases for Semi-Lock when messages get lost. *Case 1*: The hash message is lost but the plain-text message is received. In order to differentiate this situation from the cheats, the peer will send out a verification request to other peers which includes the plain-text message. The other peers compare the plain-text message with their valid message and send back the verification confirmation. If the majority of other peers confirm the validation, the plain-text message can be correctly executed. *Case 2*: If the hash message is received, but the plain-text message is lost, the peer can retrieve the valid plain-text message from other peers excluding the source peer. *Case 3*: Both hash message and plain-text message are lost. In this case, the peer still can reconcile the game state with other peers by retrieving the valid messages from other peers. Therefore, Semi-Lock can provide consistent game states to all peers even in network environments with packet losses.

3.2 Concealing Rollback

The other concern is how to conceal the visual artifacts that may result from the rollback operations of Semi-Lock. Occasionally, rollbacks will cause some drastic changes, such as the player in a first person shooting (FPS) game coming back to life when he is thought to be killed. One approach to minimize the occurrence of these artifacts is to classify the messages into different levels of significance. We delay the execution of significant messages such as a player's death in case there is a rollback.

4 Performance Evaluation

In this section, we evaluate Semi-Lock under different parameter settings. Two existing cheat-proof protocols, namely Lockstep [2] and NEO [4] are compared with Semi-Lock in the performance evaluations.

4.1 Experiment Setup

We design a trace driven simulator to evaluate the performance of Semi-Lock. Because there is no peer-to-peer game available in the Internet, we use Quake III [9] which is a popular first person shooting game based on client-server architecture to collect the trace data. We use five Quake III clients to connect to one Quake III server in the Internet and record the game traffic locally with tcpdump. We then use Ethereal [10], which has a built-in packet decoder for Quake III, to filter out everything except the game messages sent out by our client. In these trace files, there are 30-50 action messages per second that are generated by clients and sent to the server. We use the trace data in 270 seconds from game start time of each trace file to simulate a game session that lasts for 270 seconds.

In our simulator, the Transit-Stub method of GT-ITM model [7] is used to generate a hierarchical interconnecting network. Similar to SimMud [5], we use Pastry peer-to-peer overlay [6] to support peer-to-peer routing and also use Scribe that is built on top of Pastry to provide application level message multicast in our simulations.

4.2 Experiment Results

In each of the following experiments, if there are n peers in one game session, they are randomly selected from 1600 nodes in the simulated network. 10 experiments with different random seeds are conducted, and the average result of these experiments is recorded as one final result. The primary metric we use to measure the performance is the message response time which is the time from when a peer first sends out action message to when the message is executed and displayed on the screen of the other peers.

Basic Semi-lock vs Optimized Semi-lock. In this experiment, we explore the performance of the basic Semi-Lock, say *SemiLock(B)*, under different frame intervals and number of peers, and it is compared with optimized Semi-Lock, say *SemiLock(O)*. We change the game frame interval, FI, of each peer and evaluate the message response time and the number of rollbacks of Semi-Lock under different number of peers in the game session.

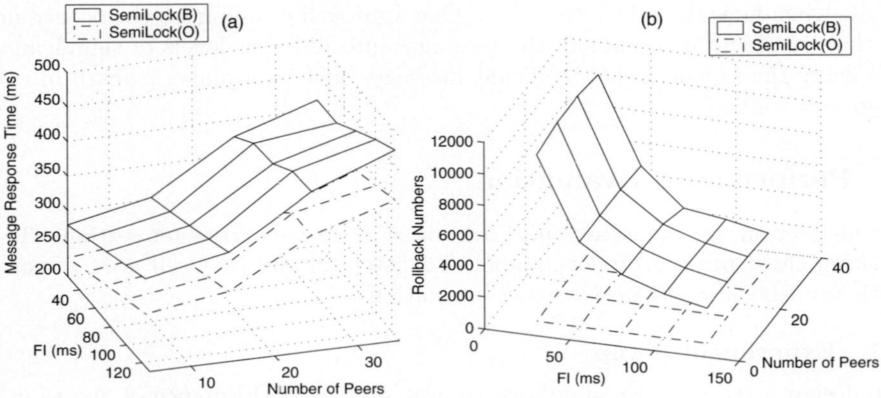

Fig. 3. Performances under different frame intervals and number of peers

As shown in Figure 3(a), the message response time is reduced as the frame interval decreases, but it increases as the number of peers increases in one game session. This is because when the FI decreases, each message needs to wait for less time for execution after being received by the destination peer. The increasing of number of peers incurs the increase of maximal link latency, D_{max}, among peers in one game session which leads to the increase of message response time. Figure 3(a) also shows that the optimized Semi-Lock algorithm reduces the message response time by about 50 ms.

Let the rollback number be the number of rollback operations that are executed in one peer in one games session of 270 seconds. In Figure 3(b), the rollback number drops as the frame interval increases, and slightly increases as more peers participate in one game session. As FI increases, more messages will be synchronized in one frame interval, so less misording messages need to be corrected by rollback operations. This results in the drop of rollbacks. As shown in Figure 3(b), the optimized Semi-Lock significantly reduces rollback operations as compared to the basic Semi-Lock. In simulations, we use the Scribe [3] multicast protocol to multicast the game messages, and all peers in the game session join one multicast group. In Scribe, a multicast tree is built among all peers to disseminate the messages in one group, so every multicast message is routed to the root node of the multicast tree, then sent to other peers. So the minimal delay D^i_{min} of each peer P_i is the delay between P_i and the peer that is closest to root of the multicast tree. Since the optimized Semi-Lock algorithm reduces the waiting time of each message by minimal delay D^i_{min} for each peer P_i, it makes all message arrive the root peer in the same sequence as the messages were generated, thus few rollbacks are needed to correct the misording messages.

Different Message Rates. In this experiment, we compare Semi-Lock with NEO and Lockstep under different message rates with five peers in the game session. We set the round time of NEO is 100 ms in the experiment. Since Quake III game has a high message rate, each player generates about 30-50 messages per second. We measure that the average interval between two consecutive messages is around 38 ms based on the measurement of 45 trace files we got. In order to evaluate the performance of each scheme under different game message rates, we vary the message rate by delaying each message multiple times of the original message interval.

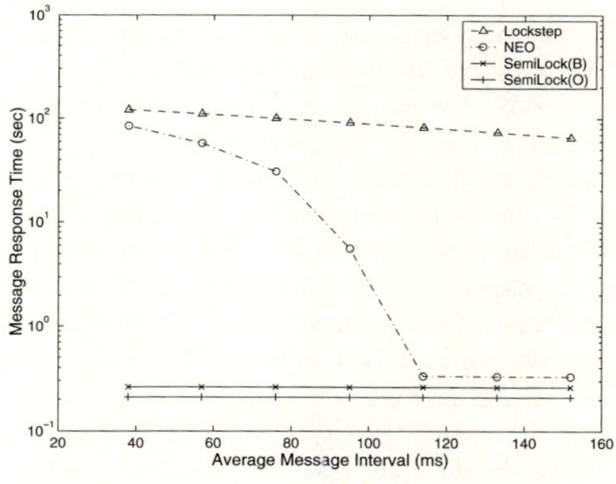

Fig. 4. Different message rates

As shown in Figure 4, Lockstep has the worst response time performance under different message rates. NEO has similar message response time as Semi-Lock at the low message rates. When the message rate increases, (i.e., average message interval decreases), the message response time of NEO significantly increases, especially, when average message interval less than 100 ms. Whereas Semi-Lock constantly has low message response time under different message rates. This is because Semi-Lock allows sending multiple messages in one frame interval. However, NEO allows only one message sending in each round so that messages are congested when the message interval is less than the round duration. Although we can reduce the round duration of NEO to relieve the congestion, this will lead to more misording messages. In Lockstep, each peer needs to receive all committed messages from other peers and then sends out the plain-text message, which results in poor message throughput. Therefore, we conclude that the Lockstep and NEO protocols are not suitable for the game with high message rate.

5 Conclusions

In this paper, we addressed two important issues in the design of peer-to-peer game systems: message synchronization and cheat proof. A novel scheme called *Semi-Lock* is proposed to support message synchronization and prevent protocol level cheats while providing low latency for peer-to-peer game systems. Trace driven simulations are conducted to verify the performance of Semi-Lock. Simulation results show that the Semi-Lock significantly outperforms two existing algorithms in message latency and synchronization with little more computation overhead on each peer. In our future work, we plan to evaluate the performance of Semi-Lock in packet loss network environments. Investigating Semi-Lock in support of massively multiplayer games is also part of our future work.

References

1. M. Allman and V. Paxson, "On Estimation End-to-End Network Path Properties", *In Proc. of ACM SIGCOMM'99*, September 1999.
2. N.E. Baughman and B.N. Levine,"Cheat-proof Playout for Centralized and Distributed Online Games", *IEEE INFOCOM*, 2001.
3. M. Castro, P. Druschel, A-M. Kermarrec, and A. Rowstron,"Scribe: A Large-scale and Decentralized Application-level Multicast Infrastructure", *IEEE Journal on Selected Areas in Communications (JSAC)*, 20(8) pp. 100-111, October 2002.
4. C. GauthierDickey, D. Zappala, V. Lo, and J. Marr,"Low Latency and Cheat-proof Event Ordering for Peer-to-Peer Games", *ACM NOSSDAV'04*, June 2004.
5. B. Knutsson, H. Lu, W. Xu and B. Hopkins,"Peer-to-Peer Support for Massively Multiplayer Games", *IEEE INFOCOM*, 2004.
6. A. Rowstron, and P. Druschel,"Pastry: Scalable, Decentralized Object Location and Routing for Large-Scale Peer-to-Peer Systems", *Proc. of IFIP/ACM Intl. Conf. on Distributed Systems Platforms (Middleware 2001)*, Heidelberg, Germany November 2001.
7. Ellen W. Zegura, Kenneth Calvert, and M. Jeff Donahoo, "A Quantitative Comparison of Graph-based Models for Internet Topology" *IEEE/ACM Transactions on Networking*, December 1997.
8. http://www.dfcint.com/game_report/Online_Game_toc.html
9. id Software, 'Quake'. http://www.idsoftware.com/.
10. Ethereal Network Analyzer, http://www.ethereal.com/

A Case Study on Message-Oriented Middleware for Heterogeneous Sensor Networks*

Sangim Ahn and Kiwon Chong

Department of Computing Soongsil University
1 Sangdo-5Dong, Dongjak-Ku, Seoul, Korea 156-743
{siahn69, chong}@ssu.ac.kr

Abstract. Needs of interoperability are getting increased since there have been some issues in heterogeneous wireless sensor networks such as information exchange, network protocol conversion, and integrity among multi-vendor products. We propose message-oriented middleware to make use of an intelligent bridge for information exchange in heterogeneous constraints. It includes middleware architecture, a message format and message types, and rule handling. We present the results of a case study in details to do demonstrate the feasibility of our approach. These are composed of three parts: First, we build a scenario based on an information exchange between wireless sensor networks in home environment so that it shows roles of a bridge, handling sensed events. Second, we define a process of information exchange using UML sequence diagram. Third, we represent soap messages which contain methods and data defined in advance. We confirm effectiveness of information exchange mechanism with extensibility and flexibility through the case study.

Keywords: Intelligent Bridge, Middleware, Heterogeneous Wireless Sensor Networks.

1 Introduction

Wireless sensor network is initiatively designed to detect events or phenomena, to collect and process data, and to transmit sensed information to interested users. According as home networks become a practical reality, wireless sensor network is applied to monitor and control environmental conditions at home. Needs of interoperability are getting increased since there have been some issues in heterogeneous wireless sensor networks such as information exchange, network protocol conversion, and integrity among multi-vendor products. The solution of these issues can be the most important part of the many competing standard researches in wireless sensor network [1][2].

We propose message-oriented middleware to make use of an intelligent bridge for information exchange in heterogeneous constraints. It includes middleware architecture, a message format and message types, and rule handling. The architecture

* This work was supported by the Soongsil University Research Fund.

E. Sha et al. (Eds.): EUC 2006, LNCS 4096, pp. 945 – 955, 2006.

makes an intelligent bridge through a home server in home networks, and the home server can help to exchange information among wireless sensor networks. The intelligent bridge carries out roles of a mediator between middlewares in heterogeneous wireless sensor networks. The rule handling is the most important function of the intelligent bridge which takes charge of possessing information, analyzing input data, searching rules, interpreting selected rule, and controlling statuses of all wireless sensor networks. A message format is composed of message type, destination identification, source identification, the sequence number of message, and contents. The message types are classified by six categories such as request, response, query, notify, control, and acknowledge. The message types are necessary when message elements are analyzed. We present the results of a case study in details to do demonstrate the feasibility of our approach. These are composed of three parts: (1) We build a scenario based on an information exchange between wireless sensor networks in home environment so that it shows the roles of a bridge which handles sensing events. (2) We define a process of information exchange using UML sequence diagram. (3) We represent soap messages which contain methods and data. We confirmed effectiveness of information exchange mechanism with extensibility and flexibility through the case study.

The rest of the paper is organized as follows: In Section 2, we discuss interoperable middleware architecture, including a message format and message types, and rule handling technique. In Section 3, we present the results of a feasibility study based on information exchange between heterogeneous wireless sensor networks. In Section 4, we describe related works with requirements on wireless sensor network middleware, the other bridge researches, and SOAP. Finally, in Section 5, we draw some conclusions and discuss research issues for future work.

2 Middleware Architecture with Interoperability

2.1 Middleware Architecture

Middleware provides a mechanism through which application specific code can be injected and triggered inside the network, allowing energy efficiency in data dissemination and increasing the wireless sensor network performance and time life. Middleware also enables the generation and communication of high level tasks, as well as the coordination of such tasks among nodes, even if the nodes have heterogeneous features. In order to suit to the wireless sensor network resource constraint and fault prone, this middleware is designed to be robust and fault tolerant, keeping the messages exchanged as short as possible.

The ultimate objective of our approach is to overcome communication problem related to heterogeneous configuration items such as different network protocol, different embedded operation system and different manufacturers. To solve them through the use of standard protocol in the middleware layer, we propose middleware architecture with interoperability between heterogeneous wireless sensor networks by a mechanism of information exchange. This architecture makes an intelligent bridge using a home server in home networks, and the home server can help to exchange information among wireless sensor networks. A home server generally integrates home appliances, and manages various services of network, security, and remote control in home networks. In our approach, a home server performs the role of an administrator to manage rules corresponding properly request and response messages that is passed from each sensor nodes, as well as the role of a gateway for information exchange.

The main internal components of middleware architecture are composed of the SOAP engine, a set of handlers, and user interface module. The SOAP engine acts as the main entry point into the SOAP module. It is responsible for coordinating the SOAP message's flow through the various handlers. Handlers are composed of a transport handler, a message build handler, a logic handler, and a rule handler. First, the transport handler carries out sending and receiving messages through networks. There are two main modules in the transport handler. One is Message Receiver (MR) which takes charge of analyzing request messages transmitted from sender and transferring a message to an actuator if it is necessary. The other is Message Sender (MS) which delivers events to a home server and responds to request messages. Second, the message build handler is building blocks inside the SOAP module. Third, the logic handler carries out processing functional logic. Finally, the rule handler exists only in a home server. It takes charge of possessing information about main roles and functions of each wireless sensor network, analyzing information that is transmitted and controlling wireless sensor networks according to rules.

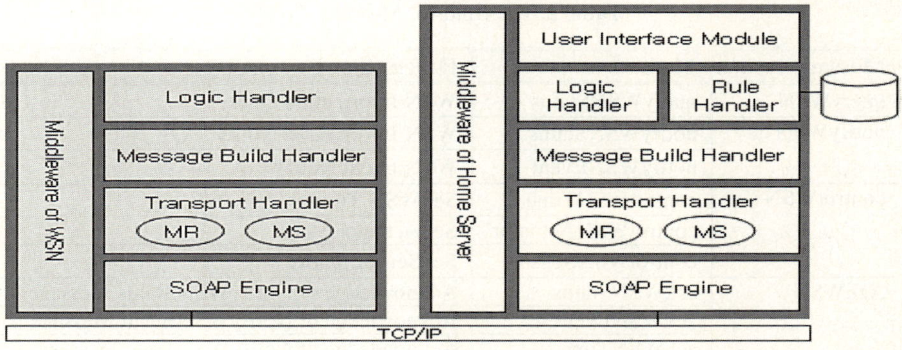

Fig. 1. Middleware Architecture

2.2 A Message Format and Message Types

Information exchange of middleware architecture is composed of three factors: a message format, a message style, and a message transmission protocol. The message format is a standard form of messages. Elements of the message format consist of message type, destination identification, source identification, the sequence number of a message, and contents to exchange information between middleware of the home server and middlewares of wireless sensor networks. The message style is a way which information is given, we use a XML document. It allows users to create their own customized tags, definition, transmission, validation, and interpretation of data between applications. Many documents and data have been expressed by XML because they easily and dynamically converted to another type documents. Therefore, XML is very suitable to express information in the network environment participated in various nodes. As the message transmission protocol, we use SOAP. SOAP is a lightweight XML-based messaging protocol to encode the information for request and response messages. There are a number of merits because SOAP is a text-based protocol using XML. First, it can be easily implemented. Second, Debugging is easy because of text forms that a person can read. Third, it can be used widely because compatibility is high. Hence, we can extend interoperable middleware architecture to web service using mobile equipment since the proposed architecture has adapted XML and SOAP with flexibility and extensity to exchange information.

Table 1. Elements of Message Format

Elements	Tags of Element	Description
Message type	<MessageType>	The type of a message
Destination ID	<To>	The target identification of a message
Source ID	<From>	The source identification of a message
No. of sequence	<MsgNo>	The sequence number of a message
Contents	<content>	The content of information exchange

Table 2. The Kinds of Message Type

Message type	Method	Description
queryWSN	queryWSNStatus	WSN Information Query
notifyWSN	notifyWSNStatus	WSN Information Notify
	notifyWSNEvent	WSN Event Notify
controlWSN	controlWSNTime	Set WSN Time
	controlWSNActuator	Set Actuator Status
	controlWSNSensor	Set Sensor Status
AckWSN	ackWSNStatus	Acknowledge of NotifyWSNStatus Message
	ackWSNEvent	Acknowledge of NotifyWSNEvent Message
	ackWSNTime	Acknowledge of NotifyWSNTime Message
RequestWSN	requestWSNxxx	Direct Message Delivery Request
ResponseWSN	responseWSNxxx	Direct Message Delivery Response

The message type is classified by six categories such as request, response, query, notify, control, and acknowledge. The message type is necessary when message elements are analyzed. Request and response message type are related to information exchange among middlewares in wireless sensor networks directly. Query and notify message type are related to information exchange between middleware in wireless sensor network and a home server. Especially, an event message is one of notify messages types. The objective of Control and acknowledge message type is to control statuses of wireless sensor network according to rules established in advance. We make a number of methods as the following table 2. The meaning of Content is different according to message types [3][4].

2.3 Rule Handling by an Intelligent Bridge

The intelligent bridge in a home server carries out the role of a mediator between middlewares in heterogeneous wireless sensor networks. The rule handler is the most important function of the intelligent bridge.

The rule handler takes charge of possessing information about main roles and functions of each wireless sensor networks. The information is used to make rules in rule repository. These rules are updated periodically. There are five main functions by the rule handler: (1) It analyzes input data which are sensed events from wireless sensor networks. (2) It searches rules corresponding with each event. (3) It carries out interpreting the selected rule. (4) It provides proper commands to middleware in wireless sensor network. (5) It also controls statuses of all wireless sensor networks to sustain home environment.

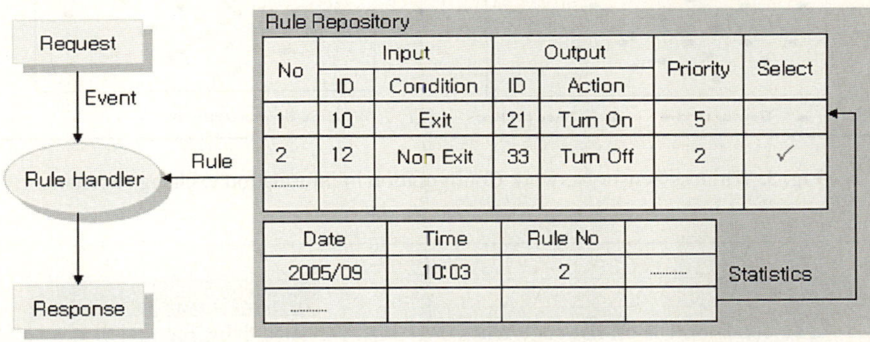

Fig. 2. A Process of the Rule Hander

3 A Case Study

3.1 A Scenario for Indoor Environment Control

We performed a case study based on an information exchange between wireless sensor networks with heterogeneous network protocol in order to demonstrate the feasibility of our approach. This section shows a scenario of information exchange which is an indoor environment monitoring with the following characteristics.

First, there are two wireless sensor networks. Each sensor network is formed by a group of sensor nodes that can monitor variables such as temperature and location-based context-aware. Wireless sensor network 1(WSN1) is responsible for monitoring location-based context-aware and wireless sensor network 2(WSN2) is responsible for monitoring temperature. WSN1 uses zigbee for a network protocol and WSN2 uses Bluetooth. Therefore, it isn't possible to communicate directly between WSN1 and WSN2. Second, all sensor nodes are grouped according to function of sending sensed events to own sink node. A base station accomplishes the role of a sink node, and it can afford to communicate with a home server by SOAP because of enough computing resources. Third, a home server was already installed to manage home network. The home server is a bridge between WSN1 and WSN2. It also can control two wireless sensor networks to integrate them. It manages all wireless sensor networks at home.

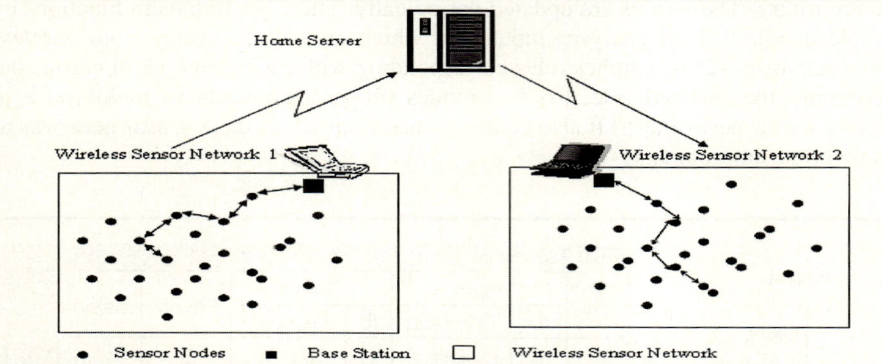

Fig. 3. Wireless Sensor Network Configuration in information exchange Scenario

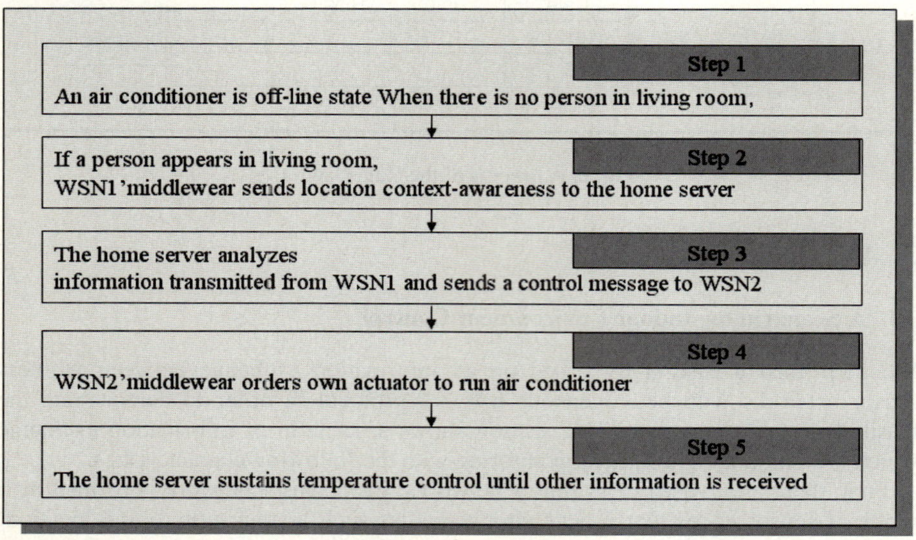

Fig. 4. The sequence and activities of A Scenario

In this environment, we execute a case study so that temperature can be controlled automatically when a person appears in living room. The sequences of scenario are as followings. At first, there are no people in the living room and an air conditioner is off-line state. After no long time, a person appears in the living room and middleware in WSN1 sends location context-awareness to the home server. The home server analyzes information transmitted from WSN1, and it sends a control message to middleware in WSN2 so that air conditioner is run because a person exists in the living room. Then, middleware in WSN2 orders own actuator to run air conditioner. The home server sustains continuously temperature control until other information is received.

3.2 A Process of Information Exchange

This section shows a process of information exchange using UML sequence diagram with objects and methods. We divide a process to three cases such as notify status, notify event, and request delivery to present effectively whole process.

Information exchange is begun from that middleware in WSN1 and middleware in WSN2 send own information to the home server. Hence, a MsgSender object of middleware in WSN1 uses firstly a notifyWSNStatus method to send own information to the home server. At this time, the home server updates information of each wireless sensor network in a repository. The information is statuses and these are utilized for a rule handler to control wireless sensor networks.

Next, a sensor node sends the event to a related sink node (is the same of a base station) by defined routing mechanism when a sensor node in WSN1 is sensing the event that someone is in the living room. At this time, the MsgSender object of middleware in WSN1uses a notifyWSNEvent method to send the event to the home server. It also receives an acknowledgment from the home server. After the location context awareness event is arrived from middleware in WSN1, the home server searches rules related to the event message in the repository and makes a decision tocontrol wireless sensor network. These functions are accomplished by a RuleManager object of middleware in the home server. The MsgSender object and the

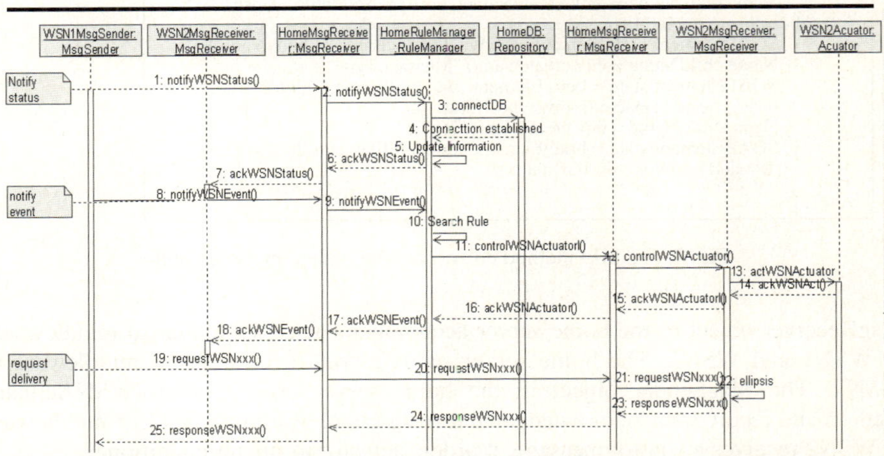

Fig. 5. A Process of information exchange in UML Sequence Diagram

```
<?xml version="1.0" encoding="UTF-8"?>
< SOAP-ENV:Envelope
  xmlns:soapenv="http://schemas.xmlsoap.org/soap/envelope/"
  xmlns:xsd="http://www.w3.org/2001/XMLSchema"
  xmlns:xsi="http://www.w3.org/2001/XMLSchema-instance">
  < SOAP-ENV:Body>
    <msg:queryWSNStatus xmlns:nsg="http://hocalhost/simple">
                <MessageType>queryWSN</MessageType>
       <To> wsn2</To>
       <From> home server</From>
       <No>1024</No>
       <Content></Content>
    </msg:queryWSNStatus>
  </ SOAP-ENV:Body>
```

Method

Data

Fig. 6. A SOAP message for server query about information in WSN2

```
    public void queryWSNStatus(SOAPEnvelope env, String stMsgType, String
stDest, String stSrc, String stMsgNo, String stContent) throws
javax.xml.soap.SOAPException    {
          StatusImpl statusImpl = new StatusImpl();
          StatusBean statusBean = null;
          String msgtypeOfStatus = null;
          String destOfStatus = null;
          String srcOfstatus = null;
          String noOfstatus = null;
          String contenOfstatus = null;
          try
          {  msgtypeOfStatus = statusImpl.getStatusInfo();
             msgtypeOfStatus = statusBean.getMsgType();
             destOfStatus = statusBean.getDest();
             srcOfStatus = statusBean.getSrc();
             noOfStatus = statusBean.getNo();
             contenOfStatus = statusBean.getContent();          }
          catch (Exception e)         {
             msgtypeOfStatus = e.toString();        }
          SOAPBody body = env.getBody();
          Name bodyName =  env.createName("notifyWSNStatus", "msg", "
http://hocalhost/simple ");
          SOAPElement bodyElement = body.addBodyElement(bodyName);
          Name childName = env.createName("MessageType");
          SOAPElement state = bodyElement.addChildElement(childName);
          msgType.addTextNode(msgtypeOfStatus);
          Name childName = env.createName("To");
          SOAPElement state = bodyElement.addChildElement(childName);
          dest.addTextNode(destOfStatus);
    .......
```

Fig. 7. A notify method corresponding with a query method

MsgReceiver object in the home server accomplish each role similar to middlewares in WSN1 and WSN2. The home server sends a control message to middleware in WSN2. The MsgSender object in the home server uses a controlWSNActuator method and receives an acknowledgement from middleware in WSN2. If middleware in WSN2 receives a control message, it orders actuator to run air conditioner.

Finally, a request delivery process is carried out in case that middleware in WSN1 wants to send directly to middleware in WSN2. In such case, the rule handler doesn't interfere in the message delivery control between wireless sensor networks. It only helps to bypass the message.

3.3 SOAP Messages

This section shows an example of SOAP message for information query. The SOAP message contains envelope, body, and header element. Methods and data of a message which we have already defined, are in the body part. Figure 6 represents a queryWSNStatus method that is used when the home server sends a query to update information of middleware in the repository. Figure 7 represents a notifyWSNStatus method that is used to response for a query message.

4 Related Works

Requirements on Wireless Sensor Network Middleware. Middleware in wireless sensor network should support all sorts of services that need in various application system development based on heterogeneous sensor nodes, maintenance, installation, and accomplishment. In order to support these purposes, middleware should provide a lot of functions which make suitable information for high level application by mixing sensing data, conduct data fusion, transfer them, and finally report data to user. Middleware should also accommodate needs of sensor network with efficient utilization of limited energy, network steadiness, and network extensibility [5][6]. We concentrated on abstraction of sensor node's heterogeneity among various roles of wireless sensor network. We build a bridge as a mediator in our architecture and integrate these middlewares.

Researches Related to Bridge Technique. Researches related to bridge techniques have started in home networks. Existing home applications are based on a large number of different APIs that are often proprietary, incompatible, and normally just address subsets of the devices that exist in a home. This leads to a demand for a general API giving standardized access to all home devices independent of the network type used. Open Service Gateway Initiative(OSGi) [7] specifications define a standardized, component oriented, computing environment for networked services. Adding an OSGi Service Platform to a networked device, enables the capability to manage the life cycle of the software components in the device from anywhere in the network. TinyLime[8] presented bridging the gap between the applications and the hardware. TinyLime uses middleware as solution. TinyLime must be specialized to the qualities of sensor networks, especially energy consumption. TinyLime presents both the model and the implementation of middleware incorporated with the Crossbow Mote sensor platform. FMS[9] proposed a service-based middleware system as comprising of heterogeneous devices assisting to a large range of applications. FMS addresses the specific requirements of wireless sensor network and FMS is based on the concept of services. Services are defined as the data provided by the sensor nodes and the applications to be executed on data. Our approach is motivated by the fact that current works on wireless sensor network don't consider such a technology in the design of heterogeneous wireless sensor network despite of the advantages related to information exchange. We propose an interoperability layer of middleware for heterogeneous wireless sensor networks. It can be more extensible by an intelligent bridge. It is also generic and flexible, providing the basic functional message required for any wireless sensor network.

SOAP, a Lightweight XML-Based Messaging Protocol. Simple Object Access Protocol is a lightweight XML-based messaging protocol used to encode the information in Web Service request and response messages before sending them over a network. The SOAP protocol extends XML so that computer programs can easily pass parameters to server applications and then receive and understand the returned semi-structured XML data document [10]. The SOAP protocol is responsible for defining exchanging rules and messages format in our architecture. The SOAP module in our architecture is composed of two main components: the SOAP engine and a set of handles. The SOAP engine acts as the main entry point into the SOAP module. It is responsible for coordinate the SOAP message's flow through the various handles. Handles are the basic building blocks inside the SOAP module and they represent the messages processing logic.

5 Conclusion and Future Works

We propose message-oriented middleware to make use of an intelligent bridge for information exchange in heterogeneous wireless sensor network. We present the results of a case study in details to do demonstrate the feasibility of our approach. Our approach offered two contributions to the study of information exchange in heterogeneous constraints. First, we described a rule management technique with interoperability in an intelligent bridge. Second, we defined general message exchange mechanism. We confirmed effectiveness of information exchange mechanism with extensibility and flexibility through the case study. Hence, it can be possible to extend home environment to ubiquitous environment as any control server carries out the same role of the home server.

We are working on identifying general message types and methods in details. We will make lots of efforts to extend this architecture to mobile equipments. We will also add QOS management into interoperable middleware architecture as described in this paper. We hope that the future works' results prove the total energy spent in transmission and processing do not overcome the values found in current wireless sensor network.

References

[1] Ilyas, M., Mahgoub, I.,: Handbook of Sensor Networks:Compact Wireless and Wired Sensing Systems. CRC Press (2005)

[2] Hac, A.: Wireless Sensor Network Designs. Jon Wiley & sons (2003)

[3] Lee, T., Jeong, C.: Service-Oriented Home Network Middleware Based on OGSA. Lecture Notes in Computer Science, Vol. 3480 (2005), 601–608

[4] Park, J.: The technique of interoperable middleware between electronic appliances. TTA journal (2004)

[5] R¨omer, K., Kasten, O., Mattern, F.: Issues in Designing Middleware for Wireless Sensor Networks.IEEE Network (2004)

[6] R¨omer, K., Kasten, O., Mattern, F.: Middleware Challenges for Wireless Sensor Networks. ACM Mobile Computing and Communications Review, Vol. 6 (2002)

[7] http://www.osgi.org/osgi_technology

[8] Curino, C., Giani, M., Giorgetta, M., Giusti, A.: TinyLIME: Bridging Mobile and Sensor Networks through Middleware. The 3rd IEEE International Conference on Pervasive Computing and Communications (2005)

[9] Delicato, F.: A Flexible Middleware System for Wireless Sensor Networks. IFIP International Federation for Information Processing (2003)

[10] Monson, R.: J2EE Web Service. Addison Wesley (2003)

A Proxy-Enabled Service Discovery Architecture to Find Proximity-Based Services in 6LoWPAN

Shafique Ahmad Chaudhry, Won Do Jung, Chaudhary Sajjad Hussain, Ali Hammad Akbar, and Ki-Hyung Kim*

Graduate School of Information and Communication
Ajou University, Suwon, Korea
{shafique, yarang, sajjad, hammad, kkim86}@ajou.ac.kr

Abstract. Recent advances in wireless communication and sensor and actuator technologies have played an essential role to realize the envisioned ubiquitous world. Wireless sensor networks (WSNs) have emerged as a great catalyst for morphing personal area networks (PANs) into low power personal area networks (LoWPANs) which itself is a channel to achieve higher degrees of ubiquity and pervasiveness. These LoWPANs need to be connected with other wireless and wired networks in order to maximize the utilization of information and other resources which are mainly associated with the IP networks. Interworking of LoWPANs with IP networks brings in many challenges for service discovery and network selection. A great problem in this scenario is to find and use services in the closest proximity of the user. In this paper we propose novel service discovery architecture and algorithms that help proximity based service discovery and network selection within an IP network and LoWPAN interworked environment. The results show that our architecture helps finding and using the closest services from inside as well as outside the LoWPAN. It also reduces the traffic overhead for service discovery considerably as compared to other protocols.

1 Introduction

Low power wireless personal area networks (LoWPANs) conform to the IEEE 802.15.4-2003 standard [1]. The IEEE 802.15.4 devices are characterized by low power, low bandwidth, short range, and low cost. While IEEE 802.15.4 provides specifications for physical and link layers, other alliances like ZigBee [2] are striving for defining the upper layers over IEEE 802.15.4. The 6LoWPAN [3], a working group of the Internet Engineering Task Force (IETF) [4], standardizes the use of IPv6 over IEEE 802.15.4. The internet draft [5] describes the overview of 6LoWPAN. It portrays the problems, assumptions and the goals for transmitting IPv6 over IEEE 802.15.4 networks. A frame format for IPv6 transmission over IEEE 802.15.4 networks is presented in [6].

* Corresponding author.

E. Sha et al. (Eds.): EUC 2006, LNCS 4096, pp. 956 – 965, 2006.

6LoWPANs need to be connected with each other and with other wired networks in order to maximize the utilization of information and other resources which are mainly associated with IP networks. This integration will help realizing ubiquity by allow users to access the services across LoWPANs and IP networks. Interworking of 6LoWPANs with IP networks brings in many challenges for service discovery and network selection. In an environment where IEEE 802.15.4 networks, which generally have a large number of lower power nodes, will help rendering numerous services across the 6LoWPAN and IP networks, the manual configuration for each service is a burdensome rather an impractical solution. In a ubiquitous and pervasive environment, a service must be searched and configured autonomously with the least user intervention. To provide such a self-configuration environment in 6LoWPANs an intuitive service discovery and selection mechanism is needed.

Both the technologies have drastically big differences in terms of devices' processing power, memory resources and data rate etc, therefore, there are several issues to be resolved to apply the IP based service discovery schemes to IEEE 802.15.4 networks. The limited packet size of 6LoWPANs is one of them; given that in the worst case the maximum size available for transmitting the IP packets over the IEEE 802.15.4 frame is 81 octets, and that the IPv6 header is 40 octets, (without optional headers), this leaves only 41 octets for the upper-layer protocols, like UDP and TCP. UDP uses 8 octets in the header, thereby leaving 33 octets for data, like service discovery mechanism, over UDP. An IP based service discovery mechanism, like simple service discovery (SLP) [7], message could easily be greater than these remaining octets, and it should be transmitted as multiple packets, causing traffic overheads to 6LoWPAN. These limitations require a light-weight service discovery protocol to discover, control, and maintain services provided by devices in 6LoWPAN.

In a 6LoWPAN environment it is better, in most situations, to find and use the nearest service as similar services may be scattered throughout the network. Finding and utilizing the nearest service is not supported by existing service discovery protocols. While using SLP or Simple Service Location Protocol (SSLP) [8] a user may get the list of available services (and their IP addresses) and can communicate with them. The IP address does not mention anything about the physical location. Two consecutive IP addresses in the network may be physically far away from each other. Summing up, an IP address provides no information about the closest service with respect to the user. The proximity of the service is an essential attribute and it must be integral part of service discovery mechanism.

In this paper we present a service discovery architecture that is based on directory proxy agent (DPA) that acts as a proxy to the directory agent (DA) in SSLP. We exploit on the fact that the IEEE 802.15.4 devices are inexpensive and put multiple DPAs within a 6LoWPAN. These DPAs are responsible to maintain and provide proximity-based service information within the 6LoWPAN. The users and service nodes are connected to the nearest DPA that help users find closest services. The connectivity between 6LoWPAN and IPv6 makes the users to find and use local LoWPAN services as well as the services available in external IP networks. Our simulation results show that proposed architecture not only helps finding and using the closest services in inter-network environment but also considerably reduces the traffic overhead, as compared to other protocols, for service discovery.

The rest of the paper is as follows. In Section 2, we review existing service discovery protocols and related work with an emphasis on 6LoWPANs. Different service discovery scenarios for 6LoWPAN have been conversed in Section 3. We describe our proposed service discovery architecture in Section 4. In Section 5 we present performance and evaluation of our scheme and section 6 concludes the paper.

2 Related Work

There are many proven approaches and technologies for IP networks but the service discovery in 6LoWPANs is in its infancy. In this section, firstly, we shall describe the service discovery mechanisms for IP networks and their limitations for 6LoWPAN. Secondly, we shall mention the available service discovery mechanisms for 6LoWPAN.

Jini [9], a product of Sun Microsystems, is an extension of the Java programming language. Jini allows platform independence through Java Virtual Machine environment. This feature limits Jini's applicability in smart environments, which are characterized by heterogeneous device capabilities; and lack of support for Java technology. Universal Plug and Play (UPnP) [10] uses simple Service Discovery Protocol SSDP [11] and extends Microsoft's Plug and Play® technology to the scenarios where devices are reachable through a TCP/IP network. There is a technological conflict between the address-centric nature of UPnP and address-agnostic feature of smart spaces. A framework that mitigates such a limitation of UPnP is still awaited. Bluetooth [12], a joint effort of Microsoft and Intel, is also poised for discovery, but does not elaborate device or service accessibility and usage procedures. The SLP supports a framework by which client applications are modeled as User Agents (UA) and services are advertised by Service Agents (SA). A third entity, called a Directory Agent (DA) provides scalability to the protocol by providing directory services for the network. The UA issues a service request on behalf of the client application, specifying the characteristics of the service which the client requires. The UA receives a service reply from DA specifying the available services in the network which satisfy the request. SLP is used in IP networks for access to information about the existence, location, and configuration of networked services. SLP is well operating in IP networks, but it cannot be applied directly to 6LoWPAN because of the limited resources at 6LoWPAN. The modifications for SLP, to be used over IPv6, have been presented in [13]. This standard describes the use of SLPv2 over IPv6. But there is no provision for use of SLP over LoWPANs.

After describing all these works, we state that currently there is no considerable service discovery architecture for 6LoWPANs except SSLP. SSLP supports the same framework as SLP, i.e., based on UAs and SAs. The DA functions as a database of the services. Besides, SSLP introduces Translation Agent (TA) which performs the translation of messages for the interoperability with SLPv2. The TA must work on a machine, called a gateway, which reaches both an IP network and a 6LoWPAN. When a TA receives either an SLP message from an IP network or an SSLP message from a 6LoWPAN, it performs the translation operation to make the messages recognizable to the agents in the other network. This operation is essential for SSLP to be interoperable with SLP and vice versa. With the help of the TA, a UA can

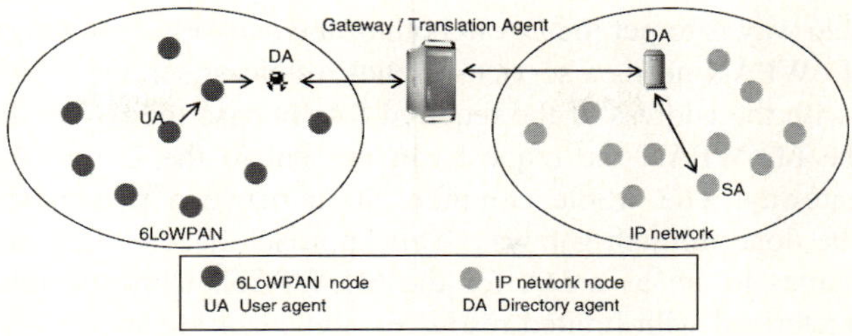

Fig. 1. Integrating 6LWPAN with IP networks

discover and control services in 6LoWPAN regardless of whether they are located inside the 6LoWPAN or outside. The figure 1 depicts a scenario where a 6LoWPAN is connected to an external IP network through a gateway. Both the networks have their DAs which communicate using the TA.

3 Service Discovery Scenarios for 6LoWPANs

In this section we shall describe the possible scenarios for service discovery and network selection for a UA in a 6LoWPAN, while integrating the LoWPANs and IPv6 networks. We assume 6LoWPAN supports SSLP for service discovery whereas IP network supports SLPv2.

First, we consider that both the networks are working without DAs. A UA, in 6LoWPAN, that wants to use a service, will broadcast a service request *SREQ* within its local network to find the service. In case the service is available in the local network the respective SA will reply with an *SREP* to the UA. If the service is not available within the local network, service request may be forwarded to other network through gateway after translating the message from SSLP to SLPv2. The service request will be broadcasted in the IP network and if the required service is available, respective SA will respond to the UA, using the TA. As the whole mechanism is based on broadcast, huge amount of traffic is generated that puts heavy overhead on the network. This overhead is definitely not tolerable in 6LoWPANs, which already have very limited data rates.

Second, only one of the 6LoWPAN and IP network has a DA. When there is a DA in IP Network, and not in 6LoWPAN, the UA broadcasts the *SREQ* and gets a *SREP* from the SA if the service is available within the local network. Otherwise, the request is sent to the DA in IP network through the gateway. The service discovery process within 6LoWPAN still has a broadcast and must be mitigated. In case, only 6LoWPAN has a DA, the situation becomes cumbersome. If a UA from 6LoWPAN needs to discover a service it will send a unicast *SREQ* to the DA, which will reply with the address for the service, if the required service is available within 6LoWPAN. In case the service is not available, the service request can be sent to the IP network, directly by the UA or by the DA, through gateway. This request will then be broadcast though IP network to find the service. The SA in the IP network needs to send the reply to the UA in 6LoWPAN and it's a bit complex. This situation is quite complex as there is no direct route setup between the UA and SA which are in different networks and an overhead of going through gateway is always involved.

Third possible way is to put the DA in both of the networks. In such case whenever a UA in the 6LoWPAN needs a service it sends a unicast service request to the DA, which replies with the address of the required SA. In case the required service is not available in the 6LoWPAN the request can be sent to the DA in the IP network through the gateway. The whole communication between two nodes in different networks can be done through gateway. This approach needs a dedicated node with sufficient resources to act as a DA for the 6LoWPAN. Unfortunately, 6LoWPAN nodes are characterized with limited resources, thus, lack the capability to work as a dedicated DA.

As we have discussed all the apparent scenarios with certain advantages and disadvantages, we insist there is a need of a better architecture for service discovery and selection in 6LoWPANs. There is a need for an architecture that can work as a trade-off between flooding and putting dedicated DAs within a 6LoWPAN.

We propose an architecture that mitigates the traffic overhead for service discovery and network selection and at the same time eliminates the need of a dedicated DA within 6LoWPAN. We introduce Directory Proxy Agent (DPA) to be deployed in 6LoWPAN rather than placing a DA. As the name suggests, DPA is a node working as a proxy for the DA. It gets services information, from DA and peer DPAs, and caches it to use in the local PAN. Exchange of directory information between DPAs in respective networks makes the approach proactive.

We exploit the fact that 6LoWPAN nodes are inexpensive: we suggest putting multiple DPAs, each responsible for a certain area, within a 6LoWPAN. These DPAs cache the information for the services within 6LoWPAN as well as the services within the IP networks accessible through gateway. These DPAs are connected with each other in a hierarchical manner. This approach reduces the traffic overhead for the whole system and does not require dedicated nodes for the role of local DA as the role of DPA can be rotated among the nodes.

4 Detailed Architecture

Before we discuss the detailed architecture, consider a scenario for a building with multiple floors, with many rooms at each floor. There are many available services that are distributed within the building. The whole building can be considered as a big network. We distribute multiple DPAs within the building; putting one DPA in a certain area, e.g. in each room. Each DPA acts, within its limited proximity, as a proxy for the DA. As mentioned before, it is feasible to have many DPAs within a network. Each DPA gets the services information from the DA and maintains a cache in order to provide directory service to the nodes within its proximity. Each DPA periodically advertises itself and the SAs within this DPA's proximity register their services with it. These DPAs could be arranged in a hierarchical way i.e. they can communicate with their peer DPAs as well as central DAs which might be the part of external IP network. The architecture is depicted in figure 2.

Our architecture is independent of the underlying routing algorithms and can be implemented on any routing algorithm with minimal changes. We have evaluated its performance with AODV, however, we believe that availability of a hierarchical routing mechanism e.g. HiLoW [15] as underlying routing algorithm, will further improve its performance. The major strength of using HiLoW is that if 16-bit address of the service or destination node is known, it can be reached without using a routing table. Once a UA knows the 16-bit address of the DPA or SA, it can start communicating with that, without finding a route to the DPA or SA.

DPAs share their caching information with each other periodically. This sharing of information allows knowing about the services registered wit the neighbor DPAs. This periodic sharing of information reduces flooding which, otherwise, will be required to find services from the neighboring networks. The connectivity of a DPA with the DA of IP network through the gateway facilitates to find services from IP networks. DPAs may exchange the services information with central DA as well, in order to maintain the information consistency.

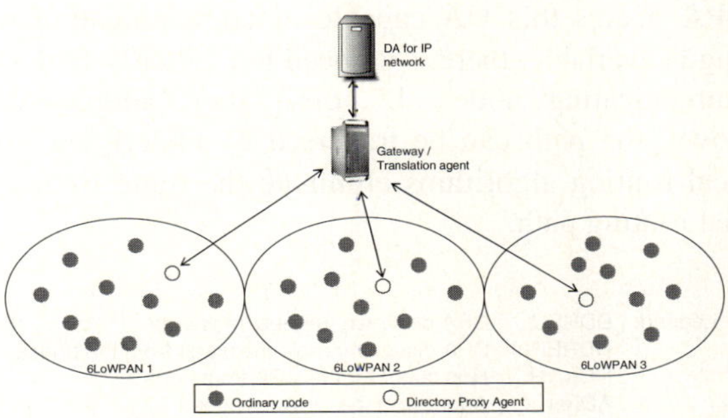

Fig. 2. Scenario for proposed architecture

4.1 Proximating the Services

To access the closest services we make it essential that a UA is connected to the nearest DPA. This condition is required to ensure that the service request is sent to the closest DPA, which then replies with the nearest service's information. To realize this condition we propose neighbor assisted DPA discovery protocol that uses the following messages.

- *DDREQ*: The request message is used to ask the neighbors about their respective DPAs. Initiated as a one hop-broadcast by the UA that needs to find the closest DPA.
- *DDREP*: This is the reply message in response to a ***DDREQ*.** It contains the address of the DPA as well as distance to the DPA in terms of hop count.

The protocol works as follows. Whenever a UA needs to send a request to DPA, it checks with its single hop neighbors, by broadcasting *DDREQ* in one hop, the closest DPA in terms of hop count. The neighbors reply with *DDREP* that contains the address of closest DPA and distance to it in hop count. The nearest DPA, in terms of hop count, is considered as the closest DPA. Once the address of DPA is known, hierarchical routing makes it possible to send unicast messages between the UA and the DPA. Whenever a UA needs a service, it sends a unicast *SREQ* to the DPA. If the required service is registered with DPA, DPA responds with an *SREP*. UA then starts communicating with SA to use the service. Neighbor assisted DPA discovery algorithm helps in handling mobility of the UA as well. This protocol makes sure that the UA stays connected with the existing DPA as long as it is the nearest one, even when UA is moving. Figure 3 illustrates the algorithm.

Whenever a node wants to join a 6LoWPAN, it first tries to discover an existing 6LoWPAN. IEEE 802.15.4 specifies active and passive scanning procedures for this discovery operation. By following either one of the scanning procedures, the new device determines whether there is a 6LoWPAN in its personal operating space. Once a PAN is found, next step is to connect with the DPA. After getting the address of the DPA, the UA must find a route to DPA if an on-demand routing algorithm like AODV is being used. In case a hierarchical routing algorithm being used, knowing the address of DPA makes this UA capable of communicating with DPA. As the hierarchical routing is available, there is no need to explicitly find and maintain routes between the communicating nodes. If 16-bit short address of a node within 6LoWPAN is known, the path can be traversed by underlying routing mechanism. Though hierarchical routing algorithms eliminate the route finding process, they do not provide optimal routing path.

```
Legend: DDREQ      : DPA discovery request message
        DDREP(i)   : DPA discovery reply message from the node i
        HC(i, di)  : Hop count for the DPA from node i
        AD(di)     : Address of the DPA for node i

begin procedure
    broadcast DDREQ message in one hop
    closest ← -1
    dp ← -1
    for each neighbor node i
        on receiving DDREP (i)
        if (HC (i, di) < closest) then
            closest ← HC (i, di)
            dp ← AD(di)
        end if
    next
end procedure
```

Fig. 3. Neighbor assisted discovery protocol

5 Performance Evaluation

We have implemented our routing protocol in network simulator-2 [NS-2] by modifying the AODV implementation. We have used AODV to evaluate our architecture. Table 1 shows the list and values of parameters for the simulation setup. The results show that our architecture improves the service discovery time, mitigates the broadcasting overhead, saving the nodes' energy.

Table 1. List of simulation parameters

Parameter	Measurements
Area	380 * 60 Meters
Number of nodes	3hop 15 nodes 30hop 150 nodes
Total time of simulation	100s
Node's transmission range	15m
Protocol	AODV
Traffic type	CBR
Inter-packet transmission delay	0.05 ~ 0.5s
Node transmission power	0.28J

We evaluated our architecture's working under different scenarios by varying the DPA's advertisement interval, which is the time between two consecutive advertisement broadcasts by the DPA. In the same way nodes try to discover a service after certain time, we call it service discovery interval. Originally AODV does not provide a service discovery mechanism but we have used it to find a specific node that may host an SA.

5.1 Number of Generated Control Packets

We define control packets as sum of total number of route request (*RREQ*), route reply (*RREP*) and route error (*RERR*) messages. We varied the service discovery interval to examine its effect on control traffic. The results show that AODV generated more control traffic as compared to our architecture. As depicted in Figure 4, increase in service discovery interval increases then number of control packets in case of AODV. This is mainly because of the fact that when service discovery interval is increased, the existing routing table entries for the SAs remain no more valid. This causes new routes to be discovered and during the process considerable control traffic is generated.

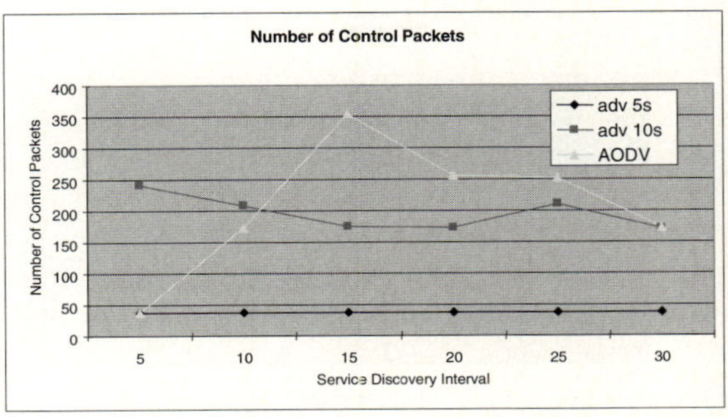

Fig. 4. Number of control packets

5.2 Service Discovery Time

We define service discovery as the time interval from making SREQ to sending first data packet in order to invoke the service. It includes the time to receive a SREP from DPA and finding a route to the SA. Figure 5 shows the service discovery time for our protocol when used with AODV. The difference between service discovery times is significant because our architecture is working as an overlay on AODV.

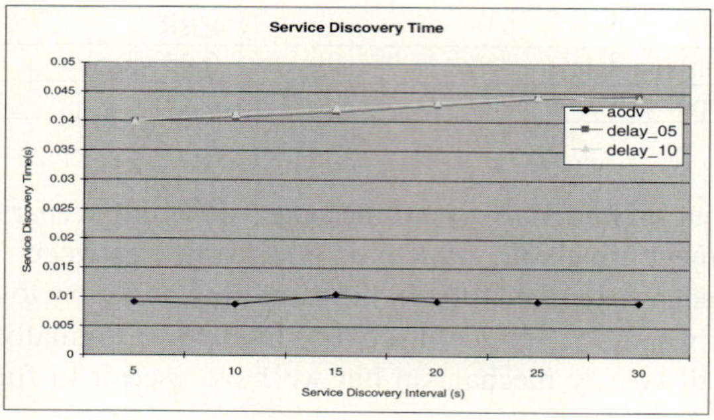

Fig. 5. Service discovery time

5.3 Energy Consumption

We have also analyzed the energy consumption of the nodes and the Figure 6 shows the results. All the nodes started with similar energy levels and we checked the remaining energy at the end of the simulation time. For this analysis, we examined the energy level with DPA advertisement interval being 5 seconds and 10 seconds. For this simulation the service discovery interval is 15 seconds. The results show that AODV causes more energy consumption as compared to DPA-based architecture. This fact can be explained with the fact that AODV generated more control traffic.

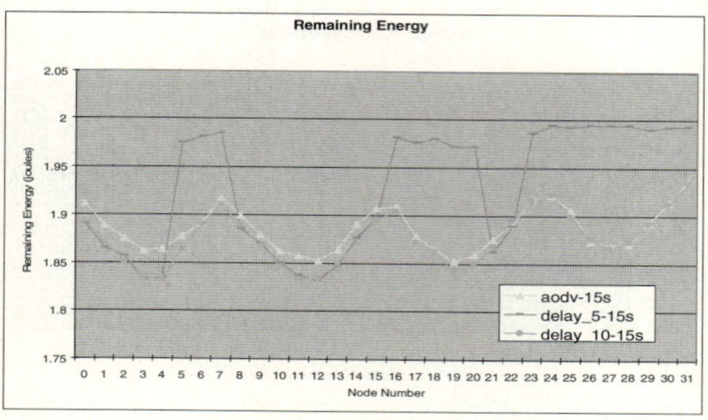

Fig. 6. Remaining node energy

6 Conclusion

With the rapid emergence of LoWPANs, it is needed to interwork them with other LoWPANs and with IP network. This integration requires robust and novel architectures for efficient service discovery that can find the services within the close proximity of the user. Existing architectures either don't provide such information or cannot be applied directly to 6LoWPANs. We propose service discovery architecture, based on Directory Proxy Agent (DPA). Our architecture not only finds inter-network services in closest proximity but also relaxes the need of a dedicated DA for LoWPAN. The results show that our architecture reduces the traffic overhead for service discovery considerably, helps finding and using the closest service, and enables users to discover and use inter-networks services.

References

1. IEEE LoWPAN Standard 802.15.4.
2. ZigBee Alliance, http://www.zigbee.org
3. IPv6 over Low Power WPAN Working Group, http://www.ietf.org/html-.charters/6lowpan-charter.html
4. Internet Engineering Task Force, http://www.ietf.org/
5. Kushalnagar, N., Montenegro, G.: 6LoWPAN: Overview, assumptions, Problem Statement and Goals. draft-ietf-6lowpan-problem-02 (2006)
6. Montenegro, G., Kushalnagar, N.: Transmission of IPv6 Packets over IEEE 802.15.4 Networks, draft-ietf-6lowpan-format-02 (2006)
7. Guttman, E., Perkins, C., Veizades, J., Day, M.: SLPv2: Service Location Protocol Version 2, RFC 2608 (1999)
8. Kim, K., Yoo, S., Kim, H., Park, S.D., Lee J.: Simple Service location Protocol for LoWPAN, draft-daniel-6lowpan-sslp-00 (2005)
9. http://www.jini.org/
10. Universal Plug and Play, http://www.upnp.org/
11. Yaron, Y., Goland, T.C., Paul, L., Ye, G., Shivaun A.: Simple Service Discovery Protocol, draft-cai-ssdp-v1-03 (1999)
12. http://www.bluetooth.com
13. Guttman, E.: Service Location Protocol Modifications for IPv6, RFC 3111 (2001)
14. Kim, K., Yoo, S., Park, J., Park, S.D., Lee, J.: Hierarchical Routing over 6LoWPAN, draft-daniel-6lowpan-hilow-hierarchical-routing-00 (2005)

PosCFS: An Advanced File Management Technique for the Wearable Computing Environment

Woojoong Lee, Shine Kim, Jonghwa Shin, and Chanik Park

Department of CSE/GSIT Pohang University of Science and Technology,
San 31 Hyoja-dong Pohang, Kyungbuk, Korea
{wjlee, postshin, shinjh00, cipark}@postech.ac.kr
http://sslab.postech.ac.kr

Abstract. In the ubiquitous computing environment, wearable computers are becoming more and more important because they provide an interface between human and computers. However, there are many challenges that come from its distributed, dynamic, heterogeneous computing environment. Most of all, an wearable computer has limited I/O devices for user interface. Thus, there are many context-aware applications to provide convenience for users. But each application should suffer from finding corresponding data. So, it is very important to support context-awareness in a file service for these applications through maintaining user's activities and metadata derived from them.

In this paper, we present a context-aware file service suitable for the wearable computing environment to provide a convenient data sharing service among devices and users. To realize our work, we present an ontology based file metadata management scheme for context awareness.

Finally, we implement the early prototype by using the UPnP [7] and WebDAV [8] technologies and define source ontology by OWL [9] and are still refining the system design. We believe that this work could be a predominant reference for a new generation of file management technology in the ubiquitous computing environment.

1 Introduction

In the ubiquitous computing environment, various devices are connected through a heterogeneous network and communicate with each other constantly. Therefore, an wearable computer as an interface between human and computers is becoming more and more important in the environment. Through the interface, users can collect and exchange information. However, due to the dynamic, distributed and heterogeneous computing environment, such an information network is difficult to construct.

Currently, we have various distributed file systems such as NFS [12], AFS [13], CODA [14] and Microsoft DFS [15], but they are not suitable because they work by a static mount mechanism and depend on a specific platform. Additionally, another critical problem is that wearable computers have limited I/O devices.

E. Sha et al. (Eds.): EUC 2006, LNCS 4096, pp. 966–975, 2006.

This affects user's ability to browse data. To provide a convenient data browsing and managing method for the user, it is very useful to support context-awareness on a file service layer.

In this paper, we present a novel distributed file service which is not only platform independent but also applicable to an ad-hoc network environment. We also present an ontology-based file metadata management scheme for context-awareness support on a file service layer. Then, we and apply them to the file service.

We summarize details of the characteristics of our file service below.

- **Heterogeneous network and platform support:** In the wearable computing environment, not only are there diverse gadgets running on specific operating systems such as Linux, MS Windows, Palm OS and so on, but also networks based on specific network protocols such as Bluetooth, IEEE 802.11b and so on.
- **Network Plug-and-Play support:** In order to provide convenient file access for users of wearable computers, a network plug-and-play and self-configuration mechanism must be supported.
- **Mobility support:** Mobility support must be provided by the file service because users wander move constantly.
- **Context-awareness support:** As we mentioned above, an wearable computer has limited I/O devices for user interface. Thus, there are many context-aware applications to provide convenience for users. But each application should suffer from finding corresponding data. So, it is very important to support context-awareness in a file service for these applications through maintaining user's activities and metadata derived from them.

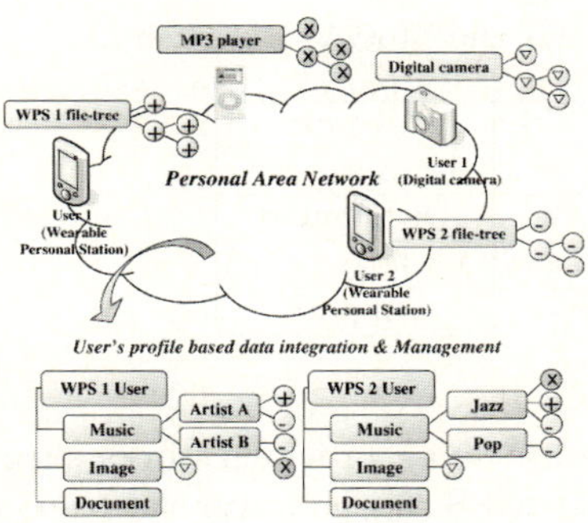

Fig. 1. Integrated data management in PAN

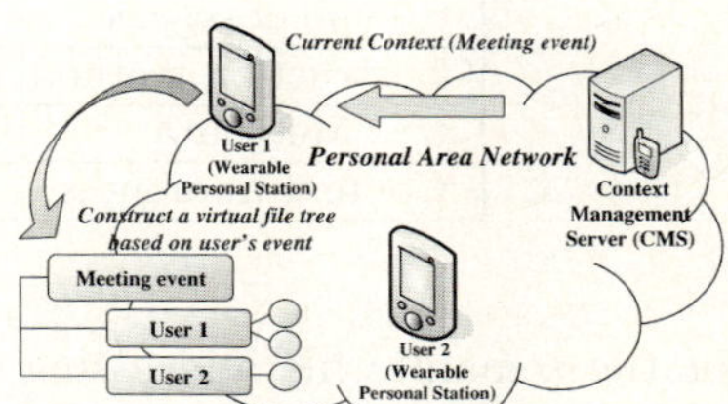

Fig. 2. File browsing based on user's event

In this paper, we present two use case scenarios to show how our file service works. The first scenario shows a feature of an integrated data management based on a user's profile. In this scenario, a user can manage his data in PAN with his profile. For example, if the user wants to browse his music files by a categorizing rule, 'genre-artist-album', our file service will provide a virtual file tree by the manner. See Figure 1.

The second scenario shows a case of context-aware file browsing. In this scenario, our file service provides a virtual file tree based on user's events such as a project meeting. See Figure 2.

The rest of this paper is constructed as follows. Works related to our research are described in Section 2. The key issues for context-awareness support are clarified and our proposed file service is introduced in Section 3. We describe the details of the service in Section 4. Finally, in Section 5, we present our concluding comments and describe future works.

2 Related Works

In this section, we describe the state of the art of context-aware data management technologies. The GAIA's context-aware file system [1] proposed by the System Software Research Group at university of Illinois was the first approach which tried to adapt a context-aware concept to a file system. It not only provided a novel concept as a well-defined middleware component but also was applicable to diverse computing environments. However, it is not suitable to the wearable computing environment because of its centralized construction mechanism and lack of representations for describing file metadata. The MoGATU system [2] proposed by UMBC provides an intelligent data service. (i.e. no file I/O interface) It keeps track of a user's situation and gathers information corresponding to the situation. Finally, the information is provided for the user according to his preference. We summarize details of the characteristics of these systems below.

Table 1. Characteristics of GAIA's CFS and MoGATU system

	GAIA's CFS	Mogatu
Type of service	File service	Data service
Construction method	Centralized	Distributed
Metadata	Keyword based	Ontology based
Context-awareness	support	support

For the semantic file addressing [3], there are some previous works such as SFS [3], LISFS [4], CONNECTIONS [5] and LIFS [6]. However they are not suitable to the wearable computing environment because of the lack of the important fuctionalities such as platform independency and network plug-and-play.

3 Concept of the Context-Aware File Service

As we mentioned before, one of the most important challenges in the wearable computing environment is to make a system correspond with a users context (situation or intention). In order to realize this, integration of context information must be achieved. Through this, a service or application can interact with users of the wearable computers.

In terms of file service, the integration is more important than other services in the environment because it lays the groundwork for realizing an intelligent file search and retrieval mechanism. In this section, we define and describe the concept of our context-aware file service and file metadata management scheme.

3.1 Concept of the Context-Aware File Service

The purpose of our file service is to provide an intelligent file search and retrieval mechanism for a user or an application. Thus, it is very important to keep track of the user's context. However, we focus on the viewpoint of the file service interacting with it.

For example, When a user comes home, the context management server becomes aware of his entrance with RFID sensor and notifies the current context information to all nodes of Personal Area Network (PAN). If the user says, "I'd like to listen to music." the home theater generates a file request with the current context information and the user's preferences. This simple scenario clearly illustrates our goal and why a novel concept of file request is required. In the remainder of this section, we show other concepts which must be specified to realize our ideals. For more details, please refer to [16].

3.2 Ontology-Based File Metadata Management

In this section, we present how to describe metadata for files using ontology and how to manage them. First of all, we define the source ontology for our file service using W3Cs OWL [9].

For our concept map of file metadata, please refer to [16]. It can be classified into two parts. One is a group of concepts related to the file (e.g. file name, file size, creation time, file path, and information extracted from standard file meta-tag like the ID3 of the mp3), the other is a group of concepts related to user (e.g. user profile, user preference, emotional status). We name the former passive metadata and the latter active metadata.

There is a radical difference between managing passive and active metadata.

Passive Metadata: The passive metadata is extracted from file system attributes and standard file meta-tag like ID3 of the mp3 format during file creation. Then, it is assigned to the file based on our source ontology. In this paper, we implement a metadata generator which is able to extract metadata from various file formats such as mp3, ppt, doc, jpg, mpeg and so on.

Active Metadata: The active metadata is constantly changed by user activities such as accessing, copying and registering files on his schedule.

For instance, when a user copies or moves a file from a source directory to a destination directory, an active metadata can be extracted from its destination directory or neighbor files - Most users usually want to manage files in the same directory, if they have a similar semantics. In the case of registering a file on a schedule, the event information can be added to the files metadata as an active metadata.

In brief, we define two types of metadata. These metadata are stored and managed in a metadata repository. One of the notable features of our work is that user activity is reflected in it.

3.3 File Browsing and Searching Mechanism

Since file metadata is managed as a form of ontology and can reflect user activity as stated above, we can search for a file corresponding with the current context. In this section we demonstrate how these files are retrieved.

Query Language: This feature is not fully implemented currently and we are still refining it. In our implementation of prototype, we use RDQL [11]. However, as we mentioned in Section 3.2, users cannot input a semantic addresses which are fully expressed by ontology or complex query language such as RDQL. Thus, another special form to describe these semantic addresses is required. Additionally, the query language is able to specify dynamic file graph construction rule.

Below we briefly describe our query form with some examples.

a) Music (type = music & artist = Ella Fitzerald & album = *)
b) Music (type = music & artist = Ella Fitzerald)
c) Presentation (type = presentation & author = wjlee) & Event (name = project meeting or name = conference)
d) Event (person (name = wjlee) & time = * & location = home)

These query examples show the same semantics of the conventional ontology languages such as DAML+OIL or OWL. Additionally, it contains file graph construction rule. In case of a) and b) above, there is a subtle difference. The result set of files is same each other. However, the former make a file graph categorized by a rule, type = music and artist = Ella Fitzerald and her albums on run-time. The latter does not contain the albums on the graph.

Initialization Step: In the initialization step, each device exchanges its service description which contains person, device information and a category list being able to provide to other devices. Through this step, a file search query can be only delivered to some corresponding devices.

Dynamic File Graph Construction and File Browsing: In this section, we present our browsing manner with the context-aware file service. Figure 3 shows the construction mechanism of a virtual file tree. The tree represents a semantic space for data browsing, which is generated on run-time by a user's intention. Using the mapping table of (node, category list), a query is sent to corresponding nodes and the results are returned to the request device by a form of a graph. Then, the results are merged based on its query form. The example in Figure 3 shows the processing of a query, Music (type = music & artist = Ella & album = *). From the construction rule in the query, the result is generated and categorized by order of the sequence, music, artist and album.

This mechanism is very useful for browsing data in wearable computing environment. if we want to show all files by a view, person and device, we can just use the query form, Person (name = *) & Device (name = *).

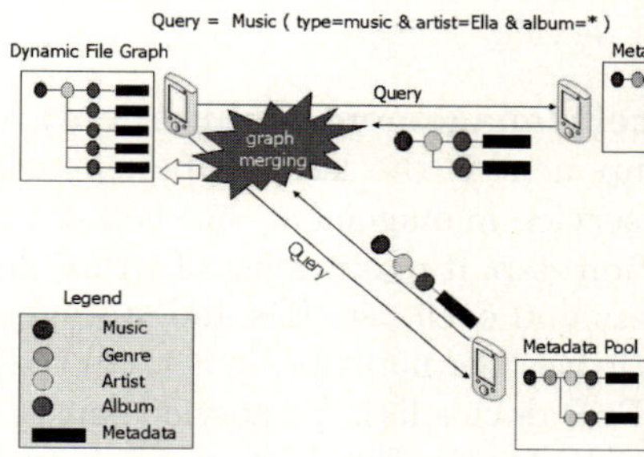

Fig. 3. Virtual file tree construction

File Searching with Current Context: The current context gathered from sensing information, user request, and user preference can be transformed to a file request. For example, a query, Presentation (type = presentation) & Event (location = Conference Room 222) reflects the aspect.

In our approach, every context is defined by an event. In order to get files corresponding current context, the current context information must be transformed to a query form described above. Then, the query is transferred to other devices which were selected by the mapping table of (node, category list).

As we mentioned, the query processing is performed by selecting sub-category graphs and by merging them. However, if it was requested by an application, only one file should be selected. In this case, we can use the user preference to choose one from the files maintained in the merged graph and to decide the order of precedence among them.

4 Implementation of the Context-Aware File Service

4.1 PosCFS Architecture and Implementation

We implement a prototype of our file service named PosCFS on Linux. The details of our implementation environment appear in Table 2.

Figure 4 shows the PosCFS Architecture. Our service is implemented as an UPnP service and WebDAV technology is used to support a platform-independent file I/O mechanism.

Table 2. Implementation environment

Platform	Sharp Zaurus SL-5500
CPU	206MHz Intel StrongARM
Memory	64MB DRAM, 16MB Flash, 512MB CF-Type SDRAM
OS	Linux Kernel 2.4.6
Library	libupnp 1.2.1, Apache mod_dav, ixml parser v1.2, librdf, sqlite3
Compiler	GNU G++ 2.95

Distributed File Service API: It describes an interface between applications and the context-aware file service.

Distributed File Service Management Component: The Distributed File Service Management Component is the key component which takes charge of system initialization, file service management and context-aware file I/O management. At the initialization step, it makes a list of UPnP devices in the PAN by the UPnP discovery process and exchange IDs and storage service information. When a new device joins/leaves the network, it detects the device and updates information such as its UPnP device list, file service status, et al.

It also provides an interface for the File I/O service between PosCFS services as an UPnP service. Through the interface, a file request is sent to a remote file service and its results are returned.

Storage Service Component: The Storage Service Component manages low-level file I/O, file metadata and a file cache. The Storage Service consists of two sub-components, the File I/O Service and the WebDAV Service. The File I/O Service manages file metadata which is stored in local system, and provides a cache management service. The WebDAV Service provides a low-level network file I/O based on the WebDAV protocol. The low-level network file I/O is used for file transmission.

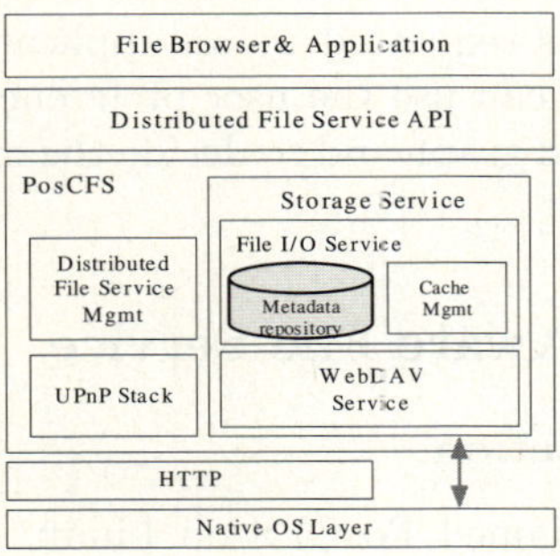

Fig. 4. PosCFS Architecture

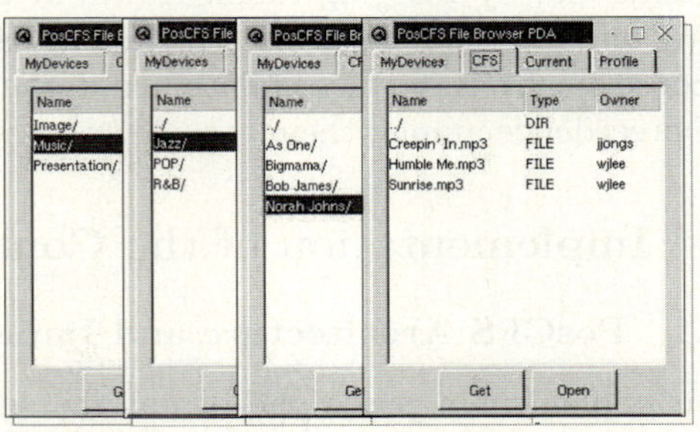

Fig. 5. PosCFS File Browser

4.2 CFS Browser

We design and implement a file browser named CFS Browser as a user interface. The CFS Browser is implemented on top of Embedded/QT 2.3.7. Figure 5 shows our CFS Browser.

There are four kinds of operating modes in our CFS Browser - My Device, CFS, Current and Profile. In the 'My Device' mode, the CFS browser provides a view of files in PAN with devices which belong to a user. In this mode, a user can export or import his/her files and attach events. If files are exported, they can be shared and managed by our semantic rules. The metadata, ontology instances extracted from files, are created at that time and maintained by the CFS.

The 'CFS' mode provide a view of integrated data management based on user's profiles. See Figure 5. a user can edit his profile and manage his/her files based on the profiles.

In the current context mode, the CFS browser provides a view of files corresponding with the current context. For the details please refer to the Section 3.

5 Performance Evaluation

In this section, we present performance evaluation focused on the devices discovery time (initialization time) and query response time. For the evaluation, we use four Jaurus-SL5500 PDAs, three PCs (800Mhz Duron, 512MB RAM) and two laptop computer (1.8 GHz P4, 512 MB RAM). Figure 6 shows the result of device discovery time. From the result, we see that device discovery time is convergence to 7 seconds regardless of the number of devices. Because it depends on the expire time of the UPNP discovery process.

Figure 7 shows our results for the query processing time. In the figure, we show the increase response time as increasing the number of devices. From these evaluations, we show our approach is acceptable to real environment. However, the query processing overhead should be reduced for scalability.

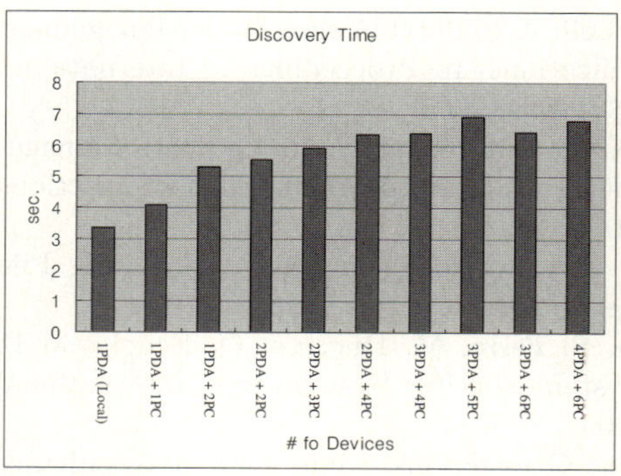

Fig. 6. Device discovery time

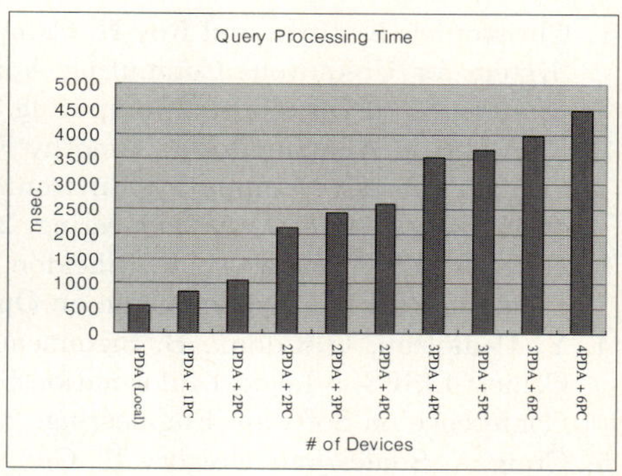

Fig. 7. Query processing time

6 Conclusions and Future works

In conclusion, we have proposed a ontology-based metadata management scheme and a context-aware file service suitable for the wearable computing environment.

Currently, there are many efforts to enhance ubiquity in this area. However, researches related to file services are just beginning despite their importance to the infrastructure of wearable computing.

As an interface for a context-aware network, our context-aware file service provides a data service which adapts to the context of the user or application through the file service interface.

We believe that our work will be a predominant reference for a new generation technology of file management in the ubiquitous computing environment. However, it is a preliminary implementation to achieve a basic concept of a context-aware file service. Therefore, our implementation has some limitations. For instance, it not only includes some restricted concepts related to a user profile and a mandatory file metadata, but also is implemented without a full consideration of efficiency. Furthermore, there are also many other important issues such as mobility support, privacy guarantee and data security. Thus, we will develop a more specific and efficient metadata management scheme which is adaptive to real-world conditions and study about the issues we mentioned above.

Acknowledgement

This research was supported in part by the wearable personal station project from the Ministry of Information and Communication and in part by the grant number IITA-2005-C1090-0501-001. This research was also supported in part by the BK21 program from the Ministry of Education of Korea.

References

1. Christopher K. Hess, and Roy H. Campbell: A Context-Aware Data Management System for Ubiquitous Computing Applications. In Proceedings of International Conference on Distributed Computing Systems, 2003.
2. Filip Perich, Anupam Joshi, Timothy Finin, and Yelena Yesha: On Data Management In Pervasive Computing Environments. In Proceedings of IEEE Transactions on Knowledge and Data Engineering, 2004.
3. Gifford, D.K., Jouvelot , P., Sheldon, M.A., O'Toole, Jr., J.W.: Semantic File Systems, 13th ACM Symposium on Operating Systems Principles, 1991.
4. Y. Padioleau, O.Ridoux, B. Sigonneau, S. Ferre, M. Ducasse, O. Bedel and P. Cellier: LISFS: a Logical Information System as a File System, 28th International Conference on Software Engineering, 2006.
5. Craig A. Soules and Gregory R. Ganger: Connections: using context to enhance file search, 20th ACM symposium on Operating systems principles, ACM Press, pp.119-132, 2005.

6. Alexander Ames, Nikhil Bobb, Scott A. Brandt, Adam Hiatt, Carlos Maltzahn, Ethan L. Miller, Alisa Neeman, and Deepa Tuteja: Richer file system metadata using links and attributes. In Proceedings of the 22nd IEEE / 13th NASA Goddard Conference on Mass Storage Systems and Technologies, Monterey, CA, April 2005.
7. UPnP Forum: UPnP: Universal Plug-and-Play, http://www.upnp.org
8. IETF: WebDAV: Web-based Distributed Authoring and Versioning, RFC 2518.
9. W3C: OWL Web Ontology Language, http://www.w3.org/TR/owl-features/
10. W3C: RDF: Resource Description Framework, http://www.w3c.org/RDF
11. W3C: RDQL: A Query Language for RDF, http://www.w3.org/Submission/2004/SUBM-RDQL-20040109/
12. IETF: Network File System (NFS) version 4, RFC 3530.
13. John H. Howard: An Overview of the Andrew File System CMU_ITC-88-062
14. Peter J. Braam: The Coda Distributed File System. Linux Journal 1998
15. Microsoft: Microsoft Distributed File System http://www.microsoft.com/windowsserver2003/ technologies/storage/dfs/default.mspx
16. Jonghwa Shin, Woojoong Lee, Shine Kim and Chanik Park: PosCFS: A Context-aware File Service for the Wearable Computing Environment, In Proceeding of Next Generation PC International conference, 2005.

Control of Information Appliances Using Instant Messaging

Seong Joon Lee and Kwang Seon Ahn

Department of Computer Engineering, Kyungpook National University
1370 Sankyuk-dong, Buk-gu Daegu 702-701, Korea
{imggaibi, gsahn}@knu.ac.kr

Abstract. Many of the systems developed to date for controlling home appliances remotely from outside have used a web server as the interface between the home network and the users. Although the user interface (UI) that uses a web server offers many advantages, this approach requires a fixed IP (Internet Protocol) address and does not have a push function. Moreover, until the user gets reconnected to the web server, he or she cannot know the result of a submitted order. In particular, internet-based applications using web browsers still require considerable time to execute the initialization process for acquiring state information on home appliances from the home server. To solve these problems, we propose an application for home automation that can efficiently control and monitor home appliances using an instant messaging system (IMS) with real time communication. The proposed system has not only the advantages of the web server method, but also with additional advantage that the homeowner does not need to continually reconnect to the home server, and that the home server does not need to have a fixed IP address. Our application can be applied using middleware technologies.

1 Introduction

The smart home (SH) is a house or living environment in which devices or services are networked together. If a SH is linked to the Internet, authenticated users can remotely control home appliances. To achieve this networking, home work, home server, and remote control devices are required. The home network is the internal network formed by various appliances and services in the house. To implement this network, appliances must have the computational power to perform predefined functions and the networking ability to share information with other appliances. Appliances with these capabilities are called information appliances or network appliances [9, 10]. Recently developed middleware for building home networks have typically utilized well-known middleware technologies such as uPnP [11], Jini [12], Havi [15], and OSGi [16]. These middleware technologies provide protocols for discovering available services in the network and for distributing required information. The home server acts as a gateway to connect the home network to the Internet and as a server to connect and manage the appliances within the home. Homeowners can remotely control and monitor home appliances through this home server. Remote control devices

E. Sha et al. (Eds.): EUC 2006, LNCS 4096, pp. 976–986, 2006.

are the tools used to control and monitor home appliances from distant locations; these devices can be used either when the user is at home or outside. Recently, a key issue in the implementation of SHs has been how to control and monitor home appliances from outside the home. Various methods have been proposed to efficiently solve this problem.

Recent advances in Internet technologies have prompted the development of various Internet-based remote controlling and monitoring of SHs [17-19], most of which adopt a web server as the interface between the homeowner and the home network. Although the use of a web server offers many advantages in terms of the UI, researchers have encountered problems in regard to issues such as fixed IP (fixed internet protocol, real internet protocol) addresses used in web servers and the lack of a push function for notification. To operate a server, the legacy system must have a fixed IP. However, home asymmetric digital subscriber line (ADSL) services offer the possibility of using a dynamic IP service, where the dynamic host configuration protocol (DHCP) server allocates a fixed IP during the lease time. Because a client does not always receive the same IP address in this dynamic IP system, it is impossible to use this system as a server.

Another problem is the push technology. Using this method, users who are subscribers to a server are able to automatically receive up-to-date information from the server. Therefore, mobile users can efficiently obtain the latest information anytime and anywhere, using any available device. Recently, several proposed systems have been worked on to integrate the push technology with various communication technologies. The best-known methods include Short Message System (SMS), Wireless Application Protocol (WAP), or Session Initiation Protocol (SIP), developed within the Internet Engineering Task Force (IETF) Multiparty Multimedia Session Control (MMUSIC) working group. SMS allows mobile phone subscribers to send and receive alphanumeric messages of up to 160 bytes in length in a store-and-forward fashion via an SMS center (SMSC). However, the SMS system allows users to send only one message at a time, and, due to technical restrictions, only short text messages, ring tones, and small graphics can be sent [6, 8]. Above all, SMS is not so much real-time as an immediate data transfer method.

In order for SIP- or WAP-based systems to control and monitor home appliances, each client must first download all the state informations on home appliances, or the file for Common Gateway Interface (CGI) scripts because they use the web serve In addition, the provider must develop various interfaces for the user. Therefore, most systems require complex hardware to reduce the technical complexity facing the user, and users spend considerable time initializing and downloading the related CGI file.

In this paper, we present an efficient real-time solution for home automation systems by using Jini network technology and instant messaging system (IMS) method. This System provides a uniform graphic UI (GUI) for end users. It immediately sends state information from the home network to the homeowner via the Internet. Homeowners with the appropriate IM installed on their mobile phones can remotely control and monitor their home appliances, anytime and anywhere. Furthermore, the system is lightweight, flexible, and extensible. The proposed system is convenient because it can sends a completion or alarm message to a manager via push functionality (NOTIFY message), even if the manager does not reconnect to the home network after it finishes setting the device. The GUI program can be used in other platforms without any changes.

2 Background

2.1 Push Technology

There are two traditional approaches to distribute information in an environment. In traditional client-server model, the client can only receive the information after connecting to the server. That is, until the connection between the server and the client has been made, the server cannot send any data to the client. This well-known method is the pull technology. On the contrary, in the push technology, the server can send any data to a client without establishing a connection.

(a) Pull technology (b) Push technology

Fig. 1. Pull Technology vs. Push Technology

2.2 Instant Messaging Systems (IMSs)

IMSs have long been one of the most popular applications on the Internet; they allow real-time exchange of messages, independent of locale [21]. Also, IMS merges e-mail, SMS function of mobile phones, multimedia communication, and file transfer. There are two features that make instant messaging unique: rapid-fire asynchronous messaging, and real time presence information. It allows near real-time communication, message interchange with little delay, and lightweight software compared to a web server. IMSs can be implemented on small Internet-enabled devices, such as mobile phones, PDAs, and set-top-boxes.

In this paper, we propose an IMS-based method for continuously controlling home appliances. The main goal was to verify that the proposed system could efficiently operate on different platforms without additional expense. To achieve this, we designed the user interface not only operates in specific environments, but also in others. In existing legacy system, the memory of most clients is too small to use Java. Even though there were many advantages of JAVA APIs, such as JMS APIs and RMI APIs, we did not consider JMS as a communication protocol for client-server interactions because of the reasons mentioned above.

2.3 Jini Network Technology

Jini network technology, a java-based middleware technology developed by Sun Microsystems, provides a set of APIs and high level network protocols that facilitate the development of distributed systems. Jini provides a simple way to perform the tasks of discovering, registering, and removing devices and services on home networks.

First, Jini creates a software infrastructure, called federation of services, to share access to services, and then engages in interactions without any prior knowledge of the other systems or any need for human intervention [13]. Figure 2 shows a simplified schematic of the process involved in using a Jini service.

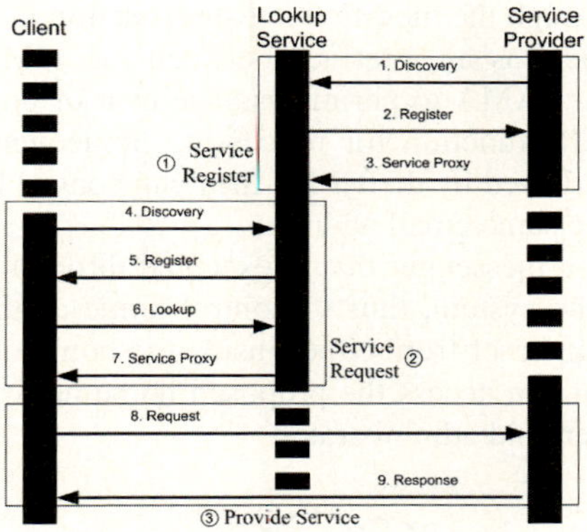

Fig. 2. Jini Technology

The system for enabling Jini service consists of three protocols including discovery, join, and lookup that provides dynamic configuration, and must first make a network service available. When a service is plugged into the Jini network, it uses a multicast request to find the local lookup service through the discover protocol and then registers the proxy service object in the lookup table via the join protocol (step 1 in Figure 2). Clients can also use the discovery protocol to find the lookup service. Subsequently, when a client requests a search for a service, the lookup service returns matching proxy service objects to the client (step 2). Finally, the object downloaded from the lookup server communicates directly with the service provider (step 3) [14].

3 HAMSuIM

The HAMSuIM system is based on the Internet/Intranet architecture, the Jini technology, and the IMS. To implement the HAMSuIM, we assume that the home network uses Virtual Private Network (VPN) and that the IP address of the residential gateway is not fixed. In the proposed system, three main agents are involved in the implementation of application programs: the Mobile Manager Agent (MMA), Home Messenger Agent (HMA) and Information Appliance Manager Agent (IAMA). Each agent must operate well even if the structure of the other two agents changes. To achieve this, we designed and implemented agents that do not depend on the environment of the other two agents. Figure 3 shows a block diagram of the system architecture.

First, the main objective of the IAMA is to create the object necessary for connecting with middleware using messages transmitted from the HMA, and then to monitor the appliances. Therefore, when the homeowner makes a request, the IAMA must rapidly seek out the information required by the homeowner and attempt to complete the specified task. If a problem is encountered, it must transmit an urgent error message to the homeowner. If a task is completed, it must send a result message to the homeowner stating that it is completed. All of this must be performed as quickly as possible. To perform its functions, the IAMA must be able to track all the changes and breakdowns of each appliance. To directly manage the Lookup table, we designed the IAMA to include the Lookup server of Jini. The appliance services are registered at the Lookup server through the modified register function in the IAMA.

Second, the HMA acts as an interface between the MMA and the IAMA. The HMA hooks up with the IAMA to permit management of home appliances and contains the register_owner() function for processing homeowner authentication. Once homeowners are authenticated by the HMA, they can control home appliances, whenever they wish, using the same email address.

Finally, the MMA is a messenger that is executed through a device that allows the homeowner to access the system, thus to control home appliances connected to the home network, via the Internet from either inside the home or from another location. The type of devices that can access the proposed home network is divided into three groups: user, homeowner, and administrator.

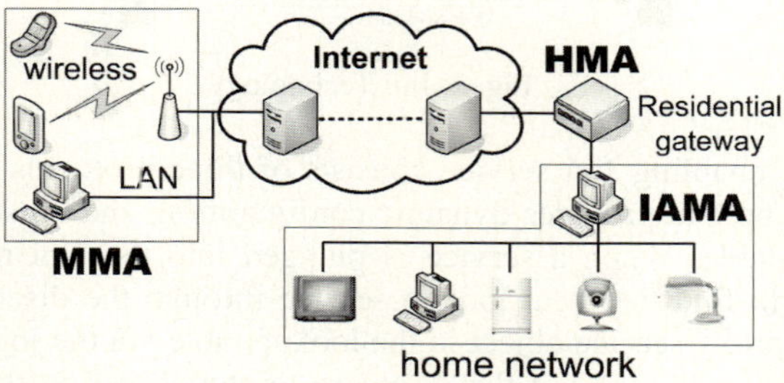

Fig. 3. Overall Software Interaction

The user group comprises all the devices onto which the IMS is installed. Members of this group are candidates for the homeowner group and acceptable to HAMSuIM but cannot control or monitor any of the home appliances. The homeowner group is defined as the device that is registered with the HMA as a friend. Once a device is added as a friend, the device can control and monitor all home appliances when needed. Finally, if the Medium Access Control (MAC) address using the registration function is enrolled to the administrator list in the HMA, the device is assigned to the administrator group. Administrator functions can only be executed within the home.

3.1 Homeowner Registration

To control home appliances on a home network, the MMA must be enrolled on the list of friends. The homeowner registration process uses the MAC address that is returned by the ARP Protocol. The advantage of such protocol is that each MAC address on a subnet is unique, and the MAC address cannot be delivered from devices that are outside the home. This method based on the ARP protocol has the disadvantage that administrators cannot add a homeowner in other subnets; however, it protects against access by unauthorized users.

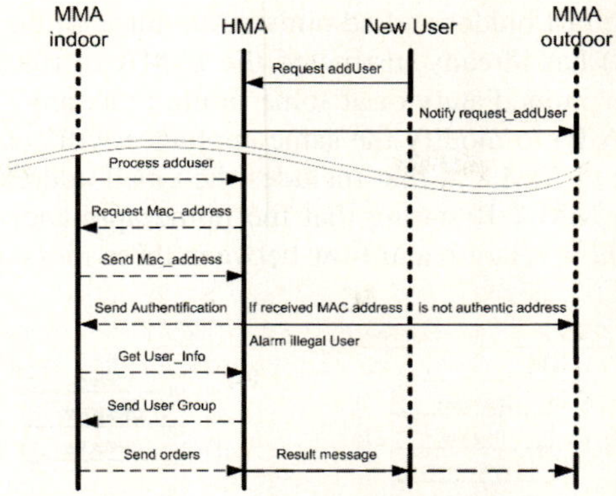

Fig. 4. The Algorithm for Adding a Homeowner

For example, if a user submits a request to register as a homeowner to the HMA, the HMA transmits this registration request to the other administrators. Such requests can only be handled by the administrator situated within the house. If the administrator operates the homeowner manager function, the HMA asks the administrator for the MAC address using the ARP protocol. If the returned MAC address is found on the administrator list, the HMA sends the administrator a list of e-mail addresses of users wishing to become homeowners. If the administrator agrees to any of these user requests, the HMA then sends a list of the e-mail addresses of new homeowners to all existing homeowners. Figure 4 shows the homeowner registration process.

After a user is enrolled as a homeowner, that homeowner receives various messages from the HMA. The types of message are classified below: information message (DESKEY, NEWDEVICE, UPDATE, and NOTIFICATION), execution message (DIRECTIVE), and emergency message (ALARM). When using IMS, The messages to be interchanged between clients are not encrypted. Therefore, we designed all messages to encode and to send. To achieve this, the MMA receives a key to use for cryptograph from the HMA by using *DESKEY message*. This key that is to be used as message encryption is periodically delivered from the HMA. And the MMA receive of the metadata list of modified home appliance using *UPDATE message*. If a new home appliance is detected, *NEWDEVICE message* is delivered to the MMA. This message consists of program layout. When the Homeowner tries to modify state variables in the IA which can be found in the metadata list (UPDATE message), the MMA receives modified state information from the HMA using *NOTIFICATION message* before the set-up window pops up.

The unique message that states the MMA notifying the HMA is the *DIRECTIVE message*. It can be classified into two orders: get_attribute to require the HMA to send the state variable of IA, set_attribute to control the home appliance. The HMA receives the DIRECTIVE message from the MMA, verifies it, and then forwards the message to the IAMA. Then, the IAMA creates a new object, begins the operation, and returns the completed result to the HMA. According to this result, the HMA sends either an ALARM or NOTIFICATION message to the MMA.

Finally, *ALARM message* is not encoded by 3DES to ensure processing without delay. When an error or fault occurs in the home appliance, the IAMA transmits an urgent message to the last bidder and administrators through the HMA. In addition, if one MMA (MMA A) has already instructed the IAMA to run a modification of the home appliance either immediately or at some future time, any subsequent attempt by another MMA (MMA B) to modify the same appliance will cause the IAMA to send an ALARM message to MMA A that includes the email address of MMA B, and an ALARM message to MMA B stating that the home appliance was not modified as instructed. Figure 5 show relation and flow between these messages.

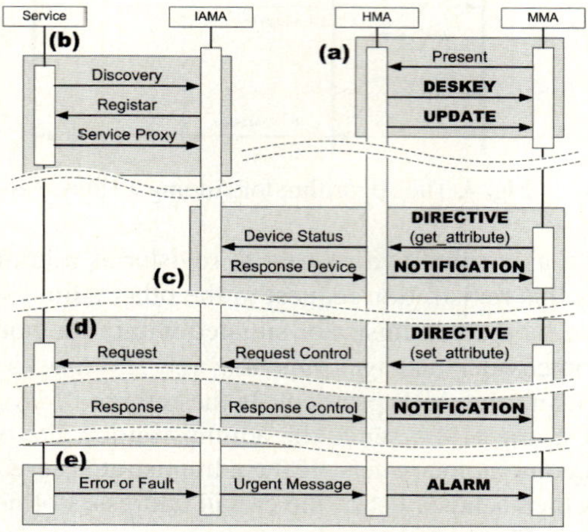

Fig. 5. Relation and Flow between Messages

4 Implementation

The aim of this research was to develop a system for controlling and managing home appliances using a home automation system onto which an IMS was installed. To implement this system, we used Jini middleware to establish an efficient home network and MSN Messenger to connect to the home server. We defined the various types of messages that are used in communication between the MMAs and the HMA.

Prototype implementations of the three agents have been developed on Java2 v1.4. We referred to the MSN analysis document [25] for creating a MSN clone, and the J-Sim Library to implement the ARP protocol. J-Sim Library is an object-oriented library written in Java for network simulators [24]. Jini API is designed to enable the simultaneous control of multiple information appliances.

In the proposed system, the MMA has a cache directory in which state information passed to the MMA by the HMA is stored. The state information stored in this directory is kept as consistent as possible with the true current state of the system. In addition, the MMA deletes data from the cache if that data has not been updated within a pre-specified time. The developed HAMSuIM has the ability to fully control and manage all appliances within the house when using Jini-enabled devices. The detailed architecture of the HAMSuIM is shown in Figure 6.

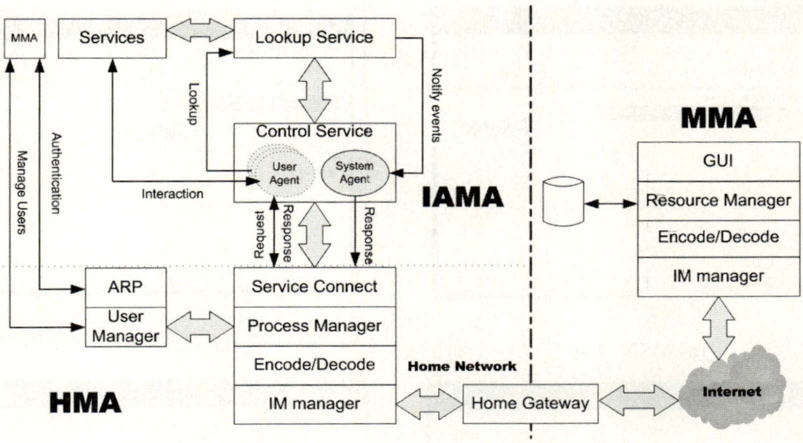

Fig. 6. Overall Architecture of the HAMSuIM

A homeowner accesses the HAMSuIM after completing the logon process. (Figure 7-a) shows the main GUI window for a MMA. If the item (HOME_SERVER) is selectable, double clicking this item will cause monitor windows to be displayed on the user screen (Figure 7-b). The homeowner is then able to control and monitor his or her home appliances. In the monitor window, the left pane is called the appliance list and the right pane is called the attributes window. If a MMA clicks a home appliance in the appliance list, all state variables of that home appliance will appear in the attributes window.

When a new appliance is enrolled into the appliance list by receiving NEWDEVICE message, the label <<new>> appears beside the name of that home appliance for 24 hours. When setting a home appliance, the homeowner can double clicks on the attributes window, and the resource manager of the MMA will search the updated metadata list stored in cache directory. If the appliance is included in the list, the MMA send DIRECTIVE message for receiving modified state variable. And, the setup window will be popped up (Figure 7-c). The setup window is configured by XML code which describes new devices that will be included to a NEWDEVICE message. In the setup window, the MMA homeowner can insert values for the attributes that he or she wishes to control. When the send button is clicked, a DIRECTIVE message is prepared and sent to the HMA. A type of control word is defined by immediate_run if the value of the timer included in the message is less than or equal to the current system time of the HMA, or by reserve_run if it is greater than the current system time of the HMA. The process manager of the HMA analyzes the received message and, if it does not identify a fault, it uses a NOTIFICATION message to broadcast updated attributes to the other homeowners. The homeowner who performed the update will also receive this message, causing his or her cache directory to be updated and his or her window to be refreshed (Figure 7-d). In brief, the DIRECTIVE message does not update the cache directory; only the NOTIFICATION message can update the cache directory.

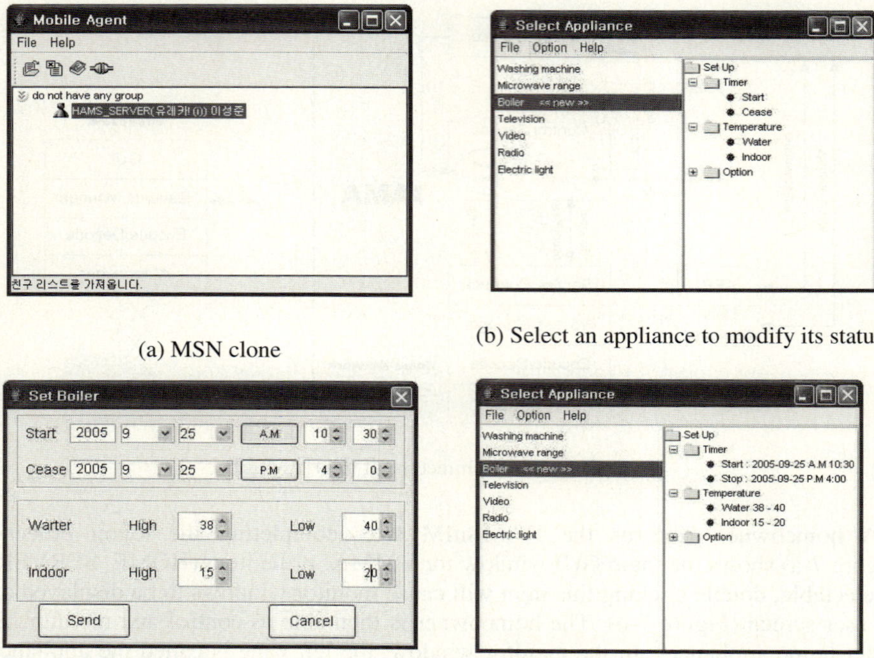

(a) MSN clone

(b) Select an appliance to modify its status

(c) Change the attributes of the selected appliance

(d) Display with new status

Fig. 7. Home Automation Management System Interface

5 Conclusions and Future Work

In this paper, we have proposed a system that supports remote control and monitoring of home appliances on a home network through an IMS with real time communication. The advantage of the proposed system is to transfer changed state of IA spontaneously. That is, it can receive messages described IA state information without reconnecting to the Home Server. This eliminates the disadvantage of the administrator needing observe information appliance attentively. And, it can increase access security, because it will make use of the system with dynamic IP as Home server. Finally, since this system is a light-weight process, it can be ported to mobile phones easily. In addition, the proposed system can implement more convenient systems by using the add-on functions of IMSs, such as voice chatting, SMS, and multimedia. In summary, the proposed system can be ported to any networked legacy system, and can control and monitor home appliances anytime anywhere. The only disadvantage of the proposed system is that it processes incoming packets from the home server without the user's request.

In the future, we plan to implement an interface with a sentence-based and speech recognition interface.

References

1. Daqing Zhang, Zhengning Dai, Xiaohang Wang, Xiao Ni, Song Zheng, "A new service delivery and provisioning architecture for home appliances," *Consumer Electronics*, 2003. ICCE. 2003 IEEE International Conference on 17-19 June 2003 Page(s): 378 - 379.
2. M. Rahman, C. Akinlar, I. Kamel, "On secured end-to-end appliance control using SIP," *Networked Appliances*, 2002. Liverpool. Proceedings. 2002 IEEE 5th International Workshop on 30-31 Oct. 2002 Page(s): 24 -28.
3. M. Nikolova, F. Meijs, P. Voorwinden, "Remote mobile control of home appliances," *Consumer Electronics*, IEEE Transactions on, Feb. 2003. Vol. 49, Issue 1, pp. 123 – 127
4. IRENE C. Y. MA, J. IRVINE, "Characteristics of WAP traffic," Wireless Networks, Jan 2004, Vol. 10, Issue 1, pp 71 - 81
5. E.M.C. Wong, E.M.C, "Phone-based remote controller for home and office automation," *Consumer Electronics*, IEEE Transactions on, Feb. 1994. Vol. 40, No. 1, pp. 28 -34
6. Ghaderi, M., Keshav, S., "Multimedia Messaging Service: System Description and Performance Analysis, " *Wireless Internet*, 2005. Proceedings. First International Conference on, 10-15 July 2005, pp. 198 - 205
7. Ismail Coskun and H. Ardam, "A Remote Controller for Home and Office Appliances by Telephone," *Consumer Electronics*, IEEE Transactions on, Nov. 1998. Vol. 44, No. 4, pp. 1291-1297
8. Ivanov, R.S, "Controller for mobile control and monitoring via short message services," *Telecommunications in Modern Satellite, Cable and Broadcasting Service*, 2003. TELSIKS 2003. 6th International Conference on, Vol. 1, 1-3 Oct. 2003, pp.108 - 111
9. Li Jiang, Da-You Liu, Bo Yang, "Smart home research," *Machine Learning and Cybernetics* 2004. Proceedings of 2004 International Conference on, Vol. 2, 26-29 Aug. 2004 Page(s): 659 - 663
10. Neng-Shiang Liang, Li-Chen Fu, Chao-Lin Wu, "An integrated, flexible, and Internet-based control architecture for home automation system in the Internet era," *Robotics and Automation*, 2002. Proceedings. ICRA '02. IEEE International Conference on, Volume 2, 11-15 May 2002 Page(s): 1101- – 1106.
11. B.A. Miller, B.A., T. Nixon, C. T., Tai, C., M.D. Wood, M.D., "Home networking with Universal Plug and Play," *Communications Magazine*, IEEE, Vol. 39, Issue 12, Dec. 2001 Page(s): 104 - 109.
12. K. Arnold, A. Wollrath, B. O'Sullivan, R. Scheifler, and J. Waldo, "The Jini Specification," Reading, MA: Addison-Weslley, Reading, MA, USA, 1999.
13. D. Reilly, D., A Taleb-Bendiab, A., "An Jini-based infrastructure for networked appliance management and adaptation," *Networked Appliances*, 2002. Liverpool. Proceedings. 2002 IEEE 5th International Workshop on 30-31 Oct. 2002 Page(s): 161 - 167.
14. Q.H. Mahmoud, Q.H., "Using Jini for high-performance network computing," *Parallel Computing in Electrical Engineering*, 2000. PARELEC 2000. Proceedings, International Conference on 27-30 Aug. 2000 Page(s): 244 - 247.
15. R. Lea, R., S. Gibbs, S., A. Dara-Abrams, A., E. Eytchison, E., "Networking home entertainment devices with HAVi," *Computer*, Vol. 33, Issue 9, Sep 2000 Page(s): 35-43.
16. P. Dobrev, D. Famolari, C. Kurzke, B.A. Miller, "Device and service discovery in home networks with OSGi, " *Communications Magazine*, IEEE, Vol. 40, Issue 8, Aug. 2002 Page(s): 86-92.
17. K. Tan, T. Lee and C. Yee Soh, "Internet-Based Monitoring of Distributed Control Systems--An Undergraduate Experiment," *IEEE Transactions on Education*, Vol. 45, No. 2, May 2002.

18. Chi Chung Ko, Ben M. Chen, Shaoyan Hu, Vikram Ramakrishnan, Chang Dong Cheng, Yuan Zhuang, and Jianping Chen, "A Web-Based Virtual Laboratory on a Frequency Modulation Experiment," *IEEE Transactions on Systems, Man, and Cybernetics-Part C: Application and Reviews*, Vol. 31, No. 3, pp. 295-303, August 2001: 295-303.
19. N. Swamy, O. Kuljaca and F. Lewis, "Internet-Based Educational Control Systems Lab Using Net-meeting," *IEEE Transaction on Education*, Vol. 45, No. 2, pp. 145-151, May 2002: 145-151.
20. Peng Gong, Feng-jiao Qiu, Meng Liu, "A new algorithm based on DES and ECC for CSCW," Computer *Supported Cooperative Work in Design*, 2004. Proceedings. The 8th International Conference on,Volume 1, 26-28 May 2004 Page(s): 481-486. Vol.1
21. Christian Dewes, Arne Wichmann, Anja Feldmann, "Applications: An analysis of Internet chat systems," October 2003. Proceedings of the 3rd ACM SIGCOMM conference on Internet measurement.
22. John Stone, Sarah Merrion, "Features: Instant Messaging or Instant Headache?," April 2004. *Queue*, Vol. 2, Issue 2.
23. Sun Microsystems Inc., "Jini Architecture Specification," Downloaded from, http:// ww.sun.com/ software/jini/specs
24. J-Sim Org., "J-Sim API Specification," Downloaded from http://www.j-sim.org/
25. MSN Messenger Protocol Documentation. Downloaded from http://www.hypothetic.org/docs/msn
26. Seong Joon LEE, Gwang Seon Ahn, "Remote Control for Information Appliances Using Instant Messenger," June 2005. Proceedings of the 2005 International conference on Embedded System and Applications.

Hybrid Dissemination Based Scalable and Adaptive Context Delivery for Ubiquitous Computing

Lenin Mehedy, Md. Kamrul Hasan, Young Koo Lee*,
Sungyoung Lee, and Sang Man Han

Real Time & Multimedia Lab, Department of Computer Engineering,
Kyung Hee University, 449-701, Republic of Korea
{lenin, kamrul, sylee, i30000}@oslab.khu.ac.kr,
yklee@khu.ac.kr

Abstract. Context delivery is an inevitable issue for ubiquitous computing. Context-aware middlewares perform all the functions of context sensing, inferring and delivery to context-aware applications. But one of the major issues for these middlewares is to devise a context delivery scheme that is scalable as well as efficient. Pure unicast or pure broadcast based dissemination can not provide scalability as well as less average latency. In this paper we present a scalable context delivery mechanism for context-aware middlewares based on hybrid data dissemination technique where the most requested data are broadcasted and the rest are delivered through unicast. Our scheme is adaptive in the sense that it dynamically differentiates hot (most requested) and cold (less requested) data according to request rate and waiting time. Inclusion of lease mechanism and bandwidth division further allows us to reduce network traffic and average latency. We validated our claim through extensive simulation.

1 Introduction

Context awareness is the ability to sense, interpret and respond to the situation of an entity (e.g. user, application) [2]. Often, the term "Context-aware Computing" is used synonymously to Mark Weiser's revolutionary concept of Ubiquitous Computing [1] as every future application will have context-awareness. Context-aware middleware performs all the functions of context sensing, inferring and then delivers to smart applications (see [4] for a survey). Thus every context-aware middlewares usually have the following three main phases of execution: a) Acquisition of raw sensor data, b) Context inference from the sensory data, c) Context delivery to applications. This paper focuses on the context delivery mechanism for such middlewares.

Our work is motivated by the unavoidable need of scalable context delivery in large smart environments (such as a corporate office, academic building, shopping complex etc.) where numerous context-aware applications (we interchangeably use client or receivers), running on mobile devices like PDA or stationary devices (desktop PC), frequently request for various contexts to the middleware. If the context information of interest is same among different clients, traditional unicast (point to

* Corresponding author.

E. Sha et al. (Eds.): EUC 2006, LNCS 4096, pp. 987 – 996, 2006.

point or pull based) connection-oriented data services are uneconomical because it incurs a lot of unnecessary traffic from clients to server and vice versa. Even if the current technology allows us to have high network bandwidth and server capacity, most of it would be underutilized and wasted during non-peak periods. Broadcast (push based) is an efficient and scalable dissemination method in a connection-less mode to any number of clients with no significant performance degradation in terms of access latency[5]; but a major concern for the success of such system is broadcasting the right set of data. Because, broadcasting less important data may cause network overload. On the other hand, in on-demand broadcast (pull-push) method, the server aggregates the requests of clients and broadcast the data. But broadcasting the context with lowest request rate (cold item) may also increase network traffic. So hybrid approach combines the benefit of broadcasting hot context data (having higher request rate) and that of unicasting the cold context data (having lower request rate) [6]. Even with this suitable and scalable approach, we have the problem of differentiating hot and cold context data and formulate a suitable delivery mechanism for quick response time.

By the term "efficient delivery" we mean that the mechanism should cause less network traffic, provide quick response time and deal with dynamic nature of ubiquitous environment (i.e. clients appear and disappear in an unpredictable manner). Unavailability of such comprehensive solution motivates us to propose a context delivery mechanism for context aware middlewares in ubiquitous computing domain that is scalable as well as adaptive to request pattern. Our solution is an effort towards developing a robust and comprehensive context delivery mechanism for the middleware CAMUS (Context Aware Middleware for Ubiquitous System) [3], [17].

This paper is organized as follows: Section 2 describes related works. Section 3 explains the proposed method of context delivery. Section 4 presents the performance evaluation and Section 5 concludes with some future works.

2 Related Work

To the best of our knowledge, the researches in context delivery of the middlewares have not addressed so far the scalability issue where contexts are to be efficiently delivered to large number of mobile or static clients in ubiquitous environment. The most related research to ours is the Context Discovery Protocol (R-CDP) [13] that has been implemented and evaluated in "Reconfigurable Context Sensitive Middleware" (RCSM) [14]. The fundamental difference between R-CDP and our work is that R-CDP uses broadcast to request for a context and the middleware unicast the data to the requester, which is completely opposite to our mechanism as we use unicast for request and combination of broadcast and unicast for delivery. We use the technique of RxW algorithm [11] to prioritize the delivery where they use *Refresh Priority* that is based on the divergence of contexts and energy consumption of "Provider". We also perform bandwidth division for hot and cold items for optimal average latency. The similarity with their work is that the motivation of their *Neighbor Validation Beacons (NVB)* is same as that of our Lease Renewal and we also have the way of specifying the *update threshold* for context update notification. However, they do not use context ontology for semantic interpretation. Moreover, R-CDP has not been tested for scalability [13], which we believe an important performance issue for large scale deployment of smart applications.

The idea of Hybrid data dissemination technique was first used in the Boston Community Information System [8] by combining broadcast and interactive communication to provide most updated information to an entire metropolitan area. This scheme is also adopted in [5], [6], [7], [8], [9], and [10] where the issue of mixing push and pull web documents together on a single broadcast channel was examined. But the document classification problem was introduced in [6] and later document classification along with bandwidth division was resolved in [7]. We employ these ideas of hybrid dissemination, scheduling, classification of data, bandwidth division etc. for scalable and efficient delivery of context for ubiquitous computing environment. Though our approach is very similar to [7], but we differ in calculating the popularity of an item not only on the total request but also on the longest waiting time of any outstanding request according to RxW as RxW does not suffer from starvation of request for cold item [11]. Moreover we also employ lease mechanism to reduce the periodic request (polling).

3 Proposed Scheme

Before introducing our context delivery scheme, let us assume that the clients request context information using context ontology for semantic interoperability (e.g. Contel [12] [17]). We use hybrid dissemination scheme [6] for the context delivery in ubiquitous environment. But this scheme introduces three inter-related data management problems at the middleware: First: the middleware must dynamically classify the requests between hot and cold context data and schedule the delivery according to priority or popularity (*Prioritization*). Second, the middleware should divide dynamically its bandwidth between unicast pull and multicast push for optimal use of bandwidth to ensure low *average latency* (*Bandwidth Division*). Third, as the hot context data are broadcast, some clients may receive the information passively in the sense that they do not send any request for that data and we call them "passive client". Therefore, the middleware lacks a lot of invaluable information about the data requirement and fails to appropriately estimate the hotness and coldness of data items (*Push Popularity Problem [7]*). The *average latency* for a data item on the push channel is half of the period of the broadcast cycle if we assume that the items are broadcast sequentially. However, the latency for pulled items are totally different because if an item i of size S_i is queued at the server for transmission, the corresponding queuing delay is either $O(S_i)$ or unbounded [7].

3.1 Message Format

All the clients request for context information according to the context ontology. Clients specify the type of context (e.g. Temperature) and as well as the entity of which this context is related (e.g. Room). "Lease Duration" and "Update Threshold" are also to be specified if a client needs a context for a certain amount of time to avoid polling. Thus the *Request* message contains the following information: Context Type

(CT), Entity Type (ET), Entity Id (EID), Lease Duration (LD) and Update Threshold (UT) (see Table 1). If any client does not need periodical update notification, it should specify the "Lease Duration" field and "Update Threshold" field as zero. *Reply* message contains CT, ET, EID, value (V), Maximum Lease Duration (MLD), Minimum Update Threshold (MUT) and Report Probability (RP). RP is discussed in section 3.4 in detail.

Table 1. Message Format

Type	Content
Request	{CT, ET, EID, LD, UT}
Reply	{ CT, ET, EID, V, MLD, MUT, RP }

3.2 Prioritization

The middleware enqueues the requests according to different context groups and maintains the following information for each of the groups:

- Total Leased Request (TLR): Total number of leased requests for this specific context. This value is used in determining whether this data should be scheduled for broadcast (hot item) or unicast (cold item).
- Leased Request List (LRL): This list contains the ids (IP address) and lease durations of leased clients.
- Max Lease Duration (MLD): Maximum lease duration among the leased duration. This information is also sent along with the data to let the clients know how long this data will be delivered. If any client is receiving the data passively and wants to use longer than this time, it will renew the lease for longer duration.
- Total Pending Request (TPR): This field denotes the total number of requests that have been received but no delivery of the context has been done yet. This field is reset to zero after each delivery of the context and incremented after receiving of each new request for this context. The larger the value of this field, the higher the priority of delivery of this context should be.
- Pending Request List (PRL): This list is similar to LRL but contains the requesters' ids (IP address) and requested lease duration of the pending requests. After the delivery, the requests with lease duration greater than zero will be added to the LRL and TLR will be updated accordingly.
- First Arrival Time (FAT): This is the arrival time of the first request which is still pending. Longest waiting time (LWT) of any pending request for this context is the difference of current time and FAT. FAT is reset to zero after each delivery and set to the arrival time of the first request as it is queued. The larger the value of this field, the higher the priority of this context should be for delivery.
- Last Delivery Time (LDT): The most recent time when the context was delivered. The difference between current time and LDT is the longest waiting time of the leased clients.

- Min Update Threshold (MUT): The minimum of update threshold values among the requests. If the context is changed by this amount, it is then scheduled for delivery.
- Candidate for Scheduling (CS): This is a binary value. If the amount of change exceeds the Min Update Threshold (MUT), the value of this field becomes one (true) and implies that this data should be delivered. This field becomes zero (false) with the next delivery of the context data.

To set the priorities of the requested context data, we use the total number of requests (R) and longest waiting time of the outstanding request (W) for that item and it is motivated by RxW algorithm [11]. In RxW algorithm, the item with higher R*W value has higher priority. Thus we prioritize a data either because it is very popular or because it has at least one long-outstanding request. We consider both Total Pending Request (TPR) and Total Leased Request (TLR) when CS is one (true) to be the total number of request (R), otherwise we only consider TPR to be the R value for the context item (see equation 1). This is because TLR comes into account as soon as the amount of change exceeds Min Update threshold (MUT) and CS becomes one (true). Similarly, as long as CS is zero, difference of current time (CT) and FAT (First Arrival Time) is the value of longest waiting time (W); but as soon as CS becomes one, the longest wait time (W) is the difference of CT and LDT (Last Delivery Time) as all the leased requests have been waiting since LDT. Hence we define RxW with the following equation:

$$RxW = \left(TPR + CS * TLR\right) * \left(\left(CT - FAT\right)\left(1 - CS\right) + CS\left(CT - LDT\right)\right) \quad (1)$$

We calculate RxW value of each group (data item) and sort them in descending order. We update the list each time a request comes and use the same data structure proposed in [11] for efficient maintenance of such list. The RxW value of i th group is denoted as popularity (or priority) p_i in the following sections.

3.3 Bandwidth Division

The motivation of bandwidth division comes from the fact that the *average latency* (L) of a data item is less when hot items are assigned to broadcast, cool items to unicast pull and the bandwidth is divided appropriately between the two channels. We used the bandwidth division algorithm similar to that is suggested for web server in [7]. But, we use the prioritization described in section 3.2 rather than using the prioritization based on request rate only as it is used in [7]. The bandwidth division algorithm uses the sorted list of items with decreasing order of popularity, i.e. $p_i \geq p_{i+1}$ $\left(1 \leq i \leq n\right)$, where n is the current size of the list. It is intuitive that if item i is pushed, then $j \leq i$ should also be pushed. So, the algorithm tries to partition the list at index k such that the push set $\left\{1, 2, ..., k\right\}$ minimizes the latency L given a certain bandwidth B. The optimal value k^* is found by trying all possible values of L and finally the algorithm determines the pull bandwidth $\alpha \sum_{i=k+1}^{n} \lambda p_i S_i$, which leaves bandwidth $pushBW = B - \alpha \sum_{i=k+1}^{n} \lambda p_i S_i$ for the push channel and average latency for the pushed documents is then $\sum_{i=1}^{k} \frac{S_i}{2\,pushBW}$. Here λ and S_i denote request rate and size of the item respectively. The algorithm runs in $O(n)$ as it performs binary search over all possible values of L and maintains an internal array that stores the total size of each possible partition using binary tree techniques [7].

3.4 Push Popularity Problem

As the data is broadcast, some clients may not need to send any explicit request. This will misguide the middleware to identify most requested item and thus it introduces the "*push popularity problem*". We can not expect to solve this push popularity problem completely as it will require all the clients to send requests explicitly and hinder the benefit of broadcast. So, a portion of the clients that are passively accessing data should send requests even though the data is ensured to be delivered. The middleware sends a report probability (RP) with the data and client submits an explicit request for this data with probability RP. It is proved in [7] that RP should be set inversely proportional to the predicted access probability for that data and the equation to calculate RP is:

$$RP_i = \begin{cases} \frac{\beta}{\lambda p_i k}, & if\, \lambda p_i k > \beta \\ 0.2, & otherwise \end{cases} \tag{2}$$

Where β is the difference of Maximum acceptable TCP connection and request arrival rate, λ denotes aggregate request rate and p_i denotes the priority (or popularity) of group i based on total request and k denotes the current number of broadcast items. Here we notice that if $\lambda p_i k < \beta$, the probability will exceed one and hence we specified RP to be 0.2 as a default. It should also be noted that whenever the client sends a request, it sends a complete request with its desired update threshold (UT) and desired lease extension (LE). LE denotes the desired extension after the expiry of current MLD. The same request format is also used for lease renewal when the lease expires.

4 Performance Evaluation

In order to establish the potential of our proposed context delivery mechanism, we have built a simulation model of the proposed system and evaluated using the simulation tool OMNET++ [16]. All the graphs presented here are generated using the PLOV tool of OMNET++.

4.1 Simulation Model

In our client-server model the server (our middleware) acts as a data server and delivers self identifying context data items of equal size either by broadcast or unicast upon explicit request. The clients request an item according to Zipf distribution [15] and the time of requests is exponentially distributed with mean M , where $\frac{1}{M}$ is the average request rate of each client. We present the analysis of average latency and network traffic of the proposed system in the following sub-sections. Table 2 presents all the simulation parameters. Here the pull over-provisioning factor α and the tolerance factor ε are used by the bandwidth division algorithm described in [7].

Table 2. Simulation Parameters

Parameter	Value
Total Client	3000
Total Item, N	50
Size of Each Item	200 bytes
Zipf parameter Θ	1.5
System Bandwidth	512,000 bits/sec
Exponential mean M	12
α	2
ε	0.005
Lease Duration of a client	10~ 100 ms (uniform)
Lease Renewal Probability	0.7
Update Threshold	0.5~2 unit (uniform)

4.2 Average Latency

Let $G(k)$ be the average latency (T_{avg}) if the k most popular items are broadcasted. The function $G(k)$ is a weighted average of the average latency of pushed items $T_{push} = \sum_{i=1}^{k} \frac{S_i}{2\,pushBW}$ and the average latency for the pulled items $T_{pull} = \frac{1}{\mu - \left(\sum_{i=1}^{N} \lambda_i - \sum_{i=1}^{k} \lambda_i \right)}$, where λ_i is the Poisson request rate for each item i [6], [7]. Our result is shown in Fig 1. Notice that the minimum of $G(k)$ is to the left of the intersection (at k=10) of the push and pull curves though theoretically it should be on the right side of the intersection [6]. The minimum of $G(k)$ occurs at a relatively small value of k and precedes the intersection due to two complementary reasons. First, the most popular items are chosen for push and are also those to which a Zipf distribution gives substantially more weight. So, if an item is delivered using broadcast, it will also have the largest impact on the globally average delays. As the numbers of the most popular items are small and are broadcasted first, the overall minimum delay occurs for small values of k. Second, pull delays are actually minimized at the points k' where the pull-curve flattens out. However k' precedes the intersection in our graph, and so the overall minimum occurs before that intersection.

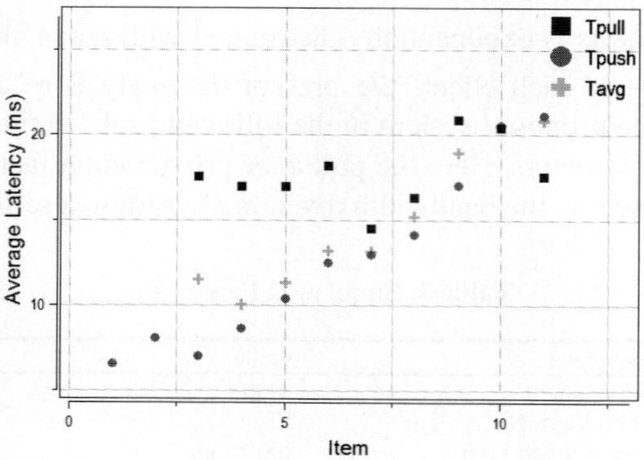

Fig. 1. Relation of average latency of Push and Pull as the number of broadcast items changes according to our experiments. Here the intersection of T_{push} and T_{pull} occurs at $k = 10$ and before k=3, T_{pull} grows arbitrarily large.

4.3 Network Traffic

Fig 2 and Fig 3 presents our simulation result regarding network traffic. Here we can see in Fig 2 that in the beginning of time, the number of request is high. But as the server starts to deliver items, the number request decreases due to two reasons. First,

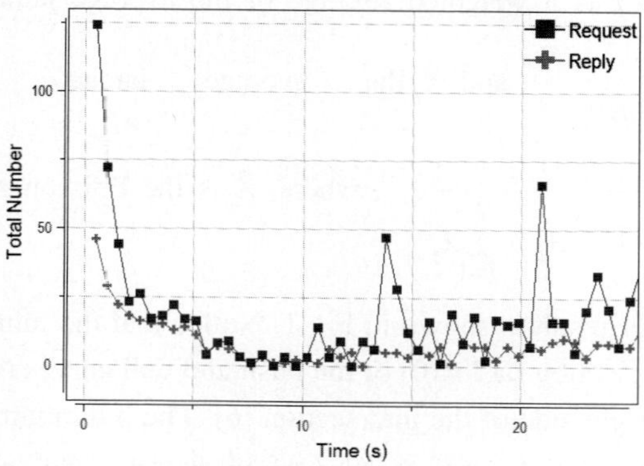

Fig. 2. Number of request and reply with change of time using our approach. The number of reply denotes total number of broadcast and unicast items.

the replies contain the maximum lease period and minimum threshold value for the context items and the clients do not need to send explicit request again until the lease expires. Second, as the most popular items are broadcast, the clients that also need the data do not send request but uses the data passively. But we can see some spikes in the request graph because of the lease renewal requests and the requests sent by the passive clients due to *Report Probability* as we have already discussed. Here we see that incorporation of lease mechanism and threshold reduces overall network traffic from client as well as from server (Fig 3).

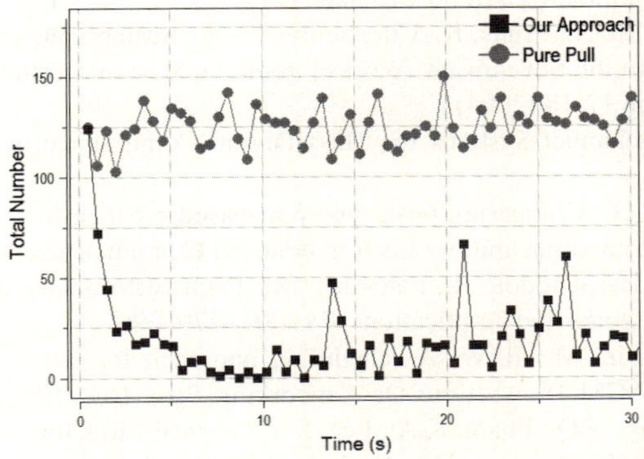

Fig. 3. Number of requests in our approach and in pure pull approach. Simulation results show that our approach causes fewer requests as it avoids polling and uses lease mechanism.

5 Conclusion and Future Work

In this paper we present a scalable context delivery mechanism for context-aware middlewares based on hybrid data dissemination technique where the most requested data are broadcasted and the rest are delivered through unicast. Bandwidth division and lease mechanism are two notable properties of our approach that reduce average latency and network traffic respectively. Correlation of contexts, real time delivery, predictive broadcast, secure delivery etc. are some of the interesting approaches to extend this work.

Acknowledgement. This work was supported by IITA Professorship for Visiting Faculty Positions in Korea from Ministry of Information and Communications.

References

1. Weiser, M.: The Computer for the 21st Century. In: Scientific America, Sept. 1991, pp. 94-104; reprinted in IEEE Pervasive Computing, 2002, pp. 19-25
2. Dey, A.K, Abowd, G.D.: Towards a Better Understanding of Context and Context-Awareness. In Proc. of the 2000 Conference on Human Factors in Computing Systems, The Hague, The Netherlands, (April 2000)

3. Hung, N.Q., Shehzad, A., Kiani, S.L., Riaz, M., Lee, S.Y.: Developing Context-Aware Ubiquitous Computing Systems with a Unified Middleware Framework. In: Proc. of Embedded and Ubiquitous Computing: EUC 2004, LNCS Volume 3207, Springer-Verlag (2004), pp. 672 – 681
4. Baldauf, M., Dustdar, S.: A Survey on Context-aware systems. Int. J. of Ad Hoc and Ubiquitous Computing, forthcoming
5. Acharya, S., Franklin, M., Zdonik, S.: Balancing push and pull data broadcast. In *ACM SIGMOD*, (May 1997)
6. Stanthatos, K., Roussopoulos, N., Baras, J. S.: Adaptive data broadcast in hybrid networks. In the 23rd Int. Conf. on VLDB, 30(2), (Sep. 1997)
7. Beaver, J., Morsillo, N., Pruhs, K., Chrysanthis, P. K.: Scalable Dissemination: What's Hot and What's Not. In the Seventh Int. Workshop on the Web and Databases (WebDB 2004), Paris, France, June 17-18 (2004)
8. Gifford, D.: Polychannel Systems for Mass Digital Communications. *CACM*, 33(2):141-151, (Feb. 1990)
9. Hall, A., Taubig, H.: Comparing push- and pull-based broadcasting or: Would "microsoft watches" profit from a transmitter? Lecture Notes in Computer Science, 2647 (Jan. 2003)
10. Triantafillou, P., Harpantidou, R., Paterakis, M.: High performance data broadcasting systems. Mobile Networks and Applications, 7 (2002) 279–290
11. Aksoy, D., Franklin, M.: RxW: A scheduling approach for large-scale on-demand data broadcast. IEEE/ACM Transactions On Networking, 7(6) (Dec. 1999) 846-860
12. Shehzad, A., Hung, N.Q., Pham, K.A., Lee, S.Y.: Formal Modeling in Context Aware Systems. In Proc. of Workshop on Modeling and Retrieval of Context, CEUR, ISSN 613-0073, Vol-114, Germany (2004)
13. Yau, S.S, Chandrasekar, D., Huang, D,: An Adaptive, Lightweight and Energy-Efficient Context Discovery Protocol for Ubiquitous Computing Environments. In the 10th IEEE International Workshop on Future Trends of Distributed Computing Systems (FTDCS'04)
14. Yau, S.S, Karim, F, Wang, Y, Wang, B., Gupta, S.: Reconfigurable Context-Sensitive Middleware for Pervasive Computing. IEEE Pervasive Computing, 1(3), July-September (2002), pp.33-40.
15. Wentian Li, References on Zipf's Law. URL: http://www.nslij-genetics.org/wli/zipf/
16. OMNET++, URL: http://www.omnetpp.org/index.php
17. Shehzad, A., Hung N.Q., Anh, K.P.M. , Riaz, M., Liaquat, S., Lee, Y.K, Lee, S.Y: Middleware Infrastructure for Context-aware Ubiquitous Computing Systems. CAMUS Technical Report (TR-V3.2). February 2005. http://oslab.khu.ac.kr/camus

A Neuroscientific Approach to Emotion System for Intelligent Agents

Gunn-Yong Park[1,2], Seung-Ik Lee[1,2], and Joong-Bae Kim[1]

[1] Intelligent Robot Research Division,
Electronics and Telecommunications Research Institute,
P.O.B. 161, Gajeong-dong, Yuseong-gu, Daejeon, Korea
{pgy64257, the_silee, jjkim}@etri.re.kr
http://www.etri.re.kr
[2] Computer Software Engineer Division,
University of Science and Technology,
P.O.B. 52, Aueun-dong, Yuseong-gu, Daejeon, Korea
http://www.ust.ac.kr

Abstract. For an agent to be believable, emotion is an essential part of the human-computer interaction. In this paper, we propose a dynamic affective system, inspired from neuroscience. The system comprises four modules: an appraisal module, an emotion-generation module, an emotional expression module, and a long-term memory (LTM). The appraisal module gathers environmental stimuli and evaluates them to see if they are rewarding or punishing. Based on the results of the appraisal module and the agent's internal stimuli, the emotion-generation module generates the affective states of the agent. The emotional expression module combines and expresses emotional behaviors in accordance with the affective states. As a result, the proposed affective system can generate various emotions simultaneously and produces emotional life-like expressions.

1 Introduction

There have been several efforts to build a life-like agent for our convenience, such as the ubiquitous robotic companion [1], the visual software agent [2], and the power wheelchair for the physically handicapped persons [3]. For an agent to be more life-like and believable, an emotion is an essential part, because affective states affect rational decision-making, perception, learning, and other cognitive functions of a human [4]. According to the somatic marker hypothesis [5], the marker records emotional reaction to a situation. We learn the markers throughout our lives, and use them for our decision-making. Therefore, a believable agent needs an affective system to synthesize and express emotions. Due to the importance of the emotion in the human-computer interaction (HCI), there have been several attempts to build an emotional agent, such as Sony's 'Aibo' [6], MIT's 'Kismet' [7].

Most of the previous work to build emotional agents was inspired by ethology, and used an affect space to produce emotion. For example, Aibo has six emotions based on the affect space, called Takanishi's model [6], and generates appropriate emotional reactions to a situation. Because the emotions in the affect space have a competitive

E. Sha et al. (Eds.): EUC 2006, LNCS 4096, pp. 997 – 1006, 2006.

relationship with each other, the agent based on the affect space expresses only one emotion can be expressed at a time. For example, Aibo expresses only one affective state from its six emotions: happy, sadness, fear, disgust, surprise, and angry. However, contrary to the previous work, humans can have several emotions simultaneously and can express them in various ways.

According to neuroscientific studies, because of the considerable developments in temporal lobe and prefrontal cortex, a human emotional processing is more complicated than the affect space. Therefore, humans can generate and express a large range of emotion from happiness to anger. Furthermore, because people feel more comfortable with a human-like agent [4], a human-oriented agent should have an emotion generation process similar to that of a human. Hence, we propose an affective system for intelligence agents based on a neuroscience research.

This paper is organized as follows. Next Section presents the human emotion process in the aspect of both neuroscience and cognitive science. Section III describes the proposed affective system based on Section II. The experimental result and the conclusion are presented in Section IV and Section V, respectively.

2 Affective System in a Human Brain

Humans have quite well developed temporal lobe and the prefrontal cortex. Literatures [8, 9] have discovered that the development has contributed to the human's simultaneous expression of emotions and the ways they are expressed. In this section, we briefly introduce neuroscientific approaches to understanding human affective system.

Since the triune brain model [4] had been proposed, many people assumed that the limbic system is the source of emotions. However, according to the recent neuroscientific studies [8, 9, 10], emotion involves not only with the limbic system but also with the neocortex such as the orbitofrontal cortex. The amygdala and the orbitofrontal cortex are responsible for the perception, appraisal, and learning of environmental stimuli such as visual or acoustic sensory stimuli. The hypothalamus is in charge of homeostasis – maintaining the body's status quo. It controls body temperature, hunger, thirst, and other circadian cycles, and alters the affective state to obtain the desired stimuli.

Fig. 1 shows how the primate brain responds to environmental stimuli. In primates, external stimuli are decoded as a reward or a punishment. Rewards are stimuli for which an animal will work, whereas punishers are stimuli that the animal will work to avoid [8]. In the primate taste system, for example, the reward decoding occurs after several processing stages. The first stage is the primary taste cortex, that identifies the taste. Based on that result, the secondary taste cortex in orbitofrontal cortex evaluates its reward value. This value is decreased by feeding to satiety, since neurons in the orbitofrontal cortex decrease their responses as the reward value of the food decreases.

Rewards and punishers can be defined as reinforcers, because they change the probability of behavior [8]. There are two types of reinforcers: primary and secondary reinforcers [9]. The primary reinforcer (e.g., the taste of food or pain) is unlearned,

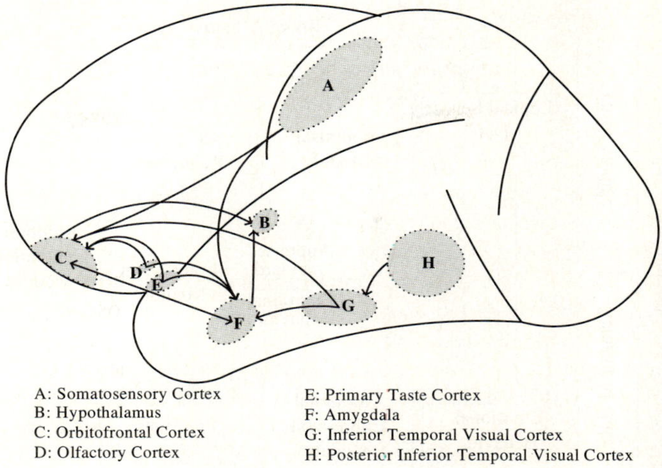

Fig. 1. Brain of the macaque monkey

and has innate reinforcing properties. The secondary reinforcer (e.g., the auditory or visual stimulus) develops its reinforcing properties through learning its association with primary reinforcement. For example, fear might be produced by a sound (i.e., the conditioned stimulus) that has been previously associated with a painful stimulus (i.e., the primary reinforcer). This type of learning is referred to as "stimulus-reinforcement association learning," [9] and involves with the amygdala and the orbitofrontal cortex.

According to neuroscientific studies, emotions are defined as affective states produced by rewards and punishers [8]. An animal changes its affective state and performs any actions to obtain rewards or to avoid punishers. For example, happiness could be produced by the occurrence of rewards such as an admiration of others or a pleasant touch; and frustration or anger could be produced by the termination of rewards such as the death of a loved one. As shown in these examples, the human emotional processing is involved in the occurrence, termination, or omission of the rewards (or punishers).

The affective states are classified as primary and secondary emotions [4]. The primary emotions are innate, and involve the primary reinforcers. For example, when you are surprised by a loud noise, the surprise involves with the primary reinforcer such as an acoustic sensory stimulus. On the other hand, the secondary emotions involve with the secondary reinforcers, and depend on the result of the stimulus-reinforcement association learning.

As described above, the environmental stimuli are evaluated as the primary or secondary reinforcers, and then the affective states depend on these reinforcers. For example, in the amygdala, the association learning is realized as modifiable synapses between visual (or auditory) neurons and neurons from taste, olfactory or somatosensory primary reinforcers [9]. However, since the cognitive ability of intelligent agents is still far behind that of humans, this learning mechanism is difficult for an intelligent agent to adopt. Hence, we adopt a cognitive appraisal model as the stimulus-reinforcement association learning in the affective system.

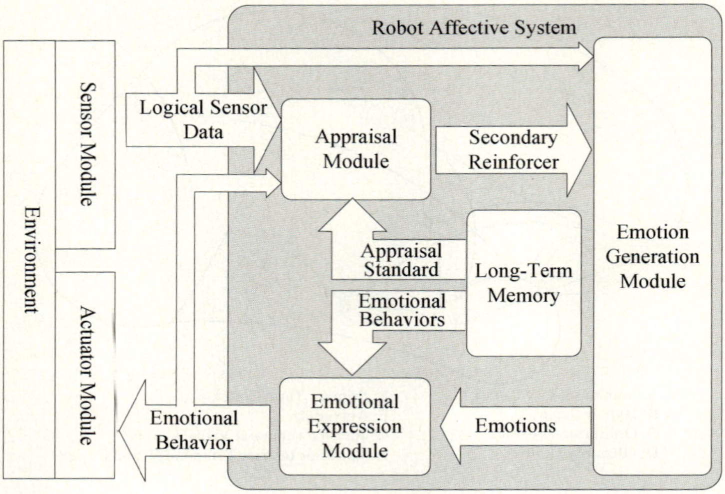

Fig. 2. Framework for the affective system

3 Affective System Framework

To make an agent more user-friendly, the architecture of the system is based on neuroscience studies on primate's brains. Our affective system is shown in Fig. 2. The sensor module translates external stimuli into logical sensor information. The logical sensor data is an abstraction of the external stimuli, such as the name and position of an object. Emotional behaviors of the agent are realized by the actuator module. The affective system has a responsibility for generating and expressing affective states in according to the external or internal stimuli.

Inside the affective system, there are four modules: an appraisal module, an emotion generation module, an emotional expression module, and a long-term memory (LTM). The appraisal module describes the stimulus-reinforcement association learning of the secondary reinforcers. The function of producing affective states of the amygdala, the orbitofrontal cortex, and the hypothalamus, is implemented in the emotion generation module. The emotional expression module controls the sequential or parallel execution of emotional behaviors. These behaviors include, for example, the facial expressions of the agent or text-to-speech. Lastly, the LTM contains appraisal standard and emotional behavior for the appraisal module and the emotional expression module.

3.1 Appraisal Module

As shown in Fig. 3, the appraisal module comprises a cognitive appraisal model, a short-term memory, and an external LTM. The LTM contains a standard list and a desired object list for the cognitive appraisal model. The standard list and the desired object list are an appraisal reference for the praiseworthiness of the actions and the appeal of the objects, respectively.

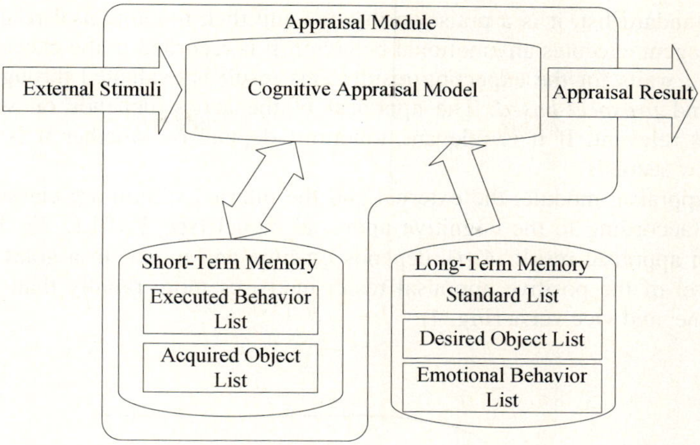

Fig. 3. Appraisal module of the robot affective system

The short-term memory contains an executed behavior list and an acquired object list. All the emotional behaviors executed by the agent are included in the executed behavior list. This module examines whether the result of the listed behaviors is received within the specified time interval. The acquired object list maintains the visual properties (placement, color, and name) of the recognized object. The agent obtains the physical changes – velocity, direction of moving objects – by comparing the data of objects from sensors with these of the short-term memory.

The cognitive appraisal model assesses external stimuli in accordance with the LTM and the short-term memory. For example, the facial expressions of users and the recognized objects determine the emotions related to the *fortunes of others* and *attraction* in Table. 1, respectively. When a recognized object is in the desired object list, the appraisal result is love. The action of the agent is related to the *attribution* in Table. 1. It depends on the praiseworthiness of the action of the agent. If the action

Table 1. Assessment result of the cognitive appraisal model

Category of Appraisal Result		Appraisal result	
		Positive	Negative
Attraction		Love	Hate
Attribution		Pride	Shame
Fortunes of Others		Happy for	Resentment
Prospect Relevant		Joy	Fear
Prospect-Based	Confirmed	Satisfaction	Fear-Confirmed
	Disconfirmed	Relief	Disappointment

is in the standard list, it is a praiseworthy one and then the appraisal result is pride. When the agent executes an emotional behavior, it is recorded in the executed behavior list, and waits for the expecting result. This result is evaluated through *prosepct relevant* and *prospect-based*. The appraisal of the action depends on whether the prospect is relevant. If it is relevant, emotions depend on whether it is confirmed within a few seconds.

In the appraisal module, the external and the internal stimuli are classified into 6 categories according to the cognitive appraisal model (see TABLE. 1). The energy level of an appraisal result, $A_n(t)$, depends on time and mood. In a good mood, the energy level of the positive appraisal result increases more rapidly than that of the negative one, and vice versa (Fig. 4).

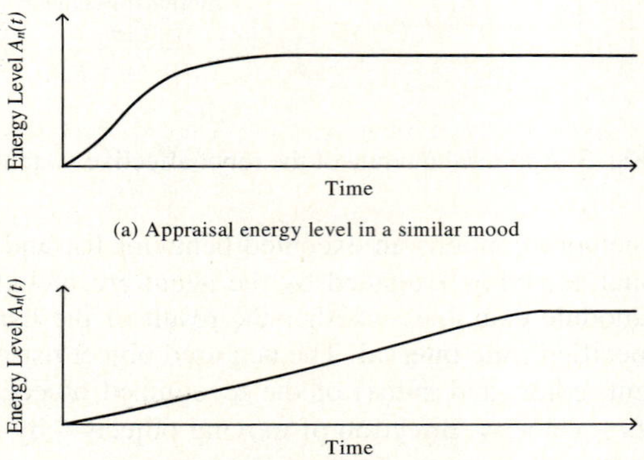

(a) Appraisal energy level in a similar mood

(b) Appraisal energy level in a different mood

Fig. 4. Characteristic graph of moods

The mood *Mood(t)* is defined as follows:

$$Mood(t) = \sum_{k=1}^{A} e_k \times E_k(t-1) , \tag{1}$$

where $E_k(t)$ is the activation level of the k_{th} emotion, A is the number of emotions, and e_k is the gain parameter of the k_{th} emotion. If $E_k(t)$ is positive, then e_k is also positive, and vice verse. When *Mood(t)* is positive, the system is in the positive mood.

3.2 Emotion Generation Module

According to Ekman's research on emotion [11], we express our elemental emotions in the same ways, and can recognize these emotions in the face of another: anger, disgust, fear, joy, sorrow, and surprise. Therefore, we propose that the affective state of the agent is the blending of the six basic emotions. In the emotion-generation module, the activation level of each emotion is continuously updated. When the activation level exceeds a threshold value, the emotion is activated. All emotions above the

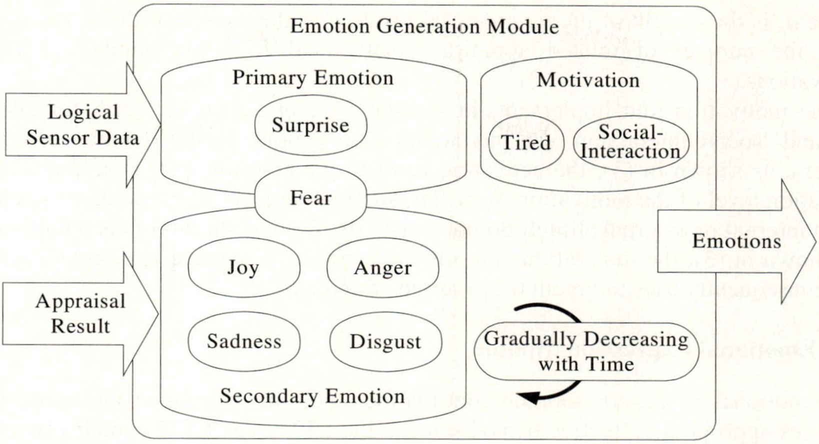

Fig. 5. Emotion–generation module of the robot affective system

thresholds are active in contrast to the winner-take-all scheme that allows only one emotion to be active at a time.

The emotion-generation module comprises three units: the primary emotion unit, the secondary emotion unit, and the motivation unit (Fig. 5). The primary emotions involve the primary reinforcers. They are linked directly to the logical sensor data, because the primary reinforcers are unlearned stimuli. On the other hand, the secondary emotions involve the secondary reinforcers. Therefore, they depend on the results of the appraisal module. The motivation module implements homeostatic regulations in the hypothalamus, such as 'tired' and 'social interaction.'

The activation level of the i_{th} primary emotion $E_i(t)$ at time t depends on the level of logical sensor data, and defined as follows:

$$E_i(t) = E_i(t-1) + \sum_{m=1}^{M} w_m \times S_m(t) - \delta(t)\,, \tag{2}$$

where S_m is the level of the m_{th} logical sensor data, w_m is the weight of the m_{th} sensor data, $\delta(t)$ is the decay factor of the emotion, and M is the number of logical sensors related to the emotion. For example, if the emotion 'surprise' depends on the microphone level, the agent is surprised by a loud noise. In this system, the elements of the surprise are a loud noise and an abrupt change in the visual stimulus.

On the other hand, the secondary emotions depend on the appraisal result of the appraisal module, since it is related to the stimulus-reinforcement association learning. The activation level of the j_{th} secondary emotion at time t, $E_j(t)$, is affected by the energy level of appraisal result $A_n(t)$ and that of the motivation $M_l(t)$, as follows:

$$E_j(t) = E_j(t-1) + \sum_{n=1}^{N} a_n \times A_n(t) + \sum_{l=1}^{L} c_l \times M_l(t) - \delta(t)\,, \tag{3}$$

where a_n is the weight of the n_{th} appraisal result, c_l is the weight of the l_{th} motivation, N is the number of related appraisal results, and L is the number of related motivations.

The motivation unit implements homeostatic factors, such as 'tired' for taking a rest and 'social interaction' for interacting with people. In the emotion-generation process, as shown in (3), the activation level of the emotion $E_j(t)$ is affected by the activation level of the motivation $M_l(t)$. The motivation level $M_l(t)$ increases gradually when internal or external stimuli do not satisfy the desired stimuli of each motivation. As shown in (3), the motivation controls the emotion to execute appropriate actions, and consequently tries to obtain the required stimuli.

3.3 Emotional Expression Module

The emotional expression module controls the emotional actions of the agent. It determines appropriate affective behavior using the LTM. The LTM contains two types of emotional behaviors: concurrently executable behaviors, and sequentially executable behaviors. An execution of a sequential behavior depends on which activation level of the emotion is the highest. That is, the emotional behavior related to the highest level has priority over the others. In the concurrently executable behaviors, all behaviors that exceed the thresholds are performed.

The emotional expression module should deal with competing rewards, goals, and priorities. Furthermore, the selection process among the emotional behaviors can respond to many different types of reward. Therefore, the emotional behavior has properties, such as the expected result, if any; the processing type (e.g., sequential execution or parallel execution); and the waiting time. The expected result is the available stimulus from the emotional behavior, and the waiting time is the maximum time allowed to receive the expected stimulus from the environment.

4 Experimental Results

To evaluate the proposed system, it was applied to the Philips iCat, which is an experimentation platform for HCI. The iCat has four touch sensors, two microphones, a CCD camera, and 13 servos for facial postures. The affective system runs on a 3 GHz PC running Windows, and communicates with the iCat through a USB port. The affective system produces the agent's emotional states in accordance with the internal and external stimuli, such as interactions between the user and the iCat. Fig 6 illustrates the basis facial postures based on emotional states.

As shown in Fig. 6, the LTM contains eight basis facial postures, each of which represents a designated emotion. The agent's facial expression is defined as a blending of basis facial postures (Fig. 7). For example, at the beginning of (2) in Fig. 7 (a), the intelligent agent detects a desired object, and the activation level of joy increases. The facial expression of joy is in (2) of Fig. 7 (b). As depicted in (3) of Fig. 7 (a), disgust is activated because of the recognition of a hateful object or the execution of a blameworthy action, and the facial expression in (3) of Fig. 7 (b) is a blending of two basis facial postures (joy and disgust). As shown in (4) of Fig. 7 (a), when the desired

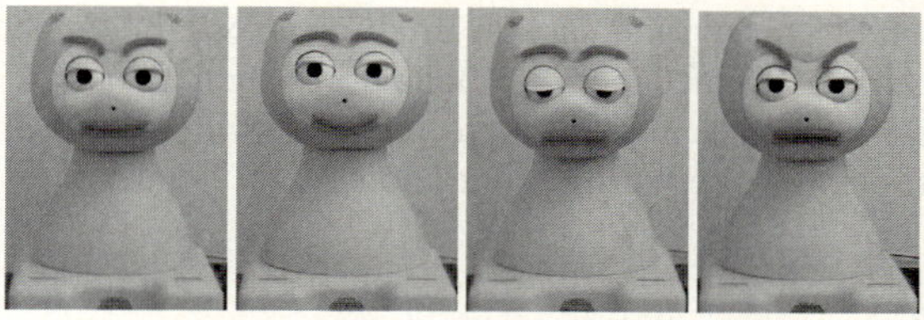

(a) Calm (b) Joy (c) Sadness (d) Anger

(h) Disgust (i) Fear (j) Surprise (f) Tired

Fig. 6. The basis facial postures of the iCat

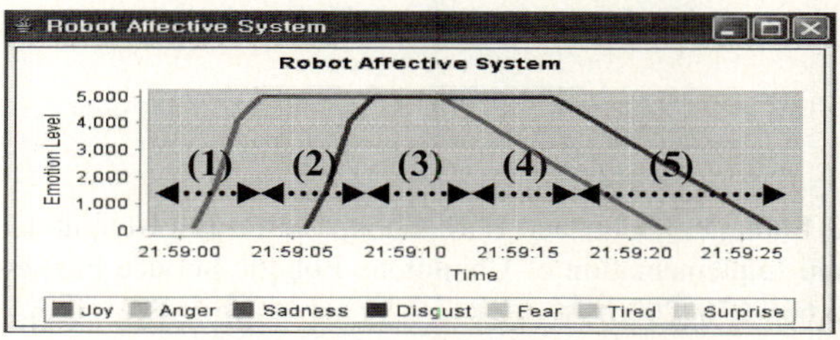

(a) Activation level of joy (red) and disgust (blue)

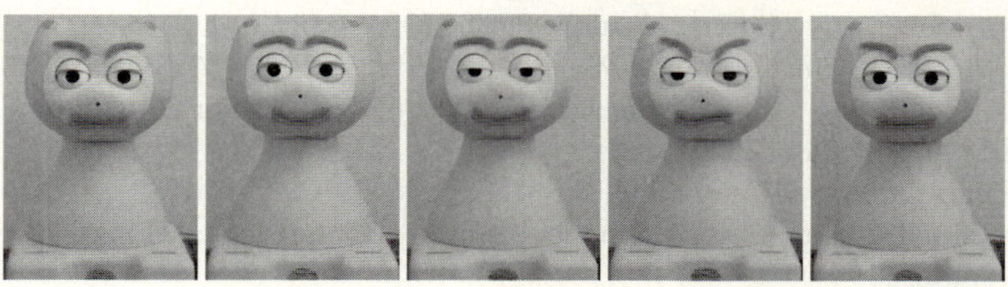

(1) (2) (3) (4) (5)

(b) Sequence of facial expression in accordance with (a)

Fig. 7. The activation level of emotions and facial postures.

object has disappeared or has been perceived for a long time, the activation level of joy decreases, and the emotional expression is in (4) of Fig. 7 (b).

As described above, the facial expression of the iCat is a blending of basis facial postures. In this system, external stimuli are evaluated according to the emotional reactions and each emotional expression is generated in accordance with the emotion activation level. There are two types of emotional expression: a sequential or parallel behavior. According to the affective states of the agent, the agent performs sequentially executable behaviors, such as emotional exclamations or simple text-to-speech, or a linearly combined parallel behaviors, such as facial expressions, and sequential behaviors. Hence, in contrast to previous work, the proposed system can generate and express various emotions continuously.

5 Conclusion

We have presented an affective system based on neuroscience and cognitive theory. The proposed affective system evaluates which external stimuli are rewarding or punishing. According to the appraisal result, this system generates and expresses various emotions simultaneously. Therefore, the emotional behavior, such as facial expressions, is not a predefined emotional behavior, but the blending of concurrently executable behaviors or the sequential execution of sequentially executable behaviors. Hence, the agent can produce human-like emotional expressions continuously.

In future, we intend to implement personality and association learning of the secondary reinforcer. Personality has an important role in emotion processing and can change the emotional reaction to the environment. Therefore, the believable agent should have characteristic personality. Furthermore, we will also focus on the association learning for the emotional response of newly discovered objects.

References

1. Y. G. Ha, J. C. Sohn, Y. J. Cho, and H. S. Yoon, "Towards a Ubiquitous Robotic Companion: Design and Implementation of Ubiquitous Robotic Service Framework," ETRI Journal, vol.27, pp.666-676 (2005)
2. Y. Nozawa, H. Dohi, H. Iba and M. Ishizuka, "Humanoid Robot Presentation Controlled by Multimodal Presentation Markup Language MPML," IEEE Int'l Workshop on Robot and Human Interactive Communication, Japan (2004)
3. K.H. Kim, H. K. Kim, J. S. Kim, W. H. Son, and S. Y. Lee, "A Biosignal-Based Human Interface Controlling a Power-Wheelchair for People with Motor Disabilities," ETRI Journal, vol.28, pp.111-114 (2006)
4. R. W. Picard, Affective Computing, the MIT Press, USA (1997)
5. A. Damasio, Descarte's error: Emotion, reason and the human brain, NewYork, NY: Harper Collins (1994)
6. R. C. Arkin, M. Fujita, T. Takagi, R. Hasegawa, "An Ethological and Emotional Basis for Human-Robot Interaction," In Proceedings of the IEEE/RSJ Int. Conference on Intelligent Robots and Systems (2002)
7. C. Breazeal, Sociable machines: Expressive social exchange between humans and robots, Ph.D. dissertation, Dept. Elect. Eng. And Computer. Sci., MIT, Cambridge (2000)
8. E. T. Rolls, "The neural basis of emotion," International Encyclopedia of the Social and Behavioral Sciences, Eds. N. J. Smelsner and P. B. Baltes, Pergamon: Amsterdam, pp.4444-4449 (2002)
9. E. T. Rolls, "Vision, emotion and memory: from neurophysiology to computation," Cognition and Emotion in the Brain, Eds. T. Ono, G. Matsumoto, R. R. Llinas, A. Berthoz, R. Norgren, H. Nishijo, and R. Tamura, Elsevier Science: Amsterdam, pp.547-573 (2003)
10. S. Greenfield, Brain Story, BBC World Wide Publishing (2000)
11. P. Ekman, "Are there basic emotions?" Psychological Review, 99, pp.550-553 (1992)

Automatic Decision Method of Effective Transform Coefficients for Face Recognition

Jean Choi[1,2], Yun-Su Chung[1,2], Ki-Hyun Kim[2], and Jang-Hee Yoo[2]

[1] Department of Information Security Engineering
University of Science & Technology
52 Yeoeun-dong, Yuseong-gu, Daejeon 305-333, Korea
[2] Biometrics Chipset Research Team
Electronics and Telecommunications Research Institute
161 Gajeong-dong, Yuseong-gu, Daejeon 305-350, Korea
{jchoi, yoonsu, kihyun, jhy}@etri.re.kr

Abstract. In this paper, we propose a novel face recognition method using the effective transform coefficients of face images. The method is based on extraction of effective vector in Discrete Cosine Transform (DCT) domain and Linear Discriminant Analysis (LDA) of effective vector. In general, face images have characteristics that they show larger energy congestion in horizontal frequency coefficients than in vertical or diagonal frequency coefficients. However, many previous methods have shortcomings that they don't utilize the facial energy characteristics. To overcome shortcomings above, the proposed method selects the effective coefficients of the face in DCT domain and then extracts feature vector through LDA analysis on DCT coefficients. Experimental results show that our method has improvements of recognition performance over the previous methods.

1 Introduction

In face recognition, feature extraction is one of the most important steps and it performs the reduction of high dimensional image data into low dimensional feature vectors. Dimensionality reduction is essential for extracting effective features and reducing computational complexity in classification stage. In feature extraction, there are two approaches; it is a method in spatial and frequency domain. In spatial domain, the most frequently used techniques are Principal Components Analysis (PCA) and Linear Discriminant Analysis (LDA), but the way of dimensionality reduction based on PCA or LDA is also high computational cost and needs the large number of training samples [1-3]. To overcome these weaknesses, the concerns and works about feature extraction using Discrete Cosine Transform (DCT) in frequency domain has been growing for the last several years.

Over the past few years, a several number of works have been conducted on face recognition method using DCT. Recently, DCT has been employed in face recognition for dimensionality reduction by Hafed and Levine [4]. Next, Jing and Zhang introduced feature extraction method based on selection of DCT frequency bands with

E. Sha et al. (Eds.): EUC 2006, LNCS 4096, pp. 1007 – 1016, 2006.

favorable linear separability [5]. Recently, Er, Chen and Wu also presented a way using DCT coefficients by zigzag-scanning [6-7]. These methods assumed that energy aggregated uniformly in the low-frequency region; so to speak, it is a distinction of non-face images rather than face images. Therefore these methods have shortcomings that can't utilize energy characteristics of face images. To overcome the shortcomings above, energy characteristics of face images unlike non-face images need to be checked and utilized. As a result, we propose a new feature extraction method using the energy characteristics of face images.

The proposed method consists of three steps. First, face image is transformed into the frequency domain using DCT. Second, *Energy Probability (EP)* is calculated for the dimension reduction and optimization of valid information, and then *Energy Map (EM)* is created. Finally, in order to obtain the most significant and invariant feature of face images, LDA is applied to the data extracted using the EM. Throughout the experiments, our method has shown improvements on the dimension reduction of feature space and the face recognition over the previously proposed methods.

The organization of the paper is as follows. In Section 2, we define an EP as magnitude of effective coefficients and explain the creation process of the energy map using EP. and describes the face recognition procedure by our method, which is based on the EP and energy map. In addition, we interpret the background of DCT and LDA. Experimental results are presented and discussed in Section 3. Finally, Section 4 concludes this paper.

2 Face Recognition Using Effective Transform Coefficients

In this section, energy probability is defined as criterion of effective information and the creation process of energy map using energy probability is explained.

2.1 Background

If we transform face images and non-face images into the frequency domain, then we can observe differences between both in the frequency distribution pattern. In order to represent data in the frequency domain, some transform such as Discrete Sine Transform, Discrete Sine Transform, and Discrete Wavelet Transform is needed[8-11]. Here, the chosen one is the DCT as an instance. The Fig.1 (a) and (c) show the general image and the face image. In Fig. 1(b) and (d), we see diagrams about coefficients used the DCT. As shown in the Fig. 1(b), the DCT coefficients with large magnitude are mainly uniformly situated in the upper-left corner of the DCT matrix. Compared with Fig. 1(b), the DCT coefficients in Fig. 1(d) are more left located in the upper-left corner of DCT matrix. Generally, horizontal frequencies increase from left to right, and vertical frequencies increase from top to bottom. To select optimal region including this distinction, we need to define a criterion of effective information. In this paper, energy probability is used as the criterion of effective information.

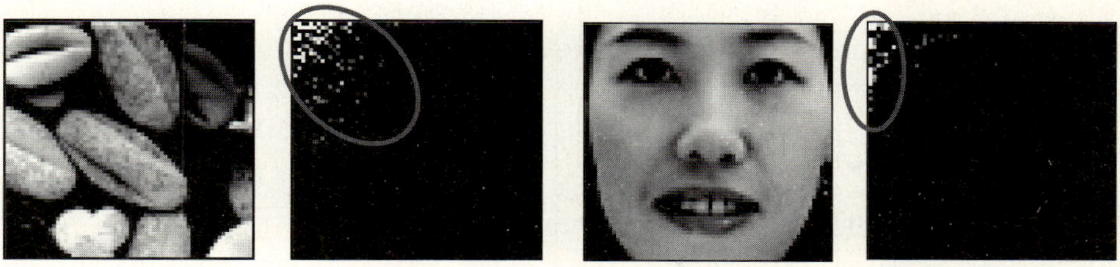

(a) (b) (c) (d)

Fig. 1. Example of a non-face image (a) and its DCT transformed image (b), and example of face image (c) and its DCT transformed image (d)

The energy is frequently utilized in signal processing domain such as audio and video coding and it means characteristics of images[8]. Given a result of DCT transformed from the image, *F(u, v)*, size *N×N*, the energy using DCT coefficients is defined as follows:

$$Energy_F = \sum_{u=1}^{N}\sum_{v=1}^{N}|F(u,v)|^2 \tag{1}$$

An important point to emphasize is the fact that $Energy_f$ is only one value, concerned with one image. It means it can be each property of each image. However, it cannot be suited our purpose, dimension reduction and optimization of valid information. For the extracted features of face, we should define Energy Probability, *EP(u, v)* and it is defined by:

$$EP(u,v) = \frac{|F(u,v)|^2}{Energy_F} \tag{2}$$

The magnitude of *EP(u, v)* is used as criterion of valid coefficients. The total number of *EP(u, v)*, N^2, indicates the ratio of an energy value holding a whole face image to an energy value held a pixel of position *(u, v)*. Hence, we can say that the large value *EP(u, v)* means more valid information than face features have.

Energy Map(EM) represents the distribution location of the effective coefficients measured by the EP. Assuming that one EM is generated from one face image, it is only optimized valid location related to the one face image rather than the general face image. Thus, if we can not only create the EM from one face image, but also create the EM from many face images, then it would be created from the general face image. The choice in the former or the latter depends on a design of systems. In this article, we limit the discussion to the EM formation about one face image.

Figure 2 summarize the generation procedure of EM. We assume that *N* is the width and height of images. The face image is transformed through DCT. The *EP*, 2-D vector of size *N*×*N*, is converted into the column vector *S,* length of N^2. *S* is arranged by the value of *EP* in descending order. We assume that the value of *S(k)* is *K*. If we select the *k*-th EP, then we will be remained 1 from the first to *k*-th value. Otherwise set the value of $EP(u,v)$ to change to zero by the following equation:

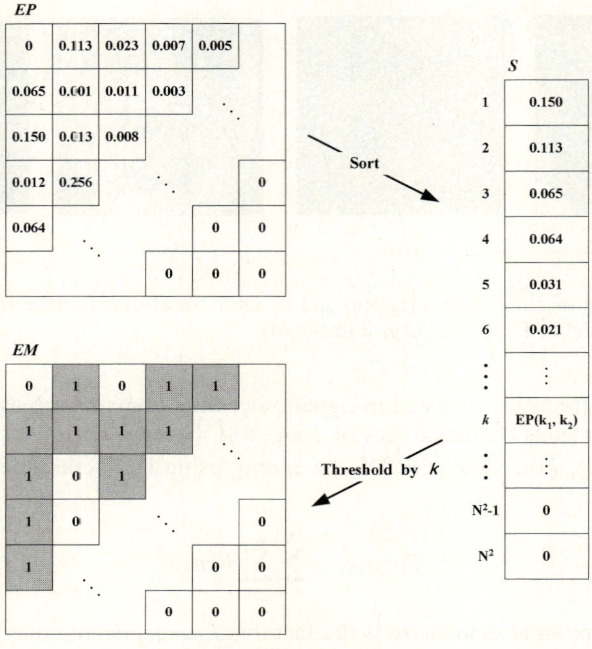

Fig. 2. The creation procedure of energy map

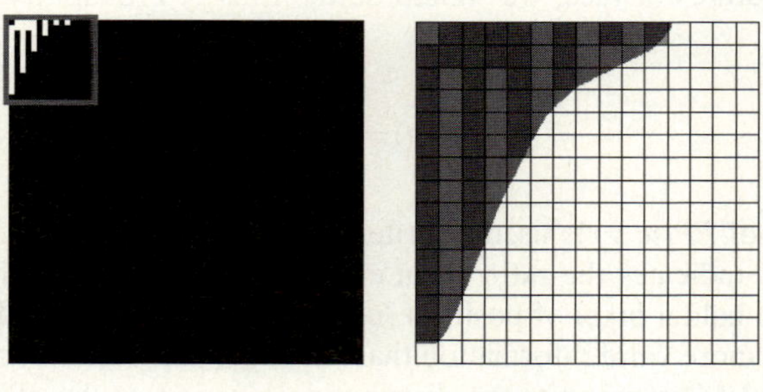

Fig. 3. (a) is the *Energy Map* and (b) is magnification of 15×15 block

$$EM(u,v) = \begin{cases} 1, & \text{if } EP(u,v) \le K \\ 0, & \text{otherwise.} \end{cases} \tag{3}$$

Figure 3 shows the *EM* and its magnification of 15×15 block. These diagrams represent that the lengthwise extended shape has a characteristic of large horizontal variation in face images. Universal face images have a distinguishing mark of these shapes.

2.2 Face Recognition

In this paper, face recognition procedure consists of three steps; 1) preprocessing, 2) feature extraction, and 3) classification. First, original images are divided into two categories, the first is the training image set and the second is test image set. Then, each image set is transformed into the frequency domain using DCT. Second, EP is calculated for the dimension reduction and optimization of valid coefficients, and then EM is generated. Next, to obtain the most significant feature of face images, LDA is applied to the data extracted from EM. Finally, to determine the recognition rate, we perform classification by the Nearest Neighbor classifier. The Euclidean Distance is employed as a similarity criterion.

In order to explain the preprocessing, we must refer to DCT. It is frequently used solution of various problems in image and signal processing. It expresses data as the sum of cosine function for reduced size of data. Under the assumption that gray scale matrix of face image as *f(x, y)* of size $N \times N$, its DCT as *F(u, v)* of size $N \times N$, is calculate from:

$$F(u,v) = \alpha(u)\alpha(v)\sum_{x=1}^{N}\sum_{y=1}^{N} f(x,y) \times \cos\left[\frac{(2x+1)u\pi}{2N}\right]\cos\left[\frac{(2y+1)v\pi}{2N}\right] \tag{4}$$

where,

$$\alpha(u),\alpha(v) = \begin{cases} \sqrt{\dfrac{1}{N}}, & u,v=1 \\ \sqrt{\dfrac{2}{N}}, & otherwise \end{cases} \tag{5}$$

with *u, v, x, y=1,2,3,…,N*, where *x* and *y* are coordinates in the spatial domain, and *u* and *v* are coordinates in the frequency domain[1].

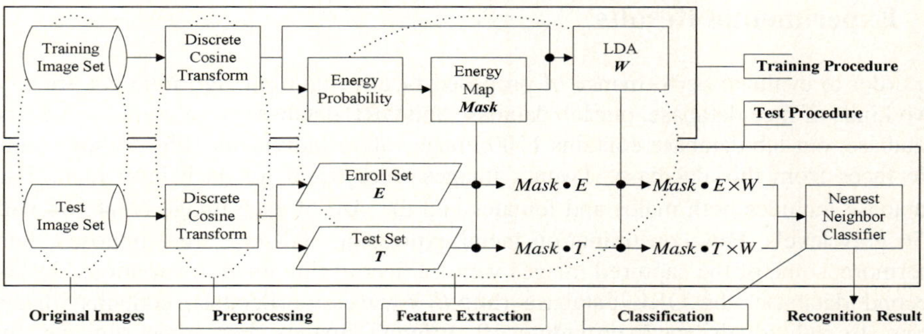

Fig. 4. Face Recognition Procedure

The first element, $F(1, 1)$, is the average of all the samples in the input image and is called Direct Current (DC) component. The remaining elements in $F(u, v)$ indicate the amplitude corresponding to the frequency component of $f(x, y)$, and are define as Alternate Current (AC) coefficients. It is well-known that the DC coefficient only depends on the brightness of the image. Consequently, it becomes DC-*free* (i.e., zero mean) and invariant against uniform brightness change by simply removing the DC coefficient [3]. The proposed method sets zero-valued DC coefficient and the remaining AC coefficients for eliminating illumination characteristic of the image.

Figure 4 appears the entire procedure of face recognition. First, face images are transformed into DCT domain through DCT. Second, DCT domain acquired from face image is applied on EP for the purpose of dimension reduction of data and optimization of valid coefficients. The EP is defined as criterion of effective facial features in section 2.2. Third, in order to obtain the most invariant feature of face images, the LDA is applied in the data extracted from the EM. It can facilitate the selection of effective coefficients for image recognition, because all the pixels are not useful in classification. At last, linear discriminative features are extracted by LDA and classification is performed by the nearest neighbor classifier. We divide original images into two parts of the training and test image set. The training image set is applied to DCT and it is computed EP. Then, we generate the EM. When the number of valid coefficients of EM is n and the number of training images is M, it creates *Mask* vector of size $n \times M$.

In feature extraction, The LDA is one of the most popular linear projection methods for feature extraction. It is used to find a linear projection of the original vectors from a high dimensional space to an optimal low dimensional subspace in which the ratio of the between-class scatter and the within-class scatter is maximized. The W is the LDA optimal projection matrix and calculated by *Mask* vector. In the same way, the test image set is applied to DCT and divide test image set into two parts of the enroll set E and test set T. $Mask \bullet E$ denotes E applied on the frequency mask. The extracted final feature vector is $Mask \bullet E \times W$ and $Mask \bullet T \times W$ and is calculated the Euclidian distance between them.

3 Experimental Results

In order to evaluate performance of proposed face recognition algorithm empirically, two kinds of face database, our lab database and ORL database were used. 1) The first database, our lab database contains 1100 images of 55 individuals. Fig. 5 shows sample faces from this database. Twenty images were taken for each individual. This database includes both males and females and the size of each image is 64×64 with 256 gray levels. Few constraints on facial expression and pose were imposed. Furthermore, some of the captured images were subject to illumination variations. 2) The second database, the ORL database (http:// www.cam-orl.co.uk), contains images from 40 individuals, each providing 10 different images. For some subjects, the images were taken at different times. The facial expressions (open or closed eyes,

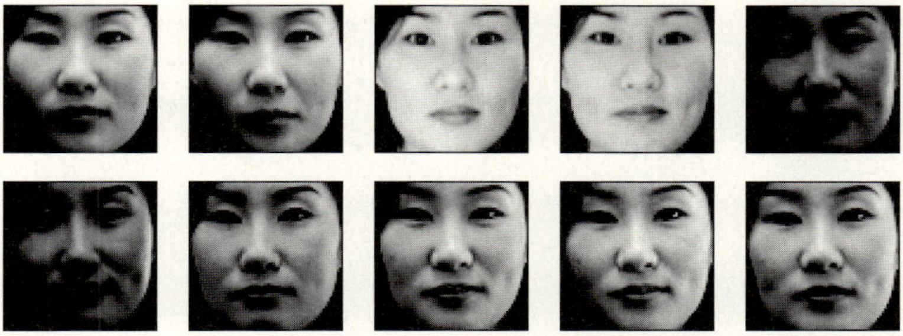

Fig. 5. Example faces in the first database

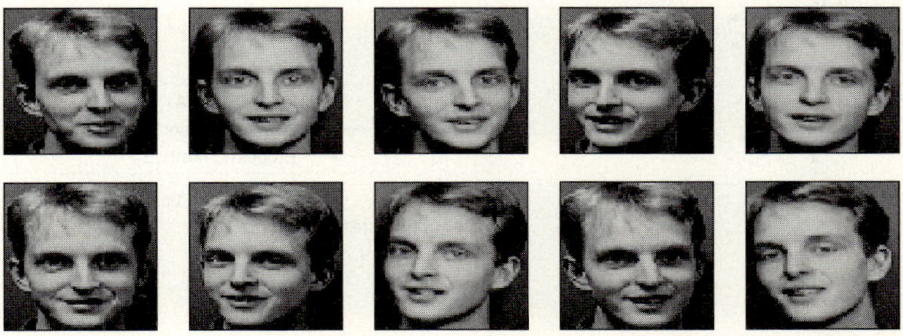

Fig. 6. Example faces in the second database (ORL database)

smiling or nonsmiling) and facial details (glasses or no glasses) also vary. The images were taken with a tolerance for some tilting and rotation of the face of up to 20 degrees. Moreover, there is also some variation in the scale of up to about 10 percent. All images are grayscale and normalized to a resolution of 92×112 pixels and each image is scaled to 64×64. Ten sample images of one person from the ORL database are shown in Fig. 6.

In the experiments, ten training images and ten test images per person are selected from the first database, and a training set of 550 images and a test set of 550 images are decided for the following experiments. In the second database, it is choose as five training images and five test images per person, and each set has 200 images. That is to say, the training images and test images is not overlapped between the two sets in both cases. Finally, the nearest neighbor classifier is used for classification.

The proposed method is compared with the results from the following conventional feature extraction methods: PCA + LDA and DCT coefficients + LDA. Fig. 7 and Fig. 8 show that is altered the number of reduced effective coefficient and fixed the number of extracted valid vector by LDA. The number of extracted feature used in LDA is 30 and 20 in the first and second database.

Figure 7 and 8 appear recognition rate with the increments of the number of the dimension reduction data and the final features applied to the LDA with fixed number. For the rank 1, the best recognition rates of PCA + LDA, DCT coefficients + LDA, and proposed method are 90.0%, 94.4%, and 96.8% in the first database

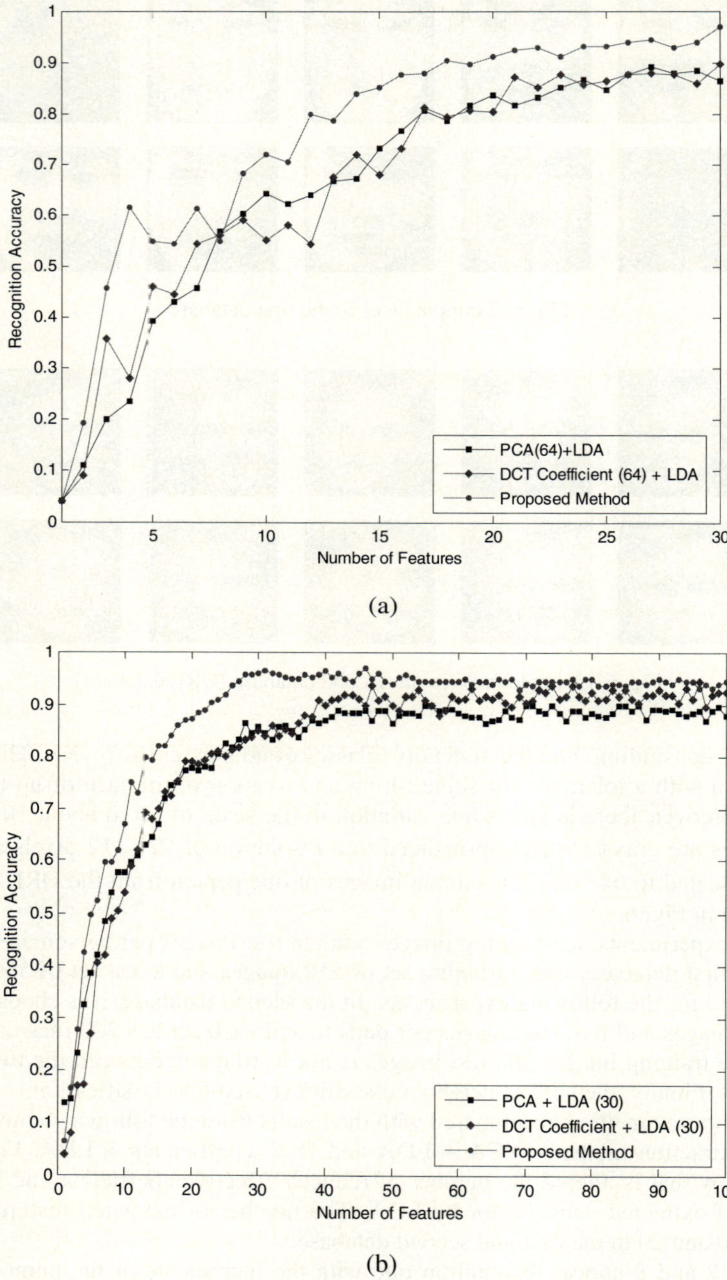

Fig. 7. (a) is recognition accuracy with the number of reduced data, 64 and the increments of the number of extracted features (b) is recognition accuracy with the increments of the number of reduce data and number of extracted features, 30

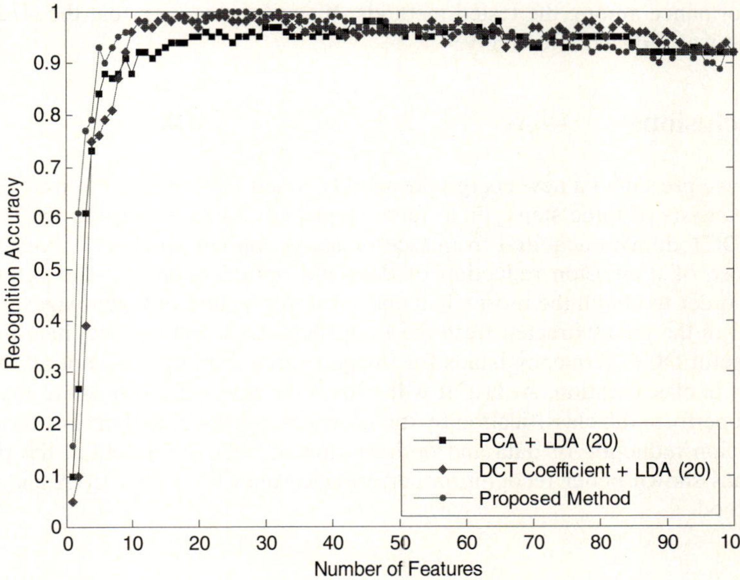

Fig. 8. The recognition accuracy with the increments of the number of reduce data and number of extracted features, 20

Table 1. Comparison of classification performance usign the ETRI database

Methods	PCA + LDA	DCT Coefficient + LDA	Proposed method
Number of Reduced Data	74	96	46
Number of Extracted Feature	29	30	30
Recognition Accuracy (%)	90.0	94.4	96.8

Table 2. Comparison of classification performance usign the ORL database

Methods	PCA + LDA	DCT Coefficient + LDA	Proposed method
Number of Reduced Data	46	23	23
Number of Extracted Feature	20	20	19
Recognition Accuracy (%)	98.5	99.0	100.0

(Table1) and 98.5%, 99.0%, and 100% in the second database (Table 2), respectively. Accuracy is computed by the number of reduced data in the second row and the number of extracted features in the third row in Table 1 and 2. The recognition accuracies in the forth row are the minimum number of reduced data with the best performance. By fixing the shortcomings of conventional methods, proposed methods showed the best performance among the tested methods. It can be also seen that the size of data dimension was reduced effectively.

4 Conclusions

In paper, we presented a new energy probability based feature extraction method. Our method consists of three steps. First, face images are transformed into DCT domain. Second, DCT domain acquired from face image is applied on energy probability for the purpose of dimension reduction of data and optimization of valid information. Third, in order to obtain the most silent and invariant feature of face images, the LDA is applied in the data extracted from the frequency mask that can facilitate the selection of useful DCT frequency bands for image recognition, because not all the bands are useful in classification. At last, it will extract the linear discriminative features by LDA and perform the classification by the nearest neighbor classifier. For the purpose of dimension reduction of data and optimization of valid information, the proposed method has shown better recognition performance than PCA plus LDA and existing DCT method.

References

1. A. Martinez and A. Kak: PCA versus LDA. IEEE Trans. on Pattern Analysis and Machine Intelligence, Vol. 23, no. 2. (2001) 228–233
2. H. Yu and J. Yang: A direct LDA algorithm for high-dimensional data with application to face recognition. Pattern Recognit., Vol. 34, no. 12. (2001) 2067–2070
3. J. Lee: Automatic Video Management System Using Face Recognition and MPEG-7 Visual Descriptors. ETRI Journal, Vol.27, no.6, (2005) 806-809
4. Z.M. Hafed and M.D. Levine: Face Recognition Using the Discrete Cosine Transform. International Journal of Computer Vision, Vol. 43, no.3, (2001) 167–188
5. X. Jing and D. Zhang: A Face and Palmprint Recognition Approach Based on Discriminant DCT Feature Extraction. IEEE Transactions on Systems, Man, and Cybernetics-part b: Cybernetics, Vol. 34, no. 6 (2004)
6. M. J. Er, W. Chen, and S. Wu: High-Speed Face Recognition Based on Discrete Cosine Transform and RBF Neural Networks. IEEE Transactions on Neural Networks, vol. 16, no. 3 (2005)
7. M. J. Er, and S. Wu: PCA and LDA in DCT domain. Pattern Recognition Letters, Vol. 26. (2005) 2474-2482
8. G.H. Park and K.H. Kim: Adaptive Scanning Methods for Fine Granularity Scalable Video Coding. ETRI Journal, Vol. 26, no.4, (2004) 332-343
9. S. Koç, E. Erçelebi : Image Restoration by Lifting-Based Wavelet Domain E-Median Filter. ETRI Journal, Vol.28, no.1, (2006) 51-58
10. W.H. Kim, S.Y. Jeong and K.H. Kim: Scalable Interframe Wavelet Coding with Low Complex Spatial Wavelet Transform. ETRI Journal, Vol.28, no.2, (2006) 145-154
11. W. K. Pratt: Digital Image Processing. John Wiley & Sons, Inc., New York (2001) 173-181
12. Gordon E. Carlson: Signal and Linear System Analysis. John Wiley & Sons, Inc., New York (1998) 152-163
13. R. C. Gonzalez and R. E. Woods: Digital Image Processing. Addison Wesley, Massachusetts (1992) 472-47713.

Finding the Perfect Projection System – Human Perception of Projection Quality Depending on Distance and Projection Angle

Jochen Ehnes and Michitaka Hirose

Hirose, Hirota & Tanikawa Lab, RCAST, The University of Tokyo,
Tokyo, Japan
{ehnes, hirose}@cyber.rcast.u-tokyo.ac.jp
http://www.cyber.rcast.u-tokyo.ac.jp

Abstract. In this paper we describe our approach to find the most suitable among several projection based Augmented Reality systems to display information on moveable objects in real time. After an introduction to the scenario, we describe our approach to estimate the Quality of Projection that each individual projection system can achieve. After that we describe how we compared these estimates to the perception of human beings. Finally we present the results, which includes a new estimation function.

Keywords: Perceived Projection Quality, User Tests, Projection Based Augmented Reality, Spatial Augmented Reality, Application Roaming, Distributed Augmented Reality, Multi Projection System, Projector Camera System.

1 Introduction: Projector Based Augmented Reality

Aiming for a technology that supports the user without being a hinderance, we developed an Augmented Reality (AR) system based on a combination of a video projector and a video camera mounted on a pan and tilt device. Using this technology, we built a system that can project augmentations on fixed as well as movable objects around the projection device. However, the nature of the projection introduces some limitations: Objects have to be close enough to the AR-projection system so that the system can detect the markers and the resolution of the projection is still high enough to be readable. Surfaces that shall be augmented have to face the projector. While certain angles between the surface normal and the direction of projection can be compensated by pre-distorting the projected augmentation, the quality of the projection decreases with increasing angles. At 90 degrees a projection becomes impossible. Finally, the augmentation may be shadowed by objects between the projector and the augmented surface. While it does not seem viable to overcome these limitations with a single projection system, it becomes possible by using several similar, networked AR-projection systems. The challenge hereby is to coordinate the different systems, to find the system with the 'best view', and to switch to a

E. Sha et al. (Eds.): EUC 2006, LNCS 4096, pp. 1017–1026, 2006.

different system if the augmented object is moved in a way that makes an other system have the 'best view' on it.

2 Previous and Related Work

This work builds on our previous work, mainly [2], [3]. The essential parts are summarized in section 2.1 and 2.2. Other controllable projector camera systems have been presented in [7] and [5]. In [8] the usage of several I/O-Bulbs (projector/camera systems) has been described as well. However, these systems all project on fixed surfaces such as tabletops ([7] and [8]) or a predefined set of fixed surfaces ([5]). While several projection systems are used in [8], their projection areas do not overlap. The systems all project on to different tabletops. Consequently there was never the need to decide which projector to use to augment a certain surface at runtime. In [4] a system is presented that eliminates the shadows cast by persons in front of a screen by using several projectors. However, this system requires exact calibration of the projectors, cameras and the display screen, something that is not possible when everything is movable. Furthermore, the requirement that only projectors may be occluded while the camera needs to be able to observe the whole screen at all times is something that contradicts with our basic idea of projector and camera forming one unit, being together as closely as possible. Different aspects that affect the quality of the projected augmentations have been researched before as well. The accuracy of optical tracking systems (in that case ARToolKit) depending on camera distance and relative camera angle has been examined in [1]. An other important factor for the perceived quality of a projection is the projection surface. In [6] the usability of interfaces projected onto real world objects has been tested.

2.1 Projected Applications (PA) and Application Roaming

While conventional applications communicate with the user via windows and widgets on a computer's screen, our *Projected Applications* (PA) use tracked objects for interaction. The AR-system can be regarded as an operating system that loads projected applications (identified by the marker on the tracked object) from an application server and executes them. Currently an application can output its data only to the projector of the system it is running on. This keeps the implementation of the applications simple and seemed appropriate since the jitter from the tracking system does not permit to match two projections on an object exactly. Besides serving PA for marker IDs, the application server keeps the states of the PA while they are not executed on any system. It also ensures that all PA are executed on only one AR-system at a time in order to keep their states consistent. To do so, it grants the display rights for an application to the first projection system that request them and waits until they are returned from there with the modified state. Only then they may be sent out to another system together with the new state.

2.2 Optimizing the Quality of Projection

In order to maximize the visible quality of the projected augmentation, as well as to make the transition between two projection systems as smooth as possible, we extended the management of the display rights. The application server can withdraw display rights and give them to better suited projection systems. In order to decide which system is suited best, we introduced a scalar *quality value* (section 3) that is provided by every projection system that detects the relevant tracked object. The system with the highest quality value is considered the best and consequently is assigned the display rights. The projected applications implement a function that calculates the quality value, since the criteria for quality can be very task specific.

3 The "Quality Value"

A crucial point in order to find the optimal projection system is the estimation of the quality of the projection that each system is able to achieve. It is not necessary to calculate an absolute quality level. The only requirement for quality values is that they can be compared with each other and that a greater value means a better quality. The quality of a projection as perceived by a human user depends on many factors. The surface material is one of them ([6]). However, that does not change at runtime. Since we only need to consider things that change at runtime, our quality value depends only on the geometric relation between projector/camera and the tracked object. We assumed that the perceived quality of projection would be better the higher the resolution is. The first two sketches of figure 1 illustrate the reduction of the number of projected pixels from moving the object further away. Since this reduction of the resolution appears horizontally as well as vertically, the aspect ratio of the pixels stays the same. A quality value that corresponds to the number of projected pixels can be calculated using equation 1.

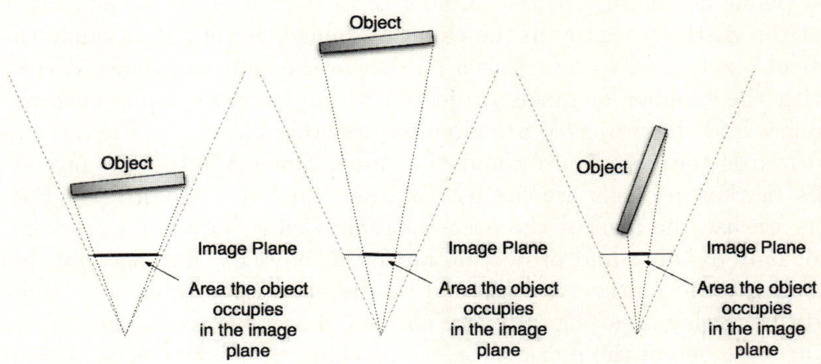

Fig. 1. A reduced area in the image plane results in fewer pixels projected onto the object

$$QV_{Distance} = \left(\frac{Const}{Distance}\right)^2 \tag{1}$$

A useful value for *Const* seemed to be the minimal distance between projection system and projection surface, as that normalizes the resulting quality values. However, that is just cosmetic, since quality values are not restricted to lay within a certain range. The first and the third sketch illustrate the effect of rotation on the number of pixels used for an augmentation. Accordingly the quality value depending on the rotation can be calculated as

$$QV_{Rotation} = dot(\widehat{N_{surface}}, -\widehat{Dir_{projection}}) \tag{2}$$

With $N_{surface}$ being the surface normal and $Dir_{projection}$ the direction of projection. The pixels are stretched perpendicular to the axis of rotation and usually change their aspect ratio. In that sense the effect of rotation is different from the change of distance. That prompted us to also consider an alternate formula to calculate the effect of distance on the perceived quality that takes into account only one dimension.

$$QV_{Distance1Dim} = \frac{Const}{Distance} \tag{3}$$

The shadowing of the augmentation also depends on the spatial relationship between projector and the augmented surface. However, it also depends on the position and shape of other objects, which are usually unknown to the projection system. Consequently the shadowing of the augmentation can not be taken into account for the quality value properly. As long as the marker of an object is visible, we assume that the projection surface is unobstructed as well. By using several markers around the projection surface, a system can assume partial occlusion if only some of the markers are detected.

In order to augment tracked objects, $QV_{Distance}$ and $QV_{Rotation}$ can be multiplied to get a combined quality value QV. This QV basically correlates to the number of projected pixels. An alternative and more *pragmatic approach* of a Quality Value correlating to the number of projected pixels is the area in pixels that the markers occupy in the camera's image. Hereby we assume that the number of pixels used to represent a marker in the camera's image corresponds well with the number of pixels projected to augment the same surface, since the camera and the projector are mounted together closely, so the distance and angle towards the object are about the same. Since AR-ToolKit provides the size of a marker in pixels, we can use that as a quality value directly. For multi markers we use the sum of the areas of their visible individual markers. This way not only distance and projection angle can be taken into account, but also if some of the sub markers are blocked by the user. By placing several markers around the display area (e.g. at every corner), a user blocks the line of sight towards at least one of the markers before blocking the display area. This results in a lower total marker area (= quality value) compared to a system that does not get blocked and thus the non obstructed system would be chosen. Example applications where tracked objects are augmented can be seen in figure 2.

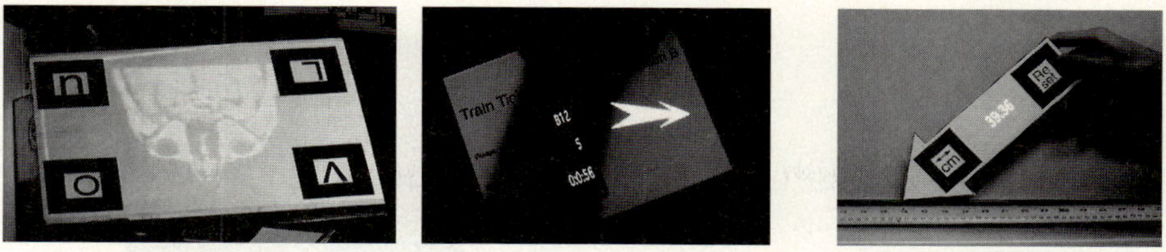

(a) Volume Slicer. (b) Guiding Ticket. (c) Distance Arrow.

Fig. 2. Example applications augmenting tracked objects

Since we found several formulas to calculate the quality value, which all rely on certain assumptions, we decided that we would have to conduct some user tests to evaluate the different approaches.

4 The User Test

Our approach of using the marker area as quality value worked well. The switching of projection devices would often go unnoticed since it was less visible than the permanent jitter produced by the optical tracking system. It became more obvious the greater the difference in distance between the object and the projection systems. This raised the question if it was due to the different natures of distortion originating from changes in distance (pixels scale in both dimensions) versus changes in angle (pixels scale perpendicular to the axis of rotation, they don't remain squares anymore), or if it was partly due to a flawed calculation of quality values. We decided to examine the exactness of our estimations more closely by comparing these quality values to the quality of projection as perceived by human beings. Since the experience of using our system depends on several other factors such as the tracking system, we decided that we could not do the tests using the AR-system itself.

4.1 Preparations for the Test

In order to make the tests reproducible, to make it easier for the test subjects and to eliminate other factors such as the performance of the tracking system, we decided to take pictures of an augmented object in a set of distances and under several angles of projection while recording the tracking information. We showed pairs of images to test subjects, making them rank the images according to the perceived quality of augmentation. Later we would compare the subjects' ranking of these images to the rankings based on our quality values. To take the pictures, we mounted a digital camera on a tripod on a board as shown in figure 3. The camera pointed at the tracked object that was also fixed on the board. We choose our 'Guiding Ticket' demo PA, since it displays text (the track where the train is leaving on, and how much time till the train leaves), as well as graphics (an arrow pointing in the direction to walk). We disabled the application's logic for the test, so that the augmentation stays the same for all

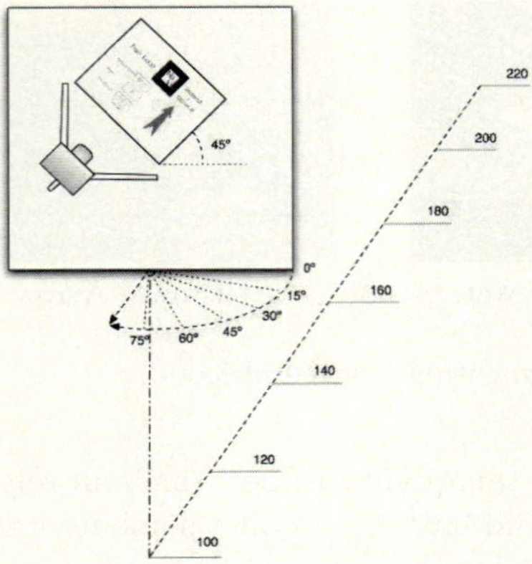

(a) Setup sketch

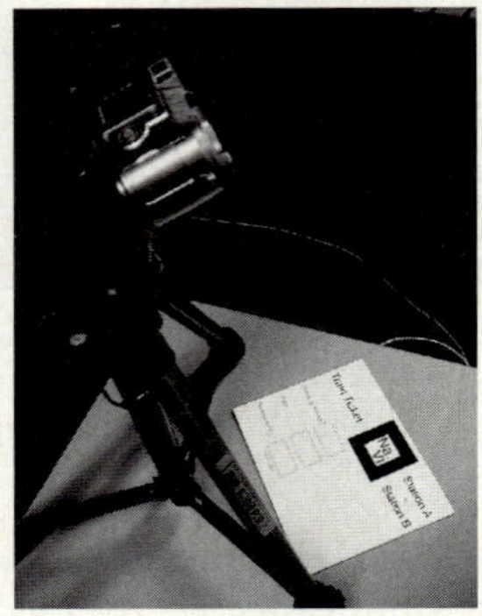

(b) Camera mount

Fig. 3. Mounting of Camera and augmented object on a board which would be rotated to different angles towards the projector at different distances

the pictures we take. We rotated the object 45 degrees so that the rotation of the board affects both dimensions of the augmentation on it. To conduct our tests, we developed an application. One module of that application was made to support the collection of the sample data. It connects to the modified 'Guiding Ticket' PA via sockets and guides the user through the collection of samples. It shows the distance and the angle in large characters on screen, so the operator can operate it from afar while holding the board in place. Once the board is in the right place, the operator starts the sampling by pressing the button on a wireless mouse. The test application then communicates with the 'Guiding Ticket' PA, gets the latest transformation matrix and the marker area of the tracked object and makes the PA use the same values for five seconds. This gives the operator enough time to take a picture without jitter and ensures that the picture and the sampled tracking values fit together exactly. After all samples are taken, the images are transfered to the computer. They are then moved into the correct data-sets of the test application. For our test we use distances from 1.0m to 2.2m in 0.2 m increments. At each distance, the object was sampled facing the projector directly and rotated away by 15, 30, 45, 60 and 75 degrees.

4.2 Evaluation of Quality Values

As defined in section 3, quality values do not have a unit of measurement and are not required to lie in a certain range. $QV_{Distance}$, $QV_{Distance1Dim}$ and $QV_{Rotation}$ as introduced in that section for example lie in the range between 0.0 and 1.0. The marker area on the other hand is an integer value that is usually much bigger than 1. As such, it does not make sense to compare these values directly. Instead we want to evaluate their ability to generate a linear order from the multidimensional tracking values and how well this order corresponds to the human perception of quality.

Our test application provides the functionality to sort all samples according to these quality values. Alternatively it can also sort the samples based on a human test subject's judgement of the images. Therefore the subject is presented pairs of images as shown in figure 4. The subject selects which one of the two

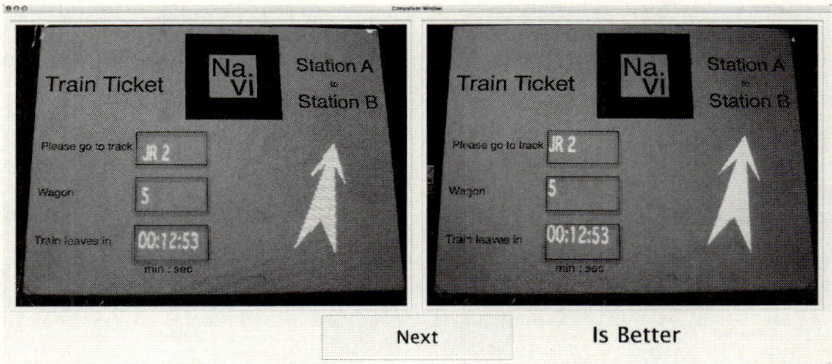

Fig. 4. During the user test the subject is presented pairs of images and has to select the better ones. In this case the subject chose the right image.

pictures shows the better augmentation and then presses the 'Next' button. The application uses the sort by insert algorithm, starting with a sorted list that contains only one sample. Then it picks a new sample, displays its image on the right side and shows the image of the sample from the middle of the sorted list on the left side. Depending on the subject's choice, the search is continued in the lower or upper half of the sorted list until the insertion point for the new sample is found. This continues until all photos have been sorted according to the quality as perceived by the test subject. In our case of 42 samples, the subjects took between 10 and 20 minutes for that test.

After the samples have been sorted accordingly to the quality values or human perception, the samples are ranked by their position in the sorted array. In order to compare these rankings, we generate tables consisting of ranking values in which the columns represent the different angles and the rows different distances. After importing these tables into Excel, we can visualize them. The contour chart turned out to be very useful. It generates a surface from the ranking values. This surface is viewed from above and different heights of the surface are represented by different colors. Figure 5(a) illustrates this type of graphics with a 3D view.

The rankings produced by our test subjects were all different from each other. That demonstrates that it often is a difficult decision to choose the better one of two pictures, one that different people make differently. In conclusion we believe that it would not be of any benefit to reduce the step size for the angles and distances any further. Looking at the average and median (figure 5) however reveals that they both are very similar. That makes us confident that the basic characteristics actually reveals something about the way humans make their decisions. The variance diagram shows that the biggest discrepancies in judgement

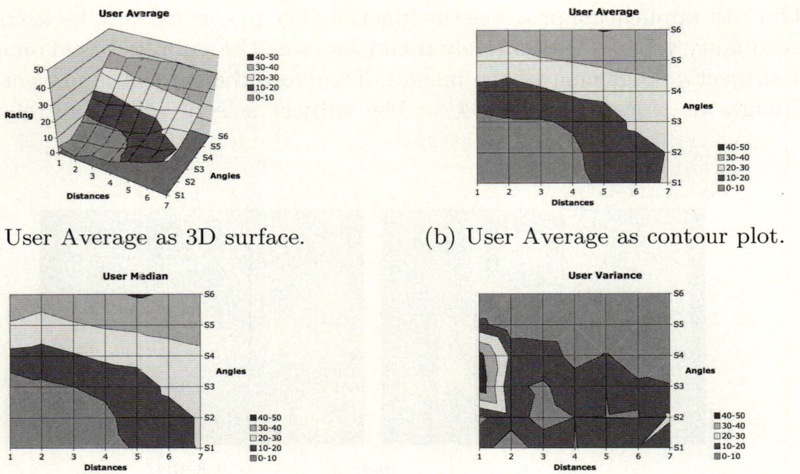

(a) User Average as 3D surface.
(b) User Average as contour plot.

(c) User Median.
(d) User Variance.

Fig. 5. Visualization of statistical data from the rankings made by 13 persosn

happened at the second and third rotation in the position closest to the projector. In these samples the tracking/calibration was off by about one cm, which resulted the augmented text to lie on the border of the text boxes printed on the 'Train Ticket'. Although the subjects were told to ignore tracking inaccuracies and judge only the projection quality, some must have taken these offsets into account for their ranking, leading to these huge differences. On the other hand it becomes very clear that all subjects agreed in their judgment of the augmentations from an angle of 75 degrees (S6). In fact all but two subjects ranked these augmentations on the last seven positions (35 to 41).

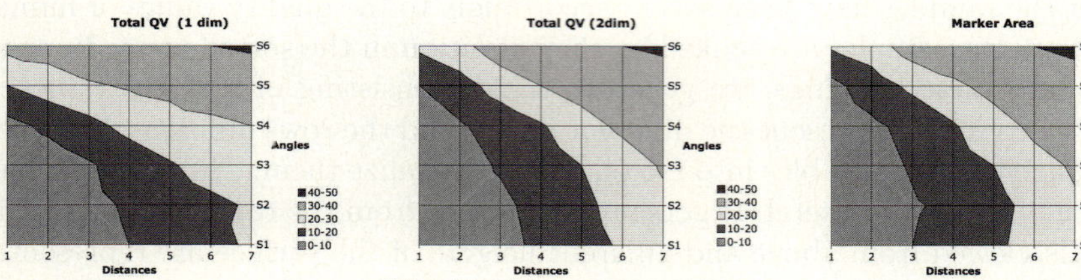

(a) $QV_{Dist1Dim} * QV_{Rot}$
(b) $QV_{Dist} * QV_{Rot}$
(c) Marker Area

Fig. 6. The Quality Values described before

The ranking diagrams generated from the Quality Values (figure 6) are quite similar, especially (b) and (c), which both correspond to the amount of pixels used for the augmentation. The offset of the camera only leads to a slight preference of the 15° samples (S2) over the 0° (S1) ones in case of the marker area.

Compared with the human ratings however, the differences are quite apparent. For once, the human subjects evaluated the samples projected from an angle of 75° as much worse, than the quality values computed using the equations presented earlier. The top edge in the diagrams 5(b/c) is completely green, whereas the yellow and red band goes much higher up in the quality values' diagrams. On the other hand the quality values evaluate the increasing distance as much worse than the human subjects, which can be seen from the blue area being much less wide in the quality values' diagrams. It turns out that the quality value $QV_{Distance1Dim} * QV_{Rotation}$ is closer to the user's rating than the other two. However, it is still quite different. The borders of the three regions follow the curve of a cosine function while especially the border of the blue area in the user averages is nearly horizontal and then becomes nearly vertical at the fourth distance step. This led us to the conclusion that the quality as perceived by humans may depend mainly on the factor that has the bigger effect on the resolution. A quality value

$$QV_{min} = \min(QV_{Distance1Dim}, QV_{Rotation}) \tag{4}$$

has this property as illustrated in figure 7(a). It is important to note that in this case the value of $Const$ in equation 3 becomes significant. We used 1500 (mm) for figure 7(a).

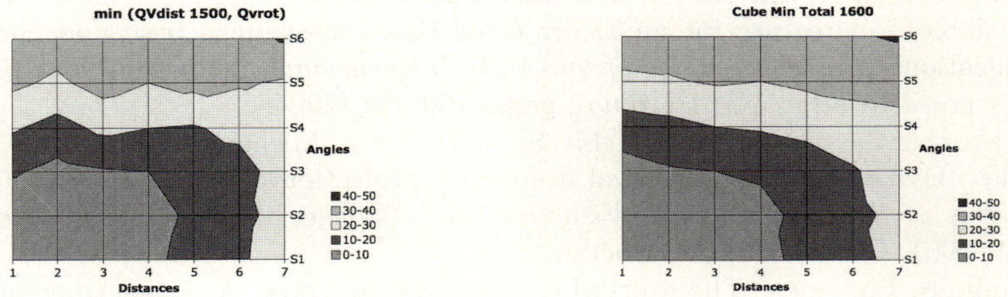

(a) $QV_{min1500}$ (b) QV_{result}(equation 5)

Fig. 7. Quality values that use the minimum of $QV_{Distance1Dim}$ and $QV_{Rotation}$

While figure 7(a) clearly is very different from the figures 5 (b) and (c), we can combine QV_{min} with other functions we used before to get a resulting quality value

$$QV_{result} = QV_{min1600}^3 * QV_{Dist1Dim} * QV_{Rot} \tag{5}$$

that estimates the projected quality according to human perception pretty well.

5 Results

In this paper we described how we conducted user tests to determine the perceived quality of projected augmentations depending on different distances between the object and the projector, as well as different projection angles. We illustrated how we compared these findings with our previously used functions to estimate the projected quality. After detecting a mismatch, we refined our formula to calculate quality values. As a result the projection quality of augmentations from our network of AR-Projection systems is optimized more accurately.

6 Future Work

We realize that it would be more exact if we had taken rotations around different axes into account. However, it would have multiplied the number of samples to be taken and to be sorted by every test subject. Consequently the number of steps in each dimension would have to be reduced.

References

1. Daniel F. Abawi, Joachim Bienwald, and Ralf Dörner. Accuracy in optical tracking with fiducial markers: An accuracy function for artoolkit. In *ISMAR*, pages 260–261, 2004.
2. Jochen Ehnes, Koichi Hirota, and Michitaka Hirose. Projected applications - taking applications from the desktop onto real world objects. In *HCII2005 Conference Proceedings [CD Rom], Lawrence Erlbaum Associates*, 2005.
3. Jochen Ehnes, Koichi Hirota, and Michitaka Hirose. Projected augmentation ii - a scalable architecture for multi projector based ar-systems based on "projected applications". In *Proceedings of the ACM International Symposium on Mixed and Augmented Reality (ISMAR 2005)*, pages 190–191, 2005.
4. Christopher Jaynes, Stephen Webb, R. Matt Steele, Michael Brown, and W. Brent Seales. Dynamic shadow removal from front projection displays. In *VIS '01: Proceedings of the conference on Visualization '01*, pages 175–182, Washington, DC, USA, 2001. IEEE Computer Society.
5. Claudio S. Pinhanez. The everywhere displays projector: A device to create ubiquitous graphical interfaces. In *UbiComp '01: Proceedings of the 3rd international conference on Ubiquitous Computing*, pages 315–331, London, UK, 2001. Springer-Verlag.
6. Mark Podlaseck, Claudio Pinhanez, Nancy Alvarado, Margaret Chan, and Elisa Dejesus. On interfaces projected onto real-world objects. In *CHI '03: CHI '03 extended abstracts on Human factors in computing systems*, pages 802–803, New York, NY, USA, 2003. ACM Press.
7. John Underkoffler and Hiroshi Ishii. Illuminating light: An optical design tool with a luminous-tangible interface. In *CHI*, pages 542–549, 1998.
8. John Underkoffler, Brygg Ullmer, and Hiroshi Ishii. Emancipated pixels: real-world graphics in the luminous room. In Alyn Rockwood, editor, *Proceedings of the 26th annual conference on Computer graphics and interactive techniques*, pages 385–392. ACM Press/Addison-Wesley Publishing Co., 1999.

Context Reasoning Technologies in Ubiquitous Computing Environment

Sun Jie and Wu ZhaoHui

College of Computer Science, Zhejiang University, Hangzhou, Zhejiang, China 310027
{sunjie, wzh}@zju.edu.cn

Abstract. Context-aware computing is a hot area in ubiquitous computing. There are several challenges to be covered. This paper focuses on context reasoning, which means deducing higher context from raw sensor data. The context reasoning problem is discussed on two different levels: context inference/recognition concerning the generation of context atoms from raw sensor data, and context reasoning concerning the composition of context atoms and deduction of higher-level context. In this paper, we discuss some commonly used reasoning technologies in context-aware systems, including rule-based logics and machine learning methods. Besides, a clustering algorithm, the Symbol Clustering Map, is introduced to learn the current context.

1 Introduction

Mark Weiser first introduced the term ubiquitous computing in 1991[1]. The ability to compute anywhere, anytime in any way is the distinct characteristic. The use of context as an input is one of the major characteristics of ubiquitous computing and the research on this topic is context-aware computing. Context-aware computing is a computing paradigm in which applications can sense, react and adapt to their environment.

In a context-aware system, the most important information is the state of the environment, the devices and the users, which we call context. Context is any information that can be used to characterize the situation of an entity. [2]

For context-aware computing, there exist many challenges to be covered, such as: context acquisition, context modeling, context reasoning, context distribution and utilization. Context acquisition focuses on how to deal with heterogeneous, mass and ambiguous sensor data and gain useful information. Context modeling is to specify the intrinsic properties of and relationship among contexts. Context distribution use some subscription/ publishing and event triggering mechanism to distribute context throughout the system. The utilization of context is different in the existent projects. Context can be utilized in different granularity or level, such as the application level, the device level and the component level.

From the 80's to now, many projects are developed or in the progress, such as [3, 4, 5], which lay emphasis on the infrastructure of context acquisition, utilization, representation and model of context. However, little emphasis has been laid on context reasoning.

E. Sha et al. (Eds.): EUC 2006, LNCS 4096, pp. 1027 – 1036, 2006.

The reasoning technology has a long history in AI. Most context-aware projects pick some technology of AI to do simple reasoning. In our opinion, although AI and context-aware computing are similar in the sense of discovering and reasoning of knowledge, they are two different domains. The requirements and characteristics of context-aware system must be mentioned. In this paper we present the reasoning in context-aware system and introduce an algorithm Symbol Clustering Map (SCM) improved by us.

The remainder of this paper is organized as follows: in section 2 we list the related works applied in context-aware systems. Section 3 gives an introduction of context reasoning. In section 4 we introduce the algorithm of SCM. Section 5 shows the experiment and the result. We conclude the paper in section 6.

2 Related Works

The reasoning technologies generally used in context-aware system include rule-based logic, Bayesian network and neural network.

FOL is the most commonly used logic in context-aware projects. The typical one is GAIA [4]. It represents context as first-order predicates in the form of Location (chris, entering, room 3231) and uses rules to infer higher level context. Many other logics are applied, such as fuzzy logic used in [6], description logic used in [7] and temporal logic used in [8]. In most cases logic is powerful for reasoning with context knowledge, but its power is weakened when dealing with discrete unprocessed sensor data.

Bayesian network is a probability-based reasoning method. CORTEX [5] applies Bayesian network to context fusion and the conditional rules are used. [9] uses a naïve Bayes classifier to recognize raw context and reason higher-level context from context atoms. [10] takes advantage of Bayesian network to predict the next room a user will visit. Bayesian network is useful to model the uncertain nature and reason the probabilistic occurrence of a context.

Neural network is commonly used in context recognition and prediction. [11] combines KSOM and probability model to learn the user's activity. In [12] neural network is used to learn and predict user's context. [13] uses SOM to recognize different context.

For the development of ontology theory, many context-aware systems adopt ontology-based context model, such as CoolAgent [14], which use RDF to model context and Prolog Forward Chaining to reason context. Many middlewares support OWL-based context modeling and reasoning.

3 Context Reasoning

The research of context reasoning can be divided into two levels: the lower level and the higher level, which we call context inference and context reasoning respectively. There are different challenges and problems in the two levels.

3.1 Context Inference

This is the lower level of context reasoning, which lay emphasis on generating the current context of the user. We acquire the context of the user and the environment from sensors. We use a vector $S_1 \times S_2 \times \cdots \times S_n$ to denote the sensor readings at time t: $< s_1 \times s_2 \times \ldots \times s_n > \in S_1 \times S_2 \times \ldots \times S_n$.

In order to process the raw sensor data into context information, we need to solve the challenges such as: how to process the sensor data? How to deal with the conflictive information from multiple sources? How to match the raw data into context? We will discuss these in detail.

(1) The sensor data preprocessing

The sensor data are enormous, heterogeneous and nonstandard, which makes it hard to harness these data directly. So before the further process we must use different technologies to preprocess the sensor data. We reduce the data amount by sampling and using average or variance over a time to substitute the raw data. We rescale the sensor range to smooth the data diversity.

(2) Sensor fusion

Sensor fusion aims at integrating the information from multiple sensors. There are three kinds of fusion: competitive fusion, complementary fusion and cooperative fusion. The competitive fusion combines sensor data that represent the same measurement to reduce uncertainty and resolve conflicts. It is a basic fusion type. The fusion function always takes the form of weighting average. The complementary fusion combines incomplete sensor data do not dependant on each other directly to create a more complete model. The cooperative fusion combines sensor observations that depend upon each other to deduce higher-level measurement. The commonly used sensor fusion methods include classical inference, Bayesian inference, Dempster-Shafer theory, voting and fuzzy logic.

(3) Context matching

The raw sensor data is not sufficient for the context-aware system. We must derive knowledge about the user/device/environment context from it. The following steps are applied: feature extraction, classification, labeling.

From raw sensor data, specific data values will be extracted, which are called features. After the sensor data preprocessing, the average $\bar{s}$ or deviation σ can be used as features for time series of numerical data. We use a feature vector $< f_1, f_2, \ldots, f_n >_t \in F_1 \times F_2 \times \ldots F_n$ to denote the feature at time t.

Classifying the extracted features into clusters is to find the common pattern of the feature vectors. Using the pattern we can classify the feature vectors into clusters, in which each cluster is a context class. Each context class is assigned a certain membership $c_i : F_1 \times F_2 \times \ldots \times F_n \to C^m$. The commonly used clustering algorithms include Kohonen Self-Organizing Map (SOM), the Recurrent Self-Organizing Map (RSOM), K-Means clustering, Hartigan's sequential leader clustering, neural gas, and growing neural gas (GNG).

For each clustering, a descriptive name must be assigned for users to utilize context. Labeling maps context classes into a set of names: $C^m \to N$, where N is name of semantic meaning. The name comes from the ontology library which is domain-specific. This is valuable in context sharing and cooperation.

In many papers research on context recognition are described. We think that the two are the same thing in respect that they are all deducing context atoms from sensor data.

3.2 Context Reasoning

This is the higher level of context reasoning, which lay emphasis on deducing higher level context from lower level context. The reasoning technologies taken in context-aware system can be grouped into two categories: logic and learning mechanism.

Logics are very powerful tools for reasoning with context knowledge, and they are sufficient for general pervasive context aware systems .The system can reason about context using rules written in different logics such as first order logic, temporal logic, and description logic. FOL is the most classic logic. Temporal logic extends conventional proposition logic in adding special operator that can specify the objects to behave as time progresses. Using temporal logic the specification of an object can define the attribute and relation of the past, present and the future. Description Logics are subsets of first order logic, and can be viewed as providing semantics for much network-based object-orientated formalism. They serve to disambiguate imprecise representations that these formalisms permit. Description Logics are the most expressive decidable logics with classical semantics, and usually are used in ontology reasoning.

Learning mechanisms are also generally used in context reasoning such as neural networks and Bayesian network. Neural networks are a classic learning mechanism which will converge to a stable state after a period of training. The network will output the state of the system whenever the contexts are input into the network. SOM is the most popular unsupervised neural network that can adjust the weight coefficient of the neuron to simulate the input signal pattern in an adaptive way. Bayesian network focuses on the representation and reasoning of uncertain knowledge. It is a directed acyclic graph with a conditional probability table associated with every node.

SCM is a kind of learning mechanism, too. SCM is an unsupervised clustering and recognizing algorithm of symbol string. We use SCM in our system for the following advantages:

Autonomy: the algorithm is unsupervised and does not need the user interaction. The initialization can be of any random state and the system input samples of the environment automatically.

Noise resistance: the signal is sampled in the real world and so the noise is inevitable. SCM works well with noise and the performance will not be affected.

Simplicity: the algorithm must be simple enough to avoid heavy operations on the feature vectors.

SCM are presented as an algorithm for the unsupervised clustering of symbol string data based on adaptive learning and the application into context-aware system are also mentioned as a method of context recognition in [15, 16]. However, there are some problems in practice: the node strings can not converge to a stable state and the algorithm does not take into account the different source of context. So we improve the algorithm in the computation of similarity and the updating rules. The following sectors will describe the algorithm of SCM in detail.

4 The Algorithm of SCM

The basis of SCM is using symbol sets to represent the state of the system. We mention that context can be easily and completely represented by symbol strings. For example, we enter a shop. If we represent each type of commodities as $\psi_i \in \Psi$, in which Ψ is the summary of commodities in the shop and $\Psi = \{\psi_1,...,\psi_N\}$, the shopping basket of customer i can be represented by a symbol string: $S_i = \{s_1, s_2,..., s_n\}, s_j \in \Psi, j = 1,..., n(i)$. It is a simple, natural and general form to represent a context by a symbol or a symbol string. We describe the idea in a formalized way in the first subsection and the algorithm in the second subsection.

4.1 The Symbol Strings of Context

With the symbol string, we can describe the two most important properties of context:
(1) Hierarchical
The context is hierarchical essentially.

$$S_j^i = \{s_{j,1}^i, s_{j,2}^i, \dots, s_{j,N_j}^i\} \tag{1}$$

We use S_j^i to denote the context state of context source j at level i., in which every context includes N_j properties. The context at level 0 is the raw sensor data.

The higher level context is the composition of the lower level context. The context at level i+1 can be deduced from the context at level j.

$$S_j^{i+1} = \{s_1^i, s_2^i, \dots, s_{N_{i+1}}^i\} \tag{2}$$

(2) Temporal
The output of a context source will vary with the time. We call the output of the context source varying with time the state of context. We use $S_j^i(t)$ to denote a context state, in which the meaning of superscript and subscript is same as above.

We can fusion the context of different sources at the same time to deduce new context. This is the most general reasoning in context-aware system. The order of symbols in the sequence does not matter.

$$S_j^{i+1}(t) = \{s_1^i(t), \dots, s_n^i(t)\} \tag{3}$$

We can fuse the context of the same sources during the sequential time to deduce new context. This is often referred to as context prediction. The order of symbols in the sequence is of great importance.

$$S_j^{i+1}(t_{l+m}) = \{s_j^i(t_1), s_j^i(t_2), \ldots, s_j^i(t_{l+m})\} \tag{4}$$

Using the symbol string to describe the properties above, we gain the context states sequence of context source j at level i:

$$\{s_j^i(t_1), s_j^i(t_2), s_j^i(t_3), \ldots\} \tag{5}$$

4.2 The Algorithm

The basic structure of SCM is a two dimension lattice with M*M nodes. There are a symbol string $S_k(t)$ and a weight vector $X_k(t)$ associated with each node k, where $S_k(t) = \{s_1^k(t), s_2^k(t), \ldots, s_n^k(t)\}$, $s_j^k(t) = (s_{j,1}^k, s_{j,2}^k, \ldots, s_{j,n(k,j,t)}^k)$. Here the superscript is used to denote the current node k. $s_{j,i}^k$ is the ith context state from source j at time t. $n(k, j, t)$ is the number of symbols of context source j of node k at time t. Initially $s_k(t)$ is a string of single symbol selected randomly and $n(k, j, t)$=1. $X_k(t) = \{x_1^k(t), x_2^k(t), \ldots, x_n^k(t)\}$, $x_j^k(t) = (x_{j,1}^k, x_{j,2}^k, \ldots, x_{j,n(k,j,t)}^k)$. Each $x_{j,i}^k \in [0,1]$ and is directly associated with $s_{j,i}^k$. The two sets are initialized to random values.

As other neural networks, the training similarly consists of two steps: 1) finding the best-matching unit for the input and 2) adaptation of the models.

The input string at time t is $\hat{S}(t) = \{\hat{s}_1(t), \hat{s}_2(t), \ldots, \hat{s}_{n(t)}(t)\}$. For each node we calculate the similarity between the input string and the node string using a function,

$$A_k(t) = \frac{\left(\sum_{i=1}^{\hat{n}(t)} \sum_{j=1}^{n(k,t)} \hat{\delta}_{k,i}(t)\delta_{k,j}(t)\right)^2}{n(k,t)\hat{n}(t)}, \text{ where}$$

$$\delta_{k,j}(t) = \begin{cases} 1, s_j(t) \in S_j^k(t) \\ 0, s_j(t) \notin S_j^k(t) \end{cases}, \text{ and } \hat{\delta}_{k,j}(t) \text{ is defined in the same way.}$$

After the calculation, a node with the most similarity is selected as the winner node, which is the one that most matches the input and can best describes the input:

$$v(t) = \arg \max_{1 \le k \le M \times M} A_k(t).$$

The updating rules for the node string $S_k(t)$ and the weight vector $X_k(t)$ are:
For each node k=1,2,…,M*M,

(1) If $s_{j,i}^{k}(t) \in \hat{S}(t)$, $x_{j,i}^{k}(t) = x_{j,i}^{k}(t) + \alpha(t) h_m(dl)(1.0 - x_{j,i}^{k}(t))$

(2) If $s_{j,i}^{k}(t) \notin \hat{S}(t)$, $x_{j,i}^{k}(t) = x_{j,i}^{k}(t)(1.0 - \alpha(t) \mid h_m(dl)$

(3) If $\hat{s}_j(t) \notin s_j^k(t)$ and $h_m(dl) > 0, n(k, j, t) = n(k, j, t) + 1$,

$s_{j,n(k,j,t)}^{k}(t) = \hat{s}_j(t)$, $x_{j,n(k,j,t)}^{k}(t) = \alpha(t) h_m(dl)$

(4) If $x_j(t) < \beta(t)$, $n(k, j, t) = n(k, j, t) - 1$.

In which the function $h_m(dl)$ is Mexican hat:

$$h_m(i) = (1 - a * b * i_2) \exp(-a * i^2),$$

and the parameter dl is the Euclidean distance between the winner node v(t) and the node k being updated.

In this algorithm we take the context type into account and the matching of symbols must happen between contexts of same type. This guarantees the clustering of training data with the same environment information.

5 The Experiment

The experiment shows how we use symbol string clustering algorithm to recognize and deduce the higher level context.

Firstly we gain context data from sensors. We equip six kinds of sensors, including temperature, humidity, light, microphone, accelerometer and a cell phone with GSM positioning service. We define six types of context atom classes: temperature, humidity, light, loudness, speed and location. For each context atom we define a symbol which is unique as shown in table 1:

Table 1. Context atoms and the symbols assigned

Context atom class	sensor	Context atom
temperature	temperature	1=hot,2=warm,3=cool,4=cold,5=Unknown
Humidity level	Humidity	6=humid, 7=normal, 8=dry, 9= Unknown
Loudness level	microphone	10=loud,11=normal,12=murmuring,13=silent,14= Unknown,
Light type	Ambient light	15=bright, 16=normal, 17=dim, 18=dark,19= Unknown
Speed level	accelerometer	20=fast,21=normal,22=low,23=walk fast,24=walk slowly,25= still,26= Unknown
location	GSM	27=home, 28=workplace, 29=marketplace,30=Unknown

Table 2. The experiment scenarios

scenario	activity
1:working	Sitting
	Walking around
	Discussion
2:shoppingl	Walking around
	Stand still
	Conversation
3:in the street	By bus
	Walking
	Run
4:home	Sitting
	Cooking
	Watching TV

Here we assign unique symbol for each atom in respect that the context recognizing is done through symbol matching between the node string and the input string. Hence the similarity is calculated and the winner node is selected. So the symbol assigned to each context must be unique. Here we use integer for its simplicity. For the future research on context uncertainty, we leave a value Unknown to represent the occasion the sensor data is ambiguous or vague. The speed is divided into six levels, which the first three are used to denote the speed of user in the vehicle, such as the bus, while the next three are used to denote the walk speed. As for the location we only emphasize three positions and the left can be extended easily.

The experiment focus on four scenarios: at working, shopping, in street and at home. Each of them involves different activities as shown in table 2:

Each activity will last for 2 minutes and will be repeated 10 times. So there will be 1200 symbol strings for each activity. For the whole experiment the sum will be 14400 symbol strings.

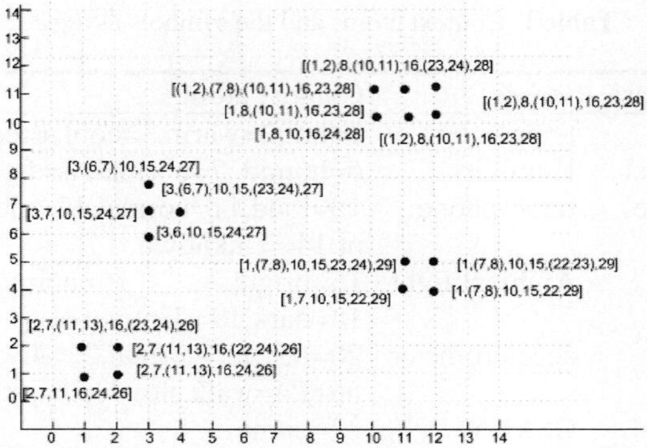

Fig. 1. The experiment result: symbol strings for nodes of the SCM. The nodes converge to 4 clusters corresponding to the 4 scenarios.

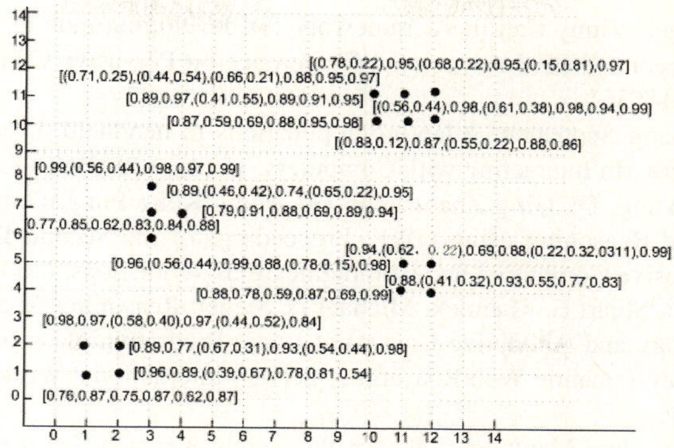

Fig. 2. The experiment result: the corresponding weight vectors associated with the symbol strings of each node of the SCM

We use a lattice of 15×15 nodes. The node strings and the associated weight vectors are randomly initialized. The resulting clustering distribution is shown in figure 1 and figure 2.

6 Conclusion

Context reasoning is one important problem in the research of context-awareness, but it is not laid enough emphasis on. Although it is similar in the sense of knowledge discover and learning with AI, the difference must be specified.

This paper discusses context reasoning in two levels: the lower level is context inference/recognition, which focuses on generating context atoms from raw data, and the higher level is context reasoning, which focuses on the composition of context atoms and deducing context of higher abstract level.

We describe the technologies used in context-aware systems and introduce an improved algorithm SCM used to adaptively learn the current context. The algorithm does not need any user intervention and is suitable for mobile devices. SCM has been applied in real-time recognition. It is proven feasible to separate different context scenarios using SCM.

References

1. Mark Weiser: The Computer for the 21st Century. Scientific American, (1991) 94-100
2. Anind K. Dey: Understanding and Using context. Personal and Ubiquitous Computing, Vole 5, Issue 1, (2001).4-7.
3. Anind K. Dey: The Context Toolkit: Aiding the Development of Context-Aware Applications. Workshop on Software Engineering for Wearable and Pervasive Computing , Limerick, Ireland (2000).
4. Anand Ranganathan, Roy H. Campbell: An infrastructure for context-awareness based on first order logic. Personal and Ubiquitous Computing , Vol. 7 , Issue 6 (2003).

5. Gregory Biegel, Vinny Cahill: A framework for developing mobile, context-aware applications. In Second IEEE International Conference on Pervasive Computing and Communications (2004) 361.
6. Mantyjarvi, Jani, Seppanen: Adapting applications in handheld devices using fuzzy context information. In Interacting with Computers, 15 (4) , (2003)521-538.
7. Xiao Hang Wang, Da Qing Zhang, Tao Gu, Hung Keng Pung: Ontology Based Context Modeling and Reasoning using OWL. Proceedings of the Second IEEE Annual Conference on Pervasive Computing and Communications Workshops, (2004)18.
8. Hongwei Zhu, Stuart E. Madnick, Michael D. Siegel: Reasoning About Temporal Context Using Ontology and Abductive Constraint Logic Programming. proceeding of Principles and Practice of Semantic Web Reasoning: Second International Workshop, PPSWR 2004 , (2004)90-101.
9. Panu Korpipaa, Jani Mantyjarvi, Juha Kela, Heikki Keranen, Esko-Juhani Malm: Managing Context Information in Mobile Devices. Pervasive compuoting, July-September Vol. 2, No. 3 (2003) 42-51.
10. Jan Petzold, Andreas Pietzowski, Faruk Bagci, Wolfgang Trumler, Theo Ungerer: Prediction of Indoor Movements Using Bayesian Networks. First International Workshop on Location- and Context-Awareness (LoCA 2005), Oberpfaffenhofen, Germany (2005).
11. Kristof Van Laerhoven, Ozan Cakmakci: What Shall We Teach Our Pants?. Proceedings of the 4th IEEE International Symposium on Wearable Computers (2000).
12. Jong-Hwa Choi, Soon-yong Choi, Dongkyoo Shin, Dongil Shin: Research and implementation of the context-aware middleware based on Neural network. In proceeding of AIS 2004, Jeju Island, Korea, (2004)295-303.
13. Kristof Van Laerhoven, Kofi Aidoo: Teaching Context to Applications. Personal and Ubiquitous Computing, Vol.5, Issue 1, (2001) 46 – 49.
14. Harry Chen, Sovrin Tolia, Craig Sayers, Tim Finin, and Anupam Joshi: Creating Context-Aware Software Agents. First GSFC/JPL Workshop on Radical Agent Concepts, Greenbelt, MD, USA (2001).
15. John A. Flanagan: Unsupervised Clustering of Symbol Strings. In proceeding of International Joint Conference on Neural Networks (IJCNN 2003), Portland, Oregon, USA, (2003) 3250-3255.
16. J. Himberg, J. A. Flanagan, J. MÄantyjÄarvi: Towards context awareness using Symbol Clustering Map. In Proceedings of the Workshop for Self-Organizing Maps 2003 (WSOM2003), Kitakyushu, Japan, (2003) 249–254.

X-Tree Diff+: Efficient Change Detection Algorithm in XML Documents*

Suk Kyoon Lee** and Dong Ah Kim

Division of Information and Computer Science, Dankook University
San 8, Hannam-dong, Youngsan-gu, Seoul, 140-714, Korea
{sklee, dakim70}@dankook.ac.kr

Abstract. As web documents proliferate fast, the need fo real-time computation of change (edit script) between web documents increases. Though fast heuristic algorithms have been proposed recently, the qualities of edit scripts produced by them are not satisfactory. In this paper, we propose X-tree Diff+ which produces better quality of edit scripts by introducing a tuning step based on the notion of consistency of matching. We also add copy operation to provide users more convenience. Tuning and copy operation increase matching ratio drastically. X-tree Diff+ produces better quality of edit scripts and runs fast equivalent to the time complexity of fastest heuristic algorithms.

1 Introduction

Computing change (edit script) between documents draws much attention from Computer Science research community. It is because version management becomes important, as Internet is crowded with excessive information. Version management is based on the algorithm of computing change between web documents [10]. It is also used in the real-time detection of hackers' defacement attacks [14]. In this paper, we present an efficient change detection algorithm X-tree Diff+ for tree-structured documents such as HTML, XML documents. Difference (change) between documents can be viewed as a sequence of edit operations (called edit script). Researches on change detection for tree-structured data such as XML/HTML documents have been carried out since late 1970s [1,2,3,4,5,6,7,8,9,10,11,12]. Early works focused on computing the minimal cost edit script for tree-structured data [2,3,4]. The general problem on change detection for tree-structured data is known as *NP*-hard [6]. So, recently, heuristic algorithms have been proposed to meet the demand. XyDiff [10] is designed for XML data warehouse and versioning. This algorithm uses hashing to represent the contents and structure of subtrees, and the notion of weigh in matching process. It achieves $O(n \log n)$ complexity in execution time. X-Diff+ [11] uses hashing to represent the contents and structure of subtrees. X-Diff+ computes the edit distance between two documents, and produce reasonable good edit scripts. But the time cost of X-Diff+ is not acceptable for real-time application. X-tree Diff [14] is designed to detect hackers' defacement attacks to web sites. X-tree Diff is simple and runs fast in

---

* The present research was conducted by the research fund of Dankook University in 2005.
** Corresponding author.

E. Sha et al. (Eds.): EUC 2006, LNCS 4096, pp. 1037 – 1046, 2006.

$O(n)$. XyDiff and X-tree Diff are quite efficient in execution time. However, the quality of edit scripts produced by them is not good enough.

In this paper, we propose X-tree Diff+ based on X-tree Diff. It produces better quality of edit scripts and run in $O(n)$. We introduce the notion of consistency of matching to tune ineffective matches. Also, we add Copy operation as a basic edit operation. With these, X-tree Diff+ increases matching ratio and produce better edit scripts. We present the change representation model in Section 2, and X-tree Diff+ algorithm in Section 3. We analyze the time complexity of X-tree Diff+ in Section 4.

2 The Model for Representing Changes in XML Documents

2.1 X-Tree

X-tree is a labeled ordered tree. The logical structure of a node of X-tree consists of nine fields shown in Figure 1. *Label*, *Type* and *Value* fields are used to represent an element of XML documents. *Index* field is used to distinguish sibling nodes in X-tree that have the same label, while *nMD*, *tMD*, *iMD*, *nPtr* and *Op* fields for matching process in X-tree Diff+. iMD field is added in the X-tree in X-tree Diff+. A node in an XML document is represented by an X-tree node. For each XML text node, the value 0, the string "#TEXT" and the text content of the node are stored, respectively, in the Type field, the Label field and Value field of the corresponding X-tree node. For each XML element node, the value 1 and the name of the node is stored in the Type field, the Label field of the corresponding node. For an XML element node with a list of attributes, the list of each pair of attribute name and attribute value is stored as a text in the Value field. For sibling nodes whose Label fields have the same value, their Index fields are set to the numbers such as 1, 2, 3, …, according to the left-to-right order to distinguish these sibling nodes.

Label	Type	Value	Index	nMD	tMD	iMD	nPtr	Op

Fig. 1. Logical structure of a node of X-tree

The iMD field represents ID attribute value for a node in XML documents. ID attributes, if used with Label, can uniquely identify each node in an XML document. The iMD, nMD and tMD fields are used for efficient comparison between two X-trees $\mathcal{T}$ and $\mathcal{T}'$, converted from two XML documents. The nMD field of an X-tree node *N* contains the hash value for information of node *N* and the tMD field of node *N* the hash value for information of the node *N* and its descendents. For the notational simplicity, a field name of X-tree node is used as a function taking X-tree node as an input and returning the corresponding field value. iMD(*N*), nMD(*N*) and tMD(*N*) are defined as follows:

iMD(*N*) = hash(Label($\mathcal{T}_i$) ⊕ 'ID attribute value')

nMD(*N*) = hash(Label(*N*) ⊕ Value(*N*)) **tMD(*N*)** = hash(nMD(*N*) $\bigoplus_{x=1}^{n}$ tMD(C_x(*N*))) where $\oplus$ is a string concatenating operator, n is the number of child nodes of node N, and $C_x(N)$ returns xth child node of node N. Note that tMD(N) reflects the structure and contents of a subtree rooted at node N. Therefore, if the roots of two X-trees have the same tMD, these trees are assumed to be *identical*.

2.2 Edit Operations and the Notion of Matching

Applying an edit script to the old version of an X-tree produces the new version from the old version. In this paper, we consider five edit operations such as *INS*, *DEL*, *UPD*, *MOV*, and *COPY*. These edit operations are defined as follows:

- DEL(N): delete a node N from X-tree T.
- INS(l, v, N, i): create a new node with the value l for the Label field and the value v for the Value field, then insert the node to X-tree T as the ith child of node N.
- UPD(N, v'): update the Value field of a node N with the value v'.
- MOV(N, M, j): remove the subtree rooted at a node N from T, and make the subtree being the jth child of M.
- COPY(N, M, j): copy the subtree rooted at a node N to the jth child of M.

Copy operation is added in X-tree Diff+. Copy operation is useful when same subtrees are scattered in duplicate around an X-tree. It allows users to use copy operations instead of a sequence of insert operations. In addition, we also use *NOP* in matching process, a dummy operation for nodes with no change occurred. Matching two nodes means that these nodes are made to correspond to each other with some edit operation involved in the match. For a pair of matched nodes N_i, N_j with operation e, it is said that that node N_i are matched with node N_j using edit operation e. Also, it is represented by a triple (N_i, N_j, e) or $N_i \xrightarrow{e} N_j$. When e is NOP, e is often omitted. Let's define several functions. For a node N, $M(N)$ and $P(N)$ return the matching node and parent node of node N, respectively. $ST(N)$ returns a subtree rooted at node N. If tMD(N_i) = tMD(N_j), then matching between the subtree rooted at N_i and the subtree rooted at N_j may be represented as $ST(N_i) \rightarrow ST(N_j)$.

3 X-Tree Diff+: Change Detection Algorithm

In this section, we explains X-tree Diff+. In Figure 2, X-tree $\mathcal{T}$ is an old version, and X-tree $\mathcal{T}'$ a new version. The number beside a node of these X-trees represents the order of visiting the node in post-order traversal. These numbers are used to identify each node in the tree. For example, $\mathcal{T}_1$ represent the leftmost node in $\mathcal{T}$.

3.1 Preprocessing

Step 0 (Build up X-Trees): We convert XML documents into X-trees $\mathcal{T}$ and $\mathcal{T}'$, and generate hash tables. During this process, all the fields of X-tree nodes are properly initialized. In addition, for each X-tree node, nMD, tMD and iMD values are computed and stored in the nMD, tMD and iMD fields, respectively.

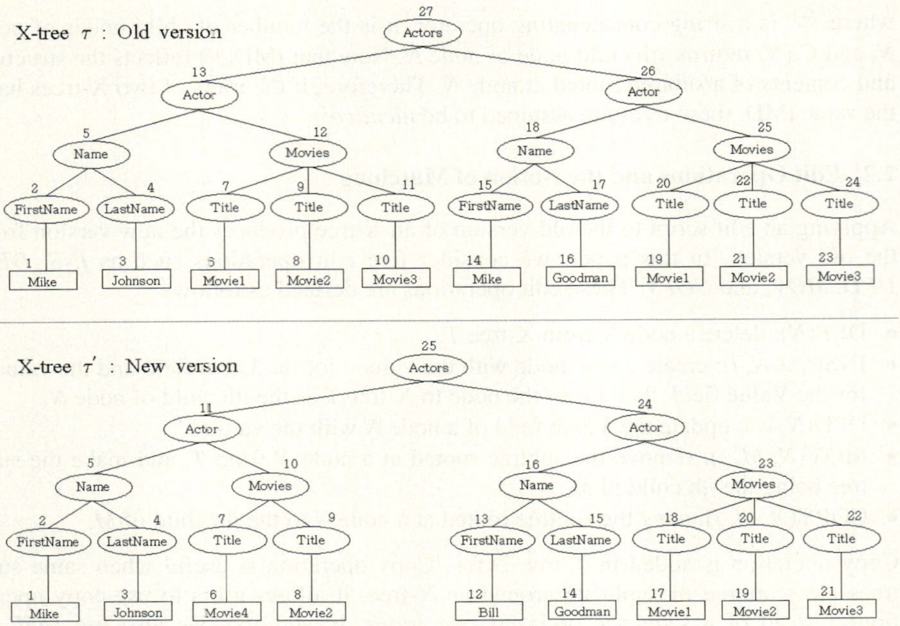

Fig. 2. Examples of X-tree

Three hash tables O_Htable, N_Htable, and N_IDHtable are generated. Entries for first two hash tables are of tuples consisting of the tMD and pointer of an X-tree node, with tMD as the key. All the nodes with unique tMD value in τ' are registered to N_Htable, while all the nodes with non-unique tMD in τ are registered to O_Htable. N_IDHtable is an hash table for nodes with ID attributes in X-tree τ'. The entry consists of iMD(as a key) of a node and a pointer to the node.

3.2 X-Tree Diff+ Algorithm

Step 1 (Match identical subtrees with 1-to-1 correspondence and match nodes with ID attributes): First we repetitively find a pair of identical subtrees one from τ and another from τ', and match them using NOP. The algorithm in Figure 3 describes this process. *N* and *M* represent the roots of subtrees in τ and τ', respectively. At the end, the algorithm computes the list of matches, called *M_List*, which is the input data for Step 2. Note that, after finding a match, we don't visit their subtrees for matching, due to the characteristics of tMD. For the details, refer to [14,17]. The matches found in this process have one-to-one correspondence.

After having finished the previous sub-step, we try to match nodes with a same iMD values. While traversing X-tree τ in breadth-first order, if unmatched node with ID attribute is found, then look up an entry in N_IDHtable with the same iMD value. If the lookup succeeds, then match them with NOP.

```
For each node N in T { /* Visit each node of T in breadth-first order */
  If any entry of O_Htable does NOT have the same tMD value that the node N has then {
      If some entry of N_Htable has the same tMD value that the node N has then {
          Retrieve the node M from N_Htable;  Match the nodes N and M using NOP;
          Add the pair (N, M) of nodes to M_List;
          Stop visiting all the subtrees of the node N, then go on to next node in T ;  }
      Else Go on to next node in T ;     }
  Else Go on to the next node in T ;
} // For
```

Fig. 3. Matching identical subtrees with one-to-one correspondence

In Figure 2, since both ST(τ_5) and ST(τ_{17}) are unique in τ, they can be matched with ST(τ'_5) and ST(τ'_{15}) of X-tree τ', respectively. So matches such as ST(τ_5)→ST(τ'_5) and ST(τ_{17})→ST(τ'_{15}) are produced. Also, one of ST(τ_{12}) and ST(τ_{25}) can be matched with ST(τ'_{23}). But since ST(τ_{12}) and ST(τ_{25}) are not unique in the X-tree τ, this match cannot be determined at this step.

```
/* Propagate each matching from M_List to its parents */
For matching (A, B) in M_List from Step 1 and 2 {
  pA = Parent(A); pB = Parent(B)
  While TRUE {
      /* None of parents have been matched. */
      If nPtr(pA) == NULL AND nPtr(pB) == NULL then {
          If Label(pA) == Label(pB) then {
              Match pA and pB using NOP;  pA = Parent(pA);  pB = Parent(pB);  }
          Else Break;        }
      Else Break;
  } // While
} // For
```

Fig. 4. Propagate matching upward

Step 2 (Propagate matching upward): In this step, we propagate matching from matches found in step 1 upward to the roots. For each matching *A*→*B* determined in step 1, we need to decide whether the parent (*P*(*A*)) of *A* can be matched with the parent (*P*(*B*)) of *B* based on their labels. The algorithm is shown in Figure 4.

In the example shown in Figure 2, we propagate the matching $\tau_5 \rightarrow \tau'_5$ found in step 1 upward. Since their parent nodes have the same label, a matching $\tau_{13} \rightarrow \tau'_{11}$ is made in this step. Again, since parent nodes of nodes in $\tau_{13} \rightarrow \tau'_{11}$ have the same label, then a matching $\tau_{27} \rightarrow \tau'_{25}$ is determined. In similar way, from the matching $\tau_{17} \rightarrow \tau'_{15}$ from Step 2, $\tau_{18} \rightarrow \tau'_{16}$ and $\tau_{26} \rightarrow \tau'_{24}$ are produced.

Step 3 (Match remaining nodes downwards): In this step, downwards from the roots, we attempt to match nodes remaining unmatched until Step 3 begins. While visiting nodes in $\mathcal{T}$ in depth-first order, we repeat the following:

(1) Find a matched node *A* in $\mathcal{T}$ which has unmatched children. Let *B* be *M*(*A*), the m atching node of *A*. For *A* and *B*, let *cA*[1..*s*] denote the list of unmatched child nod es of *A*, and *cB*[1..*t*] the list of unmatched child nodes of *B*, where *s* is the number of unmatched child nodes of *A* and *t* is also similarly defined.
(2) For *A*, *B*, *cA*[1..*s*], and *cB*[1..*t*], perform the algorithm in Figure 5.

In the implementation of Step 3, two hash tables are used. When a node *A* is found in $\mathcal{T}$, all the unmatched child nodes *cA*[1..*s*] are registered to both hash tables, where one hash table uses the tMD values of nodes as the key, and the other the Label and Index values as the key. These hash tables are used to find matching for each unmatched child node *cB*[*j*] of node *B* in $\mathcal{T}'$.

```
For j in [1..t] {   /* For each cB[j] */
  If there is a cA[i] where tMD(cA[i]) = tMD(cB[j]) then
      Match ST(cA[i]) with ST(cB[j]) using NOP;
  Else If there is a cA[i] where Label(cA[i]) = Label(cB[j]) and Index(cA[i]) = Index(cB[j]) then
       Match cA[i] with cB[j] using NOP;
  }    } // For
```

Fig. 5. Match remaining nodes downwards

In the example in Figure 2, while visiting nodes in $\mathcal{T}$ in the depth-first order, we first find an matched node $\mathcal{T}_{13}$ where $\mathcal{T}'_{11} = M(\mathcal{T}_{13})$. Nodes $\mathcal{T}_{13}$ and $\mathcal{T}'_{11}$ have unmatched child $\mathcal{T}_{12}$ and $\mathcal{T}'_{10}$, respectively. Because these children have the same label, then a mach $\mathcal{T}_{12} \rightarrow \mathcal{T}'_{10}$ is made. Similarly, node $\mathcal{T}_{12}$ has unmatched children($\mathcal{T}_{7}, \mathcal{T}_{9}, \mathcal{T}_{11}$) while node $\mathcal{T}'_{10}$ have unmatched children($\mathcal{T}'_{7}, \mathcal{T}'_{9}$). First of all, because node $\mathcal{T}_{7}$ and node $\mathcal{T}'_{7}$ have the same label and index values, then a match $\mathcal{T}_{7} \rightarrow \mathcal{T}'_{7}$ is generated. Also, from this match ($\mathcal{T}_{7} \rightarrow \mathcal{T}'_{7}$), $\mathcal{T}_{6} \rightarrow \mathcal{T}'_{6}$ is produced, because all text nodes have the same label (TEXT). Second, since $\mathcal{T}_{9}$ and $\mathcal{T}'_{9}$ have the same tMD, therefore a match $ST(\mathcal{T}_{9}) \rightarrow ST(\mathcal{T}'_{9})$ is produced. Similarly, we can easily derive matches such as $\mathcal{T}_{15} \rightarrow \mathcal{T}'_{13}$, $\mathcal{T}_{14} \rightarrow \mathcal{T}'_{12}$, $ST(\mathcal{T}_{25}) \rightarrow ST(\mathcal{T}'_{23})$.

Step 4 (Tune existing matches): We analyze the quality of matches and tune some ineffective matches. The quality of matching for a node *N* is analyzed in terms of how much a match of *N* is consistent with matches of children of *N*. For a node *N*, we define the number (*P#*) of positive children's matches, the number (*N#*) of negative children's matches, and the degree of consistency of matching *Con#*(*N*) as follows:

$P\#(N)$ = the number of child C_k satisfying $[P(M(C_k(N))) = M(N)]$
$N\#(N)$ = the number of child C_k satisfying $[P(M(C_k(N))) \neq M(N)]$
$Con\#(N) = P\#(N)$ /the number of children matched $= P\#(N)/(P\#(N)+N\#(N))$

P#(N) implies the number of children satisfying that the parent of the matching node of a child of node *N* is equal to the matching node of node *N*, while *N#(N)* shows the number of children not satisfying the same condition. *Con#(N)* implies the fraction of children contributing positive effects to the current match of *N*. In order to tune ineffective matches, we need to know alternative matches for a node. The list of alternative matches for a node (*lAM*) is defined as follows.

$$lAM\ (N) = \{<K, \text{the number of child } C_i> \mid Label(N)=Label(K) \wedge K \neq M(N) \wedge K=P(M(C_i\ (N))) \text{ for some child } C_i(N)\ \}$$

With *lAM* (*N*), we can find a node that can be matched with node *N*, and also the number of children contributing positive effect to this possible match, which is called the supporting degree for the match. Among the set of pairs represented by *lAM* (*N*), let *fN(N)* denote the node with highest supporting degree and *fV(N)* the supporting degree. The tuning process begins with traversing τ in post-order. The algorithm is presented in Figure 6.

```
For each node N in τ                    // traverse in post-order
  If Con#(N) < 0.5 then {
    Compute lAM (N);
    If fV(N) > P#(N) + P#( fN(N)) then
      {Revoke the current match of N; Revoke the current match of fN(N); Match N with fN(N);}
  }
```

Fig. 6. Algorithm for Step 4

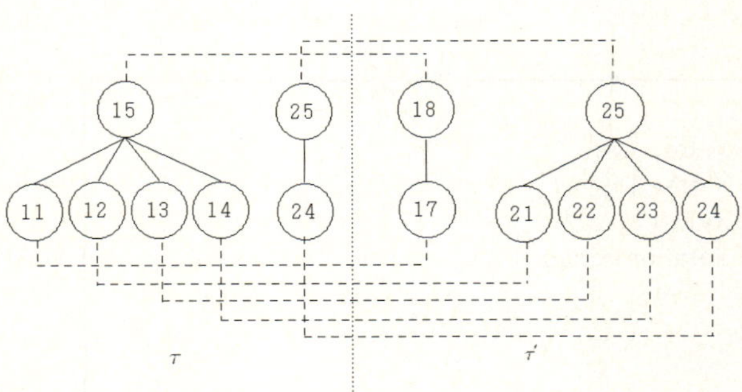

Data of τ_{15} for tuning

$P\#(\tau_{15})$	1
$N\#(\tau_{15})$	3
$Con\#(\tau_{15})$	1/4 = 0.25

Data of τ_{25} for tuning

$P\#(\tau_{25})$	1
$N\#(\tau_{25})$	0
$Con\#(\tau_{25})$	1/1 = 1.00

Fig. 7. An example for Step 4(tuning existing matches)

Figure 7 shows parts of two X-trees. Doted lines represent existing matches. Tables show *P#*, *N#*, *Con#* for nodes τ_{15} and τ_{25}. Note that *Con#*(τ_{15}) < 0.5. Since from the *lAM*(τ_{15}), *fN*(τ_{15})= τ'_{25} and *fV*(τ_{15})=3 > P#(τ_{15}) + P#(τ_{25}), we replace τ_{15} 's current match ($\tau_{15} \rightarrow \tau'_{18}$) with new one ($\tau_{15} \rightarrow \tau'_{25}$).

Step 5 (Match remaining identical subtrees with move and copy operations): Among unmatched nodes in $\mathcal{T}$ and $\mathcal{T}'$. Among them, we try to match identical subtrees, which have not been matched in Step 1, with move and copy operations.

In order to achieve this task, we find unmatched nodes from $\mathcal{T}$ and $\mathcal{T}'$ in breadth-first order traversal, and produce two hash tables, S_Htable for $\mathcal{T}$ and T_Htable for $\mathcal{T}'$. The entry structure for these hash tables is (tMD value *t*, a list of nodes (LN)) where tMD value is a hash key and the list of nodes (LN) have the same tMD value *t*. The matching process proceeds as follows.

(1) For each entry (h_key$_p$, T_LN$_p$) in T_Htable, look up S_Htable with h_key$_p$. If this lookup fails, then go on to the next entry in T_Htable. (2) In case of the successful lookup, from the list of nodes S_LN$_q$ of the entry looked up in S_Htable and the list of nodes T_LN$_p$, get pair (*N*, *M*) of nodes with the same position in both list and match *ST*(*N*) with *ST*(*M*). Suppose the length of T_LN$_p$ be *lnT* and that of S_LN$_q$ *lnS*. If $lnS \leq lnT$, we match the first m nodes from S_LN$_q$ with the first *lnS* nodes from T_LN$_p$, respectively. Then match the last node in *lnS* with the rest of nodes in T_LN$_p$ using Copy operation. In case of $lnS > lnT$, we match the first *lnT* nodes from S_LN$_q$ with the first *lnT* nodes from T_LN$_p$ using move operation respectively. Then leave the rest of nodes in S_LN$_q$ unmatched.

4 Algorithm Analysis and Experiments

In this section, we present the time complexity of X-tree Diff+ and the result of experiments. $|T|$ denotes the number of nodes in tree *T*. In this paper, since Steps 0-3 are similar to those in X-tree Diff, we just show that the time complexity of Steps 0 – 3 is $O(|T_{old}|+|T_{new}|)$. For the details, refer to the paper [17].

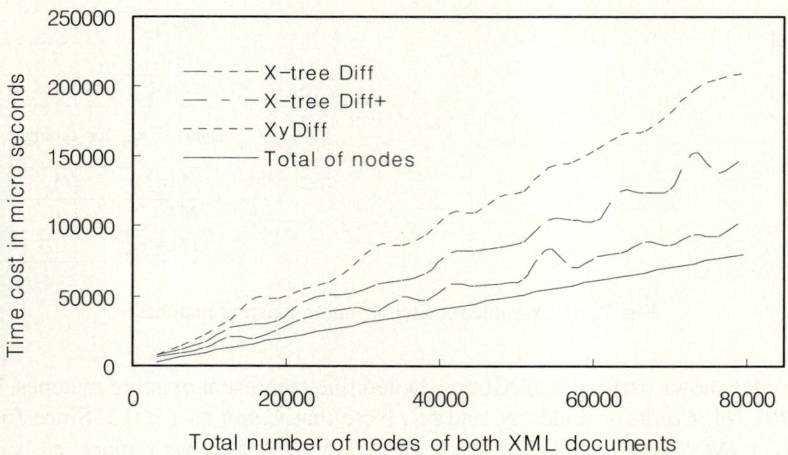

Fig. 8. Measuring the execution time for each algorithm

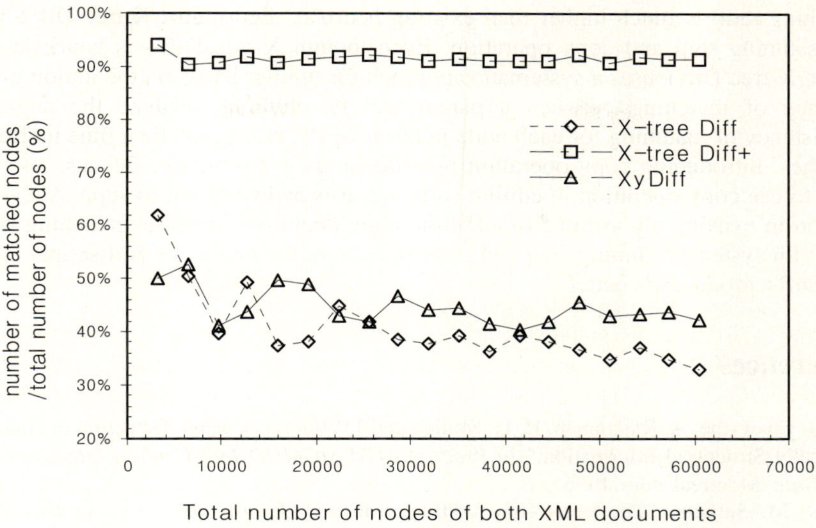

Fig. 9. Matching ratio of each algorithm

In Step 4, we traverse all the nodes in $\mathcal{T}$ in post-order way. When a node *N* is visited, we compute *P#(N)*, *N#(N)*, *Con#(N)*, *lAM(N)*. The cost of computing these functions, revoking a match and rematching is $O(1)$. All the nodes in $\mathcal{T}$ are counted once as a child during the traversal. Therefore, the cost of Step 4 is also $O(|T_{old}|)$. Step 5 requires traversing $\mathcal{T}$ and $\mathcal{T}'$, and also building hash tables S_Htable and T_Htable. This task costs $O(|T_{old}|+|T_{new}|)$. Matching process using these hash tables costs also $O(|T_{old}|+|T_{new}|)$ in worst case implying all the nodes in both X-trees are considered. The time cost of Step 5 is $O(|T_{old}|+|T_{new}|)$.

The cost of generating edit scripts is also to $O(|T_{old}|+|T_{new}|)$[14]. In conclusion, the time cost of X-tree Diff+, even in worst case, is $O(|T_{old}|+|T_{new}|)$. It is equal to that of fastest heuristic algorithms for tree-structured documents. Figure 8 shows the execution time in matching nodes for X-tree Diff, XyDiff, and X-tree Diff+. Y-axis in the graph represents the total execution time except Step 0. The lines for X-tree Diff and X-tree Diff+ are linear, as we analyzed above. In the aspect of efficiency, X-tree Diff is the best, X-tree Diff+ next, XyDiff last. The test data is produced by Synthetic XML Data Generator[15,16]In Figure 9, we show the matching ratio which is the ratio of the number of matched nodes to total number of nodes. The matching ratio of X-tree Diff+ is much higher than those of other two algorithms. It is because of introducing tuning step and copy operation.

5 Conclusion

In this paper, we propose X-tree Diff+, which is fast and produces reasonably good quality of edit scripts. The time complexity of X-tree Diff+ is $O(n)$ in worst case. Its matching ratio is much higher than existing heuristic algorithms. X-tree Diff+ introduces tuning step and copy operation. Even though X-tree Diff+ is heuristic algorithm, X-tree Diff+ uses a systematic approach for tuning; based on the notion of consistency of matching between a parent and its children, analyze the degree of consistency of matching for each node in terms of P#, N#, Con#, then tune ineffective matches. Introducing copy operation provides users convenience. Because users get used to use copy operation in editing software, it is awkward not to support copy operation in existing algorithms. In addition, copy operation increases matching ratio a lot. With systematic tuning step and copy operation, the quality of edit scripts that X-tree Diff+ produces is better.

References

1. S. Chawathe, A. Rajaraman, H. G. Molina and J. Widom, "Change Detection in Hierarchically Structured Information," *In Proc. of ACM SIGMOD Int'l Conf. on Management of Data*, Montreal, June 1996.
2. S. M. Selkow, "The tree-to-tree editing problem," *Information Proc. Letters*, 6, pp. 184-186, 1977.
3. K. Tai, "The tree-to-tree correction problem," *Journal of the ACM*, 26(3), pp.422-433, July 1979.
4. S. Lu, "A tree-to-tree distance and its application to cluster analysis," *IEEE TPAMI*, 1(2), pp.219-224, 1979.
5. J. T. Wang and K. Zhang, "A System for Approximate Tree Matching," *IEEE TKDE, 6(4)*, pp.559-571, August 1994.
6. S. Chawathe and H. G. Molina. "Meaningful Change Detection in Structured Data," *In Proc. of ACM SIGMOD '97*, pp.26-37, 1997.
7. S. Chawathe, "Comparing Hierarchical Data in External Memory," *In Proc. of the 25th VLDB Conf.*, pp.90-101, 1999.
8. S. J. Lim and Y. K. Ng, "An Automated Change-Detection Algorithm for HTML Documents Based on Semantic Hierarchies," *The 17th ICDE*, pp.303-312, 2001.
9. Curbera and D. A. Epstein, "Fast Difference and Update of XML Documents," *XTech '99*, San Jose, March 1999.
10. G. Cobéna, S. Abiteboul and A. Marian, "Detecting Changes in XML Documents," *the 18th ICDE*, 2002.
11. Y. Wang, D. J. DeWitt, J. Y. Cai, "X-Diff : An Effective Change Detection Algorithm for XML Documents," *the 19th ICDE*, 2003.
12. K. Zhang and D. Shasha, "Simple fast algorithms for the editing distance between trees and related problems," *SIAM journal of Computing*, 18(6), pp.1245-1262, 1989.
13. R. Rivest, "The MD4 Message-Digest Algorithm," *MIT and RSA Data Security, Inc.*, April 1992.
14. D. A. Kim and S. K. Lee, "Efficient Change Detection in Tree-Structured Data," In Human.Society@Internet Conf. 2003, pp.675-681, 2003.
15. A. Aboulnaga, J. F. Naughton, and C. Zhang. "Generating Synthetic Complex-structured XML Data." In Proceedings of the Fourth International Workshop on the Web and Databases, WebDB, 2001.
16. NIAGARA Query Engine, http://www.cs.wisc.edu/niagara/ .
17. D. A. Kim, “Change Detection and Management in XML Documents” Ph.D. thesis, Dankook University, Korea, 2005.

wear-UCAM: A Toolkit for Mobile User Interactions in Smart Environments*

Dongpyo Hong, Youngjung Suh, Ahyoung Choi, Umar Rashid, and Woontack Woo

GIST U-VR Lab.
Gwangju 500-712, Korea
{dhong, ysuh, achoi, urashid, wwoo}@gist.ac.kr

Abstract. In this paper, we propose a toolkit, wear-UCAM, which can support mobile user interactions in smart environments through utilizing user's context. With the rapid developments of ubiquitous computing and its relevant technologies, the interest in context-aware applications for mobile/wearable computing also becomes popular in both academic and industrial fields. In such smart environments, furthermore, it is crucial for a user to manage personal information (health, preferences, activities, etc) for the personalized services without his or her explicit inputs. Regarding reflection of user's context to context-aware applications, however, there are only a few research activities on such frameworks or toolkits for mobile/wearable computers. In the proposed wear-UCAM, therefore, we focus on a software framework for context-aware applications by taking account of how to acquire contextual information relevant to a user from sensors, how to integrate and manage it, and how to control its disclosure in smart environments.

1 Introduction

In recent years, with the development of ubiquitous computing enabled technologies and their rapid deployment, there has been an increased interest in context-aware applications on mobile/wearable computing [1,2]. In ubiquitous computing, it is generally required to install various sensors in environments in order to serve users [2]. Consequently, it is not easy for a user to manage personal information from the environmental monitoring [3].

In mobile/wearable computing, however, personal information can be retrieved from various wearable/mobile sensors, analyzed and used in services through explicit controls of a user rather than that of environments [3,4]. In this regard, a user interface for mobile/wearable computers should support users' personal information to be controlled by users themselves as well as manage their preferences to have quality of services. This is the reason that mobile/wearable computing has become a focus of attention in the era of ubiquitous/pervasive computing. In addition, mobile/wearable computing complements the inherent limitation of ubiquitous computing such as cost for infrastructure construction, privacy from environmental monitoring and so on.

---

* This was supported by Seondo project of MIC, Korea.

E. Sha et al. (Eds.): EUC 2006, LNCS 4096, pp. 1047 – 1057, 2006.

Nonetheless, there have been only a few research activities on context-aware application development toolkits for a mobile/wearable computing compared to those for ubiquitous computing [5-7]. Furthermore, most of the existing context-aware applications exploit only a few contextual cues such as location, identity and time [1]. On the other hand, it is burdensome for developers to adopt toolkits for ubiquitous computing into mobile/wearable computing because toolkits for ubiquitous computing include complicated mechanisms for sensors to detect where we are, what we want etc. Therefore, it is necessary of a toolkit to support acquisition of contextual information from wearable sensors, management of user's profile for feedback, and disclosure control of user's personal information for a proper service.

In this regard, we propose wear-UCAM, which is a toolkit for the rapid application development that supports mobile user interactions for personalized services in smart computing environments. The proposed wear-UCAM provides developers with methods for acquiring personal information from wearable sensors, methods for manipulating and analyzing the acquired information, and methods for processing flows of contextual information in applications for personalized services. In particular, the proposed wear-UCAM has the following three characteristics: 1) Acquisition and analysis of the user's physiological signals, 2) User profile management from the extracted and analyzed information, and 3) Control mechanisms for disclosure of personal information. In addition, any application based on wear-UCAM is split into *wearSensor* and *wearService* in order to support independence of sensors and services. This separation of sensors and services is also a key feature of ubiquitous computing [7]. Thus, there are many components in wear-UCAM to support extracting and analyzing a user's context from various sensors, which we explain in Section 2. To show the effectiveness of wear-UCAM, we utilize a physiological sensor and a indoor location tracking sensor as wearable sensors.

This paper is organized as follows. In Section 2, we sketch the overall architecture and design issues of wear-UCAM and its components briefly. In Section 3, 4 and 5, we explain the implemented components for context integration, context management and information disclosure control, respectively. The experimental setup and result with detailed analysis of wear-UCAM are described in Section 6. Finally, we discuss the proposed wear-UCAM as a toolkit for mobile user interactions and future works in Section 7.

2 wear-UCAM

wear-UCAM requires application developers to split an application into *wearSensor* and *wearService* and to connect *wearSensor* with *wearService* via the communicator (a networking interface) as shown in Figure 1 (a). Through this separation into sensor and service in the application, we can utilize not only wearable sensors on a user but also other sensors which probably have more computational power in environments. This mechanism can be crucial especially for resource restricted computing platforms like wearable and mobile computing. However, personal context, being highly relevant to personal privacy, is protected from other wearable computers and environmental monitoring by the explicit controls of the user. For context-aware applications

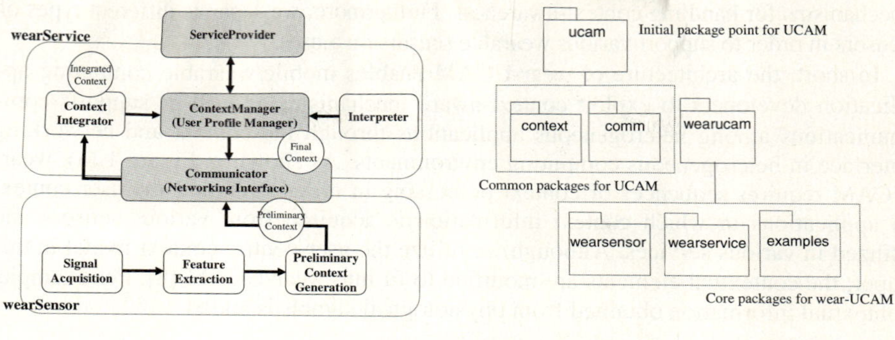

(a) (b)

Fig. 1. (a) Software Package Structure (b) Conceptual wear-UCAM Architecture

in future computing environments, application developers should be able to manipulate user's context easily. However, application developers need not know low-level details of context-aware mechanisms for implementing context-aware applications.

As illustrated in Figure 1 (b), wear-UCAM includes the following common packages: **context** package for context model, and **comm** package for a networking interface. Specifically, sensors and services are able to communicate with each other using a common context data format due to **context** and **comm** packages. The key packages of wear-UCAM are **wearsensor**, **wearservice**, and **examples**. Table 1 shows the core components for user's context processing with respect to sensor and service.

Table 1. Functionalities of components in wear-UCAM

wear-UCAM	Component	Functions
wearSensor	*Sensor**	Basic functions of wearSensor (signal processing, feature extraction, preliminary context)
Networking	Communicator	Dynamic connection among sensors and services
wearService	*Service**	Basic functions of wearService (service classification, register ServiceProvider)
	ContextIntegrator	Generates integrated context by analyzing preliminary context
	ContextManager	Generates final context by manipulating user's preference and the integrated context
	Interpreter	User's conditional context provision
	*ServiceProvider**	Basic interfaces for developers who develop context-aware application

* *Abstract Class*

The package of **wearucam** includes various classes to support sensors and services which are applicable in mobile/wearable computing environments. For instance, *wearSensor* extracts signals from sensors and constructs a preliminary context by analyzing retrieved signals. Therefore, developers are able to implement their applications in mobile or wearable computing without taking care of the details of context-aware mechanisms for handling context-awareness. Furthermore, we separate different types of sensors in order to support various wearable sensors on a user.

In short, the architecture of wear-UCAM enables mobile/wearable computing application developers to exploit context-aware mechanisms as well as supports communications among heterogeneous applications through the context and networking interface in heterogeneous computing environments. As shown in Figure 1 (a), wear-UCAM requires sequences of context processing in order to exploit the user context in applications in which context information is acquired from various sensors and utilized in various services. Although we utilize the user-centric context model in this paper, the contextual elements are modified to fit into wear-UCAM [8]. For example, contextual information obtained from physiological signals is added.

3 Context Acquisition and Integration on Physiological Signals

In this section, we introduce the way how we can obtain the personal information from wearable sensors and integrate the contexts through the proposed wear-UCAM. *wearSensor* transfers acquired signals into preliminary contexts which include some elements of 5W1H. The first step of *wearService* is the integration of preliminary contexts. Thus, the role of *ContextIntegrator* in wear-UCAM is to fill out each contextual element (5W1H) by using the preliminary context obtained from various sensors. Namely, it creates the integrated context from the preliminary contexts which have several blanks in contextual elements because a sensor cannot fill out all contextual elements. In this Section, we focus on 'how' and 'why' contextual elements to integrate the preliminary context from physiological sensors, which delivers body conditions of a user such as heart rate, temperature and skin humidity. The 'why' contextual element gives information about higher level context of user's internal states (intention, attention, emotion, etc) by inferring, interpreting and analyzing other contextual elements (who, when, how and what). The overall procedure of acquisition and analysis for physiological signals in wear-UCAM is illustrated in Figure 2.

The *ContextIntegrator* in wear-UCAM basically has two kinds of fusion methodologies; temporal fusion and spatial fusion. These fusion functions are applied in each 5W1H field fusion. The temporal fusion reduces the burden of real-time data processing from various sensors to make one integrated context by using a voting algorithm

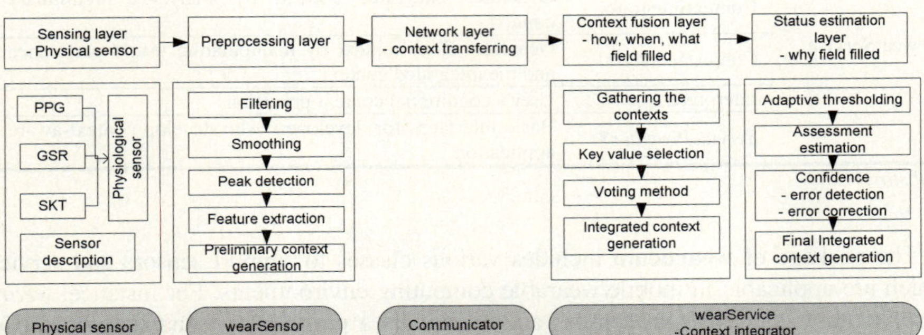

Fig. 2. The steps of acquisition and analysis of physiological signal in wear-UCAM

which selects the maximum number of key-value. For the voting algorithm, we use representative criteria to integrate the preliminary contexts under multiple hierarchies of context. For the spatial fusion methodology, the *ContextIntegrator* module supports the personalized analysis of physiological signals by adaptive thresholds. In 'why' fusion module, we use spatial fusion for user adaptive analysis of physiological signals, such as tension, stress, emotion, etc. In this paper, we analyze the tension level with GSR (Galvanic Skin Response) signal. Measurements of GSR reflect the amount of humidity in skin surface and are used to analyze the states of tension with a user-adaptive threshold [9, 10].

4 Context Management for User Profile

In general, context management is a key factor to utilize the processed contextual information in context-aware applications. The *UserProfileManager* (UPM) generates the final context by comparing the integrated context and the conditional context. Firstly, UPM receives the integrated contexts from *ContextIntegrator*. Then, it compares the integrated context with the conditional context, which consists of the user conditional context and the service conditional context. At last, it generates the final context and sends it to *ServiceProvider*. The role of UPM is to learn the preferences of a user to a certain service so that it can provide a personalized service. Specifically, it generates the user conditional contexts and disseminates them into the given service environment while automatically updating them.

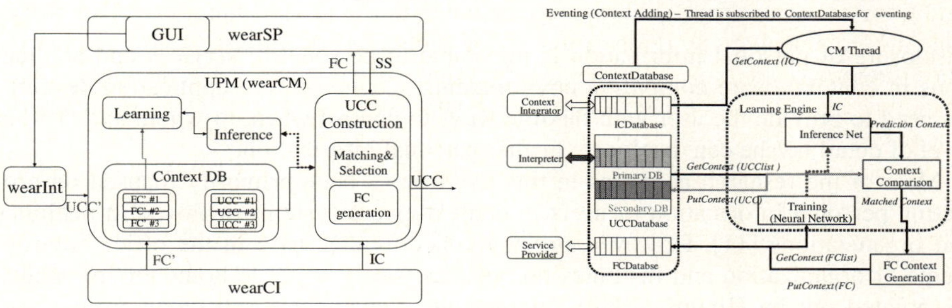

(a) (b)

Fig. 3. (a) User Profile Manager in wearService (b) User Profile Handling Module

Figure 3 (a) shows the flows of contextual information in UPM, where IC is the integrated context, FC is the final context, SS is service status, and UCC is the user conditional context. In addition, FC' and UCC' are the results processed from the given FC and UCC. Specifically, user profiles are described in 5W1H of the user conditional context (UCC), 'who' being as a focal factor. Each element of 3W1H ('where', 'when', 'how', 'why') in UCC represents where a user is, when he/she enjoys a specific service, which gesture he/she makes, and what his/her stress level is. In UCC, 'what' element denotes what kind of services he/she likes to enjoy. The final context (FC) contains the results of service execution which a user desires. Thus, we can acquire the service-specific user preferences which are dynamically changed by collecting the final context from services. After learning and matching contexts, we can update the user conditional context (UCC), which represents a user's indirect intention to enjoy a specific service, so that users can be provided with personalized services.

Figure 3 (b) illustrates the process of constructing UCC and disseminating it into the environment through a network. The procedure of UCC construction and dissemination is as follows. First of all, we construct a primary database in UCC database from static user-related information provided through a GUI. Then, FCs are aggregated at a periodic interval and stored in the FC database. At a regular pace, the UPM analyzes and learns the dynamic user-related information from FCs. At last, through context matching process, the UPM generates a new UCC, updates a secondary database in the UCC database with it, and sends it to other services.

Although users new in smart environments can provide their personal information and service-specific preferences through a GUI offered by *Interpreter* in wear-UCAM, it is necessary to automatically update a user's service-specific preferences when a user's command is not explicitly provided. And what if users want to enjoy a service for which they have not initially set their preferences through the GUI? For these situations, it is also necessary to learn a user's service usage history to infer service-specific preferences, so that results of learning can be reflected into the dynamic update of user profile.

5 Personal Information Disclosure Management

Disclosure of personal information is inevitable to personalize services and applications in context-aware computing environments. Context-aware application developers need to provide the user with flexible ways to control when, to whom and at what level of detail he/she can disclosure his/her personal information.

Most of the research activities in this realm have been primarily focused on protecting personal information of users in context-aware systems deployed in institutes and organizations [11]. However, privacy concerns that arise in the office environments of organization and institutes do not necessarily apply to home environments. As pointed out by Hindus (1999), "homes are fundamentally different from workplaces", "customers are not knowledge workers", and "families are not organizations" [12]. Family members living in the same home are more closely knit than colleagues in a workplace, and privacy from other family members is not as big an issue as it is for an enterprise. However, while family members in a smart home may be quite frank to share the personal information with each other, they may desire to keep certain elements of the personal information obscure from context-aware services in a smart home. This signifies the need for mechanisms that provide the family members with the flexibility to adjust the granularity of context information disclosed to service providers.

In this regard, we illustrate this phenomenon with the model scenario of a context-aware movie service [13]. We draw inspiration for this service from the context-aware Movie Player system and physiological signal sensor. The movie service provides the user with appropriate movies based upon the detail level of context information he/she discloses to the service. The user can choose and assign priorities to his/her preferences for movies in “what” element of 5W1H in user conditional context (UCC), via a Graphical User Interface (GUI) offered by *Interpreter*. For example, if the user does not want to disclose some of his/her preferences to the service, he/she can set the value to “0” for those elements as shown in Table 2.

Table 2. User’s preference on the context-aware movie service

Preference	Priority
SF	10
Horror	0
Drama	7
Comedy	5
Animation	3

There is a tradeoff between user’s privacy and utility of service. The more a user discloses personal information, the more customizable and beneficial the service becomes. The more specific the user is in revealing his/her personal context information to context-aware service, the more relevant movies he/she is likely to receive from the service. In this way, wear-UCAM provides the user with the option to fine-tune disclosure of his/her personal information and avail the service in relation to the disclosed information.

6 Experimental Result

Figure 4 illustrates the interaction scene between wear-UCAM and services in ubiHome test-bed, where we use a PDA-based wear-UCAM simulator. We use 2

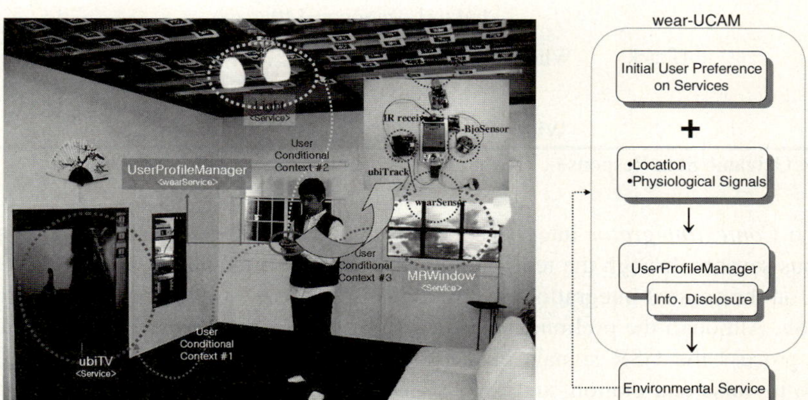

Fig. 4. Experimental setup and interactions between wear-UCAM and services

services, *MRWindow* and *ubiTV*, which can provide multimedia services based on user's preferences.

As shown in Figure 4, a user disseminates his or her preferences (initial user preference, i.e., UCC) in order to use services in ubiHome. However, the user can control the dissemination of his or her contextual information, i.e., whether to send it to services or not. Based on his or her preferences, a corresponding service is triggered. While the user is using the service, location and physiological signals are acquired from sensors. In this experiment, we exploit the processed physiological sensor which tells whether a user is in tension or not, and location sensor, called ubiTrack [14], which tracks a user's location in ubiHome. Any change of these signals and service is contextualized and reflected to user's preference. Through this procedure, the user can interact more naturally with services in smart environments.

In order to acquire contextual information relevant to a user, we employ two kinds of sensors; a wrist type physiological sensor and an IR (infrared)-based location sensor. In this experiment, we implement *BioSensor* and *ubiTrack* sensor module from *Sensor* class because this sensor class in wear-UCAM provides the necessary procedures for generating preliminary context. Table 3 shows generated preliminary context.

Table 3. The generated preliminary context from sensors

	Component		Contextual Information	Note
sensor	BioSensor	Who	Name=Dongpyo, Priority=4	Preliminary context
		What	SensorID=1, SensorType=BioSensor	
		How	GSR.mean=14.37 GSR.var=3.0 PPG.HR_mean=63.0 PPG.HR_var=3.4 PPG.HR_LF_power=70.0, PPG.HR_HF_power=62.0 SKT=36.5	
	ubiTrack	Who	Name=Dongpyo, Priority=4	
		Where	IndoorLocation.x=140 IndoorLocation.y=160 SymbolicLocation=TV Direction=0.0	
		What	SensorID=2, SensorType=LocationSensor	

*GSR(Galvanic Skin Response), PPG(photoplethysmogram), SKT(skin temperature)

The *ContextIntegrator* integrates a set of the generated preliminary contexts from various sensors through the temporal and spatial fusion methodologies. In the experiment on the context integration, we find that GSR can be used to analyze the states of tension. Although the preliminary context from *BioSensor* has 3 kinds of signals, we only process the GSR signals in the *ContextIntegrator* because PPG signal is not stable in noise and motion, and SKT signal is almost invariant. As a result, the integrated contextual information is used in updating user's preference while the user is using a service as shown in Table 4.

Table 4. The integrated context from ContextIntegrator

Component		Contextual Information	Note
service ContextIntegrator	Who	Name=Dongpyo, Priority=4	Integrated context
	When	130527(hh:mm:ss)	
	Where	IndoorLocation.x=140 IndoorLocation.y=160 SymbolicLocation=TV Direction=0.0	
	What	-	
	How	GSR.mean=14.37 GSR.var=3.0	
	Why	Tension=0	

Table 5. The final context from ContextManager

Component		Contextual Information	Note
service ContextManager	Who	Name=Dongpyo, Priority=4	Final context
	When	130640(hh:mm:ss)	
	Where	IndoorLocation.x=140 IndoorLocation.y=160 SymbolicLocation=TV Direction=0.0	
	What	ServiceName=ubiTV Parameter={"SF", 10} Function=Play	
	How	GSR.mean=14.37 GSR.var=3.0	
	Why	Tension=0	

With the integrated context and the initial user preference (UCC), UPM finds a matched service from the given service environment. Since UPM makes UCCs which reflect the user's preferences that suit him best, it can play a key role in providing personalized services in the environment. After a corresponding service is executed, UPM keeps updating user's preferences based on the integrated context from wearable sensors and the feedbacks from the service.

The final context is generated as shown in Table 5. When the final context is disseminated to the service, an altering message is displayed to a user which asks the user whether he or she wants to the service or not. In this experiment, the user discloses his or her preference on SF movie to *ubiTV* service because he/she sets the value to "10". Thus, the user does not have to take any action to have the service.

7 Discussion and Future Work

In this paper, we proposed the wear-UCAM as a rapid context-aware application development toolkit to support mobile user interactions. Through the wear-UCAM, a user is able to use contextual information obtained from physiological sensor and location sensor for his or her preference. In addition, the user can update his or her preferences on certain services with the contextual information and feedbacks from other services. Finally, the user can control whether to fine-tune disclosure of his or her personal context information or not. The proposed wear-UCAM can provide appropriated services to the users based on their preferences by retrieving personal information from sensors, processing it, and analyzing it. However, wear-UCAM is not yet fully experimented in an actual user study due to unstable physiological signals from user's movements. Moreover, the modeling of contextual information should be considered closely. Additionally, it is required to conduct experiments on the enhancement of sensing physiological signals.

References

1. Mari Korkea-aho, "Context-aware Application Survey," available in http://users.tkk.fi/~mkorkeaa/doc/context-aware.html
2. Guanling Chen, and David Kotz, "A Survey of Context-Aware Mobile Computing Research," Technical Report TR2000-381, November, 2000.
3. Bradley J. Rhodes, Nelson Minar and Josh Weaver, "Wearable Computing Meets Ubiquitous Computing: Reaping the best of both worlds," Proc. of The 3rd International Symposium on Wearable Computers (ISWC '99), San Francisco, CA, October 18-19 1999, pp. 141-149.
4. Jennica Falk,Staffan Bjork, "Privacy and information integrity in wearable computing and ubiquitous computing," Conference on Human Factors in Computing Systems archive CHI '00, pp.177-178, 2000.
5. Brown, P.J., Bovey, J.D., Chen X., "Context-Aware Applications: from the Laboratory to the Marketplace," IEEE Personal Communications, vol.4, no.5, pp. 58-64, 1997.
6. Hull, R., Neaves P. and Bedford-Roberts J., "Towards Situated Computing," 1st International Symposium on Wearable Computers, Cambridge, Massachusetts, October 13-14, 1997, pp. 146-153.
7. Anind K. Dey and Gregory D. Abowd, "The Context Toolkit: Aiding the Development of Context-Aware Applications," In the Workshop on Software Engineering for Wearable and Pervasive Computing, Limerick, Ireland, June 6, 2000.
8. S.Jang, W.Woo, "Unified Context Representing User-Centric Context: Who, Where, When, What, How and Why," ubiComp Workshop (ubiPCMM), pp.26-34, 2005.
9. B. Elie and P. Guiheneuc, "Sympathetic skin response: normal results. in different experimental conditions," Journal of Electroencephalography and Clinical Neurophysiology, vol. 76, pp. 258–267, 1990.
10. A.Barreto and J. Zhai, "Physiological Instrumentation for Real-time Monitoring of Affective State of Computer Users," WSEAS Transactions on Circuits and Systems, vol. 3, pp. 496-501, 2003.

11. Jason I. Hong, James A. Landay, "An Architecture for Privacy Sensitive Ubiquitous Computing," Second International Conference on Mobile Systems, Applications and Systems, pp. 177-189, 2004.
12. D. Hindus, "The Importance of Homes in Technology Research," 2nd Int'l Workshop Cooperative Buildings (CoBuild 99), LNCS, vol. 1670, Springer-Verlag, Berlin, pp.199-207, 1999.
13. Y.Oh, W.Woo, "A unified Application Service Model for ubiHome by Exploiting Intelligent Context-Awareness," Ubiquitous Computing Systems (LNCS), vol.3598, pp.192-202, 2005.
14. W.Jung, W.Woo, "Orientation tracking exploiting ubiTrack," ubiComp05, pp. 47-50, 2005.

A Sensing Resolution-Based Energy Efficient Communication Protocol for Wireless Sensor Networks*

Poyuan Li, Soon-Gyu Jeong, and Sang-Jo Yoo

Graduate School of information Technology & Telecommunication, Inha University,
253 Yonghyun-dong, Nam-gu, Incheon 420-751, Korea
Li_py@hotmail.com, na@sgyu.com, sjyoo@inha.ac.kr
http://multinet.inha.ac.kr

Abstract. In this paper, we propose a Sensing Resolution-based Energy Efficient (SREE) communication protocol for wireless sensor networks. SREE is intended for meeting the application's sensing objectives, where sensor nodes are densely deployed and have the determinate accuracy requirement. The primary contribution of this paper is active group head node selection with round-robin procedure, which increases the sensing accuracy and distributes the nodes energy consumption. The second contribution is using energy efficient intermediate node selection by considering both group size and energy consumption. We present the design of SREE and provide simulation results.

Keywords: Wireless Sensor Networks, Network Lifetime, Sensing Resolution, Energy Efficiency, Grouping.

1 Introduction

Wireless sensor networks (WSN) are expected to be used in a wide range of applications, especially in the military applications, it is required the network deployed rapid, self-organization, and fault tolerance [1]. This network typically have numerous sensor devices, they work together in an ad hoc multi-hop fashion.

Some common WSN protocols consider the lifetime, scalability and fault tolerance. LEACH [2-3], provides a combined TDMA/CDMA based MAC approach. The entire network is divided into non-overlapping clusters, inside the cluster using the TDMA scheme it allows to let the node directly communicate with the dynamically elected cluster head. The cluster head relays the data to the base station directly using a fixed spreading code and CSMA. For low power, short range sensors, and direct communications are not always practical.

The sensor nodes are usually operated by batteries and left unattended after deployment, so the energy consumption is the crucial factor in sensor network design. This may lead to sensor network protocols which prioritize energy savings over network throughput and packet latency. We propose a group-based communication

* This research was supported by the MIC(Ministry of Information and Communication), Korea, under the ITRC(Information Technology Research Center) support program supervised by the IITA(Institute of Information Technology Assessment) (IITA-2005-C1090-0502-0030).

E. Sha et al. (Eds.): EUC 2006, LNCS 4096, pp. 1058 – 1067, 2006.

protocol that can simultaneously achieve high energy efficiency, high network throughput, low packet latency, and fault tolerance.

The rest of this paper is organized as follows. Section 2 gives the definition of redundant node and sensing region. Section 3 presents the protocol design. Section 4 provides simulation experiment results. Finally, the paper concludes with Section 5.

2 Definitions

Sensor networks are typically consisted of very large number of low cost sensor nodes which collaborate among each other to enable a wide range of applications. In the CSMAC [4], they proposed the concept of the *Sensing Resolution* (SR), which denotes the sensing accuracy desired by an application. In the SR, the redundant nodes are forced to turn off themselves, and the battery power of these redundant nodes can be preserved for future use.

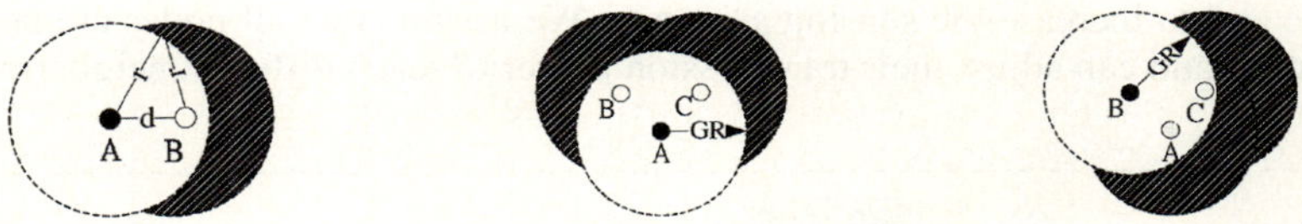

(a) Redundant node (b) Node A is active (c) Node B is active

Fig. 1. Sensing Resolution

In Figure 1-(a), where *d* is distance between node A and B. The *d* is smaller than the *sensing resolution r*. If node A keeps active, then node B is the redundant node, in the CSMAC, node B is the backup node to node A and will decide whether it should take over the node A when it finds the energy level of the node A is bellow certain threshold. The disadvantage of it is that can cause sensing accuracy loss. When node A works, the shadow area is beyond the sensing area of the node A.

From the mathematics we can get the area of the shadow part (sensing accuracy loss), and the proportion to the area of *sensing resolution* decided (πr^2) is:

$$1-\frac{1}{\pi r^2}-\left[4\times\left(\frac{\arccos\left((d/2r)\times\pi r^2\right)}{2\pi}+\frac{d}{2}\times\sqrt{r^2-\frac{d^2}{4}}\right)+2\times\left(\frac{d}{2}\times\sqrt{r^2-\frac{d^2}{4}}\right)\right] \quad (1)$$

After some simplification we obtain:

$$1-\frac{\arccos(d/2r)}{\pi/2}-\frac{d\times\sqrt{r^2-(d^2/4)}}{\pi r^2} \quad (2)$$

If an application requires r = 2m, d = 1m, the proportion is 31.41%. The value is increasing with the increasing of *d*, the extreme situation is $d = r$, the proportion can reach 60.89%. This means that if only take the redundant node as the backup node to the active node as CSMAC, the accuracy loss will be a problem in a densely deployed network, because so many backup nodes are inactive all the time before the active node is run out of battery.

We propose a round-robin based grouping method. The group radius (GR) is based on the SR. Nodes within the GR will make a group. At each round the active node is rotated within the group, which will increase the sensing accuracy at some degree, even though this way still can't solve the accuracy loss completely. Figure 1-(b) and (c) shows the sensing resolution extension in accordance with active node rotation. We can also evenly distribute energy consumption inside the group by this way. By changing the active node each round, we can avoid the situation that the sensing accuracy of the node is loss forever when a node is run out of battery.

3 The Proposed SREE Protocol

The proposed SREE protocol is targeted to meet the following requirements. In the densely deployed networks, the node densities may be as high as 20 nodes / m^3 [6], in which there will be existed so many redundant nodes in a network. Energy consumption should be evenly distributed in the sensor networks to extend network life time and to increase the sensing accuracy. We assume that all nodes are normally static nodes and can adjust their transmission power to reach different neighbors.

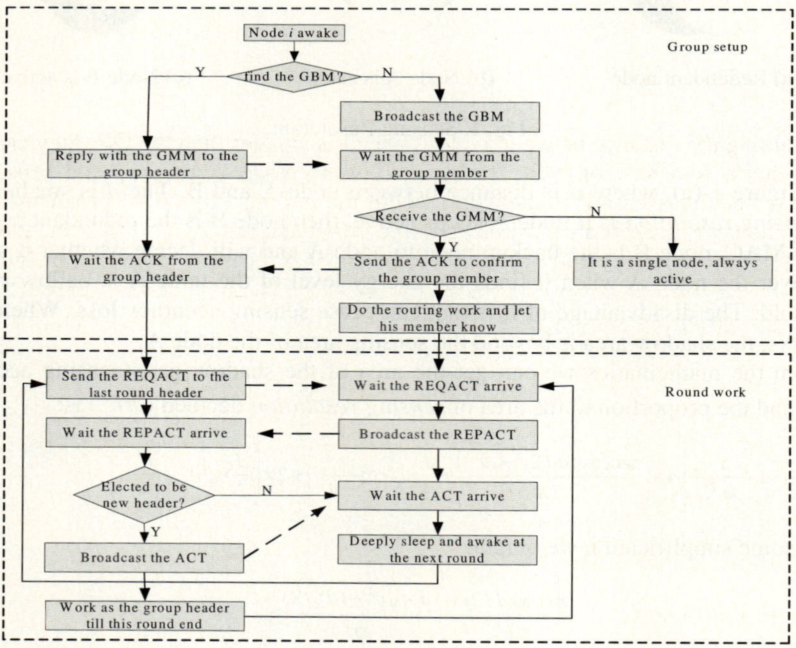

Fig. 2. Flowchart of the SREE at each node

The SREE has 3 procedures: group setup, optimal neighbor selection for packet forwarding, and group header change. Figure 2 shows the group setup and header change flows at each node.

3.1 Group Set Up

After the node deployed, the group set up phase is followed. Nodes would randomly awake and sense the channel whether there is a group broadcast message (GBM) or not. If not, it will work as the group header (GH), whose task at this phase is broadcasting the GBM with the small transmitting power (group power, which only covers the pre-determined group radius area). To avoid collision and save energy, all the communications are done with this power at the group set up phase. This message will be broadcasted periodically and continued during a relative long time (T_W) to make sure all nodes in a group radius can successfully join the group. When a node receives the GBM, it replies the group member massage (GMM) and waits the ACK from the GH to make confirm. Figure 3 shows MAC message exchanges for the group set up.

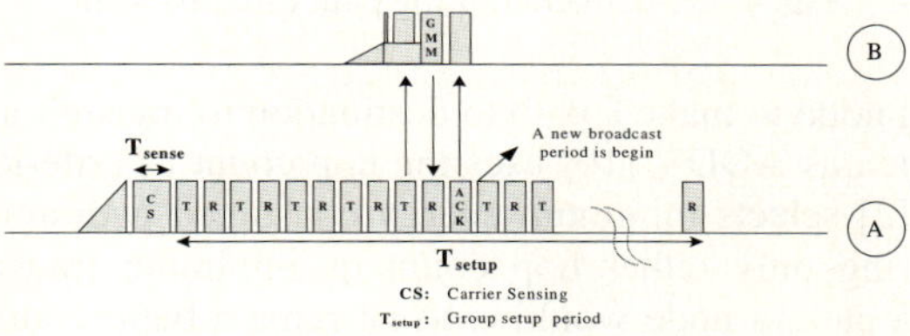

Fig. 3. Message exchanges for group set up procedure

Assuming the distance between node A and B is smaller than the GR, they can hear each other's transmission with the group power. Node A awakes and senses the channel, finds it is idle, it immediately begin the periodically GBM broadcasting, in some time later, node B awakes, receives the GBM and replies a GMM, the node like node B who sent the GMM is called a group member (GM). After A receiving the GMM, it adds B to the group list (GL) and sends back an ACK to let B know that it is in the group. At the same time, the broadcast also needs to continue for that more nodes can join in the group, during T_w period.

If a node in its broadcast period can not receive any GMM, it means that there are no redundant nodes in its GR area. We call it as single node that should be always active. The GMs already confirmed by the GH enter the periodically sleep mode and they become inactive nodes, only group header (or single node) is working. as an active node.

3.2 Optimal Path Selection

In wireless networks, transmission power between two nodes is proportional to d^k, where d is the distance between two nodes and k is the path loss that can vary from 2 to 6. Increasing the distance, required energy to communicate between the nodes is exponentially increased and then through the relay node which uses minimum transmission power between the nodes, it can reduce the consumed energy than direct transmission [7-8].

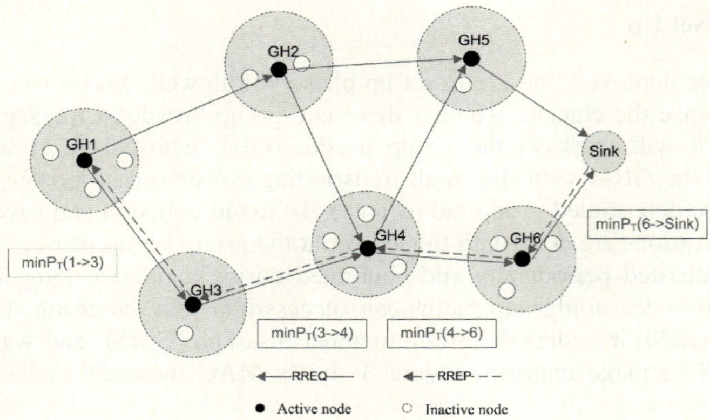

Fig. 4. On-demand routing path establishment

It is needed for a node to make a path to destination to transmit a packet. An ad hoc routing protocol such as AODV [10] uses the hop count as criterion to select a path, and MTE routing [2] selects minimum energy consumed path among various paths. However, considering only either hop count or minimum transmission energy as criterion to select a path, a node would exhaust remain battery and the node can not work anymore. At that situation network partitioning can be happened and sensing accuracy of particular region is also decreased. For solving the problems, based grouping mechanism, we propose the optimal path selection algorithm to reduce transmission energy and make consumed energy evenly for each node in a group.

As shown in figure 4, GH1 that made a sensing event initiates *path discovery* process by broadcasting a RREQ (route request) to neighbor nodes using pre-defined transmission power (maximum power) and limiting the hop count to maximum value to avoid loop problem. Whenever each neighbor node receives a RREQ, it rebroadcasts the RREQ if the node is not sink node and the RREQ is not duplicated. The RREQ contains the following information: 1) Minimum required transmission power from node *i* to *j* ($minP_{T(i\rightarrow j)}$), where node *i* denote current node and node *j* denote previous node, 2) The number of group nodes of group header *j* (G_{Nj}), where $minP_{T(i\rightarrow j)}$ is minimum transmission power of node *i* that node *j* can receive a data from node *i* correctly.

The minimum transmission power, denoted $minP_{T(i\rightarrow j)}$, to be transmitted by node *i* to conserve power while still maintaining required E_b/N_o at the receiver is given by:

$$minP_{T(i\rightarrow j)} = \frac{P_{max}}{P_{Rj}} \times R_{thresh} \tag{3}$$

where P_{Rj} is the received power by node *j* when node *i* transmits at the maximum power level (P_{max}), and R_{thresh} is minimum required power level, achieving certain E_b/N_o, at the receiver.

The group header node receiving the RREQ can respond by a RREP (route reply) if the node is sink node. Before transmitting a RREP, sink node waits certain time (T_w) to collect enough RREQs which took a different route and then it selects an optimal path. The optimal path is an energy efficient path and determined by:

$$P_{Ck} = \sum \frac{P_{Ti} + P_{Pi}}{G_{Ni}} \tag{4}$$

where,

P_{Ck} = path cost of path k.

P_{Ti} = minimum transmission power of node *i* on the path *k*

P_{Pi} = processing power of node *i* on the path *k*, processing power includes receiving power, we assume that processing power of each node is the same, so that the P_{Pi} is already known by sink node.

In this paper, we employ a cost function determined by dividing transmitting and receiving power by the number of group nodes of a group as Eq. 4. The group header is changed in a group through round-robin, being bigger group (many nodes are in a group) average consuming energy of each node is decreasing because the nodes share the energy consuming. A group that has a few nodes would exhaust ahead of a group having many nodes, then entirely network life time is decreasing and a region that died node used to cover can not be sensed, which is lowering the sensing accuracy.

Sink node selects the optimal path k^* among all paths using calculated P_{Ck} as Eq. 5 and unicasts a RREP on the selected path.

$$k^* = \arg\min_{\forall k} \{P_{Ck}\} \tag{5}$$

All nodes, including the sink node, unicast the RREP containing $\min P_{T(i \to j)}$ that is recorded in their power table on the path *k**. Therefore, when a node wants to transmit a data, they can adjust transmit power to minimum as known in power table to reduce energy consumption.

3.3 Group Header Change

At the end of each round, GH waits for the GM periodically awake, after the GM awake they use the CSMA/CA method to transmit the request to active message (REQACT) to the header, in the REQACT has the counter (*n*), which indicates how many times this node has been header, and the node remaining energy (E_{remain}), the round group header needs this information to decide which node to be the header at the next round. After an election time, the header compares the value of *n* in each received REQACT. If it can find a unique node with minimum *n*, the GH broadcast the reply to active message (REPACT), in it has the decision that the node with the minimum *n* will work as a header at the next round. If the minimum is not exclusive, after comparing the node's remaining energy, the node that has maximum residual energy will become the header at next round.

The current round header during the election time may receive the REQACT from all his GM, or can not receive any REQACT. If it receives nothing, it should work as a group header at the next round. And for the consideration of fault tolerance, if group member nodes that send REQACT cannot hear any REPACT from the current group header during the pre-determined rounds (e.g., three rounds), each member node will work as a group header.

The group node that was elected as a group header for the next round broadcasts the active message (ACT) with its biggest transmit power to announce that it will

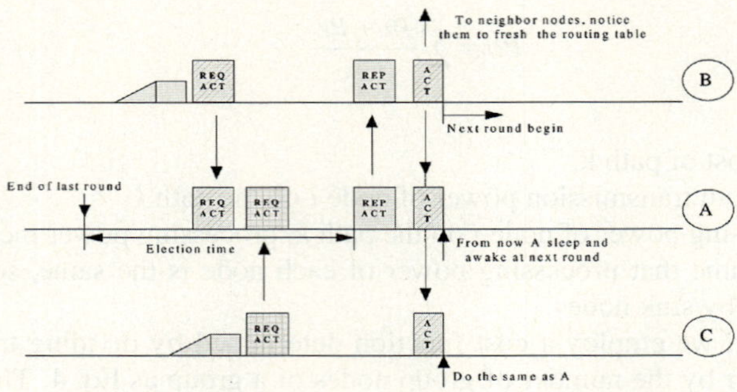

Fig. 5. Group header change

replace the last round header's work. The last round header keeps work until it receives the ACT from the new header, then it enters sleep mode and at the end of the new round it wakes up and sends the REQACT to the new header. The neighbor group headers who receive the ACT will replace the last group header with the new group header in their routing table. Figure 5 shows the proposed group header change procedure.

4 Simulation Experiment Results

In this section, we compare the performance of SREE and MTE (Minimum Transmission Energy) [5-6] by computer simulation. In MTE routing, the path that has the minimum total transmission energy is selected to send sensing data. The number of nodes we used is 100 and 150, where nodes were randomly distributed between (0, 0) and (100, 100) with the BS (base station, sink) at location (50, 175). The group radius increases from 2 m to 7 m. Each node has initial 2J energy and sends 525 bytes packet to the BS at each round. The communication energy consumption model is adopted from [3] with the same parameters.

Table 1. Parameters for energy model

Parameter	Attribute	Values
E_{elec}	Electronics energy	50 nJ/bit
ε_{fs}	Free space transmit amplifier	10 pJ/bit/ m^2
ε_{mp}	Multipath transmit amplifier	0.0013 pJ/bit/ m^4

Both the free space (α =2) and the multipath fading (α =4) channel models were used. If the distance is less than a threshold d_0 (we set d_0=1m), the free space (fs) model is used; otherwise, the multipath (mp) model is used. Thus to transmit an l-bit message a distance d, the radio expends

$$E_{TX}(l,d) = E_{TX-elec}(l) + E_{TX-amp}(l,d) = \begin{cases} lE_{elec} + l\varepsilon_{fs} d^2, \ d < d_0; \\ lE_{elec} + l\varepsilon_{mp} d^4, \ d \geq d_0 \end{cases} \tag{6}$$

and to receive this message, the radio expends:

$$E_{RX}(l) = E_{\text{RX-elec}}(l) = lE_{elec} \tag{7}$$

Figure 6 shows the relationship of system lifetime with GR and the node density. When the node density is fixed, for the bigger GR that means the smaller number of groups, shows the longer network lifetime so that the performance improvement is more significant. When the GR is fixed (e.g., GR=3m), for the higher node density network, we can get the better result as Figure 6-(b). And in the Figure 6-(a) also tells us when the node density is small, and the GR is small like 2-3m, the performance of the SREE is almost same as the MTE, because the number of group nodes is little. When there exist more groups (node density increasing or large value of GR), the performance of the SREE is more outstanding.

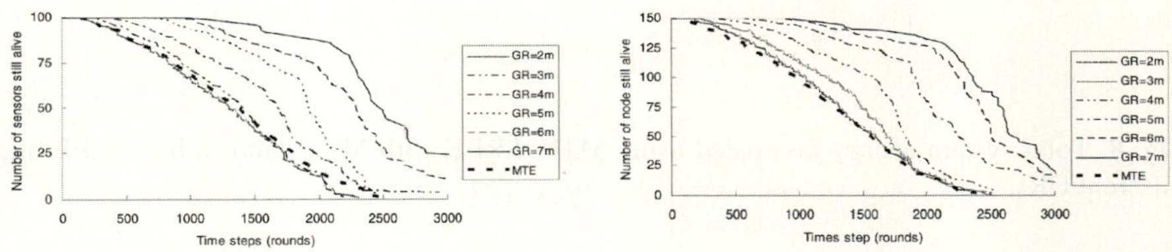

(a) 100 nodes random deploy (b) 150 nodes random deploy

Fig. 6. System lifetime using MTE routing and SREE under different GR

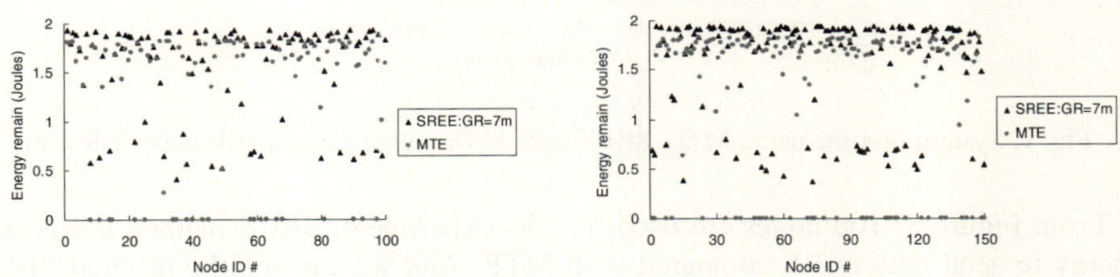

(a) 100 nodes random deploy (b) 150 nodes random deploy

Fig. 7. Remain energy level of each node after 800 rounds

To evaluate how the SREE distributed the energy cost among the network, we choose a big value of GR (7m) and relatively long time (800 rounds) to observe remain energy of each node. Figure 7 shows there are more nodes alive with the SREE than MTE routing. To evaluate the proposed optimum path selection method, we compared three methods:

- MTE: There is no grouping and sensing data is delivered to BS with minimum transmission energy routing.

- SREE with MTE: With the proposed group header selection method, grouping and group header change are performed. But routing path between group headers is determined with MTE.
- SREE: The proposed group header selection and optimal path selection are used.

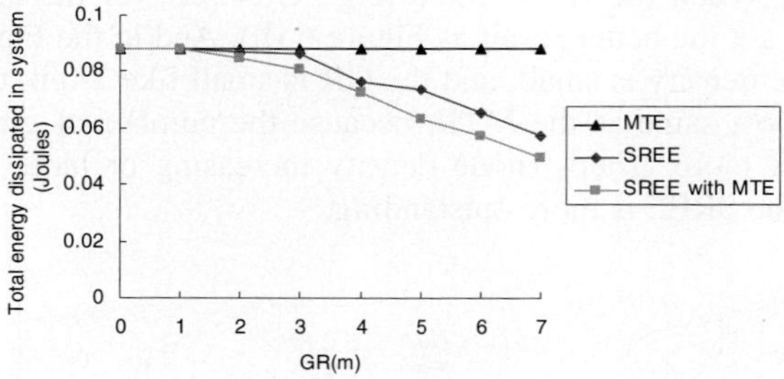

Fig. 8. Total system energy dissipated using MTE, SREE with MTE and original SREE under different GR

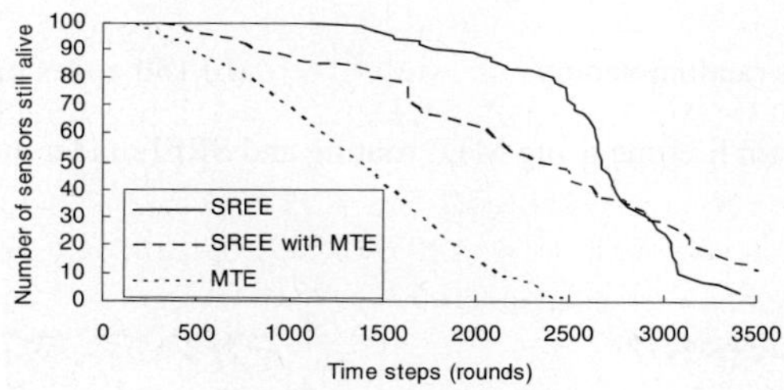

Fig. 9. System lifetime using MTE, SREE with MTE and original SREE under GR=7m

From Figure 8, 100 nodes are used for this experiment, SREE method needs less energy to send data to BS compared with MTE. And we can see the original SREE consumes a little more energy than the SREE with MTE, because SREE aim to extend the lifetime of the total network. When SREE chooses the intermediate nodes, it uses the cost function that considers not only energy consumption, but also fair energy consumption in the network. As shown Figure 9, the lifetime of the network is better indication of the advantage of SREE, because the SREE through the optimal choosing the intermediate nodes, avoids the single node energy exhausting so early, and also distributes the energy consumption among the network nodes.

5 Conclusion

When designing a protocol for wireless sensor networks, it is important to consider the required sensing accuracy, energy consumption, and network lifetime. These features lead us to design SREE, which uses grouping method and lets the redundant nodes into sleep mode to reduce energy consumption for application specific sensing accuracy. Changing group header by round-robin procedure in each round, we could get the result that energy consumption of each nodes is distributed and prolong the network lifetime. Proposed optimal routing algorithm distributed the energy consumption and reduced energy consumption that nodes send to the sink node on the optimal path than sending directly.

The simulation results shows that proposed SREE protocol, many nodes were in a group by increasing either node density or group radius made a good result that nodes can reduce energy consumption and distribute the energy consumption evenly compared with MTE routing.

References

1. Ames, B.: Electronics are central to 21st century warfare tactics, Military and Aerospace Electronics, (2004)
2. Heinzelman, W. R., Chandrakasan, A., Balakrishnan, H.: Energy efficient communication protocols for wireless microsensor networks, In proc. of the Hawaii International Conference on Systems Sciences, vol.2 (2000) 10-19
3. Heinzelman, W., Chandrakasan, A., Balakrishnan, H.: An Application-Specific Protocol Architecture for Wireless Microsensor Networks, IEEE Transactions on Wireless Communications, Vol. 1, No. 4 (2002) 660-670
4. Muqattash, A., Krunz, M.: CDMA-Based MAC Protocol for Wireless Ad Hoc Networks, In proc. of MobiHoc'03 (2003) 153-164
5. Liu, B.H., Bulusu, N., Pham, H., Jha, S.: A Self-Organizing, Location-Aware Media Access Control Protocol for DS-CDMA Sensor Networks, In proc. of 1st IEEE Conference on Mobile Ad Hoc and Sensor System (2004) 528-530
6. Shih, E., Cho, S.H., Ickes, N., Min, R., Sinha, A., Wang, A., Chandrakasan, A.: Physical Layer Driven Protocol and Algorithm Design for Energy-Efficient Wireless Sensor Networks, In proc. of ACM MobiCom '01 (2001) 272–286
7. Ettus, M.: System capacity, latency, and power consumption in multihop-routed SS-CDMA wireless networks, In proc. of Radio and Wireless Conf. (RAWCON) (1998) 55–58
8. Shepard, T.: A channel access scheme for large dense packet radio networks, In proc. of ACM SIGCOMM (1996) 219–230
9. ElBatt, T. A., Krishnamurthy, S. V., Connors, D., Dao, S.:. Power Management for Throughput Enhancement in Wireless Ad-Hoc Networks, In proc. of IEEE International Conference on Communications (2000) 1506–1513
10. Perkins, C. E., Royer, E. M.: Ad hoc on-demand distance vector routing, In proc. of IEEE Workshop on Mobile Computing Systems and Applications (1999) 90-100

Impact of Node Cheating on Gossip-Based Protocol

Nan Zhang, Yuanchun Shi, and Bin Chang

Dept. of Computer Science and Technology, Tsinghua University,
Beijing, China
{z-n04@mails, shiyc@, cb99@mails}tsinghua.edu.cn

Abstract. Gossip-based protocol has been widely adopted by many large-scale multicast applications. In this paper, we study the impact of node cheating on decentralized gossip-based protocol. We mainly focus on two cheating strategies, one is to increase the subscription request sending times, and the other is to increase the *PartialView* size. We establish a cheating model of nodes for gossip-based protocol, and evaluate the system performance when node cheating happens. In the simulations, we analyze the impact of node cheating on a representative gossip-based protocol, SCAMP (Scalable Membership Protocol, a decentralized, gossip-based protocol). The results show that node cheating makes considerably negative effects on the system performance, and there exists a delicate relationship between the percentage of cheating nodes in the system and the benefit they can gain. The study results also show that cheating behaviors should be paid much more attention during the gossip-based protocol design in future.

Keywords: ALM, gossip-based protocol, node cheating, reliable.

1 Introduction

The innovation and progress of Internet-wide distributed applications is driving the need for scalable multicast mechanism which can provide a reliable group communication [1]. There exist two kinds of multicast technologies: one is IP multicast [2], which achieves in the network-level, and is not currently widely deployed. The other is Application Level Multicast (ALM), which achieves in the application-level, without any support from the network. So ALM has been proposed mainly as a way to alleviate to the lack of deployment of IP multicast, and has been an active research issue at present.

Unlike IP multicast, ALM replicates and forwards data in application level, and uses unicast to a group of receivers. So there is a trade-off between the efficiency of IP multicast and the ease of deployment of group communication [3]. Compared with IP multicast, ALM is more scalable and can provide more semantics. Therefore, it is feasible to design suitable models and management protocols to achieve large-scale reliable multicast.

Existing ALM management protocol can be divided into two categories: one is tree-based management protocol, which constructs a multicast delivery tree among end hosts [4], [5], [6]. This kind of topology is easy to manage, and the control

E. Sha et al. (Eds.): EUC 2006, LNCS 4096, pp. 1068 – 1077, 2006.

overhead is also quite low. However, it is not robust under the situation that group membership changes frequently. The other kind of management protocol is gossip-based, where each member is in charge of forwarding each message to a set of other, randomly chosen, group members. And each member can receive messages from more than one node [7], [8], [9]. This mechanism using of redundant messages provides the reliability in face of node crashes and high packet loss rates in the network. It has been proven that the load on each node increases only logarithmically with the size of the group, so gossip-based ALM protocol becomes an attractive alternative to achieve a scalable and reliable ALM.

In gossip-based ALM protocol, new nodes join the group by sending a subscription request to an arbitrary member. Each participant member in the protocol maintains two lists: one list of nodes it sends gossip message to and the other list of nodes that it receives gossip message from. Obviously, less the size of the former list is, less cost it will pay for maintaining the information as well as replicating and forwarding data; and larger the size of latter list is, more message providers the node will have, which means it will receive messages with less delay, and obtain a higher quality of service.

The important point here is that there is an opportunity for nodes to try and improve their performance in the gossip-based ALM system by sending more subscription requests during its joining process, and rejecting more subscription requests from others as many as possible. So as to increase the size of list of nodes that it receives gossip message from, diminish the size of list of nodes it sends gossip message to, and minimize its replication burden. These cheating behaviors may cause the structure change and thus the low performance of the management protocol. It also affects the normal propagation of multicast data, leads to more control overhead of computation, storage and communication.

In the rest of this paper, we will study the effects of cheating strategies on the gossip-based ALM protocol. In Section 2, some related works are reviewed. In Section3, the cheating model we defined will be introduced in detail. Section 4 presents our simulation study, while Section 5 concludes with a summary of our observation and some recommendations.

2 Related works

The impact of node cheating on tree-based ALM protocols has been greatly discussed recently. This section will give a brief overview of some analyses which have been done.

Authors in [3] study the impact of cheating nodes in four representative tree-based ALM protocols: HBM (a protocol based on a centralized approach), TBCP (a distributed, tree first protocol), NICE (a distributed, tree first protocol based on clustering) and NARADA (a mesh first protocol). They focus on selfish nodes acting independently, cheating about their distance measurements during the constructing the tree. They choose the *stress_ratio* and *stretch_ratio* as indicators to characterize the intrinsic performance of the ALM protocols. The simulation results show that simple cheating strategies always have negative impact, either on the performance of the tree as perceived by its nodes (both cheats and honest nodes), or on the underlying physical network, or both.

Receiver cheating also brings considerably negative effects on the stability of ALM tree [12]. Dan Li established a cheating model and discussed the relationship between receiver cheating and the ALM tree's stability in detail. According to the simulation results, receiver cheating will not only cause much additional overhead for ALM to reconstruct the multicast tree, but also add more burdens to honest receivers, especially the source node.

Node cheating has become an important issue in the ALM researches, both tree-based ALM protocols and gossip-based protocols. However, as far as we know, compared with many discusses on the impact of node cheating on the tree-based ALM protocol, there is no research on the impact of node cheating on the gossip-based one. In this paper, this topic will be discussed in detail.

3 Cheating Model for Gossip-Based ALM Protocol

In this section, we first introduce the mechanisms of decentralized gossip-based ALM protocol briefly, and then present the cheating model we defined for analyzing the impact of node cheating on gossip-based ALM protocol in detail.

3.1 Decentralized Gossip-Based ALM Protocol

Gossip-based protocol uses randomization to reliably broadcast messages in the group. It has been used in various applications such as live media streaming [10], publish-subscribe systems [13] and so on. It provides probabilistic guarantees of delivery which degrade gracefully in the presence of loss links or fail nodes. By the difference of control manner, there are centralized gossip-based protocol and decentralized gossip-based protocol two types. The centralized means that each node should have global knowledge of membership, which greatly affects its scalability. While decentralized gossip-based ALM protocol only has to provide each node with a partial random view of the system. It requires less on memory and synchronization, which is much more scalable than centralized one, and is adopted by most large-scale multicast applications. In this paper, we analyze the impact of node cheating strategies on a simple and fully decentralized gossip-based protocol, SCAMP [8], which is also a representative one.

In SCAMP, a node maintains two lists:

- *PartialView* – records nodes it sends gossip messages to.
- *InView* – records nodes it receives gossip messages from.

New nodes subscribe (join) the group as follows: New nodes send a subscription request to an arbitrary member, called a *contact*, they start with a *PartialView* consisting of just their contact. When a node receives a new subscription request, it forwards the new node-id to all members of its own *PartialView*. It also creates c additional copies of the new subscription and forwards them to randomly chosen nodes in its *PartialView*. When a node receives a forwarded subscription, provided the subscription is not already present in its list, it accepts the new subscriber in its *PartialView* with a probability P which depends on the size of its view ($P = 1/(1 + \textit{size of PartialView})$). If it doesn't keep the new subscriber, it forwards the subscription to a node randomly chosen from its *PartialView*. These forwarded subscriptions may be kept by the neighbors or forwarded, but are not destroyed until some nodes keep them.

The earlier work [11] shows that the probability that a notification reaches everyone exhibits a sharp threshold at $\log(n)$. And SCAMP is proven to has the following desirable properties: If new nodes join by sending a subscription request to a member chosen uniformly at random from existing members, then the system configures itself toward *PartialView* of $size\,(c+1)\log(n)$ on average (*n* is the number of nodes in the system). Therefore, SCAMP can guarantee the message to be reliably propagated to all group members.

Messages are propagated as follows: When a node generates a massage, it sends it to a random subset of nodes in its *PartialView*. When any node receives a message for the first time, it does the same. Obviously, larger size of *InView* and smaller size of *PartialView* is the thing every node desires, because it enables the node not only to obtain a high quality of service with low delay, but also not to provide much to others.

For the sake of gaining more benefits, nodes may make cheating in the joining process, and we refer this kind of nodes as "cheats". In this paper, the cheating strategies adopted are as follows: When sending subscription requests, cheats will subscribe more than once, so as to largen the *InView* size and to get a reliable service. Similarly, on receiving a subscription request, cheats make cheating in the *PartialView* size, so as to reduce the probability of becoming the provider of other nodes and have less replicating and forwarding burden. This paper will discuss the impact of these two cheating strategies in detail. For ease of exposition, we establish a cheating model to quantify it.

3.2 Cheating Model

Here we make some definitions as follows:

Definition 1. Subscription Cheating Degree. When a new node sends subscription request to join the group, the increased time to the actual time (once), is defined as Subscription Cheating Degree, which is denoted by *s*.

Definition 2. PartialView Cheating Degree. When receiving a subscription request, the node calculates the acceptance probability by the size of its *PartialView* ($P = 1/(1+size\ of\ PartialView)$), the increased value of its *PartialView* size to the actual value is defined as PartialView Cheating Degree, which is denoted by *p*.

Definition 3. System Cheating Degree. In the gossip-based ALM system, the percenttage of cheats out of all nodes is defined as System Cheating Degree, which is denoted by *t*.

Obviously, $s \geq 1$, $p \geq 1$, and $0 \leq t \leq 100\%$, different *t* with different *s* and *p* will lead to different impacts on the protocol. We denote this gossip-based ALM protocol system with cheats as $G(n,s,p,t)$, where *n* is the number of nodes in the system. To have a better view of the impact of node cheating on gossip-based ALM protocol, we divide nodes into a group of cheats and a group of honest nodes, and then analyze each group separate.

Cheat group will destroy the balance of the whole system, in order to seek their benefit. In the gossip-based ALM protocol system, the *InView* size of nodes can be considered as a measurement of the service quality it gains, and the *PartialView* size can be considered as a measurement of the service it should provide. Therefore, the "Benefit" cheat group gains can be defined as follows:

Definition 4. Cheat Group Benefit Degree. In a $G(n,s,p,t)$, we define $\sum_i (sizeof\ InView_i - sizeof\ PartialView_i)$ as Cheat Group Benefit Degree, denoted by $\theta(n,s,p,t)$, where *i* is the number of cheats in the group, *i=tn*.

Based on definition 4, $\theta(n,s,p,t)<0$ shows that cheat group does not gain any benefit from the cheating behaviors, but a victim instead. Less $\theta(n,s,p,t)$ is, more damage the cheat group suffers. On the contrary, $\theta(n,s,p,t)>0$ means that the cheat group gets benefit from the cheating behaviors. More $\theta(n,s,p,t)$ is, more it benefits, then more damage the honest group suffers.

4 Simulations

We have tested 25 groups of 50,000 nodes each in a gossip-based session. The results are the average values of all the 25 groups. Each group was tied with a subscription cheating degree *s* of 5, 10, 15 and 20 respectively, a PartialView cheating degree *p* of 10, 20 and 50 respectively, and a system cheating degree *t* of 0%, 20%, 40%, 60%, 80% and 100% respectively. To study the impact of node cheating on gossip-based ALM protocol, we show the distributions of *PartialView* size, and *InView* size of a 50,000 node gossip-based ALM protocol SCAMP system with no cheats first.

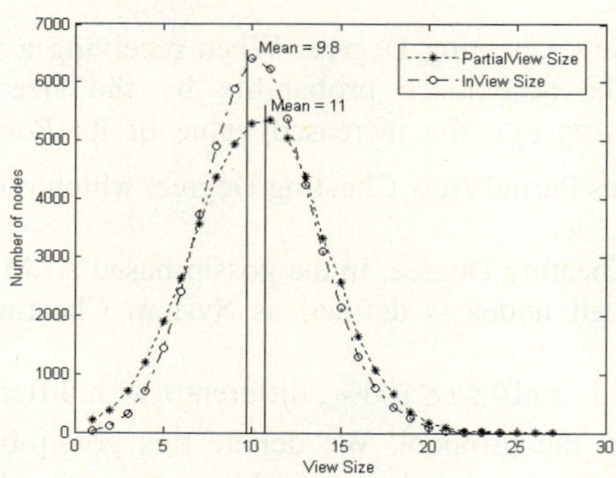

Fig. 1. Distribution of the PartialView size and InView size of a 50,000 node SCAMP system

From Fig. 1, we find that the SCAMP system with no cheats can achieve an average *InView* and *PartialView* size of $\log(n)$, where n is the size of the group ($\log(50000) = 10.8$). It is similar with the result in [9]. The earlier work [11] has shown that a *PartialView* size of this order can ensure that gossip is successful with high probability. Then what will this gossip-based ALM system be when node cheating happens?

We analysis the *InView* size, *PartialView* size of cheat group and honest group respectively, as well as cheat group benefit degree $\theta(n, s, p, t)$, against different node cheating parameters.

4.1 Subscription Cheating Degree Impact

The value of cheat *InView* size, *PartialView* Size and $\theta(n, s, p, t)$ of the gossip-based ALM protocol against *s* and *t* when $p = 20$ are illustrated in Fig 2 (a) to (c).

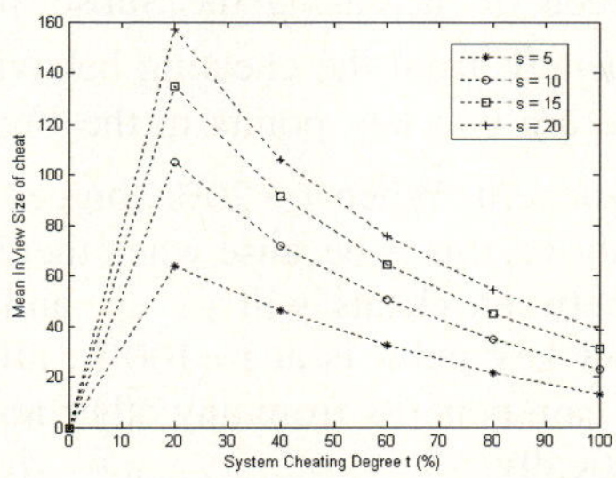

(a) Mean *InView* Size of Cheat

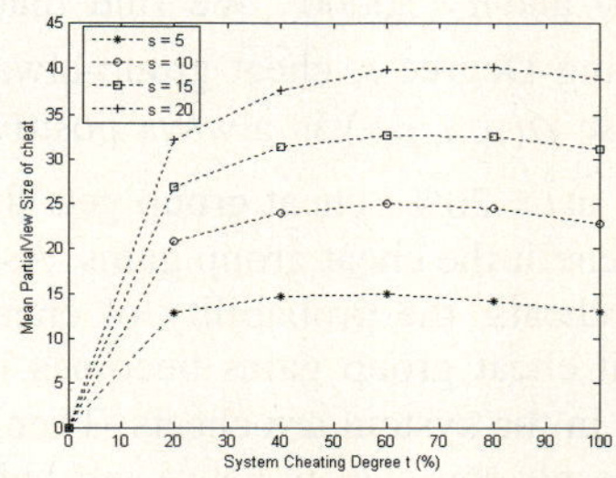

(b) Mean *PartialView Size* of Cheat

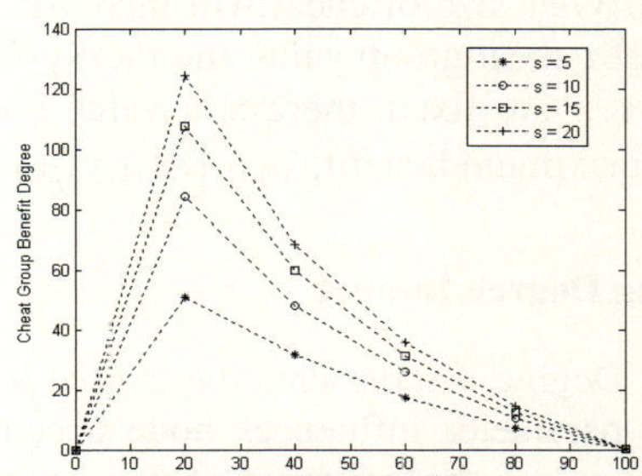

(c) Cheat Group Benefit Degree

Fig. 2. The Subscription Cheating Degree Impact

As shown in Fig. 2 (a), with a fixed *t*, cheat *InView* Size increases as *s* grows. It is because that cheat sends more subscription requests, more nodes will accept the requests and become a member of its *InView*. However, we find that with a fixed *s*, the mean *InView* Size of cheat increases when $0\% \le t \le 20\%$, and when $t > 20\%$, the mean *InView* size of cheat goes down. This can be explained as follows: When the System Cheating Degree t is small, a majority of nodes are honest nodes, who integrate the new subscriber in their *PartialView* with an honest probability, P. So bigger t is, more honest nodes will be caught with chaff, and the cheat chance will go up rapidly. However, when $t > 20\%$, most nodes are cheats, the probability of cheat behavior between cheats will go up, which will counteract the cheating effects to some extent. Many subscription requests cannot be accepted by any nodes, and finally be discarded (To avoid a subscription is forwarded an infinite number of times, we limit that when a node has received the same request more than 10 times, it simply discards the thread, same as [8]). So the mean *InView* size of cheat decreases.

From Fig. 2 (b), we find that when t is settled, the mean of cheat group *PartialView* size grows as s increases, which is similar to Fig. 1 (a). But as the System Cheating Degree t is higher, the mean of *PartialView* size does not have much change. The reason is that the factor that influences the node *PartialView* size, PartialView Cheating Degree p, is fixed in this simulation groups.

Fig. 2 (c) shows the Cheat Group Benefit Degree $\theta(n,s,p,t)$ against s and t when $p=20$ and $n=50000$. We find that by the method of increasing the Subscription Cheating Degree s, cheat group always can get benefit from the cheating behaviors, because $\theta(n,s,p,t)$ is always positive. And there are two key points in the Figure: one is at $t=20\%$, cheat group gets the maximum benefit. When $t > 20\%$, bigger t is, less benefit the cheat group gains. As mentioned above, this is because when there are more cheats, the probability of cheat behavior between cheats will go up, and the benefit cheat group gains becomes less. The other key point is at $t=100\%$, all the nodes in the system are cheats. Then they cannot gain benefits from any other nodes. As a result, this system gets a self-balance automatically.

As a whole, we conclude that cheat group can get benefit by adjusting the Subscription Cheating Degree s, which influences the cheat *InView* size directly. Bigger the s is, more the *InView* size of cheat will increase. From Fig. 2 (a) and (c), we also know that the benefit cheat group gains and the System Cheating Degree t do not direct ratio. When n, s, p are fixed, there is a value for t ($0\% < t < 100\%$) that makes cheat group have a maximum benefit, $\max\{\theta(n,s,p,t)\}$.

4.2 PartialView Cheating Degree Impact

The PartialView Cheating Degree p represents the degree which cheats magnify the *PartialView* size to. This parameter influences node acceptance probability to the subscription requests. We analyze the influence of parameter p brings to the gossip-based protocol system from honest group point of view. The value of honest group *InView* size, *PartialView* Size against p and t when $s=10$ are illustrated in Fig. 3 (a) and (b). Then the representative parameter Cheat Group Benefit Degree $\theta(n,s,p,t)$ is also analyzed in Fig. 3 (c).

From Fig. 3 (a), we find that when p is fixed, the mean *InView* size of honest node first increases when $0 \le t \le 20\%$, then decreases as t grows. This is because that cheat sends more than one subscription requests during joining group ($s=10$), and

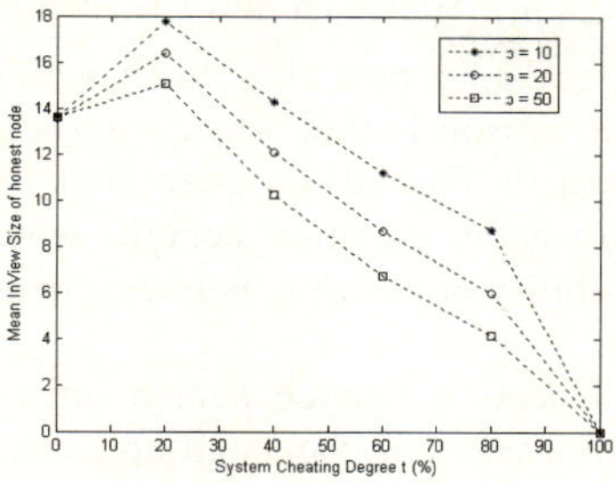

(a) Mean *InView* Size of honest node

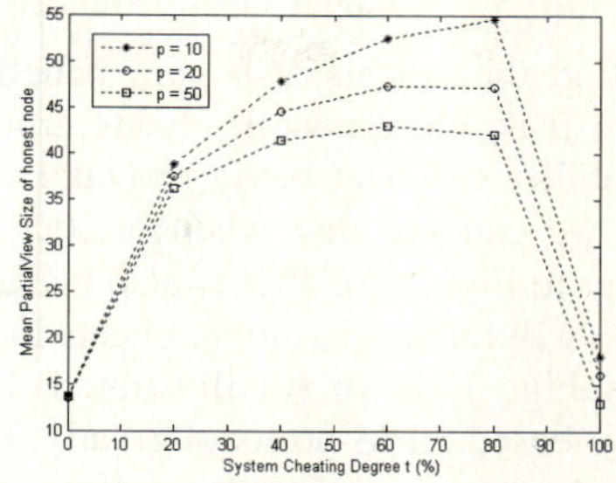

(b) Mean *PartialView Size* of honest node

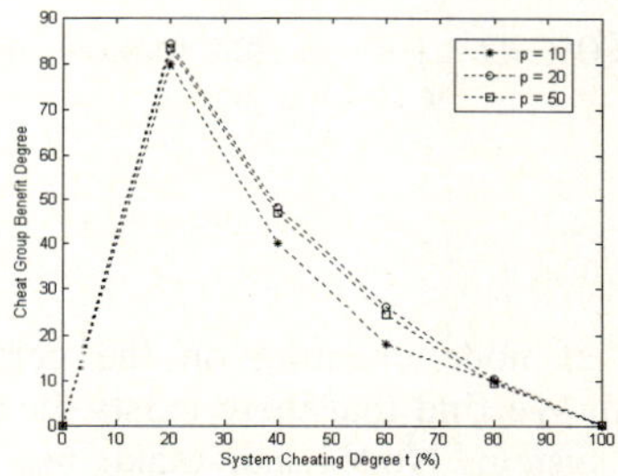

(c) Cheat Group Benefit Degree

Fig. 3. The PartialView Cheating Degree Impact

increases its *PartialView* size to decrease the probability being a provider for others ($p > 1$). In this circumstance, honest nodes are more likely to be providers, so its *PartialView* size will become much bigger than normal. Then when an honest node is going to join the group and sends a new subscription request to an arbitrary member, likely an honest one. According to the gossip-based protocol, the request will be replicated and forwarded to all the members in the receiver's own *PartialView*. For the *PartialView* size of honest node is larger than usual under this situation, the subscription request will be forwarded more times. As a result, the *InView* size of the new coming honest node increases (see Fig. 3 (a),when $0 \le t \le 20\%$). When *t* grows bigger, the mean *InView* size of honest node goes down. The reason is that when most of nodes are cheats who are prone to redirect the requests, the number of nodes willing to be providers becomes less. The subscription request is more likely to be discarded, so the honest node *InView* size decreases. In Fig. 3 (a), we can see that with a fixed *t*, the mean *InView* size of honest node decreases as *p* grows up, which is contrary to the effect of Subscription Cheating Degree *s* makes. The reason is that bigger *p* is, more likely node redirects the request.

Fig. 3 (b) shows the mean *PartialView* size of honest node against parameter *p*. We can see that when $0\% < t < 80\%$, the mean PartialView size of honest node goes up as *t* increases. When $t \ge 80\%$, the value decreases. This can be explained that when there are more cheats in the system, the probability of cheating behavior between cheats will increase, so the damage the honest node suffers goes down.

In Fig. 3 (c), Cheat Group Benefit Degree $\theta(n,s,p,t)$ against p and t is illustrated. We find that cheats also gain benefit from this cheating behavior. With a fixed t, bigger p is, more benefit cheats group gains. The reason is that when p grows, the probability of cheat being provider decreases, then its *PartialView* size goes down. Also we can see that when $t = 20\%$, cheat group gains maximal benefit, which is similar to Fig. 2 (c). This is also because the probability of cheating behavior between cheats will increase as more cheats in the system.

As Fig. 3 (a) to (c) illustrated, PartialView Cheating Degree p also influences gossip-based ALM protocol greatly. Bigger p is, more benefit cheats group gains, and more damage honest nodes suffers. Therefore, cheats always have the motivation to cheat more, so as to benefit more. Like parameter s impact, System Cheating Degree t and Cheat Group Benefit Degree $\theta(n,s,p,t)$ also have a delicate relationship. There exists a given value for t ($0\% < t < 100\%$) that makes cheat group get a maximum benefit.

5 Conclusion

In this paper, the impact of node cheating on the performance of gossip-based protocol system is analyzed. We find that there exists the severe potential trouble of trust on the gossip-based system. Nodes can make use of some simple cheating strategies to improve its performance, and lead more burdens to honest nodes. That also jeopardizes scalability of the gossip-based protocol. We establish a cheating model to analyze cheating behaviors impact, and find that node cheating has considerably negative impact on the gossip-based protocol system. Therefore, node cheating should be paid much more attention during gossip-based protocol design.

As future work, we will try to design some cheat detection or prevention techniques to discover the cheating behaviors, avoid the negative impact of node cheating.

Acknowledgments. This research is supported by NCET-04-0079 (Program for New Century Excellent Talents in University, China).

References

1. K.P. Birman. The process Group Approach to Reliable Distributed Computing. *Communications of the ACM*, 36(12): 37-53, December 1993.
2. S. Deering and D. Cheriton. Multicast Routing in Datagram Internetworks and Extended LANs. *ACM Transaction on Computer Systems*, 8(2): 85-110, May 1990.
3. L. Mathy, N. Blundell, V. Roca, and A. EI-Sayed. Impact of Simple Cheating in Application-Level Multicast. In *the Proceedings of IEEE INFOCOM 2004*, March 2004.
4. D. Pendarakis, S. Shi, D. Verma and M. Waldvogel. ALMI: An Application Level Multicast Infrastructure. In *proceedings of the 3rd USENIX Symposium on Internet Technologies and Systems (USITS)*, March 2001.
5. S. Banerjee, B. Bhattacharjee, and C. Kommareddy. Scalable Application Layer Multicast. In *Proceedings of ACM SIGCOMM*, August 2002.

6. B. Zhang, S. Jamin, L. Zhang. Host Multicast: A Framework for Delivering Multicast to End Users. In *Proceedings of IEEE INFOCOM 2002*, June 2002.
7. K.P. Birman, M. Hayden, O. Ozkasap, Z. Xiao, M. Budiu, and Y. Minsky. Bimodal Multicast. *ACM Transaction on Computer Systems*, 17(2): 41-88, May 1999.
8. A.J. Ganesh, A.-M. Kermarrec, and L. Massoulié. Peer-to-Peer Membership Management for Gossip-Based Protocols. *IEEE Transactions on Computers*, 52 (2), February 2003.
9. Q. Sun and D.C. Sturman. A Gossip-Based Reliable Multicast for Large-Scale High-Throughput Applications. In *Proceedings of IEEE International Conference on Dependable Systems and Networks (DSN2000)*, July 2000.
10. X. Zhang, J. Liu, B. Li, and T.-S.P. Yum. CoolStreaming/DONet: A Data-driven Overlay Network for Live Media Streaming. In *Proceedings of IEEE INFOCOM2005*, March 2005.
11. A.-M. Kermarrec, L. Massoulié and A.J. Ganesh. Probabilistic Reliable Dissemination in Large-Scale Systems. *IEEE Transactions on Parallel and Distributed Systems*, 14(3), March 2003.
12. D. Li, Y. Cui, K. Xu, and J. P. Wu. Impact of Receiver Cheating on the Stability of ALM Tree. In *Proceedings of GLOBECOM 2005*, November 2005.
13. P. Eugster, S. Handurukande, R. Guerraoui, A.-M. Kermarrec, and P. Kouznetsov. Lightweight Probabilistic Broadcast. In *Proceedings of IEEE International Conference on Dependable Systems and Networks (DSN2001)*, 2001.

Energy-Efficient Clustering Algorithm in Wireless Sensor Networks*

DaeHwan Kim[1,2], SangHak Lee[1], and We Duke Cho[2]

[1] Intelligent IT System Center, Korea Electronics Technology Institute,
#68 Yatap-dong, Bundang-gu, Seongnam-si, Gyeonggi-do 463-816, South Korea
{kimdh, shlee}@keti.re.kr

[2] Department of Electrical and Computer Engineering,
Ajou University, Suwon, 443-749, South Korea
chowd@ajou.ac.kr

Abstract. Wireless sensor networks is a key technology for new ways of interaction between computers and the physical environment. However, the energy constrained and limited computing resources of the sensor nodes present major challenges in gathering data. Since sensor nodes are densely deployed, redundant data may occur. While cluster-based data gathering is efficient at energy and bandwidth, it's difficult to cluster network efficiently. In this work, a new distributed clustering algorithm for ubiquitous sensor network is presented. Clustering is based on the distance between nodes and the number in a cluster for wireless sensor networks. Simulation results show that the proposed algorithm balances the energy dissipation over the whole network thus increase the amount of data delivery to the sink.

1 Introduction

A sensor network is composed of a large number of sensor nodes that are densely deployed either inside the phenomenon or very close to it [1]. The number of sensor nodes in a sensor networks can be several orders of magnitude higher than in an ad hoc network [2]. This factor contributes to a drastic increase in traffic of sensor network protocols [3]. Thus it may cause explosive traffic without in-network data processing, e.g. data aggregation. The effective strategy to solve above described problem is cluster-based routing and data aggregation [4]. However, the algorithmic complexity of clustering is known to be NP-hard for finding c optimal clusters in network while it is efficient at energy and bandwidth. Thus, it is difficult to find optimal solution, and consequently clustering is usually performed by some heuristics. The problem we address is to cluster the network distributedly to balance the energy consumption over the whole network while minimizing the overhead of clustering, thus to increase the energy efficiency.

* This research is supported in part by the Ubiquitous Computing and Network (UCN) Project, the Ministry of Information and Communication (MIC) 21st Century Frontier R&D Program in Korea.

E. Sha et al. (Eds.): EUC 2006, LNCS 4096, pp. 1078–1088, 2006.

To achieve this goal, we analyze the difference in energy consumption between nodes according to node proximity to its neighbors and propose a new distributed clustering algorithm.

The rest of the paper is organized as follows: in section 2, related works, we survey the previous works related to clustering network. In section 3, we determine the cause of difference in energy consumption between nodes, then get the criteria. Section 4 defines the problem and presents the proposed clustering algorithm. Section 5 discusses detailed experimental results. Finally, Section 6 gives concluding remarks and directions for future work.

2 Related Works

In this section, we discuss related works for clustering of sensor network. There are already a lot of works related to clustering network. LEACH [5] analyzes the performance of cluster-based routing mechanism with in-network data aggregation. LEACH leverages balancing the energy load among sensors using randomized rotation of cluster heads, but it does not guarantee good clustering head distribution. In ACE [13], the author clusters the sensor network in constant number of iterations using the node degree as the main parameter. In HEED [14], they show a distributed clustering algorithm which selects clusterheads based on residual energy of each node. However, they require too much iteration with transmitting the control packets. V. Mhatre and C. Rosenberg [11] formulated the required number of clusterheads and the required battery energy of nodes for both single hop and multi-hop communication mode.

GAF [6], SPAN [7], and ASCENT [8] tried to select a minimum number of nodes which join the multi-hop infrastructure. GAP, SPAN, and ASCENT share the same objective of using redundancy in sensor networks to turn radios on and off, thus prolong network lifetime. It does not guarantee optimal c clusterheads. In CLUSTERPOW [10], nodes are assumed to be non-homogeneously dispersed in the network. A node uses the minimum possible power level to forward data packets, in order to maintain connectivity while increasing the network capacity and saving energy.

Recently, T. J. Kwon *et al.* proposed passive clustering (PC) which does not run clustering algorithm periodically but uses piggybacking with on-demand routing in ad hoc network or sensor network [9]. In [12], authors proposed the division and merger based clustering in ad hoc networks. However, they did not consider the optimal number of clusters. The above two clustering algorithms intends to maintain the connectivity and to reduce the communication cost in networks in which nodes move. However, mobility of nodes in sensor network is rare. They do not take account for aggregating data and balancing energy consumption. Sensor networks require balancing the energy consumption, since data generated in a sensor network are too much for an end-user to process and data from close sensors may be highly correlated [4]. Thus methods for clustering the network well distributedly and combining data into a small set of meaningful information are highly required.

In this paper, we will show a clustering scheme which achieves the well distributed clustering over the whole network by using the nodes' remaining energy and the number of nodes within a cluster.

3 Analysis of Energy Consumption

In this section, to address our problem, we define simple network model and analyze the source of difference in energy consumption between nodes in case of cluster-based network. Then we propose a new clustering algorithm to balance energy consumption taking advantage of the analysis results.

Our network model is that sets of sensors are homogeneously dispersed on a regular field. Network has following properties:

(i) Network is consist of homogenous nodes.
(ii) The nodes are quasi-stationary after deployment.
(iii) All nodes have equal initial energy and similar capabilities.
(iv) Each node has a fixed number of transmission power levels and can control the level.
(v) Each node functions as either a clusterhead or an ordinary sensor node.

To analyze the main cause of difference in energy consumption between nodes, we build a simple network communication model similar to the one in [5] in which the amount of energy required to transmit a packet over distance d is given by $l + \mu d^k$, where l is the amount of energy spent in the transmitter electronics circuitry, while μd^k is the amount of energy spent in the RF amplifier to counter the propagation loss. Network consists of nodes, N, and the actual number of clusterheads, c, become clusterheads in each round. Each node become clusterhead once every $\frac{N}{c}$ round, receive data from its cluster member sensor, and transmit the aggregated data to the sink. Otherwise, nodes join the nearest clusterhead and transmit acquired sensor data to it every $\frac{N}{c} - 1$ rounds.

The nodes consume their energy differently in cluster-based network depending on their role: when they are clusterhead and when they are ordinary sensor nodes.

First, we analyze the maximum difference of energy consumption when nodes are clusterheads. If nodes are dispersed homogeneously and clustering is well distributed, one clusterhead contains $\frac{N}{c} - 1$ sensor nodes. The energy consumption of receiving data at clusterhead: $(\frac{N}{c} - 1)l$, the energy consumption of aggregating data: $(\frac{N}{c} - 1)DA$ where DA is the energy on data aggregation, the energy consumption of transmitting data to the sink: $l + \mu d^k$. The distance of the farthest node from the sink: d_{max}, the distance from the nearest node from the sink: d_{min}. The difference in energy consumption between two nodes in case of clusterhead, D_{CH}, is defined as follows:

$$D_{CH} \approx \mu({d_{max}}^k - {d_{min}}^k) \quad (1)$$

We simply set the size of sensor field to [0, 0] to [A, A] and the sink located on the end of the sensor field. Since the maximum distance in this field is assumed $\sqrt{2}A$, the greatest difference in energy consumption is approximately $\mu(\sqrt{2}A)^k$.

Second, we calculate the greatest difference of energy consumption when nodes are ordinary sensor nodes. The energy consumption of each node as an ordinary node is $(\frac{N}{c} - 1)(l + \mu d^k)$. The energy of consumption varies depending on the distance of the nearest $\frac{N}{c} - 1$ nodes which become clusterheads in turn. Since we assume the size of sensor field is A^2 and nodes are dispersed homogeneously, the coverage of each node is $\frac{A^2}{N}$ and the radius of each node is $\frac{A}{\sqrt{\pi N}}$. The distance between two neighbor nodes is $2\frac{A}{\sqrt{\pi N}}$. The transmission range which contains $\frac{N}{c} - 1$ nodes is as Fig. 1 (a).

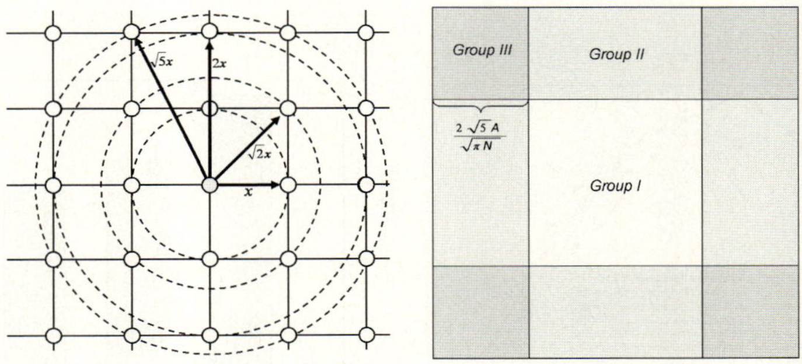

Fig. 1. (a)Numbers of neighbor per transmission range (b)Group classified by location within sensor field

We substitute x for $2\frac{A}{\sqrt{\pi N}}$. In case of transmission range x, $\sqrt{2}x$, $2x$, and $\sqrt{5}x$, the numbers of neighbor are 4, 8, 12, and 20 respectively. The numbers of neighbor node within certain range depends on the relative location within the sensor field. We categorize the nodes into three groups: the first group, called Group I, is located at the center of sensor field, the second group, called Group II, is located at which half of node's transmission range is out of sensor field, and the third group, called Group III, is located at which three-quarters of node's transmission range is out of sensor field. If the location of a node is $n_i = (x_i, y_i)$, N is 100, A is 100, and c is 5(5%), the transmission range is $\frac{2\sqrt{5}A}{\sqrt{\pi N}}$ and each group is as follows. We substitute α for $\frac{2\sqrt{5}A}{\sqrt{\pi N}}$. Fig. 1 (b) shows the location of each group.

- Group I: $(\alpha \leq x_i \leq (A - \alpha)) \wedge (\alpha \leq y_i \leq (A - \alpha))$
- Group II (two cases):
  $((0 \leq x_i < \alpha) \vee ((A - \alpha < x_i \leq \alpha)) \wedge (\alpha < y_i < (A - \alpha))$
  $((0 \leq y_i < \alpha) \vee ((A - \alpha < y_i \leq \alpha)) \wedge (\alpha < x_i < (A - \alpha))$
- Group III:
  $((0 \leq x_i < \alpha) \vee ((A - \alpha) < x_i \leq \alpha)) \wedge ((0 \leq y_i < \alpha) \vee ((A - \alpha) < y_i \leq \alpha))$

The most difference in energy consumption between Group I and Group III nodes, D_{ORD}, is defined as follows:

$$D_{ORD} \approx \mu \left(\left(\frac{\sqrt{40A}}{\sqrt{\pi N}} \right)^k - \left(\frac{\sqrt{10A}}{\sqrt{\pi N}} \right)^k \right) \tag{2}$$

We simulate energy consumption of sensor network. Network consists of 100 nodes, network field is 100×100, every node start at same energy level, 2J, and the sink located from (50, 175) to (50, 225). Protocol runs clustering at every 20s and 5% of all nodes are selected as clusterheads using a heuristic algorithm, the simulated annealing [15], to build well-distributed clustering. After 20 rounds in which every node become a clusterhead at once, we get the residual energy of each node.

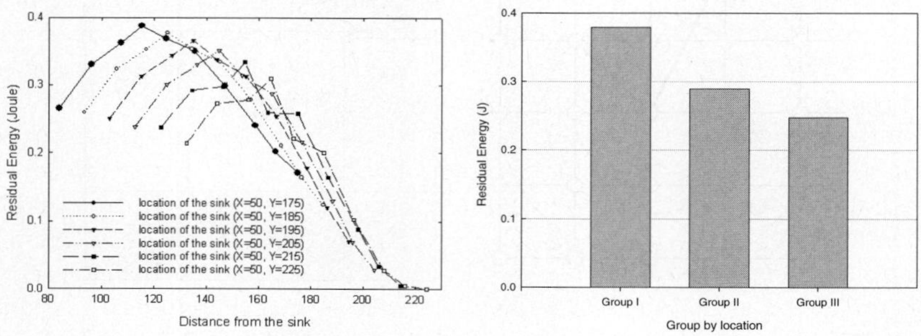

Fig. 2. (a)Residual energy per distance from the sink (b)Residual energy per group

Fig. 2 (a) shows the residual energy per the distance from the sink. The simulation results reflect that the distance between neighbors affects the energy consumption more than the distance between node and sink. The remaining energy does not decrease linearly since nodes in the middle of network have more neighbors than nodes in the fringe of sensor field. Fig. 2 (b) shows the average residual energy per above described group. Network consists of Group I: 24 nodes, Group II: 45 nodes, and Group III: 31 nodes.

In this section, we analyze the cause of difference in energy consumption between nodes in the case of single hop with clustering. We conclude that it is not effective that nodes become equally clusterhead in turn and node proximity to its neighbors affects difference more than distance between node and sink. Thus we choose the remaining energy of nodes, the distance between nodes within a cluster, and the number of nodes in a cluster as clusterhead selection criteria to balance energy consumption between nodes thus increase the amount of data delivery.

4 Proposed Clustering Algorithm

In this section, we describe our clustering algorithm, called Cluster-based self-Organizing Data Aggregation (CODA) in detail. First, we define the clustering problem we should address. Then, we propose a novel clustering algorithm based on previous analysis.

The clustering algorithm we introduce should meet the following requirements:

(i) Clustering is performed distributedly. Each node independently makes its decision based on local information.
(ii) Clustering terminates within a fixed number of iterations.
(iii) After clustering, each node is either a clusterhead or an ordinary node that belongs to one clusterhead.
(iv) Clusterheads are well-distributed over the network field.

Clustering is basically time-based operation. Thus all nodes in the network are synchronized and participate in the clustering at periodic intervals. In the pervious section, we show that clustering in which all nodes become clusterhead once in fixed period results in unbalanced energy consumption. Thus we do not restrict that all nodes should become clusterhead once in fixed period. We use the remaining energy of nodes, distance between nodes in cluster, and the number of nodes in a cluster as parameter for selecting clusterhead. The algorithm consists of three phases - the first elects clusterhead candidates based on the remaining energy and reelect clusterhead which have minimum distance cost within cluster ($Init$), the second merges clusters which have members below the lower threshold ($Merge$), and the third partitions clusters which have members over the upper threshold ($Partition$). In $Init$ phase, each sensor i elects itself to be a clusterhead at the beginning of $Init$ phase with probability $P_i(t)$. When there are N nodes in the network, $P_i(t)$ is as follows:

$$P_i(t) = \frac{E_i(t)}{\sum_{j=1(j\in N(i))}^{n} E_j(t)} \times \frac{n}{N} \times k \tag{3}$$

where $E_i(t)$ is node i's remaining energy, n is the number of neighbor in fixed transmission radius, and c is the expected number of clusters. If $P_i(t)$ is over the random number in [0, 1], node i is a candidate for clusterhead. Each candidate broadcasts advertisement message and then ordinary nodes join the nearest candidate. If ordinary node does not receive advertisement message, it become a clusterhead by itself. Candidate clusterhead calculates the intra-cluster cost for each member node. Intra-cluster cost for member node j is defined as follows.

$$Intra\_Cluster\_\_Cost_j = \sum_{k\in Cluster(i)} ((x_j - x_k)(x_j - x_k) + (y_j - y_k)(y_j - y_k))\,.$$

Candidate clusterhead promotes the least cost node as new clusterhead if the node's remaining energy is over the average in the cluster. The flowchart of this procedure is shown in Fig. 3.

We introduce the $Merge$ and $Partition$ phase since the probabilistic clusterhead election does not guarantee the expected number of cluster overall network and well-distributed cluster. After $Init$ phase, the $Merge$ phase starts if there is a cluster which has the member nodes below the lower bound ($Thresh_{Lower}$).

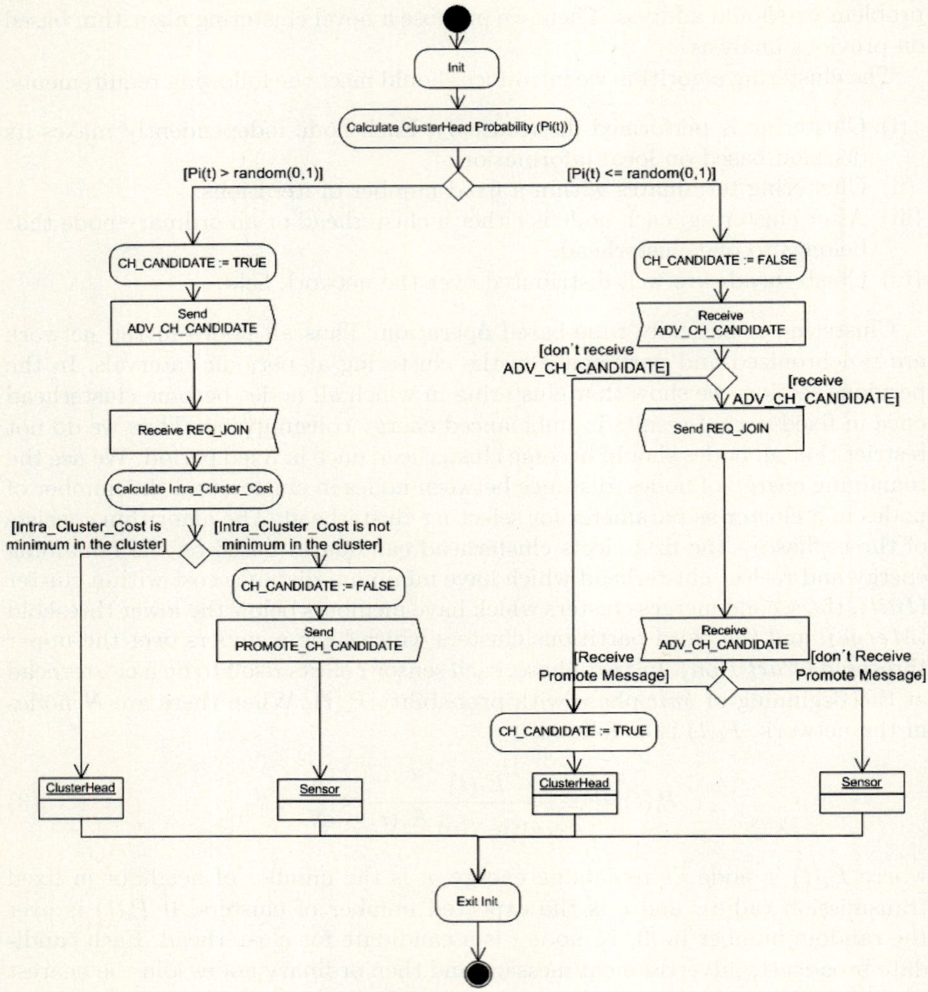

Fig. 3. Flowchart of the *Init* procedure

A candidate clusterhead which has to be merged broadcast the request message (REQ_MERGE) and then neighbour candidate clusterheads which do not need to be merged reply (ACK_MERGE) to the request message. Then merged candidate clusterhead send the merge request message (REQ_CH_MERGE). If there is no response, it diverge two case. If the cluster has member nodes, it fixes it's $P_i(t)$ as 0.5 then processes the reelection. If the cluster do not have member nodes, it generates the random number in [0, 1] to decide whether it is still a clusterhead. When there is no neighboring candidate, it means that any nodes do not become the candidate clusterhead during previous *Init* phase. The flowchart of *Merge* is shown in Fig. 4 (a).

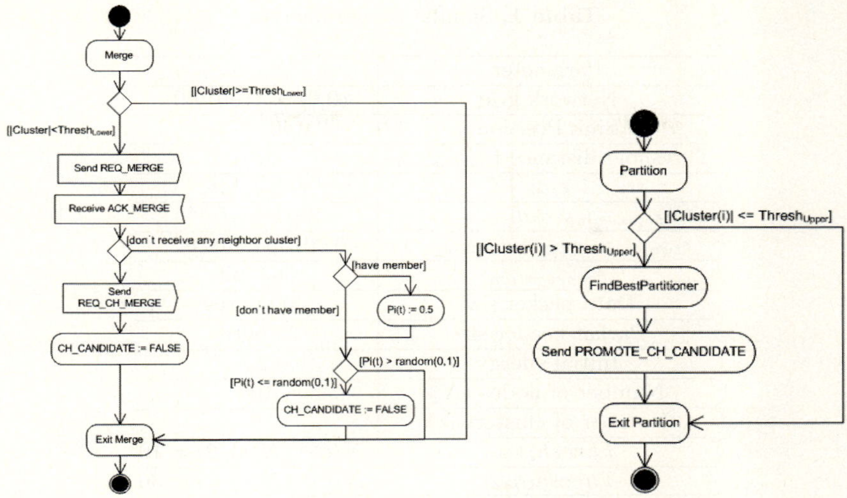

Fig. 4. (a)Flowchart of the *Merge* procedure (b)Flowchart of the *Partition* procedure

After the *Merge* phase, candidate clusterhead which has the number of member node over the upper bound ($Thresh_{Upper}$) partitions the cluster. A candidate clusterhead chooses an additional candidate clusterhead which partitions the cluster more evenly. The selection function, CH_{PART}, is defined as follow:

$$CH_{PART} = \arg \min_{j \in cluster(i)} ||Cluster(i)| - |Cluster(j)|| \tag{4}$$

where $|Cluster(i)|$ is the number of nodes in cluster i. If the number of nodes in new cluster is below the lower bound ($Thresh_{Lower}$), existing candidate clusterhead do not progress the partition. This is to prevent clustering from going back to Merge condition. The worst case occurs when there is only one candidate clusterhead over the whole network. However, the Partition process will produce c clusters in $\log_2 k$. Therefore the clustering algorithm terminates in fixed iterations. The flowchart of *Partition* is shown in Fig. 4 (a). To show the energy efficiency of the proposed algorithm, we simulate a system of 100 nodes on a 100 $\times$ 100 grid and analyze the results from several different points of view in the next section.

5 Performance Evaluation

In this section, we evaluate the performance of the proposed algorithm via simulation. We use the same parameters defined in [5], shown in Table 1.

We measure two metrics to analyze the performance of clustering algorithm: **Network lifetime** measures the time of FND (First Node Die) and LND (Last Node Die). This metrics indicates how well balance the energy consumption over the whole network. **Data Delivery** is the total amount of data received

Table 1. Simulation parameters

Parameter	Value
Network grid	(0,0) $\times$ (100,100)
Sink Position	(50, 175)
Threshold distance ($d_{crossover}$)	87m
ϵ_{elec}	50nJ/bit
$\epsilon_{friss-amp}(< d_{crossover})$	10pJ/bit/m^2
$\epsilon_{two-ray-amp}(\geq d_{crossover})$	0.0013pJ/bit/m^4
$\epsilon_{aggregation}$	5nJ/bit
Data packet size	500 bytes
Packet header size	25 bytes
Initial energy	2J
Number of nodes (N)	100
Number of clusters (c)	5
$Thresh_{Lower}$	$(N/c - (N/c)/2) = 10$
$Thresh_{Upper}$	$(N/c + (N/c)/2) = 30$

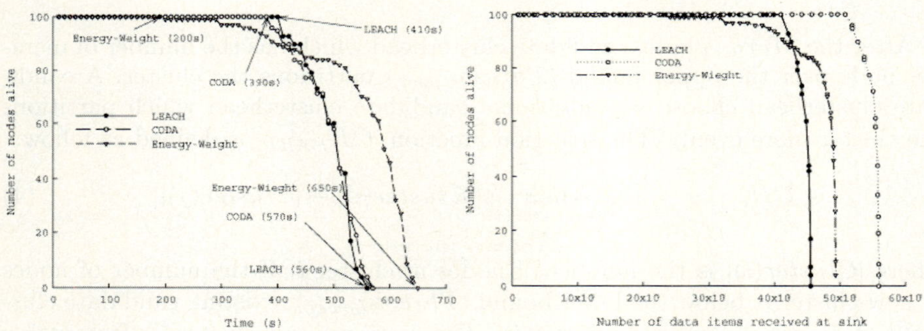

Fig. 5. (a)Number of nodes alive over time (b)Number of nodes alive per amount of data sent to the sink

at the sink. This metrics defines the network efficiency (Data received / Total energy spent). In addition, we observe the average number of cluster and average number of member.

We compare the CODA to the LEACH and Node-Weight (by remaining energy) clustering in terms of the above metrics. In LEACH every node becomes a clusterhead only once in $\frac{N}{c}$ round and Node-Weight selects a node which has the most remaining energy as a clusterhead in fixed radius. Fig. 5 (a) and Fig. 5 (b) show the total number of nodes that remain alive over the simulation time and per amount of data received at the sink. While nodes remain alive for a long time in Node-Weight, time of FND (First Node Die) is earlier than any other method. This is because it keeps clusterheads having a regular distance but it consider only in fixed range. We see that nodes in CODA deliver 23% and 13% more data than LEACH and Node-Weight for the same number of node

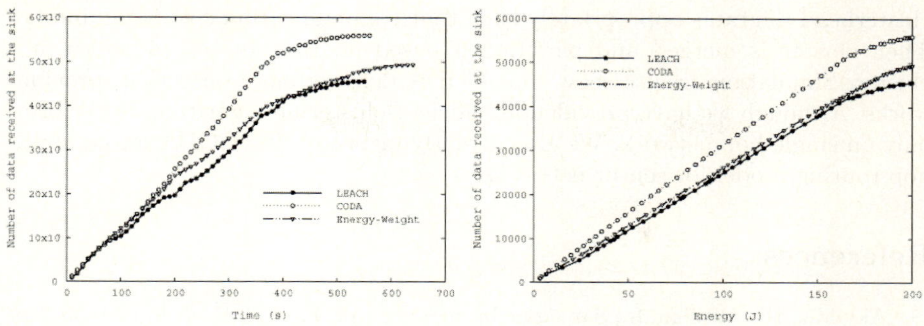

Fig. 6. (a)Total amount of data received at the sink over time (b)Total amount of data received at the sink per given amount of energy

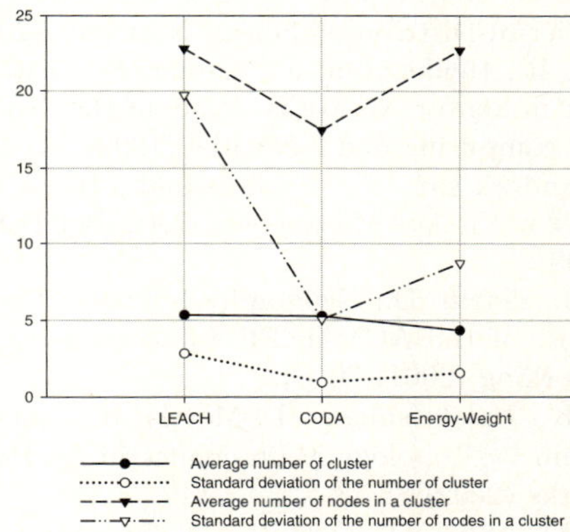

Fig. 7. Average number of cluster, Standard deviation of number of clusters, Average number of nodes in a cluster, and Standard deviation of number of nodes in a cluster

deaths respectively. Fig. 6 (a) and Fig. 6 (b) show the total number of data received at the sink over time and for a given amount of energy. Fig. 7 shows that CODA sends much more data to the sink in the simulation time than LEACH and Node-Weight. It indicates that CODA can build more efficient cluster over the whole network. Fig. 7 shows the reason why clustering performs differently. Distance-based re-electing, merging, and partitioning enable CODA to achieve a better cluster than LEACH and Node-Weight.

6 Conclusions

In this paper, we have introduced a new energy-efficient clustering algorithm for wireless sensor networks. Our approach is to balance the number of nodes in a cluster. Clusterheads are randomly selected based on their residual energy and clusterhead migrates appropriately such that communication cost is minimized. Then cluster is merged and partitioned based on the number of nodes in a cluster. Simulation results show that CODA delivers more data than previous works. Although we have provided an efficient clustering algorithm, it performs only on single-hop network. We are currently incorporating CODA into a multi-hop routing model for sensor networks.

References

1. Akyildiz, IF., Weilian, S., Sankarasubramaniam, Y., Cayirci, E.: A Survey on Sensor Networks. IEEE Comm. Mag (2002) 102–114.
2. National Research Council: Embedded, Everywhere: A Research Agenda for Networked Systems of Embedded Computers. National Academy Press (2001)
3. Ganesan, D., Cerpa, A., Ye, W., Yu, Y., Zhao, J., Estrin, D.: Networking Issues in Wireless Sensor Networks. Journal of Parallel and Distributed Computing(JPDC) Special issue on Frontier in Distributed Sensor Networks (2003) 799–814
4. Estrin, E., Govindan, R., Heidemann, J., Kumar, S.: Next Century Challenges: Scalable Coordination in Sensor Networks. Proc. of the 5th Annual International Conference on Mobile computing and Networks (1999) 263–270
5. Heinzelman, W., Chandrakasan, A., Balakrishnan, H.: An Application-Specific Protocol Architecture for Wireless Microsensor Networks. IEEE Trans. on Wireless Comm. (2002) 660–669
6. Xu, Y., Heidemann, J., Estrin, D.: Geography-Informed Energy Conservation for Ad Hoc Routing. Proc. of the ACM/IEEE International Conference on Mobile Computing and Networking (2001) 70–84
7. Chen, B., Jamieson, K., Balakrishnan, H., Morris, R.: Span: an Energy-Efficient Coordination Algorithm for Topology Maintenance in Ad Hoc Wireless Networks. ACM Wireless Networks (2002) 85–96
8. Cerpa, A., Estrin, D.: ASCENT: Adaptive Self-Configuring Sensor Networks Topologies. Proc. of IEEE INFOCOM (2002) 1278–1287
9. Kwon, T., Gerla, M., Varma, V., Barton, M., Hsing, T.: Efficient Flooding with Passive Clustering-An Overhead-Free Selective Forward Mechanism for Ad Hoc Sensor Networks. Proc. of the IEEE (2002) 1210–1220
10. Kawadia, V., Kumar, P.: Power Control and Clustering in Ad Hoc Networks. Proc. of IEEE INFOCOM (2003) 459–469
11. Mhatre, V., Rosenberg, C.: Design guidelines for wireless sensor networks: communication, clustering and aggregation. Elsevier Ad Hoc Networks (2003) 45–63
12. Tomoyuki, O., Shinji, I., Yoshiaki, K., Kenji, I.: An Adaptive Multihop Clustering Scheme for Ad Hoc Networks with High Mobility. IEICE Trans. on Fundamentals (2003) 1689–1697
13. Chan, H., Perrig, A.: ACE: An Emergent Algorithm for Highly Uniform Cluster Formation. 2004 European Workshop on Sensor Networks (2004) 154–171
14. Younis, O., Fahmy, S.: Distributed Clustering in Ad-hoc Sensor Networks: A Hybrid, Energy-Efficient Approach. IEEE INFOCOM 2004 (2004) 629–640
15. Kirkpatrick, S., Gelatt, C., Vecchi, M.: Optimization by Simulated Annealing. Science (1983) 13–22

Enhanced Multipath Routing Protocol Using Congestion Metric in Wireless Ad Hoc Networks

Chunsoo Ahn[1], Jitae Shin[1], and Eui-Nam Huh[2]

[1] School of Information and Communication Engineering, Sungkyunkwan University
300 Cheoncheon-dong Suwon, Korea
{navy12, jtshin}@ece.skku.ac.kr
[2] Department of Computer Engineering, Kyung Hee University
1 Seocheon, Giheung, Yongin, Gyeonggi, Korea
johnhuh@khu.ac.kr

Abstract. Transmission over wireless ad hoc networks is a challenging problem, because the wireless channel is characterized by limited bandwidth, multi-hop connectivity, mobility of nodes, and dynamically varying network topology. Current unipath routing protocols result in performance degradation in mobile networks due to unreliability of the wireless infrastructure and mobility of nodes. Multipath routing is an attractive alternative for scalable and multiple sub-streamable multimedia traffic under highly error-prone and resource-depleted network environments. However, existing multipath-capable routing protocols cannot split a single data flow into several sub-flows over a multipath, because these routing protocols use, mostly, an alternate path scheme that provides a secondary path in the event of link failure of the primary path. The Split Multipath Routing (SMR) protocol, which is a major multipath routing protocol based on Dynamic Source Routing (DSR) and uses decentralized transmission over multipath. In enhanced performance, Split Equal-cost Multipath Routing (SEMR) based on SMR is proposed, by introducing 'congestion path metric' as a novel metric, which can identify whether the path contains a bottleneck node and guide the selection of other non-congested paths in the path-selecting process. In using proposed concept, superior performance in comparison with SMR and DSR, can be achieved.

1 Introduction

Mobile Ad Hoc Networks (MANETs) consists of a collection of wireless mobile nodes which dynamically exchange data among themselves without reliance on a fixed base station. MANET nodes have a high degree of mobility and are typically distinguished by limited power, processing, and memory resources. In such networks, wireless mobile nodes may enter and leave the network dynamically. Due to the limited transmission range of wireless network nodes, routing is a crucial issue in the design of MANETs.

Previous unipath routing protocols, such as DSR[2], AODV[3], TORA[4], and ROAM[5], in MANETs do not solve load balancing, fault-tolerance, and route resilience problems. However, the multipath routing protocol provides various advantages

E. Sha et al. (Eds.): EUC 2006, LNCS 4096, pp. 1089 – 1097, 2006.

in addition to solving the problems of the unipath routing protocol. The multipath routing protocol is able to support superior performance in mobile network conditions [1]. Multipath routing protocols based on AODV (e.g., AODV-BR[6] or AOMDV[7]), or based on DSR (e.g., MSR[8] or MDSR[9]), contain a primary path and one or more alternate paths. Although the primary path may be broken, the connection is maintained by using an alternate path, resulting in an improvement in overall performance. However, multipath routing algorithms using an alternate path, provide fault-tolerance, not load balancing. In addition, because there are many link failures in high-mobility or in highly node-densed networks, previous multipath routing algorithms are not effective in terms of path maintenance. Hence, an equal-cost multipath routing algorithm such as split multipath routing (SMR) is proposed in order to solve both load balancing and fault-tolerance problems. [10]

In this paper, a new path metric (so called congestion path metric) is presented and applied to the equal-cost multipath routing algorithm by enhancing the SMR algorithm. It is called Split Equal-cost Multipath Routing (SEMR). SEMR reduces the congestion degree by dispersing a traffic-stream into multiple paths. Therefore, overall network performance in high-mobility networks is enhanced.

The subsequent sections of this paper are organized as follows. In Section 2, a review of SMR, as a referenced equal-cost multipath routing algorithm, is provided. In Section 3, a multipath routing algorithm where a new congestion path metric is applied, is presented. In Section 4, a performance evaluation is presented. This paper is concluded in Section 5.

2 The Problems of SMR as an Equal-Cost Multipath Routing

SMR, based on DSR, is a reactive multipath source routing protocol and equal-cost multipath routing protocol. SMR has superior throughput over DSR, because it uses maximally disjoint two paths in MANETs, so that data connections are maintained. SMR has a greater initial path configuration time and control packets than DSR, and has, lower end-to-end delay and overhead than DSR. The basic idea of SMR is similar to DSR, and is used to construct maximally disjoint paths. Unlike DSR, intermediate nodes do not maintain a route cache, and do not reply to Route Request (RREQ) messages. This allows the destination to receive all possible paths so that it can select maximally disjoint paths. The destination uses the shortest delay path metric. The first path is the shortest delay path, and the second path is a maximally disjoint path. SMR is suitable for high-mobility networks, because link failures often occur in high-mobility networks. In SMR, fault-tolerance is enhanced by selecting the maximally disjoint path. In addition, higher load balancing performance through split data transmission is demonstrated.

As a general routing protocol in MANETs, SMR selects the shortest delay path and maximally disjoint path. Therefore, it may create a bottleneck in terms of considering many data sessions. A data session includes the total multiple paths for multiple data sub-streams per each user connection. For example, if one node belongs to the shortest delay path, there is a high probability that the node belongs to the shortest delay path of another data session. Therefore, it is required to consider avoiding congested nodes so that transmission errors can be reduced. Therefore, the SMR algorithm is modified to enhance network performance.

3 Proposed Split Equal-Cost Multipath Routing (SEMR)

In SMR, it may be true that data paths are concentrated on one node in highly nodedensed networks, due to using the shortest delay path metric such as DSR. To overcome these challenges, SEMR uses the least congestion path metric instead of the shortest delay. The congestion at each path can be estimated, as the congestion degree in each node in the path is known.

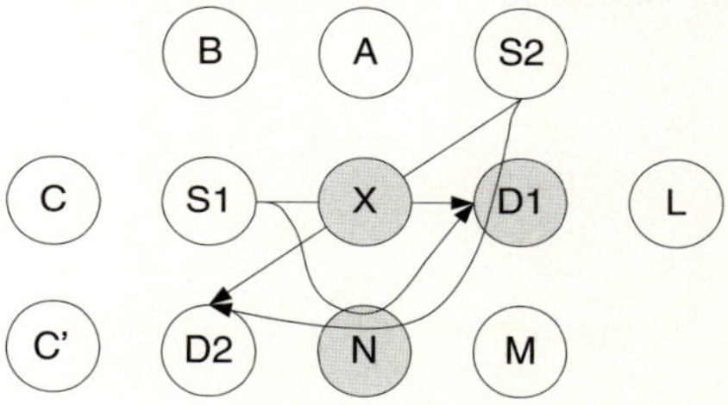

Fig. 1. Path Selection in SMR

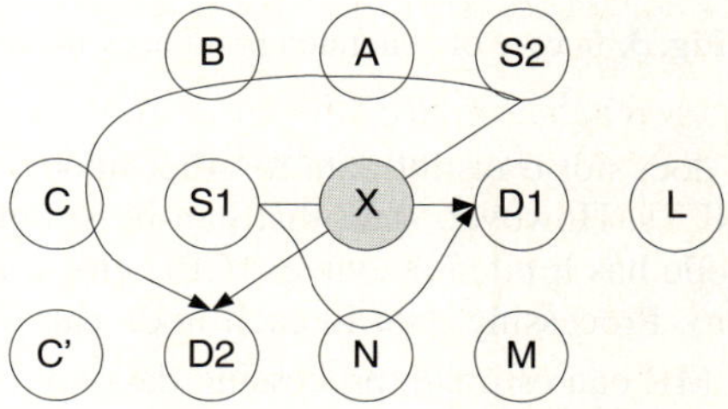

Fig. 2. Path Selection in SEMR

As conceptual diagrams, Fig. 1 and Fig. 2 demonstrate congestion nodes when selecting two paths in SMR and SEMR, respectively. There are two data sessions, i.e., (S1, D1) and (S2, D2), and each one has two paths. Both SMR and SEMR transmit data through two paths (S1-X-D1 and S1-N-D1) as a first data session. The second data session is established from S2 to D2. SMR selects the S2-X-D2 path as the first path of the second data session, and S2-D1-N-D2 as the second. Therefore, there are three congested nodes (X, D1, and N node) in SMR. (See Fig. 1). SEMR selects the S2-A-B-C-D2 path as the first path, because the S2-X-D2 path is a congested node (X node). The S2-X-D2 path, is a maximally node-disjoint path, is selected as the second path. Therefore SEMR selects the S2-A-B-C-D2 path in Fig. 2, instead of the S2-X-D2 path in Fig. 1. This results in SMR containing three congested nodes, and SEMR only containing a single node. It means that SEMR has lower probability than SMR, when network congestion occurs. Therefore, SEMR enhances load balancing, fault-tolerance, and overall performance.

3.1 Congestion Path Metric

When data is transmitted from source to destination node, all data is passed through intermediate nodes in each path. If the shortest delay is used as a path metric, the path containing the smallest hop count is selected. This means that if many paths will be concentrated on one node, the probability of congestion is high. For example, if the shortest delay is considered as a path metric, connection pairs (A →A', B →B', C →C', and D →D') cerate the X node congestion node, as presented in Fig. 3. Therefore SEMR minimizes the bottleneck probability using a congestion path metric.

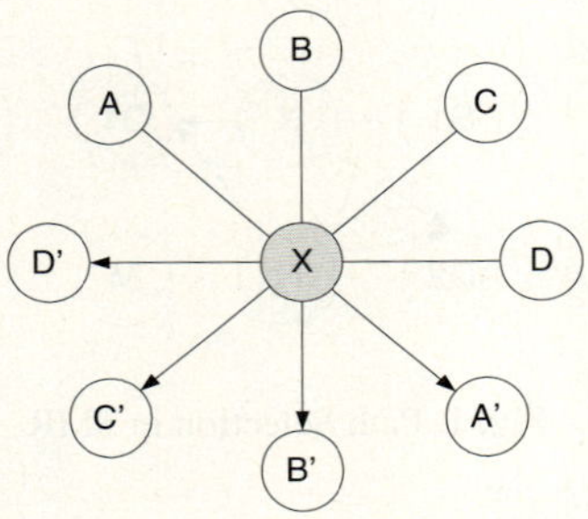

Fig. 3. In case of generated bottleneck node

Although each node does not transmit data to other nodes, it plays a role in intermediate nodes in MANETs. However, data that can be simultaneously processed is limited, because each node has limited resources (CPU clock, bandwidth, propagation range, power, and so on). Processing data in each node can be called Node Congestion (NC). NC in SEMR can estimate processing data not only at the current time, but also in the future. (Refer to Section 3.2) In addition, Path Congestion (PC) is computed using NC . PC , containing *n* intermediate nodes is,

$$PC = \sum_{i=1}^{n} NC_i \, . \tag{1}$$

where NC_i is the node congestion value of ith node.

In Eq. (1), the PC value of each path can be expressed as a summation of NC s in the intermediate node. A high PC value means that the probability of a bottleneck is high, because the PC value is directly proportional to the future transmitted data size. Therefore, SEMR can select a path that has the smallest PC value, as the smallest bottleneck probability. That is one of the different features in comparison with DSR or SMR.

3.2 Path Establishment

SEMR, based on SMR, is an equal-cost multipath routing protocol. The source generates the RREQ message to be transmitted to the destination when there is no path information, which is similar to SMR. The flooded RREQs are duplicated by intermediate nodes. Many RREQs reach the destination node, and the destination selects the least congested path and multiple node-disjoint paths. The Route Reply (RREP) messages are transmitted back to the source node via the chosen paths.

RREQ Propagation: RREQ messages in SEMR are modified from previous RREQ messages in AODV or DSR, by adding flow and congestion fields (See Fig. 4). Flow and congestion fields are used to calculate PC as a path metric. The source node initializes the flow field transmitting data size and congestion field to zero, when creating RREQ messages. When RREQs arrive in intermediate nodes, the flow value in RREQs is saved in the Congestion Cache. The congestion value in RREQ is updated by the flow value in the Congestion Cache (Refer Eq. (1)). SEMR does not use the Route Cache for various paths, similar to SMR. The Congestion Cache in Fig. 5 is created in each node in order to save NC temporarily. Every node, temporarily preserves RREQ information in the Congestion Cache. Intermediate node store the source node address, destination address, sequence number, arrival time, and flow value in the RREQ, in Src Addr, Dest Addr, Seq., and Flow field, respectively.

Previous RREQ Format	Flow	Congestion

Fig. 4. Modified RREQ message

Src Addr	Dest Addr	Seq.	Time	Flow	Check

Fig. 5. Congestion Cache

Finally, if each node receives a RREP as a reply from RREQ, the Check field is set as TRUE, otherwise it is set as FALSE. In the case the check field is set as TRUE, the data is transmited through a correspondent node because the destination node selects a path that includes the correspondent node. In addition, in the case it is set as FALSE, although RREQ is not received currently, it can be assumed that data, having flow size, will be transmitted. In addition, SEMR uses RREP_TIME_OUT to maintain the Congestion Cache. If an intermediate node does not receive a RREP during RREP_TIME_OUT, it regarded as not selecting the correct path belonging to the node. Data is deleted if the check field has a value of FALSE.

For example, suppose that the source will transmit 512 bytes of data to the destination node. First, the source node RREQ flow and congestion fields are initialized to 512 and zero, respectively. The RREQ is flooded into neighboring nodes. If a neighboring node is already received as containing an identical RREQ, it discards RREQ. RREQ information is preserved in the Congestion Cache. At this point, the check field is set to FALSE. In addition, if the same RREQ data already exists in the Congestion Cache, the neighboring node does not preserve the Congestion Cache and simply floods RREQ into other neighboring nodes. Finally, NC is calculated by summing all flow values in the Congestion Cache. NC is accumulated into the congestion field in the RREQ, and the RREQ is flooded into neighboring nodes. Therefore, a congestion value in RREQ is the PC, which is the accumulated NC. The destination can then select a path with the lowest PC.

Path Selection Method: In SEMR, the destination selects two paths. The destination waits a certain duration of time for another RREQ. The destination selects the first path that contains the lowest PC. If one or more paths containing the same PC exists, the destination selects the path arriving earlier. Then, the second path is selected as a maximally node-disjoint path of the first path. If there are two or more paths that are maximally node-disjoint with the first path, the path with the shortest hop count is chosen. If there are still multiple paths meeting the condition, the quickest path delivering the RREQ to the destination is selected. The destination then transmits RREP to the source via first and second paths selected.

Previous RREP Format	Seq.

Fig. 6. Modified RREP message

SEMR also modifies the previous RREP message by adding the Seq. field (See Fig. 6). RREP is transmitted to the source via the source routing path. When RREP arrives in the intermediate node, the intermediate node updates the check field of the Congestion Cache. If RREP arrives during RREP_TIME_OUT, the check field is updated from FALSE to TRUE. This means that the path which the node belongs to is selected by the destination.

3.3 Path Maintenance

SEMR selects the second path that is maximally node-disjoint with the first path. The term, node-disjoint, means that, if possible, overlapping nodes with previous paths are avoided. In other words, although the path cannot be used because of node mobility, collision, or power consumption, it is possible to transmit data using another path. Therefore, if one path is broken, SEMR attempts to find another path. If another path exists, data is transmitted. In the event that all paths are broken, path re-configuration is executed. In addition, when a node receives a ROUTE ERROR (RERR) message, the data field in Congestion Cache that includes RERR information is deleted in order to reduce NC. The RREQ can be supported by the Congestion Cache, which is updated periodically. It is possible to estimate congestion not only at the current time, but also at a future time, by using the reliable congestion path metric. From a traffic allocation point of view, the simple per-packet round robin scheme is used. It is possible to find the most effective traffic allocation scheme, however this is out of the scope of this paper.

4 Performance Evaluation

The simulation modules are implemented in the Global Mobile Simulation (GloMoSim) library [11]. The simulation modeled a network of 30 mobile nodes placed randomly within a 300 meter × 300 meter area. Each node has a radio propagation range of 75 meters and the channel capacity was 2Mbps. Each run is executed over 300 seconds of simulation time. A free space propagation model with a threshold cutoff [12] was used in the experiments. In the radio model, it is assumed that the ability of a radio can lock onto a sufficiently strong signal in the presence of interfering signals. The IEEE 802.11 Distributed Coordination Function (DCF) [13] is sued as a medium access control protocol. A traffic generator was developed to simulate constant bit rate sources. Ten data sessions were created, and the sources and destinations were randomly selected with uniform probabilities. The size of the data payload was 512 bytes. The random waypoint model [2] was used as the mobility model. Various mobility degrees were generate using different pause times. The minimum and the maximum speed were set to zero and 10 m/s, respectively.

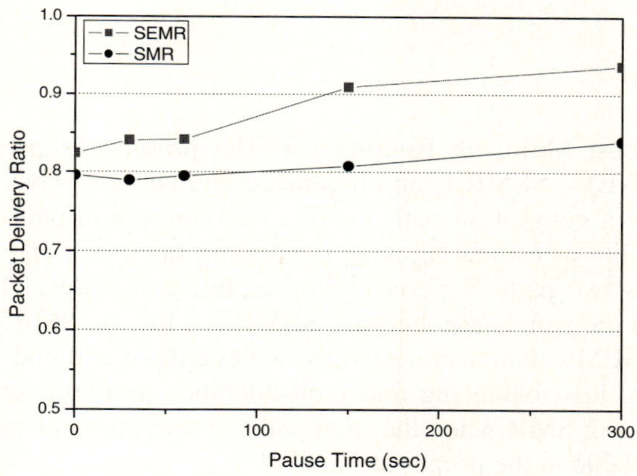

Fig. 7. Throughput

High node-density and high-mobility are considered in the simulation. The simulation compares performance of SEMR (using the least congestion path metric and two multipath) with SMR (using the shortest delay path metric and two multipath). The performance factors are throughput and end-to-end delay.

Fig. 7 presents the throughput of each protocol in the packet delivery fraction. The packet delivery ratio is obtained through dividing the number of data packets that correctly received by the destinations, by the number of data packets of the originating sources. Because SMR uses the shortest delay path metric, many congestion nodes are generated. It is confirmed that the throughput of SMR is lower than SEMR.

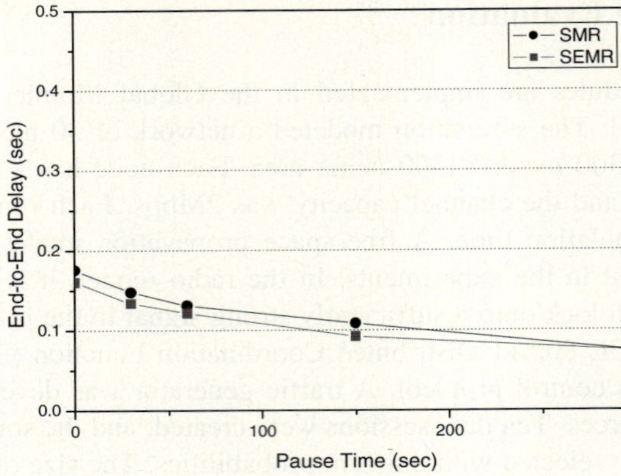

Fig. 8. End-to-end delay

Fig. 8 presents the end-to-end delay. SEMR has the shorter end-to-end delay than SMR, because it simultaneously considers both node mobility and congestion.

5 Conclusion

The Split Equal-cost Multipath Routing (SEMR) protocol is presented for highly node-densed MANETs. SEMR is an on-demand and an equal-cost multipath routing protocol that uses a congestion path metric. The congestion path metric is used to enable the possibility of estimating node congestion in current and future periods. In addition, it selects two paths for considering mobility of nodes. The performance is similar to SMR in the worst case, because SEMR is based on SMR. In a highly node-densed network, SEMR demonstrates superior throughput and end-to-end delay over SMR. In addition, load balancing and fault-tolerance problems can be much more relieved than existing SMR when the multipath routing protocol with a new congestion metric is available in the proposed SEMR.

However, there are some points to discuss for further enhancement. In perfect solution of congestion path, the combined path metric is required in order to consider both proposed congestion metric and available link capacity of the link layer. The issue of how to decide the effective traffic allocation scheme still remains. The scheduling scheme that disperses traffic is an important topic in multipath routing. In future work, the cross-layer approach in multipath routing using multiple path metrics will be evaluated. For example, the user profile in the application layer, and environment of network or channel condition, will be used, adapted for QoS routing.

Acknowledgements

This work was supported by grant No. (R01-2006-000-10556-0) from the Basic Research Program of the Korea Science & Engineering Foundation.

References

1. Pham, P.P., Perreau, S.: Performance Analysis of Reactive Shortest Path and Multi-path Routing Mechanism with Load Balance. IEEE INFOCOM, (2003)
2. D.Johnson, D.Maltz: Dynamic Source Routing in Ad Hoc Wireless Networks. Mobile Computing, T.Imielinski, H.Korth, Eds. Norwell, MA: Kluwer (1996)
3. C.E. Perkins, E.M. Royer: Ad-hoc On-demand Distance Vector Routing. IEEE WCNC (2000) 90-100
4. V.D. Park, M.S.Corson: A Highly Adaptive Distributed Routing Algorithm for Mobile Wireless Networks. IEEE INFOCOM (1999) 1405-1413
5. J.Raju, J.J.Garcia-Luna-Aceves: A New Approach to On-demand Loop-free Multipath Routing. IEEE ICCCN (1999) 522-527
6. S. J. Lee, M.Gerla: AODV-BR: Backup Routing in Ad Hoc Networks. IEEE WCNC (2000) 1311-1316
7. Marina, M.K., Das, S.R.: On-demand Multipath Distance Vector Routing in Ad Hoc Networks. Proceedings of the International Conference for Network Protocols (2001)
8. L.Wang, L.Zhang, Y.Shu, M.Dong: Multipath Source Routing in Wireless Ad Hoc Networks. IEEE Electrical and Computer Engineering 2000 Canadian Conference, Vol. 1 (2000) 479-483
9. A. Nasipuri, S.R.Das: On-demand Multipath Routing for Mobile Ad Hoc Networks. IEEE Computer Communications and Networks (1999) 64-70
10. S.J.Lee, M.Gerla: Split Multipath Routing with Maximally Disjoint Paths in Ad Hoc Networks. IEEE ICC2001, Vol. 10 (2001)
11. UCLA Parallel Computing Laboratory and Wireless Adaptive Mobility Laboratory: GloMoSim: A Scalable Simulation Environment for Wireless and Wired Network Systems, http://pcl.cs.ucla.edu/projects/domains/glomosim.html
12. T.S.Rappaport: Wireless Communications: Principles and Practice, Prentice Hall. (1995)
13. IEEE Computer Society LAN MAN Standards Committee, Wireless LAN Medium Access Protocol (MAC) and Physical Layer (PHY) Specification, IEEE Std 802.11 (1997)

Virtual Hierarchical Architecture Integrating Mobile IPv6 and MANETs for Internet Connectivity*

Hyemee Park, Tae-Jin Lee, and Hyunseung Choo**

School of Information and Communication Engineering
Sungkyunkwan University
440-746, Suwon, Korea
Tel.: +82-31-290-7145
{hyemee, tjlee, choo}@ece.skku.ac.kr

Abstract. As the demands for Internet connectivity of ad hoc networks are consistently increasing, the interconnection of Mobile Ad hoc Networks (MANETs) to fixed IP networks is emerging as an issue with considerable attention in the literature [2,3,4]. Here, we focus on connecting MANETs to the Internet by integrating Mobile IPv6. Many previous studies are suffered from some limitations that the dynamic addressing and routing protocol are not suitable in high mobility MANETs. The proposed scheme is based on the prefix delegation method in order to reduce tunneling overhead by ingress filtering and avoid unnecessary address changes. By using this method, MANETs organize a virtual hierarchical architecture for efficient gateway discovery and the optimal routing in high mobility. Comprehensive computer simulation presents that the newly proposed scheme shows up to about 50% better performance in terms of delay and signaling overhead in comparison with existing protocols.

1 Introduction

An ad hoc network is a collection of wireless mobile hosts forming a temporary network without the support of any centralized administration. These mobile nodes have routing capabilities that allow them to create multihop paths connecting nodes which cannot directly communicate. Previous work has concentrated on the development of optimal routing protocols for efficient communications among Ad hoc devices. These protocols do not consider global connectivity. Currently, as the requirement for Internet connectivity of ad hoc networks is consistently increasing, the interconnection of MANETs to fixed IP

* This research was supported by the Ministry of Information and Communication, Korea under the Information Technology Research Center support program supervised by the Institute of Information Technology Assessment, IITA-2005-(C1090-0501-0019).

** Corresponding author.

E. Sha et al. (Eds.): EUC 2006, LNCS 4096, pp. 1098–1107, 2006.

networks becomes increasingly important. Users with portable devices in ad hoc networks can access useful information on the Internet. The data collected from ad hoc nodes is available in central systems of the Internet for various purposes. Therefore, this study can be extended to many applications, including Sensor Networks, Home Networks, Telematics, and so on.

The Mobile IPv6 [1] is a protocol which allows mobile nodes to have seamless access to the Internet while moving between different networks. Today it provides an important global mobility solution. Since nodes in ad hoc networks are inherently mobile, it seems inevitable that some of these nodes are likely to move between different ad hoc networks and to other parts of the Internet as well. Hence, we focus on connecting MANETs to global IPv6 networks, while supporting the mobility of ad hoc nodes by integrating Mobile IPv6 and MANET. In such integrated scenarios, mobile nodes can easily be deployed and expanded through existing infrastructures. For seamless communications with Internet hosts, some ad hoc nodes act as gateways to be traversed by other nodes. The gateway discovery mechanism has an impact in terms of overall performance, and it is a key component in providing interoperability with fixed networks. Furthermore, connecting an ad hoc network to the Internet brings up several issues regarding routing and how to provide nodes in an ad hoc network with IP addresses that are routable to the fixed Internet. These are the most relevant elements to guarantee smooth interworking.

Our proposed scheme is based on the prefix delegation method to avoid unnecessary address changes in high mobility situation. It also avoids some routing problems and tunneling overhead by ingress filtering. The control message transmitted from the gateway initially contains the gateway and prefix information. By propagating this message to the overall network, MANETs automatically organize a virtual tree topology for efficient gateway discovery when unpredictable topological changes occur. The overall overhead is reduced by integrating the addressing auto-configuration information into gateway discovery messages. In addition, MANETs based on tree topology provide the optimal routing protocol for access to the Internet and reduce the handoff cost as well. By the comprehensive computer simulation, we compared the proposed scheme with existing schemes in terms of handoff delay and signaling overhead. Simulation results show that the newly proposed scheme shows up to about 50% better performance than the others.

The rest of this paper is organized as follows. In Section 2, related works are introduced with some discussion. Section 3 presents the proposed scheme integrating Mobile IPv6 and MANET. The performance of the proposed scheme is evaluated in Section 4. Finally, we conclude in Section 5.

2 Related Works

One of the first proposals by Broch *et al.* [2] is based on integration of Mobile IP and MANETs based on DSR. In order for a Mobile Node (MN) within an ad hoc network to communicate with a destination node outside the ad hoc network, it simply initiates route discovery of DSR. When a gateway receives this Route Request (RREQ), it transmits a proxy reply containing itself and the destination node's address as the final point in the route instead of the destination node. If the MN moves from another network, it will transmit agent solicitation piggybacked on RREQ to discover its Foreign Agent (FA). When the FA receives a solicitation, it unicasts an agent advertisement in Route Reply (RREP). After this message reaches the MN, the MN registers to the FA and its Home Agent (HA). Then, the MN's HA will forward packets for the MN to the FA and the FA will deliver them locally to the MN using DSR.

Jonsson *et al.* [3] propose a method, called MIPMANET, to connect an ad hoc network to the Internet using Mobile IP with FA's Care-of Address (CoA) and reverse tunneling. MIPMANET combines the use of Mobile IP protocol and AODV. In MIPMANET, nodes in the ad hoc network that require Internet access, register with the FA and use their Home Address (HoA) for all communications. The MNs tunnel all packets to their FAs, which decapsulate the packets and forward them to their destinations. The packets from hosts on the Internet addressed to MNs are delivered to the FA, using the ordinary Mobile IP protocol. Then, the AODV protocol is used to deliver packets to the MNs in the ad hoc network. Moreover, as for handoff, MIPMANET utilizes a mechanism called MIPMANET Cell Switching (MMCS), which allows the MN to determine when it should register with another FA.

Almmari *et al.* [4] analyze the performance of mobile gateways in a MANET based on the DSDV routing protocol. This paper proposes an approach which integrates the MANET and the Internet into a hybrid unified network. The hybrid network assists MANET nodes to obtain Internet connectivity through a special entity set called mobile gateways. These gateways are arranged at the second layer between the fixed FA of the first layer and MANET nodes of the third layer. As a result, this will shorten the paths between them and act as a means to widen the coverage range of FAs in a transparent manner. Some MANETs may be far away from fixed Internet gateways, known as FAs, because MANET nodes move frequently in a random fashion. This approach is based on mobile gateways instead of fixed gateways.

Since these proposals are based on existing protocols, they are limited in supporting all routing protocols and do not provide scalability in heterogeneous network environments. The gateway discovery function of them is done proactively or reactively by using any routing protocol. It suffers from the flooding overhead for rediscovering a default route toward the gateway whenever handoff is performed. In addition, addressing protocol of these schemes cannot solve the ingress filtering problem in MANETs with multihop routing. It incurs the routing overhead by reverse tunneling, since the packet size is increased in each hop.

3 The Proposed Scheme

3.1 Virtual Hierarchical Architecture for Mobility Management

In this paper, we consider the special property of the MANETs with the dynamic multihop topology and focus on the issue that the protocol overhead should be kept at minimum due to the scarcity of resources. To reduce the routing overhead by ingress filtering, the prefix delegation mechanism is proposed. This technique is also used to create virtual trees which are dynamically maintained and updated when unpredictable topology changes occur. In this section, we describe how to form and maintain a virtual tree with minimum overhead, and provide the optimal gateway discovery and efficient addressing mechanism based on the tree topology.

1) Prefix delegation: Prefix delegation is a method where all nodes of the MANET share the same prefix advertised from the Access Router (AR), to reduce the tunneling overhead according to ingress filtering. It is assumed that AR and MANET nodes operate under the IPv6 protocol, therefore all entities broadcast periodically the Router Advertisement (RA) message to their neighbors. Based on that, the solution uses the RA message, so that nodes can simply relay the prefix without any special control message or operation. Unfortunately, the multi-hop nature of an ad hoc network makes it impossible to use the advertisement message defined in IPv6. Therefore, the original RA message is extended to propagate over multiple hops through the ad hoc network and to share a common global network prefix using MANET nodes. The added fields in the prefix information option are represented as follows.

- The M flag means that this message is relayed over multi-hops.
- Hop count is the distance (in hops) from the gateway to the sender node.
- The IP address of the gateway is contained and the prefix length field represents the length (in bits) of the prefix part of this address.

The gateway advertises the RA message containing its prefix and setting the M flag. In addition, the initial distance transmitted by the gateway must be zero. When a node receives this message, it increments the hop count one and forwards an updated version of the RA message to its neighbors. All other message fields remain unchanged. The gateway information contained in the RA message is therefore propagated in a hop-by-hop manner, until all nodes of the ad hoc network share the gateway IP and global network prefix.

2) Virtual tree topology configuration and management: The proposed prefix propagation method leads to the creation of the virtual tree topology of the ad hoc network. Each virtual tree is rooted at a gateway, and it is formed by nodes using the global network prefix advertised by the gateway. In the proposed scheme, an AR acts as the gateway. We consider that a MANET connects to the Internet via the AR. The AR is a method of supporting Internet connectivity at the point of attachment between the Internet and MANET nodes. This overcomes the limitation that a MANET node with low power should play the role of the gateway.

In order to configure the virtual tree topology, each node tries to establish a parent-child association with its neighbor using 3-way handshake. Control packets of the procedure consist of the RA message disseminated for prefix delegation,

PARENT REQUEST, and PARENT REQUEST ACK. When a node receives the RA message from a neighbor, it generates its global IP address with the prefix of the RA message. Then, it sends back a PARENT REQUEST to notify that it is selected as a parent node. As the parent node sends the ACK with the Tree ID as a logical address, parent-child association is established. The parent node keeps its children in the table to manage. After establishing parent-child association, each node keeps a default route toward the gateway. That is, a new node can easily discover the gateway without flooding message for route rediscovery of existing routing protocols.

A node may receive one or more RA messages from its neighbors. In this case, it selects the most appropriate node as a parent from among the messages and sends a PARENT REQUEST back. In the proposed scheme, the desirable algorithm for selecting the parent node is that the node keeps its current prefix as long as it has neighbors with the same prefix, *i.e.*, until it cannot find the neighbor that uses the same network prefix. The main advantage of this algorithm is that it can minimize the number of prefix changes. This greatly reduces the overhead induced by the sending of BU messages when the node changes its global address. And, the node chooses the parent node that advertises the shortest distance to a gateway, to maintain the shortest path. They ensure that one node does not concurrently generate multiple associations and avoids a tree loop. When a child node is established with a parent node, it ignores the RA message transmitted by other neighbors as long as it maintains the association.

In order to maintain the virtual tree topology, each node periodically checks its neighborhood. The nodes can detect the loss of its parent or child nodes using RA and Router Solicitation (RS) in the Neighbor Discovery Protocol (NDP) of IPv6. If a child node does not receive the RA message from its parent within a predefined time, it assumes that its parent node has moved away. In this case, as the node transmits the RS message to its neighbors, it should restart the 3-way handshake procedure to select another parent. However, if a parent node does not receive the RA message from its child and the timer associated to it is expired, the parent node releases the resource and logical address assigned to the child. Therefore, in the proposed scheme, the RA message disseminated by the node allows its parent and children to simultaneously detect its existence.

3) IP address configuration and Tree ID assignment: Each mobile node should configure its IPv6 global address to connect the Internet. In the proposed scheme, MANET nodes generate a global address with the prefix advertised by a gateway and its EUI-64 (Ethernet Unique Identifier) as the interface ID. In additional, the MANET node is proposed to have its Tree ID as a logical address, other than global IP addresses, to provide efficient routing. The logical Tree ID indicates the location of nodes on the tree topology. This is a routing information to deliver the packet between the gateway and nodes.

In the parent-child establishment process, when the parent receives the PARENT REQUEST from the child node, it selects the address which is not assigned yet in its child table and sends with the response message. The parent keeps the Tree ID and corresponding MN's address in its child table in order to perform an optimal routing and manage them easily. For example, if the parent node using ID 1.2.1 receives a request message from the child node, it selects a random number(x) from 1 to 255, which is not used by other children. Then, the ID of the child node is set to 1.2.1.x and the parent node uses the response message for notification it. The parent adds the ID and the node's address to its table.

If the parent does not have an available ID, it must ignore the request so that the child chooses another parent. However, if the child moves away, it releases the resource and the Tree ID used by the child and deletes the entry of the child in its table. The reason why the Tree ID is not used as a global address of a node, is to consider the high mobility in MANETs. When an ad hoc node changes its point of attachment within the MANET tree, it must replace the global address based on Tree ID. It requires significant cost with regard to handoff. The Tree ID which is separated from the global IP addresses is proposed, in order to optimize routing in busy mobile environments.

3.2 Routing Protocol

We propose the routing protocol based on the virtual tree topology for communication with the Internet hosts. Depending on the routing protocol in use within the ad hoc network, ad hoc nodes must also be configured to be able to communicate with the Internet. Therefore, this work aims to propose a method that is independent of the underlying routing protocol, as our proposal can be used with both proactive and reactive routing protocols. In addition, the protocol does not require an additional overhead for Internet access, since it does not need to find routing path on demand. All traffic between ad hoc nodes and Internet hosts are forwarded along the path configured by parent-child association.

When the MANET node wants to transmit the packet to the Internet host, it transmits the data packets to the gateway using the IPv6 routing header. The extended routing header contains the final destination address, *i.e.*, the address of the Internet host, and the destination field of the IPv6 header contains the gateway address. If intermediate nodes from the ad hoc node to the gateway receive the packet with the destination field set to the gateway IP, they forward it to their parent node recursively. Only the ad hoc node with the IP address contained in the destination field of the IPv6 header can examine the routing header of this packet. Once the packet arrives at the gateway, the packet uses the address of the routing header as the destination field of header and the routing header is removed. The modified packet is then forwarded to the Internet host.

In contrast, if the gateway receives the packet from the Internet host to the ad hoc node, it adds the hop-by-hop option to the original IPv6 packet. It first searches its cache for the corresponding Tree ID of the destination address (MN's IP). Then, the Tree ID is inserted into the hop-by-hop option. As a result, intermediate nodes from the gateway to the ad hoc node check this option for routing and deliver the packet to the child node selected by the longest prefix matching algorithm. This algorithm is used to determine how to forward the packet to its destination using the Tree ID. Since the proposed scheme uses the Tree ID and the parent-child association based on tree topology, it can reduce the routing overhead.

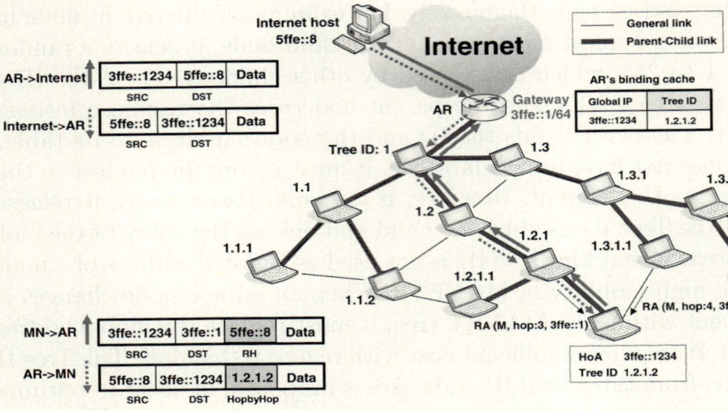

Fig. 1. The routing protocol based on virtual tree topology

3.3 MIPv6 Support for MANET Handoff

The proposed scheme supports seamless mobility of MANET nodes by integrating the Mobile IPv6 and ad hoc network. We consider that the global address acquired by an ad hoc node should be used as the Mobile IPv6 CoA of the node. Each change of global address in the ad hoc network will trigger the sending of at least one BU message. However, when the Tree ID changes, a new local registration between the gateway and node is performed to immediately provide an optimal routing.

If the ad hoc node moves from another MANET or changes its point of attachment within the network, it performs a 3-way handshake procedure to reconfigure the tree structure as it can no longer contact with its parent node any more. As a result, it has a new Tree ID. Then, it transmits the registration message to the gateway in order to update the new ID. As the receiving gateway rewrites

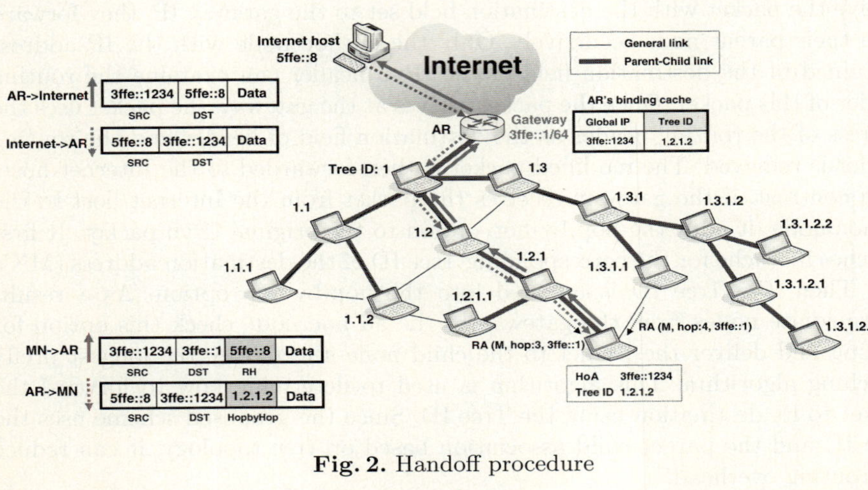

Fig. 2. Handoff procedure

its cache entry, the gateway can insert the exact information in the hop-by-hop option when it is added to the packet transmitted by the CN. This registration signal is also delivered along the parent-child path to the gateway.

In the case of internal movement within a network, the MN only changes only its Tree ID, not its global IP CoA. Therefore, as it performs a light-weight registration procedure with the gateway, it does not require the route rediscovery mechanism of previous schemes between the gateway and the MN. Therefore it can reduce the flooding overhead of the proactive or reactive protocol. However, when an MN moves to a foreign network, it first reconfigures a new global IP which will become its CoA. After a 3-way handshake, it performs the BU to its HA and CN as well as registration of the Tree ID with the gateway. Using the method, the ad hoc MN has seamless access to the Internet while performing handoff.

4 Performance Evaluation

In this section, the performance of the proposed scheme is evaluated in comparison with integrating the Mobile IPv6 and existing routing protocol, AODV, DSR, DSDV. In order to evaluate these schemes, simulation implemented in C is conducted. Our simulation models a wireless network of 25 $\sim$ 100 mobile nodes placed randomly within a $150m \times 100m$ area. Radio propagation range for each node is $30m$. We measure the total delay required when the node performs handoff and the overhead of the gateway discovery. Performance is evaluated under various mobility rates and numbers of nodes, to analyze the performance of mobility and node density effect.

4.1 Handoff Delay

The average total delay of the proposed and other schemes is first compared for various handoff rates. This simulation varies the handoff rates between 0.1 and 0.9. The network has 50 nodes. In addition, the node moves from another network or changes its point of attachment within the network, and it is placed randomly. The total delay is measured and the delay between two nodes is represented as follows.

$$Total\ Delay = \#\ of\ Hops(Transmission + Propagation + Processing) \quad (1)$$

The total delay is the summation of transmission, propagation and processing time in each hop between two end nodes. This is calculated as follows. Table 1 represents the detailed simulation parameters. Based on these values, the average total delay of four schemes is measured in our simulation.

$$Transmission_{wireless} = \frac{S_{pkt}}{B_{wl}}, \quad Transmission_{wired} = \frac{S_{pkt}}{B_{wd}} \times H_{avg}$$

$$Propagation_{wireless} = \frac{D_{wl}}{P}, \quad Propagation_{wired} = \frac{D_{wd}}{P} \times H_{avg}$$

$$Processing\ delay = T_{BU} + T_{RDP} + T_{TU} + ... \quad etc.$$

Table 1. Simulation Parameters

Parameter	Description	Value
P	Propagation speed (m/sec)	2×10^8
B_{wd}	Wired transmission Speed (bit/sec)	10^8
B_{wl}	Wireless transmission Speed (bit/sec)	10^7
T_{all}	Processing time of all procedures (sec)	0.00001
H_{avg}	Average number of hops in wired networks	10
D_{wd}	Average distance per hop in wired networks (m)	10000
D_{wl}	Average distance per hop in wireless networks (m)	30

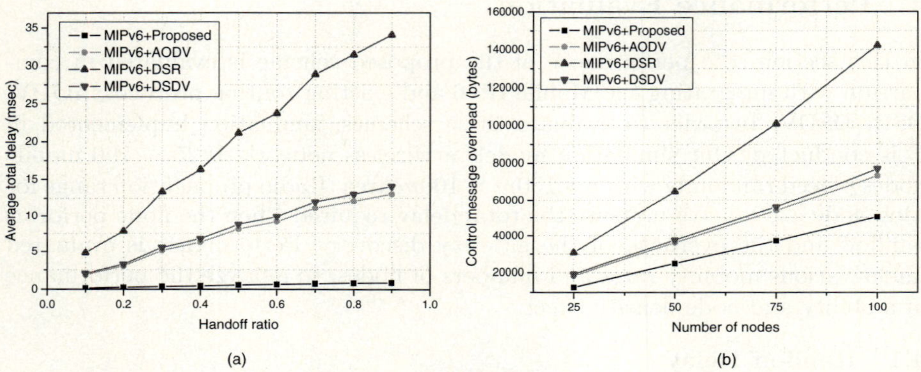

Fig. 3. Simulation results of four schemes (a)Handoff delay, and (b) Gateway discovery overhead

Fig. 3(a) presents the simulation results for the variation of handoff ratios. As shown in Fig. 3(a), our proposed scheme has better performance than other schemes. In the reactive protocol of AODV and DSR, the route discovery protocol is conducted other than NDP, BU procedures when a node performs handoff. Therefore, the RREQ message is forwarded by all nodes until the gateway is discovered and RREP is then delivered by the gateway. In particular, the DSR approach has higher handoff overhead than AODV, because the size of the control message is consistently increasing for source routing. However, the proactive protocol of DSDV updates its routing table by adding a new node entry. Though the route discovery procedure is not required, it must transmit table information to all neighbors in order to notify the new node.

4.2 Gateway Discovery Overhead

The overhead of the gateway discovery is evaluated for various network sizes in each scheme. In this simulation, the overhead is defined as the total bytes of the control message when a network is configured and initially attempts to connect with the Internet. That is, it is the sum of all control messages delivered until the gateway discovery is completed. We measure the overhead of 3-way handshake, route discovery and table update of these schemes as the network size is increasing. The simulation result is presented in Fig. 3(b). The result represents that the proposed scheme can reduce the control overhead in large scale networks.

5 Conclusion

In this paper, we present a protocol that builds a virtual trees, where each tree if formed by nodes that share a common global network prefix. By using the tree topology, an efficient gateway discovery and optimal routing is proposed in high mobility MANETs. In addition, this connectivity method is not dependent on a particular routing protocol. Therefore, it provides the optimized communication as well as scalability in heterogeneous network environments and backward compatibility with existing mechanisms.

Our simulation represents advantages of the proposed scheme compared to integrating MIPv6 and the existing routing protocols - AODV, DSR, DSDV. According to the simulation results, our newly proposed scheme shows up to about 50% of performance improvements in comparison with other schemes. Thus our solution provides Internet connectivity of ad hoc nodes with minimum routing overhead and delay in large-scale, high mobility MANETs.

References

1. D. Johnson, C. E. Perkins, and J. Arkko, "Mobility Support in IPv6," IETF, RFC 3775, June 2004.
2. J. Broch, D. A. Maltz, and D. B. Johnson, "Supporting Hierarchy and Heterogenous Interfaces in Multi-Hop Wireless Ad Hoc Networks," IEEE International Symposium on Parallel Architectures, algorithms and Networks, June 1999.
3. U. Johnsson *et al.*, "MIPMANET-Mobile IP for mobile ad hoc networks," IEEE Proc. of MobiHoc'00, August 2000.
4. H. Almmari and H. El-Rewini, "Performance Evaluation of Hybrid Environments with Mobile Gateways," 9th International Symposium on Computers and Communications, June 2004.

A Comprehensive Study on Handover Performance of Hierarchical Mobile IPv6

Youn-Hee Han[1] and Dongwon Jeong[2]

[1] School of Internet-Media, Korea University of Technology and Education, Cheonan, Korea
yhhan@kut.ac.kr

[2] Department of Informatics and Statics, Kunsan National University, Gunsan, Korea
djeong@kunsan.ac.kr

Abstract. Recently, IETF has standardized Mobile IPv6 (MIPv6) and Hierarchical Mobile IPv6 (HMIPv6) for supporting IPv6 mobility. Even though existing literatures have asserted that HMIPv6 generally improves MIPv6 in terms of handover speed, they do not carefully consider the details of the whole handover procedures. In this paper, based on the current IETF standards of both MIPv6 and HMIPv6, we conduct a comprehensive study of all IP-level handover procedures. We also provide a mathematical analysis on MIPv6 and HMIPv6 performance in terms of handover speed, and reveal that the average HMIPv6 handover latency is not always lower than the average MIPv6 handover latency. A vital finding of our analysis is that some optimization techniques for movement detection and duplicate address detection are essential to increasing the benefit of HMIPv6.

1 Introduction

To support Internet mobility, a lot of research has been studied so far. IETF Mobile IPv6 (MIPv6) [1,2] is one of the most important protocols to accommodate the increasing demand of end-to-end mobility in IPv6 Internet. In MIPv6, a mobile node (MN) is always addressable by its home address (HoA), which is the IPv6 address assigned within its home network. When an MN is away from its home network, packets can still be routed to it using the MN's HoA. Whenever an MN moves to a new subnet, it typically acquires a temporary address, called care-of address (CoA), through the address auto-configuration according to the methods of IPv6 neighbor discovery [3,4]. Through the binding update procedure, an MN registers its temporal location to its home agent (HA) in its home network and all correspondent nodes (CNs) every time it moves. So, support for the route optimization is built in as a fundamental part of the protocol.

Even though MIPv6 provides the optimal packet routing, it requires high signaling cost and long handoff latency so that MIPv6 is not appropriate for environments in which MNs frequently change their point of attachment to the network. IETF Hierarchical Mobile IPv6 (HMIPv6) [5,6] is an enhanced MIPv6 to minimize the signaling cost and the latency of updating the location of MN

E. Sha et al. (Eds.): EUC 2006, LNCS 4096, pp. 1108–1118, 2006.

by using a local anchor point called Mobility Anchor Point (MAP). The MAP is intended to limit the amount of MIPv6 registration signaling outside the local domain. Domain can be an ISP network, a campus network, a company network, a set of LANs, or even a single LAN.

In this paper, we focus to qualitatively and quantitatively study the performance of MIPv6 and HMIPv6 in terms of handover speed. Recent IETF RFC 4140 [5] where the protocol of HMIPv6 is minutely described, firmly assures that MIPv6's handover latency is reduced by HMIPv6 since HMIPv6's registration procedure is mostly conducted within a domain. But, we have been wondering whether or not the average of HMIPv6's handover speed is really faster than the one of MIPv6's handover speed. A mathematical analysis is described in this paper to gratify the curiosity based on the recent IETF RFCs [1,3,4,5]. The analysis points out that the average HMIPv6 handover latency is not always lower than the average MIPv6 handover latency. Furthermore, even the intra-domain handover latency of HMIPv6 is not much small compared with MIPv6 handover latency. We reveal that some optimization techniques for movement detection and duplicate address detection are required to shorten HMIPv6 handover latency and increase the benefit of HMIPv6.

This paper is organized as follows. In Section 2, we represent our system architecture and provide the parameters and metrics for our performance analysis. In Section 3, we analyze MIPv6 and HMIPv6 handover procedures. Section 4 conducts the performance evaluation about handover latency comparison between MIPv6 and HMIPv6. Finally, concluding remark is given in Section 5.

2 System Architecture and Performance Metrics

We consider an IPv6-based mobile system described in Fig. 1. The home network is where an MN gets its permanent IP address (home address). A foreign domain network (or a domain) can be a campus network, a company network, or a public access network. A domain is comprised of a border gateway (BG), access routers (ARs), and wireless point of attachments to which an MN can make a connection. Between a BG and ARs, there may be some intermediate routers. We assume that each AR has an interface with connection to a distinct set of wireless point of attachment. It also assigns only one network prefix per such an interface. The same network prefix cannot be assigned to the different AR's interface.

When MN moves to new subnet while preserving communication with a CN, MIPv6 and HMIPv6 usually assume that the network-layer handover procedure is initiated only after the link-layer handover procedure comes to end. We thus define *handover latency* as the elapsed time after the link-layer handover comes to end (MN re-establishes its connection to a new point of attachment) until MN receives the first data packet of ongoing session through the new AR of the new network.

To describe an analytical model, let us define the following parameters:

- a - average number of hops between AR and MAP;
- b - average number of hops between MAP and HA;

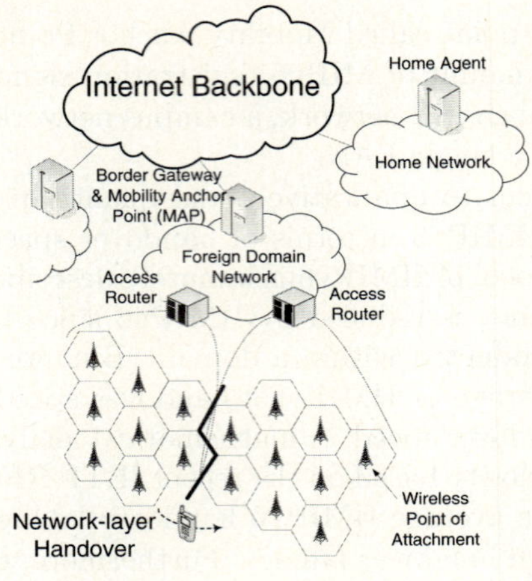

Fig. 1. Reference system architecture

- c - average number of hops between MAP and CN;
- d - average number of hops between HA and CN;
- t_α - latency of an IP packet delivery between MN and AR (over wireless and wired medium);
- t_β - latency of an IP packet's one hop delivery only through wired medium;
- t_H - latency of a packet delivery between MN and HA ($t_H = t_\alpha + (a+b)t_\beta$);
- t_N - latency of a packet delivery between MN and CN ($t_N = t_\alpha + (a+c)t_\beta$);
- t_L - latency of a packet delivery between MN and CN via HA ($t_L = t_\alpha + (a+b+d)t_\beta$);
- t_M - latency of a packet delivery between MN and MAP ($t_M = t_\alpha + at_\beta$).

The beginning procedure of network-layer handover is to determine whether or not it moves to a new IP subnet. This is called the *movement detection (MD)* procedure. The changes on the underlying link-layer status of MN might be locally relayed to network-layer of MN in the form of *link-up event notification.* Although such link-layer event trigger can facilitate MD procedure, it is not always available at all types of MNs. In this paper, the latency of MD procedure will be denoted T_{MD}. If it is decided to move to a new subnet, MN should generate a new CoA by using IPv6 stateless or stateful address auto-configuration. To verify the uniqueness of this CoA, MN should run *duplicate address detection (DAD)* procedure, before assigning the address to its interface.

The two procedures, MD and DAD, are the common parts in both MIPv6 and HMIPv6 handover procedures. After the two procedures come to an end, the location registration procedure starts. In fact, it is the location registration that differentiates HMIPv6 from MIPv6. We will use T_R to denote the latency of MIPv6 registration procedure. On the other hand, T_{HR} will denote the latency of HMIPv6 registration procedure. Using the defined symbols, the average handover latencies of MIPv6 and HMIPv6 are defined as follows:

$$\overline{T}_M = T_{MD} + T_{DAD} + T_R. \quad (1)$$

$$\overline{T}_H = T_{MD} + T_{DAD} + T_{HR}. \quad (2)$$

In the following sections, each latency parameters, T_{MD}, T_{DAD}, T_R, and T_{HR}, will be analyzed and concretized.

3 Analysis of MIPv6 and HMIPv6 Handover Procedures

3.1 Movement Detection Analysis

A complete MD analysis and its results are presented by [7], which is a outcome of our preceding research. In this paper, therefore, we give a concise description of them. For further details, refer to [7]. In IPv6-based mobile systems, MD usually relies on the reception of the router advertisement (RA) message [4] from a new AR. An RA message includes the AR's network prefix information from which an MN can determine if it moves to a new network. An AR sends (pseudo) periodic unsolicited RA messages to its all nodes. Whenever such an RA is sent from an AR, a timer is reset to a uniformly-distributed random value between the router's configured *MinRtrAdvInterval* and *MaxRtrAdvInterval*, which are respectively symbolized by R_m and R_M in this paper. When the timer is expired, new unsolicited RA is again sent. Movement is confirmed by the receipt of a new RA from a new AR. Let us assume T denotes the time interval between link-layer re-establishment and MN's first reception of a new RA. Using the equations introduced by [7], we can get the expectation of T as follows:

$$E_T = \frac{R_M^2 + R_M R_m + R_m^2}{3(R_M + R_m)} + t_\alpha. \quad (3)$$

There is another method to conform the movement with network-layer movement hint. MIPv6 specification [1] defines a new *RA interval option*, which is used in RA messages to advertise the interval at which the AR sends unsolicited RAs. An MN can keep monitoring for periodic RAs and interpret the absence of the exiting RAs as a movement hint. The indicated interval is equal to the router's configured value, *MaxRtrAdvInterval*. To differentiate new AR's *MaxRtrAdvInterval*, the old AR's *MaxRtrAdvInterval* will be symbolized by R_L. An MN may implement its own policy to determine the number of missing RAs needed to interpret that as a movement hint. In this paper, just one missing is assumed a movement hint. On receiving such a movement hint, MN can send the router solicitation (RS) message [4] to the all-routers multicast address. A new AR receiving such RS responses it by sending its RA message to the all-nodes multicast address. Movement is finally confirmed by the reception of such solicited RA from the new AR. Let us assume S denotes the time interval between the link-layer re-establishment and the receipt of the new solicited RAs. We can get the expectation of S as follows:

$$E_S = \frac{R_L}{2} + 2t_\alpha. \quad (4)$$

In order to get the average latency T_{MD}, we calculate the probability $P\{S < T\}$ that an MN first gets a solicited RA by noticing the existing RA's absence prior to get a new unsolicited RA. It is as follows:

$$P\{S<T\} = \int_{t_\alpha}^{R_M+t_\alpha} P\{S < T|T = t\} f_T(t)dt = \int_{t_\alpha}^{R_M+t_\alpha} F_S(t) f_T(t)dt$$
$$= \int_{t_\alpha}^{2t_\alpha} F_S(t) f_T(t)dt + \int_{2t_\alpha}^{R_M+t_\alpha} F_S(t) f_T(t)dt = \int_{2t_\alpha}^{R_M+t_\alpha} F_S(t) f_T(t)dt \quad (5)$$

Then, we can finally acquire T_{MD} as follows:

$$T_{MD} = P\{S < T\} \cdot E_S + P\{S \geq T\} \cdot E_T. \quad (6)$$

Some MN can accelerate MD procedure by using the link-layer trigger [8,9]. That is, the changes on the underlying link-layer status can be relayed to IP layer in a form of link-layer event notification, such as *link-up event*. On receiving such a link-up notification, the network-layer of MN can expedite (or optimize) MD procedure by sending RS message to get a solicited RA. A new AR receiving such RS responses it by sending RA message to the MN. Movement is finally confirmed by the reception of such solicited RA from the new AR. So, if MD procedure is executed with the link-layer notification, the optimized MD latency will be $T_{MD} = 2t_\alpha$.

3.2 Address Configuration Analysis

The current and simplest form of DAD was laid out as part of RFC 2462 "IPv6 Stateless Address Autoconfiguration" [3]. When a node wishes to create a new address on an interface, it combines the network prefix with a suffix generated from its interface identifier (IID). The IID can be either obtained from the interface hardware or generated randomly. This address is referred to as the *tentative address*. The node sends a neighbor solicitation (NS) message from the unspecified address to the tentative address. If the address is already in use by another node, that node will reply with a neighbor advertisement (NA) message defending the address.

Once a node has sent such an NS, it should waits for *RetransTimer* (=*RT*) milliseconds to see if a defending NA is forthcoming, and this solicit-and-wait process is repeated *DupAddrDetectTransmits* (=*DTimes*) times. During this process, the node cannot communicate with a node. As a result, with the assumption that there is no colliding node in the same subnet, DAD latency T_{DAD} is simply as follows:

$$T_{DAD} = RT \cdot DTimes. \quad (7)$$

According to [3], the default value of *RetransTimer* is 1000 ms, and by default the process is only done once, resulting in T_{DAD} = 1000 ms. Thus, the DAD procedure of RFC 2462 [3] is obviously a big factor to deteriorate the performance of MIPv6 and HMIPv6, particularly when MN in need of seamless handover runs it. So, some DAD optimization schemes have been suggested to reduce this problem [10,11]. Optimistic DAD (oDAD) [10] is proposed based on the premise that DAD is far more likely to succeed than fail. An optimistic MN starts communication without RFC 2462 DAD procedure. oDAD modifies its IPv6 neighbor discovery protocol [4] while keeping backward interoperability. On the other hand, advance DAD (aDAD) [11] is a solution of pessimistic approach for IPv6 address conflict. In aDAD, each AR reserves a bunch of unique CoAs in advance and allocates one of them into a newly connected MN. Both schemes, oDAD and aDAD, do not cause any latency. So, if these DAD optimization schemes are applied to MIPv6 and HMIPv6, DAD latency will be written by $T_{DAD} = 0$.

3.3 Registration Procedures

MIPv6 Registration Procedures: In MIPv6, an MN registers its temporal location to its HA in its home network and all CNs every time it moves. Each CN can have its own binding cache where HoA plus CoA pairs are stored. So, CN is able to send packets directly to an MN when it has a recent binding entry for the MN in its binding cache. The achieved route optimization improves data transmission rates between the MN and the CN. The time to complete MIPv6 registration procedure actually depends on how to fast update CN's binding cache with new CoA.

To prevent attackers from sending false BU messages, the BU should be authenticated using a cryptographic binding management key. The process to create the key value is referred to as the *return routability* procedure. For the details of return routability process, refer to [1]. As a result, MIPv6 handover latency is further increased by the time needed for the return routability as well as the BU procedures. Assuming $c < b + d$ (refer the parameter list in Section II), MIPv6 registration latency T_R is given by:

$$\begin{aligned} T_R &= max\{2t_L,\ 2t_N\} + 2t_N \\ &= 2t_L + 2t_N = 4t_\alpha + 2(2a + b + c + d)t_\beta. \end{aligned} \tag{8}$$

HMIPv6 Registration Procedures: In HMIPv6, an MN gets two CoAs: an on-link CoA (LCoA) and a regional CoA (RCoA) when it enters into a new domain. The former is the on-link CoA configured on an MN's interface based on the prefix advertised by its default AR, while the latter is an address on the MAP's subnet. The prefix used to form RCoA is usually advertised by MAP to all routers and MNs in the same domain through the dynamic MAP discovery scheme using MAP option [5].

For the location registration, an MN uses *local binding update (LBU)* as well as BU. LBU is sent only to the domain MAP and specifies the binding between MN's RCoA and LCoA. On the other hand, normal BU specifies the binding between MN's HoA and RCoA. It is sent to the HA and each of CNs outside

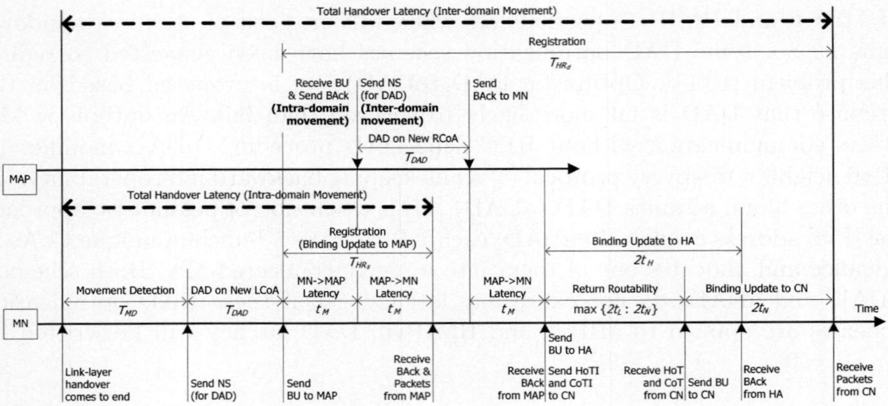

Fig. 2. Handover Procedure and Timing Diagram in HMIPv6

the domain. When an MN moves within the domain and attaches to an AR, it configures new LCoA by using the on-link prefix advertised by the AR. It should be noted that RCoA remains constant in this intra-domain movement. MN then sends LBU to MAP. No BU message is sent outside domain. After MAP receives LBU from MN, all packets destined to the MN will be rightly transferred. Let us denote by T_{HR_s} the registration latency of intra-domain movement. It is simply given by:

$$T_{HR_s} = 2t_M = 2t_\alpha + 2at_\beta. \tag{9}$$

When MN moves into a new MAP domain and attaches to an AR, it configures new RCoA as well as new LCoA. RCoA is usually auto-configured by MN using the advertised MAP option. Then, it sends LBU to MAP. Only if the uniqueness of RCoA is confirmed from RFC 2462 DAD procedure, MAP records this binding in its binding cache, and sends a binding acknowledgement (BAck) message to MN. After receiving BAck from MAP, MN also sends normal BUs to its HA and CNs. Like MIPv6, the return routability procedure is still required to authenticate the BU message. Let us denote by T_{HR_d} the registration latency of inter-domain movement. Assuming $c < b + d$, it is as follows:

$$\begin{aligned} T_{HR_d} &= 2t_M + t_{DAD} + max\{2t_L,\ 2t_N\} + 2t_N \\ &= 6t_\alpha + (6a + 2b + 2c + 2d)t_\beta + RT \cdot DTimes. \end{aligned} \tag{10}$$

If a DAD optimization scheme, such as oDAD or aDAD, is used for RCoA configuration, it will be written by:

$$T_{HR_d} = 6t_\alpha + (6a + 2b + 2c + 2d)t_\beta. \tag{11}$$

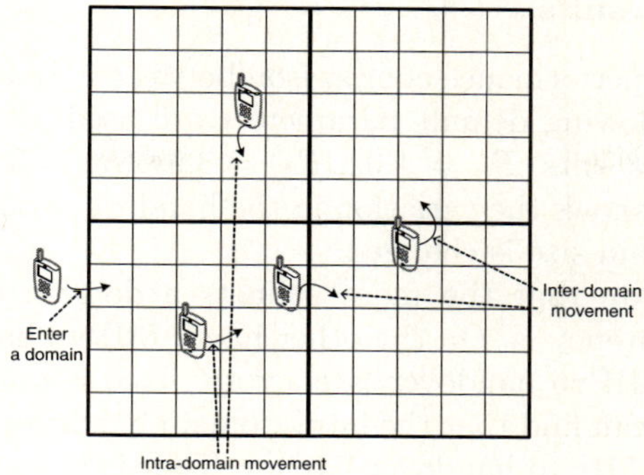

Fig. 3. Our subnet and domain overlay structure

4 Performance Evaluation

4.1 System and Mobility Models

The system architecture described in Section II is modeled as follows. Our model is similar to the one described in [12]. But, we slightly change it and include a new concept of subnet and domain overlay structure by which the service area is assumed to be covered (see Fig. 3). In the overlay architecture, the lower layer is comprised of subnets and the higher layer represents domains. For simplicity, we assume all domains overlay the same number of subnets. We also assume the homogeneous network of which all subnets in a domain have the same shape and size of mesh plane.

Let us assume that MN resides in a subnet for a period and moves to one of its four neighbors with the same probability, i.e., with probability 1/4. A domain is referred to as an *n-layer domain* if it overlays $4n^2 - 4n + 1$ subnets. We define a random variable M so that each MN moves out of a domain network at M's subnet movement. Then $E[M] = 1$ when $n = 1$. For $n \geq 2$, the expected number of M in a n-layer domain is computed as:

$$E[M] = \sum_{k=1}^{\infty} \sum_{y=0}^{2n-3} \sum_{j=0}^{2n-3} q_{(n-1,y)} p_{k,(n-1,y)(n,j)} k. \quad (12)$$

The detailed description of (12) can be found in [13], which is other outcome of our preceding research. By using (12), the latency of HMIPv6 registration procedure is more completely written as follows:

$$T_{HR} = \frac{(E[M]-1)T_{HR_s} + T_{HR_d}}{E[M]}. \quad (13)$$

4.2 Analytical Results

We demonstrate the performance comparison between MIPv6 and HMIPv6. For our analysis, the following default parameters are used: $a = 3$, $b = 7$, $c = 6$, $d = 3$, $t_\alpha = 3ms$, $t_\beta = 2ms$, $R_m = 1.0s$, $R_M = 3.0s$, $R_L = 3.0s$, $RT = 1.0s$, and $DTimes = 1$. Fig. 4 shows the variation in the handover latencies of MIPv6 and HMIPv6 as the domain size is changed.

The results indicate that the more subnets a domain contains, the lower HMIPv6 handover latency is. On the other hand, MIPv6 handover latency and the intra-domain HMIPv6 handover latency are fixed regardless of the domain size. In addition, we can find that the intra-domain handover latency of HMIPv6 is always lower than MIPv6 handover latency. That is to say, if MN moves only within a domain, HMIPv6 always outperforms MIPv6 in terms of handover speed. However, it is noted that the intra-domain handover latency of HMIPv6 is not much low compared with MIPv6 handover latency unless both MD and DAD optimizations are supported. The intra-domain HMIPv6 handover reduces MIPv6 handover latency just by about 3% at the case (see Fig. 4 (a)). Only with MD optimization and only with DAD optimization, it reduces MIPv6 handover latency just by about 8% and 6.5%, respectively (see Fig. 4 (b) and (c)).

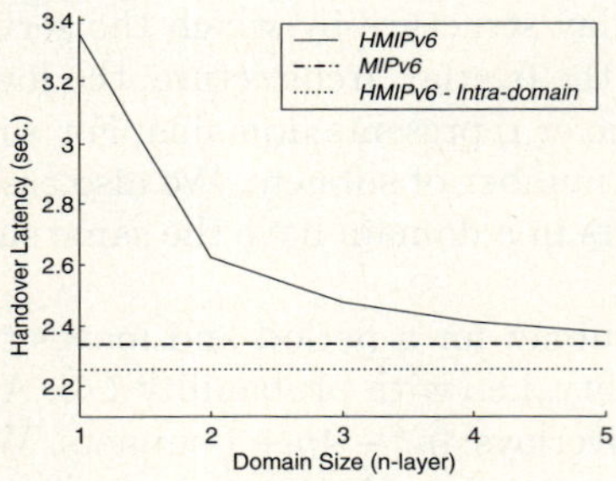

(a) No MD and DAD optimizations

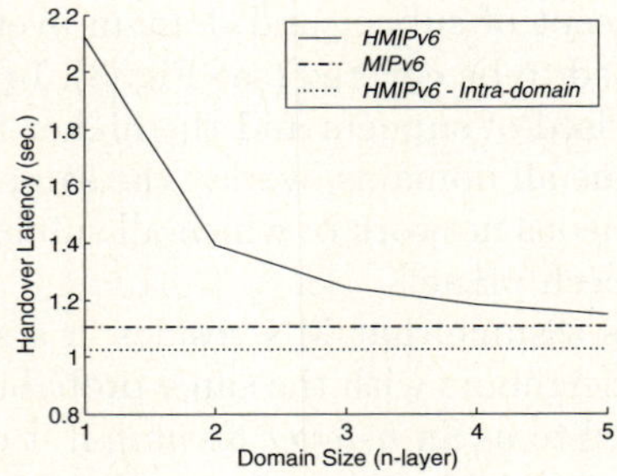

(b) Only MD optimization

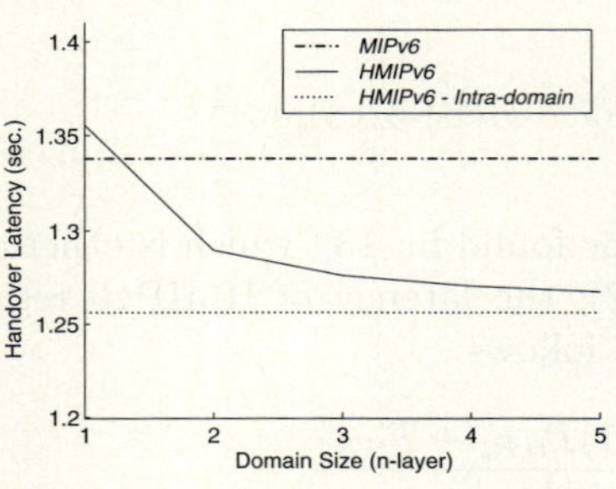

(c) Only DAD optimization

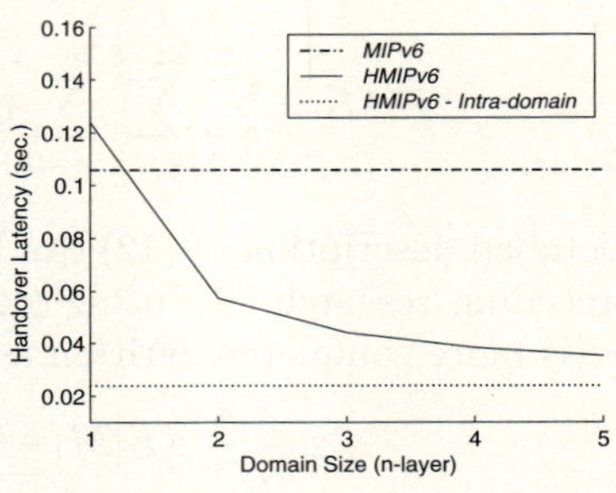

(d) Both MD and DAD optimization

Fig. 4. Handover latency comparison

Another surprising results are seen from Fig. 4 (a) and (b) which report that the average HMIPv6 handover latency is always higher than the average MIPv6 handover latency unless DAD optimization is supported. This is justified by noting that HMIPv6 requires DAD procedure for RCoA as well as DAD procedure for LCoA when MN moves to a new domain. Although inter-domain handover does not frequently occur, its latency becomes so long due to the DAD procedures for both LCoA and RCoA. On the average, therefore, HMIPv6 handover latency becomes longer than MIPv6 handover latency.

Fig. 4 (c) and (d) show that HMIPv6 can outperform MIPv6 in terms of handover latency if DAD optimization is used for CoA configuration in MIPv6 and HMIPv6. Only with DAD optimization, however, we see from Fig. 4 (c) that HMIPv6 handover latency is not much reduced. Compared with MIPv6 handover latency, there is only about 6% decrease when the domain layer is 3, 4, and 5 (each number of subnets in a domain is respectively 25, 49, and 81). It explains that, although DAD latency is diminished, MD latency is still a dominating factor of the whole handover latency. Of more practical and remarkable interest shown by Fig. 4 (d) is the case that both MD and DAD optimizations are supported. In this case, on the average, HMIPv6 handover latency can theoretically becomes below 50 ms when the domain layer is above three. We can also know that, compared with MIPv6 handover latency, there is about 50 $\sim$ 60% decrease. In particular, the intra-domain handover latency of HMIPv6 is very low (reduction by about 79% compared with MIPv6 handover latency). It means HMIPv6 can nicely support a real-time application like VoIP in terms of handover speed, if both MD and DAD optimizations are supported.

5 Conclusions

In this paper, we studied the details of MIPv6 and HMIPv6 handover procedures based on the recent IETF RFCs. While existing literatures have asserted that HMIPv6 generally improves MIPv6 in terms of handover speed, we revealed that the average HMIPv6 handover latency is not always lower than the average MIPv6 handover latency. Furthermore, even the intra-domain handover latency of HMIPv6 is not much small compared with MIPv6 handover latency unless both MD and DAD optimizations are supported. In order to increase the benefit of HMIPv6 and make HMIPv6 appropriate to a real-time application requesting considerably short handover latency, both MD and DAD optimizations are essential requirements.

References

1. Johnson, D.B., Perkins, C.E., Arkko, J.: Mobility Support in IPv6. IETF RFC 3775 (2004)
2. Vaughan-Nichols, S.J.: Mobile IPv6 and the Future of Wireless Internet Access. IEEE Computer **36**(2) (2003) 18–22
3. Thomson, S., Narten, T.: IPv6 Stateless Address Autoconfiguration. IETF RFC 2462 (1998)

4. Narten, T., Nordmark, E., Simpson, W.: Neighbour Discovery for IP version 6. IETF RFC 2461 (1998)
5. Soliman, H., Castelluccia, C., Malki, K.E., Bellier, L.: Hierarchical Mobile IPv6 Mobility Management (hmipv6). IETF RFC 4140 (2005)
6. Castelluccia, C.: HMIPv6: A Hierarchical Mobile IPv6 Proposal. ACM Mobile Computing and Communications Review **4**(1) (2000) 48–59
7. Han, Y.H., Hwang, S.H.: Movement Detection Analysis in Mobile ipv6. IEEE Communication Letters **10**(1) (2006) 59–61
8. Yegin, A.: Link-layer Event Notifications for Detecting Network Attachments. IETF Internet draft, draft-ietf-dna-link-information-01.txt (work in progress) (2005)
9. Choi, J., Daley, G.: Goals of Detecting Network Attachment in IPv6. IETF RFC 4135 (2005)
10. Moore, N.: Optimistic Duplicate Address Detection. IETF Internet draft, draft-ietf-ipv6-optimistic-dad-05.txt (work in progress) (2005)
11. Han, Y.H., Hwang, S.H., Jang, H.: Design and Evaluation of an Address Configuration and Confirmation Scheme for IPv6 Mobility Support. In: Proc. of IEEE Wireless Communications and Networking Conference (WCNC). (2004)
12. Akyildiz, I.F., Lin, Y.B., Lai, W.R., Chen, R.J.: A New Random Walk Model for PCS Networks. IEEE Journal on Selected Areas in Communications **18**(7) (2000) 1254–1260
13. Hwang, S.H., Han, Y.H., Min, S.G.: Performance Analysis of IPv6 Mobility Protocols over IEEE 802.11 Network. IEICE Transaction on Communication **E87-B**(9) (2004) 2613–2625

Adaptive Error Recovery in cdma2000 1xEV-DO Mobile Broadcast Networks

Kyungtae Kang, Yongwoo Cho, Hosang Park, and Heonshik Shin

School of Electrical Engineering and Computer Science
Seoul National University, Seoul, 151-744, Korea
{ktkang, xtg05, phosanna, shinhs}@cslab.snu.ac.kr

Abstract. We analyze the performance of MAC-layer Reed-Solomon error-recovery in the cdma2000 1xEV-DO Broadcast and Multicast Services (BCMCS) environment, with respect to the size of the error control block (ECB) and the air-channel condition, and establish the relationship between ECB size, error-recovery capacity and service latency. Real-time traffic, such as voice and video streaming, is very sensitive to delay, but can stand a certain level of packet loss. We therefore propose an adaptive error-recovery scheme which adjusts the size of the ECB to reflect the environment of the mobile nodes so as to meet the required service quality (target bit error-rate), while reducing the latency of real-time applications, decoding complexity, and memory requirement. Extensive simulation results show the effectiveness of our adaptive approach compared to the current static scheme. Our scheme achieves near-optimal service latency while meeting the target service quality criterion, and also reduces energy consumption during error recovery.

Keywords: cdma2000 1xEV-DO BCMCS, Adaptive error-recovery, Reed-Solomon, error control block, service latency.

1 Introduction

Work has begun, in both the Third Generation Partnership Project (3GPP) and the 3GPP2 group, on enhancing 3G networks to support broadcast and multicast services (BCMCS) [1] [2] [3]. The 3GPP2 group recently baselined the specification for the cdma2000 high-rate broadcast packet-data air interface [4] [5]. In order to provide a high-speed broadcast service in the BCMCS environment, the efficient handling of data transmitted over wireless radio channels must be considered.

In general, a wireless radio channel has a much higher error-rate than that expected on a wired link. Additionally, errors occur in clusters or bursts, with relatively long error-free intervals between them. BCMCS therefore use Reed-Solomon [6] coding as a forward error-correction scheme, which can efficiently conceal error clusters. Usually, the Reed-Solomon scheme is combined with an appropriate data interleaving mechanism to increase performance. In BCMCS, this interleaving is controlled by the size of the ECB (error control block). Bursty

E. Sha et al. (Eds.): EUC 2006, LNCS 4096, pp. 1119–1128, 2006.

errors can be corrected much more efficiently with a larger ECB. But, as the size of the ECB increases, mobile node have to buffer a lot of data. This delays the applications that access this data, and increases the memory required at the mobile node and the computational complexity of the decoding process [4]. Reducing delay is very important for real-time applications, such as voice and video streaming, but a certain level of packet loss is tolerable. On the basis of extensive simulation, we derive the performance of Reed-Solomon coding with respect to error capacity and service delay as the size of the ECB changes, within the current cdma2000 1xEV-DO broadcast environment.

Additionally, we propose an adaptive error-recovery scheme for cdma2000 1xEV-DO broadcast networks. Our scheme varies the ECB size to suit changing channel conditions at the mobile nodes. Its aim is to achieve the smallest ECB necessary to meet the required level of service while controlling the latency. The condition of the stationary channel, which drives adjustments to the ECB, is obtained from heuristics which use a moving average (MA) or a weighted average (WA) to flatten out large fluctuations in the bit error-rate.

2 Background

2.1 Error Recovery in Current BCMCS

Unlike the unicast cdma2000 1xEV-DO standard [7], BCMCS do not use an error-control scheme based on ARQs (automatic repeat requests), because there is no reverse link to carry the ACK/NAK signal from the access terminal to the access network. Instead, error control is provided by a forward error-correcting product code, comprising an inner turbo code and an outer Reed-Solomon code. The broadcast framing protocol fragments higher-layer packets at the access network; the broadcast security protocol provides encryption of framing packets; and the broadcast MAC (medium access control) protocol defines the procedures used to transmit over the broadcast channel and specifies an additional outer code which, in conjunction with the physical layer turbo code, forms the product code. As already mentioned, Reed-Solomon was chosen as the outer code for cdma2000 BCMCS, and the broadcast MAC layer packets have a fixed size of 125 bytes. The protocol is completed by the broadcast physical layer, which provides the channel structure for the broadcast channel [4] [5].

Each logical channel uses error control blocks (ECBs) with M MAC packets per ECB row. The variables N and K represent the number of octets and security-layer octets in a Reed-Solomon code word. R is the number of parity octets: the Reed-Solomon decoder can recover up to R octet erasures in each code word. Reed-Solomon coding is applied to the columns of the ECB, and then the data is transferred row by row to the physical slot, where it forms one or more physical-layer packets. The ECB is designed to provide a structure such that, in the event of a physical-layer packet erasure, octets in the same position are lost from all affected Reed-Solomon code words. The data octets which have been successfully received are simply forwarded to the upper layer of the BCMCS protocol suite. The possible values of N in BCMCS are 32, 16 and 1,

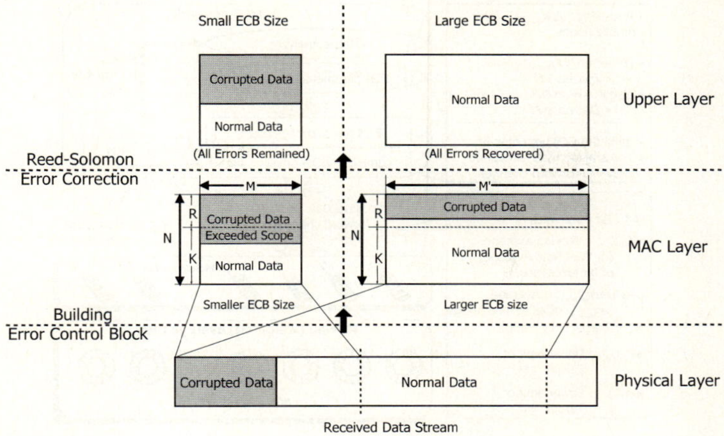

Fig. 1. Correlation between ECB size and error-recovery capacity

and K can take a value of 28, 26 or 24 when $N = 32$, or a value of 14, 13 or 12 when $N = 16$ [4] [5].

One of the most significant environmental factors affecting channel condition is fading. This is correlated with the burstiness of errors. In slow-moving conditions, the error occurrence pattern tends to be more bursty than in fast-moving conditions. A Reed-Solomon code of (N, K, R) cannot recover any lost data if the corrupted portion of a code word is larger than R. For this reason, the performance of error correction will drop if the burst length of errors becomes so large that the ECB cannot interleave them sufficiently. This situation is shown schematically in Fig. 1. The burstiness of errors caused by bad channel conditions can be an important factor in selecting an appropriate data interleaving interval, determined by the width of the ECB, which is $M \times 125$ octets. The value of M for a given ECB has to be less than or equal to 16. As the value of M increases, the time-diversity also increases and thus a mobile node which is in a time-varying shadow environment is able to recover more corrupted data. However, the amount of storage required at the mobile node also increases. Therefore, the value of M is an important consideration in achieving better error-recovery capacity for mobile nodes with less system resource.

3 Proposed Adaptive Error Recovery Scheme

As explained in the previous section, the bit error-rate after Reed-Solomon decoding can be controlled by adjusting the value of M. In current BCMCS, this value is fixed, generally to 16, to increase the error recovery capacity without considering the service delay. However, we can reduce the average service delay by dynamically reconfiguring the Reed-Solomon ECB according to the channel condition of the mobile nodes. Ideally, adapting the value of M to the current

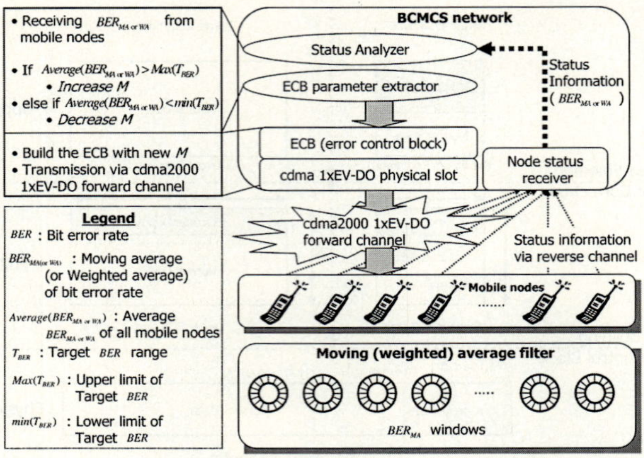

Fig. 2. Service implementation scenario

network environment in this way would provide a full solution, reducing the service latency while guaranteeing the target bit error-rate. However, in reality it is not possible for the network to sense the environment around the mobile nodes directly. Instead, to detect the tendency of the current environmental status of the mobile nodes, we use a feedback mechanism in which each node reports its bit error-rate as an indicator of its receiving channel environment. Because the status of each mobile node depends on its previous situation, prediction of subsequent status can be achieved by the heuristic feedback algorithm which we will go on to describe.

Fig. 2 shows the service scenario with which we have experimented. The BCMCS network broadcasts a data stream to the mobile nodes via the cdma2000 1xEV-DO forward traffic channel. Each mobile node records its error count at a predefined interval as a BER_{MA} or BER_{WA} (moving average or weighted average of the bit error-rate), implemented as a circular queue. Each node periodically reports the moving average (MA) of the bit error-rate at a window, or the weighted average (WA), to the network via the cdma2000 1xEV-DO reverse channel. The network then selects a new value of M on the basis of the average of the status information collected from the nodes. An $Average(BER_{MA})$ or $Average(BER_{WA})$ larger than the maximum boundary of the target BER range ($Max(T_{BER})$) suggests that the environmental status in the current service area is unsatisfactory. In this case, the network increases M in order to improve its capability to conceal errors. Conversely, an $Average(BER_{MA})$ or $Average(BER_{WA})$ that is lower than $Min(T_{BER})$ indicates that the current network status is more than sufficient for the required level of service, and that M can be reduced so as to reduce the total latency of service, the memory required and the computational complexity. The network then builds a new ECB in the MAC layer of cdma2000 1xEV-DO, using the adjusted value of M. The data-stream built by this procedure is transferred across the cdma2000

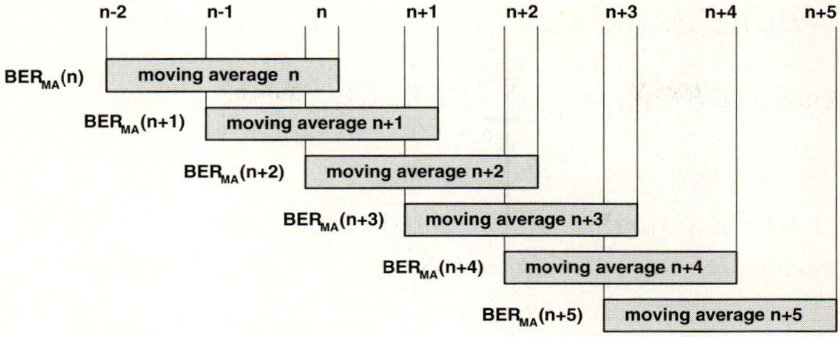

Fig. 3. Simple moving average

1xEV-DO forward channel. By repeating these procedures, the network can adapt its transmission configuration to suit the environmental situation.

To control the size of the ECB according to the average channel condition of mobile nodes, we employ the MA as a low-pass filter, and its output is used to determine the appropriate ECB size. By damping changes in the BER, it can be used to determine the channel condition more reliably. Fig. 3 shows the basic idea of an MA with a given window size w, which is calculated as follows:

$$\begin{aligned} BER_{MA}(\tau_j, n) &= \frac{1}{w} \sum_{i=n-w+1}^{n} BER(\tau_j, i) \\ Average(BER_{MA}) &= \frac{1}{\eta} \sum_{j=0}^{\eta-1} BER_{MA}(\tau_j, n) \\ BER(\tau_j, i) &:= i^{th} \text{ BER of } \tau_j \\ BER_{MA}(\tau_j, n) &:= n^{th} \text{ moving average of } \tau_j \\ Average(BER_{MA}) &:= \text{average } BER_{MA} \text{ of all mobile nodes} \\ \eta &:= \text{number of mobile nodes.} \end{aligned} \tag{1}$$

Each node feeds back recent information about its environmental condition, measured as a value of BER_{MA}, to the network, which then determines the general status of the mobile nodes by averaging the BER_{MA} values. If the general status of the network environment is getting worse, then M will be increased; if the situation takes a favorable turn, then M will be reduced so as to shorten delays in the system. However, it takes a long time for the value of M to decrease once it has increased following the deterioration of the channel condition, and in the meantime the service latency will become longer. We therefore deploy another method, a weighted average, which works to reduce a large value of M more quickly, by giving more priority to the tendency of the recent BER values reported by the mobile nodes. This weighted average (WA) can be calculated as follows:

$$
\begin{aligned}
BER_{WA}(\tau_j, n) &= \omega \cdot BER_{WA}(n-1) + (1-\omega) \cdot BER(\tau_j, n) \\
Average(BER_{WA}) &= \frac{1}{\eta} \sum_{j=0}^{\eta-1} BER_{WA}(\tau_j, n) \\
BER(\tau_j, i) &:= i^{th} \text{ BER of } \tau_j \\
BER_{WA}(\tau_j, n) &:= n^{th} \text{ weighted average of } \tau_j \\
Average(BER_{WA}) &:= \text{average } BER_{WA} \text{ of all mobile nodes} \\
\omega &:= \text{weight}.
\end{aligned} \tag{2}
$$

4 Performance Evaluation

4.1 Simulation Environment

In our experiments, we used QPSK modulation with a 1228.8 kbps data rate forward channel. We also used the simple threshold model suggested by Zorzi [8] to simulate the behavior of errors which arise in data transmission over fading channels. This model can be represented as a binary Markov process [9] in which the receiver is deemed to have received a data bit when the fading envelope of that bit is more than some threshold value. If the fading envelope is below the threshold, receipt fails. A first-order two-state Markov process can simulate the error sequences generated by data transmission on a correlated Rayleigh fading channel: these errors occur in clusters or bursts with relatively long error-free intervals between them.

By choosing different values for the physical-layer bit error-rate ($\varepsilon_{physical}$) and for f_dT (the Doppler frequency normalized to the data-rate), we can model different degrees of correlation in the fading process of radio channels. The value of f_dT determines the correlation properties, which are related to the mobile speed for a given carrier frequency. When f_dT is small, the fading process has a strong correlation, which means long bursts of errors (slow fading). Conversely, the occurrence of errors has a weak correlation for large values of f_dT (fast fading). A value of f_dT of 0.00001 is taken to correspond to slow fading; and values of 0.00002 and 0.00003 are taken to correspond to fast fading. In computing the MA and WA, we set the values of $Min(T_{BER})$ and $Max(T_{BER})$ to 1% and 3% respectively, the size of the window to 10, and the weight (ω) to 0.7. We varied the value of $\varepsilon_{physical}$, while fixing the RS code at (16,12,4). These settings were then applied to simulation scenarios in which ten mobile nodes move around a service area in a pattern that yields values of f_dT between 0.00001 and 0.00003.

4.2 Experimental Results

Performance Analysis of Reed-Solomon Coding with Respect to M. Our first experiment investigated the relationship between the average value of $\varepsilon_{recovered}$ and the number of MAC packets per ECB (M) in a cdma2000 1xEV-DO broadcast environment. We will use $\varepsilon_{physical}$ to denote the physical-layer bit

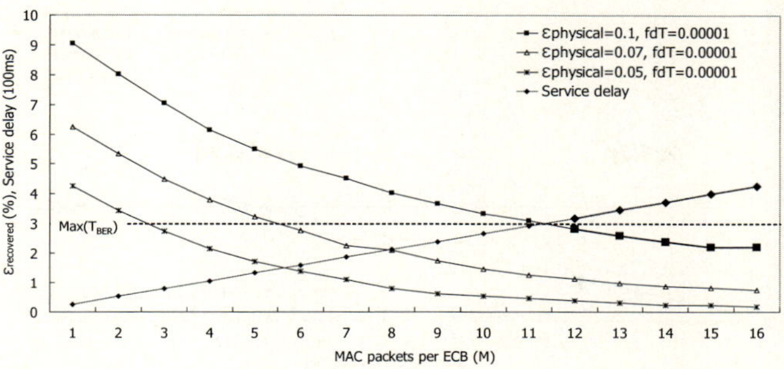

Fig. 4. Average $\varepsilon_{recovered}$ when $f_dT = 0.00001$

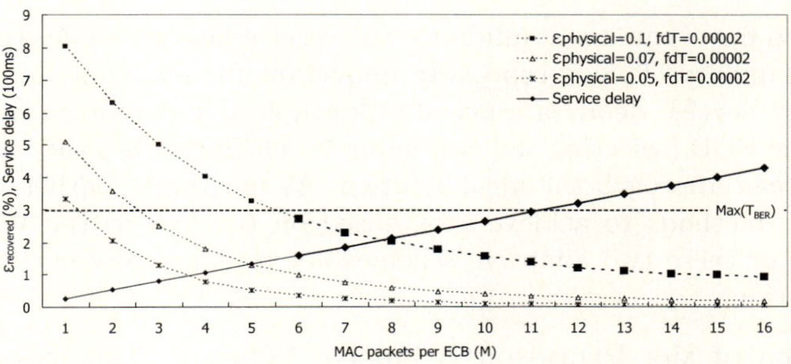

Fig. 5. Average $\varepsilon_{recovered}$ when $f_dT = 0.00002$

error-rate, and $\varepsilon_{recovered}$ to denote the bit error-rate of data carrying (excluging parity-carrying packets) after Reed-Solomon decoding. For each $\varepsilon_{recovered}$ and f_dT, the average $\varepsilon_{recovered}$ using Reed-Solomon coding is inversely proportional to M. Additionally, the rate of reduction of the average value of $\varepsilon_{recovered}$ is greater in fast fading, because the error bursts are shorter than they are in slow fading. Bursts of errors can be sufficiently interleaved in an ECB when their lengths are short, and thus the average $\varepsilon_{recovered}$ increases considerably with even a small increase of M. Because M is related to service latency and the memory requirement, both latency and storage must be sacrificed to reduce the average value of $\varepsilon_{recovered}$. The service delay increases linearly with the size of the ECB, as shown in Figs. 4, 5 and 6.

However, if we abandon a fixed value of M, and instead control M dynamically to suit the channel condition of the mobile nodes, while also satisfying the target bit error-rate, then we can reduce the average $\varepsilon_{recovered}$ with relatively little service delay. For example, a target BER ($Max(T_{BER})$) can be satisfied if the value of M is more than 12, as represented by the bold line in Fig. 4. Therefore, if we set M to 12, we can minimize the service delay while guaranteeing the required service quality. When $M = 12$, the service delay is about 100ms less than it is when $M = 16$. Another example, in Fig. 5, shows that $\varepsilon_{recovered}$ is less than $Max(T_{BER})$ when M is more than 6. Thus, by constructing an ECB

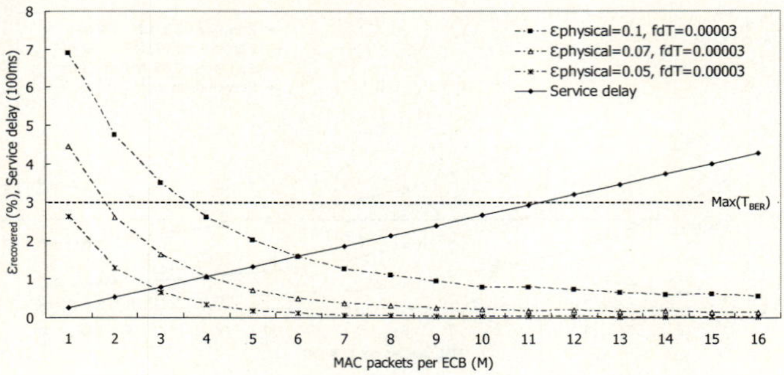

Fig. 6. Average $\varepsilon_{recovered}$ when $f_dT = 0.00003$

with M set to 6, we can again minimize the service latency while still achieving the required quality. This is especially important for real-time applications in which a short service delay is especially desirable. By dynamically optimizing the size of the ECB (selecting the minimum M which satisfies the target service quality), we can approach the ideal solution. As mentioned earlier, we propose two heuristic methods to achieve this, based on the MA or the WA, and the performance of these two adaptive schemes is experimentally evaluated in the following section.

Performance of the Proposed Adaptive Scheme. This experiment was conducted to show that our adaptive schemes, using either the MA or the WA method to adjust M, achieve results close to the ideal solution. This 'ideal solution' is computed using a minimum value of M chosen so that the average value of $\varepsilon_{recovered}$ corresponds to T_{BER} even though the channel condition changes.

Figs. 7 and 8 show that the value of M in our proposed scheme follows the values arrived at by the ideal solution. From Fig. 7, we can see that the MA scheme requires more time to accommodate to changes in channel condition than the ideal solution. However we see from Fig. 8 that M decreases as quickly as it does in the ideal solution, because the WA method adapts to a more recent channel condition of the mobile nodes. A moving average is a statistical technique used to predict the tendency of a stochastic process, and tends to eliminate short-term fluctuations in a time series and to highlight long-term trends. Thus an MA provides an effective way to predict the occurrence of errors in wireless communication, provided that they have a continuous stochastic pattern. Conversely, a weighted average emphasizes recent movements rather than overall low-frequency trends; it is sensitive to high-frequency fluctuations and is therefore more agile. However, the methods will tend to converge if the recent weight of the WA and the window period of the MA are reduced.

Fig. 9(a) shows that the average value of $\varepsilon_{recovered}$ achieved by our proposed schemes and by the ideal solution both satisfy the target BER. In Fig. 9(a), the average value of $\varepsilon_{recovered}$ is lower than that of $Max(T_{BER})$, and our scheme's average $\varepsilon_{recovered}$ is close to that for the ideal solution. Fig. 9(b) shows the average service delay generated by the proposed adaptation methods and by the

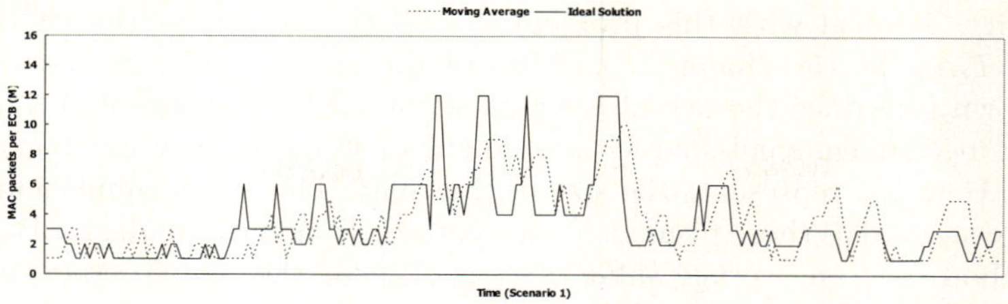

Fig. 7. MAC packets per ECB (M) with the MA method and the ideal solution

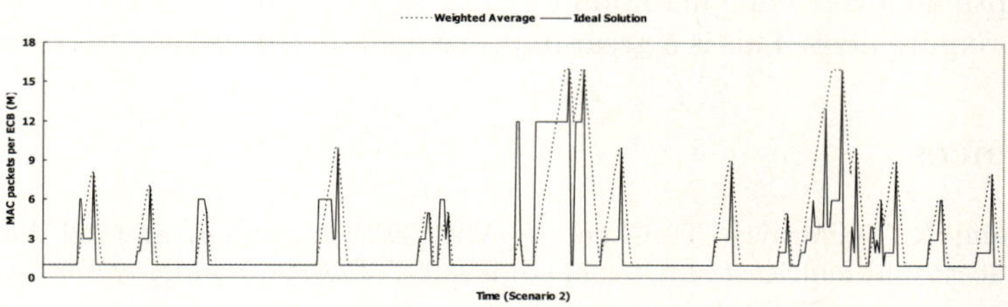

Fig. 8. MAC packets per ECB (M) with the WA method and the ideal solution

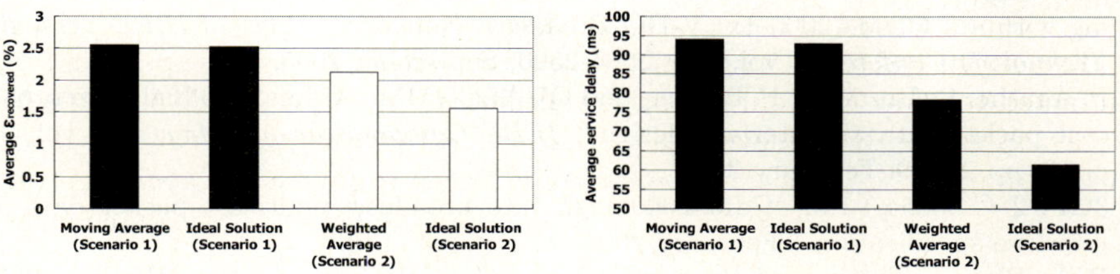

(a) Average $\varepsilon_{recovered}$ (b) Average service delay

Fig. 9. Average $\varepsilon_{recovered}$ and service delay of all mobile nodes

ideal solution. We can see from this figure that our proposed heuristic methods provide a near-optimal reduction in service delay, without compromising quality. The differences in average $\varepsilon_{recovered}$ and average service delay between the MA and WA methods stem from the different experimental scenarios.

5 Conclusions

The Reed-Solomon error-correction scheme uses data interleaving mechanisms to increase error-recovery performance. This can be achieved in current BCMCS by adjusting the size of the error control block. By increasing the size of the ECB, we can recover from bursty errors efficiently; however, a larger ECB means increased service latency, an increased memory requirement, and increased computational complexity. To deal with this problem, we adapt the size of the ECB to the value of T_{BER} as the channel condition of the mobile nodes varies. This has been shown to reduce the overall average service delay. We adopted a heuristic feedback mechanism combined with a moving or weighted average to generate a value of M which represents the size of the ECB. This gives simulation results which are as good as those from an ideal solution. To determine the ECB size, our MA method uses an average value of $\varepsilon_{recovered}$ for the mobile nodes obtained from a window of size w, while our WA method uses a statistical approach which reflects more recent changes in $\varepsilon_{recovered}$. We have observed that the these approaches to the dynamic variation of ECB size reduce average service delay to a near-optimal level, while maintaining $\varepsilon_{recovered}$ within T_{BER} and reducing the memory requirement. This is a great improvement on the use of a fixed-size ECB.

References

1. J. Wang, R. Sinnarajaj, T. Chen, Y. Wei, E. Tiedemann, and QUALCOMM, "Broadcast and multicast services in cdma2000," *IEEE Communications Magazine*, vol. 42, no. 2, pp. 76-82, February 2004.
2. 3GPP2 X.P0019 v0.1.3, "Broadcast-multicast services (bcmcs) framework draft doument," August 2003.
3. K. Kang, Y. Cho and H. Shin, "Performance analysis of dynamic packet scheduling within a CDMA2000 1xEV-DO Broadcast Network," *Proc. of IEEE Vehicular Technology Conference*, vol.4, pp.2586-2590, September 2005.
4. P. Agashe, R. Rezaiifar, P. Bender, and QUALCOMM, "Cdma2000 high rate broadcast packet data air interface design," *IEEE Communications Magazine*, vol. 42, no. 2, pp. 83-89, February 2004.
5. 3GPP2 C.S0054 v1.0, "Cdma2000 high rate broadcast-multicast packet data air interface specification," February 2004.
6. R. E. Blahut, *Theory and Practice of Error Control Codes*, Addison-Wesley, 1983.
7. 3GPP2 C.S0024 33.0, "Cdma2000 high rate packet data air interface specification," December 2001.
8. M. Zorzi, R. R. Rao, and L. B. Milstein, "Error statistics in data transmission over fading channels," *IEEE Transactions on Communications*, vol. 46, no. 11, pp. 1468-1477, November 1998.
9. H. S. Wang, "On verifying the first-order Markovian assumption for a Rayleigh fading channel model," *IEEE Transactions on Vehicular Technology*, vol. 45, pp. 353-357, May 1996.

A Novel Approach for Sharing White Board Between PC and PDAs with Multi-users

Xin Xiao[1], Yuanchun Shi[2], and Weisheng He[1]

[1,2] Department of Computer Science and Technology, Tsinghua University
100084, Beijing, China
{xiaoxin00, hws99}@mails.tsinghua.edu.cn, shiyc@tsinghua.edu.cn
http://media.cs.tsinghua.edu.cn/~pervasive

Abstract. White board sharing between PC and PDAs is a typical interactive application between PC and mobile device in ubiquitous environment. Due to the limited size of PDA' s screen, when a large amount of clients simultaneously use PDAs to share the server's screen while their viewed areas (or *viewports*) are different in size and position, the server must transform the viewports to fit the size of PDA for each client and thus will suffer from heavy burden. A novel approach is proposed in this paper to reduce the burden of the server and provide the clients with real time white board sharing. Instead of zooming the viewport to fit PDA's screen for every user, it only zooms the screen nine times; then, chunked encoding is adopted to reduce the cost for encoding the overlapped area of different viewports. The experiment results have demonstrated the efficiency and effectiveness of our approach.

Keywords: white board sharing, mobile device, multi-users.

1 Introduction

In recent years, mobile devices such as PDA, Smart Phone have been experiencing a significant growth, which considerably affect people's life. Especially, they are widely used in interactive applications with PC, such as SlideShow Commander [5], whiteboard-based interactions [3], VNC-based access to remote computers [12] and so on. Currently, in our SEMIC [6] project, we are exploring the following area in mobile environment: screen or white board is shared between PC and multi-PDAs so that the underlying scenarios can be achieved: a large amount of remote students could browse the PowerPoint screen of the Smart Classroom [7, 8] by PDA in any places; we could hold Smart Phones to continue our discussion by means of white board sharing on our way home and so on.

In order to achieve these goals, many problems need to be overcome. Among them, the crucial challenge is how to enable multi-users with mobile devices to simultaneously share the same remote screen while their viewed areas (or viewports) are different in size and position. Unlike the traditional desktop PC, mobile devices have much smaller display area, e.g. PDA only has the resolution of 240×320 pixels, therefore, the viewed range of the remote screen and the image clarity are conflict with each other on mobile devices. On one hand, the whole remote screen sometimes needs to be zoomed to fit the size of the mobile device so that the user could have an

E. Sha et al. (Eds.): EUC 2006, LNCS 4096, pp. 1129 – 1138, 2006.

overview of the entire remote screen. However, in this way the image on the mobile device is much smaller than its original size, preventing the user from clearly watching the content. On the other hand, sometimes an area with the same size as the mobile device screen may need to be captured from the remote screen and delivered to the users so that they can see a clear image. However, in this situation the users can just see a part of the remote screen. Hence, the above two schemes are not sufficient to provide users with satisfactory vision experience. Instead, if a series of viewports with gradually changed size captured from the remote screen can be provided, the user can choose a preferred one. E.g. if an area with resolution of 480×640 pixels captured from the remote screen is zoomed to 240×320, it could provide clearer image than the scheme zooming the whole screen to 240×320; and compared with the scheme only capturing 240×320 from the remote screen, it can make the user see larger area of the remote screen.

If there are many users, however, the following problem arises: each user has its own preference for the size and position of the viewport from the remote screen. This brings us great challenge to meet all users' needs. On one hand, if the whole screen is sent to the users and zoomed on the mobile devices, it will result in both the redundant network load and extra time expenditure on mobile devices. On the other hand, if the server captures each user's the required area one by one and sends them to the remote users, it will suffer from heavy burdens when there are many users.

A novel approach is proposed in this paper to cope with the above problem, which aims to reduce the burdens on both the server and the client sides and to provide the remote users with real time screen/white board sharing. The theoretic analysis and experiment result show that our approach is efficient when multi-users share the remote white board with PDAs.

The rest of the paper is organized as follows: in section 2 we introduce the related work; then details of our approach are presented in section 3 and 4. We present the experiment result and evaluation in section 5. Section 6 concludes the paper and outlines our future work.

2 Related Works

In literature [1], a Rapid Serial Visual Presentation (RSVP) based approach is proposed to enable automatic browsing of large pictures on mobile devices. Firstly, an image attention model, which manipulates each region-of-interest in the image separately, is employed to illustrate the information structure within an image. Then, an optimal image browsing path is calculated based on the image attention model to simulate the human browsing behaviors. However, the concept "region-of-interest" may not always hold. For instance, if it is a PowerPoint slide, the whole image usually contains evenly distributed information, thus it's difficult to tell which regions are of interest. Besides, it just focuses on how to browse large pictures on local mobile device.

There have also been several research results on shared white board applications [2][9][10][11], among which, PebblesDraw [2] allows all of the users to draw simultaneously on different PDAs while sharing the same PC display. This project explores the field that multi-users with PDAs interactive with PC through white board sharing. However, it still does not take into account how to deliver viewports with different sizes and positions captured from the same white board to remote users. Therefore, the users can't choose the browsing resolution and position as they like.

SVNC [12], a VNC[4]-based application, enables users to access and control remote computers from cellular phones. SVNC makes some efforts to solve problems inherent to the cellular phone's small screen. For instance, frequently used screen area can be assigned and restored quickly by using the *Shortcut* function. Also, the viewport can be widened (zoom out) to browse its contents and narrowed (zoom in) to see the display in greater detail. In our work, we expand zoom out and zoom in to gradually change in viewport's size which will be described in detail in the next section.

As is discussed above, there are already some works concerning about large image's browsing on PDA, white board sharing between PC and PDAs. They don't consider, however, the problem of multi-users' share of the same screen while each user's viewport is different; and accordingly say nothing of how to improve the efficiency of the server to achieve this goal. Hence, we propose a novel approach to solve the problem.

3 Classification of Users and Screen Snatch Based-On Viewports' Sizes

Our approach can be divided into two parts, whose first part—classification of users and screen snatch based on viewports' sizes will be described in this section and whose second part—chunked encode of viewports will be described in section 4. Here we must point out that we assume the resolution of the PC is 1024×768 pixels and 240×320 for PDA in the following sections.

Recall that to meet the needs of multi-users with different viewports, a possible solution is to send the encoded whole screen to all of them and then decode the received data, capture the required viewport from the screen and zoom the viewport to fit the size of the mobile device. However, this approach has obvious shortcomings: since each user only needs to browse part of the whole screen, it wastes network bandwidth and CPU time to process the unnecessary data. Moreover, the PC server is much more powerful than the PDA client in CPU speed, memory capacity and bandwidth, which makes it unrealistic for the client to keep up with the server. Instead, in our approach, the server processes the captured screen and only sends the necessary parts to the clients to reduce the extra cost and to make the clients synchronous with the server.

Step 1: our approach firstly defines nine gradually changed sizes (width×height) of viewports on the white board so that the size of each user's viewport belongs to one of them:

$$\{240\times270,\quad 288\times324,\quad 346\times389,\quad 415\times467,\quad 498\times560,\quad 598\times672,\quad 718\times768,\quad 862\times768,\quad 1024\times768\}$$

Two neighbored sizes have the relation that:

$$\begin{bmatrix} Width_{n+1} \\ Height_{n+1} \end{bmatrix} = f * \begin{bmatrix} Width_{n} \\ Height_{n} \end{bmatrix} \tag{1}$$

Here, f is so-called *Gradient Factor (GF)*. In our approach we set it to 1.2 to gain the effect of gradual change in size among different groups of viewports and we found in our experiment that users could have a very natural experience when browsing the white board with f =1.2. Besides, when we use the program "Windows Picture and Fax Viewer" in Windows XP to zoom out or zoom in a picture, we find the variation is also 1.2 times. Here, we must point out that the first group has size 240×270 but not 240×320 because 320 is the height of PDA's whole screen; then, the available height of the application is 270 with the heights of title and menus deducted.

Users can choose what sizes of area to be viewed. If a user chooses group n, he means to view an area with size $Width_n \times Height_n$ on remote screen. Finally, after our approach completes, his required viewport is zoomed to 240×270 to be sent to his PDA. Figure 1 illustrates the effect of the nine gradually changed sizes zoomed to fit the PDA's screen.

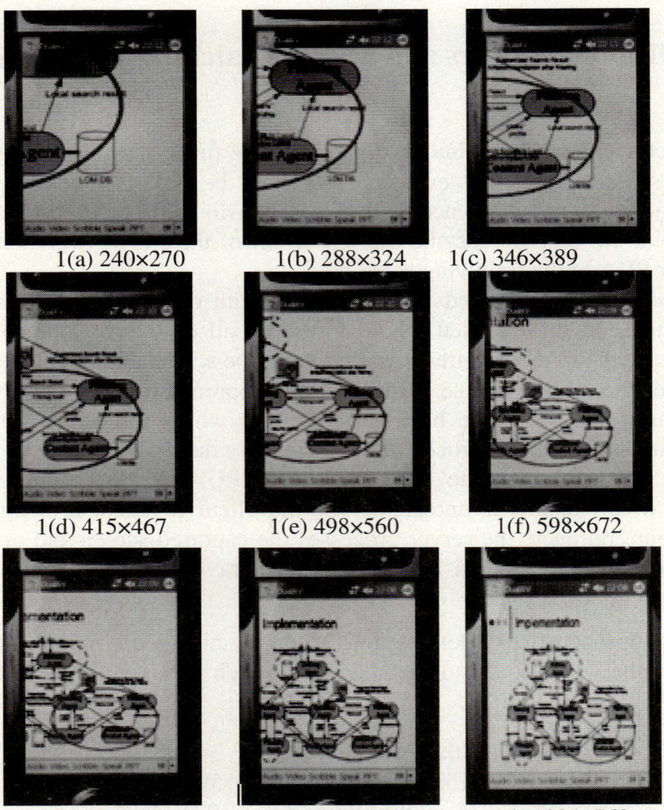

1(a) 240×270 1(b) 288×324 1(c) 346×389

1(d) 415×467 1(e) 498×560 1(f) 598×672

1(g) 718×768 1(h) 862×768 1(i) 1024×768

Fig. 1. Nine viewports with gradually changed sizes zoomed to fit PDA's screen. The original sizes of these viewports are marked in the figure.

Note that although we just present the algorithm for PDAs, it's quite similar for other mobile devices with different screen sizes. For example, for a mobile devices with screen size 160×120 pixels, the gradually changed viewports are with size

$$\{160\times120,\ 192\times144,\ 230\times173,\ 276\times208,\ 331\times250,\ 397\times300,\ 476\times360,\ 571\times432,\ 685\times518,\ 822\times622,\ 986\times746,\ 1024\times768\}$$

Step 2: zoom the screen nine times and fetch a specific area with size 240×270 from one of the zoomed screens for each user:

In the first step, we have defined nine groups of gradually changed sizes of viewports on the remote screen, and the size of each user's viewport must belong to one of the groups.

If we capture, zoom and encode the required area for each user, the cost (on average 32 ms per time for a user in our experimental environment, in which the time spent zooming plays a crucial role) will be high if the count of users is large. Alternatively, our approach only zooms the whole screen nine times. More specifically,

- Firstly, for users with the same viewport size, it zooms the whole screen to a specific size so that their viewports are zoomed to 240×270. For instance, for the users whose viewed areas are 346×389 on the remote screen, since their viewed areas will be zoomed to 240×270, the whole screen should be zoomed to:

$$\frac{1024}{346/240}\times\frac{768}{389/270}=711\times533\cdot$$

  Figure 2 illustrates how to zoom the whole screen to specific sizes. Because there are totally nine groups of gradually changed viewport sizes, the server only zooms the screen for nine times rather than n times (n is the count of users).

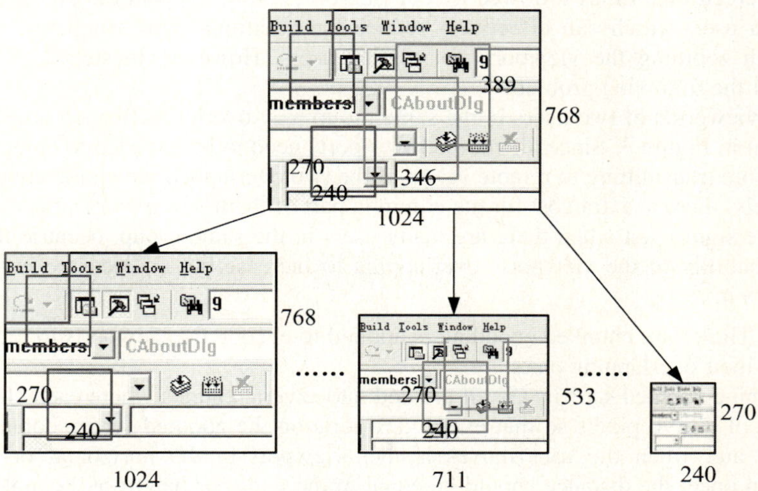

Fig. 2. Zoom the whole screen to nine different sizes. Colored rectangles are the required viewports by the users. The rectangle on the top is the original screen; the rectangles at the bottom are zoomed from the original screen. Note, the original required viewports are all zoomed to 240×270.

- Then, it just needs to copy the zoomed viewports from the zoomed screen and to encode them(on average 6 ms per time for a user to copy and encode in our experimental environment).

Note that for the approach zooming the viewport for every user, if there are 100 users, it needs to zoom 100 times; and for our approach, it only needs to zoom nine times. Also note, zooming a viewed area to 240×270 takes much more time than copying an area with 240×270 from the zoomed screen. Suppose there are n users, the former approach will cost time T_1:

$$T_1 = t_1 * n \tag{2}$$

where t_1 is the time to capture, zoom and encode the required area for each user. And our approach will cost time T_2:

$$T_2 = \tau + t_2 * n \tag{3}$$

where τ is the time spent on zooming the whole screen for nine times and t_2 is the time to copy and encode an area of 240×270 for each user. We find in our experiment that $t_1 \approx 32ms$, $\tau \approx 150ms$ and $t_2 \approx 6ms$. With the increase of n, our approach will be significantly faster than the former one because it reduces the zooming times.

In the following section, the last step (step 3), which can further improve the efficiency of our approach, will be explained.

4 Chunked Encode of Viewports

In last section, we classify the users according to their viewports' sizes and zoom the whole screen nine times followed by copying only 240×270 from the zoomed screen for each user, which can effectively reduce the additional cost compared with the approach zooming the viewports for all the users. However, in step 2, it doesn't consider the following problem:

The viewports of two users in the same group may overlap with each other, which is shown in Figure 3. Since all zoomed viewports need to be encoded to compress the data before transmitting to remote PDAs, if the two overlapped viewports are encoded separately, there is extra cost for the common part of them. Even worse, the extra cost might be significant when there are many users in the same group, because it causes the probability of the viewports overlapping to increase but no measure is taken to deal with it.

Step 3: Therefore, chunked encoding is applied to encode the viewports to reduce the cost for their overlapping parts:

The nine zoomed screens are all divided into several chunks where each chunk has the size of 80×90 pixels so that every viewports on the zoomed screen contains 3×3 chunks, and when the user moves his/her viewport in the horizontal or vertical direction once, the distance should be equal to the width or height of a chunk, which is illustrated in Figure 3. Although this way makes the movement of the viewports non-continuous, the user will not feel any big difference when watching due to the small size of a chunk.

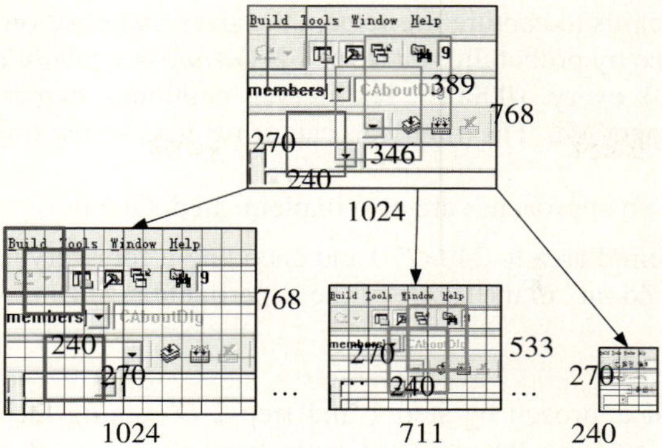

Fig. 3. Chunked encoding

When encoding a user's viewport, our approach is implemented as follows:

```
for each of the 3*3 chunks of the viewport do
begin
   if the chunk has not been encoded then
         encode it;
   else begin  /* it has been encoded when
                    encoding other users' viewports */
              doesn't encode it again and just use the encoded data;
   end-if
 end-for
```

In this way, much time spent in encoding the overlapping parts is saved.

Finally, after processing all the nine chunks, the server can send the chunked encoded data to the user. And when the user's PDA receive these data, it decodes for every chunk and displays viewports on the screen.

5 Implementation and Evaluation

We have implemented our approach for white board sharing between PC and PDAs in our SEMIC project. To demonstrate the efficiency and effectiveness of this approach, two experiments are carried out. The server runs on a PC with CPU Pentium 4, frequency 1.4GHZ; memory 512MB; operating system Windows XP; and the PDAs are HP 5550 and Lenovo TJ 218. The two experiments are carried out as follows:

5.1 Experiment One

Initially, the server records 100 users' information in its *user-info-list*. Their viewports' sizes are evenly distributed on the nine groups defined in step 1. Since we don't have 100 PDAs at hand currently, 98 of them are simulators and 2 of them are real devices.

After the server begins to capture the screen, the sizes and positions of these users' viewports change once by probability P (we call P *Variation Probability*, which varies from 10% to 100%) every 1000ms. The server continues capturing screen and implementing our approach. The time for capturing and generating the frames is measured.

In contrast, other two approaches are also implemented. One is:

- Zooming the required area to 240×270 and encoding it for every user. We call this approach "DirectZoom" in the figure of the experiment result.

and the other is:

- Implementing our approach by step 1 and step 2 (Zooming the captured screen nine times, then copying the required parts from the zoomed screen for every user), but not adopting chunked encoding. We call this approach "GroupZoom" in the figure of the experiment result.

The experiment result is illustrated in Figure 4(a).

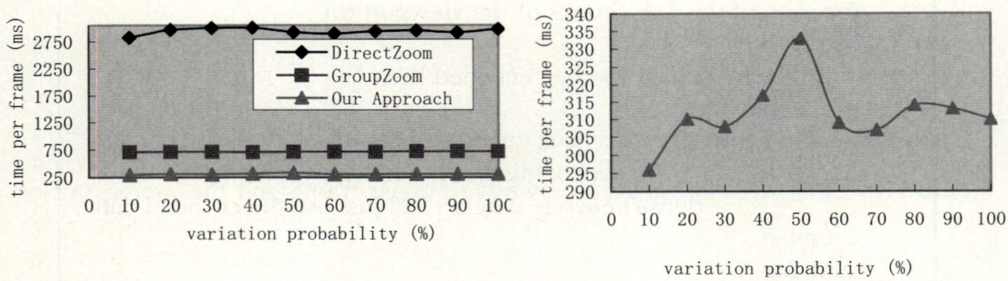

4(a) 4(b)

Fig. 4(a). Average time-per-frame with 100 users; **4(b).** Average time-per-frame with 100 users for our approach

From Figure 4 (a), we can see that our approach is much faster than Approach "DirectZoom" and Approach "GroupZoom" when user count equals 100. Compared with Approach "DirectZoom", it saves time 89.4%; and compared with Approach "GroupZoom", it saves time 56.4% per frame.

An interesting phenomenon occurs when running our approach: the maximum value of time-per-frame occurs at *variation probability* P equals 50% rather than 100% or other values (see Firugre 4(b)). Intuitively, we may think the maximum value of time-per-frame should occur when every user's viewports change (at this time P equals 100%). The explanation to this phenomenon is as follows: although previous overlapped areas don't exist any more when every user changes his viewed area (P=100%), it may lead to many new overlapped areas of the new viewports. In contrast, if P equals 50%, there are only approximately half of the users changing their viewports, which leads to less overlapped areas of the new viewports and the amount of previous overlapped areas also decreases. Since chunked encoding is adopted in our approach, it takes less time when P equals 100%.

5.2 Experiment Two

Experiment two is somewhat similar to experiment one, but the *variation probability* P is fixed to 50% and the user count varies from 10 to 1000. Figure 5 showes us the results.

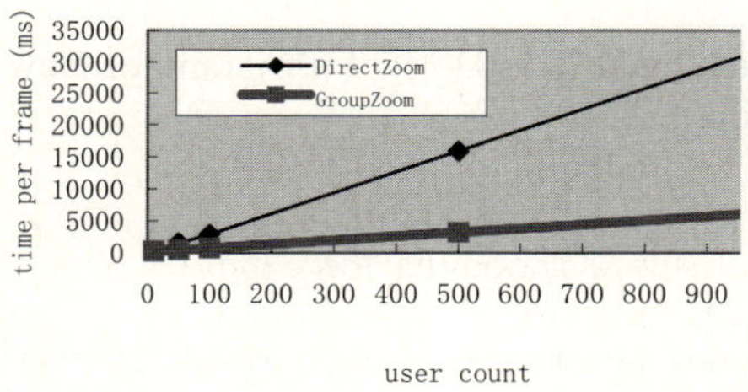

5(a)

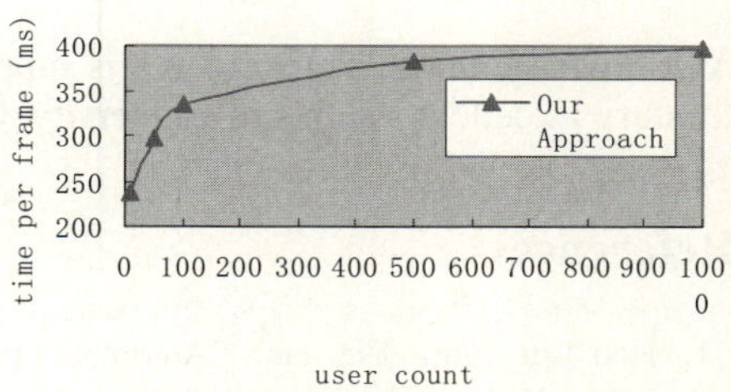

5(b)

Fig. 5(a). Average time-per-frame for Approach "DirectZoom" and "GroupZoom" when P=50%; **5(b).** Average time-per-frame for our approach when P=50%

From Figure 5(a) we can see that the time-per-frame is indeed linear to user count in Approach "DirectZoom" and Approach "GroupZoom", which is in accord with equation (2) and (3). When user count is large, time spent generating a frame for everyone is accordingly significant.

Figure 5(b) illustrates the relation between time-per-frame and the user count of our approach. With the increase of user count, time-per-frame increases slowly. Even if there are 1000 users, only 397ms needs to be spent generating the frame for all of them. At this time, the frame rate is about 2.5 frame/s. When user count is smaller, say, less than 100, the frame rate is higher than 3 frame/s. In general, the content displayed on the white board (such as PowerPoint, electronic map, etc.) doesn't vary as fast at the video, therefore, this rate is sufficient to provide the users with high quality.

In a word, the results of experiments 1 and 2 demonstrate the efficiency and effectiveness of our approach for white board sharing between PC and PDAs with multi-users. Compared with two other approaches, it avoids the linear increase of time-per-frame with the increase of user count and meets the need for frame rate in our application scenario described in the Introduction part. This approach has been used in out SEMIC [6] project. In this project, based on this approach users can also annotate on the shared white board on their PDAs.

6 Conclusion

In this paper, we present a novel approach for white board sharing application between PC and PDAs with multi-users in ubiquitous environment. It enables a large amount of users to simultaneously browse viewports with different sizes and positions on the white board. The experiment result shows its efficiency and effectiveness.

Our future work will continue in two aspects. Firstly, we will utilize a user model to simulate the user behavior when they browse the remote screen so that a new experiment based on the user model can be carried out to test our approach. Secondly, in the current implementation, we use our own encode module. In future, we'll replace it with a mature encode tool to improve the efficiency of our approach.

Acknowledgments. This research is supported by NCET-04-0079 (Program for New Century Excellent Talents in University, China).

References

1. Hao Liu, Xing Xie, etc., "Automatic Browsing of Large Pictures on Mobile Devices", MM'03, November 2-8, 2003, Berkeley, California, USA
2. Brad A. Myers, Herb Stiel, Robert Gargiulo, "Collaboration Using Multiple PDAs Connected to a PC", submitted for publication
3. Jun Rekimoto, "A Multiple Device Approach for Supporting Whiteboard-based Interactions", SIGCHI conference on Human factors in computing systems, 1998, pp. 344~351
4. Tristan Richardson, Quentin Stafford-Fraser, Kenneth R. Wood, etc., "Virtual Network Computing", IEEE Internet Computing, January and February, 1998, pp. 33~38
5. BRAD A. MYERS. "Using Handhelds and PCs Together", COMMUNICATIONS OF THE ACM. November 2001. Vol.44, No.11, pp34-41.
6. http://media.cs.tsinghua.edu.cn/~pervasive/projects/semic
7. Y.C. Shi, W.K. Xie, G.Y. Xu, etc. "The Smart Classroom: Merging Technologies for Seamless Tele-Education." Pervasive Computing. April-June 2003. pp47-55.
8. W.K. Xie, Y.C. Shi, G.Y. Xu and Y.H. Mao. "Smart Platform - A Software Infrastructure for Smart Space (SISS)" , ICMI'02, October 14 - 16, 2002. Pittsburgh, Pennsylvania. p. 429.
9. Bier, E.A. and Freeman, S. "MMM: A User Interface Architecture for Shared Editors on a Single Screen," in Proceedings UIST'91. Hilton Head, SC: pp. 79-86.
10. Pederson, E., et al. "Tivoli: An Electronic Whiteboard for Informal Workgroup Meetings," in Proceedings INTERCHI'93: Human Factors in Computing Systems. 1993. Amsterdam, The Netherlands: pp. 391-398.
11. Stewart, J.E. "Single Display Groupware," in SIGCHI'97 Adjunct Proceedings: Human Factors in Computer Systems, Extended Abstracts. 1997. Atlanta, GA: pp. 71-72.
12. Buntarou Shizuki, Masato Nakasu, and Jiro Tanaka, "VNC-BASED ACCESS TO REMOTE COMPUTERS FROM CELLULAR PHONES", Proceedings of the IASTED International Conference on Communication Systems and Networks (CSN 2002), pp. 74-79

Semi-soft FMIPv6 for 802.11 Network

Hyon-Young Choi[1], Sung-Gi Min[1,⋆], Youn-Hee Han[2], and Hee-Jin Jang[3]

[1] Dept. of Computer Science and Engineering, Korea University, Seoul, Korea
{neongas, sgmin}@korea.ac.kr
[2] School of Internet-Media, Korea University of Technology and Education, Cheonan, Korea
yhhan@kut.ac.kr
[3] Samsung AIT, Giheung-ci, Kyungki-do, Korea
heejin.jang@samsung.com

Abstract. Mobility support in the wireless network enables us to be served continuous service. Fast Handover for Mobile IPv6 (FMIPv6) is proposed to support a faster handover than that of Mobile IPv6. Unfortunately, FMIPv6 shows too long handover latency to serve smooth video traffic flows. We proposed semi-soft FMIPv6 handover to minimize the handover latency to serve video traffic efficiently. The proposed scheme clarifies the handover procedure by separating the handover preparation and the actual handover. We also clarify the use of L2 triggering by introducing four triggers and triggering time scheme. With our experimental implementation, the proposed scheme has shortened the handover latency below 50ms and this low handover latency helps to reduce the buffered packet size in access routers.

1 Introduction

Mobility support is a key feature in wireless network environment. Mobility support provides continuous service for mobile nodes when they move from one wireless point of attachment to another in a different subnet. In IEEE 802.11 wireless network, communication disruption period exists between current attachment point and new attachment point. And additional process time to update mobility information is required according to mobility support protocol. Handover latency is a traditional metric that measures network disruption period.

Mobile IPv6 (MIPv6)[1] is a well-known protocol to support mobility in IEEE 802.11 wireless network. Handover latency in MIPv6 is more than one second excluding layer 2(L2) handover latency and it is considered too long to serve multimedia service such as video traffic. Fast Handover for Mobile IPv6 (FMIPv6)[3] is proposed to shorten the handover latency as a micro-mobility approach. FMIPv6 provides a faster handover than MIPv6. According to [6], handover latency in FMIPv6 is about 160ms. FMIPv6 has reduced the handover latency, but the handover latency still has to be reduced further to serve multimedia service such as

⋆ Corresponding author.

E. Sha et al. (Eds.): EUC 2006, LNCS 4096, pp. 1139–1147, 2006.

video smoothly. Moreover, buffering in an access router to provide seamlessness needs to be minimized.

In this paper, we propose semi-soft FMIPv6 handover to minimize the handover latency to support video traffic smoothly. In semi-soft FMIPv6 handover, we separate handover preparation and actual handover clearly. We can configure the address configuration and tunneling setup before actual handover is occurred during handover preparation phase, so we call semi-soft FMIPv6 handover. We perform experiment to verify the operation of proposed handover procedures in test bed.

2 Semi-soft FMIPv6 Handover

2.1 FMIPv6

FMIPv6 is proposed to reduce the handover latency of MIPv6. FMIPv6 predicts mobile movement and prepares the movement before actually the movement occurs. Fig. 1 shows the sequence of message for FMIPv6. In FMIPv6 over IEEE 802.11 network, FMIPv6 handover procedure is as follows:

1) MN performs a scan to see which APs are available. The result of the scan is a list of APs including physical layer information, such as signal strength. MN selects one or more APs by its local policy.
2) MN exchanges Router Solicitation for Proxy (RtSolPr) and Proxy Router Advertisement (PrRtAdv) with the current AP to get the new subnet prefix of the selected AR.
3) MN itself configures its prospective new CoA (NCoA) based on the new subnet prefix.

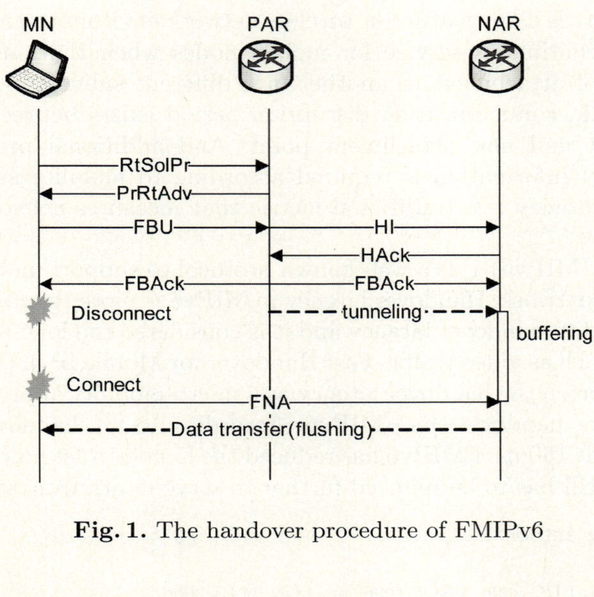

Fig. 1. The handover procedure of FMIPv6

4) MN sends Fast Binding Update (FBU) to current(previous) AR (PAR) to tunnel packets from PAR to new AR (NAR).
5) PAR exchanges Handover Initiation(HI)/Handover Acknowledgement (HAck) message with NAR. After receiving HI, NAR does Duplicate Address Detection(DAD) and protects the NCoA from other nodes in the subnet until MN arrives this subnet. In addition NAR prepares to buffer tunneled packets from PAR.
6) MN should wait Fast Binding Acknowledgement(FBAck) message, if possible, when it still presents on the previous subnet. If MN receives FBAck in the previous subnet, it should move to NAR as soon as possible. If the MN does not receive FBAck in the current subnet and cannot sustain current association (e.g., signal strength is very low), MN should move to NAR without waiting FBAck.
7) After PAR sends FBAck, PAR forwards every packet towards MN to NAR, and NAR starts buffering. Buffering continues until NAR receives Fast Neighbor Advertisement(FNA).
8) When MN moves into new subnet, it sends FNA to NAR and receives buffered packets in NAR.

FMIPv6 uses predictive scheme to reduce handover latency and also uses tunneling and buffering to support seamlessness. With buffering, the handover latency is critical to NAR. Large handover latency for high volume traffic flow may cause buffer overflow. If there are several such flows in a MN or several MNs does handover to NAR simultaneously, this situation can be very serious.

2.2 Semi-soft FMIPv6 Handover

To use FMIPv6, it must be considered practical issues. The issues are as follows:

1) FBU causes HI/HAck. Because DAD procedure in NAR takes one second, HI/HAck exchanges consume at least one second. According to [3], FBU can be considered as handover signal to network. If the MN is disconnected from current AP as soon as FBU is sent, all packets arrived before receiving HAck are lost due to non-existence of the forward tunnel. If packets, which are sending from PAR after FBU received, are buffered in NAR, this may cause excessive burden to NAR buffer.
2) How a MN knows candidate APs without communication disruption with one antenna?
3) In [3], the use of L2 trigger is strongly recommended. But [3] does not mention when the L2 trigger occurs because this is implementation issue.

1) may cause excessive delay for real time traffic in FMIPv6, and 2) and 3) are implementation issues.

The delay problem is caused by the unclearness of preparation phase and handover phase in FMIPv6. If FBU is sent too early, all packets are forwarded to NAR so the MN cannot receive packets from PAR anymore and the buffering overhead of NAR is increased due to long buffering time. On the other hand, sending FBU too late may cause incomplete fast handover process and packet is lost because the link is disconnected before tunnel is set up. This phenomenon is due to the dual usages of FBU as preparing handover and handover signal. It is much better to sperate FBU's two functions into two signals. One is used to prepare handover - doing HI/HAck and tunneling setup and the other is actual handover signal. We restrict FBU function as the first role and propose new messages called Movement Notification (MvNoti) and Movement Acknowledgement (MvAck) to do the second function. This makes the separation of handover preparation and actual handover phases much clear in FMIPv6. Because FMIPv6 uses predictive method, we consider that the separation of handover preparation and actual handover is more desirable.

Even if the handover preparation is done before actual handover, the number of messages to be used in handover must be minimized as well. The needs of RtSolPr/PrRtAdv exchange is to generate NCoA based on NAR's RA by the MN. If network allocates NCoA rather than the MN, this exchange is not required. In semi-soft FMIPv6, RtSolPr/PrRtAdv exchange is eliminated and NAR allocates NCoA. The information sent in RtSolPr is included in FBU. PAR selects the NAR using its CAR (Candidate AR) table based on information sent in FBU. When NAR receives HI message from PAR, NAR allocates pre-configure duplicate-free NCoA address to MN in order to avoid DAD procedure. The NCoA is sent back to PAR using HAck. PAR uses the NCoA for tunneling preparation and gives it to the MN via FBAck. The allocation of duplicate-free address using advance DAD[5] instead of DAD is optional. The option is used to reduce DAD delay in HI/HAck exchange. When the preparation phase is end, the forwarding path setup is completed. We call this status as Semi-soft.

In FMIPv6, it uses L2 triggers to the starting point of preparation and actual handover procedure. [3] mentions that a MN must prepare the scan list of APs before starting FMIPv6 procedure. Unfortunately, IEEE 802.11 network adapter has only one antenna and it cannot usually be used to scan after an association with an AP is made. Therefore to scan APs, the association must be terminated and made re-association after scanning APs. This means current connections may disconnected due to scanning. This is unpractical. To solve this problem we use two antennas in one interface. One is used for communication and the other is used to scan APs passively. This does not violate any current IEEE 802.11 specification. Passive scanning antenna does not send any messages, so the power consumption will be minimal. The role of passive scanning module is selecting a candidate AP based on incoming signal strength and triggering L2 signaling for FBU and MvNoti. The triggering time is equivalent to RtSolPr and FBU in FMIPv6.

To make L2 triggering time for each step clear and to make handover procedure stable, we introduce four triggers: 1) Link Quality Cross the Target(LQCT), 2) Link Going Down(LGD), 3) Link Switch(LS) and 4) Link Up(LU) triggers. LQCT, LGD, and LU triggers are sent from L2 layer and LS trigger is sent to L2. L2 maintains neighbor AP list from periodical passive scanning. The entry of neighbor AP list contains all information about neighbor AP such as AP's MAC

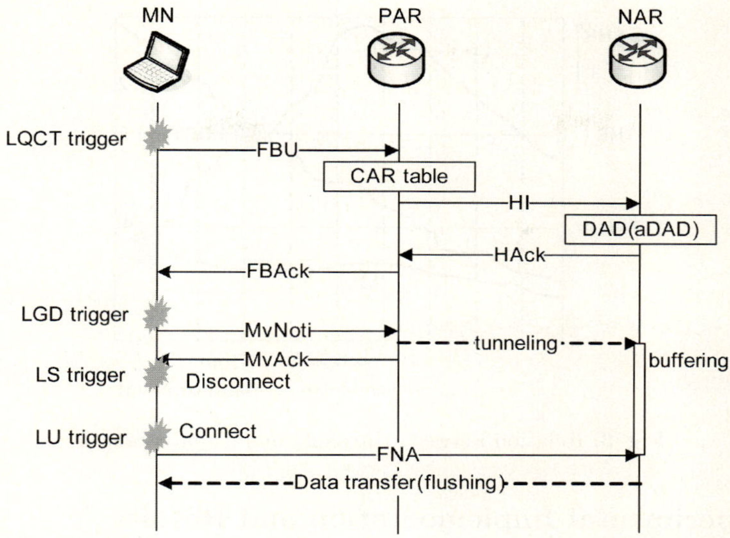

Fig. 2. The handover procedure of semi-soft FMIPv6 handover

address and signal strength. Neighbor APs are divided into candidate APs list and detected APs list. An AP in candidate APs list has enough signal strength that the MN can do handover to it. Among candidate APs, the AP having the highest signal strength becomes the target AP. LQCT trigger is generated when the signal strength of currently associated AP crosses that of the target AP. This cross point is called as THR I. The signal strength of any AP is varying, so THR I cannot be a fixed value. The second threshold, THR II, is set to certain signal strength as high as MvNoti can be surely sent before the association is terminated with current AP. When the signal strength of the current AP is going down to THR II, LGD trigger is sent to semi-soft FMIPv6 handover. When LGD is received, semi-soft FMIPv6 sends MvNoti to PAR. If semi-soft FMIPv6 receives MvAck, LS trigger is sent to L2 layer to start L2 handover. In FMIPv6, FMIPv6 does not mentioned when L2 layer should perform L2 handover. We make it clear by sending LS. When L2 handover is completed LU trigger is sent to semi-soft FMIPv6. LU trigger cause semi-soft FMIPv6 to send FNA to NAR. When NAR receives FNA from MN, it flushes all buffered packets. After this, the process of semi-soft FMIPv6 handover is done and the MN in new subnet can receive data packets and starts L3 handover using MIPv6. Fig. 2 shows semi-soft FMIPv6 handover flows including triggers.

Fig. 3 shows an example of the relation between two thresholds and signal strength. AP1 is currently associated AP, and AP2 and AP3 are neighbor APs. AP2 can be selected as the target AP and AP3 is a detected AP. LQCT trigger is occurred when the signal strength of AP1 and AP2 is crossed. As scanning is performed periodically, the actual trigger may not exactly matches the cross point. LGD is triggered when the signal strength of AP1 is below the THR II.

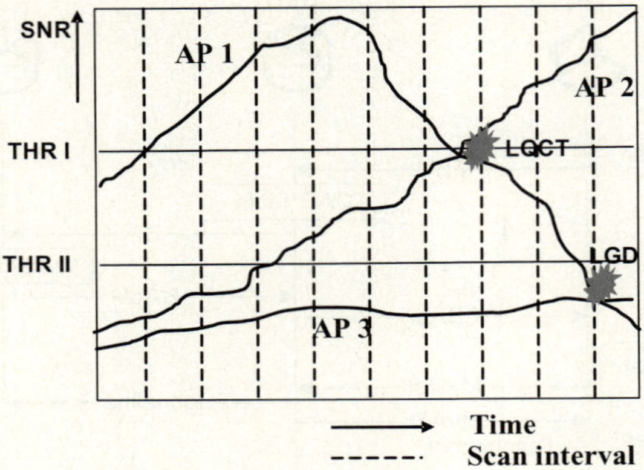

Fig. 3. Relation between threshold and signal strength

3 Experimental Implementation and Results

We perform experiment to verify the operation of semi-soft FMIPv6 handover procedures in test bed and to estimate the performance. Fig. 4 shows the network configuration of experimental environment. There are two client systems perform as a MN and a CN. The CN is fixed PC system and the MN has *Samsung Atmel* WLAN adapter for data communication and *Lucent Orinoco USB client silver* WLAN adapter for passive scanning. As the device driver of Atmel WLAN

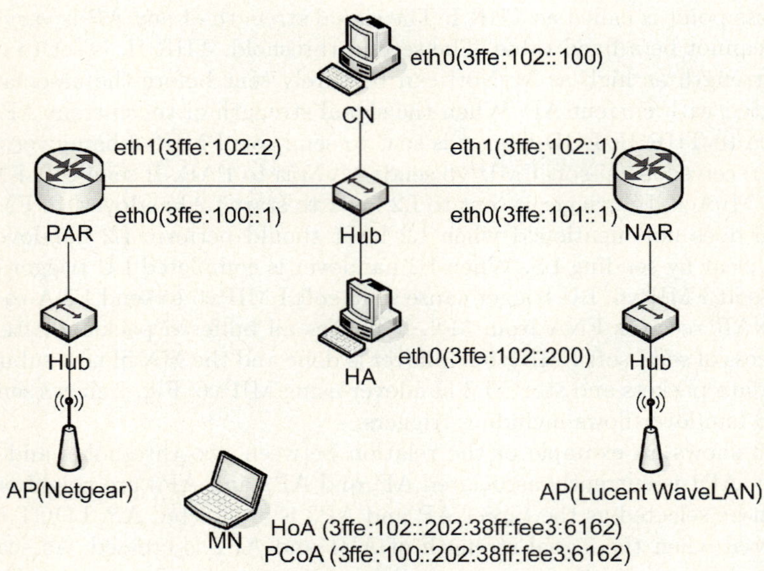

Fig. 4. Experiment test bed setting

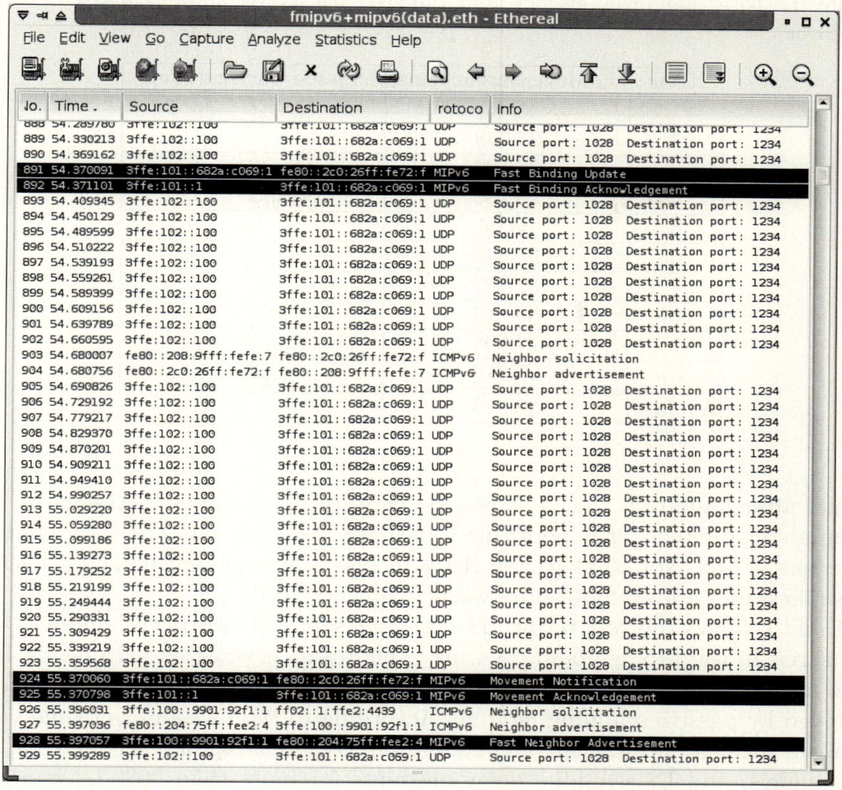

No.	Time	Source	Destination	Protocol	Info
888	54.289780	3ffe:102::100	3ffe:101::682a:c069:1	UDP	Source port: 1028 Destination port: 1234
889	54.330213	3ffe:102::100	3ffe:101::682a:c069:1	UDP	Source port: 1028 Destination port: 1234
890	54.369162	3ffe:102::100	3ffe:101::682a:c069:1	UDP	Source port: 1028 Destination port: 1234
891	54.370091	3ffe:101::682a:c069:1	fe80::2c0:26ff:fe72:f	MIPv6	Fast Binding Update
892	54.371101	3ffe:101::1	3ffe:101::682a:c069:1	MIPv6	Fast Binding Acknowledgement
893	54.409345	3ffe:102::100	3ffe:101::682a:c069:1	UDP	Source port: 1028 Destination port: 1234
894	54.450129	3ffe:102::100	3ffe:101::682a:c069:1	UDP	Source port: 1028 Destination port: 1234
895	54.489599	3ffe:102::100	3ffe:101::682a:c069:1	UDP	Source port: 1028 Destination port: 1234
896	54.510222	3ffe:102::100	3ffe:101::682a:c069:1	UDP	Source port: 1028 Destination port: 1234
897	54.539193	3ffe:102::100	3ffe:101::682a:c069:1	UDP	Source port: 1028 Destination port: 1234
898	54.559261	3ffe:102::100	3ffe:101::682a:c069:1	UDP	Source port: 1028 Destination port: 1234
899	54.589399	3ffe:102::100	3ffe:101::682a:c069:1	UDP	Source port: 1028 Destination port: 1234
900	54.609156	3ffe:102::100	3ffe:101::682a:c069:1	UDP	Source port: 1028 Destination port: 1234
901	54.639789	3ffe:102::100	3ffe:101::682a:c069:1	UDP	Source port: 1028 Destination port: 1234
902	54.660595	3ffe:102::100	3ffe:101::682a:c069:1	UDP	Source port: 1028 Destination port: 1234
903	54.680007	fe80::208:9fff:fefe:7	fe80::2c0:26ff:fe72:f	ICMPv6	Neighbor solicitation
904	54.680756	fe80::2c0:26ff:fe72:f	fe80::208:9fff:fefe:7	ICMPv6	Neighbor advertisement
905	54.690826	3ffe:102::100	3ffe:101::682a:c069:1	UDP	Source port: 1028 Destination port: 1234
906	54.729192	3ffe:102::100	3ffe:101::682a:c069:1	UDP	Source port: 1028 Destination port: 1234
907	54.779217	3ffe:102::100	3ffe:101::682a:c069:1	UDP	Source port: 1028 Destination port: 1234
908	54.829370	3ffe:102::100	3ffe:101::682a:c069:1	UDP	Source port: 1028 Destination port: 1234
909	54.870201	3ffe:102::100	3ffe:101::682a:c069:1	UDP	Source port: 1028 Destination port: 1234
910	54.909211	3ffe:102::100	3ffe:101::682a:c069:1	UDP	Source port: 1028 Destination port: 1234
911	54.949410	3ffe:102::100	3ffe:101::682a:c069:1	UDP	Source port: 1028 Destination port: 1234
912	54.990257	3ffe:102::100	3ffe:101::682a:c069:1	UDP	Source port: 1028 Destination port: 1234
913	55.029220	3ffe:102::100	3ffe:101::682a:c069:1	UDP	Source port: 1028 Destination port: 1234
914	55.059280	3ffe:102::100	3ffe:101::682a:c069:1	UDP	Source port: 1028 Destination port: 1234
915	55.099186	3ffe:102::100	3ffe:101::682a:c069:1	UDP	Source port: 1028 Destination port: 1234
916	55.139273	3ffe:102::100	3ffe:101::682a:c069:1	UDP	Source port: 1028 Destination port: 1234
917	55.179252	3ffe:102::100	3ffe:101::682a:c069:1	UDP	Source port: 1028 Destination port: 1234
918	55.219199	3ffe:102::100	3ffe:101::682a:c069:1	UDP	Source port: 1028 Destination port: 1234
919	55.249444	3ffe:102::100	3ffe:101::682a:c069:1	UDP	Source port: 1028 Destination port: 1234
920	55.290331	3ffe:102::100	3ffe:101::682a:c069:1	UDP	Source port: 1028 Destination port: 1234
921	55.309429	3ffe:102::100	3ffe:101::682a:c069:1	UDP	Source port: 1028 Destination port: 1234
922	55.339219	3ffe:102::100	3ffe:101::682a:c069:1	UDP	Source port: 1028 Destination port: 1234
923	55.359568	3ffe:102::100	3ffe:101::682a:c069:1	UDP	Source port: 1028 Destination port: 1234
924	55.370060	3ffe:101::682a:c069:1	fe80::2c0:26ff:fe72:f	MIPv6	Movement Notification
925	55.370798	3ffe:101::1	3ffe:101::682a:c069:1	MIPv6	Movement Acknowledgement
926	55.396031	3ffe:100::9901:92f1:1	ff02::1:ffe2:4439	ICMPv6	Neighbor solicitation
927	55.397036	fe80::204:75ff:fee2:4	3ffe:100::9901:92f1:1	ICMPv6	Neighbor advertisement
928	55.397057	3ffe:100::9901:92f1:1	fe80::204:75ff:fee2:4	MIPv6	Fast Neighbor Advertisement
929	55.399289	3ffe:102::100	3ffe:101::682a:c069:1	UDP	Source port: 1028 Destination port: 1234

Fig. 5. Packet flows of semi-soft FIMPv6 handover with a single handover

adapter did not supply enough information to do scanning manually, we have to use different adapter instead of using the same two Atmel WLAN adapters. The device driver of Orinoco WLAN adapter included in Linux kernel 2.4.20 is modified not to receive any packets and to do scanning periodically. PAR and NAR are modified to include semi-soft FMIPv6 handover functions and advanced DAD module based on Linux kernel 2.4.20 and for L3 handover, we used MIPv6 supplied by Samsung AIT. The test was performed using VLC streaming client[8] on MN and CN. We used the video stream sent from CN. The stream was transferred with UDP over RTP and the transmission speed of video was 300 Kbps.

We measured the handover latency in the MN and buffered packet count in NAR. The handover is performed periodically from AR1 to AR2 and AR2 to AR1; the MN moves between two APs periodically. The measurement of handover latency is done by capturing data with ethereal[9] at MN and calculating the time differences between last data packet before handover and first data

Table 1. Total handover latency and buffered packet count of semi-soft FMIPv6 handover

Trial	Handover latency(ms)	Buffered packets(count)
1	22.89	3
2	27.748	4
3	26.592	8
4	23.206	2
5	33.03	16
6	31.245	15
7	31.982	9
8	35.814	2
9	24.808	9
10	26.816	17
Average	28.413	8.5

packet after handover. Fig. 5 shows the captured packets with ethereal at MN when a single handover is performed. It shows the semi-soft FMIPv6 handover processes of MN. Note that HI and HAck messages are not shown in fig. 5 because these messages are exchanged between PAR and NAR.

Table 1 shows the test result. The average semi-soft FMIPv6 handover time measured in the MN is about 28.4 ms. This result is possible because L2 layer does not perform any scanning but it just tunes to the specific channel which is supplied by passive scanning module. According to [7], L2 handover time varies between 53.3ms and 420.8ms depending on WLAN adapters, AP makers, and AP models, and L2 scanning delay accounts for more than 90% L2 handover time. Therefore semi-soft FMIPv6 handover delay takes nearly a half of the best L2 handover time. Semi-soft FMIPv6 handover delay includes all semi-soft FMIPv6 handover delay and L2 handover time. The average buffer packets in NAR is 8.5 packets per 28.5ms. If the handover latency is one second, the average buffer packets should be 298 packets for 300Kbps flow. If several handovers with one second handover time had occurred simultaneously, NAR must have faced serious buffering problem.

4 Conclusion

Mobility support in the wireless network enables us to be served continuous service. Fast Handover for Mobile IPv6 (FMIPv6) is proposed to support a faster handover than that of Mobile IPv6. Unfortunately, FMIPv6 shows too long handover latency to serve smooth video traffic flows.

We proposed semi-soft FMIPv6 handover scheme. FMIPv6 may be unsuitable for video traffic due to excessive handover delay. The excessive delay is caused by unclearness of handover preparation and handover itself. Semi-soft FMIPv6 handover makes the separation of preparation and handover phase clear and optimizes message flows. In addition, we clarify the use of L2 triggering by introducing four triggers and triggering time scheme. Our test result shows the handover latency of semi-soft FMIPv6 handover is about 28.4ms. The latency is less than a half of most L2 handover latency of various WLAN devices.

With semi-soft FMIPv6 handover procedure, video traffic can serve more smoothly and the overhead of buffering at access routers also reduced so that access routers can support handover more efficiently.

References

1. D. Johnson, C. Perkins and J. Arkko, "Mobility Support in IPv6," RFC3775, June 2004.
2. S. Sharma, N. Zhu and T. Chiueh, "Low-Latency Mobile IP Handoff for Infrastructure-Mode Wireless LANs," IEEE Journal on Selected Areas in Communications, May 2004.
3. R. Koodli, Ed., "Fast Handovers for Mobile IPv6," RFC4068, July 2005.
4. S. Thomson and T. Narten, "IPv6 Stateless Address Autoconfiguration," RFC2462, December 1998.
5. Y. Han, "Advance Duplicate Address Detection," Internet Engineering Task Force (IETF) draft-han-mobileip-adad-01.txt, July 2003.
6. N. Montavont and T. Noël, "Analysis and Evaluation of Mobile IPv6 Handovers over Wireless LAN," Mobile Networks and Applications, December 2003.
7. A. Mishra, M. Shin, and W. Arbaugh, "An Empirical Analysis of the IEEE 802.11 MAC Layer Handoff Process," ACM SIGCOMM Computer Communications Review, April 2003.
8. VideoLan Client, Available from http://www.videolan.org/vlc
9. Ethereal, Available from http://www.ethereal.com

An Optimized Scheme for Mobile IPv6 Handover Between Domains Based on AAA*

Seonggeun Ryu and Youngsong Mun

School of Computing, Soongsil University,
Sangdo 5 Dong Dongjak Gu, Seoul, Korea
sgryu@sunny.ssu.ac.kr, mun@computing.ssu.ac.kr

Abstract. When Mobile IPv6 is deployed in commercial network, a mobile node needs AAA services for authentication, authorization and accounting. AAA and Mobile IPv6 are operated independently. Hence schemes which merge these protocols have been emerged. These schemes enable the mobile node to establish a security association between the mobile node and a home agent, and to perform a home binding update during AAA authentication procedure. But these schemes introduce lots of signal messages and long handover latency during the handover, since Route Optimization mode for Mobile IPv6 is performed using Return Routability procedure. To solve this problem, we propose an optimized scheme which performs Route Optimization mode via the AAA infrastructure between the home agent and a correspondent node instead of Return Routability procedure. For performance evaluation, we analyze handover latency in three scenarios. We then show that the proposed scheme reduces handover latency like the average of 58% compared with the existing scheme.

1 Introduction

As mobile devices like laptops and PDAs are improved and wireless/mobile communications and networking were propagated widely, mobile users for Internet access have increased. Hence mobility support between administrative domains is required, since these users want to use a high-quality Internet service at any administrative domain.

Mobile IPv6 [1] which supports mobility of a mobile node (MN) in IPv6 networks has been standardized by Internet Engineering Task Forces (IETF). When Mobile IPv6 is deployed in commercial network, the MN needs AAA services for authentication, authorization and accounting. AAA and Mobile IPv6 are operated independently. Hence schemes which merge these protocols have been emerged. Frank Le's scheme [2] among these schemes can support a fast handover, since it enables the MN to establish a security association between the MN

* This research was supported by the MIC(Ministry of Information and Communication), Korea, under the ITRC(Information Technology Research Center) support program supervised by the IITA(IITA-2005-C1090-0502-0009).

E. Sha et al. (Eds.): EUC 2006, LNCS 4096, pp. 1148–1157, 2006.

and its home agent (HA), and to perform a home binding update during AAA authentication procedure. However, this scheme introduces lots of signal messages and long handover latency during the handover, because Route Optimization mode for Mobile IPv6 is performed by using Return Routability procedure. Return Routability procedure consists of Home of Test Init (HoTI) / Home of Test (HoT) and Care-of Test Init (CoTI) / Care-of Test (CoT) messages which cause long handover latency.

To solve this problem, we propose an optimized scheme for Route Optimization mode by using the AAA infrastructure between the HA and a correspondent node (CN) instead of Return Routability procedure. When the MN performs AAA procedure, it embeds a home Binding Update (BU) message and the CN's information (address and the Network Access Identifier (NAI) [3]) in a request message of AAA procedure. The BU message and the CN's information are delivered to the HA through AAA procedure. After the HA performs the home binding update, it creates a BU message to the CN for Route Optimization mode. The HA then sends the BU message to the CN via the AAA infrastructure between itself and the CN.

The proposed scheme can reduce signal messages and handover latency during the handover, because Return Routability procedure for Route Optimization mode is not performed. The proposed scheme also can get a security benefit, since it uses the AAA infrastructure which is secured by IPsec [6] and TLS [7].

The rest of this paper is organized as follows: in section 2, basic protocols and Frank Le's scheme are presented as related works. The proposed scheme is described in section 3, and in section 4 the proposed scheme is evaluated through analysis of handover latency. Finally, in section 5 we conclude discussion with future study.

2 Related Works

Mobile IPv6 protocol enables an MN to keep connections to an HA and a CN, although the MN changes a point of attachment to network. In Mobile IPv6 the MN has two addresses of a home address (HoA) and a care-of address (CoA). The HoA is generated in a home network, which never be changed although the MN moves into another network, and hence the HA and the CN identify the MN as the HoA. The CoA is generated in a visited network whenever it moves, and represents a current location. Mobile IPv6 protocol binds the CoA to the HoA. In Mobile IPv6 the MN uses Route Optimization mode consisting of Return Routability procedure and a binding update to the CN to communicate with the CN directly. Return Routability procedure consists of HoTI/HoT and CoTI/CoT message, and it generates a key between the MN and the CN, and then a BU message to the CN is authenticated by the generated key. Whenever the MN moves between networks, a process for mobility support is required and is called a handover. The handover consists of a movement detection, an address configuration, a home binding update, Return Routability procedure, and a binding update to the CN. The MN cannot communicate with the CN during the handover.

When Mobile IPv6 is deployed in commercial networks, the MN needs AAA [4] services to allow it to access to any service provided by an administrative domain different from its home domain. AAA supports authentication and authorization for the MN and collects MN's accounting information [5]. AAA is a distributed security model which consists of distributed clients and central servers. In AAA, all of connections between entities are secured by IPsec and additionally by TLS.

When the MN moves into a foreign domain, it needs authorization to attach to the foreign domain. Hence AAA is required to enable the MN to get access to the foreign domain. After getting the access permission to the foreign domain through AAA, Mobile IPv6 is performed to support mobility. These two protocols are performed in order, so signal messages and handover latency are increased. Schemes which merge two protocols have studied to solve these problems. This paper is based on Frank Le's scheme among these schemes.

In Frank Le's draft, he specifies a new application to Diameter [8] that enables Mobile IPv6 to roam between administrative domains, and provides a solution for Mobile IPv6 and AAA interworking. Besides supporting authentication and authorization for the MN, the AAA infrastructure can also be used for distributing the security association which is necessary to support mobility. Optionally, the AAA infrastructure can be used to optimize authentication, authorization and mobility in a common procedure. In this paper, we focus on the optimization scheme in Frank Le's draft.

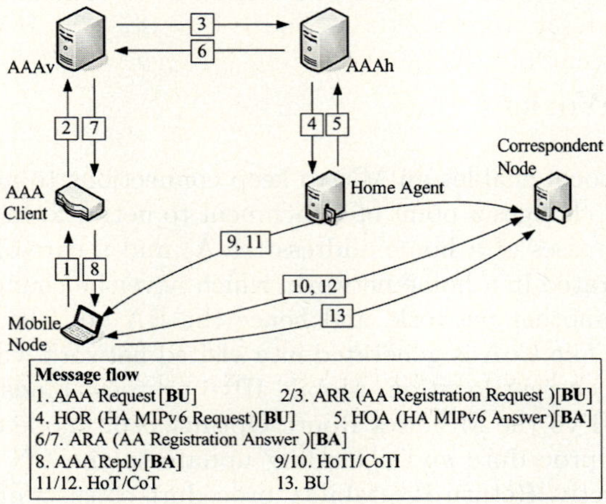

Fig. 1. Message flows of Frank Le's scheme

Figure 1 shows message flows of Frank Le's scheme, and the numbers in Fig. 1 are the order of flows. When entering a foreign administrative domain, the MN receives router advertisements and it retrieves the local challenge, the visited network identifier and the information to derive a CoA. The MN computes the CoA and creates the request message with the CoA as the source IP address, the AAA Client address as the destination IP address, the NAI, the long-term security key shared with its AAAh, and other parameters. The MN creates the BU message, which will be embedded in the request message. The BU message will be forwarded to the designated HA via the AAA infrastructure. The MN then sends the request message to the AAA Client. Frank Le's draft does not define how the authentication information is exchanged between the MN and the AAA Client. This may be performed using the protocol defined by the PANA working group in IETF.

When the AAA Client receives the request message, it converts this message to the AA Registration Request (ARR) message. The ARR message includes the MN's NAI, MIP-Home-Binding-Update AVP containing the BU message and other AVPs. The AAA Client sends the ARR message to the AAA home server (AAAh) via the AAA visited server (AAAv). When receiving the ARR message from the AAAv, the AAAh verifies the message coming from a valid AAAv. The AAAh then authenticates the user using the NAI provided by the MN. The AAAh forwards the MIP-Home-Binding-Update AVP to the HA in the HA MIPv6 Request (HOR) message. If the MN asks for some security keys, the AAAh performs the appropriate steps and eventually sends the corresponding messages in order to achieve the key distribution.

Upon receipt of the HOR message, the HA verifies the message. It processes the MIP-Home-Binding-Update AVP, updates the Binding Cache Entry (BCE), and then creates the Binding Acknowledgement (BA) message. If the MN requests key distribution, the HA computes the key for the security association with the MN from the received data. The HA creates the HA MIPv6 Answer (HOA) message including the MIP-Binding-Acknowledgement AVP containing the BA message, and it then send the HOA message to the AAAh.

After receiving the HOA message, the AAAh verifies the message. The AAAh then creates the AA Registration Answer (ARA) message including MIP-Binding-Acknowledgement AVP and other AVPs, and sends the message to the AAA Client via the AAAv. When receiving the ARA message from the AAAv, the AAA Client converts the message to a reply message and sends the reply message to the MN.

When receiving the reply message from the AAA Client, the MN authenticates the network according to the network authentication data sent by the AAA Client. If the MN requested the key distribution, it creates the security associations from the received keying material. The MN then processes the BA message, and it performs Return Routability procedure, which the HoTI/HoT and CoTI/CoT messages are exchanged between the MN and the CN. The MN then creates a BU message and sends the BU message to the CN. When receiving the BU message from the MN, the CN updates the BCE for the MN. Finally, the handover is completed and the MN and the CN can communicate directly.

3 The Proposed Scheme

Frank Le's scheme can optimize a handover, since the AAA infrastructure can be used to support mobility procedures and to optimize authentication, authorization and mobility in a common procedure. However, Frank Le's scheme must perform Return Routability procedure for Route Optimization mode. Therefore, handover latency is long because of messages used in Return Routability procedure.

To solve this problem, we propose an optimized scheme for Route Optimization mode by using the AAA infrastructure between the HA and a CN instead of Return Routability procedure. When the MN requests AAA authentication, it embeds a home BU message and the CN's information (address and NAI) in a request message of AAA procedure. When the HA receives the BU message and CN's information via the AAA infrastructure, it performs the home binding update and creates a BU message to the CN. The HA then sends the BU message to the CN via the AAA infrastructure between itself and the CN.

For the proposed scheme, we assume the followings. The proposed scheme is based on Frank Le's scheme, and the CN must be supported by AAA. When the MN sends the request message to an AAA Client, the CN's address and NAI must be able to be embedded in the message. The MN must have known the CN's NAI using an appropriate manner in advance. The CN's address and NAI will be forwarded from the MN to the HA via the AAA infrastructure. The HA must be able to create an AAA message like as the ARR message, and then an MIP-CN-Binding-Update AVP containing a BU message for the CN must be included in the created message. We define the MIP-CN-Binding-Update AVP like as the MIP-Home-Binding-Update AVP in Frank Le's scheme. The CN must be able to process the MIP-CN-Binding-Update AVP.

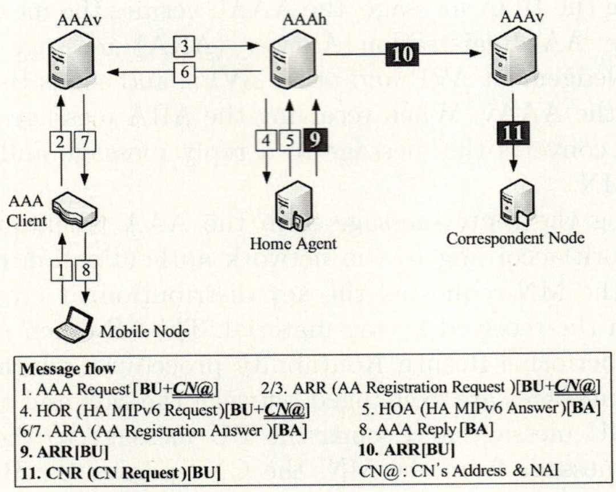

Fig. 2. Message flows of the proposed scheme

Figure 2 shows message flows of the proposed scheme, and the numbers in Fig. 2 are the order of flows. In the proposed scheme the processes from the number 1 to the number 8 in Fig. 2 are the same as Frank Le's scheme except the case that the CN's address and NAI are included in the AAA request.

When receiving the HOR message from AAAh, the HA processes MIP-Home-Binding-Update AVP and creates a BA message. The HA then creates a BU message for the CN with the MN's CoA as the source IP address, the CN's address as the destination IP address, and the MN's HoA as the home address option. The BU message is converted into a MIP-CN-Binding-Update AVP. The HA then sends the ARR message including the MIP-CN-Binding-Update AVP to CN's NAI. Upon receipt of the ARR message, the CN processes the MIP-CN-Binding-Update AVP, and then BCE for the MN is updated. Finally, Route Optimization mode is completed and the MN and the CN can communicate directly.

The proposed scheme does not need Return Routability procedure for Route Optimization mode, because the mode is completed via the AAA infrastructure. Therefore, the proposed scheme can reduce signal messages and handover latency.

4 Performance Evaluations

In this section we make an analytic comparison of Frank Le's scheme with the proposed scheme in terms of handover latency. The handover latency consists of link layer establishment delay and signaling delay. We focus on signaling delay, since protocols of link layer are various. Hence, we define a period of handover latency as one from a moment of the movement detection to a moment of Route Optimization mode. For simplicity we consider the model illustrated in Fig. 3 referring to [9].

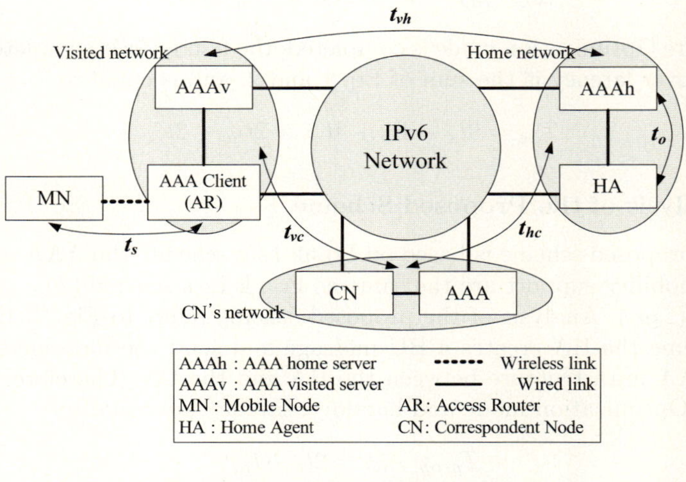

Fig. 3. A simple model for analysis

The notations in Fig. 3 are used as the followings, referring to [9], [10]. The delay between the MN and the AAA Client is t_s, which is the time to send a message over the subnet via wireless link. Also, the delay between entities in a same network is t_o , which is the time to send a message over one hop via wired link. The delay between the entities in the visited network and the entities in the home network is t_{vh}, the delay between the entities in the home network and the entities in the CN's network is t_{hc}, and the delay between the entities in the visited network and the entities in the CN's network is t_{vc}. In this paper we only consider the scenario where the CN is in its home network, although the CN is a mobile node. In general, we assume that the processing and queuing times are negligible, since these times are much shorter than above times [10].

4.1 Analysis of Frank Le's Scheme

We analyze Frank Le's scheme referring to Fig. 1. In Frank Le's scheme AAA procedure and mobility support are performed in a common procedure. Therefore, the time for the AAA authentication and mobility support is given by

$$T_{Le-AAA-BU} = 4t_s + 4t_o + 2t_{vh}. \tag{1}$$

$T_{Le-AAA-BU}$ is a transmission time consisting of transmission times for Router Solicitation(RS)/Router Advertisement(RA) messages and messages from the number 1 to the number 8 in Fig. 1.

After the home binding, the MN performs Return Routability procedure for Route Optimization mode. In the procedure HoTI/HoT and CoTI/CoT messages are exchanged between the MN and the CN referring to Fig. 1. The MN then creates a BU message and sends the message to the CN. Therefore, Route Optimization mode is completed and the time for this procedure is given by

$$T_{Le-RO} = 5t_s + 2t_{vh} + 2t_{hc} + 2t_{vc}. \tag{2}$$

When Route Optimization mode is completed, the handover is completed. Therefore, handover latency is the sum of Eq. 1 and 2, and is equal to

$$T_{Le} = 9t_s + 4t_o + 4t_{vh} + 2t_{hc} + 2t_{vc}. \tag{3}$$

4.2 Analysis of the Proposed Scheme

Since the proposed scheme is based on Frank Le's scheme, the AAA authentication and mobility support are the same as Frank Le's scheme ($T_{Le-AAA-BU} = T_{prop.-AAA-BU}$). Analysis of the proposed scheme refers to Fig. 2. In the proposed scheme the HA creates a BU message and send the message to the CN via the AAA infrastructure between the HA and the CN. Therefore, the times for Route Optimization mode and handover latency are equal to

$$T_{prop.-RO} = 2t_o + t_{hc}, \tag{4}$$

$$T_{prop.} = 4t_s + 6t_o + 2t_{vh} + t_{hc}. \tag{5}$$

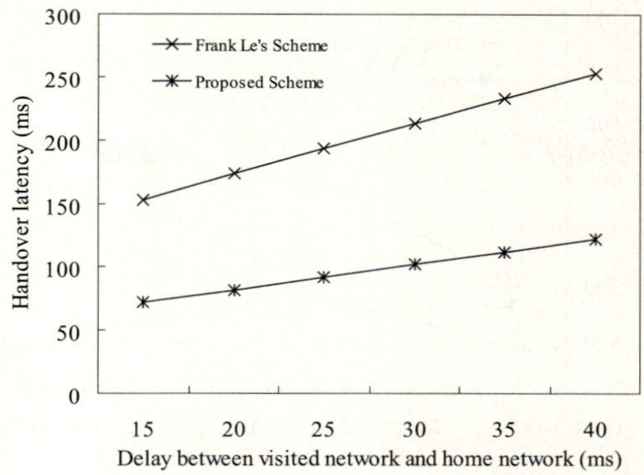

Fig. 4. Handover latency vs. delay between the MN and its home network

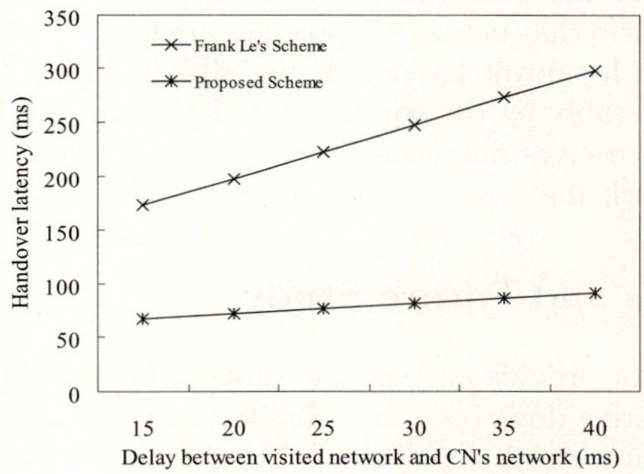

Fig. 5. Handover latency vs. delay between the MN and the CN

4.3 Numerical Results

In this section we present some results based on the previous analysis. We assume $t_s = 10ms$ and $t_o = 2ms$ as in [9], considering relatively low bandwidth in the wireless link. Handover latencies for two schemes are calculated by Eq. 3 and 5 in three scenarios, respectively.

Impact of the delay between the MN and its home network. We set $t_{vc} = 5ms$ and $t_{hc} = 10ms$, since we assume in this scenario that the distance between the visited network and the CN's network is close. Figure 4 shows handover latencies according to t_{vh}, and it shows that the proposed scheme reduces handover latency in comparison with Frank Le's scheme.

Impact of the delay between the MN and the CN. We set $t_{vh} = 0$ and $t_{vc} = t_{hc}$, since we assume in this scenario that the MN is in its home network. In Fig. 5 handover latencies of the proposed scheme hardly increase according to t_{vc}, since Route Optimization mode for the proposed scheme does not use networks between the MN and the CN.

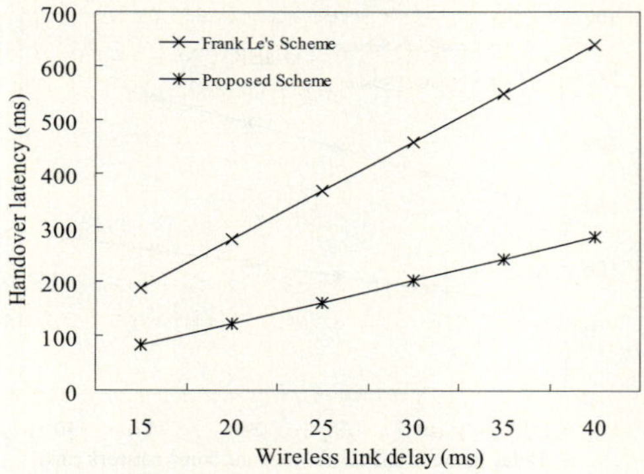

Fig. 6. Handover latency vs. wireless link delay

Impact of the wireless link delay. We set $t_{vh} = t_{hc} = t_{vc} = 10ms$, since we assume in this scenario that network topologies are fixed. The wireless link delay has an influence on handover latency. Especially, in Fig. 6 Frank Le's scheme is influenced considerably by the wireless link delay, since in Frank Le's scheme the MN sends and receives many messages via the wireless link in comparison with the proposed scheme.

5 Conclusions and Future Study

Mobile IPv6 does not provide any specific support for mobility passing through different administrative domains, which limits the applicability of Mobile IPv6 in a large scale commercial deployment. For Mobile IPv6 to be deployed in commercial networks, there therefore has to be AAA support for the protocol. Frank Le's scheme provides a solution for Mobile IPv6 and AAA interworking. It also can support a fast handover, since it enables an MN to establish a security association between the MN and an HA, and to perform a home binding update through AAA procedure. However, Frank Le's scheme introduces a lot of signal messages and long handover latency during the handover, since Route Optimization mode is performed using Return Routability procedure.

To solve this problem, we propose an optimized scheme for Route Optimization mode that the HA performs the binding update for a CN by using the AAA infrastructure between the HA and the CN instead of Return Routability procedure. The proposed scheme can reduce handover latency during the handover, because Return Routability procedure for Route Optimization mode is not performed. The proposed scheme also can get a security benefit, since it uses the AAA infrastructure which is secured by IPsec and TLS. We have shown that the proposed scheme reduces handover latency like the average of 58% by comparison with Frank Le's scheme.

Fast Handovers for Mobile IPv6 (FMIPv6) [11] and Hierarchical MIPv6 (H MIPv6) [12] have been standardized in IETF. FMIPv6 is a enhanced handover scheme for Mobile IPv6, as portions of layer 3 handover are peformed layer 2 handover. HMIPv6 reduces location updates, since mobility is managed locally. Therefore, the proposed scheme can be considered to be used in FMIPv6 or HMIPv6, since these mechanisms have enhanced Mobile IPv6.

References

1. Johnson, D., Perkins, C., and Arkko J.: Mobility Support in IPv6, RFC 3775 (2004)
2. Le, F., Patil, B., Perkins, C., and Faccin, C.: Diameter Mobile IPv6 Application, Internet-Draft (2004)
3. Aboba, B. and Beadles, M.: The Network Access Identifier, RFC 2486 (1999)
4. Laat, C. de, Gross, G., Gommans, L. Vollbrecht, J., and Spence, D.: Generic AAA Architecture, RFC 2903 (2000)
5. Glass, S., Hiller, T., Jacobs, S., and Perkins, C.: Mobile IP Authentication, Authorization, and Accounting Requirements, RFC 2977 (2000)
6. Kent, S. and Seo, K.: Security Architecture for the Internet Protocol, RFC 4301 (2005)
7. Blake-Wilson, S., Nystrom, M., Hopwood, D., Mikkelsen, J., and Wright T.: Transport Layer Security (TLS) Extensions, RFC 3546 (2003)
8. Calhoun, P., Loughney, J., Guttman, E., Zorn, G., and Arkko, J.: Diameter Base Protocol, RFC 3588 (2003)
9. Kwon, T., Gerla, M., Das, S., and Das, S.: Mobility Management for VoIP Service: Mobile IP vs. SIP, IEEE Wireless Communications (2002) 66-75
10. Fathi, H., Prasad, R., and Chakraborty, S.: Mobility Management for VoIP in 3G Systems: Evaluation of Low-Latency Handoff Schemes, IEEE Wireless Communications (2005) 96-104
11. Koodli, R.: Fast Handovers for Mobile IPv6, RFC 4068 (2005)
12. Soliman, H., Castelluccia, C., Malki, K., and Bellier, L.: Hierarchical Mobile IPv6 Mobility Management (HMIPv6), RFC 4140 (2005)

Interoperation of Home and Mobile Network Devices Employing a Jini-Agent System

Sang Tae Kim and Hyun Deok Kim

Dept. of Electronic Engineering, Kyungpook National University, Daegu 702-701, South Korea
hyundkim@ee.knu.ac.kr

Abstract. The interoperation of home electronic devices and mobile devices has been demonstrated employing a Jini-agent system. The agent system enables a resource-limited mobile device to support a Jini network service by using a web browser of the mobile device without any additional client program installation in it. It provides the lies of services existing on different networks simultaneously, which facilitates the users to utilize various Jini network services in real time and enables the interworking between home and mobile networks.

1 Introduction

As the mobile devices become more powerful enough to support much more sophisticated applications, the interoperation between mobile devices and other devices become more important. The mobile device should be able to interact with other mobile devices and even with non-mobile devices anytime and anywhere in the world to provide seamless interworking services. The agent system plays a key role to realize such an interoperation since the devices may employ different operating systems, different platforms and different protocols [1].

Though various middlewares are available at this moment, it is not easy to realize the interoperation between the traditional networked devices such as personal computers and home electronic devices and the mobile devices since the resource of the mobile devices may not be sufficient to operate a middleware required for the interoperation. For example, the Jini is one of the widely used middlewares for the interworking between the home network devices and the home appliances. However, the Jini network technology cannot be applied directly to the mobile devices since the resources of the mobile device such as a processing power and a memory size are not sufficient to support a Java virtual machine (JVM) [2]. Most of middlewares have similar problems since they have been developed originally as a part of the desktop applications and thus they are too heavy to apply directly to the mobile devices [3]-[4].

It is also important to provide the users a user-friendly interface on the mobile device to facilitate the uses of the interworking services through the mobile device. The web browser has been one of the most widely used user interfaces even in the mobile devices. The users can utilize any service on the network through the web browser. Thus the web browser is a very promising user interface to

E. Sha et al. (Eds.): EUC 2006, LNCS 4096, pp. 1158–1165, 2006.

implement an interworking service between mobile devices and other electronic devices.

In this paper, we demonstrate a web-based Jini agent system employing Jini network technology to provide a seamless interworking service between the wired network elements and the mobile devices. The web-based Jini agent system enables the resource-limited mobile device to participate in Jini network without any additional client program installation in the device. The interworking service is provided through a web browser, which enables the users utilize any service on the Jini network through a user-friendly interface of the mobile device. In the section 2, we will briefly review the Jini network technology. After that we will describe the web-based Jini agent system in section 3 and the experimental results in section 4. The conclusion will be given in section 5.

2 Jini Network Technology for Mobile Devices

The Jini network technology is built around the Java programming language and environment. It provides an object-oriented distributed network where the devices and the applications are treated as services. The users can easily utilize the services through the network without any changing of the specific configuration of the client. In addition, there is no need to install any additional programs such as device drivers into the client. It is easy to manage the network dynamically since the Jini network is a distributed network. The Jini network technology supports a plug and play operation when a device or an application is added to the network. The Jini network components are composed of a service provider, a client and a lookup service as shown in Fig. 1. The Jini network components transmit and receive the Proxy, also known as Java objects, which simplify the network management and enable the plug and play operation [5].

The plug and play operation of the Jini network is a very important feature since it facilitates the internetworking between devices even in different networks. Namely, the user can easily add or remove devices of applications without any

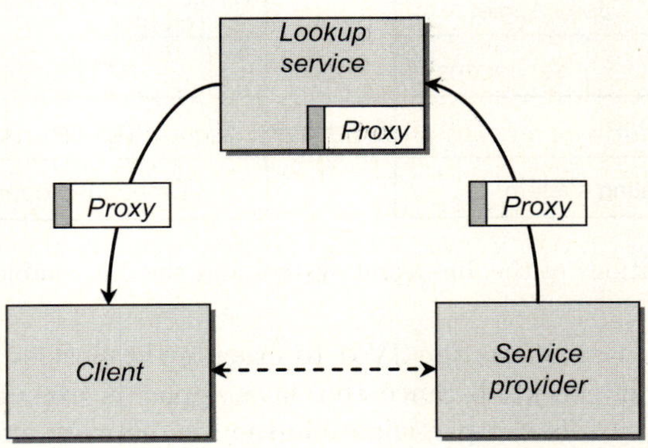

Fig. 1. Jini network components

information on the devices and the applications. However, the Jini network requires a Java platform. There are three platforms in Java, Java Standard Edition (J2SE), Java Enterprise Edition (J2EE) and Java Micro Edition (J2ME). The JVM is used to operate a Java program and the J2SE and the J2EE uses JVM, while the J2ME uses other virtual machines such as a kilobyte virtual machine (KVM) and a classic virtual machine (CVM) [6].

The Jini network technology is originally developed for a desktop environment and implemented by using a JVM. However, the mobile devices such as cellular phones and portable digital assistants (PDAs) have insufficient resources and suffer from the problems in performing the operations related a floating point, a reflection and an error processing. Namely, it is difficult to apply the Jini technology to a mobile device since the mobile device may not support the JVM due to a resource limitation. Thus, it is important to develop a Jini agent which enables a mobile device to participate in the Jini network even when the resources of the device are insufficient. To realize the interoperation between home electronic devices and mobile devices we implemented a web-based Jini agent system, which enables the resource-limited mobile device participates in the Jini network without the JVM.

3 Jini Agent Systems

Recently, the web browsers are widely used in various electric devices such as a workstation, a personal computer (PC) and even a mobile device. Thus we have implemented the Jini agent system based on a web browser, which will facilitate the users to utilize the Jini network services by using a user-friendly web browser of the mobile device. The configurations of the web-based Jini agent system and the Jini-enabled mobile device are shown in Fig. 2.

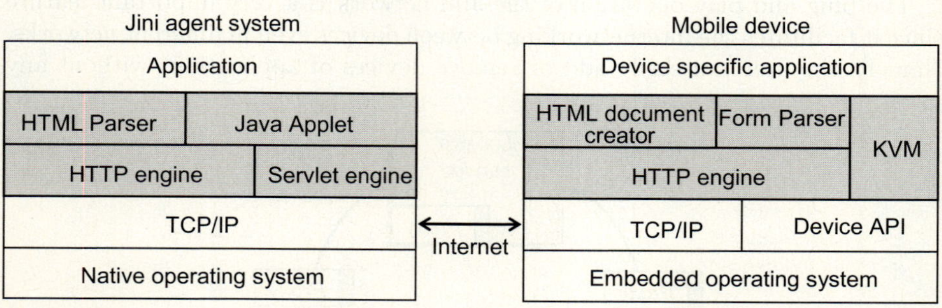

Fig. 2. Configurations of the Jini agent system and the Jini-enabled mobile device

The Jini agent system has the JVM to execute the Servlet engine on which the Java Applet is executed. Since the Java applet is executed in the agent system the agent system can participate in the Jini network and utilize the Jini network services. The agent system also has a HTTP engine and HTTP Parser to support a web-based service. Since the Java applet is executed in the agent system, there is no need to install JVM in the mobile device. The mobile device has been implemented by using the KVM which is widely used in mobile devices to support Java environments.

The mobile device has a HTTP engine and a HTML document creator to support a web browser. The web browser of the mobile device is used to access the Jini agent system by using a HTTP protocol. If the mobile device is accessed to the agent system, Java Applet of the agent system is downloaded to the mobile devices. Thus, the users can access the Servlet engine of the agent system through the web browser of the mobile device. The Form Parser of the mobile device converts the Java message transmitted from the agent system to a proper one readable via the HTML. The connection between the Jini agent system and the mobile devices is established by using a TCP/IP interface. Other devices are also connected to the Jini agent system through the TCP/IP interface.

4 Experimental Results

To evaluate the validity of the proposed web-based Jini agent system, we implemented a Jini network with the agent system. The network configuration is shown in Fig. 3. The client mobile device was connected to a public internet service provider (ISP) network though a wireless access local access network (LAN) and the web-based Jini agent system located on a home network which was connected to the public ISP network through Ethernet interface. The home network devices were a personal computer (PC) with a file server, a printer and a scanner. The client mobile device was a PDA (*Compaq iPAQ PocketPC H*4700). The operating system of the PDA was Microsoft Windows for Consumer Electronics (CE). The version of the Java was J2sdk 1.3.1.

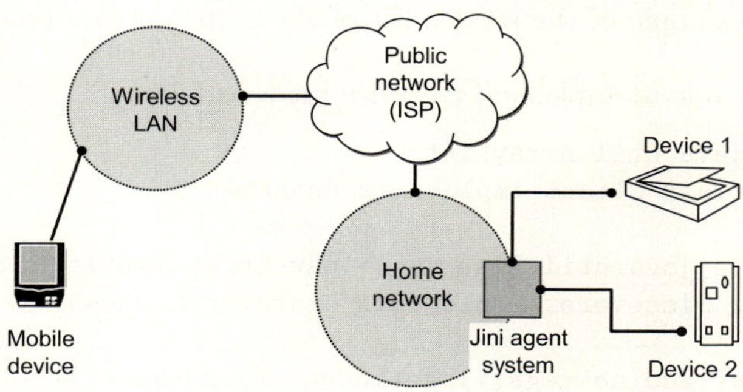

Fig. 3. Jini network with web-based Jini agent system

Both the browsers of the mobile device and the web-based Jini agent system were Microsoft Internet Explorer. The user interface of the mobile device was implemented by using a Java applet and the web server of the agent system was implemented by using a Servlet. It is notable that we installed Jeode virtual machine into the client to support a Java applet since the Microsoft Internet Explorer included in the Windows CE does not support a Java applet [7].

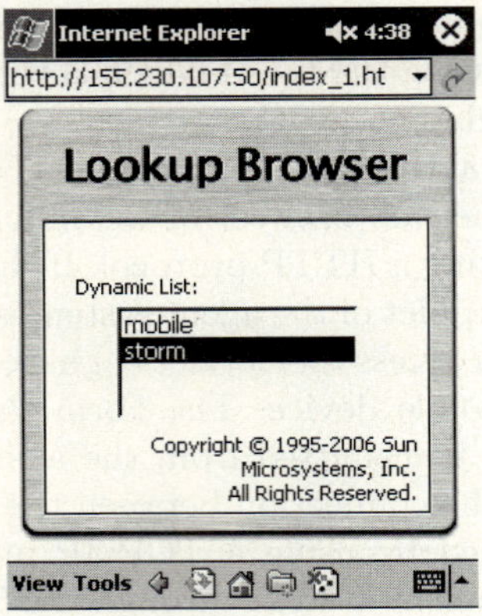

Fig. 4. The service list available on the network

The web-based Jini agent system was implemented to provide a service list available to the client and thus the users can easily search the services available in the Jini network. The servlet of the agent system receives the proxy ID and the service ID of the specific service registered to the Jini network from the Jini Lookup Service. The servlet lists up the available service list form the proxy ID and the service ID and provides the service list available to the mobile device. The process of the service list provision is as follows. The constructor of the service list initializes the user interface and sets up all the objects required for the client to participate in the Jini network. It also creates a `Discoverer`, which tries to discover the services available through a `DiscoveryListener` on a `LookupDiscovery` instance. Finally, the constructor display `ServiceItem` to the user. An example of the service list of the mobile device (client) is shown in Fig. 4.

The source code to implement a service list is as follows:

```
import java.util.ArrayList;
public class Client implements Runnable
 {
  private java.util.List vec = new ArrayList();
   class Discoverer implements DiscoveryListener
    {
      vec.add(newregs[i].getLocator().getHost()+" ");
        for(int j = 0; j < vec.size(); j++)
        {
           dic += (String)vec.get(j);
        }
    }
 }
```

Jini network technology provides a security policy by using Java2 security mechanisms, which grants the client the right to access a specific service provider.

Each client should have the security policy file denoting the right of access and the client should submit the policy file through a `java.security.policy property` property to the lookup server to utilize any Jini service. The lookup server examines the policy file submitted from the client and determines whether to allow or to deny the access requested by the client. We have created two policy files, one for the agent system and the other for the mobile device. Two files are similar but the policy file of agent system denotes the right to access the Jini network, while the other policy file denotes the right to access only the agent system. The policy files include a security file as a subset. Following is the context of the security file of the mobile device.

```
grant { permission java.security.AllPermission; };
```

The policy file was registered in `java.security.policy` of mobile device and the context of the policy file as follows.

```
policy.url.3=file:/Windows/lib/security/mypolicy
```

We have demonstrated two exemplary services, a file download service and a printing service. The selection process of the file to be downloaded from the file server on the Jini network is shown in Fig. 5(a) and the downloading process is shown in Fig. 5(b). If the user select a file server from the service list through the web browser of the client, the client sends the proxy ID and the service ID of the file server to the agent system. The agent system searches the file server and informs the client of the usability of the file server. After receiving the message, the client accesses the file server and the user can download the files in the file server. Since the Java applet is downloaded from the agent system in initial connection, the user can download the file by executing the Java applet through a web browser. Thus there is no need to install the Java applet in the mobile device, which makes it possible to utilize a Jini network service with a resource-limited mobile device.

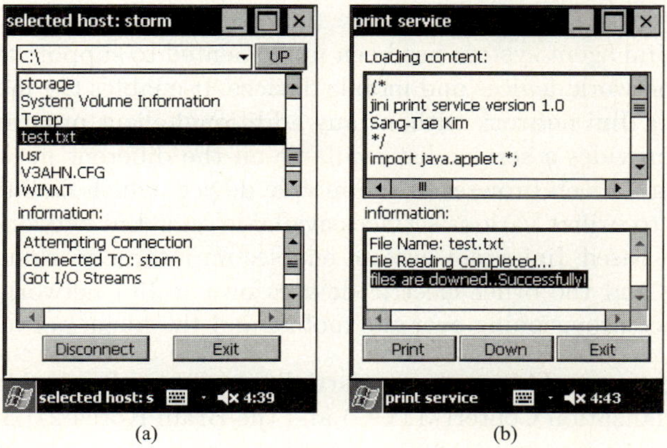

Fig. 5. File download service (a) a file search and (b) a file download

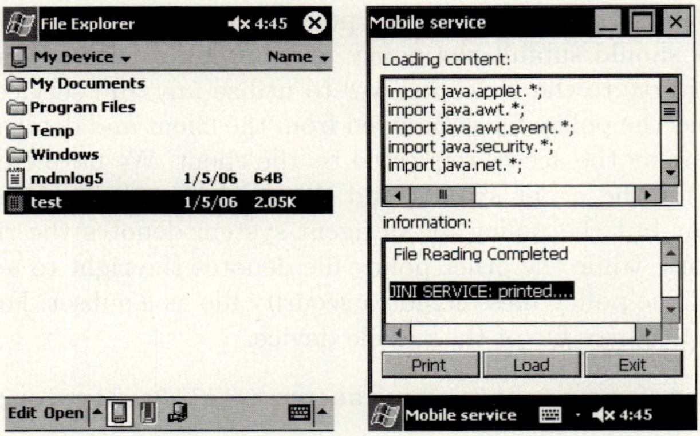

(a) (b)

Fig. 6. Printing service (a) a file search and (b) a file print

After reading a downloaded file (test.txt), we have the file to be printed by using another service provider (a printer). The file selection process to be printed and the print process are shown in Fig. 6 (a) and (b), respectively. If the user execute the printing service through the web browser of the mobile device, the client sends the proxy ID and the service ID of the printer to the web-based Jini agent system. The agent system searches the printer and informs the client of the usability of the printer.

After receiving the message, the client transmits data to the printer to execute a file printing. When the file printing service has been completed the printer server sends a message to the Jini Lookup service to inform the client has completed the use of the service. It is notable that there is no need to install any printer driver in the client to use a file printing service.

5 Conclusion

A web-based Jini agent system has been implemented to support the interoperation of home network devices and mobile devices. It enables the mobile device to participate in a Jini network without any additional client program installation in it. It also provides a service list available on the different networks simultaneously through a web browser of the mobile device, which facilitates the users to search and to utilize various services available on a Jini network in real time. Since the web-based Jini agent system enables an internetworking between the mobile device and the other electric devices over a Jini network, it enables a seamless service provisioning over the mobile and the home networks.

Acknowledgement. This work was partially supported by the Mobile Technology Commercialization Center(MTCC) and the Brain Korea 21(BK21) Project.

References

1. Sang Tae, Kim., Byoung Ju, Yun., Hyun Deok, Kim.: Mobile Agent System for Jini Networks Employing Remote Method Invocation Technology. KES (2005)
2. Landis, S., Vasudevan, V.: Reaching out to the cell phone with Jini. System Sciences (2002)
3. Sing, Li.: Professional Jini. Wrox Press Ltd (2000)
4. Gupta, R., Talwar, S., Agrawal, D.P.: Jini home networking: a step toward pervasive computing. IEEE (2002)
5. Sun Microsystems.: Java Object Serialization (1998)
6. Sun Microsystems.: Java 2 Platform Micro Edition. http://java.sun.com/j2me/index.jsp (2002)
7. Insignia.: Jeode Platform White Paper (2001)
8. John, W., Muchow.: Core J2ME. Sun Microsystems Press (2002)
9. Hinkmond, Wong.: Developing Jini Applications Using J2ME Technology. Addison Wesley (2002)
10. W. Keith, Edwards.: Core JINI. Sun Microsystems Press (2002)
11. Michael, Jernimo., Jack, Weast.: UPnP Design by Example. Intel Press (2003)
12. John, Hyde.: USB Design by Example. Intel Press (2002)
13. McDowell, C., Shankari, K.: Connecting Non-Java Devices to a Jini Network. Proceedings of the Technology of Object-Oriented Languages and System (2000)

Author Index

Abbas, Cláudia J. Barenco 844
Ahn, Chunsoo 1089
Ahn, Kwang Seon 976
Ahn, Sanghyun 652
Ahn, Sangim 945
Ahn, Sunshin 785
Akbar, Ali Hammad 956
Amvame-Nze, Georges 844
An, Sunshin 601
Aoki, Terumasa 519

Bae, Jongwoo 805
Bae, JungSook 591
Baek, Jonghun 509
Baek, Sung-Hoon 795
Bai, Zhiquan 224
Baik, MaengSoon 183
Biaz, Saâd 630
Byeon, Okhwan 682
Byun, EunJoung 183

Cam, Hasan 121
Cao, Jiannong 580
Cao, Liqiang 529
Chae, Yohan 864
Chan, Alvin 580
Chan, Chi-Shiang 469
Chang, Bin 1068
Chang, Chih-Hao 57
Chang, Chin-Chen 469
Chang, Jyh-Huei 874
Chang, Kisoo 914
Chang, Rong-Guey 35, 297
Chaudhry, Shafique Ahmad 956
Chen, Chao-Lieh 620
Chen, Chih-Yuan 297
Chen, Han 479
Chen, Hsin-Pei 662
Chen, Jia-Ming 57
Chen, Yung-Yuan 754
Cheng, Ray-Guang 824
Cheng, Wen-Hsin 620
Cheung, Ronnie 580
Chi, Chi-Hung 328
Cho, Eunhee 234
Cho, Gihwan 79
Cho, Hyeonjoong 274
Cho, Jinsung 15
Cho, Namho 254
Cho, We Duke 1078
Cho, Yongwoo 415, 1119
Cho, Yookun 336
Choi, Ahyoung 1047
Choi, Bong Dae 884
Choi, Eunmi 365
Choi, Hyon-Young 1139
Choi, Jean 1007
Choi, Kwonhue 924
Choi, SungJin 183
Chong, Kiwon 141, 945
Choo, Hyunseung 345, 1098
Chou, Paul B. 479
Chung, Hyun-Yeol 549
Chung, Kwangsue 254
Chung, Min Young 345
Chung, Tae-Sun 394
Chung, Yun-Su 1007

Das, Sajal K. 935

Edwards, Stephen A. 449
Ehnes, Jochen 1017
Ewe, Hong Tat 834

Fan, Yi-Hsuan 469
Fayziyev, A. Sh. 924

Gao, Zhigang 426
Gil, Joon-Min 183
Goh, Hock Guan 834
Goo, SooJin 183
Guo, Yang 732

Han, Jong-Wook 131
Han, Sang Man 987
Han, Seok Bung 692
Han, Sung-Kook 151
Han, Taisook 742
Han, Youn-Hee 1108, 1139

Hasan, Md. Kamrul 987
He, Weisheng 1129
Hirose, Michitaka 1017
Hong, Dongpyo 1047
Hong, In-Pyo 459
Hong, Jiman 264
Hong, Kwang-Seok 539
Hong, Sung Je 308
Horng, Mong-Fong 620
Hsu, Jang-Pong 620
Huang, Su-Shun 662
Huh, Eui-Nam 1089
Hung, Jia-Yang 824
Hussain, Chaudhary Sajjad 956
Hwang, Buhyun 570
Hwang, Chong-Sun 183
Hwang, Jin-Bum 131
Hwang, Joo-Young 795
Hwang, Seok Joong 785
Hwang, Wen-Jyi 776

Inoue, Koji 722
Ip, Nicholas Jun Hao 449
Ito, Megumi 287

Jan, Rong-Hong 874
Jang, Hee-Jin 1139
Jang, Ik-Jin 509
Jensen, E. Douglas 274
Jeon, Yang-Seung 151
Jeong, Dongwon 1108
Jeong, Jongpil 345
Jeong, Soon-Gyu 1058
Jeong, Young-Sik 151
Ji, Aiming 766
Ji, Yiming 630
Jie, Sun 1027
Jin, Yier 766
Jung, ChangWoo 479
Jung, Ho-Youl 549
Jung, Won Do 956

Kang, Hyun-Soo 509
Kang, Kyungtae 415, 1119
Kang, Mikyung 264
Kang, Woo Shik 785
Kim, Andrew 479
Kim, Byung Chul 591
Kim, Cheolgi 914
Kim, Cheolmin 264
Kim, DaeHwan 1078
Kim, Daein 570
Kim, Dong Ah 1037
Kim, Dong-Hoi 642
Kim, Dong Phil 244
Kim, Dongshin 652
Kim, Dongsun 437
Kim, Eunkyo 652
Kim, Gunwoo 742
Kim, Hongjoong 884
Kim, HongSoo 183
Kim, Hyeokman 652
Kim, Hyun Deok 1158
Kim, Ikchan 264
Kim, Jong 308
Kim, Joong-Bae 997
Kim, Joongheon 652
Kim, Juil 141
Kim, Jung-Hyun 539
Kim, Kang Chul 692
Kim, Ki-Hyun 1007
Kim, Ki-Hyung 956
Kim, Kyong Hoon 308
Kim, Min-Joung 549
Kim, Sang Tae 1158
Kim, Sang Wook 244
Kim, Seon Wook 785
Kim, Seong-Whan 162, 560
Kim, Shine 966
Kim, SooYeon 479
Kim, SungHo 601
Kim, SungSuk 610
Kim, Sung Won 214
Kim, Tae Ok 884
Kim, Taeyeon 79
Ko, Hyun Jin 14
Ko, Ki-Hong 162
Kobayashi, Kazutaka 712
Koh, Seok Joo 244
Kong, Junguk 682
Koo, Jihun 785
Koo, Si-Gyung 785
Koo, Yongbon 69
Kowalik, Uwe 519
Kumar, Mohan 935
Kuo, Yau-Hwang 620
Kwak, Kyungsup 224
Kwon, Younggoo 864

Lee, Bih-Hwang 662
Lee, Dong-Ho 394
Lee, Giljae 682
Lee, Hyung-Kyu 131
Lee, Jae Yong 591
Lee, Jenq-Kuen 57
Lee, Jin Wook 121
Lee, Joon Goo 785
Lee, Joonho 415
Lee, Joonwon 69
Lee, Junghoon 264
Lee, Junsoo 884
Lee, KangYoon 479
Lee, Keon Myung 89
Lee, Kwangyong 141
Lee, Min-Gu 904
Lee, Minsun 682
Lee, SangHak 1078
Lee, Sang-Ho 89
Lee, Sang-Won 394
Lee, Seong Joon 976
Lee, Seong-Won 805
Lee, Seung-Ik 997
Lee, Seungwon 336
Lee, Suk Kyoon 1037
Lee, Sunggu 904
Lee, Sungyoung 15, 987
Lee, SunWoo 479
Lee, Tae-Jin 1098
Lee, Wonjun 318, 652
Lee, Woojin 141
Lee, Woojoong 966
Lee, Yann-Hang 121
Lee, Yong-Joo 459
Lee, Yong-Surk 459
Lee, Young Koo 987
Leu, Kuen-Long 754
Li, Hong 426
Li, Minglu 204, 375
Li, Poyuan 1058
Li, Tun 732
Li, Xi 489
Lim, Chang-Gyoon 692
Lim, Seung-Ho 795
Lin, Frank Yeong-Sung 894
Lin, Man 110
Lin, Shun-Chieh 499
Lin, Tzong-Yen 35
Liu, Lin 328
Liu, Meilin 25, 405
Liu, Xingwu 529
Liu, Yao-Yuan 824
Lo, Chia-Tien Dan 776
Lu, Kuo-Shiang 620

Ma, Joongsoo 914
Ma, Tianyi 702
Mehdipour, Farhad 722
Mehedy, Lenin 987
Men, Chaoguang 99
Min, Sung-Gi 1139
Mun, Hyung-Jin 89
Mun, Youngsong 1148
Murakami, Kazuaki 722

Nakajima, Tatsuo 287
Narazaki, Shuji 712
Noori, Hamid 722

Oikawa, Shuichi 287
Ou, Chien-Min 776

Parameswaran, Sridevan 45
Park, Bok-Nyong 318
Park, Chang-Sup 385
Park, Chanik 966
Park, Dong-Joo 394
Park, Gunn-Yong 997
Park, Gyung-Leen 264
Park, HarkSoo 183
Park, Hosang 1119
Park, Hyemee 1098
Park, Jin Soo 884
Park, Jong-Hyun 264
Park, KeeHyun 509
Park, Kyu-Ho 795
Park, Kyung Ho 785
Park, Neungsoo 805
Park, Sangwon 394
Park, Sooyong 437
Park, Soyeon 385
Penz, Stefan 672

Qi, Bing 630
Qiu, Meikang 25, 405
Quinn, John 110

Rammig, Franz J. 2
Rashid, Umar 1047
Ravindran, Binoy 274
Reason, Johnathan M. 479
Rhim, JiHye 479

Roan, Huang-Chun 776
Ryu, Seonggeun 1148
Ryu, Seungwan 591

Sedighi, Mehdi 722
Seo, Euiseong 69
Seo, Jeeyoung 234
Seok, Woojin 682
Seol, Jae-Min 560
Sha, Edwin H.-M. 25, 405
Shao, Zili 25, 375, 405
Shen, Haibin 766
Shen, Huaping 935
Shi, Yuanchun 1068, 1129
Shih, Wei-Kuan 57
Shin, Christian 318
Shin, Heonshik 415, 1119
Shin, Jitae 1089
Shin, Jonghwa 966
Shin, Kang G. 1
Sim, Moh Lim 834
Son, Choonho 742
Song, Eun-Ha 151
Song, Ha-Joo 394
Song, Minseok 193
Su, Chien-Chung 620
Suh, Youngjung 1047
Suk, Soo-Young 549

Tan, QingPing 732
Tran, Doan Thanh 365
Tseng, Cheng Yao 854
Tseng, Shau-Yin 57

Villalba, L. Javier García 844

Wang, Dongsheng 99
Wang, Gicheol 79
Wang, Jhing-Fa 499
Wang, Jia-Ching 499
Wang, Shao-Yang 297
Wang, Xinglan 702
Wang, Zhijun 935
Wen, Yean-Fu 894
Wenig, Martin 672
Willow, Charles C. 171
Wojciechowski, Paweł T. 355
Wong, Danny 479
Woo, Woontack 1047
Wu, Haisang 274
Wu, Hui 45
Wu, Shaoen 630
Wu, ZhaoHui 426, 1027

Xiao, Bin 375
Xiao, Xin 1129
Xu, Cheng-Zhong 814
Xu, Li 110
Xu, Shaoyi 224
Xue, Chun 25, 405

Yamasaki, Ryosuke 712
Yan, Bo 15
Yang, Hsueh-Wei 499
Yang, Jie 15
Yang, Jun 489, 702
Yang, Laurence T. 110, 489
Yang, Sun Ok 610
Yang, Wenlu 204
Yao, Gang 580
Yasuda, Hiroshi 519
Yeh, Chao-Sung 754
Yoo, Jae Hung 692
Yoo, Jang-Hee 1007
Yoo, Sang-Jo 234, 1058
Yoshida, Norihiko 712
You, Rongquan 766
Yu, Chang Wu 854
Yu, Jiadi 375
Yu, JinShan 732
Yu, Xiaoyin 328
Yun, Byoung-Ju 509
Yun, Jeong-Han 742

Zakaria, Nurul Azma 712
Zamani, Morteza Saheb 722
Zha, Li 529
Zhang, Chongqing 204
Zhang, Nan 1068
Zhang, Weihua 224
Zhao, Yunlong 99
Zhou, Haojie 529
Zhou, Xiaobo 814
Zhu, Angela Yun 489
Zhuge, Qingfeng 25

Lecture Notes in Computer Science

For information about Vols. 1–3999

please contact your bookseller or Springer

Vol. 4048: L. Goble, J.-J.C.. Meyer (Eds.), Deontic Logic and Artificial Normative Systems. X, 273 pages. 2006. (Sublibrary LNAI).

Vol. 4047: M. Robshaw (Ed.), Fast Software Encryption. XI, 434 pages. 2006.

Vol. 4046: S.M. Astley, M. Brady, C. Rose, R. Zwiggelaar (Eds.), Digital Mammography. XVI, 654 pages. 2006.

Vol. 4045: D. Barker-Plummer, R. Cox, N. Swoboda (Eds.), Diagrammatic Representation and Inference. XII, 301 pages. 2006. (Sublibrary LNAI).

Vol. 4044: P. Abrahamsson, M. Marchesi, G. Succi (Eds.), Extreme Programming and Agile Processes in Software Engineering. XII, 230 pages. 2006.

Vol. 4043: A.S. Atzeni, A. Lioy (Eds.), Public Key Infrastructure. XI, 261 pages. 2006.

Vol. 4042: D. Bell, J. Hong (Eds.), Flexible and Efficient Information Handling. XVI, 296 pages. 2006.

Vol. 4041: S.-W. Cheng, C.K. Poon (Eds.), Algorithmic Aspects in Information and Management. XI, 395 pages. 2006.

Vol. 4040: R. Reulke, U. Eckardt, B. Flach, U. Knauer, K. Polthier (Eds.), Combinatorial Image Analysis. XII, 482 pages. 2006.

Vol. 4039: M. Morisio (Ed.), Reuse of Off-the-Shelf Components. XIII, 444 pages. 2006.

Vol. 4038: P. Ciancarini, H. Wiklicky (Eds.), Coordination Models and Languages. VIII, 299 pages. 2006.

Vol. 4037: R. Gorrieri, H. Wehrheim (Eds.), Formal Methods for Open Object-Based Distributed Systems. XVII, 474 pages. 2006.

Vol. 4036: O. H. Ibarra, Z. Dang (Eds.), Developments in Language Theory. XII, 456 pages. 2006.

Vol. 4035: T. Nishita, Q. Peng, H.-P. Seidel (Eds.), Advances in Computer Graphics. XX, 771 pages. 2006.

Vol. 4034: J. Münch, M. Vierimaa (Eds.), Product-Focused Software Process Improvement. XVII, 474 pages. 2006.

Vol. 4033: B. Stiller, P. Reichl, B. Tuffin (Eds.), Performability Has its Price. X, 103 pages. 2006.

Vol. 4032: O. Etzion, T. Kuflik, A. Motro (Eds.), Next Generation Information Technologies and Systems. XIII, 365 pages. 2006.

Vol. 4031: M. Ali, R. Dapoigny (Eds.), Advances in Applied Artificial Intelligence. XXIII, 1353 pages. 2006. (Sublibrary LNAI).

Vol. 4029: L. Rutkowski, R. Tadeusiewicz, L.A. Zadeh, J. Zurada (Eds.), Artificial Intelligence and Soft Computing – ICAISC 2006. XXI, 1235 pages. 2006. (Sublibrary LNAI).

Vol. 4028: J. Kohlas, B. Meyer, A. Schiper (Eds.), Dependable Systems: Software, Computing, Networks. XII, 296 pages. 2006.

Vol. 4027: H.L. Larsen, G. Pasi, D. Ortiz-Arroyo, T. Andreasen, H. Christiansen (Eds.), Flexible Query Answering Systems. XVIII, 714 pages. 2006. (Sublibrary LNAI).

Vol. 4026: P.B. Gibbons, T. Abdelzaher, J. Aspnes, R. Rao (Eds.), Distributed Computing in Sensor Systems. XIV, 566 pages. 2006.

Vol. 4025: F. Eliassen, A. Montresor (Eds.), Distributed Applications and Interoperable Systems. XI, 355 pages. 2006.

Vol. 4024: S. Donatelli, P. S. Thiagarajan (Eds.), Petri Nets and Other Models of Concurrency - ICATPN 2006. XI, 441 pages. 2006.

Vol. 4021: E. André, L. Dybkjær, W. Minker, H. Neumann, M. Weber (Eds.), Perception and Interactive Technologies. XI, 217 pages. 2006. (Sublibrary LNAI).

Vol. 4020: A. Bredenfeld, A. Jacoff, I. Noda, Y. Takahashi (Eds.), RoboCup 2005: Robot Soccer World Cup IX. XVII, 727 pages. 2006. (Sublibrary LNAI).

Vol. 4019: M. Johnson, V. Vene (Eds.), Algebraic Methodology and Software Technology. XI, 389 pages. 2006.

Vol. 4018: V. Wade, H. Ashman, B. Smyth (Eds.), Adaptive Hypermedia and Adaptive Web-Based Systems. XVI, 474 pages. 2006.

Vol. 4017: S. Vassiliadis, S. Wong, T.D. Hämäläinen (Eds.), Embedded Computer Systems: Architectures, Modeling, and Simulation. XV, 492 pages. 2006.

Vol. 4016: J.X. Yu, M. Kitsuregawa, H.V. Leong (Eds.), Advances in Web-Age Information Management. XVII, 606 pages. 2006.

Vol. 4014: T. Uustalu (Ed.), Mathematics of Program Construction. X, 455 pages. 2006.

Vol. 4013: L. Lamontagne, M. Marchand (Eds.), Advances in Artificial Intelligence. XIII, 564 pages. 2006. (Sublibrary LNAI).

Vol. 4012: T. Washio, A. Sakurai, K. Nakajima, H. Takeda, S. Tojo, M. Yokoo (Eds.), New Frontiers in Artificial Intelligence. XIII, 484 pages. 2006. (Sublibrary LNAI).

Vol. 4011: Y. Sure, J. Domingue (Eds.), The Semantic Web: Research and Applications. XIX, 726 pages. 2006.

Vol. 4010: S. Dunne, B. Stoddart (Eds.), Unifying Theories of Programming. VIII, 257 pages. 2006.

Vol. 4009: M. Lewenstein, G. Valiente (Eds.), Combinatorial Pattern Matching. XII, 414 pages. 2006.

Vol. 4008: J.C. Augusto, C.D. Nugent (Eds.), Designing Smart Homes. XI, 183 pages. 2006. (Sublibrary LNAI).

Vol. 4007: C. Àlvarez, M. Serna (Eds.), Experimental Algorithms. XI, 329 pages. 2006.

Vol. 4006: L.M. Pinho, M. González Harbour (Eds.), Reliable Software Technologies – Ada-Europe 2006. XII, 241 pages. 2006.

Vol. 4005: G. Lugosi, H.U. Simon (Eds.), Learning Theory. XI, 656 pages. 2006. (Sublibrary LNAI).

Vol. 4004: S. Vaudenay (Ed.), Advances in Cryptology - EUROCRYPT 2006. XIV, 613 pages. 2006.

Vol. 4003: Y. Koucheryavy, J. Harju, V.B. Iversen (Eds.), Next Generation Teletraffic and Wired/Wireless Advanced Networking. XVI, 582 pages. 2006.

Vol. 4001: E. Dubois, K. Pohl (Eds.), Advanced Information Systems Engineering. XVI, 560 pages. 2006.